D1294003

# ENCYCLOPEDIA OF
# AMERICAN
# ARCHITECTURE

**McGraw-Hill Books of Related Interest**

BREEN AND RIGBY • *Waterfronts: Cities Reclaim Their Edge*

HARRIS • *Dictionary of Architecture and Construction,* Second Edition

KATZ • *The New Urbanism*

SHOPSIN • *Preserving American Mansions and Estates*

SIMONDS • *Garden Cities 21*

WOLFE • *New York: A Guide to the Metropolis,* Second Edition

# ENCYCLOPEDIA OF
# AMERICAN
# ARCHITECTURE

---

*Robert T. Packard, AIA*

*Balthazar Korab, Illustration Editor*

Second Edition

**McGraw-Hill, Inc.**

New York  San Francisco  Washington, D.C.  Auckland  Bogotá
Caracas  Lisbon  London  Madrid  Mexico City  Milan
Montreal  New Delhi  San Juan  Singapore
Sydney  Tokyo  Toronto

Somerset County Library
Bridgewater, NJ 08807

**Library of Congress Cataloging-in-Publication Data**

Packard, Robert T.
    Encyclopedia of American architecture / Robert T. Packard.
Balthazar Korab.—2nd ed.
        p.      cm.
    Rev. ed. of: Encyclopedia of American architecture / William
Dudley Hunt, Jr. c 1980.
    Includes index.
    ISBN 0-07-048010-9
    1. Architecture—United States—Dictionaries.    I. Korab,
Balthazar.    II. Hunt, William Dudley, Encyclopedia of American
architecture.    III. Title.
NA705.P3   1994
720′.973—dc20                                          94-13941
                                                            CIP

Copyright © 1995, 1980 by McGraw-Hill, Inc. All rights reserved. Printed in
Hong Kong . Except as permitted under the United States Copyright Act of
1976, no part of this publication may be reproduced or distributed in any form
or by any means, or stored in a data base or retrieval system, without the prior
written permission of the publisher.

1 2 3 4 5 6 7 8 9 0   1IMP/1IMP   9 0 9 8 7 6 5 4


ISBN 0-07-048010-9



The sponsoring editor for this book was JOEL STEIN,
the editing supervisor was JANE PALMIERI,
the designer was SILVERS DESIGN,
and the production supervisor was SUZANNE BABEUF.
It was set in Aldus by SILVERS DESIGN.
Printed and bound through Print Vision, Portland, OR.



All photographs by Balthazar Korab unless otherwise credited.
Mr. Korab's photographs are available through Balthazar Korab Studios,
Troy, Michigan, 810-641-8881.

# CONTENTS

# PREFACE

The first edition of the *Encyclopedia of American Architecture* was published by McGraw-Hill in 1980. The author was William Dudley Hunt, Jr., and preparation of the book occurred over a period of several years. I came to know Dudley and Gwen Hunt while he was editor for architectural books for John Wiley and Sons. He was my editor for the seventh edition of *Architectural Graphic Standards*, which was prepared at the American Institute of Architects in Washington, D.C. During this time we had several long conversations about his work in progress—the *Encyclopedia of American Architecture*. After Dudley's death in 1983, his friends agreed that a new edition of the *Encyclopedia* would be a suitable recognition of his friendship to so many in the architectural profession. Gwen Hunt agreed, and with McGraw-Hill's cooperation, work on the present edition began in 1991.

As William Dudley Hunt, Jr., stated in the preface to the first edition, "this book presents, in words and pictures, the vast breadth of American architecture. It is intended to be of interest and use to people who want to know about the culture and the environment in which they live, and how it came to be that way." The book provides interest and value to students, as well to other people with involvement and interest in buildings. The book is also intended for those who must know about architecture, such as landscape architects, engineers, interior designers, city planners, building owners and developers, real estate people, artists, contractors, product manufacturers, government officials, and building managers. Although specialists may find the overview articles for their field too basic to be of use, articles on other subjects should be useful.

This book is nontechnical, and specialized terms are defined where used. Architectural libraries at universities and at the American Institute of Architects in Washington, D.C., contain relatively complete information on all aspects of American architecture, and further reading suggestions refer to current sources for further study. Most titles listed are still in print, or may be easily found in libraries. The growth of the architectural press suggests new books relevant to the material presented in the *Encyclopedia of American Architecture* will continue to be published. This book should be recognized as a general overview, with individual articles presenting sufficient material for supplying basic facts, but not so detailed that only experts would require or understand the information.

Subjects implied in the previous edition, but expanded now, include the impact of computer use on the profession of architecture, a new look at energy conservation, accessible design, and a recognition of changes in design thinking and practice. Events such as the prolonged recession of the early 1990s after the overbuilding of the 1980s and the devastating earthquakes and flooding experienced in the United States have resulted in greater emphasis on these design issues.

The new edition was based on a study of changes in architecture since 1980. New articles have been added for such subjects as vernacular buildings, patrons of architecture, international practice, as well as new biographies of several leading individuals and firms.

The last 15 years have been a maturing period in American architecture. The leaders of the past generation, many European bred, included Ludwig Mies van der Rohe, Walter Gropius, Marcel Breuer, Richard Neutra, Josep Lluis Sert, Eliel and Eero Saarinen, and Louis Kahn. American designers became trailblazers in ideology and aesthetics. Major commissions came from the oil-rich countries, but also from Europe, Australia, and the Pacific rim. The United States changed from importers to exporters of design.

Frank Lloyd Wright has been the subject of so many books that it is obvious that he remains the public image of the greatest American architect. In this edition we have selected a representative collection of his work for illustration, more than that for any other architect.

Perhaps the most evident contrast between editions is in the use of color photographs, many taken specifically for publication here. One of the great pleasures in preparation of the new edition has been the enthusiastic cooperation of the internationally famous architectural photographer Balthazar Korab as illustration editor for this edition. My choice of illustration editor fell on Balthazar Korab due to his familiarity with the subject matter beyond just his photographic skills and the benefit of a file of 40 years of practice. Several trips were taken to add photographs to what was already a major resource in Balthazar's files. More photographs were considered than could be used in this book, and modern technology has resurrected early color photographs such as those by Julius Shulman in the Richard Neutra article. We have selected photographs in varying weather and lighting conditions. We have elected to show build-ings in their environment, sometimes with people rather than unpopulated as often seen in the architectural press. With a few exceptions, current views have been selected over frequently published archival sources. The preservation of our architectural heritage is well illustrated in the new photographs of historic buildings and sites.

The interest in the "greening" of architecture has encouraged the illustration of more gardens, parks, and landscape architecture. Where possible, illustrations indicate the surrounding plant materials, even in urban settings. Some well-known Frank Lloyd Wright buildings are so shielded with plant materials that they are almost impossible to photograph except in closeup details.

A large number of photographs of buildings constructed since 1980 result in a more varied geographical selection of building types and sizes. The newer buildings represent the continuing work of many styles, including Modernism, and the experiments with post-Modern design, contextualism, and deconstructivism. It is a stimulating period in architectural theory, and shows promise for a more public-spirited architecture to come.

# ACKNOWLEDGMENTS

Born in Hungary in 1926, Balthazar Korab studied architecture at the Polytechnicum of Budapest, graduating from the École des Beaux Arts in Paris. His early experience included employment with Backström Renius in Stockholm and Le Corbusier in Paris. In 1955 he joined the Eero Saarinen office in Bloomfield Hills, Mich., working with such currently prominent architects as Kevin Roche, Cesar Pelli, and Gunnar Birkerts. It was in this creative atmosphere, while pioneering the use of photography in design, that he initiated his new career specializing in photography and architectural journalism. His work, in addition to the ongoing service to the architectural press, includes historic studies from Italy and the United States, in particular Columbus, Indiana, and Cranbrook Academy. He is the author of the article on architectural photography in this book. The *Encyclopedia of American Architecture* is the largest group of Balthazar Korab's photographs published in a single book, and for this reason will be of interest to many architects. Designers of many of these buildings, although not the subject of articles, are the probable leaders of the future.

The support by McGraw-Hill for this well-illustrated book has made relations with the publisher a pleasure. Our thanks to our editor Joel Stein and publisher Sybil Parker for taking time to view presentation of the photographs and for supporting an all-color book. Others to be mentioned with thanks include Jane Palmieri, editing supervisor; Suzanne Babeuf, production supervisor; Tom Kowalczyk, production manager; and Scott and Caryl Silvers, Silvers Design, for the book's excellent design.

On a personal note, I have been entertained and given access to Dudley Hunt's files by Gwen Hunt at her home. Monica and Balthazar Korab have been generous in their hospitality to me during several trips to Michigan. Throughout my writing my wife Anne has patiently read and commented on work in process, and kindly listened to my long monologues on architecture. I have had the pleasure of selecting my hometown of Reston, Va., as an example of a planned community. This book has been a stimulating and gratifying effort.

*Robert T. Packard*

**ADAPTIVE USE** Refers to the adaptation of existing buildings for new uses. Buildings have been adapted since early times, but in current usage the term includes specific requirements to make older buildings usable as museums, housing, work spaces, stores, or restaurants. In general, older buildings are structurally sound, and often have amenities not found in new construction, such as decoration, high ceilings, and operable windows. What older buildings lack is adequate electric power, air-handling systems, fire protection, plumbing, handicapped access, and occasionally fire-rated stairs and exits. Thus savings in structure and minimal demolition expense are frequently offset by the introduction of new systems. The challenge has been to improve the building use to justify the costs of adaptive use. The first step in analyzing old buildings is to record the present state of the building and inventory the interior spaces. The use of stereophotogrammetry has proven effective to record existing conditions. Inspection and repair of the exterior may include replacing or partially replacing old materials in favor of new. Structural cracks in masonry need special attention, which requires a good understanding of building materials and procedures.

Original-use buildings which have been successfully adapted include warehouses, railway stations, houses, religious buildings, and schools. One adaptation was prompted by the wide support for saving the old Post Office on Pennsylvania Avenue in Washington, D.C., producing a much-needed adaption of the building for restaurants and shops within easy reach of the Mall. In New York, the International Design Center (1978) designed by Gwathmey Siegel is housed in four former industrial warehouse buildings. Some other projects are described in the following text and illustrations.

**Industrial Buildings and Warehouses** Perhaps the best-known adaptive use of industrial buildings is the old mill town of Lowell, Mass. The underutilized early American stone mills have been restored for use by research and development firms and for offices. The historic area is managed by the National Park Service and has revitalized the town.

**ADAPTIVE USE** Union Terminal (1908, 1984), Washington, D.C. Railway station converted into retail space. *[1908 architect: Daniel Hudson Burnham; 1984 adaptive use architect: Ben Thompson]*

1

**ADAPTIVE USE** Farmhouse (19th century; 1984), Kresge Foundation Headquarters, Troy, Mich. Farmhouse and yard converted into offices. *[Adaptive use architects: William Kessler Assoc.]*

A large warehouse in Minneapolis dating from 1906 and abandoned in 1964 was remodeled into an office-retail space surrounding a central atrium. The architects for the 1974 Butler Square renovation were Miller Hanson Westerbeck Bell Architects, Inc.

Examples of adaptive use of early American warehouses include Faneuil Hall Market in Boston, which was transformed from freight use to a popular waterfront series of shops and restaurants designed by Ben Thompson. Another example is the Candlestick warehouses in Baltimore adjacent to the new baseball stadium at Camden Yards for the Baltimore Orioles; the warehouses have been adapted for use as offices and restaurants for this in-city project, designed by HOK. See the article entitled preservation for a description of tax credits available for reuse of older buildings.

**Railway Stations** The redundancy of older railway stations has resulted in some interesting and effective adaptation for a new life as restaurant, theater, or shopping. The success of the Union Terminal project in Washington, D.C., has salvaged a much-abused landmark of the city. Originally designed by Daniel H. Burnham in 1908, the restoration work and new adaptation was another project of the Ben Thompson firm. Another adaptive use railway station is the St. Louis Union Station remodeled by HOK. The renovated building included a hotel, a covered shopping mall and restaurants, and a lake.

The Cincinnati railway station has been twice remodeled, most recently as an arts center.

**Housing** Old houses of architectural interest have been salvaged in a number of communities for use as professional offices, town offices, and, in a smaller group, as museums. The best examples are not treated as decorative highpoints but are integrated into larger neighborhoods. Careful economic and social planning are required to maintain old buildings in the housing stock.

An example of a museum adaptation is the Hackerman House in Baltimore, restored and adapted to house the Oriental collection of the Walters Art Gallery in Baltimore. Architects for the adaptation for museum use were Grieves, Worrall, Wright and O'Hatni. Another building saved from destruction was the historic 1803 Octagon House, now operated as a museum by the

American Institute of Architects (AIA) Foundation. Originally designed by William Thornton, the house was purchased by the AIA in 1902 and restored in 1902, 1954, and 1968. The current, and fourth, extensive exterior restoration was completed in 1993, and the interior will be completed in 1994. The restoration architects are Mesick Cohen Waite Architects. The preservation of other historic buildings for public use is discussed in the article entitled preservation.

**Other Building Types** Surplus schools in several communities have been adapted successfully for housing. Churches and synagogues have been converted to other uses. An example is the headquarters of the Missouri Historical Society which saved the former 1925 United Hebrew Temple on the edge of Forest Park in St. Louis. This project was originally designed by Gabriel Ferrand for the architectural firm of Maritz & Young. Conversion architects, including an addition, are Murphy, Downey, Wofford & Richman. The adaptive reuse allowed the repair and decoration of the dome over the former sanctuary, now adapted as the library for the Historical Society, and much of the rest of the structure was modified for office use.

**Additional Reading** Kay, Gersil Newmark: *Mechanical and Electrical Systems for Historic Buildings*, McGraw-Hill, New York, 1992; Robert, Philippe: *Adaptations: New Uses for Old Buildings*, Princeton Architectural Press, New York (copyright 1989 by Editions du Moniteur, Paris); Weaver, Martin E.: *Conserving Buildings: A Guide to Techniques and Materials*, John Wiley, New York, 1993.

**Sources of Additional Information** See article entitled preservation.

**ADHESIVES** In recent decades adhesives have been increasingly applied in building construction. Chemical advances have allowed design of adhesives for specific applications. A recognized definition of an *adhesive* is a substance capable of holding materials together by surface attachment. Adhesives are also used in the manufacture of sealants.

Materials used include organic polymers and elastomers. Natural polymers have been used since early times. Such adhesives have been made from animal, casein, blood, starch, dextrin, and cellulosic adhesives. Natural rubber is another polymer that has had long use. Although some of these traditional materials are still used, the greatest group of adhesives are now made by using synthetic polymers.

**Organic Polymers** The organic polymers include both thermoplastic and thermosetting types. Thermoplastic materials soften and flow with heat and harden when cooled. These materials include polyvinyls, acrylics, polystyrenes, and polyamides. Thermosetting polymers make good adhesives because they undergo chemical change on application of heat. They have high strength, resist deterioration, and can be used for long-term loads without deforming. Thermosetting polymers include resorcinolic, amino, and epoxy resins. The thermosetting polymers are used to make structural adhesives. Most adhesive products are combinations of several materials in various ratios to achieve the desired strength, durability, and adhesiveness. In addition, such materials as fillers can be used to reduce the cost of adhesives.

**Advantages** The advantage of adhesives is that they can be matched to the stresses and environment of the application, resulting in a stronger connection than can be achieved using mechanical fastenings. New composite products have been developed using the capabilities of adhesives. Examples of these include laminated timber, plywood and chipboards, honeycomb or foam assemblies using aluminum or hardboard surfaces. Often the resulting product is made of low-cost materials which take on new attributes in the final product. Other common uses include installation of carpet and other floor coverings, wall coverings, and countertops. The list of products using adhesives is constantly increasing.

**Application** Careful application under controlled conditions is required to achieve proper adhesion, and improper adhesion can require discarding otherwise sound materials. Careful consideration is needed for surface preparation and application of adhesive, including control over time, temperature, and relative humidity. Often pressure must be applied, with or without heat, to achieve proper adhesion. The cost of the application procedures must be taken into account to ensure proper use of adhesives.

Surfaces to receive adhesives should be clean and smooth. In construction, adhesives are required to adhere differing materials and surfaces. Wood is the most complex material for adhesion, and metals require the most careful preparation.

**Limitations** One problem with the widespread use of adhesives is the release of gases such as formaldehyde which can cause irritation or more serious inflammation or allergic reactions. Solvent-based adhesives may present a fire risk if improperly stored. Regulations now require that products be carefully labelled with application instructions to reduce exposure to risk. Some adhesives to be avoided break down under specific conditions, and may release potentially dangerous toxic materials.

**Uses** Adhesives can be used in the manufacturing plant, or in the field in the form of mastics and sealants. Sealants are used to close joints which move under stresses anticipated in construction. Such factors as dimension and spacing of sealed joints determine the desired physical characteristics of the sealant. Very specific evaluation of the sealant selected would include adhesion and cohesion, hardness, elastic recovery, permanent set, compression set, and the effects of ultraviolet exposure. The newer polymers, although more expensive than traditional materials, will give more satisfactory performance in use. The detailing of the joint is an important issue.

**Behavior** The action of adhesives has been analyzed for physical behavior. These bonding mechanisms include forces produced by the interactions of atoms, ions, and molecules that exist within and at the surfaces of the adhesive and the materials being adhered. Some surfaces will not bond effectively if too hard and smooth. For adhesives to work properly, the surfaces to be coated must be wetted to allow molecules of the adhesive to diffuse over or into the surfaces to make contact with the molecular structure of the surface. When the adhesive becomes heavily viscous or hardens to resist sheer and other forces tending to separate the surfaces, proper adhesion is obtained. This change in the state of the adhesives may occur by drying, chemical change, or cooling. The analysis of an adhesive joint is a complex subject.

**Sealants** Sealants have been developed for use in waterproof joints required by the movement of structures. The dimension and placement of joints determine the materials used. Sealants can be grouped as rigid or flexible and nonhardening types, although specialized sealants have been developed for unusual conditions. The selection and installation of modern sealants is a technically complex subject, which will be described only briefly here.

**Types of Joints** Construction joints are used to divide large areas of concrete or masonry. This allows contraction and expansion and limits the location of cracks. Expansion and isolation joints are used to separate walls from floors or roofs, around columns penetrating slabs, etc. Movement joints are used to seal joints subject to movement as temperature rises or falls. They are generally designed as sliding surfaces. Joints are either butt or lap joints.

**Movement of Buildings** All building materials expand and contract at different rates relative to temperature. Materials are rated by their coefficients of linear expansion. Clay masonry products are relatively stable compared to metals or plastics which move more than other materials. It is possible to estimate the relative movement of materials for the design of a particular joint over a temperature range that can be expected.

Modern sealant materials include butyl, LP polymers: high sulphur, silicones, polythioethers, polyurethanes, and acrylics. Butyls and synthetic rubber are frequently used in glazing applications.

The design of joints includes preparation of joint surfaces, the use of bond breakers and backup materials, the use of fillers, and primers. Sealants are often extruded under pressure from a nozzle. With experience, application will result in a neat joint. Cleanup of equipment and tools avoids the problem of hardened sealants. Special solvents may be used as recommended by the manufacturer of the sealant material. Further development of sealant materials and installation details may be expected in the future, just as current materials have replaced the earlier putty. Currently the polyurethanes have become the most widely used of the sealant materials, with silicones retaining their place in the market. Polysulfides are now less used.

**Further Reading** Panek, J. R., and J. P. Cook: *Construction Sealants and Adhesives*, 2d ed., John Wiley, New York, 1984.

**Sources of Additional Information** American Society for Testing and Materials (ASTM), Philadelphia, Pa.; Forest Products Laboratory, USDA Forest Service, Madison, Wis.

**AESTHETICS** Pertains to the nature of beauty or the nature of art, including architecture. Aesthetics (also spelled *esthetics*) is concerned with experiencing beauty and with that which constitutes beauty. It is concerned with the essential character of beauty and the perception of, response to, and judgment of beauty. Thus aesthetics is one of the most important considerations in architecture.

A considerable amount of confusion exists about aesthetics, perhaps because of its subjective nature. What is beautiful? Why is something beautiful? How does one know it is beautiful? Questions such as these have no simple responses. Yet aesthetics attempts to answer these questions, a difficult task for professional aestheticians, who devote their careers to such studies.

**Definitions** In this subject so essential to architecture, vast differences of opinion exist. Some define aesthetics as a science, along with mathematics, physics, chemistry, and so on. Others define it as a branch of philosophy, which they define, in turn, as the science of the principles and truths of reality, knowledge, and human nature and conduct. There is some difference of opinion about the nature of philosophy itself, some maintaining that it should be subdivided into three major fields: natural, moral, and metaphysical, the study of the nature of reality. Others hold that all philosophy is metaphysical. Still another view is that the division must be four parts: metaphysics; logic, the study of correct reasoning or validity; epistemology, the coordination of knowledge with the natural world; and axiology, the study of values in such concepts as art, morals, and religion. Thus axiology includes both ethics—the study of moral character, principles, quality, and practice—and aesthetics.

Further confusing the issue, philosophy is usually classified today not as a science but as one of the humanities, along with music, literature, religion, and art, including architecture. In this way, aesthetics may be thought of as closely allied to the arts, the very subjects into which it attempts to impart meaning. However, some maintain that aesthetics must be restricted to the study of the fine arts, usually, but not always, considered to include painting, drawing, and architecture, to which are often added, music, dance, drama, poetry, and other literature. Others believe even this extended list is too restrictive and should include such activities as industrial design; printmaking, such as engravings, woodcuts, silkscreen prints or serigraphs, etchings; and motion pictures.

In such a state of affairs, it is not surprising that those who are called upon to design buildings so often find confusion, uncertainty, and controversy surrounding their architecture, the central essence of which is aesthetics. No wonder that the principles of aesthetics design are so hard to formulate, to teach, and to put into practice by architects, so nearly impossible to explain to clients and others, and so often impossible for architecture critics to deal with.

Yet architects must deal with aesthetics if they are to create architecture, no matter how its aesthetic qualities be defined or codified. Aesthetics crosses many of the lines of other disciplines. The social sciences, such as history, archeology, sociology, anthropology, help to explain how the arts are related to human beings and how people live. Psychology helps in the understanding of how human beings think, perceive, feel, learn, and act when creating art, when thinking about it, and when experiencing it. Many other disciplines, including the natural sciences, are helpful in the study of aesthetics.

**Branches** Aesthetics is often divided into five major branches: psychology of art, the study of human behavior when creating, contemplating, or experiencing art; sociology of art, the study of how art affects and is affected by human activities in religion, government, and so on; aesthetic morphology, the study of forms and styles in art; aesthetic value theory, the study of the functions of art and principles for its judgment; and aesthetic semantics, the study of the language used in describing and discussing art.

**Philosophies** Sometimes aesthetics is divided into two major philosophies: the objective, which maintains that beauty is contained or is inherent in the art object itself, such as a building or painting, and the subjective, which maintains that beauty is contained not in the object but in the observer's perception of the object. Needless to say, there are many gradations and variations of belief between the two extreme positions.

**Functions** In any case, the functions of aesthetics involve several types of activity, including the collection, organization, and interpretation of information. Aesthe-

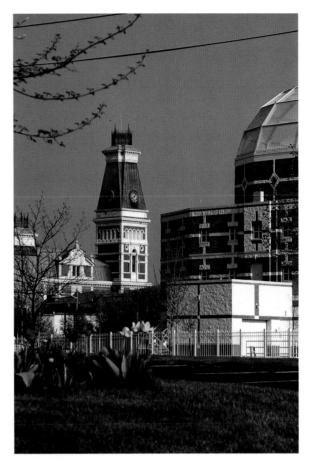

**AESTHETICS** Contextualism: Bartholomew County Law Enforcement Building (1990) *[Architect: Don M. Hisaka]* and Bartholomew County Courthouse (1874), Columbus, Ind. *[Architect: Isaac Hodgson]*

ticians attempt to discover how artists work, use their imaginations, and make their performances, how people use and enjoy art, and how they feel about it. Aestheticians also study the principles of beauty, what makes one object beautiful, another not. And they study the moods, beliefs, and attitudes of artists and the people who experience artists' creations. Other specific subjects for study are perception, the awareness of consciousness in the mind of a person whose senses are stimulated by an object; aesthetic value, the property of an object that allows it to be perceived with pleasure or displeasure; and taste, the quality of being able to express preferences among aesthetic values, based on sensitiveness to perceptions caused by stimulation of the senses by objects.

The principles and theories of aesthetics require considerable study, and not a little contemplation, if they are to be understood and translated into buildings that are great architecture; if they are to be meaningfully and justly criticized by architecture critics; and if they are to be understood and appreciated by those interested in art, architecture, and their environment.

**History** From its beginnings, the history of aesthetics, irrespective of how it is classified today, has been part of the history of philosophy and therefore the province primarily of philosophers. The great ancient Greek philosopher, Aristotle (384–322 B.C.), originally named Aristocles, was deeply concerned with aesthetics as well as with other aspects of philosophy. Since that time, aesthetics has been of concern to a number of philosophers, although it was not actually called by that name until the 18th century.

Beginning late in the 18th century, a number of great philosophers wrote important books on aesthetics. Among them are two Germans, Immanual Kant (1724–1804), who wrote *Critique of Judgment*, published in 1790, a valuable book, though less well known than his earlier work, *Critique of Pure Reason*, 1781, and George Wilhelm Friedrich Hegel (1770–1831), whose *Philosophy of Fine Arts* was published after his death. Englishman Roger Eliot Fry (1866–1934) wrote *Vision and Design*, 1920. The Italian philosopher Benedetto Croce (1866–1952), wrote several books on aesthetics, including *Aesthetic*, published in 1921. George Santayana (1863–1952), a Spanish philosopher educated at Harvard University and professor of philosophy there from 1889 to 1912, wrote a number of books on aesthetics, including *The Sense of Beauty*, 1896, and *Reason in Art*, 1905. Since 1952, when the two giants of aesthetics, Croce and Santayana, both died, no philosophers of aesthetics have reached the heights they occupied.

**Related Articles** ARCHITECTURE; ART IN ARCHITECTURE; BOOK, ARCHITECTURAL; CRITICISM, ARCHITECTURE; DESIGN, ARCHITECTURAL; SOCIAL SCIENCE.

**Further Reading** Berlyne, D. E.: *Studies in the New Experimental Aesthetics—Steps Toward an Objective Psychology of Aesthetics: Appreciation*, John Wiley, New York, 1974, available through Books on Demand, UMI, Ann Arbor, Mich.; Scruton, Roger: *The Aesthetics of Architecture*, Princeton University Press, Princeton, N.J., 1979.

**AIRPORT** An architectural complex consisting of runways, buildings, and related facilities for the takeoff, landing, and handling of airplanes and other aircraft and their crews, passengers, and cargoes.

**Types** There are three major types of airports: air carrier, general aviation, and military. Air carrier airports are designed for use by scheduled airlines. General aviation airports are for all types of civilian aircraft, except those of the airlines. Business, pleasure, and charter aircraft use general aviation airports, as do air taxis that fly to air carrier airports and between small towns. Facilities for general aviation are also provided at air carrier airports, often in buildings separated from the passenger terminals. Military airports are for the armed services, including the U.S. Air Force, Army, Navy, and Marines. These airports are also used by Reserve and National Guard units of the services. The major military airports are operated by the armed services, but they sometimes use facilities at commercial airports.

Air carrier airports serve various kinds of airlines and are classified by size, with the smaller airports providing service to hub airports at major centers of population. These hub airports in turn offer service to other hub airports or to the large airports at major urban centers. With the deregulation of the U.S. airlines, several have gone out of business, and routes have been taken over by the surviving airlines. A number of U.S. airlines offer service to foreign airports.

In 1991, fewer passenger miles were flown than in the previous year due to the recession of the early 1990s. Scheduled service at smaller airports has increased after an earlier decline. Growth of hub airports follow demographic changes—John Wayne Airport serving Orange County, Calif., is an example.

General aviation airports are classified into basic utility for small airplanes, general utility for larger propeller airplanes, basic transport for small jets, and general transport for larger jets. Special types of general aviation airports are heliports for helicopters, which can land in small areas, including the tops of buildings, and the seaplane bases for seaplanes and amphibians, which can land on both land and water. In later years, short takeoff and landing (STOL) aircraft and vertical takeoff and landing (VTOL) aircraft have been developed. If they should come into widespread use, special airports may be provided for them.

The United States houses over 12,000 airports, most of which are relatively small. Only about 1,000 can be used by aircraft that carry 20 or more passengers. And only slightly over 500 are used by scheduled airlines. Although very few new airports are being built, continuing changes in aircraft and increases in their size, range, speed, and numbers cause existing airports to become obsolete much faster than most other building types. Airports' modernization and replacement, therefore, and the design of a few new ones make airports not only an important building type but one that is interesting and challenging to architects.

**Elements** The major elements of an air carrier airport are air-traffic control and navigational facilities, runway and taxiway systems, ground handling systems, passenger handling systems, and ground transportation systems. Although airport design involves all these systems, the major portions handled by architects are those having to do with passenger handling and ground transportation. The other elements are primarily handled by engineers who specialize in such design.

**AIRPORT** Interior, Centralized Terminal Building, Lambert-St. Louis (1956), with later additions, St. Louis, Mo.
[*Architects: Hellmuth, Yamasaki and Lienweber; additions: Hellmuth, Obata and Kassabaum*]

Sometimes the term *airside* or *fieldside* is used to indicate runways for takeoffs and landings and for other facilities required by the aircraft themselves. The term *landside* is often used for facilities required by passengers and their luggage, freight, and mail. Often engineers design the airside and architects the landside. However, engineers and architects must work closely together if the design of an airport is to be a success. They must also work with the airlines, often called the "carriers," and with those who will operate the airport.

**Design** In the design of an air carrier airport, primary consideration must be given to the relationships between the apron, the terminal, and ground transportation. The apron is the area between the airside, or runway-taxiway, part of the airport and the terminal, the building in which the requirements of passengers and other functions are handled. On the apron, aircraft arrive and depart, load and unload at connections with the ter-

minal called "gates," and here the aircraft are serviced with fuel, passenger meals, and so on. In the terminal, passengers check baggage, purchase tickets, and so on. In the ground transportation area, provisions are made for arriving and departing passengers, sometimes called "deplaning" and "enplaning" passengers, to reach the terminal by automobile, limousine, bus, taxicab, or on foot. Parking lots and sometimes garages are provided for short-term and long-term parking by passengers, visitors, and employees.

At the junction of the apron with the terminal, the gates allow passengers to enplane or deplane, or to board or depart from the aircraft. There are four major methods of providing gates. The simplest, used at small terminals, is the linear method in which the gates are placed on the side of the terminal facing the apron. For larger terminals, piers, sometimes called "fingers," project from the terminal proper, and aircraft are parked along-

**AIRPORT** International Terminal (1993), O'Hare International Airport, Chicago, Ill. *[Architects: Perkins and Will]*

side; the third method uses satellite buildings which are smaller elements located away from the main terminal and connected to it with corridors or concourses. The fourth type, not used to any great extent so far, is the transporter method, which utilizes mobile lounges. In this case, aircraft are parked at some distance from the terminal, and passengers are transported to and from the terminal in vehicles that resemble buses and that can be driven in either direction and have special provisions for connecting to the terminal building and satellite terminals. An example of this type of airport is Dulles International Airport, Chantilly, Va.

**The Terminal** In some air carrier airports, a single terminal building is used by all the airlines. In other airports, there may be a group of terminal buildings, each used by one or more airlines. In any terminal, there are several kinds of space: passenger and public areas; management offices; areas used by the airlines; special facilities such as the control tower, from which aircraft air and ground traffic are directed, a weather station, and, for international airports, customs, health, and immigration services.

In any terminal, an important design problem is the flow of passengers from ground transportation to baggage check-in to ticket counters to the departure lounge at the gate. In recent years, this flow has become even more complicated by the need for security checks to prevent hijacking and other threats. For *deplaning* passengers, the flow is from the lounge at the gate to baggage claim and to ground transportation. In addition, most airports make provisions for many other needs and wishes of passengers and visitors, including rest rooms, newsstands, restaurants, bars and lounges, banks, shops, and in some cases even hotels and motion picture houses. Freight, or air cargo, including mail, is often handled along with passenger luggage at small airports. In larger ones, special provisions must be made, including separate terminals designed specifically for freight. At almost all airports, except the very smallest, hangars are provided for the maintenance of aircraft.

General aviation, whether located at an air carrier airport or at a general aviation airport, utilizes many of the same elements as the air carriers, runways, taxiways, and so on. However, runways are usually shorter and terminal provisions much simpler. For these purposes, an individual or organization called a "fixed base operator" provides flight and weather information, fuel, hangars and tie-down space for aircraft, and maintenance.

Airports, particularly air carrier airports, confront architects and engineers with very complex design problems. Because of the interrelationships among the com-

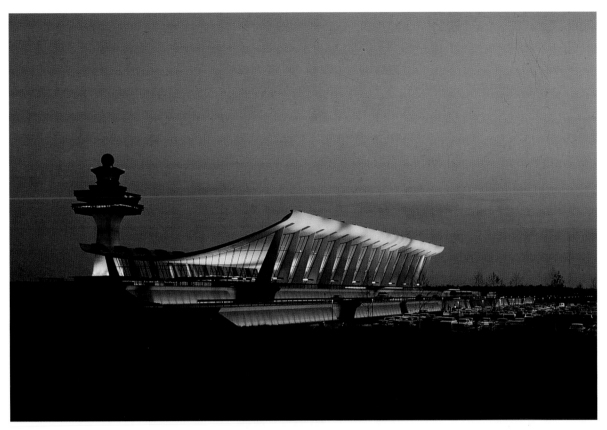

**AIRPORT** Dulles International Airport (1963), Chantilly, Va., near Washington, D.C. *[Architect: Eero Saarinen in association with Ellery Husted]*. The original mobile lounges are being replaced with people movers as part of an expansion (1994). *[Architects: Skidmore, Owings and Merrill]*

plicated requirements of the airlines, management, passengers, and visitors; and the extremely high degree of technological requirements of the aircraft, including servicing, maintenance, and control; the need for safety and security; and the great and growing number of people using airlines; the design of airports has become highly specialized. Most airport design is therefore handled by architects and engineers with the experience, knowledge, and foresight to design facilities that will function properly for the aircraft and the people who will use them some 10 years later, when their construction has been completed.

**History** The history of airports is relatively short, beginning with the work of the Wright brothers, Orville (1871–1948) and Wilbur (1867–1912), that resulted in the first flight on December 17, 1903, at Kitty Hawk, N.C. For many years, airports were pastures or fields level enough for the early airplanes to take off and land. Barns were used as hangars and any gas pump served for refueling. As time went on, improvements were made in the form of dirt (later asphalt and concrete) airstrips and mats. In 1925 the first scheduled airline was started. By that time, there were about 1,000 airports in the United States, most of them quite primitive. By the beginning

of World War II, their number had more than doubled. Today there are more than 12,000 U.S. airports and their number is still growing.

**Related Articles** GARAGE; ROAD AND TRAFFIC DESIGN.

**Further Reading** Horonjeff, Robert M., and F. X. McKelvey: *Planning and Design of Airports*, 3rd ed., McGraw-Hill, New York, 1983; Jahn, Helmut: *Airports*, Birkhauser, Boston, 1991.

**Sources of Additional Information** Air Transport Association of America, 1709 New York Ave., N.W., Washington, D.C. 20006; Aircraft Owners and Pilots Association, 421 Aviation Way, Frederick, Md. 21701.

**ALUMINUM** A lightweight, silvery-colored, nonmagnetic metal used extensively in buildings, in extruded, forged, stamped, rolled, and cast form, for windows, doors, roofing, wall covering, wiring, hardware, and a host of other purposes. Called aluminium in England, Canada, and some other countries, aluminum is one of the most versatile of metals.

**Extraction** Aluminum is a very abundant element, occurring in almost all soils and rocks, but only in compounds, not as a native metal. Bauxite ore, composed primarily of alumina, or aluminum oxide, and other oxides,

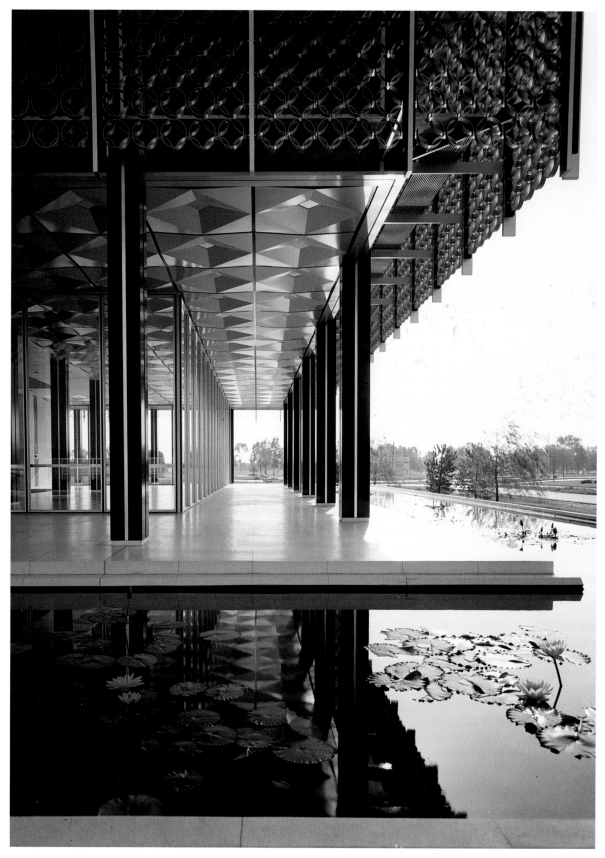

**ALUMINUM** Reynolds Aluminum Building (1959), Detroit, Mich. *[Architect: Minoru Yamasaki]*

is the source of the metal. The separation of aluminum from the other materials in bauxite ore is a two-stage process. In the first stage, bauxite is crushed, mixed with lime, soda ash, and hot water and pumped into digester tanks. There the action of the chemicals and the introduction of steam dissolves the alumina, leaving the other materials as solids, which are filtered out. In a precipitator, the dissolved alumina cools and precipitates into crystals, from which the water is removed in a rotary kiln, leaving pure alumina. During the process the alumina changes into sodium aluminate, aluminum hydrate, and back into alumina.

In the second stage, the alumina is dissolved in cryolite, a compound of sodium, fluorine, and aluminum, in an electrolytic cell, through which current is passed to break down the alumina into carbon dioxide and molten aluminum, which is approximately 99 percent pure. Once started, the second stage is continuous, aluminum being removed periodically and alumina, cryolite, and other materials added. The molten aluminum is siphoned off into large ladles and either poured directly into molds to form pigs weighing 50 pounds each or fluxed, skimmed, and cast into ingots. For most architectural uses, pig or ingot aluminum is remelted and alloyed before further processing into various products.

**Properties** Among the properties of aluminum that make it so important in architecture is its lightness, about one-third that of other common metals, and its easy workability by most methods, including, most importantly, extrusion, a process involving drawing the metal through dies to produce shapes. Other properties include resistance to corrosion through the formation of aluminum oxide on the surface which then resists further deterioration, relatively high conduction of both heat and electricity, and reflection qualities. Aluminum is nonpoisonous and nonflammable, though it does have a relatively low melting point. While pure aluminum is soft and has relatively low strength, both properties may be improved considerably by proper alloying and various metalworking techniques.

Aluminum for use in architecture may be obtained in bars, rods, wire, cable, plate, sheet, foil, pipe, and structural shapes, and in complete products such as nails, rivets, hardware, windows, doors, and many others. Such products may be made by all the major production methods: forging, casting, extrusion, pressing, molding, stamping, cold or hot rolling, and so on. Aluminum may be fastened in many ways such as nailing, riveting, welding, brazing, and soldering, and adhesion with glues or other adhesives.

**Alloys** Aluminum alloys are available in great variety. Among the major metals with which aluminum is alloyed are copper, manganese, silicon, magnesium, and zinc. Among the large number of alloys are types suitable for a host of architectural purposes. Special alloys are available for producing plate, sheet, and other shapes by rolling—forcing hot metal between rollers; others are for extrusion—forcing hot metal through dies; others are made for casting—pouring the molten metal into molds of sand, cast iron, or steel; and still others for forging—utilizing forging presses or hammers to form the metal. The choice of an alloy for a specific architectural purpose is heavily dependent on the forming method to be used.

The choice of an alloy for a specific architectural purpose is also dependent on the function to be served. For example, the alloys used most often for structural members are usually quite different from those used for other purposes. Aluminum structural members are often alloys with copper or with a combination of magnesium and silicon, while hardware is often made of alloys with magnesium alone. Aluminum manufacturers and suppliers furnish information on the various alloys and their uses.

Aluminum is widely used without the addition of finishes, other than various surface textures. Many people find the natural color pleasing and, under most conditions other than near bodies of salt water, the metal is resistant to corrosion. However, aluminum may also be finished with a number of materials, including wax, plastic coating, paint, plating of other metals, and porcelain enamel. By making a selection from the types of finishes available, it is possible to obtain aluminum in plain, textured, highly polished, or matte finishes, exposing the color of the natural metal or in a variety of colors. A most important aluminum finishing method is called anodizing. This is an electrolytic process which builds up a clear protective coating of aluminum oxide on the surface of the metal. The color of anodized aluminum depends on the alloy used and includes a range of grays. Color anodizing produces a range of colors in the aluminum oxide coating by means of dyes or by adding various metals in small quantities.

**Architectural Products** Any list of architectural products made of aluminum would be a very long one. Among the major products are structural members, including beams, tees, angles, channels, zees, and square, rectangular, and round pipe; roofing and siding, including flat, corrugated, and other shapes; roofing, including crimped, shingles, and others; flashing, copings, gravel stops, gutters, and downspouts, or leaders; windows and doors; curtain walls and storefronts; railings, stair treads, and fences; insect screens; ceiling products; movable partitions; heating and air-conditioning ducts; hardware; and others. Such products come in a great variety of sizes, alloys, finishes, and colors. Aluminum is also used for wiring and, in the form of foil, for insulation and vapor barriers and under plastic laminated materials for countertops to make them resistant to heat, including

**ALUMINUM** Detroit Receiving Hospital (1979), Detroit, Mich. *[Architect: William Kessler with Zeidler Roberts partnership]*

damage from cigarettes. Powdered aluminum, actually miniscule flakes, is sometimes used in paints.

Aluminum appeals to architects as a material because of its inherent characteristics and properties and for its versatility. Particularly appealing is the ease of extrusion of the metal, using low-cost dies that make special applications economically feasible that might not be if other metals were used. Also of appeal is the variety of surface textures, as well as the great number of colors, available through color anodizing at relatively low costs.

When selecting products of aluminum, architects and other environmental designers should make sure the proper alloys, forming methods, and finishes are used for the specific purposes intended. Designing special products or usages of aluminum requires considerable knowledge of its properties and characteristics, and those of its alloys, and its fabrication and finishing. When designing structures of aluminum, careful attention must be paid to the properties and characteristics of aluminum that are quite different from those of other structural materials.

**History** Although natural compounds containing aluminum were used for various purposes in ancient times, the metal itself was not separated from the compounds until the 19th century. And aluminum did not make its appearance in architecture until the late 19th century, making it one of the very few really modern building materials. The discovery of aluminum and its later extraction and development was an international effort.

In 1809 the English chemist Sir Humphrey Davy (1778–1829) first demonstrated that alum contained an unknown metal, which he named aluminum. The Danish physicist Hans Christian Oersted (1777–1851) produced the first aluminum powder in 1825. A German chemist, Friedrich Wöhler (1800–82), made the first aluminum particles in 1845 and discovered the properties of the metal, including its light weight. In 1854 a French chemist, Henri Étienne Sainte-Claire Deville (1818–81), developed a method for melting the particles to produce bars of the metal. In the same year a German chemist, Robert Wilhelm Bunsen (1811–99), accomplished the same feat. The new metal was then more costly than gold. Emperor Napoleon III (1808–73) of France had a set of aluminum tableware made for his most honored guests; his less important guests dined with gold and silver tableware.

In 1884 the first aluminum to be used in architecture was the 6-pound cap of the Washington Monument, Washington, D.C., designed by Robert Mills (1781–1855). The price of aluminum had come down from that of the time of Napoleon III, when it was about $550 per pound, to about $12, which was still too expensive for most uses. In 1886 the twenty-two-year-old American chemist Charles Martin Hall and the French metallurgist Paul Louis Toussaint Héroult independently developed methods for the electrolytic production of aluminum, the basis of the methods still used today. Within six years, the price per pound had dropped to about 60 cents, and the future of aluminum as a material for architectural and other purposes was ensured.

The major uses of aluminum in the early 20th century were for such purposes as cooking pots and pans and other small utensils and devices. The first structural uses were in dirigibles and these were followed by widespread uses in the aircraft industry. By the beginning of the second quarter of the 20th century, aluminum began to be used in buildings, on a somewhat tentative basis at first. As time went by, its use spread rapidly, not only to a great number of architectural elements, including curtain walls, but also to many other industries, including aircraft, automobiles, bridges, and others. Today aluminum is used in many ways in architecture and has become one of the most important materials.

**Related Articles** Various articles on structures, components, and systems in architecture.

**Further Reading** Hornbostel, Caleb: *Construction Materials—Types, Uses and Applications,* 2d ed., John Wiley, New York, 1991.

**Sources of Additional Information** Aluminum Assoc., 900 19th St. N.W., Suite 300, Washington, D.C. 20006; Architectural Aluminum Manufacturers Assoc., 2700 River Road, Suite 118, Des Plaines, Ill. 60018.

**APARTMENT** Originally a dwelling room, now usually a group of rooms used as a dwelling, or an apartment building or apartment house which contains a number of such groups of rooms. Apartment buildings assumed importance in the United States as cities became more crowded, causing land values to increase and available land to decrease. Apartment buildings are enjoying increasing acceptance by those who choose to live in close proximity to other people, shops and stores, and often jobs and recreational facilities, with relative safety and ease of maintenance. An apartment often provides increased living space and more amenities than a single-family house that costs the same amount of money. Because of their popularity and increasing numbers in suburbs as well as in urban areas, apartment buildings have become one of the major building types in architecture today.

**Types** There are several different kinds of apartment buildings. A garden apartment, usually found in the suburbs and one to three stories in height, is an apartment building in which some or all of the individual units have private gardens of limited size or share an outdoor garden area. In some cases, each garden apartment unit occupies only a single floor, but in others the units have two stories. When similar apartment buildings are located in more highly populated areas, as in cities, they are frequently called townhouses.

Often the terms *high-rise* and *low-rise*, and sometimes *medium-rise*, are applied to apartment buildings. There is little agreement about the exact definition of these terms. However, it is generally accepted that any apartment over three, or possibly four, stories in height must be served by elevators, while the lower buildings may be walk-up apartments. If low-rise apartments are defined as walk-ups, perhaps medium-rise might mean those from about five to nine stories; and high-rise, those more than nine. If an apartment building requires elevators, its design and construction will differ markedly from those that only require stairs.

An apartment hotel combines some of the qualities of both hotels and apartments. For example, it might have more or fewer permanent residents as in an apartment, but might provide public spaces for dining and other purposes and maid and maintenance service as in a hotel.

Formerly, all apartments were rented or leased by the occupants. Such apartment units are available furnished, with all major pieces of furniture and furnishings provided and sometimes with such things as dishes and linen. Unfurnished apartments usually have only the major kitchen equipment, the remainder of the furniture and furnishings to be supplied by the occupants. In later years, there has been a growing tendency toward ownership of some apartments by their occupants. Occupant-owned apartments may be condominiums or cooperatives.

**Ownership** A condominium is an apartment building, in which the occupants own their own individual apartment units and share ownership with all other occupants of common areas, such as halls, elevators, swimming pool, outside areas, and so on. In a condominium, the maintenance and upkeep of these common areas and of the overall building are usually performed by people who handle the work for the benefit of all occupants, who pay a fee for these services. In some cases, the occupants also pay an additional fee for which they receive janitorial, maintenance, and other services within their apartments.

In a cooperative, the occupants share ownership in the entire apartment building, but do not own their individual apartment units, leasing their units from the cooperative in which they are stockholders. As in a con-

**APARTMENT** Dakota Apartments (1884), New York, N.Y. *[Architect: Henry J. Hardenbergh]*

dominium, cooperative apartment occupants usually pay a fee for upkeep, maintenance, and so on. Also property taxes are paid on the entire building and prorated among the owners.

The most obvious advantage of both condominiums and cooperatives is that of ownership as opposed to renting. With this comes the advantages that other homeowners have of acquiring equity and various tax advantages. Since cooperatives and condominiums are generally nonprofit, their occupant-owners can ordinarily afford nicer apartments than they might in a rental apartment building.

**Unit Variations** Apartment units vary considerably in size, number of rooms, and degree of luxury. The smallest, an efficiency apartment, has a single major room for living, dining, and sleeping; a kitchen; and a bathroom. Larger apartments, like single-family houses, may have any number of rooms, large or small. Apartments of all sizes may range from somewhat simple, utilitarian types to the utmost in luxury, with costs and rentals reflecting the various degrees between. Apartment units may occupy one floor, two floors, or sometimes more. If a unit occupies two floors, it is called a duplex apartment, not to be confused with a duplex house, which means a double house for two families. If

the apartment unit occupies three floors, it is called a triplex.

**Building Complexes** At one time, the most usual apartment development consisted of a single building placed on a single site. Such a building might contain a few individual units or hundreds. Of increasing importance are complexes consisting of two or more apartment buildings on one site, with landscaped areas, automobile parking spaces, and sometimes recreational facilities, such as swimming pools and tennis courts, shared between them. In some cases, the development goes much further, providing on a single site a shopping center, a motion picture house, and other amenities. A further development is the multiuse center which not only contains elements of this kind but also may provide hotel or motel facilities, a convention center, and offices. In most cases, this multiplicity of usage is provided in a group of buildings, designed and constructed in such a way as to complement each other. In some cases, though, many of these uses may be combined into a single high-rise building.

In the last few years, another method for providing housing has been the planned unit development. Such developments provide open spaces, recreation facilities, churches, schools, and shops, as well as dwellings, for a

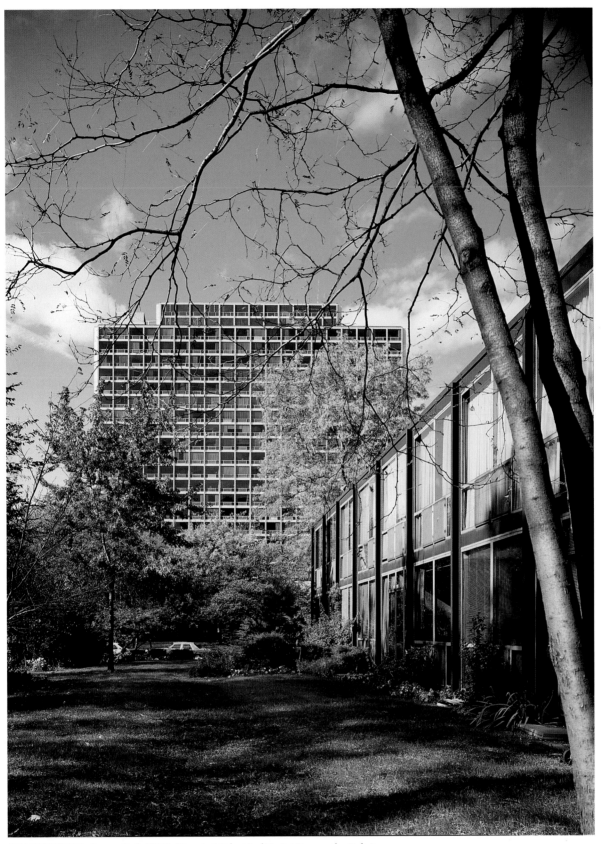

**APARTMENT** Lafayette Park (1959), Detroit, Mich. *[Architect: Mies van der Rohe]*

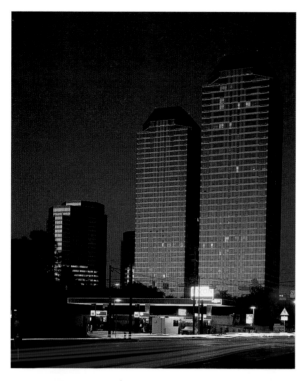

**APARTMENT** Four Leaf Towers (1979), Houston, Tex. *[Architect: Cesar Pelli & Assoc.]*

relatively large number of families. A typical planned unit development might include multifamily residences, such as high-rise apartments and townhouses as well as single-family and two-family homes.

**Elements** The planning of apartment buildings involves three major elements: private areas, public areas, and administration-service areas. The private areas are the apartment units. These ordinarily contain rooms or spaces, as in a single-family house, for sleeping, dining, food preparation, and so on. The public area includes the lobby or vestibule, stairs and elevators, corridors, parking facilities, and sometimes a mailroom. Also often included are other shared facilities, such as laundry rooms, bulk storage for tenants, recreational facilities, and community rooms for games and dining. There may be shops and service establishments in the building. The administration-service area includes office space for the management, storage rooms, and space for mechanical equipment and sometimes maintenance shops.

**American Development** In colonial America, land was plentiful and inexpensive, and most people lived in single-family houses. As land became less available and more expensive, construction of apartments began, first in New York City in the mid-19th century and later in

**APARTMENT** Greenway Gables (1981), Loring Park, Minneapolis, Minn. *[Architects: Frederick Bentz/Milo Thompson/Robert Rietow]*

other large cities. Prior to about 1870, these buildings were tenements, which originally simply meant apartments but which came to mean buildings for housing great numbers of poor families in large cities. Often shabbily built, overcrowded, unsafe, and unsanitary, the tenements were not desirable places to live. The conditions of the tenements and their eventual deterioration into slums slowed the development of more suitable forms of multiple housing for many years.

In spite of the bad reputation of tenements, the continuing growth of city populations gradually led to construction of better apartment buildings, beginning about 1875 in New York City and a few years later in Chicago. The evolution of the modern apartment had begun. Technological developments, including steel-framed structural systems, electric lighting, and greatly improved elevators, helped speed the evolution. Better planning of apartment buildings and individual apartment units soon followed. Early in the 20th century, passage of laws protecting the safety and health of apartment dwellers gave a tremendous boost to the development of apartments. This led to a great boom in apartment construction in larger cities after 1921, a boom that spread to the smaller cities and towns and then to the suburbs. In most urban areas today, single-family houses have largely been supplanted by apartments. And apartment living has come to be very acceptable, even desirable, for a large number of people. With the continuing scarcity and high cost of land, the trend can be expected to continue.

**Related Articles** HOUSE; HOUSING.

**Further Reading** Nolan, John and Duo Dickinson: *Common Walls, Private Homes; Multiresidential Design,* McGraw-Hill, New York, 1990; Macsai, John, Eugene P. Holland, Harry S. Nachman, and Julius Y. Yacker: *Housing,* 2d ed., John Wiley, New York, 1982.

**ARCH** A structural element that usually supports the weight of a building or other structure above a door, window, or other opening in a wall. Originally, arches were constructed from a number of small wedge-shaped masonry units, of brick, stone, or tile called *voussoirs,* set in such a way as to form an opening that curved upward from the sides. Curved arches may take many forms, including semicircle, horseshoe, and lancet (pointed). Arches may also be flat.

Masonry arches derive their strength by transferring weight, or thrust, laterally from unit to unit starting at

**ARCH** Chicago Stock Exchange (1893), detail, Art Institute of Chicago, Chicago, Ill. *[Architect: Louis Sullivan]*

**ARCH** Tunnel between Detroit Receiving and Harper Hospitals (1978), Detroit, Mich. *[Architect: William Kessler and Assoc.]*

the crown in the top unit, the keystone, down the sides or haunches to the bottom of the arch to what is called the spring line. At the spring line, the weight, or thrust, is transferred from the arch to a wall or other structural element. This may be a pier, which is a heavy type of column designed to take the thrust. The pier may be assisted in this by a buttress, another structural element placed to help take the thrust. An arcade is a line of arches resting on columns, arranged so that the thrust at the bottom of each arch is resisted by the thrust from the arches on either side.

**Elements of an Arch** The rise of an arch is the height from the springer to the keystone and the span is the width between springers. An archivolt is an ornamental molding on the face of an arch, and an extrados is the line or surface of the exterior of an arch at the outside edge of the units or voussoirs. This is the line which the archivolt follows. An intrados is the line or surface at the interior of an arch at the inside edge of the voussoirs. A springer, or skewback, is the unit at the bottom of the side of an arch.

Today arches are also made of wood, steel, space frames, and reinforced concrete, utilizing many of the same principles but with the lateral thrust at the spring line reduced to a minimum so that heavy piers or buttresses are not required.

**History** The principles of the arch were discovered in Mesopotamia at least 6,000 years ago. The ancient Babylonians and Egyptians used arches, as did the Greeks. The Romans developed arch design to a high level, especially in the semicircular form. In the Gothic architecture of the Middle Ages, the pointed arch was widely used and highly developed. In Renaissance buildings, there was a return to the round form.

**ARCH** Components of masonry segmental types.

ARCH Masonry types.

**American Development** The Spanish began using masonry, including arches, in St. Augustine in 1565. Early in the 17th century, perhaps as early as 1610 at Jamestown, the manufacture of brick in the English colonies in America began, and stone quarrying soon followed. The masonry arch then followed and has been an important structural element of American architecture ever since. At first, masonry buildings and arches were relatively uncommon in the colonies. Later the use of stone and brick became widespread not only for large, important buildings but also for houses. Today arches of masonry are still used in buildings, but arches of the newer materials of laminated wood, steel, space frames, and reinforced concrete are more prevalent.

**Related Articles** BRICK; CONCRETE: DOME; MASONRY STRUCTURE; STONE; TILE; VAULT; WOOD.

**ARCHITECTURE** A profession in the same sense as engineering, law, or accounting. Architecture differs from other professions in that it is directed more to client service than to business. Law is perhaps closest in this regard. Engineering is more regulated by codified scientific data and legal regulations and is more business centered. Accounting would be heavily dependent on standard accounting rules and is most business oriented. A definition of a profession is one which requires licensing under state law. The justification for such requirements is based on the states' responsibility for public health, safety, and welfare.

Architects normally receive their education at schools of architecture associated with universities, which offer programs resulting in a variety of degrees. After several years of experience working with professionals, the individual is eligible to take licensing exams which must be successfully completed before the title of architect may be used. Historically, some individuals have been licensed solely on the basis of extensive experience.

The architect provides expert knowledge in design and construction. This problem-solving attribute is a service rather than goods or products. Architecture requires technical knowledge, good judgment, and artistic ability. All professionals require successful relationships with people and information.

**History** The history of the architectural profession can be traced to early beginnings in ancient Egypt and Greece. The attributions of expert knowledge and creative talent have been consistent throughout history. Egyptian architects could have great power in the society, but Greek architects were less highly placed. Architecture is inseparable from the act of building, and the complexity of ancient monuments reflects the quality of architectural design. The ancient Egyptian temples and tombs and the Greek temples remain high points of architectural history. One of the earliest surviving books on architecture is *The Ten Books on Architecture* by Marcus Vitruvius Pollio, known as Vitruvius, about 25 B.C. in Rome. This book is still read, and translations remain in print.

During the medieval period, the church was client for most major building, employing artisans and master craftspeople. In the Renaissance, architects such as Brunelleschi and Palladio began to separate design from construction. The increased technical knowledge required to build great structural spaces such as the dome of St. Peter's in Rome required a broad education.

The term *profession* came into use during the 16th century. The initial professions were law, medicine, the clergy, and perhaps the military. Architecture, along with dentistry, civil engineering, and accounting were established professions soon after. The ties of these professions with the universities tended to restrict them to the higher level of society. Those interested in using architects were the wealthy landowners, the church, and state.

In America, architects were closely tied to British examples in the east and Spanish influences in the west. Later the French École des Beaux Arts became a major influence. Architects were trained by apprenticeship to other architects. In the 1850s, the American architects Richard Morris Hunt and H. H. Richardson opened ateliers for educating architects based on their experiences at the École des Beaux Arts. The American Institute of Architects was founded in 1857, and the first architecture school started in 1865 at the Massachusetts Institute of Technology. The first requirement for licensing was adopted by Illinois in 1897. Since 1951 architects have been licensed in all 50 states.

**Influences** The profession of architecture is continually evolving. Clients are becoming more knowledgeable about building and require more specialized services.

Rehabilitation and remodeling of existing buildings have been an increasing part of construction in contrast to new construction. The press is increasingly addressing the architect's work, reflecting public interest in the profession. Public awareness has brought a greater involvement of the public in decisions on the built environment. Increased professional liability has affected all professions as the public increasingly expects services to be performed without error.

**Response** The architectural profession has responded to societal changes by increased specialization of practice, collaboration of design professionals with others of the building team, increased attention to the management of firms, and a greater diversity of firms offering specialized services. Opposed to this tendency is the perception that small general firms are more likely to provide innovation in architecture. In an attempt to improve compensation, more architects are seeking profitability. Demonstrating the value of their services to the client and better firm management have improved income. There is evidence to indicate that architects' incomes are about one-half that of lawyers and one-quarter that of physicians.

The profession is growing, exceeding the growth of other professions. Competition for jobs will increase as the graduates of architecture enter the job market. This growth in the profession is affected by economic cycles but still exceeds the level of construction, implying a growth in related services.

**The Profession** The unique aspect of architecture compared with other professions is its relationship to the arts and to the creativity central to design. This importance of design is close to the center of architecture and is reflected in the fact that many practitioners feel architecture is a calling rather than a business.

Some studies indicate that architecture ranks high in terms of prestige but lags other professions in years of education, income, and proportion of members belonging to professional societies. Architecture, once a purview of the wealthy, has become a service to a wider spectrum of the population. Further changes in the profession can be envisioned with the increasing number of women and minorities entering the field.

The health of the profession is closely tied to the economic well-being of the construction industry. Periods of economic downturn have been difficult to manage and contrast with periods of growth. Since years of great growth early in the century, construction has declined proportionally to the national economy. Growth of the architectural profession has exceeded the growth of construction, indicating new roles and markets for services. Specialization means that more professionals are involved in the building team. The profession tends to organize in divisions of support personnel, administra-

tors, and leaders. The support personnel would include drafters and junior design and production people. The administrators include the principals and senior designers and project managers, and leadership can refer to the famous architects whose work often establishes precedents for others. Also the leadership category might include educators, critics, and theorists of design.

The firms with large numbers of employees earn the greatest share of professional fees. This group represents less than 20 percent of architectural firms, as contrasted with the majority of smaller, less financially rewarding practices. The larger firms organize in a series of specializations, with complex organizational structures. This stratification of personnel causes tensions within the firms, but the most successful are able to give adequate attention to the varying interests of their employees.

As with all professions, the architect is educated in the universities by others in the profession. There is a public expectation of professional expertise. The architectural programs in the universities are accredited by the National Architectural Accreditation Board (NAAB), with visiting teams taken from the membership of related organizations including the American Institute of Architects (AIA), the American Institute of Architecture Students (AIAS), and the National Council of Architectural Registration Boards (NCARB).

As with other professions, architects are increasingly expected to continue in further study. This continuing education emphasis will take on increasing importance in the maintenance of licenses to practice.

Licensing of architects is controlled by the states or territories of the United States under their constitutional authority to protect the public health, safety, and welfare. All states have established statutes and administration governing the licensing process. The profession of architecture has an obligation to contribute active participation in the establishment of standards and in evaluating candidates for licensing.

Before applying for admittance to the licensing exam, the candidate must complete a period of practical training. Historically informal, this process has been largely replaced by the Intern Architect Development Program (IDP) developed by the AIA and NCARB.

The licensing exam is developed by NCARB and is administered by the states. The exam is in several parts and is taken over a period of several days. The broad scope of the exam is to establish basic competence, and each candidate must pass all sections of the exam. Because of the wide acceptance of standardized testing, an architect licensed in one state may apply for licensing in other states.

Most states require that building projects of even moderate size require licensed architects. Architects have major roles in setting and administering licensing standards. Professional conduct is monitored by the states under regulations governing professional conduct. The courts through the years have defined the professional's responsibilities to the public.

Architects may be called to be expert witnesses in legal proceedings to assist in defining the architect's reasonable standard of care applicable in a particular situation.

The profession of architecture will continue to respond to changes in society. In certain periods, the public's desire to influence professionals has increased the rate of change in the profession. The late 1960s and 1970s was such a period of public participation, and many regulatory boards now have positions for public members.

**Related Articles** Various articles focus on major aspects of architecture and of the profession and practice of architecture. Several historical articles trace the history of architecture in America, and many articles on other subjects contain historical information. Articles are also included on the lives of notable American architects. The functions of architects are discussed in articles on various phases; see, for example, articles entitled design, architectural; programming; specification; working drawing. A number of articles are included on other aspects of architecture; for example,

see computer; drafting; model making; rendering. See also articles entitled career; education; engineering; landscape architecture; planning, city. Various articles cover the important materials, equipment, and systems used in architecture.

**Further Reading** *Architects Handbook of Professional Practice*, latest edition, American Institute of Architects, Washington, D.C.

**Periodicals** *Architecture*, 1515 Broadway, New York, N.Y. 10036; *Architectural Record*, 1221 Avenue of the Americas, New York, N.Y. 10020; *Progressive Architecture*, 600 Summer Street, Stamford, Conn. 06904.

**Source of Additional Information** The American Institute of Architects, 1735 New York Avenue, N.W., Washington, D.C. 20006.

**ART IN ARCHITECTURE** Paintings, sculpture, and other art forms enhance the aesthetic effect of architecture. From the time prehistoric humans first decorated the walls of caves, art has been an integral and important aspect of architecture.

The fine arts are often defined as painting, drawing, sculpture, and architecture and sometimes include poetry, music, dance, and drama. While the latter four arts are often enjoyed in or near buildings, art in architecture

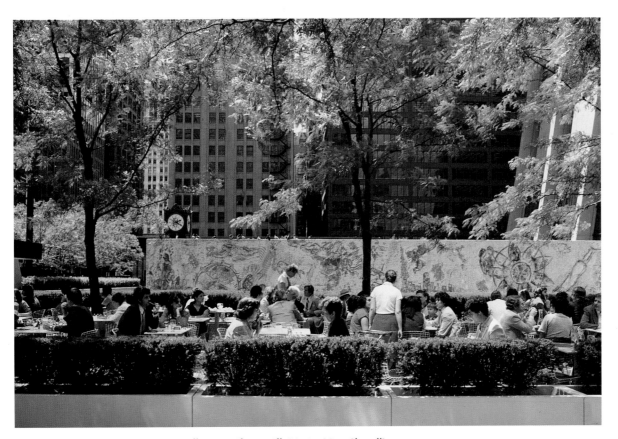

**ART IN ARCHITECTURE** Mosaic Wall (1974), Chicago, Ill. *[Artist: Marc Chagall]*

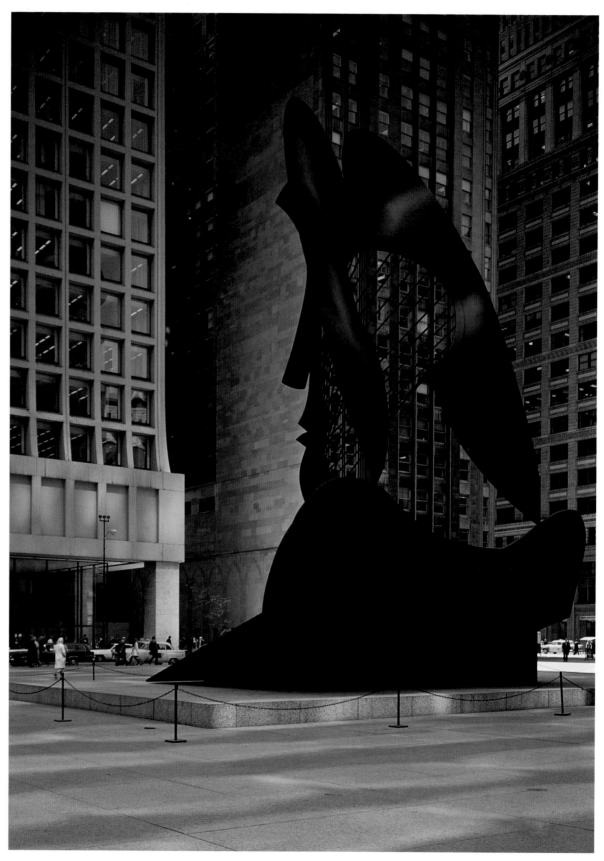

**ART IN ARCHITECTURE** Head of a Woman (1967), Chicago, Ill. *[Artist: Pablo Picasso]*

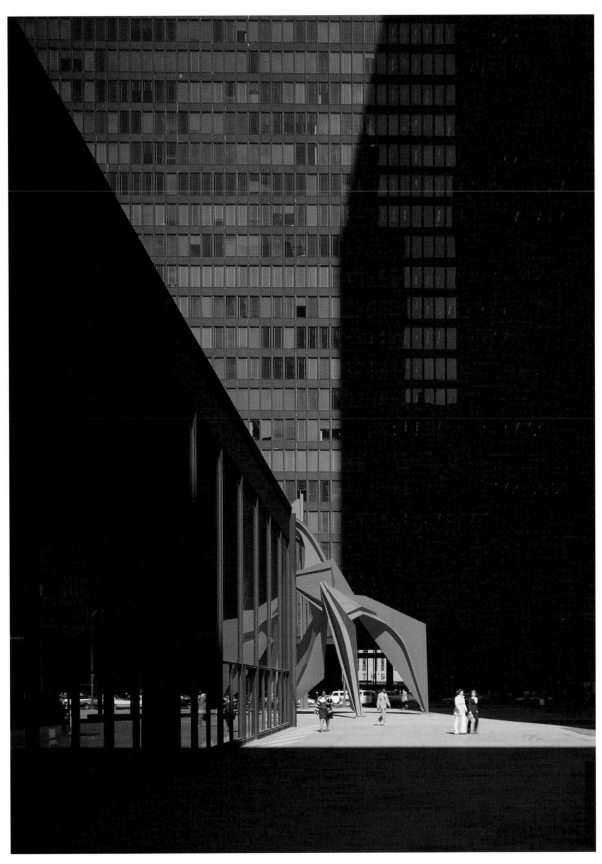

**ART IN ARCHITECTURE** Stabile (1969), Chicago Government Center, Chicago, Ill. *[Sculptor: Alexander Calder]*

usually means the visual arts, mainly painting and sculpture, but often includes such useful arts as furniture, furnishing, and industrial design.

**Types** Art in architecture, fine arts and others, can be classified into four major types: those that are attached to and are, to an extent, integral with buildings, for example, walls with murals or carvings; independent artworks placed in buildings, for example, paintings on canvas or freestanding sculpture; architectural ornament, which is integral with buildings; and architecture itself as sculptural or other art forms.

Art in architecture may be attached to, located in or on, or integrated with every conceivable architectural element, including walls, floors, ceilings, fireplaces, chimneys, grilles or screens, doors, windows, towers, and exteriors of buildings and their sites. Other elements of architecture, such as landscaping, furniture and furnishings, lighting, fabrics, and graphic arts, may be used in conjunction with art in architecture and, in some cases, may be works of art in themselves. Works of art today may be created in almost every conceivable material and combination of materials: aluminum, brass, brick, bronze, ceramics, concrete, copper, glass, iron, plastics, stainless and other types of steel, stone, terracotta, terrazzo, tile, and wood. Some artists have gone even further, working with light or with sand or soil.

Among the major types of art intended to enhance architecture and sculpture—freestanding, integrated into walls and other elements, relief carving and engraving, constructions, and mobiles; painting, both independent paintings and those on walls—murals and frescoes; stained glass; mosaics of tile, glass, and other materials; and various structures, including the buildings themselves or such elements as bell towers, fountains, and reflecting pools. In many cases, artists work with mixed media, for example, a combination of painting and sculpture; and in others they combine major elements to produce a complete work of art, such as sculpture in conjunction with a fountain.

**Acquisition** Artworks for placement or integration into architecture may be acquired in two ways: direct purchase of existing works or commission of new works made especially for specific buildings. In either case, the art to be acquired must meet certain standards of taste, economics, and function. Taste in art varies as much as it does in architecture. Therefore, art forms that please an owner may not please the architect. Decisions on such matters are not always easy and must be handled with tact and diplomacy. Sometimes the architect and owner defer such decisions to museum directors or art professors, or they may be asked to aid in directions.

In any case, artworks should be compatible with the buildings in which they will be located; architectural settings must be appropriate; the medium or media must be correct. In addition, a work of art should serve a purpose as an important, strong focal point in a building, a somewhat incidental ornament, or any other. Although not all would agree, many would consider the most important attribute to be that the art should exist in harmony with the architecture, enhancing it rather than competing with it.

The economics of art in architecture are also important. Works of art, especially those by established dead or living artists, can be very expensive. Complete understanding on this subject between owners and architects is essential. While works of art may be profitable in financial investments, the first consideration should be the pleasure and fulfillment that can come from art. However, from an owner's point of view, the financial investment may be of considerable importance. Works of lesser known, often younger, artists may well fulfill the purposes of art in architecture at relatively low costs. It should also be remembered that works of art may be imported from foreign countries, under the proper circumstances, without payment of import duties.

Should the decision be made to acquire the art by direct purchase, additional factors should be taken into consideration. Existing works are ordinarily for sale in any of the media mentioned above, with the exception of those that are integrated directly into the architecture of the building, such as wall carvings or murals. In addition, one may purchase drawings or original prints, such as etchings, lithographs, wood engravings, woodcuts, engravings, or silk-screen prints (serigraphs). Original prints, as distinguished from reproductions, are conceived and executed by artists in limited quantities, after which the etching plates, lithograph stones, silk screens, and so on are defaced or destroyed.

In purchasing works of art, consideration should also be given to the intended locations in buildings and to whether the locations will be permanent or temporary. Some architects and owners prefer to rotate works of art, displaying them for a time and then replacing them with others. Some art museums and other institutions lend or rent works of art, thus making it possible to show and rotate examples in buildings, without making an actual purchase. Some also offer lease-purchase plans, in which rental fees may later be applied to purchases. In the purchase of artworks, the integrity of art dealers or other sources is of utmost importance. Thus not only the works of art but the reputation of the dealer should be acceptable. Certificates of authenticity should be required, signed by experts who guarantee the works.

When works of art are specifically commissioned for buildings, additional considerations must be made. First, there should be complete understanding between owners and architects on the works to be commissioned, artists to be selected, and costs of the artworks. Artists may be

**ART IN ARCHITECTURE** Interior "Garden Game" (1984), Lake Cook Office Center, Chicago, near Northbrook, Ill. [*Fabric sculptor: Gerhardt Knodel*]

selected directly by the architect or owner; by the two together, by an art committee that might include the owner, architect, and experts from museums, universities, or other institutions; or by competitions, in which a few artists are asked to submit conceptual drawings or models. In competitions, it is customary to pay fees to the artists for their submissions. The winners may be required to apply the fees toward the total cost of the works.

In addition to the quality of work, an artist should be selected for compatibility, competence, and dependability. The artist must be expected to perform properly and, most importantly, must work smoothly and creatively with the architect. However, it would be self-defeating if an adequate degree of creative freedom were not granted the artist.

Firm agreements should be reached at the beginning, regarding location, size, materials, scale, cost, and schedule for completion of the artwork. In addition, agreements should be reached on detailed specifications for the work; submissions by the artist of preliminary models or sketches; their approval by the owner and architect; and periodic visits to the artist's studio by the archi-

tect to determine progress and problems and to aid the artist in the work and arrangements for installation of the art in the building. Guarantees should be required, often for two years, of the permanence of the materials and other factors. All the factors listed and any others that apply in individual cases should be made part of written agreements between owners and artists.

Architects sometimes design works of art that are to be executed by others or, in a few cases, by the architects themselves. In all cases, architects must provide the proper physical environment for works of art, which are often affected, sometimes extremely, by humidity, ventilation, temperature, light, and other conditions. In some cases, as in weathering steel or bronze sculptures, the gradual change in the surface or the acquiring of patina are normal and expected. In other cases, the conditions in which a work of art exists can cause it to deteriorate or eventually to be destroyed. The requirements for each work of art in architecture must be individually determined and provided for.

**History** The earliest known art forms are from the Paleolithic or Old Stone Age, about 20,000 B.C. These are

25

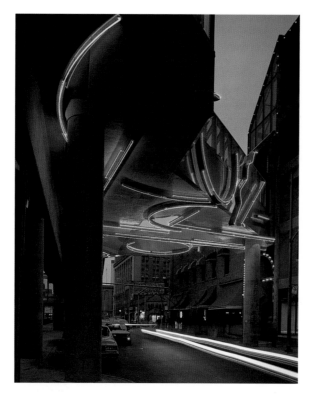

**ART IN ARCHITECTURE** People mover (1987), Greektown Station, Detroit, Mich. [*Artist: Stephen Antonakos*]

common stone tools into which ornament was chipped by hand. The earliest known art in architecture, dating from about five centuries later, is found in various European caves. Both the tools and the cave art show a sophistication indicating that they evolved from earlier and more primitive efforts.

In the caves, art of about 15,000–10,000 B.C. includes the marvelous cave paintings at Altamira, Spain, and Lascaux, France; the rock carvings at La Magdeleine Cave, Penne, France; and the rock engravings in the Cave of Addaura, Monte Pellegrino, Palermo, Italy. Not very much is known about art in architecture in the New Stone, or Neolithic, Age, which began about 8000 B.C., because by that time humans had begun to build tents and huts, none of which has survived. However, some of their other art forms, such as tools, have survived.

In ancient Egypt, Mesopotamia, and other parts of the Middle East and Mediterranean area, beginning sometime between 5000 and 4000 B.C., more permanent buildings were constructed and ornamented with various art forms. These included wall paintings, now known as mural paintings or murals; freestanding sculpture; sculpture on walls, either with raised figures or in intaglio, incised into the wall surfaces; and engaged sculpture, in which figures are almost freestanding but are partly attached to walls or other architectural ele-

ments. The sculpture of these cultures was mostly in stone and many examples have survived.

Wall paintings were usually on stone and some of these also still exist. Another form of art in architecture of the era was the use of sculptural ornament on columns, both freestanding and attached to buildings or engaged, and on their tops or capitals, and for other architectural elements of buildings, thus beginning a tradition that has persisted almost until the present time. In addition, other types of art were integrated into the buildings, including sculptured walls of glazed brick, copper sculptures, and mosaics, ornamental areas made by arranging small pieces of stones or tile or other material to form decorative patterns.

**Early Art Forms** The names of the artists who created the great variety of art forms in architecture of these early times are unknown. So many great examples of their work have survived that only a few can be mentioned here: in Egypt—the temples of Karnak (*c.* 1500–300 B.C.) and Luxor (*c.* 1400–1300 B.C.) at Thebes, Queen Hatshepsut (*c.* 1500 B.C.) at Deir el-Bahari, Abu Simbel (*c.* 1300 B.C.) and Edfu (*c.* 300 B.C.); in Assyria—the city of Khorsabad (705 B.C.), Iraq, including the Temple of King Sargon II (722–705 B.C.); in Crete—the Palace of King Minos (*c.* 1600 B.C.), Knossos. Many art objects that were originally parts of ancient buildings and also others have been removed from their original sites and are now in museums around the world. For example, the great sculptured brick walls of the Ishtar Gate (*c.* 575 B.C.), originally in Babylon of King Nebuchadnezzar II (605–563 B.C.), were removed to the State Museum of Berlin, Germany, where they were restored and reconstructed.

The ancient Greeks performed prodigious feats in the incorporation of art, particularly sculpture, into their buildings. Some of the sculptures were free standing; others are integral parts of the buildings they adorn. The Greeks were particularly fond of ornamenting certain parts of their buildings with sculpture, believed to have been originally painted in bright colors. They ornamented the tops, or capitals, of columns with stylized sculpture; the triangular gable ends, or pediments, with sculptured groups; the portions of buildings between the tops of columns and the undersides of roofs, or friezes; and other parts of their buildings. An interesting Greek form employed sculptured female figures, called caryatids, as columns to support the roofs in certain buildings. It is known that the Greeks employed wall paintings in buildings, but none has survived.

The great surviving examples of Greek art in architecture would make a very long list. Some of the most important are the buildings on the Acropolis, Athens, including the Parthenon (*c.* 432 B.C.), by the architects Iktinus and Kallikrates (both 5th century B.C.); the

Propylaea (*c.* 432 B.C.) by Mnesicles (5th century B.C.), who also designed the Erechtheion (*c.* 405 B.C.), together with the caryatids of its Porch of Maidens; and the little Temple of Athena Nike (*c.* 427 B.C.), probably by Callicrates.

It is thought that the incomparable sculptor Phidias (*c.* 500–432 B.C.) created a great sculpture of Athena that was placed in the center of the Parthenon and another Athena nearby and that he may have contributed to the sculptures of the friezes and pediments of the Parthenon. The *Athena* sculptures disappeared long ago, and no other works by Phidias are known to exist. This was almost the fate of a later great sculptor, Praxiteles (*c.* 370–330 B.C.); only a few of his works still exist, including *Hermes*, at Olympia, where it was found.

It is a wonder that anything remains of the buildings on the Acropolis, when it is remembered that the Persians tried to destroy it in 480 B.C., that the Parthenon was converted first into a Byzantine and then into a Roman Catholic church and finally into a mosque by the Turks, who came close to destroying it when gunpowder stored in it exploded in 1687. And then in 1803, Englishman Thomas Bruce, Lord Elgin (1766–1841), removed much of the remaining sculpture from the Parthenon and shipped it to the British Museum, London, where today it remains as a spectacular exhibit called the Elgin marbles.

The Etruscans (forerunners of the Romans) used art in architecture, including wall painting, wood carving, and sculptured terra-cotta. The best-preserved examples are at Tarquinia, Italy, where the *Tomb of Hunting and Fishing* (*c.* 520 B.C.) wall paintings are thought by some authorities to be similar to the lost ones of the Greeks.

The Romans continued the use of art in architecture, though much of it was derived from the Greeks who are better known for artistic ability than are the Romans. The Romans ornamented the capitals of columns and other elements of buildings, placing on them sculptures of various sorts, including friezes, mosaics, and wall paintings or murals. They also further developed sculptured plaster, which had been used to some extent by earlier cultures. The Romans are believed to have developed true fresco painting, a method in which the paints are applied to wet, lime-plastered walls. Other types of fresco painting, utilizing dry plaster with binders to make paint adhere to it, had been used in more ancient cultures. Many of the Roman works of art were by Greek artists, but their work is not the equal of that of earlier times. The Romans erected many monuments and memorials, which appeared everywhere in honor of almost every historical event and included columns, obelisks, and triumphal arches. Most of these were highly decorated with sculpture and other ornamental forms.

Many examples of Roman art in architecture have survived, including some triumphal arches and other monuments. Among the most notable examples in Rome are the Arch of Titus (A.D. 82), the Column of Trajan (A.D. 113), the Column of Marcus Aurelius (A.D. 174), and the Arch of Constantine (A.D. 312), all erected to memorialize Roman emperors. The most striking examples of Roman wall paintings are in the ancient cities of Pompeii and Herculaneum, buried by an eruption of Mount Vesuvius in A.D. 79, and preserved under the cinders and ashes until their rediscovery in the 18th century. Many examples of Roman sculpture have also been preserved there.

Art in architecture continued to be used in Early Christian and Byzantine churches, and included wall and ceiling paintings, mosaics, ornamented architectural elements, sculpture, frescoes, and encaustic, a painting method utilizing a binder of wax or wax and resin to make the paint adhere. Although used earlier in the Orient, bits of colored glass were used, in Early Christian and Byzantine churches, for the first time in Europe, becoming the forerunner of the great stained-glass windows. Among the important buildings containing art of the times are the Byzantine churches of Santa Sophia (536), also called Hagia Sophia, in Istanbul, and San Marco (1085, with later additions), Venice.

**Middle Ages** At the beginning of the Middle Ages, Romanesque architecture laid the groundwork for the great development of art in architecture that came to fruition in the Gothic style, particularly in monumental sculpture, mostly in stone. Other types of art in both eras were bronzes in sculptures, sculptured doors, other architectural elements, and stained glass, which was developed to a very high point. Much of the great Romanesque and Gothic art in architecture was of a religious nature, and appeared mostly in and on the great churches and cathedrals of the time.

While a list of the best examples would be very long indeed, some must be mentioned. Among the most notable churches and cathedrals are: in France—Abbaye-aux-Hommes (1086), Caen; Notre Dame de Paris (1163–1250); Saint Madeleine (1206), Vezelay; Chartres (1194–1260), with north tower later; Rheims (1211–90), towers later; and Amiens (1220–88); in England—Durham (1093–1133) and Salisbury (1220–70); in Germany—Cologne (1248–1880); in Italy—Pisa (1092); Monreale (1182); Palermo (1170–85); and Florence (1296–1462), designed by Arnolfo di Cambio (1232–*c.* 1300), with great dome added later by Filippo Brunelleschi (*c.* 1377–1446).

Many nonreligious buildings of the Middle Ages also contain notable examples of art in architecture. These buildings and the churches and cathedrals, with

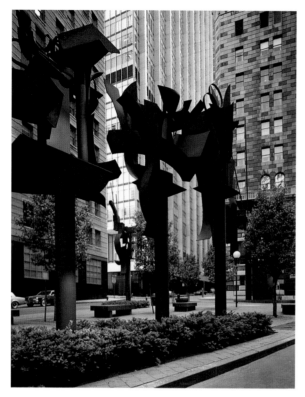

**ART IN ARCHITECTURE** Nevelson Plaza, New York, N.Y. [*Artist: Louise Nevelson*]

some exceptions, were designed by master builders and their art created by unknown artists. This is very unfortunate since they created not only some of the greatest buildings of all times but some of the greatest art in architecture.

During the Middle Ages, and even earlier, some notable artists created a number of important works of art in architecture. Among the many works are the religious frescoes (1306) of the painter, sculptor, and architect Giotto di Bondone (*c.* 1276–1337), usually called Giotto, in the Arena Chapel (1305), Padua, Italy. In a secular vein, Ambrogio Lorenzetti (*c.* 1300–1348) painted *Good and Bad Government* (1340) in the Palazzo Pubblico (1309) in Siena, Italy. Among the many great sculptures of the time are the pulpit (1260) by Nicola Pisano (1220–84), in the Baptistery (1278) at Pisa, Italy. In 1310, his son, Giovanni Pisano (1245–1314), architect, sculptor, and painter, created another sculptured pulpit for the nearby Cathedral of Pisa (1092). Also in this building group is the campanile (1174), the famous leaning tower of Pisa. Sculptured bronze doors, called the *Gates of Paradise*, were completed in 1447 by Lorenzo Ghiberti (1378–1455) for the Baptistery of the Cathedral of Florence, Italy. Another famous masterpiece is the Ghent Altarpiece (1432), by the brothers van Eyck, Hubert (*c.* 1366–1426) and Jan

(*c.* 1370–1440), in Saint Bavon Church (14th century) at Ghent, Belgium.

**Renaissance** During the Renaissance, the tradition of art in architecture was continued and developed to a high point, not only because of the interest in art among the nobility and the wealthy but many of the greatest architects of the time were also among the greatest artists in other media, particularly in painting and sculpture.

The magnificent works of art in architecture during the Renaissance form a very long list. Only a few can be mentioned here. First among them must be the sculptures of Donatello (*c.* 1386–1466), particularly those for the Cathedral and other churches in Florence. Among the greatest frescoes are those of Giovanni da Fiesole (1387–1455), known as Fra Angelico, in the Monastery of San Marco (1450), Florence; the *Last Supper* (1498) of Leonardo da Vinci (1452–1519) in Santa Maria della Grazie (15th century), Milan; the frescoes (1511 and 1513) of Raphael Santi (1483–1520), known as Raphael, in the Vatican and the Villa Farnesina (1511), both in Rome; those of Tiziano Vescelli (1477–1576), known as Titian, in San Nicolò dei Frari (1526) in Venice; and the wall and ceiling frescoes (1512) and *The Last Judgment* (1541) by Michelangelo Buonarroti (1475–1564) in the Sistine Chapel (begun 1508) at the Vatican, Rome.

Among many later important works are the frescoes (1525) of Antonio Allegri da Correggio (1494–1534), known as Correggio, in the Parma Cathedral and in other buildings in Parma; the frescoes of Jacopo Robusti (1518–94), known as Tintoretto, in several churches in Venice; and the great sculptured throne of Saint Peter (1666) by Gian Lorenzo Bernini (1598–1680) in the Cathedral of Saint Peter (1506–1667), Rome. Architecture of the Renaissance not only formed a background for works of art but was itself richly ornamented.

Toward the end of the Renaissance, the ornamentation of buildings increased to a point that, beginning with the Baroque style and especially the Rococo that followed it, the art in architecture cannot really be separated from the architecture itself. By the 18th century, in buildings such as the Kaisersaal (1744), in the Palace, Wurzburg, Germany, by Balthasar Neumann (1687–1753), the murals by Giovanni Battista Tiepolo (1696–1770) and other ornament almost succeed in hiding the building itself.

During the 18th and 19th centuries, the use of ornament in buildings continued but became more subdued and more architectural. The great era of integration of art into architecture that developed during the Renaissance was superseded by times in which many architects sought to integrate art into their work but not always with the great success of the past. Murals and sculpture were often used, but now in many cases, the works of art were accomplished independently of buildings in which they were then placed. Freestanding works of art, such as memorials and monuments, were prevalent, and architects and sculptors often worked together on these.

**Modern Movement** During the late 19th century, with the beginning of the modern movement in architecture, deliberate efforts were made by many architects to eliminate ornament in an attempt to make their buildings look more functional. Some architects, including Louis Henri Sullivan (1856–1924), attempted to integrate ornament with modern buildings. But these were not the highly ornamented exteriors and interiors of what is probably the last ornamented building of its kind, the Paris Opéra (1874), by Jean Louis Charles Garnier (1825–98).

A few other attempts were made in the late 19th and early 20th centuries to bring art back into an integral relationship with architecture. One involved the undulating and sinuous lines of the Art Nouveau style, exemplified by the Tassel House (1893) in Brussels, Belgium, by Victor Horta (1861–1947). Art Nouveau, however, never really became well-established in architecture. Another attempt was in the sculptural building designs of the great Spanish architect, Antoni Gaudí, whose most notable buildings are the Casa Milá (1910) and the Church of Sagrada Familia (1926), both in Barcelona. For the most part, architects of the modern movement avoided everything that resembled ornament and turned away from other forms of art in architecture.

**U.S. Art Programs** Some attempts were made in the United States beginning in the 1930s to restore art to a place in architecture. A few architects designed buildings in which works of art were placed. At the time, the U.S. government gave art in architecture considerable impetus with its Public Works of Art Project, part of the Work Projects Administration. Almost 4,000 artists were paid by the government to produce paintings and sculpture, some 16,000 pieces in public buildings, mostly post offices, and others that were donated to public institutions.

In 1962 President John F. Kennedy (1917–63) instituted another program to bring art into the architecture of the federal government, authorizing the payment of up to 1 percent of the cost of government buildings for works of art. The actual percentage allowed is 0.5 percent. A number of cities, including New York and Philadelphia, instituted similar allowances for artwork. Another federal government boost to art, including art in architecture, was the establishment in 1965 of the National Foundation of Arts and Humanities. One of its branches, the National Endowment for the Arts, provides grants to artists for the furtherance of their creative work. The other branch, the National Endowment for Humanities, provides similar grants in its field.

Private, corporate, and institutional clients of architects have become increasingly interested in art in their buildings in recent years. Today many companies make allowances for art in building budgets, as do many individuals. Because of this growing interest, the number of buildings with integrated art is growing rapidly. Some buildings, and groups of buildings, now look almost like art galleries.

For example, Lincoln Center for the Performing Arts (1968), New York City, has an array of art by leading artists of the time, including sculptures by Englishman Henry Moore (1898–1986) and by Americans Alexander Calder (1898–1977) and Richard Lippold (1915–    ); murals by Frenchman Raoul Dufy (1877–1953) and Russian Marc Chagall (1887–1985); and a bronze fountain by American architect Philip Cortelyou Johnson (1906–    ).

The United Nations Headquarters (1953), New York City, also contains a sizable collection of art in architecture, including murals by Frenchman Fernand Léger (1881–1955), American Fritz Glarner (1899–1972), and Brazilian Candido Portinari (1903–62); and stained glass by Chagall. The Graduate Center, Harvard University, Cambridge, has sculpture by Lippold, a mural by the Spaniard Joan Miró (1893–1983), wood relief sculptures by Frenchman Jean Arp (1887–1966), and a sculptured brick chimney by German-American Josef Albers (1888-1976).

Many other works of art are to be found in recent buildings all over the United States: public buildings, schools and universities, churches, shopping centers, airports, office buildings, and almost every other building type. Although a great deal of progress has been made, many people think there has not been enough. One who has actively attempted to improve the situation for many years is Polish-American architect, watercolorist, and writer Louis Gordon Redstone (b. 1903), whose book *Art in Architecture* was published in 1968.

**Related Articles** AESTHETICS; DESIGN, ARCHITECTURAL; GARDEN; HISTORY OF ARCHITECTURE; MUSEUM.

**Further Reading** Janson, H. W.: *History of Art: A Survey of the Major Visual Arts from the Dawn of History to the Present Day*, 3d ed., Harry N. Abrams, New York, 1986.

**Sources of Additional Information** American Federation of Arts, 41 E. 65th St., New York, N.Y. 10021; National Endowment for the Arts, 1100 Pennsylvania Ave. N.W., Washington, D.C. 20506; National Institute of Arts and Letters and American Academy of Arts and Letters, 633 W. 155th St., New York, N.Y. 10032.

**ASSOCIATION, BUILDING INDUSTRY** An organization of people with some common interest. Sometimes called business, professional, or trade associations, organizations of this type are nonprofit; their major purpose is the accomplishment of important goals for members that they cannot accomplish as individuals. Such goals often include promotion of the services or goals of the members to the public; cooperation with other organizations; influencing legislation; maintaining good relations with governments; education, ethics, and public relations; and ensuring the competence of members and others.

It is estimated that there are over 6,000 organizations of this type in the United States, ranging in size from very small to very large and representing almost every conceivable interest. Some organizations are composed of individual members; others of corporations, companies, or groups.

In the building industry, there is a large number of such organizations. In addition, there is an even larger number whose goals and work affect the building industry in some way. Some of these are listed in individual articles in this book. The most important ones may be divided into major groups in much the same manner that the building industry may be divided, for example, design, construction, ownership, finance, real estate, and regulation. The other group deeply involved in building, the users, have no associations to represent them, unless some of the consumer groups might be considered as performing this task.

Building industry designers are those who design and perform professional services for buildings and other structures: architects, engineers, landscape architects, planners, interior designers, and technicians.

**The AIA** The most important association in architecture is the American Institute of Architects (AIA). Founded in New York City in 1857 by 13 architects led by Richard Upjohn (1802–78), who served 18 years as its first president, the AIA was the second national organization of architects in the United States. The first was the American Institution of Architects, founded in 1836 in New York City, which lasted only a few years. Since architecture was in the beginning stages of becoming a profession in the United States, the AIA grew very slowly until 1867, when the first local chapter was organized in New York City. Other chapters soon followed, and membership grew, but it still numbered only a few hundred in 1887, over 30 years after its founding.

In 1884, a rival organization, the Western Association of Architects was founded, and in 1889 it merged into the AIA. Membership continued to grow slowly until 1920, when it had reached about 1,500. Growth was somewhat more rapid from that year until the end of World War II, when the membership was slightly more than 5,000. Then membership growth accelerated until it reached about 12,000 in 1957, a hundred years after the founding of the AIA. Today the membership is about 57,000 in all classes of membership, including associate, intern, allied, emeritus, and honorary members.

The organization of the AIA includes the national body, which is governed by national officers who are elected at large by delegates to national conventions and by members of the board of directors who are elected from the 18 regions, each composed of one or more states. In addition, some states have state associations with their own officers and directors. The lowest echelon consists of chapters, which operate on local levels and have their own officers.

Membership in the AIA consists of individuals who, with a few exceptions, are all registered or licensed architects and who were formerly called "corporate" members but now simply are members. The AIA associate members are not registered or licensed architects, but they work for architects or in fields related to architecture. Members of both classifications are not only national members but also members of state associations, where they exist, and local chapters. There are also local memberships, of chapters only, for newly registered architects and those in related fields. The category of student members, intended for students in architectural schools, has a local and national organization of its own. Every prospective member is expected to declare intention of complying with the bylaws and the 1992 Code of Ethics and Professional Conduct of the AIA.

Management of the AIA is conducted by a national organization staff, headed by an executive vice president, located in Washington, D.C., who acts as the chief executive officer of the AIA executive management committee. Other members of this committee include the chief financial officer, general counsel, group vice presidents for membership services, institute services, business centers, practice/education, human resources, and external affairs. Also a member of this committee is the president of the American Architectural Foundation, which, in addition to its many programs, operates the Octagon House in Washington as a museum.

On the state association and chapter levels, management is provided by small staffs headed by component executives who are often called "executive directors." The work of the AIA goes on at all levels, national, state, and chapter. In addition to the functions performed by staff members, a large number of professional interest areas are represented by committees and corresponding members. These interest areas include building codes and standards, corporate architects, design, emeritus members forum, environment, facility management, health-care facilities, historic resources, housing, interiors,

**ASSOCIATION, BUILDING INDUSTRY** Headquarters of the American Institute of Architects (1972), Washington, D.C. *[Architects: The Architects Collaborative]*

international, justice systems facilities, practice management, public architecture, and specifications technology.

The AIA performs many services for its members: maintenance of liaison with other organizations in the building industry and with governments; publication of newsletters, studies, books, and contracts and other legal forms; provision of insurance programs; continuing education; and others. *Architecture, Incorporating Architectural Technology,* is the magazine of the American Institute of Architects, now published by BPI Communications in New York.

The AIA on the local, state, and national levels presents a number of awards to architects and those in related fields each year. A fellowship is the highest award that can be given to a member for accomplishments, except for the Gold Medal, which may be given to only one architect a year. Members ordinarily use the letters *AIA* after their names, unlike doctors and other professionals, who use the initials of their professional degrees. Fellows of the AIA use the initials *FAIA.*

**Other Associations** Associations that represent the interest of other professionals who perform portions of

the design services for buildings offer services to their members that are similar to those of the AIA, though the services may differ in some details. The more important of these, in the order of their founding, are: American Society of Civil Engineers (ASCE) founded in 1852, divided into divisions, of which the most important to architecture are structural, sanitary, soil mechanics and foundations, and surveying; American Society of Mechanical Engineers (ASME), 1880; Institute of Electrical and Electronics Engineers (IEEE), organized in 1884 and merged with radio engineers in 1963; American Society of Landscape Architects (ASLA), 1899; Illuminating Engineering Society (IES), 1906; American Planning Association (APA), 1978, incorporating the American Institute of Planners (AIP), 1917; Acoustical Society of America (ASA), 1929; National Society of Professional Engineers (NSPE), 1934; Construction Specifications Institute (CSI), 1948; and American Society of Heating, Refrigerating and Air Conditioning Engineers (ASHRAE), 1956, incorporating earlier associations dating back to 1894.

Owners of buildings are represented by the Building Owners and Managers Association International (BOMA), 1908, and by other groups. Financiers have a number of associations, of which the most important to the building industry are American Bankers Association, founded in 1875, and the Mortgage Bankers Association of America, 1914. Real estate interests are represented by a number of associations. The most important to the building industry are American Society of Real Estate Counselors, founded in 1953, and the National Association of Realtors, 1908.

The regulators formulate and enforce codes and standards for the building industry and are government employees. Many of them, along with others interested in this work, belong to associations. Among the most important of these associations are National Fire Protection Association (NFPA), founded in 1896; American Society of Testing and Materials (ASTM), now called ASTM (Testing) (ASTM), 1898; Building Officials and Code Administrators International (BOCA), 1915; International Conference of Building Officials (ICBO), 1922; and the Southern Building Code Congress, International (SBCCI), 1940.

The names and addresses of the associations discussed above, as well as many others, are listed at the end of articles on related subjects.

**Related Articles** Many articles in this book discuss subjects related to building industry associations, including BUILDING CODES AND STANDARDS; ELECTRICAL ENGINEERING; ENVIRONMENTAL PROTECTION; MECHANICAL ENGINEERING; PLANNING, CITY.

**Sources of Additional Information** See articles on specific subjects.

# B

**BACON, HENRY** American architect (1866–1924). If he had not designed another building, Henry Bacon would be remembered for the Lincoln Memorial (1922), Washington, D.C. This monumental building brought him world fame when it was finished shortly before he died and has come to be one of the most respected and loved structures in the United States.

Equally respected and loved is the great sculpture in the building of the seated Abraham Lincoln (1809–65) by the noted sculptor Daniel Chester French (1850–1931). This collaboration between architect and sculptor culminated an association between the two men that had lasted a great number of years and produced more than 50 monuments located in many parts of the United States.

Bacon designed a great number of other monuments, including some for which the sculptor was the noted Augustus Saint-Gaudens (1848–1907). All Bacon's monumental works were in the Eclectic Beaux Arts style so popular at the time. His buildings were in the same mode. Many of them were considered very distinguished at the time they were constructed, but later generations have tended to regard them as merely representative of the Beaux Arts tradition of the time, not the finest buildings of that time.

**Lincoln Memorial** Henry Bacon's masterpiece, the Lincoln Memorial, was a hit from the first and has become even more so with the passing years. So impressed were his fellow architects that they staged its dedication like a latter-day grand opera which might have been composed by Richard Wagner (1813–83). It began on May 18, 1923, during the convention of the American Institute of Architects (AIA), with the annual banquet at tables set along the reflecting pool in front of the Memorial.

At the end of the banquet, as the architects and their guests stood alongside the reflecting pool, a decorated barge with a great yellow sail, drawn by ropes by architecture students, slowly made its way toward the Memorial, which was illuminated from within with violet-colored lights. At the foot of the Memorial waited officers and former officers of the AIA, bearing colorful banners. Waiting with them were the president of the United States, Warren Gamaliel Harding (1865–1923),

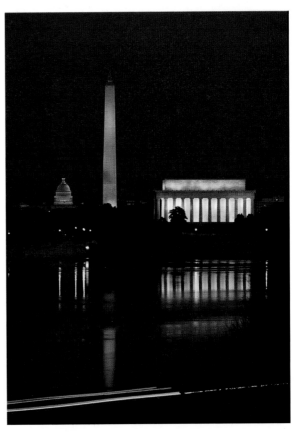

**BACON, HENRY** Lincoln Memorial (1922), Washington, D.C.

and former president William Howard Taft, then chief justice of the Supreme Court, standing between incense-burning braziers.

On the barge were the architect Henry Bacon, the sculptor Daniel Chester French, and members of the U.S. Marine Corps Band, all dressed in colorful medieval cloaks, illuminated by what was called the "fire in inspiration." From muted trumpets came "Walther's Prize Song" from Wagner's opera *Die Meistersinger.* After disembarking from the barge, Henry Bacon received from President Harding the Gold Medal of the American Institute of Architects, its greatest honor for an architect. The Memorial was then dedicated as a national shrine. The ceremonies ended with the playing of the national anthem by the Marine Band and the bursting high overhead of a single star shell.

**Life** Henry Bacon was born at Watseka, Ill., on November 26, 1866, the son of an engineer. In 1881 he entered the Chauncey Hall School in Boston, and after graduation entered the architectural school of the University of Illinois, Urbana, in 1884. After staying

**BANK** Norwest Center (1988), Minneapolis, Minn. *[Architect: Cesar Pelli].* The Federal Reserve Bank (1972) by Gunnar Birkerts is on the edge of the image.

only a year, Bacon went to work in an architectural office in Boston and then went to New York City to work for McKim, Mead and White, where he came under the influence of their eclectic architecture, which was based on the principles of design of the École des Beaux Arts in Paris. In 1889, Bacon won the important Rotch Traveling Scholarship and went to Europe for two years to study and travel. After returning to New York City, he again entered the office of McKim, Mead and White in 1891 and stayed there until 1897, when he opened his own office. During his professional career, he designed buildings of many types, including churches, hospitals, libraries, banks, railroad stations, schools, and office buildings. He was best known for his designs for monuments and memorials. Bacon designed the base of the Sherman monument in New York and the Parnell monument in Dublin, Ireland. The sculptures were by Augustus Saint-Gaudens. With Daniel Chester French, Bacon designed a number of settings for sculpture. They were not as successful as the collaboration on the Lincoln Memorial.

Toward the end of his life, Bacon received many honors, including membership in the National Academy of Arts and Sciences and the National Institute of Arts and Letters. As mentioned previously, he also won the Gold Medal of the American Institute of Architects in 1923 for his design for the Lincoln Memorial. Less than a year later, on February 14, 1924, Henry Bacon died. It was a tragic year for architecture. On April 14 Louis Henri Sullivan died, and 10 days later Bertram Grosvenor Goodhue died.

**Related Articles** ART IN ARCHITECTURE; BEAUX ARTS, ÉCOLE DES; CAPITAL, UNITED STATES; CRAM, GOODHUE AND FERGUSON; ECLECTIC ARCHITECTURE; McKIM, MEAD AND WHITE; MONUMENT.

**BANK** A type of building, or portion of a building, in which financial transactions are performed, including receiving, protecting, and lending money. Several other types of financial institutions whose functions resemble those of banks are sometimes called banks. A credit union is a cooperative that receives funds for deposit and makes loans to its members. Land banks lend money on real estate, as do mortgage companies; investment banks distribute corporate securities.

**Types** Banks provide a number of services, including savings accounts, checking accounts, loans, safety deposit boxes and vault storage, and trust management. A commercial bank usually performs all these and other functions. Commercial banks may be either national or state banks, according to which governmental body charters and supervises them. Savings banks, chartered and supervised by the states, perform more limited services, mostly confined to savings accounts and loans. Trust

**BANK** National Farmers Bank (now Northwest Bank Owatonna) (1907), Owatonna, Minn.
*[Architect: Louis Sullivan]*

companies, most of which are banks, manage trusts, receive deposits of money or other valuables, and make loans. Central banks are owned and operated by the government, such as the 12 Federal Reserve Banks of the United States. These banks perform services for other banks, such as issuing bank notes, clearing and collecting checks, making loans to the banks, and acting as depositories for government funds.

**Elements** The major elements of banks are public spaces, operations departments, and the executive suite. Other elements are the legal department, the mailroom, and data-processing (computer) facilities. The public spaces include the lobby where tellers are located for easy accessibility to the customers; the officers' area where bank officials are available for consultation, making loans, and other functions; and the safety deposit vault located conveniently nearby. The public spaces also include the drive-in and sidewalk, or walk-up, tellers' windows and the automated banking system where customers may activate computers to make transactions.

The operations departments are behind the scene to customers. They include bookkeeping, data-processing, clerical, mail, records, and employees' areas. The trust department and often an auditorium for meetings are included. The executive suite contains offices for the offi-

cers of the bank and their assistants, and conference rooms. Many banks also have building departments used by the people who maintain the building and handle the renting of office space to other businesses.

**History** Banking has existed since ancient times, first practiced by money changers and money lenders who later received deposits of money from their customers to hold for safekeeping. The first bank, in the modern sense of the word, was the Banco di Rialto in Venice, Italy, established in 1587. In 1694 the Bank of England was established and the business of banking has continued to grow ever since. With the growth of banking came the establishment of bank buildings as an important building type.

**American Development** In colonial times, attempts were made to establish banks, but none succeeded. There were loan offices but no real banks. The first commercial bank in the United States, the Bank of North America, was established in Philadelphia in 1781 by Robert Morris, who was superintendent of finance for the colonies. The first state-chartered bank, the Bank of Massachusetts, was established in Boston in 1784. The First Bank of the United States (1798), in Philadelphia, was the first bank in which the U.S. government had a financial interest. Its architect was Samuel Blodget. The

**BANK** Irwin Union Bank and Trust (1954; 1973), Columbus, Ind. *[Architect (1954): Eero Saarinen; 1973 Addition: Kevin Roche John Dinkeloo & Assoc.]*

Second Bank of the United States (1818), also in Philadelphia, was designed by William Strickland (1787–1854). The original buildings of the last two banks are still in existence.

Over the years, banks have continued to add new services and new buildings have been built to accommodate them. In 1816, the first savings bank was established; in 1822, the first trust company; and in 1910, the first postal savings bank. In 1946 the first drive-in bank was built in Chicago, a trend that has continued in complete drive-in banks and as one of the services of regular banks. A recent development has been the automated teller system, by means of which check cashing, deposits, and other transactions may be handled by a computer activated by the customer's identification and instructions.

Over the years, the design of banks has greatly changed. Now banks tend to be as open, spacious, and well furnished as any other commercial establishment that hopes to attract customers. Just a few years ago, most banks were austere, the tellers hiding in forbidding cages instead of working at open counters as they now do. Another somewhat recent development is the construction of banks in large office buildings, portions of which are used for banking operations, with other spaces occupied by other businesses.

In recent years, many banks have been consolidated into regional banking organizations. The result has been a greater competition coupled with the closing of redundant branch banks.

**Further Reading** *Money Matters: A Critical Look at Bank Architecture*, McGraw-Hill, in association with the Museum of Fine Arts, Houston, and Parnassus Foundation, New York, 1990.

## BAUHAUS, STAATLICHES (STATE BUILDING SCHOOL)

Famous German school of architecture and other design arts. From 1919, when it was founded by architect Walter Adolph Gropius, the Bauhaus has had an important influence on design of buildings, furniture, manufactured products, and other arts. The original Bauhaus was formed by Gropius, who became its director, by combining two other schools in Weimar, Germany; the Grand Ducal Saxon School of Applied Arts and the Grand Ducal Academy of Arts.

**Principles** The Bauhaus was founded in a time of eclecticism in architectural and other design. The modern movement, then in its infancy, was deeply affected by this new school that revolutionized the principles of design and their teaching. The most important principles were: the machine and industrial production are the new media of design and designers must understand and exploit the media; to accomplish this, designers and others involved must collaborate rather than working only as individuals; all elements of design are completely interdependent on one another; education of designers must integrate practical training in workshops actually engaged in production with sound training in the theoretical aspects of design. As Gropius said, "The object of the Bauhaus was not to propagate any 'style,' system or dogma, but simply to exert a revitalizing influence on design."

**Curriculum** For the new school, Gropius devised a new curriculum that required all students to take a preliminary course in the fundamentals of design that are common to all of the arts. Their interrelationships were studied in a broad way that would prepare students, as whole designers, to further pursue specialized studies within an overall system. Each student then entered a workshop of his own choosing, where the studies were taught by two masters: one in handcrafts and one in design. The workshops served as laboratories in which students could develop their own ideas, with help from the staff masters and from visiting experts. After the first three years, students were required to pass a difficult examination before being allowed to proceed to building training. For those who went on, the training included practical work in building sites and materials, drafting, engineering, and design. Those who finished the course were awarded the Master Certificate of the Bauhaus, and went on to become architects or designers in other fields.

**Masters** To ensure that the instruction and other work at the Bauhaus would be of the highest order, Gropius attracted top-quality teachers, or masters, to the faculty. The list sounds like a who's who of modern design and the arts. Among those who became the most famous are Josef Albers (1888–1976), German painter, graphic artist, and educator; Herbert Bayer (1900– ), Austrian graphic artist; Marcel Lajos Breuer (1902–81), Hungarian architect; Lyonel Feininger (1871–1956), American painter; Wassily Kandinsky (1866–1944), Russian painter; Paul Klee (1879–1940), Swiss-German painter; Ludwig Mies van der Rohe (1886–1969), German architect; and Lazlo Moholy-Nagy (1895–1946), Hungarian designer and artist. All these masters except Kandinsky and Klee later came to America to live and work.

With a superior faculty and a strong curriculum, the Bauhaus had great success with its students. Starting in 1919, all went well for several years, but Weimar, the capital of Germany after World War I, became one of the first cities to feel the growing reaction in Germany to the continuing inflation and political problems that later would bring the Nazis into power. The reaction was felt in attitudes toward the arts and architecture as well.

**Later History** In 1925 Gropius moved the school to Dessau where the political atmosphere was better, and there designed new buildings (1925) which were among his best ever. The growing unrest in the country forced Gropius to resign as director in 1928 and go back into private practice. A faculty member, Hannes Meyer (1889–1954), became director and served until 1930, when Ludwig Mies van der Rohe took over. Mies was the director until 1932 when the Dessau school was closed and in temporary quarters in Berlin until the school was permanently closed by the Nazis in 1933.

A total of only about 1,250 students had attended the Bauhaus, but its influence went much further than the numbers would indicate. One of the former faculty members, Moholy-Nagy, continued the programs in the United States through the establishment of a school in Chicago, the Institute of Design, which was called the New Bauhaus. Gropius went to Harvard University in 1937 and became chairman of the department of architecture, and in 1938 Marcel Breuer joined him as a design professor. That same year, Mies went to the Armour Institute in Chicago, later renamed Illinois Institute of Technology, to become director of architecture.

Through the efforts of such people as these, the principles of the Bauhaus were preserved, further developed, and disseminated to thousands of future architects and other designers.

**Related Articles** BREUER, MARCEL LAJOS; EDUCATION; GROPIUS, WALTER ADOLF; MIES VAN DER ROHE, LUDWIG.

**Further Reading** Wingler, Hans M.: *The Bauhaus—Weimar, Dessau, Berlin, Chicago*, MIT Press, Cambridge, Mass., 1968.

**BAUHAUS, STAATLICHES** School Building (1925), Dessau, Germany. *[Architect: Walter Gropius (photo of restored building: Gregory Wittkopp)]*

**BEAUX ARTS, ÉCOLE DES** Famous French school of the fine arts—architecture, painting, and sculpture—located in Paris. Although the Paris school is the one usually referred to in architectural circles, there were schools of the same name located in eight other French cities.

The École des Beaux Arts and its predecessors dominated the teaching of architecture in France for almost 300 years, from 1671 until 1968. They also dominated the teaching of painting and sculpture and, later, of related arts during the same period. In addition, this influence was international. Students from countries other than France were freely admitted and, beginning in the middle of the 19th century, a large number of American architects were educated there. These architects came back to the United States, trained young people in the principles of the Beaux Arts, and founded American architectural schools. Gradually, the influence of the Beaux Arts philosophy spread and deepened until it dominated American architectural education well into the 20th century. Architectural schools taught Beaux Arts principles; and design problems, to be solved by students, were prepared and judged by Beaux Arts architects. This became the accepted tradition in American architectural education until the 1930s, when Walter Adolf Gropius (1883–1969) began to divert the architectural school at Harvard University, Cambridge, Mass., away from Beaux Arts philosophies toward those of the Bauhaus, the school he had founded in Germany. Other American schools later followed the lead of Harvard toward teaching modern principles, but the Beaux Arts system did not die out in the United States until after World War II.

Thus it may be seen that the philosophy of the Beaux Arts was a dominant factor in American architecture for approximately 100 years. Although the philosophy of the École changed somewhat over the years of its existence, it was in the main academic and conservative. In its later years, some of its professors and graduates turned toward the modern movement in architecture, but education in the École was primarily based on scholarly study of the architecture of the past. For some years, the style most emulated was that of Classical Greece. Later, all styles of the past were embraced and students began to design buildings in eclectic styles, but always based on proper scholarship.

**Composition** The central and all-important theme in Beaux Arts architecture was composition, which was the essential act of architectural design or making a whole, as in a building, of its parts. Composition in this sense has several elements, including proportion, scale, contrast, balance, rhythm, unity, and character.

Proportion means the relationship of one part of a building to the whole building and to the other parts.

**BEAUX ARTS, ÉCOLE DES** Grand Central Terminal (1913), New York, N.Y. *[Architects: Reed and Stern and Warren & Wetmore; sculptor of clock and sculpture group: Jules Coutan]*

Scale is the factor that permits comparisons of proportions in relation to one another and to some abstract unit of measurement, such as the human figure. Contrast means differences in parts of buildings, as in form, mass and shape, line size, tone, and so on. Balance means a state of equalization or equilibrium in the form of a building and its parts and may be symmetrical, having identical forms on both sides of an axis, or asymmetrical, in which balance is obtained with forms that are not identical on the sides of an axis. Rhythm means the organized repetition of elements so that they flow from one to the other with regularity and accents; in music, rhythm is produced by sounds; in architecture, mostly by forms. Unity involves bringing together all the elements of architecture into a harmonious whole. Character is the aggregate of the elements of a building that makes it individual or unique.

**Education** Although changes were made in education at the École des Beaux Arts over the years, in the important things it remained much the same as when it was founded. In general, the requirements for admission were simple: attainment of age fifteen and no more than thirty, and the successful completion of oral and written entrance examinations in mathematics, descriptive geometry, history, drawing, and architectural design. Entrance was open to all male students, regardless of nationality; in 1900 the first women were admitted. Although there was no tuition, students were charged rent for the studios in which they studied, fuel for heating, and oil for lighting; some students paid fees to the design professors.

Upon passing the examinations, an applicant, called an *aspirant*, was admitted to the second, or *seconde*, class. Attendance at lectures was optional and no examinations were given except in scientific subjects. Each new student, or *nouveau*, was also admitted to a studio, or *atelier*, of a practicing architect called a *patron*, in which to learn architectural design, or composition as it was usually called. In an *atelier* the *nouveau* learned by designing series of projects, or *projets*, in competitions, or *concours*. These projects were generally of two types: sketches, or *esquisses*, which lasted 12 hours and required one drawing, and rendered projects, or *projets rendus*, which lasted about two months and usually required three large drawings or renderings. Students could participate in as many *concours* as they wished, with a minimum of two a year, and after receiving an adequate number of points, called *valeurs*, in the competitions and in mathematics, construction, and perspective, a *nouveau* could enter the first, or *première*, class and become an old student, or *ancien élève*. Completion of the *seconde* class usually took from two to four years.

Work in the first class could also be done at a student's own pace. There were six *esquisses* and six *projets rendus* each year and a student could participate in any or all of these. At first, there was no official graduation. Students simply stayed as long as they wished and left the school when they wanted to. However, they were not eligible to remain in the École after age thirty. After 1867, students could participate in an annual special competition for diplomas.

In all the competitions, awards were made to students who did the best work. In some, these were medals, or *médailles*; in others, *mentions*. Money prizes were also awarded. The highest prize of all was the *Grand Prix de Rome*, a special competition held each year for French students only. This was the ultimate honor at the École. The winner received all expenses for study at the French Academy in Rome for four or more years at first, and later for two years of study and two of travel.

Work in the *ateliers* was the most important part of education at the École. *Ateliers* varied in size from only 1 student to 100 or more, with the average size about 20 in the middle of the 19th century. Some of these were *ateliers officiels*, in which the fees of the *patrons* were paid by the government. Others were *ateliers libres*, in which *patrons* were paid by the students. The *ateliers* were governed by the students, each group electing one of its members, called a *massier*, to take charge of its common fund. The *patron* regularly gave instructions and the students helped each other, the *anciens élèves* by criticizing the work of the *nouveaux*, who in turn helped the older students make their drawings and renderings.

In general, a student participated in competitions, or *concours*, by choice. If the student decided to participate, a separate enrollment was required for each *concours*. After the student had signed in, a copy of the program for the *concours* was furnished. The student then went into a small cubicle, or went *en loge*. Twelve hours were allocated for study of the problem and preparation of a sketch, called a *parti*, showing ideas for solution of the problem. At the end of the allotted time, the student signed out and turned in the sketch, retaining a copy.

Returning to the *atelier*, the student developed the idea, with critical help from the *patron*, and prepared drawings and submitted them to the school on the scheduled completion day for judgment. If the student's drawings did not reflect the original ideas of the *parti*, the submission was declared out of competition, or *hors-concours*, and no credit was given. As time for submissions approached, students usually worked day and night to complete their drawings. On the last day, their drawings were transported to the school on hand-drawn carts, called *charrettes*. Thus the last struggle to complete the work came to be called a *charrette* and a student so engaged was said to be *en charrette*.

Although the École des Beaux Arts no longer exists and architecture and architectural education have changed radically, many of the old French terms are still in use in the United States and elsewhere today.

**American Students** Before the closing of the École, a great many Americans were educated there. The first was Richard Morris Hunt (1827–95), who went to the École in 1846. Some of the most notable of the later students were Henry Hobson Richardson (1838–86), Charles Follen McKim (1847–1909), Louis Henri Sullivan (1856–1924), Ernest Flagg (1857–1947), John Merven Carrère (1858–1911), Thomas Hastings (1860–1929), Bernard Maybeck (1862–1957), Whitney Warren (1864–1943), Chester Holmes Aldrich (1871–1940), John Russell Pope (1874–1937), William Adams Delano (1874–1960), Paul Philippe Cret (1876–1947), Raymond Mathewson Hood (1881–1934), and George Howe

**BEAUX ARTS, ÉCOLE DES** Municipal Building (1914), New York, N.Y. *[Architects: McKim, Mead and White]*

(1886–1955). Julia Morgan (1872–1957) was the first American woman to graduate from the Beaux Arts.

**History** The École des Beaux Arts, together with its predecessors, had a long and often turbulent history that lasted almost 300 years. In 1648, the Royal Academy of Painting and Sculpture in Paris was founded. The Royal Academy of Architecture, founded in 1671, had as its first professor and director François Blondel (1617–86). It had a curriculum consisting of theory of architecture, mathematics, mechanics, military architecture, perspective, and stonecutting. Some years later, building construction was added. Early in the 18th century, competitions were instituted, in which students vied for prizes. The first regular annual competition was held in 1720 and this started a tradition that was to be followed, with some breaks in continuity, for almost 250 years. The annual competition came to be called the *Grand Prix* and later the *Grand Prix de Rome*, since its award brought with it a scholarship to the French Academy in Rome. The annual competition, and others, became the most important factor in architectural education in France for almost as long.

Other than the institution of competitions, the curriculum in the academy, including lectures and student design problems, changed very little until the advent of the French Revolution. Beginning in 1789, the famous French painter Jacques-Louis David (1748–1825) led a fight to abolish the academies along with other royal institutions. The fight was successful and the royal academies were abolished in 1793, only to be reconstituted a short time later without the royal designation. Architect Julien-David Leroy (1724–1803), who had taught at the architectural academy since 1762 and was well thought of by the painter David, was appointed head of the new academy and served in that capacity until his death. In 1795 the academy was renamed the Special School of Architecture and joined to the also newly renamed Special School of Painting and Sculpture.

During the years since its beginning, the École des Beaux Arts did not have many students, for example, only 28 in 1717, and 47 in 1746. During the period Leroy was its head, 1793–1803, a total of only 37 students were admitted. The curriculum remained very much like it had been before the Revolution, consisting of lectures, monthly student design problems, and the annual competition for the *Grand Prix de Rome*. The design philosophy of the school was based on the architecture of ancient Greece.

In another school in Paris, the École Polytechnique, some architectural courses were taught but never a full program as in the special school. The professor of architecture at the École Polytechnique was Jean-Nicolas-Louis Durand (1760–1834), who espoused free use of all architectural styles. After the death of Leroy, Léon Dufornoy (1754–1818) became the head of the Special School and continued the Greek classical tradition started by Leroy. Annual enrollments began to increase, from 6 in 1803 to 38 in 1818.

In 1814 the monarchy was reestablished in France under Louis XVIII (1755–1824). In 1816 the King ordered the special schools to be combined under the name of the École Royale et Spéciale des Beaux Arts. The decree became official in 1819 and the school's name was modified to École Royale des Beaux Arts. Nothing much, other than the name, was changed until 1863. By 1851 the student body in architecture had grown to 281. In 1846 the first American student, Richard Morris Hunt, enrolled in the École, and was subsequently followed by other American students. In 1848 the second French Republic was established with Charles Louis Napoléon Bonaparte (1808–73), a nephew of the first Emperor Napoléon (1769–1821), as president. In 1852 Louis Napoléon was declared Emperor Napoléon III.

For some time previously, controversy had raged concerning the orthodox teaching of architecture at the École. The opposition to the teaching was led by Henri Labrouste (1801–75) and later by Eugène Emanuel Viollet-le-Duc (1814–79). Finally, mostly because of the campaign of Viollet-le-Duc against the orthodoxy of the school, Napoléon III ordered a reform of the policies in 1863. The school was then reorganized. Some professors were dismissed and others appointed to take their places. The admission age for students was changed. The judgment of the competition for the *Grand Prix de Rome* was changed and the prize itself became two years in Rome and two years for travel. Lecture courses were made mandatory rather than optional. The most far-reaching change was that the school was placed under the direction of the government of France rather than under the appointed academy members. The academy members protested vehemently and brought suit. The students rioted and the professors were embroiled in controversy. As a result of the uproar, most of the reforms were gradually rescinded.

It was another development in 1867 that changed the nature of architectural education at the École more than all the reforms of 1863. This was the institution of a diploma to be given to graduates who successfully completed a special competition. Few students attempted the competition and the diploma was largely ignored until 1887, when the government awarded a diploma to each living winner of the *Grand Prix de Rome*. Students now remained at the École from five to seven years, though theoretically the diploma was available after two years, seeking the award of an Architecte *D.P.L.G.* (*diplôme par le gouvernement*). Thus a certain consistency and continuity, which had not existed before, was established in the educational process of the École.

By 1890, there were 606 students enrolled in architecture at the École; by 1906, 950 students; and by 1920, 1,100 students. By that time, architecture that seemed to have been designed on the basis of the principles of the École was called Beaux Arts architecture. After World War I, the school's philosophies were vigorously opposed by architects of other countries, particularly Walter Adolf Gropius and the others of the Bauhaus in Germany and the great Swiss architect practicing in France, Charles Édouard Jeanneret, called Le Corbusier (1887–1965). These and other men were engaged in developing what came to be called modern architecture and in pioneering educational principles for architectural schools. The academic classicism of the Beaux Arts was anathema to them.

World War II, when France was mostly occupied by the Germans, brought further problems. The postwar years were not much better. The French economy was depressed and money was scarce. In the 1950s, when the economy began to recover, inflation set in. In spite of these problems, the architectural enrollment of the École rose to 2,780 in 1967. In 1968 student rioting broke out at the University of Paris and spread to the Sorbonne and then to the École. In June 1968, students were evict-

ed and locked out of the École; during that summer the students prevented the competition for the *Grand Prix de Rome* from being held and in the fall prevented the school from reopening.

In December 1968 President Charles de Gaulle (1890–1970) reorganized architectural education in France. The *Grand Prix de Rome* was abolished. The École was replaced by a number of schools called pedagogical units in various parts of France, including eight in Paris. Each unit now teaches architecture in its own manner. The grand and controversial history of the École des Beaux Arts and its predecessors, which had lasted almost 300 years, had come to an end.

**Related Articles** BAUHAUS, STAATLICHES; CRET, PAUL PHILIPPE; DESIGN, ARCHITECTURAL; ECLECTIC ARCHITECTURE; EDUCATION; HOOD, RAYMOND MATHEWSON; HUNT, RICHARD MORRIS; MAYBECK, BERNARD; McKIM, MEAD AND WHITE; MORGAN, JULIA; POPE, JOHN RUSSELL; RICHARDSON, HENRY HOBSON; SULLIVAN, LOUIS HENRI.

**Source of Additional Information** National Institute for Architectural Education, 30 W. 22d St., New York, N.Y. 10010.

**BELLUSCHI, PIETRO** Italian-American architect (1899–1994). Particularly noted for his religious buildings and for his masterful use of wood, Belluschi spent much of his career in and around Portland, Ore. And a full and influential career it was.

After receiving engineering degrees, never having had any formal architectural education, and immigrating to the United States, speaking little English, Belluschi spent 18 years in a Portland architectural office that produced eclectic work in many styles. He instituted a modern design philosophy. The changes he made had a quiet drama about them, just as much of his later work would have that quality.

**Regional Characteristics** Beginning in the late 1930s and early 1940s, Belluschi developed an architecture that nestled into its Pacific Northwest setting as if it had grown there. Using wood, often combined with stone which he remembered with pleasure from his boyhood in Italy, he designed buildings, in particular houses and churches, that were closely related to the climate, landscape, materials, needs, and qualities of the region in which they were built. Along with a few other Northwest architects of the time, he created a truly regional architecture in a part of the world that was quite different from that in which he grew up. Yet he never allowed himself to become stereotyped. At the time when he was designing wood houses and churches with regional character, he also designed office buildings and other types that were quite different—modern skeleton structures with plain geometric surfaces of thin stone, glass, and aluminum. His ability to design buildings to fit their purpose and to integrate them into their setting continued in his later work.

Belluschi's houses have been highly praised for their functional plans and human qualities as well as their regional characteristics. Partaking of the same qualities, his many churches are even more admired. As he stated on many occasions, Belluschi tried all of his life to achieve an architecture of attainment and restraint. Most who have experienced his buildings would agree that he succeeded admirably. And his architecture and philosophy have had considerable influence on the work of other architects.

**Academic Career** Belluschi also deeply influenced architects and architecture through his academic career. For 15 years, he was dean of the School of Architecture and Planning of the Massachusetts Institute of Technology, Cambridge, and lectured at many other schools. His philosophy of a quiet architecture, that is, original and of high quality, yet attainable and harmonizing with its setting, was imparted to a great number of students at MIT and to many young architects who worked for or were associated with him. And other people who have become familiar with his work and philosophy have learned a great deal about what constitutes the finest architecture.

**Buildings** The first important building by Belluschi was the Portland Art Museum (1932), designed when he was working in the firm of Albert E. Doyle. He added a wing in 1939 and another in 1970. When the first two wings had been completed, the museum brought Belluschi considerable recognition, as did the Finley Mortuary (1937), also in Portland. During the depression years few buildings were completed, but beginning about 1940, Belluschi began designing a great number. Over the years, he designed houses, churches, office

**BELLUSCHI, PIETRO** St. Mary's Cathedral (1971), San Francisco, Calif. *[Architects: Pietro Belluschi with McSweeney, Ryan & Lee; structural engineer: Pier Luigi Nervi]*

buildings, banks, stores, shopping centers, schools, hospitals, fountains, and many other types, including a drive-in restaurant.

Among the best of his buildings were houses, the most notable of which are: Sutor (1938), Portland; Meyes (1940), Seattle; Joss (1940), Portland; Kerr (1941), Gearhart, Ore.; Coats (1941), Tillamook, Ore.; and Menefee (1948), Yamhill, Ore.

**Churches** There is widespread agreement that Belluschi's finest designs were for religious buildings. Starting with his first church, the St. Thomas More Chapel (1941), Portland, still considered one of his best, he gained an international reputation for buildings of this type. Some of his finest churches are: Zion Lutheran and Central Lutheran, both completed in Portland in 1951; First Presbyterian (1941), Cottage Grove, Ore.; Central Lutheran (1952), Eugene, Ore.; Episcopal Church of the Redeemer (1959), Baltimore, in association with Rogers and Taliaferro; Trinity Episcopal Church (1963), Concord, Mass.; and St. Mary's Cathedral (1971), San Francisco, in association with McSweeney, Ryan and Lee and the great Italian engineer Pier Luigi Nervi (1891–1979).

**Office Buildings** In the design of office buildings, Belluschi was a leader in a way that was different from his work with houses and churches. In his first important office building for the Oregonian Publishing Co. (1948) in Portland, he made a design for a simple rectangular mass, faced with marble and granite, and with large expanses of windows. The design of this building was completely overshadowed by that of another finished in the same year, the Equitable Building, now the Commonwealth Building, also in Portland. Here, in a 12-story office building, Belluschi produced what many think is a masterpiece of modern architecture. This office building, with a curtain wall of tinted glass and aluminum and with the structure expressed on the exterior, has been called the logical conclusion of the trends in tall building design started by Major William Le Baron Jenney (1832–1907) and the other talented members of the Chicago school of architecture in the late 1800s.

Belluschi never did another office building that excelled in the way the Equitable did. Later, with Walter Adolf Gropius (1883–1969), he acted as design consultant on the Pan American Building (1963), New York City, by architects Emery Roth and Sons, but it was not considered up to the standards of either consultant. He also was associated as design consultant, with the firms of Wurster, Bernardi and Emmons, and Skidmore, Owings and Merrill, for the design of the Bank of America headquarters (1971) in San Francisco, a much better designed building.

**Life** Pietro Belluschi was born in Ancona, Italy, on August 18, 1899. When he was six years old, his family moved to Rome, where he spent most of his early years. As a boy, he was interested in drawing and in high school he became interested in architecture. At seventeen, he enlisted in the Italian Army in World War I, and served three years. Belluschi entered the school of engineering of the University of Rome and graduated in 1922, with a doctor of engineering degree. In 1923, as an exchange student, he came to the United States and entered Cornell University, Ithaca, N.Y., and received a civil engineering degree in 1924.

After leaving Cornell, Belluschi worked for a while in Idaho as an electrician's helper and then went to Portland, Ore., where he was employed in 1925 by the well-established and successful office of the eclectic architect Albert E. Doyle (1877–1928). When Doyle died two years after Belluschi began work in the office, several other members of the firm left. In 1928 Belluschi became chief designer of the firm and in 1932, a partner. During this period of his life, Belluschi was deeply affected by the philosophy of Harry Wentz, a Portland artist and art teacher who was inspired by the regional qualities of the Northwest and by Japanese architecture. In 1929 Belluschi became a naturalized U.S. citizen.

In 1931 Belluschi designed his first important building, the Portland Art Museum, and gained a measure of national recognition for his effort.

In 1934 Belluschi married Helen Hemmila and they had two children. That same year, he went to Europe where he studied the modern architecture being built and the old medieval churches and villages. On his return, he decided to design buildings that would be expressions of their own time, but founded in the great cultural traditions of the past.

After becoming chief designer, Belluschi produced a steady flow of well-designed buildings. In 1943 he had become so successful that he acquired the Doyle firm and changed its name to his own. The good designs continued and brought him an international reputation as a designer and as one of the foremost proponents of regional architecture.

In 1951 Belluschi decided to devote much of his time and energies to education and became dean of the School of Architecture and Planning of Massachusetts Institute of Technology. Leaving Portland, he formed an association with Skidmore, Owings and Merrill, one of the greatest and most successful of American architectural firms. In spite of Belluschi's deep involvement in architectural and planning education, he still managed to design many buildings, often in association with other architects. During his very prolific career, the total reached well over 1,000 buildings.

In 1962 Belluschi's wife died. He continued at MIT until 1965, when he retired. In that same year, he married Marjorie Bruckner. After retirement from the deanship, he became more active in architectural practice and later moved back to Oregon. Pietro Belluschi received many honors, including a number of honorary doctor's degrees, election to fellowship in the American Academy of Arts and Sciences and to membership in the National Institute of Arts and Letters. In 1972 the architects of his adopted country awarded him their highest honor, the Gold Medal of the American Institute of Architects. Belluschi died February 14, 1994.

**Related Articles** CONTEMPORARY ARCHITECTURE; EDUCATION; JENNEY, WILLIAM LE BARON; MODERN ARCHITECTURE; RELIGIOUS BUILDING; SKIDMORE, OWINGS AND MERRILL.

**BIRKERTS, GUNNAR** American architect, born in Riga, Latvia, and resident in the United States since 1949, Gunnar Birkerts practices internationally. His work carries on the Modern movement in sensitive design of a wide variety of projects.

**Work** Perhaps his most famous buildings are the Federal Reserve Bank of Minneapolis (1973) and the fluid form of the addition to the Museum of Glass in Corning, N.Y. (1980). He has designed a wide variety of projects, including religious buildings and fittings, apartments, office buildings, educational buildings, banks, recreation facilities, museums, libraries, and public buildings. With offices in Birmingham, Mich., Gunnar Birkerts has produced many projects in Michigan and surrounding states. He is particularly adept at planning expansion of existing buildings, often in underground structures, such as for the University of Michigan Law School (1981) in Ann Arbor, Mich., or for the recently completed Library Addition (1993) at the University of California in San Diego.

One of his clients has been Domino's Pizza, for which he made a master plan for Domino's Farms in Ann Arbor, Mich., and he designed the Domino's Pizza Headquarters building, the Special Designs building (1986), and Exhibition Building (1987), and other projects.

For IBM, Gunner Birkerts designed the Corporate Computer Center (1972) at Sterling Forest, N.Y., and several projects in Michigan. His international work includes the U.S. Embassy Office Building in Caracas, Venezuela, the Novoli Multi-Use Center in Florence, Italy, the National Library in Riga, Latvia, and a Sports Center in Venice, Italy.

Gunnar Birkerts has been involved in a number of special projects, such as the design of furniture for the Papal visit (1987) to Michigan and interiors for many of his projects. His design for the woodwork for the Holzman & Silverman Office Building (1989) is illustrated in the article entitled woodwork.

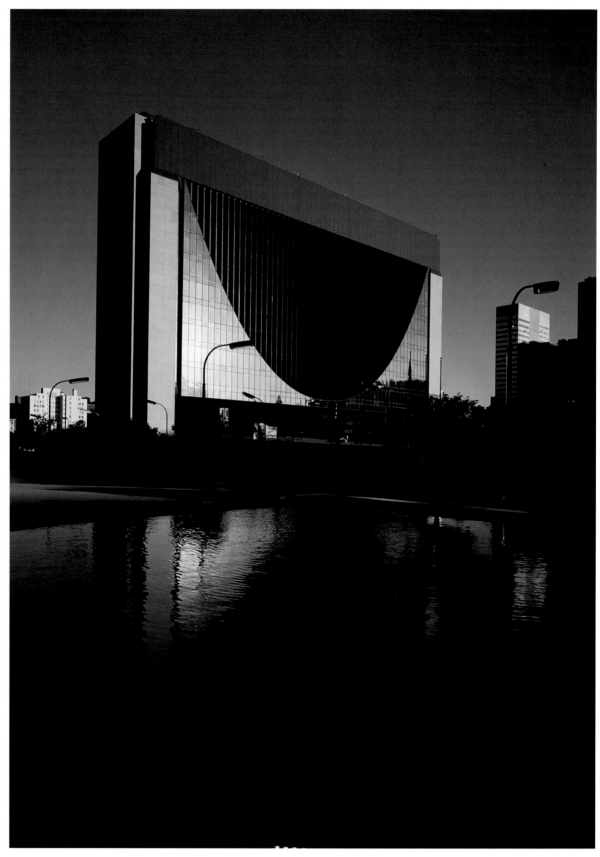

**BIRKERTS, GUNNAR** Federal Reserve Bank (1972), Minneapolis, Minn.

**BIRKERTS, GUNNAR** The Corning Museum of Glass (1980), Corning, N.Y.

**Life** Gunnar Birkerts was born in Riga, Latvia, on January 17, 1925, the son of Marija Shop Birkerts and the educator Peteris Birkerts, who had studied in the United States. During World War II Latvia was occupied by the Germans from 1941 to 1944 and was then annexed by Russia. In 1944, Gunnar Birkerts left Latvia and went to Germany; he was granted a displaced persons status, which made him eligible for education at the Technische Hoschschule in Stuttgart. After receiving his *Diplomingenieur-Archtitekt* degree in 1949, he emigrated to the United States. He worked briefly for the firm of Perkins and Will in Chicago and then joined the office of Eero Saarinen in Bloomfield Hills, Mich., in 1951. In 1956 he joined the office of Minoru Yamasaki, and in 1959 he opened his own office (Birkerts and Straub) in Birmingham, Mich., later renamed Gunnar Birkerts and Associates.

Gunnar Birkerts has taught at the universities of Michigan and Illinois and was architect in residence at the American Academy in Rome in 1976. He has received the Arnold W. Brunner Memorial Prize in Architecture (1981) from the American Academy and Institute of Arts and Letters. He has also been named an honorary fellow of the Latvian Architects Association and was honored by the Association for the Advancement of Baltic Studies. Many of his projects have received design awards. Now in his late sixties, he continues an extensive practice.

**Related Articles** Saarinen, Eero; Yamasaki, Minoru.

**Further Reading** Kaiser, Kay: *The Architecture of Gunnar Birkerts*, The American Institute of Architects Press, Washington, D.C., 1989.

**BOGARDUS, JAMES** American inventor (1800–74). As an inventor, James Bogardus originated a great number and variety of devices, including clocks, cotton spinning machinery, engraving machines, gas meters, and mechanical pencils. Some of these were important contributions and were quite successful.

**Cast-Iron Buildings** In architecture, Bogardus is remembered for other reasons. He was the first American to develop practical methods for the construction of skeleton frames of cast iron for buildings. And he was the first to prefabricate almost every part of a building, transport the parts to the site, and erect the building in record time, sometimes in a few weeks. Whereas cast iron had been used previously, starting in England, for the construction of portions of the frames of buildings and bridges, Bogardus was the first to develop a system for an entire building: a five-story factory he built for himself in New York City in 1849. This building had

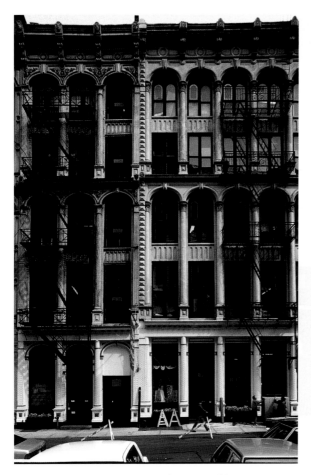

**BOGARDUS, JAMES** 85 Leonard Street Building (1860), New York, N.Y.

prefabricated cast-iron columns, piers, beams, and wall panels and was constructed in a few weeks. Some 10 years later, it was disassembled.

Thus Bogardus accomplished the early pioneering work that led eventually to wrought-iron and later steel skeleton-framed buildings and to the tall buildings, or skyscrapers, of today. His earlier buildings were not completely framed with cast iron. Eventually, Bogardus developed methods for making cast-iron fronts for buildings, another element of architecture that soon spread from New York City, where he first used it, to other parts of the country. These fronts might be considered the forerunners of the curtain walls of metals and other materials in use today.

After his first cast-iron building, Bogardus built others in many places, including Baltimore, Washington, Chicago, and Cuba. But he did more of them in New York City than anywhere else. Most of his buildings were demolished long ago. In New York City the only examples that remain are two warehouses in very poor condition on Leonard Street, one of which Bogardus built for himself. Another interesting structure thought to be by Bogardus that still exists is a cast-iron watch-tower (1857), or fire tower, in Mount Morris Park, New York City. Another of his New York City works, the Laing Warehouses (1949), later known as the Bogardus Building, was torn down in the 1960s, after the cast-iron wall panels had been carefully removed. The panels were stolen; how and by whom has never been established.

**Life** James Bogardus was born in Catskill, N.Y., on March 14, 1800. He did not do well in school, attending only at irregular intervals until he was fourteen years of age. Then he was apprenticed to a watchmaker. He never went back to school. After completing his apprenticeship in his early 20s, he went to New York City where he embarked on a life of invention.

When Bogardus was twenty-eight years old, he received a considerable amount of publicity by winning a gold medal for his invention of an eight-day clock. He continued to invent devices of many kinds for the rest of his life. In 1831 he married Margaret Maclay, the daughter of a minister. They had children, but none survived to adulthood.

Starting in the 1840s, Bogardus developed systems for the use of cast iron in buildings, some of which were inventions that he patented. Much of the remainder of his life was spent designing and constructing cast-iron buildings and other structures and further developing inventions of this sort. He became a successful manufacturer of cast-iron systems and parts for buildings, which were used by others in their buildings, and a very successful designer and constructor of buildings.

In his lifetime, Bogardus did not receive much credit for pioneering skeleton-frame construction for buildings and prefabrication. After his death, on April 13, 1874, he gradually slipped into relative obscurity, his name but an occasional footnote in books and other references on architecture.

**Related Articles** IRON; JENNEY, WILLIAM LE BARON; MODERN ARCHITECTURE; STRUCTURE.

**BOOK, ARCHITECTURAL** Although other meanings have been used in past eras, the word *book* today commonly means a work of considerable length, about 96 pages or more, printed on paper which has been assembled and bound into a cover. From very early times, a great number of architectural books have been written and published for use by both professionals in architecture and laypeople. Many of these books, some by architects, have greatly and even profoundly influenced architecture.

**Composition** Books are classified as "softbound," with flexible covers usually of heavy paper, or "hardbound," with stiff covers usually of cardboard covered with cloth, paper, leather, or other materials. Each leaf of paper in a book has two sides, or *pages*. The top of a book, of its pages, is the *head*; the bound edge is the *back*; the opposite edge is the *front*; and the bottom is the *foot*. The area in which type and illustrations occur on a page is the *type page* and the space around it, the *margins*. The inside edge at the binding is the *gutter.* Often included on the pages are the titles of chapters or other information; if at the top of pages, these are called *running heads*; if at the bottom, *running feet.* Also on the pages are page numbers, or *folios*.

Upon opening a book, the first double sheet is ordinarily attached to the inside of the front cover, and the last, to the back cover. These are the *endpapers* and may contain illustrations or other decorative matter. The first printed page other than the endpapers is the *half-title page,* which contains only the title of the book. This is the first page of a series called the *front matter.* The second printed page is the *title page,* which contains not only the title but the author's name, the publisher's name, the place of publication, and sometimes other matter. On the back of the title page is the *copyright page,* which usually includes other information, such as a Library of Congress number and an International Standard Book Number (ISBN). The next page or sometimes several pages in the front matter is usually called the *table of contents.* There may then be a list of illustrations, an enumeration and background of contributors, a dedication page, a foreword written by someone other than the author, and a preface written by the author to explain the reasons for the book and to acknowledge those who helped in its preparation. If many people have to be acknowledged, an acknowledgment page follows the preface. There may be other pages in the front matter.

After the front matter comes the *text,* or main body of the book. This is usually divided into chapters but may be divided into parts which are subdivided into chapters. Notes may be placed at the end of each chapter or footnotes at the bottom of text pages, particularly in scholarly books.

After the main body of a book comes the *back matter.* This may consist of appendixes to furnish supplementary information to the main text, often a bibliography, and, most important, an index. In some architectural books, more than one index is used for clarity and usefulness to readers. For example, there might be a general index plus indexes of architects, buildings, places, and so on.

The covers of books are ordinarily stamped with the titles, authors' names, and publishers on the back, sometimes called the *shelf-back* or spine, and sometimes these are also stamped on the front. Most stamping is with colored ink; however, in blind stamping, only an impression is made without using ink. Most books have *jackets,* sometimes called *dust jackets,* which are printed separately and folded around the book.

**Classifications** Books are classified into four major kinds: trade, including novels and others intended for the general public; textbooks, intended for instruction in schools, colleges, and universities; reference books, including dictionaries, encyclopedias, and the like; and professional books, for specialized use by those who need them in their vocations. Most architectural books fall in the professional category and in the reference group. There is also a fifth category, reprint books, usually less expensive versions of published books. Reprints may be made from all kinds of books. A recent type of book is the monograph of the work of an individual architect or even an individual building. Often these books contain mostly photographs of the work involved.

As in many other categories of professional books, architectural books are often written by people whose main occupation is other than writing, including the teaching and practice of architecture professions. Thus writers of architectural books are often members of their own audience.

**Launching a Book** An architect, or a person in a field related to architecture, who wants to write a book usually starts by preparing an outline of the book, together with a prospectus telling the purpose or objective of the book, what is to be included, the audience for whom it is intended, how the writing will be accomplished, the intended length of the manuscript, the number and character of the illustrations, and schedule for completion of the work.

With this information in hand and perhaps with the addition of sample chapters, a publisher can decide about the feasibility of publishing the book. During the writing of the book, an editor works with the author to assist with problems that may arise. Architect-authors often make their own drawings or have them prepared under their supervision. When the manuscript and illustrations are ready and accepted by the publisher, the book is put into production. The book is styled by a designer; a copy editor corrects the manuscript; the materials are typeset; the author and proofreader read the galleys— long sets of typeset matter not yet divided into pages— for errors; the corrected galleys are returned to the compositor to effect necessary changes and to be divided into pages; page proofs are sent to the author and editors who read them for errors.

After some time, usually a matter of months after the start of production, everything is ready for printing. The printed sheets are folded and then gathered into signatures which are groups of 16, 32, or 64 consecutive pages and the signatures are arranged in the proper order, or collated; the book is then bound. The book is inserted into a jacket and is now ready to be marketed. For most architectural books, marketing is effected by advertising in architectural and related magazines, by direct mail promotion, and, in the case of textbooks, by salespeople, called college travelers, who call on educators and bookstores.

**Purposes of Architectural Books** Books have exerted a powerful influence on architects and their architecture from the time of the Romans. Books have deeply affected architectural design. They have been used for the espousal of architectural philosophies and for education, not only in schools, colleges, and universities but for self-education. In the early days of American colonial architecture, books were the training source of many gentlemen-architects, who had no other way to learn about architecture. Since that time, a major purpose of architectural books has been the continuing education of architects after they have entered practice. This list of purposes of architectural books might be expanded considerably.

Hundreds of thousands of architectural and related books have been published and new ones appear every year. Although many architectural books are mentioned or listed in other articles in this book, it is impossible to do justice to their scope, breadth, and impact. However, some books have had such a powerful effect on architecture that they must be mentioned here.

**Influential Architectural Books** The first great architectural book, still of considerable influence today, was *De architectura*, written by Marcus Vitruvius Pollio, usually called Vitruvius, a Roman architect of the first century B.C., about whom very little is known. In this book, not published until 1486, Vitruvius attempted to analyze the elements of good architecture. His principles are still quoted. Another book of importance to architecture was the *Historia Naturalis*, written by scholar Gaius Plinius Secundus (A.D. 23–79), usually called Pliny the Elder. This monumental work, the only one of Pliny's many books that is still in existence, discussed architecture, along with all the known sciences of the time.

During the Renaissance a number of Italian architects wrote important books. The first architectural book printed from movable type was *Architecture in Ten Books* by Leon Battista Alberti (1404–72), published in 1485. Giacomo Barozzi da Vignola (1507–73) wrote *The Five Orders of Architecture*, published in 1563. These books greatly influenced later architects who designed in the Classic Revival and Eclectic styles.

Another important book was *Lives of the Most Eminent Painters, Sculptors, and Architects*, published in 1550, by Giorgio Vasari (1511–74), who was a painter as well as an architect. Although not gathered into a book, the engravings of Giovanni Battista Piranesi (1720–78) presented the most complete view of Roman architecture of his time and of the past. Perhaps the most important book of all was *The Architecture of*

*A. Palladio*, by Andrea Palladio (1518–80), first published in 1570 and translated into English in 1716. This book became the most used guide to classical architecture for the architects who later designed Classic Revival buildings.

Many other architects wrote books about classical architecture. Among the most important were those by the English architects—James Gibbs (1682–1754), who wrote *Book of Architecture*, 1728, and *Rules for Drawing the Several Parts of Architecture*, 1732; and Inigo Jones (1573–1652), who wrote *Designs*, a two-volume book published in 1770. Also of importance were books by Scottish architects, in particular, those of the brothers Adam, the first of which was *Ruins of the Palace of Diocletian in Dalmatia*, by Robert Adam (1728–92), published in 1764; equally important is *Works in Architecture of Robert and James Adam*, in three volumes published in 1773, 1779, and 1822, and written by Robert Adam and his brother, James Adam (1730–94). Another ambitious publishing project was the *Vitruvius Brittanicus*, published in five volumes, 1715–71), the first volume by Colen Campbell (*c.* 1676–1729), the next four by other authors. One of the many important books by French architects is *L'Architecture Français* by Jacques François Blondel (1705–44), published in four volumes, 1752–56.

Many architects and others wrote books of importance in the era of Gothic Revival architecture and later. Among the most influential are those of the Pugins, father and son. The father, Augustus Charles Pugin (1762–1832), wrote *Architectural Antiquities of Normandy*, 1828, *Examples of Gothic Architecture*, vol. 1, 1828, and in collaboration with his son, Augustus Welby Northmore Pugin (1812–52), *Examples of Gothic Architecture*, vol. 2, 1838. The younger Pugin wrote other books, including *The True Principles of Pointed or Christian Architecture*, 1841. The books of the French architect Eugène Emmanuel Viollet-le-Duc (1814–79) were also noteworthy; his most important was the 10-volume *Dictionary of French Architecture*, published in 1854–69. Also important were those of the Englishman Batty Langley (1696–1751), including his *Gothic Architecture Improved by Rules and Proportion*, published in 1742.

English critics produced evaluative works. John Ruskin (1819–1900) wrote *Seven Lamps of Architecture*, 1849, and *Stones of Venice*, published in three volumes, 1853. The English critic and painter Sir Charles Lock Eastlake (1793–1865) wrote *A History of the Gothic Revival in England*, published in 1872.

A great number of books on architecture and related subjects were published in the late 19th and in the 20th centuries and many new ones are constantly being published. Some of the most influential have been written by architects, including Louis Henri Sullivan (1856–1924), Ralph Adams Cram (1863–1942), Walter Adolf Gropius (1883–1969), Eliel Saarinen (1873–1950), and Frank Lloyd Wright (1867–1959). Two influential books of the 20th century are *The International Style* by Henry-Russell Hitchcock and Philip C. Johnson (1932) and *Complexity and Contradiction in Architecture* by Robert Venturi (1966), both originally published by the Museum of Modern Art, New York. Some important works have been written by architecture critics and historians, including works by Montgomery Schuyler (1843–1914) and Lewis Mumford (1895–1990). Far too numerous to mention here, many relevant works are discussed or listed in other articles in this book.

**History** The forerunners of books, clay tablets with symbols, existed in Mesopotamia from about 50 centuries before the birth of Christ. Beginning about the 25th century B.C., the Egyptians used a paperlike substance, papyrus, made from the bark of a plant, instead of clay. Papyrus was usually made into long sheets or rolls, called scrolls. Although papyrus was a better writing material than clay, it decayed quickly. The ancient Greeks also used papyrus scrolls. The Romans invented a new kind of writing material, parchment, made from untanned skins of animals. For the finest work, they used a top grade of parchment called vellum. At first, parchment or vellum was made into scrolls, but beginning about the second century A.D., sheets of vellum were folded, gathered, and sewn together very much like the pages of a modern book. Such a gathering was called a codex. During the Middle Ages, vellum was used extensively by monks who copied books by hand.

**Inventions** In China two more important inventions eventually revolutionized the making of books. In the 2d century A.D. the Chinese invented paper, and about the 9th century they printed the first book from type made of baked clay. It is thought that paper was introduced into Europe in the 12th century by merchants who had traveled to China. However, printing with movable type was developed independently in Europe, probably by Johann Gutenberg (c. 1397–1468). One of the world's most famous books is Gutenberg's *Latin Bible*, printed about 1456 with movable cast-lead type. Originally known as the *Mazarin Bible*, it is now generally called the *Gutenberg Bible*. More than 40 copies are still in existence.

After the invention of movable type, the growth of printing and the publication of books was very rapid. Early books, printed before the 16th century, are called *incunabula*, from the Latin word for cradle. By the 16th century, many books were published, some of them among the most beautiful examples of book design, printing, and binding of all time. Woodcuts, carved designs on blocks of wood, usually by hand, came into use for printing illustrations. Woodcuts were cut into the side grain of woodblocks. This process was followed by wood engraving, cut into the end grain of wood blocks, first by hand and then by machine, allowing more detail than in woodcuts. Later in the 15th century, engravings were made on copper, allowing still more detail and a longer useful life. In the 19th century, engravings were often made on steel, further extending the number of printing impressions that could be made from a single plate. All these and other methods are still in use by artists today, but in book printing they have been supplanted by new methods.

For more than 300 years after the invention of movable type, books were printed in much the same manner, with hand-cast type, set by hand, printed on handmade paper on hand-operated wooden presses. This is how the books of the first American printer, Stephen Daye (c. 1594–1668), were produced in Cambridge, Mass., starting in 1640. In the early 18th century machines were invented for making paper, and in the early 19th century an all-metal press was developed. Soon afterward, a machine-driven press was developed and in 1845, a revolving cylinder press. In 1865 a web press, using paper in rolls rather than in single sheets, was invented. These were the last great improvements in printing machinery until the 20th century.

Other inventions improved the type used for printing. First, in 1725 came the stereotype, a device for casting type in large plates, in molds usually made of paper pulp, and still in use today mostly by newspapers. Then in 1839 stereotypes were mostly superseded by the invention of the electrotype, a method of casting type in metal-coated wax molds made by electroplating.

In 1852 a new process was developed for printing illustrations and other content. The photoengraving process involves exposing a photographic negative against a metal plate, coated with a substance that may be hardened by light. Then the metal plate is exposed to acid that eats away the parts of the plate not covered by the coating. A line engraving, or line cut, is an engraving of line drawings or similar matter and shows only the lines without shading. A halftone engraving is photographed through a screen that produces small dots, which show tones or shading when printed. Halftones are used for photographs and similar matter.

All these developments helped in the growth of printing and book publishing. Another development in 1884 speeded up the growth considerably; this was the invention of the Linotype, a machine for setting type and still in use today, by Ottmar Mergenthaler (1854–99). This was closely followed in 1887 by another machine for this purpose, the Monotype, also still in use.

**Other Improvements** The 20th century has seen a number of improvements in printing methods, including in 1902 methods for controlling the cleanliness, humidity, and temperature of the air in printshops, problems that had always made consistent printing difficult. Then in 1904 the offset press was invented, utilizing the techniques of photolithography. Heretofore, printing was done by letterpress. In the new method, called "offset printing," printing plates are made by sensitizing metal, to which the matter to be printed is then transferred by a photographic process. On the press, this printing plate transfers the inked image to a rubber cylinder which in turn transfers the image to the paper or other material.

The offset method of printing is based on the principles of lithography, or stone printing, invented in 1796. The original form of lithography, still used by artists, involves drawing on a porous stone (found chiefly in Germany) with greasy crayon, ink, or pencil, wetting the stone with water and inking the stone with greasy ink which adheres only to the drawing, not to the other parts of the stone. Paper is then printed by pressing it on the inked stone. At first, offset printing could not achieve the quality of the letterpress, but in recent years it has been greatly improved and has become the most important method for printing books and many other materials.

Color printing can be accomplished on either letterpress or offset press. For such work, separations must be made dividing the material to be printed into its component colors, usually four—black, magenta (red), yellow, and cyan (blue)—for most work. For special printing such as reproduction of great paintings, more than four colors are often used. From each color separation, a separate plate is made and each is printed in succession.

Other 20th-century developments of importance in printing include the invention of xerography, or photocopying, in 1937, a form that requires no ink; and the invention of cold setting of type, starting with the first commercial phototypesetting machines in 1947. Another development is setting type by computer, which began in 1962.

All these developments have contributed to the great flow of books of all kinds, including many on architecture, in the 20th century.

**Related Articles** CRITICISM, ARCHITECTURE; GRAPHIC DESIGN; LIBRARY; MAGAZINE, ARCHITECTURAL.

**Sources of Additional Information** American Institute of Architects Library, 1735 New York Avenue, N.W., Washington, D.C. 20006; Avery Library, Columbia University, New York, N.Y. 10027; Library of Congress, 10 First St., S.E., Washington, D.C. 20540.

**BOTANICAL BUILDING** A structure for shelter and display of plants for scientific, educational, and artistic purposes. The botanical building is often located in a botanical garden, an outdoor area in which plants are grown for the same purposes, or in an arboretum, an

**BOTANICAL BUILDING** Interior, Climatron (1960), Missouri Botanical Garden, St. Louis, Mo. *[Architects: Murphy and Mackey; Dome, R. Buckminster Fuller]*

outdoor area in which trees, shrubbery, and other woody plants are grown. Sometimes botanical and zoological gardens, or zoos, are combined.

**Functions** Botanical gardens and buildings are often located in universities or other institutions where plants are studied. Various functions are performed, including collection and cultivation, classification, breeding and hybridization, and research and experimentation of plants. Botanical institutions often maintain libraries of books and other information on plants and present educational programs for adults and children. Permanent displays are usually available, in which plants are labeled with their common and scientific names. In many botanical gardens and buildings, plants are displayed in areas that approximate their natural habitats, such as temperate, tropical, or desert zones. In others, plants are arranged according to cultural requirements as indoor, rock, or aquatic gardens.

Although botanical buildings are not an important building type in terms of the number built, they do represent an interesting architectural challenge. They must be designed in such a way that climatological conditions found in nature may be duplicated artificially. The sun must be controlled, along with the humidity, tempera-

**BOTANICAL BUILDING** Rainbow Center Mall and Winter Garden (1977), Niagara Falls, N.Y. [*Architect: Cesar Pelli at Gruen Associates*]

ture, soil conditions, insects, and plant diseases. These conditions are provided by such architectural means as the conformation, orientation, and placement of the buildings, and by mechanical and electrical systems designed to produce requisite environmental states.

**Greenhouse** A special kind of botanical building in increasingly widespread use is the greenhouse, a glass or plastic enclosed building in which plants may be grown under controlled conditions the year round. Greenhouses are used in botanical gardens, by commercial growers, and by individuals who like to grow things as a hobby or for the table. Greenhouses usually have shading devices to control the sun and range from simple types to those with built-in heating and ventilating equipment and piped-in water supplies. They range in size from small units that attach to a window to commercial units covering acres of ground. Greenhouses may be framed with wood, steel, or aluminum; many prefabricated types are available.

**Development** One of the earliest botanical, and zoological, gardens in Europe, the *Jardin des Plantes*, Paris, was established in 1626 and is still one of the best and most extensive institutions of its kind in the world. Another famous one that still survives is the Royal

Botanic Garden, known as Kew Gardens, established in 1760 in Surrey, just west of London. In 1728 American botanist John Bartram (1699–1777) established the first botanical garden in Philadelphia and built his house there in 1731. Both garden and house still exist and, now known as Bartram's Gardens, are open to the public. There are a number of botanical gardens all over the United States, including the Brooklyn Botanic Garden; the New York Botanical Garden, New York City; the Missouri Botanical Garden, St. Louis; and the U.S. National Arboretum, Washington, D.C.

**Related Articles** GARDEN; ZOOLOGICAL BUILDING.

**BREUER, MARCEL LAJOS** Hungarian-American architect (1902–81). After having been a student and a faculty member at the Bauhaus in Germany, Marcel Lajos Breuer came to the United States in 1937 to join Walter Adolf Gropius (1883–1969) on the faculty of Harvard University and as a partner in architectural practice.

**Assessment** Breuer had a brilliant career in education and in furniture design, but he was first and foremost an architect. And his architecture is thought by many to embody all the elements that the best architecture must contain. His buildings solve the problems contained in their programs. The materials used are a

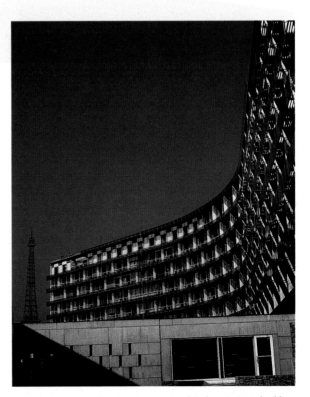

**BREUER, MARCEL LAJOS** Exterior detail, UNESCO building (1953–57), Paris, France. [*Architects: Marcel Breuer, Bernard H. Zehrfuss and Pier Luigi Nervi*]

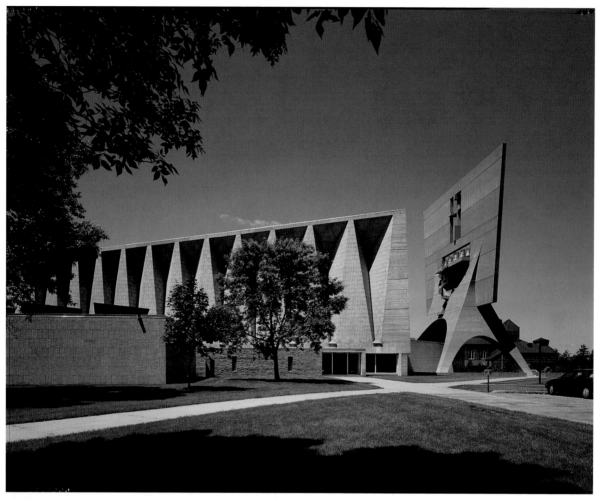

**BREUER, MARCEL LAJOS** Exterior, St. John's University Church (1958), Collegeville, Minn.
[*Architects: Marcel Breuer, Hamilton P. Smith, assoc.*]

combination of the traditional such as wood and brick with newer types such as concrete and metal. The designs are inventive, without gimmicks, and strictly of their time rather than some past era. There is a naturalness about his buildings, a neatness in their form and appearance. Somehow, they always seem to combine a sort of quiet excitement with serene contentment, an accomplishment not often achieved in the architecture of today.

**Works** Starting with his early work in Germany and other parts of Europe, Breuer produced a steady stream of notable buildings, almost all of the highest quality. His first building was a house in Germany in 1932. This was followed by an apartment building (1933) in Zurich, Switzerland, for Dr. Sigfried Giedion (1888–1968), the eminent art and architecture historian and critic, who wrote one of the most influential books on architecture of all time, *Space, Time and Architecture*, first published in 1941 and still in print, in a fifth revised edition (Harvard University Press, 1967).

After coming to the United States, Breuer continued to design houses and other residential buildings exclusively until he was almost fifty. His first American buildings were designed in partnership with Gropius in and around Cambridge. Among these were the house for Gropius (1937; illustrated in Gropius article) and that for Breuer himself (1939), both in Lincoln, Mass.; the University House (1938), Cohasset, Mass.; and the Aluminum City Terrace Housing (1941); New Kensington, Pa., near Pittsburgh.

After leaving Gropius to start his own firm, Breuer continued to design houses, including the Geller House (1945), Lawrence, N.Y., and the Robinson House (1947), Williamsburg, Mass., and had continued to design houses ever since. Breuer also designed a house which was constructed in the garden of the Museum of Modern Art, New York City, in 1949. This house brought him to the attention of architects and the general public as nothing had before. He soon received commissions for other houses and for larger buildings.

**BREUER, MARCEL LAJOS** Whitney Museum of American Art (1966), New York, N.Y. *[Architects: Marcel Breuer, Hamilton P. Smith]*

Notable buildings by Breuer include the Ferry Cooperative Dormitory (1951), Vassar College, Poughkeepsie, N.Y.; the UNESCO Headquarters (1958), Paris, designed in association with Pier Luigi Nervi (1891–1979) and Bernard Zehrfuss (b. 1912); the IBM Building (1962), La Gaude, France; Whitney Museum of American Art (1966), New York City; St. John's Abbey Church and College buildings (1967), Collegeville, Minn.; the U.S. Department of Housing and Urban Development Building (1967), Washington, D.C.; New York University Technology buildings (1969); and the Murray Lincoln Center (1973), University of Massachusetts, Amherst, Mass.

**Life** Marcel Lajos Breuer was born in Pecs, Hungary, on May 22, 1902. After graduating from school in Pecs, he enrolled in 1920 in the Bauhaus founded by Walter Adolf Gropius in Weimar, Germany. In 1924 he received his degree and joined the faculty as a master of carpentry, remaining there until 1928. In 1926 he married Martha Erps; the marriage ended in divorce. While at the Bauhaus, he designed several modern chairs and other furniture, using bent, tubular steel frames for the first time.

In 1928 both he and Gropius left the Bauhaus faculty, and Breuer established an architectural practice in Berlin. In 1931, when the worldwide Depression and the Nazi influence had almost brought architectural com-

missions to a halt, he managed both to practice and to travel in other parts of Germany and Europe and in North Africa. While in Berlin, he designed interiors, a few houses, and an apartment building. He also designed more chairs, of plywood and metals, which are still considered among the best examples of modern furniture. In 1935 he went to England, where Gropius had set up a practice, and formed a partnership with F. R. S. Yorke (1906–62) which lasted until 1937.

Soon after Gropius arrived at Harvard University in 1937 to assume the chair of the department of architecture, Breuer joined him on the faculty as a design professor and stayed until 1941. Also in 1937 the two architects started an architectural practice in Cambridge that lasted until 1942. In 1940 Breuer married Constance Leighton.

In 1942 Breuer organized his own practice in Cambridge and in 1946 moved his office to New York City. He retired in 1977 and died in 1981. Breuer received many honors for his contributions to architecture and for his significant building designs. These included several honorary doctors' degrees, including one from Harvard. He was elected a member of both the American Academy of Arts and Sciences and the National Institute of Arts and Letters. In 1968 he received the highest award of the architects of his adopted country, the Gold Medal of the American Institute of Architects. In 1975 he had the honor of having his tubular chair of 1929 again put into production by a leading furniture manufacturer, certainly an indication of the lasting freshness and originality of his designs.

**Related Articles** BAUHAUS, STAATLICHES; CONTEMPORARY ARCHITECTURE; EDUCATION; FURNITURE; GROPIUS, WALTER ADOLF; MODERN ARCHITECTURE.

**BRICK** A masonry unit usually made of kiln-burned clay, but sometimes of other materials, used in architecture for construction of walls and other purposes. From the earliest times to today, brick has been one of the most important building materials. The major type of brick used today and the one most frequently referred to when using the word *brick* is made of clay fired in kilns to impart hardness, strength, and resistance to moisture. Other types include cement, sand-lime, and adobe brick types. Cement brick, sometimes called concrete brick, is made of portland cement and aggregates, very much like other types of concrete. Adobe brick is very much like that used by ancient people, and is made of sun-dried clay.

**Kiln-Burned Brick** This brick is usually made by the stiff-mud process, in which just enough water is added to the ground clay to allow it to be extruded through a die into a ribbon. The ribbon is then sliced with wires to form bricks. Sometimes a vacuum pump is used to remove air from the clay to make the bricks stronger. The shaped bricks are dried at 100 to 300°F (38 to 149°C) and then burned in kilns at 1600°F (871°C) or higher. Other methods for making brick include the soft-mud process, in which a greater quantity of water is used with the clay, and the dry-press process, in which almost no water is used.

The two most important types of kiln-burned bricks are building brick, sometimes called "common brick," and facing or face brick. The main differences between the two types are appearance and use; face brick has a better appearance and is used for exposed brickwork left in its natural state; building brick is used mostly for hidden work or for exposed work where appearance is unimportant or the brickwork will be painted. Building brick comes in three grades: SW, MW, and NW; SW for conditions of heavy rainfall and freezing, MW for moderate conditions, and NW for minimal conditions. Face brick also comes in three grades—FBX, FBS, and FBA—generally denoting the degree of perfection of the bricks, from the most perfect to the least. All grades of both

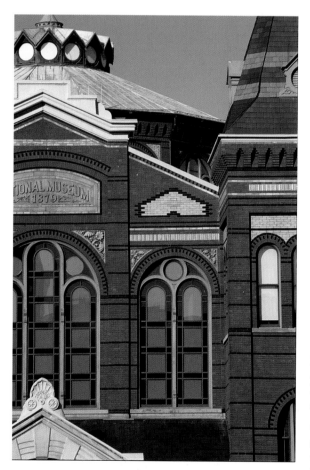

**BRICK** Detail, Arts and Industries Building (1881), Smithsonian Institution, Washington, D.C. *[Architects: Cluss and Schulze after plans by Montgomery C. Meigs]*

types of brick generally have high strength against crushing (compression) and bending, but less strength against stretching (tension). All are relatively impervious to water penetration and are incombustible. However, bricks with various degrees of strength and other characteristics may be obtained. Both building and face brick may be obtained either solid or cored, with vertical holes through the centers.

Other important types of kiln-burned bricks include glazed, flooring, and paving. Glazed brick, solid or cored, is face brick which has a surface glaze produced by gases or with ceramic materials. It comes in two grades, S (select) and SS (select sized), in which face dimension variations are minimal. These bricks may be obtained with either one of two faces glazed. Flooring brick is hard and dense and is used in buildings, such as factories, in which floors must resist heavy wear and hard treatment. Flooring brick comes in several grades for various uses. Paving brick is also hard and dense, and may be used in buildings of all types.

Special types include fire, refractory, and acid. Firebricks are made of special clays that are resistant to heat for such purposes as lining the interiors of fireplaces. Refractory bricks are similar but will withstand even higher temperatures, such as those in industrial furnaces. Acid bricks are produced for use in chemical plants, laboratories, and the like. Also available are thin-brick veneers used to simulate real walls.

Bricks may be preassembled into panels with cement plastic mortar which has high tensile strength, but the more general method involves laying them in mortar, one by one. Bricks may also be obtained in special shapes for making arches, trim around windows and doors, and other purposes. Such shapes are usually made in molds. Various surface textures are available, including smooth; grooved, or scored; scratched, or combed; roughened; water-struck, in which molds have been wetted; and sand-struck, in which sand was used on the sides of molds. Bricks may also be obtained in a variety of earth colors, and glazed bricks in additional colors.

**Sizes** Regular brick comes in a variety of sizes in addition to the usual nominal size of about 4 by 8 by slightly more than 2 inches. In general, there are two systems for brick sizes: the modular and the nonmodular. The modular sizes differ from the others in that they produce even multiples of 4-inch increments, or modules, including the mortar joints that separate the bricks. Thus a brick that is nominally 4 inches deep and 8 inches long will actually be slightly less than those dimensions, to allow for the width of the mortar joints. A regular modular brick has a nominal size of 4 by 8 by 2⅔ inches, if it is to be laid with ⅜-inch mortar joints. The actual dimensions of the brick will be smaller so that a brick, with its mortar joint, will be an even 8 inches in

**BRICK** Cleo Rogers Memorial Library (1969), Columbus, Ind. *[Architect: I. M. Pei]*

length; and three brick courses in height, including mortar joints, will be an even 8 inches high. Nonmodular bricks come in sizes that do not produce even dimensions when laid in walls or other structures.

In addition to the regular-sized bricks, there are a variety of other sizes, all nominal, including Norman brick, 12 inches long; Roman brick, 12 inches long but only 2 inches high; and jumbo brick, 12 inches long, 4 inches high, and 6 or 8 inches thick. Flooring and paving bricks come in various sizes, from about 1/2 to 2 1/2 inches thick, and from 4 to 16 inches in the other dimensions. Paving brick may be obtained in rectangular, square, and hexagonal shapes.

**Brick Laying** Bricks are usually laid in a manner that allows their joints to be staggered to produce stronger walls or other building elements. This is ordinarily accomplished by placing individual bricks in different positions, to produce a bond. The two most common ways of placing bricks in walls are with the long side showing, in which a brick is called a stretcher, and with the end showing, in which it is called a header. By alternating headers and stretchers in various ways, good bonds are produced, along with ornamental patterns. The most commonly used bonds in the United States are

the English, in which courses are alternately composed of stretchers and headers; the Flemish, in which stretchers and headers alternate in courses; and the common, or American, in which every fifth or sixth course is composed of headers, while others are stretchers. A number of other bonds are also used and sometimes bonding is accomplished by means of metal ties. Where only

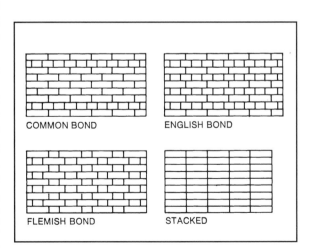

**BRICK** Several types of bonds.

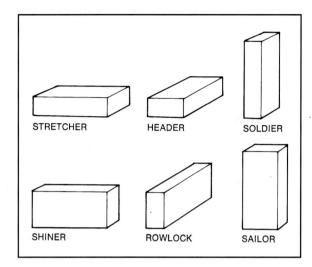

STRETCHER    HEADER    SOLDIER

SHINER    ROWLOCK    SAILOR

**BRICK** Names of brick positions.

stretchers are used with both horizontal and vertical mortar joints continuous, the brick is said to be stacked. This method is not usually employed for structural building elements unless bonded with ties.

Brick floors may be laid flat or on edge. A number of patterns may be used, including running, in which bricks, flat or on edge, are laid like stretchers in a wall, for example, along a walk; and cross, in which the bricks are laid with their long dimensions at right angles to a walk. Brick floors may also be laid in other patterns, such as herringbone, basket weave, and diagonal.

**Other Types of Bricks** Cement, or concrete, and sand-lime bricks are generally available in sizes similar to those for kiln-burned brick. Both types are naturally gray, but other colors may be introduced by adding various mineral pigments. These colored types are not recommended for use in sunlight because of fading. Adobe bricks, used mostly in arid climates such as the Southwest, are generally the colors of the clays from which they are made. Adobe bricks are usually larger than regular brick and may only be used for buildings of one to a few stories in height. They must be laid on top of waterproof foundations, must be protected from precipitation by overhangs and finishes of plaster or adobe, and must be laid with mortar made of adobe.

While regular bricks are relatively impervious to water infiltration, some types are often treated with silicone or other materials to increase resistance. Joints are also important in preventing water from entering. Another problem that sometimes occurs is discoloration, called efflorescence, caused by salts within the brick or mortar that are brought to the surface by water action. Efflorescence can also cause deterioration of brick and the mortar joints. To avoid this problem, brick should be carefully selected and mortars carefully formulated and applied. If efflorescence occurs, it can be removed by

scrubbing with dilute hydrochloric acid followed by rinsing with clear water. However, no method to completely stop efflorescence is known.

Bricks of so many varied sizes, colors, shapes, and types are available that architects and other environmental designers have a wide selection at their disposal. Types should be selected according to the function, textures, and colors desired; the bonds to be used; and other technical and design considerations. Brick is widely used in many ways in both exteriors and interiors of buildings today. Many people think it one of the finest materials for imparting warmth, texture, and other desirable qualities into architecture.

**History** Other than wood and mud, brick is the oldest material used in architecture. When bricks were first made has not been established, but brick fragments made about 4000 B.C. have been found in Mesopotamia. It is believed that brick making began many centuries before that time. In this area, the principle of the corbel for spanning an opening is thought to have been developed. A corbel, thought to be the forerunner of the arch, vault, and dome, was constructed by projecting each higher course of brick, or stone, slightly farther out from the sides until the highest courses met in the middle.

The earliest bricks were made by fashioning clay into shapes and drying them in the sun. Fire-burned brick making developed somewhat later, first utilizing open fires into which the formed bricks were placed and later using kilns. Fire-burned bricks were mostly used for special purposes such as facings for walls. The process of applying impervious coatings, often in color, fired on bricks in kilns, called glazing, was also discovered very early. Plain and glazed bricks were often laid in bitumen.

Brick was widely used in Mesopotamia because of the shortage of lumber and stone. In ancient Egypt and Greece, brick was also used, usually without mortar, but only to a limited extent since other materials were available. The Romans used both sun-dried and kiln-dried bricks, leaving them exposed in modest buildings and covering them with stone or plaster in more important ones. The Romans sometimes laid brick without mortar, but also often used mud, lime mortar, or lime, with crushed tiles or sand, for that purpose. Roman bricks were usually wider and longer than those of today, but thinner to resist warping and cracking. Brick walls were bonded, much as they are today.

Brick was widely used in Early Christian and Byzantine architecture, often left exposed in the former and frequently highly ornamented with marble or other stone or with glass mosaics in the latter. Romanesque architecture utilized brick in many buildings. During the Middle Ages brick was no longer used extensively. However, brick was an important element of architecture, especially in France and Germany where it was often molded or carved into ornamental shapes and laid in widely varied patterns. Brick was also used in Italy and to some extent in England. By the 16th century, English brick sizes had been standardized, generally at $4\frac{1}{2}$ inches thick, by 9 inches long, by 2 inches high. Before standardization, sizes had varied from 8 to 11 inches long and of various thicknesses. English brickwork generally utilized English bond, with alternate courses of headers and stretchers, but sometimes used Flemish bond, with stretchers and headers alternated in each course. Since bricks were often misshaped or distorted, they were usually laid with thick mortar joints.

By the time of the Renaissance, good brick in standard sizes had become widely available and was used in buildings of all types. Some of the finest buildings were of brick or brick combined with stone. While brick is often thought of as a less costly material than stone, this was not always the case in this period, except in areas where no local stone existed. By the 16th and 17th centuries in Europe, brick had become less expensive and was used more extensively. By the 18th century, brick was plastered or stuccoed, painted, and scored to resemble stone.

**American Development** Although wood was the prevalent material for buildings in early colonial America, brick was also widely used. Bricklayers and brick makers were among the first colonists at Jamestown, and it is believed that they constructed kilns and made brick early in the 17th century, possibly about 1610, three years after the colony was founded. The Spanish had made brick in St. Augustine, Fla., and other colonies much earlier.

Brick has always been produced locally, partly because of difficulties in shipping the relatively heavy and bulky materials and partly because the raw materials are found almost everywhere. In spite of this, bricks for a few buildings in the colonies were imported from England and other places. Both sun-dried and kiln-dried bricks were used in the colonies, the former mainly in the Southwest and the latter elsewhere.

Bricks were molded by hand usually in wooden molds and then dried. For the most part, except in the Southwest, they were then burned in kilns of various types, usually fueled with wood. Colonial bricks varied in size from place to place. However, most were of excellent quality, comparable to bricks made in Europe. American bricklayers were, for the most part, also as capable as those in the countries from which they had emigrated. Bricks were usually laid in English bond, but later Flemish bond became quite popular and other bonds were also used. Bricks were generally laid in mortar composed of sand and lime, often obtained from oyster shells in the coastal colonies.

By the middle of the 18th century, bricks for sale were made in many locations in the colonies. And bricks were also made on or near the sites of many individual buildings and were widely used for buildings of all types. All this brick was molded by hand. About the end of the 18th century, attempts were made to produce brick-making machines, and, by the second quarter of the 19th century, a few bricks were produced in machines that mixed the ingredients, extruded the mixture through dies into ribbons of clay, and then cut the ribbons into individual bricks. By the end of that century, almost all bricks were made by machine. Essentially, this established the method used for the manufacture of brick today.

From the beginning of brick making in America to the present, brick has been an important building material in every era. Some of the finest houses and buildings of other types were constructed of brick. Brick continues to be an important building material today, particularly in houses and other buildings of relatively small size. Brick is also sometimes used very effectively in larger buildings, but the last use for bearing walls in a tall building was in the Monadnock Building (1891), Chicago, designed by Burnham and Root. This 16-story building has 6-foot brick walls in the first story.

**Related Articles** Arch; Dome; Fireplace; Masonry Structure; Tile; Vault; Wall.

**Further Reading** Ambrose, James: *Simplified Design of Masonry Structures*, John Wiley & Sons, New York, 1991; Beall, Christine: *Masonry Design and Detailing*, 2d ed., McGraw-Hill, New York, 1987.

**Sources of Additional Information** Brick Institute of America (BIA), 11490 Commerce Park Dr., Reston, Va. 22091; International Masonry Institute, 823 15th St., N.W., Washington, D.C. 20005.

**BRIDGE** A structure that spans a river, a depression, or some other space, usually providing a passageway for people, automobiles, or other vehicles. Although many bridges would not be considered architecture by most people, and engineers rather than architects now usually design them, there are numerous notable bridges which many observers consider architecture of high excellence.

**Types** Bridges may be fixed or movable. Fixed bridges are built permanently in place; movable bridges, sometimes called drawbridges, are designed so that portions may be raised or moved aside to allow ships to pass unobstructed. The major types of movable bridges are swing, lift, and bascule. A portion of a swing bridge may be turned to a position approximately at a right angle to the bridge proper, allowing ships to pass through. A lift bridge can be raised with counterweights, between two towers, allowing ships to pass underneath. A bascule bridge has counterweights on one end that allow the other end to be raised as if the bridge were on a pivot. A special kind of bridge is a viaduct, used for carrying automobiles or trains over low-lying ground, valleys, or other obstructions.

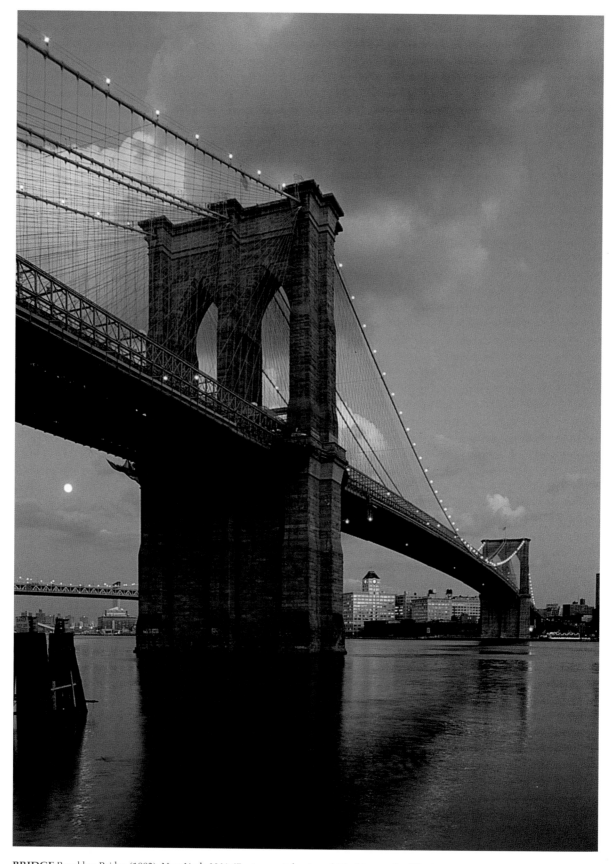

**BRIDGE** Brooklyn Bridge (1883), New York, N.Y. *[Engineers: John A. and Washington Roebling]*

**BRIDGE** Walker Art Center Garden bridge (1988), Minneapolis, Minn. *[Sculptor: Siah Armajani (Photo: Christian M. Korab)]*

**BRIDGE** Cranbrook Trellis Bridge (1993), Bloomfield Hills, Mich. *[Architect: Daniel Hoffman; engineer: Ted Galante]*

Bridges may be constructed of most structural materials, including wood, stone, cast or wrought iron, aluminum, steel, and reinforced concrete. The earliest bridges were wood, a material now little used except for small footbridges. Stone and wrought and cast iron, in their time the most important bridge materials, have been largely supplanted by steel and reinforced concrete.

**Structural Systems** Three major structural systems are used in bridges: beam, arch, and suspension. A beam structure can range from the smallest and simplest, for example, a log spanning a stream, to a large reinforced concrete bridge system with many spans resting on vertical supports, called piers, set on foundations in a river or lake bottom. An advanced use of the beam for relatively long spans utilizes trusses, made up of steel components joined together to form strong rigid frames. Arched bridges, originally of masonry but today of steel or reinforced concrete, are curved to allow the higher portions to be supported by the lower, transferring the weight down to piers or the ground. Suspension bridges are hung on towers, originally with vines, then with ropes, and later with chains. Today such bridges are suspended with great cables made of steel wire.

A more unusual structural type is the pontoon bridge, supported on floats and used for temporary pur-

59

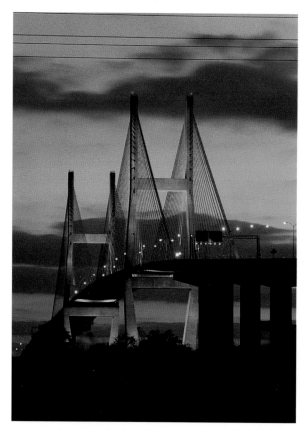

**BRIDGE** New Route 17 bridge over the Savannah River (1991), Savannah, Ga. *[Engineers: Parsons, Brinkerhoff, Quade & Douglas; Georgia Dept. of Transportation Designer: Mike Davis]*

are of one piece or monolithic, and the entire structure acts together to support the weight.

**History** The earliest bridges, in prehistoric times, were probably trees that fell across steams or depressions. These were followed by bridges constructed of logs and by ropes made of twisted vines in pairs, one to walk on and one to hold on to. Masonry bridges of brick and stone are known to have been constructed in the Middle East at least as early as 4000 B.C. Many of these used arched construction, a method later highly developed by the Romans. Stone has continued to be used to some extent well into the 20th century. In medieval Europe, stone bridges were often picturesquely lined with small shops. Metal bridges, of wrought or cast iron, both arch and suspension types, were first built in Europe in the late 18th century.

**American Development** The first bridges in colonial America were built of wood. This tradition continued for some time. Some of the most pleasant examples were covered bridges, a type that had its origins in other countries. The architect and bridge engineer Ithiel Town (1784–1844) built a large number of wood bridges between 1816 and 1825, obtaining patents for his designs. Later stone was used for bridges, but the most significant developments were in metals. Architect Henry Hobson Richardson (1838–86) designed a fine, small stone bridge (1811) in the Fenway, Boston. Architect Paul Philippe Cret (1876–1947) designed a number in and around Philadelphia.

An early pioneering steel-arched bridge is the Eads (1874) in St. Louis, designed by and named for engineer James Buchanan Eads (1820–87). But it is in steel suspension bridges that American bridge design talent has been at its best. First developed in Europe, steel suspension bridges, each seemingly more daring than the last, have been built in the United States since the late 19th century. One of the earliest and best is the Brooklyn Bridge (1883), New York City, designed by John Augustus Roebling (1806–69), a German-American engineer, with its construction directed by his son,

poses, such as military operations. A special type of beam, the cantilever, is sometimes used in bridges. A cantilever is a beam so constructed as to project beyond the pier that supports it. Cantilever bridges usually have two cantilever spans with their ends anchored on the banks of the water body. Their cantilevered ends ordinarily do not meet but instead support a third span suspended between them. Another special type of beam bridge utilizes a fixed frame, sometimes called a portal frame. In this type of frame, the beam and its supports

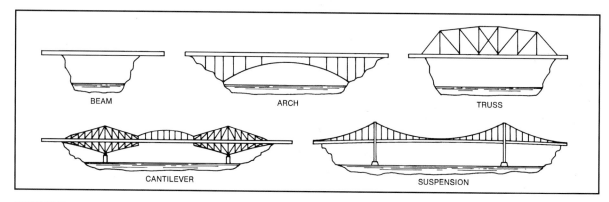

**BRIDGE** Types.

Washington Augustus (1837–1926), also an engineer. This bridge was followed by the George Washington Bridge (1931), New York City, designed by Swiss-American engineer Othmar Hermann Ammann (1879–1965), with Cass Gilbert (1858–1934) as consulting architect; the Golden Gate Bridge (1937), San Francisco, by engineer Joseph B. Strauss (d. 1938), with Ammann as a consulting engineer and Irving F. Morrow as consulting architect; and the Verrazano-Narrows Bridge (1964), New York City, with the longest span in the world, 4,260 feet, also designed by Ammann. Americans have not done so well with the design of reinforced concrete bridges. Although pioneering designs were made in the early 20th century by European engineers and architects, the Swiss engineer Robert Maillart (1872–1940) was the acknowledged master of their design. During the 1940s Frank Lloyd Wright (1869–1959) proposed daring designs for reinforced concrete bridges, including one between San Francisco and Alameda. It would have had a garden in the center between the roadways, but, like others he proposed, it was never built.

**Related Articles** Arch; Cret, Paul Philippe; Engineering; Gilbert, Cass; Richardson, Henry Hobson; Structure; Town, Ithiel; Wright, Frank Lloyd.

**Further Reading** Mock, Elizabeth B.: *The Architecture of Bridges*, reprint of 1949 edition, Ayer Co., Salem, N.H., 1972; Plowden, David: *Bridges—The Spans of North America*, Norton, New York, 1988, also published by the American Society of Civil Engineers (ASCE), New York, 1984.

## BUCKLAND, WILLIAM

English-American architect (1734–74). Many colonial architects prepared designs for buildings as an avocation while supporting themselves by some other unrelated trade or profession. Others, including William Buckland, were builders by trade who prepared designs for buildings and erected them. Buckland, trained in London as a carpenter and joiner, worked as designer and builder, interior designer, and wood-carver on his buildings. The interiors for Gunston Hall, Fairfax Co., Va., was his first job in the colonies, starting in 1755. After working on other buildings nearby, of which little is known, he moved to Annapolis, where he designed a number of notable houses. The best-known and most noted is the Hammond-Harwood House (1774). Georgian in style, this house has been called the finest colonial town house in America. The fine details, inside and out, show it to be the work of a talented architect and builder, who was totally involved in all the parts of the house, in the manner in which the parts relate to each other and to the whole building. While the design shows indications of adaptation from influential architectural books of the time, it also shows the architect to have been a creative, trained craftsman who made adaptations with an originality and freedom not often found in the work of the more academic architects of the period.

**Works** William Buckland's career as an architect and builder lasted less than 20 years, from 1755 to the year of his death, 1774. It is assumed that he designed a number of buildings, but only about 10 have been attributed to him with any accuracy. Among these are Strawberry Hill (about 1766) near Annapolis; Raspberry Plain (1771), Loudoun Co., Va.; and the Chase-Lloyd House (1774), Annapolis; only the Chase-Lloyd House still exists. Three other great Annapolis houses, on which Buckland is known to have worked and is believed to have been the architect, are the Paca House (1763), the Ridout House (1763), and the Brice House (about 1770).

**Life** William Buckland was born on August 14, 1734, in England. At about fourteen, he was apprenticed to his uncle in London to learn the joiner's and carpenter's trade. Six years later, he came to America as an indentured servant to George Mason, owner of Gunston Hall. Buckland designed some exterior details for this house, and the interiors which have become known as among the most beautiful in any colonial house. While indentured, and for a while after being released, he worked on buildings by other architects and, later, on buildings for which he was the architect and builder. About 1770 he moved to Annapolis and established his own workshop, which he operated until his death in December 1774, at age forty.

**Related Articles** Colonial Architecture; Georgian Architecture.

**Further Reading** Beirne, Rosamond Randall, and John Henry Scarff: *William Buckland, 1734–1774: Architect of Virginia and Maryland*, Maryland Historical Society, Baltimore, 1958.

## BUILDING, VERNACULAR

Architects were not licensed in the United States until 1897. Although the American Institute of Architects was founded in 1857, the first American architectural school was established at the Massachusetts Institute of Technology in 1865. Prior to that time, any architect had received training in Europe, often at the French École des Beaux Arts or by working in the office of such an individual. Richard Morris Hunt was the first American to study in Paris, enrolling in the École in 1846 and completing his studies in 1852. Thus much of early American building was built without architects, and this work is called *vernacular building*, native to America.

One of the reasons so much competent work was built was due to the publications known as "pattern books." They were used to communicate practical design and construction information to carpenter-builders and archi-

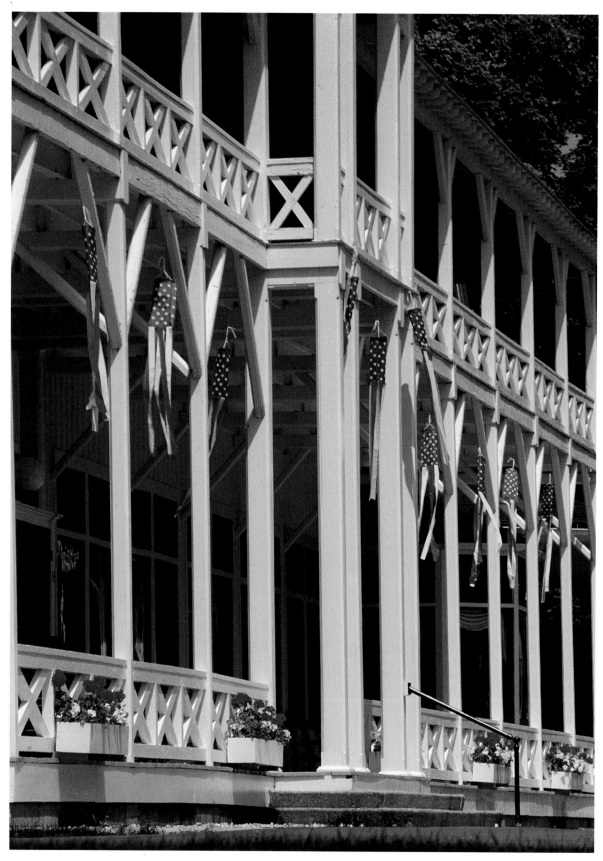

**BUILDING, VERNACULAR** Chicago Club House (1881), Charlevoix, Mich.

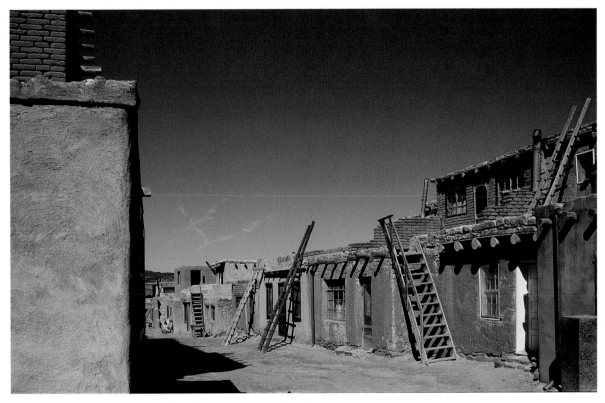

**BUILDING, VERNACULAR** Detail, "Sky City" Acoma, N. Mex.

builders. The books were used before the legal distinction between an architect and a builder was defined.

The earliest books used in colonial America were published in Great Britain beginning in 1733. These early books were not written for the problems facing

**BUILDING, VERNACULAR** Mystic Seaport (19th century), Mystic, Conn.

American builders, and it was not until 1797 that Asher Benjamin published *Young Country Builder's Assistant,* a more practical guide for American use. Others followed quickly, and part of the interest in looking at vernacular building is to trace the influence of such work.

The use of these books was most common from 1800 to 1840 and promoted the Greek revival throughout America. Some of these books stayed in print from 20 to 40 years. Between 1790 and 1840 the population increased almost 5 times, and by 1860 it had doubled to 34.1 million, which resulted in a building boom.

By the early 19th century, sawmills were producing lumber, and machine-manufactured nails were widely used by the 1830s. Balloon framing, developed in Chicago in 1833, made building simpler and faster, and the finished product used less material than products built with earlier construction methods. This plus the development of the railway ensured quick adoption of this framing type nationwide.

By 1830 Asher Benjamin published *The Practical House Carpenter,* and this demonstrated a shift in pattern books from a builder's aid to an architect addressing a carpenter. By the time the profession began to organize, pattern books were of this type. By 1855, 20 volumes showing a variety of plans, elevations, and perspectives using variant materials were published. By 1895 the average published life of this type of book was

**BUILDING, VERNACULAR** Watts Towers (1921–54), Los Angeles, Calif. *[Artist: Simon Rodia].*
The most famous example of U.S. folk-art.

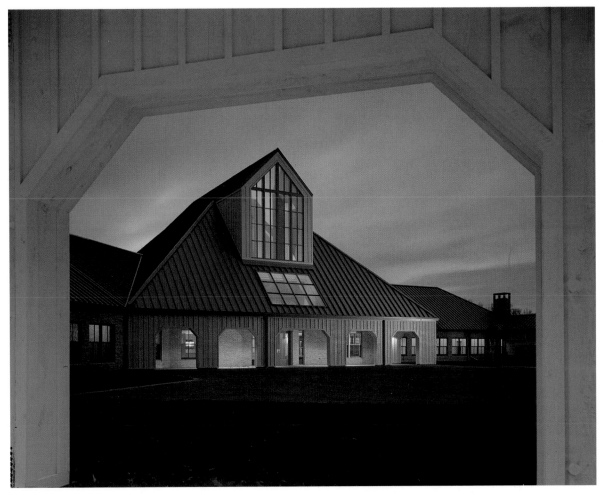

**BUILDING, VERNACULAR** Regional vernacular inspiration: Trinova County, Toledo, Ohio (1992).
*[Architect: Charles Moore (Photo: Gary Quesada/Korab Ltd.)]*

an estimated 4.34 years. One of the more successful such books was published by Palliser, Palliser & Company under the title *Palliser's New Cottage Homes and Details* (1887) and is familiar Victorian style simplified for American residential use. This book also promoted the use of professional architects by the reader.

The manufacturing and standardization of building products promoted a better lifestyle. One well-known book which used perspectives by the talented illustrator and architect Alexander Jackson Davis for Andrew Jackson Downing's *The Architecture of Country Houses* (1850) went through nine printings by the end of the Civil War. This book illustrated the work of several architects.

Thus the earlier books changed from information on design and building into presentations of illustrations of fine homes, reflecting the change to architect-approved houses successfully marketed to the public.

An effort to find a truly American style was slow in coming. As early as 1843 Horatio Greenough (1805–52) was calling for a new style for the country. Thomas

**BUILDING, VERNACULAR** Regional vernacular inspiration: Apache Visitor's Center (1991), Montezuma's Castle, Ariz. *[Architect: Denis Numkena]*

**BUILDING, VERNACULAR** Regional vernacular inspiration: Residence of Alexander Girard, Santa Fe, N. Mex. *[Architect: Alexander Girard]*

Jefferson (1743–1826) had suggested a Roman style as suitable, but the Greek revival became dominant. Some see the open green lawn at Jefferson's University of Virginia (1825) as an American invention, and others would credit the new factories of the 1830s as being the beginning of a truly American style. Certainly the emphasis on practicality and technology resulted in such truly American structures as the new building in Chicago after the fire in 1871, and the Roeblings' Brooklyn Bridge completed in 1883.

**Further Reading** Benjamin, Asher: *The American Builder's Companion*, 1827, reprint, Dover Publications, New York, 1969; Crosbie, Michael J.: "Pattern-book Architecture," *Encyclopedia of Architecture, Design, Engineering & Construction*, Vol. 3, John Wiley, New York, 1989; Downing, Alexander Jackson: *The Architecture of Country Houses*, D. Appleton and Co., 1850, reprint, Dover Publications, New York, 1969; Fitch, James Marston: *American Building: The Historical Forces That Shaped It*, Shocken Books, New York, 1973; Gifford, Don, Ed.: *The Literature of Architecture: The Evolution of Architectural Theory and Practice in Nineteenth-Century America*, E. P. Dutton, New York, 1966; Mumford, Lewis: *Sticks and Stones*, W. W. Norton & Co., New York, 1934; Palliser, Palliser & Company, *Palliser's New Cottage Homes and Details*, 1887, reprint, Da Capo Press, New York, 1975.

**BUILDING CODES AND STANDARDS** In law, a code may refer to any law or statute, but more properly means a collection of statutes on a subject. A standard is a rule, usually part of a set of rules, established by an authority but having no legal standing except when referenced or cited in a code or other statute.

**Range of Regulations** Architecture today is subject to a vast set of codes and statutes which govern many aspects of the methods, materials, systems, types, and sizes of buildings, and almost every other facet of design and construction. In general, these codes and statutes are part of the laws of states, counties, and municipalities, but some are federal laws effective throughout the country. Most of them include certain standards by reference. Other standards also affect architecture, though they are not regulatory in a legal sense. These are standards developed by insurance companies and lending institutions to control certain aspects of the buildings that they insure or finance. Another example is the kind of standards of design and construction required by such organizations as hotel, food, or automobile service station chains.

**Governmental Regulations** In general, architects and others participating in building design and construction must abide by the provisions of the codes, statutes, and regulations of the municipalities, counties, and states in which their buildings will be constructed. First, they must comply with zoning codes that determine which buildings may be built where, including land uses, sizes and bulks of buildings, densities or how many families or people will be permitted per acre, provisions for light and air, and parking. Next there is the subdivision ordinance or code which governs how land may be subdivided. The third major type, the building code, determines how buildings may be constructed, including many details of construction, materials, fire-resistant qualities, exits, stairs, floor and roof load capacities, and many others. In addition, there may be separate housing codes for single-family and multifamily dwellings. There are also other types of codes, including those for plumbing, electrical work, and fire safety. In addition, building construction must be in conformance with a number of federal statutes: the Occupational Safety and Health Act (OSHA); the Architectural Barriers Act, governing design for the disabled in federal buildings and those financed by the federal government; the Americans with Disabilities Act (ADA) covering all public accommodations and commercial facilities, as well as state and local government services; and the National Environmental Policy Act, governing the effects of construction on the environment.

In addition, construction with loans insured by the Federal Housing Administration (FHA) of the U.S. Department of Housing and Urban Development (HUD) must conform to the property standards of the FHA; and those guaranteed by the Veterans Administration, to its construction standards. Hospitals must be constructed in conformance with regional, state, and federal statutes; schools, colleges, and universities, with state educational statutes; and so on.

Taken together, the codes, standards, statutes, and regulations affecting architecture contain a bewildering array of legal requirements that sometimes seem to threaten to drown architecture in a sea of red tape and bureaucracy. No reasonable person would argue with their intent: the preservation of health, safety, and welfare of those who occupy or use the buildings, and the protection of their surroundings and the environment.

However, many think that much of their content could be considerably simplified or even eliminated. And some believe that a part of the content may even be detrimental.

**Authoritative Organizations** Although some local codes have been prepared individually to answer specifically local needs, many are based on one or more national model codes and standards. These are codes and standards prepared by national authoritative organizations and kept up to date at intervals. Other than the federal government and its publications, the more important of these organizations and their more important publications include: American National Standards Institute (ANSI)—*ANSI Standards*; American Society for Testing and Materials (ASTM)—*ASTM Standards*; Building Officials and Code Administrators International (BOCA)—*BOCA National Building Code, Mechanical Code, Plumbing Code, Fire Prevention Code*; International Conference of Building Officials (ICBO)—*Uniform Building Code, Uniform Mechanical Code, Uniform Plumbing Code, Uniform Sign Code, Uniform Fire Code*; National Fire Protection Association (NFPA)—*Life Safety Code, National Electric Code, Fire Prevention Code*; and the Southern Building Code Congress International (SBCCI)—*Standard Building Code, Standard Mechanical Code, Standard Plumbing Code, Standard Fire Prevention Code*.

All these organizations publish codes and/or standards other than those mentioned, including ones on housing, gas uses, types of construction, and other subjects. Some codes and standards of these organizations, such as those of ANSI and NFPA, are incorporated into statutes of localities all over the United States; others such as those of BOCA, ICBO, and SBCCI are used only in certain regions of the country, for example, the SBCCI codes in the Southern states.

Architecture and building construction are certainly made more difficult by the mass of regulations contained in codes, statutes, and other laws. Just how difficult can be gathered from a typical situation, in which an architect might design 10 single-family houses for a builder who has a small firm. For this project, the architect and builder will have to deal with at least 15 major codes, ordinances, and standards if the houses are to be VA and FHA approved. And in some building projects, additional statutes would apply in certain cases, including those concerned with environmental impact, water pollution, air pollution, and wetlands conservation and protection.

To the extent that these codes and ordinances and standards contribute to health, wealth, and safety and to the protection of the environment, both the architect and the builder, whoever they may be, would probably agree that the time, money, and effort spent to meet the requirements were well spent.

**History** In very early times, humans made laws governing conduct even before they developed writing. The earliest laws appear to have included architecture and building construction. One of the most important discoveries of all time was the finding in 1901 of the stone slab upon which was carved the Code of Hammurabi, who was king of Babylon for 43 years during the 18th century B.C. This code contains some 300 legal provisions concerning the rights of people under the authority of the law. The code is thought to have been based on still older laws of the Sumerians and Akkadians. Among the subjects covered are tariffs, wages, trade, military service, and business.

One important part of the Code of Hammurabi contains laws concerning land and building construction. Hammurabi expected good building construction, for one of his provisions was: "If a builder has built a house for a man and his work is not strong, and if the house he has built falls in and kills the householder, that builder shall be slain." Evidently Hammurabi took the responsibilities of builders and, by implication, of architects quite seriously.

Other ancient civilizations developed laws, including those for building construction, most of which were concerned with safety. The Romans devised many types of building regulations, and some of these have survived, in particular those having to do with fire safety. The first real legal profession began in Rome and in the fifth century B.C. an important set of laws was developed, called the Law of the Twelve Tables. Another important development was the codification of Roman law in the *Corpus Juris Civilis,* under Emperor Justinian I (A.D. 483–565). This code laid the foundation for the laws of most European countries.

During the Middle Ages canon law, the legal system of the Roman Catholic Church, took the place to some extent of Roman law, and the Germanic codes also were important. During the Renaissance, Roman law was revived and, along with canon and Germanic law, it influenced the development of new codes of law. The most important was the Code Napoléon, a system developed and codified by a group of experts appointed by Emperor Napoléon (1769–1821). The Code Napoléon had great influence on the laws of European countries.

The laws of the United States generally follow the English system of common law, which is based on judicial decisions rather than on statutes. An exception is Louisiana, in which much of the law is still based on the Code Napoléon. In states that were originally settled by the Spanish, such as Texas and California, some vestiges of Spanish law still remain.

In all the above systems of law, there have been provisions for regulating architecture and building construction. For example, the Code Napoléon contains an article that says in effect that if a building should fall, either in whole or in part, within 10 years after its construction, because of bad workmanship or bad soil, its architect and workmen shall pay for the loss. Many other regulations of architecture and building construction had been made into law earlier. For example, the London Building Act of 1667, passed after the great fire a year earlier which had almost destroyed London, prohibited timber-framed houses in the city and contained a number of other safety provisions, such as minimum wall thicknesses and requirements for noninflammable roofs.

**American Development** In the English colonies in America, common law was in effect. This situation still exists today, though, starting in the early 19th century, various statutes have been adopted and collected into codes to supplement the common law. In the Spanish and French colonies in America, codes were also established. Some of these early codes regulated buildings, though they were not so highly developed and complete as the building codes of today. New York City passed the first housing code in 1867 and the first zoning code in 1913.

Great numbers of statutes affecting architecture and building construction have since been passed all over the nation by municipal, county, state, and federal governments. Building codes exist in almost every town and city in the United States, and some also exist for counties and for over 30 of the states. Zoning codes are in existence in most jurisdictions. For many years, Houston, Tex., was known for being the only major U.S. city without a zoning code, but Houston now has adopted zoning.

**Related Articles** DESIGN, ACCESSIBLE; ECOLOGY; FIRE PROTECTION; GOVERNMENT; LIGHTNING PROTECTION; PRACTICE OF ARCHITECTURE; SEISMIC DESIGN.

**Further Reading** *An Architect's Guide to Building Codes & Standards,* 3rd ed., American Institute of Architects, Washington, D.C., 1991. Various codes and standards listed in this article are published by organizations listed below.

**Sources of Additional Information** American Institute of Architects, 1735 New York Ave., N.W., Washington, D.C. 20006; American National Standards Institute, 1430 Broadway, New York, N.Y. 10018; American Society for Testing and Materials, 1916 Race St., Philadelphia, Pa. 19103; Building Officials and Code Administrators International, 4051 W. Flossmoor Rd., Country Club Hills, Ill. 60477-5795; Environmental Protection Agency, 401 M St., S.W., Washington, D.C. 20460; International Conference of Building Officials, 5360 S. Workman Mill Rd., Whittier, Calif. 90601; National Fire Protection Association, 470 Atlantic Ave., Boston, Mass. 02210; Southern Building Code Congress, 3617 Eighth Ave. S., Birmingham, Ala. 35222; U.S. Department of Commerce, National Institute of Standards and Technology, Gaithersburg, Md. 20899; U.S. Department of Health and Human Services, Commissioner, Administration on Developmental Disabilities, 200 Independence Ave., S.W., Washington, D.C. 20201; U.S. Department of Housing and

Urban Development, 451 Seventh St., S.W., Washington, D.C. 20410; U.S. Department of Labor, Occupational Safety and Health Administration, 200 Constitution Ave., N.W., Washington, D.C. 20210.

**BUILDING INDUSTRY** The loosely knit, diverse group of individuals and organizations that performs the many functions necessary to bring buildings into being. Often thought of as only consisting of those who design buildings and those who construct them, the building industry is actually much more complex. The major elements include designers, constructors, owners, users, financiers, real estate agents, and regulators. All are essential in transforming a need for a building from an idea to a completed structure.

**The Designers** Buildings and their surroundings are designed by a group of professionals: architects, engineers, planners, landscape architects, interior designers, and others. Technicians, drafters, specification writers, and others assist them, working together with the professionals to create building designs and to prepare working drawings and specifications that indicate what is to be constructed, and coordinating the work so that the actual construction will conform to the intent of the working drawings and specifications. Ordinarily, an architect has the overall responsibility for these activities. And the architect has the specialized responsibility for the concept of the building or its design. The engineers, usually working in architects' offices or as consultants to them, are responsible for their own specialized activities: the structural engineer for the structure, the electrical engineer for electrical systems, and the mechanical engineer for mechanical systems such as plumbing and heating. The planners, usually called city planners, are responsible for the design of the city or part of the city in which buildings are to be located. Sometimes they work on an area in which only a relatively small number of buildings are to be placed in a group. Landscape architects are responsible for the design and coordination of the exterior areas around the buildings, interior designers for the interiors, road and traffic designers for provisions for automotive requirements. At times, the services of other professionals are required, for example, in a theater, an acoustical or lighting expert, or both. An industrial designer may be called upon if specialized equipment is to be designed into a building. Various combinations of these professionals may be required on buildings of varying sizes, purposes, and complexity. For a small single-family house, for example, the architect and the technicians might perform all or most of the functions named.

**The Constructors** The people who actually construct buildings are contractors, manufacturers, and the building trades. Contractors, sometimes called builders for houses, manage the actual construction work: general contractors or builders having responsibility for the entire building, subcontractors for specialized portions such as plumbing, electrical, or roofing work. The most usual method for accomplishing this work is the general contract method, in which a general contractor signs a contract with an owner, for an agreed-upon price, to construct a building in a manner required by the working drawings and specifications prepared by the architect and other design professionals. The general contractor makes contracts with the subcontractors needed to perform specialized phases of the work. The contractors then proceed to construct the building utilizing the abilities of those in the building trades, the carpenters, electricians, plumbers, roofers, and so on who actually perform the labor.

In a more recent variation of this process, the owner employs a project, or construction, manager who performs duties similar to those of the general contractor, but for an agreed-upon fee or salary instead of a price for the entire construction work. Advantages claimed for this method are faster completion of the building at a lower cost to the owner.

Other important constructors are the manufacturers, sometimes called producers, who produce and distribute building materials and equipment. In a way, they function in a role similar to that of the other constructors, except that their work is accomplished in factories rather than on building sites. With the growth of prefabrication, the assembly of smaller parts into large assemblies or systems, such as a whole wall, in factories, the role of producers and production trades has grown while that of contractors and building trades has diminished.

**The Owners** Of great importance are the owners, without whose needs and requirements for buildings and furnishing of capital for their design and construction there would be no building industry. In general, an owner may be an individual, as the owner of a private house, a private group, as a corporation or partnership that owns an office building, or a government representing its constituents, as a post office. The owner, called the client by the architect and other design professionals, is the individual or group who makes contracts with them and with the constructors for the design and the construction.

**The Users** The needs and desires of people who actually use buildings, whether they be workers in offices, salespeople and customers in stores, tenants in public housing, or others, have not always been given serious consideration by the other groups in the building industry. Recently, users have come to be considered of prime importance and in some cases have been given a role in the design and construction decisions that affect their lives and welfare. In fact, a movement called advocacy architecture or planning has come into being, in which architects and other professionals devote their professional practice or a portion of it to the representation of the rights of those who use buildings.

**The Financiers** This group furnishes the capital in the form of money and credit, and is an important element of the building industry. While such needs are often supplied in part by owners, it is common practice for a large percentage of the money for buildings to come from investors, banks, insurance companies, savings and loan organizations, and other investors. They finance the purchase of the land, furnish money on a short-term basis or interim financing, during the construction process, and make long-term loans to owners, usually taking a mortgage on the building and the land on which it is located. As a result of their investment policies, such financiers exert a strong influence on building construction. The government strongly influences financing of buildings through its Federal Housing Administration and Veterans Administration guarantees of private loans and through the activities of various regulating agencies.

**The Real Estate Agents** Through their active participation in the buying, selling, leasing, and development of land and buildings, the real estate agents perform important functions in the building industry.

Real estate brokers find buyers for those who wish to sell property and manage the transactions. Developers, sometimes called entrepreneurs or promoters, assemble land on which buildings can be constructed to meet needs and procure financing for the projects, often taking a financial interest themselves. Real estate appraisers estimate the value of land and buildings; counselors advise owners and investors; managers administer leasing, maintenance, and other business matters for buildings.

**The Regulators** On every governmental level, from that of the smallest township to the federal, an important element of the building industry is the regulator, who formulates and enforces the rules for building design and construction. The federal government affects building construction by such means as the Occupational Safety and Health Act (OSHA) which governs the safety and health of those who work on and in buildings. The National Environmental Policy Act regulates construction that may affect the quality of the environment. The regulations of the Federal Housing Administration (FHA) govern the construction of houses for which it guarantees loans. On state, county, and local levels the use of land is governed by regulations of land-use agencies. The size and other factors of buildings allowed to be constructed on individual sites are regulated by zoning laws and their construction, by building codes.

**American History** In the earliest times in America, there was no building industry as such. If a person decided to build a house, he simply cleared a site, cutting trees that were then worked into lumber with hand tools, and started the construction of the building. Such a house was not really designed but rather grew out of the needs of the family that would occupy it and the available materials and labor, usually members of the family and neighbors; its plan and appearance reflected houses in the builder's native country.

Soon after the founding of the first English colonies in the early 17th century, artisans and craftsmen arrived from Europe. These carpenters, joiners, bricklayers, painters, and plasterers performed much of the construction work. Designs for houses and other buildings were made by amateur gentlemen-architects who learned from books and by craftsmen-architects who learned from practicing their trades as well as from books. Most of these early architects acted as their own engineers, and in the case of the craftsmen-architects, as the constructors of the buildings as well. Many of the craftsmen-architects were master carpenters. And master carpenters usually directed the work of construction for buildings designed by the gentlemen-architects.

The manufacturing of building products began early, brick making as early as 1610 in Jamestown, Va., and 1629 in Salem, Mass. Water-powered sawmills for processing lumber were established about the same time in Maine as well as near Jamestown. Other industries, including the quarrying of stone and the making of window glass, followed soon after.

By the middle of the 18th century the functions of designers and constructors were beginning to become established. This trend continued into the 19th century with an accelerated pace brought on by industrialization, invention, and education. By the beginning of the 20th century most of the present-day elements of the building industry were established and recognized. The architects had organized a national association, the American Institute of Architects, in 1857; the civil engineers had founded the American Society of Civil Engineers in 1852, in spite of the fact that the functions of architects and engineers were not really separated until the late 19th century and have continued to overlap to this day.

**Labor Groups** Labor movements had existed in one form or another from colonial days; by the beginning of the 20th century they had achieved a solid place in the building industry mainly through the efforts of the American Federation of Labor, founded in 1886, which represented the interests of the craftsmen who worked on buildings. Although the Associated General Contractors of America was not founded until 1918, there had been an organization of master craftsmen who directed the work of building construction as far back as 1724. This was the year of the founding of the Carpenters' Company of the City and County of Philadelphia, an organization still in existence. This group, with a membership of master carpenters who directed the construction of buildings, and many of whom acted as architects, might be called a link between the guilds of the Middle Ages and the labor unions and contractors of today.

Paralleling the development of the designers and constructors has been that of the other important elements of the building industry, the owners, financiers, realtors, and regulators. And the users are finally coming into their own position of importance.

**Related Articles** ARCHITECTURE; ASSOCIATION, BUILDING INDUSTRY; BUILDING CODES AND STANDARDS; BUILDING TRADE; CARPENTERS' COMPANY; CONSTRUCTION, BUILDING; ELECTRICAL ENGINEERING; FINANCE; GOVERNMENT; INTERIOR DESIGN; LANDSCAPE ARCHITECTURE; MECHANICAL ENGINEERING; PLANNING, CITY; ROAD AND TRAFFIC DESIGN; STRUCTURAL ENGINEERING; SURVEYING.

**BUILDING TRADE** One of the specialized types of work performed by workers who construct buildings and other structures. The major building trades today are bricklayers, carpenters, electricians, ironworkers, painters, plasterers, plumbers, steam fitters, and roofers.

Bricklayers lay brick and other types of masonry products. Carpenters are divided among rough carpenters, who build wood frameworks for buildings and wood forms for concrete work; and finish carpenters, who handle such work as hanging doors, installing windows, putting hardware in place, and installing wood baseboards and other trim. Electricians install wiring, switches, outlets, switchboards, and other electrical equipment. Ironworkers erect beams, trusses, columns, and other parts of the structural frames of steel buildings. Painters apply paints and other finishes to the interiors and exteriors of buildings. Plasterers apply and finish plaster and related products in the interiors of buildings. Plumbers install water, gas, and sewer piping; and bathroom, kitchen, laundry, and other equipment. Steam fitters install heating, ventilating, and air-conditioning equipment and ductwork and related items. Roofers install roofing and related items.

Members of the building trades usually work for general contractors, or builders, who are responsible for the complete construction of building projects; or for subcontractors, who are responsible for portions of it, such as mechanical, electrical, or painting work. Workers in the building trades often become general contractors or subcontractors after having gained knowledge and experience.

**Trade Unions** Today most building trade work in the United States is handled by members of trade unions. Labor unions are divided generally into craft unions and industrial unions. A craft union includes all workers employed in a single craft. Most of the building construction unions are craft unions, such as the electricians, carpenters, plumbers, and so on. An industrial union includes all workers employed in a single industry, such as automobile manufacturing or mining. Industrial union members participate in the building industry because ordinarily they fabricate parts and components, such as structural steel, windows, hardware, and so on in factories. They also become involved in a larger way when building components or whole buildings are prefabricated or preassembled in factories.

Labor unions control most of the training of young people who wish to become master or journeyman workers in the crafts and industries. This is often accomplished through apprenticeship programs, which specify schedules of study and experience. To qualify for apprenticeship, a young person must ordinarily be between age sixteen and twenty-four, a high school graduate, and often must pass tests or have other qualifications. The young person must also join the union which administers the apprenticeship program. Apprentices then follow prescribed training schedules that include working in a single craft, study, and often courses in a technical school. The period of apprenticeship varies but the normal time is approximately four years before an apprentice can complete the training. To prepare for careers in given crafts, many young people take vocational courses in secondary schools or attend trade or vocational schools after graduation from high school. For people who like to work with their hands, constructing portions of buildings and other structures, careers in the building trades can be very satisfying.

**History** In ancient times, the concept of labor was based on the use of slaves to do the work. In ancient cultures, including Greece and Rome, this was most often the case. During the Middle Ages, with the decline of slavery and the spread of Christianity, laborers gained status and became respected community members. Skilled craftsmen and artisans formed guilds which fixed prices, set standards and wages, and determined who could practice the crafts, much as do the labor unions of today. Workers were classified according to their knowledge and abilities as apprentices, those learning a craft; journeymen, those who were proficient in it; and masters, those who were highly skilled. Some labor unions still follow this practice today. The guild system began to die out with the end of the Middle Ages and the advent of capitalism, which required free markets in goods and labor.

In Europe as well as in colonial America the status of workers declined after the Middle Ages. Workers were expected to work long hours in unhealthy environments for low wages. And child labor was accepted as a normal state of affairs.

**American Development** In colonial America, there were attempts to induce Indians to act as laborers but to no avail. The colonists then turned to other involuntary laborers: slaves, convicts, and debtors. Another source of labor was indentured servants, people brought from Europe who had agreed to work for a period of time, often seven years or more, in return for their passage to America and freedom at the end of the indentured period. Another method was cooperative effort, such as people joining forces in raising a barn. In time, skilled artisans and craftsmen were brought to American from Europe and they trained others. Some of the early American architects were craftsmen, who had been trained in their crafts rather than in architecture.

Apprenticeship was also widespread in early American colonies. Young boys were apprenticed to masters of various trades, by whom they were instructed. Unlike apprentices of today, those of colonial times often lived with their masters and worked for them for periods of seven years or more, for no wages, in return for the training and upkeep received. After that, the apprentice could become a journeyman and later a master.

The first real labor union in the United States was that of the shoemakers, founded in 1792 in Philadelphia. The Carpenters' Company had been founded in that city in 1724, but it functioned more like a medieval guild than like a modern union. In the 1800s many local unions were founded, and in 1852 the first national union, the International Typographical Union, was started; it exists to this day. The American Federation of Labor (AFL) was founded in 1886 and the Congress of Industrial Organizations (CIO), in 1938. These two organizations merged into the AFL-CIO in 1955. This union includes in its membership those who work in the building trades. Working conditions and pay scales in the building trades have been vastly improved during the 20th century, primarily due to the efforts of the unions.

**Related Articles** BUILDING INDUSTRY; CARPENTERS' COMPANY; CONSTRUCTION, BUILDING.

**Source of Additional Information** American Federation of Labor and Congress of Industrial Organizations (AFL-CIO), 815 16th St., N.W., Washington, D.C. 20006.

**BULFINCH, CHARLES** American architect (1763–1844). Born into a prominent and wealthy Boston family, and educated at Harvard, though not in architecture, Charles Bulfinch occupied city and later national government positions most of his life. This did not prevent him from becoming an architect; many think him one of the greatest. That he considered himself an architect and that others accepted him as one is certain. Other American architects of Bulfinch's time and before were either architect-builders who primarily constructed buildings, with the design secondary, or amateur gentlemen-architects who designed buildings as an avocation

while pursuing some other career. Bulfinch, though he certainly started out as the latter kind, soon found himself almost totally involved with architecture.

**Architectural Plans** Bulfinch was one of the first American architects known to have used drawings extensively for the construction of buildings. Before him such drawings were few and sketchy. Perhaps even more importantly, Bulfinch also used drawings to study the design of the building. Thus he took a giant step toward becoming what would now be called a professional architect. He seems professional in other ways too. Bulfinch was deeply concerned in the everyday operations in constructing buildings. His involvement was not that of an architect-builder who actually worked on buildings but much more like that of later professional architects who supervised the construction to ensure that designs were carried out properly and that the workmanship was acceptable.

Although self-taught from books, as were the other colonial architects, Bulfinch was not satisfied with the design of buildings by adaptation of elements of architecture selected from books. As have architects who came after him, Bulfinch attempted to understand the

**BULFINCH, CHARLES** First Otis House (1796), Boston, Mass.

buildings, their materials, the methods by which they were constructed, and their functions. And also like later architects, he became aware of the importance of the surroundings of the buildings, that is, their relationship to streets and walkways, parks and city, and other buildings in their vicinity.

**Boston** It has been said that Bulfinch changed Boston from a provincial town with meager buildings and meandering streets into a city of taste, of handsome buildings placed in a setting of parks and trees and plantings. In the 30-odd years he practiced in Boston, Bulfinch accomplished much that merits such an accolade. Part of the reason was the excellence of his buildings, but of almost equal importance was his involvement in every aspect and activity of the city through civic work, as a member, and chairman, of the board of selectmen. In this capacity, he came to understand Boston and its needs thoroughly.

The early work of Bulfinch was Georgian in character, though late Georgian as influenced by the brothers Adam. His later buildings demonstrate a maturing process that led him more toward the Classic Revival style that had come to be the preferred style of such architects as Thomas Jefferson and Benjamin Henry Latrobe. In his first major buildings, the Federal Street Theater and Franklin Crescent houses (1794), Bulfinch demonstrated his concern with the totality of architecture and its surroundings. This was ambitious architecture indeed for its time, the late 18th century, and place, provincial Boston. As might a present-day architect, Bulfinch conceived the design as a master plan for two curved buildings each of which would contain 16 connected houses, placed at opposite sides of a landscaped oval park. At one end was the theater, forming a focal point for the whole composition. All three buildings were to be brick and were designed to complement each other in style and scale. Only one of the crescent buildings and the theater were actually built. Where the other crescent would have been, detached houses by Bulfinch were substituted. Neither the theater nor the crescent building has survived.

The architect's next major building, the Massachusetts State House (1798), has survived in good condition, though it is now only a part of a much larger complex, having been added on to several times. The State House is a simple rectangular building in plan and exterior, two stories high with a basement, and a porch or portico in front, the whole crowned by a dome. The walls are of brick, the portico and columns of wood, and the dome of wood boards, matched and worked to fit tightly against each other. The elegant proportions of the building, the use of arches with slender columns above, the relationship of the dome to the other elements, and the spacious and richly ornamented interiors

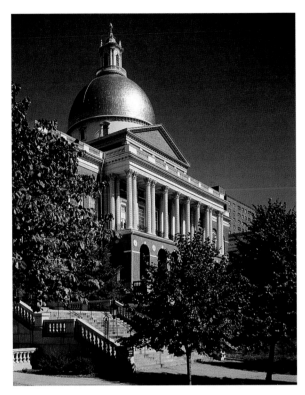

**BULFINCH, CHARLES** Massachusetts State House (1798), Boston.

caused the building to be called a masterpiece immediately upon its completion. It is still considered one of the greatest American buildings and a very high point in Bulfinch's architectural career.

**Other Works** After this triumph, Bulfinch went on to design some 40 other public buildings and churches. Among the most important public buildings still in existence are the Old Connecticut State House (1796), Hartford; the Old Maine State House (1829), in Augusta, and now much altered; University Hall, Harvard University (1815), Cambridge; and the Massachusetts General Hospital (1820), Boston, a building now called the Bulfinch Pavilion and a relatively small part of a large hospital complex. This was the architect's last building in Boston, the city upon which his buildings had so great and lasting an effect. Of the five Bulfinch churches in Boston, only New North Church (St. Stephen's Catholic), completed in 1804, remains. It is not considered one of Bulfinch's best designs and has been much modified and was even moved back for a street widening. Fortunately preserved is the church which is considered the architect's best, some think his best building of any kind, the Lancaster Meeting House (First Church of Christ) built in Lancaster, Mass., in 1817.

Charles Bulfinch designed a number of houses, many of them on or around Beacon Hill in Boston. Their

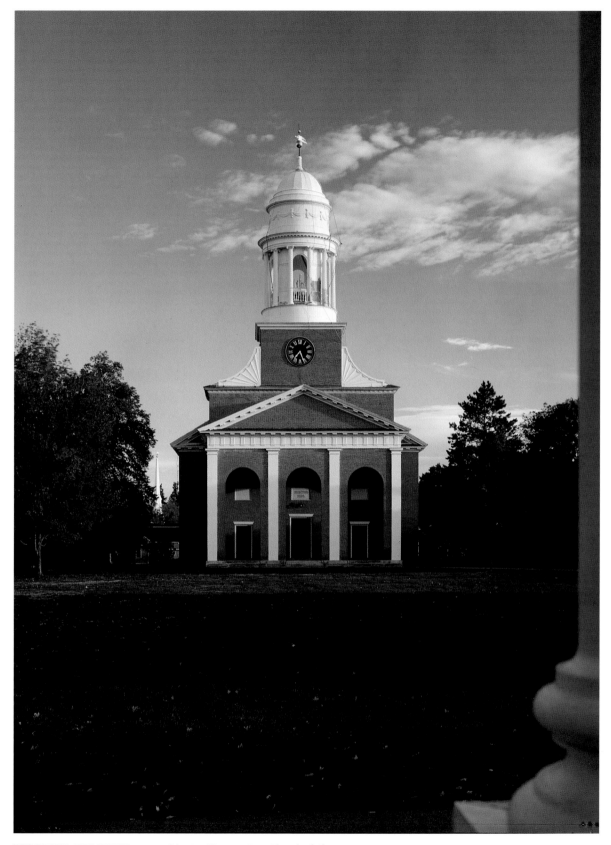

**BULFINCH, CHARLES** Lancaster Meeting House or First Church of Christ (1817), Lancaster, Mass.

impact on Boston was probably stronger than that of his public buildings or even his churches since the houses and their settings established an atmosphere of charm and beauty which has been preserved in the Beacon Hill area to this day. Bulfinch designed both single detached houses and row or attached houses. Most of the latter are now gone but a notable exception is the Chestnut Street block containing numbers 13 to 17. Several of his detached houses still exist in Boston as well as in other Massachusetts towns. Among the finest are the three houses he designed for Harrison Gray Otis, a prominent and powerful Boston politician. These houses are the First Otis House (1796), the only one with the original interiors; the Second Otis House (1800), usually considered the finest of the three; and the Third Otis House (1806), the architect's last great house in Boston.

**Life** Charles Bulfinch was one of the first great American-born architects. Born in Boston, on August 8, 1763, into a well-to-do and prominent family, he was graduated from Harvard in 1781, one of the first American architects to complete a college education. His interest in architecture seems to have been awakened when he spent two years (1785–87) touring France and Italy, at the suggestion of Thomas Jefferson, and England. Upon his return from Europe, he entered the accounting room of a Boston merchant, a position which left him time to study architectural books and to dabble in design and construction much as did other amateur gentlemen-architects.

As early as 1787, soon after his return from Europe, Bulfinch gave an indication of his future dedication to architecture by submitting the first plans for a new Massachusetts State House, a project that was to elude him until he was selected to design the building in 1795. During these early years, he also designed other important buildings, but continued to have only a casual involvement in architecture until he went bankrupt in 1796.

In 1791 he was elected to the board of selectmen of Boston, a position in which he served, except for four years, until he left for Washington in 1817. For the last 18 of these years, he was the board's chairman, a position not unlike that of a mayor. At about the time of his bankruptcy, he resigned from the board to devote himself fully to architecture. Returning to the board in 1799, he soon found himself deeply involved in all of the governmental, commercial, and financial affairs of Boston. From that time, his civic work and his architecture went hand in hand and complemented each other. As an architect, he designed government buildings, churches, wharves, warehouses, schools, markets, prisons, banks, hospitals, theaters, multifamily houses, and numerous single-family houses. In addition, he planned portions of Boston.

His city honored him for his civic work and for his architecture early in life and this appreciation was to continue. His civic work primarily belonged to Boston, but his architecture came to belong to the country. In 1817 James Monroe (1758–1831), newly inaugurated President of the United States, appointed him to replace Benjamin Henry Latrobe (1764–1820) as architect in charge of rebuilding the U.S. Capitol (see the illustration in article capital, United States), burned by the British in 1814. Bulfinch continued in this position until 1829. During this time he joined the two wings with a central dome and designed the west portico with steps and terrace forming the approach to it, completing the building for the first time since its construction had begun. Bulfinch's dome was later replaced by a larger and grander one, but the west front remains. After 1830 Bulfinch returned to Boston where he lived in retirement until his death on April 4, 1844.

**Related Article** CAPITAL, UNITED STATES; CLASSIC REVIVAL ARCHITECTURE; COLONIAL ARCHITECTURE; GEORGIAN ARCHITECTURE.

## BURNHAM AND ROOT

American architectural firm. This partnership, formed in 1893 by Daniel Hudson Burnham (1846–1912), architect and city planner, and John Wellborn Root (1850–91), architect, became one of the most prominent and successful in America in its time. It was the ideal partnership. The two architects shared a mutual respect and affection. And the talent of one complemented those of the other perfectly. Burnham was good-natured, energetic, practical, and a good executive. He brought commissions into the office and was master of the technical, utilitarian, and financial aspects of architecture. On the other hand, Root was a dreamer and artist, creative and deeply interested in culture. It has been said that Burnham saved Root from becoming a dilettante-architect and in turn was saved from being only a businessman-architect. In any case, they were a good team and went on to design a great number of distinguished buildings.

**Firm's Works** During the first years of the firm's existence, Burnham and Root did mostly houses. The first big commission was for the Montauk Block (1882), now demolished, followed by the Calumet Building (1884), both in Chicago, composed of masonry with cast-iron columns. These were followed by other masonry buildings in Chicago, the most notable being the Rookery (1886), named for its site where flocks of pigeons had formerly roosted, and the Monadnock Building (1891; see illustration in article modern architecture), the last tall building, 16 stories, with brick bearing walls. Then came the first all-steel skeleton-framed building, the Rand-McNally Building (1890), since

**BURNHAM AND ROOT** Interior of lobby, The Rookery (1886), Chicago, Ill. *[Photo: Nick Merrick/Hedrich-Blessing]*

demolished. In Chicago the firm did several metal skeleton-framed buildings that were designed before Root's death and constructed afterward. Among these were the Great Northern Hotel (1892) with a wrought-iron and steel frame and the Masonic Temple (1892) with a steel skeleton and at the time the tallest, 20 stories, building in the world. Both were later demolished.

Considered the finest by the firm is the Reliance Building (1895), the design for which had begun before Root's death and was completed by Charles B. Atwood (1848–95), who was in charge of the design department. In this building came the logical conclusion in the design of Chicago skyscrapers. The structural skeleton is steel and the walls are terra-cotta and glass, expressing the structure underneath. The proportions and details are skillfully handled and balanced.

After the untimely death of Root in 1891, Burnham changed the firm's name to D. H. Burnham and Company and continued in practice. The practice grew, but the design was never quite the same. Burnham produced a great number of buildings, many of them very good ones. But now they were in eclectic styles, particularly the Renaissance, which were popular in the Eastern United States. None approached the invention and daring of those of Burnham and Root. Among the most notable are Field Museum of Natural History (1900), the Fisher Building (1896), and the Railway Exchange Building (1904), all in Chicago; and the Flatiron, formerly Fuller, Building (1902) in New York City.

In his later years Burnham became seriously interested in city planning. With Root, he had designed the master plan for the World's Columbian Exposition (1893; see illustration in article exposition) in Chicago. As early as 1897, he had begun thinking about a great plan for the development of the Chicago lakefront in collaboration with Edward H. Bennett and Jens Jensen (1860–1951). Later with Jensen as the landscape architect, Burnham was to see his work result in the construction of Grant Park and the other great Chicago parks beginning in 1904 and, ultimately, in his widely admired Chicago Plan of 1909. He made other plans for a number of other cities, including Baltimore, Duluth, and San Francisco, and for Manila and Baguio, the Philippines.

Burnham had said, "Make no little plans; they have no magic to stir men's minds." In everything he did, in architecture, planning, and practice, he followed his own dictum.

**Burnham's Life** Daniel Hudson Burnham was born near Henderson, N.Y., on September 4, 1846, and moved to Chicago with his family when he was nine years old. An indifferent student, he graduated from Central High School with a poor record, except for freehand drawing in which he excelled. After failing the entrance examina-

**BURNHAM AND ROOT** Flatiron, formerly Fuller, Building (1902), New York, N.Y. *[Architects: D. H. Burnham and Co.]*

tions of both Harvard and Yale, he tried one thing after another, all for short periods, working as a clerk in a retail store, mining in Nevada, running for the Illinois senate, a race in which he was defeated, working in the architectural office of William Le Baron Jenney (1832–1907), and attempting to start his own office.

In 1872 he went to work in the Chicago architectural office of Carter, Drake and Wight. He admired Peter B. Wight (1838–1925), who taught him a great deal about buildings. Having had no academic training in architecture and a short apprenticeship, Burnham formed a partnership in 1873 with a man who had both the training and the experience, John Wellborn Root. Both were working in the office of Carter, Drake and Wight at the time. The partnership, after a slow start, flourished and grew. One of its first draftsmen was William Holabird (1854–1923), who later made a reputation in his own right. The partnership lasted until Root's death and produced a number of notable buildings.

In 1876, Burnham married Margaret Sherman, the daughter of his first important client, wealthy Chicago

**BURNHAM AND ROOT** Union Station (1908), Washington, D.C. *[Architect: D. H. Burnham and Co.]*

stockyard executive John B. Sherman. Two years earlier, Burnham and Root had completed a large and fashionable house for Sherman. Within ten years after the marriage, Daniel and Margaret Burnham had two daughters and three sons born to them. Two of the sons, Hubert and Daniel, Jr., eventually became architects and joined their father's firm.

After Root's death, Burnham began to broaden his interests. He was named chief of construction and then chief consulting architect for the World's Columbian Exposition. During this period another architect destined for success, Dwight Perkins (1867–1941), ran the office, and Charles B. Atwood was in charge of design. His office grew to be the largest in Chicago and he established branch offices in New York and San Francisco. He became quite active in the work of his profession, serving in a number of capacities, including that of president of the American Institute of Architects, 1894–95. He worked diligently, along with Charles Follen McKim (1847–1929) and others, for the establishment of the American Academy in Rome.

After 1900 the administration of the firm was under Ernest Robert Graham (1868–1936), who had joined it in 1888. Burnham died on June 1, 1912, in Heidelberg, Germany, and Graham continued the firm in partnership with Burnham's sons, Hubert and Daniel, Jr. This

was a productive firm and was later continued as Graham, Anderson, Probst and White.

**Root's Life** John Wellborn Root was born on January 10, 1850, in Lumpkin, Ga., of a well-to-do family. As a child, he showed great interest in nature and talent in the arts, beginning serious study of drawings when he was seven and the piano at twelve. General William Tecumseh Sherman's troops drove Root's family out of their home when he was fourteen. He was then sent to school in Liverpool, England, where he studied architecture and music and further developed his interest in the other arts.

In 1866 Root entered New York University from which he was graduated in 1869 with a B.S. in civil engineering and a brilliant record. He had also distinguished himself in drawing and music, composing and playing both the piano and organ. After graduation, he entered the office of James Renwick (1818–95), the noted Gothic Revival architect in New York City, staying there in 1869 and 1870. He was strongly influenced by Renwick, and Gothic details were to appear in all his buildings. In 1871 he went to Chicago to work in the office of Carter, Drake and Wight, where he met Daniel Hudson Burnham, the man who would most influence the rest of his career. In 1873 the two formed a partnership that produced many fine buildings and lasted until Root's death.

Root's interest in the arts continued throughout his life. In Chicago, he produced amateur plays, concerts, and recitals and even achieved something of a professional status as a critic, reviewing concerts and operas for the *Chicago Tribune*.

In 1880 Root married Mary Louise Walker, who died of tuberculosis six weeks after the wedding. In 1882 he married Dora Louise Monroe. Their son, John Wellborn Root (1887–1963), became a successful architect. Root's sister-in-law, Harriet Monroe (c. 1860–1936), became well known both as the founder of *Poetry* magazine, which published most of the great American poets of the day, and as the biographer of her brother-in-law.

Root practiced architecture fewer than 20 years. He died on January 15, 1891; though only forty-one, he had accomplished a great deal. He had pursued the ideas of the Chicago school to a high peak of excellence.

**Related Articles** HOLABIRD AND ROCHE; JENNEY, WILLIAM LE BARON; MODERN ARCHITECTURE.

# C

**CAPITAL, UNITED STATES** The seat of the federal government in Washington, District of Columbia. Washington and the District of Columbia are unique in many ways, not the least of which is in the architecture.

**Residence Act** In 1790 the U.S. Congress passed the Residence Act authorizing President George Washington (1732–99) to select a site of not more than 100 square miles on the Potomac River for the location of a federal district to be used as the nation's capital. In 1791 Washington chose the present site of exactly 100 square miles, 10 miles on each side, incorporating the existing Maryland towns of Georgetown, Carrollsburg, and Hamburg, and a portion of Virginia. Later that year he received approval from Congress to add the town of Alexandria, Va., to the district, but Alexandria was ceded back to Virginia in 1846.

Early in 1791 Washington appointed Major Pierre Charles L'Enfant (1754–1825), French engineer who had served in the Continental Army during the American Revolution, to survey, map, and make plans for the city to be built in the federal district. After he had prepared excellent plans for the city, still much admired today, L'Enfant was dismissed in 1792, but not before he had indelibly stamped the city with the pattern that has lasted ever since. For illustration of original 1791 plan see article entitled planning, city. Work began on the laying out of the city, its streets and buildings. And this work has been going on ever since.

**Design Competitions** In 1792 competitions were held for the design of the two most important buildings, the Capitol and the President's House, as the White House was known then, and construction began on the White House the same year and on the Capitol the following year. Of all the important government buildings in Washington, these two have had the longest and most interesting histories.

When the competition for the Capitol was held in 1792, there were 17 entries and the winner, who submitted his entry three months late, was a doctor of medicine and amateur architect, William Thornton

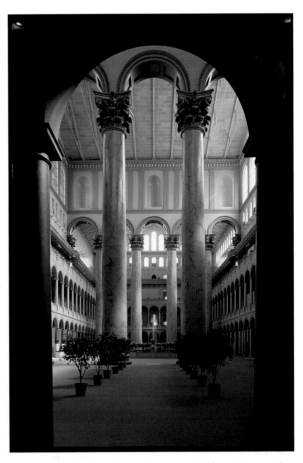

**CAPITAL, UNITED STATES** Interior, Building Museum, former Pension Building (1883), Washington, D.C. *[Architect: Gen. Montgomery Meigs]*

(1759–1828). When it became apparent that Thornton was unqualified to construct the building, a French architect, Stephen Hallet (1755–1825), the runner-up in the competition, was employed, but after disagreements with Thornton and the Commissioners of the Federal Buildings, he was dismissed in 1794. An Irish architect, James Hoban (c. 1762–1831), who had won the competition for the President's House, was given the title of surveyor of public buildings and replaced Hallet, who remained as his assistant. By 1800 they had finished the north wing, and Congress moved in for the first time.

In 1803 Benjamin Henry Latrobe (1764–1820), who had come to America from England five years before, was given the appointment by President Thomas Jefferson (1743–1826) that had been Hoban's, and the south wing was started. This wing was finished by 1807 and the north wing altered. Latrobe also had his problems with Thornton and later on with Jefferson. In 1812, after funds for the work had run out, Latrobe left his position.

During the War of 1812, on August 24, 1814, the British burned the Capitol, along with the White House and other Washington buildings. In 1815 Latrobe was again appointed to his old position and took on the job of rebuilding the Capitol. He restored the building and designed many of the interiors, and then, under pres-

sure, resigned his position in 1817. Charles Bulfinch (1763–1844) was then appointed and during his tenure, which lasted until 1829, the central link between the wings was completed along with a dome, designed by him generally following the Thornton scheme. In 1836 Robert Mills (1781–1855) was appointed architect of public buildings, which included work on the Capitol, and served until 1851.

In 1850 a competition was held for the design of a new dome. It was won by Thomas Ustick Walter (1804–87), who then became architect of the Capitol, replacing Mills. During Walter's tenure, not only was the present dome completed but the wings were extended for both the House of Representatives and the Senate. After the completion of Walter's work on the Capitol in 1865, little was done other than remodeling, plumbing, and electrical work and construction of related buildings until the middle of the 20th century. In 1962 the east front was extended outward some 30 feet after a bitter struggle involving the government and preservationists. In 1970 George Malcolm White (1920– ) became architect of the Capitol. His proposal to extend the west front of the Capitol was rejected in favor of the restoration of the Bulfinch design, completed in 1987.

The White House, designed by James Hoban, went into construction in 1792 shortly after the architect won

**CAPITAL, UNITED STATES** United States Capitol Building (begun 1793), Washington, D.C. *[Architects: William Thornton, Benjamin Henry Latrobe, Charles Bulfinch, Robert Mills, Thomas Ustick Walter, and others]*

the competition. The runner-up was Secretary of State Thomas Jefferson, who had submitted an anonymous design. In 1800, with the building still incomplete, President John Adams (1735–1826) moved in with his family. In 1807, after Jefferson had become president, Latrobe added terrace pavilions on both sides, worked on the interiors, and designed porticoes. In 1814 the White House was burned by the British but was saved from total destruction by a thunderstorm. The president at the time, James Madison (1751–1836), and his family moved into the Octagon House (1800), designed by Dr. William Thornton for Col. John Tayloe III (1771–1828) and now owned by the American Institute of Architects. By 1815 the White House had been rebuilt. In 1824 Hoban added the south portico that Latrobe had designed and in 1829, the north portico.

In 1849 landscape architect Andrew Jackson Downing (1815–52) redesigned the grounds and also worked on those of the Capitol and the Smithsonian Institution. Subsequently, few changes were made except the installation of plumbing and electricity. In 1902 the White House was extensively remodeled by McKim, Mead and White, and the East Gallery and Executive Office Wing were added. While Harry S Truman (1884–1972) was president, the White House was badly in need of repairs, and much of the structure of the building was removed and replaced with steel framing. The exterior walls were not changed, and the interiors were reinstalled.

**Government Buildings** In Washington there are significant buildings of many kinds and eras, some of which are discussed elsewhere in this book. The buildings of the U.S. government alone make the city a virtual museum of the history of architecture in this country after colonial times. The Capitol and the White House are the oldest government buildings. Many of the other early buildings are now gone. Those still in existence

**CAPITAL, UNITED STATES** White House (begun 1792). *[Architects: James Hoban, Benjamin Henry Latrobe, and others]*

include the Navy Yard buildings (1804) by Latrobe and the Marine Barracks (1805) by George Hadfield (c. 1764–1826). In the old Congressional Cemetery, established in 1807, architects Thornton, Hadfield, and Mills are buried, surrounded by the tombs of senators and congressmen and by a number of monuments designed by Latrobe.

Among the later government buildings are the Old City Hall (1850) by Hadfield, now the D.C. Courthouse; the Old Patent Office (1867), restored (1969) as the National Portrait Gallery; the Old Post Office (1869), later restored as offices and shops; and the Treasury Building (1869), the last three by Mills. Still later are the Old Pension Building (1883), now the National Building Museum, by General Montgomery Meigs (1816–92); the Old State, War and Navy Building (1888), now the Executive Office Annex, by Arthur B. Mullet (1834–90); and another Old Post Office (1899) by Willoughby J. Edbrooke (1843–96), one of the few Romanesque Revival buildings in Classic Revival Washington.

Early in the 20th century congressional office buildings were built, designed by Carrère and Hastings, who divided the work between them, John Merven Carrère (1858–1911) assuming responsibility for the Old Senate Office Building (1909) and Thomas Hastings (1860–1929), for the Old House Office Building (1908).

In the 1920s and 1930s a large group of buildings for various departments of the government were built in an area that was cleared and is now called the Federal Triangle. All of the buildings are Eclectic Classic Revival and seem like throwbacks to an earlier era. During the same period the Supreme Court Building (1935) was designed by Cass Gilbert (1859–1934). In 1937 the Federal Reserve Building, designed by Paul Philippe Cret (1876–1945), was built. These buildings were the last great examples of the academic phase of Classic Revival architecture in Washington.

Although it took a long time coming, modern architecture finally arrived in official Washington. Modern buildings, constructed in the past few years, include the New Executive Office and Court of Claims buildings (1968), designed in conjunction with the restoration of the buildings around Lafayette Square, across from the White House, by John Carl Warnecke (1919–    ). Other buildings include the Office of the Department of Housing and Urban Development (1968), designed by Marcel Lajos Breuer (1902–1981) in association with James A. Nolen (1913–    ) and Herbert H. Swinburne (1912–    ), and the International Monetary Fund Building (1973), designed by Vincent Kling (1916–    ).

**Smithsonian Institution** One of the most interesting groups of buildings in Washington, really not a group since they are scattered, are the buildings of the Smithsonian Institution. It was founded in 1846 with a bequest, in 1829, of some $550,000 from an Englishman, James Smithson (1765–1829), who had never seen the country to which he left his money. The Smithsonian has since grown to include a number of activities and buildings in Washington and in other locations. The first building was designed by James Renwick, Jr. (1818–95) in Gothic Revival style and was completed in 1849. Another Renwick building, the Old Corcoran Gallery (1859), later used by the Court of Claims, was restored in 1972 and renamed for its architect as the Renwick Gallery. The first Smithsonian building was followed by another Gothic Revival design for the Arts and Industries Building (1880) by Cluss and Schulze.

In later years other buildings were constructed, including the Museum of Natural History (1910) by Hornblower and Marshal, the Freer Gallery (1923) by Charles A. Platt (1861–1933), and the National Gallery of Art (1941) by John Russell Pope (1874–1937). After some years of building inactivity, the Smithsonian constructed the Museum of History and Technology (1964) by McKim, Mead and White, and Steinmann, Cain and White. The newer buildings are the Hirshhorn Museum (1975) by Skidmore, Owings and Merrill and the Air and Space Museum (1975) by George F. Hellmuth (1907–    ), Gyo Obata (1923–    ), and George E. Kassabaum (1920–82). The Air and Space Museum is the most-visited museum in the United States, and a glass-walled cafeteria and restaurant addition has been added. In 1969 the Old Patent Office (1867), designed by Robert Mills, was restored and converted into the National Portrait Gallery, adjoining the National Museum of American Art. More recently, the National Museum of African Art and the Arthur M. Sackler Gallery were built under the Enid Haupt garden adjoining the Freer Gallery. Designed by Shepley, Bulfinch, Richardson and Abbott, the museums were completed in 1987. The next museum planned is the National Museum of the American Indian. Washington's newest museums are the Holocaust Memorial (1993), designed by James Freed of Pei, Cobb, Freed & Partners, and the Postal Museum (1993) in the old postal building near Union Station.

In addition to the museums and galleries, the Smithsonian directs the activities of the National Zoological Park, founded in 1890, and the John F. Kennedy Center for the Performing Arts (1969), designed by Edward Durell Stone (1902–78).

One of the most famous buildings of recent years was the East Wing extension (1978) of the National Gallery, designed by Ieoh Ming Pei. It provides Washington with one of its greatest public spaces.

In addition to the monuments and other public buildings, the District of Columbia has a group of interesting buildings not owned by the government. Among

these are the foreign embassies, many of which are located along Massachusetts Avenue. Several of these were fine old homes converted to embassy use.

**Related Articles** PUBLIC BUILDING; Individual architects and firms; Various building type articles.

**CAREER** The estimated total of licensed architects in the United States is currently 75,000. There are more than 35,000 students in architectural schools, and some 4,000 are graduated each year. The architectural graduate has two options: to pursue traditional practice or to seek other sources of employment. This article discusses several of the options open to the architectural graduate both in and out of architects' offices.

The public may believe that the architect is competent in all areas, but this is not true. The typical architectural graduate has a good general education with perhaps a specialized ability. As the student accumulates experience, the typical individual may become a specialist. The intern architect will be exposed to all the office functions in preparation for a licensing exam. The Intern Development Program materials developed jointly by the American Institute of Architects (AIA) and the National Council of Registration Boards (NCARB) address all functions of the architectural office, and the program is recommended to or is a requirement for the architectural graduate.

**Architectural Practice** Studies of architectural practices by the American Institute of Architects, and others, suggest the following needs, which occur in all offices. The larger firms may employ people who specialize in one or more of the listed functions.

**Marketing** Finding new work for the office has become a time-intensive activity not only for the management of the firm but also by people on at least a part-time basis to follow up leads, schedule initial contacts, and follow through. Frequently the needed marketing skills may be other than those of an architect or architectural graduate.

**Communicating** This area involves preparing marketing tools such as brochures, proposals, and slide presentations. Such a position involves developing relationships with newspapers, magazines, radio and television, and arranging for principals of the firm to speak to public audiences. This position would maintain project histories, photo and slide collections.

**Programming** Refers to the need to clarify the owner's needs and the scope of the work. It may involve researching the specialized needs of the users of buildings. The more experienced clients will provide the architect with much of the needed information, but serious problems in client relations and in the building constructed have occurred where proper attention has not been given to this area.

**Designing** The process where the program solution is conceptualized. For buildings, it may involve locating the building on a site, organizing spaces, establishing circulation, establishing appearance, and selecting materials. There are two parts to this effort, schematic design and, after owner approval, design development. Architectural education addresses the integration of various disciplines such as structural, mechanical and electrical systems, and materials. The designer may also apply knowledge of architectural practice, history, and theory to this process. Design is the art of architecture and is very close to the center of the profession.

The designer may also make illustrations of the proposed building, called "renderings," and be involved in the making of models. Both these activities are useful for design study but have an additional role in client presentation and promotion. The ability of some computer graphics programs used to incorporate photographs of a model into a photograph of the actual site has resulted in photographs of new projects where it is not possible to visually differentiate between existing and proposed development.

**Technical Staff** The production of contract documents requires technical abilities. At the entry level, these people would not be licensed, or are support personnel such as secretarial, clerical, or office assistant. The architectural graduates would likely enter office work at this level as junior drafters and designers. With experience, these people reach an intermediate level, with less supervision and greater self-determination and responsibility. Some professionals may become specialists or move into management of the project. At this point, graduates would become licensed and have contacts with clients and some supervision responsibility. The senior technical staff are frequently licensed professionals who are highly skilled specialists, job captain, senior designer, draftsperson, specifier, or construction administrator. One option conferred by licensing is to leave the firm and become an independent architect. If remaining in the firm, the architect or engineer in a firm may reach a level to be credited in public recognition of her or his role in the project, although this is unfortunately a rare occurrence.

**Managing the Project** Management was typically a function of the ownership of a firm, but the client and public demand a closer accounting of quality, cost, and time schedules than the partners of a firm have time to monitor, leading to the specialized positions of project managers. Well-managed projects can make the reputation of the firm.

**Managing the Business** Personnel and payroll, finance, legal concerns, and insurance are major concerns for all firms, leading to positions in many firms of business manager. In the larger firms, this area may be assigned to those who have special aptitude and interest in this area. Architectural students at some universities are able to take business courses in management of architectural firms.

**Writing Specifications** Specifications define the desired quality of materials and workmanship for a project. A good specification writer has a knowledge of the technical side of building materials, products, and equipment, and a good writing ability. With the current computerized master specifications, accuracy and speed have been greatly improved, with a lesser cost for this frequently in-house operation.

**Estimating and Cost Control** A firm has need for accurate cost projections because clients normally have fixed budgets. Management of costs and their control involve knowledge of current material and labor prices, a sense of the bidding climate, and knowledge of delivery times which often controls the construction schedule. Some firms may use cost consultants for this work, particularly in times of high inflation.

**Contract Administration** This area of work involves frequent field visits to monitor work in process and includes paperwork for payment certification, review of material samples and shop drawings, and processing of change orders if needed. Some individuals enjoy this direct involvement in the construction process.

**Specialization** Some firms and individuals may specialize in particular building types or in historic preservation, adaptive reuse of older buildings. Evaluation of old buildings in itself may be a specialized practice, particularly as requirements for building inspection legislation call for architectural inspection. The list of specialization can be expanded, and many such specialties are discussed elsewhere in this book.

**Other Career Options** Some architects have earned additional degrees in other fields, such as business management and law. Although some are employed in firms, some have become active in their new fields serving these needs for several firms or others. The following careers are more common, and attract many architects.

**Architects in Education** Teaching in architectural schools has been a long tradition for architects. Some practitioners have taught for a number of years, some returning to private practices at a later time. Other architects make their entire careers teaching. Some 3,000 individuals are primarily occupied in teaching architecture at about 90 schools. Others teach at junior or community colleges and in other nonprofessional programs.

**Architects in Government** Service in government is appealing to those who wish to guide public policy in the areas of planning, design, and construction and to be involved in construction. Architects may work for semi-autonomous public authorities involved in major construction programs or work as facilitators of policy and process rather than being directly involved in design. An architectural license is valuable in government service but is not a requirement for federal agencies. Unless the architect is at the higher levels, influence may be limited to the supervisor. Becoming an administrator may remove the architect from direct involvement in architecture.

**Architects in Industry** Many architects are employees in the facilities, real estate, construction, or manufacturing divisions of a corporation, often as a member of a corporate management team. In these positions, they influence long-range planning, site selection, and programming, selection of the architect and other consultants, and coordinating of entire projects. Salaries are often higher than in private practice. Again, moving into management may remove the architect from direct involvement in building.

**Other Related Fields** Some architects have built practices in fields which relate to architecture. Emerging areas would include design for the handicapped, involvement in public transportation facilities and planning, computer applications, or energy use in building. The following list of related fields is a sample of possible careers.

**Interior Design** Interior design has become a separate area of business. Architectural firms may hire firms that specialize in this area or employ staff with expert knowledge of interior design. Often interior design firms may have a specialty such as hotels and restaurant interiors, furniture design, retail store design, application of historical styles and preservation. Some architects have been involved in the design of stage and movie sets, ships and aircraft interiors. The industry has its own organizations which have promoted licensing of interior designers.

**Industrial Design** Architects have been involved in the design of furniture and accessories as well as ornamental ironwork, light fixtures, and other items to furnish buildings. Such famous architects as Robert Adam (1728–92), Charles McKim (1847–1909), Charles MacIntosh (1868–1928), Louis Sullivan (1856–1924), Frank Lloyd Wright (1867–1959), Bertram Goodhue (1869–1924), Charles Eames (1907–78), George Nelson (1908–86), Eliot Noyes (1910–77), and, in the current generation, Robert Venturi (1925– ), Frank Gehry (1929– ), Michael Graves (1934– ), Richard Meier (1934– ), and Charles Gwathmey (1938– ), have been commissioned for industrial design.

**Planning and Urban Design** Although architects are frequently involved in planning and urban design decisions, the planner is more involved with economics, demographics, and ecology. The urban designer is involved with the three-dimensional aspects of outdoor spaces and buildings. Most planners are employed by government agencies.

**Landscape Architecture** Architects have always been interested in the relationship of buildings to the site and often either hire consultants or add landscape architects to their office staffs. Concerns of land planning and use, including evaluation of slopes, soil patterns, vegetation, wildlife, geology, surface and subsurface water, and climate, lead landscape architects to appropriate decisions for site development. Some landscape architects work for government agencies active in parks, recreation, and urban planning.

**Graphic Design** Designers in this field are typically educated in art or design programs at the university level. In addition to building and site signage, many complex sites and buildings require well-designed directories and graphics to guide the visitor to the desired location. Graphic designers can create public images for corporations through publication and packaging design. Graphic designers work in publishing and advertising. Such designers as Ivan Chermayeff (1932– ) and Paul Rand (1914– ) have had great influence on the appearance of everyday objects.

**Lighting Design** Lighting design has become a separate area of practice and is important to the appearance and quality of light in buildings and their exteriors. The integration of daylighting and the increase in number of lamps and fixtures makes this a creative area of practice closely linked to electrical engineering. In addition to architects, interior designers or industrial designers have been attracted to this field.

**Acoustical Design** The importance of acoustics in concert halls and churches is only an aspect of acoustical design, which is important in all building types. Acousticians are often consultants to architects. In addition to acoustical behavior of materials, the acoustician is expected to be expert in electronic systems for control of sound and the physics of soundwaves.

**Engineering** Although structural engineering is closest to architecture, the mechanical and electrical systems of buildings are becoming an increasing percentage of the cost of building. Engineers are licensed by the states, and must have degrees from accredited engineering programs and several years of relevant experience. Some firms specialize in one field of engineering. The larger architectural firms may have engineering departments; others may be consultants to architects.

**Construction Management** Construction management firms are either parts of larger architectural firms or of general contracting firms. Knowledge of construction, production schedules, materials, the various trades involved suggests that management experience in administration of a wide range of building projects is a necessary background for this important field.

**Facilities Management** Facilities management includes planning new construction and maintaining inventories of space, furniture, etc. available for possible alteration or adaptive use. Computer software has been developed to assist the facilities manager in maintaining close control of maintenance and operation of buildings.

**Historic Preservation** The maintenance and restoration of older buildings has become an important specialty. Several universities offer courses and degree programs in this field.

**Specialized Careers** Architects have had rewarding careers in other fields. Architects have been authors, editors, and critics. Several has served as editor of professional journals, author, editor, or publisher of books on architecture and design, or critic on a newspaper or weekly magazine. Architectural photographers are important communicators to the public and the profession. Several photographers have a background in architecture. Architectural editorial consultants are freelance writers and editors working for government, foundations, corporations, and professional and trade associations.

Architects have worked in helping firms achieve better-managed practices. In seminars or in-house educational programs, they can advise on business and project management, professional liability, ownership transition, marketing, and personnel management.

Some government and quasi-government agencies have funded architectural research, and architects have also been employed in research at universities and for manufacturers and trade associations.

The professional societies employ architects on national, state, and local levels to coordinate the volunteer time contributed to the profession and manage the support services for the profession.

An increasing number of the nation's museums are involved in collections and exhibitions of photographs of buildings, including original drawings and models for exhibitions and archives. Although job opportunities are few, architects can find a rewarding career.

One of the riskier but potentially profitable areas for architects is real estate development. The largest successful firm involved in this work is that of John Portman in Atlanta, Ga. The architect-developer can bring design quality to real estate development.

Involvement in community concerns has led several architects to become candidates for public office, and several have continued in political life on local and state levels. The ability to influence and promote legislation in such areas as housing, health care, education, and urban planning can benefit the society as a whole.

**Related Articles** ARCHITECTURE, BUILDING INDUSTRY; CONSTRUCTION, BUILDING; EDUCATION; ENGINEERING; INTERIOR DESIGN; LANDSCAPE ARCHITECTURE; PLANNING, CITY; PORTMAN, JOHN; PRACTICE OF ARCHITECTURE; Also articles on architectural practice, such as design and drafting.

**Further Reading** *NCARB Architectural Registration Handbook—A Test Guide for Professional Examination Candidates,* current edition, McGraw-Hill, New York; *Architect's Handbook of Professional Practice,* current edition, The American Institute of Architects, Washington, D.C. The American Institute of Architects also publishes surveys of firms.

**Sources of Additional Information** The American Institute of Architects, Association of Collegiate Schools of Architecture, National Architectural Accrediting Boards, Inc., National Council of Architectural Registration Boards, all at 1735 New York Ave., N.W., Washington, D.C. 20006; American Association for Counseling and Development, 5999 Stevenson Ave., Alexandria, Va. 22304; National Institute of Architectural Education, 30 W. 22d St., New York, N.Y. 10010.

**Periodicals** *Journal of Architectural Education,* 1735 New York Ave., N.W., Washington, D.C. 20006; *Career Development Quarterly,* 5999 Stevenson Ave., Alexandria, Va. 22304.

**CARPENTERS' COMPANY** An organization of builders and architects, founded about 1724 by master carpenters and still in existence. The full name of the organization is the Carpenters' Company of the City and County of Philadelphia. The Company is a sort of combination of a medieval guild with a modern labor union and a professional association. It was modeled after the Worshipful Company of Carpenters, London, under whose rules many of the Philadelphia carpenters had served their apprenticeships.

**Company Controls** For a long time after its founding, the Company dominated building, construction, and architecture too, for its members were master builders, or builder-architects, who both designed and constructed structures. Controls over construction were exercised in various ways. The Company strictly limited the number of its members and the members controlled the selection of those allowed to join. Starting with 10 to 15 members, the Company had grown to a membership of about 60 by the middle of the 18th century. It was the custom at this time for sons of deceased members to join without paying entrance fees. Thus membership became something of a family affair.

Members of the Company were close to government officials in the city and, through their influence, obtained preferential treatment when construction projects were contemplated. Company members were the chief employers of other construction craftsmen and laborers. In addition, the Company obtained a considerable amount of control of the pricing of construction and maintained secret price books. One of these books, first published in 1786, was republished in 1971. However, the Company never did gain real control of the building industry.

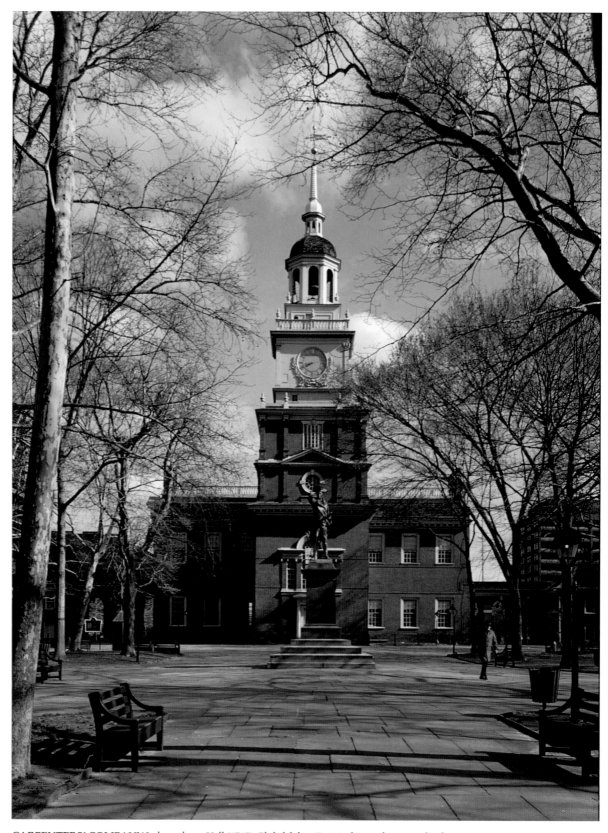

**CARPENTERS' COMPANY** Independence Hall (1745), Philadelphia, Pa. *[Architect: design credited to Andrew Hamilton, built by many including the carpenter Edmund Woolley]*; spire reconstruction (1828). *[Architect: William Strickland]*

A rival organization, the Friendship Carpenters' Company of Philadelphia, was founded in 1769. For some years the two companies competed, while making some halfhearted attempts to cooperate with each other. In 1785 the newer organization was merged into the older. The Carpenters' Company provided education for and assistance to its members. Although it never had an organized apprenticeship system, its individual members trained new craftsmen. And when the Library Company was formed in 1732, some of its new members who were also Carpenters' Company members saw to it that the first books purchased were concerned with architecture.

**Accomplishments** The greatest accomplishments of the Carpenters' Company are to be found in the buildings its members designed and constructed in late-18th-century Philadelphia. The earliest builder-architect was James Portues, sometimes spelled Porteus (*c.* 1660–1737). He designed and built a number of houses in and around the city, most of which were later demolished. A masterpiece, believed to have been built from his design, is Christ Church (1744) which still stands. Two other Company members, John Harrison, Jr. (d. 1760) and Robert Smith (1722–77), added a steeple in 1754. Smith, a most successful member of the Carpenters' Company, designed and built a number of notable buildings in Philadelphia, among them several houses and a dormitory (1763) at Philadelphia College, now the University of Pennsylvania, and the Walnut Street Prison (1776), both demolished. He also designed Nassau Hall (1756) at Princeton University and University Hall (1771) at Brown University, then called Rhode Island College, in Providence, both still standing, and the Mad House (1769) at Williamsburg, Va., since demolished. One of Smith's most distinguished buildings is Carpenters' Hall (1773), which he designed for the Company. This building was used for the meetings of the First Continental Congress in 1774.

The crowning achievement of the great era of the Carpenters' Company is Independence Hall (1745), formerly the State House of the Province of Pennsylvania. Here were held the Second Continental Congress, starting in 1775, and the Constitutional Convention, starting in 1787. And in this building, the Declaration of Independence was debated and signed and the Constitution drafted, debated, and signed. Independence Hall, formerly Old State House, was started in 1731 to a plan by Andrew Hamilton, Speaker of the Assembly, but is also credited to the chief carpenter, Edmund Woolley. In addition to the carpenters, brickmasons, a marble worker, woodcarvers, a joiner, plasterers, and glazier were employed in construction. The building was in use from 1736 but was not completed until 1745. The steeple of 1753 was removed in 1781 and replaced in 1828 to

designs by William Strickland. The building has undergone extensive restoration.

By the end of the 18th century, the grand era of the Carpenters' Company was drawing to a close. Architects not members of the Company, and even from places other than Philadelphia, were now called upon to design many Philadelphia buildings.

**Related Articles** BUILDING INDUSTRY; COLONIAL ARCHITECTURE; GEORGIAN ARCHITECTURE.

**CEILING** The overhead interior surface of a building or room. In times past, ceilings were often highly ornamented, important determinants of architectural design. Today, except for those ceilings in which the roof structure is exposed or expressed, ceilings are usually designed to be as plain, simple, and unobtrusive as possible.

**Types** Other than those with exposed roof structures, ceilings are usually one of two types: ceilings fastened to the undersides of roof structures; or suspended or hung from the structures. In buildings today, though ceilings are not as important design elements as in the past, they are of more importance functionally since they are often acoustically treated; have thermal insulation above them, particularly in flat-roofed buildings; and often house air-conditioning and heating diffusers, ductwork, electrical wiring, and light fixtures. In a suspended ceiling system, all such devices and systems may be easily installed below the structure and then may be concealed above the ceiling, if required. Suspended ceilings are often made so that there is easy access to the space over them for repairs, maintenance, and modifications. In ceilings attached directly to the underside of structures, ducts must be run alongside beams or joists or through them.

**Finishes** Today finishes for ceilings, suspended or not, are usually plaster, gypsum board, acoustical tiles, or other materials, and sometimes wood. Ceilings are generally painted; wallpapered; stained, in the case of wood; or furnished with factory-applied coatings or primers, as in the case of acoustical tile.

Suspended ceilings can be obtained in a number of types of integrated systems, utilizing metal channels, hangers and runners to support acoustical tiles, lighting fixtures, and heating and air-conditioning diffusers. These are complete systems in which acoustical tiles of various kinds may be clipped or otherwise attached. Insulation and vapor barriers may be supported above them if required. Acoustical tiles of various materials are available, either made with quite porous textures or with holes in them. They include tiles made from wood; mineral or glass fibers, either plain or perforated; and perforated metal, above which is placed the acoustical material. Acoustical ceilings made of mineral fibers and binders or other materials may also be sprayed on or applied with trowels like plaster. A limited number of ceilings, such as a curved surface, an ornamental ceiling, or an auditorium ceiling, may be finished with plaster, often called the "wet system," troweled onto metal or gypsum lath. Plaster may be applied in two coats: the scratch coat and the brown coat. Three-coated plaster is recommended and is required over metal lath. In addition to the other coats, it has a third or finish coat. Scratch and brown coats are usually composed of portland cement, lime, and sand mixed with water. Finish-coat plaster is often composed of a special material (gauging plaster, or Keene's cement), lime, and water. Infrequently, acoustical materials may be substituted for the sand in plaster.

In the more common dry systems, boards of gypsum with surfaces of paper are often used. They are ordinarily nailed or screwed in place, and are available with depressed edges that allow for taping and filling with special cements or joint compound to conceal joints. Other dry systems include paneling of plywood or sometimes solid wood and boards made from various wood and other vegetable fibers. Ceiling products containing asbestos are no longer used.

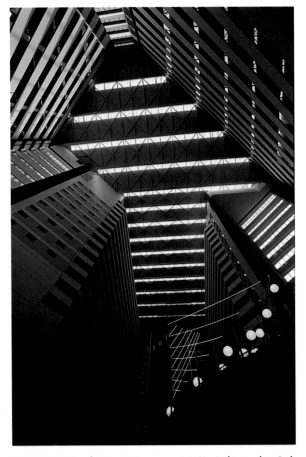

**CEILING** Mixed; Hyatt Regency (1982), Indianapolis, Ind. *[Architect: CRSS]*

**Lighting** Fixtures are available in sizes to fit properly into suspended ceiling systems. The light fixture is supported on the suspension grid for the ceiling, and the fixture is installed above the grid. In some cases the spaces above ceilings are divided in such a way that they act as ducts for warm-air heating, with the ceilings acting as radiant panels. In other types, copper tubing, through which hot water flows, or electrical cables are embedded in the ceilings for the same purpose. Ceilings have been developed in which all of the aspects of heating and cooling, lighting, acoustics, and so on are integrated. Ceiling materials and construction are governed by applicable building and other codes, particularly where they are used for fire protection of structures.

**History** The first ceilings in buildings constructed in ancient times were the undersides of animal skins, brush, or thatch used to cover primitive huts or tents. Such ceilings, if so they can be called, exposed both structures, the limbs of trees or poles and the undersides of roofs. Thus began a tradition that lasted thousands of years until about the beginning of the Renaissance.

By about 3000 B.C. in the civilizations around the Mediterranean Sea, ceilings were often treated as major architectural elements and highly ornamented. Coffered ceilings, with deeply recessed panels and often highly ornamented, were introduced at this time. Both exposed ceilings and coffering became traditions that have lasted until today. The early Persians used exposed roof structures with beams and brackets and with planks, all highly ornamented, while the Mesopotamians often used vaults. The ancient Greeks also utilized coffered ceilings of wood, with the roof structures exposed. They often painted the ceilings in several colors. They also constructed roofs and ceilings of stone, often coffering them to resemble wood construction; sometimes they used no ceiling at all, only the undersides of sloping roofs.

For the most important buildings, the Egyptians used stone in roof structures, often coffered below and painted in various colors. The Romans also used coffered ceilings, sometimes of stone, carved with patterns, and at others of stucco, modeled with patterns of foliage and other forms and sometimes also ornamented with paint. In Byzantine architecture, the undersides of domes were often entirely covered with mosaics.

In Gothic architecture, ceilings were usually the undersides of vaults, often unornamented except for the forms of the ribs where vaults intersected, or exposed wood structures, especially in England, that often were highly ornamented with carvings. During the Renaissance, ceilings were generally constructed under roof structures, completely concealing the structures from view. Ceilings were generally flat or vaulted and almost always highly ornamented in the more important buildings. During this period, coved ceilings, those that

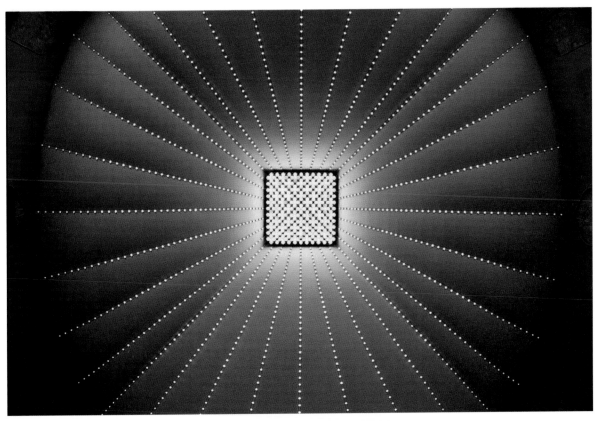

CEILING Fabric; King's Pavilion (1984), Jhiddah Airport, Jhiddah, Saudi Arabia. *[Architect: Minoru Yamasaki]*

have decorative elements at the line of junction of ceilings with walls, were also used. Often curved or angular, the coves were usually highly ornamented. Coffered ceilings were also used. Many ceilings of the era were elaborately ornamented with wood carvings, plaster forms, gilding, or murals. After the Renaissance, in the

CEILING Plaster; Wayne County Courthouse, Detroit, Mich.

Baroque period of architecture, ceilings were given a profusion of paintings and carved and molded forms in plaster and other materials, completely hiding the structural and functional aspects. This was the ultimate stage of a philosophy of design that had started during the Renaissance.

By the 18th century, the design of ceilings had begun to move away from the elaborate and sometimes unrestrained ornament of Renaissance and Baroque architecture. Instead, refined, often delicate forms, derived from Classical architecture, came into use in the United States as well as in Europe.

**American Development** In the earliest colonial times, ceilings in America had been quite plain and utilitarian for the most part. By the beginning of the 18th century, they followed the models in use in Europe. During the Classic and Gothic Revival periods of architecture, ceilings in America were usually derived from those of these past periods. In the Eclectic period, ceilings were derived from those of any of the past periods upon which the styles of individual buildings were based. There was also a return to highly ornamented ceilings.

With the beginning of the modern movement in architecture in the 19th century, ceiling design went in two widely varied directions: one toward completely plain, unornamented flat ceilings, and the other toward the exploitation of structure by exposing it in the interiors of buildings. Both trends continue today, simple flat ceilings being used in most of the usual types of skeleton-framed buildings and in houses, and exposed structural systems in the ceilings of buildings with advanced structural systems, such as space frames and folded plates.

**Related Articles** ART IN ARCHITECTURE; CONCRETE STRUCTURE; FIRE PROTECTION; HEATING, VENTILATING, AND AIR CONDITIONING; LIGHTING; MASONRY STRUCTURE; ORNAMENT; ROOF; SOUND CONTROL; STEEL STRUCTURE; WOOD-FRAME STRUCTURE.

## CLASSIC REVIVAL ARCHITECTURE

A movement, or style, in architecture that used forms derived from the architecture of the classic periods in Greece and Rome. Sometimes called the "neoclassic style," the movement began in the United States toward the end of the American Revolution, when architects turned away from the Georgian style architecture of England. In its place, they espoused an architecture they considered more appropriate for a new republic and turned to the Greeks and Romans for inspiration. This article includes the Federal style as a prelude to the Classic Revival.

**The Federal Style** This style, which began about the time of the Revolution and lasted into the 19th century, was not radically different from Georgian architecture (see the article entitled Georgian architecture). Some maintain that the Federal style was actually a continuation of the Georgian, varying only in relatively small details and in the scale of buildings. Some of these details, derived from the work of Robert Adam (1728–92) in England, include the giant portico, the doors with narrow flanking sidelights, and elliptical fanlight above, the curved or polygonal bay window, the balustrade or parapet placed over the eaves, graceful spiral stairways in the entrance hall, and the delicate-scaled ornament in wood or plaster. The Federal style, conservative as it was, produced some notable architecture, in particular that of Charles Bulfinch (1763–1844) and Samuel McIntire (1757–1811).

**The Classic Revival** The new nation continued to reflect architectural developments in Europe. Thomas Jefferson (1743–1826) visited several new buildings in France and England as well as antiquities such as the Maison Carré in Nimes, France, dating from 16 B.C. Jefferson's architectural work shows the continuation of the prevailing Classic detailing as seen in the current work abroad. The Roman style filtered through the work of Palladio (1508–80) was his favored style. Jefferson was particularly interested in buildings set in rural environments and their formal lawns and gardens which he felt was appropriate to the new nation. Whereas the Federal style was conservative and traditional, Jefferson's Roman style was individualistic. Sometimes called the "idealistic" phase of the Classic Revival movement, the Roman phase is considered to have begun with Jefferson's Virginia State Capitol (1791), Richmond, loosely derived from the Roman Maison Carré (c. 16

**CLASSIC REVIVAL ARCHITECTURE** Gore Place (1804), Waltham, Mass. *[Architect: unknown]*

**CLASSIC REVIVAL ARCHITECTURE** City Hall, New York, N.Y. (1811; later addition). *[Architects: Mangin and McComb]*

B.C.), Nimes, France. The Roman style reached its peak about 1820, but continued to be an important influence until the beginning of the Civil War.

Typical of the Roman style architecture were such forms as columns, or orders; large imposing porticoes; gable roofs, with great pediments; and domes. All Jefferson's greatest buildings are in the Roman style, notably the Rotunda, derived from the Pantheon (A.D. 124), Rome, Italy, and other buildings at the University of Virginia, Charlottesville. In his own great house, Monticello, in Charlottesville, Jefferson provided a masterful example of the change from the Georgian to the Roman Revival style. Construction, tearing down, and rebuilding of this house continued from about 1770 to almost the end of his life. By 1775 the house was virtually completed in the Georgian style, but Jefferson soon started to remodel and rebuild it in the Roman style, essentially completing this work in 1808. The Monticello of today, in Roman style, is quite different from the first version.

The Roman style was used for a great number of important buildings. Considered by many the greatest of these is the U.S. Capitol, upon which construction began in 1793. Other notable buildings in this style include the White House, begun in 1792 and designed by James Hoban (*c.* 1762–1820). The style was also used for many great houses in various parts of the United States, sometimes in various combinations with the Greek Revival style. At the time that Jefferson was calling for a Roman style as the source for a new Republican architecture, other voices were calling for a more indigenous style, less based on European precedent. Such voices as the revolutionist Thomas Paine (1737–1809), the younger Ralph Waldo Emerson (1803–82), and Horatio Greenough (1805–52) called for a new architecture suit-

**CLASSIC REVIVAL ARCHITECTURE** Oak Alley or *Bon Sejour* (1839; later alteration and addition), Vacherie, La. *[Architect: Joseph Pilie; restoration: Koch & Wilson]*

**CLASSIC REVIVAL ARCHITECTURE** Stanton Hall (1857, restoration), Natchez, Miss. *[Architect: Thomas Rose]*

able for American society. Instead, Greek Revival became the preferred style.

**The Greek Revival Style** This style, occasionally called the American Greek Revival architecture, is thought to have begun in the United States with the Bank of Pennsylvania (1801), Philadelphia, designed by Benjamin Henry Latrobe (1764–1820). Although the architect used the Greek Ionic order and other Greek details, the essential character of this building, with vaults and a dome, was Roman. Other later Greek Revival buildings, and there were many of them, including houses and commercial, public, and other types all over the United States, were more purely Greek in derivation. Greek Revival became more firmly established in American architecture than did Roman and persisted until the Civil War and afterward to an extent, into the present century. Two of the earliest proponents of the style were both former employees of Latrobe, Robert Mills (1781–1855) and William Strickland (1787–1854). Strickland designed what many believe to be the first purely Greek Revival building in America, the Second Bank of the United States (1824), Philadelphia, and went on to design many others. Mills also became committed to the style and designed numerous Greek Revival buildings, including the Treasury building (1842), Washington.

**CLASSIC REVIVAL ARCHITECTURE** Nathanial Russell House (c. 1811), Charleston, S.C. *[Architect: unknown]*

As time went by, the Greek Revival style became predominant, though Roman forms and details were sometimes combined with it. Most of the greatest U.S. architects of the first half of the 19th century designed buildings in this style, including John Haviland (1792–1852), Thomas Ustick Walter (1804–87), Isaiah Rogers (1800–69), Ammi B. Young (1798–1874), and Gideon Shryock (1802–68). Some of these and other architects of the time were dedicated to the Greek Revival style, and many sometimes worked in other styles.

Greek Revival architecture soon became familiar to most educated people in the United States and was as greatly admired as were the principles of Greek democracy. This was the first style to become almost completely acceptable in all parts of the country for buildings of various kinds. Buildings designed like Greek temples, with classic orders, porticoes, and pediments, were constructed everywhere. Books of details were published showing the orders and other parts of the style, and these became familiar to the carpenters as well as the architects of the time.

By the beginning of the Civil War, the style had been completely accepted by most architects and their clients. Not only were standard details available but standard columns and other elements were being manufactured. About 1840, some architects turned away from the Classic Revival toward other styles; see, for example, articles entitled eclectic architecture; Gothic revival. After the Civil War, Classic Revival buildings continued to be designed even into the 20th century, but the style never again had the force and vitality it had once had, particularly from about 1820 to 1860.

A very large number of Classic Revival buildings are still in existence all over the United States. A complete listing would be very long indeed. The growing interest in historic preservation has helped to preserve this part of our heritage. In addition to those mentioned above, others buildings are discussed in articles on various architects of the period and in other articles in this book.

**Principles of Classicism** The Classic Revival period in architecture was one of deep beliefs in the principles of classicism: in reason, ideals, and analysis; with what were considered to be universal truths; and in the good and the beautiful, meaning that which was clear, symmetrical, reposeful, and derived from traditional classical forms. With the beginning of Gothic Revival architec-

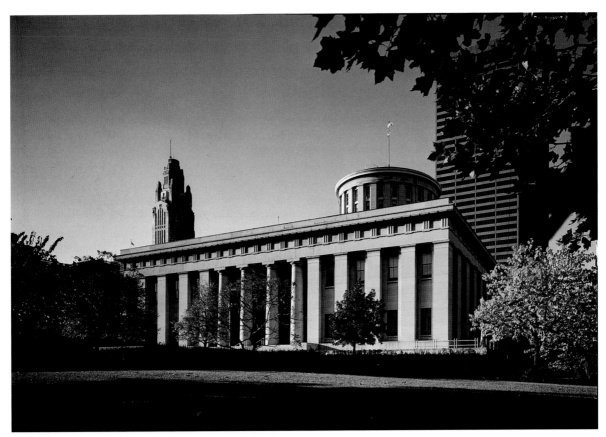

**CLASSIC REVIVAL ARCHITECTURE** State Capitol (1839–61), Columbus, Ohio. *[Architects: Henry Walter, W. R. West, Nathan B. Kelly, Isaiah Rogers; consulting architects: Alexander Jackson Davis, Thomas U. Walter, Richard Upjohn (Photo: Gary Quesada/Korab Ltd.)]*

ture, architects and others turned away from classical principles to those of romanticism, in many ways the antithesis of the classical ideals. This led first to the Gothic Revival style and then to the many others that are spoken of collectively as the "Eclectic architecture" of the second half of the 19th and the early part of the 20th centuries.

**Related Articles** COLUMN, ECLECTIC ARCHITECTURE; GEORGIAN ARCHITECTURE, HISTORY OF ARCHITECTURE; JEFFERSON, THOMAS; LATROBE, BENJAMIN HENRY; PRESERVATION; Various articles on other Classic Revival architects.

**Further Reading** Hamlin, Talbot: *Greek Revival Architecture in America*, Oxford University Press, London, 1944, available in a reprint from Dover Publications, New York; Kennedy, Roger G.: *Greek Revival America*, A National Trust for Historic Preservation Book, Stewart Tabori & Chang, New York, 1989. See also listings in articles entitled colonial architecture, Georgian architecture, and history of architecture.

**Sources of Additional Information** See listing in the article entitled history of architecture.

**CLIMATE** Over a period of many years, the weather conditions that exist in an area, such as a continent, a country, a city, a building site, or even a portion of a site. The climate in which a building will be placed is one of the major considerations in architecture. Climatology is the science of climate and its relation to animal and plant life. Climate is concerned with long-term conditions; and weather, with short-term conditions. Both climate and weather are concerned with five major conditions: temperature, wind, sun, humidity, and precipitation in the form of rain, sleet, snow, and hail.

**Determinants and Zones** The major determinant of climate is the distance of an area from the equator, or its latitude. Other important determinants include an area's altitude, terrain or topography, prevailing winds, and proximity of water bodies, particularly oceans. Climates are often classified into five major zones, based on the relation of the climate to the vegetation in the area. The zones are rainy tropical, dry or desert, warm-temperate, cool-snow-forest, and polar. Climates may also be classified into nine zones: rainy tropical; alternately wet and dry tropical; semiarid; desert; warm rainy; dry summer, rainy winter; cold moist; polar; and ice cap. Often zones are spoken of in other terms, such as the equatorial zones or doldrums, which have high temperatures and heavy rainfall; subtropical; or the horse latitudes, usually taken to be in the neighborhood of 30° latitude, north or south. Another zone which has a dry, mild climate is sometimes said to have a Mediterranean type of climate and is found on the west coasts of continents, north of the subtropical zone. It is

characterized by mild temperatures, with moderate rain in winter and dry summers.

**U.S. Zones** In architecture, all climate zones are important. The United States has almost all zones, the major ones being warm, rainy in the Southeastern states; cold moist in the Northern states and much of Alaska; semiarid in the Western states; warm with dry summers and rainy winters on much of the West Coast; and desert in the Southwestern states. In addition, the Pacific Northwest and the coastal lands of Alaska have warm, rainy climates; northern Alaska's climate is polar in nature; and Hawaii has a mild, rainy climate, with little seasonal change in temperature. American architects design buildings to be constructed in all these areas. And many of them design buildings to be constructed in foreign countries where other zones, such as rainy tropical, are to be found.

**Effects on Architecture** The determinants of climate, latitude, altitude, terrain, prevailing winds, and water bodies deeply affect architecture. The latitude of a building site affects the path of the sun from sunrise to sunset, the height to which it will rise at noon, and the length of days. These factors in turn determine the heating effect of the sun and the hours of daylight. For example, in the north middle latitudes between the tropical and polar zones, the sun usually rises toward the southeast, reaches its highest point in the southern sky at noon, and sets toward the southwest. On the day of the summer solstice, about June 21, the sun rises at the point farthest north of east that it will have all year, progresses to its highest point of the year in the southern sky, and sets at the point farthest north of west of the year. This is also the longest day of the year, the daylight hours exceeding those of the night. After the summer solstice, the sun rises farther to the south, reaches a lower point in the sky at noon, and sets farther to the south with each succeeding day until the winter solstice, about December 21, is reached. On that day, the sun rises at its most southeasterly position, progresses to its lowest point in the southern sky at noon, and sets in its most southwesterly position of the year. This is the shortest day of the year, with the nighttime hours exceeding those of the day. After the winter solstice, the process repeats itself, in reverse, the sun rising more toward the northeast each day, climbing higher in the sky, and setting more toward the northwest until the summer solstice is again reached. On two days of the year, the vernal equinox, about March 21, and the autumnal equinox, about September 21, the sun rises in the due east and sets in the due west, providing days and nights of equal length.

While the latitude of an area is the most important determinant of climate, altitude, or elevation above sea level, is also important, since temperatures are usually colder at higher than at lower altitudes. Also lower barometric pressures at higher elevations have some effect, and rainfall tends to increase with increases in altitude up to about 6,000 feet above sea level and then to decrease above that level.

Terrain has considerable effect on climate. Some surfaces, such as sand, rock, and pavement, absorb more heat than do water, forests, and meadows. Thus sand, rock, and pavement give off more heat to the lower atmosphere than do water, forests, or meadows. Mountains or hills generally receive more rainfall than flat areas, since moist air carried past the highest terrain feature is forced to rise, becomes cooler, and cannot hold as much moisture as warm air.

Mountains block winds and valleys channel them, thus affecting the flow of cool or warm air toward various areas. These and other conditions determine prevailing winds, the normal direction of wind flow, in various areas. Water bodies also have a considerable effect on climate. The larger the body of water, the greater will be its effect. Water bodies do not become as cold in winter as the land adjacent to them, or as warm in summer. Water bodies therefore have a moderating effect on the land areas near them, producing milder climates in coastal areas than in those farther inland. On the west coasts of continents, where prevailing winds are usually from the west, climates are usually mild. They are often rainy because the winds bring moisture from the ocean. West coastal mountain areas are often very rainy since the winds bring considerable moisture which is forced to fall when the winds rise to pass over the mountains.

Most of the foregoing discussion is particularly directed to the climates of relatively large areas, which are often called macroclimates. But the same conditions also affect smaller climates, often called microclimates, as might exist on a specific building site, or even in one area of the site, such as a sunny patio or a shaded backyard. Architecture is affected by both macroclimates and microclimates. In addition to the conditions already discussed, microclimates are affected by such conditions as relatively small terrain features: rocks, banks, surrounding buildings or other structures, and trees and other vegetation.

**Building Types** Climate affects architecture in a number of ways. Since it affects animal and vegetable life, it affects the lives of human beings and the living things with which they surround themselves. One of the most important social questions related to architecture is concerned with differences in the way people live and act in different climates and methods by which architecture can serve their varied needs. Meeting such needs requires considerable variation in the types of buildings constructed in various regions. Thus at the risk of oversimplification, building forms throughout history have tended to vary in design according to the climates in which they were built, becoming closed-in insulated structures, with few small openings and pitched roofs in cold areas; structures with heavy walls, small openings, and flat roofs in hot, arid zones; open structures with pitched roofs in hot, humid areas; and so on. Climate continues to affect the form of buildings today as it did in the past. Architects must study climatic effects on their designs to produce solutions that properly meet the requirements of various climates. Climate also affects other architectural considerations in buildings, such as plans, which, for example, can be more open in temperate than in colder climates.

**Weather Controls** Climate also deeply affects architecture in another way: the control of its effects on buildings. Such controls fall into three major categories: provision of more desirable climates within buildings, portions of them, and on their sites; protection of buildings and their occupants from extreme climatic or weather conditions, such as hurricanes and floods; and production of energy for use in buildings from climatic phenomena, such as solar radiation and the force of winds. For further discussion on protection from climatic conditions, see the article entitled weather protection; and on production of energy, the article entitled energy.

Control of climates within buildings may be classified into two major types: those of an engineering nature and those of an architectural nature. Engineering controls include mechanical and electrical systems employed to create artificial climatic conditions within buildings. This subject is discussed in the article entitled heating, ventilating, and air conditioning.

Perhaps the most important architectural control is building orientation, the placement on a site to take advantage of desirable climatic conditions, such as the heat of the sun in winter and prevailing winds in summer, and to minimize undesirable effects of the sun in summer and cold winds in winter. Proper orientation also may reduce the amount of heating and air conditioning required and have other desirable effects, such as improvement of the quality of lighting in buildings. Some architects maintain that the walls of buildings should be considered as filters. In this view, walls, together with their openings and other devices, act to allow wind, heat, light, and so on to enter buildings when needed or to be excluded when they are not. Such a filter may also modify entry, such as in heat-absorbing glass which allows light to enter or louvers which permit wind to enter but direct its flow.

Other important architectural controls include materials and systems. Horizontal and vertical sunshades can aid in controlling the entry of sun into buildings, allowing it to come in during winter and excluding it during summer. Trees and other vegetation may also be used for the same purpose, and in addition may serve to channel winds in desirable directions or act as windbreaks. Garden walls or other structures may serve the same functions. Insulation retains heat inside in winter and blocks it from entry in summer. Double or triple glazing of windows, or storm windows and doors, serves a similar purpose while also minimizing entry of drafts.

In addition, the major building materials used have a considerable impact on the control of climate in buildings. Heavy masonry walls tend to block the entry of heat more than thin metal or wood-framed walls. On the other hand, masonry walls also retain the heat they absorb longer than the other types, radiating it back after the air cools.

From the foregoing discussion, it may be seen that the proper handling of climatic considerations in architecture involves a number of factors and complications. Proper handling must begin with the programming phase, in which accurate information, both macroclimatic and microclimatic, is gathered and analyzed, and continue during the design phases. If the right decisions are made in these first phases, it will be easier to make decisions during the preparation of working drawings and specifications.

**Data-Gathering Techniques** A number of techniques have been derived for study of the effects of climate on buildings and their occupants, and a considerable amount of data is available. After obtaining accurate data on a specific site for a building, architects and other design professionals use a number of tools for their analysis and for proper climatic design of buildings and other structures. Charts and tables of climatic data are available, including sun charts and tables that contain information on the timing and paths of the sun relative to the earth for various latitudes and times of the year.

Calculators and other devices may be used for this and other purposes. Formulas also have been derived for calculations of such information. Thus a choice of methods is available to an individual user. Some experts believe that calculations of this sort should be worked out with formulas, while charts, tables, and other devices serve only for quick approximations and for checking the results derived from the calculations. Some experts recommend the use of models for checking the effects of the sun and wind.

**History** Although weather changes take place on a regular basis, sometimes very rapidly, changes in climate occur very slowly. It is thought that climate has changed very little during the period of recorded history. Before that, great changes took place during what is called the Pleistocene Epoch, sometimes called the Ice Age, when sheets of ice, or glaciers, moved down from the polar regions into the areas south of them.

Beginning about 2 million years ago, there have been four major periods of the Ice Age. Each lasted many thousands of years and was separated from the next by a warmer period in which the ice melted. In North America the Ice Ages, or glaciation periods, from the oldest to the latest, are the Nebraskan, Kansan, Illinoisan, and Wisconsin. The warmer periods between, the interglacial periods, from first to latest, are Aftonian, Yarmouth, and Sangamon. The first Ice Age in North America, the Nebraskan, started about 600,000 years ago and lasted about 64,000 years. The Aftonian interglacial period started about 536,000 years ago and lasted 60,000 years. The latest North American period of glaciation, the Wisconsin, began about 115,000 years ago and ended more than 10,000 years ago.

Since the end of the Wisconsin glaciation period, no great climatic changes have occurred. However, there have been periods, lasting from 35 to 100 years, when general warming or cooling trends have been recorded. Some scientists believe that these climatic cycles occur on a regular basis. In any case, from about the middle of the 19th to the middle of the 20th centuries, somewhat higher temperatures have been observed, particularly in the middle and higher latitudes of the Northern Hemisphere.

Climate-related environmental concerns of the last decades of the 20th century include the presumed tendency to global warming, the greenhouse effect and acid rain caused by pollution of the atmosphere, changes in the size of openings in the ozone layer, continuing destruction of tropical rainforests, and the lingering effects of natural phenomena such as volcanic ash in the upper atmosphere.

**Related Articles** DESIGN, ARCHITECTURAL; ELECTRICAL ENGINEERING; ENERGY; HEATING, VENTILATING AND AIR CONDITIONING; INSULATION, THERMAL; LIGHTNING PROTECTION; MECHANICAL ENGINEERING; PROGRAMMING; WATERPROOFING; WEATHER PROTECTION.

**Additional Reading** Arnonin, Jeffrey E.: *Climate and Architecture*, 2d ed., Van Nostrand Reinhold, New York, 1984; McHarg, Ian L.: *Design with Nature*, 1969, reissued by John Wiley, New York, 1991; Olgyay, Aladar, and Victor Olgyay: *Solar Control and Shading Devices*, Princeton University Press, Princeton, N.J., 1957, available from Books on Demand, UMI, Ann Arbor, Mich.; Olgyay, Victor: *Design with Climate—Bioclimatic Approach to Architectural Regionalism*, Princeton University Press, Princeton, N.J., 1963.

**Sources of Additional Information** U.S. Department of Commerce, National Weather Service, National Oceanic and Atmospheric Administration, National Meteorological Center, 5200 Auth Rd., Camp Springs, Md. 20746.

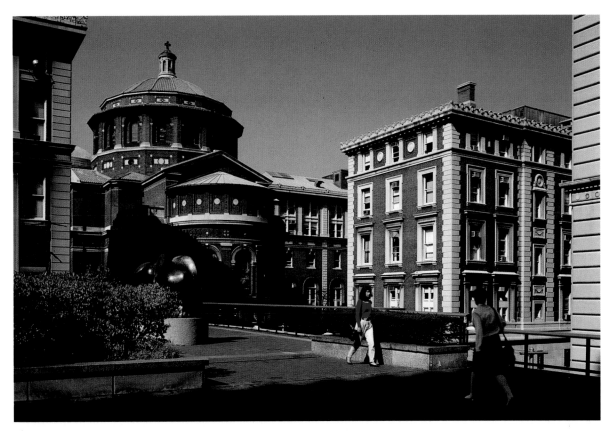

**COLLEGE AND UNIVERSITY BUILDING** General view, Columbia University (begun 1897), New York, N.Y. *[Architects: Campus Planning, Charles Follen McKim of McKim, Mead and White; St. Paul's Episcopal Chapel (1907), Howells and Stokes]*

**COLLEGE AND UNIVERSITY BUILDING** A building in an institution for higher learning and research, located on a campus. A college is an institution dedicated to only one branch of knowledge, such as a liberal arts or medical college. A university is an institution dedicated to many branches of knowledge. These individual branches within a university are also referred to as colleges. Special types are junior colleges which ordinarily offer only freshman and sophomore courses, and community colleges which offer courses to students who usually live at home and commute to the colleges. There are also undergraduate, graduate, and professional colleges.

**Campus Size** Many colleges in the past were small and had all their facilities in one or a few buildings. Today some universities have student bodies numbering in the tens of thousands and have campuses that provide all the facilities of a small city, in addition to classroom and other educational buildings. Some universities have branches located in various parts of their states, thereby bringing higher education to students in the various localities, allowing for some specialization among the branches, and avoiding the problems of one campus

becoming too large for proper education. In spite of this, some campuses have move than 50,000 students. In comparison, many of the smallest colleges have fewer than 100 students. In the past, there were colleges for men and women, but the current trend is toward coeducational colleges.

**Operation** Colleges and universities are operated by private or governmental groups. Private colleges and universities are sometimes sponsored by religious groups, sometimes by other groups, often with the help of endowments, money given by philanthropists. Government-sponsored colleges and universities include state universities; community colleges, sponsored by state or local governments; and those sponsored by the federal government, such as the armed services academies. Governing the affairs of most colleges and universities are boards of trustees or regents, elected or appointed by the sponsors.

**Organization** A college or university is organized with an administration, a faculty, a student body, and a maintenance group. The administration ordinarily consists of a president or chancellor, along with other executives who have duties as deans, controllers, and so on.

The faculty consists of the professors of various ranks and instructors, organized into a department, such as biology or mathematics, with a chairman of each department. In a university, each college usually has a dean, who is its administrative head. Members of the student body enroll and take courses in the individual colleges. Maintenance includes grounds keeping, janitorial services, repair shops, and the like.

**Campus Buildings** Although all the buildings on a college or university campus are involved in the education of students in some way, the elements may be divided into those that are primarily educational, such as classroom buildings; residential, such as dormitories; administrative, such as offices; athletic, such as gymnasiums; and miscellaneous, such as cafeterias. In addition to regular classroom buildings, many other types of educational facilities may be provided, including laboratory and research buildings, theaters, auditoriums, and computer centers. Some of these buildings may also be used for administrative, recreational, or other purposes.

Residential facilities include dormitories, which usually have been restricted to men or women but today also include coed buildings, in which each sex occupies a separate wing or an alternate floor. Although some dormitories have single rooms, most have double rooms for

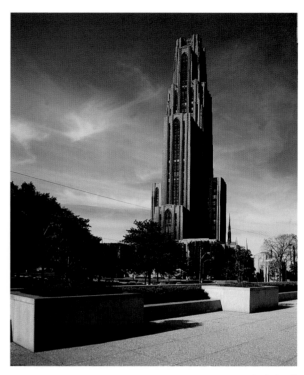

**COLLEGE AND UNIVERSITY BUILDING** Cathedral of Learning (1937), University of Pittsburgh, Pittsburgh, Pa. *[Architect: Charles Klauder]*

**COLLEGE AND UNIVERSITY BUILDING** Alumni center (1984), University of Michigan, Ann Arbor, Mich. *[Architect: Hugh Newell Jacobson]*

two students. Three-student rooms have been used, but were not successful. In some cases, two or more rooms are organized into suites, often with shared baths. In other cases, baths for a relatively large number of people, or gang baths, are provided. This is not considered to be the best planning solution but may be dictated by economy. Dormitories often have communal areas used by some or all of the occupants, including lounges, libraries, mailroom, dining or vending facilities, laundry rooms, and date rooms. On some campuses, apartments are provided for married students, and facilities are available for mobile homes and trailers. Fraternity and sorority houses often have dormitory rooms in addition to other facilities for members.

Administrative facilities in colleges and universities often include separate buildings for the office of the president and other officials as well as offices in the educational buildings for the college deans and others. Also provided are shops for repair and maintenance work, and often a communications center.

Athletic buildings provide for several types of activity: physical education, intramural sports and games, intercollegiate sports, and recreation. Outdoor areas are also required, including such facilities as stadiums, practice fields, tennis courts, golf courses, swimming pools, and playing fields. Some of the buildings are gymnasiums for physical education and sports; field houses for dances, assemblies, and other events as well as athletics; and specialized buildings for indoor swimming, handball, and so on.

Important miscellaneous buildings are the cafeterias and other dining facilities for students, faculty, and administrators. Also of great importance is the library, without which a college or university cannot operate properly. Other buildings often provided are chapels, observatories, and student unions. In fact, buildings of almost every type may be found on campuses, for example, hospitals in medical schools, farm buildings in agricultural schools, churches in theological schools, and so on.

There are more than 2,200 colleges and universities in the United States with student bodies of 200 or larger. Of these, about 100 have colleges of architecture. The construction of new colleges and universities accelerated after World War II, but has now declined. However, the remodeling and replacement of older buildings and the construction of new buildings on existing campuses make this an important building type. And design of a college or university campus, or a building on a campus, is one of the most interesting and gratifying commissions to an architect.

**History** Early colleges came into existence first in Italy, including one founded at Salerno in the 9th century that specialized in medicine and one founded at

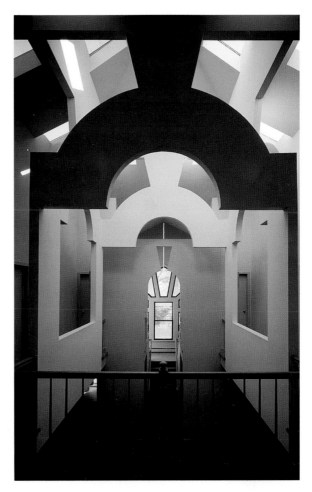

**COLLEGE AND UNIVERSITY BUILDING** Detail, Sammis Hall (1981), Cold Spring Harbor, N.Y. *[Architects: Moore, Grover, Harper]*

Bologna in the 12th that specialized in law. The first universities included these two, a few hundred years later, and also the University of Paris and the Universities of Oxford and Cambridge in England, all founded in the 12th or early 13th century. The first in America was the University of Santo Domingo, founded in 1538, in what is now the Dominican Republic; and it was followed by the universities of Mexico, Mexico City, and San Marcos, Lima, Peru, both founded in 1551.

**American Colonial Universities** The first university in the English colonies in America was planned to be built near Richmond, Va., in 1619, but the project was abandoned. The first actually built was Harvard College, now University, in Cambridge, Mass., in 1636, followed by the College of William and Mary, Williamsburg, Va., in 1693. Other early American universities were Saint John's (1696), Annapolis, Md.; Yale (1701), New Haven, Conn.; Princeton (1746), Princeton, N.J.; Columbia (1754), New York City; and Pennsylvania (founded as a charity school, in 1740), Philadelphia.

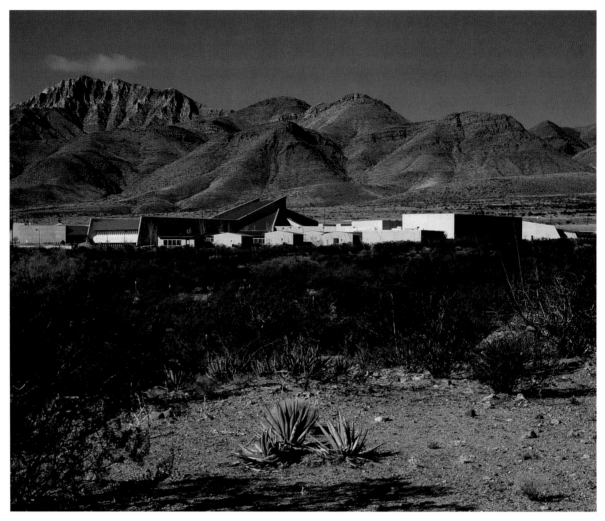

**COLLEGE AND UNIVERSITY BUILDING** El Paso Community College (1980), El Paso, Tex.
*[Architects: Fouts Gomez Architects]*

Since the founding of Harvard, a very large number of architects, including some of the greatest, have designed campuses and their buildings. The earliest American college building still in existence is the so-called Wren building (1695) at William and Mary, its design traditionally attributed to the great English architect, Sir Christopher Wren (1632–1723).

**Further Reading** Dober, Richard P.: *Campus Design,* John Wiley, New York, 1992.

**Sources of Additional Information** American Association for Higher Education; Association of State Colleges and Universities; Association of American Universities; American Association of Community and Junior Colleges, all at 1 Dupont Circle, N.W., Washington, D.C. 20036

**COLONIAL ARCHITECTURE** The architecture of the colonists in America, beginning with the rude structures of the earliest settlers and continuing to the time of the American Revolution. Although architecture of this period is sometimes spoken of as the Colonial style, the phrase is a misnomer. There was no such single style, but a number of different styles, varying considerably between the English, Dutch, Spanish, French, and other colonists, at various periods of time and between the various geographical regions.

**Early Colonization** The time of the founding of the earliest colonies that eventually became the United States is often taken to mark the beginning of the colonization of America. Actually, of course, the process began much earlier, with the colonization of Greenland by the Norseman Eric the Red, about 985. The mainland is believed to have been discovered by Leif Ericson, son of Eric, about the year 1000, and colonized a short time later. Leif Ericson named the land he found Vinland, variously held to have been Newfoundland, Labrador, or New England. The Greenland colony lasted several hundred years and then died out and that in Vinland only a few years. Theories have been advanced, but remain unproven, that Irish adventurers, and possibly others, reached North America about the same time or earlier.

The first colony in America after the time of the Norse efforts was established by Columbus, during his voyage in 1492, on the island of Española, now the Dominican Republic. The colony had disappeared when he returned the following year. He established another colony in 1493, near where the first one had been. In 1496 this colony was moved to Santo Domingo, and became the first permanent colony in America. Other colonies, in various locations in the Caribbean and in Central and South America, soon followed. The earliest colony directly related in any way to the future United States, San Juan, Puerto Rico, was founded in 1521.

**U.S. Settlements** The first permanent settlement in what became mainland United States was founded by the Spanish in St. Augustine, Fla., in 1565, six years after an earlier attempt had failed at Pensacola, Fla. The first Spanish missions in the Southwest date from 1598 in New Mexico. The first permanent English settlement was made at Jamestown, Va., in 1607, following an earlier colonization effort at Roanoke Island, N.C., in 1584, which disappeared with scarcely a trace. Beginning in 1620 at Provincetown, Mass., seven New England colonies were established within 20 years. In 1626 the Dutch founded New Amsterdam, now New York City, and the Swedish had founded, in 1638, Fort Christian, which later became Wilmington, Del. After several earlier attempts had failed in other locations, the French finally established permanent colonies at Mobile, Ala., in 1710 and at New Orleans, La., in 1718. Following these early colonies, others were established in many parts of what are now the United States.

**Early Structures** The first settlers in America generally constructed buildings much like those they had known in the countries from which they had come, with materials most easily obtained. Thus half-timbered houses were built in Jamestown soon after it was founded. In Spanish Florida wood was used along with brick; and in the Spanish Southwest, mostly adobe. In New England and the other English colonies, wood was used at first and later brick. While many of the earliest colonial houses resembled those in the home countries of the settlers, numerous houses were much more primitive, a fact that has been somewhat overlooked in histories of the period.

Many of the early settlers lived in caves, either natural or dug into the sides of hills. Others lived in huts, the lower halves of which were pits dug into banks or cliffs, the upper halves of limbs and brush, sometimes covered with mud or sod, and with roofs of limbs covered with tree bark, sod, or brush. In other cases, the settlers constructed houses copied from the wigwams of the Indians. Chimneys were often constructed of fieldstone or of a combination of sticks, grass or brush, and clay. Contrary to popular belief, the use of log cabins did not originate in America but in the northern countries of Europe. The first log cabins in America were constructed by the Swedish settlers in Delaware, beginning about 1638. Later, German immigrants to Pennsylvania and other places also built log cabins. Still later, pioneers built log cabins in the West. Another type of early building was the sod house, constructed of dirt and used mostly in the Midwest. Although it is not widely known, many Americans still lived in such primitive dwellings at the time of the Revolutionary War and even later.

For the most part, the settlers soon moved out of their first primitive dwellings into more permanent types, modeled after those in Europe. Most of the more permanent houses were quite modest in size, had few rooms, and were constructed of materials easily obtainable locally. In time, mainly because of differences in climate, materials available, national origins and preferences of the colonists, regional styles of architecture became established.

**Regional Styles** The major early styles in the English colonies were Northern, or New England, Colonial; the Southern Colonial. Another major style

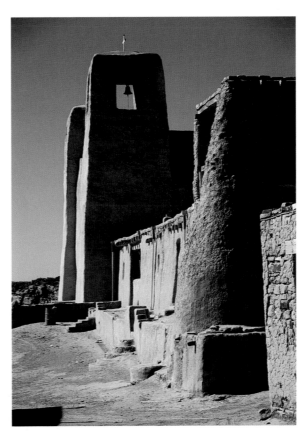

**COLONIAL ARCHITECTURE** San Estévan del Rey (c. 1642), Acoma, N. Mex. [Architect: unknown]

101

**COLONIAL ARCHITECTURE** Old Ship Meeting House (c. 1681), Hingham, Mass. [Architect: unknown]

and Louisiana and up the Mississippi River to St. Louis, during the 18th century. Much of the colonial architecture before the end of the 17th century, and even afterward in some instances, was designed by architects whose names are unknown.

**New England Colonial Style** Early New England Colonial structures were built almost entirely of wood, except for fireplaces and chimneys which were usually of stone. Most had heavy, half-timber frames which were filled in with wattle and daub, a mixture of clay or lime with straw. In other cases, the frames were covered with clapboard. Chimneys were usually built inside houses for additional warmth. Most of these early houses were derived from English rural architecture of the time. At first, only one room was provided on the ground floor with a sleeping loft above, but later houses had several rooms on each of two floors. Roofs over the main portions were gable types, and often one-story kitchens were built on the back sides and covered with lean-to roofs. Windows were small because of the severity of the winter, and houses were usually compact, without porches, for the same reason. Sometimes the second story projected out beyond the first-story wall. In time, buildings other than houses were also built in New England. Notable among them were religious

from the early 1600s to well into the 1800s was Dutch Colonial, mostly in what is now New York City and its environs and northern New Jersey. In the areas that became the State of Florida and the Southwestern states, Spanish Colonial was the prevailing style from the time of the earliest settlements until almost the middle of the 19th century. The French Colonial style, originally established in the area that became Canada, prevailed in the areas that became southern Mississippi, Alabama,

**COLONIAL ARCHITECTURE** John Turner House, also known as the House of Seven Gables (1668; later alteration and addition), Salem, Mass. [Architect: unknown]

buildings, meeting houses, which were also built of wood until late in the 17th century, when brick and stone came into use.

Unlike the South, where brick was used much earlier and nearly all the early 17th-century wooden buildings have long since disappeared, a number of early wooden buildings still exist in New England. Unlike those in the South, they were protected from deterioration by the colder, drier climate. Among the existing 17th-century Colonial buildings, some of the most notable houses are Fairbanks House (1636), Dedham, Mass.; Whipple House (c. 1639), Ipswich, Mass.; Scotch-Boardman House (c. 1651), Saugus, Mass.; Richard Jackson House (1664), Portsmouth, R.I.; The House of the Seven Gables (c. 1669), Salem, Mass., made famous in the book of that title by Nathaniel Hawthorne (1804–64); the Paul Revere House (c. 1676), Boston, equally famous as the home of the great silversmith and patriot, Paul Revere (1735–1818); and the Parson Capen House (1683), Topsfield, Mass. The only 17th-century meeting house still in existence, considered by many as one of the finest buildings in the United States, is the Old Ship Meeting House (1681; see illustration), Hingham, Mass. Another interesting early building is the Jail (1652) in York, Maine.

**Southern Colonial Style** In the English colonies that later became the Southern states, Southern Colonial architecture was, like that of New England, derived from English rural architecture. At first of wood, later often of brick, the earliest buildings were quite similar to those of New England: small with one or a few rooms and sleeping loft, with small windows, but with chimneys usually attached to exterior walls. Later, houses became much more open in plan because of the milder climate, and much larger and more imposing than most of those in New England. In the South, the early great houses were mostly located on plantations of many acres, owned and operated by gentlemen-planters, while New England houses were more typically located in towns and owned by merchants. In the South, other types of buildings were also constructed, the most important of which were churches. Though almost all of the early Southern Colonial buildings were destroyed long ago, several remarkable examples still exist relatively small distances from each other in tidewater Virginia.

The oldest, and possibly the oldest English colonial building in America, is St. Luke's Church (1632) in Isle of Wight County, near Smithfield, Va. Almost as old and possibly the oldest existing English colonial house is the Adam Thoroughgood House (c. 1636), near Norfolk, Va. Both of these buildings are quite Gothic in character. Perhaps the last surviving house in America in the Jacobean style, named for King James I (1566–1625) of England, is in Surry, Va. It is now called Bacon's Castle

(c. 1655), after Nathaniel Bacon (1647–76), who led an ill-fated rebellion against the English in 1676. At one point during the rebellion, Bacon's followers seized the house and it has been called by his name since that time. Bacon's Castle gives early and considerable indication of the grandeur of future Southern plantation houses that followed it. Not far away, another building, the Thomas Rolfe House (1652), is more typical of the residential architecture of its time. It is much smaller, having only four rooms, and unpretentious.

**Dutch Colonial Style** Dutch Colonial buildings were derived from those in the Netherlands, from which the settlers had come. Dutch Colonial houses were of two major types: one had steep, double-pitched, modified gambrel roofs with overhangs, or eaves, only on the front and back and with chimneys on both ends; the other type was similar, but had gable roofs with flared eaves. Gambrel roofs were sometimes used in early New England and in the South, but these are thought to have been borrowed from the styles of the Dutch. Dutch Colonial buildings were generally of wood at first, but later stone was often used. Although the Dutch colonists often used solid doors, they became noted for the so-called Dutch door, divided horizontally in the middle so that either the top or bottom half could be opened independently of the other.

Only a moderate number of Dutch Colonial houses exist today. Some of the most notable are Pieter Claessen Wyckoff House (c. 1641), Brooklyn, New York City, probably the oldest building in the state; Ackerman House (1704), Hackensack, N.J.; Bries House (1723), Greenbush, N.Y.; Dyckman House (c. 1783), New York City; and Vreeland House (1818), Englewood, N.J. Settlers from many other countries eventually affected Colonial architecture, particularly in the middle colonies of Maryland, Pennsylvania, Delaware, and New Jersey. In addition to the English and Dutch who settled in some of these places, Swedish, German, Scottish, and Welsh immigrants also settled there. None of them established strong styles as did the English and Dutch, but they nevertheless stamped their architecture with their own traditions.

**Spanish Colonial Style** Spanish Colonial architecture began in Central and South America, earlier than in the areas that later became the United States. However, it soon spread to what became the State of Florida and along the Gulf Coast to the Southwest to California, and eventually to New Orleans. Spanish architecture in the colonies was mainly of brick, or adobe, after the time of the earliest wood buildings. It was unlike other architecture in America at that time. The English and Dutch settlers based their buildings on rural types in their homelands, and produced buildings that were mostly medieval, or Gothic, in character. The Spanish, on the

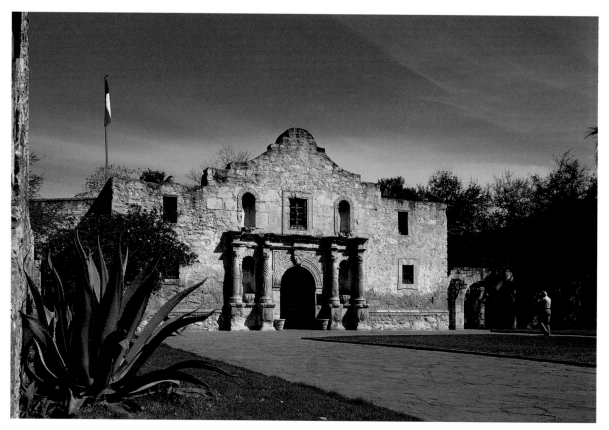

**COLONIAL ARCHITECTURE** The Alamo, also known as Mission San Antonio de Valero (1777, partly restored), San Antonio, Tex.

other hand, produced a more exuberant architecture more akin to the Baroque style then in favor on the European continent. However, Spanish Colonial architecture was never as dramatic and ornamented in what became the United States as it was in Mexico and other places farther south.

Many Spanish Colonial buildings are still in existence, primarily forts (see the article entitled military building), churches, and government buildings. In St. Augustine, in addition to the fort and a few other old buildings, is located the oldest Spanish Colonial house, now called the Spanish Treasurer's House (c. 1695). Its first story is built of coquina, limestone from fossil seashells, and the second, of wood. In New Orleans are located some important Spanish Colonial buildings, including the old Spanish Town Hall, the Cabildo (1795), and the nearby Presbytere (1794–1813), both now used as museums, and the Cathedral of St. Louis (1794, and later remodeled).

The greatest collections of existing Spanish Colonial buildings in the United States exist in the Southwest and in California. In the Southwest, some of the most notable churches include San. Estévan (c. 1642), Acoma, N. Mex.; Nuestra Señora de la Asunción (1692), Zia Pueblo, N. Mex.; San José (1706), Old Laguna Pueblo, N. Mex.; San José y San Miguel de Aguayo (1731), San Antonio, Tex.; The Alamo (1757), San Antonio, the scene, in 1836, of the great battle for Texas independence from Mexico; San Francisco (c. 1772), Ranchos de Taos, N. Mex.; and San Xavier del Bac (1797; see illustration), Tucson, Ariz. Among the most notable California Spanish mission churches are San Carlos Borremeo (1797), Carmel; San Juan Capistrano (1806); and Santa Barbara (1820). A number of other Spanish Colonial buildings still exist in California and in the Southwest. Among the most interesting are the Governor's Palace (1614), Santa Fe, N. Mex., and the Governor's Palace (1749), San Antonio, Tex.

**French Colonial Style** Early French Colonial architecture in what eventually became the United States, like that in the other colonies, reflected the buildings the settlers had known in Europe. At first very primitive and impermanent, French Colonial architecture soon progressed to better designed and constructed and more permanent types. Several things made French Colonial architecture quite different from that in the other colonies. One was a system called *briquette entre poteaux*, which employed structures of wood, with the spaces between filled in with brick and the walls stuccoed.

Other differences came from the hot, humid climate and the heavy rainfall of Louisiana and the Mississippi

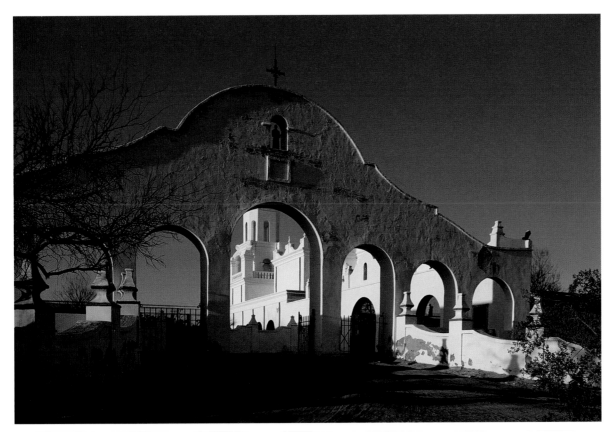

**COLONIAL ARCHITECTURE** San Xavier del Bac (*c.* 1797), Tucson, Ariz. *[Architect: unknown]*

River Valley. One answer to this problem was the provision of considerable numbers of large windows, surrounded by great verandas that not only shaded the windows and walls from the sun but provided protected outdoor living space. Another answer was the construction of raised cottages, which have the main living areas on the second floor and other floors above, while only service and storage areas are located on the ground floor. Thus the early permanent French Colonial buildings, while derived from those in France, soon developed into a regional style, well adapted to the habits of their occupants and the climate of the area in which they were built.

While French Colonial buildings still exist in a number of places, the greatest number are in Louisiana, including New Orleans and the bayou country. The great era of French Colonial architecture in New Orleans began with the founding of the city in 1718 and continued until 1769, when Louisiana was ceded to Spain. Louisiana came back to France in 1799, but only for four years until the Louisiana Purchase in 1803. The French Colonial style continued to influence the architecture of New Orleans and other places in Louisiana for many years after that date.

In New Orleans, there are a number of French Colonial buildings, including examples of many types,

such as small houses and plantation houses. Some of the most important are Ursuline Convent (*c.* 1727); Madame John's Legacy, a house thought to be the oldest in the Mississippi Valley and to have been built in the early 18th century; Lafitte's Blacksmith Shop, thought to be almost as old and to have been occupied by the pirate, Jean Lafitte (*c.* 1780–1826); and the Spanish Customs House (*c.* 1784), actually a relatively small plantation house built during the Spanish regime but French Colonial in character.

Outside New Orleans, several great plantation houses of the era still exist. Among the most notable are Ormond Plantation (*c.* 1790), St. Charles Parish; Parlange Plantation (*c.* 1750), Pointe Coupee Parish; Voisin Plantation (*c.* 1785), St. John the Baptist Parish; and Rienzi (*c.* 1800), Lafourche Parish.

Beginning in the early part of the 18th century, architecture in the English colonies and in the former Dutch colonies, by then also English, gradually changed from the colonial styles of the past to the style then most important in England, the Georgian (see the article entitled Georgian architecture). Other styles continued in these colonies for quite a long time, but the Georgian eventually prevailed. In the French and Spanish colonies, which became states later, the early colonial styles continued until well into the 19th century. And Dutch

**COLONIAL ARCHITECTURE** John Whipple House (1640), Ipswich, Mass. *[Architect: unknown]*

Colonial also continued to an extent, alongside the Georgian, in parts of New York, New Jersey, and other places settled by the Dutch.

The 13 original states had all started out as either proprietary colonies, those controlled by individuals under grants from European rulers, or as corporate colonies, controlled by groups chartered by the rulers. By the beginning of the Revolutionary War, eight of the colonies had become what were called Royal Colonies, under the direct control of the king of England. They were Georgia, Massachusetts, New Hampshire, New Jersey, New York, North Carolina, South Carolina, and Virginia. Maryland, Pennsylvania, and Delaware remained proprietary. Connecticut and Rhode Island were still corporate colonies.

Very little architectural construction took place during the Revolution. Afterward, the new states turned away from the Georgian of the English toward other styles thought to be more appropriate to the newly formed republic. For a discussion on the new kind of architecture, eventually called Classic Revival, see the article entitled classic revival architecture.

**Related Articles** CLASSIC REVIVAL ARCHITECTURE; GEORGIAN ARCHITECTURE; HISTORY OF ARCHITECTURE; PRE-COLUMBIAN ARCHITECTURE; PRESERVATION; Various articles on colonial architects.

**COLUMN** In the trabeated, or post and lintel, structural system, a structural member that is usually relatively long and slender, vertical, and supports weights and other loads above it. Columns are sometimes called "posts" or "pillars." A *pier* is like a thick column, relatively short usually, which supports very heavy loads such as those of arches, vaults, or domes. Columns and piers may be either freestanding or attached to walls, the latter often called "engaged." A rectangular column or pillar attached to a wall is often called a "pilaster."

**Functions** Columns have been one of the most important elements in architecture since ancient times. They have functioned as vertical structural members carrying loads from the structures above them from the time of the earliest civilizations. Columns continue to perform this important function today. In the past, the major materials for columns were wood, stone, and later cast and wrought iron. Today wood is still important, but steel and reinforced concrete have virtually replaced the other materials.

Until the end of the 19th and the beginning of the 20th century, columns performed another immensely important function, as one of the primary determinants of architectural design. In every era, from the beginning of architecture to the 20th century, the aesthetic design of columns and their uses as ornament have deeply affected the overall appearance, architectural effects, and other qualities of buildings. Today the ornamental functions of columns have virtually disappeared, leaving as their only function that of structural members.

**History** Little is known about the first uses of columns in buildings. However, by the beginning (about 3000 B.C.) of the ancient civilizations around the Mediterranean Sea, in the Middle East, Egypt, Crete, and other islands of the Aegean Sea, and on the mainland of Greece, columns had come to be used extensively, and in some cases as very important elements of architecture.

The Mesopotamians did not use columns to any extent, but the Persians developed highly ornamental columns of wood and stone, with tops, or capitals, and scrolls and brackets above depicting bulls, sometimes with human heads, and dragons. In Crete and in the early years on the mainland of Greece, square stone columns were used, but the most common type was round, made of wood and usually tapered, with a capital similar to that of later Greek Doric columns. In Egypt, square pillars of stone and round columns were used. Ordinarily, the columns were built up in sections, or drums, each placed on top of the one below. Column shafts were often ornamented, as were capitals, the major types of which had stylized versions of papyrus bundles in bell or bud shapes, lotus flowers, or palm leaves. Sometimes the heads of gods were used on capitals, and sometimes their figures were used for entire columns. Some column shafts were simple cylinders, and others were fluted.

Most of the styles of columns of these ancient civilizations have had little effect on the architecture in America. An exception is the Egyptian style, which was used sometimes on certain buildings of the Eclectic era and a few earlier and later ones.

**Greek Columns** The design of columns was a great accomplishment of the ancient Greeks. Eventually, they refined their designs to a very high degree of excellence, which have been models for architects ever since. Also they produced a system with three types, called "orders," for the design of columns and related elements. The later Greek columns were of marble, constructed by placing a series of drums in layers.

**Orders** The three Greek orders, from the simplest to the most ornamental and from the earliest to the latest developed, are the Doric, Ionic, and Corinthian. An order is considered to consist of the shaft of the column, with its top, or capital, and its base, if it has one, together with the horizontal structural member, or entablature, it supports. The entablature is divided into three parts, the lowest being the architrave, the middle part the frieze, and the highest the cornice. Very definite proportions and forms for all these elements and for the relationships between the elements were established. The orders

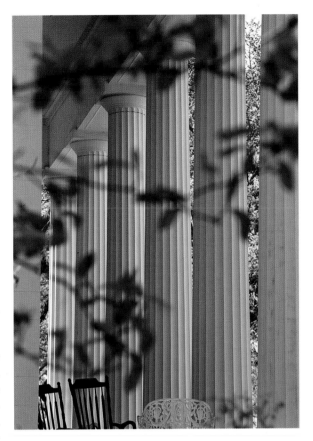

**COLUMN** Classic Revival, D'Evereux (1840), near Natchez, Miss. *[Architect: James Hardie]*

played a very important role in Greek architecture, becoming the single most important element that determined the appearance of buildings. Although the Greek orders are often thought of as comprising a rigid standardized system, they never were that to the Greeks, who varied them considerably in every building they designed and constructed.

The Doric order was relatively plain and dignified. Without a base, the columns were generally fluted, but not always, tapered toward the simple capital and entablature above. The Ionic order, more slender and somewhat more ornamental than the Doric, was also fluted and tapered to a capital with volutes similar to those of the spiral structure of some seashells. Almost always, the volutes were placed on the insides and outsides of the capitals, except at corners of buildings. The Corinthian orders were similar, except that in the Corinthian, columns were even more slender than those of the Ionic.

The Greeks were masters of architectural design. To make sure that buildings and their elements had the proper appearance, they introduced methods of design which corrected for optical errors inherent in the human eye. The major methods involved the subtle curving of

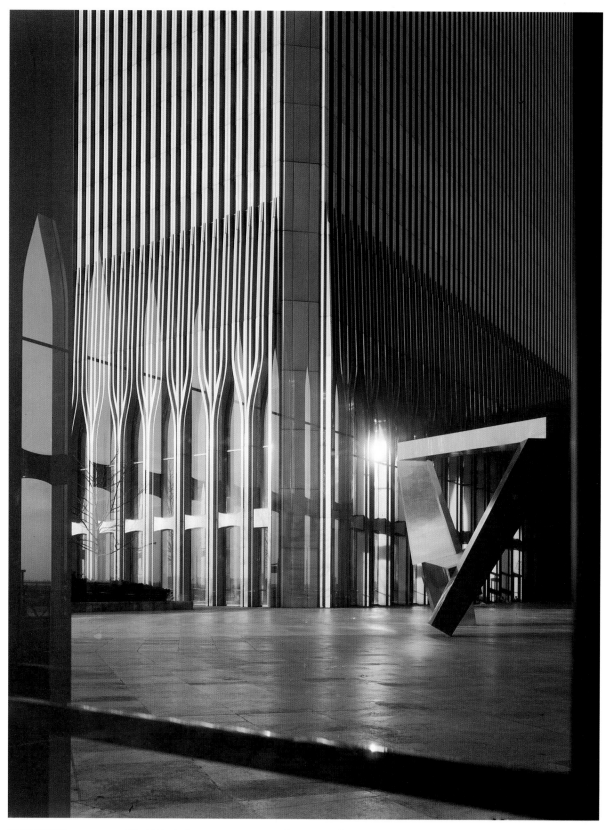

**COLUMN** Contemporary, World Trade Center (1973), New York, N.Y. *[Architects: Minoru Yamasaki and Emery Roth and Sons]*

**COLUMN** Roman Order, Tuscan. (*Andrea Palladio:* The Four Books of Architecture, *Dover Publications*)

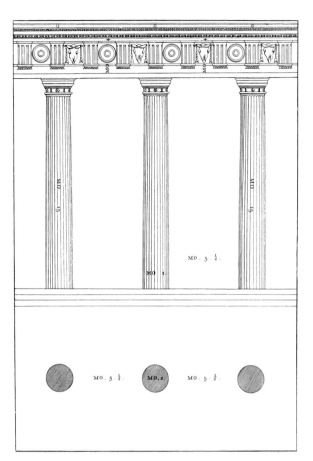

**COLUMN** Roman Order, Doric. (*Andrea Palladio:*The Four Books of Architecture, *Dover Publications*)

horizontal and vertical lines to make them appear straight to viewers and the inclination of vertical elements to make them appear to be absolutely vertical rather than as if they were leaning. In columns, optical corrections were made by subtly curving the shafts, giving them what is called "entasis."

**Roman Columns** The Romans used columns which they adapted from those of the Greeks, changing them to meet their own purposes. Although Greek columns of fine marble were generally fluted, the Romans usually eliminated the flutes, finding them unsuitable for the granite and other stones at their disposal. Their columns were made in one piece, that is, monolithic. The Romans also placed lines of columns, or colonnades, over other colonnades, or superimposed them, something the Greeks rarely did. The Roman taste for grandeur and ornament is reflected in their columns. The original Greek Doric order was modified, making the column shafts taller and more slender, and bases were added. The Ionic order was made less refined and more ornamented, eventually having capitals with volutes on all four sides. Neither order gained the acceptance with the Romans of

the Corinthian, which was their favorite, and which they developed to a highly ornate state. The Romans occasionally used an order called the Tuscan, similar to the Doric, which they adapted from the architecture of the Etruscans, who were the early inhabitants of west-central Italy. More to their liking, and highly ornamented, was a new order, the Composite, which they developed by combining some of the characteristics of the Ionic with those of the Corinthian.

The columns, and the complete orders, of both Greece and Rome have had great influence on subsequent architecture, including that of the Renaissance and the Classic Revival and Eclectic periods that followed, in America as well as in Europe.

**Early Christian and Byzantine Columns** In the architecture of the years immediately following the Roman era, columns in both the Early Christian and Byzantine buildings generally utilized the Roman orders. In fact, many of the columns in Early Christian churches were actually removed from older Roman buildings. Byzantine architecture soon discarded the old orders to develop newer types better suited for the sup-

**COLUMN** Roman Order, Ionic. (*Andrea Palladio:* The Four Books of Architecture, *Dover Publications*)

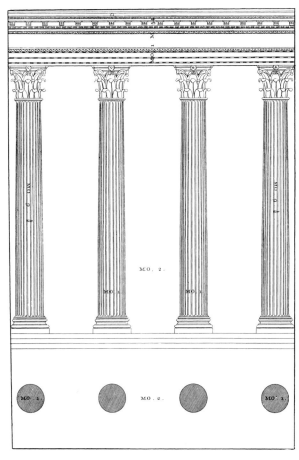

**COLUMN** Roman Order, Corinthian. (*Andrea Palladio:* The Four Books of Architecture, *Dover Publications*)

port of arches and domes. Capitals became very ornate; some prevalent types were the bird and basket and the cushion. During the Romanesque period, columns in Italy were often monolithic, as they had been in Roman times, but were usually made up from smaller pieces of stone in other countries. Romanesque columns or piers were generally heavy and large, somewhat crudely made, often relatively short, with capitals adapted from those of Rome. Sometimes several columns were grouped in a sort of cluster. The columns of none of these eras have deeply affected those in America.

**Gothic Columns** The opposite is true of the Gothic era, which followed the Romanesque. Architecture in Europe as well as in America has been deeply affected by the Gothic, particularly in the design of churches in the Gothic Revival and Eclectic periods. Gothic columns or piers came in a great variety. Some were simple, cylindrical shafts, with or without capitals, and others utilized various kinds of clusters with highly ornamented capitals.

Designs of columns varied so much from country to country during the Gothic era and between buildings and at different times, it is impossible to generalize about them. In England, for example, columns varied

from short cylinders with unornamented square capitals to tall, slender types in the shape of octagons and other polygons, with designs on the shafts and highly ornamented capitals with foliage forms.

**Renaissance Columns** During the Renaissance, architects turned away from the column forms used in Gothic times back to those of the classical era, in particular to the classic Roman orders. Columns were used structurally or purely for decorative effects, whether freestanding or engaged. Two widely divergent philosophies of column design seem to have existed during the Renaissance: one that produced a variety of types with various kinds of ornament not only on the capitals but also on the shafts, and another that attempted to codify and standardize designs, based on the five Roman orders.

**Standardization** The move toward standardization was probably started by the first publication in Latin, in 1486, and subsequent publication in Italian in 1521, of a book written in the 1st century B.C. by a Roman architect of that era, Marcus Pollio Vitruvius. The thoughts of Vitruvius, including those on the orders, had a considerable effect on Renaissance architects. The move toward standard design of columns was accelerated by

**COLUMN** Roman Order, Composite. (*Andrea Palladio:* The Four Books of Architecture, *Dover Publications*)

the publication of two books by two Italian architects who were contemporaries, Giacomo Barozzi da Vignola (1507–73) and Andrea Palladio (1508–80). Palladio's book, published in 1570, greatly influenced architects of the Classic Revival era, including Americans, even more. Vignola's book, published in 1562, also influenced architects of the time, and later in the Classic Revival era. Particularly influential were his standardized designs and proportions for the classical Roman orders.

**American Development** From the time of the early colonies, the design of columns generally followed the prevailing styles in Europe, in wood at first and later in wood or stone. The books of Palladio and Vignola were used for inspiration and information as were others on similar subjects published mostly in England, including those of Inigo Jones (1573–1652), Colen Campbell (1673–1729), and James Gibbs (1682–1754). Many early American architects learned architecture from studying such books and went on to design buildings using the orders much as they were presented in the books.

As was the practice elsewhere, many American architects did not slavishly copy the orders as standardized by the authors of such books. Although an American, upon occasion, would copy a column design and an order for a given building straight from a book or from some specific classic or Renaissance building, many of the buildings they designed employed columns that were inspired or derived from books or older buildings. In this way, a vast vocabulary of column types, roughly identifiable as having been derived from the orders, appeared in American buildings, particularly up to the end of the Classic Revival period. The columns for Gothic Revival buildings in America were designed in a similar manner. After that, during the Eclectic period, column designs were derived or reproduced from a variety of sources and styles, including Egyptian, Muslim, and other styles. Some column types were so popular that they became widely available as stock items in wood.

In the latter half of the 19th century with the beginnings of what became the modern movement in architecture, the use of ornamental columns declined and was replaced by use of types that were frankly only structural in function. An exception was the attempt by some architects to reproduce in cast-iron and wrought-iron columns the designs of the classic orders. Thus iron columns on buildings looked superficially like Greek, Roman, and Renaissance forms. Because of their extremely slender shafts and other factors inherent in the nature of iron as a material, these columns actually appeared quite different. Iron columns were also often offered as stock items. However, an era of structural design of columns, without regard to their ornamental effect, had begun, and it eventually brought the use of ornamental columns, except for an occasional resurgence, virtually to an end in the 20th century.

**Related Articles** ART IN ARCHITECTURE; BOOK, ARCHITECTURAL; DESIGN, ARCHITECTURAL; HISTORY OF ARCHITECTURE; MOLDING; ORNAMENT; Various articles on phases of American architectural history.

**COMMUNICATION SYSTEM** In buildings, communication systems refer to provisions for delivering information from person to person or place to place. Important types include intercommunication systems, commonly called "intercoms," telephones, data communications, and electronic mail, commonly called "E-mail," systems, which combine text, graphics, and audio segments, and teleconferencing. Other systems include alarm, sound, and security systems. Several of these systems may be combined for computer monitoring and control. (See articles entitled fire protection; security systems.)

Many people would agree that the highest form of communication between persons takes place in conversation, face to face. In the complex world of today, face-to-face conversation is not always possible. Therefore a vast array of types of communication devices and systems has been developed. All are important in architecture. Although some people may believe it possible to communicate directly from person to person through extrasensory perception (ESP), most communication systems used in architecture today rely on the senses, in particular those of sight and hearing. Architects and other environmental designers must be familiar with these systems and provide for their proper design and installation when and where they are needed in buildings.

**Sound Systems** The simplest communication systems used in buildings are those that rely on sounds from bells, buzzers, horns, or chimes to relay certain simple messages. Perhaps the simplest of all is a door knocker that tells people that a visitor or some other person has arrived at a house, apartment, or other building. A door-bell system serves the same purpose and requires only the provision of a simple button, a transformer, low-voltage wiring and a bell, buzzer, or chime to announce the visitor. Equally as simple are such devices as horns to communicate simple facts, such as the end and start of work shifts in factories. Such communication systems may be manually operated or automatic.

In schools, colleges, and universities similar systems are used to signal the end and beginning of class periods, lunch hours, and other activities. These systems are usually automated by tying them in with clock systems that not only give the time in various areas but automatically trip the bells or other sound devices at the proper time. Often called clock and program systems, a communication system of this type may be controlled by a master clock. Another type operates in a similar manner, but does not have a master clock. In either case, the system may have only a single scheduled program or several. If more than one is required, a program instrument is used. A variation of such systems is a complete sound system, which allows for paging, music, and other transmissions, in addition to signaling the ending and beginning of class periods.

Other sound systems, similar to those already discussed, include paging, nurses' call, and similar types. Some of these systems require wiring, microphones, loudspeakers, and other equipment. In others, such as doctors' call systems, radio transmissions are used to activate devices, some of which are portable and may be carried in a pocket or on a belt, which signal to a person that a telephone call should be placed to a paging center. Another relatively simple system, sometimes installed in large homes or other buildings, uses annunciators, devices that register numbers indicating the location of a person who wishes assistance or service.

**Telephones** In the last few years, great changes have occurred in this form of communication. In addition to wiring systems, the growth of cellular phones, dedicated lines for information transmission, and the proliferation of specialized equipment have transformed the industry.

Automation of office operations has increased the need for in-building computer networking. The need for flexibility and growth has changed the concept of phone service for larger buildings. The phone company brings lines to the building, but the interior of the building wiring systems and equipment are the responsibility of other designers and contractors. In a multistory building, vertical risers and distribution from floor panels allows integration of power, lighting, and communication connections at each work location either from overhead or in the floor construction. Often coaxial cable is used to connect computers, and phone line connections using modems and facsimile (Fax) machines allow outside communication. Radio communication devices can also be integrated into a building's communication systems. Many in-office systems are now wired with fiber optic cables.

**Building Automation** This term refers to central building automation monitoring and operation of the systems in a building or group of buildings. The central computer's monitor screen can indicate detailed information about any system or any area of a building such as a floor. The computer can keep track of heating, ventilating and air conditioning, energy use, lighting loads, fire alarm systems, security systems, water use, and elevator operations. The system arrangements are monitored at several levels which may be described on a scale from 5 to the highest 1.

The fifth level is automated operation of passive sensors, such as flame, smoke, ionization, temperature and water flow connectors, smoke and fire door position sensors, and manual fire alarm pull stations.

The fourth level provides operators or actuators for such items as fire and smoke door actuators, smoke vent controls, sprinkler system valves, and fan override switches. The third level may represent a floor, zone, or other area control, with programmable controls depending on the system complexity. This level receives information from the lower levels, processes it, returns control information to the third level, and sends alarm condition information to the second level. It may also be used to reset alarms or reprogram systems.

The highest and first level is the computer console. This level receives status reports on individual devices, or sections of the building and subsystems, and each system separately. Printouts can be made on alarms and status reports. Systems can be controlled in preprogrammed alarm modes, with manual override possible. In a fire emergency, the HVAC, elevator, security, water, electrical and lighting systems may be controlled from a central computer console. Computers activate exhaust and pressurizing fans, and deactivate supply fans, place elevators in fire-evacuation mode, override access barriers to permit evacuation, connect fire pumps to emergency power feeders, disconnect high-voltage feeders, and activate emergency lighting. The computer can be used to override any of these actions. Other complex reports, such as energy use, can be produced in great detail. The complexity implied in this description may not be needed in simpler buildings.

**Intelligent Buildings** The building automation monitors described above are included in the definition of intelligent buildings, but they also involve individual systems for computer networking, etc. Provisions for empty ducts and conduit implies that most speculative office buildings will not contain any more than needed to rent the space, while privately owned buildings may require extensive consideration of flexibility and integration of systems. Special factors are the need to separate communication systems cables from electrical devices and radios. Building codes require that vertical shafts be fire-protected at each floor. Since many of these systems may be proprietary and subject to rapid obsolescence, good judgment is needed to design with foresight.

**Specialized Sound Systems** Another kind of communication system often used in buildings is a sound system, over which public address announcements, music, and sometimes other types of communication may be broadcast in buildings. Systems of this type may be quite simple or very complex, ranging from a public address system in a school auditorium, consisting of a microphone, or more than one, an amplifier, and loudspeakers, to a complete system in a multiuse recreational building, with the equipment named and in addition, record players, radio receivers, tape players, and other equipment. In some of the most completely equipped buildings, motion picture and television facilities are also provided. In some buildings, music is piped to various rooms. In others, such as schools or colleges, special provisions are often made for listening or viewing by individuals or small groups. Closed-circuit television is also sometimes provided. Central antenna systems may be required in buildings such as hotels and others.

In specialized buildings, such as theaters, opera houses, concert halls, and the like, very complete sound systems with very high-quality components such as those named are usually required, along with complex instrument panels, or consoles, from which the various components may be controlled. Motion picture houses have their own special requirements and most other types of theater and music buildings require facilities for showing motion picture film.

The design and installation of such audio, video, and audiovisual systems are quite complex and grow more complex with time. Provision for such systems must be made in many building types; for example, in theaters or concert halls such provision is a major consideration. Today numerous community auditoriums and similar buildings are being constructed. In many of these, hockey, basketball, tennis, and other athletic events are staged, along with dance recitals, plays, rock groups, symphony orchestras, and other types of entertainment. Not only are effective sound systems required for such buildings but they must have extreme flexibility. In all but the simplest of sound systems, specialists are required for proper design and installation.

**Monitoring and Control** Another major type of communications system used in buildings involves the monitoring and control of various functions. For example, in hospitals, remote systems are required for monitoring the vital signs of patients in intensive care wards. Closed-circuit television is often used in hospitals for observation of such patients and is used in many other ways in other types of buildings. Processes in chemical plants or within furnaces in factories may be monitored by television, when no other visual method would be possible. Children in nursery schools may be similarly monitored during free play periods. Many other uses may also be made of such systems.

**Resident Systems** While houses and other residential buildings are often thought of as relatively simple building types, in actuality they are not, since they combine facilities under one roof for so many varied kinds of human activities. Communication systems in houses and other residences may also be quite complex and complete. In addition to the usual door-bell and telephone requirements, houses and other residences often have smoke detectors; burglar alarms; intercom systems, including instruments outside for identification of callers; closed-circuit television for monitoring nurseries, for example; rooftop antennas, some of which are electrically operated; maid call annunciators; telephone systems utilizing master stations and jacks for portable instruments; radio and television sets; and often very complete sound and music systems with amplifiers, tape decks, radio receivers or tuners, record changers and players, microphones, and elaborate speaker systems.

**Written Communications** In this time of electronics, it is easy to forget that written communications have existed for a much longer time than the electronic. The major written communications used in architecture involve both outside and internal services. In single-family houses, a mailbox usually suffices for the former and perhaps a bulletin board for the latter. In apartment houses and some other building types, such as small office buildings, banks of mailboxes may be provided. In other larger buildings, mailrooms are ordinarily required for the receipt and sending of mail. Mail chutes for letters and bundle drops for packages are used for mailing articles. Sometimes, in very large buildings, conveyors are installed to transport mail from floor to floor.

Internal, sometimes called interoffice, written communications within buildings are often handled, routed, and carried to their destinations by the same people who handle the incoming and outgoing regular mail, using the same mailrooms. For a small business or other organization, a mailroom may be quite simple in design and small in size; but for larger ones, mailrooms may require a considerable amount of equipment for receiving, sorting, temporary storage, and delivery of mail. In some cases, such mailrooms may also be quite large in size. In any case, architects and other environmental designers must provide proper facilities and equipment for mail. Before proceeding with such designs, it is necessary to check the relevant regulations and other requirements of the U.S. Postal Service as well as the requirements of the users of buildings.

A method for handling written communications in buildings, used widely in the past but less so today, is a pneumatic tube system. Used in such building types as department stores, transportation buildings, factories, and hospitals, pneumatic tube systems consist of tubing connecting various areas of a building, through which small carriers travel propelled by air pressure or vacuum. In addition to written communications, some pneumatic tube systems have the advantage of being able to transport small articles that can fit into carriers of up to about 3 by 11 by 16 inches in size.

In practice, most electronic communication systems are designed by electrical engineers, particularly those who specialize in such work. Complete sound and music systems are often designed by other specialists. Both mechanical and electrical engineers are involved in the design of control systems. In the design of all such systems, the engineers must work closely with each other and with architects.

**History** In the earliest primitive times, communications between people in buildings could only be accomplished by speaking to each other face to face or, later, by written communications that were hand delivered from one person to another. Still later, communications were printed and the first practical typewriter, invented in 1867, made private business communications fast and efficient. Other communication devices included mechanical bells and speaking tubes that carried the voice through piping or tubing. The real history of intercommunications in buildings begins with the invention of the telephone in 1876, by Alexander Graham Bell (1847–1922). A few years later, there were more than 1,000 telephones in the United States.

In 1878 the first telephone exchange, serving 21 customers, was installed in New Haven, Conn. Long-distance calling began in 1881 between Boston and Providence, R.I., and in 1884 a line was opened between New York City and Boston. Transcontinental calls between New York City and San Francisco began in 1913, transatlantic calls via radiotelephone between New

York City and London in 1927, and long-distance calls by coaxial cable between New York City and Philadelphia in 1936. Many improvements have since been made in telephone instruments, lines, and equipment until today the telephone is the most important communication system used in architecture, for both internal and external messages.

Other communication systems used in architecture include radio, first used in 1895 by Italian engineer Marchese Guglielmo Marconi (1874–1937) and considerably improved during the 20th century, and television, first developed in the 19th century but not used commercially until the 1930s and not widely accepted until after World War II. Television now includes closed-circuit broadcasting and international broadcasting via satellite. Computers have had wide applications in communications in the second half of the 20th century (see the article entitled computer). Computer and other electronic communication systems are being rapidly improved and expanded today and new developments of importance in architecture can be expected to continue.

**Related Articles** Computer; Electrical Engineering; Electric Power and Wiring; Fire Protection; Security Systems; Sound Control; Theater.

**Additional Reading** Stein, Benjamin, and J. S. Reynolds: *Mechanical and Electrical Equipment for Buildings*, 8th ed., John Wiley, New York, 1992.

**Source of Additional Information** Institute of Electrical and Electronics Engineers (IEEE), 345 E. 47th St., New York, N.Y. 10017.

**COMPLEX, ARCHITECTURAL** A group of buildings, for single or multiple purposes, on one site. Architectural complexes have been designed by architects for a very long time in such projects as colleges and universities, schools, apartments, and shopping centers. See articles entitled apartment; college and university building; school; shopping center.

**Categories** Architectural complexes fall into two major categories: the type for which master plans are made by an architect or other design professionals for long-term development, often with buildings by other architects; and the type for which both the master plan and the buildings are made by one architect. For example, many colleges and universities have had master plans and buildings designed by one architect, while in others the master plan was made and buildings added later by the same architect, by another architect, or by several architects. In the case of a university that has been in existence a long time, one architect may have made the original master plans, to be followed by buildings by various architects, designed over a period of time ranging up to 300 years or more in the United States. In such a case, it is not uncommon for the original master plan to have been revised or redesigned one or more times by other architects.

In any case, the design of architectural complexes, of whatever type, involves more than just the design of a single building. The relationships between the buildings and the open spaces around them, the landscaping, and other elements they share, must all be designed properly if success is to be achieved.

**Single-Purpose Complexes** Many of the architectural complexes in the United States are designed for a single or related purpose. Industrial and commercial buildings are gathered into industrial or office parks. Shopping centers and malls in many communities have replaced separate shops and stores. College buildings have been grouped on campuses, buildings for music and drama into cultural centers, and so on.

Many U.S. cities have developed cultural centers. New York City's Lincoln Center for the Performing Arts includes the New York State theater (1964) designed by Philip C. Johnson with Richard Foster, the Metropolitan Opera House (1966) designed by Wallace K. Harrison, the Vivian Beaumont Theater (1965) designed by Eero

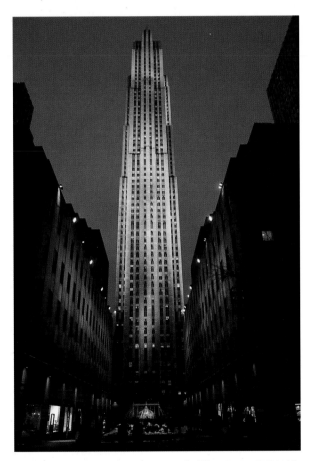

**COMPLEX, ARCHITECTURAL** Rockefeller Center (1931–40), New York, N.Y. *[Architects: Reinhard & Hofmeister; Corbett, Harrison & MacMurray; Raymond Hood, Godley & Fouilhoux]*

Saarinen and Assoc., the Avery Fisher Hall (1962) concert hall by Max Abramovitz, later remodeled in 1976 by Johnson-Burgee with Cyril Harris as acoustical engineer. The complex adjoins the Julliard School of Music (1968) designed by Pietro Belluschi with Eduardo Catalan and Westerman & Miller. The New York complex has been criticized because of the design limitations imposed on the designers, for the lack of public transportation, and for its conservative design.

Dallas, Tex., has cleared portions of a 60-acre site for an Arts District. The cultural complex includes the Dallas Museum of Art (1984) designed by Edward Larrabee Barnes and the Myerson Symphony Center (1989) designed by I. M. Pei.

Denver, Colo., has developed a cultural center near the center of the city. Beginning with the 1907 Auditorium Theater, the 12-acre site has progressively developed under a master plan (1973) by Kevin Roche John Dinkeloo Associates. The firm designed the Helen Bonfils Theatre (1979). The Boettcher Concert Hall (1978) was designed by Hardy Holzman Pfeiffer Associates, and, in 1979, Muchow Associates added an eight-level parking structure. The most recent addition was the Temple Hoyt Buell Theatre (1992) designed by Beyer Blinder Belle and van Kijk, Pace, Westlake & Partners. The complex contains a multilevel galleria linking the various elements.

A recent major complex for the arts scheduled for completion in 1994 is the J. Paul Getty Center in the Santa Monica mountains near Los Angeles, Calif., designed by Richard Meier. Buildings include the Center for the History of Art and the Humanities, the Getty Museum, Trust Offices and Auditorium, restaurants, gardens, and an amphitheater. All these facilities are reached by tramway from the reception area and parking in the valley below.

**Mixed-Use Centers** A later development has been mixed-use, or multiuse, sometimes called "MXD," centers. In these centers, many kinds of functions can be served, including hotel and motel lodging, convention facilities, apartments and other housing, offices, shopping, and cultural activities.

The pioneering mixed-use center is Rockefeller Center, New York City, completed in 1940, and designed by an association of three architectural firms: Reinhard and Hofmeister; Corbett, Harrison and MacMurray; and Hood and Fouilhoux. In Rockefeller Center are to be found such uses as offices, restaurants, theaters, recreational facilities, stores, exhibition rooms, broadcasting stations, and museums.

Some years later, architects and others began to think about providing mixed-use centers in other cities. It was felt that the segregation of complexes by a single type of function was not always the best solution. The

**COMPLEX, ARCHITECTURAL** Lincoln Center for the Performing Arts (1962–68), New York, N.Y.
*[Architects: Wallace K. Harrison (Metropolitan Opera), Philip C. Johnson and Richard Foster (New York State Theater), Max Abramovitz (Avery Fisher Hall), Eero Saarinen and Assoc. (Vivian Beaumont Theater), and Skidmore, Owings and Merrill (Library and Museum of the Performing Arts, N.Y. Public Library)]*

downtown areas of cities had traditionally been places where many functions were served in close juxtaposition to each other. Why not try to bring this idea back into new projects in urban locations? In the middle 1950s some attempts were made to accomplish this, the most notable being the Back Bay Center proposal made for Boston in 1954. Architects Pietro Belluschi (1899– ), Walter Bogner (1899– ), Carl Koch (1912– ), Hugh Stubbins (1912– ), and The Architects Collaborative set up a separate office to design the center. The proposal met with great critical acclaim but was never built.

Other mixed-use centers, with office, shopping, and transportation functions, were proposed about the same time, including Penn Center, Philadelphia, designed by Vincent Kling (1916– ), and Place Ville Marie, Montreal, Canada, by Ieoh Ming Pei (1917– ), both finished in the 1960s.

Battery City at the southern tip of Manhattan in New York City has been developed as a new city within the city. It includes housing, waterfront park, and retail and office structures linked by a large winter garden. Architects for the mixed-use development include Cesar

Pelli for the four-tower World Financial Center complex (1987). Two pedestrian bridges cross West Street providing a connection to the remainder of the city.

Many other mixed-use centers have been proposed and built in recent years in cities all over the United States. Today most mixed-use centers encompass a large number of functions that reflect the life of the central city. The centers' designs are based on the principle of fully integrating the various functions into the buildings and other spaces rather than simply placing each function in a separate building within the group.

**Edge Cities** A recent recognition of the tremendous scale of suburban development adjacent to older urban cores has been described as "edge cities" by the journalist Joel Garreau. His definition of each of these developments includes: over 5 million ft² of leased office space, 600,000 ft² of retail (a major shopping mall), known as more of an employment than a residential center, recognition as a destination for jobs, shopping, and entertainment, and built on previously undeveloped land. By this definition, there are such suburban centers near most major urban areas in the United States. Many of these

**COMPLEX, ARCHITECTURAL** Embarcadero Center (1981), San Francisco, Calif. *[Architect: John C. Portman, Jr.]*

suburban developments provide more office space than the older central business districts. The projects have been developer-generated in response to economic forces. Each edge city is supported by large residential areas, some of which predated the development of new centers, resulting in shifting transportation patterns and further development.

There is considerable ambivalence among urban planners and environmentalists concerning these centers, but they are widely supported by the public. Criticism of the edge city include the low density, the lack of cultural advantages compared to the center city, the fact that pedestrians are limited to shopping malls, the limited provision of public transportation, and the dependence on the automobile. The desire to preserve wetlands and open acreage for the public benefit and the lack of adequate roads have motivated opposition to development. The edge city developments depend on the automobile, the jet airplane, and computer technology. The ability to move people and data quickly from one place to another has allowed the decentralization of corporations and support services. The social impact of these new centers has not been fully assessed, but it is apparent that the poor tend to be left in the central city.

Some interesting alternative developments have been built, including the first phase of a new town center (1990) for the new town of Reston in Fairfax County, Va., which attempts to provide the advantages of the central business center where none previously existed and to provide for future controlled growth. Designed by the Baltimore, Md., architectural firm of RTKL on land owned by Reston Land Corporation, the center, within easy reach of Washington, D.C. airports, was planned to include housing, hotels, mid-rise office towers, shopping, theaters, parking structures, and landscaped plazas served by existing and new road construction.

The future growth of cities will certainly include new patterns of mixed-use centers. Even more certain is the growth of suburban centers.

**Related Articles** APARTMENT; HARRISON, WALLACE KIRKMAN; PLANNING, CITY; PRACTICE OF ARCHITECTURE; Articles on other individual building types.

**Further Reading** Garreau, Joel: *Edge City: Life on the New Frontier*, Doubleday, New York, 1991; Witherspoon, Robert E., Jon P. Abbott, and Robert M. Gladstone: *Mixed Use Developments—New Ways of Land Use*, Urban Land Institute, Washington, 1976, available from Books on Demand, UMI, Ann Arbor, Mich.

**COMPUTER** A machine or device that handles information through calculation and measurement. Computers have many uses in architecture and related fields. Sometimes their functions are called "automatic data processing" (ADP) or "electronic data processing" (EDP).

**Types** There are two major types of computers: analog and digital. Analog computers, which measure quantities in terms of other quantities, have been used in architecture for many years and are still widely used today. A slide rule, for years used for making numerical calculations by distance measurements, is an analog computer. So is an alcohol, or mercury, thermometer which measures temperature in terms of the length of a fine line of one of the fluids.

A more recent development is the digital computer, which makes calculations by counting numbers, or digits. Digital computers in the past, such as adding machines and cash registers, did the counting by movements of wheels, drums, or other mechanical means. Electronic analog and digital computers were developed in the 20th century, starting about 1930, and have been vastly improved over the years. Electronic analog computers operate by the measurement of electrical currents and are mostly used for special purposes. They are not as accurate as electronic digital computers, which may be used for special purposes, but are mostly general-purpose types that can be used for numerous applications. A very common type is the hand-held, or pocket, calculator which has largely supplanted the slide rule. Other electronic digital computers are much larger, more complex, and capable of many types of activities. In some ways, they have revolutionized architecture, as they have other fields of endeavor. And as improvements continue to be made, they can be expected to contribute to further changes.

**Function** Digital computers function by counting binary numbers, those which have only two digits. Examples of binary situations are those which can be expressed by yes or no, on or off, up or down, right or left, and so on. Decimal numbers have 10 digits, from 0 to 9, but binary numbers have only two, 0 and 1. A typical binary number is 10011 which equals 19 in the decimal system. In the binary number 10011, the first digit on the right stands for $1x2^0$, or 1 in the decimal system; the next digit stands for $1x2^1$, or 2; the next for $0x2^2$, or 0; the next for $0x2^3$, or 0; and the digit on the extreme left stands for $1x2^4$, or 16. By adding, the decimal number is found to be 1+2+0+0+16=19. Digital computers operate by binary means that involve electrical currents that are on or off, magnetization that is north or south, switches that are open or closed, or other processes of this sort that represent the two digits of the binary numbers. In this way, great quantities of binary numbers may be counted very accurately and rapidly by computers.

Computer technology has brought with it a new set of terms. One of these is bit which stands for 1 binary digit; another is byte which stands for 8 bits. Digital computers handle calculations by counting large numbers of bits and bytes.

Digital computers come in various sizes and capacities. The smallest can perform arithmetic calculations with reasonable speed and have limited logical or reasoning capabilities. Larger machines calculate faster than small ones, have greater logical capabilities, and have storage and printing capabilities. The largest machines calculate still faster, have larger storage capacities, and may have capabilities for performing several calculations at once, for graphical displays, and for communicating with other computers.

**Basic Components** In all computers, of whatever size, there are five basic components: input unit, which sends data and instructions; memory unit, which receives and stores data and instructions; control unit, which takes instructions from the memory and transmits them to the arithmetic unit; the arithmetic unit, which performs the mathematical functions; and output unit, which records or delivers the results or information to the user.

**Operation** A computer operator operates and controls a computer from a unit called a console. Data and instructions, or input, are given to the computer in various ways. The operator may set switches or push buttons, a method that is very slow, only about 2 characters per minute; or a typewriter may be used, raising the speed to about 300 characters per minute. One of the most common input methods was by means of punched cards, in which holes have been made on keypunch machines, very much like typewriters, operated by keypunch operators. The cards are read into the computer by a card reader that can handle 1,000 or more cards a minute. Input from magnetic tape, which is very similar to that used in tape recorders, can reach speeds up to 100,000 characters per minute.

Other types of input methods include punched paper tape, magnetic ink as used on bank checks, and optical scanners that work somewhat like the human eye. For computer graphical work and drafting, two input methods are in use: a light pen with which the operator may draw on the face of a cathode-ray tube, and a digitizing table which contains a grid of wires activated by drawing on it with a stylus.

**Memory Storage** Memory units utilize storage of four types. The basic type is a core which contains thousands of little rings that may be magnetized in a clockwise or counterclockwise direction. A core is usually used for the working memory storage, but it is expensive, has a small capacity, and is slow. For larger amounts of information, drums, disks, or magnetic tapes are used. Transfer of information between the different types is efficient and easy.

Output from computers may take a number of forms such as punched cards or tape, magnetic tape, automatic typewriting, automatic typesetting, high-speed printing, drawings, images on screens similar to those of television sets, and so on. The output of a computer may also be transmitted by radio or telephone to other computer equipment in distant places.

**Computer Language** In order for people to give data and instructions to computers, it is necessary to translate ordinary human language into computer language. Computer languages must be based on the binary system. To do this, a program is written for the computer using certain words or symbols. The first type used was called machine language and involved programs using the binary digits, 0 and 1; this was slow and cumbersome. Other computer languages have been developed, including assembly or symbolic, and compiler, using only simple words which the computer translates into binary machine language. A later language is called problem-oriented and uses ordinary English phrases. Typical compiler languages include common business-oriented language (COBOL), used for business transactions, and formula transaction (FORTRAN), used in problem solving. Others are also available for specific purposes.

To prepare a program or a set of instructions for a computer, a computer programmer starts with the selection of the proper computer language for the task that the computer will perform and with a description of the task, including the input information required, processing to be performed, and the required output. Sometimes such information is prepared by system analysts. From this information, a systems flowchart may be prepared, indicating how the various activities involved will pass through the computer operations. From the flowchart, the programmer then prepares coding sheets of the program in computer language. From these coding sheets, cards may be punched, and, if required, the cards may be read by a machine that transmits the information to units that record it on magnetic tape.

**Architectural Uses** In architecture, a great many important functions may be vastly improved and speeded up by the use of digital computers. Among them are engineering design and calculations, including structural, mechanical, electrical, and others; cost estimating and control; specification writing and printing; accounting and bookkeeping; management of offices and projects; systems analysis; programming; design; analysis of specific building types; drafting; preparation of working drawings; and project scheduling. Another important use of computers in architecture, not fully developed so far, is in storage and retrieval of information on building systems, materials, products, design factors, and the like.

The growth of computer technology and usage has created many career opportunities. Most require college education, with emphasis on mathematics and computer courses. Some of the jobs are systems analyst, who studies uses, programming, and operation of computers; design engineer, who performs research, development, and design work on computers; computer programmer, who prepares programs; computer operator, who operates the machines; and service engineer, who maintains and repairs the machines.

Architectural, engineering, and other professional schools now offer courses in computer programming and operation as part of their regular curricula, thus providing their graduates with some knowledge and experience in computer capabilities and uses. There are also opportunities in architectural, engineering, and other related offices for career programmers and operators.

**History** A device using beads for solving arithmetic problems, called an abacus, is probably the earliest form of computer. In various forms, it was used by the ancient Chinese, Egyptians, Greeks, and Romans. Other devices were developed later, including the slide rule which makes calculations by the positioning of sliding or revolving scales. The modern slide rule was invented in the middle of the 19th century and was based on a logarithmic scale made by English mathematician Edmund Gunter (1581–1626), who pioneered many surveying instruments.

The first mechanical digital computer was developed in the early 1800s by the Englishman Charles Babbage (1792–1871). He called it an analytical engine, but never completed building it after the English government turned it down. Not much happened in the field for almost 100 years, until 1928, when American electrical engineer Vannevar Bush (1890–1974) developed the first electronic analog computer; he called it a differential analyzer. In 1944 a mechanical-electrical digital computer was developed at Harvard University, and in 1946 the first one using vacuum tubes was built at the University of Pennsylvania. During the same period, the principles of computer memories were introduced.

People in the computer industry call the computers of various eras "generations" of computers. The first generation appeared on the market during the 1950s, using electronic circuits controlled by vacuum tubes. The second generation came on the market in the early 1960s. They were more dependable and faster, as much as 10 times faster, than those they superseded, mainly because they used transistors instead of vacuum tubes. The third generation, using miniature electronic circuits, were introduced in the late 1960s and are sometimes 100 times faster than those of the second generation.

Computers have caused many great changes in the ways people do business and live their daily lives, and in architecture. One of the most spectacular results of their use has been the space program. With the aid of computers, Alan B. Shepard, Jr. (1923–  ), was the first American in space on May 5, 1961; John H. Glenn (1921–  ) was the first to orbit the earth on February 20, 1962; and Neil Armstrong (1930–  ) was the first man on the moon on July 20, 1969. Possibly more spectacular achievements may be made in the future, with the aid of computers. Certainly computers will continue to deeply affect people's lives and architecture.

**Recent Developments** In the last decade, computer use has revolutionized the architect's office as computers have become more powerful and prices have dropped to a fraction of former prices. As more students are trained to use computers for design and drafting, the use of computers has increased dramatically, particularly in the larger firms. Applications for computers in architectural offices are most often for word processing, spreadsheets, specification writing, computer design and drafting (CADD), and financial management. Other uses of computers are for desktop publishing, payroll and personnel records, marketing, scheduling and personnel time records, energy analysis, and facility management.

The future directions of computer use suggest that small firms will be able to take on larger projects and that quality of information will be improved as all members of the building team share common electronic data. Most experts see the day when increasingly powerful and low-cost computers are on every architect's desk.

**Related Articles** Construction Contract Administration; Cost Control; Design, Architectural; Drafting; Electrical Engineering; Mechanical Engineering; Practice of Architecture; Programming; Specification; Structural Engineering; Working Drawing.

**CONCRETE** An important building material, usually consisting of portland cement, aggregates, and water which, when mixed together and poured into forms, set into a hard strong material that resembles stone. Earlier, concrete, mostly made with natural cements, was generally used without reinforcement. Today the material most widely used is reinforced concrete, which has steel bars or mesh embedded in the other materials for added strength.

**Uses** Concrete, usually reinforced, has wide uses in architecture, including foundations, floor slabs, structures, piping, sidewalks, roads, parking lots, and driveways. Portland cement also has many other uses, for example, for making mortar for brick and stone masonry; in plaster; for finishing interior walls and ceilings; in stucco for finishing exterior walls; in the production of planks and boards, shingles, and other products; in terrazzo flooring; for making concrete, or cement, brick and concrete block; and in paints.

**Composition** Concrete is composed of four major ingredients: cement, most often portland cement today; fine aggregates, mostly sand; coarse aggregates, such as gravel; and water. The types of materials used, their proportions, or mixes, and the ratio between the cement and water, called the water-cement ratio, are the major determinants of the strength and other properties of concrete. In addition, in reinforced concrete, the steel bars or mesh determine certain strength and other properties.

**Portland Cement** This cement is manufactured, under highly controlled conditions, from about 60 percent lime, 25 percent silica, 10 percent alumina, and smaller quantities of iron oxide and gypsum, the latter to control the hardening or setting time of the cement. The manufacture of portland cement involves mixing, crushing, and grinding the raw materials and burning them in a kiln, in which they are placed dry or mixed with water. The burning produces marble-sized clinkers, which are ground, often with added gypsum, to a fine powder ready to be used.

Eight types of portland cement are used in architecture. Type I is for general use; II for slower setting and less generated heat, in massive structures such as large retaining walls or dams; III, high early strength; IV, low heat slow setting; and V, called sulfate-resisting, for uses in which the concrete must resist damage from alkaline water or soils. The other three types, IA, IIA, and IIIA, are similar in composition to I, II, and III, but are air-entrained cements and have a great number of entrapped air bubbles. The air-entrained types have increased resistance to freezing and thawing.

Special types of portland cement include white, waterproof white, pozzolanic, and blast-furnace slag cements. Other cements that are employed in architecture include aluminous, for use where extremely high temperatures are to be encountered; plastic, with plasticizers added to types I and II portland cement, for use in mortars, plaster, and stucco; Keene's cement, for hard-finish coats of plaster; and oxychloric, for floors.

**Aggregates** Fine aggregates for concrete, mortar, and plaster are usually sands of various kinds, with granules ranging from $1/16$ to $1/4$ inch in diameter. They must be free of organic or other harmful materials, and are usually washed, graded for size, and may be otherwise treated before being used in concrete. Coarse aggregates used in concrete, but not in mortar or plaster, are over $1/4$ inch in diameter and include natural materials, such as gravel or crushed stone, and manufactured materials, such as expanded blast-furnace slag or expanded burned clay or shale. The manufactured kinds are considered lightweight aggregates, and are used in applications in which that characteristic is important, together with insulating qualities. Other lightweight aggregates include minerals, such as vermiculite, perlite, and diatomite. Lightweight concretes made with such aggregates vary considerably in shrinkage, strength, and insulating qualities. Those made with expanded shale or clay are relatively the strongest and shrink the least. Next in strength are concretes made with expanded clay or shale, and the weakest are those made with diatomite, vermiculite, or perlite, which have the highest insulating qualities.

**Water-Cement Ratio** In addition to the selection of the proper types of portland cement and aggregates, the correct water-cement ratio for various purposes must be selected. The water-cement ratio determines the strength of the concrete, other than that derived from reinforcement, its durability, and other qualities. In concrete, the compressive strength or ability to resist forces that push upon it, developed in 7 and 28 days after placement, are usually specified, based on building and other codes and accepted practices. The water-cement ratio largely determines such strengths. Such ratios vary widely, from about 1.0, with equal parts, by weight, of water and cement, developing a compressive strength of 1,750 lb/sq in, in 28 days, to 0.40, 40 percent as much water as cement, by weight, which produces 6,000 lb/sq in, in the same time. Data of this sort may be accurately obtained by testing actual specimens. On building sites, the usual method is a slump test, which involves filling a standard metal cone on a flat surface with concrete mix. The mix is rodded with a standard-sized rod and the cone raised to release the concrete. The empty cone is then placed adjacent to the concrete and the distance from the top of the cone to the top of the concrete measured. The distance indicates the water-cement ratio.

**Placement** Concrete in architecture is usually poured in place on building sites or precast, either in manufacturing plants or on the sites. In either case, it is generally poured into molds or forms made of wood, metal, or plastic, and sometimes reinforced paper for columns. Concrete can also be set into place in other ways, by using special machinery. Forms for precast concrete and other standard applications are often made of metal and are reusable. In other cases, special forms must be designed. Since they must carry the load of the concrete until it has cured, such forms are usually designed by structural engineers.

The placing of concrete must be strictly controlled. Either very hot or very cold temperatures will affect curing and ultimate strength. Regular testing of sample cylinders are made during the pouring of concrete, in a manner specified by building and other codes. Most concrete poured on building sites comes ready-mixed in trucks. They must not be allowed to transport the mix too far. The concrete must be placed carefully in layers and each succeeding layer must be placed before the previous one starts to set. The concrete must not be allowed to drop very far, no more than about 5 feet for hidden work and 3 feet for exposed. Sometimes vibrators must be used to ensure proper placement in the forms. In cold weather, calcium chloride is sometimes used to hasten setting, and the concrete is covered with insulating materials. Another method, more often used today, involves heating the materials and the space around the poured concrete. Many other approved methods and precautions must be taken to ensure proper placement and curing of concrete.

Many types of finishes may be given to concrete. Textures may be obtained by lining forms with materials, such as sandblasted plywood, plastics, rubber mats, and hardboard. Aggregates of various kinds, such as marble and granite, may be exposed on the surface of concrete. The surfaces of concrete may also be finished by various processes, such as grinding, bushhammering, sandblasting, or polishing. In addition, various pigments may be added to concrete mixes to produce a range of colors.

**Versatility** Concrete is a very versatile material and as such is widely used in architecture for many purposes. Many architects and other environmental designers prefer concrete as a material, because it is plastic and may be formed in the manner they wish, to materials such as steel that come in stock sizes. The plasticity and workability of concrete can also cause difficulties in design if it is used in ways not appropriate to its nature, for example, in certain extreme forms or as fake stone. Concrete must be designed, mixed, placed, and otherwise cared for properly if it is to perform properly. Thus, for all but the simplest applications, concrete structures and many other types of uses require the attention of highly qualified structural engineers to perform design, detailing, and other professional services.

**History** Cements, materials such as mud and clay, which when placed wet, dry to form hard adhesives, were used in architecture from early primitive times. The use of gypsum followed. All of the early uses were as mortar for use in masonry buildings. The time of the first use of concrete for structural purposes has not been determined, possibly as early as 1000 B.C.

The first recorded uses of concrete as a structural material were made by the Romans, beginning about 200 B.C. It soon became their favorite structural material for buildings, aqueducts, bridges, and other purposes. Roman concrete was made with a natural cement, called pozzolana, a volcanic ash found at Pozzuoli, Italy, near Mount Vesuvius. Mixed with slaked lime, or water and lime, pozzolana formed a quite strong cement mortar with which concrete could be made. This was called hydraulic mortar because it was virtually waterproof and could be used for buildings and other structures, including those placed under water.

As aggregates in concrete, the Romans used a variety of materials, including broken stone, brick, or other clay objects. Instead of mixing the aggregate with the other materials and water, as is the practice today, the Romans usually placed the aggregate where they wanted it and then covered it with mortar, repeating the process as required by the structure being built. Large-sized, heavy aggregates were usually placed in the lower part of a structure, such as a wall, covered with mortar, and then followed by alternating layers of aggregate and mortar, with the smaller and lighter aggregates toward the top.

Roman concrete was used as a compressive material, one that can withstand weights that push on it. Centuries passed before reinforcing allowed concrete to be used in other types of structures. Roman concrete structures were often very large and massive, as required by the compressive forces, and well engineered. In addition to walls, the Romans built arches, vaults, and domes of the material. They knew how to use formwork to hold the concrete in place while it was curing. They often made the framework out of durable materials, such as brick, and left it in place instead of removing it as is the practice today. Although Roman concrete was often left exposed, the more usual procedure, especially in important buildings, was to cover it with a veneer of brick, stone, or stucco. Before the end of their era, the Romans exploited mass concrete to the ultimate, producing large, daring, and well-engineered structures of many kinds.

In addition to pozzolana cement, the Romans sometimes used other natural types. And lime mortar, used as a cementing material long before, was sometimes employed. However, lime mortar is relatively weak and, not being waterproof, must be protected. The Romans therefore preferred the other material. After the era of the Romans, the use of concrete in architecture virtually came to a halt.

During the Middle Ages, concrete was used only on rare occasions. Instead, lime mortar was often used for such purposes as the construction of rubble-stone cores of structural members that were then covered with finished stone. It is believed that the rubble was laid as stone is today, by placing a layer of mortar upon which the stones were then placed, instead of in the opposite manner used by the Romans. During the Renaissance, lime mortars were used but cement mortars, only very rarely. Such was the situation until the 18th century.

In 1752 an English engineer, John Smeaton (1724–92), rediscovered the making of hydraulic cement and used it first as mortar for a stone lighthouse in 1759, which he designed for Eddystone, England. After that, several other people developed cements. The first portland cement, named for Isle of Portland stone and for which it was at first considered a substitute, was patented by an English bricklayer, Joseph Aspdin (1779–1855), in 1824. For some years, it was used only in mortar for masonry work and mass concrete. But the beginning of the modern use of concrete had been assured.

American architects and engineers excelled in innovation and invention using structural steel, beginning in the 19th century. Innovation and invention in concrete, beginning in the same century, was almost exclusively the province of European architects and engineers for many years. Precast concrete was made in England about 1832. Reinforced concrete was patented by a Frenchman, Joseph Monier (1823–1906), in 1857. Prestressed concrete was used in Germany as early as 1886, but its uses in architecture were pioneered by a French engineer, Eugéne Freyssinet (1879–1962), in the 1920s and 1930s.

Many other great contributions of the development of concrete in architecture were made during the first half of the 20th century by such people as the French architect Auguste Perret (1874–1954), the Swiss-French architect Le Corbusier (1887–1965), the Swiss engineer Robert Maillart (1872–1940), the Italian engineer Pier Luigi Nervi (1891–1979), and the Spanish architect Felix Candela (b. 1910).

In later years, American architects and engineers have also been quite inventive and innovative in the use of concrete. Among them are architect Frank Lloyd Wright (1867–1959) and engineer Othmar Hermann Ammann (1879–1965). Others have been involved in the development of structural concrete, and their work is discussed in various articles in this book.

**Related Articles** Bridge; Concrete Structure; Dam; Fire Protection; Foundation; Masonry Structure; Structural Engineering; Structure; Various articles on architects and building components and systems.

**Sources of Additional Information** American Concrete Inst., P.O. Box 19150, Detroit, Mich. 48219; Portland Cement Assoc., 5420 Old Orchard Rd., Skokie, Ill. 60077.

**CONCRETE STRUCTURE** A building or other structure in which the structural frame, columns, joists, beams, girders, floors, and roof, and sometimes walls, elevator shafts, and vent shafts, are of concrete, which is usually reinforced with steel bars or mesh. Although used to some extent before, concrete first became a popular structural material during the time of the Romans, when it was used in mass without reinforcement. After the time of the Romans, concrete was used very little in architecture until the 18th century. Beginning in the late 19th century, with the development of reinforced concrete, its use in architecture has grown until the present time, when it is one of the most important materials for structures and other purposes.

Concrete is used today in mass, without reinforcement, in dams and other heavy construction. For the most part, reinforced concrete is used in buildings for such purposes as structures, walls, foundations, floors, walkways, driveways, roads, parking lots, and roofs. For

**CONCRETE STRUCTURE** Close-up, Salk Institute (1965), La Jolla, Calif. *[Architect: Louis I. Kahn]*

the general subject of concrete, including portland cement and fine and coarse aggregates from which it is made, see the article entitled concrete. Uses other than for structural frames of buildings, such as walls, foundations, paving, concrete or cement, brick, and concrete block masonry are discussed in articles in this book on various building components and systems.

**Reinforced Concrete** In addition to foundations (see the article entitled foundation), major structural uses of reinforced concrete are made in architecture. Reinforced concrete may be poured in place on building sites or precast, either on the sites or in manufacturing plants. Poured-in-place concrete is placed in forms in buildings in the exact locations where it will remain. Precast concrete is also placed in forms, but after curing it is moved into the final locations in buildings. The major advantage of precast concrete is that it can be poured under controlled conditions on the ground or on tables in standard, often reusable forms, that do not need structural supports while the concrete is curing. Poured-in-place concrete, on the other hand, except for floor slabs on grade or other similar applications, must be supported until it cures, with often elaborate, strong, engineered formwork and shoring. Thus precast concrete may often be considerably less expensive than poured-in-place concrete.

Poured-in-place concrete can be used for any structural purpose for which concrete is suitable. Precast concrete is often used for relatively small components, such as stair treads, curbs and gutters for roadways, and curtain-wall panels. A great number of structural components are precast today, including columns, joists, beams, girders, and decking units for floors and roofs. Such components are available in most localities in a limited range of sizes and strengths. For relatively large buildings, special sizes may be produced.

Precast concrete may also be used for very large structural components, such as entire walls or floors. For entire walls or portions of them, a system called tilt-up is often employed. Tilt-up construction consists of precasting a wall, or portion of one, on the ground in special forms, allowing the concrete to cure, and then tilting the entire assembly into place in a building, usually with the aid of cranes. Tilt-up walls may be structural, or load-bearing, or nonloadbearing. With this system, it is possible to cast walls with windows, doors, and other components in place. In tilt-up work, it is necessary to coat the forms with a bond-breaking agent, such as wax, paraffin, oil, paper, or others, to allow the precast walls to be detached easily from the forms.

Another technique for precasting entire floors and roofs, or large portions of them, is the lift-slab method. In general, the lift-slab method involves the erection of columns for a building, pouring a slab on grade around the columns, and then pouring additional slabs on top of the first, with bond-breaking materials between them. Each slab is then lifted into place with powerful jacks attached to columns, the columns being extended as required. The lift-slab system has the advantages of simple formwork, no need for shoring, work performed on the ground level, and speedy erection.

**Steel-Reinforcing Types** Reinforced concrete may be either poured in place or precast. The major structural principle of reinforced concrete is the combination of the high compressive strengths, resisting forces that push on it, of concrete with the high tensile strength, resisting forces that pull, of steel reinforcing. Steel reinforcing for use with concrete is of three general types: bars, often called rebars; welded wire mesh; and wire rope or cable. Rebars are available in a number of sizes, plain or deformed. The deformed bars have raised projections for better bonding with the concrete, and are designated by numbers, from the smallest number, 3 (about $3/8$ inch in diameter) to the largest number, 18 (about $2\frac{1}{4}$ inches in diameter). Rebars are used for reinforcing beams, girders, columns, and other structural members. Welded wire mesh, sometimes called welded wire fabric, consists of wires welded to each other, at right angles, or sometimes welded to form triangles. Welded wire fabrics, made from wire of various gauges ranging from about 0.06 inch in diameter to about 0.5

**CONCRETE STRUCTURE** St. Francis de Sales Church (1966), Muskegon, Mich. *[Architect: Marcel L. Breuer]*

inch, is used for reinforcing floors, roofs, walls, and similar structural components. Wire rope or cable is used for reinforcing prestressed concrete components.

The most widely used method for placing reinforcement in concrete structures involves locating carefully designed rebars or mesh, or both, in forms, supporting and tying them together properly, and then pouring concrete around them to make the proper bond and develop the required strength. Another method, often used today, is prestressing, which involves stretching the reinforcing steel to place it in tension, thereby placing the concrete in compression, before the building loads are placed on it. Prestressing has several advantages, including reduced sizes of structural members, use of lesser quantities of reinforcing steel and concrete, and resistance to cracking. Prestressing is accomplished by two methods: pretensioning and posttensioning. In pretensioning, the reinforcing is prestressed and then the concrete is poured around it. When the concrete has cured, the steel is released and the bond between steel and concrete maintains the tension in the one and the compression in the other. In posttensioning, tubes or other devices are placed in the form and the concrete poured around them. After the concrete has cured, reinforcing is inserted in the tubes, tensioned and anchored at the ends of the members. Both prestressing methods are widely used, sometimes in combination.

In reinforced concrete work, there are strict requirements of building and other codes and good practice for overlapping of bars or other reinforcing for the bending of bars, tying of reinforcing, amount of coverage of reinforcing by concrete, and many other factors. There are also strict requirements for joints between concrete pours, called construction joints, and for expansion joints. Construction joints must be designed and located properly and the concrete pours keyed to each other properly. Expansion joints are usually located at points where cracks are likely to occur, such as the intersections of wings of a building, and are also provided in long walls or other building elements. Expansion joints must also be designed and located properly.

In addition to the usual ingredients in concrete (portland cement, fine and coarse aggregates, and water), other materials, called admixtures, are often used for special purposes. Many types of admixtures are available, including those that retard the time of hardening, those that accelerate it, those that make concrete more waterproof, and those that make concrete mixes more workable.

**Shapes** Concrete is a plastic material and as such may be used to produce a great many shapes. The most common shapes are square or round columns, rectangular beams and girders, and flat slab floors and roofs. However, columns and other structural members may

be formed in many other shapes. They may also be reinforced in only one direction, called a one-way system, as is usual in beams and girders and sometimes used in slabs; or in two directions, two-way systems, as most often used in slabs.

A form of slab often used is ribbed and consists of tee-shaped beams placed in a series, and either poured in place or precast. A variation of this, often referred to as a waffle, flat-plate slab, has ribs in two directions at right angles to each other. These slabs are poured over series of square forms.

Many other shapes are possible with reinforced concrete, including arches, vaults, and domes. Often used in buildings today are various shapes usually classified as thin shells. These shells may be designed in a number of shapes and can be very thin as compared to other structures, since reinforced concrete in the shells transmits direct compressive stresses throughout their entire areas. Often only enough concrete is required for the minimum allowable covering of the reinforcing, some-

**CONCRETE STRUCTURE** Tougaloo College Library (1972), Tougaloo, Miss. [*Architect: Gunnar Birkerts*]

times as little as a few inches in a very large shell, with some thickening near columns or other supports.

One of the simplest, thin-shell structures is called a folded-plate roof. It consists of thin-shell concrete plates connected together to form a series of triangles or other shapes when viewed from the end. Other types of thin-shell concrete structures include domes, barrel and other vaults, and hyperbolic paraboloids. While most thin-shell structures of these types are usually poured in place, precast units are sometimes available.

Tables of properties and characteristics of commonly used concrete structural members can be easily obtained. However, the use of such members and the design of more complex ones and of buildings with reinforced concrete structures require the services of skilled and talented structural engineers. As a plastic material which can be controlled and formed almost at the will of architects and engineers, reinforced concrete is very versatile. Since it can be controlled and formed so readily, many architects and other environmental designers prefer it for many uses in buildings and other structures to any other structural material. The previous discussion of the properties and uses of concrete is general and can only be considered as a guideline. In practice, the design of reinforced concrete structures must follow the applicable building and other codes and the principles of good engineering, architecture, and construction.

**History** During the Roman period, and even earlier, concrete was used as a structural building material. The early uses were all in mass as a structural material dependent on its strength in compression. After the time of the Romans, concrete was no longer used to any extent as a structural material until the 18th century, when it again began to be used in mass as a compressive material. During the 19th century, reinforced concrete was developed.

Today mass concrete is sometimes used for such purposes as the structures of dams. In architecture, concrete has come into its own only in the reinforced and prestressed types.

Many of the early innovations in concrete were made in Europe; for further discussion see the article entitled concrete. In the United States, architects and engineers of the era were primarily concerned with steel structures. They still are to some extent, but interest in concrete as a structural material has grown rapidly in the United States in recent years. Reinforced concrete has been used in the United States as a structural material since about the beginning of the 20th century. None of the early American reinforced concrete buildings were as daring and innovative as those being built in Europe at the same time.

Later, American architects and engineers began to design innovative reinforced concrete structures. Some of the notable examples are the State Fair and Exposition Buildings (1955), Raleigh, N.C., designed by Matthew Nowicki (1910-49) in association with William Henry Dietrick (b. 1905) and with Frederick Severud (b. 1899); the Administration Building (1939) and Research Building (1950) for S. C. Johnson and Sons Company, Racine, Wis., by Frank Lloyd Wright (1867–1959); and the Hayden Planetarium (1935), New York, N.Y., Trowbridge and Livingston. In the post–World War II years, concrete structures became widely used. Examples of important concrete buildings include Lambert Airport (1955), St. Louis, by Hellmuth, Yamasaki and Leinweber; the Guggenheim Museum (1959), New York City, by Wright; several buildings by Eero Saarinen (1910-61) including the TWA Terminal (1962), New York City; several by Ieogh Ming Pei (1907-  ) including Kips Bay Plaza (1957), New York, N.Y., the Dallas City Hall (1967), Dallas, Tex., the New York University Towers (1967), New York, N.Y., the East Wing, National Gallery of Art (1978), Washington, D.C., and the Javits Convention Center (1986), New York; and others by Paul Rudolph (1918-  ) including the Art and Architecture Building (1963), Yale University, New Haven, Conn., and the New Haven Parking Garage (1963), also in New Haven. Possibly the most recognized is the Salk Institute (1965), designed by Louis I. Kahn (1901–74).

Today American architects and engineers continue to be interested in reinforced concrete and to use it in relatively high-rise buildings such as Marina City (1967), and River City (1985), both in Chicago, Ill., designed by Bertrand Goldberg and Assoc. Other concrete systems of interest include folded plates, domes, and prestressed structures.

**Related Articles** BRIDGE; CONCRETE; DAM; STRUCTURAL ENGINEERING; STRUCTURE; Various articles on building components and systems.

**Further Reading** Parker, Harry, and Harold D. Hauf: *Simplified Design of Reinforced Concrete*, 5th ed., John Wiley, New York, 1986; Wilby, C. B.: *Concrete Materials and Structures: A University Civil Engineering Text*, Cambridge University Press, New York, 1991.

**Sources of Additional Information** American Concrete Inst., P.O. Box 19150, Detroit, Mich. 48219; Concrete Reinforcing Steel Inst., 933 Plum Grove Rd., Schaumburg, Ill. 60173; Portland Cement Assoc., 5420 Old Orchard Rd., Skokie, Ill. 60077.

**CONSTRUCTION, BUILDING** The construction of a building is the visible activity of the construction industry. In addition to the trucks, cranes, deliveries of materials, and workers of various trades, there is a large group of workers who are not seen at the site of building but work in architectural and engineering offices, estimating and purchasing, and material manufacturing plants. The actual construction is headed by a contractor, although many contracts and contractors may be employed for the purpose of building complex buildings. The term *builder* refers to those who construct buildings, usually housing, for sale to the general public when the building is finished.

**General Contractors** A general contractor is a firm which is hired for construction of a specific project, supplying all materials, labor, and equipment to produce a finished project ready for use. Not all workers need to be hired by general contractors; some may work for a subcontractor employed for a specific trade. Examples of such subcontractors might include steel erectors, plumbing, or electrical firms. On large projects, many additional subcontractors may be employed for such specialties as electronic controls or alarm systems. The general contractor is responsible for the performance, scheduling, and coordinating the work of all trades and managing the project so that design objectives and specified construction quality are achieved at a profit.

General contracting or building firms are organized in two major ways. One type of organization is large and complete, and usually constructs the basic parts of buildings, foundations, structure, carpentry work, and so on, with its own employees using its own machinery and equipment, subcontracting only the specialty trades such as electrical, heating and air-conditioning, and plumbing work. A second type of organization for general contractors or building firms has little or no machinery or equipment and few employees—mostly management and supervisory people—and subcontracts almost all the phases of the work.

**Construction Managers** An alternative to the general contractor is the employment of a firm for management only. Often multiple contracts for construction are awarded, whose work is directed by the construction manager. Separate contracts may be awarded for earth moving, concrete work, etc.

**Developers** Much construction is built without a specific owner or user involved. Such operations are headed by firms known as developers. A typical example would be housing development where the marketing effort occurs after construction is started.

**Subcontractors** Many construction workers are employed by subcontractor firms for specific trades. Such firms may be employed by general contractors or may be directly employed under separate contracts by construction management companies.

**Construction Workers** Construction workers, particularly in urban areas, are usually members of trade unions. The unions have a role in bargaining for wages, working conditions, worker safety, and other benefits. Unions may train new workers and act as a central source for skilled and unskilled labor.

As more building parts are prefabricated or assembled far from the building site, union workers may not be involved. The nonunion workers are protected by many laws regarding hours of work, pay, and safety measures, and these laws resulted from union efforts.

**Manufacturers** Construction specifications are organized around materials. The Construction Specifications Institute (CSI) has published *Masterformat,* widely used as a classification system for building materials. The McGraw-Hill company publishes collections of manufacturer's catalogs using the same classification system. The collection is called *Sweet's Catalog Files.*

Most construction materials are manufactured other than at the building site, unlike earlier times. Windows and doors are factory produced, as are many building and site structures. Materials may be purchased as manufactured or may be produced for a particular building. The expertise of the manufacturer is an important contribution to the construction industry.

**Construction Contracts** Contracts for building construction are awarded in two ways: by competitive bidding or by negotiation. For competitive bidding, the owner ordinarily receives bids from several prospective general contractors, often ones who have been prequalified by the owner and architect for competence, financial status, and other requisites. The contract is ordinarily awarded to the low bidder, although it need not always be if the bid is not responsive to the owner's original bidding instructions. In a negotiated award, the owner, with the counsel of the architect and often other consultants, awards the contract after negotiating the price of the contractor thought to be the best choice for the job. In either case, the contract is between the owner and the contractor. Subcontracts for various portions of the work may be included in the total price of the general contractor. For most public work, laws require that bids must be solicited by advertising or by invitations to contractors.

**Construction Process** After the contract has been signed and the necessary building permits have been obtained, the actual construction of the building can begin. The general contractor oversees and manages the work, often by employing superintendents to perform these functions. Subcontractors manage their own work under the overall direction of the superintendent. The construction work of the project goes forward, usually starting with site work that may include grading and excavation, proceeding to foundation work and then to framing the building. During these phases, some subcontractors start their work, at the stage called "roughing-in," by putting in the first portions of piping, ductwork, electrical conduits, and so on. Gradually the structure proceeds, and the exterior covering of the walls begins. The last structural member at the top of the building is raised into place, and the building is said to have been "topped out." The covering of the exterior is then completed, and the roofing is installed. At this point, the building has been completely enclosed, or weathered-in. Interior work begins; the subcontractors proceed with their work; windows, doors, and other items are installed. Finally, after some months for a small building or years for a large one, the building is completed.

During the construction the architect, engineers, and other consultants, or technicians representing them, will have made regular visits to the work to check its construction and progress. Periodically, usually at the end of each month, the contractor will make an application for progress payments, which the architect, after having reviewed them in comparison to his or her site visits, will then certify for payment by the owner.

Many other functions will probably have been performed by the architect, engineers, and other consultants, such as examination of material samples, tests, and reports; checking of shop drawings made by subcontractors or suppliers to indicate exactly how they will fabri-

cate or construct parts of the building; and checking and processing of change orders.

At the end of construction, the contractor delivers warranties, guarantees, maintenance schedules and instructions, and other pertinent information to the architect for the owner. The contractor receives the final payment, and the owner receives the keys to the building.

Sometimes, particularly for projects in which there have been substantial changes during construction, the architect, engineers, and other consultants may prepare record drawings, showing the actual construction. These are based on a set of construction documents, maintained at the site by the contractor, on which all changes are noted. If defects appear during the guarantee or warranty periods for the whole building or any of its parts, the contractors are required under their contracts to correct the defects.

For a single-family house, only a few workers may have been involved in the construction; a high-rise office building or skyscraper may involve thousands. But each building will have been constructed of thousands of items of materials and products, each studied, designed, and painstakingly put into place.

Construction work done by contractors or construction managers appeals to many people who like to work on the construction of buildings and other structures and who like some sedentary office work, some active on-the-job work, and combining business principles with the chance to create something. Many are drawn to construction because it offers a chance for a degree of independence, to work for oneself and to become an owner of a business.

In the past, many contractors came from a background of work in the building trades and others from engineering or sometimes architecture. Today many of the people who eventually become contractors or construction managers are graduates of building construction programs in colleges. Often four years in duration and attached to architectural schools, building construction curricula usually offer BS degrees to students who complete the prescribed general courses and the specialized courses in such fields as building materials, structures, systems and equipment, architectural drafting, economics, business law, construction administration, estimating, scheduling, and procedures.

**History** Humans have constructed structures from the earliest primitive times. From the time of the most ancient cultures, the design and construction of buildings were considered to be related parts of a single function. Those identified as architects in antiquity and through the medieval period were often named only and not easily distinguished from those who built the building. During the Renaissance the architect became a recognized figure, and many also were leaders in other

**CONSTRUCTION, BUILDING** Reorganized Church of Latter Day Saints (1992), Independence, Mo. *[Architects: Hellmuth, Obata and Kassabaum]*

fields such as painting and sculpture. It was during the 19th century when the architect became a professional and formal architectural education was established. Prior to that time, architects learned by working for other architects. The concept of an architect as a professional separate from those who constructed a building became established by the efforts of such persons as Sir John Soane (1753–1837) in England, who earned his living from architecture. The Institute of British Architects was founded in 1834, and a royal charter was issued in 1837.

**American Development** In colonial America, many of the early builders designed their own buildings, and some of them became accomplished architects as well as craftsmen. As was happening in Europe, some architects in America had learned their architecture from books and others did the actual construction from their designs, or they were builder-architects or craftsmen-architects, who had learned their architecture from actual construction experience and generally designed and built their own projects. By the 18th century the time of the builder-architects was almost past, and by the 19th century it was gone. Since then, design has been the province of professional designers, architects, engineers, and others, and construction, the province of constructors, builders, and contractors. The debate continues as to whether the architect is an artist, a businessperson, a technician, an entrepreneur, or a bit of each.

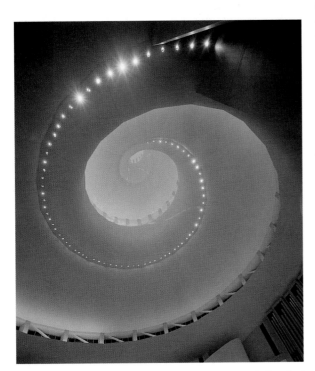

**CONSTRUCTION, BUILDING** Interior, Reorganized Church of Latter Day Saints (1992), Independence, Mo. *[Architects: Hellmuth, Obata and Kassabaum]*

The building team consists of the architect, consulting engineers, such as structural and mechanical engineers, building contractors, and subcontractors or specialty contractors. Others might include suppliers and manufacturers of building products. As has been implied, contractual arrangements between clients and the building team may take a number of forms.

**Further Reading** Clough, Richard H.: *Construction Contracting*, 5th ed., John Wiley, New York, 1986; Merritt, Frederick S., ed.: *Building Design Construction Handbook*, 4th ed., McGraw-Hill, New York, 1982.

**Periodicals** *Constructor*, 1957 E St., N.W., Washington, D.C. 20006; *NAHB Journal of Homebuilding*, 15th and M Sts., N.W., Washington, D.C. 20005; *Professional Builder*, 5 S. Wabash Ave., Chicago, Ill. 60603.

## CONSTRUCTION CONTRACT ADMINISTRATION

The roles of architect, contractor, and owner are defined in contracts between the parties. Construction contract administration refers to the period after contracts between the owner and contractor are signed. In cases where a construction manager is involved, responsibilities between the parties to contracts may differ from traditional construction practices described here.

**Selecting the Contractor** There are two ways of selecting contractors: The first is the negotiated contract, and the second is competitive bidding, required for public works and preferred by many other clients. The advantage of the negotiated contract is that the selected contractor may be called to consult during the design and construction document phases. In this manner, the owner will be able to determine that the project scope and quality is within budget. It is the owner's responsibility to determine the insurance and bonding requirements in consultation with legal counsel.

For competitive bidding, the owner reserves the right to reject the bids, an important consideration if the project is over the project budget. In public work, there is no limit on the number of bidders, although credit checks on the ability of a contractor to complete the work are needed. Private projects may have a restricted list of bidders who have been selected after checking their financial standing and experience. Advertisements to bid are published for public work, and invitations to bid are sent to selected bidders, and the specifications and drawings are issued. Included in the specifications are bidding requirements, including the advertisement or invitation to bid, instructions to bidders (standard instructions), supplementary instructions to bidders (specific to the project), the bid form, and other sample bidding and contract forms. The specifications and drawings are distributed to bidders. Some cities have public plan services where the bidding documents may be consulted by subcontractors and suppliers.

Usually the bidding period is limited, and bids are opened at one time and tabulated. Sometimes additional prices are requested for alternative bids or unit prices so that the owner may add or delete work. These prices add confusion to the bidding, in that selection of alternative bids or unit prices may affect the lowest project cost.

**Project Conferences** It is normal to have a conference before construction starts to resolve and open questions regarding construction. Good communication between the parties at this time can prevent misunderstanding, and errors or inconsistencies can be corrected. Further clarification may be required if omissions are found.

The architect's visits to the site may vary depending on the firm's practice and the size of the project. The intention of the architect should be made clear to the contractor and owner. Reports of each visit should be written to the owner, with copies to the contractors and others involved. The architect's responsibility is limited by the conditions of the construction contract, and these limitations should be strictly observed.

**Consultants** Engineers and other consultants to the architect have responsibility during the construction period as defined in their contracts with the architect, and these responsibilities may involve site visits and review of shop drawings. In some cases, consultants are employed directly by the owner and work in cooperation with the architect.

**Construction Insurance** Advice from legal and insurance advisors is required to be sure that construction projects are properly covered by insurance and bonds. Certificates of insurance, including continuing coverage, are required as may be specified for a particular project.

**Site Observation** Services provided by the architect during construction are many and varied. Visits to the site may vary in frequency depending on the size and complexity of the project. The purpose of site visits is to become aware of the progress of the work, to be assured that the final project will agree with the requirements of the contract documents. The typical contract between owner and contractor requires that they will communicate with each other through the architect. The architect will certify payments due to the contractor, review shop drawing as specified, and accept or reject samples and product data. Insurance certificates and warranties from the contractor to the owner are transmitted by the architect.

**Bonding** A construction bond is a three-party agreement where the surety or guarantor guarantees the completion of the project by the contractor as a protection to the owner. This instrument may be inadequate protection from a contractor in poor financial condition.

**Shop Drawings** The submittal of shop drawings and related material is specified in the contractor's contract.

Often these drawings are needed for fabrication by suppliers of material to the project. The consultants to the architect may review shop drawings related to their area of responsibility, although the architect should also review these drawings to be sure that clearances from other construction are adequate. As an example, there could be a problem with recessed ceiling lighting fixtures below pipes, ducts, and structural members. Formal records of receipt and action taken is an important aspect of this work, and letters of transmittal should be copied to the owner. Shop drawings may require revision and be resubmitted. However, the architect should not use shop drawings to change contract requirements. Corrections should be minor, or a change order, as described below, should be issued.

**Payment Certifications** The contractor makes application for payment which is sent to the architect for approval. The architect certifies that work has progressed as far as the application states. Withholding certification in whole or in part may be required to protect the owner. The contractor must be informed of such withholding. The danger of certifying in advance of actual work is that the contractor will be paid in advance for work not done and may never complete the project. Final payments are not made until the owner is satisfied that the work is complete and that no outstanding claims exist.

**Change Orders** Change in the scope of work is accomplished by change orders on the basis of prices prepared by the contractor and accepted by the owner. Change orders may require the preparation of additional documents by the architect and may increase or decrease the total cost of the project. Change orders may also change the completion date of the project. Minor changes in contract documents by the architect should be the subject of a change order to preclude uncertainty as to the cost of such changes, if any.

**Owner Responsibilities** As this article indicates, the owner has multiple responsibilities during construction. The owner is expected to act promptly, to provide information to the contractor for such items as land surveys and information about any government limitations on the site; to sign contracts; to purchase insurance and bonds; and to make payments. The owner also has the right to stop the work if the contractors do not properly perform. The owner may employ another contractor or separate contractors to complete the project. If the owner feels insecure, a project manager may be employed to act on the owner's behalf. If the owner so decides, different contracts with the architect, the contractors, and the owner are required to include the role of a project manager.

**Contractor Responsibilities** The contractor, upon being awarded a contract, is responsible for performing the work, including supervision and direction of the acts of employees and subcontractors, to enforce discipline on the job, to inspect the work of each trade, to pay for all labor and materials and related items. The contractor is responsible for the means, methods, techniques, sequences, and procedures for coordinating the work. The contractor is responsible for providing safeguards and warnings and for establishing an accident prevention program. The contractor is expected to proceed with the work on schedule by assigning adequate personnel, supplying materials, and providing supervision. The normal project will have a construction superintendent to manage the project, keep daily construction logs, and to notify the architect and owner of any unforeseen conditions affecting the project. The contractor's superintendent also is responsible for obtaining tests and inspections of the work by authorized personnel.

For projects where there are multiple contractors, the owner signs contracts requiring cooperation among the contractors. For demolition or remodeling, special attention must be paid to removal of hazardous materials. Since this work is not usually covered by liability insurance, the owner will normally need to engage specialty contractors for removal of hazardous materials from the site.

The construction contract provides a warrant or guarantee that the work is properly constructed. Such assurance is limited in time, often one year, but during the guarantee period corrections to the work are the responsibility of the contractor. Certain aspects of the work may have longer warranties, such as roofing, and sometimes bonds are issued to provide funds for needed repairs over the warrantee period.

**Construction Disputes** Construction contracts provide for the resolution of disputes. The authority of the architect in matters relating to aesthetic effect are final and not subject to arbitration or court cases. The architect may order minor changes in the work not involving changes in cost and consistent with the intent of the contract documents.

Other causes of possible dispute may involve sureties providing performance and labor and material payment bonds. These may be resolved without further involvement of arbitration or court cases. Many contracts provide for arbitration and mediation of other unresolved disputes. The contractor is required to continue work on the project without waiting for an arbitration decision unless all parties agree to stop the work. Fortunately, most disputes can be resolved by agreement between the parties.

This article has provided only a general overview of issues concerned with the construction period.

**Related Articles** BUILDING INDUSTRY; Various articles on building materials and systems.

**Further Reading** American Institute of Architects: *The Architect's Handbook of Professional Practice*, latest edition, AIA Press, Washington, D.C.; O'Leary, Arthur. F.: *Construction Administration in Architectural Practice*, McGraw-Hill, New York, 1992.

**Periodicals** *Constructor*, 1957 E St., N.W., Washington, D.C. 20006; *NAHB Journal of Homebuilding*, 15th and M Sts., N.W., Washington, D.C. 20005; *Professional Builder*, 5 S. Wabash Ave., Chicago, Ill. 60603.

**Sources of Additional Information** American Subcontractors Assoc., 1004 Duke St., Alexandria, Va. 22314; Associated General Contractors of America, 1957 E St., N.W., Washington, D.C. 20006; National Association of Home Builders of the U.S., 15th and M Sts., N.W., Washington, D.C. 20005.

**CONSTRUCTION MATERIALS** Because of the broad and almost all-encompassing nature of architecture, it is hard to conceive of a material that serves no useful purpose in architecture. However, some of these uses are relatively minor. The major materials of architecture can be classified into the natural, those that may be used in buildings without significant changes, and those that come from nature but must be considerably modified before being used. Materials may be ranked by the amount of energy consumed in their processing and the cost of delivery to the building site. The major natural materials used today are stone and wood. The major modified or man-made materials include metals, such as aluminum, copper alloys, iron, and steel; ceramic materials, such as brick, glass, and tile; concrete; and plastics. A host of other materials are also of importance in architecture.

Construction materials then are the stuff from which buildings are made. They are used in structures, without which buildings would not stand. They are used in enclosures, such as walls and roofs, without which buildings would offer little shelter to humans. They are used for the manufacture of the myriad pieces that go to make up complete buildings, together with their systems. They are used for making ornamental features. Thus it may be seen that knowledge of the properties, applications, and economics of materials is absolutely necessary in architecture. And every person who contributes to the creation of architecture must have such knowledge.

Many architects maintain that materials, in addition to their important technical functions, are one of the primary determinants of architectural design. They believe that building designs, in order to produce excellent architecture, must utilize materials in a manner that fully exploits their unique characteristics and that fully expresses those characteristics. Although an oversimplification, it might be said that in this view, stone, a material that efficiently resists compressive forces (those that push on it) but is relatively inefficient in resisting tensile forces (those that pull), should be used in a manner that exploits and expresses the compression forces. And in

**CONSTRUCTION MATERIALS** 2x4 lumber in a lumberyard.

addition, stone should be used in a manner that exploits and expresses its nature as a material that can be sawed or carved but cannot be extruded into long, thin pieces as can a material like aluminum.

Other characteristics of stone should also be expressed and exploited. Most of all, the stone must look like what it is, not like some other material with different properties and characteristics. The proper expression and exploitation of materials goes much further, into what some have called "honesty of use," into good craftsmanship, and even into advanced philosophical theories of the nature of materials and their uses.

The view of materials as one of the primary determinants of architectural design was essentially developed in the late 19th and 20th centuries. In earlier periods, architects do not seem to have been too concerned with this principle. The architects of ancient Greece used stone in a trabeated, or post and lintel, structural system, one with vertical members, posts, or columns supporting horizontal members, lintels, or beams. The result is considered to be excellent architecture. On the other hand, the master builders of the Middle Ages used stone to produce great cathedrals, also considered to be of great excellence, with an arcuated structural system, based on the principles of the arch. It is difficult to determine which method properly expressed and exploited the nature of stone. From the earliest times, buildings with structures of one material have been covered, or veneered, with another. For example, the Romans habitually constructed buildings of brick or concrete and covered them with stone or plaster. Many other examples could be cited in later periods.

Today many architects believe that the proper use of materials in architecture involves truthfulness to their innate natures, insofar as possible. Thus reinforced concrete, with which, unlike stone, great spans may be achieved, is used in a manner that expresses that fact. And concrete, as is fitting to a manmade material, is finished to look like concrete not like imitation marble or granite. Some architects do not agree with this position.

In any case, the selection of materials for use in architecture involves a number of considerations, including quantitative factors such as size, weight, and shape; chemical and physical properties such as strength, workability, durability, hardness and rigidity, compatibility with other materials, quality, and appearance; and a much more elusive factor, the character imparted by materials to buildings or portions of them.

For further discussion on all major materials used in architecture, see articles entitled aluminum; brick; concrete; copper alloy; glass; iron; plastics; steel; stone; tile; wood. Some discussion is also included in the articles on building components and systems, in which various materials are used.

**Minor Materials** However, a number of others, though not considered major materials, do have important functions in architecture. These include asphalt, coal tar, gypsum, lead, Monel metal, terneplate, porcelain enamel, rubber, sand, gravel, slag, paper, and textiles. Many other metals and materials are also used in conjunction with architecture, in alloys of other metals; as ingredients of paints, coatings, and adhesives for plating or other coatings of materials; and many other uses.

Asphalt and coal tar are bituminous products, natural or manufactured, mostly derived from coal or petroleum. Both are used for waterproofing, for paving streets and highways, in the construction of built-up roofs, as ingredients in certain paints and coatings, and in the manufacture of such products as resilient flooring, paving blocks, and building papers or felts.

Gypsum is a mineral that when heated, or calcined, loses most of the water it contains, and then cements together in any shape desired when water is added to it. Most gypsum is used in architecture for important functions, such as a major ingredient of plaster, plaster lath, and gypsum board, sometimes called sheet rock; in roof decking, both precast and poured; in tile, boards, and blocks for partitions; and for fire protection of columns and other structural elements.

Lead is used in architecture, mainly because of its heavy weight and softness, for such purposes as special flashing; rough hardware items, such as expansion shields for anchoring bolts or screws in masonry; equipment in laboratories; and as a shield against the radiation of atomic reactors and x-rays. It is also used in coatings for other materials, in exterior paints, and in alloys with other metals.

Monel metal is an alloy composed of 66 percent nickel, 31.5 percent copper, and 2.5 percent iron, manganese, silicon, and other ingredients. It is very resistant to corrosion and does not stain most other materials. Relatively expensive, Monel metal is used mostly for laboratory sinks and other equipment and for high-quality roofing and flashing. Terne is an alloy of 80 percent tin with 20 percent lead, used to provide a protective coating for steel, in a product called terneplate. Terne-coated stainless or copper-bearing steel is called short terne and is used for roofing, flashing, gutters, and downspouts, or leaders. Terne-coated steel of other types, called long terne, is used for doors, door frames, and roofing. The stainless steel type need not be painted, but painting is recommended for the others.

Porcelain enamel, which is neither a porcelain nor an enamel, is composed of metal, usually steel or aluminum, on which vitreous surfaces have been fused by high heat. The vitreous, glasslike finishes make the metals highly impervious to moisture, chemicals, pollution, and other hazards, except direct impact or bending.

The base metals impart considerable strength to the material. Porcelain enamel may be obtained in a great variety of colors and in various sizes of sheets, panels, and other forms. The material is used mostly for exterior and interior wall panels and for kitchen and other equipment.

Rubber is made from a milky secretion, or latex, about 99 percent of which is obtained from rubber trees (*Hevea brasiliensis*), though other trees and plants also produce latex. Some 90 percent of the world's supply of rubber comes from Malaysia, Indonesia, and other countries in the Far East. Rubber has many uses in architecture: for resilient flooring, gaskets, and glazing strips; in paints and other coatings, and toppings for concrete floors; and as adhesives. Today many synthetic rubbers are used for similar purposes; one of the best known and most widely used is neoprene.

Sand, gravel, and slag (a by-product of blast-furnace production of iron) have a number of uses in architecture. Sand is a major ingredient of concrete, mortar, plaster, stucco, and terrazzo and is used for other purposes, such as fill. Gravel is used as an aggregate in concrete; for setting beds under concrete slabs; for finishing built-up roofs; for fill around buildings, particularly where good drainage is required; and for walkways and roadways. Slag is used for similar purposes and also in the manufacture of portland cement, mineral wool, and concrete block.

Paper is used quite often in building construction, in such products as building and roofing papers and felts; flashing; coverings for other materials, such as gypsum board; and wall coverings. Paper forms are often used for pouring concrete columns. In combination with other materials, such as asphalt, coal tar, plastics, and the like, papers are often used for waterproofing and similar purposes. Textiles are also used extensively in architecture, not only in interiors for carpeting, curtains, furniture upholstery, and the like but outside as outdoor carpeting and for awnings. Textiles are also used for roofing structures that are supported by air.

**Historical Development** In prehistoric times, humans lived in natural caves or those they dug. When humans began to construct rudimentary shelters, they turned to the materials that were close at hand and easy to work with. Thus the first man-made shelters are believed to have been rude huts made of poles covered with brush, leaves, or thatch; or tents made with poles covered with animal skins. Since these early buildings were made of organic materials that disintegrated very quickly, almost no remains of them have been found. However, it is known that the first building materials were mostly wood, which has continued to be an important building material ever since. Another early building material was mud.

Later, when more elaborate structures were constructed, wood was most likely to be used in areas where trees were plentiful. Elsewhere, early builders turned to other materials that were plentiful, including turf, mud, and adobe. Thus the concept of using materials that were available locally was established very early and became a regional tradition in architecture, which has lasted, though it has not always been honored, to the present time.

In the Neolithic period, European buildings continued to be constructed mostly of wood which was plentiful and well adapted to the climate. Early buildings in the Middle East and in Egypt utilized wood as a material, but the limited supplies were soon exhausted, and some wood was imported. Since the supply of clay in those areas was almost inexhaustible, most buildings were constructed of sun-dried brick, though wood continued to be used in a limited way. In time, bricks were burned in kilns improving their strength, making them more uniform in size and shape, and improving their resistance to water penetration. Brick, like wood, thus was established as an important building material in early times and has continued to be important to the present day.

In the Middle East, with little wood and almost no stone, brick has continued to be the major building material to this day. In Egypt, on the other hand, ample supplies of stone allowed the more important buildings to be constructed of that material. Terra-cotta was used after methods of glazing this material and brick were developed. Other materials also came into use, including bitumen for waterproofing and plaster made of clay or mud.

Although the ancient Greeks first constructed buildings of wood and then of brick, they had an abundance of fine stone, primarily limestone and marble. During the classical period in Greece, all the important buildings were of stone. At first, limestone with a rough surface was used with a covering of plaster made of burned limestone. Later buildings were of marble cut with precision, smoothly finished, and erected with accurate joints. Iron had been available as a building material for a long time, but was not much used until the time of the Greeks and then for only minor purposes, such as attachment of sculpture to buildings. Roofs were generally of marble or terra-cotta tiles. By the time of the construction of the Parthenon (432 b.c.), the Greeks had begun using some wrought-iron beams in their structures.

The Romans continued the use of stone as a building material, quarrying it not only in Italy but in Greece and other places. They also used brick extensively in their buildings and other structures. The most striking development by the Romans was the widespread use of concrete for buildings and other purposes. Roman concrete was composed of a natural volcanic earth, called pozzolana, found near Naples and in other places in Italy.

Pozzolana was mixed with burned, slaked lime to form a good, strong cement. Cement mortar was then made into concrete by combining it with broken bricks or stones. Most of the concrete used in buildings was then plastered or covered with thin sheets, or veneers, of marble.

After the 1st century A.D., the Romans used concrete more often than any other building material. They continued to use stone, especially for covering concrete walls and other structures. They also used wood for framing walls and roofs and for floors. Wood-framed Roman buildings are not so well known as those of other materials since none of them has survived. The most used roofing materials were terra-cotta tiles, but stone slates were also used for this purpose. Glass was used in windows by the Romans beginning about the middle of the 1st century B.C. The first glass was colored, but later the Romans discovered a method of making relatively clear glass. Their method was later lost and was not rediscovered until the 15th century.

For various parts of buildings, the Romans used other materials, including wood for doors and bronze for both windows and doors, and, in a few cases, for columns and other structural purposes. Iron was sometimes used for structural members.

After the era of the Romans, few innovations were made in building materials for quite a long time. By the 7th century, both tin and lead were sometimes used for roofs, and iron was used for hardware and grilles. Other than these, the most prevalent building materials were those that had been used in the past. During the Middle Ages, the use of stone increased, particularly in important buildings such as cathedrals. These usually were of stone, with wood-framed roof structures. In England, brick making resumed in the 13th century, after a lapse of more than 800 years. Glass also began to be more widely used in windows, not only of churches and cathedrals but in larger houses. The glass was thick, uneven, and greenish, and came only in small pieces that were held together with strips of lead. Wood was also extensively used in the Middle Ages, a time when methods for framing heavy timbers were developed. Also half-timber structures were constructed. These employed heavy timbers in their structural systems with plaster filling the spaces between the timbers. Concrete fell into disuse during the Middle Ages.

During the Renaissance, few innovations were made in building materials. Architects of the period seemed content to stay with materials that had been used before, but with increasing refinement in their treatment. Stone continued to be the most important building material for all but the simplest buildings, but wood and brick were used extensively. Concrete was used sparingly, but iron came to be used more often than before, especially for structural members. Window glass was improved considerably and was used in buildings of all types. Renaissance architects made great progress in the use of traditional materials in innovative structural ways, but developed no important new materials.

After the Renaissance, building materials were mostly brick, stone, and wood, varying between localities mainly because of availability. In cities, because of fire hazards, stone was the favored material and brick was also used. Beginning in the early 19th century, a number of people developed artificial cements, whose manufacture was not dependent on natural materials, such as pozzolana. The most successful came to be called portland cement, because it was supposed to produce a concrete that could be substituted for Isle of Portland stone. Invented by an English mason and builder, Joseph Aspdin (1779–1855), this cement in time revolutionized building construction and remains a very important material today. With the advent of artificial cement, concrete began to be used more extensively in buildings and other structures.

Although it had been used to some extent much earlier, iron started to become an important building material during the 18th century and came into its own during the 19th. Both wrought and cast iron were utilized, first for the structures of bridges, then for those of buildings. Later, both materials were used for other architectural purposes, such as in decorative ironwork and even for entire fronts, or facades, of some buildings. Although steel had been manufactured in relatively small quantities for several centuries, it was only used for minor parts of buildings until the late 19th century, when the architects of the so-called Chicago school began to design steel-framed tall buildings. The use of steel in structures has since become standard practice everywhere.

Concrete had been extensively used by the Romans, fell into disuse for an extended period, then once again became an important building material in the 19th century. Until that time, it was always used as mass concrete, which had great strength in compression but much less in tension. In the 19th century, various experiments were made involving the embedding of iron rods in concrete to improve its tensile strength. This marked the beginning of the development of reinforced concrete.

Beginning in the 19th century and continuing to the present time, many other materials have been developed and are now used in buildings. Almost every material known has some usefulness in building construction. Most types of metals are used to some extent. Composite materials, in which two or more materials are combined, are used extensively. Plastics have assumed an important position in building construction. Research and development continues at the present time, and it can be expected that new materials will be forthcoming as well as new uses for older types and new uses of materials in combinations.

**American Development** The history of materials in building construction in America generally parallels that elsewhere. In early colonial days, the materials used were those available locally, wood generally in the Eastern and Southern states, brick and other clay products in the Southwest. Stone also began to be used early in American history. It was plentiful in some areas and quarrying was started early. For many years, stone was the preferred material for the most important buildings.

As cast and wrought iron became available, American architects turned to those materials, with which they pioneered in the design of tall buildings. They also pioneered in the use of steel in tall buildings. Reinforced concrete became an important American building material. And American architects have been enthusiastic users of most other new materials that have been developed. Today the most important materials used in American architecture are aluminum, brick, concrete, copper, glass, iron, miscellaneous metals, plastics, steel, stone, tile, and wood.

**Related Articles** DESIGN, ARCHITECTURAL; STRUCTURE; Various articles on specific materials, structural methods, and building systems and components.

**Further Reading** Brady, G.: *Materials Handbook,* 12th ed., McGraw-Hill, New York, 1985; Hornbostel, Caleb: *Construction Materials—Types, Uses and Applications,* 2d ed., John Wiley, New York, 1991.

## CONTEMPORARY ARCHITECTURE For the

purposes of this book *contemporary architecture* is defined as American work produced after 1970. Two major architects of the modern movement died in 1969: Ludwig Mies van der Rohe (1886–1969) and Walter Gropius (1883–1969). Both these architects had come to the United States from Germany. Two other major figures had died earlier, the Swiss-French architect Charles-Édouard Jeanneret called Le Corbusier (1887–1965) and the American Frank Lloyd Wright (1867–1959). All these figures strongly influenced the architecture of the United States, and their influence can be traced in later work.

The 1970s have been described as a decade of new directions after the death of the great modern architects. The 1980s has been described as a decade of inflation and excess, with a proliferation of design directions, whereas the early 1990s appears to be a period of withdrawal and reflection. A common assessment is that modernism failed to reach the idealistic goals associated with the early years of the century. A look at the United States would show that in residential architecture, the modern house was the exception, and commercial office buildings tended to become repetitive copies of the work of famous buildings. Nevertheless, several of the best-received current works can be described as modern, and the short-

lived Postmodern style has been critically dismissed. Deconstructivism is a contemporary concept where buildings are visually pulled apart or distorted to achieve new effects. Past buildings are quoted in much contemporary work, while others embrace the American love of wood construction or treat buildings as art objects in the landscape.

Societal influences include a widespread concern for the environment, financial restraints, client attitudes, the rapid integration of computers in all areas of society, the willingness of the public to trust architects to make proper decisions, and the larger role of the architect in society.

The role of the critic and architectural historian in shaping public perceptions of architecture is another influence on contemporary work. This period has seen an increase in the number of newspapers, magazines, and television programs which address the art of architecture. Architects must cope with the rapid increase in technology of construction. The client expects the architect to design buildings that function properly and that are adaptable to changing needs. Sociologists study the effectiveness of buildings from the point of view of their users and provide meaningful information for the architect. Refer to the article entitled social science. Building construction is expected to be rational, and government regulations have been imposed to protect the public health, safety, and welfare. The interest in our past has led to a new respect for historicism, resulting in preservation, restoration, or adaptive reuse of older buildings. A common criticism of some modern work is that it was not responsive to the regional differences in climate and history, and architects are now expected to be more sensitive to regional influences. New buildings that are respectful of the existing community are considered successful, or in context. Buildings by law must be accessible to the handicapped, and the architect is now more concerned with the public experience of building. Changes in political opinions and programs impact architects by shifting emphasis on the need for particular building types to the preservation of existing buildings. Architects in turn can influence the political community in support of quality design. The words used to describe architecture in themselves influence design concepts and perhaps explain the constant search for new terms for new approaches to design. Urban affairs are continually discussed in architectural terms. New towns, developing suburbs and satellite communities, transportation issues, and survival of older communities become regional issues, profoundly influencing architecture. Refer to the article entitled planning, city. It is apparent, particularly in residential design, that there is a public desire for tradition and increased quality of life carefully studied by builders and adapted to various eco-

**CONTEMPORARY ARCHITECTURE** Piku Residence (1992), Orchard Lake, Mich.
*[Architects: Dennison Luchini Architects]*

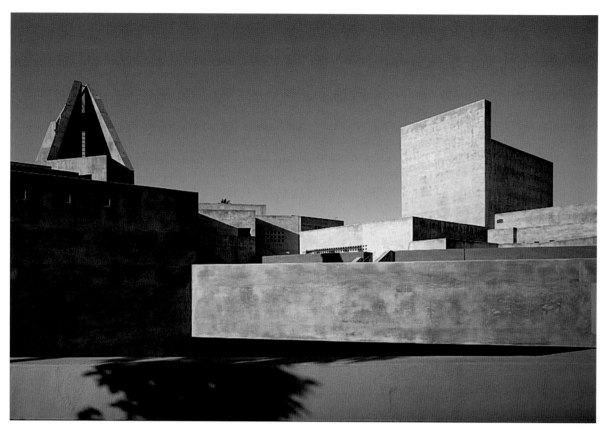

**CONTEMPORARY ARCHITECTURE** Museum (1989), University of Arizona, Tempe, Ariz.
*[Architect: Antoine Predock]*

nomic levels. This evocation of past societies is reflected in the work of many architects as well as developers, and interior designers and manufacturers supply a ready source of adaptions of historic furniture, fabrics, and accessories. Contemporary architecture is a rich amalgam of the described forces and directions, and architectural styles are influenced by these larger forces. Since the terms modern and *contemporary* overlap, the definitions used here are somewhat arbitrary. Also the eras overlap, since many of the architects practicing today or who practiced recently were already in practice before the death of the last master.

**Contemporary Architects** Some notable architects born early in the 20th century are still in practice, including Philip Cortelyou Johnson (1906– ), who in 1992 opened a new office in New York at the age of eighty-six; see article entitled Johnson, Philip Cortelyou. Others of the older generation include Marcel Lajos Breuer (1902–81), Wallace Kirkman Harrison (1895–1981), Louis Isadore Kahn (1901–74) and Minoru Yamasaki (1912–86); see the articles entitled Breuer, Marcel Lajos; Harrison, Wallace Kirkman; Kahn, Louis Isadore; and Yamasaki, Minoru. Other important contemporary architects born in the early decades of the 20th century and still in practice or who practiced until

recently include Paul Schweicker (1903– ), Paul Albert Thiry (1904– ), John Lyon Reid (1906–82), Cloethiel Woodard Smith (1910–93), Hugh Stubbins (1912– ), Bertrand Goldberg (1913– ), Ralph Rapson (1914– ), Edward Larrabee Barnes (1915– ), Harry Weese (1915– ), John Johansen (1916– ), Paul Rudolph (1918– ), and John Carl Warneke (1919– ).

Important contemporary architects who emigrated to the United States include Josep Lluis Sert (1902–83), from Spain; Ieoh Ming Pei (1917– ), from China; Ulrich Franzen (1922– ) from Germany; Kevin Roche (1922– ), from Ireland; Gunnar Birkerts (1925– ), from Latvia; and Cesar Pelli (1926– ), from Argentina.

Other contemporary architects of importance include Fay Jones (1922– ), Victor Lundy (1923– ), Gyo Obata (1923– ), John Calvin Portman (1924– ), Charles Willard Moore (1925–93), Robert Venturi (1925– ) and his wife Denise Scott-Brown (1931– ), Frank Gehry (1929– ), Stanley Tigerman (1930– ), Peter Eisenman (1932– ), Michael Graves (1934– ), and Richard A. Meier (1934– ). A slightly younger group would include Eric Owen Moss (1943– ) and Stephen Holl (1947– ). Among the firms whose award winning work is of importance today are Davis and Brody; Esherick, Homsey, Dodge and Davis; Gwathmey and

**CONTEMPORARY ARCHITECTURE** Cholla Branch Library (1974; alteration and addition 1991), Phoenix, Ariz. *[Addition Architect: William P. Bruder]*

Siegel; MLTW/Turnbull; Hartman and Cox; McCue, Boone and Tomsick (MBT); Geddes, Brecher, Qualls and Cunningham; Hardy, Holzman, Pfeiffer; and Mitchell and Giurgola. Other newer firms to be mentioned are Arquitectonica and Morphosis, each of which have been the subject of recent monographs.

**Firms** Today a number of relatively large firms offer not only basic architectural services but engineering and various combinations of landscape architecture, interior design, graphic design, construction management, and other services. Some of these firms have been in existence for a long time. One of the oldest is Shepley, Bulfinch, Richardson and Abbott, which grew out of the practice of Henry Hobson Richardson (1838–86), established in 1865. The firm, in spite of a number of name changes, still practices in Boston. Perhaps the oldest firm still in practice, established in 1853, also has had a number of name changes—Smith Hinchman and Grylls, of Detroit, whose president for a number of years was Robert Frank Hastings (1914–73). Perkins and Will, in Chicago, was founded in 1935 by Lawrence Bradford

Perkins (1907– ) and Philip Will (1906– ); Skidmore, Owings and Merrill (SOM) in New York and other offices was founded in 1936 by Louis Skidmore (1897–1962), Nathaniel Alexander Owings (1903–84), and John Ogden Merrill (1896–1975). Welton Becket and Associates, in Los Angeles, Calif., and other offices, was founded in 1933 by Welton David Becket (1902–69) and Walter Wurdeman (1902–48); Caudill, Rowlett and Scott (CRSS), Houston, Tex., was founded in 1946 by William Wayne Caudill (1914–83), John Miles Rowlett (1923–78), and Wallie Eugene Scott, Jr. (1921– ). The Architects Collaborative (TAC), Cambridge, Mass., was founded in 1946 by Walter Adolf Gropius and a group of young architects; and Hellmuth, Obata and Kassabaum was founded in 1955 by George Francis Hellmuth (1907– ), George Edward Kassabaum (1920–87), and Gyo Obata (1923– ). Of course, there is not sufficient space to list the many other excellent American architects and firms practicing today. However, the work of quite a few is shown in the many illustrations in this book.

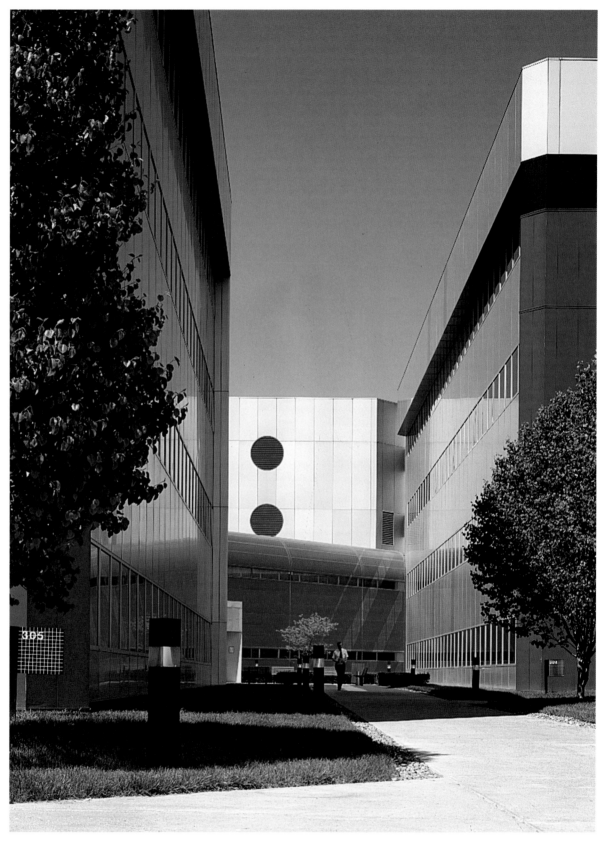

**CONTEMPORARY ARCHITECTURE** McDonell Douglas Missile Systems (1983), St. Louis, Mo.
*[Architects: Hellmuth, Obata and Kassabaum]*

**CONTEMPORARY ARCHITECTURE** Addition to Los Angeles Art Museum (1986 and later), Los Angeles, Calif. *[Architects: Hardy, Holzman, Pfeiffer]*

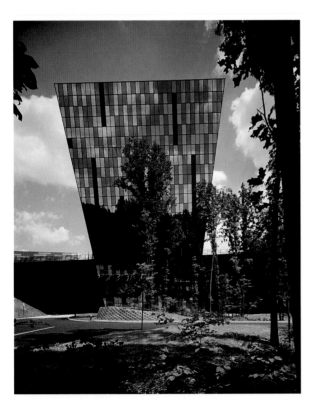

**CONTEMPORARY ARCHITECTURE** Center for Innovative Technology (1989), Fairfax County, Va. *[Architect: Arquitectonica (Photo: Greg Hursley)]*

**Building Designs** Many architects are producing very competent, often excellent, building designs. They have learned how to exploit the great technology of the time in daring structures, masterful use of materials, and sophisticated and efficient systems, such as heating and air conditioning, lighting, and so on. They know how to produce comfortable interiors, and, above all, many have learned to provide for the sociological, humanistic, aesthetic, and other needs of the people who occupy or use the buildings. Nevertheless, there is unrest among architects today. The critics and others who attempt to analyze and draw conclusions about the architecture of today often add to the unrest. No wonder that owners and users are perplexed.

**Current Labels** To gain some appreciation of the problems, it may help to look at some of the phrases or labels being attached to the architecture of today. Many of these terms are of short life, not receiving wide acceptance. One such label is Postmodernism, a word meaning simply after, or later than, Modernism. This implies that the Modern movement has ended. In its turn, some critics have declared Postmodernism dead. *Deconstructivism* is a term still in favor and has been increasingly influential as a freeing from the rigidity of rectangular forms. Humor in architecture is expressed in several buildings for Disney and has been labelled the "Disneying" of architecture.

In spite of all the confusion, many individual architects and firms continue to design excellent buildings that serve their purposes, function well, serve the needs and desires of the people who use them, and fulfill the requirements of their owners. Many of these building projects are large and complex; many are composed of several buildings and related areas; some are for multiple uses, requiring unusual skills in handling relationships between elements. Undoubtedly, such architects will continue to design excellent buildings and young architects are ready to perform just as well and even better. In time, also, an analysis of and conclusions about the present era will be possible, and the era will take its proper place in the history of architecture.

**Related Articles** ECLECTIC ARCHITECTURE; HISTORY OF ARCHITECTURE; MODERN ARCHITECTURE; Various articles on modern and contemporary architects.

**Further Reading** See listings in articles entitled history of architecture; modern architecture.

**Periodicals** *Architecture,* published by BPI Publications, 1515 Broadway, New York, N.Y. 10036; *Architectural Record,* 1221 Avenue of the Americas, New York, N.Y. 10020; *Progressive Architecture,* 600 Summer St., Stamford, Conn. 10904; various foreign architectural magazines.

**CONTEMPORARY ARCHITECTURE** State of Illinois Center (1985), Chicago, Ill. *[Architect: Helmut Jahn of Murphy/Jahn]*

**CONTEMPORARY ARCHITECTURE** Haskel Botanical Garden (1991), San Antonio, Tex. *[Architect: Emilio Ambasz (Photo: Greg Hursley)]*

**COPPER ALLOY** An alloy made from copper with tin, zinc, or other metals. Used in architecture for a great many purposes, the major copper alloys include true bronze, containing tin; bronzelike alloys, containing one or more other metals, such as zinc, lead, or nickel, and nonmetallic elements, such as silicon; brass, containing zinc, and sometimes lead, tin, manganese, or silicon. Other alloys include copper-nickels; nickel silvers, with copper and the other two metals; and leaded coppers. Pure copper has a minimum of 99.3 percent copper.

**Properties of Copper** Copper has high electrical and thermal conductivity. It is extremely ductile, capable of being stretched without breaking, and malleable, capable of being shaped or otherwise worked without breaking. It is nonmagnetic, highly resistant to corrosion by air or salt water, but not resistant to acids and alkalies. When exposed to air, copper and its alloys acquire a coating, called a patina, that protects them from further corrosion. Admired by many as an admirable property of copper and its alloys, patinas gradually change the surface colors to grayish green in about six years of exposure. Copper and its alloys can be efficiently worked by all the current metalworking methods, including casting, extrusion, bending, drawing, forging, welding, brazing, and soldering.

**Properties of Copper Alloys** Copper alloys generally have properties and characteristics similar to those of copper. However, some alloys are strong enough to be used for certain structural purposes and have other properties and characteristics that vary somewhat from those of copper. A great number of copper alloys are available today. Some of those most used include commercial bronze, with 90 percent copper, 10 percent zinc; red brass, 85 percent copper, 15 percent zinc; cartridge brass, 70 percent copper, 30 percent zinc; Muntz metal, 60 percent copper, 40 percent zinc; architectural bronze, 57 percent copper, 40 percent zinc, 3 percent lead; silicon bronze, 97 percent copper, 3 percent silicon; nickel silver, 65 percent copper, 25 percent zinc, 10 percent nickel; and leaded nickel silver, 45 percent copper, 42 percent zinc, 10 percent nickel, 2 percent manganese, 1 percent lead. As may be seen, the so-called commercial and architectural bronzes of today are actually brasses, since they contain zinc rather than tin. Silicon bronze is not a true bronze either, since it contains no tin. The only true bronze used in architecture today is statuary bronze, composed of copper, tin, and various combinations of other metals, including zinc, lead, and nickel. Different alloys, all containing tin, yield varying characteristics and colors. Statuary bronze is used in architecture for such purposes as sculpture, ornament, and hardware.

**Uses** Pure copper is used for many purposes in architecture, including roofing, flashing, insect screening, hardware, piping, and electric wiring. Copper alloys are used for an even greater variety of purposes, including curtain walls, storefronts, doors and frames, plumbing fixtures, windows, furniture, flag poles, railings, and many other kinds of equipment for buildings. Copper is also used in other ways, for example, as an alloying metal in steel to improve its corrosion resistance, as a pigment in coatings, for the plating of other metals, and as a wood preservative.

**Production** Copper is produced by several processes, including a type that involves crushing and grinding the ore in a mill, with water, into slurry; mixing the slurry with oil and chemicals in a floating tank, which causes the copper-bearing particles to rise to the surface, forming a froth of copper concentrate which is about one-third or less pure copper; after the froth has been scraped off, the concentrates are again ground, passed through flotation tanks, and filtered. From the mill, the copper concentrate goes to a smelter where it is heated in a reverberatory furnace, forming copper matte, still quite impure. It is then put into a converter, where silica is added and air is forced through the molten copper matte, producing blister copper which has a purity of 97 percent or more. The blister copper is then placed in a fire-coating or electrolytic furnace for further refining. About half the copper used in the United States comes from recycled products. Copper in products to be recycled has a value of as much as 90 percent of that of the primary metal.

**Finishes** Copper alloys may be obtained with a number of different kinds of finishes, including as-fabricated; buffed, the result of grinding, polishing, and buffing; directional textured; and nondirectional textured. Directional-textured finishes are available in five grades, from the finest to the coarsest, called fine satin, medium satin, coarse satin, uniform, and brushed. A relatively expensive finish is the hand-rubbed. Nondirectional textured finishes come in fine, medium, and coarse matte. Copper alloys may also be colored with chemicals, laminated with protective plastics, or coated with plastic coatings.

In using copper alloys in architecture, care must be taken not to connect them directly to other metals and not to place copper alloys where water can run off them onto other metals. Because of galvanic action or electrolysis, copper alloys, low in the galvanic scale, will cause deterioration, or even destruction, of most other commonly used metals. Copper alloys should never be used where sulfur is present and should be used with care where acids and alkalies are present. Moisture runoff from copper alloys may stain some kinds of stone and other materials.

Copper and its alloys are very important in architecture, particularly those cases which call for high-quality materials. In many instances, and for many functions, copper and its alloys are considered the best choices possible.

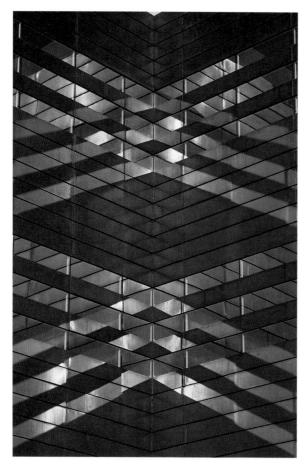

**COPPER ALLOY** Detail of copper and glass curtain wall, Michigan Library and Historical Center (1989), Lansing, Mich. *[Architect: William Kessler & Assoc.]*

**History** Some doubt exists about which metal, gold or copper, was first used by humans and when. Both occur naturally, gold almost always in veins, lodes, or placer deposits; and copper in particles, nuggets, and sometimes masses. Since many other metals are found only in ores or in combination with other minerals, it is understandable that gold and copper, followed by silver and lead, were the first usable metals.

It is believed that the first copper was used by humans during the Neolithic, or New Stone, Age, beginning about 5000 B.C. Some believe the metal may have been used 3,000 years earlier. However, no objects made of the metal at that time have been found.

There is little evidence that any considerable progress was made in the use of copper until about 3000 B.C., which is assumed to be the beginning of the Bronze Age. About that time, various methods of extracting copper from ore were developed, along with the process of annealing by heating the metal. As time went on, methods for melting, casting, and other techniques were developed, along with methods of extracting already alloyed bronze. By about 1400 B.C., methods for alloying copper with tin to produce bronze had been discovered.

Most of the early uses of copper and bronze were for relatively small, functional articles, such as tools and containers for food and drink, and later for weapons, armor, and works of art. The first use of copper or bronze in architecture has not been established. However, the use of these metals for ornamental sculpture, furniture, and small hardware and fittings certainly began about 1000 B.C., for doors shortly afterward, and was well established by about 600 B.C. in the Middle East as well as in Egypt. Between those dates, alloying copper with zinc to form brass was discovered. From that time, copper alloys have been important architectural materials. And bronze has been considered, in almost every era, to be one of the finest architectural and sculptural materials. In the earliest days, the main source of copper was on the island of Cyprus, Cyprium in Latin, from which came the Latin word *cuprum* or, in English, copper. Today the United States leads the world in mining copper, over half of it coming from Arizona.

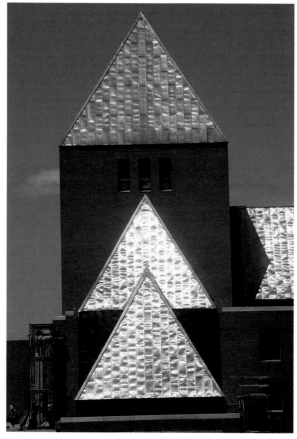

**COPPER ALLOY** Roof, St. John's College Student Union (1993), Collegeville, Minn. The new copper roof shown will accumulate a copper oxide patina with age. *[Architects: Rafferty, Rafferty, Mikutowski, Roney & Assoc.]*

The ancient Greeks used bronze for sculpture, for fittings to hold sections of columns together, and for attaching various architectural elements to buildings. The Etruscans also used bronze for sculpture and other purposes. The Romans used copper and bronze extensively in architecture and for sculpture, ornament, roofing, doors, furniture, candelabra, fittings for stone and brick elements, and many other purposes. In the Pantheon (A.D. 124), the Romans used bronze girders, since removed, for the structure of the roof of the portico and gold-plated copper or bronze tiles, later replaced with lead, for the roofing of the dome. After the Romans, copper production came almost to a halt and the small amount produced went mostly into utensils and ornaments for religious purposes.

During the Renaissance, copper alloys were used extensively. Bronze was a preferred material for sculpture, including sculptured doors, other ornamental purposes, and parts of furniture. Other copper alloys were widely used for many purposes similar to those of today. Since the Renaissance period, in America as well as in other places copper alloys have continued to be of great importance in architecture.

**Related Articles** ART IN ARCHITECTURE; DOOR; ELECTRIC POWER AND WIRING; HARDWARE; ORNAMENT; PLUMBING; ROOFING; WATERPROOFING.

**Source of Additional Information** Copper Development Assoc., 2 Greenwich Office Park, Box 1840, Greenwich, Conn. 06836.

**COST CONTROL** The process undertaken to ensure that the amount of money spent for a building or other structure will be kept within its budget or other proper limits. Control of costs of architectural and related services and actual construction has always been an important consideration in architecture. Since costs of construction have been rising rapidly for many years, it is even more important to keep costs under strict control. And it can be expected that continued inflation will cause construction costs to rise further in the future, making controls increasingly important.

Proper cost controls start at the beginning of an architectural project, when a need for a building or other structure has been identified. They should continue through all the phases of architectural and related services, through the construction, and, according to some experts, through the whole life of a building or structure. Good cost control requires that reliable data be available and that the data be interpreted properly by trained, intelligent cost experts, using up-to-date methods for analysis and projections. While architects and other design professionals may not be legally responsible for the construction costs of projects, they have responsibilities for keeping their clients informed

of probable costs and for having clients approve their estimates.

**Estimates** An estimate is an approximate calculation of the costs of construction of a building. Architects, other design professionals, and others in the building industry utilize estimates of two major types: unit estimates and quantity estimates. Unit estimates are based on the principle of establishing a price for each unit of a certain kind that will go into a building or other structure, such as square feet of floor area. The unit price multiplied by the total number of units establishes the total cost. Quantity estimates are based on the principle of actually determining the exact number of items to go into a building or other structure, such as doors, windows, cubic yards of concrete, and so on, and then determining the complete cost of these items as constructed into the building or structure, including purchase price, delivery to the site, labor, overhead, and profit of contractors. These prices are then added to establish an estimated total cost. In an inflationary era, this total estimated cost must then be projected to the time of actual construction to determine what the total estimated cost will be when the effects of inflation have been considered.

Unit estimating is not as accurate or reliable as quantity estimating. Some unit-price estimating systems, beginning with the least reliable and proceeding to the most reliable, are the area, or square-foot, method; volume, or cubic-foot method; and the unit-of-use method, which uses, for example, the estimated cost per hospital bed or school pupil. While all these methods are frequently employed, they are, at best, only useful for early, very rough estimates of construction costs. Another method, more refined than the others, is the unit-of-enclosure system, which requires determination of the total quantity of construction: walls, floors, roofs, and so on enclosing a building. This quantity is then multiplied by a unit rate, derived from reliable data. The quantity estimating method, called quantity surveying in England and sometimes in this country, is the most reliable and accurate current method.

For estimating by means of the area and volume unit methods, systems have been established for the relative values given to areas and volumes of various types. While practices vary, a typical square-foot system might assign full value to ordinary floor areas in buildings measured from exterior wall to exterior wall; and for special areas, decreased values such as $2/3$ of regular floor areas to heated garages, enclosed walkways, and porches; $1/2$ value to unheated garages and penthouses; $1/3$ value to carports, nonenclosed porches, and walkways; and $1/4$ value to roof overhangs.

After the determination of the number of square feet of area for each of the elements of the structure listed above, each total is multiplied by its proper fractional value, and the gross area determined. The gross total, in square feet, is then multiplied by an estimated cost per square foot to determine the total estimated cost of the building. The cost per square foot to be used is usually derived from published cost indexes for specific building types, modified by as much applicable information as can be gathered. Some of the modifiers might include the area of the country in which the building site is located, inflation and other cost-increasing factors during the time between the estimate and that of construction, seasonal cost factors such as the possibility of slowdowns because of bad weather, the effect of unusual design factors, and so on.

In a similar way, the other unit estimate methods entail totaling the units and multiplying them by unit prices to determine the gross total estimated costs of buildings. Quantity estimating also makes use of unit prices, but in this case they are prices for relatively small elements of buildings and therefore may be more accurate.

Quantity estimating is more accurate in another important way since it involves actually counting the materials, equipment, and so on that will go into a building and then establishing a unit price for each that may then be multiplied by the total quantities. While the other methods might be called rule-of-thumb methods, a quantity estimate, if done properly, will result in an accurate list of everything that will go into the construction of a building.

Quantity estimating begins with a takeoff: a list of all the materials, equipment, and other items in a building. An estimator usually develops a takeoff from working drawings and specifications either in their completed form or in some intermediate stage before completion. It is also possible to take off quantities, approximately, before the working drawings and specifications have been prepared. However, the more complete the information available, the more accurate the takeoff and therefore the estimate that can be made.

Experienced estimators stress the necessity of an orderly, methodical approach to takeoffs. Although procedures may vary, one method is to prepare takeoffs for general construction work in an order similar to the following: concrete work, masonry work, carpentry work; finishing work; excavation; and site work. To these must be added the takeoffs of specialized work, including such items and systems as plumbing, heating and air conditioning, electrical work, structural steelwork, and others. After the takeoff has been completed, an estimate of the cost of each group of items may be made. Then the overall estimate may be prepared, including labor and materials for each of the categories in the takeoff, to which are added the prices of subbids, if any, and the contractor's overhead and profit.

**Estimators** Making of reliable estimates depends on many things. First, of course, it depends on good estimators, who not only know construction and architecture but have inquisitive attitudes that lead them to investigate every possible source of pricing information. And they must approach estimating jobs as controllers as well as evaluators of costs. A good estimator is always on the lookout for information on such factors as wage scales; labor problems; local material prices; special work rules; special building code requirements; shortages of labor or materials; degree of competition among contractors, suppliers, and others; and any other information that may be of help in the estimating process.

In addition to information of this sort, estimators use data from other sources, including national and other cost indexes, unit price manuals of various types, and valuation and appraisal manuals. A large number of these are available today. Price indexes showing relative changes in costs of construction over the years can be obtained from several sources. One of the leading ones is published by *Engineering News-Record* magazine. Some architects prepare their own indexes.

Estimating is the most important tool of cost control. Estimates may be of several kinds. General contractors make estimates, using quantity takeoffs to price their bids on construction projects; as do subcontractors for their bids on specialized portions of the construction, such as electrical work, plumbing, heating and air conditioning.

Architects and other design professionals use estimating as a tool with which to control the costs of construction so that the buildings they design can be built within the budgets or other limits established by owners. This entails beginning the cost control program at the beginning of the performance of architectural services, or even before. Most contracts or agreements between owners and architects require that architects perform certain cost control activities as part of their basic services. Usually, these activities include preparing for the owner statements of probable cost during the schematic design phase, updated versions during the design development phase, and further refined versions during the construction documents phase. All these statements should be based on the best information and estimates possible at each phase. Some believe that proper cost control should begin even before the schematic phase, at the time of program preparation, and that cost control does not end until the construction has been completed within the budget or other amount to which an owner has agreed.

Unit estimating methods are widely used in the early phases of architectural services, while quantity estimating is generally used in the construction document phase. Some architects believe that unit pricing methods should not be the basis of the early estimates, but should only be used as rules of thumb. In their place, they suggest that quantity takeoffs can be made even in the earliest stages if they are approached with knowledge, imagination, and creative ability. It is obviously more difficult, and less accurate, to make a takeoff of a building when only preliminary design drawings have been made. However, some architectural offices do just that.

**Budget Estimates** Cost control begins with the preparation of a budget estimate, which must be made at a time when only the building program, and perhaps some early sketchy ideas of the building concept, are available for estimating. Thus budget estimates must be based on data that are ordinarily much less reliable than that of quantity takeoffs. In order for a budget estimate to be as realistic and reliable as possible, it must be made by expert cost control people who use every device at their disposal, including their knowledge of the type of buildings the firm produces as well as cost data. As in other types of estimates, those for budgets require orderly, methodical processes.

Although the process may vary somewhat, budget estimates ordinarily include separate items for the costs of site work, structure, exterior and interior finishes, electrical work, plumbing, heating, air conditioning, fire protection, elevators, and the like. They also include estimated costs of special work required by unusual site or soil conditions, special equipment, provisions for future alterations or expansion, construction schedules, type of construction contracts, landscaping, signs, art allowances, and so on. In addition, in order to furnish owners with budgets for entire project costs and not just those of the construction, budget estimates include the cost of architectural and other professional fees, surveys, insurance, legal fees, financing costs, and any other costs directly related to projects. From a budget estimate, a project budget can be prepared for the approval of the owner. Ensuring that the project costs stay within a budget then becomes the goal of all further cost control efforts.

During the schematic design phase, budget estimates can be considerably refined. Although unit estimating may be the basis, a quantity takeoff may be started to help in the refinement of the earlier estimated costs. Cost controls practiced by designers and others involved in the work may be directed toward ensuring that the project can be constructed within the budget. The estimate made at this time indicates budgetary problems, if they exist, and often indicates the building elements in which the problems occur.

During the design development phase, further efforts to keep the costs under control are made by designers, project architects, and others working on projects. A more refined estimate can now be prepared,

based on more complete information than was previously available. Additional quantity takeoffs may be made of certain elements of the proposed building. While the working drawings and specifications are being prepared, further refinements may be made in the estimate and after these documents have been finished, the takeoffs may be completed and a further refined estimate made. During this phase, controls of costs may be more difficult because of the great number of specific decisions that must be made and because a number of people may be working on the job.

Cost control during the construction contract administration phase is mainly devoted to keeping changes from being made in a building. Such changes may result from various causes. The worst, from a cost control standpoint and for other reasons, are changes made necessary by errors or omissions in the working drawings or specifications, or changes made necessary by misunderstandings between the architect and owner. Obviously, the need for such changes must be eliminated in the preceding phases of the work, before construction begins. Other changes during construction may be initiated by the owner, contractors, or architect. Regardless of the source of the ideas for such changes, they must be dealt with firmly. If they will result in sufficient benefits in the building, are economically feasible, and are approved by the owner, such changes may be justified. Otherwise there is a risk of exceeding a budget that has been carefully guarded by all the cost control activities in the phases that preceded construction.

**Construction Variables** It has often been said that the three variables in building construction work are quantity, quality, and cost. For example, if a building of a certain size, or quantity, is required at a certain specific cost, the quality of the building will be determined by the other two factors. Of course, this can work in several ways: any of the variables can become fixed, while the other two vary; any two can be fixed, and so on. But it is not possible to fix all three.

Recently, a fourth variable, the time of construction, has become of extreme importance because of rising costs of construction due to inflation and other factors. This has resulted in a situation that causes a building designed at a certain time to cost considerably more if it is built some years later. This situation makes estimating and cost control more difficult since factors have to be applied to today's costs to determine those of tomorrow. In addition, the actual time required to design a building, prepare construction documents, take bids, and construct it will greatly affect the cost. In general, the faster these phases can be accomplished, the lower will be the cost of the building. This situation has produced some new ways of handling the phases of architectural services and construction.

**Architectural Service Methods** Today the most used method of architectural services is still the traditional one, beginning with schematic design and ending with construction contract administration. However, two other methods, the phased system, sometimes called fast-track, and the design-build system, have come into use. In the phased system, after schematic designs have been approved, the project work is separated into what are sometimes called bid packages. Design development and construction contract documents are prepared for each package, and each is then contracted for, without waiting for completion of the documents for the other packages. Thus construction can begin on site work, foundations, and so on, long before construction documents have been completed for work that comes later. Considerable time may be saved on certain architectural projects, with requirements that fit into this system, by allowing the design and construction-document phases to overlap to some extent with the construction phases.

The design-build system is essentially a method of placing complete responsibility for architectural and related services and construction on one organization, that of an architect, contractor, or construction manager. Often used for technically complex projects, such as petrochemical plants, the design-build system also allows projects to be separated into packages as in phased construction and also makes time-savings possible in the overall process. Variations of these systems are sometimes used; one is the turnkey system, which is quite similar to the design-build system.

**Work Schedule Systems** The new systems all have as their major purpose the saving of building costs through acceleration of the processes required to produce a building. Another aspect of cost control and saving money are systems for scheduling the work. In the past, such systems were primitive, mostly dependent on bar charts upon which the various activities could be shown. Bar charts are still used to some extent, but they have been joined by much more sophisticated methods and techniques for scheduling the work.

One of the most widely used techniques is known as the critical path method (CPM). The critical path method utilizes diagrams upon which lines are placed, each representing a task or activity that must take place in the construction of buildings. CPM diagrams are also used for scheduling activities involved in architectural services and for many other purposes. Each line on a CPM diagram represents one activity and each is connected in order to the activity that follows it. Arrowheads are placed at the ends of all lines, indicating the order in which the activities take place and the end of each activity. Each arrow is labeled with the title of the activity it represents and the arrowheads are numbered with event numbers. At the midpoint of each arrow, the normal time, in days, to complete the event is placed. A complete CPM diagram is called a network. The critical path consists of the sequence of activities representing the minimum length of time in which the project may be completed.

The CPM system allows projects to be properly scheduled, gives indications of possible problems, and allows actual problems to be identified early, thus helping to keep projects on schedule and to control their costs. The use of CPM is more complicated than is indicated by the short description given here, but the system is not overly complicated and can be used either manually or with the aid of a computer. Another system, with some similarities to CPM, called program evaluation and review techniques (PERT), was developed by the U.S. Navy in connection with its Polaris missile project. PERT can be used as a cost control system without networks, and some think it superior to CPM for continuous project cost control. Other methods are also available, and it may be expected that new ones will be developed in the not too distant future.

**Other Techniques** A number of other systems and techniques have been developed to aid in cost control. One of these is value engineering, developed about the end of World War II. Value engineering is a technique for determination of the lowest costs for the proper accomplishment of the function of anything, such as a building project. This technique attempts to eliminate unnecessary costs by examining each item on the basis of what the item is, what it will do, what it will cost, what other item or items will do what the first does, and at what cost.

Another comparatively recent technique is life-cycle cost analysis. This system involves not only the cost of construction or even the cost of completely producing a project but the total cost of a building throughout its useful life from start to finish. Life-cycle costing takes into consideration the costs of architectural and related services and construction, together with costs for capital, financing, both interim and long term; costs of use, operations, heating, cooling, alterations, repairs, improvements, replacement, and delays in use caused by weather or strikes; and lost revenues if a project is not constructed. From this list, it may be seen that life-cycle analysis is complex and demanding. However, in no other way can owners or investors completely understand the total costs involved in building projects.

All the cost control techniques described are now mostly prepared using computers. The ability to access data banks of current cost information allows for more accuracy in estimating.

Formerly, the people most directly involved in cost control in architectural and other design offices were estimators. For a very long time, much of the public and many clients of these professionals believed that the estimators and the architects they worked for did not really do a very good job. One of the harshest, and most frequently heard, criticisms of architects was their often seeming disinterest in cost control and their inability to perform architectural services which would ensure that buildings could be constructed within their budgets.

Today the situation has changed. Estimators still perform important functions in cost control, but architects generally cannot be satisfied with anything less than the best cost controls. Therefore it has become necessary for all the people who perform any of the functions in architectural and related services to become cost conscious and to participate in cost control. The estimator of the past has had to change into the cost manager of today. Often in the past, estimators were trained on the job in construction under experienced estimators. Some of the cost managers of today have been trained in the same manner, but they have also had to learn many new techniques and to develop attitudes that enable them to perform positive, creative functions in the production of building designs and buildings.

**Related Articles** COMPUTER; PRACTICE OF ARCHITECTURE; Articles on various phases of architectural services.

**Further Reading** Parker, Donald E., and Alphonse J. Dell'Isola: *Project Budgeting for Buildings*, Van Nostrand Reinhold, New York, 1991.

## CRAM, GOODHUE AND FERGUSON American architectural firm. Founded in 1899 as a successor to Cram and Wentworth, Cram, Goodhue and Ferguson established themselves as the leading church architects in the United States and as the foremost proponents of the Eclectic Gothic style. The partners were Ralph Adams Cram (1863–1943), Bertram Grosvenor Goodhue (1869–1924), and Frank Ferguson (1861–1926).

With two talented designers, Cram and Goodhue, and Ferguson to run the office, the new firm made rapid progress. Soon numerous commissions for important buildings came in. Some of these were from clients who were impressed with the firm; others came as a result of the publicity gained from Cram's books and, in particular, his lectures. Others were won in competitions. Soon the firm had become a great success that lasted for more than a decade.

At the beginning, the working relationships between the two major partners, Cram and Goodhue, were excellent. Cram usually initiated the design, plans, and overall appearance of buildings. Then Goodhue took over, developing details and ornament. The two partners complemented each other very well. As time went on, each began to design his own buildings and, in some cases, each developed a design for a single building, presenting

both to a client or in a competition. Although their predominant style was Gothic, they did buildings in Colonial, Georgian, and other styles.

Goodhue eventually became disenchanted with the dedication of his partner to Gothic architecture. Competition between the two men grew. After Goodhue moved to New York in 1903 to start a branch office, the rift widened. Finally, in 1914 Goodhue left to start his own practice in New York City. And Cram went on practicing in Boston with Ferguson, under the name of Cram and Ferguson.

**Works** The first commissions of the firm were for small, insignificant work, remodeling and the like. This did not last long and soon they were being chosen for, or winning in competitions, a large number of important buildings. Beginning with All Souls Church (1894), Ashmont, Mass., the first in Gothic style, produced when the firm name was Cram and Wentworth, the architects designed many other churches. Among the best were All Saints (1895), Brookline, Mass.; St. Stephen's (1900), Cohasset, Mass.; First Baptist (1909), Pittsburgh, Pa.; the U.S. Military Academy Chapel (1910), West Point, N.Y.; Park Avenue Christian Church

**CRAM, GOODHUE AND FERGUSON** Exterior, St. Thomas's Episcopal Church (1914), New York, N.Y.

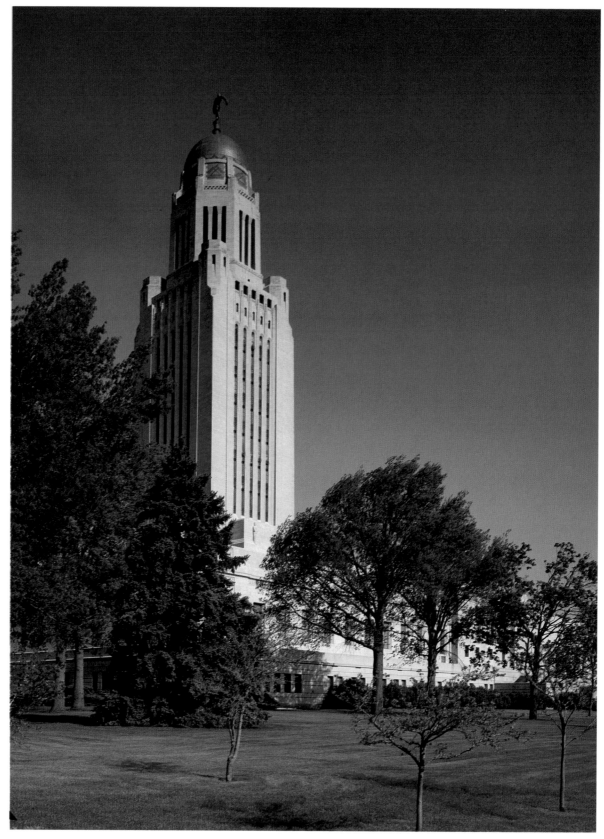

**CRAM, GOODHUE AND FERGUSON** Nebraska State Capitol (1928), Lincoln, Neb.
*[Architect: Bertram Grosvenor Goodhue]*

(1911), New York City; Euclid Avenue Presbyterian (1911), Cleveland; Fourth Presbyterian (1912), Chicago; and Hope Presbyterian (1912), St. Paul, Minn.

The firm's most significant buildings, other than churches, were at West Point, where Cram, Goodhue and Ferguson designed a number of buildings beginning in 1903. Appropriately, their last building together was a church, St. Thomas's, New York City, completed about 1914, the year Goodhue left.

**Cram's Life** Ralph Adams Cram was born in 1863, in Hampton Falls, N.H., the son of a Unitarian minister. After graduating from high school, he toured Europe. Interested in many cultural subjects, including art and architecture, he went to Boston where he wrote articles on art for the *Boston Transcript*, and in 1881 he joined the firm of Rotch and Tilden as an apprentice, staying there until 1885.

After participating in competitions in which he did well but did not win, he again went to Europe, this time specifically to study buildings. Coming back greatly impressed with Gothic architecture and the medieval spirit, he started his own architectural practice in Boston in partnership with Charles Wentworth (1861–97). Their first commissions were for modest houses and remodeling. In 1891 Bertram Grosvenor Goodhue joined the firm and in 1897, became a partner. In 1899 Frank Ferguson joined, to take care of the business end of things, and the firm was renamed Cram, Goodhue and Ferguson.

Cram was a prolific writer and speaker. In his lifetime, he wrote 24 books on a variety of subjects, including art, architecture, philosophy, and religion. The books and speeches brought the firm to the attention of potential clients all over the country and soon commissions started to come into the office in increasing numbers. Cram, and the firm, became the foremost proponents of Gothic architecture of the time. Their architectural work was mostly Gothic, and Cram's books and speeches espoused the cause of that style.

In 1903 Goodhue went to New York City to open a branch office for the firm. After that, the two partners drifted apart, not only because of the physical separation of the offices but because of competition between the two and Goodhue's increasing unhappiness with the Gothic style.

In 1889 Cram and Goodhue had submitted separate designs in the competition for the Cathedral Church of St. John the Divine (begun in 1892 and still incomplete) in New York City. Neither won, the commission going to Heins and La Farge. In 1911 Cram was appointed architect for the building and remained in that position until 1942, when he died. He managed to complete a major portion of the cathedral during his lifetime, and succeeded in changing its design from the Romanesque-

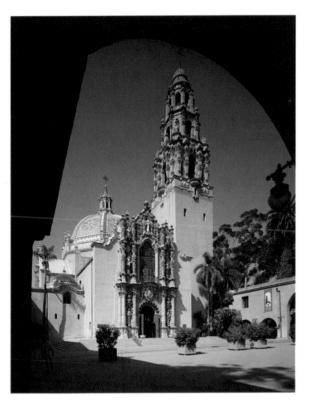

**CRAM, GOODHUE AND FERGUSON** California Building, now Museum of Man (1915), Balboa Park, San Diego, Calif. *[Architect: Bertram Grosvenor Goodhue]*

Byzantine style of his predecessor to Gothic. Although Cram and Ferguson designed other buildings after 1911, the cathedral occupied most of Cram's time for the remainder of his life. At various times, Cram acted as supervising architect at Princeton University and Bryn Mawr, Mount Holyoke, and Wellesley colleges. On September 22, 1942, Ralph Adams Cram died, having been one of the most successful architects of his era and certainly the most dedicated to medievalism.

**Goodhue's Life** Bertram Grosvenor Goodhue was born in Pomfret, Conn., on April 28, 1869. He was educated at the Collegiate and Commercial Institute, New Haven, Conn., but left in 1884, when he was only fifteen to go to work in New York City for James Renwick, Jr. (1818–95), a famous architect who designed buildings in the Gothic Revival style. Within two years, Goodhue had become the chief draftsman for the firm. Thoroughly indoctrinated in the design of Gothic Revival buildings and an accomplished draftsman, in 1891 Goodhue left Renwick to join the firm of Ralph Cram in Boston, and in 1897 he became a partner. In 1914 Goodhue left to start his own office in New York City.

Goodhue practiced as an individual architect for another 10 years. He was one of the finest draftsmen of his time and designed a number of distinguished buildings in many eclectic styles, including Spanish Colonial Revival, sometimes called Spanish Baroque; Gothic Revival; and a style that was almost modern but still derivative from the past.

After leaving Cram, Goodhue was appointed chief architect for the Panama-California Exposition (1915) in San Diego, Calif. He was successful in making the architectural theme of the fair the Spanish Colonial, or Spanish Baroque, Revival style. In addition, he designed buildings for the fair, some of which, including the California Building, still exist.

During his remaining years, Goodhue produced a number of other important buildings, all of them eclectic, including the Church of St. Vincent Ferrer (1918) and St. Bartholomew's Church (1923), both in New York City; the Los Angeles Public Library (1924); and the Rockefeller Memorial Chapel, University of Chicago, finished in 1928 after the architect's death. Also completed in 1928 was the building generally considered his best, the Nebraska State Capitol, Lincoln. Toward the end of his life, Goodhue seemed to be progressing toward an architecture that would be more specifically modern. But this was cut short by his death at fifty-five, on April 21, 1924.

**Related Articles** BOOK, ARCHITECTURAL; ECLECTIC ARCHITECTURE; EXPOSITION; GOTHIC REVIVAL ARCHITECTURE; RENWICK, JAMES, JR.

**Further Reading** Whitaker, Charles H., ed.: *Bertram Grosvenor Goodhue—Architect and Master of Many Arts*, DaCapo Press, New York, 1976.

**CRET, PAUL PHILIPPE** French-American architect (1876–1945). As a practicing architect for more than 40 years and as a teacher of architecture for more than 30, Paul Philippe Cret strongly influenced the design of buildings, not only those of his many students and associates but those of other architects of the time. A talented designer and teacher, Cret was a man of high principles and deep knowledge. He was respected and revered by all who knew him.

Cret was an eclectic architect, a very talented one, who designed excellent buildings in styles derived from the great buildings of the past. Trained at the École des Beaux Arts in Paris, his whole philosophy was imbued with Beaux Arts traditions. He taught Beaux Arts design by Beaux Arts methods and he designed buildings in the same manner. He was not an innovator, and his whole career was spent outside the mainstream of what became modern architecture. Nevertheless, he designed a number of fine buildings in various styles that are still well thought of today and transmitted to his students a knowledge of good architecture and a sensitivity to its design.

**Works** His first commission in America was the Pan American Union Building (1907), formerly called the International Bureau of American Republics, in Washington, designed in association with Albert Kelsey. Many consider this his best building, a Classic eclectic design with fine detailing and a beautiful garden with a reflecting pool. In any case, it was the forerunner of the kind of designs that would flow from his office afterward. His next important work was the Public Library (1915), Indianapolis, Ind., for which he won a competition in association with the firm of Zantzinger, Borie and Medary, and this was followed by the Detroit Institute of Fine Arts (1922), designed in association with the same firm. Both buildings are notable examples of his eclectic architecture.

Over the years, Cret designed several houses, though they were a small part of his work. On the other hand, he designed a great number of monuments and memorials, several of them in Europe in commemoration of World War I. Others of importance are the Washington Memorial Arch (1912), Valley Forge, Pa.; Providence War Memorial (1927), Providence, R.I.; and the Gettysburg Peace Memorial (1938), Gettysburg, Pa. He also designed a number of bridges. In fact, it is hard to cross any body of water in Philadelphia without using a Cret bridge. Among the most notable are the Delaware River Bridge (1922), the University Avenue Bridge (1925), and Henry Avenue Bridge (1927). Two bridges in Washington are also of note: Klingle Valley (1931) and Calvert Street (1933).

Paul Cret designed many other kinds of buildings, including museums, libraries, government buildings, apartments, university buildings, and courthouses. He even designed interiors for many of the great railroad trains of his era, including the Zephyrs, the Santa Fe Super-Chief and the Silver Meteor, and the Empire State.

Cret continued to practice architecture until he died, producing designs of good taste and refinement. Some of the most important buildings are the Rodin Museum (1928), Philadelphia; Folger Shakespeare Library (1929), Washington, D.C.; and the Federal Reserve Building (1935), Washington, D.C.

**Life** Paul Philippe Cret was born in Lyons, France, on October 21, 1876. At an early age, while working in the architectural office of his uncle, Johannes Bernard, he seems to have decided to become an architect. Entering the École des Beaux Arts in Lyons, he won an important prize for his work and a scholarship to the École des Beaux Arts in Paris. A good student, he won many prizes there. American students at the École, who had previously attended the University of Pennsylvania, recommended Cret for a position teaching design at the

**CRET, PAUL PHILIPPE** Pan American Union, now Organization of American States (1907), Washington, D.C.

latter school. He accepted and came to Philadelphia in 1903 to join the faculty, a position he held, with the exception of the World War I years, until 1937.

Soon after arriving in America, Cret went back to France to marry Marguerite Lahalle in 1904. The next few years were devoted to teaching until he won (with Albert Kelsey) a major competition for the design of the Pan American Union Building (1907) in Washington. During his career, he won six additional major competitions. The Pan American Union Building started his architectural practice, but he designed only a few other buildings before World War I. Still a French citizen, he was called into the French army in 1914 and after the war, came back to the University of Pennsylvania in 1919. He had been decorated for his service and had partly lost his hearing.

Soon after the war, General John J. Pershing appointed him first consulting architect to the American Battle Monuments Commission, a post in which he served the rest of his life. This began an important part of Cret's architectural practice, the design of memorials, three of them for the commission and a number of others. Other important building commissions came his

way and the small office Cret had started grew to 25 people, almost all of them his former students. Four students became partners in the firm, though it was always called simply by his name until his death. The partners were John Harbeson, William Hough, William Livingston, and Roy Larson.

The work of the firm was varied, from the usual architectural types—residences, libraries, office and commercial buildings—to monuments and bridges, and from 1933 on, interiors of railroad trains. Cret continued to teach, in his office, as well as classes at the university. He was known by students, clients, and employees as a kind and gentle man, devoted to those with whom he was associated. He was witty and well read. Dedicated to architecture, he spent most of his time in the drafting rooms where the work was going on rather than in his private office. His deafness did not slow his interests and activities. Later in life, after he lost the use of his voice from cancer of the throat, he carried a pad and pencil with which he communicated.

The architecture of Paul Cret was widely admired and brought him many honors, including the Gold Medal of the American Institute of Architects in 1938.

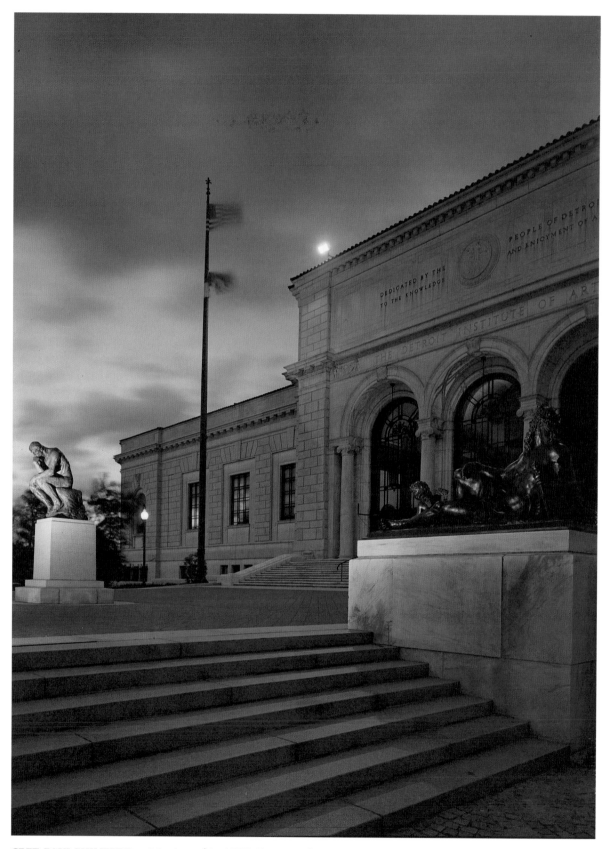

**CRET, PAUL PHILIPPE** Detroit Institute of Art (1922), Detroit, Mich.

After his death on September 8, 1945, his partners continued his firm under the name of Harbeson, Hough, Livingston and Larson.

**Related Articles** ECLECTIC ARCHITECTURE; EDUCATION.

**Further Reading** White, Theo B. ed.: *Paul Philippe Cret—Architect and Teacher*, the Art Alliance Press, Philadelphia, 1974.

**CRITICISM, ARCHITECTURE** The act or skill of analyzing and judging architecture. Although perhaps not as highly developed or as widely practiced as criticism of art, music, drama, or literature, architecture criticism today often makes valuable contributions to architecture.

In architecture, the word *criticism* has several meanings. In architectural schools, students receive criticisms which are analyses and judgments, positive and negative, of their design work by their professors, who in this case are called "design critics." In a similar sense, the word can be used to denote other actions, such as the criticism of a designer's work in an architectural office by an architect-principal or chief designer or criticism of an architect's work by clients or by users of buildings. Although all these interpretations are extremely important, the type of criticism under discussion here is that performed by architecture critics, amateur and professional.

**Purposes of Criticism** Critical writings on architecture can come in many forms, from short articles or essays that appear in magazines and other places to books. Although open to considerable interpretation, the avowed purposes of most critics are the analysis and understanding of architecture, identification and judgment of what is good and bad in it, interpretation of architecture's effects on society and the environment, and provision of guidelines by which architecture might be made better. By providing insight and information of these kinds, a critic expects to influence architects and other designers; clients and other consumers of architecture; and government, real estate, and financial forces toward the goal of better architecture and ultimately a better environment. Furthermore, critics believe they may discover something of the nature of future issues and solutions of problems caused by them.

**Types** Criticism may be divided into two major types: objective, sometimes called "normative," in which a work of architecture or other art object is judged on the basis of criteria or doctrines that are as free of personal bias as possible; and impressionistic, sometimes called "interpretative," in which works are judged by their effect on the critic. A review is a form of criticism usually written soon after a book has been published, a play has opened, or a building has been completed. Some reviews are impressionistic, some are descriptive, mentioning only the facts without making judgments about the subject of the review.

Some believe that architecture criticism should be concerned with the totality of buildings, that is, with their functions or purposes; their structure and mechanical and electrical systems; their effect as real property that adds value to the land on which they are built; their environmental impact; and their social, cultural, and symbolic meaning as well as their aesthetics.

In practice, such comprehensive criticism of total buildings is very rare. Many critics, even though they may be considered authorities or experts, are not really expert in all these aspects of architecture. Their jobs are made even more difficult by the fact that architecture, unlike music, drama, painting, and so on, is a functional art. In architecture, the art and science of buildings must become so intermingled that one cannot be separated from the other without destroying the total concept of the buildings. Many an architect has struck back at many a critic, saying in effect that the critic could not know what the architect had in mind, could not understand the total problem and therefore had written only superficial criticism. The views of critics have been called biased, invalid, narrow-minded, and inconsequential; the critics have been called vandals, parasites, and worse. In an extension of the old saying—"those who can, do; those who cannot, teach"—comes a third part: those who cannot teach become critics. To these charges, critics reply that they are, by their nature, experts who can take a broad overview of architecture and contribute to its understanding, based on valid information, their experiences, and their imaginations.

Objectively approached, criticism has had considerable influence on the arts for a very long time. Perhaps this is more the case in certain arts, such as literature, painting, drama, and poetry, but architecture criticism does go back a long way.

In architecture as well as in the other arts to some extent, critics very seldom make criticism their sole activity. In fact, it is rare for architecture criticism to be the prime activity of most critics. Instead, they are mostly writers, historians, aestheticians, teachers, editors, and even cartoonists who also write criticism. In literary criticism, almost all advanced college literature courses might be considered preparation for critical writing, and in most of the other arts, advanced history courses in specialized fields might also be considered in the same manner. In architecture, the situation is quite different. Only a few universities offer courses in architecture criticism and these are electives; there are no complete curricula for people who would like to make careers of architectural criticism.

Another factor that prevents architecture criticism from becoming more widespread and effective is that only a few magazines and newspapers publish architecture criticism on a regular basis. In contrast, critics of music, drama, and other forms have a great number of outlets for their work. Because of the paucity of architecture-focused popular media, most people rarely read any architecture criticism; it is hidden away from the average person in professional and scholarly magazines and books.

**History** Criticism of the arts is generally thought to have been started by the ancient Greek philosophers, Plato (c. 427–347 B.C.), originally named Aristocles, and Aristotle (384–322 B.C.), both of whom wrote criticism of poetry. A large number of critics of literature and the other arts have since received acclaim. In the 20th century, they have included such American literature critics as William Dean Howells (1837–1920), Van Wyck Brooks (1886–1963), Thomas Stearns Eliot (1888–1959), and John Anthony Ciardi (1916–  ). All did other kinds of writing. In drama criticism, noted Americans included Henry Louis Mencken (1880–1956), an editor and journalist; Joseph Wood Krutch (1893–1970); and Brooks Atkinson (1894–1988), a journalist and foreign correspondent. American music critics include Deems Taylor (1885–1966) and Virgil Garnett Thompson (1896–  ), both of whom were also composers. An interesting American critic of the 20th century was Gilbert Vivian Seldes (1893–1970), who wrote criticism of what he called the seven lively arts: motion pictures, comic strips, vaudeville, musical comedy, radio, popular music, and ballroom dancing.

The first art and architecture critic is usually thought to have been the Italian architect and painter Giorgio Vasari (1511–74), who wrote *Lives of the Most Eminent Painters, Sculptors, and Architects*, published in 1563.

Many other critics followed, including the Englishmen, John Ruskin (1819–1900), Walter Horatio Pater (1839–94), and Roger Eliot Fry (1866–1934), who was also a painter. Two Americans of importance are Bernard Berenson (1865–1959) in art criticism and Montgomery Schuyler (1843–1914) in architecture criticism.

Influential critics of the 20th century include the Swiss historian Sigfried Giedion (1888–1968), who wrote *Space, Time and Architecture*, the German-born English historian Sir Nikolaus Pevsner (1902–83), the Italian historian Bruno Benedetto Zevi (1918–  ), and the Australian Robin Boyd (1919–1971); each has written a number of important books. The dean of American critics was Lewis Mumford (1895–1990).

Writers such as Wolf von Eckardt (1918–  ), of the *Washington Post*, Ada Louise Huxtable (1921–  ), of *The New York Times*, and Alan Temko of *The San Francisco Chronicle* wrote about buildings being planned as well as those actually built. Other well-known critics include Henry-Russell Hitchcock (1903–87), Peter Blake (1920–  ), and Walter McQuade (1922–  ). One of the most incisive architecture critics was Alan Dunn (1900–74), longtime cartoonist of the *New Yorker* and *Architectural Record* magazines.

Today, architecture criticism is published regularly in New York, Boston, Los Angeles, Miami, Philadelphia, and Dallas. Paul Goldberger of *The New York Times* won the 1984 Pulitzer Prize for his writing. Recently Goldberger has been joined by the younger Herbert Muschamp.

**Related Articles** AESTHETICS; ARCHITECTURE; BOOK, ARCHITECTURAL; DESIGN, ARCHITECTURAL; MAGAZINE, ARCHITECTURAL.

**Further Reading** Attoe, Wayne: *Architecture and Critical Imagination*, John Wiley, New York, 1978, available through Books on Demand, UMI, Ann Arbor, Mich.

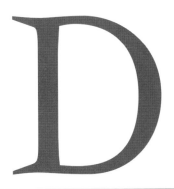

**DAM** A structure placed across a river or other body of water to stop or control its flow. Although most dams would not be considered architecture by many people, and architects are not often involved in their design, there are some notable exceptions. The purposes of dams include storage of water for drinking, irrigation, and other uses; control of water flow to stop erosion and flooding; and production of electric power through water-flow operation of hydraulic turbines. In addition, dams can form lakes for the benefit of wildlife and for recreational purposes. Major dams are among the great achievements of 20th century engineering.

**Construction Materials** Dams may be constructed from many materials, including timber, earth, rock, masonry, and combinations of these elements. Timber is used only for relatively small dams and does not last long. The timber is usually weighted down with rock. Embankment dams are raised structures made of earth, rock, or other fill materials. An earth-fill dam is constructed of fine earth in the center, coarser earth or rock on the outside, with a core of concrete or other means of waterproofing. Rock-fill dams are similar but constructed of heavy rock and boulders. The side of the dam facing the water is covered with concrete or some other waterproofing material. Earth and rock are used together in earth-and-rock-fill dams.

Masonry dams are constructed of cut stone or blocks of concrete. These may be gravity dams, which resist water pressure by their own weight; or arch dams, single or multiple, with structures designed to resist pressures. A single-arch dam is usually constructed in a narrow canyon or gorge and gains its strength from the curved conformation of the arch. A multiple-arch dam may be considerably wider and derives its strength from the shape of the arches and from extra supports called buttresses. Important parts of dams are spillways which allow bypassing of water, valves and gates for releasing water, and powerhouses.

**History** Dams have been constructed from very early times, at first of timber and later of earth and rock. Ruins and other traces of ancient dams have been discovered in the Middle East and in Egypt. The Romans built quite large masonry dams, many of which are still in use, all over their empire.

**American Development** In colonial American, modest dams were built. The second quarter of the 20th century saw the great era of dam building. Then came great dams such as the Hoover (1936) in Arizona but only 25 mi from Las Vegas, Nev.; Bonneville (1937), about 40 mi east of Portland, Ore.; and Grand Coulee (1942), about 90 mi northwest of Spokane, Wash.

At the same time most of these dams were under construction, the greatest dam project of all time, the Tennessee Valley Authority (TVA), began in 1933. In all, 20 dams were completed in 20 years along the Tennessee River. Also constructed were eight steam plants and a number of bridges, office buildings, visitor centers, and other structures. As great as were the engineering and construction accomplishments of TVA, many observers also consider the dams and other structures of considerable architectural significance. The architectural success of TVA must be attributed, in large part, to the architects who worked on the project, and especially to the head architects, Roland A. Wank (1898–1972), Rudolph Mock, and Harry Bird Tour (1899–    ). Another architect who consulted on the design of dams, including the Libby Dam (1976), Libby, Mont., was Paul Albert Thiry (1904–  ) of Seattle. Many other U.S. dams have been built by the Bureau of Reclamation and the Army Corps of Engineers, often for irrigation and flood control programs.

**Related Articles** Arch; Engineering; Structure; Vault.

**DAVIS, ALEXANDER JACKSON** Lyndhurst (1842; addition, 1867), Tarrytown, N.Y.

**DAVIS, ALEXANDER JACKSON** American architect and illustrator Alexander Jackson Davis (1803–92) was one of the most inventive architects of his time.

**Works** Davis practiced architecture from 1829 to 1878, a period of 49 years, and saw the change from Greek Revival to post–Civil War eclectic design. Davis designed in Greek Revival, Gothic, Italianate, and Egyptian styles. In association with Ithiel Town, he designed public buildings, commercial ventures, churches, and houses from mansions to country cottages. He experimented freely in architectural design. The firm Town and Davis designed mostly in the Greek Revival style. See the article entitled Town, Ithiel for a description of some projects undertaken by the firm during its existence (1829–35). Davis is credited with the more dramatic qualities of the firm's work and taught drawing and architecture to several students including the talented James H. Dakin (1806–56), who later joined the firm as partner during 1832–33. Dakin went on to have a notable practice in New Orleans, La., Mobile, Ala., and Baton Rouge, La.

Davis's design for Colonnade Row (1836) in New York used a giant Corinthian colonnade over a ground floor base, an imposing effect comparable to contempo-rary work in Britain. To allow daylight into the temple-form buildings, Davis introduced what he called the "Davisean" window between columns or pilasters.

Davis's most important Gothic style house (1847) was started for Philip R. Paulding, near Tarrytown, N.Y. Later, for George Merritt, this house was enlarged (1867) by Davis and has been preserved as Lyndhurst, now open to the public. It was his cottage designs in the Gothic manner which had the biggest impact and for which Davis is remembered.

**Life** Andrew Jackson Davis was born in New York in 1803 but spent his boyhood years in Newark, N.J., and upstate New York at Utica and Auburn. At age 15 he was sent to Alexandria, Va., to learn the printing trade. In 1823, Davis was in New York, supporting himself by typesetting and studying at the American Academy of Fine Arts, the New York Drawing Association, and the National Academy of Design. The artist Rembrandt Peale advised him to concentrate on architecture, and A. J. Davis became well known for his pictures of buildings in New York and New England.

His art training led to his interest in design rather than structure or theory. In 1826, he began architectural drafting for several New York architects and builders.

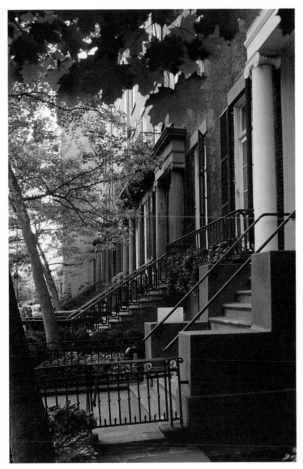

**DAVIS, ALEXANDER JACKSON** 21-26 Washington Square North (*c.* 1831), New York, N.Y. *[Architect: Martin E. Thompson of Town and Davis]*

Davis was attracted to the architectural books in Ithiel Town's office and spent time at the Boston Athenaeum on two occasions during 1827–28.

He set up his office while still exhibiting at the American Academy. His first built project was an imposing house for James A. Hillhouse near New Haven (1831), which brought him recognition in New Haven society. Ithiel Town (1784–1844) invited Davis to join him as partner in 1829, which gave the younger man great opportunity in a leading firm under the direction of the experienced Ithiel Town.

After the firm was dissolved in 1835, Davis and Town remained friends. Davis briefly worked with Russell Warren of Providence, R.I., and he designed several buildings that year, including the Dutch Reformed Church in Newburgh, and the Gothic first Unitarian Church (1838) in New Bedford, Mass. After this, Davis practiced alone except for his few collaborations with Town and the revived partnership in 1842–43.

Practicing independently, Davis's work was more and more residential in scale. His Gothic cottage designs inspired Andrew Jackson Downing, and from 1839–50,

Davis collaborated with Downing on his books and the *Horticulturist* magazine published by Downing. A. J. Downing (1815–52), was an American horticulturist, author, and after 1850, in partnership with Calvert Vaux (1824–95), an architect. Widely known through his publications based on English prototypes, he promoted the picturesque residential style, particularly the work of Davis, who supplied examples of his designs and prepared drawings for Downing's books, in particular *The Architecture of Country Houses* (1850). The influence these publications had on American taste was immense, and they were kept in print long after Downing's untimely death by drowning in the Hudson River after the boat he was on caught fire. Readers of Downing's books were frequently referred to A. J. Davis, who greatly benefited from this work.

For more than 20 years Davis was the leading American architect of romantic country houses, designing many of the finest examples. It is known that over one hundred of these houses were built. Few survive, although two are known, one in Rhinebeck (1844) and one in New Bedford, Mass. (1847?). He designed some thirty Italianate style houses in the period just before the Civil War. The Civil War effectively ended his successful practice, and younger architects came into their own. Davis kept his office open until he was seventy-five in 1878, and in 1890 he moved to Llewellyn Park, where he died in 1892.

**Related Articles** GOTHIC REVIVAL ARCHITECTURE; STRICKLAND, WILLIAM; TOWN, ITHIEL.

**Further Reading** Peck, Amelia, ed., with introduction by Jane B. Davies: *Alexander Jackson Davis: American Architect 1803–1892*, The Metropolitan Museum of Art, Rizzoli, New York, 1992.

**DESIGN, ACCESSIBLE** Accessible design is an important architectural consideration, not only in buildings specifically for the disabled but in barrierfree architecture in all buildings. About 15 percent of all the people in the world have some kind of disability. In the United States, disabled people constitute about 12 percent of the population. Of these, about 6 out of 10 are capable of leading normal productive lives.

The words describing this subject have changed from *handicapped* to *disabled* to *barrierfree* to the presently favored term *accessible design*. The problems experienced with the word *handicapped* relate to the presumption that this term refers to those in wheelchairs. As the federal regulations have evolved, the needs of many other segments of the population have been addressed. Currently, the term *accessible design* is taken to benefit the entire population.

Some persons with physical limitations who cannot lead normal productive lives are cared for at home by their children, parents, or others. Many are cared for in such institutions as long-term hospitals and special homes. The majority of the disabled lead productive lives, live in houses or apartments, work in offices or other buildings, shop in stores and shopping centers, go to restaurants, stay in hotels, and use other buildings in much the same way as do nondisabled people. Obviously, specialized buildings for the handicapped must be designed with their disabilities in mind. Until about the end of World War II, it may have been obvious that other buildings should be designed for use by the handicapped, but almost none were so designed.

Today accessible design has become a very important part of architecture, and, because of federal and state regulations, has become a legal responsibility of architects and others in the building construction industry.

**Disabilities** The American Institute of Architects publishes a list of organizations entitled *National Resources on Employing People with Disabilities*. This listing of organizations groups disabilities under the following titles: across-disability; developmental disability; hearing impairment; learning disabilities; mobility impairment, illness- and injury-related disabilities; psychiatric disabilities; vision impairment; rehabilitation; independent living; employment; and technology.

People with disabilities generally include those whose disabilities have resulted from birth defects, accidents, or illness. The major disabilities are hearing impairment, vision impairment, crippling, and mental disability.

A new building type is housing for those terminally ill with AIDS. Experience with this provides lessons applicable to other building types, such as hospitals and nursing homes. The use of computers and other technology for training or for providing special aids for the severely handicapped has enriched many lives.

**Barrierfree Design** The primary purpose of barrier-free design is to overcome problems in the physical environment of people with major disabilities. Disabled people are also protected by law against discrimination in employment and in many cases by federal and state laws concerning architectural barriers. Major disabilities are only part of accessible design, since many other people have handicaps of other kinds, including those of children because of their age and handicaps relating to obesity; physical size or stamina; and lack of coordination. People become disabled temporarily at times, for example, because of pregnancy, fractured bones, convalescence from accidents and illnesses, and other causes. And in the end, everyone who lives long enough becomes handicapped by the infirmities of old age. Accessible design does not have to be only a passive response to existing physical or mental disabilities but may be an active one in the prevention of accidents that cause disabilities. In other words, accessible design leads to better, more comfortable, safer environments for all people.

**Barriers** Certain common barriers which accessible design attempts to deal with: those of building sites, exteriors, interiors, rest rooms and bathrooms, kitchens, and services. Common problems include narrow parking spaces, curbs or other obstructions, narrow doors, unsafe stairs, steep ramps, too-long ramps, narrow corridors or work areas, slippery or varied-level floors, small toilet stalls, fixtures such as water fountains and telephone booths that are too small or in positions hard to reach, kitchen equipment that impedes use, and many others. Requirements to overcome these barriers are addressed in the current standards and laws.

The objectives of accessible design include proper design of the sizes, shapes, and positions of architectural elements of buildings and their sites, including the larger elements such as room, furniture, and equipment and the smaller elements such as doorknobs, water fountains, and kitchen, bath, and restroom appliances and equipment. In addition, limits must be placed on the amount of effort and energy required to use the various elements of buildings and their sites. Finally, signs and other signals, including an alarm or warning system, should be specifically designed for quick understanding and ease of use.

**Problems** Accessible design has come a long way in a relatively short time, but some problems still need to be solved. Some will require a considerable amount of study and research. Some architectural problems will not be solved until designers repudiate the approaches of the past and attack the problems in a free and creative manner.

Some of the current problems in accessible design include products that operate in ways that make them difficult to use; specialized safety problems, such as the exit from a burning building of people with limited mobility; and making existing buildings accessible. Providing ramps for wheelchair-bound people and eliminating curbs provides problems for blind people with their canes or their guide dogs.

The National Association of Homebuilders has questioned the additional space required in residential structures by the code-required stair riser and tread limitations designed to reduce the hazards of stairs. In residential construction, the effect of accessible design is to widen corridors, doors, and provide more clear floor space and safety features in bathrooms and knee room under sinks. The cost of accessible architecture is difficult to determine. Some analyses have indicated that the cost of providing accessible environments in new buildings might be as little as 0.5 percent of the total construction costs, in other words, $5,000 for a $1 million building. If these analyses are correct, this seems a small price to pay for the great benefits to be derived from accessible design.

**History** In prehistoric times and in the early historical eras, handicapped people were thought to be threats to the societies in which they lived because they did not contribute to the welfare or safety of their communities. Such people were often abandoned or driven out by nomadic people. The ancient Greeks abandoned deformed babies; in Rome, it was legal for parents to drown these babies. During the Middle Ages, handicapped people were reviled and ridiculed or treated as objects of entertainment. Many were burned to death.

It was not until the 19th century that handicapped people were cared for and became accepted by society. In the 20th century, progress has continued, accelerating with World War I. World War II and the Korean War resulted in great numbers of casualties, including a large percent of disabled people, again bringing about progress in the status of the disabled; this progress has steadily grown.

**U.S. Standards and Laws** Since the early 1960s, much progress has been made in barrierfree architecture. In the United States, this started with the formulation of standards in 1961 by the American National Standards Institute, Inc. (ANSI). The ANSI standards have since been the basis of federal and state legislation on the subject. The first major federal law was the Vocational Rehabilitation Act of 1965, since amended. This act dealt with employment discrimination against the disabled on federal government work or by those doing business with the government. This was followed by the Architectural Barriers Act of 1968, the creation of the Architectural Barriers Compliance Board in 1973, and the Rehabilitation Act of 1973. A majority of the states have passed building code requirements or other legislation dealing with the subject. In 1980 ANSI issued revised standards for barrierfree architecture. The comprehensive Americans with Disabilities Act (ADA), 1990, requires that any building available to the public be accessible to all. Buildings designed in accordance with the Uniform Federal Accessibility Standards are understood to fulfill the requirements of the law. Further guidelines and standards may be anticipated in the future.

**Related Articles** BUILDING CODES AND STANDARDS; DESIGN, ARCHITECTURAL; GOVERNMENT; HOSPITAL; HOUSING; Other articles on building types and systems.

**Further Reading** Barrier Free Environments Inc.: *The Accessible Housing Design File*, Van Nostrand Reinhold, New York, 1991; Bednar, Michael J., ed.: *Barrier Free Environments*, Van Nostrand Reinhold, New York, 1982; Evan Terry Assoc.: *Americans with Disabilities Act Facilities Compliance Workbook*, John Wiley, New York, 1992; Goldsmith, Selwyn: *Designing for the Disabled*, 3rd ed., RIBA Publications, London, 1977, available through International Specialized Book Services, Portland, Ore.;

Perritt, Henry H., Jr.: *Americans with Disabilities Act Handbook*, 2d ed., John Wiley, New York, 1991; Perry, Lawrence: *BOMA International's ADA Compliance Guidebook: A Checklist for Your Building*, BOMA International, Washington, 1991.

**Sources of Additional Information** American Institute of Architects, 1735 New York Ave., N.W., Washington, D.C. 20006; American National Standards Institute, Inc., 1430 Broadway, New York, N.Y. 10018; The Committee on Barrier-free Design, 111 20th St., N.W., Washington, D.C. 60601; National Center for a Barrier-Free Environment, 7315 Wisconsin Ave., N.W., Washington, D.C. 20014; National Easter Seal Society, 40 E. Lake St., Chicago, Ill. 60601; National Information Center for Children and Youth with Handicaps, P.O. Box 1492, Washington, D.C. 20013; U.S. Department of Health and Human Services (HHS), 200 Independence Ave., S.W., Washington, D.C. 20201; U.S. Department of Housing and Urban Development (HUD), 451 Seventh St., S.W., Washington, D.C. 20401.

**DESIGN, ARCHITECTURAL** The process of developing a mental concept of a building and its parts and expressing the concept in drawings and sometimes in models and written matter. The result of the process, the concept, is also called an architectural design. Those who perform the process are called architectural designers. It has become commonplace that not all architectural design involves new buildings but may include a wide variety of projects. This article describes the process for a new building. Refer to the article entitled practice of architecture for a wider view of architectural design.

Actually, architectural design is much more difficult to define than any phrase commonly used in architecture. For centuries, architects, philosophers, psychologists, and others have attempted definitions, none universally accepted and certainly not by architects. Architectural design has been called problem solving, the creation of something new, the changing of human-made things, or the changing of the environment. A long list of other definitions of architectural design and ideas and beliefs about its nature might be cited. Architects, architectural theoreticians, and critics today discuss the real nature of design whenever they have a chance and often argue about it, too.

New research into the practice of architecture brings insights into architectural design. The complexity of architectural practice is well understood, and attempts to define the attributes of a firm which produces excellent architecture is under study.

**Design Phases** In any case, architectural design is the creative process used to translate the problems, needs, and aspirations of potential building owners and users into drawings and other documents that depict

**DESIGN, ARCHITECTURAL** Organization plan sketches made on the flight back to the United States after visit to Singapore, Embassy of Singapore (1993), Washington, D.C. *[Architects: RTKL Associates, Inc.]*

possible answers to needs and aspirations and eventually translate them into buildings. In architects' offices, architectural design begins after research into the needs, problems, and aspirations of clients, a process called "programming"; see the article entitled programming. The next part of the process is the schematic design phase. During this phase, along with consultation with the client, studies and analysis of all the most important aspects of the proposed building are made. This is recorded by drawings and information that illustrate a design concept, sometimes with alternative concepts of

**DESIGN, ARCHITECTURAL** Three-dimensional form adding the circular geometry overlay, Embassy of Singapore (1993), Washington, D.C. *[Architects: RTKL Associates, Inc.]*

**DESIGN, ARCHITECTURAL** Further three-dimensional development of the building, Embassy of Singapore (1993), Washington, D.C. *[Architects: RTKL Associates, Inc.]*

**DESIGN, ARCHITECTURAL**  Isometric, Embassy of Singapore (1993), Washington, D.C.
*[Architects: RTKL Associates, Inc.]*

the proposed building, including floor plans, appearance, and other important aspects.

After approval of the schematic design by the client, before which further studies often must be made, the process continues in the design development phase. In this part of the process, the schematic concepts are further studied in greater detail, and the drawings and other information produced, illustrating more definitively how the floor plans are to be arranged, the appearance of the building, the materials to be used, its structure, and its mechanical, electrical, and other systems. During either or both of the design phases, study renderings or models, or both, and other specific proposals may be made. See articles entitled model making; rendering.

After the design development drawings and other materials have been approved by the client, the process proceeds into the construction document phase; see articles entitled specification; working drawing. Although a major portion of the architectural design work will have been completed previously, the design of many details of buildings and relatively small or minor elements and components often continues to the end of the construction document phase, and even during construction.

Along with the architectural design of buildings, other types of design must be performed, including the engineering design of structures, mechanical and electrical systems, and landscape design. Although architects sometimes handle such design activities, particularly for

**DESIGN, ARCHITECTURAL** Floor plan of garden level, Embassy of Singapore (1993), Washington, D.C.
*[Architects: RTKL Associates, Inc.]*

relatively small, simple building types such as single-family houses, structural design is usually the province of structural engineers; mechanical systems design, of mechanical engineers; electrical systems design, of electrical engineers; landscape design, of landscape architects; and so on. In small offices, architectural design is often performed by one or more of the architect-principals. In large firms, design may be performed by one or more of the principals or under their direction by architects or others employed as architectural designers.

In all but the smallest firms, most architectural designers are specialists. In very small firms, architect-principals and architect-employees alike often perform more than one function. For example, an individual might be involved not only in design but in some of or all the other functions, such as obtaining clients for the

**DESIGN, ARCHITECTURAL** Floor plan of entry level, Embassy of Singapore (1993), Washington, D.C. *[Architects: RTKL Associates, Inc.]*

firm, management of the office, production of working drawings and specifications, and administration of construction contracts. In most larger firms and many smaller ones, a single individual architectural designer has responsibility for one or more projects, working closely with other architects, production people, engineers, and so on in the design of the buildings. Many influences, such as client input, affect the design.

**Design Methods** Architectural design today is an incredibly complicated and complex process. So many elements are involved that architectural designers must use every means possible in analyzing the problems of proposed buildings and solving them through design. Traditionally, the major means of architectural design have been study drawings or sketches that begin with simple diagrams of relationships between elements and

**DESIGN, ARCHITECTURAL** Floor plan of third level, Embassy of Singapore (1993), Washington, D.C.
*[Architects: RTKL Associates, Inc.]*

proceed to more elaborate and definitive drawings. Sometimes study models have also been constructed to allow designers to examine relationships of elements in three dimensions. Such methods remain the primary means of architectural designers today. In addition, many other aids are used, including computers for analysis of data, comparisons of proposed solutions, and other purposes. Computers may be utilized for both written and graphic studies; see the article entitled computer.

**Scientific Method** A great many systems of problem solving, often computer-aided, have been developed. All are based on the scientific method, believed to have been first used by the Italian scientist Galileo Galilei (1564–1642), usually called Galileo. The scientific method has five steps that are intended to lead to orderly problem solving; see the article entitled programming. Based on the steps of the scientific method, many theorists have proposed architectural problem-solving methods. In general, these methods involve (1) definition of the problem, (2) establishment of objectives, (3) collection of data, (4) analysis of the problem, (5) consideration of possible solutions, and (6) solution of the problem. Although the steps may overlap in a given situation

**DESIGN, ARCHITECTURAL** Floor plan of fourth level, Embassy of Singapore (1993), Washington, D.C
*[Architects: RTKL and Associates, Inc.]*

and their order of performance may be changed at times, in architecture, steps one through four are generally called "programming" and steps five and six, "design."

**Principles and Rules** In the past, architectural design could be systematized in a manner that, though not always entirely satisfactory, furnished designers with principles and rules that were useful and generally reliable. Some believe that the same principles may be applied to architectural design today and that when the principles are ignored or the rules broken, excellence in architectural design cannot be achieved. Others argue that principles are subject to change and that rules are

made to be broken. In any case, no theory that seems valid for today's architecture has come along to take the place of the set of principles and rules that evolved through centuries of architectural design. And even if principles change and rules are broken, it seems necessary to know and understand the principles before changing them and the rules before breaking them. Without discussing them in detail, some of the principles and rules are enumerated here. In the broadest sense, they include four general areas: (1) needs and desires of people, (2) influences on architecture, (3) major requirements of architecture, and (4) design elements of architecture.

167

**People's Needs** The major needs and desires of people are physical, intellectual, aesthetic, and emotional. Obviously, all humans need, in their buildings, physical attributes that provide comfort and adequate space in which to live or perform tasks and other functions. People need to understand the buildings they occupy or use. People need beauty in their buildings and environments conducive to their emotional well-being. The desires of people often far exceed their actual needs; for example, great spaces, when smaller ones might do, and ornament, when the building would function just as well, physically, without it.

**Influences** The influences on architecture may be divided into three major types: natural, cultural, and technological. Natural influences on architecture include climate, geography, and geology. Climate affects the proper form, placement on sites, use of windows, insulation, and heating and air conditioning of buildings. Geology affects the design of buildings in their relation to the region or area in which they are to be constructed, to their neighborhoods, and to their actual sites. Geology affects the design of buildings in many ways, including their structures, form and drainage needs. Cultural influences affect the design of buildings in the large sense of their locations in various countries, states, cities, and so on and in the smaller sense of their exact sites and neighborhoods. Cultural influences include religion, politics, and others and the ideals of the owners and users of buildings and the cultures in which they live. Technological influences are the materials, structures, and systems.

**Architectural Requirements** The four major requirements of architecture include function, strength, aesthetics, and economics. Obviously, a well-designed building should function properly for the use to which its owners and occupiers will put it. It must be strong enough to withstand the uses and outside influences, such as weather. A well-designed building must satisfy the aesthetic standards of the owners and users, and often architects try to exceed the standards of the owners and users. And finally, a building must be designed so that it can be constructed for the stipulated amount of money, or within its budget, and to be an economically sound investment for its owners.

**Design Elements** The design elements of architecture include plans, form, and composition. Most, though not all, architects believe that the problem-solving process of design begins with the establishment of the elements that compose the plans of a building and the relationships between them. This involves the functions of spaces, their sizes and shapes, their juxtaposition, and, most important, circulation, the movement of people and sometimes things within and between the plan elements. Stated simply, a floor plan of a house should be designed, for example, so that the front entrance is prop-

erly located, circulation moves smoothly from that point into the house and into living areas that are of the proper sizes and shapes. Private areas of the house, such as bedrooms and bathrooms, should also be properly sized and shaped. Other relationships in houses must also be studied and designed properly.

In some past eras of architecture, the proper form of buildings was thought to be almost synonymous with their mass or bulk. Today the mass of buildings is still considered important, but their volumes or enclosed spaces are usually considered more important. It is in the volume or space of buildings that people live and function. Mass contributes heavily to the appearance or aesthetics of buildings, as does volume. In conjunction with the architectural design of the mass and volume of buildings, other important related considerations include structures, protective elements such as walls and roofs, materials, and ornamental features.

As in the other fine arts, composition is the process in architectural design involved in combining all the elements into a coherent whole or design. In the past, the principles of composition in architecture were followed very closely at times, as in the Renaissance, and followed scarcely at all in others, as in the revolt against Renaissance principles, called Mannerism, in the 16th century. The same is true today. There are six major considerations in architectural composition: proportion, scale, contrast, balance, rhythm, and unity. The end result of the combination of such principles of composition establishes the character of a building design.

Proportion is concerned with relationships, or ratios, in size and shape of the various geometric parts of a building to each other and to the building as a whole. Scale refers to the relationships, or ratios, between the sizes and shapes of various parts of a building to the size and shape of the human body in order to produce unity or harmony between them. Contrast refers to the design of various elements of building in order for them to have interesting and pleasing differences. Important types of architectural contrasts include lines, areas, volumes, masses, sizes, textures, colors, materials, and tones (shades from light to dark).

Balance involves the provision of a state of equilibrium in a building design, not only in actuality but visually. The two types of balance are symmetrical, in which identical parts appear in identical positions on either side of an axis, and asymmetrical, in which the parts are balanced by ones that are not identical. Rhythm means a regular repetition, according to some system, of elements, such as windows or columns and the spaces between them. Unity means the combination of all the elements into a systematic, identifiable whole.

When all the elements of architecture have been brought into proper relationships with each other and with the whole building or group of buildings, the result is architectural character. Some believe that there are intrinsic qualities in the character of buildings that cause churches to look like churches or office buildings to proclaim themselves as such. Others do not agree.

To many people, architectural design is exactly what architecture is all about. Some even go so far as to say that architectural design is architecture and all the other functions are supportive. In any case, design is the central theme of architecture and is probably the only activity in architecture in which the knowledge and talents of architects are unique. For those with such talents and knowledge, architectural design offers exciting, creative, and fulfilling careers. Most architectural designers today have become registered or licensed architects after completion of college professional training, experience requirements in architects' offices, and examinations. Others are architectural graduates who have not yet been registered or licensed to practice on their own. In the past, some architectural designers started out in drafting or other work, learned on the job and through independent study, and eventually became designers. Today there are few, if any, opportunities to become designers in that manner.

**Issues in Design** Analysis indicates that architecture tries to unite the contradictory issues of art and business. Many participants are involved in design decisions, and the architect must respond to an unlimited number of interests and concerns. The architect is acting in an uncertain environment which leads to the frequent observation that each project is unique and that the outcome of architectural design is not certain. The contest of power between client and architect and the architect's relationship with consultants may make assigning responsibility for design decisions difficult. When the outcome of design is uncertain, determining the effort and time required for the project may be difficult. Buildings have major impact on the lives of people who plan them and who use them. This sense of serious effect may reveal discrepancies in attitudes between architect, client, financial source, consultants, neighbors, and users. Any of those affected by design are likely to feel strongly about the result. This real-life view of the design environment is in contrast to the academic theory of design as taught in the schools of architecture.

**Related Articles** AESTHETICS; ARCHITECTURE; ENGINEERING; INTERIOR DESIGN; LANDSCAPE ARCHITECTURE; MODEL MAKING; PRACTICE OF ARCHITECTURE; PROGRAMMING; RENDERING; SITE PLANNING; WORKING DRAWING; Various other articles.

**Further Reading** Cuff, Dana: *Architecture: The Story of Practice*, MIT Press, Cambridge, Mass., 1991; *The Architect's Handbook of Professional Practice*, latest edition, The American Institute of Architects Press, Washington, D.C.; Saint, Andrew: *The Image of the Architect*, Yale University Press, New York, 1983.

**DOME** A curved roof structure usually, but not always, in the form of a hemisphere or other portion of a sphere. The structural principle on which a dome is based is the same as that of the arch and vault. In fact, a dome might be thought of as a special kind of arch, pivoted along its centerline and spun around to form a partial sphere on a circular base.

**Construction** Originally of masonry, brick, stone, or tile, domes were constructed with wedge-shaped units of these materials laid in rings, of decreasing diameters, one upon the other from their bases toward their tops. As in an arch or vault, a dome exerts great lateral pressure, or thrust, toward the outside at its base. This thrust must be opposed by heavy, thick walls or buttresses. A masonry dome is usually supported on a pendentive, a structural element that is a segment of a vault situated in such a way as to provide for the transition from the round base of the dome to a square or polygonal structure supporting it below.

An opening in the middle of the top of a dome is called an eye or oculus. Some domes have lanterns, sometimes called cupolas, small rooms, usually round or polygonal in plan, on their tops. A round or polygonal ring between the base of a dome and the pendentives or other supports is called a drum. Domes may be either smooth-shelled or ribbed and of uniform or varying thicknesses. Also domes can be constructed with one shell or with more. Two shells, one inside the other, were often used to allow different architectural treatment of the interior and the exterior. Sometimes domes are constructed with three shells, with the middle shell supporting the lantern.

Although they may be constructed of masonry and other materials, most domes today are of steel or reinforced concrete, utilizing principles similar to those of masonry, but designed with strong compression rings to resist the outward thrust at the base. A geodesic dome is a special type invented by Buckminster Fuller. Such domes may be constructed from relatively small elements of a variety of materials; see articles entitled botanical building; Fuller, Richard Buckminster.

DOME WITH PENDENTIVES

DOME WITH PENDENTIVES SUPPORTING DRUM

**DOME** Masonry types.

**DOME** Styling Dome, Chrysler Technology Center (1992), Auburn Hills, Mich. *[Architects: CRSS Architects; interiors: Harley Ellington Pierce Yee Assoc.; lighting: IlluminArt Lighting Consultants]*

**History** The use of domes began in Mesopotamia some 6,000 years ago, soon after the development of the arch and vault. Primitive domes were used in ancient Assyria and Persia and in the tholos or beehive tombs in Greece. The Romans carried on the development of the dome to a very high level of sophistication, culminating in the great dome of the Pantheon at Rome (2d century A.D.), still the largest masonry dome (spanning almost 143 feet) in the world. It remained for the Byzantine architects to solve the problem of the pendentive, as in the Hagia Sophia in Istanbul (A.D. 532–37), and the use of the dome spread not only into the rest of Europe but into Turkey, India, Egypt, and North Africa.

The dome was not an important structural element during the Middle Ages, a time which saw great development in the use of vaults, particularly in the Gothic and later churches. Domes again became popular during the Renaissance and later were further developed in such churches as Michelangelo's St. Peter's in Rome, finished in 1590, and Sir Christopher Wren's St. Paul's in London, finished in 1710, the first with double masonry shells, the second with triple shells.

**American Development** The introduction of the dome into American architecture came later than the arch and vault, and its use developed more slowly. The early settlers perceived no real need for the great monumental spans of domed roofs and indeed did not have the means to construct them. The use of domes became

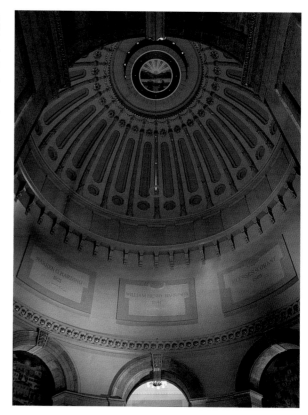

**DOME** Ohio State Capitol Dome (1839–61), Columbus, Ohio. *[Architects: Henry Walter, W. R. West, Nathan B. Kelly, Isaiah Rogers; consulting architects: Alexander Jackson Davis, Thomas U. Walter, Richard Upjohn]*

more widespread, especially for churches, state capitols, and other monumental buildings, during the Classic Revival and Eclectic periods of the 19th century and continued into the 20th. Today domes are still widely used, usually of steel or reinforced concrete construction, for such buildings as stadiums in which large areas must be enclosed with a minimum of obstructions, such as columns.

**Related Articles** ARCH; BRICK; CONCRETE; FULLER, RICHARD BUCKMINSTER; MASONRY STRUCTURE; STEEL; STONE; VAULT.

**DOOR** An entrance into a building or room; also called a "doorway." The word *door* is also used for the movable portion of a doorway. Doors and doorways have been important elements of architecture since the earliest primitive times. The functions of doors include building security, weather protection, privacy, and smoke and fire protection. In major buildings, multiple doors are needed to accommodate the large number of users.

Doors and doorways have an important symbolic role in architecture because of their function as ceremonial points of entry. Some famous historical examples are well known, but even the typical building visually emphasizes the location of the entrance. Visitors can be confused when such signals do not exist. Architectural solutions to identifying points of entry is an interesting study, and architectural critics comment if entrance doors are hard to find.

Studies of urban crime suggest that entrance doors visible to the street are safer than those out of view from public streets. Good lighting and well-lit vestibules can improve security. See articles entitled communication system, fire protection, and hardware.

**Classification** Doors today are classified in two major ways: by the methods in which they open and close and by the material of which they are made. The major types of door operation are swinging, on hinges or pivots; sliding, on tracks, rollers, or slides; folding, with tracks, rollers, or slides, and also those that fold like an accordion; overhead, ones that swing, roll, or fold up; revolving, like four doors on a central pivot; and bypassing, which open with narrow panels that slide over each other to the side of the doorway.

**Types** Doors may be placed singly, in pairs, or in multiples. A Dutch door has two leaves, one over the other, making it possible to open half the doorway without opening the other. A French door is made of wood, or other material, with glass inserted from near the top to near the bottom; French doors often come in pairs. A door may have louvers inserted into it for ventilation and would be called a louver door if the louvers extend from near the top to near the bottom. If the louvers are movable, it may be called a shutter door. If the shutters are of glass, it may be called a jalousie door. If a door has insect screening, it is called a screen door. A door with a window over it is said to have a transom. A storm door is a additional door used in conjunction with a regular exterior door to help retard the loss of heat from the interior in winter and to help prevent cold drafts from entering a building. In general, most doors today are either flush, those with plane surfaces, or paneled.

**Materials** A great number of materials may be used for doors and door frames, the assemblies into which doors fit; the most important are wood, plastics, steel, and aluminum. Glass is used extensively in doors and some doors, made of tempered glass, may have no frames. Wood doors may be solid or built up with layers of wood and other materials; they come in exterior grades and interior grades that may be hollow-core or solid-core. Metal doors are generally hollow, sometimes with insulation or other materials inside. Other door materials often used are bronze, stainless steel, and plastics. Many doors are composites, built up of two or several materials, such as a wood flush door with a core of particle board or some other material. Many different types of hardware may be used on doors, ranging from ordinary hinges, locksets, and so on, to door operators that open and close them by means of mechanical or electrical devices. See the article entitled hardware.

**Special Types** There are a number of special types of doors, including those shielded against the radiation of x-rays, atomic radiation, and so on, and fire-resistant doors. The former ordinarily use lead, steel, or concrete to resist radiation. Fire-resistant doors, which are required in buildings where walls, partitions, and other construction must meet fire-resistance codes, are labeled according to the places where they may be used in buildings, the labeling being based on tests by organizations,

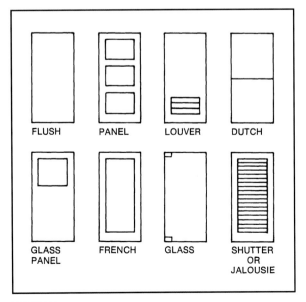

**DOOR** Contemporary types.

such as the Underwriters Laboratories. Another special kind of door is the type often used in entrances to stores and other commercial buildings. These doors are usually metal-framed glass or all glass and are often combined into storefront systems that also include show windows. They are usually of aluminum or stainless steel, but other materials, such as bronze, may be used. Doors of other types may also be obtained, including insulated ones.

An ordinary swinging door is often spoken of as a left-hand or right-hand door. When such a door is viewed from what is usually considered its outside, a left-hand door has hinges on the left and opens on the right toward the inside; a right-hand door is just the opposite. A left-hand reverse door has hinges on the left and opens toward the outside, while a right-hand reverse door does the opposite. In a door, vertical parts on the edges are called the hinge stile, where the hinges are located, and the lock stile on the other side, where the lock goes; the horizontal edges are the top and bottom rails; a center, or lock, rail is a horizontal member in the door at the height of the lock. These are parts of every door; in paneled types they may be seen, but in flush types they are hidden inside.

Although doors of various types are generally used for specific purposes for which they are designed, for example, overhead doors for garages and storefront doors for commercial buildings, architects today sometimes use them in ways that were not originally intended. For example, almost all types have been adapted to uses in houses, including overhead doors for the protection of vacation houses after the season ends.

Doors can be obtained in many sizes, types, and finishes. Many are stock items, while others are available on special order or may be custom designed to fit a purpose. Many doors, of wood, plastic, and metal, are available already mounted in frames, sometimes with all hardware already in place. Frames may be obtained precut but unassembled.

**History** Although the remains of none of the most primitive doors constructed by ancient people have been found, it is thought that they were rudimentary types of brush or animal skins. In Mesopotamia, doorways were often high with semicircular arches over them. Some doors were made of wood, often with bands of metal, such as bronze; others were thin slabs of stone, paneled to reduce their weight. In Egypt, doorways were rectangular in shape and usually fitted with wooden doors with pivots that acted like hinges. Ancient Greek doors, none of which is known to have survived, are thought to have been of paneled wood and sometimes of metal. Greek doorways were used sparingly and were almost always rectangular, but sometimes were narrowed at the top. Some simple ornament was used on both doors and

doorways. An important element of Greek architecture is the colonnade, or peristyle, a row of columns with openings between them but no doors.

The Romans used doorways that were rectangular and others that had semicircular arches at their heads. Doors for important buildings were often of paneled wood covered with bronze that had been hammered into ornamental designs; others were of hollow bronze. In Byzantine architecture, similar doors were used. Notable Roman examples still in existence are on the Pantheon (A.D. 124), Rome; and Byzantine examples on Santa Sophia, or Hagia Sophia (A.D. 537), Istanbul, Turkey. For less important buildings, wood was the door material most often used. A distinguished feature of Roman architecture is the arcade, a row of arches supported on columns or piers with openings in between but without doors. In Early Christian and Romanesque architecture, doorways were often spanned by semicircular arches, as in Roman times, and doors were of wood or metal and, in some cases, stone such as marble. Some doors were ornamented with carving or other patterns and often doorways were also ornamented.

In Gothic architecture, doorways were ordinarily spanned by pointed arches and were often highly ornamented with moldings or, especially in France, with sculptured likenesses of saints and human figures. Doors were placed where needed, without great regard for symmetry. They were generally made of heavy, vertical wood planks, often ornamented with wrought-iron work, some of it in conjunction with hinges, which were used for the first time in this era. Notable examples include those on the Cathedral of Notre Dame (1163–1250) in Paris. Arcades were used frequently, mostly at first with pointed arches but later with three-centered and four-centered arches, which have several curves of varying radii. The Dutch door is thought to have been developed in northern Europe during the Gothic era for use in houses.

During the Renaissance, door designs were based on those of the classical periods, particularly Rome. Doorways were generally designed with arched heads, and arcades were used extensively. Sometimes arcades

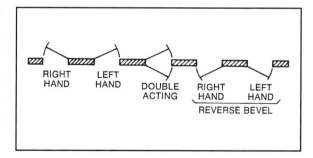

**DOOR** Identification by swings.

were superimposed, one above the other. Arrangements were usually formal and symmetrical, with doorways often ornamented with flanking columns or with architraves, systems of moldings. Along with fine murals, sculpture, and other art produced by Renaissance architects and artists, doors were an important art form in buildings of the era. Perhaps the most famous doors in the world are those of the Baptistery (6th–16th centuries), Florence, Italy, by Andrea Pisano (c. 1270–1348) and Lorenzo Ghiberti (1378–1455), Pisano's southern door completed in 1336 and Ghiberti's northern in 1424 and eastern in 1447. These doors are of solid bronze, highly sculptured, and became the models for monumental doors of many churches of the Classic Revival and Eclectic eras that followed. Doors for more modest buildings were generally of wood.

After the Renaissance period, doors and doorways were generally derived from those of past eras of architecture, until about the 19th century when the modern movement began. Innovations were made in types of doors, in hardware, and in materials used, but about the only entirely new design was the flush door, a plain type with a flat surface and no ornament. Flush doors, along with a few standardized paneled types, and glass doors of various kinds have become the norm in the architecture of today.

**Related Articles** ART IN ARCHITECTURE; CLIMATE; GLASS; HARDWARE; INSECT PROTECTION; INSULATION, THERMAL; ORNAMENT; SECURITY SYSTEMS; WALL; WEATHER PROTECTION; Various articles on building materials and systems.

**Source of Additional Information** Door and Hardware Inst., 7711 Old Springhouse Rd., McLean, Va. 22102.

**DRAFTING** The process of making drawings. The major uses of drafting in architecture and related fields are in the preparation of conceptual sketches and other drawings for study and design purposes, in the making of drawings or renderings to depict the plans and appearance of buildings to clients and others, and in the preparation of working drawings depicting how buildings are to be constructed.

In 1991 a survey of architectural firms determined that 80 percent used computers, and of this group, about 50 percent used computers for design and drafting. The larger the firm, the more likely that drawings are prepared with computers. Of those firms using computer-aided design and drafting (CADD), productivity has increased an estimated 40 percent. A growing number of firms require that all new people hired have experience in CADD. For further information refer to the article entitled computer. The remainder of this article describes the traditional pencil-dominated procedures for drafting.

A person who makes a career of drafting is called a "draftsman," or sometimes today, a "drafter." However architects and others also make such drawings. People who make renderings are usually called "renderers," or delineators, instead of drafters. People who make design drawings are usually called "designers"; see articles entitled design, architectural; rendering.

**Uses** Drafting can be considered the true language of architects. They use drawings or sketches to establish relationships between various elements of building designs, to aid in the thought processes of design, to depict buildings in a manner that will be understood, and to prepare working drawings, which are used as guides to the construction of buildings. Drafting is also an important part of the services of other design professionals, such as landscape architects, engineers, and interior designers. Material and equipment suppliers use drafting as an aid in manufacturing and assembly of building products and for the preparation of large-scale shop drawings for the fabrication of other building components and systems.

One of the highest compliments that may be paid to an architectural technician is to be called a "good drafter," one who produces excellent working drawings. And one of the highest compliments that can be paid to an architectural designer is the same, except that in this case, it means skill in the delineation of sketches and renderings.

**Types** Architectural drawings may be divided into three major types: conceptual, presentation, and construction. Although the first two types utilize some principles of drafting, such drawings are more closely associated with drawing, painting, and other techniques of the fine arts. Conceptual drawings are usually freehand, sketchy, made with pencil, charcoal, conté crayons, or in other media used by artists. For further discussion on conceptual drawings, see the article entitled design, architectural.

Presentation drawings or renderings primarily depict the designs of buildings for clients and others. This may be accomplished in various ways, as by presentation of the drawings or rendering themselves; by presentation of photographs of the drawings; or by reproduction of the drawings in booklets (brochures), magazines, books, or newspapers; and by slide or filmstrip presentations. For further discussion of various aspects of presentation drawings, see articles entitled graphic design; photography, architectural; practice of architecture; rendering.

The third major use of architectural drawings, the one most people mean when they speak of drafting, is in the preparation of working drawings to be used in the construction of buildings. This kind of drafting is factual, intended to furnish construction information but not

**DRAFTING** Principles of orthographic projection.

necessarily to depict the appearance of buildings. Therefore it utilizes many techniques, tools, and instruments to produce precise drawings with all the dimensions and other information needed by the contractors and material suppliers and those who will construct buildings.

**Drawing Systems** Many systems have been devised for drafting. Only a few are used in architecture, mainly perspective drawing, isometric drawing, and orthographic projection. The first two are included in techniques that are often called "pictorial drawing" systems because they attempt to depict in two-dimensional drawings how three-dimensional objects, such as buildings, appear to the human eye. Orthographic projection attempts to depict the exact shape of objects, such as buildings, together with their sizes or dimensions. Perspective drawing is used mostly for conceptual sketches and drawings and for presentation drawings or renderings. Isometric drawing may also be used for such purposes. For a discussion of computer-generated presentation drawings, see article entitled rendering. Orthographic projection is the system used for the preparation of working drawings.

The theory of orthographic projection may be understood by imagining a building enclosed in a clear plastic box. By looking in the front of the box, an observer sees a vertical front view of the building, and by moving around the box, clockwise, the observer may see in turn, the left end view, the back view, and the right end view. These are called the front, side, and back elevations of the buildings. By looking down on the box, the observer sees a view of the roof, called the roof plan. By taking a horizontal slice through the walls of the build-ing and looking down, the observer may see the floor plan. The observer then imagines that the major points of one of the views, for example, the front elevation, are projected out from the building horizontally and at right angles to the front until these points intersect with the front sheet of plastic. If a drafter connects the points on the plastic with a pencil, a front elevation drawing of the building will have been made, using the principles of orthographic projection. The other views may be drawn by similar means. On working drawings, drafters show floor plans, roof plans, and elevations, complete with dimensions and other information, along with drawings of other types, including additional plans, such as the site, interior elevations, sections, and details. Sections are made by slicing through the building as in the drawing of floor plans, but the slices may be made horizontally or vertically and may cut through the entire building or any of its parts. Details are drawings, usually in larger scale than those of floor plans or elevations, which contain more information about a building part or component than could be shown otherwise. Working drawings usually contain other information. See the article entitled working drawing.

**Instruments and Equipment** In making conceptual or presentation drawings, drafters use many of the instruments and pieces of equipment used for working

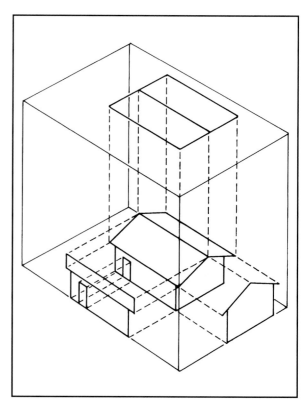

**DRAFTING** Three orthographic views.

drawings. In addition, these types of drawings utilize materials, such as paints or pastels, not ordinarily required for working drawings. Many types of drafting instruments and equipment exist. Some of the items are ordinarily not used by architectural drafters but may be used by engineers or others involved in architecture. For example, a drafting machine is like several pieces of drafting equipment, including a T square, scales, triangles, and protractors, combined into one device. Architects very seldom use drafting machines, but engineers frequently do. Many people are familiar with drafting instrument sets, which contain a number of instruments that are commonly a vital part of mechanical drawing courses in secondary and technical schools. Engineers often use sets of instruments such as these, but architects mostly do not, preferring to use only a few instruments selected individually.

The largest piece of equipment is a drafting table, usually made with a drafting surface, or drafting board, that may be raised or lowered and set at various inclines, and ordinarily covered with light-green linoleum, vinyl, or plastic-coated paper to form a surface upon which drawings of good quality may be accomplished easily. A book or storage space should be adjacent, as should a layout table for reference materials. Good overall lighting is a necessity, as are individual flexible lights on drafting tables. Some drafters prefer two-tube fluorescent fixtures; others, incandescent lights.

For generations, T squares were used for drawing horizontal lines. Much preferred today are parallel rulers, like T squares without heads, which are attached to drafting tabletops with cables. The cables are arranged in such a way that their geometry causes the rules to move up and down drawing boards, always ending in positions parallel to each other. For lines that are vertical or at standard angles, plastic triangles are used, the most common types having one 90° angle with the other two angles either both 45° or 30° and 60°. For angles other than these, adjustable triangles are used. Protractors are used for angular measurements and French curves, together with some special instruments, for drawing irregular, curved lines. For circles, compasses are used, the most popular being bow compasses for most circles and drop compasses for smaller ones. For very large circles, beam compasses are used.

Formerly thumbtacks were used to hold drawings down on drafting boards, but these badly damaged the boards. Today drafting tape is used, a special type much like masking tape but not as sticky. Drafting brushes, sometimes called crumb brushes, are used to keep drawings clean, as is drafting powder. Soft pink rubber erasers or other special types that are less likely to damage the drawings are used for correcting mistakes. Erasing

shields have slits through which erasing may be accomplished while the area surrounding the slit protects the remainder of the drawing. Electric erasers are also available but must be used with extreme caution, since they cut through drawings very rapidly. Lettering triangles have holes through which pencils may be inserted for making guidelines for lettering on drawings. There are many types of templates, plastic devices with precut slits for drawing circles, plumbing fixtures, kitchen equipment, furniture, and many other items.

Another type of drafting equipment for special purposes is lettering sets. Although architectural working drawings are not ordinarily drawn in ink today, some engineering drawings may be inked, and ink is often used for certain kinds of presentation drawings. The old nib-type drawing pens widely used in the past have now been replaced by much more efficient and easier to use fountain drawing pens.

Of utmost importance to drafters are scales of various kinds. Resembling rules, scales are devices with divisions along their edges indicating the size of the drawings in relation to the actual size of buildings. Two major types are used in architecture: a civil engineer's scale and an architect's scale. A civil engineer's scale is divided into tenths, twentieths, and so forth of an inch and is used for large area drawings, maps, and similar purposes. When using one, the scale of drawing is said to be, in the case of the twentieths scale, 1:20, or 1 in on the scale equals 20 ft on the actual site or area. An architect's scale is divided into eighths, fourths, and so on and is used for most architectural working drawings. When using an architect's scale, a drawing is said to be, for example, in the case of the one-eighth portion, in the scale of $1/8$ in/1 ft or $1/8$ in on the drawing equals 1 ft on the actual building. Architects learn to think in scale, mentally projecting themselves inside buildings they are drawing as if they could experience them at the drawing sizes and scales. For metric drawings, engineers and architects use the same scales, divided into subdivisions of a meter. Common scales are 0.01 or 1:100, or 1 centimeter on the scale equals 1 meter in the building. Drawings in this scale approximate the $1/8$-in scale on a conventional architectural scale. Other common metric scales include 0.0125 or 1:80, 0.02 or 1:50 (approximates the $1/4$-in scale), 0.025 or 1:40, 0.03 or 1:33 ($1/3$), or 0.05 or 1:20.

Undoubtedly, the single most important instrument for a drafter is the common pencil, though drafting pencils are quite different from the ordinary lead pencil. Today wood-encased drafting pencils have been superseded by mechanical holders in which leads may be replaced. The several types of holders include one that has a single lead of a size similar to that in wood pencils

**PLANS AND SECTIONS**

EARTH

FILL (STONE OR GRAVEL)

ROCK

LIGHTWEIGHT CONCRETE

STRUCTURAL CONCRETE

BRICK

CONCRETE MASONRY UNITS

CUT STONE

MARBLE

RUBBLE STONE

SLATE, BLUESTONE SOAPSTONE, FLAGGING

STRUCTURAL CLAY TILE

METAL (LARGE SCALE)

METAL (SMALL SCALE STRUCTURAL & SHEET)

PLYWOOD (LARGE SCALE)

FINISHED WOOD

ROUGH WOOD

GLASS (LARGE SCALE)

INSULATION (RIGID)

INSULATION (LOOSE OR BATT)

ACOUSTIC TILE

CERAMIC TILE

GYPSUM WALLBOARD

PLASTER, SAND CEMENT, GROUT

RESILIENT FLOORING

TERRAZZO

CARPET

**ELEVATIONS**

CONCRETE, PLASTER

MARBLE

SHEET METAL

GLAZING

BRICK

CERAMIC TILE

STEEL STUDS

WOOD STUDS

SPECIAL FINISH

**DRAFTING** Material indications for architectural drawings.

and another that stores supplies of very thin leads which need little or no sharpening. For the single-lead holder, electric and manual rotary sharpeners are available. Lead comes in many grades, ranging in hardness from the very hard, 9H, through 18 degrees to the very softest, ExB. For architectural working drawings, only a few grades are generally used, H, 2H, and 3H, and perhaps HB, being sufficient for most tasks. For drafting on plastic film, 6 degrees are available usually marked in a dif-

ferent manner, from softest to hardest, 1 to 6, with letter prefixes that vary among manufacturers. The proper hardness to be used depends on several variables, including type of drawing paper or film, relative humidity in the drafting room, and touch of individual drafters.

**Drafting Rudiments** It takes a great deal of training, practice, and experience to become an established drafter. The subject is too large for other than a cursory discussion here. But it should be pointed out that the rudiments consist of the ability to draw lines properly, without which no one can master architectural drafting. At the risk of oversimplification, it must be pointed out that a parallel rule is used for horizontal lines, with the sharpened point of the pencil pulled along it from left to right by right-handed people. As the pencil moves, deliberately and at an even speed, it is held always in a position slanted to the right and is rotated between the fingers to keep the point sharp. Similarly vertical lines are drawn by right-handed people from the front of the drafting board toward the rear along the left side of a triangle resting firmly against a parallel rule, with the pencil slanted toward the back of the board and rotated. Left-handed people draw horizontal lines from right to left and vertical lines along the right side of a triangle. Drafters must also learn to draw lines in a variety of weights, or thinnesses, and of several types, including full and broken, or dash, and other types. Another all-important, rudimentary part of good drafting is proper freehand lettering. Architects usually use roman letters, those with their vertical strokes straight up and down, but many engineers use italic lettering with slanted vertical strokes. Both employ guidelines for lettering.

A great number of new techniques have recently been developed to make drafting more efficient and faster, to take some of the drudgery out of the work, and for other purposes. The first innovation was printing drawing sheets of standard sizes with borders, title blocks, and other standard items. Later developments include paste-up drafting, rub-on techniques, typesetting methods to replace some hand lettering, freehand detailing, half-size techniques, photodrafting, and computer drafting. For a fuller discussion of these techniques, see the article entitled working drawing.

Many architects and other design professionals perform drafting work, particularly in the years just after graduation and when they have recently established their own practices. Some of these professionals continue to do drafting, but the more usual case is for technicians to perform this work. Drafting work requires not only skill in the mechanics and techniques of making working drawings but a considerable knowledge of buildings, including their design and construction. Drafting technicians usually obtain the knowledge and experience they need by attending architectural or other design schools, by training in technical schools, and by on-the-job training in offices of architects or other design professionals. Even with some formal training in architectural drafting, some years of broad and diversified experience usually are needed before a person can master the craft. For those who would like to participate in important ways in the creation of

buildings and related structures without becoming professionals in one of the fields, careers as drafters can be challenging and rewarding. Many drafters go on to become chief drafters or other managers in architectural offices, and in the past some eventually become registered architects after gaining sufficient experience and passing architectural registration or licensing examinations.

**History** Since drawings of buildings have been made by humans from the earliest times, it might be said that there have been architectural drafters for a time equally as long. In a sense, this is true. However, it is not really known when the first drawings were used for construction of buildings. Since the earliest architects were master builders who actually worked in construction, they seem to have had little need for elaborate drawings. In any case, judging by examples of architectural drawings from ancient architects and those of the architects of the Middle Ages, such drawings consisted of very little more than rudimentary floor plans and elevations, most of them drawn by the architects, or master builders.

The major change in drafting in the Renaissance was the introduction of perspective drawings, which helped depict buildings realistically. Although most Renaissance architects and those following in later years did not actually help construct buildings, they were ordinarily available almost constantly to explain to workers what they had in mind.

Not until the late 18th or early 19th century did architects begin to prepare more elaborate sets of drawings. A set of working drawings might consist of floor plans, the most important elevations, and a section, all drawn in a rudimentary way at small scales and often with imprecise dimensions. About the middle of the 19th century, architects began to produce sets of drawings more like those of today.

Young people who aspired to become architects often did the drafting work in offices, a practice that still exists today. And about that time, people began to make careers as drafters, as they do today. In the intervening years up to the present time, working drawings have become more and more complex, now consisting of a large number of drawings that can reach a total of 300 sheets or more for a large and complex building. Until the last few decades, drafting techniques lagged behind the changes in working drawings, remaining approximately the same as they had been in the mid-19th century. During later years, methods, instruments, and equipment changed radically.

One thing that has not changed much is drawing lines with a pencil. For years, students in architectural schools have been told that they should learn to think with their pencils, which might be considered extensions of their arms, which were in turn extensions of their brains. Architects still think with their pencils, but it appears the day will come when computers will finally replace the lowly pencil.

**Related Articles** CAREER; COMPUTER; DESIGN, ARCHITECTURAL; ENGINEERING; GRAPHIC DESIGN; INTERIOR DESIGN; LANDSCAPE ARCHITECTURE; PHOTOGRAPHY, ARCHITECTURAL; PLANNING, CITY; PRACTICE OF ARCHITECTURE; RENDERING; WORKING DRAWING.

**Further Reading** French, Thomas, et al.: *Engineering Drawing and Graphic Technology,* 12th ed., McGraw-Hill, New York, 1978; Helper, D., and P. Wallach: *Architecture: Drafting and Design,* 5th ed., McGraw-Hill, New York, 1987; Liebing, Ralph W.: *Architectural Working Drawings,* John Wiley, New York, 1990.

# E

**ECLECTIC ARCHITECTURE** A style or movement in which forms and details are selected from any of the styles or buildings of the past. In more extreme examples, forms or details selected from more than one building or style of the past are combined into a single building design. The movement began about the middle of the 19th century and has continued into the 20th in the United States and elsewhere.

**Melange of Styles** Prior to the U.S. Civil War, Classic Revival and Gothic were the preferred styles. Architects of that time also experimented with other styles. Thomas Ustick Walter (1804–87) built the Moyamensing Prison (1832), Philadelphia, in a Gothicized style. His addition of the Debtor's Wing (1835) to the prison was in an Egyptian-inspired style. John Haviland (1792–1852) used a similar style for the Tombs Prison (1840), in New York City, later demolished. Perhaps the earliest real eclectic architect was John Notman (1810–65), who designed buildings in Gothic, Romanesque, Renaissance, Baroque, and other styles. Eclectic architecture became more prevalent after the Civil War and, before it faded in the 20th century, produced a great number of styles. Some of these were the Italianate, Queen Anne, Stick, Victorian, French Second Empire, Romanesque Revival, Shingle, Eclectic Gothic Revival, Eclectic Classic Revival, also called "Classic Eclecticism," Renaissance Revival, Colonial Revival, Baroque Revival, Jacobean, Eastlake, Beaux Arts, and many others. Many of these styles were short-lived fads.

The post–Civil War preference for Italianate buildings had its beginnings in the prewar period. A fine surviving early example of the Italianate villa is the Victoria Mansion (Morse-Libby House) (1859–63) designed by Henry Austin as a summer house for Ruggles S. Morse in Portland, Maine. Beginning in 1848, cast-iron buildings and building fronts were manufactured in America.

By the end of the Civil War, cast-iron buildings were the structures of choice. Peaking about 1865 in New York, these buildings continued to be built in many cities into the 1870s. The ability of cast iron to reproduce classic detailing led to the use of stacked stories of cast-iron columns. Cast-iron columns remained important until the introduction of steel made it economical.

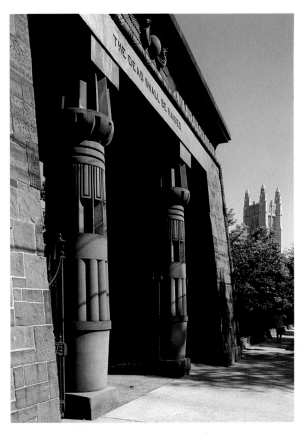

**ECLECTIC ARCHITECTURE** Egyptian style gates, Grove Street Cemetery (1848), New Haven, Conn. *[Architect: Henry Austin]*

Another style emerged, known as the Stick style in contrast to earlier Colonial or Greek style houses. The Stick style house was derived from A. J. Downing's cottage houses as shown in his *The Architecture of Country Houses* (1850) and popularized in William E. Bell's *Carpentry Made Easy* (1858). The Stick style house was picturesque, using siding framed in vertical panels. These houses usually were asymmetrical in plan and featured verandas. An example is Richard Morris Hunt's J. N. H. Griswold house (1862) in Newport, R.I., or the Sturtevant house of 1872 in Middletown, R.I., designed by Dudley Newton (1845–1907). Attempts to attribute the Stick style to the Englishman Charles Lock Eastlake, author of *History of the Gothic Revival*, published in 1872, are inaccurate, and his name is no longer applied to the style. In vernacular construction, the balloon frame house was perfected, allowing vast tracts of housing to be erected quickly using semi-skilled labor.

In 1857 the American Institute of Architects was founded. Many of the original members had been trained at the École des Beaux Arts in Paris. The architects of the eastern United States brought new sophistication to America in contrast to the builder's utilitarian approach. The leading architect of this period was Richard Morris Hunt (1827–95). Trained in the French Renaissance style, he was architect to the wealthy at Newport, R.I. (1878 and later), and for George Vanderbilt at "Biltmore" in Ashville, N.C. (1890). The influence of the French Second Empire could be seen on new office buildings and public buildings. Good examples are Philadelphia's City Hall (1871–81) designed by John McArthur, Jr. (1843–90) and Thomas U. Walter

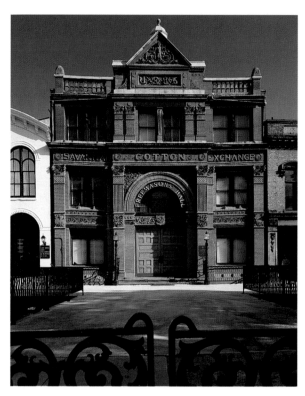

**ECLECTIC ARCHITECTURE** Cotton Exchange (1887), Savannah, Ga. *[Architect: William Gibbons Preston]*

(1804–87), and the State, War and Navy Department Building (1871–75) in Washington, D.C., designed by Alfred B. Mullet. At the time of completion, this was the largest office building in America. During this period, cast iron was slowly replaced by structural steel, making possible higher buildings. The invention of the elevator was necessary to the success of these buildings.

The influence of the Englishman John Ruskin (1819–1900), a supporter of polychrome Gothic, was important in the United States for church and educational buildings after the Civil War. His books *The Seven Lamps of Architecture* (1849) and *The Stones of Venice* (1851–53) were frequently reprinted and studied. The most accomplished Gothic work, which nevertheless compares poorly to Gothic revival work in England, was built later in the century, designed by the architect Ralph Adams Cram (1863–1942) and his partner Bertram G. Goodhue (1869–1924).

The late 19th century in America could be described as unregulated laissez-faire. Construction technology advanced, with economical steel, elevators, balloon frame, and machine-made nails all delivered on the nation's railways. Railways, mines, and steelyards brought great fortunes; the power of money was everywhere. This tended to be expressed in large, elaborately decorated and imposing buildings, in interior design, and in the lifestyles of the wealthy.

**ECLECTIC ARCHITECTURE** Longwood (1860), near Natchez, Miss. *[Architect: Samuel Sloan]*

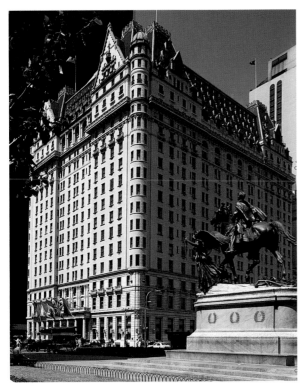

**ECLECTIC ARCHITECTURE** The Plaza Hotel (1907), New York, N.Y. *[Architect: Henry J. Hardenbergh]*

A counter movement was architect versions of vernacular buildings for the wealthy, known as the Shingle style. It was an escapist fashion, suitable for vacation houses, and recalled preindustrial building. The Shingle style was related to the British Queen Anne style. This was the time when new interest in colonial America was first reflected in house designs.

Urban America developed along with heavy industry. It was the period of worker housing, urban parks, and, with the growth of railways, the development of the suburbs with their detached one-family homes. The period after the financial crisis of 1873 to the first world war has been called the "age of energy." Cities vied for the tallest buildings, and the design issues of large buildings received critical attention. The work of Boston architect Henry Hobson Richardson (1838–86) was the first American architect to have an international reputation. His Romanesque-inspired Trinity Church, Boston (1873–77) is perhaps his most famous, but important work of his short career included libraries, churches, houses, city halls, the Allegheny County Courthouse in Pittsburgh (1884–88), office buildings, Sever Hall at Harvard University, Cambridge, Mass. (1878–80), train stations, and the Marshall Field Wholesale Store (1885–87) in Chicago. Charles F. McKim (1847–1909) worked for Richardson, but by the mid-1880s became the leader of the reaction against Richardsonian design.

McKim, with his partners Mead and Stanford White (1853–1906), became the leading firm in New York City. The new work in Chicago following the fire of 1871 has been identified as the beginning of modern architecture and is described in the article of that name.

Perhaps the most original eclectic architect was Frank Furness (1839–1912). He was trained in the office of Richard Morris Hunt and practiced in the Philadelphia area. Other eclectic architects of importance include George Brown Post (1837–1913), Cass Gilbert (1859–1934), and John Russell Pope (1874–1937). These were graduates of the École des Beaux Arts, and their and their fellow graduates' work has at times been called the Beaux Arts style.

For many years after the Modern movement in architecture had begun, the architects who created Eclectic architecture were denigrated, even reviled. Needless to say, eclectic architecture was quite different from the functional architecture that followed. Eclectic work has been severely criticized as being irrelevant, derivative, dishonest, unfitted to its purposes, sentimental, even undemocratic. In many cases, some of these accusations may be true, at least in part. But what has become increasingly evident, as the century nears its end, is the excellence of some of the buildings of the Eclectic era and the proficiency and talent of some of the architects. Fortunately the importance of many of their buildings has been recognized, and the buildings will be protected for future generations. See the article entitled contemporary architecture for comment on post-modern interest in historic prototypes.

**Related Articles** BEAUX ARTS, ÉCOLE DES; CLASSIC REVIVAL ARCHITECTURE; COLONIAL ARCHITECTURE; CONTEMPORARY ARCHITECTURE; GOTHIC REVIVAL ARCHITECTURE; HISTORY OF ARCHITECTURE; PRESERVATION; Various articles on Eclectic architects.

**Further Reading** See listing in the article entitled history of architecture.

**ECOLOGY** The branch of biology that is concerned with the relationships between living things and their environment. While architecture might be said to have always been concerned with the ecological results of what is built, the concern has deepened in the past few decades. Not only are human beings affected by ecological considerations but the rest of nature is also affected when buildings and other structures are constructed.

**Branches** The science of ecology may be divided into two major branches—plant and animal—but some think this unnatural because plants and animals ordinarily live together in an environment. Another division sometimes used is that of terrestrial or land ecology; and marine or sea and ocean ecology. All the branches of ecology deal with such subjects as how living things adapt, anatomically, physiologically, and in other ways, to environmental conditions, such as moisture, light, temperature, winds, solar conditions, and interrelations of various plants and animals.

Ecology is also concerned with what are called successions: series of stages of changes that take place in the kinds of animals and plants that live in a specific environment. As an example, in an area that has lost its plant life as the result of some disaster, such as fire or flooding, the succession that follows may vary but would generally include the stages of first flowers, and then grasses, then trees. The final stage of succession is called a climax which produces a climax community. In a climax community, animal and plant life remain relatively stable and unchanging for very long periods of time, thousands of years. In all the stages, the geographical area in which specific animals and plants live is called their range; and the kinds of places in which they prefer to live within the ranges are called their habitats.

**Life Zones** Environments that exist on land are usually classified as seven types, or life zones, which are different from each other in major ways, and which stretch from the poles to the equator. In the United States, starting from the North Pole, there are six regions: arctic; tundra; taiga, sometimes called boreal, or northern, forest; deciduous forest; prairie, sometimes called grassland, steppe, veldt, or pampas; and desert. The seventh, tropical rainforest, is found south of the United States, in Central and South America.

The arctic zone is an area in which few animals or plants live on the land, though abundant life exists in the seas. The tundra is the area south of the arctic, in which there are no trees, but in which animals and some plants live. The taiga is an area of evergreen trees, called conifers, and of other plant and animal life. The deciduous forest zone is the next most northerly area and contains deciduous trees, sometimes called hardwoods, and other plant and animal life. The prairie zone has a heavy growth of grasses and a variety of animal life. The most southerly zone in the United States is the desert, an area in which the climate is hot and dry and in which cacti and a few small trees grow, along with mostly nocturnal or night-moving animals. The tropical rainforest is an area of hot temperature and heavy rainfall, in which many trees, plants, and animals live.

**Ecological Concerns** Some of the major ecological concerns of architects and other environmental designers are with populations; for example, how many animals, including human beings, or plants can live together without doing harm to each other or to their environment. Ecological population studies are also concerned with the removal or reduction in the numbers of harmful plants and animals, such as rats and mice, insects, and poisonous plants.

Another important ecological consideration of architects and other designers is the study of the interactions between plants and animals, including human beings, and also among animals and among plants. Two or more dissimilar organisms living in a close relationship that benefits each of them is called symbiosis. Many architects and other professionals today believe symbiosis to be one of the most important goals in the design of buildings and other structures.

Finally, architects and other design professionals are greatly concerned today about the conservation of natural things, not only land, air, and water but also the important ones that exist in the multitudinous forms of animal and plant life and the human race.

**Related Articles** ENVIRONMENTAL PROTECTION; LANDSCAPE ARCHITECTURE; PARK; PLANNING, CITY.

**Further Reading** Colvinaux, Paul A.,: *Ecology,* John Wiley, New York, 1986; Knowles, Ralph L.: *Energy and Form—An Ecological Approach to Urban Growth,* MIT Press, Cambridge, Mass., 1974; Naser, Jack L., ed.: *Environmental Aesthetics,* Cambridge University Press, New York, 1988.

**EDUCATION** To practice architecture in the United States, the individual must be licensed in one of the 50 states, the District of Columbia, Puerto Rico, or island possessions (Guam, Northern Mariana Islands, Virgin Islands) of the United States. State laws regulating practice determine education, training, and examination requirements. The combination of education and practical experience has been the historic route to the profession. The purpose of architectural education may be stated as the ability to make appropriate decisions, a trait shared with all professions.

The student's interest in architecture may originate in drawing, photography, or computer graphics, or in building and its relationship to the natural world. Interested students are encouraged to have conversations with an architect and can learn from visiting an architectural office. Reading architectural magazines and architectural articles in newspapers is another way to learn about the profession. A visit to schools and universities offering architectural programs and talks with faculty members and students are desirable. Some architecture schools offer summer programs for high school students. Tests and counseling can help clarify abilities and interest and focus the student on career choices. At the end of this article is a listing of organizations which can provide information about architecture.

**Schools** There are more than 90 architecture programs offered in the United States. These are accredited programs evaluated by the National Architectural Accrediting Board (NAAB). Schools offer several different types of programs, requiring 2 to 4 years after earning another degree, or the more typical 5-year programs leading to Bachelor of Architecture degree. The differences can be described as the contrast between general education and professional education in the 5-year programs, or for the student the conflict between architecture and other interests, often leading to a specialized field for those who enter architectural programs after earning other degrees. There are variations of these programs offered, allowing those working in related fields, such as construction and building, to enter professional schools. Some schools offer work-study programs.

**Curriculum** Professional education courses include design, theory and history, technology, practice, and general education courses. A feature of architectural education is the design studio where students investigate and discuss architectural issues and propose buildings and other projects. The design projects become progressively complex as the student develops critical judgment and the ability to make informed decisions. Each architectural school varies from others in many ways, including faculty, location of the school, urban or rural setting, and how courses combine with landscape architecture, interior design, planning, fine arts, or engineering. The prospective student should consider these differences in deciding where to apply.

**Licensing** The U.S. Constitution reserves to each state and territory the power to protect the health, safety, and welfare of its citizens. State regulations vary but may define architectural practice, the use of the title *architect*, the process for becoming registered, standards for licensure, use of the architect's seal, disciplinary powers and procedures, and penalties. Some states merely regulate the use of the title *architect*, and regulations vary from state to state. A model registration law has been prepared by the National Council of Architectural Registration Boards (NCARB) in an attempt to standardize the requirements for licensing. The registration board in each state carries out the registration law in that state. All boards require satisfaction of an education standard, training standard, and examination standard.

The National Council of Architectural Registration Boards was established to provide a degree of uniformity across the country. The Council develops and recommends standards for practicing architecture and requirements to be met by an applicant for registration, providing a process for certifying to registration boards the qualifications of an architect licensed in another state, and represents the interests of the member state boards before other groups.

**Internship** The internship period normally starts upon graduation from an accredited architectural program and lasts until the intern passes the registration examination. State laws vary on the definition of required practical experience. The most easily acceptable

experience is as an employee in the office of a registered architect. The typical period required for internship is 3 years. A few states allow an extended internship period to substitute for education requirements.

The Intern-Architect Development Program (IDP) was established by the American Institute of Architects (AIA) and the National Council of Architectural Registration Boards (NCARB) to define appropriate experience for admission to licensing. Some states require satisfying the IDP requirements for internship.

**Professional Examination** Upon fulfilling the state's requirements for education and experience, the intern can apply to the state registration board for admission to the examination. The NCARB exam, the Architect Registration Examination (ARE), is used nationwide in all states except California, which has its own examination. The ARE is given annually on the same date nationally in each jurisdiction. The exam lasts four consecutive days, and covers nine areas: predesign; site design; building design; structural technology—general and long span; structural technology—lateral forces; mechanical, plumbing, and electrical systems; materials and methods; and construction documents and services.

The candidate must receive a passing score for each section of the examination. Credit for passing parts of the exam exempt the candidate from taking those parts again, although there may be limits on the time for which credit can be kept. Upon satisfactorily completing the examination, a license is issued by the state. Fees to maintain the license are charged by the states.

Since many architects wish to practice in more than one state, reciprocal arrangements between states have been established. To simplify this process, the architect may apply for NCARB certification, and, if NCARB requirements have been met, a certificate is issued, and upon request, NCARB will transmit to the member board a copy of the qualifications of the architect with a recommendation that the individual be licensed in that state. Additional requirements may be demanded by some states, and, in these cases, the architect must meet these additional requirements to be licensed. Thus the NCARB certificate is not a national license.

**Professional Development** Most professions require continuing education, but architecture has been an exception except in a few states. The changes in practice and developments in technology have increased the need for continuing education, and seminars and courses have been developed by schools of architecture, the American Institute of Architects, and other groups. The AIA is studying the values of mandatory versus voluntary continuing education as a requirement for AIA membership.

**American Development** In the colonial era, there were no architectural schools in America. The earliest

American architects were trained either by participation in the actual construction of buildings or by study of books and travel. Architectural students were then trained as apprentices in the offices of practicing architects. A large number of important American architects were trained in this manner until late in the 19th century. About the middle of the 19th century, architectural students went to Europe to study, particularly in the École des Beaux Arts in Paris. The first American to enter this school, in 1846, was Richard Morris Hunt (1827–95), who became one of the most noted architects of his time. Many other American architects were trained at the Beaux Arts and in the ateliers of architects who had trained there, well into the 20th century. The first American woman graduate of the Beaux Arts was Julia Morgan (1872–1957).

The first architectural school in the United States was founded in 1868 at Massachusetts Institute of Technology, Cambridge, with nine students, by architect William Robert Ware (1832–1915), follower of Hunt and acknowledged as the father of architectural education in this country. Ware also started a tradition in American architecture in which many practicing architects devote part of their time to teaching and many architectural teachers, to practice. Since that time, there has been a distinguished list of architect-teachers. The first woman to graduate from M.I.T. was Sophia Hayden (c. 1868–1953).

Other architectural schools quickly followed, at the University of Illinois, Urbana, and Cornell University, Ithaca, N.Y., both in 1870, and at Syracuse University, Syracuse, N.Y., in 1873. In 1881 Ware established another architectural program at Columbia University, New York City, in, of all places, the School of Mines. All these schools are still in existence; by 1896 nine schools existed in the United States, with a combined total of 273 regular students. Now there are more than 90 accredited architectural programs in many locations in the country, with over 30,000 full-time students.

During the early years, the first architectural schools in the United States were under the influence of the architects who had been educated at the Beaux Arts. Some of these men founded an organization dedicated to these principles, the Society of Beaux Arts Architects in 1894, in New York City. In 1916 the Beaux Arts Institute of Design was founded in New York City, and this organization dominated the teaching of architectural design in schools all over the United States, through the medium of standard design problems which students solved and which were then graded, according to Beaux Arts principles, by juries chosen from the membership of the Institute.

In the late 1930s Walter Adolf Gropius (1883–1969) brought the more modern philosophy of another famous school, the Staatliches Bauhaus, from Germany to Harvard University. One by one, other schools around the country deserted the Beaux Arts system, until soon after World War II, that system had become only a memory. The Beaux Arts organization then changed its name to the National Institute for Architectural Education; its major purpose today is providing grants and scholarships for higher architectural education and travel.

Architectural education has been undergoing considerable change in the recent past, reflecting greater concern with the people who use buildings, the new technology, conservation and preservation, and the sociological aspects of architecture.

Licensing of architects has been required in all the states since 1951. Corporate practice of architecture has been allowed, but all states require that a licensed architect must be in direct control and responsible for the performance of architectural services and that the corporate structure cannot shield the individual from liability.

**Related Articles** BAUHAUS, STAATLICHES; BEAUX ARTS, ÉCOLE DES; CAREER; CONSTRUCTION, BUILDING; ENGINEERING; GROPIUS, WALTER ADOLF; HUNT, RICHARD MORRIS; INTERIOR DESIGN; LANDSCAPE ARCHITECTURE; PLANNING, CITY.

**Further Reading** *Architect's Handbook of Professional Practice*, The American Institute of Architects, Washington, D.C.; *Barron's Profiles of American Colleges*, latest edition, Woodbury, N.Y.

**Periodicals** *ACSA News and Journal of Architectural Education*, 1735 New York Ave., N.W., Washington, D.C. 20006.

**Sources of Additional Information** The American Institute of Architects, Association of Collegiate Schools of Architecture, National Architectural Accrediting Boards, Inc., all at 1735 New York Ave., N.W., Washington, D.C. 20006; National Institute for Architectural Education, 19 W. 22d St., New York, N.Y. 10010.

**EISENMAN, PETER** Peter Eisenman (1932– ) is an architect, educator, and theoretician. He is a chief proponent of the Deconstructivism movement in architecture. He was one of the so-called New York Five, on the basis of a publication of young architects in 1972. His early years were limited to residential design and teaching, and recent years have produced commissions for larger buildings, often in association with others.

**Work** Eisenman's early houses were studies in abstract design and were often clients' second homes. Conceived in the abstract, they have no clear relationship to the sites on which they were built. These studies are identified by Roman numerals, and House X was published as a book in 1982. The closely reasoned design process described in this book has had considerable influence; Eisenman describes the dialogue between abstract geometric form and the preexistent concept of spaces

**EISENMAN, PETER** Wexner Center for the Visual Arts (1989), Ohio State University, Columbus, Ohio.
*[Architects: Eisenman Architects and Richard Trott and Partners]*

which may have multiple functions. He points out that these expected spatial entities are cultural concepts and not universal. This process of a search for a new architecture has led to the term *deconstruction.*

It is in the larger buildings that Eisenman's shift to site-specific buildings can be shown. Also, in his earlier houses, the interiors were equally abstracted, whereas in his public buildings the interiors are by necessity more accommodating to the program needs.

The most famous of his buildings is the Wexner Center for the Visual Arts (1989) at Ohio State University, Columbus, Ohio, with Richard Trott and Partners. An addition to and inserted between two existing auditoriums, the building contains four galleries and a number of smaller exhibition spaces, a film and video theater, performing space, video and audio laboratories, the University libraries for fine arts and communications, a cafe and bookstore, storage, exhibition preparation and administration. The design is derived from a shift in the street grid as it meets the campus and from the Gothic style armory previously demolished.

The space between the two earlier auditoriums becomes an entranceway to the new construction, and is marked by a large elevated white grid structure establishing the shifted grid. The entrance is marked by frag-

ments of brick tower forms recalling the former armory. This new entrance gives access to the entire facility, including the existing auditoriums. The disturbing offset grid and elements of structure where columns fail to meet the ground stimulate the visitor to consider the future direction of the arts. The building has been well received by the University, the students, and the architectural press.

Another building of note is the Koizumi Sangyo Building in Tokyo, Japan, a cooperative design by Peter Eisenman and Kojiro Kitayama of K Architects in Tokyo. K Architects designed a medium-rise office building, and Eisenman designed a series of cubic interruptions to the basic building. These cubes include shifted window walls tilted from the building grid and similarly skewed in plan. The impact of these interruptions creates a different plan on each floor. The client's lighting and furniture products are effectively displayed in these highly colored spaces. The exterior makes a lively landmark in the restless streets of Tokyo.

**Life** Peter Eisenman was born on August 11, 1932, in Newark, N.J. He received his Bachelor of Architecture degree from Cornell University, Ithaca, N.Y., in 1955, and a M.S. Arch. at Columbia University in New York in 1960. He received his M.A. in theory of design in 1962, and a Ph.D. in 1963 from Cambridge University in the United Kingdom. Peter Eisenman is married to Elizabeth Henderson, and they have two children, Nicolas and Julia. In his early years, Peter Eisenman worked for Percival Goodman in New York and the Architects Collaborative in Cambridge, Mass. His teaching included positions at Cambridge University, Princeton University, and Cooper Union in New York. He was architect in residence at the American Academy in Rome in 1976. He was the founder-director of the Institute for Architecture and Urban Studies in New York (1967–82) and was editor of *Oppositions* magazine (1973–82). He has continued to teach, lecture, and write articles on architecture.

Peter Eisenman's current firm is Eisenman & Robertson. Earlier the firm was known as Eisenman Architects. They have frequently associated with other firms for specific projects. In recent years Peter Eisenman has received an increasing number of commissions. His work has been widely exhibited, including the 1991 Venice, Italy, Biennale. His sketches have been sold by art galleries.

**Related Articles** CONTEMPORARY ARCHITECTURE; GRAVES, MICHAEL; MEIER, RICHARD.

**Further Reading** Eisenman, Peter: *House X*, Rizzoli, New York, 1982; Eisenman/Trott: *Wexner Center for the Visual Arts, The Ohio State University*, Rizzoli, New York, 1989.

**ELECTRICAL ENGINEERING** A major branch of engineering that deals with distribution, controls, and use of electricity in buildings. An electrical engineer is a person who has been registered or licensed to perform professional services on work of this type.

Working closely with the architects and coordinating the work with that of the other engineers and consultants, an electrical engineer is primarily responsible for the design of the electrical systems in a building; preparation of the construction documents, drawings, and specifications for their construction; making estimates of construction costs; and inspecting the electrical work to ensure that it is properly constructed.

**Systems** The major systems in the building for which electrical engineers are responsible are electrical service and distribution, lighting, electrical heating and cooling, communications, and electrical generation and transmission. Electrical service and distribution includes the wiring, meters, conduits, controls, switches, and other devices required to bring electrical power into a building and distribute it properly and safely. Lighting includes the design or selection of fixtures and other equipment for proper illumination, exterior and interior, and for lighting for ornamental, safety, and other purposes. Lighting is sometimes designed by specialists, who may or may not be electrical engineers. Electrical

heating and cooling includes self-contained electrical fixtures and equipment for these purposes, and for snow melting and freeze control. Communications includes systems and equipment for telephones, telegraphs, radio and television, public address and paging, alarms, and the like. Electrical generation and transmission includes motor-powered or turbine-powered generators, overhead or underground transmission lines, and related equipment and systems.

In addition, electrical engineers are responsible for special systems, such as lightning protection and emergency light and power. Elevators and other conveying systems, automated systems, and data-processing systems are often handled by electrical engineers, in many cases by specialists in these fields.

Electrical engineering has increased rapidly in importance since the beginning of the 20th century, as electric power became available all over the country. New inventions and the widespread availability of electrical laborsaving devices and equipment have contributed heavily to its importance in architecture. Today most buildings are full of electrical appliances and equipment; many of them were luxuries just a few years ago but are now considered necessities by most people. Electrical work in buildings consumes an ever-larger portion of construction budgets as time passes. Electrical systems in buildings are also among the most important consumers of energy, and electrical engineers have an important function in the provision of efficient means both to use and to conserve energy.

**Work Phases** The professional work of electrical engineers is ordinarily divided into phases that are the same as those for architectural and other engineering work: schematic, design development, construction document, and construction administration. Electrical engineers make studies of the site, utilities, building programs, and important problems during the schematic phases, and produce preliminary drawings, specifications, and cost estimates for the electrical work. The problems are further studied during the design development phase and the drawings, specifications, and estimates are refined. During the construction document phase, drawings and specifications, from which the electrical work will be constructed, are prepared, along with further refined cost estimates. In the construction phase, electrical engineers assist the architects in the administration of the work and inspect it to ensure that it conforms to the construction documents and good practices.

In addition to the major functions of their work, electrical engineers are often required to prepare revised drawings and specifications, to make as-built drawings after a building is complete, and other services. In all their work, electrical engineers work closely with the architects and other engineers and consultants to achieve the purposes of the total building as well as the purposes of the systems for which they are primarily responsible.

The education, registration or licensing, and practice of electrical engineers today parallels that of the other professional engineers; for further discussion, see the article entitled engineering.

**Related Articles** Building Codes and Standards; Building Industry; Communication System; Cost Control; Drafting; Electric Power and Wiring; Energy; Engineering; Lighting; Lightning Protection; Specification; Working Drawing.

**Further Reading** See the article entitled engineering.

**Periodicals** *Actual Specifying Engineer,* 5 S. Wabash Ave., Chicago, Ill. 60603; *Electrical Consultant,* 1760 Peachtree Rd., N.W., Atlanta, Ga. 30309; *IEEE Spectrum,* 245 E. 47th St., New York, N.Y. 10017.

**Sources of Additional Information** Illuminating Engineering Society, 345 E. 47th St., New York, N.Y. 10017; Institute of Electrical and Electronic Engineers, 345 E. 47th St., New York, N.Y. 10017; see also list in the article entitled engineering.

**ELECTRIC POWER AND WIRING** The systems that provide and distribute an important source of energy, electricity, in buildings. Electrical energy is such an integral part of architecture today, and of the lives of the people who occupy or use buildings, that it seems unbelievable that electricity was completely unavailable for such uses until about 100 years ago. Electricity is the energy that powers almost all of the great number of kitchen appliances in buildings, including ranges, ovens, dishwashers, garbage grinders, trash compactors, knife sharpeners, can openers, hot plates, and mixers. Electricity also powers laundry washers, irons, dryers, and other appliances. Electric power is used for pumping water and for television sets, radios, electric blankets, vacuum cleaners, and a great array of other items. For extremely important uses of electricity, see articles entitled communication system; fire protection; heating, ventilating, and air conditioning; lighting; security systems; vertical transportation. For a discussion of electric signs, see the article entitled graphic design.

**Composition of Matter** Although various theories of the characteristics of matter have been held at various times in the past, scientists today generally agree that all matter is composed principally of electrical particles. These particles, called protons (positively charged), electrons (negatively charged), and neutrons (no charge), in various combinations make up the atoms of elements. Hydrogen atoms are the simplest, ordinarily having one electron and a nucleus of one proton. This is the ordinary or neutral (uncharged) state of an atom, when the number of protons in the nucleus and the total number

**ELECTRIC POWER AND WIRING** High-tension lines.

of electrons are equal. Elements, other than hydrogen, have nuclei of more than one proton, along with neutrons and sometimes electrons. These elements also have varying numbers of free electrons. When it loses free electrons, an atom becomes positively charged. When it gains free electrons, it becomes negatively charged. Such charged atoms are called ions, and it is the property of losing or gaining electrons that causes electric currents to flow in materials.

Some elements, such as metals, have greater numbers of free electrons than others, and therefore are better passages, or conductors, for electric currents. In metals, the electrons flow from atom to atom, the positive charges being attracted to the negative and vice versa. In liquids and certain gases, ions flow in a similar manner. Although it is common to consider electricity as flowing from positive to negative in construction and other industries, it is now believed that electrons actually flow from negative to positive.

**Electrical Current** Electrical energy flows through good conductors very rapidly, at almost the speed of light, 186,282 mi/s (299,792 km/s). This produces an electrical current which powers all the appliances and

187

other electrical equipment. Electrical current is measured by the amounts of electrons that pass a given point in a given period of time. Sometimes referred to as the intensity or rate of flow, the amount of current is measured in amperes (A). The pressure or potential of electricity that causes it to flow, is measured in volts (V). The resistance of the material, through which the current flows, to the flow is measured in ohms ($\Omega$). These three variables were named for physicists who worked with electricity: André Marie Ampère (1775–1836) of France, Count Alessandro Volta (1745–1827) of Italy, and Georg Simon Ohm (1787–1854) of Germany.

Ohm discovered the basic relationship between the three characteristics of electricity and expressed it in what is now called Ohm's law: the current in amperes is equal to the potential in volts divided by the resistance in ohms. The power of electrical current is measured in watts (W) and is equal to volts times amperes. The watt was named for the Scottish mechanical engineer James Watt (1736–1819), who invented many machines utilizing power, particularly steam. Delivered electrical energy is measured in terms of power in a certain unit of time, such as watt-hours (W•h), or more commonly 1,000 watt-hours, or kilowatt-hours (kW•h). In the International system, the SI units are the joule (J) and 1 million ($10^6$) joules, called a megajoule (MJ). One kW•h equals 3.6 MJ.

**Production** Electricity may be obtained in several different ways. One is a battery which utilizes the action of chemicals on metals to produce electric current. Thermocouples, consisting of two dissimilar metals attached together, produce electricity when heated. Photoelectric cells, sometimes called electric eyes, produce electricity from rays of light. Solar cells produce electricity by use of the rays of the sun. All these devices have uses in architecture and are discussed elsewhere in this book. The major source of electric current for most of the applications in architecture is huge generators powered by steam, waterpower, or other means. See the article entitled energy.

The electric energy produced by generators is transmitted from the places where it is produced to various areas of the country and finally to the sites of buildings. The electric currents produced are either direct current (dc), which flows at a fixed time rate in one direction in a circuit, or alternating current (ac), which has a varied time rate and flows alternately in two directions in a circuit. In ac, one time interval of flow in one direction plus one in the other is called a cycle. One cycle per second is called a hertz (Hz). Ordinarily, ac systems today operate at 60 Hz, or 60 cycles per second. The generators for ac are often referred to as alternators, and when dc is changed to ac, the device for this accomplishment is called a rectifier.

Ac and dc electricity are both used in architecture, the ac for most purposes and dc for such purposes as powering elevators, telephone equipment, certain controls and other devices, and for standby or emergency electrical systems. Although electricity usually is generated and transmitted at very high voltages, transformers are used to reduce the voltage for use in buildings, most of which are supplied with 120/208 V or 120/240 V systems. In such cases, the 120-V current is available for purposes such as lighting, and the 208 or 240 V for large motors, cooking ranges, water heaters, and other machinery.

**Electric Service** The electric current enters buildings through an electric service, which may be overhead, wires strung between poles, or underground, cables or wires, often in pipe or other containers. Because of the unsightly appearance of overhead systems, many architects and other environmental designers often specify underground systems. In some locations, underground systems are required by building or other codes. However, underground systems are much more expensive than overhead ones and much harder to maintain and repair. Ordinarily the utility companies furnish the service facilities up to the meter loops of buildings. However, in some building developments, underground services are constructed with a special system, called underground residential (UR) distribution, which uses direct burial high-voltage cables. Such systems require small transformers that may be installed indoors or outside. Often developers share the costs of such systems with the utility companies.

Where electric services enter buildings, meter loops with utility company meters are installed, usually one in a single-family house or other small building, but more than one in larger, more complex building types. The meters register the amount of electricity that passes through them into the buildings in kW•h. From these measurements, checked periodically by meter readers, the utilities bill for the electricity consumed. Electric utility rates, governed by various laws and regulations, are quite complex. The basic charge is a certain number of cents per kW•h, often with lower rates for commercial, industrial, and other large consumers, and sometimes sliding scale rates for quantities above certain levels. Many variations in these rates may occur, including those based on the relative costs of fuels used to generate the electricity; relative demands for power, such as the increased demand in summer because of air conditioning; and time of use, with higher rates during peak demands during days and lower rates during low-demand hours at night. The only method by which architects and other environmental designers may project the costs of electricity in their building designs is by calculation of amounts of electricity that will be required, or electrical loads, combined with a complete analysis of the various rates of the utilities that will supply the power.

**Equipment** From meters, electric current passes through various pieces of equipment, called switchboards or panelboards. Each is equipped with a service switch that disconnects all electric service into a building, except that required for emergencies. For small, relatively simple types of buildings, panelboards are ordinarily used. They are small boxes with the service switch and arrangements for the incoming service to be directed into various individual circuits of the building. While fuses have often been used in panelboards in the past, more prevalent today is the use of circuit breakers. These devices, unlike fuses which protect electrical circuits with metal parts that melt under high loads, are tripped by heat or magnetic forces. Since circuit breakers may be reset after tripping, they need no separate switches. Panelboards may be surface-mounted on walls or recessed into walls so that their faces are flush with the planes of the walls. In addition to the main panelboards at the electrical service entrance of buildings, auxiliary panelboards may be located within buildings for such purposes as the protection of groups of motors or other devices.

Switchboards are used for relatively large and complex buildings for purposes similar to those of panelboards. Usually freestanding and often quite large, switchboards contain fuses, switches, circuit breakers, and so on for the control and protection of large electrical systems with numerous circuits. A unit substation, sometimes called a transformer load center, is another relatively large assembly, installed indoors or outside, which not only contains equipment as in a switchboard but also meters, controls, transformers, and other electrical devices required in large and complicated buildings.

From panelboards, switchboards, or unit substations, electric power is directed into distribution systems that carry it to various parts of buildings and ultimately to appliances, lights, motors, and other devices. This is accomplished with electrical conductors, usually made of copper or aluminum. Large conductors (usually rectangular in section and insulated), called busways, are used for heavy power loads. For smaller loads, insulated wire or cable is used. The sizes of busways in gauges of wire in cables for carrying loads of various amounts are specified in electrical, building, and other codes. Cables that are ordinarily used include a type armored with flexible steel covering, called BX; and NM or NMC cable sheathed with plastic or rubber coverings, called Romex. Neither may be embedded in concrete or similar materials. High-voltage cables are available, as are other special types. Codes also govern their uses.

**Raceways** Electric cables are often installed in buildings in raceways, devices for the containment and pro-

tection of electrical wiring. Raceways of many types and sizes can be obtained, including conduits, which may be rigid or flexible steel types; thin-wall (EMT) steel types, plain or coated with plastic; and aluminum, plastic, and fiber types. Larger raceways may be obtained in square or rectangular surface-mounted metal types and floor raceways. The latter includes metal types that may be installed in floor structures, with their top surfaces flush with the finished floor surfaces. Also available are cellular metal and precast concrete types that serve not only as raceways but as the structural systems of floors in buildings. Raceways are also provided in integrated floors and ceilings, along with the structure; lighting, heating, and air-conditioning distribution systems; and telephone systems. The other types of raceways may also be used for telephone and other communication and sound installations.

**Other Devices** In addition to the cables, busways, and raceways required in electrical systems in buildings, a great variety of fittings and other devices are used. There are various kinds of connectors, including types that are clamped, screwed, bolted, or otherwise affixed to connect electrical conductors. Soldering is still used for large cables, and welding is used sometimes. Various types of conduit and raceway connectors are used, including outlet and junction boxes. Many electrical appliances and devices, such as light fixtures, are wired directly but for many others, receptacles of various types are used. The most common is the duplex, which accommodates two caps, or plugs, from the usual types of movable fixtures, such as table or floor lamps. A duplex outlet has two parallel slots for each plug, along with a third hole for the ground. A triplex outlet takes three appliance plugs. Special outlets of various kinds include locking types, waterproof types with covers, safety types, and clock outlets.

In addition, various types of switches and other devices are used. Switches have ampere ratings and sometimes also horsepower ratings. The proper types must be used for given purposes. Many switches close or open circuits by simple metallic contacts. Others use electromagnets, the small ones called relays, to operate the switches; throwing the handle activates the relay by means of low-voltage current, and the relay opens or closes the switch. Such switches may be used in low-voltage wiring systems, which are much more flexible than regular types. For example, with such a system, one light fixture may be turned off and on from a number of locations by means of small-gauge wiring carrying low-voltage, usually 12 or 24 V dc, current to activate the single relay required. If more than two such switches were required for a fixture in the usual system, the wiring would not only carry the regular voltage current but would be extraordinarily complex. To finish outlets and switches, wall plates are generally used. A single-gang plate is used for a single outlet or switch; a double-gang plate, for one with two switches or outlets; and so on. Plates come in metals or plastics and various finishes.

**Design Requisites** The design of electrical power and wiring systems for buildings can be quite complex. The main principles are to provide complete systems that will be adequate for the needs of building occupants, designed for expansion for future needs and with flexibility for changing needs. Systems must be safe and reliable, yet economically feasible. They must provide for the necessary uses in building, such as lighting; heating and air conditioning; vertical transportation; kitchen equipment; communication; plumbing equipment; sound and warning system; fire, security, and other hazards; motors; and other uses of electricity, some quite special in certain building types. In addition, special provisions must be made in many buildings types, such as hospitals, and for certain building functions, such as elevators, emergency lighting, and so on, and also in many other types, for standby or emergency power systems. Emergency equipment often consists of standby generators or battery systems.

The various steps in the design of electric power and wiring systems vary somewhat for buildings of different types, complexities, and sizes. However, general steps include determination of an estimate of the expected electrical power loads for lighting, equipment, and so on; power requirements in various locations in the building; requirements of the utility for service and related factors; and determination of the required electrical equipment, including switchboards, panelboards, and other items and their locations in the building. Based on such data, the design of the electrical system may proceed, including lighting circuit layouts; circuits required for other purposes; special layouts for communications, sound, warning, and other systems; electrical appliances and equipment, together with raceways, conduits, fittings, and other devices required.

In addition to spaces for panelboards or switchboards, unit substations, and transformers, space must be provided for special equipment and controls in what are called electric closets, located in convenient positions in the building. All must be protected with proper circuit breakers or other devices. The major circuits up to circuit breakers or other protective devices are called feeder circuits. From that point on, circuits are called branch circuit. Spare circuits must be provided for future uses. And the entire electrical system must be properly grounded. In addition, some systems are so complex that computers are used to control them.

Because of the great importance of electricity in the buildings of today and the relatively high expense of systems installations and operation, which consume a large portion of every building construction and operation dollar, the need for conservation of energy and other reasons, the proper design of electrical systems is all-important. Their design is usually performed by electrical engineers, some of whom specialize in building design rather than in more esoteric fields of electronics. Working closely with architects, engineers, and other environmental designers, electrical engineers can provide efficient, functional, safe systems in the buildings of today.

**History** The time that humans first learned about electricity has not been established. It is known that the Greek philosopher and scientist Thales (c.640–546 B.C) discovered that rubbing a piece of amber with a cloth produced static electricity. Not much progress was made with electricity for more than 2,000 years, until about the 16th century, when the English physician and physicist William Gilbert (1540–1603) experimented with static electricity and magnetism. Many scientists experimented with electricity and made important discoveries after.

The discovery in 1831 of the principle of generation of electricity with magnets and coils of wire was made independently by an English scientist, Michael Faraday (1791–1867), and an American scientist, Joseph Henry (1797–1898). This was the fundamental discovery that eventually led to the widespread use of electricity today. Generators were developed soon afterward and by 1882, a generating station was supplying power to private consumers in London. In the same year, the first generating plant in the United States was built in New York City by American inventor Thomas Alva Edison (1847–1931), who had invented in 1879 a practical incandescent light bulb. For some years previously, electric arc lights had been in use in limited installations, such as in lighthouses and for street lighting.

The early generating plants all produced direct current. In 1886 American inventor and industrialist George Westinghouse (1846–1914) built the first alternating current generating plant. Since that time, thousands of generating plants have been built in the United States, and electricity has become the most important type of energy used in architecture for such purposes as lighting and others. Today some 2,000 generating plants are operating in the United States, utilizing mostly steam, gas, or water turbines, called hydroelectric, sources for electrical production. Since the first atomic plant was established in 1951, others have been built in many places in the United States, but they produce only a small portion of the total output.

Most of the electricity produced in the United States comes from privately owned plants, but the federal government owns and operates a large system, including the Grand Coulee plant in the state of Washington and the sprawling system of the Tennessee Valley Authority (TVA), which was built beginning in the

1930s along the Tennessee River and tributaries in portions of Tennessee, Alabama, Georgia, Kentucky, and Virginia.

Over the years, many developments in the use of electricity in architecture have taken place. Electric lighting got off to a slow start in the late 19th century and little progress was made until the 20th, when a spectacular increase in electric lighting and in the use of electricity for other purposes took place. Today electric lighting is utilized all over the United States, with very few exceptions in extremely remote locations. Great improvements have been made in light bulbs and in lighting fixtures, and newer types such as fluorescent, sodium-vapor, and mercury-vapor lights have been developed.

Electric appliances are widely used in architecture today. Electric elevators are commonly used in buildings of more than a few stories, and escalators are used in others. Electric heating has become important, and electricity is the main type of energy used for air conditioning. New appliances and other applications of electricity are developed each year, and the end seems nowhere in sight.

In the 1960s electric use in the United States was projected to increase annually, but electric use has tended to remain fairly constant in recent years thanks to better understanding of efficiency in the design of electric systems. Computerized management of buildings may be used to control unnecessary use of electric power. Timers may be used to operate electric equipment during nonpeak hours of electric use. Daylight analysis may reduce the need for electric lighting, the greater use of ambient and task lighting, and general reduction of wasteful lighting levels helps to control electric use. The inclusion of better thermal insulation and the recapture of the heat generated from electric lighting and more efficient electric fixtures, lamps, and appliances have all contributed to the efficiency of electrical systems.

**Related Articles** COMMUNICATION SYSTEM; COMPUTER; ELECTRICAL ENGINEERING; ENERGY; FIRE PROTECTION; SECURITY SYSTEMS; VERTICAL TRANSPORTATION.

**Sources of Additional Information** Institute of Electrical and Electronic Engineers (IEEE), 345 E. 47th St., New York, N.Y. 10017; National Fire Protection Assoc. (NFPA), 1 Batterymarch Park, P.O. Box 9101, Quincy, Mass. 02269-9101.

**ENERGY** The rate of power used; may be expressed as energy (or work) equals power multiplied by time. This article describes the sources of power and the energy needs of buildings.

**Fossil Fuels** The principal source of energy for buildings is fossil fuels. Fuels may be coal, oil, or gas. Historically, wood has been used as a fuel, and newer sources include trash and coal-water mixtures.

Heat energy is supplied through combustion of hydrocarbon fuels. The utilization of these fossil fuels requires a combustion chamber into which a fuel-air mixture is introduced. When the mixture is ignited, oxidation of the carbon content releases heat. To improve efficiency, flue gases may be used to heat air or water, including steam.

Fossil fuels are also widely used in the production of electric power, although other energy sources may be used to operate the engines or turbines required to operate the alternators used to produce alternating power (ac). Direct current is supplied by batteries or by converting alternating current to direct current. The cost of electric power is a major expense in the operation of buildings and includes the 3 percent distribution loss experienced to bring electric power to the building. Analysis shows that production of electricity is inefficient, with the waste of 45 percent of the fuel consumed. The efficiency of electric resistance heating may be only 27 percent of the fossil fuels consumed, although more efficient furnaces are now available, reducing the inefficiency to that experienced in the electric power plant.

Building mechanical systems typically use fossil fuels or electricity. Traditionally, heat energy has been supplied by the combustion of hydrocarbon fuels, coal, oil, and gas. Combustion requires adequate air to release heat. Electricity is used for operating motors, control devices, and transportation systems. Resistance heating and almost all refrigeration devices rely on electricity.

**Geothermal Energy** Geothermal sources have been utilized as an energy source for the production of electricity, hot water, or direct heating of buildings. The water from hot springs may be highly corrosive, and the source must be near the point of use. Beginning in 1904 in Italy, geothermal generation for electricity has increased steadily in many parts of the world. Geothermal resources may be categorized into four types: hydrothermal (water or steam), geopressured (water pressurized by overlying sedimentary rock), hot dry rock, and magma (molten rock). These sources produce a small portion of the electricity in the United States.

**Nuclear Power** Use of molecular fusion has become an important new source for electricity, although safety has been an issue. The failure of the Chernobyl plant near Kiev in the Ukraine in April 1986 was the most serious accident to date, spreading radiation over a large area. The worst commercial accident was at Three Mile Island, Middletown, Pa., in March 1979.

The United States and France are the largest producers of nuclear energy. There are 110 operating nuclear plants in the United States, producing 21 percent of the nation's electric power. Because of public concerns for safety, no plant has been ordered since 1978, except for

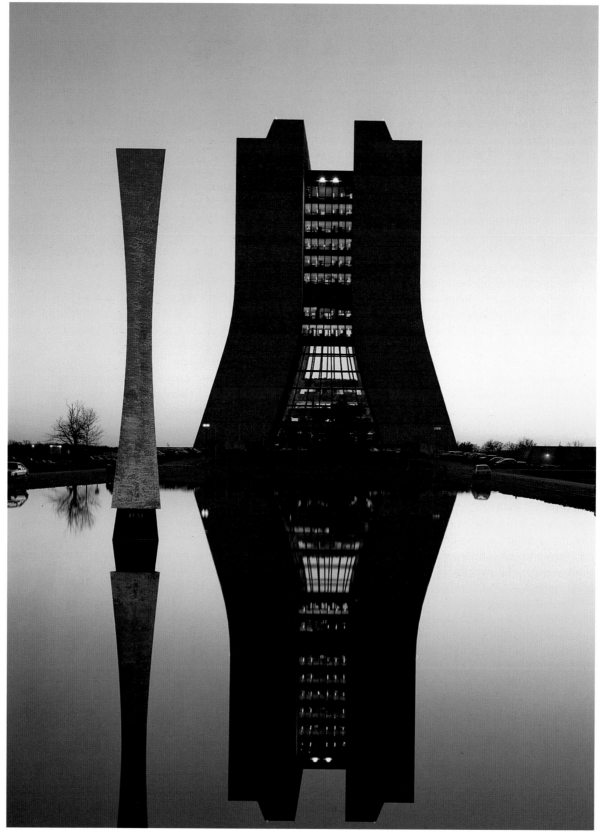

**ENERGY** Enrico Fermi Nuclear Power Plant (1979) in Illinois. *[Architects/Engineers: Daniel, Mann, Johnson, & Mendenhall (Photo: Timothy Hursley/Korab, Ltd.)]*

those being constructed by the Tennessee Valley Authority. As a federal agency, the TVA is exempt from state regulation. Smaller, safer, and less costly nuclear plants are under development.

**Solar Energy** Solar energy has been of continued interest for lighting and heating systems, although in many locations back-up systems are needed to maintain comfort. In areas with long periods of cloud cover, solar energy may be inefficient compared to areas of clearer skies such as the southwestern United States. For residential use, solar energy is a viable consideration for heating hot water and providing at least some of the heat. Solar cells have been developed for producing electricity, particularly valuable in remote locations. Building design utilizing daylighting has been used to reduce electrical loads in many building types. This reduction results in further potential savings in power needed for heating and air conditioning.

**Wind Power** Alternative sources of power include wind energy systems. The old windmills of historic periods have given way to technically advanced wind energy systems which have the potential of producing increasing percentages of needed electrical power. Historically, wind has been used for sailing ships since ancient times. Although fossil fuels have largely replaced wind, future shortages will support the use of this widely available source of power.

**Water Power** Historically important for industrial plants placed along rivers, water-powered turbines are used in producing electric power in conjunction with dams. Another use of water in production of electricity is the cooling of nuclear plants where large volumes of water are raised in temperature before being returned to streams.

**Other Energy Sources** Heat pumps are used to take advantage of the differential temperatures between air, water, or ground and the desired temperature in the interior of the building. The most common systems use air-to-air operation, although in favorable locations, water systems can be used for heating or cooling.

A potential source of energy is tidal action, although this may cause ecological damage at estuaries. Tidal systems typically involve the construction of a dam in a bay where naturally high tides occur. The systems can be designed to operate while the tide is rising or dropping, or both. The largest such facility is on the Rance River in France, although smaller tidal power systems operate elsewhere, including the United States. Other potential concepts include obtaining heat from sea water taking advantage of temperature differential between surface and deep water. Wave energy systems have been investigated but are hampered by variations in wave action and the inability of equipment to withstand the destructive forces of storms.

**Future Trends** Projections of fuel supplies suggest that oil and gas will become depleted, although U.S. coal supplies will be available well through the next century. Future growth in the use of nuclear power, solar power, wind, and biomass (wood and waste) may be anticipated. There will be a reduction in the use of fossil fuels from the 1989 figure of 85.9 percent of total energy supplied to something less than 50 percent during the next few decades. With increased energy efficiency, the total energy sources consumed is expected to experience little or no growth in contrast to the earlier projections of unlimited growth.

**Uses of Energy** In the years following World War II, energy was inexpensive, and developing technology allowed occupancy of spaces sealed off from the natural world. The recommended levels of heating and lighting for buildings increased dramatically. The energy shortages of the 1970s brought a realization that fuel sources are finite and that in the interest of conserving energy many assumptions of the designer would need modification. As the years passed, the concept of energy-efficient building resulted in extensive research and applications in building design. Energy use in new buildings is now regulated by law. Refer to the article entitled building codes and standards. The subject is complex because many factors must be considered, several of which are briefly described here. Earlier assumptions regarding energy use proved unreliable after careful analysis. Now a number of computer software programs can analyze the energy use in design and in actual operations of a building. The typical building will consume more energy in operation than was used in its construction.

A worldwide concern is the degradation of the earth's atmosphere. The use of energy by automobiles, industrial plants, as well as buildings are major air polluters. The resulting acid rain has degraded the forests and water supplies of the earth, and the release of pollutants has contributed to the greenhouse effect which has long-range implications for world climate.

Water is essential to life, and water pollution has increased. Treatment of raw sewage and other waste is needed to preserve water quality as populations grow. The run-off from fertilized lawns and fields adds to water pollution. In many areas food supplies from the rivers, lakes, and oceans has been affected. The continuing destruction of tropical rain forests results in climatic changes which may be detrimental to human life.

The use of finite fuel supplies brings into question future sources of energy. By-products of petroleum may be more valuable than its use as fuel. There has been increased interest in taking advantage of renewable energy sources, such as solar energy, wind and water.

All building materials come from the earth. Without regard to transportation, it is possible to rank materials as to their energy costs. Additional transportation and handling costs can be added depending on the location of the building site being considered. Such items as stone, clay, and the use of adobe and rammed earth are the least energy-intensive building materials. Wood and gypsum are the next level of products requiring lesser amounts of energy, and the metals are the most energy-intensive to produce. Aluminum in particular requires large amounts of energy to refine.

Building use requires light and power. The effective use of daylighting may reduce the need for lighting, although solar gain and heat loss are factors needing analysis. Power to operate buildings may be reduced by using energy-efficient equipment and taking into account solar energy, or using air, soil, and water as sources of heat or cooling. Electric generation using wind or water systems may be used where the geography and climate allow. The use of natural ventilation can reduce the demand for cooling. Waste products may be another source of energy.

Transportation is a greater user of energy than buildings. In particular, the automobile is an extravagant user of fossil fuels. Public transportation is more efficient, and in some places bicycles are efficient means of transportation. Thus the location of a building in relation to transportation is a factor in total energy consumed.

Conserving energy is a complex subject in building design. The designer must now consider how to conserve energy, to take advantage of natural lighting and solar heating in response to varying climatic conditions, to select products which require less energy to produce as well as to be maintained. Frequently, adaptive use of older buildings may be more energy efficient than replacing the building with new construction. The preservation of older buildings in the United States has been encouraged by tax policy, and there is a wide public interest in historic preservation. New buildings can be designed to adapt to the changing needs of the user. One admired example of a user-friendly building is the Centraal Bebeer, Apeldoorn, in the Netherlands, an office building where the occupants are encouraged to modify their own spaces.

The use of gardens, parks, and natural areas left undisturbed is another contemporary trend. Atrium buildings can be designed to be energy-efficient as well as provide pleasant interior spaces. One of the more interesting approaches to energy-efficient design is a series of underground or earth-sheltered buildings. In some of the buildings the entire site remains useful for other purposes. The use of roof gardens can increase the amount of planting in an urban area while giving pleasure to the occupants.

Study of the lifestyle in extreme climates can give clues to energy efficiency. The use of tents by nomadic peoples shows how to respond to climate with minimal materials or effect on the fragile, temporary site. Caves have been adapted for housing, and the Chinese were among the first to build underground houses. The use of materials found on the site have produced some interesting houses, and another ancient approach is to minimize ground contact and improve air movement by raising buildings on posts above the natural terrain. In fact, until the invention of electricity, architects were concerned with designing buildings responsive to their sites and with achieving comfort with minimal use of energy. The ability to illuminate interior spaces led to a conceptual as well as physical separation of the building from its climatic environment.

The design of what is called "green" architecture can be most easily obtained with relatively small buildings on open sites. However, urban building has an inherent advantage in reducing transportation costs. The implications for zoning and regional land use planning are extensive, but controls have not been well received by the public in many urban areas. Even in large buildings, attention to the considerations listed in this article is resulting in buildings more responsive to their locations and more enjoyable to their inhabitants.

**Related Articles** ADAPTIVE USE; ELECTRIC POWER AND WIRING; HEATING, VENTILATING, AND AIR CONDITIONING; LIGHTING; PRESERVATION; UNDERGROUND BUILDING.

**Further Reading** McHarg, Ian L.: *Designing with Nature*, 1969, reprinted by John Wiley and Sons, New York, 1991; Szokolay, S. V.: *Solar Energy and Building*, Halsted Press, New York, 1977; Szokolay, S. V.: *Climatic Data and Its Use in Design*, Specialized Book Services, Portland, Ore., 1988; Vale, Brenda: *Green Architecture: Design for an Energy-Conscious Future*, A Bulfinch Press Book, Litte, Brown and Company, Boston, 1991; American Society of Heating Refrigeration and Air Conditioning Engineers and the Illuminating Engineers Society joint publication: ASHRAE/IES 90.1-1989.

**Sources of Additional Information** Association of Energy Engineers, 4025 Pleasantville Rd., Suite 420, Atlanta, Ga. 30340; U.S. Department of Energy, 1000 Independence Ave., S.W., Washington, D.C. 20585; American Solar Energy Society, 2400 Central Ave., B-1, Boulder, Colo. 80301 (affiliate of the International Solar Energy Society, National Science Foundation, P.O. Box 52, Parkville, VIC 3052, Australia).

**ENGINEERING** The profession that deals with the science involved in the design, construction, and operation of buildings and other structures, machines, systems, and devices used by humans. An engineer is an individual who is licensed or registered to practice the profession of engineering. Since others, such as boiler operators and locomotive drivers, are sometimes called engineers, those licensed or registered to practice professional engineering are usually called professional engineers.

**Branches** Today the major branches of engineering are civil, chemical, electrical, mechanical, mining, and metallurgical. Civil engineering is concerned with the design, planning, and construction of structures, including buildings, dams, docks, railroads, tunnels, highways, canals, bridges, and water and sewage systems. Civil engineering therefore has a number of specialty fields, including structural, highway, transportation, sanitary, hydraulic, and city planning. Chemical engineering is concerned with the design, construction, and operation of industrial plants in which raw material are changed into other products by chemical processes. Electrical engineering is concerned with the design, construction, and operation of structures, devices, and systems for the production, transmission, distribution, control, and uses of electricity. Specialty fields within electrical engineering include electronics and illuminating engineering. Mechanical engineering is concerned with the design, construction, and operation of engines and other machines and mechanical systems. Specialties include aeronautical or aerospace, automotive, and heating and air conditioning. Mining and metallurgical engineering are concerned with the discovery, removal from the ground, and processing of minerals. Petroleum engineering is a special branch that deals with oil and natural gas. Other types of engineering include agricultural, nuclear, and textile.

Many of the engineering specialists participate, to some extent, in the design and construction of buildings, including civil engineers who specialize in soils and foundations or in sanitary engineering, the specialty that deals with water and sewage systems. However, the major types of engineering involved in the design and construction of buildings are structural (a branch of civil), electrical, and mechanical engineering. Sometimes these specialties, taken together, are called architectural engineering when applied to building design. Structural engineers design the structures of buildings. Electrical engineers design the electrical, and often the lighting, systems. Mechanical engineers design the heating, ventilating, and air conditioning; plumbing; and other mechanical systems.

Engineers may work in special fields, such as research, development of devices or products based on research, testing, construction of buildings and other structures, sales or service functions, teaching, production functions, or in the operation of machinery, factories, or specialized devices.

**Firms** The most important function in architecture is the engineering design and planning of buildings and other structures. Design or planning engineers often have their own firms and perform engineering services for buildings for several architects. In such cases, they are often referred to as consulting engineers. Some engineers work for consulting firms. In other cases, engineers are employees of architectural firms and perform services only for those firms. Engineers may also be partners or stockholders in architectural firms. In these cases, the firms may be called simply architects, but are often called architects and engineers, referred to as A-E firms. Sometimes, if engineering comprises a relatively large part of a firm's work as compared to its architecture, the firm is called an E-A firm, or engineers and architects.

In all cases, the engineers work closely with the architects in the design of buildings, each specialist group designing the parts of the building and the systems for which it is primarily responsible and each coordinating this specialized work with that of the architects and other engineers to produce the proper results in the totality of the building.

Engineering offers a great diversity in the kinds of work performed. Some engineers work indoors primarily, others outdoors, or in some combination. Some engineers perform research and studies in a quiet, introspective manner; others spend their time in more active pursuits, such as inspection of the construction of high-rise buildings. Some work in cities, others in rural areas, still others in foreign countries around the globe. Accordingly, the opportunities for careers in engineering are numerous and diverse. For people who are naturally curious, imaginative, industrious, and responsible, engineering careers offer a great deal of satisfaction.

**Education** To prepare for careers in engineering, young students should demonstrate aptitudes and interest in mathematics and the sciences. In addition to the usual college-preparatory secondary school courses, students should prepare for engineering school with four years of mathematics and science if possible. In college, engineering students ordinarily take courses in humanities, social sciences, mathematics, sciences, and basic engineering. These are followed by courses concentrated in the areas of choice, such as mechanical, supplemented by fundamental courses in the major fields. Upon successful completion of four or five years, students are awarded bachelor's degrees. Some students earn master's degrees, usually requiring an additional year or more, and a few earn doctor's degrees, requiring two or more years past the master's level.

People interested in an engineering career have a wide choice of educational institutions. There are more than 150 accredited engineering schools offering bachelor's degrees in the United States. In addition, there are many colleges and institutions that offer the first two years of education in preengineering courses. The schools of engineering are located in universities all over the country and preengineering courses are offered in many junior, community, and other types of colleges in many localities.

For people who would like to do engineering work without becoming professional engineers, many technical school and institutions offer courses for engineering technicians. Engineering technicians assist professional engineers in their work, often performing such functions as drafting, specification writing, and field supervision.

**Registration** To call themselves professional engineers and to practice professional engineering, graduates must be licensed or registered, thus establishing their competence to perform engineering that will safeguard the health, safety, and welfare of the public. To accomplish this, they must meet the requirements of the registration or licensing board of one of the states or territories. Upon successful completion of the requirements, they are granted licenses or registrations allowing them to call themselves professional engineers (P.E.'s) and to practice engineering. The general requirements of all the states and territories are good character, U.S. citizenship or a declaration to become a citizen, a minimum age (usually twenty-five), and a high school diploma.

In addition, candidates for registration or licensing as professional engineers must have had a minimum combination of engineering education and experience acceptable to the board. The usual combination is graduation from an accredited engineering school and four years of experience that is acceptable toward the development of professional judgment, capacity, and competence to practice. Various other combinations of education and experience may be accepted by boards, such as eight years of experience with no college. Laws vary between the states and territories. For example, some allow older, experienced candidates to become registered or licensed without written examinations.

The practice of an engineer is often not confined to one state. In general, the states and territories allow engineers registered in other states to practice in their jurisdictions temporarily, for periods of 30 days or more. An engineer may also obtain reciprocal registration or licensing in other states by endorsement, a process that waives another examination, but may require an interview or other action. The National Bureau of Engineering Registration issues Certificates of Qualification to engineers, attesting to their prior registration or licensing and other qualifications. These are usually accepted for reciprocal registration or licensing by states and territories.

The written examinations required for registration or licensing of professional engineers are generally divided into two parts, the first on fundamentals and engineering sciences, lasting eight hours or more; and the second on professional engineering subjects in the candidate's specialty and related specialties. The first-day examination covers such subjects as mathematics, sciences, economics, professional ethics, and contract law. The second-day examination covers all the specific areas of specialty, such as civil engineering for civil candidates, and certain areas of related specialties, such as mechanical and electrical engineering. The examination for mechanical engineers includes, in addition to mechanical subjects, certain areas of civil, electrical, and metallurgical engineering. The electrical examination, in addition to electrical subjects, includes civil and mechanical engineering.

The two parts of the written examination may be taken at different times. The first fundamental part may be taken immediately after graduation, under a program called Engineers in Training, when most people are best prepared for the examination, or it may be taken later. The second part must be taken after completion of the required years of practical experience.

**History** The history of engineering goes back to prehistoric times when humans first made tools, tents, and other devices. For many centuries, engineering was performed by people who were not specialists in the field. Architecture and engineering were parts of the work of the person whom the Mesopotamians called *batu*, the builder, and the Egyptians called the master builder. Many of the great works of these earlier cultures, often referred to as architecture, such as the pyramids, aqueducts, and other structures, were as much engineering as architecture, or more. In ancient Greece the master builder became known as the *architekton*, arch technician or builder. In Rome the master builder was called an *architectus*, an architect who was also an engineer. In ancient Greece, engineering feats were accomplished in such fields as tunnels, water supply systems, harbors, city planning, mining, and buildings, even though they were not called engineering at that time. The Romans were great engineers, excelling in the design and construction of roads, bridges, aqueducts, mines, harbors, buildings, and other structures.

Many ancient Greeks and Romans made inventions and otherwise contributed to what later became engineering, but they were scientists or philosophers and cannot be called engineers. About the 3rd century A.D., a war machine was called an *ingenium*, an invention of genius, and later the word *engin* came into use for such machines. It was not until the Middle Ages that a person who designed, constructed, or operated such machines came to be called an *ingeniator*, an engineer. Thus the first use of the word *engineer* was applied to the work of the military engineer.

Most other work involving engineering, including military engineering, continued to be performed by master builders. By the time of the Renaissance, the role of master builders changed, dividing along the lines of those who constructed buildings, the builders, and those who designed them, the architects. And architects designed not only buildings but other structures, including war machines and fortifications. Many of the architects were also artists.

Engineering and architecture continued to be practiced simultaneously until the 17th century, when some distinction was made between military engineers and architects. Sébastien Le Prestre, Marquis de Vauban (1633–1707), became a great engineer in France, designer and builder of many forts, and dedicated himself to the profession of engineering. He has been called the first engineer. In the 18th century, modern engineering had its beginnings in France. At that time, civil engineering of structures, such as bridges, canals, and water supply systems, was often handled by men who specialized in such work.

By the end of the 18th century, civil engineering had become partly separated from architecture in both France and England, but the real separation was not to be accomplished until near the end of the 19th century. Since then, the two professions have continued to overlap in important ways. In 1750 the great English engineer John Smeaton (1724–92) first used the term *civil engineer* to describe his work. Others began to call themselves civil engineers and later organized an engineering society in England. In 1818 the Institution of Civil Engineers was founded in London and a few years later the Société des Ingénieurs Civils de France was founded in Paris. Soon afterward, lectures in engineering were delivered in French and English universities, and in 1840 a professorship in engineering was established at Glasgow University, Scotland.

**U.S. Schools and Societies** Civil engineering became established in the United States in the early 19th century. The American Society of Civil Engineers was founded in 1852. At first its title included "and Architects," but that portion was dropped in 1869. The first engineering school in the United States was the U.S. Military Academy, West Point, N.Y., which started teaching engineering when it was founded in 1802 and has continued to do so every since. Rensselaer Polytechnic Institute, Troy, N.Y., was the second, beginning in 1824, and it granted the first engineering degree in 1835.

Mechanical engineering had its beginnings with the start of the industrial revolution in the 18th century but did not come into its own until the 19th. The American Society of Mechanical Engineers was founded in 1880. Electrical engineering began in the 19th and came into its own in the 20th century. The Institute of Electrical and Electronics Engineers was founded in 1884. Structural engineering, as one of the specialties of civil engineering, started in the 19th century and became solidly established in the 20th.

**Related Articles** ARCHITECTURE; BUILDING CODES AND STANDARDS; BUILDING INDUSTRY; ELECTRICAL ENGINEERING; MECHANICAL ENGINEERING; PLANNING, CITY; ROAD AND TRAFFIC DESIGN; SURVEYING.

**Periodicals** *Consulting Engineer,* 217 Wayne St., St. Joseph, Mich. 49085; *Engineering News-Record,* 1221 Avenue of the Americas, New York, N.Y. 10020; *Professional Engineer,* 2029 K St., N.W., Washington, D.C. 20006.

**Sources of Additional Information** American Consulting Engineers Council, 1015 15th St., N.W., Washington, D.C. 20005; Accreditation Board for Engineering and Technology, 345 E. 47th St., New York, N.Y. 10017; American Association of Engineering Societies, 111 19th St., N.W., Suite 608, Washington, D.C. 20026; National Council of Examiners for Engineering and Surveying, P.O. Box 1686, Clemson, S.C. 29633; National Society of Professional Engineers, 1420 King St., Alexandria, Va. 22314.

**ENVIRONMENTAL PROTECTION** The guarding, preservation, and conservation of nature and natural resources, such as air, water, land, animals, plants, and natural fuels. Architecture, of necessity, changes the environment in which it is placed. Therefore architects and other environmental designers must make efforts not to destroy or deplete, any more than is absolutely necessary, nature and the natural resources affected by their buildings.

**Ecological Effects of Architecture** Architecture is so deeply involved with all aspects of nature and life that almost every decision an architect or other environmental designer makes has serious environmental implications. The manner in which a subdivision is planned affects the entire ecology of the area. The planning of a city, or a portion of one, will probably have even greater ecological effects. Such activities greatly affect the potential pollution of the air from heating systems and fireplaces, and by other means. They affect the potential pollution of rivers and other water bodies through increased needs for waste disposal. They may affect erosion by changing drainage patterns, shaping the land with machinery, destruction of trees and ground-cover vegetation, and in other ways. They may destroy the natural habitat of birds, animals, vegetation, and other forms of life. This list could be extended to embrace many other factors, including increased noise levels from automobiles and other sources and from visual or aesthetic pollution.

For many individual buildings, the environmental effects may be equally as great and in some cases, for example, factories, even greater. Therefore many architects and other environmental designers today consider environmental protection as one of their major professional responsibilities, whether required by laws or regulations or not. In their architecture, they attempt to solve the functional, esthetic, and other problems, while disturbing the environment as little as possible. Occasionally, they have even improved the environment in some respects, for example, by correcting conditions that cause erosion; by providing parks, open spaces, natural trails, and the like; by blocking noises; by conservation of natural resources, such as fuel oil and gas; and by provision for the cultural, esthetic, and psychological needs of people as well as their functional and physiological ones.

Such architects and other environmental designers have dedicated a major part of their efforts to the protection of the air, water, land, animals, birds, vegetation, natural resources, and other aspects of the environment. Some have even turned away from the more usual types of practice of their professions to become specialists in environmental fields. Other environmental specialists come from varied backgrounds and educational experiences, including science, from such disciplines as forestry, agriculture, horticulture, wildlife management, and geography.

**Environmental Laws** Architects and other environmental designers, in addition to their own professional environmental concerns, must often follow state and federal environmental laws and regulations in their work. These vary from state to state, and sometimes between localities within states. The major federal environmental law is the National Environmental Policy Act and the major federal regulatory agency is the Environmental Protection Agency (EPA). For major projects to be constructed with federal funds, EPA requires what are called environmental impact analyses (EIA) and environmental impact statements (EIS). Architects and other environmental designers are often involved in such analyses and statements when their projects may be expected to have major environmental implications.

In general, the procedure involved in the preparation of an EIA is as follows: (1) determine whether or not the project can be expected to have major effects on the environment, by comparison to lists of types of projects; (2) identify activities of the project that may have environmental effects, such as site preparation and excavation, foundations, construction materials and methods, and so on; (3) evaluate the potential impact of each activity on the environment and summarize the impacts; (4) review the alternatives; and (5) analyze the findings. If at this stage a project does not appear to have significant adverse environmental impacts, is not controversial, and is not a major federal budget item, the process stops and the results are used to verify that fact in an EIA report. If a significant adverse environmental impact does seem to exist and the project is controversial or a major budgetary item, an EIS must be filed. If the decision is made not to file an EIS for a project on the published list of those normally requiring one, a negative declaration (ND) must be filed for the public record, stating the reasons why an EIS was not filed.

If an EIS is required for a project, the contents are expected to include detailed information on the (1) project description, (2) land-use relationships, (3) probable impact of the proposed action on the environment, (4) alternatives to the proposed action, (5) probable adverse environmental effects which cannot be avoided, (6) relationship between local short-term uses of the environment and the maintenance and enhancement of long-term productivity, (7) irreversible and irretrievable commitments of resources, and (8) other interests and considerations of federal policy that offset the adverse environmental aspects of the proposed action.

**History** Until the 18th century, little thought was given to protection of the environment. As a result, timber was cut and not replanted; soil eroded; and birds and animals were killed in great numbers; for example, the passenger pigeon, once estimated to number up to 5 billion, and other birds became extinct, and the American bison or buffalo almost became extinct. Rivers became polluted, partly because water runoff from the land carried with it various harmful substances and partly because raw sewage was customarily dumped into them. The list could be extended almost indefinitely. And the situation in America was even worse than it was in Europe and other places. Some people were concerned and tried to do something about the situation. For example, Thomas Jefferson(1743–1826) and George Washington (1732–99) attempted to control erosion on their farms. But their efforts fell far short of what was needed.

Beginning in the 19th century, some people began to write about environmental subjects and make other efforts to improve conditions, including the naturalist and writer Henry David Thoreau (1817–62) and the landscape architect Frederick Law Olmsted (1822–1903). The first book to excite wide interest in conservation in the United States was *The Earth as Modified by Human Action*, written in 1864 by lawyer and diplomat George Perkins March (1801–82). The first textbook on the subject, not published until 1910, was *The Conservation of the Natural Resources of the United States*, written by geologist and college president Charles Richard Van Hise (1857–1918).

Many others worked for environmental protection and wrote about the subject, including Theodore Roosevelt (1858–1919), naturalist John Muir (1838–1914), planner Benton McKaye (1879–1972), drama critic and naturalist Joseph Wood Krutch (1885–1970), marine biologist Rachel Carson (1907–64), and U.S. Supreme Court Justice William Orville Douglas (1898–1980). The naturalist and journalist Jay Norwood Darling (1876–1962), under the pseudonym of Ding, drew cartoons to promote interest in conservation. Many others have been active in environmental protection and conservation and many are still active today.

Numerous organizations have fought and continue to fight for environmental protection and conservation; for example, the Conservation Foundation, National Wildlife Federation, Sierra Club, Izaak Walton League, National Audubon Society, American Forestry Association, Future Farmers of America, and Conservation Education Association. On the international level, conservation has been the subject of conferences of the United Nations, which also has continuing programs of studies and activities.

**U.S. Regulations** Partly because of the activities of such conservation-minded organizations and individuals, federal, state, and local governments in the United States have enacted a great number of laws and taken other actions concerned with environmental protection and conservation. Although some previous efforts had been made, the first important federal action is thought to have been the establishment of the U.S. Fish Commission in 1872. In the same year, Yellowstone National Park was established, the first of many public parks. In 1885 the U.S. Bureau of Biological Survey was established in the Department of Agriculture. In 1891 the U.S. Congress enacted a law authorizing the creation of certain forest reserves and in 1897, and later, authorized additional lands to be set aside for such purposes. In 1898 a Division of Forestry was established in the U.S. Department of Agriculture and Gifford Pinchot (1865–1946), considered the first professional forester in the United States, became its first chief.

The conservation movement in the United States greatly accelerated under the leadership of Theodore Roosevelt, while he was president (1901–09). During his tenure in office, and largely because of his deep interest in conservation, a number of progressive steps were made. The Reclamation Act was passed in 1902. The following year, Roosevelt established federal bird reservations. The U.S. Forest Service, with Pinchot as its chief, was established in 1905. Roosevelt added more acres of land to the national forests than any other president and established regulations for grazing in them. In 1908 he held the first conservation conference of state governors,

with the result that many states soon afterward created conservation commissions. In the same year, he created the National Conservation Commission, under the leadership of Pinchot.

Since the time of Theodore Roosevelt, many other laws have been enacted and other actions taken by the federal government. Among the most important were the Weeks Law, enacted in 1911, allowing purchase of lands for national forests; the establishment of the National Park Service in 1916; and the first migratory bird treaty with Canada in the same year. Federal conservation efforts lagged somewhat until 1928, when the Forest Research Act was passed by Congress.

President Franklin Roosevelt (1882–1945) gave considerable impetus to conservation during his terms in office (1933–45). From 1933 to 1942, thousands of unemployed young men joined the Civilian Conservation Corps (CCC) to work on conservation projects, including planting some 2 million acres of trees. During Roosevelt's tenure, a number of important conservation laws were sponsored by him and passed by Congress, including those creating the Tennessee Valley Authority (TVA) and the Soil Erosion Service, later called the Soil Conservation Service, in 1933. In 1934 the Taylor Grazing Act was passed; in 1935, the Soil Conservation Act; and in 1936, the Flood Control Act.

Many other laws have subsequently been passed and other actions taken by the federal government, including the Water Pollution Act of 1948, and other later acts on this subject, the Watershed Protection and Flood Prevention Act of 1954, and the Wilderness Act of 1964. Actions have also been taken in the various states for environmental protection and conservation. A leader has been the State of New York, which began conservation programs very early and now has almost 3 million acres in forest preserves in the Adirondack and Catskill Mountains. Other leaders have been the states of Michigan and California.

During the 1960s and 1970s, many people, sometimes called environmentalists, and including a number of college students and other young people, were not at all satisfied with governmental efforts in environmental protection and conservation. Together with environmental organizations, they demanded better environmental policies and controls. In 1970 the National Environmental Policy Act became law and was subsequently amended. In addition to establishing policies and criteria for environmental protection and maintenance of quality in the environment, the act provided for a Council on Environmental Quality in the Executive Office of the President, for the submission by the president of annual environmental quality reports to Congress, and for the preparation of environmental impact analyses and statements for all proposed legislation or other major actions of the federal government or by others when supported with federal funds.

In December 1970, a new Environmental Protection Agency (EPA) was created. To it were assigned the many agencies and administrations concerned with environmental problems then scattered among the Departments of the Interior; Health, Education and Welfare; and others. EPA was thus given the overall responsibility for water quality, air pollution, solid wastes, pesticides, radiation, and other environmental concerns.

Efforts to improve the quality of the environment and to protect it in the future are continuing by individuals, organizations, and federal and state governments. Many believe that the efforts made so far have not been enough and often have come too late. Some disagreements have arisen in later years between people and organizations who generally support the same or similar positions on the importance of environmental protection and conservation. One of the most serious of such disagreements has been between those who are most deeply concerned about environmental quality and those whose deepest concerns are with growing energy shortages. For example, those concerned primarily with energy often support the increased use of coal of which there are greater reserves than those of oil or other fuels. Those primarily concerned with air pollution maintain this would greatly increase that problem. People who advocate the use of nuclear electric generating plants cite their advantages in the conservation of fuels and the relatively low degree of pollution of the air. Those opposed to nuclear plants cite the dangers of accidents, radiation, and pollution by radioactive wastes. Such questions must be resolved, together with all the other important issues, if the environment is to be protected and preserved for humans and the animals and plants with which they share it. Architects and other environmental designers today are in an exceedingly good position to help bring about meaningful changes for the better.

**Related Articles** CLIMATE; DESIGN, ARCHITECTURAL; ECOLOGY; ELECTRIC POWER AND WIRING; GARDEN; HEATING, VENTILATING, AND AIR CONDITIONING; INSECT PROTECTION; LANDSCAPE ARCHITECTURE; PARK; PLANNING, CITY; PLUMBING; ROAD AND TRAFFIC DESIGN; SITE PLANNING.

**Further Reading** Angell, D. J., et al., eds.: *Sustaining Earth; Response to the Environmental Threat*, St. Martins Press, New York, 1991; Callison, Charles H., ed.: *America's Natural Resources*, rev. ed., Ronald, New York, 1967, available through Books on Demand, UMI, Ann Arbor, Mich.; Chanlett, Emil, T.: *Environmental Protection*, 2d ed., McGraw-Hill, New York, 1979; McHarg, Ian L.: *Design with Nature*, reissue of 1969 ed., John Wiley, New York, 1991.

**Periodicals** *National Parks and Conservation Magazine*, 1701 18th St., N.W., Washington, D.C. 20009; *National Wildlife*, 1412 16th St., N.W., Washington, D.C. 20036.

**Sources of Additional Information** Assoc. of Conservation Engineers, c/o Terry N. Boyd, Alabama Dept. of Conservation, 64 N. Union St., Montgomery, Ala. 36130; World Wildlife Fund, 1250 24th St., N.W., Washington, D.C. 20037; Environmental Protection Agency, 401 M St., S.W., Washington, D.C. 20460; National Parks and Conservation Assoc., 1015 31st St., N.W., Washington, D.C. 20007; National Wildlife Federation, 1400 16th St., N.W., Washington, D.C. 20036-22266; Sierra Club, 730 Polk St., San Francisco, Calif. 94109.

**ESHERICK, HOMSEY, DODGE AND DAVIS** This architectural firm was founded by Joseph Esherick in 1946. Based in San Francisco, its work represents the best California work of the post–World War II period. The firm avoids stylistic display but rather uses careful analysis of the program and site to produce its work. In addition, the influence of the firm was extended through teaching. Esherick began teaching at the University of California at Berkeley in 1952 and became department chair from 1977 to 1981. The other partners have also taught at the University. Forty years after founding, the firm was awarded the Architectural Firm Award by the American Institute of Architects in 1986.

**Work** Among the best-known projects of the firm are the Sea Ranch houses (1965) in Sonoma County, Calif., the Cannery (1966), San Francisco, Calif., and the Monterey Bay Aquarium (1984), Monterey, Calif. These projects have been widely discussed in the architectural press and have had wide influence in housing, adaptive use, and marine ecology.

The development of Sea Ranch on a spectacular site along the Pacific coast of California involved the landscape architect and planner Lawrence Halprin with Moore Lyndon Turnbull Whitaker for the first condominium units and Esherick for the Lodge and the Hedgerow houses. Appreciated for the sensitive relationship to the site, the early buildings stand in unfortunate contrast to the more intensive later development of large houses. Newer guidelines have been established to control intensity of developments. The original houses were influential, and the style was mimicked elsewhere in the country. However, the effect of Sea Ranch remains that of a lightly inhabited landscape, with about half the property not yet built on.

The Cannery project along the waterfront in San Francisco was an adaptive reuse of a series of old brick structures formerly used for a Del Monte fruit cannery. The conversion resulted in a retail center at Fisherman's Wharf. The refurbished brick walls have been kept, with

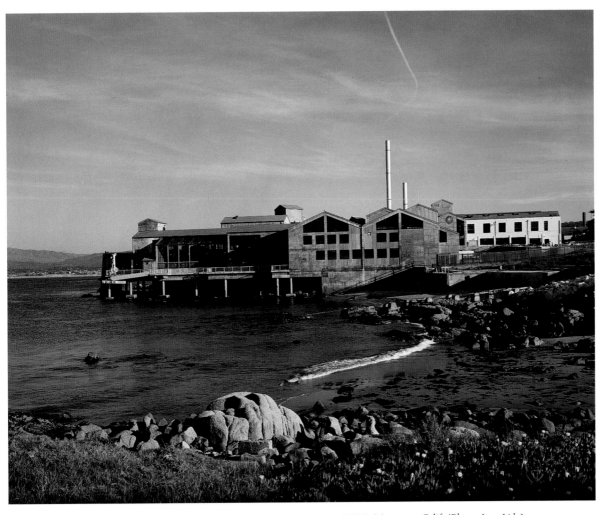

**ESHERICK, HOMSEY, DODGE AND DAVIS** Monterey Bay Aquarium (1984), Monterey, Calif. *[Photo: Jane Lidz]*

arched openings allowing movement through the many levels of the center.

Another adaptive use project was the Monterey Bay Aquarium, which made use of the abandoned Hovden cannery, a part of the historic Cannery Row. The aquarium is designed so that visitors may move freely where they wish among the old buildings and new shoreline tanks. The project was designed to focus on the marine life of the Monterey peninsula. The technology of aquariums involves careful selection of materials to survive the salt water used for the fish. Filtration systems, methods of disinfection, and other complex systems ensure the best possible environment for the sea life exhibited.

Another project of note is the Silver Lake Center, Deer Valley Resort, Park City, Utah (1981), where, as for Sea Ranch, the buildings are broken up into parts, fitting into the landscape. Materials include timber logs and heavy timber framing, rough-sawn red cedar siding, stonework, and dark clay tile roofs.

The firm's approach to design displays an unusual sensitivity to the site and the program and is well adapted to the northern California area in which the architects practice. Their work has had a major influence on environmentally concerned architects.

**Further Reading** "Esherick, Homsey, Dodge and Davis," *Encyclopedia of Architecture, Design, Engineering, and Construction*, vol. 2, John Wiley & Sons, New York, 1988.

**EXPOSITION** Educational and usually festive exhibition, often called a "fair," especially one of international scope. Most expositions and their buildings are of a temporary nature, but there are exceptions. Some of the buildings left standing, and many others that were demolished, have strongly influenced architecture. And many highly regarded architects have participated in master planning of expositions and in the design of their buildings.

It is impossible to generalize about the design of expositions, since each is a unique event, with its plan,

**EXPOSITION** World's Columbian (1893), Chicago, Ill. *[Chief Architect: Daniel Hudson Burnham (Photo: Chicago Historical Society)]*

buildings, and content, subject to the inventiveness of its promoters, exhibitors, and architects. However, there are in almost all expositions structures of four major types: buildings for display of arts, sciences, manufacturers, and so on; buildings and other structures for recreation, such as shows, rides, games, and the like; buildings for administration and maintenance; and structures that usually serve no other purpose than the symbolic.

**Origins** Expositions, as we now know them, started in England in the middle of the 18th century, but the grand era did not begin until the Great Exhibition (1851) in London. Here the famous Crystal Palace, designed by Sir Joseph Paxton (1801–65), was built of glass and iron. Its structure and size, 408 ft wide by 72 ft high by 1,848 ft long, caused a sensation and has influenced both architecture and expositions ever since. The building was moved to Sydenham, England, and was destroyed by fire in 1936. In 1853 another version of the palace was constructed at the New York City Exhibition. In 1855 in the Paris Exposition, the glass and iron Palais de l'Industrie was even larger than its London counterpart, and in 1889 the Galerie des Machines, longer.

A number of other great European expositions followed, including those in London in 1862, 1908, 1924–25, and 1951; Brussels in 1935 and 1958; Montreal in 1967; and Paris in 1855, 1867, 1878, 1889, 1900, 1931,

and 1937. All had some influence on architecture and were notable in other ways. Perhaps the most lasting and well-known structure of any of them is the Eiffel Tower (1889), erected for the Paris Exposition of that year. It was designed by engineer Alexandre Gustave Eiffel (1832–1923). An interesting building at Brussels, in 1958, was the U.S. Pavilion by Edward Durell Stone (1902–78).

**U.S. Expositions** Major 19th-century American expositions include the Philadelphia Centennial (1876) and the World's Columbian Exposition (1893) in Chicago. The latter was a showplace for eclectic architecture, its character determined by New York architects, including Charles Follen McKim (1847–1909) and Richard Morris Hunt (1827–95). Daniel Hudson Burnham (1846–1912) was its chief architect. All these architects designed buildings for the exposition as did Charles B. Atwood (1848–95), whose Palace of Fine Arts later became the still-existing Rosenwald Museum of Science and Industry. Sophia Hayden (c. 1878–1953) designed the Women's Building, the commission for which she had won in a competition. Louis Henri Sullivan (1856–1924) designed the Transportation Building, the only pioneering modern effort, but it was later destroyed.

The Chicago exposition was followed by the Pan-American (1901), Buffalo, N.Y., and the Louisiana

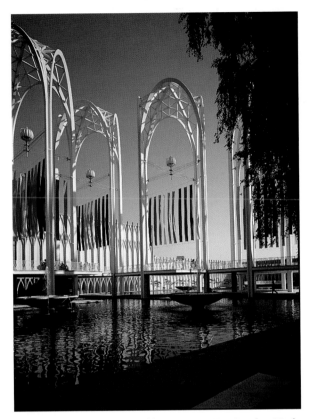

**EXPOSITION** Seattle World's Fair (1962), Seattle, Wash. *[Architect: Minoru Yamasaki]*

Purchase (1904), St. Louis. The latter leaned heavily on Beaux Arts architecture and produced a building that still exists, the Palace of Fine Arts, now the St. Louis Museum, by Cass Gilbert (1858–1934). The Panama-Pacific Exposition (1915), San Francisco, produced the Palace of Fine Arts of Bernard Maybeck (1862–1957), now reconstructed, and the Panama-California Exposition at San Diego in the same year produced an eclectic Spanish style under the design direction of Bertram Grosvenor Goodhue (1869–1924) of New York. Some of these buildings still exist. The 1933–34 Chicago exposition, A Century of Progress, with Louis Skidmore (1897–1962) as director of design, produced mostly fanciful, futuristic buildings.

The 1939–40 Golden Gate Exposition was held on artificial Treasure Island, made from earth dredged from San Francisco Bay and now the location of a naval base. Also in 1939–40, the New York World's Fair produced little in the way of architectural innovation, except the Swedish, Finnish, and Brazilian pavilions, all of which were taken down after the fair. The 1964–65 fair on the same site as the earlier fair produced several buildings still in existence, the Museum of Science and Technology, by Harrison and Abramovitz, Wallace Kirkman Harrison (1895–1981), and Max Abramovitz

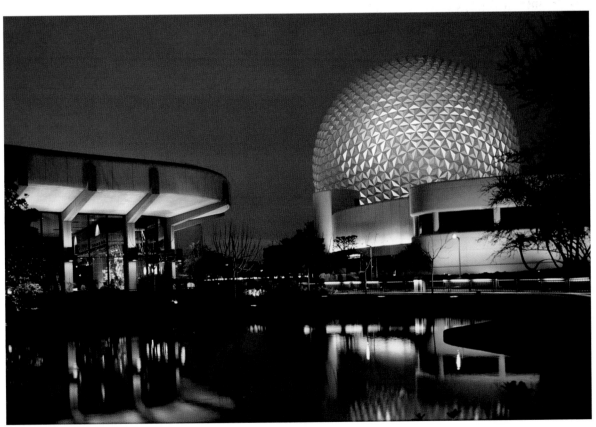

**EXPOSITION** EPCOT Center (1982), Lake Buena Vista, Fla.

(1908–    ); the United States Pavilion by Charles Luckman (1909–  ); and the New York State Pavilion by Philip Cortelyou Johnson (1906–  ).

Many smaller expositions and fairs have been held, and are still being held, all over the world. Some of them have produced innovative, even pioneering, architecture. The German Pavilion of Ludwig Mies van der Rohe (1886–1969) at the Barcelona Exposition (1929) became world-famous and deeply affected the development of modern architecture. There are many other notable examples, including the buildings (1962) at the Seattle Century 21 Exposition by Minoru Yamasaki (1912–86)

and the Berlin Congress Hall (1957) at the Berlin Exposition, designed by Hugh Stubbins (1912–  ). R. Buckminster Fuller (1895–1983) in association with Shoji Sadao designed the 250-ft diameter geodesic dome for the U.S. Pavilion at the 1967 Montreal Expo.

**Related Articles** BURNHAM AND ROOT; GILBERT, CASS; HARRISON, WALLACE KIRKMAN; HUNT, RICHARD MORRIS; JOHNSON, PHILIP CORTELYOU; MAYBECK, BERNARD; McKIM, MEAD AND WHITE; MIES VAN DER ROHE, LUDWIG; SKIDMORE, OWINGS AND MERRILL; STONE, EDWARD DURELL; SULLIVAN, LOUIS HENRI; YAMASAKI, MINORU.

# F

**FACTORY** A building, often an industrial building, or a group of buildings in which products or goods are manufactured or assembled. At one time, the word *factory* was used for any building in which people worked. By the time of the industrial revolution, the word had come to mean a place in which mostly standardized goods were manufactured as contrasted with the shops of craftsmen. Today a factory is apt to be highly organized and automated, with specialized buildings and assembly lines designed specifically for the type of goods to be manufactured. Formerly architects tended to regard factory design as nonarchitectural, but today this has become one of the most important architectural building types.

**Classifications** Factory buildings are sometimes classified by the type of industries in which they are used: heavy or light. Heavy industries are concerned with relatively large products and processes, such as steel, automobiles, aircraft, and ships. Light industries manufacture or assemble relatively small products, such as machine tools, television and other electronic items, food, and paper. Factories are also sometimes classified by their involvement in processing or assembly. Processing industries are concerned with changing natural materials into some other form, and include such activities as oil refining, papermaking, grain milling, and the like. Assembly industries are involved with combining natural or manufactured items into completely assembled products, and include textile, automobile, and baking plants.

**Elements** The major elements of factories are the areas used for manufacturing or assembly, warehousing, research and control, administration, and employee facilities. The proper relationships between these elements must be established in a well-planned factory. Of utmost importance is the layout of the spaces for the manufacturing or assembly operations. These operations are generally planned with the aid of flow diagrams, which indicate the sequence of all of the activities required from the receipt of the raw materials to the delivery of the finished products for transportation. Plant layouts are generally used in factories that produce relatively large numbers of only a few product types. Process layouts are used in plants that produce relatively small numbers of many products, all of which require similar processes.

The manufacturing or assembly areas of factories vary considerably between industries and types of products. But all must be designed for ease of operation, efficient flow of materials, flexibility, and good supervision. It is an axiom of factory design that provisions must be made for changes and expansion. Warehousing must provide for efficient storage and movement of both raw materials and finished products. The research and control areas must be designed to allow new product development and testing, and control and testing of current products. The types of laboratories and other facilities required are determined by the type of industry.

Administration areas in factories are similar to those of office buildings, but there may be some specific requirements because of the nature of the operations. Employee facilities include such areas as lounges, lockers and rest rooms, cafeterias, meeting rooms, and first aid stations.

Factories must often be designed to meet special requirements necessitated by the operations, the people who perform them, and the products. For example, in some factories natural lighting is very important and special provisions must be made for windows, skylights, and the like. In other factories artificial light may be used exclusively and no windows are required. Transportation of raw materials into factories and finished products away from them often requires special attention to rail lines and sidings, truck roadways and parking, and loading docks.

In other factories, provisions must be made for storage tanks, incinerators, and water tanks. Provisions may be required for handling dangerous wastes, materials that pollute the air or water; fire hazardous materials and operations; and operations that are noisy or produce unpleasant odors. In many industries, the requirements for heating and cooling, water distribution, electrical and other power may be quite important, complex, and costly. Many are now highly automated and use sophisticated controls and computers. Early factories, usually built in cities, were mostly three or four stories high. Today factories are often built outside cities and are generally single-story, but sometimes have two or more stories. And some multistory factories, of eight stories or more, have been built in recent years.

Recently, a trend has developed in the United States toward planned industrial districts, sometimes called industrial parks. These areas range in size from about eighty to several thousand acres. Individual sites are provided for a great number of factories in a planned area with roadways, parking, and utilities. In some industrial parks, restaurants, shops, recreational facilities, and even motels are provided.

In this postindustrial society, more manufacturing is occurring abroad, even for U.S. corporations. Some foreign corporations are now manufacturing in the United States. Also impacting new building is the declining birth rate of the 1970s which has resulted in some 8 million fewer persons entering the labor force in the 1990s compared with the earlier post–World War II baby-boom decades. Industrial buildings of all kinds, particularly factories, remain an important building type. Factory design is complex and demanding, but it is also challenging and rewarding. The number of factories built each year fluctuates because of the state of the economy, but in times of slow building activity, there are usually numerous remodeling projects and changes from one type of process or product to another. In other years, industrial buildings have comprised a large and important segment of the construction activity in the United States.

**History** Although factories of a sort have existed to some extent since the 16th century, it is only since the middle of the 18th that factories, as now known, were built. With the beginning of the use of coal, coke, and waterpower and with the increasing development of water and land transportation for materials and products, factories for the manufacture of iron and textile products were constructed first in England, then in other European countries. Matthew Boulton (1728–1809), an English engineer and manufacturer, built several innovative factories and then teamed up with Scottish inventor James Watt (1736–1819), who had invented improved steam engines, to produce the engines and to design new factories. One was a pioneering seven-story cotton mill (1801) near Salford, England. Although improvements were made in factories and in the use of power in the buildings, the design of factories for the safety and welfare of the workers lagged behind.

**FACTORY** Consolidated Diesel (1983), Rocky Mount, N.C. *[Architects: CRSS Architects]*

**FACTORY** General Motors Saturn Plant (1991), Spring Hill, Tenn. *[Architects: Argonaut (GM)]*

**American Development** In colonial America, there were no real factories. In the years before independence, most manufacturing processes were handcrafts. The only operations that used power were mills that manufactured lumber, flour, paper, and gunpowder. During the last decade of the 18th century and the first of the 19th, some 200 textile mills, many of them using steam for power, were built in New England and the Middle Atlantic states. During the next decade an industrial town was built in New Hampshire, not only with a factory but housing and other buildings for the workers, a harbinger of later company towns in many parts of the United States.

The advent of wrought, and later cast, iron for building structures changed the design of factories considerably. Now a building could be built with a frame of relatively unobtrusive metal members that did not get in the way of the processes as did the earlier heavy walls. In 1848 James Bogardus (1800–74), inventor and engineer, designed and built a five-story factory in New York City, using iron framing. This was followed by many others, in both wrought and cast iron, all over the United States. Some of the most notable were in New York City and St. Louis. Still most factories were constructed with brick walls and timber floors and roofs. The invention of the skeleton frame and steel changed factory construction drastically. And the widespread use of reinforced concrete starting in the early 20th century brought with it the virtual end of the old types of construction.

Most of the other changes in factory design were brought about by improvements required for the safety and welfare of workers and by increasing mechanization and later automation. Otherwise, factory design did not change much. Architects continued to consider it nonar-chitecture and avoided factory design or relegated it to an unimportant place in their practice. Then a few European architects, including Walter Adolf Gropius (1883–1969), began to design handsome, functional factories. And Albert Kahn (1869–1942) revolutionized factory design, first with his significant automobile plants in and around Detroit, and later in other buildings. These factories were not only efficient and functional but comfortable for the workers, and so elegant in appearance that many consider them among the best-designed American buildings. The tradition established by Kahn continues in the design of factories today.

**Related Articles** BOGARDUS, JAMES; GROPIUS, WALTER ADOLF; KAHN, ALBERT; LABORATORY; STRUCTURE; WAREHOUSE.

**FARM BUILDING** A building, or group of buildings, used for production of agricultural or horticultural products or for housing farm families. While ranchers might not readily admit it, a ranch is a special kind of farm for raising cattle or sheep. Although farm buildings do not form an important building type designed by architects, they were among the first buildings constructed in America. They were then very important in the life and progress of the country and they remain so today.

A great variety of buildings may be found on farms today, some nothing more than sheds for sheltering machinery, some very complex and specialized. First, of course, is the farmhouse, the dwelling for a farm family, and sometimes for employees, farmhands, and others who work on the farm. Farmhouses have always been very much like other houses, ranging from very modest dwellings, similar to those found in towns and cities, to

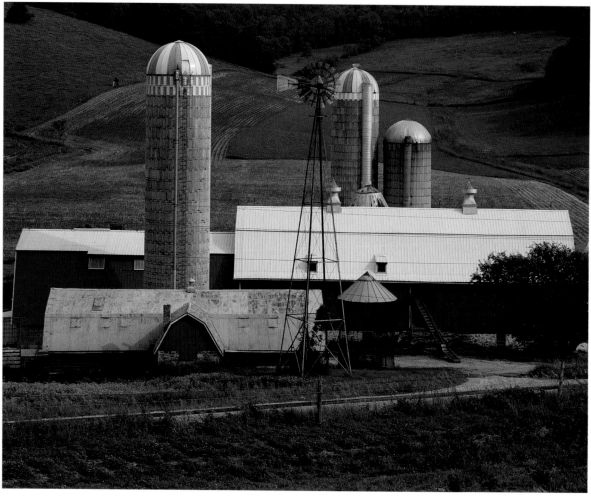

**FARM BUILDING** Farm in Wisconsin.

great plantation houses, as large and lavish as the great town houses of the same eras.

The design of farmhouses has closely paralleled the design of other houses, except that perhaps in later years it has tended to be more founded in tradition, less progressive than other house design. A family living in a city or suburb might accept a very modern design, or even prefer it, while their counterpart living in the country might choose a design adapted from a historic style from the past. In other respects, farmhouses and town houses are quite similar, except that kitchens, shared much of the time by all members of families for pursuits other than just meal preparation, have been the rule in farmhouses from the beginning. These so-called live-in kitchens, or family rooms, have only started to become popular in suburbia in the recent past.

**Building Types** The most important building on a farm, other than the house, is the barn. There are many types of barns, but the most prevalent is the general-purpose barn used to house farm animals, shelter machinery and equipment, and store feed and other sup-plies. There are many specialized barns, including those for dairy cattle, horses, and other animals. Barns are divided into spaces that are specialized by use, such as stalls for horses or dairy cattle, or pens for other animals. Dairy farms often use loose housing or stanchion barn systems. Loose housing systems have several buildings and other elements, including a building for bedding and milking cattle, one for storage, a feeding area with silo, a milkhouse, and a hay storage building. A stanchion barn, more expensive than loose housing but requiring a smaller site, incorporates all the elements into one building, with a silo nearby. Barns may be built of many materials, including wood, masonry, and metal. The most commonly used materials today are wood structures, with sides and roofs of metal or wood. A building closely associated with the barn is the silo, often a tall structure, usually round in plan, for storage of animal feed, usually called "silage."

Farms often have many other types of buildings. Storage is most important, not only for animal feed but for canned goods, root vegetables, and other food for the farm family. Root cellars for food storage have long been a fixture on farms, but today farm families often supplement them with freezers. Smokehouses and baking ovens have often been provided for food preparation.

Many specialized buildings are used on farms. Buildings for various kinds of farm animals, such as chicken houses, cattle sheds, hog sheds, and so on, are often required. In addition, many farms raise other animals, which require specialized structures, including rabbits, ducks, geese, pigeons, and turkeys, and on some farms, even catfish and crayfish. Other farms are devoted to horticulture, raising flowers and their seeds or bulbs, trees, or shrubbery. Such farms often require special buildings for handling the products and others, including greenhouses, for raising and propagating plants. Some farms have stringent requirements for cold storage of the products. Obviously dairy farms have such requirements, but so do other types, including fruit and nut farms.

As somewhat independent operating units using a great variety of machinery and tools, farms must have good provisions for the storage of these items and for their repair and servicing. Special buildings are often provided for these purposes, with spaces for storing machinery and maintenance and service parts and materials, and a shop.

One of the most important aspects of the design of farms is provision for mechanical and electrical equipment and systems. Farms require large electrical systems, not only for the usual residential services and equipment but lights and machinery in the barns and other buildings; often heat and ventilation in animal shelters, greenhouses, and other places; power for water pumps for farmhouses, animals, and sometimes irrigation of crops. Water piping runs to barns, animal houses, shops, gardens, and other locations. Sewage disposal is dependent on grease traps, septic tanks, and drainage fields. Waste disposal of other kinds must also be provided for, including animal waste, used chemicals, and so on.

All in all, farms are quite complex and would present interesting design problems to architects. For the most part, this does not happen today, for most architects never get the chance to design more than an occasional farmhouse or horse barn.

**History** Farms have a very old history, dating back to the Neolithic period, beginning about 8000 B.C. or earlier, in Mesopotamia, Egypt, and other countries of that area. During the centuries following, Neolithic people developed cultivation of barley, wheat, and other grains and domestication of cattle, sheep, goats, and pigs. Farms have been an important part of the culture of humans ever since.

**American Development** The first farms in America were established immediately after the colonists arrived, in the Upper South and East. The first farmhouses were very modest, many of them built with wood frames filled in with wattle and daub, a method using wattles, twigs, or other materials woven together and inserted into the house frame, and then covered on both sides with daub, a mixture of mud and clay with chopped straw or other materials. These were followed by farmhouses made entirely of wood and then of sun-dried brick. In the French settlements of the Deep South, New Orleans and others, wooden buildings were also erected and they were followed by a method called *briquette entre poteaux*, soft brick inserted between timbers.

Later some of the finest houses in America were built on farms, or plantations, of the South. Many were designed by talented amateur architects whose names have been lost; others by some of the best American professional architects. Beginning in the 19th century and continuing into the 20th, the design of farmhouses has often been done by builders and by farmers themselves.

**Related Articles** BOTANICAL BUILDING; HOUSE.

**FEASIBILITY STUDY** The practicality of a proposed building project, established through research and analysis of its use, financing, construction, and other aspects of importance. A feasibility study is made to determine whether or not the construction of a project is advisable.

Whenever some doubt exists about the advisability of a building construction project, a feasibility study should be prepared. While such studies might seem necessary for all projects in this category, they are absolutely essential for development projects proposed by developers, who must sell the concepts to those who will finance them and to those who will lease or buy them.

Feasibility studies of a somewhat limited sort are often done by architects for their private clients, and some architectural offices are capable of handling more complicated studies. Upon becoming involved in a development project, an architect often participates in the study of feasibility, together with other people, such as real estate counselors and mortgage bankers. For a project for a private client, the situation is relatively simple. A private owner may decide to do without a feasibility study, relying only on needs and wishes based on experience and judgment. If a feasibility study is prepared for a private owner, the decisions about whether to build or not, what to build, and so on may be made directly by the owner. For development projects and many other profit-making projects, establishment of feasibility is all-important.

Some confusion exists regarding the term *feasibility study*. The term may be used to mean a complete study of all the facets of a proposed building project, including markets for products or services; appraisal of the value of the project; analysis of the project as an investment; economic feasibility; and use of the building. Sometimes the term is applied only to an economic feasibility study, which determines the maximum project budget that will produce the return the owner expects on the investment.

Although the determination of economic feasibility is the most important single element in a complete feasibility study, only analysis of all the elements can produce a reliable basis for making all the proper decisions on real estate projects.

**Study Phases** A complete feasibility study begins with a market analysis. This analysis is concerned generally with the market, the supply and demand for particular types of real estate projects, such as shopping centers, stores, hotels and motels, speculative office buildings, housing developments, apartments, or industrial buildings. It then proceeds to the study of a proposed project. Answers must be derived to such questions as estimations of future markets, availability of transportation, population trends, rent and occupancy levels, and growth in the area in which the site is located. Changes in the 1986 tax law limiting tax shelters and overly optimistic decisions regarding real estate investment have led to widespread bank failures and collapse of development companies in recent years. Office buildings have been overbuilt in several market areas, and other proposed projects have been abandoned. These factors underline the importance of good data and decisions in preparing feasibility studies.

An appraisal of the value of a project may not be based solely on the cost of the project but also on its value in terms of the net income that it can be expected to generate. An economic feasibility study may be made, based on the appraised value of the project, together with the mortgage terms, acceptable rate of return on the equity, or ownership, investment in it. From these data, one can calculate the maximum cost of the project or budget which can be expected to produce the expected return. The cost of the project or budget in this case includes all costs, such as those for land; professional fees for architects, engineers, and others; interest; taxes; equipment; moving expenses; in addition to the actual costs of construction. A special type of economic feasibility study, called a "highest-and-best-use study," is prepared when several different uses might be made of a site. A study of this sort compares the uses to determine which will produce the maximum return on equity investment. A criticism of this approach is that often the highest-and-best-use is determined to be an office building, which contributes to the overbuilding of this building type.

In any type of economic feasibility study, the final question is whether a project is feasible, that is, whether it will produce the rate of return expected by the investor. At this point, an investment analysis may be made to determine the effects of depreciation on the project, capital gains if the project is to be sold upon completion or later, and other tax considerations. By means of such a study, the leverage of the investor may be determined. Leveraging is a technique used to create the maximum profit to an investor for the least amount of equity or investment. The higher the profit-equity ratio can be made, the better the investment. In some cases, through adroit handling of project financing, very high profits in relation to equities may be produced.

**Other Factors** Other aspects of feasibility studies should be noted. Successful real estate projects depend on such factors as their locations; control of costs by the architect, owners, and others involved; the ability to obtain good financing terms; the ability to lease or sell the projects or to operate them efficiently; and the ability to complete projects on time, including all phases, from establishment of the concepts, through feasibility studies, architectural and related services, and construction.

Thus the creation of a sound real estate investment depends on doing everything right: selecting the right site for the right kind of enterprise, making the right real estate and financial decisions, providing the right management for the right owners, and providing the right kind of architectural and other design services.

**Related Articles** BUILDING INDUSTRY; COST CONTROL; FINANCE; PROGRAMMING.

**Periodical** *National Real Estate Investor*, 461 Eighth Ave., New York, N.Y. 10001.

**Sources of Additional Information** American Society of Real Estate Counselors, 430 N. Michigan Ave., Chicago, Ill. 60611; National Association of Realtors, 430 N. Michigan Ave., Chicago, Ill. 60611-4087; Society of Industrial and Office Realtors, 777 14th St., N.W., Suite 400, Washington, D.C. 20005.

**FINANCE** The provision of capital, and its management, for the development, design, and construction of buildings. In the past, architects had little or nothing to do with the financing of buildings. Ordinarily, clients simply arranged for the financing of the amounts needed, in addition to the funds they already had available from savings, corporate capital, or otherwise, with a lending institution or private investors. Then the clients engaged architects, who proceeded with the regular architectural services.

Today the situation has changed. Some clients need assistance from their architects to obtain financing. In other cases, architectural projects are initiated and developed by people called developers, who may or may not end up as the owners or users of the buildings. In such cases, the architectural services become part of the total development scheme, thus involving the architects. In yet another type of case, the architects participate as principals in development work or initiate such projects and act as developers. To deal with situations of the sort described, and particularly to participate in development projects, architects must have knowledge of and experience in the financing of buildings. This is true of those involved in such work today and may be expected to become the case for other architects in the future. For information on development building, see the article entitled real estate.

**Ownership of Buildings** Buildings and other real estate are owned in a number of ways. The simplest, of course, is ownership by a single individual in fee simple: absolute ownership with rights to dispose of the property. Almost as simple is ownership by more than one person in joint tenancy, tenancy in common, and tenancy of the entirety. Joint tenancy is the situation that exists when two or more people own property together in such a way that when one of the joint owners dies, that share goes to the others. Tenancy in common is the situation that exists when two or more people own shares, not necessarily equal shares, in property that may be willed to people other than the surviving owners. Tenancy of the entirety, allowed in some states, treats a husband and wife as one entity, each with rights of survivorship.

The other major ways that groups own real estate is through partnerships or corporations. A partnership is a relationship between two or more people who contract together to join in business in which they share profits. The two major types of partnerships are a general partnership, in which any partner can commit the group and each partner is liable for all the obligations of the partnership; and a limited partnership, in which there must be one or more general partners and may be any number of limited partners who are not liable for the obligations of the partnerships. Limited partnerships are often used in the ownership of real estate.

A corporation is a legal entity separate from the people who own it, ordinarily called stockholders, set up to conduct business under the applicable laws of a state. Corporations are used in real estate ownership primarily because of the limited liability of the stockholders, ease of transferring portions of ownership, and the possibility of acquiring capital through sales of stock. The fact that corporations report, for tax purposes, as separate entities may be an advantage in some situations and a disadvantage in others. Another form of real estate ownership is a real estate investment trust (REIT), which allows a number of investors to pool their money to invest in real estate. A REIT is most often used to spread the risk of investment or development over a relatively large number of projects.

**Financing Types** There are two major types of financing involved in building construction: interim and long-term. Interim financing takes the form of an interim loan or loans, producing funds that are used to finance the construction of buildings. Long-term financing involves permanent loans, usually secured by first mortgages, which pledge the property and its improvements as security for debts. A second mortgage is an additional mortgage used to obtain more funds, pledging the property and its improvements as security after first mortgage claims have been satisfied. To secure an interim loan, it is usually necessary to obtain what is called a commitment, or standby commitment, from a long-term lender, agreeing to make the long-term loan. Only part of the long-term funds are usually obtained from lending institutions, the remainder, sometimes called front-end money, comes from cash or its equivalent in services from those participating in the ownership of the project and represents the value of their ownership, or their equity in the project. After a building has been completed and the long-term money received, the interim loan is paid off.

**Equity Money** The capital, equity money or its equivalent, for real estate acquisition may come from sources other than the owner or developer. Sometimes a joint venture, in which more than one person participates, is used, as are options on land, ground leases, and other types. In leasehold financing, the lessor, one who owns property, leases it to a lessee, one who uses the property. Leasehold financing is generally used when land is unusually high priced or not for sale. The lessor owns the land and the improvements made on it while the lessee has the right to its use. On this basis, long-term financing may be obtained. Equity capital may also be obtained by the process of having a lending institution become a partial owner in a joint venture. Another technique is called a sale leaseback. In this type of venture, a developer sells all, or a portion, of a project to a lending institution or other investor, who in turn leases it back to the developer to use. A sale-buyback arrangement, rarely used, entails the purchase of property by a lending institution or other investor, who then sells it back to the developer on an installment payment contract, payable over a number of years. Sometimes a contingent interest or participation system is used. This is an agreement in which the interest rate on a loan is a combination of a fixed percentage and an additional amount based on the degree of success of a project. Another method is a variable-rate mortgage, which allows interest rates to shift up or down, within fixed limits, based on the current cost of capital as determined at various times by an agreed-upon index.

A great number of other types of financing construction may be used and no doubt other types will be developed in the future. Other types used today include joint-pool financing, in which several lenders share in the loan on a project; and balloon loans, in which only partial payments are made on the loan periodically, with a relatively large final payment, called a balloon payment.

**Loans** Loans backed by mortgages for building construction and other real estate purposes may be obtained from a number of sources, including individuals, businesses, lending institutions, and governments. By far the greatest proportion of loan money comes to borrowers from intermediaries which receive the savings of savers and lend them to borrowers. In real estate, the most important are life insurance companies, saving and loan institutions, commercial banks, savings banks, and mortgage bankers, who specialize in placing mortgage loans with investment institutions of the other types. Other sources of loans for real estate investment include credit unions; Federal Land Bank associations, which lend money on farm and rural property; and the federal government, which makes loans on some types of projects, such as new communities. The federal government also makes grants of various kinds, particularly for low-rent housing for low-income families. These federal grant programs for low-income housing have varied over the years but have decreased substantially from post–World War II levels. Loan insurance programs by quasi-governmental organizations such as Fannie Mae and Freddie Mac bring stability to the home mortgage market.

Although the construction industry figures vary from year to year, some idea of the scale of the U.S. industry is that it provides an estimated 5 percent of the gross national product, including nonresidential, residential, and nonbuilding construction. The overbuilding of the 1980s means that financial constraints limit the growth of the industry in the 1990s. In addition to the financial issues, demographics suggest that residential and commercial construction will follow the variable rate of growth of the population.

Some changes during recent years have been the use of home equity loans at moderate interest rates to recapture some of the equity of existing real estate property. For the elderly, experiments have included reverse mortgages to allow a financial agency to provide monthly income to the elderly against the equity in their homes.

Surviving federal entitlement programs include rent subsidies for low-income individuals and families, home purchase loan programs, and grants to local governments which may be used for neighborhood improvements and to finance low- and moderate-income housing. The state or local governments and nonprofit housing groups have similar housing programs. All these programs are inadequate to meet the housing needs of the low- and moderate-income population.

**Long-Term Financing** Ordinarily the method of obtaining long-term financing for building projects involves preparation of materials describing the project with which to approach potential lenders, the making of applications for loans, and negotiation of the terms of the loans and mortgages. Although the details of these steps vary with different types and sizes of projects, some general principles may be enumerated. For some projects, such as single houses, presentations to lenders may be quite simple; in others, such as large-scale shopping center developments, they are quite complex. In the first case, the presentation may consist of only working drawings, specifications, and financial information. In the second kind of presentation, made before working drawings and specifications have been prepared, the materials presented might consist of general information about the proposed projects, schematic drawings, feasibility studies, outlines of materials and methods of construction, legal information, financial and economic information, surveys' lessee information, a description of the organization of the developers, and other information. These materials are submitted to potential lenders in order to determine their interest. When an interested lender has been identified, an application for a loan is made and negotiations begin on interest rates, mortgage terms, and other important matters. Today the work of analysis of a development project and preparation of a presentation to potential lenders, sometimes called the mortgage package, has been much simplified and improved through use of computers.

For architects contemplating becoming involved in financing building projects or acting as developers, knowledge and abilities are required that are not ordinarily dealt with thoroughly in an architect's education or experience. Therefore architects must turn to experts in the field, such as mortgage bankers or real estate counselors, for the knowledge and abilities needed to be successful in pursuits of this kind. For some architects, participation in such pursuits can be exciting and satisfying, architecturally as well as financially. For others, the financing and development of real estate projects might better be avoided.

**Related Articles** BANK; BUILDING INDUSTRY; COMPUTER; FEASIBILITY STUDY; GOVERNMENT; PRACTICE OF ARCHITECTURE; REAL ESTATE.

**Periodicals** *The Mortgage Banker*, 1135 15th St., N.W., Washington, D.C. 20036; *National Real Estate Investor*, 461 Eighth Ave., New York, N.Y. 10001.

**Sources of Additional Information** American Bankers Assoc., 1120 King St., Alexandria, Va. 22314; American Society of Real Estate Counselors, 430 N. Michigan Ave., Chicago, Ill. 60611; Mortgage Bankers Association of America, 1125 15th St., N.W., Washington, D.C. 20005; National Association of Realtors, 430 N. Michigan Ave., Chicago, Ill. 60611-4087; Society of Industrial and Office Realtors, 777 14th St., N.W., Suite 400, Washington, D.C.

20005; United States League of Savings Institutions, 1709 New York Ave., N.W., Suite 801, Washington, D.C. 20006; ULI—Urban Land Inst., 1625 Indiana Ave., N.W., Washington, D.C. 20004.

**FIREPLACE** An incombustible compartment in which a fire may be made, located at the base of a chimney which conducts the smoke and gases of the fire vertically to the outside.

From the earliest times, fire has had a fascination for humans unlike almost any other phenomenon on earth. Ancient cultures are known to have considered fire one of the major elements of the universe, to have believed it had mystical qualities, and to have held it sacred. Although the use of fires as direct sources of light has ended in modern times and its use for cooking and heating curtailed, the mystical qualities are still present for many people. And with the shortage of fuels, other than coal and wood, people have recently turned back to fireplaces not only for their emotional qualities but for heating as well.

**Types** Fireplaces may be large or small and of several types. They may be very plain, almost like simple openings in walls, or highly ornamented. Fireplaces may be specifically designed for the buildings into which they will go or they may be obtained prefabricated. Those specifically designed for individual buildings are ordinarily constructed of brick or concrete block, but sometimes of concrete or stone. Prefabricated types are usually made of steel or cast iron.

Fireplaces may be attached to walls or freestanding. Those attached to walls may project into rooms or be situated so that their faces are flush with the walls. Projecting types may be open only on their fronts or on the fronts and one or both sides. Freestanding fireplaces may have openings of the same kinds or on all four sides.

**Components** The usual types of fireplaces have a number of parts in addition to the fire chamber, the space in which the burning of wood or other fuels is accomplished. Above this space is a narrowed opening called the throat, in which a steel or cast-iron device, called a damper, may be placed to control the flow of smoke from the fireplace and to allow the chimney to be closed off when not in use. Above the damper is a larger space, called a smoke chamber or shelf, which helps prevent downdrafts into the fireplace and helps establish updrafts. Above is the chimney, generally of masonry, which is lined with flue liners, usually of clay tile but sometimes of double-walled metal, to form a stack up which smoke and gases rise. At the top of the chimney, clay tile chimney pots may project or openings may be made at the sides for smoke and gases to escape, with a hood over the top to help prevent downdrafts and precipitation from entering the chimney.

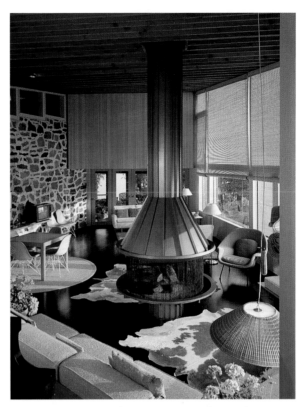

**FIREPLACE** Summer home (1950), Canada. *[Architect: Eero Saarinen; fireplace (1961) designed by Kevin Roche]*

The walls of the fire chamber are finished with materials that resist heat, usually firebrick but sometimes soapstone or other materials. Fireplaces can also be built around prefabricated liners or fireboxes of steel or iron that ensure the proper shapes and dimensions and are equipped with dampers and smoke chambers. Such prefabricated types may also be obtained with grilles that allow cold air near the floor in a room to flow past the firebox, where it is heated and then discharged into the interior of the room from high grilles.

The bottoms inside fireplaces or back hearths are usually covered with heat-resistant materials, such as firebrick, and in front of the fireplaces, other fire-resistant materials, such as clay tile or stone, form front hearths. The face of a fireplace around the opening, the surround, may be finished with any of a number of materials, including ceramic tile, marble or other stone, and wood. If wood is used, it must be held back from the sides and top of the opening for fire safety.

The complete surround of a fireplace is called a mantelpiece, and may include a shelf above the opening, called a mantel shelf or simply mantel. A hole in the back hearth may be provided for an ash dump and covered with a cast-iron, pivoted door to allow ashes to be dropped to a basement or the bottom of the chimney, where they may be removed periodically. Fireplaces usu-

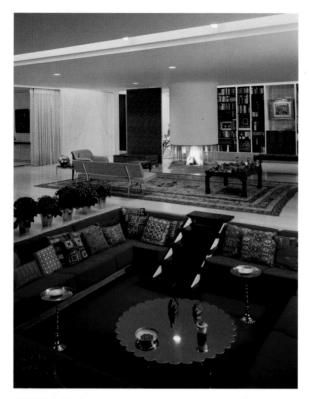

**FIREPLACE** Private residence (1956), Ind. *[Architect: Eero Saarinen; interiors: Alexander Girard]*

ally have devices called andirons placed inside, upon which logs may rest, or grates, into which coal or coke may be placed. For safety from flying sparks, they are often furnished with fire screens, usually of metal mesh that may be pulled to the side like curtains but sometimes of special glass made like doors.

**Design** For the fireplace to operate or draw properly, it must be designed properly. This means that the fire chamber, smoke chamber, flues, and so on must be in the proper sizes, in relationship to each other and to the whole fireplace, and in the proper shapes. Proper design of a fireplace starts with its opening, for which there are definite ratios of heights to widths. Depths should not be less than half the height of the opening and should not, except in very special cases, exceed 2 ft. For best radiation and for control of fires, smoke, and gases, the side walls should slant inward from front to back; back walls should be vertical to a certain point, then slant toward the front. In very large fireplaces, hoods are often used to decrease the effective openings or hearths may be raised for the same purpose. Both methods may be used purely for design reasons.

Flue sizes are directly related to fire chamber sizes and usually have an area of 10 percent of the fireplace opening. The throat should have an area equal to or larger than that of the flue; if the throat is too small, a fireplace may smoke or if too large, will waste heat.

Similarly, certain dimensions and shapes are proper for smoke chambers. To draw properly, chimneys should rise to a point at least 2 ft above the peaks of pitched roofs and 3 ft above flat ones. More than one fireplace may use a single chimney, but building codes require each to have a separate flue. Other code requirements apply to the design and construction of fireplaces and should be consulted. Proper dimensions for various sizes and types of fireplaces and their individual components are available from a number of sources and should be strictly followed.

If the established principles for their proper design and the code requirements are followed, fireplaces of many kinds can be useful, enjoyable, and important features of architecture. In addition to those specifically designed for individual buildings, some of the prefabricated types, available in several shapes and sizes, can be obtained complete with necessary accessories and with flue and chimney hood systems.

While fireplaces can be counted upon today to furnish some amount of heat in buildings, they are not really very efficient. Of all the types, the most efficient are those constructed with prefabricated liners or fireboxes with grilles; and certain prefabricated free-standing types, with openings generally on only one side. Various stoves available today, many of them based on the principles of the Franklin stove, are quite efficient. The less efficient fireplaces are generally those with more than one side open and the least efficient, the type with all sides open.

**History** The time of the first use of fire by humans is unknown. Evidence of its use has been found in all ancient cultures discovered so far. At first fires were used only out of doors, but later, it is not known when, fires were brought indoors for light, cooking, and warmth. The first fireplaces were very primitive, consisting of a shallow hole scooped out of the ground and lined with stones or clay. There was no chimney; smoke simply rose through a hole in top of the hut or tent. For safety, such hearths were usually located in the centers of huts and tents. Wood was often burned, though coal is known to have been used as a fuel from very early times.

By the time, beginning about 3000 B.C., of the great civilizations around the Mediterranean Sea, braziers of stone and metal, with pierced sides and legs, had been developed. Charcoal was often burned in them. This practice has continued until today in certain parts of the world.

In masonry buildings, hearths were sometimes placed adjacent to walls, though the central type was still used. Instead of holes in roofs, rudimentary exposed flues were used to exhaust the smoke. Andirons were developed, not only for holding logs but for supporting cooking pots; later grates were developed, along with tongs and bellows for starting fires and keeping them burning. Gradually, fireplaces that were partly enclosed, resembling to some extent those of today, were developed along with chimneys and flues.

By the time of the Romans, fireplaces were in general use. However, the Romans, dissatisfied with such a rudimentary heating system, developed the first central heating system, called a hypocaust. During the Middle Ages, in Gothic buildings, the idea of central heating was not pursued. Many buildings, including the great cathedrals, were not heated at all. In other buildings, heating was primitive, consisting of wood-burning, open hearths in the centers of rooms with louvered holes in the roofs to let out smoke. By the 13th century, fireplaces were sometimes placed against walls and furnished with flues, chimneys, and sometimes hoods. Coal was once again used as a fuel. But the older practices persisted in some places until the 16th century. Fireplaces were placed only in the most important rooms. Some Gothic buildings had ornamented fireplaces, often with arches over their openings, and were quite large.

During the early Renaissance, fireplaces, complete with chimneys, developed into the types known today. The custom was to provide a fireplace in every room, including bedrooms, rather than only in the most important rooms as in the past. As they did with other architectural elements, the architects of the Renaissance ornamented the fireplaces and often the chimneys. Some of the designs were quite elaborate. They also put ornamental firebacks of cast iron in fireplaces to protect the masonry from heat. Fireplace openings gradually became smaller than those of the Gothic period and the custom of using mantelpieces, sometimes used in the

past, became common practice. Mantelpieces were often of fine wood, marble, or other stone. In the 17th century, the first stoves for heating the interiors of buildings were developed in Northern Europe, particularly in the Scandinavian countries. Stoves thus began to replace fireplaces to some extent.

**American Development** In early colonial America, rudimentary fireplaces, of the types then in use in Europe, were the first devices for cooking and heating. Later, fireplaces became important architectural elements of American buildings, and gradually became more efficient. About the beginning of the 18th century, stoves for heating appeared and these were also gradually made more efficient. In 1740 the master of all trades, Benjamin Franklin (1706–90), invented a very efficient type that came to be called the Franklin stove. Widely copied and emulated, Franklin's invention was never patented by him. Stoves of this sort, in which coal or wood may be burned, are still available and used today. Other types of stoves and heaters were developed later, including gas and electric types.

Beginning in the 19th century and continuing during the 20th until the present time, central heating systems were developed and continuously improved, originally steam and hot-water, followed by hot-air and other types. By the beginning of the 20th century, the end of fireplaces and stoves as the prime sources of heating for most buildings was in sight. Today major buildings and many others are completely heated, and often air-conditioned, by central systems. Fireplaces have become mainly ornamental and emotional, it might even be said sentimental, vestiges of the past. Regrettably, in terms of architectural honesty and excellence, some fireplaces today hold only fake logs with gas fires issuing from them and some hold no fires at all, only electric lights that glow. With the fuel shortages of the fourth quarter of the 20th century, fireplaces and stoves of improved types, including some newer ones from Scandinavia, have made something of a comeback.

**Related Articles** DESIGN, ARCHITECTURAL; ENERGY; HEATING, VENTILATING, AND AIR CONDITIONING.

**FIRE PROTECTION** The use of devices, systems, and materials for the prevention of fires, warnings when fires occur, and saving property and life in fires. The major considerations in building design for fire safety consists of provision of fire-resistant materials and construction, provisions for fire detection and alarms, provisions for escape or refuge from fires, and provisions for bringing fires under control. Fires are sometimes caused by lightning or earthquakes; for further discussion, see articles entitled lightning protection; seismic design. Because of dangers to life and property in fires and because of the huge losses of both

**FIREPLACE** Section and elevation of typical masonry type.

each year, architects and other environmental designers must give serious consideration to fire protection in buildings. Detailed requirements for fire protection are contained in applicable building, fire, and other codes and regulations.

**Ignition Point** Various materials ignite at different temperatures; paper, for example, at about 450°F and wood at about 500°F. Fires in buildings move rapidly upward, through convention, carried by the motion of air. Fires spread more slowly horizontally. Fires can also spread by conduction, transfer of heat through solid materials, in particular metals; or by radiation, transfer by waves. Temperatures in fires may reach 1000°F or higher very quickly, igniting combustible materials at considerable distances away. Humans can only withstand temperatures of 250°F for some 15 minutes and 350°F for about 30 seconds. In spite of the inherent danger of such levels of heat, most deaths in fires result from lack of oxygen or inhalation of toxic gases and smoke.

The rate of burning of fires is controlled by two major factors: the ventilation available and the fuel load, the presence of combustible materials. If ventilation is poor, as in a closed room, and the fuel load is high, the rate of burning will be slow and the fire prolonged. If the opposite is true, as in a room with ample ventilation and a small fuel load, the rate of burning will be fast and the fire of short duration. In any fire, there is danger of flashover, the almost instantaneous ignition of all or most combustible materials in a room when air temperatures near the ceiling reach 800°F or more.

**Code Requirements** Certain factors must be taken into consideration in the proper design of buildings for fire protection. One is called the fire load, a measure of the amount of combustible materials in various types of buildings. A given fire load is the fuel contribution of the combustibles in a building converted to that of a certain number of pounds of wood per square foot (psf) of floor area. Fire loads are specified in fire, building, and other codes, and range from about 8 psf in an apartment to 36 psf in library bookstacks up to 50 psf in clothes closets and to 86 psf in file rooms.

Codes also require buildings of certain types and in certain locations to have specific levels of fire resistance. The usual classifications of fire resistance in buildings include fire-resistive, with three- to four-hour rating for primary structures, two to three hours for secondary structural members and partitions around stairways and other vertical openings and incombustible materials elsewhere; noncombustible, with fire-resistive bearing walls, floors, and roofs; heavy timber; protected combustible, with incombustible exterior walls; and unprotected combustible, or wood frame. The fire rating requirements vary considerably between building types

and between various components of each type, from four hours resistance down to none.

Fire requirements also limit the allowable heights of buildings. No limit, for fire reasons, is placed on fire-resistive construction for any type of building. Typical restrictions on other classifications are noncombustible, three stories for residential buildings, two for other types; protected combustible, four stories for residential and commercial buildings, three for factories, and two for educational buildings; heavy timber, three stories for residential, commercial, and industrial buildings, and two for educational. In some cases, restrictions are also placed on the actual heights of buildings in feet. Restrictions are also made on allowable floor areas of buildings of various types, except for fire-resistive construction upon which there is no limit. Typical limits for other types of construction include 13,200 ft² for noncombustible, 10,000 for protected combustible, and 8,800 for heavy timber residential and educational buildings. Applicable codes contain the exact requirements for various classifications of construction.

Fire, building, and other codes also contain other requirements for fire protection of buildings. For example, fire-resistive construction is the most usual requirement in central city areas, while lesser classifications are generally allowed in less congested areas, in which exposures are not considered as dangerous. Fire walls, with no openings and extending several feet above roofs, are often required between apartment units that may otherwise be of unprotected combustible construction. Tall buildings, in general, must be sealed to fire at every story and have automatic, electric motor-driven fire-resistive covers for escalators. Vertical shafts must be enclosed in fire-resistive construction. Often provisions for smoke shafts or other means for venting smoke and gases to the outside must be provided. Careful attention must be paid to electrical wiring and devices to prevent the possibility of fires originated by overloading or other malfunctions. Automatic dampers are required in heating and air-conditioning ductwork in many cases. Other important considerations are also necessary for the prevention of fires in buildings.

One of the most important considerations requires that structural components must be protected from damage from fire, which might cause them to fail. The most important methods, often used for fire-protection purposes with structural steel, involve covering the steel with prescribed thicknesses of materials, such as gypsum or other types of plaster, mineral wool, gypsum board, concrete, or other fire-resistive materials. Such materials may also be used for protecting walls, partitions, and other building components. Reinforced concrete, properly designed, is highly fire-resistive, as are brick, concrete block, and other masonry materials. Recently, the columns of some buildings have been fire-protected by water which transmits heat to a storage tank, to be vented to the outside as steam.

**Detectors** The detection of fires in buildings is usually accomplished with heat or smoke detectors. Several types are available for detection of various kinds of fires, including those that smolder or flame up, flash fires, and so on. In order to be effective, the proper types must be selected, must be located properly and in sufficient numbers, and must be properly maintained. Heat and smoke detectors may sound alarms or warnings of fires either directly from the units or through wiring to various locations in buildings. Manual alarms are also widely used in buildings. These require a person who discovers a fire to open an alarm box or break its glass cover and pull a handle. Such alarms may be uncoded, simply sounding warnings, or coded, to indicate where fires are located. Both types should be placed in obvious locations in plain view of building occupants.

**Exit Routes** Once a fire alarm has sounded, the most important aspect of human safety is the availability of safe escape or egress routes or refuges. Fire, building, and other codes specify requirements for egress and refuge. Such requirements include escape routes that are direct, unimpeded, wide enough, not too far away, and not too long. Maximum limits for travel distances to exits vary according to building types and whether or not buildings have sprinkler systems. For example, buildings with sprinklers may have the following maximum travel distances: hotels, dormitories, apartments, commercial and industrial buildings, 150 ft; most educational and assembly buildings, 200 ft; office buildings, 300 ft. Without sprinklers, these travel distances are reduced by 50 ft, except for office buildings which are reduced by 100 ft.

Exit route minimum widths are often taken to be 3 ft. The number of exits required depends on the number of people per amount of floor area, or occupant density, of various building types. Assumed occupant densities range from 15 ft$^2$ per person in assembly rooms with fixed seats, to 20 in classrooms, 30 to 60 in commercial buildings, 100 in office buildings and factories, and 200 in residential buildings. The capacity of an exit is the number of people who can pass through one unit of exit, defined as 22 in wide, in 1 minute. Exit capacities vary in different building types, from 30 people per unit of exit width in sleeping areas of institutions such as hospitals, 60 in residential buildings, to 100 in most other types.

For stairs used as exits, the exit capacities are lower: 22 people per exit unit in sleeping rooms of hospitals and other institutions, 45 in residential buildings, and 60 to 75 in most other types. To determine the required exit widths, the total area of a floor of a building is divided by the density and the exit capacity. For example, a factory with 30,000 ft$^2$ on a floor, divided by a density of 100 and by a capacity of 100 for horizontal exits, would require three exit units, totaling 66 in. For stairways, the factory would require 5 units, or 110 in.

In addition to exit width requirements, codes require fire doors of fire-resistive construction, self-closing, equipped with horizontal bars, called panic hardware, which open the doors when people press against them. Minimum stair widths, often 44 in, are required, along with approved types of handrails. Multistory buildings must have certain minimum number of stairs, protected by fire-resistive materials, extending the full heights of the buildings. Such enclosures must also be smokeproof and may be pressurized to accomplish this. Approved types of illuminated exit signs must be provided. In some cases, certain areas of buildings may be designed as safe refuge areas to which people may move until they can escape from the buildings. It is possible to enclose elevators in safe areas and pressurize them for limited use during fires by invalids or other incapacitated people and by fire fighters. A minimum of two exits should be provided on every floor leading to safe exit routes. Corridors should not dead-end, creating traps for smoke and for building occupants.

**Control Systems** A number of considerations are related to the control and extinguishing of fires in buildings. Sprinkler systems that automatically release water to extinguish fires are required in certain types of buildings and in spaces in other buildings in which high risks of fire exist. Standpipes are often provided in buildings for use by people fighting fires. A dry standpipe system is one which includes piping that usually does not contain water. Fire fighters attach hoses to the systems inside buildings and receive water, pumped by fire trucks, from hydrants on the ground level. Some of these systems are actually dry until used, while others are primed with water that is not under pressure until pumps are attached. Wet standpipe systems contain water under pressure at all times, from storage tanks located on the roof or upper floors of buildings. Water from these is available at all times to building occupants as well as to fire fighters. Sometimes wet and dry systems are used in combination. And often hose cabinets, with hoses ready to be used, are located in the corridors of buildings with wet or combination systems. Special systems include $CO_2$, foams, and halogenated agents.

In addition, fire extinguishers of various types are often provided in buildings. Fire extinguishers are classified by the types of fires they are designed to extinguish. The A type is for ordinary combustibles, such as wood and paper; the B type for flammable liquids, such as gasoline; the C type for electrical fires; the D type for combustible metals, such as magnesium. Labels on extinguishers indicate their type, and care should be taken to use each type properly. For example, an A type used on a gasoline fire will not extinguish it but may cause it to burn or spread more rapidly. On the other hand, an ABC type may be used on gasoline fires as well as ordinary combustible materials and flammable liquids. Fire extinguisher charges last from a few seconds up to about a minute and a half.

In architecture, it is also important for provisions to be made for the professional fire fighters. Adequate space should be provided on building sites for fire trucks and other equipment; an adequate number of hydrants, properly located, should be provided. Windowless buildings present great problems to fire fighters. When more than two stories high or with more than certain prescribed floor areas, windowless buildings must be sprinklered. In addition, access openings for use in fire fighting should be provided on each side of windowless buildings facing streets or other public areas on every floor.

Fire protection of buildings is one of the most important technical considerations in design and construction. While fire, building, and other codes specify certain requirements, architects and other environmental designers often consult experts and organizations that have the experience and knowledge to aid in the design of buildings that will be as fire-safe as possible. Such organizations and many of the individual experts are engaged in continuing research and testing to determine improved methods for fire safety. Advantage should be taken of their continuing important work on such matters.

**History** The threat of fire has always existed in architectural structures. In the earliest primitive huts and tents, the use of fires inside undoubtedly often led to their destruction. Lightning took its toll. The earliest primitive wooden buildings have all been destroyed by fires, weather, insects, and other disasters.

In the buildings of the ancient civilizations in Mesopotamia, Egypt, Crete, and Greece, no particular precautions against fire seem to have been taken, partly because masonry was the major material used. The Romans were much more conscious of the threat of fire to their buildings, which were very close together in towns and cities. During the 1st century A.D., after several bad fires, regulations restricted the heights of buildings, prohibited party walls between buildings, required use of fire-resistant materials, restricted use of timber, and required flat roofs from which fires could be fought. The Romans also placed roads through cities to act as firebreaks and to provide access to fires, and they established a well-equipped fire-fighting corps. In addition, the Romans had adequate sources of water for fire fighting, available from aqueducts and other systems.

During the Middle Ages and the Renaissance, fires were frequent and were not controlled or extinguished as efficiently as they had been in Roman times. Streets were often narrow and crooked, making access to fires difficult. Roof structures were often of timber, easily ignited by lightning. Water supplies were inadequate. And fire fighters were less well trained and equipped. During both periods, disastrous fires occurred in many parts of Europe. One of the worst was the Great Fire of London in 1666, which lasted four days and virtually destroyed the city.

As a result of the Great Fire, regulations for buildings were formulated in the London Building Act of 1667, prohibiting timber-framed houses, setting minimum thickness for walls, and requiring nonflammable roof coverings. In 1680 the first fire insurance company was founded and since there were no public fire fighters, the company organized its own. The fire fighters fought only the fires in insured buildings. Later other private fire-fighter companies were formed and this continued to be the practice in early colonial America.

Starting in the 18th century, with the advent of iron-framed buildings, methods for making structures fire-resistant, or fireproof as it was called then, were developed. At first earthenware pots were used but later most utilized bricks, hollow-tile or terra-cotta units to enclose structural members. In some cases, plaster was used, and sometimes brick arches were used to form floors and roofs between the iron girders.

**U.S. Fire Disasters** Many disastrous fires have occurred in America since the time of the first colonization. Among the worst were the fire in New York City in 1835, which destroyed some 500 buildings; the great Chicago fire of 1871, traditionally started by Mrs. O'Leary's cow, which destroyed the city and took 250 lives; and in the same year, a forest fire near Peshtigo, Wis., which destroyed several small towns and took 1,182 lives. In 1876 fire in a theater in Brooklyn, N.Y., claimed 295 lives; and in 1903 another in the Iroquois Theater, Chicago, 602 lives were lost. In 1904 a large portion of Baltimore burned, but no lives were lost.

**U.S. Fire Codes** In 1905 the first model fire code was produced by the National Board of Fire Underwriters, now known as the American Insurance Association, and the code was subsequently adopted by many cities and towns. In spite of the requirements of this code and others that followed it, disastrous fires have continued to occur, including that in 1942 in the Coconut Grove Club, Boston, in which 491 people died, only about a week after it had been approved in a fire inspection. In spite of increasingly stringent code and other requirements for building construction, destructive fires continue to occur with regularity, including that of the Beverly Hills Supper Club, Southgate, Ky., which took 164 lives in 1977. In the recent past, some 1 million fires, causing over $3 billion in property losses, have occurred each year.

Gradually over the years, more reliable information on fires, how they start, how they spread, how they are fueled, and so on, has been developed through research and testing. Building, fire, and other codes and standards have been improved. Fire-detection devices and fire-fighting equipment and techniques have also been vastly improved. Today rigid requirements for fire resistance in buildings are contained in building, fire, and other codes and standards, as are requirements for fire detection, fire fighting, and evacuation of people from buildings.

Because of the great frequency of fires in buildings and the devastating toll they take in human lives and property damage each year, provision of proper fire protection in buildings is one of the major concerns of architects and other environmental designers.

**Related Articles** BUILDING CODES AND STANDARDS; COMMUNICATION SYSTEM; LIGHTNING PROTECTION; SEISMIC DESIGN; Articles on various building components and systems.

**Further Reading** Egan, M. David: *Concepts in Building Firesafety*, reprint of 1978 ed., Krieger, Melbourne, Fla.; Stein, Benjamin, and John S. Reynolds: Part IV, *Fire Protection*, in *Mechanical and Electrical Equipment for Buildings*, 8th ed., John Wiley & Sons, Inc., New York, 1992.

**Sources of Additional Information** American Insurance Assoc., 1130 Connecticut Ave., N.W., Suite 1000, Washington, D.C. 20036; American Society for Testing and Materials (ASTM), 1916 Race St., Philadelphia, Pa. 19103; National Fire Protection Assoc., 470 Atlantic Ave., Boston, Mass. 02210; Underwriters Laboratories, 333 Pfingsten Rd., Northbrook, Ill. 60062.

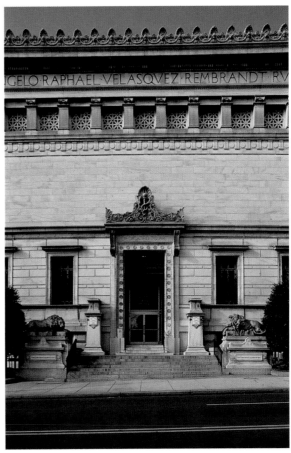

**FLAGG, ERNEST** Corcoran Gallery of Art (1897; addition, 1927), Washington, D.C. *[Architect: Ernest Flagg; 1927 addition architect: Charles Platt]*

**FLAGG, ERNEST** An eclectic American architect Ernest Flagg (1857–1947) was one of seven children of a well-known minister Jared Bradley Flagg (1820–99), who was, for a period, pastor of Grace Church, New York, and his second wife, Louisa Hart Flagg (1828–67). The family was socially well placed. His sister married the publisher Charles Scribner, and a cousin married Cornelius Vanderbilt II. These connections provided Flagg with several important architectural commissions.

**Work** Flagg's first work was encouraged by Cornelius Vanderbilt II, who was instrumental in the award of a contract in 1893 on the basis of a design competition for St. Luke's Hospital in New York. This project was followed by the new Corcoran Gallery of Art in Washington, D.C., also awarded to Flagg in 1893. He was architect for the U.S. Naval Academy at Annapolis, Md., from 1896 to 1908. The Singer Tower in New York was completed in 1908 as one of a group of buildings designed for that company. At that time the Singer Tower was the tallest building ever built, constructed in 20 months, and has the dubious record of being the tallest building ever demolished (1968). Flagg was active

in the debate resulting in the 1916 zoning laws for New York. He designed the Scribner Building (1913) on Fifth Avenue in New York as one of a group of projects for the publisher and brother-in-law. Ernest Flagg experimented with and promoted well-lit and ventilated low-cost housing in response to problems with the New York old-law tenements, was concerned by the crowding of skyscraper towers in New York, was interested in designs for suburban houses, and was the designer of the first architect-designed parking garage in New York City.

**Life** Born in Brooklyn, N.Y., on February 6, 1857, he was nine when his mother died, and the children were sent away to school or sent to live with relatives. His father resigned from Grace Church in 1863 and moved his family frequently. Ernest Flagg was educated in a number of private schools and at the age of 15 went into several business ventures, the last as a speculator in land and apartment building in New York City, then new to America. Flagg devised a plan of two-story apartments served by skip-stop elevators. Although the family invested in successful apartment developments, later ventures were less successful. In 1888, Flagg was encouraged by the Vanderbilts to attend the École des Beaux Arts in Paris.

Flagg arrived in Paris in 1888 and finished his studies by 1890, just long enough to learn the techniques and principles of the École des Beaux Arts before travelling extensively in Europe. Flagg returned to New York early in 1891 and proceeded to form a successful firm in the École des Beaux Arts tradition. A founding member of the Society of Beaux-Arts Architects, Flagg was in opposition to the schools of architecture, of which 13 were organized by 1900. Rather, the Society promoted the French style of education based on the atelier, or studio, where students were encouraged to work by themselves. This attempt to found a Beaux Arts education system developed into a debate as to whether professional educators or practicing architects should educate the next generation.

In 1899, Ernest Flagg married Margaret Elizabeth Bonnell (1882–1978). Having practiced in New York for over 40 years, Flagg was honored by the New York Chapter of the American Institute of Architects in 1945. Ernest Flagg died on April 10, 1947, at age ninety.

**Further Reading** Bacon, Mardges: *Ernest Flagg: Beaux Arts Architect and Urban Reformer,* The Architectural History Foundation, New York, and the MIT Press, Cambridge, Mass., 1986.

**FLOOR** The bottom surface within a building or room, usually but not always horizontal, on which furniture and other objects may be placed and people may walk. The term *floor* may be applied to the complete system, including its structure and surface material, or to the surface material only. Such surfacing materials are sometimes referred to as flooring. The word *floor* may also be used to denote the separation between stories of a building, as in a building with five floors or stories.

**Materials** A great variety of flooring materials are available, with many types of characteristics, useful lives, textures, colors, forms, and costs. Major materials include wood, burned-clay types, stone, terrazzo, concrete, carpeting, and resilient flooring. Flooring is usually installed on wood or concrete subfloors. For all kinds of flooring, subfloors must be properly designed and constructed.

Wood flooring comes in strips, up to $^{25}/_{32}$ in in thickness, from $1^1/_2$ to $3^1/_2$ in wide; and squares, ranging in size up to about 10 by 10 in. The squares may be laminated with veneers like plywood for less costly installations or made with solid strips, often called parquet flooring, fastened together with metal splines or other devices, for more costly work. Parquet flooring in the past was often made with chevron or other patterns.

Wood flooring is available in both softwoods and hardwoods. The former are less expensive but do not

**FLOOR** Mosaic floor, Wayne County Courthouse, Detroit, Mich.

wear as well. Softwoods include Douglas fir, pine, hemlock, and larch. Hardwoods include oak, beech, birch, and maple. Wood-strip flooring ordinarily is manufactured with tongues and grooves on the sides, which enable it to be attached to wood subflooring by blind nailing into the tongues, with the grooves hiding the nails. When wood subflooring is used, it is considered good practice to cover it with a felt fabric before the finished floor is laid. When wood-strip flooring is installed over concrete subfloors, small wood strips, called sleepers, to which finish flooring may be nailed are generally used. Parquet and other wood blocks are often laid in mastic or other adhesives.

Burned-clay flooring materials include ceramic tile, quarry and similar tiles, and brick. Stone flooring is mostly of marble or slate. Colors and textures are generally limited in all types except ceramic tile, which comes in many varied colors. All are available in squares or rectangles of various sizes and are laid in cement mortar. Terrazzo is a flooring material, which may be obtained in a number of colors and textures, composed of about two parts marble chips and one part portland cement. Terrazzo may be laid in sand beds, bonded to concrete toppings, or may be used as a thin topping for uncured concrete slabs. Divider strips are used in the sand-bed and bonded types. Terrazzo can also be precast. A type of flooring, much like very thin terrazzo, is sometimes installed with adhesives.

Concrete is often used for flooring, particularly in utilitarian buildings, such as factories. In such cases the structural concrete of floors is usually finished with a thin topping of special concrete bonded to the structural concrete before it has completely cured. Carpet can be laid, with proper precautions, on almost any kind of floor or subfloor that has been properly prepared.

The most common flooring is a group of products identified as "resilient flooring." The word *resilient* refers to the ability of these products to recover from indentation that may be created by the heel of a shoe, a table leg, or wheel. There has been a shift from the earlier linoleum and asphalt tile, which had a large part of the market earlier in the 20th century, to the most common material identified as vinyl products.

Linoleum was first produced in 1860 and remained in wide use for many decades. Linoleum was made of various fillers and binder materials culminating in the felt-based products used in residential buildings in the 1940s and 1950s. Manufacturing of linoleum was discontinued in the United States by 1974, although still produced in Europe. Imported linoleum was not used for floors but for table tops.

Asphalt tile was developed because linoleum was damaged by alkaline moisture and thus not suitable for on-grade or below-grade surfaces. First produced in 1922, asphalt tile largely replaced linoleum but was limited in colors and offered poor resistance to oils and greases. The development of vinyl asbestos tile and the current vinyl composition tile largely replaced the earlier resilient products. The polyvinyl chlorides used as binders are resistant to most acids and alkalis, including moisture, but are attacked by some organic solvents.

Asbestos was formerly used as a filler for vinyl tile and other flooring materials but because of health reasons is no longer used. Vinyl asbestos tile (VAT) was for many years the resilient flooring product of choice.

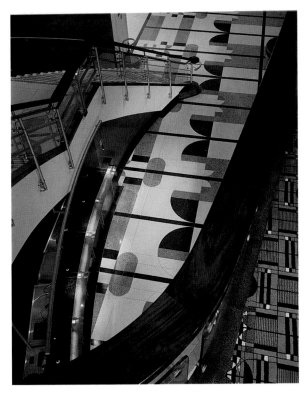

**FLOOR** Terrazzo and carpeting, North York Art Center (1993), Ontario, Canada. *[Architect: Zeidler Roberts]*

Current production of vinyl flooring products include vinyl tile, vinyl composition tile (VCT), and vinyl sheet flooring of various types. The difference between vinyl tile and vinyl composition tile is in the amount of vinyl resins. The vinyl tile might have 25 percent by weight of vinyl resin, and vinyl composition may have half as much. In addition to plasticizers and stabilizers, the largest part of the mix is fillers and pigments. Sheet vinyl may be cushioned for residential use or manufactured with a backing in several grades and often used in health-care facilities, or without any backing for commercial and institutional applications.

Rubber tile and sheet have been produced since the 1920s. Although losing market share to the vinyl products, they are now frequently selected because of the popularity of the raised disk design. Rubber tile is now primarily made with artificial rubbers of various types. These products make very durable flooring, quiet, long wearing, and are resistant to cigarette burns. They are limited in color and are subject to damage from certain asphaltic or vegetable oils, although they are more resistant to some solvents than the vinyl products.

In general, resilient tiles indent or will be damaged if loads that are too heavy are placed on them. Rubber and vinyl tile will withstand the greatest loads, followed by vinyl sheet. Vinyl composition tile can support the least amount of load. Rubber and cushioned vinyl flooring are selected for the quietness of the floor. Wear and durability of various types of resilient flooring have been ranked for use in elevator cabs with rubber tile the best, followed by vinyl sheet flooring. Linoleum is ranked better than vinyl composition tile, with asphalt tile having the shortest life. Good maintenance will greatly lengthen the life of a floor. Other conditions require careful attention such as the choice of subflooring, the need for well-cured concrete surfaces free from moisture, and the smoothness of the surfaces to receive flooring.

The resilience of flooring varies depending on the short-term versus long-term or permanent loading. Vinyl composition tile, for instance, .is excellent for short-term or moving loads but is less good for permanent loading. Recommendations are given for the loading of various flooring materials, although pressures from small-diameter forces such as the heels of women's shoes may greatly exceed the rated resilience.

Other available types of flooring include those designed for specialized or specific uses. Conductive flooring in limited colors contains conductive carbon black and is used where explosive or flammable dusts or vapors exist or where control of static electricity is needed. Slip-retardant flooring is used for ramps, wet areas, or vestibules. Raised patterns or deep embossing in combination with the addition of carborundum, quartz, or other mineral aggregates in the surface will increase the nonslip characteristics of the flooring. Heavy-duty installations where machinery or vehicles are used require special attention to the selection of flooring.

In addition to their selection for such attributes as the appearance desired, useful lives, degree of maintenance required, and costs, flooring in buildings may be designed as unobtrusive bases or backgrounds for other architectural features or may become such features themselves by the use of patterns, colors, textures, or ornamental designs, including representational as well as abstract or geometrical types. Flooring can also become the base or background for rugs or carpets, ranging from solid unobtrusive colors and weave to ornamental or pictorial qualities found in Oriental rugs or those by modern designers.

**History** No floor system was used in ancient primitive huts and tents; the ground served as both floor and flooring. Later buildings are thought to have had floors built of wood logs and branches. By about 3000 B.C., in the great civilizations around the Mediterranean Sea, floor systems of stone or brick laid on the ground and wood for upper stories had come into use. For many years, the structure of floors on the ground level was also the flooring. Wood structures of upper stories often supported wood flooring.

Later developments included the use of concrete in Mesopotamia. Made of lime, sand, and broken limestone, it was used on ground levels with waterproofing of bitumen and flooring of stone slabs. In Egypt the roofs of temples were often of cut stone, and served the additional purpose of roof terraces or floors used in ceremonies. In Crete floor structures were often rounded logs, and polished gypsum was used for flooring.

Clay tile was also an important floor material in ancient times and was used in Mesopotamia, Crete, Egypt, Greece, and Rome. However, the most important flooring material used in ancient Greece was stone, particularly marble. In addition to clay tile, the Romans used stone, wood, concrete, and mosaic, usually made by inlaying small pieces of stone into a concrete base. The Romans usually placed ground floors on bases of concrete and floors of upper stories on concrete or wood-framed structures. In Byzantine architecture elaborate mosaic floors were often used, together with flooring composed of several different colors of marble slabs.

In the Romanesque and Gothic periods of architecture, floor systems were generally of stone and wood, as was flooring. In the Renaissance, the previously available types of floor systems and flooring were used and a new type, terrazzo, was developed.

**American Development** In early colonial America, floors were tamped earth inside buildings. Later, floor systems and flooring similar to the types in Europe were used. During the revival and eclectic periods in American architecture, floor designs were generally derived from periods of the past. With the beginnings of the modern movement in architecture in the 19th century came the development of skeleton-framed, steel, and reinforced concrete construction. Floor structures were constructed of those materials, using new systems. Wood-framed floor systems were important, particularly in house construction. Floor systems of these types are still used in architecture. A vast array of flooring materials are available today, including all the types used previously.

**Related Articles** CONCRETE STRUCTURE; FIRE PROTECTION; FOUNDATION; MASONRY STRUCTURE; STEEL STRUCTURE; WOOD-FRAME STRUCTURE; Articles on various materials.

**Sources of Additional Information** Carpet and Rug Inst., P.O. Box 2048, Dalton, Ga. 30722; Ceramic Tile Inst. of America, 700 N. Virgil Ave., Los Angeles, Calif. 90029; Maple Flooring Manufacturers Assoc., 60 Revere Drive, Suite 500, Northbrook, Ill. 60062; National Oak Flooring Manufacturers Assoc., P.O. Box 3009, Memphis, Tenn. 38173-0009; National Terrazzo and Mosaic Assoc., 3166 Des Plaines Ave., Suite 132, Des Plaines, Ill. 60018; Resilient Floor Covering Inst., 966 Hungerford Dr., Suite 12-B, Rockville, Md. 20805; Tile Council of America, P.O. Box 326, Princeton, N.J. 08450; Wood and Synthetic Flooring Inst., 4415 W. Harrison St., Suite 243-C, Hillside, Ill. 60162.

**FOUNDATION** The lowest part of a building which supports the loads of the structure above and transmits the loads to the ground. Ordinarily, foundations today are constructed of reinforced concrete, though mass concrete without reinforcing is sometimes used for support of heavy walls, chimneys, or similar heavy loads. The term *foundation* is often taken to mean the entire substructure of a building, and may be partly concrete, brick, or stone masonry, while the lowest portion of reinforced concrete, resting directly on the soil, is called a footing.

Foundations and footings serve the primary purpose of supporting weights of buildings and other loads above them, but they also resist heaving of the earth caused by freezing and thawing. In buildings with basements, foundations also resist the sideways or lateral forces of the earth outside and are expected to protect the interior from water infiltration. See the article entitled waterproofing.

The design of foundations and footings for buildings and other structures must take into consideration several major factors: the loads to be carried, the characteristics of the soil on building sites, climate, and water conditions. The loads to be carried by foundations and footings are determined by the weights of the materials and construction used, the number of stories to be constructed, snow and wind loads, and the loads of people and furnishings. The determination of the loads of foundations and footings, and their design to carry the loads, is a function of a structural engineer. Sometimes simple types, such as those for single-family houses on soil with good load-bearing qualities, are handled by architects and other environmental designers. See articles entitled structural engineering; structure.

**Soil Properties** The qualities of soils on building sites are determined by the science of soil mechanics or soil engineering. Soils are the thin layer of particles of rock that cover a large portion of the land in the world. Topsoil is the uppermost, richest layer and is usually 6 in or less in thickness today. Subsoil is the next lower strata, about 2 or 3 ft deep ordinarily. Below that may be additional soil until the depth of bedrock is reached. To determine the effects of the soil on foundations and footings for a building, it is necessary to know many facts, including such things as the range of sizes of grains and their shapes, chemical makeup, and others. Of particular importance in architecture are determination of the weight or density of soil, strength of its components, cohesion of the soil, and changes that take place when forces are applied to it. Other considerations include the quantities of organic materials contained in the soil, along with quantities of such materials as limestone.

Identification of soils and their properties and characteristics is usually accomplished by borings. Building and other codes determine the minimum number of borings

**FOUNDATION** Sections of typical types.

SPREAD FOOTING

GRADE BEAM

STEPPED FOOTING

INTERIOR WALL FOOTING

for a given site; and boring depths and locations must be carefully determined. Although borings were made in other ways in the past, the usual method today utilizes a device called a boring spoon, which is driven into the ground. This produces core samples of soils in layers, and establishes the resistance of the soil to forces and the depths of underground rock and water. The test samples are then analyzed in laboratories for such properties as specific gravity, grain size and shape, ratio of voids to solid matter or void ratios, water content, strength, and others. Based on such information, proper foundations and footing may be designed and constructed.

Special problems relate to certain soil types. Expansive soils may expand when wet and shrink when dry. This movement may increase pressure on foundation walls and floor slabs and may vary if paving or planting areas adjoin the building. Collapsing soils are those with large voids, which can be identified by the light weight of the soil. Voids may collapse with wetting or shock. Fortunately, these soils are unusual. Quick soils are loose sands or silts which become quick (liquefied) if sufficient moisture is present. These are usually easily identified by routine soils investigation. Liquification applies to certain loose, cohesionless soils which tend to lose shear strength during seismic activity. These may produce disastrous results, such as the overturning of retaining walls.

If necessary, soils may be modified by compaction or densification; by adding portland cement, sand, crushed cinders, or other materials; by rolling with machinery; by reducing the water content; and by other methods. All are intended to improve the bearing qualities of the soil. It must be noted that all soils compact to some extent, and all foundations and footings therefore settle somewhat.

**Climatic Effects** The climate in which foundations and footings are to be constructed is of great importance, because of the damage that can occur from alternating cycles of freezing and thawing. The bottoms of foundations and footings must therefore be extended approximately 1 ft below the frost line, the lowest level of soil that can be expected to freeze in a given location. If foundations or footings are too shallow, damage may occur to them and to the building structures they support. In very warm places, such as southern Florida, the soil does not ordinarily freeze. For small buildings, such as single-family houses in warm locations, reinforced concrete slabs with thickened portions under bearing walls are often used. In colder areas, care must be taken to construct foundations and footings to the proper depths, which vary from about 1 in, in the lower part of the Deep South, to several feet in the upper parts of New England.

**Types** Several types of foundations are commonly used in architecture. The simplest, other than a thickened slab, is a spread footing. This type of footing is ordinarily of reinforced concrete, in a rectangular cross section, laid continuously in locations where bearing walls are to be erected, and usually in square shapes under columns. Spread footings must be considerably wider than the walls or columns they support. Sometimes they are constructed in stepped shapes, with wide portions at the bottoms and narrower portions above. Another relatively simple type of foundation is called a grade beam, usually reinforced concrete of rectangular section, only slightly wider than the walls supported. Basement walls are sometimes made of reinforced concrete in a manner similar to relatively tall grade beams, but for the most part, they are constructed on top of spread footings.

Other types of foundations and footings are sometimes used, including combined and strapped types. Combined footings are much like the spread footings used under columns, except that they support two or more columns, while spread footings support only one. In combined footings, care must be taken to ensure that the centers of gravity of the loads coincide with the actual centers of the footings. A strapped footing is similar to a combined type and is used to support two columns. Instead of being poured in one piece as in combined footings, strapped footings are poured under individual columns, with straps of reinforced concrete that act like beams connecting them. Strapped footings may be somewhat less expensive than combined types. Neither type can be used on sites with soils that are soft and wet, which have low load-bearing capacities.

For soft, wet soils, mat or raft foundations are often used. Much like concrete slabs, mat or raft foundations float on the soft, wet soil much like a raft or boat. They may be used for the support of entire buildings. Another method for soft, wet soil, with low load-bearing capacities, utilizes long structural members called piles or piling, driven or otherwise forced into the soil, after which foundations or footings are placed on top of them. Piles support the loads above them by frictional resistance along their lengths and by bearing on the soils near or at their lower ends. Bearing piles are driven down to bedrock or near it. Friction piles support loads by frictional resistance along their lengths and are assumed to have no bearing at their lower ends.

Piles may be made of a number of materials, including most kinds of timber; H piles; precast, plain, or reinforced concrete; and steel shells into which concrete is poured, the shells being either left in place or removed. Timber piles that remain wet at all times deteriorate very little, but alternating dry and wet cycles eventually cause failure. Timber piles that must extend above water levels are pressure-treated with creosote to preserve them.

Piles are usually driven into the ground by machines called pile-driving hammers or pile drivers, which hold the piles in position while the hammer rises and falls or is driven onto their tops. Sometimes piles are placed in the ground by using water jets or by other means. The load-carrying capacities of piles were often determined in the past by the resistance of the piles to the impact or driving forces of the hammers; when a pile had been driven to a depth in which a certain number of blows of the hammer were required to move it a certain additional distance into the ground, tables indicated its bearing capacity. This method is still used today, but actual tests by loading test piles are considered more reliable. Sometimes the bearing capacity is determined by computation.

Other methods sometimes used in foundation work include excavating the ground to various levels and then bracing the sides of the excavation with structural members of steel, wood, or concrete, to construct temporary, essentially watertight walls, called cofferdams. Structural members used for the walls are called sheeting or sheet piles. A caisson is like a cofferdam, but it is a complete structural shell that can sink by its own weight, sometimes aided by excavation. Caissons may also be placed in holes drilled with well-drilling machinery and by other methods.

The design of foundations and footings may be quite complex, and all but the simplest are usually designed by structural engineers and in the most complex situations, by specialists. Foundations and footings must be of adequate strength to carry the loads imposed on them, must provide controlled settlement, must resist displacement by heaving of the ground or other causes, and must not deteriorate or fail. Thus their design and construction is all-important in architecture, for if foundations and footings do not function properly, the other elements of buildings cannot.

Slabs on grade should have adequate thickness, be reinforced with mesh, have a good subbase of compacted material separated from the slab by a plastic membrane, and be provided with joints to control shrinkage cracking. Slabs are poured in small units, and joints may have keys, dowels, or waterstops where necessary. Slabs subjected to freezing and extreme temperature ranges may require expansion joints.

**History** The first buildings made by humans, huts and tents, had no foundations as such. In the masonry buildings of the great civilizations around the Mediterranean Sea, foundations sometimes were used to support the weight of the walls and other construction above. The foundations of ancient Egyptian and Greek buildings were usually of stone, while those of Rome were often of concrete, though they also used stone.

During the Middle Ages, foundations were not always as strong as earlier ones. For example, some cathedrals have foundations of layers of logs, covered with weak concrete. In others, foundations were better, consisting of concrete on compacted clay, with stone above, or of wood piling. During the Renaissance, foundations were constructed along the lines of those of the Rome era, but usually of brick or stone instead of concrete. Although most were quite strong, some of these foundations proved faulty, including those of several leaning towers in Italy.

**American Development** During the early colonial era in America, foundations were generally of brick and sometimes of stone for more important buildings. Mats of logs were sometimes used. These continued to be the practices for most buildings until the rediscovery of concrete and steel in the 18th century, and the development of reinforced concrete in the 19th.

By the late 19th century, with the advent of the modern movement in architecture, attempts were made to predict the amount of settlements to be expected in buildings and to allow for it in their design. Foundations were often of concrete or grillages of iron rails, and usually each column of tall, skeleton-framed buildings had its own separate foundation. Piling also came into widespread use, mostly of steel or concrete, and later of steel casings into which concrete was poured. Wood piling is still used, often in installations where it will remain continuously under water.

Today, with improved engineering and testing techniques, not only for foundations but in the mechanics of soils, many types of foundations, usually of reinforced concrete or piling of various kinds, are used in architecture.

**Related Articles** CLIMATE; CONCRETE; CONCRETE STRUCTURE; STRUCTURAL ENGINEERING; STRUCTURE; WATERPROOFING.

**Further Reading** Bowles, J. E.: *Foundation Analysis and Design*, 4th ed., McGraw-Hill, New York, 1988; Tomlinson, M. J.: *Foundation Design and Construction*, John Wiley, New York, 1986.

**Source of Additional Information** American Society of Civil Engineers (ASCE), 345 E. 47th St., New York, N.Y. 10017.

**FOUNTAIN** An ornamental feature of the landscaping of buildings, which produces a display with jets of water. The use of water in fountains and in other ways has been an important element of architecture since ancient times and remains so today. Although fountains and other displays of water were often very complex in the past, today they tend to be simpler but no less effective.

**Water Elements** In addition to fountains, the major ways of using water as an architectural element today include pools or ponds of various kinds, such as reflecting pools, waterfalls, and cascades. Water as an element of architecture is almost always used in conjunction with landscaping and often with sculpture. In some cases, pools or ponds and even fountains are planted with water plants to form water gardens, and often fish or other aquatic animals are part of the overall design.

In any case, water in an architectural setting seems to add something that is impossible to achieve in any other way, an almost universal aesthetic experience composed of the delights of the sound and touch of the water itself or of its humidity on the skin, the motion of the water as well as its appearance. Water is essential to life and its inclusion in an architectural setting seems to bring to the human mind and emotions a sense of tranquility, repose, peace, and restfulness.

Fountains and other water elements may be conceived of as freestanding works of art or as integrated elements of buildings. The play and motion of water may be the major aesthetic elements or they may be combined with landscaping or sculpture, or both, to achieve the desired effects. Special lighting may be provided to enhance the effects. Plantings in the water may or may not be a major part of the design. Water may be almost completely still, as in a reflecting pool, or may be continuously in motion, changing direction and height, from thin sprays that go high in the air in various patterns to simple cascades that flow slowly down from one rock or bowl to another. The variety that may be achieved is only limited by the imagination of designers and by the spaces and budgets available.

The sizes and complexities of water elements in architecture are extremely varied. A pond or pool, for example, may have only a few square feet of area in the garden of a small house or inside the house, or on a balcony or rooftop of an apartment building. Even in such a very small area, a fountain or cascade may be included. From such small and simple types, the scale increases to pools of great size and fountains of immense size and complexity. Landscaping and sculpture may become a part of both the modest type and the grand, elegant type.

**Construction Materials** For small ponds, pools, and fountains, prefabricated units, mostly of plastic, may be purchased in various sizes and shapes. Larger ponds and fountains are most often constructed of reinforced concrete, though other materials, such as brick or stone, may be used. When brick, stone, or materials other than concrete are required, they are most often used as surfacing with concrete as the structural base. Concrete is more waterproof than the other materials and need not be painted or otherwise treated. However, if plants or fish are to be introduced into a concrete pool or fountain, the material must be well seasoned to eliminate harmful lime. This is usually accomplished by filling the structure with water and letting it stand for five or more days, repeating the process several times. Then the pool or

**FOUNTAIN** Meeting of the Waters (1940), Aloe Plaza, St. Louis, Mo. *[Sculptor: Carl Milles]*

fountain is completely drained and treated with a solution of 1 part of common vinegar diluted with 10 parts of water, scrubbed with a brush, and the vinegar solution completely washed away.

For all but the simplest and smallest of pools, an overflow pipe, more than one for a large pool, should be provided along with a drainage system. If a pool is to be painted, latex or epoxy masonry paints are recommended. If plants or fish are to be introduced, a pool should be at least 2 ft in depth; if not, any depth may be used that creates the effects desired.

**Aquatic Plants** Pools may be informal, natural, or formal as determined for the effects desired. Planting, in and around pools, is often restricted to types of vegetation that might naturally grow there and to types hardy enough to survive the climate in which the pool is located. In concrete pools, water plants are usually encased in plastic containers or buckets which are then arranged in the water. The major types of aquatic plants are water lilies, lotus plants, bog plants, and floating plants. Water lilies are of two major types: hardy and tropical. Hardy lilies ordinarily bloom during the day, while tropicals may be either night or day bloomers. Hardy lilies may be left in ponds or pools during winter if their crowns and roots do not freeze. Tropical water lilies are very dif-

ficult to protect during cold winters and are therefore usually treated as annuals, with new ones planted each year. Tropical lilies come in a much greater variety of forms, colors, and types than hardy lilies. Lotuses make spectacular displays in water gardens and are hardy if the crowns of the plants are below the freezing depth of the water.

A great variety of bog plants are readily available for ponds and pools. They are easy to grow and for the most part, hardy. Some useful types are cattail, arrowhead, water canna, arum or sweet flag, marsh marigold, water plantain, water iris, and pickerel plants. Among floating plants, which are decorative and also oxygenate pools for fish, are duckweed, water chestnut, salvinia, water poppy, ludwigia, and water violet.

**Aquatic Animals** Fish and other aquatic animals, such as salamanders, tadpoles, snails, and so forth, are often introduced into pools. Not only do they add life and color to pools but they also take in oxygen from the water giving off carbon dioxide that is beneficial to plants. Fish and other aquatic animals also fertilize plants to an extent and play a very important role in controlling insect life, particularly that of mosquito larvae in the water. The most common fish used in pools are ordinary goldfish, members of the carp family. They need

**FOUNTAIN** General Motors Technical Center (completed 1956), Warren, Mich. *[Architects: Eero Saarinen and Assoc. with Smith, Hinchman and Grylls; artist: Alexander Calder]*

little care, almost no feeding (none in a balanced pool), and may be left in the water during the winter in most parts of the United States if the ice in the pond does not get too deep. Other fish may also be used in ponds but require more care and are not as hardy as goldfish.

**Recirculating Pumps** For many centuries, supplying water with adequate pressure to be sprayed out of nozzles or otherwise displayed in fountains was difficult. The pressure was strictly derived from the height of the water above the fountains and could only be achieved by having water that ran down from mountains or other high places or by lifting water to heights with mechanical devices. Today water pressure in fountains is generally supplied by recirculating electrical pumps, which are relatively simple and inexpensive. The advent of the recirculating pump has put fountains within the economic reach of almost anyone who thinks them of importance in architecture.

**Jets** In general, flowing water descends in waterfalls or in cascades or is ejected from fountains to fall into a pool or other container. All may be powered by recirculating pumps of various sizes.

Jets for fountains may be of several types, producing straight streams of water, ribbons, droplets, or other forms. The simplest is a single jet that ejects water vertically into the air to a certain height from which it falls generally straight down if no wind is blowing. In addition, such jets may be placed so that they slant inward or outward or on diagonals; they may be placed to arch from jet sources toward other areas; or they may produce many other effects.

Multiple jets produce various effects, including tiers of water and funnel shapes, and jets may be timed to produce sprays in different sequences of heights, types, and shapes. Various amounts of turbulence and movement of the water will be produced in the pool or other container below the jets. Some plants, including certain water lilies, do not survive well if subjected to great turbulence or movement of water; many others do very well under such adverse conditions.

**Design** Fountains and other water elements may be designed by several kinds of professionals, including architects, landscape architects, and sculptors. Such a wide variety of forms, types, landscaping, artworks, and other factors must be considered that it is impossible to generalize about the principles of their design, except that they are similar to designs of other architectural elements. To many architects and other design professionals, the design of fountains, pools, ponds, waterfalls, cascades, and other water elements and the landscaping and the sculpture often incorporated into their design is one of the most gratifying and fulfilling aspects of architecture. And many believe that creative use of lighting, both underwater and around water elements, can produce very satisfying architectural designs.

**History** Water has been an important element in architecture from the earliest times. Primitive communities were often established near bodies of water; pools or ponds were introduced into the architecture of the early cultures around the Mediterranean Sea. Even in the Middle East and Egypt, with only modest amounts of annual rainfall, pools or ponds were placed in gardens to relieve the effects of the arid, hot climate. The ancient Greeks used water in conjunction with their architecture, in pools and springs over which buildings were constructed.

The time of the first use of a fountain has not been established. However, the ancient Mesopotamians, Egyptians, and other cultures are known to have practiced irrigation, dam building, and piping water. They also built rudimentary machines for lifting water, the basic requirement for establishing the water pressure needed for fountains. The earliest known fountains all utilized the principle that water flowing from a high place built up pressure that would allow it to be directed into the air in sprays, jets, or in other ways to form the ornamental displays of fountains.

One of the greatest accomplishments of the Romans was their extensive water systems. For these systems, the Romans constructed many famous aqueducts but also a number of lesser known elements, such as wells, cisterns, dams, and piping or conduit systems. The most notable Roman accomplishment with water was, no doubt, the provision of adequate, reliable, safe supplies of water for drinking, public baths, irrigation, and other purposes. However, the Roman concerns with water also produced the first great era of fountain design and other architectural uses of water.

The Romans built many fountains in public areas of cities and in the courtyards and gardens of their houses. They built them everywhere, not only in Rome but in the countries they conquered. Most were powered by the pressure of the water coming down from the mountains in aqueducts, but others by lifting machinery and not a few by some natural spring or formation that allowed water to flow or fall. Many of the fountains were combined with sculpture or sculptured spouts from which the water ejected. Some Roman fountains still exist, especially in Rome. The early fountains and the great later examples of the Middle Ages and Renaissance are major elements contributing to the architectural quality of the city of Rome.

During the Middle Ages, though fountains were still important in Rome and other parts of Italy, few were constructed elsewhere in Europe. Fountain design flourished again during the Renaissance, a period when great numbers were built, including some of the most ornate and complex of all time. In Italy, fountains were built in the most insignificant little towns and in the gardens of many houses as well as in almost every public space where there was room for one. Magnificent examples were constructed on the grounds of villas.

A list of the great fountains and other architectural uses of water in Italy would be very long indeed. The greatest collection, from many eras, is to be found in Rome. However, in Tivoli, only a few miles from Rome, spectacular examples of several types are still to be seen. In Tivoli are the remains of several villas and other buildings dating from Roman times and after. The Temple of Vesta (c. 80 B.C.) still exists, as do several other buildings of the Roman era, including the Temple of the Sibyl and portions of the Villa (A.D. 124) of Emperor Hadrian (A.D. 76–138) and the Villa d'Este (1550), designed by Pirro Ligorio (c. 1520–80).

Equally as interesting as the buildings at Tivoli are the many varied uses of water as an element of architecture. Here may be seen examples of most of the important methods of architectural uses of water, ranging from the natural beauty of a great waterfall, through the several kinds of pools in Hadrian's Villa to the complexities of sprays, cascades, pools, and other water uses at the Villa d'Este. Here may be seen water in all of its moods: the tranquility of reflecting pools, the wild rush of water downward through a rocky landscape, the spectacular displays of hundreds of jets in the several types of fountains at Villa d'Este. In addition, landscaping, sculpture, buildings, and other architectural elements are combined with water in many ways to produce a great range of total effects.

Many other great fountains and other architectural uses of water were constructed during the Renaissance and after. One of the most spectacular is the great displays of water, used in many ways, designed by the landscape gardener André Le Nôtre (1613–1700) at the Palais de Versailles (1661–1756) in France. The original part of the palace was designed by Louis Le Vau (1612–70), who joined with Le Nôtre to create another great integration of architecture, landscaping, and water at the Chateau of Vaux-le-Vicomte (1661), France. At Versailles, a great complex of various fountains, pools, landscaping, and sculpture was created by Le Nôtre. The water was made to flow by raising it to a height of 500 ft with machinery.

A great number of magnificent uses of water, including fountains, exist in many places around the world, not only in many other parts of Europe but in Egypt and the Middle East, India, China, and Japan.

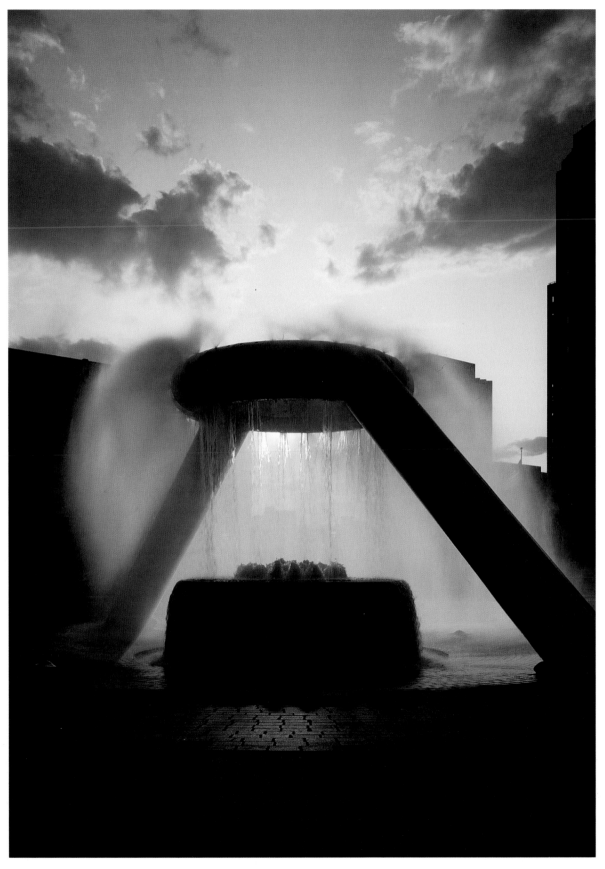

**FOUNTAIN** Dodge Fountain (1979), Detroit, Mich. *[Sculptor: Isamu Noguchi]*

**American Development** In colonial America, fountains were not important elements of architecture, partly because of the utilitarian nature of the early buildings and party because of the mechanical difficulties of raising water to heights from which it could descend to jet or cascade in fountains and other elements. By the end of the 18th century or the beginning of the 19th, the construction of great fountains and other water elements in architecture, with only a few exceptions, had come virtually to an end in Europe, with the end of building immense palaces, villas, and public buildings. With the beginning of the modern movement in architecture in the late 19th century, ornaments of all kinds, including fountains and other water elements, were gradually almost completely excluded from building designs.

During the 20th century, interest in ornamental features of architecture has been revived to an extent and with the advent of relatively inexpensive electric recirculating pumps, the technical problems of providing water pressure have been almost eliminated. Fountains and other water elements of architectural design are often relatively simple and modest in scale today, when compared to some of the most spectacular examples of past eras. On the other hand, many contemporary examples are delightful additions to the architecture, not only in great public spaces but in commercial buildings and even in the gardens of modest houses. Many examples today are combined with landscaping and many, with sculptural elements.

A list of notable examples in the United States would be too long for the space available, but a few should be mentioned to give some indication of the various types and locations. These might include the sculptured fountains by the Swedish sculptor Carl Milles (1875–1955) at the Cranbrook schools, Mich., designed in the 1930s by Eliel Saarinen (1873–1950); the Kaufmann House (1937), Bear Run, Pa., designed by Frank Lloyd Wright (1867–1959) and called Fallingwater for the waterfall over which it was built; the various pools and fountains at the Lincoln Center for the Performing Arts (1968), some with sculptures by the English sculptor Henry Moore (1898–1986); and Lovejoy Plaza (1966), Portland, Ore., a fountain made for walking in, climbing on, and bathing as well as esthetic enjoyment, designed by landscape architect Lawrence Halprin (1916–  ). Many other excellent examples of fountains and other water elements of architecture are located in many places in the United States.

**Related Articles** ART IN ARCHITECTURE; DESIGN, ARCHITECTURAL; GARDEN; LANDSCAPE ARCHITECTURE; MONUMENT; ORNAMENT.

**Further Reading** Aurand, C. Douglas: *Fountains and Pools: Construction Guidelines and Specifications*, 2d ed., Van Nostrand Reinhold, New York, 1991.

**Sources of Additional Information** American Federation of Arts, 41 E. 65th St., New York, N.Y. 10021; American Society of Landscape Architects, 4401 Connecticut Ave., N.W., Washington, D.C. 20008; National Sculpture Society, 15 E. 26th St., New York, N.Y. 10010.

## FULLER, RICHARD BUCKMINSTER

American architect, engineer, philosopher, and inventor (1895–1983). Almost impossible to categorize, Richard Buckminster Fuller had a very full and rewarding career. His inventions have challenged the imagination of people; his philosophies have stirred their minds; his books, articles, and lectures have brought his ideas to a great many, making them question the world in which they live and the way they live in it. Largely self-educated, having never finished college, Fuller has obtained a view of nature, the universe, and the minds of human beings unequaled in its time for its universality and scope.

Superactive all his life, he had been some distance ahead of his contemporaries for a long time. He had managed to influence architecture and the world in which it exists in a way that is unique. Fuller had never been an architect or an architectural designer, in the usual sense. His concerns had always been larger than life. His view encompassed all that was around him: physical, mental, and emotional. His domain was everywhere and he was deeply concerned with everything. Out of all this comes an architecture of invention that foresees the future in ways that are sometimes tangible, sometimes not. His designs have deeply affected architecture and architects. And some, such as his geodesic domes, have affected people everywhere.

**Inventions** The story of Fuller's architecture is in his inventions, primarily, rather than in individual buildings. The first important invention was the Dymaxion House, designed in 1927 in an attempt to adapt house construction to mass production in factories. Supported on a central mast and engineered like an airplane, the house was to be completely prefabricated, even to its bathroom and all its equipment. Fuller experimented with the design of these houses, gradually perfecting his ideas, for many years. The culmination was the construction of a prototype model in the Beech Aircraft Plant in Wichita, Kans., in 1945–46. The houses were to cost about $3,700 complete, when the plant had gone into full production. Orders for almost 4,000 houses were received, but the financing of the project was never worked out and the houses never produced. Fuller produced other inventions, such as a Dymaxion car (1934), based on the principles of aircraft design, and new world maps with minimal distortion.

**Geodesic Domes** Starting in 1952, Fuller began to develop what he called geodesic domes. He utilized tetrahedrons, geometrical forms with four triangular faces,

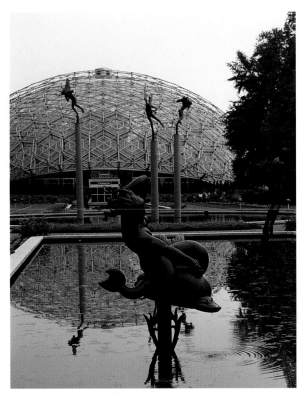

**FULLER, RICHARD BUCKMINSTER** Climatron geodesic dome (1960), St. Louis, Mo.

combining them into icosahedrons, which have 20 faces, and connecting them together so that they formed domes that closely resembled portions of spheres. He found that light, strong dome structures could be constructed in this way with relatively small pieces of aluminum or other materials. The domes could then be waterproofed with plastic, fiberglass, or other light materials.

One of the first domes was placed on the Rotunda Building (1953) of the Ford Motor Company, Dearborn, Mich. In 1954 others were designed as mobile shelters for the U.S. Marine Corps and were so light they could be transported by helicopters. Some were used to house radar installations, beginning in 1956. Still later, geodesic domes were constructed, often by unskilled workers including college students, all over the country, in every imaginable material, for example, aluminum, steel, wood, folded cardboard, and even bamboo.

Some notable uses of geodesic domes have been the Union Tank Car Plant (1958), Alsen, La., then the largest clear span (384 feet) in the world; the Climatron (1961; see illustration and article botanical garden) in the Missouri Botanical Gardens, St. Louis, designed by Joseph D. Murphy (1907–    ) and Eugene J. Mackey (1911–68); and the U.S. Pavilion (1967) at Expo 1967, the World's Fair, Montreal, Canada.

Buckminster Fuller placed his domes on many other buildings in many different locations. They have become a part of the landscape and something of a symbol of an inventive phase of American architecture.

**Life** Buckminster Fuller was born on July 12, 1895, in Milton, Mass., the son of a merchant. As a boy, he was interested in boats and boatbuilding, but not in formal education. After attending the Milton Academy from 1904 to 1913, he entered Harvard University, stayed two years, and was dismissed in 1915.

Fuller went to Canada, where he worked for a while for a machine fitter, then returned to Harvard where he was again dismissed. Except for a short course at the U.S. Naval Academy, Annapolis, Md., while he was in the U.S. Navy, 1917–19, he never again had any formal education. He thoroughly enjoyed his navy experience, learned a lot, made several inventions (harbingers of things to come), and rose to the rank of lieutenant.

In 1917 Fuller married Anne Hewlett and they had two daughters; the older died when she was five. Fuller's father-in-law was James Monroe Hewlett (1869–1941), an accomplished architect, mural painter, and stage designer. After several years in various jobs, none of them related to architecture, in 1922 with his father-in-law, Fuller started a firm to develop and manufacture a new fibrous concrete block that Hewlett had invented. In 1927 they lost financial control of the company, and Fuller started another company, called 4-D, in Chicago and embarked on his long and varied career.

His first venture was the design of the Dymaxion House in 1927, though this name was not used until 1929, which he later worked on for more than 15 years. After working on mass-produced bathrooms for the Pierce Foundation for a year, he founded the Dymaxion Corporation in 1932. He founded a number of companies, all with exotic names he invented or adapted: Dymaxion Dwelling Machines (1944–46); Synergetics, Inc. (1955–59); Geodesics, Inc.; Plydomes, Inc.; and Tetrahelix Corp.

The inventions poured from him all these years, and the companies were founded to develop, manufacture, and market them. Concurrently, Fuller kept a schedule that would have been impossible for a lesser man. He wrote numerous articles and books on many subjects, all related to his Promethean views of the universe, its present state, and what it might become. He lectured whenever there was an audience. When scheduled for an hour, he often took three or five and sometimes ended in the early hours of the morning. Never fond of education as he found it, he nevertheless accepted visiting professorships and lectureships at universities and colleges all over the world, even one at Harvard in poetry. He served as consultant, researcher, board member, or in other capacities for many companies, agencies, and organizations.

In 1959 he moved to Carbondale, Ill., to become professor of generalized design science exploration at

Southern Illinois University, a position he held until 1974. Characteristically, he built a house there in 1960 for himself, using a new wood frame and plywood dome he invented and which later was mass-produced. Later, he moved to Philadelphia.

Fuller had always been an enigma to the architectural profession and the world at large. Architects have been intrigued by him and his inventions and ideas, but they have been puzzled by the question of whether to accept him as a fellow architect. And in truth, he never had been an architect in the usual sense. He was unique. Misunderstood he might have been, but his work and ideas have challenged the minds of people, including architects, for many years. And he always seemed to keep on coming up with new ideas. In spite of his opposition to formal education in his youth, he had been the recipient of a large number of honors, including more than 25 honorary doctor's degrees and election to the American Academy of Arts and Sciences and the National Institute of Arts and Letters.

In accordance with the ambivalent nature of Buckminster Fuller's relationships with the architectural profession, a strange series of events had taken place over the years. In 1959 the American Institute of Architects (AIA) elected him an honorary member, a category reserved for nonarchitects. In 1963 it gave him its Allied Professions Medal, for nonarchitects. In 1970, while he was still an honorary member, the AIA gave him its highest honor, the Gold Medal, reserved only for architects, though Fuller was still not eligible for registration or licensing as an architect or for regular membership in the AIA. Fuller later became eligible, having received his registration, became a member, and in 1975, at age eighty, was elected a fellow of the AIA. In Europe he had been recognized earlier, in 1968, with the Royal Gold Medal of the Royal Institute of British Architects.

Whatever he might be called, Buckminster Fuller was certainly a great man of his time and one who may have seen the future. He deserves to be called architect as well as futurist, engineer, inventor, writer, and philosopher.

**Related Articles** CONTEMPORARY ARCHITECTURE; DOME; EDUCATION; MODERN ARCHITECTURE; PREFABRICATION.

**Further Reading** Fuller, R. Buckminster: *Operating Manual for Spaceship Earth,* Amerion Ltd., Mattituck, N.Y., 1968; Kahn, Peter H., and Robert D. Kahn, eds.: *R. Buckminster Fuller on Education,* University of Mass. Press, Amherst, Mass., 1979.

**FURNESS, FRANK** American architect (1839–1912). Furness' work was reviled in the early part of this century, only to survive to become recognized as the work of a major figure in American architecture. His work was

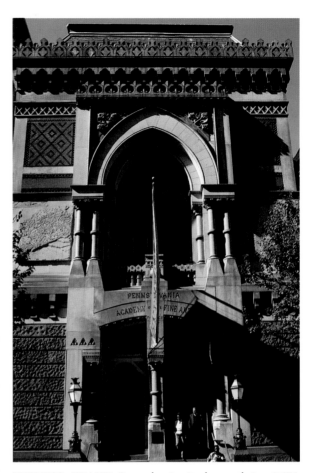

**FURNESS, FRANK** Pennsylvania Academy of Art (1876, restored), Philadelphia, Pa.

based on architectural theories advanced by Viollet le Duc (1814–79) in France, filtered through Richard Morris Hunt (1827–95), and the polychrome Gothic of John Ruskin (1819–1900) in England but has a vigor and originality that could only be American. Because his office records were destroyed, it is not certain how many of Frank Furness' buildings were built. Recent research has identified some 600 projects, most of them in or around Philadelphia. Additional projects may yet be identified.

Furness formed a partnership in 1867 in Philadelphia, his home city, that soon became successful. A brilliant Eclectic designer, he worked most often in his personal Gothic-derived style popular in the Victorian era. As times and tastes changed, his clients retired, and Eclectic Gothic style commercial and residential buildings were no longer of interest to the next generation. After about 1895, he withdrew more and more from active practice, and relatively few of his projects date from after 1900. He died in 1912, almost forgotten, and an estimated half of his buildings have now been demolished.

Furness left his mark on architecture, as a talented and inventive designer, in his important buildings that have survived, and his reputation has been restored, beginning in the middle of the 20th century. His first building was a church that has now been demolished, as has almost every other structure he did in his first 10 years of practice. Most of those remaining have been radically altered. Fortunately, one of his best of that time has been preserved, the Pennsylvania Academy of Fine Arts (1876), Philadelphia. It is Victorian and highly ornamented.

**Works** Furness designed several types of buildings, but perhaps was most recognized for his churches, banks, and houses. A number of these buildings have survived, including the interesting church he did for his father's old parish, the First Unitarian Church (1886), Philadelphia. In addition, Furness designed many other types of buildings, including offices, clubs, hotels, institutions, a number of buildings for railroads, and three buildings at the Philadelphia Zoological Gardens, all of them now gone except the gatehouse (1876).

The crowning point in the architect's career was his design of the Library of the University of Pennsylvania (1891), Philadelphia. A Victorian building with great ornamentation of the exterior and interior, the library, now renamed the Furness Building, has been considerably altered and expanded. His last known work was an alteration, as were three out of the last five of his commissions. His last complete building, a factory, has been demolished.

**Life** Frank Furness was born in Philadelphia on November 12, 1839, the last child of a Harvard-educated Unitarian minister, who was artistic and intellectual and imbued those traits in his children. Ending his formal schooling early, Furness worked for a while in the office of a Philadelphia architect, John Fraser, and decided he wanted to become an architect. Since there was no professional school of architecture in the United States then, he did the next best thing. He entered the atelier or studio of the foremost architect he could find, Richard Morris Hunt (1827–95) in New York. Here he stayed until the outbreak of the Civil War.

He enlisted in the Union cavalry in 1861. By the time he was discharged in 1864, he had been promoted to captain, a title he liked to use in later life. He had also won his country's highest military award, the Congressional Medal of Honor, refused at the time but later bestowed in 1899.

After the war, he worked for about a year in Hunt's office, but returned to Philadelphia in 1866, thoroughly indoctrinated in the Eclectic Beaux Arts–inspired architecture of which Hunt was the first acknowledged U.S. master. Furness had also discovered that he had a talent for drawing caricatures of people, which were at once comical and biting. He continued to draw caricatures all his life. Starting his own office in Philadelphia, Furness

designed a few buildings by himself, but in 1867 he formed a partnership with his former employer, John Fraser, and another architect, George W. Hewitt (1841–1916). The partnership lasted four years and established Furness as an architect. After Fraser moved to Washington in 1871, Furness and Hewitt continued to practice together until Hewitt left in 1875. During this time, in 1873, a budding young architect, Louis Henri Sullivan, aged sixteen, worked in their office for six months. Sullivan's later description of the office in his 1924 *Autobiography of an Idea* is one of the few descriptions of the Furness office.

After Hewitt left, Furness continued the growing practice under his name. In 1881 a drafter, Allen Evans (1845–1925), who had been employed in the firm for 10 years, was taken in as a partner, and in 1885, the firm was renamed Furness, Evans, and Company to reflect the fact that Furness kept taking in increasing numbers of silent partners. Good commissions continued to come in, and the firm prospered. Considered a genuine eccentric, Furness, with a red beard and drooping mustache and dressed in loud plaids, strode around the office and the town in a military manner, swearing and domineering. Among others, Sullivan was impressed by the fact that Furness could draw and swear at the same time.

In 1879 Furness began work for the Philadelphia and Reading Railroad Company and later worked for other railroads, designing hundreds of buildings and alterations all over the country. His work for the railroads continued until just a few years before he died. The practice prospered until, by 1895, it was no longer possible for Furness to control the designs and details as he had in the past. Thus much of the later work does not measure up to the earlier.

As he grew older, Furness began to dwell more and more on his Civil War record. He liked to be addressed as captain, and he accepted the congressional Medal of Honor which he had refused, at age twenty-five, when he won it in battle. Many people considered him very disagreeable, and the incoming commissions slowed almost to a halt. He spent his last years in relative obscurity, in ill health, playing old soldier and neglecting architecture. When he died, on June 27, 1912, his obituaries in the Philadelphia papers dwelt on his war record and the lives of his father and brother, hardly mentioning his buildings at all.

His architecture and his reputation remained in almost total eclipse for 40 years until the 1950s, when architects and critics began to take a new interest in the importance of his work. An exhibit of Furness buildings in 1973 resulted in further attention, and several publications have followed. This recognition of the importance of Furness as designer will help preserve the few buildings which remain.

**Related Articles** ECLECTIC ARCHITECTURE; HUNT, RICHARD MORRIS; SULLIVAN, LOUIS HENRI.

**Further Reading** O'Gorman, James F., George E. Thomas, Hyman Myers, and Jeffrey A. Cohen: *The Architecture of Frank Furness*, 2d ed., Philadelphia Museum of Art, Philadelphia, 1987; Thomas, George E., Jeffrey A. Cohen, and Michael J. Lewis: *Frank Furness—the Complete Works*, Princeton Architectural Press, Princeton, N.J., 1991.

**FURNITURE** Equipment, such as tables, chairs, and cabinets, for use in or around buildings. Furniture may be movable or built-in. Furnishings include furniture and also floor and wall coverings, curtains, and other movable articles.

In many cases, architects become involved in the selection of furniture and other furnishings for the buildings they design. In some cases, architects collaborate with interior designers who perform the interior design work, together with the selection of furniture and furnishings. In other cases, architects handle the interior design and the selection of furniture and other furnishings, or departments in their firms perform these services. A few architects today design furniture and furnishings for production and sale to the general public. And many others design custom items, in particular built-in furniture, for the buildings of their clients.

**Properties** In order to properly select or design furniture and other furnishings, the major considerations are similar to those common to other elements of architecture: function, strength, appearance, and cost. Although not always the case, most pieces of furniture or other furnishings have relatively simple functions. A chair is for sitting; a bed is for lying down; a carpet is for standing upon. These are primary functions, though each piece may have others. Each furniture or furnishing item must be strong enough to perform its function or functions. In addition, there is a need for stability. A chair may be strong enough, for example, to easily withstand the weight of a person but, at the same time, so unstable that it falls over when a person leans from it. The appearance or visual effect of a piece of furniture or furnishing item depends not only on its form, color, texture, and the like but also upon its fitness to its purpose, structure, and materials. From this it might be gathered that the most successful pieces are those that excel in all the elements mentioned. That this is not always true can be demonstrated by the simple process of sitting in some types of chairs that seem to have all the above excellent attributes, but turn out to be comfortable only if a person sits in a single position. On the other hand, so-called overstuffed chairs, though not designed in a modern manner or constructed with the latest types of materials, are often extremely comfortable.

**Types** A great variety of pieces of furniture and other furnishings are available today, including newly manufactured items, older ones, and antiques. An architect, or interior or other environmental designer, is thus faced with an often bewildering array of types, at widely varied prices. The selection therefore becomes partly a matter of taste of the owners or occupiers of buildings and the building designers. In addition, attention should be paid to other aspects of the furnishings, including function, structure, materials, and safety as well as price. The most expensive items are not necessarily the most appropriate choices.

Other materials used in furniture include glass, mostly tempered plate but sometimes other types, for tabletops, doors, and other purposes. Glass is also used in mirrors and in the form of glass fibers for reinforcing plastics and for curtain fabrics. Stone is sometimes used for tabletops and similar purposes. The most used stone is marble but others, such as granite and slate, are sometimes used. See the article entitled stone. A rather large group of additional materials are often used in furniture. See the article entitled construction materials. They include natural and synthetic rubber in foamed types for such uses as upholstery pads and in other forms for minor purposes. Textiles of many kinds and materials are widely used, not only for finish upholstery fabrics but as canvas and other materials for hidden construction in chairs, sofas, and beds. Felt, hair, down, and feathers are often used, alone or in combination with plastic or rubber foams, for cushions.

Furniture may be either movable or built-in. Most movable furniture used in architecture is selected from standard stocks of various manufacturers, though special pieces are sometimes designed by architects or other environmental designers. Built-in furniture may be selected from stock, as is usually the case with kitchen cabinets, or designed by architects or others for special applications. For further discussion of both types, see the article entitled woodwork. Movable furniture runs the gamut from the very simplest of pieces to quite complex units. For many young as well as some older people today, the less movable furniture the better seems to be the theme. Often they seem perfectly satisfied with a pad on the floor to sit on and perhaps to sleep on, and very little else.

**Systems** Most people, however, select furniture that is a bit more formal and considerably more comfortable. In addition to single, freestanding pieces of furniture, such as individual chairs, sofas, tables, and bookcases, systems of furniture are often used today. Sometimes called sectional or modular, these systems are made up of pieces that may be interconnected or placed side by side to form large units or moved apart to be used individually. Perhaps the first of such pieces were sectional

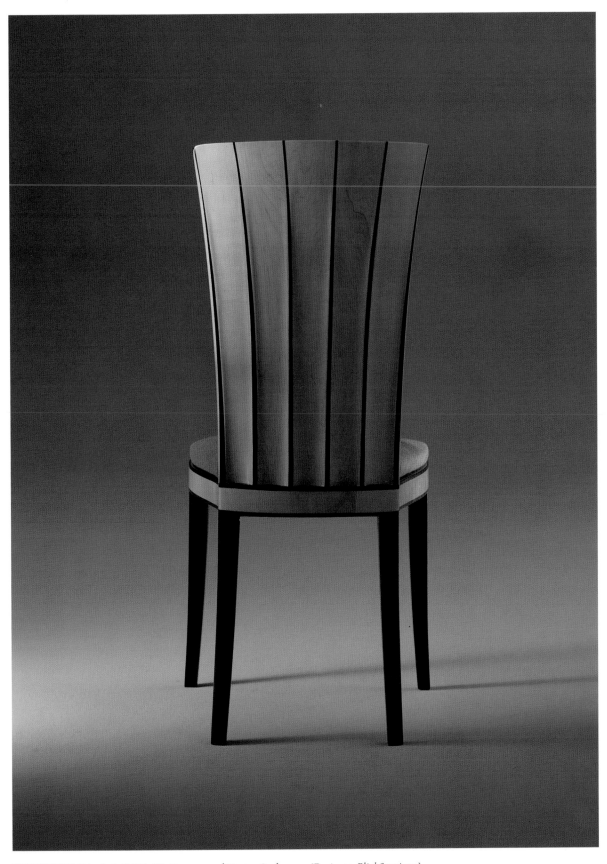

**FURNITURE** Side chair (1928–30), Company of Master Craftsmen. *[Designer: Eliel Saarinen]*

sofas and bookcases, individual pieces that may be joined together at will. A number of systems of this sort are available for use in various building types, such as houses, offices, and others. Some of the systems are quite complex. For example, in certain office systems, tables, desks, bookcases, file cases, and other elements may be joined in a great variety of combinations according to the needs of the users and the ingenuity of the designers. Some systems also serve as room dividers, creating open-planned offices or office landscaping.

Specialized furniture, and sometimes systems of furniture, are available for many building types, including hotels, hospitals, schools, libraries, and churches. Special outdoor furniture, often made of such materials as redwood, iron, and glass, may be obtained in many different designs.

To make matters more difficult, there exists the problem of compatibility between various items of furnishings. At one time, many believed that modern furniture could not be mixed successfully with furniture from other periods. Many architects and other designers today believe that good, well-designed furniture from many eras and of many styles can be successfully mixed. Perhaps heavy bulky furniture, of highly ornamented wood, from some periods may not be quite right with attenuated types made of metal, plywood, and plastics. However, the best individual pieces, particularly if they are authentic and not merely adaptations or copies, are often very much at home together. For example, Thonet bentwood rockers seem quite appropriate when used in otherwise modern interiors. So do Windsor chairs, Shaker furniture, and good pieces of many of the other furniture designers of the past.

When considering the selection of furniture and other furnishings, function is quite important. Each piece should perform its primary function well. In addition, each should be safe and easy to maintain and repair. Furniture or other furnishings should be structurally sound. This means being well made, of good design, construction, and materials. Materials must be proper for the use intended and strong enough to function properly. They should also present a pleasing appearance. The form of a piece of furniture, along with its texture, color, and other factors, join with the materials and structure to produce a visual effect that is satisfying or one that is not. Then there is the question of comfort. The piece should provide the utmost in comfort to the people who use it. Furniture and other furnishings should pass all these tests before being selected for use in well-designed buildings.

The structures of furniture today are often quite complicated, utilizing many of the contemporary construction types and techniques employed in other building elements. As pointed out previously, structures must not only be of adequate strength but must have adequate stability to resist overturning. The structural design of furniture therefore resembles that of buildings. Strength in furniture is derived from the strength of the individual parts and, very importantly, from the strength of the joints between the parts. In addition, the frame of a piece of furniture and other working parts must have complete structural integrity when joined together in a system, such as a chair.

**Structural Materials** The major structural materials used in the construction of furniture today are wood, steel, iron, aluminum, and plastics. Many other materials are often used for finishes and for other purposes, including fabrics for upholstery, other metals for hardware and similar purposes, and stone and glass for tops, doors, and the like.

In general, wood used for furniture today may be either softwood, used mostly for utilitarian purposes such as breakfast tables or for hidden parts of furniture; and hardwoods, used for exposed parts of furniture. Among the most used softwoods are various kinds of native American pine, fir, and redwood. Among the most used hardwoods are such native American woods as oak, birch, maple, and walnut, and woods from other countries, including mahogany, rosewood, ebony, and numerous others, some very ornamental and many quite rare. Although solid hardwoods were often used for furniture in the past and are still used to some extent, the more common practice today utilizes veneers of the desired woods glued to cores of less desirable species or to particle board.

Plywood is also widely used. Both veneers and plywood are currently available in a great variety of woods. Grain, color, and the like are important in wood furniture. And it should be strongly constructed with stable rigid frames, proper joints, and excellent workmanship. For a discussion of various aspects of wood for use in furniture, see articles entitled paint; wood; woodwork.

Two special uses of wood in furniture are bentwood and molded plywood. Bentwood is made by placing shaped pieces of wood in chambers where they are subjected to steam until they become flexible. They are then bent in molds to the desired forms. Molded plywood is made by placing the required number of wood plys and external veneers, with glue between them, in molds. Pressure and heat are applied to help in the process of molding and to cause the glue to set, or high-frequency radio waves can be used.

Until the 20th century, metal was used in furniture sparingly, at first for hardware and other minor purposes and later for wrought-iron or cast-iron outdoor or garden furniture. Such uses continue today. However, some of the finest modern furniture for other purposes is made, at least partly, of steel or aluminum tubing,

**FURNITURE** Tulip chair and table (1955–57), Knoll International *[Designer: Eero Saarinen]*. Prototype chairs shown were photographed in Eero Saarinen's home.

bars, sheet, or other shapes. These metals are also often used for utilitarian pieces of furniture, such as kitchen chairs. Metal furniture can be constructed with great strength and durability and often may be less expensive than comparable pieces made of fine woods. For a discussion of the various metals used in furniture today, see articles entitled aluminum; construction materials; iron; steel. For a discussion of their finishes, see the article entitled paint.

Although the first plastics had a bad reputation in architecture, perhaps because they copied, and were considered cheap substitutes for, other materials, today plastics are widely used in architecture for furniture and other purposes. In furniture, their uses include complete glass-fiber reinforced shells of chairs and other pieces; foam for pads, mattresses, and the like; woven and other flexible materials for upholstery; laminated types for tops of tables, counters, and the like; in glues and other adhesives; in finish materials such as paints and others; and for hardware. Plastics are also widely used for other furnishings, such as curtains, carpets and rugs, and other items. For further discussion of plastics, see the article entitled plastics.

**Furnishings** In addition to furniture, a large number of other types of furnishings are available today. Perhaps

the most important are floor coverings and materials for windows. Other than the more permanent flooring materials, the major floor coverings are carpeting and rugs, mostly machine-woven. Carpeting is generally used to cover entire floors of rooms in buildings, cut to size and installed more or less permanently. Rugs, sometimes called area rugs, are usually smaller than the dimensions of rooms and are not permanently left in place. Such a vast variety of fibers, colors, patterns, and textures exist in carpets and rugs that they cannot be adequately described here. In general, both carpeting and rugs are made of wool or any of a variety of synthetic fibers, often in combinations. They may be obtained with plain undersides or backs, or with various backing materials, including rubber sponge or sheet materials.

Carpeting generally is available in widths ranging from about 4 ft 6 in up to 15 ft and in any reasonable length. Special carpeting for stairs comes in smaller widths. Rectangular rugs come in sizes from about 3 by 5 ft up to 12 by 18 ft, and round rugs in diameters from about 4 ft, sometimes less, up to about 12 ft. Underlayment or pads for use under floor coverings are made of hair, fiber, rubber foam or sponge, and combinations of such materials. Plastic carpets for outdoors and indoors are generally available in 3- to 12-ft widths

**FURNITURE** Catenary chairs and table (1963), Herman Miller. *[Designer: George Nelson]*

and reasonable lengths. Both outdoor and indoor carpeting usually comes in 12-in squares for fastening to floors with adhesives. Handwoven rugs of many kinds can be obtained in a considerable variety of sizes. Carpeting is usually sold by the square yard or square meter, and rugs by the individual item.

Materials for curtains and drapery for windows are available in a great variety of fibers, textures, patterns, and colors. They may be very sheer or completely opaque, lined or unlined, in a great variety of types. They may be obtained in stock sizes or may be custom-made for individual windows. Perhaps the most important type in architecture today is the draw curtain, which is ordinarily hung from a traverse track. Pulls at the sides allow the curtains to be drawn to the sides for opening or together in the middle for closing. Traverse tracks are available for one-way, two-way, and multiple drawing, in lengths up to 30 ft or more for the one-way and two-way types and up to 60 ft or more for the multiple type. Traverse tracks can be obtained in various degrees of strength, lighter ones being used for such buildings as houses and heavier ones, for public and commercial buildings.

Other systems, often used with windows, include Venetian blinds with horizontal slats of aluminum or sometimes wood or other materials, which can be inclined at various angles to permit or prevent vision and to allow light and breezes to enter or to exclude them. Venetian blinds also may be raised to the top or lowered to the bottom of windows. The blinds come in various stock sizes, ranging up to 16 ft or more in width and 20 ft or more in height, and in several colors. Vertical blinds, like the Venetian type except with the slats vertical instead of horizontal, are often used. Made of aluminum or fabric, they come in sizes up to 16 ft in width and 25 ft in height and in several colors. Other devices sometimes used with windows include louvered blinds and roll-up shades of cloth, wood, bamboo, or other materials.

Furniture designers today come from a variety of disciplines: architecture, interior design, industrial design, and crafts. For many people, the field is exciting and fulfilling. For those who are deeply interested in design, people, and craftsmanship, careers as furniture designers offer a great deal. For architects and other environmental designers the occasional chance to design a custom piece of movable or built-in furniture represents a welcome departure from ordinary practice.

**History** From the time the first rude huts and tents were constructed by primitive humans, furniture and other furnishings have been important attributes of architecture. None of the earliest examples has survived, and almost none from the ancient civilizations in the Middle East, Crete, Greece, and Rome. The little that is known about furniture and furnishings of those early times has been learned from illustrations on vases or in paintings. The ancient Egyptians believed that various objects needed in life should accompany the dead in their afterlife. The Egyptians therefore buried furniture, furnishings, and other things with the dead. Thus objects that would have been destroyed under ordinary circumstances have been preserved and may be seen in museums today. The furniture and other objects show a high level of design and workmanship and include beds, chairs, storage cases, tables, and other useful and decorative items.

From the fall of the Roman Empire, and the beginning of the Middle Ages, furniture has been closely related to the other aspects of interiors in architecture. For a discussion of the developments from that time to the beginning of the modern movement in architecture in the 19th century, see the article entitled interior design.

Although the beginning of the modern movement in architecture is often taken to have occurred in the late 19th century, it can be foreseen in some buildings and in the design of furniture of earlier eras. Still greatly

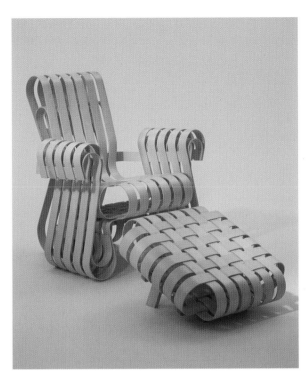

**FURNITURE** Wood chair (The Gehry Group) (1992), Knoll International. *[Architect: Frank Gehry]*

Perhaps the real beginnings of modern furniture design may be found in the work of the German furniture maker Michael Thonet (1796–1871). With his brothers, Thonet pioneered the design of molded plywood and bentwood furniture, mostly in chairs. He started manufacturing such furniture before the middle of the 19th century. Considered strictly utilitarian at first, the furniture designs were later recognized for their spare, machine-age, modern beauty and are still much admired today. Together with later designs, many are still being manufactured.

In the late 19th century, Frank Lloyd Wright (1867–1959) began to design furniture and continued to do so for certain of his buildings the remainder of his life. Wright's designs were as special and customized as the designs of his houses and other buildings and their interiors. During the same period the German architect Peter Behrens (1868–1940) designed furniture which had a more universal appeal and which deeply affected later designs. Behrens also affected the work, in architecture and in furniture design, of three architects who worked in his office at various times: Walter Adolf Gropius (1883–1970), Ludwig Mies van de Rohe (1886–1969), and Charles Édouard Jeanneret (1887–1965), known as Le Corbusier. All three designed furniture, Le Corbusier quite a number of individual pieces and a system that was the forerunner of later storage walls. Mies designed several pieces that became famous, including his Tugendhat chair in 1930, and his Barcelona chair, designed in 1929, still being produced and as handsome and admired as ever. Gropius and Mies were associated at the famous German architectural and design school, the Bauhaus, with another architect who also designed excellent furniture, Marcel Lajos Breuer (1902–81). Breuer designed many pieces of furniture over the years, including some in wood and some in other materials. His most notable designs, however, have been in bent metal tubing, an early and excellent example of which, designed in 1925, is still produced and admired today.

The furniture of the great Finnish architect Alvar Aalto (1898–1976) was first shown in the United States at the New York World's Fair in 1939. Constructed mostly of birch plywood, the furniture was widely praised at the time and today is still considered as some of the greatest modern furniture designs. In 1940 the Museum of Modern Art in New York City sponsored a furniture design competition, entered by a number of noted designers. First prizes for a molded plywood chair and modular storage cases went to two young designers, later to become famous for their work in architecture as well as in furniture design, Eero Saarinen (1910–61) and Charles Eames (1907–78). Eames later designed many notable pieces of furniture, not only in molded plastics

admired for simple, functional designs and fine workmanship is the furniture of the Shakers, a religious sect that originated in England about the middle of the 18th century and spread to America about two decades later. Another forerunner of the modern movement was the work of the English architect and interior and furniture designer William Morris (1834–96), one of the leaders of the Crafts Movement. Morris and others turned away from the heavy ornament of the Victorian era to simpler furniture designs and better craftsmanship. The work of the members of the Crafts Movement were also antimodern in that they also turned away from factory production to handcrafts.

Another movement, mostly in France and Belgium, called Art Nouveau, also turned away from the past toward nature for inspiration. The Belgian architects Henry van de Velde (1863–1957) and Victor Horta (1861–1947) and the French architect Hector Guimard (1863–1942), the leaders of the movement, not only designed buildings but also furniture and furnishings. The Scottish architect Charles Rennie Mackintosh (1868–1928) also designed furniture that presaged the coming modern movement, as did that of the Spanish architect Antoni Gaudí (1852–1926) and the Austrian architect Josef Hoffman (1870–1956). In the United States, Henry Hobson Richardson (1838–86) and Louis Henri Sullivan (1856–1924) often designed furniture for use in their buildings.

and other materials, many of which are still marketed today. Saarinen also designed excellent furniture but is best known for his designs of buildings.

Near the end of World War II, a New York City company was established to construct and market modern furniture and other furnishings by Hans G. Knoll (1914–58). The company's first designer was a Dane, Jens Risom (1916–  ), who produced a number of notable furniture designs. Later called Knoll Associates, and now Knoll Studio, a division of The Knoll Group, the company attracted many of the best designers from all over the world and has consistently produced fine pieces to this day. Several well-known U.S. architects have designed furniture for the company, including Venturi Scott Brown (1984) and Frank Gehry (1992).

The Herman Miller Company in Grand Rapids, Mich., an old-line producer of solid but scarcely modern pieces, turned to modern furniture after World War II. Architect George Nelson (1917–86) had designed, with another architect, Henry Wright (1910–86), a revolutionary system for houses called a storage wall, and with the same collaborator had written an equally revolutionary book, *Tomorrow's House*, about modern house design. Nelson became director of design for Herman Miller and proceeded to completely modernize not only its line of furniture but its promotion pieces, catalogs, and the whole image of the company. The first postwar furniture made by the company was designed by Nelson, and he continued to design other pieces and systems for them for many years. He also attracted other designers to the company, including Charles Eames (1907–78) and

Harry Bertoia (1915–78). The company is still very active today, in the design and production not only of individual furniture pieces but of systems for open-planned offices and other purposes.

During the 20th century, modern furnishings of such types as rugs and carpets, textiles for upholstery and curtains, and tapestries have been designed, and sometimes made, by many talented designers and artists in other fields. Notable examples of such furnishings are designed and manufactured today in many parts of the world. In the United States, perhaps the greatest textile designers and weavers have been Anni Albers (1899–1994) and Dorothy Liebes (1899–1972). Others, including architect Alexander Hayden Girard (b. 1907), have designed notable textiles. Incidental furnishings, such as ceramics, lamps, wallpaper, tableware, tablecloths, and cooking utensils, are available in excellent designs, made both in the United States and other countries.

**Related Articles** ART IN ARCHITECTURE; GARDEN; INTERIOR DESIGN; ORNAMENT; WOODWORK; Articles on various materials.

**Further Reading** Clark, Robert Judson, David G. DeLong, Martin Eidelberg, J. David Farmer, Neil Harris, Joan Marter, R. Craig Miller, Mary Riordan, Roy Slade, Davira S. Taragin, and Christa C. Mayer Thurman: *Design in America: The Cranbrook Vision 1925–1950*, Harry N. Abrams Inc., New York, in association with the Detroit Institute of Arts and The Metropolitan Museum of Art, 1983; Pile, John F.: *Modern Furniture*, 2d ed., John Wiley, New York, 1990.

**GARAGE** A building, or a room in a building, in which automobiles, trucks, or other motor vehicles are kept or repaired.

**Types** There are three major types of garage: residential, repair, and parking. Residential garages shelter one or more cars and are attached to or located near houses. A special type is a carport, a covered shelter for the same purpose but not closed in on all sides. Repair garages are commercial buildings in which automobiles and other vehicles are kept temporarily for service, maintenance, and repair. Residential garages and carports are elements of house design, and repair garages are most often design elements of automobile or other vehicular sales and service commercial buildings.

With the growth in automobile traffic, parking garages have become an important building type. Their function is the temporary shelter of vehicles, particularly in densely populated areas where street parking is scarce or impractical. Parking garages may be either separate structures or attached to or integrated with other building types, such as apartments, hotels or motels, and office buildings. In all cases, the principles of design are similar.

Parking garages are usually multistory. When automobiles are parked on one level, the area is usually called a parking lot and no building, except a small one for the attendants and cashier, is required. Multistory parking garages are classified by the types of floors: flat; sloping; and staggered or split-level. They are also classified according to the type of system used for traffic to and from the floors: ramps, used with flat and staggered floors; sloping floor, where the floor itself serves in place of the ramps; and mechanical, using elevators. Ramps may be straight or helical, shaped like a spiral, and may have one-way or two-way traffic. Some parking garages utilize mechanical elevators for moving automobiles into

and out of place. In some garages of this type, the automobiles must be driven on and off the elevators by attendants; in others, dollies automatically perform these functions. The elevators are counterweighted so that, in case of power failure, they will rise when empty and descend slowly when loaded with automobiles.

In addition to the parking areas and the ramps or vehicle elevators, the major elements of parking garages are the public areas, which may include waiting rooms, rest rooms, passenger elevators, and a booth for the cashier and attendants. Major considerations in their design include efficient and economical use of space to park the maximum number of vehicles safely and the problems presented by irregular and relatively small sites. Because of problems of this sort, many parking garages are designed individually, but for more straightforward sites, prefabricated buildings and systems are often used.

Other issues involved in the design of parking garages in urban locations are pedestrian safety, requiring traffic control at entrances, and the possible need for building security personnel. Another problem relating to parking garages is the possibility of long blank building walls at the street level. This may be addressed by the addition of street-level stores under the parking levels or by landscaping between the parking garage and the street. Occasionally, the roofs of parking structures may be landscaped, and they are frequently directly connected by bridges or elevators to the buildings they serve.

**History** Some sort of shelter has been used for vehicles ever since they were invented. In Europe the carriage house, and later the coach house, was used to shelter horse-drawn vehicles. Such shelters were ordinarily attached to or near private houses or built in conjunction with inns. The same practice was followed in colonial America and for many years after independence. With

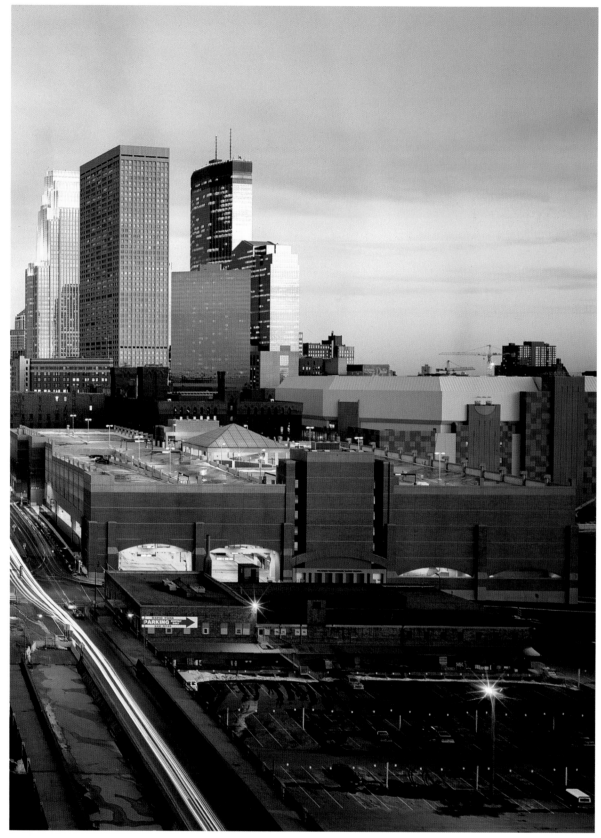

**GARAGE** 5th Street Transit Garage (1991), Minneapolis, Minn. *[Architect: Stageberg Partners (Photo: Christian M. Korab)]*

the advent of the automobile, the need for parking garages might have been foreseen, but no one seems to have predicted the phenomenal growth in both the number of automobiles and the population of cities. Thus the parking garage has only become an important building type within the last few decades.

**Related Articles** APARTMENT; HOTEL; HOUSE; HOUSING; OFFICE BUILDING.

**Source of Additional Information** National Parking Assoc., 1112 16th St., N.W., Washington, D.C. 20036.

**GARDEN** An area of ground primarily used for growing flowers, shrubbery, and trees; also an area used for growing fruits, nuts, or vegetables. Gardens for use and enjoyment are important parts of the lives of many people. While a garden of vegetables may assume aesthetic qualities, most gardens in conjunction with architecture contain ornamental plants. In addition, such gardens often contain other elements, as rocks, lawns, outdoor furniture, paving, garden houses or gazebos, water in fountains or pools, special lighting, and greenhouses.

In any case, gardens have been an important adjunct of architecture since its earliest beginnings and remain so today. Gardens come in a variety of sizes, from the smallest in a window box or planter to that in a yard of a modest house to the great gardens, often many acres in size, in public areas of cities and on large estates.

It has been said that parks should provide opportunities for visual, mental, and physical recreation. Gardens might be said to have the same functions, though not always in the same degree as parks. Activities in gardens are not usually as strenuous as in many parks. And the opportunities for quiet contemplation or reflection and the appreciation of beauty and nature may be even greater in gardens than in most parks.

**Types** Throughout history, gardens have been of two major types: those in which people are more important (or of equal importance) than plants; and those in which people are subordinated to the plants. The first type might be called a living garden and the second one, a show garden. In addition, in the past, gardens have had varying degrees of formality, ranging from completely informal, naturalistic types to rigidly formal ones. These principles are still applied to garden design today.

The two major types of gardens may be subdivided into a number of variations. One may be a general garden, with plants of many kinds; another may be special, containing only plants of certain varieties, such as a rose garden, or certain kinds of plants, such as alpine, aquatic, rock garden, and so on. They may be even more specialized, as in a cutting garden for production of flowers for display indoors. Gardens may be outdoors or indoors. They may be placed at ground level or elevated, enclosed or not, on roofs, or on level or hilly sites. They may be

enclosed in patios or courtyards or on porches. Plants may be set into the ground, or in pots or planters.

**Essentials** The primary elements of any garden are plants and people. Other essentials are natural features, such as soils, rock, water, topography, and climate, and constructed features such as structures. All these elements must be properly integrated to create a successful garden.

To meet the needs of plants and people, the ideal garden should live in harmony with nature, the soil, the sun, the weather, birds and other animals, and insects. Since ideal conditions never exist, the goal of a designer might be to create gardens in which conditions can be controlled to produce states as near the ideal as possible or practical.

For most gardens, sites that are open to the sun all day are best. Land that slopes gently provides the best drainage. Therefore, for plants that grow well in the sun, eastern and southern exposures are ideal. Trees or large shrubbery planted on the northern and eastern sides protect plants that like sun from winter winds, while those on the southern and eastern sides protect those that prefer shade from the hot summer sun. Walls, windbreaks, and proper placing of shrubbery can also help protect a garden and channel the flow of air through it or around it as desired.

**Soil** To succeed, a garden must have appropriate soil, properly drained. Rocky soil makes growing plants difficult, as does sandy or clay soil. If the soil remains too wet or too dry, the growing of many plants will be difficult if not impossible. Of course, there are exceptions, for example, many cacti prefer sandy, dry soils. If the soil in a garden site does not have the proper characteristics, they must be provided, using decayed vegetable matter, or humus, to improve sandy or clay soils and working the soil with tools to break it up. In the same way, garden sites that are too dry or too wet must be corrected by improving drainage or by provision for watering.

Another important factor in successful gardens is the acidity of soils; this may be measured with simple kits available from companies that sell plants or seeds or the tests can be made by state agricultural extension services. The measure of acidity of soils is called the pH factor, which is the symbol for the amount of hydrogen ion present. The values of pH range from 0 to 14, with 0 the most acid, 14 the most alkaline, and a value of 7 representing neutrality. Most natural soils in the United States are neutral or slightly acid, except for the Western states where soils tend to be alkaline. For many plants, a neutral or slightly acid state is ideal. For others, such as azaleas and rhododendrons, acid soils are required. After determination of the plants to be grown in a garden, along with their preferences in pH, acidity in soils may

**GARDEN** Edsel B. Ford House (1927), Grosse Pointe Shores, Mich. *[Landscape architect: Jens Jensen]*

be reduced by the addition of lime and raised by the addition of certain common chemicals.

**Water** Water is another essential of a successful garden. A sufficient quantity must be applied in the correct manner for plants to grow properly, and excessive quantities must be controlled by proper drainage. Other than in those with desert plants or other types that require only small quantities of water, gardens must receive water regularly, either through rain or other precipitation or by irrigation. While the quantities required vary for plants of different kinds and sizes, a rule of thumb often quoted calls for a minimum of an inch of water per week. A good soaking over a relatively long period is more effective than a great quantity deposited in a short time. Much of the water given too quickly runs off instead of sinking into the soil. On the other hand, an inch of water received over a longer period of time will wet the soil to a depth up to 6 in, a proper level.

Inexpensive rain gauges may be used to measure rainfall and also sprinkler water. Although not truly accurate, these gauges are adequate for garden purposes. Some experts maintain that irrigation by means of such devices as soaker hoses, ones that have a series of holes and are laid on the ground to water plants at their bases, are better for plants than sprinklers. When watering by hose, several hours may be required to apply an inch.

The time required will be shorter on light sandy soils, longer on heavy clay soils. Less water will be lost by evaporation if gardens are watered in the late afternoon or early evening, instead of during the hotter times of the day. However, some think that water left on the foliage of plants at night is conducive to diseases.

In dry weather, when gardens must be watered, it is thought that a good soaking once a week is best, rather than more frequent applications of smaller quantities. Gardens may be watered with watering cans, hoses with nozzles, soaker hoses or sprinklers. In some cases, permanent systems, with undergrounding piping, are provided, either with sprinklers attached or with soaker or trickle devices. They must be buried deep enough to prevent freezing in winter or be equipped for draining.

**Animals** Many people maintain that a garden without animals, in particular birds, is not complete. However, most would agree that animals, like insects, in gardens can be welcome additions or pests. Some harmless animals might include toads and frogs; nonpoisonous garter, king, and other snakes; and fish, tadpoles, snails, and salamanders in ponds to control mosquito larvae and other pests.

**Insects** Many varieties of insects attack plants. Without controls, they can destroy a garden very quickly. Some people advocate biological controls; others

**GARDEN** Dow Garden, Midland, Mich. *[Architect: Alden Dow]*

believe that only chemical insecticides or other devices can do the job. Many methods for biological control of insects are used today, including helpful insects, such as the praying mantis and the ladybird beetle, or ladybug, which kill harmful insects; devices that interfere with insect reproduction through sterilization or other means; plants that repel certain insects; symbiotic plant pairings that protect each other; and parasites that destroy the eggs of other insects. Some gardeners also capture harmful insects by picking them off plants or by various kinds of traps.

People who use pesticides maintain that, regardless of preference for biological or other means of insect control, nothing really works properly except chemicals. Several types are available, though some were eventually withdrawn from the market for environmental protection reasons.

Insecticides for control of various insects are available in forms that may be dusted or sprayed on plants. It is also possible to obtain some, in combination with fertilizers, which are absorbed by the roots of plants. In any case, the insecticides must be selected for their specific insect-control properties. All of them are poisons and must be handled and applied properly and with extreme caution.

Proper gardening practices can be of great aid in the control of insects. Gardens should be kept clean.

Diseased or dead vegetation should be quickly removed. Rotation of plantings may help. Proper cultivation aids in control of insects as well as in plant growth. These measures also help to control plant diseases, which can be as destructive as insects. Plant diseases are also controlled with chemicals, the most important being fungicides. Other chemicals for control of various kinds of garden pests include miticides for mites, herbicides for weeds, nematocides for nematodes (very small eelworms), molluscides for snails and slugs, and rodenticides for mice and rats. All these chemicals are poisonous and should be handled properly and with extreme caution.

**Plants** An almost endless list of plants of various types may be used in gardens to suit every purpose and whim. The major types of plants include trees, shrubbery, flowers, and vegetables. Trees may be evergreens, those with needlelike leaves that are not usually shed in winter, and deciduous trees, those with other types of leaves that are shed. Many types are available, including dwarf and regular fruit and nut trees. Shrubbery may also be evergreen or deciduous and of various sizes and habits. Some are dwarf types; others are creepers; still others grow very large. Some have flowers, and many have colorful berries that are decorative and provide food for birds.

**GARDEN** Hamilton Garden (1971), Columbus, Ind. *[Landscape architect: Dan Kiley]*

Flowers exist in an almost endless variety. For example, there are some 9,000 varieties of daffodils alone. The major types of flowers are perennials, which come back every year, and annuals, which die after one season. Biennials are flowers that take two years to mature and then die. Some flowers are grown from seeds; others, such as daffodils and tulips, from bulbs; and still others, such as gladiolus, from bulb or rootlike corms. Bulbs or corms may be hardy, those that usually live through winter in the ground, or tender, those that often do not. Many types of plants and flowers are available for specialized gardens or garden areas, such as rock gardens. Vegetables are also classified as perennials, such as asparagus, and annuals, such as peas. Vegetables are usually grown from seeds, except for bulb plants, such as onions or garlic, which can be grown from bulbs or seeds.

Plants in gardens may be arranged in various ways. When shrubbery or other plants are placed close to buildings, they are often referred to as foundation plantings. Plants may be placed in beds, in borders along walks or fences, or in other places. Larger plants in front of which smaller ones are planted are often referred to as background plantings. For embankments, under trees, and on hillsides, plants are often placed as ground covers. Climbing plants or vines are often grown on fences or walls.

**Fertilizers** All plants in gardens should be placed and planted with care, at the proper depth in the soil and in proper relationships to each other. Almost all plants require feeding from their roots as well as from the sun. Fertilizers for plants feeding should be chosen with care to ensure that they will perform properly for the specific plants to be grown. Complete fertilizers contain primarily nitrogen, phosphorus, and potash, along with traces of other elements. A set of numbers on a fertilizer bag denotes the percentages of the primary minerals it contains. For example, a common garden, all-purpose fertilizer is called 5-10-5, indicating, in order, 5 percent nitrogen, 10 percent phosphorus, and 5 percent potash. Various plants have specialized requirements for fertilizer which should be determined before application.

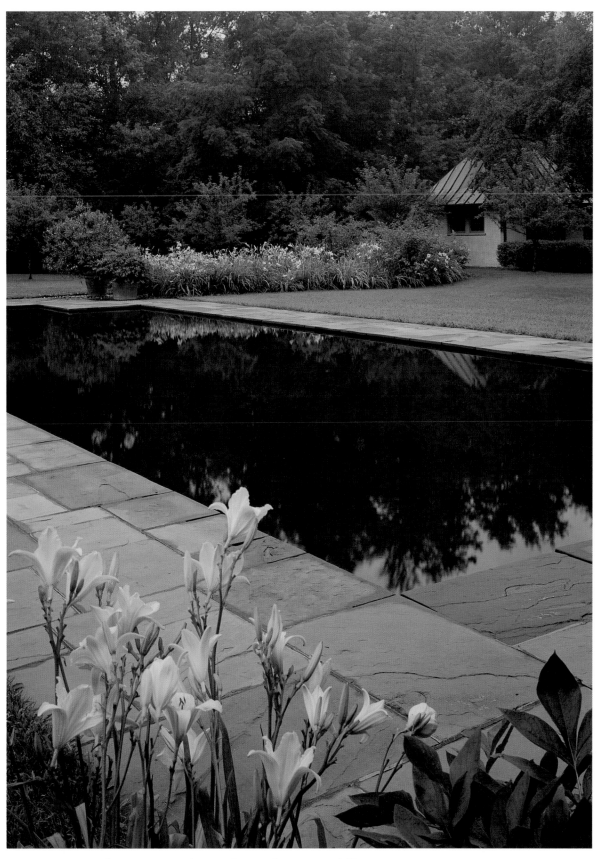

**GARDEN** Private garden (1993), Troy, Ohio. *[Landscape architect: Susan Child]*

As in the controversy between those who espouse biological control of insects and those who use insecticides, there is a division of opinion about fertilizers. Most gardeners today rely on chemical fertilizers; however, a growing number espouse the use of organic fertilizers. Organic fertilizers include well-rotted manure, leaf mold, bone meal, treated sewage sludge, peat moss, and dried animal blood. Also a good source of organic fertilizer is a compost pile, an uncovered box or other container into which kitchen scraps, leaves, and other organic materials are placed, limed to hasten rotting, and, then, when sufficiently rotted, applied to gardens.

Some plant feeding is furnished by decaying organic mulches, materials placed around plants to control weeds, retain moisture, and prevent erosion. Many materials may be used for mulches, including straw, leaves, rotting sawdust, and tree bark.

**Planting Devices** Although many gardeners start all their plants in the ground where they will remain, others use various devices for starting them, including cold frames, hot beds, and greenhouses. A cold frame is a box laid on the ground outdoors, containing soil in which seeds are planted. A plastic or glass top, hinged at one end, covers the top of the cold frame, letting sun in during the day and retaining some of its heat through the night. The top may be opened for ventilation and to let heat escape on warm days and closed on cold ones and at night. Seeds may be planted in a cold frame much earlier than in the ground and later transplanted into the garden.

A hot bed is like a cold frame, except that fresh manure is placed under the soil. As the manure deteriorates, it produces heat within the hot bed. Today electric coils may be embedded in the soil for heating. A greenhouse is like a large cold frame, a structure of metal or wood with glass or plastic panels or coverings. Greenhouses come in a great variety of sizes, from those that fit outside a standard window to very large commercial types used by horticulturists and nursery operators. Greenhouses may be fitted with equipment to control the climate inside, including fans for ventilation, heaters, and watering systems.

Materials for gardens are of two major types: natural and manufactured. Natural materials are primarily those of the soil, rocks, and water. Manufactured materials may include almost all of those used for other architectural purposes. In gardens, an attempt is often made to express the natural features and to improve upon them for esthetic and functional reasons. In addition to the plants, garden designers may use a variety of structures and devices, including benches and tables, walkways, screens, walls, embankments, lawns, paved areas, changes in levels, ramps, steps, sculpture, urns, plant containers, ponds and pools, fountains and waterfalls, garden houses or gazebos, and bird feeders and birdbaths.

**Design** The skillful design of a garden requires the establishment of the proper functional and esthetic relationships among the many elements. Garden design begins with the surroundings, the climate, and the site. In general, the climate or planting zone in which a garden exists, often called macroclimate, cannot be changed and will determine which plants can be grown successfully; smaller climates within gardens, called microclimates, can be created by skillful use of walls, trees, shrubbery, and other elements. The principles to be followed are the same as those in any other kind of landscape architecture or, for that matter, in the architecture of buildings. However, there are a few important additional principles. Unlike some other types of design, that of gardens must be more concerned with the blending of natural and manufactured elements and with the interactions between humans and the rest of nature. Gardens are often self-contained, causing the surroundings to be of lesser importance than might otherwise be the case. Such a condition may also restrict the view from and into the garden, causing it to be more intimate than other architectural forms. Nevertheless, views from the gardens of nearby buildings and from buildings into the gardens are important design considerations.

**Special Considerations** Plants are growing organisms; some grow quite rapidly. Therefore garden design must take into consideration not only the initial sizes and shapes of plants, and the relationships of these sizes and shapes to other plants and elements of the garden, but must also deal with the sizes to which the plants will eventually grow and the shapes they will take. Other special considerations in garden design include ensuring that the garden itself and nearby structures are protected from damage from such sources as flooding and wind. The maintenance of gardens is also a major consideration. Provisions must be made for receiving plant and other materials and for removal of debris. Storage for gardening tools and equipment must be provided and often space for potting plants and other functions. A watering system is a necessity, and often special lighting is placed in gardens.

**Seasonal Nature** Perhaps the most important special design consideration is the seasonal nature of gardens. All too often, a garden is designed and constructed as if it is not to exist except in spring and summer. Some experts think that the design of gardens for winters, when flowers usually cannot grow and many trees and much shrubbery have lost their leaves, is a primary consideration. Be that as it may, there are no overriding reasons why a garden cannot be attractive and functional all year. In the winter, evergreens, some with berries, can be very beautiful, especially in snow. Deciduous trees may have a stark beauty. Ground covers often stay partly green in many places, and songbirds may be attracted with feeders. In the spring, if the garden has been properly designed and planted, crocuses and other early plants begin the growing season even when snow is on the ground, to be followed by daffodils and tulips, and then an everchanging panorama of greenery, colors, and forms as successive waves of plants leaf out, bud, grow, and blossom.

In the autumn, many summer flowers are still in bloom and late bloomers, such as chrysanthemums, join them, to be followed by colchicum, the so-called autumn crocus. In a properly designed garden, autumn can also be splendid with great masses of colored leaves of deciduous plants and trees.

For many architects, landscape architects, and others, the design, planting, maintenance, and use of gardens are challenging and gratifying.

**History** The first gardens are thought to have been planted in the Neolithic period, beginning about the 50th century B.C. in the Middle East. In this period, people were becoming sedentary, instead of nomadic, settling in one place where they developed agriculture and domesticated animals. The first examples of gardens are assumed to have had only edible plants. From that period to the present, gardens have been an important adjunct of architecture.

In all the early civilizations, public and private gardens were designed and planted. The early Egyptians established gardens near their temples and homes, combining usefulness with beauty by planting a variety of edible fruits, vegetables, and herbs; trees; shrubbery; and flowers. The Egyptians developed the first irrigation systems for gardens. In the Middle East, great gardens were established, one of which, the Hanging Gardens of Babylon, constructed by King Nebuchadnezzar II (605–563 B.C.), became known among the wonders of the world.

The ancient Greeks and Romans constructed ornamental gardens, many of which contained herbs that were used for medicinal purposes. The Greeks developed the science of botany. They also planted groves of trees, called arboretums, an art that they had learned from the Persians, who had also introduced the Western world to formal planting of courtyards or patios. The Romans also built roof gardens. In other areas in the Middle East, courtyard gardens were used as well as gardens enclosed with walls to separate them from their surroundings and to insulate them from heat and the dry climate. These were rectangular gardens built along axes, containing plants, water, and paving. Early gardens were also constructed in the Far East, notably in China.

During the Middle Ages, the building of gardens languished, except for those in monasteries and castles, in which were grown fruits, vegetables, and herbs. During the Renaissance, a great wave of garden design and construction began. These were mostly gardens intended to complement the architecture. Plants were of less importance than the architectural element of the gardens: walls, terraces, paving, fountains, pools, waterfalls, and sculpture. These gardens were usually axial and formal, but with sculptural qualities. Flowers, shrubbery, and trees were planted in a very controlled manner and often clipped or shaped to resemble architectural forms rather than left in their natural state.

The design of gardens during the Renaissance began in Italy, where it has remained strong ever since, and spread throughout Europe to France, England, Spain, and other countries. In France, gardens were formal and regular; in Spain, they were mostly planted in patios or courtyards. In England, great formal gardens, ranging in size to more than 30 acres, often had covered walks, the coverings made by training the upper branches of trees to shut out the sky. And English gardens often had terraces, garden houses or gazebos, and shrubbery and trees clipped or shaped to reflect the formal characteristics of the entire garden. Many of the great public gardens of the Renaissance were not public in any real sense, but were intended for the use of the wealthy, the nobility, and sometimes certain other privileged classes.

After the Renaissance, beginning in the 18th century in England, gardens were often designed to create illusions of long ago or faraway places or of an imagined nature that was not natural but contrived to appear the way the garden designers thought it should look. The French called this type of garden *le jardin Anglais* and soon adopted the style; the idea eventually spread all over Europe. These gardens were the antithesis of the formal, axial gardens that had come before. Some gardens of the time were given a romantic, wild appearance, with irregular planting, faked dead trees, and faked building ruins. This type of garden was mostly promulgated by two English architects, William Kent (1684–1748) and Batty Langley (1696–1751), who started the trend, and by an English landscape gardener, Lancelot Brown (1716–83), known as Capability Brown. Having constructed a fake river, Brown is said to have remarked, "Alas, the Thames will never forgive me." Another English landscape gardener, Humphrey Repton (1752–1818), attempted to restore a more rational approach to the design of gardens.

Few changes have taken place in garden design since the 18th century, except for the adoption of ideas from non-European sources, notably from the Chinese, Japanese, and Muslims. A change of another sort has been in the democratization of public gardens, a process that began primarily with the work of the great American landscape architect Frederick Law Olmsted (1822–1903). Olmsted designed parks, including gardens, for private estates, but he also designed the first significant examples intended for use by all the people, not only by the privileged.

**American Development** In the American colonies, gardens were established very early. They were simple and utilitarian, geometrical in plan, and usually axial. The earliest gardens were strictly utilitarian, containing mostly fruit trees and vegetables; flowers and other ornamental plants were soon added. Later American gardens followed the various styles prevalent in Europe at the time: some formal and axial, others informal and naturalistic, and still others a combination of the two design philosophies.

Today there are gardens everywhere in America, in great public places, in parks, in botanical buildings and arboretums, on the grounds of great estates, and in the yards of more modest dwellings. They are widely varied in design and purpose, as specialized types, roof gardens, inside gardens, pot gardens, patio or courtyard gardens, and water gardens. They are a very valuable and important element of architecture.

A great many fine public gardens of all kinds, and others sometimes open to the public, exist in many places in the United States. Perhaps the greatest concentration can be found in the Southeastern states. Among those of greatest interest and beauty are the following: in Washington—the gardens of the U.S. Capitol; in Virginia—Mount Vernon and Woodlawn Plantation (both in Mount Vernon), Gunston Hall (Lorton), and the gardens of colonial Williamsburg; in North Carolina—Orton Plantation (Wilmington), Tryon Palace (New Bern), Elizabethan Garden (Manteo), and Biltmore (Asheville), designed by Frederick Law Olmsted; in South Carolina—Middleton Place, considered to be the oldest landscaped garden in the United States, and Magnolia (both in Charleston) and Brookgreen Gardens (Murrell's Inlet); in Tennessee—Cheekwood (Nashville) and Botanic Garden (Memphis); in Georgia—the gardens of Savannah and Callaway Gardens (Pine Mountain); in Alabama—Bellingrath Gardens (Theodore); in Mississippi—D'Evereux and Cherokee (both in Natchez); in Louisiana—Afton Villa and Rosedown (both in St. Francisville), Jungle Gardens (Avery Island), and Longue Vue (New Orleans).

**Related Articles** ART IN ARCHITECTURE; BOTANICAL BUILDING; ECOLOGY; FOUNTAIN; LANDSCAPE ARCHITECTURE; OLMSTED, FREDERICK LAW; PLANNING, CITY; SITE PLANNING.

**Further Reading** Church, Thomas D.: *Gardens Are for People,* 2d ed., McGraw-Hill, New York, 1983; Hay, Roy, and Patrick M. Synge: *Color Dictionary of Flowers and Plants for Home and Garden,* compact ed., Crown, New York, 1982.

**Periodicals** *American Horticulturist,* Mount Vernon, Va. 22121; *Horticulture,* 300 Massachusetts Ave., Boston, Mass. 02115; *Landscape Architecture,* 1500 Bardstown Rd., Louisville, Ky. 40205.

**Sources of Additional Information** The American Horticultural Society, 7931 E. Boulevard Dr., Alexandria, Va. 22308; American Society of Landscape Architects, 4401 Connecticut Ave., N.W., Washington, D.C. 20008; U.S. Department of Agriculture, Fourteenth St. and Independence Ave., S.W., Washington, D.C. 20250; Various agricultural extension services of states and county agents.

**GEHRY, FRANK O.** American architect (1929– ), a design leader among his generation identified with the movement labelled "Deconstructionism." Having started with a conventional practice, in mid-career he redirected his efforts to art-centered design.

**Work** Initially identified with the Los Angeles area, Gehry's noted projects have included a number of houses. Examples include the Ron Davis Studio-Residence (1972), Malibu, Calif, the Gehry House (1978), Santa Monica, Calif., and the Norton House (1984), Venice, Calif. His 1983 design of a guest house in Wayzata, Minn., is part of a compound containing a main house designed by Philip Johnson in 1952. The guest house is set apart on the property and is a grouping of forms making a small village effect. Each room is a small separate building clustered around a pyramidal form con-

**GEHRY, FRANK O.** Frank O. Gehry Residence (1978), Santa Monica, Calif.

**GEHRY, FRANK O.** Loyola Law School Campus (1983), Los Angeles, Calif.

taining a living room. The assemblage is made of differing materials which heighten the village aspect. This free assemblage is both artistic and childlike, making an interesting contrast to the main house.

His interest in buildings in process is reflected in the use of exposed stud partitions and chain link fencing in his earlier designs. His interest in the fish form resulted in a lamp design as well as restaurant decoration and museum exhibition projects. The 1987 guest house in Minnesota is consistent with his later free-form designs.

Larger projects have included the California Aerospace Museum (1984) and Loyola Marymount University's Law School (1986), in Los Angeles. The Law School consists of a campus in the middle of an area of nondescript buildings. His solution is a group of structures of varying sizes and shapes, with freestanding concrete piers recalling the classic colonnade. The acropolis grouping gave a real sense of space to the urban campus and was inspired by the classic understanding of law and the courts. The use of color enlivens the interior of the block, and street frontages are in gray stucco, fitting in with the nondescript neighborhood of low-rise buildings.

The Francis Howard Goldwyn Regional branch Library (1986), Hollywood, Calif., is a symmetrical group of buildings set behind a street wall. The tri-part composition contains two high spaces suitable for a public building.

Frank Gehry has received a number of commissions for art museums. The Vitra Design Museum of 1989 is his first completed European project. The museum is in Germany near the Swiss border and the city of Basel and is a typical example of Gehry's design. The building consists of a grouping of irregular forms relating to earlier German Expressionist structures while remaining clearly a Gehry design. The building contains an important collection of early 20th-century chair designs. The museum is set in front of a factory addition to Vitra International, the office seating manufacturer headquartered in Switzerland. The sculptural grouping of the museum leads on to Gehry's later designs.

**Life** Frank Gehry was born Frank Goldberg on February 29, 1929, in Toronto, Canada. He and his family moved from Toronto to Los Angeles in 1947. Because of the anti-Semitic prejudice he experienced in school, Gehry changed his name from Goldberg to Gehry in the 1950s.

Gehry received his architectural degree from the University of California School of Architecture in 1954. In 1955 he was in military service and was able to apply his architectural skills to interiors and furniture design. In 1956, Gehry studied at the Harvard Graduate School

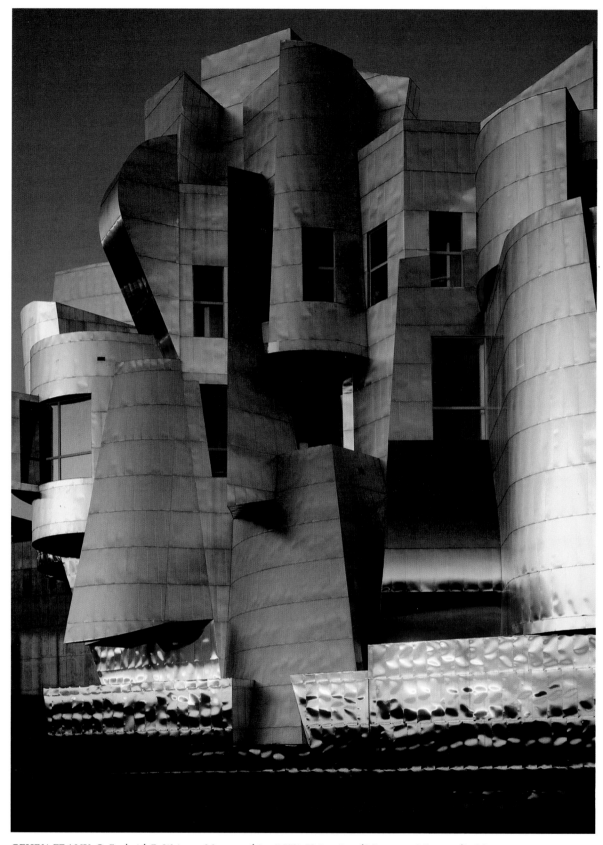

**GEHRY, FRANK O.** Frederick R. Weisman Museum of Art (1993), University of Minnesota, Minneapolis, Minn.

of Design. He also worked briefly for Hideo Sasaki and Perry, Shaw, Hepburn and Dean. In 1957 he returned to California and worked in the offices of Pereira and Luckman and for Victor Gruen. In 1960, he and his family went to Paris, where he worked for over a year in the office of André Remondet.

Gehry set up his own practice in Los Angeles in 1962. His first marriage ended in divorce in 1966, and in 1976 he married Berta Isabel Aquilera. Having practiced architecture for many years in a conventional manner, Gehry withdrew to form a personal practice, artistically motivated. Widely recognized in the press, his work has become a major influence on American architectural thinking. The first project to win national recognition was his own house of 1977–78. This and later work led to his identification as a Deconstructivist architect, and he was so identified in a 1988 exhibition at the Museum of Modern Art in New York directed by the architect Philip C. Johnson. By the end of the 1970s, Gehry had established an international reputation and commissions were awarded to him that he would never have been considered for in his earlier years. His friendships with artists and actors has resulted in commissions for buildings and some well-received exhibition installations.

Frank Gehry received the prestigious Pritzker Award in 1989. For several years, Gehry was involved in furniture designs for KnollStudio, a division of The Knoll Group. Announced with considerable publicity, the series of bentwood chairs are reminiscent of the earlier work of Thonet, Alvar Aalto, and Charles and Ray Eames but are decidedly Gehry designs. Gehry's interest in the technology of laminated wood resulted in lightweight products made of wood and glue, without the use of metal connections.

**Related Article** CONTEMPORARY ARCHITECTURE.

**Further Reading** Gehry, Frank: *The Architecture of Frank Gehry*, Rizzoli, New York, 1986; Johnson, Philip: *Deconstructivist Architecture*, New York Graphic Society Books, 1988.

**GEORGIAN ARCHITECTURE** The term *Georgian* is loosely used to describe the classicism of 18th-century architecture in England and her colonies on the eastern seaboard of North America. The period is named for the English kings, George I, II, III, and IV, who reigned from 1714 to 1830. The Georgian style was an important style in the United States before and for a short period after independence. The early American Georgian style has

**GEORGIAN ARCHITECTURE** Wren Building (1695, rebuilt later), College of William and Mary, Williamsburg, Va. *[Architect: possibly Sir Christopher Wren]*

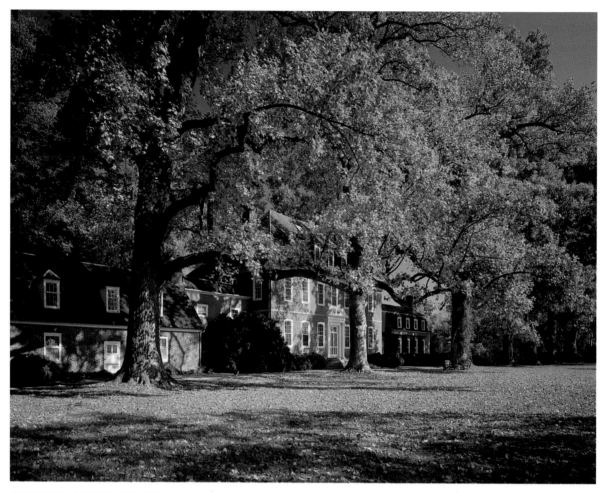

**GEORGIAN ARCHITECTURE** Westover (*c.* 1730), Charles City Co., Va. *[Architect: unknown]*

often been called "Colonial," a misnomer since Georgian was only one of a number of styles of architecture in the colonies.

Georgian architecture followed the rules of design and proportion formulated by several great English architects, including Inigo Jones (1573–1652), who introduced Italian classic detailing to England, Sir Christopher Wren (1632–1723), James Gibbs (1682–1754), and Sir William Chambers (1726–96), who were trying to create a national architectural style as the Renaissance was coming to an end in England. These architects based their concepts on those of architects of the Italian Renaissance, particularly Andrea Palladio (1508–50), who had studied classical Roman architecture and had published his concepts of the proper use of Roman details.

**Principles** These principles led to architecture which was symmetrical in plan and exterior appearance. The buildings were quiet and serene. Mostly of brick, sometimes of stone or brick with stone details, Georgian buildings are quite elegant, but subdued.

**GEORGIAN ARCHITECTURE** Drayton Hall (1742), near Charleston, S.C. A property of the National Trust for Historic Preservation. *[Architect: unknown]*

**GEORGIAN ARCHITECTURE** Gunston Hall (1758; restored), Fairfax County, Va. [Architect of interiors: William Buckland]

Typically, Georgian buildings had either simple square or rectangular plans, often with two symmetrical flanking wings, and the form was also generally rectangular. A Georgian house often had a central stair hall with high-ceilinged rooms on either side and tall windows in the rooms. The number of stories varied, but there were usually two and sometimes more. Entrances were imposing, with large, paneled doors and often with porches or projected hoods, with columns and narrow windows alongside the doors, all finely detailed. Well-proportioned chimneys, often quite large, were symmetrically placed. The edges of the roofs, or cornices, were quite ornamental and finely detailed. Inside, the walls were often of wood divided into paneled areas by ornamental moldings. At the top of the walls where they met the ceilings were rich, ornamental cornices. Fireplaces were included in all major rooms and often in most other rooms. As elsewhere, the fireplaces were finely detailed and had ornamental mantels.

Other Georgian buildings followed the design and detailing of the houses, with changes as required by their relative sizes and purposes. For example, Georgian churches often had imposing steeples or towers, designed and detailed to reflect the rules of the style as seen in the English churches of Wren and Gibbs.

**Criticism** Elegant as they were, restrained but rich, Georgian buildings have often been criticized for sometimes sacrificing function, comfort, and convenience to the demand for symmetry and to the rules of design, proportion, and correctness of form. Another criticism is that Georgian style produced clichés that were repeated over and over. The most famous is the so-called Palladian motif, introduced by Palladio into the design of an arcade for the Basilica at Vicenze, Italy, in the 17th century. The Palladian motif consists of a round-arched opening supported by columns or pilasters, with smaller rectangular openings at the sides. A well-known example is in Washington's home at Mount Vernon, Va.

**American Development** The Georgian style was brought to America during the first half of the 18th century, several decades after its beginnings in England, by emigrants who had seen or read about it in England. The first efforts to use the style in the colonies were in houses of wood, attempting to simulate the form and details of the brick and stone buildings in England. The names of architects or builders are missing for the first half of the eighteenth century. By midcentury, Palladian influence could be found in America, probably derived from books. Among the first architects of note was Peter Harrison (1716–75), who came to Rhode Island from England in 1740 and who produced a number of fine buildings in rather pure Palladian style in Newport at first in wood and later in brick. A house, Westover (c. 1730), in Charles City Co., Va., is another masterpiece. Richard Taliaferro (1705–79) was probably the architect, but that is not certain. Westover is a plantation house in a rural setting. As a contrast, the Hammond-Hardwood House (1773) Annapolis, Md., is often said to be the finest Georgian town house in America. Its architect was William Buckland (1734–74). Many American Georgian

**GEORGIAN ARCHITECTURE** Moffit-Ladd House (1764), Portsmouth, N.H. [Architect: unknown]

**GEORGIAN ARCHITECTURE** Pohick Church (1774), near Alexandria, Va. *[Architects: Credited to George Washington with William Buckland]*

buildings were derived from published designs by English architects, among them Sir Christopher Wren and James Gibbs, adapted for use in this country. This was true of Harrison's buildings and those of others. In addition, English architects sometimes prepared designs and plans for buildings to build in America, even though these architects had never been in the colonies. Thus the so-called Wren building, at the College of William and Mary, Williamsburg, Va., is widely believed to have been designed by Wren. The cornerstone was laid in 1695, and two wings were completed by 1702. The building burned in 1705 but was rebuilt, and the chapel wing was added in 1732. Fire damage occurred in 1859 and 1862. The modern restoration was based on old documents and drawings. Other Georgian buildings in America, such as the Capitol (1705), reconstructed in 1934, and the Governor's Palace (1720), reconstructed in 1932, both in Williamsburg, so resemble the other work of Wren that some historians think he may have designed them also. None of these buildings have survived in any way intact from those early years.

**History** The Georgian era is sometimes said to have begun in 1702, thus covering the reign of Queen Anne (1702–14). Some historians think of the architecture of Queen Anne's era as a separate style. Some consider the end of the Georgian style to have coincided with the end of the reign of King George III in 1820. In any case, the Georgian style was developed in England early in the 18th century and was based primarily on the work of Inigo Jones and Sir Christopher Wren, who were deeply affected by their studies of Palladio's writings even more than by his architecture. The publication of new English editions of his 1570 *The Four Books of Architecture (I Quattro Libri di Architettura)* in Leoni's 1721 edition, and again with better plates in Isaac Ware's 1737 edition, made Palladio's theories, rules, and drawings readily available.

In 1759 Sir William Chambers reformulated the principles of Palladio and other Italian architects of the Renaissance in his *Treatise on the Decorative Part of Civil Architecture,* and this was followed by Robert Adam's *Ruins of the Palace of Diocletian in Dalmatia* in 1764. Such books spread the principles widely, and they were readily accepted by many English and American architects. The Georgian style thus became a kind of literary architecture, based more on reading about past

**GEORGIAN ARCHITECTURE** John Brown House (1788; later addition), Providence, R.I. *[Architect: Joseph Brown]*

architecture than by the buildings themselves. The style also deeply affected other arts, particularly furniture design, as may be seen in the work of the great furniture makers of the time, Chippendale, Hepplewhite, and Sheraton.

Early architectural pattern books were also widely used by carpenter-builders. Some of the most popular books included Francis Price's *The British Carpenter* (1734) and Batty Langley's *Builder's Jewel* (1741). By the end of the 18th century, American pattern books began to be published more appropriate for the new nation. The first important example was Asher Benjamin's *The Country Builder's Assistant* (1797), based on earlier books of Peter Nicholson and William Chambers.

By the second half of the 18th century, the Georgian style became firmly entrenched in America for houses as well as more ambitious buildings. American architects then drew most of their inspiration, and often their forms and details, from the books they imported from England. By the end of that century, the Georgian style's popularity had begun to wane in the face of the growing preference for what was to become the Classic Revival style, and by 1830 the real end had come, though some

vestiges have persisted ever since, even into the 20th century. The real end was signaled when American architects turned away from Georgian to the Classic Revival for important public and other monumental buildings of the new republic. In fact, Thomas Jefferson (1743–1826), who had built his home, Monticello, near Charlottesville, Va., in the Georgian style in 1775, remodeled and rebuilt part of it in the Classic Revival style, beginning in 1796.

**Related Articles** BULFINCH, CHARLES; CLASSIC REVIVAL ARCHITECTURE; COLONIAL ARCHITECTURE; FURNITURE; HARRISON, PETER; HISTORY OF ARCHITECTURE; JEFFERSON, THOMAS; LATROBE, BENJAMIN HENRY; PRESERVATION.

**Further Reading** Architects' Emergency Committee: *Great Georgian Houses of America*, 2 vols., Dover, New York, 1970; see also listings in articles entitled colonial architecture and history of architecture.

**Sources of Additional Information** See the article entitled history of architecture.

**GILBERT, CASS** American architect (1859–1934). Although Cass Gilbert had very little architectural training, a year at Massachusetts Institute of Technology, a year traveling in Europe, and two years as an assistant to Stanford White (1853–1906), all of it was under the influence of the principles of design taught at the École des Beaux Arts in Paris. It is therefore only natural that Gilbert should have become an architect in the Beaux Arts tradition, designing eclectic buildings in many styles derived from the past.

Like his contemporary, John Russell Pope (1874–1937), Gilbert was very good at it. He produced buildings that were scholarly, well designed, and quite popular, but like those of Pope, something of an anachronism in the years just before World War II. He also became a very skilled draftsman, producing fine drawings and renderings to show his clients and others his proposed building designs. And his designs have long been considered among the very best of the late Eclectic period in American architecture. He had little patience with the developing modern movement in American architecture, continuing to produce eclectic buildings to the last, some of which were completed in the late 1930s, after his death.

Gilbert also became one of the most successful architects in the United States, producing a very large number of buildings during his almost 50 years of private practice. Unlike some architects of the time, who tended to design buildings only in and near the cities in which their offices were located, Gilbert built a national practice, designing buildings not only in New York City but in Washington, the Midwest, Arkansas, West Virginia, Missouri, and many other places.

Gilbert also designed a large number of building types, such as office buildings, public buildings, art museums, libraries, and banks. In addition, he planned college campuses for the University of Minnesota, Minneapolis, and the University of Texas, Austin. Gilbert also did architectural designs for bridges, including, in New York City, the Bayonne Bridge between Staten Island and New Jersey and the great George Washington Bridge between Manhattan and New Jersey, both completed in 1931, and both engineered by the noted Swiss-American engineer, Othmar Hermann Ammann (1879–1965). See article entitled bridge.

**Works** Some of the most notable of Gilbert's buildings in New York City are the U.S. Customs House (1907); the Woolworth Building (1913), the tallest building in the world when it was built; the New York Life Insurance Building (1928); the New York County Lawyers Building (1930); the North Building (1930), of the National Institute of Arts and Letters and American

**GILBERT, CASS** Woolworth Building (1913), New York, N.Y.

Academy of Arts and Sciences; and the U.S. Courthouse, completed by his son, Cass Gilbert, Jr., in 1936. His deteriorated Customs House has been restored for use as a federal office building.

Notable buildings of Gilbert's in Washington are the U.S. Treasury Annex (1919), the U.S. Chamber of Commerce Building (1925), and U.S. Supreme Court Building (see illustration), finished by his son in 1935. Important buildings in other locations include the Minnesota State Capitol (1903), St. Paul; the Festival Hall and Art Building (1904), now the St. Louis Art Museum, at the Louisiana Purchase Exposition, St. Louis; the Ives Memorial Library (1905), New Haven, Conn.; the Central Public Library (1912), St. Louis; the Detroit Public Library (1914); the Allen Memorial Art Museum (1917), Oberlin College, Oberlin, Ohio; and the Old Federal Reserve Bank (1924), Minneapolis.

**Life** Cass Gilbert was born on November 24, 1859, in Zanesville, Ohio. When he was young, his family moved to St. Paul, Minn., where Gilbert grew up and received his early education. At eighteen, he went to work for an architect in St. Paul for about a year. In 1878 he entered Massachusetts Institute of Technology, Cambridge, where he studied for a year, and in 1879 he went to Europe where he studied and traveled in England, France, and Italy.

Upon his return from Europe in 1880, Gilbert went to work for the New York City architectural firm of McKim, Mead and White, and became an assistant to one of the partners, Stanford White. After two years, Gilbert left the firm in 1882 to form a partnership in St. Paul with James Knox Taylor (1857–1939), which lasted more than 10 years. The firm was moderately successful, but Gilbert did not come into prominence until 1896 when, after dissolving the partnership, he won the competition for the design of the Minnesota State Capitol, St. Paul. In 1898 he won another important competition, that for the U.S. Customs House, New York City. After winning the second competition, Gilbert moved his office to New York City and practiced there the remainder of his life.

In 1887 Gilbert married Julia T. Finch, and they had a son, Cass Gilbert, Jr., who became an architect and a partner in his father's firm and carried on the practice after his father's death. The Minnesota State Capitol brought Gilbert considerable recognition, and soon his practice began to grow very rapidly. Eventually, he became one of the most successful architects of his time.

Gilbert was very active in civic and professional affairs, belonging to a number of organizations, including the American Academy of Arts and Letters and the National Academy of Design. He served as president of the American Academy and also, in 1908–09, of the

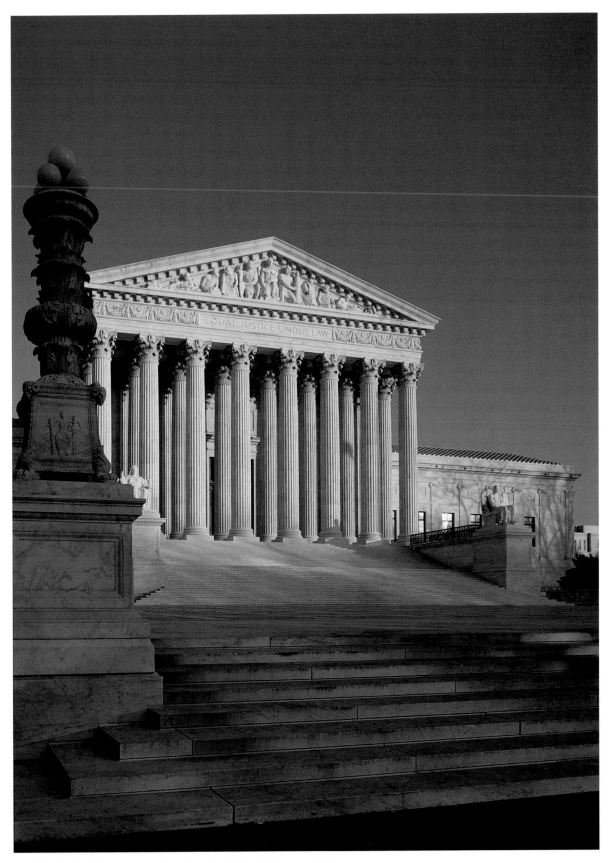

**GILBERT, CASS** U.S. Supreme Court Building (1935), Washington, D.C.

American Institute of Architects. He received honorary degrees from a number of universities. Appointed to the chairmanship of the National Council of Fine Arts by President Theodore Roosevelt (1858–1919), he later served on the National Commission of Fine Arts, 1910–18, under presidents William Howard Taft (1857–1930) and Woodrow Wilson (1856–1924). On May 19, 1934, after nearly a half-century of practice, Cass Gilbert died while on a trip to England.

**Related Articles** ECLECTIC ARCHITECTURE; McKIM, MEAD AND WHITE.

**Further Reading** Thompson, Neil B.: *Minnesota State Capitol—The Art and Politics of a Public Building,* Minnesota Historical Society, St. Paul, 1974.

**GILL, IRVING JOHN** American architect (1870–1936). In spite of having had no formal training in architecture, Irving Gill nevertheless became one of the most important pioneers of the modern movement in architecture. He developed a unique design style, apparently from study, experimentation, and participation in the construction process. He believed that the interiors and landscaping of buildings were integral parts of the architecture. He was concerned with the sociological aspects of low-cost housing. He was an experimenter, innovator, and inventor, using the newest building materials and methods. Thus his work has deeply affected architecture ever since.

A contemporary of the Greene brothers, Gill was, like them, deeply interested in good craftsmanship. This interest led the Greenes to elaborate, handcrafted details and forms, mostly in wood and other natural materials, combined into a rich and even more elaborate overall design for buildings. Gill's interest led him in the opposite direction to details and forms simplified almost to abstractions, in new materials, particularly reinforced concrete, combined into designs for buildings composed of masses that are angular, cubic solids, with broad surfaces and deep voids. To achieve a high level of craftsmanship, Gill trained his own construction crews, made up mostly of German, English, and Scandinavian immigrants. With the Greenes, everything was richly ornamented and handcrafted. With Gill, there were plain, clean surfaces, with little ornamentation.

**Experimental Materials and Devices** Gill started his own practice in 1895, and the first 10 years or so gave only a slight indication of his later development. His designs were eclectic, in a variety of styles and materials, but were also beginning to show experimentation with building materials and methods and with form. In 1907, in the Klauber and Laughlin houses in San Diego, he used concrete and hollow-tile structure. And in the latter, he used concrete floors that curved up at their edges to form smooth surfaces with the walls above. He had done this in kitchens and bathrooms before, but here he used the process throughout the house. He was experi-

menting with laborsaving devices for housewives which made his houses more sanitary than others. Among these were a disposal that dropped garbage into a basement incinerator, a vacuum cleaner system that carried dust and debris from outlets in all rooms through pipes to the furnace, rooms with no dust-catching moldings, flush doors that had invisible hinges or slid into walls, a refrigerator with a door in the outside kitchen wall for milk deliveries, and a system in the garage that sprayed an entire car for washing.

**Works** Gill continued using concrete and hollow tile in other buildings. A notable example was the five-story Wilson Acton Hotel (1908) in La Jolla, his tallest building. In 1908 he began to experiment with monolithic concrete structures in Scripps Institution for Oceanography Building (1908), the Holly Sefton Memorial Hospital (1908), Bishop's School (1909), all in La Jolla, and in the Christian Science Church (1909) and Bishop's Day School (1909), both in San Diego. All showed his progress toward near-ultimate simplification of forms.

In 1911 Gill bought, from the U.S. government, equipment for tilt-slab construction, a method of pouring concrete into steel-reinforced hollow-tile forms laid on a large table. With this equipment, a whole wall could be poured with metal door and window frames in place, and after having been cured and finished with a coating of fine cement, could be raised to the vertical by a small engine. In 1912 he used tilt-slab in the Banning House, Los Angeles, and in 1913 in the Women's Club, La Jolla. In 1914 he used tilt-slab walls 60 ft long for the Community House at Scripps Institution. Such was Gill's interest in concrete that he established a laboratory in his office for experiments and tests on concrete. He used concrete for the Walter Luther Dodge House (1916), generally considered his greatest building but now destroyed, and for the Ellen Scripps House (1916), now the Art Center in La Jolla. The latter house, now drastically altered, was the epitome of Gill's mature style.

During his whole career, Gill was deeply interested in low-cost housing for laborers, the unemployed, and others who ordinarily could not afford decent housing. He designed a number of projects of this kind, always seeking to provide economical solutions to the problems of good housing. Among his designs of this kind was Lewis Courts (1910), Sierra Madre, which he always said was his favorite design. Following this were a series of low-cost projects, including barracks for Mexican laborers and housing for resettled Indians.

After 1917, commissions became fewer as potential clients turned away from Gill's designs to the new Spanish Colonial Style made popular by the Panama Pacific Exposition of 1915. After that, he designed only two additional major works, the Civic Center,

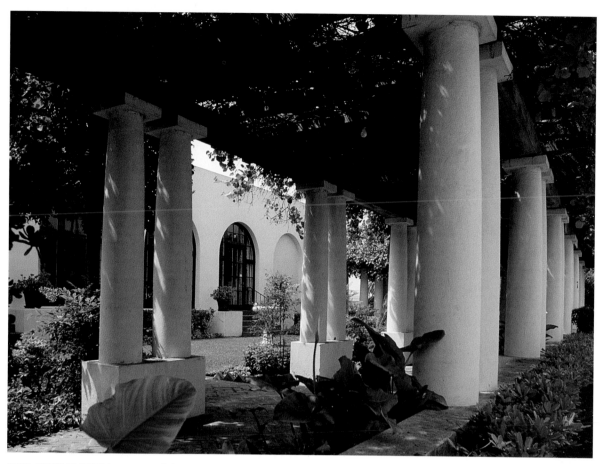

**GILL, IRVING JOHN** Women's Club (1913), La Jolla, Calif.

Oceanside, and the Christian Science Church, Coronado, both build in 1929. Neither building was experimental. Gill's pioneering of forms and materials had come to an end.

**Life** Irving John Gill was born in Syracuse, N.Y., in 1870, the son of a building contractor. He had only a high school education. His early architectural training came from his contact with his father's business and from working for a short time in an architect's office in Syracuse. Becoming aware of the work of Louis Henry Sullivan (1856–1924), Gill went to Chicago in 1890 and was hired by the firm of Adler and Sullivan, joining another young employee, Frank Lloyd Wright (1867–1959), almost three years older than Gill, who had come to this office two years earlier.

Gill worked and studied with Sullivan for two years, participating in the drawings for Sullivan's Transportation Building for the Chicago World's Columbian Exposition of 1893. Tired from overwork and ill, Gill went to California in 1892 for a rest. Arriving in San Diego, Gill was impressed by the climate, the surroundings, and the quality of the life. He decided to stay and, except for short periods, lived in California the rest of his life.

Gill's first building, the Normal School (1895) in San Diego, now demolished, was an undistinguished building with Ionic columns, a form he never used again. During the next few years, he designed other buildings in eclectic styles, including one in Gothic Revival. In 1898 he formed a partnership with W. S. Hebbard, and together they continued designing houses and other buildings in various styles. The partnership was dissolved in 1906, and Gill's buildings began to show evidence of his future directions.

Those who knew Gill thought him sincere and straightforward, with a winning personality. As a result, during the next few years, Gill's office grew and prospered until by 1911, he had six draftsmen, a field supervisor, and a secretary, a mighty accomplishment in a town of 25,000 in which contractors did almost all the design and construction of buildings. Among the draftsmen were his nephew, Louis J. Gill, John Lloyd Wright (1892–1978), the son of his former fellow-draftsman in Sullivan's office, and Hazel Wood Waterman (1865–1948). All later became noted architects.

During this period, Gill had been expected to be named chief architect of the San Diego Panama Pacific Exposition to be held in 1915. Instead, an Eastern architect, Bertram Grosvenor Goodhue (1869–1924) was selected, turning the design of the fair away from Gill's developing modernism to the eclecticism of the Spanish Colonial style. This style made an immediate hit in Southern California and, after 1915, the work of Gill's office radically declined.

The work revived somewhat when Frederick Law Olmsted, Jr. (1870–1957) and his half brother John Charles (1852–1920), son and stepson of the great landscape architect, received a commission to plan a new industrial town, Torrance, near Los Angeles. The Olmsteds promoted Gill's nomination as chief architect for the building of the town. They had met Gill some years before and in fact the architect had designed a house for John Charles in Newport, R.I. The brothers had also been instrumental in his receiving commissions for two other large houses in Rhode Island. Excited by the prospect of the new town, Gill established an office in Los Angeles to be near the work, leaving his nephew, Louis, in charge of the San Diego office. Again the architect was to be disappointed. He saw only a few small buildings, a railroad station, and a bridge of his built. Of the hundreds of houses that were planned, only 10 were built, but not as Gill had designed them. His designs for simple, economical concrete houses were rejected after having been opposed by labor for having dispensed with traditional details. In their stead were built wood houses in traditional styles.

In 1916 Gill closed the San Diego office and had little to do but remodeling work. By that time, he had designed about 100 houses and 50 other buildings in the San Diego area. After that, he designed only a few buildings, only one or two of them notable examples of his work.

In 1928, at age fifty-eight, Gill married Mrs. Marion Brashear of Palos Verdes, where he went to live, and they moved a year later to a small house in Carlsbad that belonged to his wife. Here, in 1929, he suffered a heart attack. In 1933, after a second attack, he moved to Lakeside to design and supervise the construction of cottages and a chapel for the resettlement of Indians at Rancho Barona. His last design was a small building in Redondo Beach in 1936. His client took the drawings to be blueprinted, and Gill never again saw his drawings or his client. Gill died on October 7, 1936, almost forgotten, his contributions to architecture unrecognized.

Some 34 years after his death, the Dodge House, owned many years by the city, was sold and in spite of the fervent efforts of those who wanted to preserve it, was demolished in 1970. His masterpiece is gone, but Gill's reputation as one of the pioneers of modern architecture has now been reestablished.

**Related Articles** GREENE AND GREENE; SULLIVAN, LOUIS HENRI.

**GIURGOLA, ROMALDO** American architect (1920– ), and design partner with Ehrman B. Mitchell in the firm Mitchell/Giurgola with offices in New York and Philadelphia. As a designer, the major influences on Romaldo Giurgola were his Italian education, where he became convinced of architecture as an urban activity, and a long-term friendship with the Philadelphia architect Louis I. Kahn (1902–74). The firm, formed in 1958, is famous as the designers of the Parliament House at Canberra, Australia, a commission awarded on the basis of a major international competition. Romaldo Giurgola was awarded the 1982 Gold Medal of the American Institute of Architects. Ehrman Mitchell left the firm in 1984 due to ill health.

**Work** Known for its work in urban design, campus planning, and public buildings, the firm has a long list of notable buildings. Early work included the American College in Bryn Mawr, Pa., and various projects for the National Park Service. The firm was runner-up for the Boston, Mass., City Hall in 1962 and winner of the competition entry for the American Institute of Architects National Headquarters in Washington, D.C. (not built). The firm won the commission for renovations and additions to the Wainwright Building in St. Louis, Mo., originally designed by Louis Sullivan (1856–1924). Laboratories for biology, chemistry, and health sciences include those at Columbia University and at MIT. A

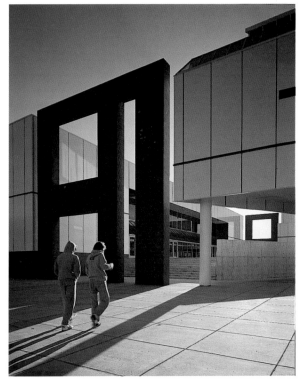

**GIURGOLA, ROMALDO** Columbus East High School (1972), Columbus, Ind. *[Architects: Mitchell/Giurgola Architects]*

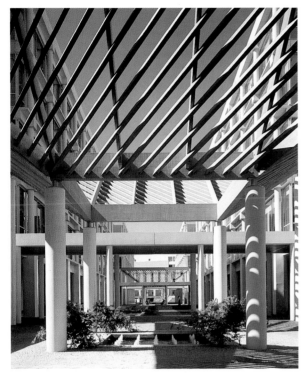

**GIURGOLA, ROMALDO** Phase I, office/parking, IBM Complex, Solana (1989), West Lake/South Lake, Tex. *[Architects: Mitchell/Giurgola, New York, with Harwood K. Smith & Partners (Photo: Hedrich-Blessing)]*

major health clinic was designed for the University of California at Los Angeles, and at Rensselaer Polytechnic Institute in Troy, N.Y., a large laboratory building for robotics, microelectronics, and computer graphics. Factories designed include those for Knoll manufacturing in East Greenville, Penn., and for Volvo in Chesapeake, Va., Udevalla, Sweden, and the master plan for the Torlanda plant in Gothenburg.

Completed in 1988, the Australian Parliament House project was one of the more important commissions of this century. Providing approximately 2.5 million ft$^2$ of offices and meeting rooms, the project is an appropriate response to the plan of the city, the land forms, and natural setting.

**Life** Romaldo Giurgola was born in Rome in 1920 and graduated from the University of Rome in 1948. He came to the United States in 1949 as a Fullbright Fellow at Columbia University, where he received an M.S. degree in architecture in 1951. Giurgola worked as an editor of the magazines *Interiors* and *Industrial Design* from 1952 to 1957. In 1954 he began teaching at the University of Pennsylvania, and after 1967 he was named chair of the architectural school at Columbia University and later Ware Professor of Architecture there.

Another position held by Romaldo Giurgola was his four years on the Philadelphia City Planning Commission as design consultant; in addition, Mitchell/Giurgola was responsible for the master plan for the U.S. Capital Grounds (1977–81).

In 1958 he formed a partnership with Ehrman B. Mitchell in Philadelphia. A second office was opened in New York in 1967. Giurgola has received awards in Italy and the United States. He is a member of the American Academy in Rome and the Accademia Nazionale di San Luca. Giurgola has now retired from his firm, which continues in the New York office. Giurgola is now living in Canberra, Australia.

**Further Reading** Giurgola, Romaldo, and Ehrman B. Mitchell: *Mitchell/Giurgola Architects*, Rizzoli, New York, 1983.

**GLASS** An important building material, glass is usually transparent or translucent, made from sand (silicon dioxide), soda (sodium oxide), and lime (calcium oxide) and used for windows and many other purposes. Glass technology is developing faster than any other building product. Glass may be selected for thermal performance, light transmittance, cooling, and sound transmittance. Products are no longer simply glass but are defined by tints, coatings, and intermediate bonding layers and insulated spaces that are available for specific locations in a building.

**Types** There are literally hundreds of thousands of kinds of glass, most of them for specialized purposes.

**GLASS** Hyatt Regency (1978), Dallas, Tex. *[Architect: Welton Beckett]*

Among the most used in architecture are flat glass, for windows, doors, and similar purposes; blown glass, for such things as light bulbs; corrugated glass; and pressed glass, as in block; and glass fibers, for such purposes as thermal insulation, textiles, and reinforcing for plastics.

The most important type used in architecture is flat glass. Float glass, developed by the Pilkington Glass Company in 1959, is now estimated at over 90 percent of the flat glass market. Previously, there were two major additional kinds: sheet and plate. Although these terms are still in use, they are most likely to be different thicknesses of float glass. All three may be used for glazing windows and similar purposes. Sheet glass, drawn molten from furnaces through rollers that flatten it, was most widely used for glazing windows, although now it is produced mostly in the less developed countries. The only polishing it received was from the fire in the furnace. Plate glass was made in a similar manner but was then ground and polished. It was also used for glazing windows and similar purposes, particularly for those, such as show windows of stores, in which exceptional clarity is required. Float glass, made by floating molten glass on top of molten metal, usually tin, has smooth, flat surfaces similar to those of plate glass but doesn't require grinding and polishing operations. Float glass is used in applications similar to those of the older plate.

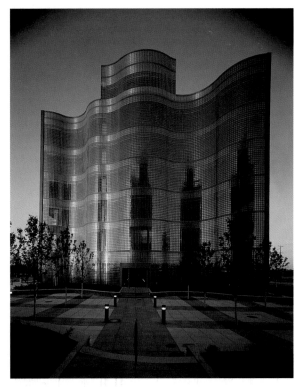

**GLASS** Liberty Center (1987), Troy, Mich. *[Architects: Rossetti Associates]*

**Flat Glass** Many special types of flat glass are widely used in architecture, including patterned, heat-strengthened, structural, laminated, tempered, tinted or heat-absorbing, reflective, and wire glass. Patterned glass is produced by rolling the molten material through rollers that have designs. Available in numerous designs, patterned glass is usually translucent and may be tempered or heat-absorbing. Heat-strengthened and structural glass are used mostly for curtain-wall panels or facings for walls or partitions. Heat-strengthened glass is about twice as strong as plate glass and has ceramic, colored glazes fused to its surface. Structural glass has integral colors produced with metal oxides. It may be heat-strengthened or tempered to improve its strength.

Laminated glass is manufactured in two major types: safety glass and bullet-resisting glass. The types are similar except that safety glass has one layer of plastic to which are laminated two layers of glass, and bullet-resisting has at least three layers of plastic and four of glass. Both types resist damage from impact and, when broken, the plastic holds the pieces of glass, preventing them from flying loose. Safety glass is available with heat-absorbing qualities, tinted, translucent, reflective, or clear. Safety glass is used in architecture where there is danger of impact, such as in sports arenas. Bullet-resisting glass is used in architecture for drive-in windows of banks and similar places where the danger of burglaries exists.

Tempered glass is heavy sheet, plate, or float glass that has been given a special heat treatment, consisting of reheating the glass and cooling it very quickly with jets of cold air. Tempered glass is quite resistant to breakage by impact. If broken, which rarely happens, it shatters into small rounded fragments that are not as dangerous as the sharp pieces of broken glass of other types. It is available in clear, tinted, reflective, and patterned forms and, in a special glazed form, is used for school chalkboards. Tempered glass is used for all-glass doors in buildings and for glazing where impact damage may be expected to occur. Tempered glass cannot be cut or drilled. Therefore it must be made in accurate sizes, with holes for hardware formed in advance.

Tinted or heat-absorbing glass may be heavy sheet, plate, or float glass. Available generally in gray, bronze-colored, or blue-green, heat-absorbing glass is used for glazing that is expected to reduce heat gains in buildings. It may be obtained in tempered, laminate, and patterned forms. Reflective, sometimes called "mirror," glass may be used for the same purpose. Coated on one side with thin-metal coatings, reflective glass reduces the amount of heat that enters buildings by reflecting it away in a manner similar to a mirror. In fact, this glass is sometimes called a "one-way mirror," because people on its darker side, inside buildings, can see through it while

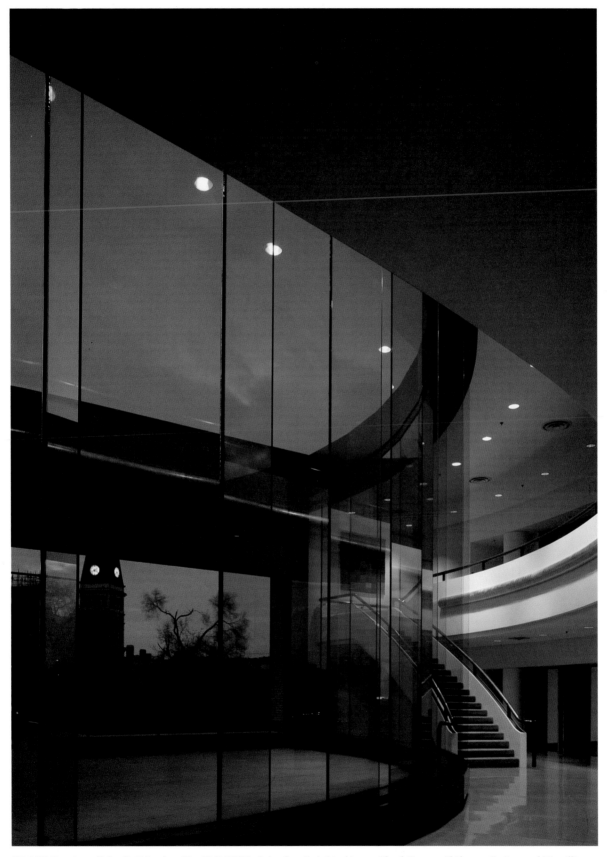

**GLASS** Curtain wall detail, Columbus City Hall (1981), Columbus, Ind. *[Architects: Chuck Bassett, Skidmore, Owings and Merrill]*

those on the brighter outside cannot. At night, in lighted interiors of buildings, the phenomenon works in reverse. Reflective glass is available in the same colors and forms as heat-absorbing glass.

Wire glass is heavy sheet, plate, or float glass in which hexagonal, square, or other forms of wire mesh are embedded. It resists damage from impact and upon breaking under heavy impact, the wire holds the pieces of glass intact. Wire glass is used when breakage from impact may be expected to occur and where the danger of flying glass must be avoided. Wire glass is also resistant to fires and may be used, subject to building code requirements, in firedoors and other places where fire resistance must be provided. It is available plain, patterned, and corrugated.

**Assembled Glass** Insulating glass is used to prevent heat gains in buildings in hot weather, and heat losses in cold. It is fabricated by joining two or three pieces of glass with air spaces between them, dehydrating the air spaces, or using an inert gas, and sealing the edges of the glass. Insulating glass is available in float glass, or formerly sheet and plate types. It can also be obtained as heat-absorbing, patterned, tempered, or laminated glass. The edges of insulating glass may be sealed in two ways: by use of molten glass to form the edges or by use of special metal alloys. Insulating glass can reduce heat losses or gains to less than half of those experienced with single panes of glass.

Glass blocks are building units that are usually a nominal 4-in thick, made by pressing glass into square or rectangular shapes that have bottoms and sides like bowls. Pairs of these shapes are then fused to form hollow units, in which the air inside has been dehydrated and partly evacuated. Glass blocks are used in interior and exterior walls, particularly in places in which control of light and good insulating qualities are required.

Glass has many other uses in architecture, including applications as glass fibers or foamed glass in thermal insulation, see the article entitled insulation, thermal. Other special types of glass include mirrors, made with thin coatings of metals, and one-way mirrors, with even thinner coatings of metal. Installed on a wall with an opening behind it, a one-way mirror allows observers on the dimly lighted back side to see into a brightly lighted space on the other side, where the glass appears to be a mirror. One-way mirrors are used in places where activities or experiments must be observed unseen by those being observed, such as nursery schools, laboratories, and psychiatric hospitals.

Other types of glass sometimes used in architecture include heat-conducting glass, treated with chemicals to conduct heat; radiation-absorbing glass, available in types that control the transmission of heat, x-rays, and other rays; and radiation-transmitting glass, in types that may allow heat but not light to be transmitted or, unlike regular glass, admit ultraviolet rays while excluding heat rays.

A recent development is the use of glass in tension with slim stainless steel rods and fittings for bracing. Glass-clad walls can achieve near total transparency. These walls require computer analysis of the stresses on the glass. Glass may also be used structurally in all-glass walls, braced with full-height sections of glass at right angles to the glass wall.

**Properties** A very large number of types and sizes of glass are available for use in architecture, with widely varied properties and characteristics. Although most types of float glass transmit 85 to 95 percent of visible light and exclude ultraviolet rays, other types are available with very different transmission properties. Most types of glass may be fabricated by such methods as pressing, blowing, rolling, grinding, polishing, and bending to no less than a 6-in radius. However, some glass, such as the tempered type, cannot be fabricated at all after it is made. The most frequently used glass is clear, but many types may be obtained in a variety of colors. The selection of specific glass types to be used for

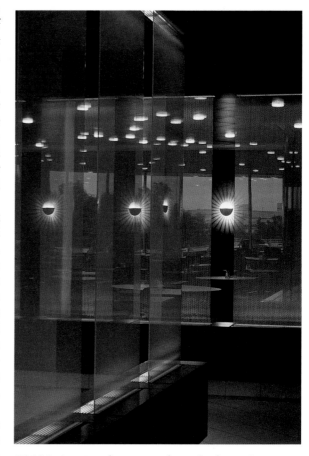

**GLASS** Interior decorative glass, Steelcase Corporation Development Center (1989), Grand Rapids, Mich. *[Architects: The WBDC Group]*

various purposes in individual buildings requires definition of the functions to be served and determination of building and other code requirements concerning glass uses, allowable sizes and conditions, and installation procedures. Float glass is available in thicknesses from $1/8$ to 1 in and in sizes up to slightly more than 10 by 25 ft. Special types of glass are available in a variety of sizes and thicknesses. Glass blocks come in nominal sizes of 6, 8, and 12 in² and 4 by 12 in, rectangular.

Information on the properties, characteristics, sizes, and other aspects of glass are available from manufacturers, along with information on proper installation. In general, glazing is usually accomplished with putties or glazing compounds specifically formulated for use with wood, aluminum, steel, and other frame materials. Another method involves the use of special gaskets made of rubber, neoprene, or plastics.

Architectural design with glass can produce results that are often quite exciting in contemporary buildings. It is very important to select the proper kind of glass, have it installed properly and in acceptable sizes, with proper clearances for expansion, and in accordance with applicable building and other codes.

**History** Glass is one of the oldest materials used in architecture and one of the best liked. The first knowledge humans had of the material came from natural glass, fused by the heat of lightning or volcanoes. When humans first made glass is not known, but it is believed that the first use was for glazes on ceramic jars or other vessels, about 3000 B.C. Glass rods and beads are also thought to have been made in Mesopotamia and Egypt about that time. The first use of glass for drinking vessels and similar purposes is thought to have occurred about 1500 B.C. in the same countries. By 750 B.C., glass was widely used in the Mediterranean civilizations. The blowing of glass began before 30 B.C.

The Romans knew how to make both important types of glass: crown and cylinder. Crown glass is made by blowing the molten material into a rough sphere, then spinning it until it is flattened into a fairly flat, round form. Cylinder glass is made by a more complicated process, which also begins with blowing the molten glass into a bulb approximately the shape of a sphere. Then the bulb is swung to give it the shape approximately, of a cylinder, after which both ends are pierced and opened wide. Again heated, the open-ended cylinder is split with a hot iron, and the glass flattened into a sheet. The Romans were skilled glassmakers and used the material extensively for many purposes, including bowls, vases, and other vessels; jewelry; and other relatively small objects. The Romans also made and used the first window glass, starting about A.D. 50, in small pieces but quite clear. After the Romans, the making and use of glass declined until about 1000, when

it was revived in Venice, Italy. Glass was also made in the Middle East.

During the Middle Ages, glassmaking was dominated by the Venetians for some time, after which the art spread throughout Europe. Both crown and cylinder glass were made and used in architecture. By about the 12th century, glass, mostly in small panes, was widely used in churches and by the 14th in important residences, such as palaces and villas. One of the glories of Gothic architecture, particularly in churches and cathedrals, is stained-glass windows. Actually, much of the so-called stained glass was colored with translucent paints. Others were colored with metallic oxides while melted, and still others were regular glass with thin layers of colored glass fused to their surfaces. The latter type was called "flashed" glass. The usual method for installing glass included shaping the pieces to size, firing those that had been painted in kilns, inserting the pieces in lead channels that were soldered together, and finally installing the assembly of glass and lead into a framework of iron.

Medieval glass had many imperfections, mostly in the form of trapped air bubbles. Although the Romans had made glass that was quite clear, the Gothic artisans were unable to duplicate the feat, their ordinary glass being somewhat colored. The art of making clear glass was rediscovered in Venice in the 15th century and was afterward widely used in buildings from the time of the Renaissance to the present. In the 16th century, Venetian glassblowers brought the art of making clear, crown glass to England, after which crown glass was widely used there until the 19th century. By that time, the use of glass in Europe had spread to modest homes, after its price came down to an affordable level. About the third quarter of the 17th century, the method of casting glass was developed in France and was subsequently widely used. Cast glass had numerous defects, but later it was considerably improved.

**American Development** Glassmaking began very early in the American colonies, a factory having been established at Jamestown, Va., in 1608, a year after the first colonists arrived. The factory closed a year later after a famine. In 1621 the Jamestown colonists tried again, but glass manufacturing ceased once again, this time mainly because of the massacre of colonists by Indians in 1622. Other glasshouses, as they were then called, were started in a number of places in the colonies. All failed soon after being founded, until an emigrant from Germany, Caspar Wistar (1696–1752), built one in New Jersey, near Philadelphia, in 1739; it operated until 1780.

Many of the earliest colonial buildings in America used oiled paper and other materials in their windows because of the shortage of glass, which continued for some years. When glass was used, it generally was nailed into window frames instead of puttied as was the customer later. During the 17th century, cast glass was first produced in Europe, and methods were later developed for grinding and polishing it. After that, few improvements were made in glass for use in architecture until just before the 20th century began.

Late in the 19th century, with the beginning of the Modern movement in architecture, glass became one of the most important building materials. The early modern architects began to use glass in large panes, often in continuous, or almost continuous, strips of windows in many of their buildings. Later the amount of glass used in each building increased even further. Such major uses of glass in architecture were made possible by the introduction of new methods of glassmaking. In 1901 the first method for making large sheets of glass, called the Fourcault process, was developed. Named after a Belgian, Émile Fourcault, the process consisted of drawing molten glass directly from a furnace through a slot. By 1917, an American mechanical engineer, Irving W. Colburn (1861–1917), had developed a glass-drawing machine for making sheet window glass. About 1887, a process for making rolled plate glass was developed in England.

Other developments in glass have since followed. In 1926 production of safety glass began, followed by the first manufactured insulating glass, or double glazing, in 1930. Glass block was introduced in 1933. Glass fibers, widely used today for insulation and other purposes, were introduced in 1938, and foamed glass, used for insulation, in 1942. Float glass was introduced in England in 1959. Float glass has very flat surfaces and a brilliant finish as if it had been polished. Beginning in the 1950s, other developments have taken place, including heat-resistant or absorbing glass, and reflective or mirror glass, both often used in building today.

In the 20th century, an important element in architecture has been large areas of glass, often fixed in place in many buildings. Very large windows were used in the Fagus Factory (1911), Alfeld, Germany, designed by Walter Adolf Gropius (1883–1969), foreshadowing curtain walls and window walls, so much a part of architecture since the late 1940s. Such walls would never have become feasible without the development of dependable and economical air-conditioning systems. However, their forerunners go back to such buildings as the glass-enclosed Crystal Palace (1851), designed by Sir Joseph Paxton (1801–65) of the Great Exhibition, London, and the Bibliotheque Nationale (1868), Paris, designed by Henri Labrouste (1801–75).

Today glass of many kinds is widely used in buildings of all types. Perhaps the most important types are float glass and glass-fiber insulation. Double and triple glazing are also important as are heat-absorbing, tempered, and reflecting glass types. Stained glass, which had been such a powerful element in Gothic architecture, was used less frequently afterward and virtually stopped being used by about the 18th century. Stained glass came back into demand during the Gothic Revival and Eclectic periods of architecture in the 19th century. Today stained glass again is used frequently in religious and other building types, some designed by great contemporary artists. In recent years, the use of large areas of glass in building has declined somewhat, mainly because of the problems of shortages and sharply rising prices of fuels used to cool and heat buildings. Building regulations now specify the maximum areas of walls to be glazed.

**Related Articles** CLIMATE; DOOR; ENERGY; FARM BUILDING; HEATING, VENTILATING, AND AIR CONDITIONING; INSULATION, THERMAL; LIGHTING; OFFICE BUILDING; RELIGIOUS BUILDING; WALL; WINDOW.

**Source of Additional Information** Stained Glass Association of America, 4050 Broadway, Suite 219, Kansas City, Mo. 64111.

## GOTHIC REVIVAL ARCHITECTURE

An architectural movement, or style, in which the forms and details of buildings were derived from the Gothic style of the Middle Ages. Beginning in Europe in the early 18th century, the movement spread to America where it strongly influenced many architects and their buildings until the end of the 19th century and afterward. Architecture in this style, during the last 60 years of the 19th century, is often called Victorian, after Queen Victoria (1819–1901), during whose reign (1837–1901) it was built. Great impetus was given the movement when the Queen insisted that architects Sir Charles Barry (1795–1860) and Augustus Welby Northmore Pugin (1812–52) use the Gothic Revival style for the English Houses of Parliament, designed in 1836 and completed in 1860.

**Characteristics** While Classic Revival architecture, which had begun earlier in America, was based on the cool, rational ideals of classicism, Gothic Revival, from about the beginning of the 18th century, was based on imagination, emotions, the unconventional, mysticism, and the implied true Christianity of medieval forms and ornament. Gothic Revival architecture got off to a rather slow start in the United States. Although a few buildings in the style were designed previously, the first of national importance was Trinity Church (1846), New York City, designed by Richard Upjohn (1802–78). This church received widespread recognition and helped greatly in the establishment of Upjohn as the dominant church architect and Gothicist of his time and one of the most successful architects of all time. It also helped greatly in establishing a tradition of Gothic Revival as the predominant style for churches, a tradition that has lasted in some degree to the present time.

**GOTHIC REVIVAL ARCHITECTURE** College buildings, Yale University, New Haven, Conn.
*[Architect: James Gamble Rogers]*

**English Influence** Gothic Revival architecture in the United States was greatly inspired and influenced by that in England and by books on the subject by English writers, including the architects Pugin and his father, Augustus Charles (1762–1832), and by the critic John Ruskin (1819–1900). Upjohn was influenced by their writings and designed a great number of church buildings, houses, and other buildings in the Gothic Revival style. Another architect who became famous for his designs in the Gothic Revival style, James Renwick, Jr. (1818–95), was also deeply influenced by such books and by Gothic architecture. However, Renwick sometimes designed buildings in other styles, such as the Romanesque. Upjohn and Renwick are usually acknowledged as the greatest Gothic Revival architects.

Another architect who approached their level, and surpassed it in residential work, was Alexander Jackson Davis (1803–92), who started out working in the Classic Revival style, but later turned to the Gothic. With his partner Ithiel Town (1784–1844), Davis designed many fine Gothic Revival houses as well as other buildings in Gothic and other styles. Another important Gothic Revival architect, who also designed buildings in other styles, was Minard Lafever (1797–1854).

By the beginning of the Civil War, the great era of Gothic Revival architecture was beginning in the United States. Its exponents had by then designed and constructed a large number of great churches in many places, together with numerous houses and buildings of other types. Upjohn had published a book of plans that were used to erect modest wood Gothic churches and other buildings in even the smallest towns in out-of-the-way places. Many people admired the mystical, ornamental, and soaring aspects of the style and many still do. The beginning of Eclectic architecture had taken place as early as the 1830s and the movement had gradually achieved some importance in the United States by the time the Civil War began.

**Amalgamation** After the Civil War, Gothic Revival architecture entered another phase, this time as one important style alongside all the rest, Romanesque, Renaissance, Colonial, Classical, and so on, that collectively are called eclecticism. From this time, for many years to come, architects would choose what they thought an appropriate style for each new building from all of those available from the past. Eventually they would employ every imaginable style, and combine several styles in single buildings, though the effect would

**GOTHIC REVIVAL ARCHITECTURE** Prouty House, (1852), Kalamazoo, Mich. *[Architect: unknown]*

**GOTHIC REVIVAL ARCHITECTURE** Washington Cathedral, Episcopal (begun 1907), Washington, D.C. *[Architects: Henry Vaughn & George Bodley; Frohman, Robb and Little; others]*

often be disconcerting, even chaotic in some cases. In others, especially when the most talented architects of the time, such as Henry Hobson Richardson (1838–86), Ralph Adams Cram (1863–1942), Stanford White (1853–1906), or Frank Furness (1839–1912), were involved, the results turned out to be architecture of the highest excellence.

**Related Articles** ECLECTIC ARCHITECTURE; HISTORY OF ARCHITECTURE; PRESERVATION; RENWICK, JAMES, JR.; UPJOHN, RICHARD; Various articles on other Gothic Revival and Eclectic architects.

**Further Reading** See listing in the article entitled history of architecture.

**Sources of Additional Information** See listing in the article entitled history of architecture.

**GOVERNMENT** The system of social control, under law. Government on every level, from the local to the federal, strongly affects architecture in many ways. Among the most important are controls on architecture

by means of codes and standards, statutes, and regulations; licensing of architects, engineers, and others in the building industry; control of financing of buildings by agencies, such as the Federal Housing Administration (FHA) and Veterans Administration (VA); and as the owners, clients of architects, of a great number of buildings and building complexes of every size and almost every type.

The role of government in architecture on every level is so all-pervasive that information on the subject is included in a number of articles in this book. Among the most important are those listed at the end of this article. Governments on all levels are very important clients of architects. There are so many variations between the ways municipalities, counties, and states handle the design and construction of buildings that no meaningful discussion is possible here. However, some information of this sort is contained in articles on various building types in this book.

**Federal Programs** The federal government has many wide-ranging programs of design and construction. While the subject is too complex to be covered in detail, federal government construction programs are of such importance to architects and other building design professionals that the major considerations should be discussed. While the number and types of buildings, and the amount of money spent on them vary considerably from year to year, the federal government, by any measure, is the biggest client for American architects. And through various programs of federal grants and subsidies for public housing, community development, and other purposes, the biggest client, in effect, becomes even bigger.

The General Services Administration (GSA), an independent agency, has the responsibility for the design, construction, operation, and maintenance of more public buildings, some 10,000, than any other federal department or agency. These include buildings of many types, other than military, and make GSA the most important federal agency to architects. GSA operates through regional offices.

Military construction is accomplished by the U.S. Department of Defense (DOD), through the services, Air Force, Army, and Navy, all of which have regional offices. Other executive departments that contract for architectural and related services are Agriculture, through its Agricultural Research Service and U.S. Forest Service, both with regions, and Animal and Plant Health Inspection Service; Health and Human Services (HHS) which has regional offices; Housing and Urban Development (HUD), also with regional offices; Interior, through its bureaus of Indian Affairs and Land Management, and the National Park Service, all with regional or divisional offices; Justice, through the Bureau of Prisons; State, in its Foreign Service and foreign civilian agency programs; Transportation (DOT), through its Federal Aviation Administration, with regions, U.S. Coast Guard, with districts, and Federal Railway Administration; and the Department of Education, established in 1979.

Two other independent agencies, each responsible for its own building design and construction program, are the U.S. Postal Service, which has regional offices, and the Veterans Administration. A few other federal agencies sometimes contract for architectural and related services, mostly for studies and research or development projects.

**Regulations** Federal contracting for architectural and related services, which in government parlance is called procurement, is subject to a host of statutes and regulations that are not only difficult to understand but which vary between types of construction and between departments and agencies. Some departments and agencies have at least a portion of their buildings designed by architects and engineers, and other design professionals who are their employees. Others contract with independent practitioners exclusively.

In addition to the statutes and regulations that apply to federal construction in general, each department or agency generally has regulations and standards of its own. These vary considerably. In general, an architect, engineer, or other design professional seeking a federal commission must submit an information questionnaire that must be brought up to date periodically. If a proposed project costs more than a certain maximum amount, it is required by law to be announced in the *Commerce Business Daily*, published by the U.S. Department of Commerce. Professionals who have current questionnaires on file are automatically considered for these commissions, if they do not involve large amounts of money in professional fees. Those without questionnaires on file must submit another kind of questionnaire for each specific project. If a proposed project will involve large amounts in professional fees, every architect, engineer, or other design professional must submit a special questionnaire for each job.

**Criteria** Certain criteria must be met in the selection of an architect, engineer, or other design professional for federal work. These include geographical considerations, requirements that a share of the work go to small businesses and to firms owned by minorities, and others, in addition to the required experience, competency, and capacity of design firms to perform the work properly.

**Work Requirements** Architects, engineers, and other design professionals who would like to be considered for federal work should obtain information about the general requirements for such work and the special-

ized requirements of the various departments and agencies. They should also submit questionnaires and should follow announcements in the *Commerce Business Daily* to determine when additional questionnaires are required for specific projects. If they are to perform professional services for federal departments and agencies, firms must be prepared to deal with a vast array of regulatory material and often with considerable red tape.

**Related Articles** BUILDING CODES AND STANDARDS; BUILDING INDUSTRY; CAPITAL, UNITED STATES; CAREER; ENERGY; FINANCE; MILITARY BUILDING; PLANNING, CITY; PUBLIC BUILDING.

**Further Reading** Publications of various government departments and agencies.

**Periodical** *Commerce Business Daily*, Superintendent of Documents, Government Printing Office, Washington, D.C. 20402.

**Sources of Additional Information** Committee on Public Architecture, c/o American Institute of Architects, 1735 New York Ave., N.W., Washington, D.C. 2006; General Services Administration, 18th and F Sts., N.W., Washington, D.C. 20405; U.S. Department of Agriculture, 14th St. and Independence Ave., S.W., Washington, D.C. 20008; U.S. Department of Defense, the Pentagon, Washington, D.C. 20301-1155; U.S. Department of Health and Human Services, 200 Independence Ave., S.W., Washington, D.C. 20201; U.S. Department of Housing and Urban Development, 451 7th St., S.W., Washington, D.C. 20410; U.S. Department of Interior, 1849 C. St., N.W., Washington, D.C. 20240; U.S. Department of State, 2201 C. St., N.W., Washington, D.C. 20520; U.S. Department of Transportation, 400 7th St., N.W., Washington, D.C. 20590; U.S. Postal Service, 475 L'Enfant Plaza, S.W., Washington, D.C. 20260-0010; U.S. Department of Veterans Affairs, 810 Vermont Ave., N.W., Washington, D.C. 20420.

**GRAPHIC DESIGN** The art and science of drawing, according to mathematical and artistic principles. Graphic design, or graphics, is important in architecture, not only in plans and other working drawings for the construction of buildings but in drawings and renderings for presentations to clients and for other purposes, in brochures showing the work of architects and other environmental designers, in books and magazine articles, and in signs and other uses in and around buildings.

All such uses of graphic design in architecture, other than for brochures and similar uses and in and around buildings, are discussed in articles listed at the end of this article. For a discussion of graphic design, along with the basic principles of printing processes, see the article entitled book, architectural.

**Functions** Other than in working drawings and similar work, architectural drawings and renderings serve

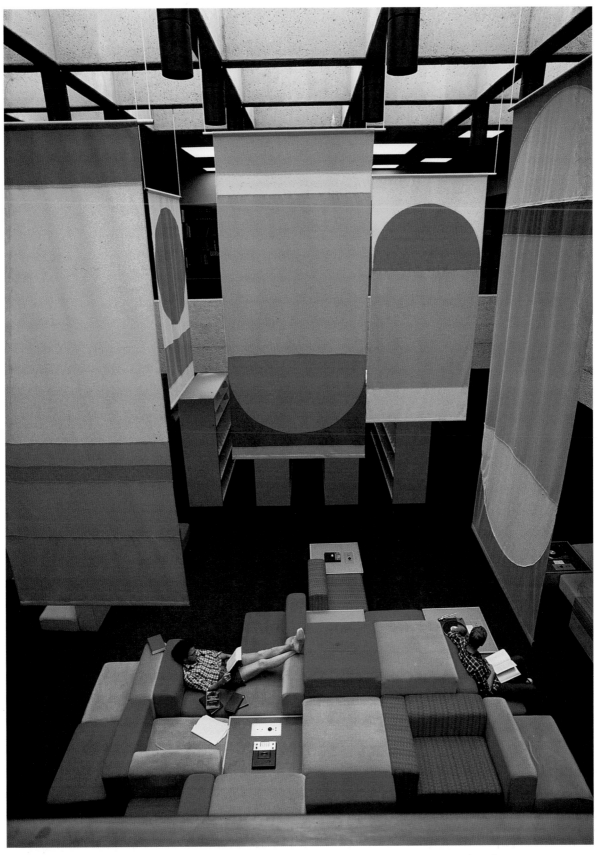

**GRAPHIC DESIGN** Oberlin College Library (1975), Oberlin, Ohio. *[Architects: Warner, Burns, Toan and Lunde]*

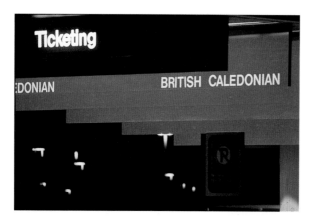

**GRAPHIC DESIGN** Hartsfield International Airport (1980), Atlanta, Ga. *[Architects: Smith, Hinchman and Grylls with Heery and Heery]*

two important functions: presentation of buildings to clients, potential clients, and others, by showing the actual drawings and renderings or photographic representations in slides; and reproduction of the drawings and renderings in brochures, magazines, and books. In many cases, architects and other environmental designers expect the same drawings and renderings to be used in all these ways. Although it is often impossible to use them for all these purposes, they can be used in most cases if drawings and renderings are prepared properly, with the various end uses in mind. This involves attention to the size and scale of drawings, use of color, gradations of tone, drawing techniques, and other factors.

For example, in preparing a drawing or rendering that will be shown to clients full-size and later reproduced in a reduced size in a brochure, magazine, or book, the need for full-size presentation must be balanced with the need for reproduction at reduced size. In general, drawings or renderings to be reproduced should be approximately 1½ to 2 times the reproduction size. If properly drawn, the reduced size of the reproduction will sharpen line and other work when it is printed. Care must be taken not to make the line and other work so detailed or complex that it will not reproduce properly. Any lettering on the rendering or drawing should be simple and large enough to be perfectly legible when it has been reduced.

Drawings or renderings in color are often reproduced in black and white. If the color will not photograph in black and white with considerable variation, or contrast, in tones of grays, the reproduction will not be satisfactory. In making a color drawing or rendering, it must be kept in mind that various colors photograph in black and white in different ways. For example, reds tend to photograph black. In order to check what may happen when a drawing or rendering is reduced for reproduction, reduced photostats may be made while it is in progress,

or a reducing glass that works like a magnifying glass in reverse may be used. If the line weights are too heavy or too light, if the lines are so close that they may fill in or so fine that they might break up, or other problems are present, the photostat or reducing glass indicates them.

**Reproduction Methods** Drawings and renderings are reproduced in brochures, magazines, books, and other places by two major methods: line drawings or halftones. Line drawings reproduce solid lines much as they exist in a drawing. In this method, tones or gradations will not reproduce, but some suggestion of them can be obtained with self-adhering plastic sheets containing cross-hatching, dots, and other graphic devices. Drawings for line reproduction are almost always made with ink.

When the reproduction of tones or gradations is required, as in most pencil drawings with shading, color renderings, and other types, halftones are generally used. Halftones involve a process of photography that breaks up the drawing or rendering into very small dots of various sizes and spacing. The larger the dots, the closer they will be to each other, thus creating relatively

**GRAPHIC DESIGN** Carver Hawkeye Arena (1983), University of Iowa, Iowa City, Iowa. *[Architects: CRSS]*

dark areas; smaller dots, farther apart, produce lighter areas. For precise work, such as floor plans, details, or diagrams, line drawings are often preferred; for more subtle work, such as perspectives of interiors or exteriors of buildings, the halftone process is usually preferred. For four-color work, halftones are mostly used, separated into four colors, magenta (red), yellow, cyan (blue), and black, and sometimes, for very fine reproductions, into additional colors.

The same principles of reproduction discussed above apply to photographs. In general, large photographs made with large cameras set on tripods reproduce better than small ones made with small hand-held cameras. Photographs with considerable contrast of grays reproduce better than those with less contrast. Color photographs, to be reproduced in black and white, must follow the same principles as color renderings. Finally, only very fine photographs, reproduced properly, show good architecture as it should be shown in brochures, books, and magazines. (See the article entitled photography, architectural.)

Not much can be said here about writing for brochures, articles, and books, except to point out that architects and other environmental designers tend to be more graphically minded than verbally minded. In addition, many are not well trained in writing. (For a discussion of some of the principles of preparing and publishing a book, see the article entitled book, architectural. Similar principles apply to the preparation of magazine articles.) To be effective, such writing should be well organized; discussions should be straightforward, without too many flourishes; and faith should be put in good editors. And one last point: many architects and other environmental designers are notoriously bad spellers. Good copy editors can help correct this, but care should be taken in spelling, especially in lettering on drawings and renderings to be reproduced.

**Typography** The typography used in the preparation of brochures and for other purposes is a complex subject. Type faces are so numerous, come in such a wide variety of sizes, and have such a diversity of uses that architects and other environmental designers must usually obtain the services of graphic designers to deal with the typography and layout of brochures and other publications. Magazine and book publishing staffs ordinarily handle these functions for their publications. However, it should be pointed out that type with serifs is generally easier to read than sans serif type. Also important for legibility and ease of reading are the size of types and faces used, the size relative to the length of lines, and the amount of space between lines, or leading, provided.

Brochures and other graphic materials should be prepared to perform their purposes effectively and power-

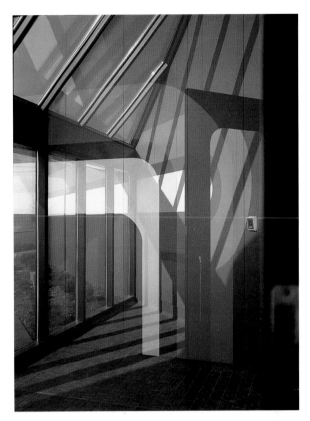

**GRAPHIC DESIGN** C.O.T.A. Bus Storage (1984), Columbus, Ohio. *[Architect: Brubaker & Brant]*

fully. They should be well organized, well designed, written for the audiences they are intended to serve or impress, well illustrated, and direct and complete. Many architectural and other design offices have found that flexible brochures, systematized so that they can be bound together in many ways for various purposes, serve their needs best. With such a system, one type of brochure might be put together for a hospital board considering the construction of a new hospital and a quite different brochure assembled for a school board. Both would contain general information on the firm, including its experience, size, staff, former clients and their buildings, and similar subjects, and specialized information on the building type proposed by a potential client.

Many architects and other environmental design professionals prepare their own brochures and other graphic materials, or have them prepared by people in their offices. Some offices have their own graphic design departments to accomplish this sort of work; a few perform such work for clients and others. For the most part, good brochures and other graphic materials are prepared by free-lance, professional graphic designers, who work as individuals or in design studios.

**Brochure Preparation** In general, a graphic designer setting out to prepare a brochure or other graphic mate-

**GRAPHIC DESIGN** Gaviidae Common (1989), Minneapolis, Minn. *[Architects: Cesar Pelli; graphic design (1991): Sessman Phrasier (Photo: Christian M. Korab)]*

rials for an architect or environmental firm would start with the purpose to be served, the audience to be reached, and the problems to be solved. A schedule for production of the finished piece might then be established. Materials to be used, such as information and existing drawings and photographs, would then be assembled. The size and shape of the piece would be determined and its format would be designed, including page layouts, title pages and the like, and cover. Type faces and sizes would be selected, including body type and, for the main text, head types and types for other purposes.

The paper, or stock, for printing would be selected, along with the binding material. After the layout has been completed, along with the writing of text and other matter and the illustrations selected or prepared, the project can be readied for printing. The text manuscript must be copy edited for factual and typographical errors, and copy-fitted to the spaces in the layout in which it will appear. Heads and other matter must also go through a similar process. Illustrations must be sized for reproduction, and portions not to be reproduced indicated by marks, or cropped. All items must be marked with instructions for the printer.

In some cases, a graphic designer will prepare, for the printer, camera-ready copy, or mechanicals, sheets on which all the type is placed in proper positions, along with the illustrations or indications of where they will be stripped in by the printer. In other cases, the graphic designer will furnish the printer with detailed layouts, called comprehensives, and the printer does the actual placement of the type and other elements. Sometimes rough sketches are furnished to printers for such purposes, but this practice should be avoided.

After the manuscript and other copy have been typeset by a compositor, galley proofs usually come back to be read for typographical and other errors. The brochure or other publication may then be set into pages and page proofs made, which are read again for errors. Finally, the publication is printed, bound, and ready for use. Many architects and other environmental design professionals consider the work of a graphic designer to be finished when a design for a publication has been submitted and approved. Such a course is not really effective, for some of the most vital services of a graphic designer are in following through on the design with the compositor, printer, binder, and others to ensure that the final product is what was envisioned and expected. In addition, graphic designers should be able to determine and control the costs of publication production and should know where best to have the work accomplished.

**Building Signs** Signs and other graphic devices in and around buildings are of considerable importance in architecture. Many years ago, the only graphic design in most buildings might consist of Roman lettering, sometimes in Latin, carved into the cornerstones or over the main entrances. Today graphic design is used for those and many other purposes in buildings. In addition, many kinds of signs are used, including types for giving directions, for identification, for warnings, for instruction, for advertising, and simply for ornament. Some considerations include lettering, colors, pictures, symbols, and lighting. Signs and other graphic devices for buildings are usually designed by specialists who work in graphic design companies or studios. Large architectural and other environmental design firms may have such specialists on their staffs.

**Education** Students who think they would like to become graphic designers should have many of the same interests as architects and other environmental designers and artists. For the most part, a general cultural course in secondary school should be pursued, followed by advanced work in an art school, college, or university. Drawing and painting courses in secondary schools vary considerably. If they are not creative, they are thought by many to do more harm than good. In urban centers and sometimes in other places, secondary school students often can take certain art and design classes at night or during summer vacations.

Higher education for graphic designers varies considerably. However, a typical course might include, in addition to the usual general and cultural subjects, courses in communication, art and design history, drawing, painting, graphic design, photography, printing processes, layout, makeup, and research. Many graphic designers today have studied such curricula, while others have come from industrial design, architectural, or art schools, and others have learned through on-the-job training.

In any case, for individuals who like the arts, particularly the visual arts, and want to work in the creation of art that can communicate ideas, graphic design offers meaningful and exciting career opportunities, not only in architecture and the other environmental design fields but in magazine or book publishing, advertising, newspaper work, and other fields.

Architects have always been interested in graphic design, and they are today. Perhaps this can be explained by the fact that although the primary function of architects is the design of buildings and other structures, graphic design, as well as the other arts, is closely and intimately related to architectural design. Another reason is that the creation of architecture is largely accomplished by graphic means, with sketches and drawings of various kinds. The presentation of architectural designs to clients and others is by graphic means, sketches and rendering. Buildings are constructed primarily from working drawings, a graphic means. Architects also often design signs and other graphic devices for buildings and they use graphic design in presentations, brochures, and exhibits.

Thus graphic design naturally pervades many of the thoughts and activities of architects and other environmental designers.

**Related Articles** ART IN ARCHITECTURE; BOOK, ARCHITECTURAL; COMPUTER; DESIGN, ARCHITECTURAL; DRAFTING; MAGAZINE, ARCHITECTURAL; PHOTOGRAPHY, ARCHITECTURAL; PRACTICE OF ARCHITECTURE; RENDERING; WORKING DRAWING.

**Further Reading** Jones, Gerre L.: *How to Prepare Professional Design Brochures*, 2d ed., McGraw-Hill, New York, 1983; Stevenson, George A.: *Graphic Arts Encyclopedia*, 2d ed., McGraw-Hill, New York, 1979.

**Source of Additional Information** Society of Environmental Graphic Designers, Cambridge, Mass.

**GRAVES, MICHAEL** An American architect. Michael Graves (1934–   ) practices internationally and is known as a post-Modern architect. Michael Graves is identified as one of the so-called New York Five, with Richard Meier (1934–   ), Peter Eisenman (1932–   ), Charles Gwathmey (1938–   ), and John Hejduk (1929–   ). The publication of the work of these thirty-year-olds (*Five Architects: Eisenman, Graves, Gwathmey, Hejduk, Meier*, Wittenborn, New York, 1972) promoted their careers. These architects rejected the social concerns of the 1960s and undertook aesthetic inquiry. Inspired by Le Corbusier, and the European work of the 1920s, they eventually moved in different directions. Graves came to feel that such pure abstractions were not understood by the public, and he moved toward a broader audience. He has been remarkably effective in this regard. Some of

**GRAVES, MICHAEL** San Juan Capistrano Library (1982), San Juan Capistrano, Calif.

Michael Graves's buildings have aroused considerable controversy, but he is recognized as a major designer of American buildings.

**Works** Michael Graves has been the architect for a large number of major buildings. The first building to bring him wide attention was the Portland Building (1980), a municipal building for the city of Portland, Ore. One of the most appreciated of his works is the San Juan Capistrano Library (1982), San Juan Capistrano, Calif. Based on his study of the Spanish mission style, the library is organized around an internal court. Lighting is introduced into the library with light monitors. There are roofed outdoor reading areas and covered walkways. Exterior materials are typical of the area, using cream-colored stucco and red tile roofs. The formality of the plan is particularly effective as an organizing feature of the library.

The Humana Building (1982), Louisville, Ky., is a 26-story building occupying its entire site near the Ohio River. The building is a transition between low older buildings and the high-rise downtown. In addition to the use of fine materials, the building is dramatic because of the projected terrace and conference room on the 25th floor.

Other projects include the Newark Museum Master Renovation Plan (1982), Newark, N.J., the Riverbend Music Center (1983), Cincinnati, Ohio, various designs for the addition to the Whitney Museum in New York, N.Y. (1985–88), the Clos Pegase Winery (1984), Napa

**GRAVES, MICHAEL** The Humana Building (1985), Louisville, Ky.

Throughout his career, Michael Graves has been active in interior design, including carpets, wallpaper, and furniture design. He has also designed dinnerware and many decorative objects in limited editions.

**Life** Michael Graves was born in Indianapolis, Ind., in 1934. He received his architectural education at the University of Cincinnati and Harvard University. He won the Rome Prize in 1960 and spent his year at the American Academy in Rome. Michael Graves has taught for many years at Princeton University and opened his office in Princeton, N.J., in 1964. Two monographs of his work have been published. He has received many awards and several honorary degrees.

**Related Articles** CONTEMPORARY ARCHITECTURE; EISENMAN, PETER; LIBRARY; MEIER, RICHARD; OFFICE BUILDING.

**Further Reading** Nichols, Karen Vogel, Patrick J. Burke, and Caroline Hancock, eds.: *Michael Graves— Buildings and Projects 1982–1989*, Princeton Architectural Press, New York, 1990; Wheeler, Karen Vogel, Peter Arnell, and Ted Bickford, eds.: *Michael Graves: Buildings and Projects 1966–1981*, Rizzoli, New York, 1981.

**GREENE AND GREENE** American architectural firm of two brothers, Charles Sumner (1868–1957) and Henry Mather (1870–1954). The Greene brothers had a remarkable life together. Born a short time apart, they went to high school and college together and remained close all their lives. Most importantly, their joint architectural practice, most of the time in Pasadena, Calif., lasted 21 years and had profound effects on modern architecture as well as on the lives of their clients and all who experience their buildings.

Trained in Classical Eclectic architecture, the brothers turned away from this foremost trend of their time to an architecture composed of good planning, fine use of materials, development of ornament, and, perhaps most important of all, excellent craftsmanship, in particular handcraftmanship. They became the foremost of American proponents of what came to be known as the Craft Movement. Begun about the middle of the 19th century in England, primarily by William Morris (1834–96), inventor of the Morris chair, an architect turned painter and promoter of handcrafted articles of wood, metals, textiles, and the like, the movement soon spread to America. The Greenes had attended a high school where they had learned and espoused craftsmanship, and had become deeply engrossed in nature, including the nature of materials. They also became deeply interested in Japanese domestic architecture and the wood houses of Sqitzerland and other European countries.

**Bungalow Style** Out of these interests came a steady stream of livable, beautifully detailed and constructed houses, admirably suited to the climate in which they were situated and molded to their sites as if they had

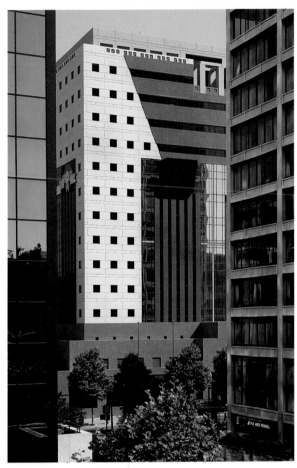

**GRAVES, MICHAEL** The Portland Building (1982), Portland, Ore. *[Photo: Greg Hursley]*

Valley, Calif., and the Crown American Building (1986), Johnstown, Pa.

Michael Graves has designed a number of buildings for Walt Disney Enterprises. Some critics have dubbed this work the "Disneying" of America. These projects include the Team Disney office building (1986), Burbank, Calif., the Walt Disney World Swan Hotel (1987), Walt Disney World, Fla., the Walt Disney World Dolphin Hotel (1987), Walt Disney World, Fla., and the Hotel New York at Euro Disneyland, France. Several of these buildings feature large decorative figures as caryatids or as roof decorations. These buildings are flamboyant and in the case of hotels, entertaining. Some critics do not consider these projects or other Disney buildings as serious design.

Michael Graves has designed a sizable number of buildings in Japan. One of these projects is the Momochi District Apartment Building (1988), Fukuoka, Japan, on a site adjoining that containing the Stanley Tigerman (1930–   ) apartment building. Other projects include a number of office buildings, such as the 27-story Portside Tower, a part of the billion-dollar Minato Mirai mixeduse development on landfill in Yokohama harbor.

**GREENE AND GREENE** Interior, David B. Gamble House (1908), Pasadena, Calif.

Pasadena; that for William R. Thorsen (1908), Berkeley; and the Pratt House (1909), Ojai. All these houses show the mature Greene style and their detailing is apparent, as is their devotion, especially that of Charles, to close work with the craftsmen and their materials, both in their shops and during the construction of the houses. The most elaborate of these houses is the Blacker, which cost $100,000 in 1907, a very large sum indeed for what is essentially a relatively small house. The Gamble House is the best place to experience the total effect of a Greene and Greene house today. Through the efforts of a group of Pasadena citizens, it has been magnificently preserved, together with its gardens and the Greene brothers' designed furniture, carpets, lighting fixtures, silverware, linens, and the like. Here, as in many of their other houses, the Greenes had designed an entire environment for the occupants.

Though their reputation was founded almost entirely on their wood houses, often redwood, the Greenes also experimented with other materials. For example, in the L. A. Robinson House (1906) in Pasadena, the ground-floor walls are brick, covered with stucco, and the second floor has an exposed wood frame with stucco panels between the timbers. In the Cornelia Culbertson House (1911) in Pasadena, they went even further; the framing is wood, but the wood is covered with sprayed-on concrete, a pioneering use of this material. With its clay-tile roof, this house does not look like other Greene brothers houses; it is in Mission style, derived from the design of California mission churches and other buildings.

If they had been able to foresee it, the Greenes might have considered the Culbertson House an omen of what lay ahead. The brothers drifted apart, not in their personal relationship but in their philosophies, into separate practices. Charles, who had become deeply interested in philosophy and art, moved to Carmel where he designed a few houses, mostly in the Mission style, and wrote, mostly about Oriental philosophy. Henry stayed in Pasadena, where he designed a few houses, mostly unlike the older work of the brothers, in stucco with tile roofs.

The great era of the brothers ended in the second decade of the 20th century. And they, along with their achievements, lapsed into obscurity. After World War II came a revitalized interest in architecture of wood, led by architects in California and the Pacific Northwest. With this resurgence came a strong, new interest in the work of those early pioneers, the Greene brothers. Called out of retirement, they were given accolades and awards from their fellow architects for their accomplishments. In one acceptance speech, Henry Greene made it clear that the brothers had lived in the right time, that for them the 20th-century practice of supervising or inspecting the work could never take the place of being

grown there. Out of it also came a proliferation of houses, many of them badly copied from the work of the Greenes and crudely constructed. This came to be called the Bungalow style, and when handled by the Greenes, was of the highest excellence; but as the building of such houses spread all over the United States, their quality worsened with time. This situation existed through the first quarter of the 20th century. But the fact that their work was badly copied and eventually became an unfortunate movement in architecture does not detract from the importance of the achievements of the Greenes, or from their part in the early development of modern architecture in this country.

The first decade of the Greene and Greene practice, from the establishment of their office in 1893, found them designing houses in many of the popular styles of the past. Later their work took on more of an open, Japanese feeling, and their interest in craftsmanship, particularly in wood, was developed. During their second decade, they produced a proliferation of good houses.

**Works** Perhaps the greatest houses were those for R. R. Blacker (1907) and David B. Gamble (1908), both in completely involved in and participating in the work of construction themselves. An era was indeed over.

**Life** The brothers Greene were born in Cincinnati, Ohio, just over a year apart, Charles on October 12, 1868, and Henry on January 23, 1870. Their lives and careers were interlocked from then on. Their family having moved to St. Louis, Mo., they attended a high school sponsored by Washington University, in which handwork in wood, metals, and other materials was stressed, along with the more academic subjects. Thus the brothers received an early knowledge of craftsmanship and acquired a love for it that they never lost. Entering the Massachusetts Institute of Technology in 1888, they received the classical tradition, Beaux Arts, education of the architecture schools of the time. Graduating in 1891, the brothers worked for a short time in Boston and then went to Pasadena, Calif., for a visit with their parents who had again moved. They never went back to Boston.

In 1893 the Greenes established their office in Pasadena, their first commission being a small house for a friend of their father's; their second, a tombstone. The next 10 years found the brothers designing houses in most of the fashionable styles of the day, eclectic in a way that reflected their classical tradition education but also giving some promise of what was to become their mature style.

Henry married Emeline Augusta Dart in 1899, and built a house for her four years later. Here their four children were raised. In 1901 Charles married Alice Gordon White, an Englishwoman, and also built a house for his family, which was eventually to include five children. Neither house was particularly notable, but Charles's house was to become so for he almost continually added to it and remodeled it, using it for studies and experiments with architectural forms and materials.

In 1903 the Greenes closed their office in Pasadena and opened one in Los Angeles. The number of their commissions in Pasadena continued to grow, however, and in 1906 they again established an office there, closing the one in Los Angeles a short time later. Their practice grew rapidly and they soon occupied additional space. As long as their partnership lasted, until 1914, they did not move their office again.

The decade ending in 1914 saw their practice flourish. It was a period in which they designed a great number of houses. Although the exact number is uncertain, it is believed that they designed 540 in Pasadena alone. This also was a period that saw their style and craftsmanship flourish in such great architectural accomplishments as the Blacker, Gamble, Thorsen, and Pratt houses. Toward the end of this era, work in the Pasadena area dropped off and the Greenes had fewer commissions. For the first time, the brothers began to practice separately, though their close personal relationship continued. Charles accepted a commission for the D. L. James House (1921), near Carmel, and captivated by that area, soon moved there. He continued to practice in Carmel, though with few commissions, until he died on June 11, 1957.

Henry continued practicing in Pasadena, under the old partnership name. After an episode of sickness that lasted four years, he again practiced for a time as an individual, first in the brothers' former Pasadena office, then in a studio at his home. As had been the case with Charles, Henry obtained only a small number of commissions after the end of the partnership. Their work as individuals never had the high degree of style, craftsmanship, and excitement of their best years, the 21 they spent practicing together. After his wife's death in 1935, Henry sold their house and moved in with his eldest son in Altadena, Calif., where he died on October 2, 1954.

The brothers left a legacy that has deeply affected architecture ever since. Quite a few of their houses still exist, and some neighborhoods of Pasadena seem to be almost entirely composed of the architecture of Greene and Greene.

**Related Article** MODERN ARCHITECTURE.

**Further Reading** Makinson, Randell L.: *Greene and Greene: Architecture as a Fine Art*, Peregrine Smith, Inc., Salt Lake City, 1977; Makinson, Randell L.: *Greene and Greene: Furniture and Related Designs*, Peregrine Smith, Inc., Salt Lake City, 1979.

## GROPIUS, WALTER ADOLF

German-American architect and educator (1883–1969). As a young man, Walter Adolf Gropius decided to become an architect, and he never swerved from the path he had chosen. It turned out to be a very good choice, for he became one of the great pioneers of modern architecture, an educator who revolutionized architectural education, and an influential social critic who affected not only architecture but life in general.

The Gropius influence was many-sided. He designed influential buildings early in his career and continued to do so all his life. He changed architectural education from the eclecticism of the 19th and early 20th centuries based on the prestige and philosophy of the École des Beaux Arts in Paris to the geometric purity, technical excellence, and functionalism of the philosophy of the Bauhaus in Germany, which he founded and directed for nine years, and in the department of architecture, Harvard University, of which he was chairman for 14 years.

The influence of the Bauhaus had a profound effect on architectural education everywhere, and the Bauhaus principles applied at Harvard marked the end of the Beaux Arts system in America. The architects and other designers Gropius attracted to the faculties of these schools have made great accomplishments on their own

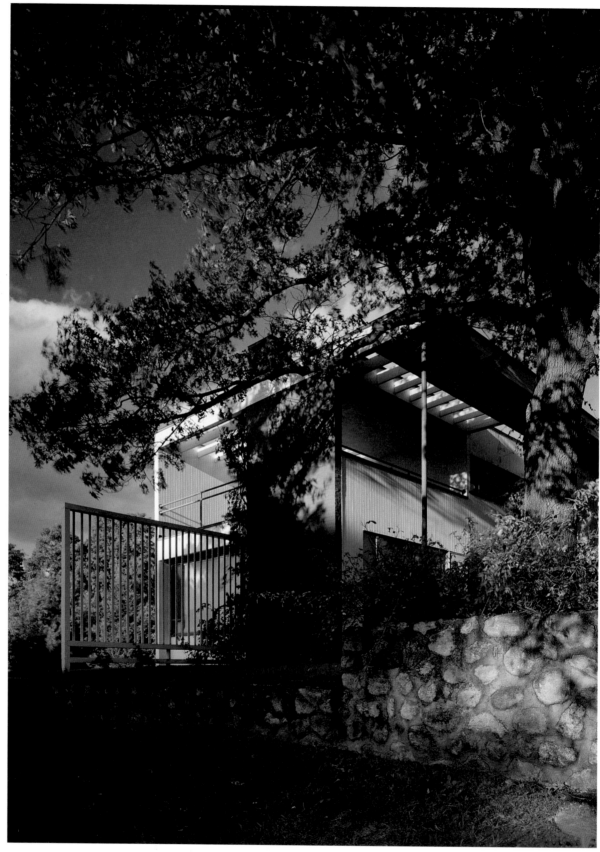

**GROPIUS, WALTER ADOLF** Gropius House (1938), Lincoln, Mass.

and have profoundly affected the design philosophies of their students, many of whom have in turn made their marks on architecture.

The sphere of the Gropius influence was enlarged beyond his own buildings and his teaching through many speeches and articles. He was never satisfied to occupy himself only with the buildings he designed. He had to go beyond that into the social implications of architecture in the society in which it exists.

**Architectural Influence** It has been said that the influence of Gropius was mostly in his teaching and philosophy rather than in his architecture. As great as his educational accomplishments were, they complement rather than overshadow his other achievements. He was one of the first to express his belief in the technology of the machine, and to act upon it. As early as 1909, he experimented with production-line panels for buildings and with the prefabrication of building parts. This interest continued throughout his career. He was one of the first to express the belief that future architecture must be the result of a group or team working together on building designs, rather than one person who acted as sole designer. He practiced with other architects almost all his life, first with Adolph Meyer (1881–1924), followed by Edwin Maxwell Fry (1899–1987), then Marcel Lajos Breuer (1902–81), and finally in a group practice with The Architects' Collaborative (TAC).

**Works** The impact of Gropius on architecture also came from his building designs. Starting with his early German work, the Fagus Factory (1911), Alfeld, on which he was associated with Adolph Meyer, the Werkbund Exhibition (1914), Cologne, and the Bauhaus buildings (1926), Dessau, his designs have had a clarity and consistency not often found in the work of other architects. The early buildings brought him worldwide recognition as a modern architect and influenced architecture everywhere.

During his Bauhaus days, Gropius designed very few buildings. Although some of those he designed were pioneering and inventive, most were never built. Two, however, were built: a prefabricated house (1927) for the Werkbund Exhibition in Stuttgart, a continuation of his interest in production line units, and the Siemensstadt Housing (1929), Berlin, a continuation of his lifelong interest in housing for large numbers of people. During his three years in England, he and Maxwell Fry designed Impington College (1936), near Cambridge.

After coming to America, Gropius and Marcel Breuer, who had been on the Bauhaus faculty and was now on that of Harvard, designed a number of houses around the Boston area, including one for Gropius (1937) in Lincoln; Aluminum City Terrace Housing (1941), New Kensington, near Pittsburgh; and buildings for Black Mountain College, Lake Eden, N.C., that were

never built. The first big project of Gropius, after he had formed the group practice, The Architects' Collaborative (TAC), in 1946, was the Harvard Graduate Center (1949), Cambridge, Mass. Like some of his other later buildings, such as the Pan American Building (1963), New York City, for which Gropius and Pietro Belluschi (1899–1994) served as design consultants, the Harvard complex has been criticized as being not up to the early standards set by the architect. The most important later Gropius-TAC buildings were the U.S. Embassy (1961), Athens, Greece; the Boston Back Bay Center (1953); the John F. Kennedy Federal Office Building (1964), Boston; and the last great design of his career, the University of Baghdad (1969), Iraq.

The Gropius philosophy and principles live on in the work of the many architects he taught and influenced. The Architects' Collaborative continues to practice as an influential and successful firm in Cambridge, which has designed such buildings as the headquarters of the American Institute of Architects (1972) in Washington. In 1979, TAC completed the Bauhaus Archive Building, Berlin, developed from a Gropius design, made some years before he died.

**Life** Walter Gropius was born on May 18, 1883, the son of an architect who held high governmental positions, into an artistic and successful family. After a boyhood spent among a congenial and intelligent family and circle of friends, he entered the University of Munich in 1903 to study architecture. His education was interrupted by a trip to Spain (1904–05) and by service in the Hussars of the German Imperial Army (1905–06). He completed his education at the University of Berlin in 1907. The next year he went to work in the office of a noted German architect, Peter Behrens (1868–1940), where he stayed three years. Behrens was one of the pioneers of modern architecture and employed three of the greatest future Modernists, Gropius, Ludwig Mies van der Rohe (1886–1969), who later distinguished himself in America, and for a five-month period beginning in the summer of 1910, the twenty-two-year-old Swiss-French architect Le Corbusier (1887–1965), whose real name was Charles-Edouard Jeanneret.

In 1910 Gropius set up his own office in Berlin. His first buildings were successful and set the stage for his designs the rest of his life. During this period, he also did industrial designs for wall hangings, furniture, and a railroad engine and car.

His career was interrupted by World War I, during which he served in the German army from 1914 to 1918. During the war, in 1916, he married the divorced wife of the composer and conductor Gustav Mahler, Alma Mahler (nee Schindler), and they had one daughter before their divorce. He married Ise Frank in 1923, and they also had a daughter. In 1918, Gropius was appointed

**GROPIUS, WALTER ADOLF** Harvard Graduate Center (1949), Harvard University, Cambridge, Mass.

director of both the Grand Ducal Saxon School of Applied Arts and the Grand Ducal Academy of Arts in Weimar. In 1919 he merged the two schools into the Staatliches Bauhaus (State Building School), an action that was destined to revolutionize architectural education and to have far-reaching effects on the design of buildings, furniture, and industrial products. In 1925, disturbed by hostility in Weimar, Gropius moved the school to Dessau. During the Weimar years, Gropius designed few buildings; he submitted a design in 1922 in the Chicago Tribune competition, which still looks fresh and modern today. The move to Dessau provided him with a great new opportunity: design of the buildings for the new school (see illustration in article Bauhaus, Staatliches).

Under political pressure, he resigned as director of the Bauhaus in 1928, visited the United States, and then resumed private practice in Berlin. In 1929 he was elected vice president of the international Congresses of Modern Architecture (CIAM), an organization started to consolidate and promote the new architecture. He served in this capacity until 1957. CIAM was disbanded in 1959.

In 1934, disillusioned and saddened by the political situation under the Nazis in Germany, Gropius went to England, where he formed a partnership in 1935 with the noted English architect Edwin Maxwell Fry. After three years in which most of the designs were for houses, in 1937 Gropius accepted an invitation to take a professorship in the Harvard University Graduate School of Design, offered by the dean, Joseph Hudnut (1886–1963), and the university president, James B. Conant (b. 1893). This was a great challenge to a man as deeply interested in education as Gropius, the chance to apply the principles of the Bauhaus in an outstanding school that, along with the others in America, was still immersed in the Beaux Arts system of architectural edu-

cation. In 1938 he became chairman of the department of architecture. Again he made educational history and remained in this position at Harvard until 1952.

**TAC Practice** In 1938 Gropius opened an architectural office in Cambridge, this time in partnership with Marcel Breuer, whom he had first attracted to the Bauhaus faculty and then to that of Harvard. They practiced together until 1943, designing mostly houses. After 1943, each went into his own private practice. In 1946 Gropius, together with several young architects, founded a group practice, The Architects' Collaborative (TAC), in Cambridge which was unique in its organization and methods. TAC was composed of partners who were theoretically equal to each other, each serving as the architect for individual buildings which were subject both to criticism by the other partners and assistance from them. This is quite different from the usual architectural partnership in which each partner specializes, at least to a degree, one in design, one in administration, and another in obtaining commissions for the firm. TAC continued to practice and grow during the lifetime of Gropius, and for many years after.

After his retirement from the Harvard faculty, Gropius devoted his time to the architectural practice of TAC. Early in his career, he had begun to make speeches and write articles, many of which were collected into books. He continued to write and speak on all the subjects that so greatly interested him: design and practice of architecture, education, and social issues. It was a fruitful time for a man who had lived a long and productive life, and had achieved the stature of a sage.

Great honors piled up. Over the years, he had been elected to Phi Beta Kappa, awarded honorary doctors' degrees from universities all over the world, including a doctor of arts from Harvard, and elected a fellow of the American Academy of Arts and Sciences. In 1956 he received the Gold Medal of the Royal Institute of British Architects and in 1959, that of the American Institute of Architects. Perhaps the ultimate was the high recognition from his native country which the Nazis had caused him to leave. In 1958 the Federal Republic of Germany awarded him the Grand Cross of Merit with Star and in 1960, the Grand State Prize in Architecture.

Respected, admired, and loved, Walter Adolf Gropius died on July 5, 1969. He had changed architecture and architectural education.

**Related Articles** BAUHAUS, STAATLICHES; BREUER, MARCEL LAJOS; EDUCATION; MODERN ARCHITECTURE.

**Further Reading** Isaacs, Reginald R.: *Gropius: An Illustrated Biography of the Creator of the Bauhaus*, Little, Brown, Boston, 1991.

# H

**HARDWARE** Products, or fittings, mostly made of metal, used in conjunction with larger parts of buildings, including such items as nails and screws, or rough hardware, and locks and hinges, or finish hardware. Rough hardware is primarily used for the general construction of buildings, including foundations, walls, structures, and so on, and is generally but not always concealed. Sometimes rough hardware items are called fasteners since so many types are primarily used for fastening two or more materials or parts together. Finish hardware is generally exposed in buildings and includes types for a great variety of purposes, such as those that enable doors or windows to operate or those for security purposes. Thousands of kinds and sizes of hardware items are available as stock items, in many metals, with various finishes and colors. Many can be obtained on special order, and some manufacturers will fabricate certain special types to order.

**Rough Hardware** The most common types of rough hardware are nails, screws, nuts, and bolts, but also turnbuckles, washers, anchors, ties, inserts, and other fasteners of every conceivable kind for every type of function. The most basic and oldest fastener is the nail, which is known to have been used in ancient building construction. There is a great variety of types of nails, in numerous shapes, materials, and sizes for many purposes. A nail has a head, a shank, and a point. Many kinds of heads are available; the two types most frequently used are the flat head on common nails, in rough carpentry and other ways; and the smaller head on finishing or casing nails, meant to be set, driven below the surface of materials with a nail set and puttied or otherwise finished. Nails are often specified by the pennyweight, as in eight penny, or 8d, which reflects the fact that several hundred years ago one hundred 8d nails sold for 8 pence in England. Common nails come in sizes from 2d, 1 in

long of no. 15 gauge wire to 60d, 6 in long of no. 2 gauge wire. Finishing nails are generally available in the same sizes up to 40d.

A variety of other nails are available for various purposes, including fence, roofing, sheet metal, flooring, lath, molding, shingle, and slating. Some nails have heads that are large and flat, double, cupped, offset, oval, or round; and nails may be headless. Special types are made for such materials as concrete or masonry. Very large nails are called spikes and come in several types, in sizes from $1/2$ to $5/8$ in$^2$, and in lengths from 3 to 12 in or more and with various types of heads. Nails may be driven by hand with hammers or other tools, or by mechanical and power-actuated devices. Most nails are made of iron or steel, plain or coated with zinc or other metals to increase their resistance to rust. Nails are also made of other metals, such as copper and aluminum.

Other rough hardware items that are often used include bolts, screws, nuts, and related types. A bolt is like a rod with a head on one end and external screw threads along its shank. Bolts are used with nuts, devices usually square or hexagonal in shape, with internal threads to mate with those of bolts. A machine bolt has a square or hexagonal head, while a carriage bolt has a rounded head with a square portion below it to keep the bolt from turning when inserted into a square hole. A stove bolt usually has an oval or a round head into which a screwdriver may be inserted. Bolts range in diameter from $1/8$ up to $1/2$ in and in some types to a full inch or more, and in lengths from about $1/2$ to 6 in or more. Nuts come in sizes to fit the bolt sizes. A special type is a lag bolt that has a tapered shank. Washers (metal disks) are often used in conjunction with bolts and nuts, and may be flat or cut, spring locking, with external teeth.

Screws are of two major types: one called a wood screw that is like a bolt but tapered toward its point to

285

allow it to be driven with a screwdriver into various materials; and another that is similar to a bolt and used for similar purposes. The two most used types of screws of the second type are machine screws, which come with round, flat, oval, or other types of slotted heads; and cap screws, which come with slotted, round, flat, hexagonal, or other heads. Slotted head screws may be driven by ordinary screwdrivers; those with two slots, by Phillips screwdrivers. Nuts may be obtained with the types of heads used for bolts and screws and as cap nuts, wing nuts, and in a great number of other forms.

Many other types of rough hardware are available for any imaginable purpose in architecture, including hangers for pipes and other elements, anchors for holding one component securely to another, ties for similar purposes, inserts that go into one material to allow another material or some device to be attached, and fasteners of every shape and kind for every problem and purpose. Among the most useful are staples, roughly U-shaped devices with two pointed ends, for fastening a variety of materials by staple guns or staple hammers; and studs, usually driven partly into materials with power-actuated or mechanically actuated guns, leaving their ends exposed for screwing on, or otherwise attaching, materials or devices. Another special device is a shield, or anchor, usually of lead, fiber, or other material, which is inserted into a material and expands when a screw is driven into it. Another device, for similar purposes, is a toggle bolt which has a flap or flaps that may be aligned with the shank while the device is inserted into a hole, after which the flaps may be caused to spread out to hold the toggle bolt in place.

**Finish Hardware** This hardware also comes in a great variety of types, sizes, finishes, and materials, and in a somewhat wider range of prices, for many architectural purposes. In some cases, finish hardware usually comes with an assembly, as in most windows today. In other cases, such as in doors, the hardware is often selected separately. So many variations are possible in finish hardware that a complete discussion is not possible here. However, some idea of the scope of the subject may be gained by examining the hardware for doors alone.

**Door Hardware** This hardware may be obtained in a number of metals, including brass, bronze, aluminum, and steel; steel may be plated with brass, bronze, or chromium or may have a prime coat of paint or other material. In addition, certain finish hardware items, such as doorknobs, may also be obtained in such materials as glass, china, and plastics. Plastics are often used for other parts of door hardware. And the various materials may be obtained in a number of textures, such as bright, semimatte, or matte (sometimes called brushed) finishes.

Many separate items of finish hardware are used with doors. Hinges may be exposed or concealed and special types are available. Doorknobs or levers may be used for opening and closing. Locks may be integral with knobs or separate; and special types, including door bolts, may be used. Thresholds or saddles are located beneath doors when they are closed and, for exterior doors, may be fitted with weatherstripping devices. Weatherstripping around the sides and heads of doors is also recommended. Push plates or bars are often used on doors, particularly in public and commercial buildings. In addition, in buildings of all types, closers which automatically close doors, holders which hold them open when desired, silencers which keep them from making noises when slammed, stops which limit the amount they may open, letter boxes, and other devices are often used. Bars which open doors when people press on them from inside, called panic hardware, are often used in buildings occupied by many people and are required by building codes in some types, such as theaters.

The types of hardware used for windows are equally as varied and numerous. And there are other types of hardware for many different purposes in buildings. Rough hardware, except in special cases, is usually considered part of the construction of the various elements and often is not made a part of the specifications for buildings, except in standards for performance. Finish hardware comes as part of assemblies, such as is usually the case in windows, or is specified in schedules of hardware included in the working drawings or specifications. Sometimes a monetary allowance is made for the total cost of all finish hardware, instead of specifying each item separately.

Since there is such a variety of hardware available today, sometimes architects obtain the services of hardware consultants, who specialize in this field, to aid in selecting and specifying the various items.

**History** It is believed that the first fasteners used by primitive humans in building construction were vines with which parts were tied together, followed by shaping wooden parts to fit into each other, as in log cabins, and by wooden stakes driven into holes to function much like nails. Metal nails have been used since very early times and were originally forged by hammering pieces of iron. Nails continued to be forged until the 18th century and some were forged in the 19th. In 1786 Ezekiel Reed, an American inventor, patented a machine that made nails out of wire. This method, though improved over the years, is still used for most nails today. Other types of rough hardware were developed when needs for them arose and have been improved over the years.

Finish hardware was also used in buildings in very early times. From about 3000 B.C. in the great civilizations around the Mediterranean Sea, hardware for various kinds of doors were developed, including pivots that acted like hinges. Later locks and other types of hardware were developed, followed by the first real hinges during the Middle Ages. Some Gothic hinges were highly ornamented features of doors. During the years following, various types of finish hardware were developed, gradually producing the vast array of types available today.

Recent developments related to hardware are the electric controls for automatically closing doors in case of fire or smoke or as a security measure in response to motion detectors. Also, doors may be unlocked remotely upon proper identification procedures seen by security personnel on a television monitor.

**Related Articles** DOOR; SECURITY SYSTEMS; WINDOW; Various articles on building materials, components, and systems.

**Source of Additional Information** Door and Hardware Inst., 7711 Old Springhouse Rd., McLean, Va. 22102.

**HARRISON, PETER** English-American architect (1716–75). The buildings of Peter Harrison occupy a very important place in American architecture. He is the first colonist known to have made designs for buildings to be erected by others. He has therefore been called America's first architect. As noteworthy as his accomplishments were, he was not really a professional architect. His vocation was that of merchant and sea captain.

Architecture, important as it must have been to him, was an avocation only. He was only slightly involved in the construction of his buildings, if at all. He had no architectural training, except what he learned from books. He also derived all his designs for buildings from books. And it is known that he never received proper professional fees for his work, only token gifts or payments instead.

However, these factors have little or nothing to do with the importance of his work, the largest number of buildings attributed to any architect of his time, at least five major buildings, a number of homes, a fort, a lighthouse, and a map of the town and harbor of Newport, R.I. For his time, he was a first-rate draftsman, something of an engineer, and a self-educated architect, possessed of refinement and taste; in short, a gentleman-amateur architect. He possessed the best architectural library of its time in the colonies, composed mostly of books collected on his trips to England as a ship captain. He was one of the first, and perhaps the most important, of the colonial architects who participated in the development of Georgian architecture in America, adapting it from books about the English style.

**Works** His first building is thought to be a large house, Shirley Place (1746), in Roxbury, Mass., designed for Gov. William Shirley (1694–1771) of Massachusetts.

**HARRISON, PETER** Brick Market (1762), Newport, R.I.

Two stories high with a basement, this house is Georgian in appearance but is constructed of wood rather than stone or brick as in English Georgian houses. Since masonry materials were unavailable, the architect used exterior wood, cut in such a way as to resemble masonry, and painted, with sand in the paint, to resemble the color and texture of masonry. This was to be the device used in his first public building, the Redwood Library (1750), Newport, R.I., named for its founder, Abraham Redwood.

Harrison's next major building, usually considered his most important work, King's Chapel (1754), in Boston, was designed to be constructed of granite from Quincy, Mass. This was the first church in America to be built of stone, but the columns and the porch or portico were built of wood and were not completed until some 30 years after the main church. The great spire of stone, which Harrison had envisioned, was never built. Although the architect's designs for the exterior were never fully realized, his designs produced the most magnificent interior space in any church in the colonies.

Other important buildings by Harrison are Christ Church (1761), Cambridge, Mass.; and Touro Synagogue (1763) and the Brick Market (1762), both in

**HARRISON, PETER** Exterior, Touro Synagogue (1763), Newport, R.I.

Newport, R.I. As was the case with King's Chapel, Christ Church was never completed. Built of wood, the exterior was to have been covered with a rough stucco intended to resemble masonry and was to have a tall steeple; neither was accomplished. Touro, the first synagogue in America, like King's Chapel, has a marvelously refined and elegant interior. So much so that the elegance seems out of place in a Jewish house of worship. Knowing nothing of the Hebrew faith, Harrison simply followed his usual procedure of adapting the design from books. The architect's last major building, the Brick Market, is an adaptation from the 17th-century Somerset House in England. It is of brick with an open-air, arcaded market on the ground floor. The two stories above, also of brick, have wooden pilasters attached.

In addition to Shirley Place, Peter Harrison designed many other houses. The number is uncertain, but some of the important ones include Vassall-Longfellow House (1760), Cambridge; Lady Pepperell House (1760), Kittery Point, Maine; and Francis Malbone House (1760), Newport. In addition, he designed a remarkable series of three houses, all different and all designed for members of one family: the first Apthorp House (1760) in Cambridge for the rector of Christ Church, the Rev. East Apthorp; the second for the minister's father (about 1763), in Brighton, Mass.; and the third for his brother in New York City (1767).

All of Harrison's major buildings as well as the houses have designs based on English books studied by the architect. Among the most important were a 1736 translation of the works of Andrea Palladio (1518–80), an Italian Renaissance architect and theorist; *Vitruvius Brittanicus,* by Colen Campbell (c. 1676–1729) and others (published 1715–71); and James Gibbs' books. Harrison has been accused by some purists of being only a literary or bookish architect. However, it must be remembered that none of the colonial architects had been formally trained in architecture. They were builders or wood-carvers or men of other vocations, who were deeply interested in architecture. And they learned what they knew from books. Harrison, it must be conceded, learned his lessons well and produced notable and important buildings with the help of his books.

**Life** Peter Harrison came to Newport, R.I., when he was about twenty-two, as a member of the crew of his brother's ship. Soon becoming a ship captain himself, he showed an early interest in drawing and architecture. Captured by the French in 1745, he was imprisoned at Fort Louisbourg on Cape Breton Island, Nova Scotia. After his release, he drew an accurate map of the fortifications which helped the colonial troops to capture the fort. Governor Shirley of Massachusetts, who instigated the attack, was so pleased with Harrison's map that he asked the young ship captain to design a house for him; this was Harrison's first building.

From this beginning, Harrison went on to become an important colonial architect. Originally a Quaker, he became a member of the Church of England soon after reaching America. Though a colonist, he considered himself an Englishman and, as the movement toward independence of the colonies progressed, was known as a Tory in politics. Toward the end of his life, he moved to New Haven, Conn., where he was appointed Customs Collector, a post most harmful to his reputation among those who opposed the English crown. After his death in 1775, on the eve of the Revolution, a mob broke into his house and burned what was one of the great architectural libraries in the colonies and all his drawings.

**Related Articles** BOOK, ARCHITECTURAL; COLONIAL ARCHITECTURE; GEORGIAN ARCHITECTURE; HISTORY OF ARCHITECTURE.

**HARRISON, WALLACE KIRKMAN** American architect (1895–1981). Although he had little formal education after age fourteen, and almost none in architecture, Harrison became an architect in the manner that many others had before him, by working in the offices of other architects and also by studying on his own.

In spite of the seeming handicaps of his lack of formal education and his childhood in a relatively small city, Wallace Kirkman Harrison eventually became an urbane and successful architect. Although he worked in offices of other architects most of his early life before becoming a partner, Harrison eventually designed a number of New York City skyscrapers and many other buildings.

Harrison also performed another role that is probably unique in architecture in America and perhaps in any other country. For a very long time, it seemed that whenever some great complex of buildings was to be designed

**HARRISON, WALLACE KIRKMAN** U.S. Steel Building (1971), Pittsburgh, Pa. *[Architects: Harrison and Abramovitz]*

and constructed by a number of architects, Harrison always turned out to be the architect who was called on to direct and administer the project, to keep the peace, and to ensure that the job was done properly. Yet he

**HARRISON, WALLACE KIRKMAN** Assembly Hall (1962), University of Illinois, Champaign, Urbana, Ill.
*[Architects: Harrison and Abramovitz; engineers: Ammann and Whitney]*

never relinquished his role as a building designer; rather, he combined the roles of designer and administrator.

**Building Complex** Harrison's first experience with a great complex came with the design and construction of Rockefeller Center, New York City (see illustrations in article complex, architectural). Although he did not direct this work, he was deeply involved and is considered one of the architects, the others being Harvey Wiley Corbett (1873–1954) and Raymond Hood (1881–1934), who contributed most to the design.

The design of Rockefeller Center began in the 1920s; its construction was started in 1931 and was not completed until 1940. The architectural work was performed by an association of three architectural firms: Reinhard and Hofmeister; Corbett, Harrison and MacMurray; and Hood and Fouilhoux.

The next complex, the United Nations Headquarters, New York City, was begun in 1947, completed in 1950. The UN Headquarters was designed by an international team of 15 architects, headed by Harrison and including Le Corbusier (1887–1965) of France, Oscar Niemeyer (1907– ) of Brazil, and Sven Markelius (1889–1972) of Sweden.

Idlewild, now John F. Kennedy, Airport (see illustration in article Saarinen, Eero) in Jamaica, near New York City, a great complex of individual terminals and numerous other buildings, was begun in 1942 and virtually completed by 1962, with Harrison as consulting architect. The terminals and other buildings were designed by a number of architectural firms to fit into the master plan. Buildings were designed by Skidmore, Owings and Merrill; Kahn and Jacobs; Tippetts, Abbett, McCarthy and Stratton; Eero Saarinen (1910–61); Edward Durell Stone (1902–78); White and Mariani; William B. Tabler (1914– ); Reinhard, Hofmeister and Walquist; I. M. Pei (1917– ); George I. Sole; Bloch and Hesse; and Edgar Tafel (1912– ).

While Kennedy Airport was under construction, Harrison received a commission to direct the design and construction of another important complex, the Lincoln Center for the Performing Arts, in New York City, begun in 1962 and completed in 1968. In this complex six buildings were designed by as many architects, including Philip Cortelyou Johnson (1906- ); Eero Saarinen (1910–61); Edward Durell Stone (1902–78); Pietro Belluschi (1889-1994); Skidmore, Owings and Merrill; Max Abramovitz (1908– ), then Harrison's partner, who did the Philharmonic Hall (1962); and Harrison, who did the Metropolitan Opera House (1966). See article entitled theater.

**Other Buildings** Harrison designed many other buildings, most of them in partnership with Max Abramovitz, including airport buildings, apartments, auditoriums, churches, museums, college buildings, and research buildings. Some of the more notable buildings

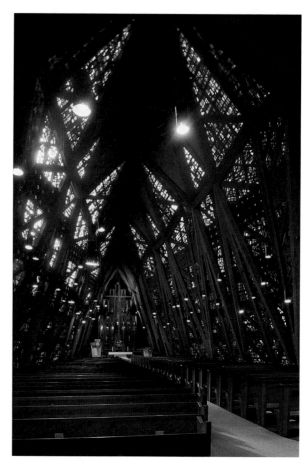

**HARRISON, WALLACE KIRKMAN** Interior, First Presbyterian Church (1958; later alterations), Stamford, Conn. *[Stained glass: Gabriel Loire]*

include the African Building (1941) at the Bronx Zoo, the New York Aquarium (1955), the Loeb Student Center (1959) at New York University, the Museum of Science and Technology (1964), and LaGuardia Airport (1965), all in New York City; the First Presbyterian Church (1958), Stamford, Conn.; and the Assembly Hall (1962), University of Illinois.

Perhaps the most notable buildings designed by Harrison and Abramovitz are office buildings, including the Alcoa Building (1952); Corning Glass (1959) and Time-Life (1960), both in New York City; and U.S. Steel (1971) in Pittsburgh.

**Life** Wallace Kirkman Harrison was born in Worcester, Mass., on September 28, 1895. Leaving school early, he went to work in 1909 at age fourteen for a contractor in Worcester but soon left to work in an architectural office there. In 1916 he went to New York, where he worked in the office of McKim, Mead and White for a short time before entering the U.S. Navy during World War I.

After the war, Harrison entered the École des Beaux Arts in Paris where he studied for a year and then remained in Europe to travel and study for a year.

Returning to the United States, he went to work in the New York City office of Bertram Grosvenor Goodhue (1869–1924). After Goodhue's death, Harrison joined Helmle and Corbett, which eventually became Corbett, Harrison and MacMurray, and participated in the design of Rockefeller Center. In 1926 Harrison married Ellen Milton, and they had one daughter. Mrs. Harrison's brother married Abby Rockefeller, and Nelson Rockefeller represented the family's interest during the construction of Rockefeller Center. The Rockefeller connection provided many of Harrison's important commissions. In 1935 Harrison formed a partnership with another architect who had worked on Rockefeller Center, J. André Fouilhoux (1879–1945). They were joined in the partnership by Max Abramovitz in 1941. After Fouilhoux was killed in a construction accident during World War II, the firm became Harrison and Abramovitz, which it remained until it was dissolved in 1977.

In his later years, Wallace Harrison was awarded honorary degrees by many universities all over the United States, including Harvard, Oberlin, Dartmouth, and Michigan. In 1967 he was awarded the highest honor for an American architect, the Gold Medal of the American Institute of Architects. At age eighty-six, Harrison died on December 8, 1981, in New York City.

**Related Articles** COMPLEX, ARCHITECTURAL; CONTEMPORARY ARCHITECTURE; MODERN ARCHITECTURE; OFFICE BUILDING; PUBLIC BUILDING; THEATER.

**Further Reading** Newhouse, Victoria: *Wallace K. Harrison, Architect*, Rizzoli, New York, 1989.

## HEALTH-CARE FACILITIES

**HEALTH-CARE FACILITIES** A growing group of building types including acute- or intensive-care hospitals, ambulatory-care facilities, continuing-care facilities, psychiatric hospitals, and rehabilitative facilities.

**Hospitals** The familiar hospital in many communities is defined and regulated by licensing and accreditation agencies that have major impact on the design of the facility. Hospitals may be classified by ownership, such as the federal government, state government, and local government, and by voluntary (not for profit) and proprietary (for profit).

Another classification grouping is the level of care provided, described as primary, secondary, and tertiary

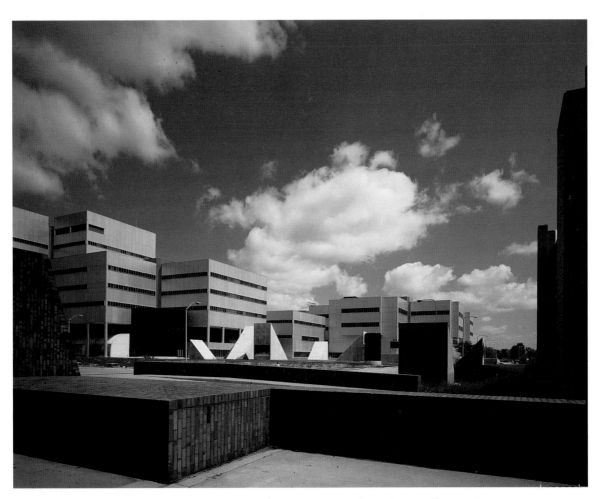

**HEALTH-CARE FACILITIES** Detroit Receiving Hospital (1979), Detroit, Mich. *[Architect: William Kessler with Zeidler-Roberts Partnership]*

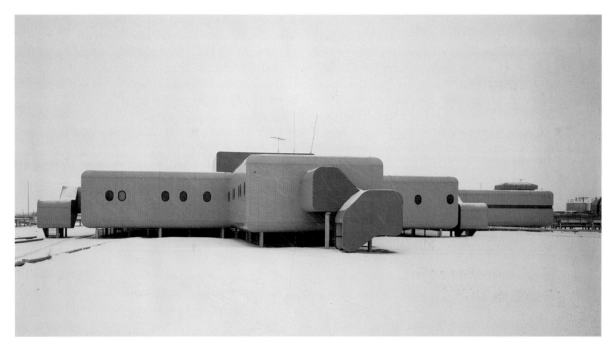

**HEALTH-CARE FACILITIES** Yukon Kuskokwin Regional Hospital (1983), Bethel, Alaska. *[Architects: CRSS]*

levels, which reflect the level of specialized care needed. For instance, primary care is the initial medical assessment, including emergency rooms. Much of this care may be given in doctors' offices or hospital outpatient departments. Secondary care involves the broad range of subspecialties in medicine and surgery. Tertiary care refers to the highest level of specialization, such as neurosurgery, cardiac surgery, organ transplants, and intensive care. Secondary and tertiary level care is usually provided on the basis of referrals from primary care.

Facilities are also defined by the patient's length of stay, with the typical hospital stay being limited to less than 30 days. Long-term facilities are markedly different from general hospitals. A special type of hospital is what is called a "teaching" hospital allied to a medical school or with an approved physician internship-residency program. Historically osteopathic facilities have been in separate hospitals, but there is a trend to include both osteopathic and medical facilities in the same building.

The need for varying types of care has led to the development of specialty hospitals. Such types include hospitals for women (maternity), children (pediatric), cancer (oncology), orthopedics, cardiovascular services, eye care, ear nose and throat (ENT), neurosensory services, burn care, rehabilitation, and osteopathic services. Most typical is the general acute-care hospital.

**Ambulatory-Care Facilities** Ambulatory care refers to medical services which do not normally require an overnight stay. Building types include medical office buildings, hospital outpatient departments, health-care centers, and specialty centers such as wellness centers, urgent-care centers, women's health centers, etc.

Ownership of these buildings may be as varied as hospitals, although more are privately owned.

**Continuing-Care Facilities** Long-term care for the elderly consists of a variety of facilities suited to the needs of an aging population. Such facilities include conventional housing, congregate housing, hospitals, retirement communities, nursing homes, and life-care or continuing-care retirement communities. The needs of the young-old (ages fifty-five to sixty-nine) differ from the needs of the middle-old (ages seventy to seventy-nine) and the old-old (age over eighty). As aging occurs, the individual moves from independent living to requiring various levels of health care. This transition can be envisioned as moving from homes or retirement communities to life-care or continuing-care retirement facilities to nursing homes for those with limited mobility. Senior centers or other adult day care are important adjuncts to housing. Specialized types of continuing-care facilities are hospices for the terminally ill and Alzheimer units for those suffering from this condition. Facilities for coma management; rehabilitation; physical, occupational, and speech therapy are specialized facilities which should be accessible to the continuing-care facilities.

The demographics of the U.S. population indicate that there will be need for many additional facilities for continuing care as the elderly population increases well into the next century. This need also reflects a shift from the traditional care in the home to a variety of newer building types. The wide variation in needs of the elderly have supported a great increase in building types which will continue into the future. Statistics indicate that better diet and exercise as well as a reduction in smoking have resulted in a healthier and less physically restricted older population.

**Psychiatric Facilities** Possibly the greatest variety of health-care facilities is required for diagnosis, evaluation, and treatment of those with mental problems. The treatment of the mentally ill has changed greatly as more is understood about mental health needs. An estimated 20 to 32 million Americans need some type of mental care at some point in their lives.

Psychiatric hospitals now try to separate adolescent care from adult care and substance abuse units. Crisis intervention is separately served. Current thinking about these facilities emphasizes the need for education opportunities and social activities as well as recreation including gymnasiums. Needed support services include food service and laundry facilities. Administrative areas include offices for patient interviews and an admitting office, as well as business and administrative offices including medical records. Other rooms may include doctors' lounge, library, meeting rooms, and a chapel for religious services. A pharmacy is another need, as well as lobby reception for visitors who must be monitored as to entering and leaving the facility.

**Rehabilitative Facilities** Rehabilitative facilities serve disabled individuals suffering from strokes, head injury, spinal cord injury, amputation, complicated fractures, arthritis, neurological degeneration, genetic disor-

**HEALTH-CARE FACILITIES** Columbus Occupational Health Association (1973), Columbus, Ind. *[Architects: Hardy Holzman Pfeiffer Assoc.]*

ders, and cardiac rehabilitation. These facilities may be offered in acute-care hospitals but may now be separate buildings for some of or all the rehabilitative functions. Needed are public and administrative areas, diagnostic and therapeutic services, and patient-care services as well as building support services.

Occupational therapy is aimed at helping the patient to become independent. Vocational training may include office settings, as well as metal and woodworking shops. Some patients need outpatient services after discharge from a hospital, sometimes for the rest of their lives.

Physical therapy makes use of hydrotherapy baths and pools, and gymnasium facilities, as well as specialized equipment. Speech and audiology testing require special rooms for patient use and staff support. Recreation needs for the long-term patient include in-hospital events as well as trips to public places that can accommodate handicapped patients.

Psychiatry and psychology programs are designed to assist the patient to cope with a disability. Specialists for neurological problems are called "neuropsychologists." Group therapy is used to share experiences in coping with disabilities.

The federal accessibility laws are making the United States a better place for those with handicaps. Refer to articles entitled building codes and standards; design, accessible.

**Further Reading** Harvey, Thomas E., Jr.: "Health Care Facilities-Acute/Intensive" and "Health Care Facilities—Ambulatory," Hawkins, H. Ralph: "Health Care Facilities—Psychiatric" and "Health Care Facilities—Rehabilitative," and Seiben, Paul G.: "Health Care Facilities—Continuing Care," vol. 2, *Encyclopedia of Architecture*, John Wiley & Sons, New York, 1988.

**Sources of Additional Information** American Assoc. of Healthcare Consultants, 11208 Waples Mill Rd., Suite 109, Fairfax, Va. 22030; American Hospital Assoc., 840 N. Lake Shore Dr., Chicago, Ill. 60611; The Forum for Health Care Planning, 1101 Connecticut Ave., N.W., Suite 700, Washington, D.C. 20036.

## HEATING, VENTILATING, AND AIR CONDITIONING

Major systems that provide proper temperatures, ventilation, and humidities for the occupants of buildings. Such systems are often called heating, ventilating, and air conditioning, or HVAC, systems. HVAC systems also help keep buildings and their furniture and furnishings from deteriorating by providing relatively constant levels of temperature and humidity. For a discussion of the requirements for human comfort, heat flow, heat losses and gains, and other principles, see the article entitled insulation, thermal.

Heating of buildings is generally accomplished by convection, the heating of air which then heats the occupants; by radiation, which does not heat the air but travels from a heat source to the persons being heated by rays or waves as in heat from the sun; or by combinations of the two. Some heating is also received from conduction, the movement of heat within a material, from molecule to molecule.

**Heating Methods** Four major methods are used for producing heat in the interiors of buildings: steam, hot water, hot air, and electric coils. Steam and hot-water types are called hydronic systems. Any of the systems can be used with unit, or space, heaters which are placed in various locations within buildings and heat only certain areas. Space heaters, such as portable electric types, are often used for temporary heating and for places, such as bathrooms, where additional heat may be required at times. Large space heaters are also often used for heating factories or warehouses. Fireplaces and heating stoves, which are actually types of space heaters, are often used for supplementary heating. See the article entitled fireplace.

Today the general method in most buildings, other than those in very warm climates, is central heating, involving a central source of heat, such as a boiler or furnace, from which air, water, or steam is pumped or blown to various locations in the buildings. Boilers may produce steam or hot water. In the past, the steam or hot water was delivered to devices called radiators, which actually heated partly by radiation and partly by convention. Today steam is usually delivered to devices called convectors, which may also be used with hot water. In addition, hot water can be delivered to baseboard heating units, which are often placed at or near the bases of walls. Baseboard units have one or more pipes surrounded by metal fins, which heat by radiation with some convention. Hot water may also be used in conjunction with radiant panels, composed of coils of piping placed in floors, ceilings, or walls through which the hot water is circulated.

Hot-air systems employ furnaces of various kinds for heating relatively large volumes of air which are then blown through a system of metal ducts to various areas of buildings. The heated air enters rooms through grilles, registers, or diffusers located in floors, walls, or ceilings and returns to the furnaces through return-air grilles or registers. In the furnace, this warm air is often combined with some percentage of fresh outside air to improve the ventilation in buildings. Return-air grilles are not installed in bathrooms, kitchens, or other places where fumes or odors might enter the system. Ductwork for warm-air heating may be installed in a number of ways, including the perimeter loop system, in which supply ducts are placed around the outside walls of buildings, and the radial system, in which supply ducts radiate to outside walls from the center of buildings.

Electric coils for radiant heating may be embedded in plaster or other ceiling and wall materials or in concrete floors. Separate controls may be installed for each space. Electric baseboard heating may also be obtained but it is practical only in relatively warm climates or in well-insulated spaces. Electric heat sources of other types are also available, including infrared lamp fixtures and panels and electric boilers.

**Fuels** In addition to electricity, the fuels most used for heating are gas, fuel oil, and coal. As is the case with electricity, gas requires no storage on building sites, except when liquefied, or bottled, gas is used in areas in which gas is not supplied from central municipal systems. Fuel oil requires storage tanks, which are often buried in the ground outside buildings and may be strapped down to concrete slabs to keep them from rising when nearly empty or sinking when full. Coal, formerly the major fuel for heating, is not used as much today. When coal is used, special containers or bins must be provided in sheltered spaces for its storage. Today coal-burning furnaces are usually fed by mechanical stokers which automatically feed proper amounts of coal to the furnaces at regular intervals.

Electricity has advantages because of the simplicity of installing systems, easy control, cleanliness, and easy maintenance; and because it does not produce pollution in buildings. Fuel oil is a very efficient source of heat in modern furnaces and boilers. It has the disadvantages of requiring storage in or near buildings, need for regular maintenance, and the air pollution produced. Gas, both natural and manufactured, is a relatively clean-burning fuel, contributing less to air pollution than fuel oil. It does not require storage, and furnaces and boilers that use it are relatively easy to maintain. Coal produces considerable air pollution, particularly the bituminous or soft type, while anthracite or the hard type produces less. Coal requires storage facilities and machinery to feed it to furnaces and boilers, which may require frequent maintenance to assure their efficiency. Coal also has the disadvantage of undependable availability at times, because of the frequency of strikes in the industry. The costs of equipment to be used with each type of fuel, supplies of the fuels over the years of operation, and maintenance should be considered when selecting the types of systems to be used in buildings.

Steam and hot-water heating systems, with convectors, are often more expensive to install than hot-air systems, but may be more efficient to operate. A problem with both types is that, since warm air rises, uneven temperatures may occur in rooms, with the area near the floors and the floors themselves difficult to heat. Also, unless strictly controlled, the air currents caused by convention may be unpleasant. Radiant heating is found to be more comfortable than other types by many people, since it causes no air waves. And because the air itself is not heated, only people and objects, a quite pleasant atmosphere is created.

**Air Conditioning** Many people consider air conditioning to be a system that only cools the interiors of buildings in hot weather. Some systems, including central systems and unit or room air conditioners, are in fact used in hot weather to cool and to remove moisture from air in interiors, or dehumidify them. They also clean the air with filters and other devices and may be used to introduce fresh air from outside. Today many systems provide air conditioning all year, performing the above functions in summer and introducing fresh air and cleaning and heating it in winter. They also provide moisture, or humidify the air, to replace the moisture lost during the heating process. Complete year-round air-conditioning systems require heat sources, such as boilers or furnaces, along with equipment for cooling air or chilling water, humidity and air-cleaning devices, and blowers or other devices to introduce heated or cooled air into the interiors of buildings.

In general, air conditioners operate by the compression and liquefaction of refrigerants, such as Freon, causing them to give off heat, and then through evaporation causing them to absorb heat. Leakage of common refrigerants into the air is a threat to the atmosphere. Alternative safer refrigerants are being introduced. The major parts of air conditioners and their operations are generally as follows: a compressor compresses the refrigerant, which then is pumped into a condenser, in which fans blow cool air or pumps circulate cool water, which liquefies the refrigerant causing it to release heat that is exhausted to the outside air or to the water; the liquid refrigerant under high pressure then flows through an evaporator, which turns the refrigerant back into a gas, which absorbs heat thereby cooling air blown over it or chilling water pumped over it. The cooled air is then blown into the interior of the building or air is blown over the chilled water coils and into interiors. In some systems, the chilled water itself is pumped to various locations in buildings, where devices, called air-handling units, are equipped with fans that blow air over the chilled water in finned coils and into interior spaces. In the case of year-round air conditioning, heated air is supplied to the interiors in the first type of system, while hot water is supplied to air-handling units in the second type during cold weather.

Many variations of the equipment discussed and the methods of heating and cooling are possible today. In the simplest systems, unit or room air conditioners, all components are contained in packaged units that may be placed in windows or built into walls. Larger, self-contained units of this sort, with greater capacities, usually stand on the floor near outside walls through which they exhaust heat. Other packaged units may be placed on roofs or under floors. Still others have all components installed inside, except for remote condensers that are placed outside. Air-cooling types are often used in conjunction with or combined with warm-air heating systems. Chilled-water types are often used in a similar manner, with steam or hot-water boilers.

While the air-cooling types require no water sources, the chilled-water types must have reliable sources of large quantities of water. Most often, the water is stored in cooling towers, which ordinarily have fans and other machinery to help cool the heated water returned to them. Cooling towers may be located on the roofs of buildings or on the sites outside. Sometimes a pond or lake is used as the source for chilled-water systems.

A special type of year-round air-conditioning system that has come into use in later years is called a heat pump. Heat pumps operate like summer air conditioners in which the processes may be reversed to extract heat from the outside in cold weather to produce heated air inside buildings. In summer, they operate in the same manner as ordinary summer air conditioners. Heat pumps are of two general types. The air-to-air type takes heat from inside air in summer exhausting it to the air outside and performs in the opposite way in winter. The air-water-air type exhausts heat from the air inside buildings in summer and passes it off into water taken from a well, or sometimes a pond; and in winter, the system extracts heat from the water and directs it into the interiors of buildings. In recent years, the reliability of heat pumps has improved.

In houses and small buildings of other types, various kinds of packaged air conditioners are installed. In larger buildings much more complicated systems are used. In addition to the compressive refrigeration types previously described, other types, including absorption and thermoelectric, are often used. Absorption types, which have fewer moving parts than the compressive types, are quieter and often require less maintenance. Instead of compressors, absorption types use tanks filled with chemical salts that soak up water from evaporators causing some of the water to evaporate, thereby cooling that remaining. Thermoelectric types are used today only for relatively small installations because of their expense. Such systems generally operate by electricity passed through thermocouples, made by joining two dissimilar metals. When direct current is passed through the thermocouples, they give off heat at one place and absorb heat at another.

**Control Devices** Controls for heating, air-conditioning, and year-round air-conditioning systems for houses and other small buildings are relatively simple. Some controls are required in connection with the operation of the equipment itself, but the only one readily apparent to building occupants is the thermostat, which controls the starting and stopping of the equipment, when heating or cooling is needed or when a sufficient amount has been supplied. Ordinary thermostats simply react to temperatures inside buildings. More elaborate types may have timers which, for example, automatically lower the amount of heat called for at night and raise it in the morning in winter. Other types have outdoor sensors that can anticipate to an extent future changes in outdoor temperatures. The controls for year-round air-conditioning and other systems in large buildings are usually very complex, and may include many types of controls, timers, gauges, switches, and other devices, not only for the operation of the central system but for sensing and controlling conditions in many parts of buildings. When various rooms or areas of a building have different heating or cooling requirements, the system is zoned to provide flexibility. Thus at a given time, one area might be receiving cooling, another heating. Some control centers or panels today have become so complex that computers are used in conjunction with them.

**Design Temperatures** In general, the selection of boilers or furnaces for heating and the design of heating systems are based on the hourly rate of heat loss to be expected from buildings and the temperatures to be maintained inside when outdoor temperatures are at certain low levels, called design temperatures. The amount of heat is generally measured in British thermal units (Btu), defined to be the amount of heat required to raise the temperature of 1 pound of water by 1°F. The rate of heat flow, loss or gain, is measured in Btu per hour (Btuh). Winter design temperatures in the United States vary from 55°F in Key West, Fla., to 5°F in New York City, to -30°F in Billings, Mont., and -57°F in Fairbanks, Alaska. Winter design conditions in other parts of the country do not depend on their latitude only, but on other factors as well. For example, Anchorage, Alaska, about 250 mi south of Fairbanks, has a design temperature of -24°F and Kodiak, another 250 mi south, 4°F. Boilers and furnaces are generally selected to replace the hourly heat losses in buildings, with somewhat more in capacities often provided for safety factors.

Heat gains in hot weather are also measured in Btus, and cooling systems are selected and designed to produce selected inside temperatures when certain summer outside design temperatures are reached. In Key West the summer design temperature is 100°F; in New York City, 90°F; and Fairbanks never reaches a level high enough to require cooling. Cooling units are sometimes rated in tons, the amount of heat, 288,000 Btu, required to melt 1 ton of ice in 24 h. A 1-ton cooler can remove this amount of heat in 24 h, or 12,000 Btu. The horsepower ratings of cooling equipment are also often cited. Small window units may be quite small, a fraction of a horsepower, while the largest may have several thousand. In addition to the heat gains or losses in heating or cooling buildings, other factors must be taken into account when designing these systems, such as air infiltration, the number of air changes per hour required inside rooms, and the effect of the sun.

In addition to the usual parts of heating and air-conditioning systems, other devices may be added, including humidifiers and dehumidifiers; several types of air cleaners which remove smoke, dust, pollen, and even bacteria from the air; and heaters for supplying hot water for various uses in buildings.

**Solar Heating** For many years, architects and other environmental designers have been interested in solar heating. Many have designed buildings that take advantage of the sun rays in winter, while excluding them in summer by architectural devices such as sunshades and roof overhangs. Some have designed systems which, at least in part, heat the interiors of buildings and provide solar cooling in hot weather. Others have designed solar systems for heating water. In the second half of the 20th century, interest in solar heating has increased considerably because of growing concern about conservation of natural resources and about increasing shortages and rising costs of fuels for heating and cooling.

Solar heating may utilize any of several methods for converting solar radiant energy into forms that may be used in buildings. The rate of delivery per square unit of horizontal surface of solar energy is called insolation. Solar cells, chemical converters that convert the radiation into electricity, and collectors of various kinds in which water, air, or other materials are heated may be utilized for converting solar energy into useful forms. Chemical converters have had no applications in architecture and solar cells, because of their cost, very few applications. However, continuing research may produce solar cells that are economically feasible.

Most solar heating systems in buildings today utilize collectors in which tubing or other channels are provided through which water or some other liquid may flow. These collectors are usually made into panels with glazing on the outside to enable radiation to enter, with a collector or absorber under the glass to trap radiation, and with insulation under the collector. Panels of this sort are placed on the roofs of buildings or in other places and oriented to receive the maximum amount of solar energy.

Water, with a liquid or substance such as ethylene glycol added if there is danger of freezing, is circulated through the collector where it is warmed by the rays of the sun. From there, the liquid is pumped to storage tanks and from them into distribution system piping to be delivered to radiators, convectors, or radiant floor heating systems. The liquid is then returned to storage and back to the collector. Many variations of such a system are possible. In some installations, in which additives such as ethylene glycol are not needed, the systems also produce hot water for bathing, dishwashing, and other purposes. In those in which antifreeze is required, heat exchangers may be installed so as to supply a separate hot-water system.

Solar collectors may also be used to heat air. Instead of piping, these systems have ductwork to carry heated air to storage, often in crushed rock or other materials with high capacities for absorbing heat. Air is blown by fans through the storage into ductwork which supplies the interiors of buildings through grilles or registers. Sometimes the heat from such storage places is used to heat water as in the system first described. Solar heating systems, in all but the warmest climates, require auxiliary heating by boilers or furnaces at times. To reduce the use of the auxiliary equipment to a minimum, various chemicals, with high capacities for heat retention, are sometimes introduced into systems, thereby often making it possible for stored solar heat to last through several cloudy winter days.

Complete solar heating systems are often quite expensive to install, when compared to systems of other types. In spite of this, many complete systems of varied types are being designed and constructed today. As the systems become more standardized and more widely used and as the technology of solar heating improves, their use may be expected to increase.

**Solar Cooling** Solar cooling systems have not been used as widely as the heating types. In general, solar cooling or air conditioning may be produced in two major ways. In the first type, solar panels are heated by the sun as in solar heating systems. Instead of circulating the heated water to heat rooms, it is used to operate an engine that in turn operates equipment, compressors, condensers, evaporators, and so on very much like a conventional air-conditioning system. In the second type, solar heat is used to operate an absorption cooler, which works like a gas refrigerator. Absorption coolers, or air-conditioning systems, may use heat from solar energy or from other sources. Absorption coolers contain refrigerant liquids which when heated vaporize. Directed into a condenser, the vapor condenses losing heat as it does so; the liquid refrigerant is then directed into an evaporator, in which it rapidly evaporates, cools, and absorbs heat from the rooms in buildings. The heated refrigerant is then pumped back into the solar collector or other heat source to repeat the process. Further research and development is being carried on in solar air conditioning and is expected to produce valuable results. Some believe this will produce a nearly perfect system that involves minimum energy uses coupled with the possibility of maximum energy collection. Others are more skeptical.

**Design** The proper design of heating, air-conditioning, and year-round air-conditioning systems is quite complex and requires a great deal of skill and knowledge. In a time of increasing shortages and prices of fuels, proper design is even more necessary than before. And the growing initial costs of such systems and the increasing amount they require out of the total budget for buildings make their proper and creative design a necessity today. Mechanical engineers, particularly those who specialize in heating, refrigeration, and air conditioning, usually design all but the simplest, packaged unit systems. They coordinate their work closely with architects, other engineers, and environmental designers to produce the best systems for the functions to be served. In the future, further improvements in heating and air conditioning may be expected.

Energy conservation calculations take into account passive solar gains in winter or losses in summer, as well as the use of natural lighting to reduce the use of electrical power. Building forms and orientation, insulation, and glazing affect the use of energy, and computer programs have been developed to assist in the complex analysis of energy-efficient buildings.

**History** Early primitive huts and tents were probably not heated at all, but in time fires were used, the smoke and gases escaping through holes in the roofs. From this rudimentary beginning was developed the fireplace which has been used in architecture ever since. With few exceptions, fireplaces were the major means of heating buildings until heating stoves were manufactured in the 17th century. Such stoves were first used in the American colonies in the following century. For further discussion on fireplaces and heating stoves, see the article entitled fireplace.

No attempt was made to provide central heating in buildings until the time of the Romans, who invented an efficient system called a hypocaust. Used for heating public baths and sometimes other buildings, hypocausts consisted of floors raised on short pillars, creating spaces through which hot air and smoke from furnaces could pass, thus heating the floors. The smoke and gases were then vented to the outside air. This was not only the first central heating system but the forerunner of radiant panel floors and ceilings of the 20th century. After the Roman era, buildings were again heated only by fireplaces, and further development of central systems ceased until the 18th century.

During the 18th and early 19th centuries, rudimentary central heating systems were developed, including a type that utilized waste steam in a factory. Also developed were gravity warm-air systems and hot-water systems with radiators. Gradually these systems were improved and stock boilers and warm-air furnaces were produced along with radiators. Artificial ventilation, using fans and other devices, was also developed. Early in the 20th century, studies began of the conditions of human comfort, eventually leading to criteria and standards for heating and air conditioning buildings. They also led to improved systems.

Natural ice and snow have been used to provide some cooling effects since the time of the Romans. In the earliest 20th century, manufactured ice, over which air was blown by fans, was used to cool motion picture houses and other buildings. The first building to be air-conditioned in the modern manner was a motion picture house in Los Angeles, completed in 1922, and the first fully air-conditioned office building was the Milam Building (1928), San Antonio, Tex., designed by George Willis. Air conditioning for buildings received its greatest impetus from the installation in Rockefeller Center, New York City, in 1932.

Before World War II, central heating had become the norm for all but the most modest houses and other buildings. After the war, air conditioning also began to have a similar wide usage. Over the years, heating and air-conditioning systems have been greatly improved in operation and efficiency and in their controls. Hot-water and steam systems are now used extensively, as are hot-air systems.

Other systems have been developed, including radiant heating, which utilizes hot water in pipes or electric coils embedded in floors, walls, or ceilings. Anther form of radiant heating utilizes baseboards, with piping or electric coils. While coal was the major fuel for heating in the 19th century, more commonly used today are fuel oil, gas, and electricity. A 20th-century heating system, called a heat pump, has had growing acceptance. Another recent development is the use of computers to control and monitor heating and air conditioning in relatively large, complex systems in buildings. Since the mid-1950s when fuel shortages started to occur, there has been considerable interest in solar heating and cooling.

**Related Articles** CLIMATE; COMPUTER; ELECTRICAL ENGINEERING; ELECTRIC POWER AND WIRING; ENERGY; ENVIRONMENTAL PROTECTION; FIREPLACE; GLASS; INSULATION, THERMAL; LIGHTING; MECHANICAL ENGINEERING; PLUMBING.

**Further Reading** McQuiston, Faye C., and Jerold D. Parker: *Heating, Ventilating and Air Conditioning—Analysis and Design*, 3rd ed., John Wiley, New York, 1988; Stein, Benjamin, and John W. Reynolds: *Mechanical and Electrical Equipment for Buildings*, 8th ed., John Wiley, New York, 1992; Szokolay, S. V.: *Solar Energy and Building*, Halsted Press, New York, 1977.

**Sources of Additional Information** American Society of Heating, Refrigerating and Air Conditioning Engineers (ASHRAE), 1791 Tullie Circle N.E., Atlanta, Ga. 30329; American Society of Mechanical Engineers (ASME), 345 E. 47th St., New York, N.Y. 10017; Plumbing, Heating and Cooling Information Bureau, 35 E. Wacker Dr., Chicago, Ill. 60601.

**HISTORY OF ARCHITECTURE** The story or record of the past of humanity as expressed in architecture, together with the understanding and explanation of the record or story. To understand and explain American architecture, it is necessary to have some understanding of that which preceded it and from which it evolved.

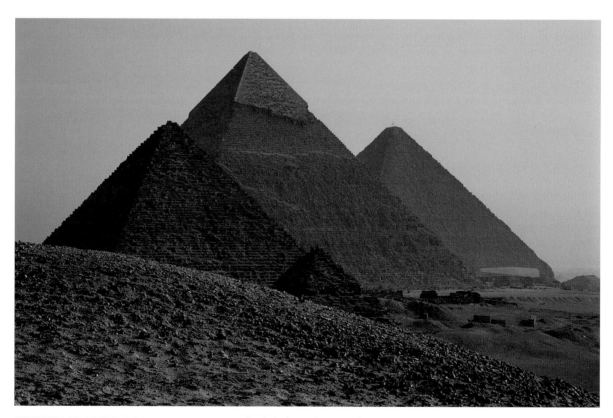

**HISTORY OF ARCHITECTURE** Egyptian, Pyramids of Chefren, Cheops, and Mykerinos (*c.* 2570–2500 B.C.), Giza, Egypt. [*Architect: unknown*]

Great architecture has been produced all over the world, including China, Japan, India, and the Islamic countries. Although it has been affected by the architecture of such countries at various times, American architecture evolved most directly and generally from that of the countries around the Mediterranean Sea and in Europe. Therefore the simplified account that follows is devoted to the direct line of evolution.

**Architectural Periods** Scholars disagree to some extent about the periods of architectural history, but for all useful purposes the major periods, starting from the earliest, may be taken to be Prehistoric, Ancient, Classical, Early Christian, Byzantine, Romanesque, Gothic, Renaissance, Baroque, Classic Revival, Gothic Revival, Eclectic, and Modern. Many of these periods may be subdivided, for example, the Renaissance into the early period, the high period, and the later period, sometimes called Mannerism. Scholars also disagree somewhat on the dates for various periods, partly because the periods do not cover the same span of years in all countries. For example, the Renaissance, which is taken to have originated in Italy about 1400 or earlier, did not spread to France until later in the 15th century and to England until the 16th.

**Prehistoric Period** Architecture may be taken to have begun in prehistoric times in the New Stone, or Neolithic, Age, starting about the 50th century B.C. or earlier. During that time, humans first left the nomadic life of wanderers and settled down to the sedentary life of villages, to domesticate their first animals and to plant their first crops. The earliest buildings were made of branches of trees, brush, mud, and other readily obtainable simple materials, constructed into rudimentary huts or tents. Remains of these early civilizations have been found in the Middle East and Egypt, but only traces of buildings. Not much is known about the progress of architecture until about the 30th century B.C., by which time advanced civilizations had been established in several places.

**Ancient Period** The major civilizations of the time were those in Mesopotamia and other areas of the Middle East, Egypt, the islands of the Aegean Sea, in particular Crete, and on the mainland of Greece in Mycenae and Tiryns. Architecture flourished in all of these civilizations, from about 3000 B.C., ending at different times.

In Mesopotamia, architecture may be divided into four major periods: the Babylonian, from the earliest times to about 1250 B.C.; the Assyrian, from about 1250 to 612 B.C.; the Neo-Babylonian, 612–539 B.C.; and the period after the conquest by Persia, 539–331 B.C. Wood and stone were used in buildings in Mesopotamia, but the major material was brick, sun-dried at first, then later burned in kilns. In the area, the two major struc-

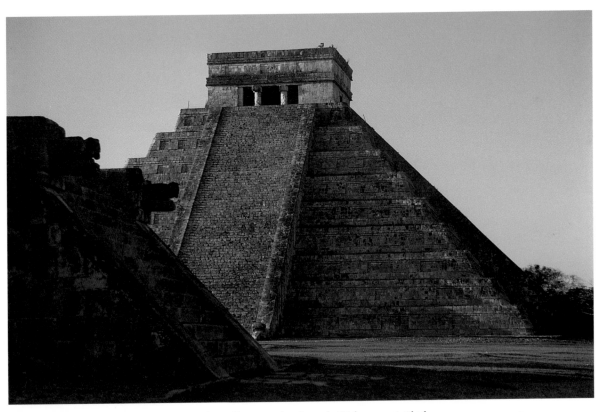

**HISTORY OF ARCHITECTURE** Mayan, El Castillo pyramid and temple (11th century), Chichen Itza, Mexico. *[Architect: unknown]*

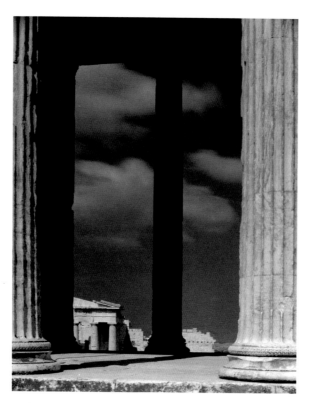

**HISTORY OF ARCHITECTURE** Greek, Parthenon (447–432 B.C.), Athens Acropolis, Greece. *[Architects: Iktinos and Kallikrates (Photo: G. E. Kidder Smith)]*

tural systems of the time were both used: the trabeated, or post and lintel system; and the arcuated, based on the principles of the arch. Thus Mesopotamian buildings were constructed with vertical and horizontal members and with arches, vaults, and domes.

Some of the important buildings, of which remains exist today, are: the Temple (*c.* 3000 B.C.), Khafaje, Iran; Ziggurat (2020 B.C.), Ur, Iraq; the city of Babylon, Iraq, first built about 2500 B.C. and rebuilt, along with the famous Hanging Gardens, by King Nebuchadnezzar II (605–563 B.C.); the Ziggurat (*c.* 1300 B.C.), near Susa, Iran, where was found the Code of King Hammurabi (18th century B.C.), the earliest legal code known, containing laws for building; the Palace (705 B.C.) of King Sargon II (722–705 B.C.), Khorsabad, Iraq; and the Palace (465 B.C.) at Persepolis, Iran.

Egyptian architecture may be taken to have begun about 3000 B.C. and to have continued until about the 1st century A.D. The history of Egyptian architecture is usually divided into three long periods covering the 30 dynasties of Egyptian rulers, or pharaohs: the Ancient Kingdom about 3000–2130 B.C., dynasties I–X; the Middle Kingdom, about 2130–1580 B.C., XI–XVII dynasties; and the New Empire, about 1580–332 B.C., dynasties XVIII–XXX. Later periods are the Ptolemaic (332–30 B.C.), named for Ptolemy (*c.* 367–268 B.C.), a

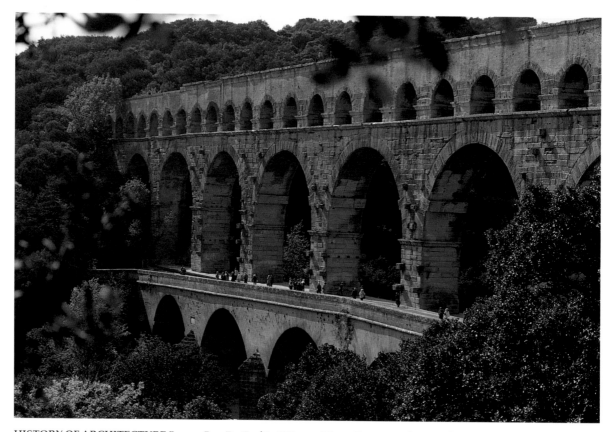

**HISTORY OF ARCHITECTURE** Roman, Pont Du Gard (*c.* 150), near Nîmes, France. *[Architect: unknown]*

general of Alexander the Great (356–323 B.C.), who ruled Egypt after Alexander's death; and the Roman period (30 B.C.–A.D. 395), when the country was ruled by Roman emperors.

Materials used in Egyptian architecture include wood, stone, and sun-dried (later kiln-dried) brick. For the most important buildings, stone was usually the major material, while the others were used for lesser structures. The mains structural system was the trabeated, post and lintel, but the arcuated system, with rudimentary arches and vaults, was sometimes employed. The Egyptians had strong beliefs in religion and in an afterlife. Their monumental architecture, massive and mysterious, reflects these beliefs, as do the many major buildings still in existence, all of which are tombs or temples.

Among the most important Egyptian buildings still in existence, at least in part, are: The Step Pyramid of Zoser (c. 2800 B.C.) and the rest of the complex of buildings at Saqqara; the Pyramids and Sphinx (c. 2700–2500 B.C.) at Giza, near Cairo; the Rock Tombs (c. 2100–1800 B.C.) at Beni Hasan; the Temple of Hatshepsut (c. 1500 B.C.), Deir-el-Bahari; the Temple of Amon (started c. 1500, completed c. 300 B.C.) and others at Karnak; the Temple of Amon (c. 1300 B.C.) at Luxor, and others; the Great Temple (c. 1300 B.C.) and others at Abu Simbel; the Temple of Horus (c. 300 B.C.) and others at Edfu; and the Temple of Isis (247 B.C.) on the island of Philae.

Aegean architecture existed from about 3000 to about 1100 B.C. and centered in the islands of that sea and on the mainland of Greece. The major materials were brick, stone, and wood and the major structural system, the post and lintel, or trabeated. Also used were rudimentary arches, vaults, and domes. The Aegean people developed a highly sophisticated architecture, often of great size and magnificence and mostly of nonreligious building types. Among the most important buildings still in existence, at least in part, are: on Crete—the Palace of Minos (completed about 1600 B.C.) at Knossos and Palace of Radamanthus (completed about 1300 B.C.) at Phaistos; the so-called Treasury of Atreus (c. 1325 B.C.), actually a tomb, and the Lion gate (c. 1250 B.C.) at Mycenae; and the Palace (c. 1300 B.C.) at Tiryns.

None of these early architectural periods influenced architecture in America to any great extent. However, they did influence the classical architecture of Greece and therefore indirectly that of America. Egyptian architecture had some influence in America, since it was one of the styles sometimes adapted by American architects, mostly in the 19th century, for the design of certain buildings, including many early prisons.

**Classical Period** The greatest influence on ancient Greek architecture was that of the Aegean, but after the end of the great Aegean period about 1100 B.C., little progress was made in architecture in Greece until about

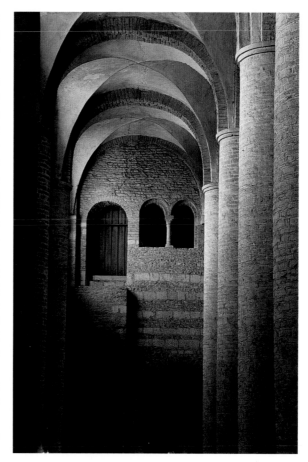

**HISTORY OF ARCHITECTURE** Romanesque, St. Philibert (1009), Tournus, France. *[Architect: unknown]*

650 B.C. This date is often taken to mark the beginning of the Golden Age, called the Hellenic period of Greek civilization. This great period is considered to have ended about 323 B.C., and was followed by the Hellenistic period which ended about 30 B.C.

The Hellenic period produced some of the greatest architecture the world has ever known, the major examples of which were religious in character. During the Hellenistic period, the quality of architectural design declined, but progress was made in the architecture of public buildings and other types and in city planning. Although the Greeks used wood, brick, and other materials, stone was the major material for important buildings. Most frequently used was the trabeated, post and lintel, structural system, but arches and vaults were used to some extent during the Hellenistic period and later.

Although the Greeks made architectural progress of many kinds, including further development of residential designs, perhaps the greatest progress was in aesthetic design refinements of monumental buildings. The Greeks not only produced buildings of excellent form and proportions but invented a system of proportions still much admired today. They also learned how to correct the forms and proportions of their buildings to

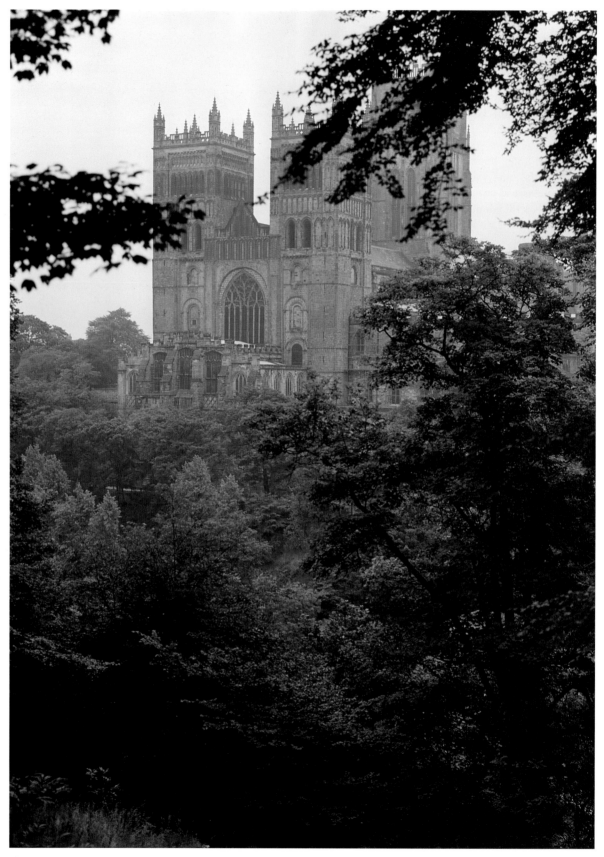

**HISTORY OF ARCHITECTURE** Norman, Durham Cathedral (1093–1133), Durham, England. *[Architect: unknown]*

**HISTORY OF ARCHITECTURE** Gothic, vaulting over choir, Cathedral (1220–54), LeMans, France. *[Architect: unknown]*

**HISTORY OF ARCHITECTURE** Chinese, Forbidden City, most existing from Ming and Ch'ing Dynasties (1368–1912), Peking (Beijing), China. Imperial Palace (1602). *[Architect: unknown]*

allow for optical distortions produced by the human eye. The Greeks also developed design systems for the columns, bases, and other elements used in their buildings. These systems, called orders, from the earliest developed and simplest in design to the latest and most ornamental, are the Doric, Ionic, and Corinthian. The orders gave the Greeks a useful system for design, but the actual appearance and proportions of the columns and other elements varied considerably from place to place, between buildings, and at different times. The Romans adapted these orders to their own uses and they were used later on, in varied forms, in Renaissance and Classic Revival architecture.

A large number of Greek buildings still exist, at least partly, not only in Greece but in many other places, including Italy and Sicily. A list of the great examples would be very long, but some of the most important are: three Temples at Paestum, Italy, the Basilica (*c.* 530 B.C.), Demeter (*c.* 510 B.C.), and Poseidon (*c.* 460 B.C.); the Treasury of the Athenians (*c.* 485 B.C.), the Theater (*c.* 510 B.C.), and other buildings at Delphi; the Choragic Monument of Lysicrates (*c.* 334) and other buildings at Athens; and the Theater (*c.* 350) at Epidaurus.

The most important architectural remains in Greece are those of the several buildings on the Acropolis in Athens, including the Erechtheion (*c.* 405 B.C.) and Propylaea (*c.* 432 B.C.) designed by Mnesicles (5th century B.C.), the Temple of Athena Nike (*c.* 427 B.C.), probably designed by Callicrates, and the crowning glory of the Acropolis, the Parthenon (*c.* 432 B.C.), designed by Kallikrates and Iktinus (both 5th century B.C.).

Traditionally, Rome has been said to have been founded by the twins Romulus and Remus in 753 B.C. At first Rome was ruled by the Etruscans, who inhabited west-central Italy. The Etruscans had a highly developed architecture that flourished from about 750 to 100 B.C. There were accomplished builders and engineers, using burned bricks, terra-cotta, and stone and are thought to have developed the first true arches. They developed a new architectural order called the Tuscan. They are also believed to have developed houses with atriums or patios.

By the start of the 3rd century B.C., the Romans were well on the way toward developing their own architecture which continued until about A.D. 365. The Romans were not great designers in the sense that the Greeks were. But they were great engineers and builders and took ideas for their architecture wherever they found them, mainly from the Middle East, the Greeks, and the Etruscans. The Romans used brick, stone, and many

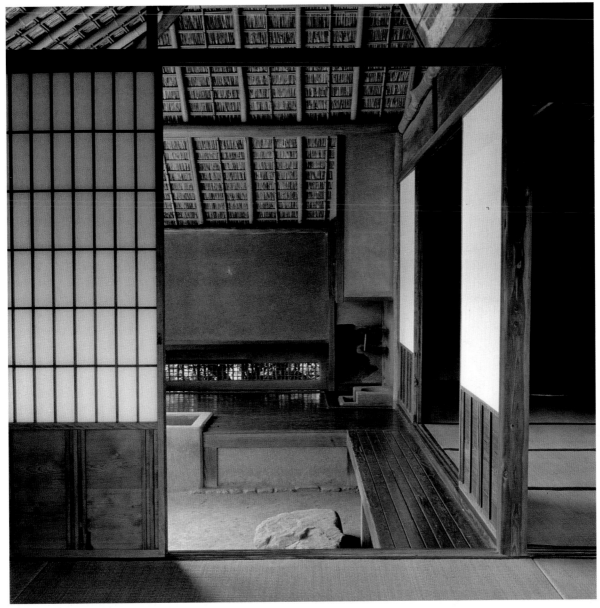

**HISTORY OF ARCHITECTURE** Japanese, Gepparo, or tearoom, Katsura Imperial Villa (1620–50), Kyoto, Japan. *[Architect: unknown (Photo: Norman F. Carver, Jr.)]*

other materials but, after a while, their favorite material was concrete, which they often veneered with stone or plastered. They were noted for the great size of their buildings and other structures and for daring engineering feats.

From the Etruscans, the Romans took the arcuated system, based on the principles of the arch, and further developed it to produce great vaults and domes. From the Greeks, they took the trabeated, or post and lintel, system, which they often combined with the arcuated. They also took the Doric, Ionic, Corinthian, and Tuscan orders, adapted them to their own ends, and elaborated upon them. One of their elaborations produced a new

order, the Composite, which has some of the attributes of the Corinthian combined with some from the Ionic.

The Romans constructed a great number of buildings and other structures in Italy and in all the countries they conquered, including France, England, Spain, Lebanon, Syria, and Germany. These included forums, temples, law and commerce buildings or basilicas, public baths, theaters, amphitheaters, palaces, houses, and other types of buildings and structures. A list of the notable examples still in existence would be quite long. Among the most important of those existing today, at least in part, are: the forums of Vespasian, Augustus, Nerva, Trajan, and Caesar, and the Forum Romanum, in Rome; temples such as Bacchus (second century B.C.), Jupiter (A.D. 10–249), and others at Baalbek, Lebanon; Portunus (31 B.C.) and Fortuna Virilis (c. 40 B.C.) in Rome; the Maison Carrée (c. 16 B.C.), Nîmes, France; the Pantheon (A.D. 124), Rome; the Basilica of Constantine (A.D. 313), sometimes called that of Maxentius, Rome; baths such as those in Rome, Caracalla (A.D. 217) and Diocletian (A.D. 302), part of which was made into the Church of Santa Maria dei Angeli in 1563 by Michelangelo (1475–1564).

Other great Roman buildings existing, at least in part, are: theaters, Marcellus (13 B.C.) in Rome and that in Orange, France (A.D. 50); amphitheaters such as the Colosseum (A.D. 82) in Rome and that in Verona, Italy, completed in A.D. 290; residences such as the Palace of Diocletian (A.D. 300) in Split, Yugoslavia, Hadrian's Villa (A.D. 124) in Tivoli, Italy, and the House of Livia (c. 55 B.C.) in Rome. The most complete groupings of Roman houses, and of other buildings and structures, exist at Pompeii and Herculaneum, Italy, both of which were covered with lava and volcanic ash by an eruption of Mount Vesuvius in 79 A.D. Both towns have been well preserved and include houses, forums, amphitheaters,

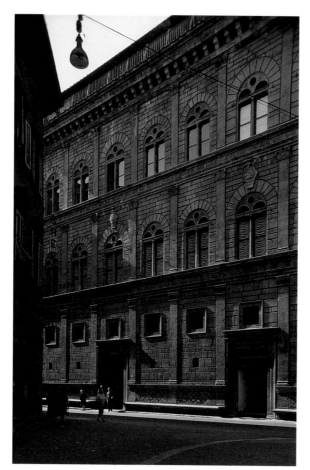

HISTORY OF ARCHITECTURE Renaissance, Palazzo Rucellai (1451), Florence, Italy. [Architect: Leon Battista Alberti]

and other buildings constructed from about the 5th century B.C. to the 1st century A.D.

The classic architecture of Greece and Rome has greatly influenced that of succeeding eras, particularly the Roman on the architecture of the Renaissance and both Roman and Greek on the Classic Revival during the 18th and 19th centuries.

**Early Christian and Byzantine Periods** Early Christian and Byzantine architecture developed side by side at the same time in history, beginning in the early 4th century. Both styles of architecture were mainly used for churches and other religious buildings. The era of Early Christian architecture is usually thought to have begun in 313, when the Roman Emperor Constantine (c. 280–337) declared Christianity to be the Roman state religion. The beginning of Byzantine architecture is taken to have been 330, when Constantine moved the capital of the Roman Empire to Byzantium, later called Constantinople and still later Istanbul, Turkey.

The major development in Early Christian architecture was the basilica church, named after the halls of justice and commerce of the Romans. Basilica churches are typically constructed of stone, with timber roof structures. The main church, or nave, is higher than the side aisles, thus making it possible for the nave section to have rows of windows, called clerestories, above the roofs of the aisle areas. Some basilica churches have post-and-lintel structural systems, some arches, and some combinations of the two types. Many of these churches are relatively simple in design. The amount of ornament varies.

Byzantine architecture took another course in church design, that of the arcuated system, mainly relying on the use of domes, the design of which the Byzantines developed into a high art. Byzantine churches were highly ornamented.

Among the important Early Christian churches are Santa Sabina (425) and Santa Maria Maggiore (432), both in Rome; Sant'Apollinare Nuovo (525) and Sant'Apollinare in Classe (539), both in Ravenna, Italy; and San Demetrius (550) in Salonika, Greece. Masterpieces of the Byzantine style include Santa Sophia (536), often called Hagia Sophia, which was converted into a mosque in 1453 and later into a museum, in Istanbul; San Vitale (547) in Ravenna; and San Marco (1085, with later additions) in Venice.

Both types of architecture have had an effect on that which came later, establishing traditions in church design some of which have come down to the present day. The end of the Byzantine era in architecture is often taken to be about 1450, or even later. The end of the Early Christian era came much earlier, with the advent of Romanesque architecture in the 9th century.

**Romanesque Period** Romanesque architecture flourished in Europe, mainly in Italy, France, Spain, Germany, and England, until about the 12th century when it was superseded by the Gothic of which it was the forerunner. Romanesque architecture was developed mainly from that of the Romans, but it was also influenced to some extent by Byzantine and other earlier types. Romanesque architecture was massive and heavy in character, utilizing stone, mostly in religious buildings, particularly in churches and cathedrals. Based on the Roman system of semicircular, or barrel, vaulting, Romanesque architecture gradually developed systems of ribs to replace the heavy groins used by the Romans where vaults crossed each other. This was the beginning of further developments to be made later in Gothic architecture.

Among the most important Romanesque buildings still in existence are: in Italy—the Church of San Miniato al Monte (1090), Florence; the Cathedral (1092), Baptistery (1278), and Campanile (1174), better known as the famous leaning tower, at Pisa; Church of San Ambrogio (1128), Milan; and Monreale Cathedral (1182), Palermo, Sicily; in France—the Church of Sainte Madeleine (1206), Vezelay; and at Caen, Saint Étienne (1086), often called Abbaye-aux-Hommes founded by William the Conqueror (1027–87) and where he is buried, and La Trinité (1140), called Abbaye-aux-Dames, and founded by William's wife, Matilda.

In Germany, notable examples are the cathedrals of Aix-la-Chapelle (Aachen, 804), established by Emperor Charlemagne (742–814) and where he is buried; Speyer (1030); Mainz (1036); and Worms (1181). In England, notable examples, sometimes called Norman in style rather than Romanesque, are Canterbury (1071–1126), Durham (1093–1133), and Peterborough (1117–93) cathedrals.

Romanesque architecture greatly influenced the Gothic that followed, having established the principles of ribbed vaulting, which were later developed to their ultimate limit in Gothic architecture. Romanesque architecture also influenced some of the architects of the 19th century, in particular Henry Hobson Richardson (1838–86), who established a revival of Romanesque principles and adapted them into designs for buildings.

**Gothic Period** Gothic architecture is thought to have started in the 12th century and to have flourished until about the 16th. Gothic architecture is arcuated, having evolved slowly from the Romanesque. The major structural change from the older type was the use of pointed arches, derived from those of Mesopotamia, instead of the round or barrel arches as in Romanesque and Roman buildings. Instead of the heavy, massive stone used in Romanesque buildings, Gothic buildings were designed with high, soaring ribbed vaults that exploit the properties of stone to their ultimate. Eventually, this resulted

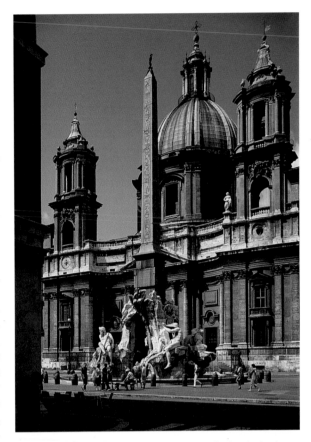

**HISTORY OF ARCHITECTURE** Baroque, S. Agnese in Agone (begun 1652), and Fountain of the Four Rivers (1651), Piazza Navona, Rome. [*Architect: Francesco Borromini; fountain sculptor: Gianlorenzo Bernini*]

in structures that, unlike the somewhat ponderous earlier Romanesque examples, seem thin, attenuated, almost lacelike. In Gothic architecture, the ribs where two vaults cross are the major structural members supporting roofs. The ribs are supported on tiers of columns.

The central portions, or naves, of churches and cathedrals are higher than the side aisles, allowing high windows to be placed over the roofs of the aisles. These windows and others are often glazed with magnificent stained glass, arranged to make patterns or to depict religious or other subjects. Stone was used with great economy in small pieces, which were accurately cut and set with thin mortar joints to form elegant and craftsmanlike building elements.

Instead of the heavy masonry buttresses used previously to resist the forces, or thrusts, of the vaults, Gothic architecture employed flying buttresses which utilized arches and piers to resist the thrusts, thereby lightening structures and making them more open.

The result is an architecture, quite unlike that of the past, composed of piers, columns, buttresses, and ribbed vaults in a structural system in which each member has been properly designed to receive and resist the thrust of others. This produced true skeleton structures, not unlike those of steel and reinforced concrete buildings today, in which the walls with their stained-glass windows were used only to enclose space rather than for structural purposes.

The crowning achievements of Gothic architecture are churches, cathedrals, and other religious buildings, of which a great number are still in existence all over Europe. Many of these required a century or more to construct and therefore various stages of the development of Gothic architecture may often be seen in a single building.

A list of significant Gothic religious buildings would be quite long. Among the most notable, still in existence, are: in France—the cathedrals of Notre Dame de Paris (1163–1250), Chartres (1194–1260), Rheims (1211–90), Amiens (1220-88), Strasbourg (1230–1365), and Rouen (1318–1515), and the church of La Sainte Chapelle (1248) in Paris; in England—the cathedrals of Winchester (1079–1235), Lincoln (1192–1320), Salisbury (1220–65), and York (1261–1324); Westminster Abbey (1055–1269), with the Chapel (1515) of King Henry VII (1407–1509), and the King's College Chapel (1519), Cambridge.

In other European countries, some examples are Saint Gudule (1220–1475), Brussels, Belgium; Antwerp Cathedral (1352–1411), the Netherlands; in Germany—the cathedrals of Cologne (1248–1880) and Ulm (1377–1492); Saint Stephen (c. 1300–1510), Vienna, Austria; Burgos Cathedral (1221–1457), Spain; and in Italy—the cathedrals of Siena (1226–1380), Milan (1385–1485), and Florence (1296–1462), the last-named designed by Arnolfo di Cambio (1232–c. 1300), with a dome added later (1434) by Filippo Brunelleschi (c. 1337–1446).

Nonreligious Gothic buildings include such types as houses, manor houses, hospitals, market halls, guild halls, forts, and castles. A number of examples are still standing, of which the following may be representative: in England—the Guildhall (c. 1529), Lavenham; Hampton Court Palace (c. 1520); and the colleges, constructed from the 12th to the 16th centuries, of Oxford and Cambridge; in France—the House of Jacques Coeur (1453), Bourges; and the Hôtel de Cluny (1498), Paris; in Italy—the Doge's Palace, Venice, started in the 9th century and completed 1550; the Palazzo Pubblico (1289–1302), Siena; and Cloth Hall (1202–1304), Ypres, Belgium.

Representative medieval forts, castles, and fortified towns still in existence include the walled city of Carcassonne (13th century), France; Caernarvon Castle (1323), Wales; the Tower of London (begun in the 11th century); Windsor Castle (begun in the 12th century),

London; Castello Nuovo (1283), Naples, Italy; and Castle Krak (1131), Jordan, built by Crusaders.

Gothic architecture deeply affected that of America in many ways. When the colonies were first founded in the New World, the Gothic was the prevailing style in England and on the continent of Europe, and thus deeply influenced the architecture of the English colonies in America. Later, American architects went back to it in the Gothic Revival style and again during the Eclectic period in architecture. The principles of stone, skeleton-framed buildings developed during the Middle Ages also contributed to the development of skeleton structural systems in iron, steel, and reinforced concrete.

**Renaissance Period** The Renaissance began in Italy in the 15th century at about the time the Middle Ages were coming to an end and spread northward to France later in that century, reaching Germany, the Netherlands, Belgium, and England in the 16th century. Turning away from the style and forms of Gothic architecture, the Renaissance adopted those of classical times, in particular the Roman, including barrel vaults and domes. Renaissance architects used all the Classic Roman orders (Tuscan, Doric, Ionic, Corinthian, and Composite) in their buildings and the first attempts to codify and standardize the orders were made by the Italian architects Andrea Palladio (1508–80) and Giacomo Barozzi da Vignola (1507–73). Their standards became those of later generations of architects, though they were not usually strictly followed.

The Renaissance was a time of great developments in architectural design, based on the old forms, but using the emerging new scientific methods in the creation of well-designed buildings. It was also a time for a return to older principles of garden and city design and to a new interest in the entire environment in which buildings exist. It was a time of ornament in and on buildings and some of the greatest buildings ever produced by collaboration of architects and artists. It was also a time when architects emerged from their former almost complete anonymity to design buildings that were constructed by others, almost in the manner of today.

The Renaissance produced a prodigious number of significant buildings, of every type imaginable, designed by a great number of talented architects. No list could do justice to the great output and to the architects who produced it. Among the greatest examples in Italy, where the period started, are the churches of San Lorenzo (1460) and San Spirito (1482) and Pazzi Chapel (1446), all by Brunelleschi; Palazzo Medici-Riccardi (1460), by Michelozzo di Bartolommeo (1396–1472); the churches of Santa Maria Novella (1470), all in Florence, and Sant'Andrea (1494), Mantua, and Palazzo Rucellai (1451), Florence, by Leon Battista Alberti (1404–72); Palazzo Strozzi (1539), Florence, by Simone Pollaiuolo

**HISTORY OF ARCHITECTURE** Baroque and Rococo, Palais de Versailles (1661–1756), Versailles, France.
*[Architects: Louis Le Vau, Jules Hardouin-Mansart, Ange-Jacques Gabriel]*

(1454–1508), known as Il Cronaca; the Tempietto (1510) by Donato Bramante (1444–1514); Palazzo Farnese (1545), Rome, by Antonio da Sangallo, the younger (1485–1546), with additions by Michelangelo Buonarroti (1475–1564), known as Michelangelo; the Villa Madama (1516), Rome, and Palazzo Pandolfini (1527), Florence, by Raphael Santi (1483–1520), known as Raphael. Many other significant examples still exist in Italy.

Beginning in the second quarter of the 16th century, Italian architects began to develop more personal styles, generally retreated from the conventional principles of design to adopt a somewhat capricious use of forms and theories. This movement has been called Mannerism and has been held by some to be similar to what they consider self-centered, idiosyncratic architecture produced by some architects today.

While there is no real agreement on the subject, Mannerism is thought to have started about 1525, in the late Renaissance, and may be first detected in the work of the great painter, sculptor, poet, and architect, Michelangelo, in his Laurentian Library (1542), Florence, later completed by another architect considered to have been Mannerist, Giorgio Vasari (1511–74), and his Medici Chapel (1532), in which are his sculptured tombs of the Medicis. Vasari also designed the Mannerist Uffizi Court (1574) in Florence and other buildings.

Other important Mannerist buildings are Palazzo Farnese (1549), Caprarola, and the churches of San Andrea (c. 1550) and Il Gesu (1584), both in Rome, by Vignola; and the Basilica (1549) and Villa Capra (1569), also known as Villa Rotonda, both in Vicenza, and the Church of San Giorgio Maggiore (not completed until 1610), by Palladio.

One of the most important of late Italian Renaissance buildings, often thought of as Mannerist, is the Basilica of Saint Peter (1506–1667) in Rome. For this great building which took more than 150 years to construct, the services of some 11 architects were required, including Bramante, Raphael, and Michelangelo.

Some of the important Renaissance buildings in France are the Chateau of Azay-le-Rideau (1527), Chateau de Blois (1524 and later), Palais de Fontainebleau (1540 and later), and the Palais de Louvre, Paris, begun in 1546 by Pierre Lescot (c. 1510–78), and, after 10 other architects, most recently modified by I. M. Pei in 1989 with the new entrance to the Louvre museum. Renaissance architecture came late to other countries in Europe and was never nearly so highly developed as it was in Italy. These countries held on to the Gothic

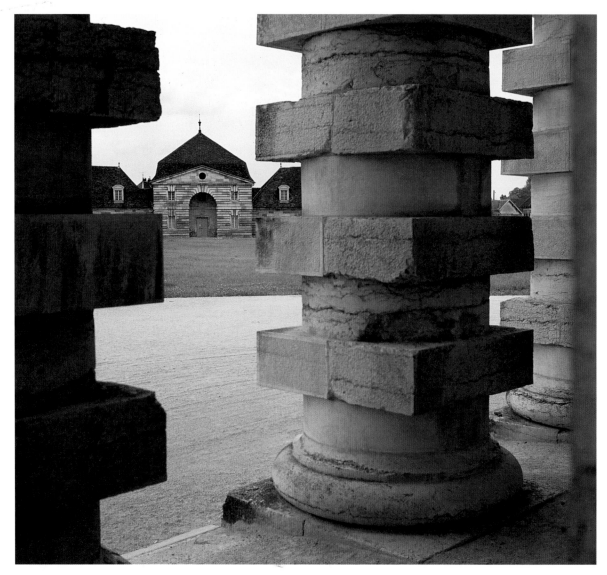

**HISTORY OF ARCHITECTURE** Classic Revival, Saltworks of Arc and Senans (1775–79), Chaux, France.
*[Architect: Claude-Nicholas Ledoux]*

style long after it had been supplanted in Italy. During the Renaissance, styles in England were usually designated by the names of the ruling monarchs at the time: thus the Elizabethan (1558–1603) for Queen Elizabeth I (1533–1603); the Jacobean (1603–25) for James I (1566–1625); the Stuart (1625–1702) for the reigns of Stuart rulers after James I; and the Georgian (1702–1830) for George I, II, III, and IV.

The Elizabethan and Jacobean styles are usually taken to coincide with the early Renaissance style in other countries and the Stuart and Georgian with late Renaissance. Elizabethan buildings include Hardwick Hall (1597), Derbyshire, by Robert Smithson (*c.* 1536–1614), and Longleat House (1580), Wiltshire, probably by the same architect. Jacobean buildings include Hatfield House (1611), Hertfordshire, and

Charlton House (1612), Kent. The Stuart era was the time of the work of one of England's great architects, Inigo Jones (1573–1652), including his Banqueting Hall (1622), Whitehall Palace, London. The towering figure of the Stuart era was Sir Christopher Wren (1632–1723), who designed more than 60 important buildings in London alone, including his magnificent Saint Paul's Cathedral (1710), London.

Renaissance architecture strongly affected that in America. The English Elizabethan, Jacobean, and Stuart styles were exported to the colonies, but never became well established on a wide scale. On the other hand, the Georgian style was the first to become deeply rooted in the architecture of the American colonies, and has been a part of American life ever since. When American architects began to move away from the Georgian style, they turned to the architecture of classical Greece and Rome to replace it, often utilizing Renaissance interpretations of those styles instead of the originals. Later in the period of Eclectic architecture, some American architects again turned to the Renaissance for inspiration.

**Baroque Period** Much of Wren's work is considered to have been in the style called Baroque, which had started in Italy early in the 17th century. Some consider the style to have started even earlier in some of the works of Michelangelo and Vignola. In any case, the Baroque style was one of great sizes, grand spaces, curved forms, complexities, rich materials, and drama.

Among the important Baroque buildings in Italy are Church of Santa Susanna (1603), Rome, by Carlos Maderna (1556–1629); churches of San Carlo alle Quattro Fontane (1641) and San Ivo della Sapienza (1650), both in Rome and by Francesco Borromini (1599–1667); and the Piazza (1667) of the Cathedral of St. Peter and the Church of Sant'Andrea al Quirinale (1670), both in Rome and by Giovanni Lorenzo Bernini (1598–1680).

Important Baroque buildings in other places include: in Paris—the Pantheon (1790), formerly the Church of Saint Geneviève, by Jacques Germain Soufflot (1713–80), where many heroes of France are buried, and the Church of Saint Louis des Invalides (1691), by Libéral Bruant (1635–97) and Jules Hardouin-Mansart (1646–1708), where Emperor Napoleon I (1769–1821) is buried.

The last phase of the Baroque, called "Rococo," is not so much a style in architecture as a method of ornamentation often utilizing seashell, rock, and scroll forms. Rococo ornament was profuse, and not always composed into an organic whole. Two important German buildings with Rococo ornament, designed by Balthasar Neumann (1687–1753), are the Kaisersaal (1744), in the Palace, Wurzburg, and the Church of Vierzehnheiligen (1772), near Banz.

In the closing years of the reign of Louis XV (d. 1774), several French visionary architects published theoretical work of considerable historical interest. One of these architects was Claude-Nicholas Ledoux (1736–1806). His last project before the revolution was the building for the saltworks in Franche-Comte (1774) near the forest of Chaux. In his book *L'Architecture Considerée sous le Rapport de l'Art, des Moeurs et de la Legislation* (1804, 1847) he expanded the saltworks into an ideal city of simplicity and grandeur based on a geometry of circles and squares without decoration.

During the period of Eclectic architecture in the United States, Baroque was one of the styles revived by American architects. However, it never became as popular as some of the other historical styles.

**American Development** In the earliest years of the colonies in America, architecture generally followed the styles of the countries in Europe from which the colonists had emigrated. Architecture in America generally lagged behind that in Europe to some extent, and was neither as large in size nor as grand in scale. There were other differences between the architecture in America and in Europe mainly due to the materials, craftsmen, and machinery available; differences in climate and social conditions; and needs for protection.

The history of architecture in America may be taken to have begun in pre-Columbian times before Europeans came to the New World. After that, the history generally parallels that of Europe, sometimes lagging behind, sometimes leading. Separate articles in this book are devoted to the various phases of American architecture. Some differences of opinion exist about American architecture historical periods. However, the subject can be covered, as in the separate articles in this book, approximately in chronological order, as follows: pre-Columbian, Colonial, Georgian, Classic Revival, Gothic Revival, Eclectic, Modern. To round out the history in America, see the article entitled contemporary architecture.

**Related Articles** ARCH; ART IN ARCHITECTURE; BOOK, ARCHITECTURAL; COLUMN; CONSTRUCTION MATERIALS; DOME; INTERIOR DESIGN; MAGAZINE, ARCHITECTURAL; PLANNING, CITY; STRUCTURE; VAULT; Various articles on American architectural periods and individual architects.

**Further Reading** Cowan, Henry J.: *Master Builders: A History of Structural and Environmental Design from Ancient Egypt to the Nineteenth Century*, reprint of the 1977 edition, Kreiger, Malabar, Fla.; Fletcher, Sir Banister: *A History of Architecture on the Comparative Method*, 18th ed., Macmillan, New York, 1975; Kostof, Spiro: *A History of Architecture: Settings and Rituals*, Oxford University Press, Inc., New York, 1985; Scully, Vincent: *Architecture: The Natural and the Manmade*, St. Martin's Press, New York, 1991; Whiffen, Marcus: *American Architecture Since 1790: A Guide to the Styles*, MIT Press, Cambridge, Mass., 1969.

**Source of Additional Information** Society of Architectural Historians, 1232 Pine St., Philadelphia, Pa. 19107.

**HOLABIRD AND ROCHE** American architectural firm. In 1883 William Holabird (1854–1923) and Martin Roche (1853–1927), American architects who had worked in the office of Major William Le Baron Jenney (1832–1907), formed a partnership in Chicago that was to last 40 years, until the death of Holabird in 1923. They became deeply involved in the movement toward functional design of tall skeleton-framed buildings, along with other architects, including Jenney, who came to be known as the Chicago school.

**Standard Forms** In their long years of practice together, they handled a very large number of commissions, consisting mostly of office and other commercial buildings. In the commercial area of Chicago alone, they did 72 major buildings. They developed the most consistent approach to the problems of tall buildings of any of the Chicago school. Attacking the problems of structure, utility, and shape of tall buildings in crowded urban areas, they developed rational methods for their design. They developed standard forms that were repeated in all their buildings with variations only to meet special problems. Thus their buildings have a family resemblance that is not always recognizable in the work of other architects. They have been criticized for both the uniformity and the lack of inventiveness of their work. Instead of allowing these characteristics to become faults, they capitalized on them by letting each succeeding design evolve from those that preceded. In the process, they achieved a consistent excellence in a great number of buildings that has seldom been equaled and never surpassed.

**Works** After some years of designing buildings that were the forerunners of their mature style, Holabird and Roche designed one that heralded the excellence to come, the Tacoma Building (1889), in Chicago. It was the first or second building to be designed with the skeleton frame supporting almost the entire exterior wall. The other was Jenney's Home Insurance Building (1885). The question of which was first has never been resolved, but the fate of both landmarks was. They were demolished in 1925 and 1927.

This was followed by the Pontiac Building (1891) in Chicago. Starting in 1894, with the construction of the Marquette Building, the firm designed a remarkable series of fine buildings in Chicago. Among the best were the Old Colony Building (1894), Gage buildings (1898), the Williams Building (1898), Crown, formerly McClurg, Building (1900), the Chicago Building (1904), the Champlain, formerly Powers, Building (1903), and the Brooks Building (1910). Their last important building together was a church with offices inside, topped by a great carillon tower and spire.

The great work of the partnership came to an end in 1923, with the death of William Holabird. Holabird's son, John Augur Holabird (1886-1945), came into the partnership and, upon the death of Martin Roche, brought in the son of another great Chicago architect, John Wellborn Root, Jr. (1887–1963), to form a successor partnership, Holabird and Root. It too became large and successful, and it is still in practice today. Firm archives are in the Chicago Historical Society's architectural collection.

**Holabird's Life** William Holabird was born on September 11, 1854, in American Union, N.Y. During his early years, he had no intention of becoming an architect. Instead he expected to have a military career and entered the U.S. Military Academy at West Point, N.Y. After two years, he resigned because he had been disciplined for aiding a sick friend. In 1875, having decided to become an architect, he went to Chicago to begin work, as a draftsman, in the office of Jenney.

In 1880 he formed a partnership with Ossian C. Simonds (d. 1931) and in 1881 brought Martin Roche, with whom he had worked in Jenney's office, into the firm which now became Holabird, Simonds and Roche. After Simonds left the firm in 1883, the name was changed to Holabird and Roche, which lasted 40 years. William Holabird died on July 19, 1923.

**Roche's Life** Martin Roche was born in Cleveland, Ohio, on August 1, 1853, and moved with his family to Chicago two years later. After a high school education, he went to work for Jenney in 1872, remaining in that office until he joined forces with Holabird in 1881. In the early years, Roche and Holabird divided the design of buildings between them, sometimes acting as codesigners on certain jobs. Roche designed the interiors for the most part. As the office grew, the partners hired other designers who worked under their direction. Martin survived Holabird by four years; he died on June 6, 1927.

**Related Articles** JENNEY, WILLIAM LE BARON; MODERN ARCHITECTURE.

**Further Reading** Blaser, Werner, ed.: *Chicago Architecture: Holabird & Root 1880–1992*, Birkhauser Verlag, Boston, 1992.

**HOOD, RAYMOND MATHEWSON** American architect (1881–1934). In 1922, when he was forty-one, Raymond Mathewson Hood burst on the architectural scene, after a life of obscurity, by winning, with John Mead Howells (1868–1959), the competition for the office building for the Chicago Tribune (1925). The design was Hood's and the resulting steel-framed skyscraper, clothed in an eclectic stone Gothic Revival exterior complete with flying buttresses, brought him worldwide renown. Though it brought its architects fame and commissions for other buildings, the Tribune Tower did not advance the art of the skyscraper design or the Modern movement in architecture, as did many of the buildings of other early Modern architects in America and Europe.

In little more than a decade, the architectural career of Raymond Hood started and ended. But it was a decade of almost unparalleled accomplishment, one that saw him develop from a provocative but largely outmoded eclectic into the leader of the New York City designers of modern skyscrapers.

**Works** Hood continued to design buildings in the eclectic manner for some time. His first tall building, in New York City, 20 stories in height, the American Radiator Building (1924), is also Gothic Revival but with more subdued forms, and ornament on the top stories is gilded.

Only five years later, again with John Mead Howells, Hood's Daily News Building (1929) became the pacesetter for tall buildings in New York City. Its simple, unadorned limestone walls are arranged in uninterrupted vertical bands from the bottom of the building to the top, expressing both the steel-skeleton structure and the essential verticality of skyscrapers. The old McGraw-Hill Building (1930) in New York City was also a pacesetter, but in this design, Hood, who always tried something new in each building design, used terra-cotta bands that are horizontal and continuous around the building.

During these years Hood played a very important role in the design of Rockefeller Center (see illustrations in article complex, architectural), for which construction began in 1931 and was not completed until 1940, some years after Hood's death. Rockefeller Center has become world famous, not only for the design of its buildings on the midtown New York City site of several blocks but for the excellence of the relationships between buildings and the open spaces between them.

Rockefeller Center was designed by an association of three architectural firms: Reinhard and Hofmeister; Corbett, Harrison and MacMurray; and Hood and Fo uilhoux. The major contributions to the design of the complex were made by Harvey Wiley Corbett (1873–1954), Wallace Kirkman Harrison (1895–1981), and Hood.

In a short time, Raymond Hood had made great progress and had accomplished a great deal. Each new building was a challenge that produced fresh design, evolving from those that preceded. If he had lived longer, Hood might have realized his seeming ability and aspiration for further evolution and accomplishment.

**Life** Raymond Mathewson Hood was born in Pawtucket, R.I., on March 2, 1881, the son of well-to-do parents. After high school, he entered Brown University in 1898, stayed two years, and then enrolled in the architectural school of Massachusetts Institute of Technology, staying two years. After leaving MIT, Hood worked as an apprentice in the office of Cram, Goodhue and Ferguson in Boston. Here he was influenced by the Gothic styles of both Ralph Adams Cram and Bertram Grosvenor Goodhue, but wanting to further his education, he stayed for only a short time.

He went to Paris, where he enrolled in the École des Beaux Arts in 1905, after having failed to be accepted on his first try in 1904. One year later, Hood was back working for Cram, Goodhue and Ferguson by midyear 1906, in their New York offices, but was fired after only a few months. He then went to Pittsburgh to work for Henry Hornbostel (1867–1961).

After much indecision, Hood went back to the Beaux Arts in 1908, and for the first time in his life seems to have committed himself to finish something he started, graduating in 1910 at age twenty-nine. After traveling for a time with his brother in Europe, Hood returned in 1911 to the Hornbostel office in Pittsburgh, this time as chief designer. He went back to New York in 1914, and set up an office with another architect, Rayne Adams. For the first years, the commissions were few and insignificant in size, mostly remodeling or alterations. Hood kept the office going by working on competitions for other architects. Hood was now more than forty years old and had not yet designed a building of any importance.

Then in June 1922, the Chicago Tribune announced an international competition for its building. A New York architect, John Mead Howells, familiar with Hood's competition work, asked him to collaborate on a design. Out of 263 designs submitted, that of Howells and Hood won the $50,000 first prize and the commission to do the building. Hood borrowed money to go to Chicago to receive the award. In 1920 Hood had married his secretary, Elsie Schmidt. When Hood returned to New York, his wife showed the check to all their many creditors.

In the years following, Hood became a very successful and influential architect. In the early 1920s, Hood

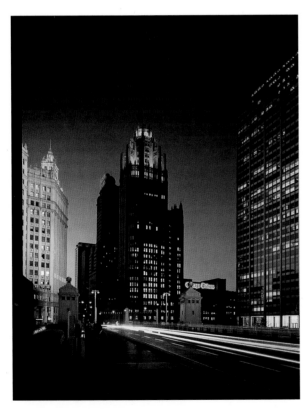

**HOOD, RAYMOND MATHEWSON** Chicago Tribune Tower (1925), Chicago, Ill. *[Architects: Hood, Fouilhoux and Howells]*

took in a French engineer, Jacques André Fouilhoux (1879–1945), as a partner and in 1924 took in Frederick Augustus Godley (1886–1961). As it turned out, Godley worked mostly on buildings of his own, rather than those of Hood, until he left the firm in 1931 to become a professor at Yale. Howells and Hood also practiced independently of each other, except for the Tribune Tower, the Daily News Building, and an apartment house.

Outside his office work, Raymond Hood pursued other interests that were almost exclusively related to architecture. He was active in the Beaux Arts Institute of Design, an organization founded by graduates of the Paris school to prepare and judge design projects of architectural students. He was also active in the Architectural League of New York, an organization of architects and artists.

Hood designed a number of other buildings, playing a key role in the Century of Progress Exposition in Chicago (1933). During the Depression, there was almost no work in the office. After almost a year of illness, Raymond Hood died on August 15, 1934, at age fifty-three. His major buildings had been done in less than 10 years. But in that short time, he had come a long way, from the Gothic eclecticism of the Tribune

Tower to the modernism of the Daily News and McGraw-Hill buildings.

**Related Articles** BEAUX ARTS, ÉCOLE DES; CRAM, GOODHUE AND FERGUSON; MODERN ARCHITECTURE.

**Further Reading** Kilham, Walter H.: *Raymond Hood, Architect—Form Through Function in the American Skyscraper*, Architectural Book Publishing Co., New York, 1973.

**HOTEL** A building in which travelers and others may obtain food and shelter, and often entertainment and other services. The forerunner of the hotel of today was the inn or colonial times. Inns were simple buildings in which travelers could find a few plainly furnished rooms, along with food and drink.

In the hotels of today, travelers find accommodations that are quite different from those of the earlier era, ranging from comfortable but somewhat utilitarian to the utmost in luxury. Rooms are larger, better furnished, better lighted, heated or cooled according to the season, and most have private bathrooms. Hotels today vary in size as they do in degree of luxury, from only a few rooms to several thousand. There is also considerable variance in the services provided. A small hotel may have a limited number of staff people, providing only the

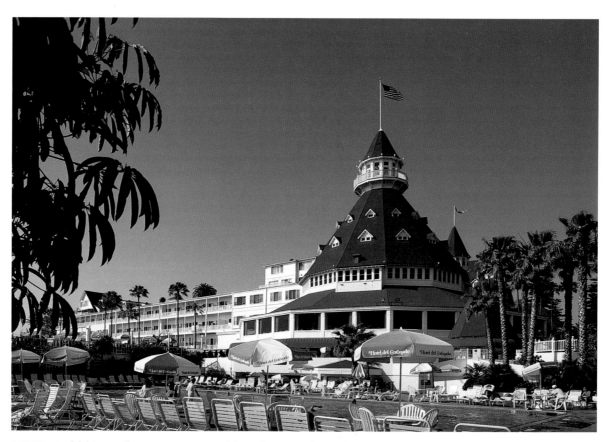

**HOTEL** Hotel del Coronado (1888), San Diego, Calif. *[Architects: Reid & Reid]*

most necessary housekeeping and maintenance work, while a very large hotel may have a staff of thousands performing a great variety of services.

In a small hotel, dining facilities may consist only of a cafeteria or limited restaurant, while a large hotel may have a number of dining facilities, ranging from relatively inexpensive coffee shops to expensive and elegant restaurants, sometimes with entertainment. Some hotels provide newsstands, flower shops, clothing shops, laundry and valet service, barber and beauty shops, and many other services for their guests. Larger hotels often have ballrooms, banquet rooms, and meeting rooms, for use by large groups of people and for conventions. Many have recreational facilities, such as swimming pools and tennis courts. Some have steam baths and saunas, and even golf courses.

**Classification** Hotels are often classified into four types: transient or commercial, motels, resort hotels, and apartment or residential hotels. A transient or commercial hotel caters to travelers who usually stay only one or a few nights. Many of the guests are business people. Others are individuals or families on a short holiday or stopping over enroute to some other place. Because of the needs of such travelers, these hotels are ordinarily located downtown in cities.

At one time a motel, then called a tourist court, was a modest building or group of cabins adjacent to a well-traveled highway which provided rudimentary lodging for travelers in much the same manner as did the earlier inns. Often poorly maintained and serviced and not very comfortable, these were replaced by better facilities that came to be known as motor courts, motor hotels, or motels. At first, motels were usually one or two stories in height, provided automobile parking near the rooms, and generally had only a few services for guests. Today the distinctions between motels and regular hotels have become blurred. Many motels are a number of stories high, with elevators, are located in cities, and provide many of the services of hotels. Motels, wherever located, continue to provide convenient parking, but now some hotels do also.

Resort hotels are located in the mountains, on the seashore, on lakes, or in other recreational areas for the use of guests on holidays or vacations. Resort hotels provide services similar to those of commercial hotels. In addition, they provide, or have nearby, facilities for golf, tennis, swimming and other water sports, horseback riding, and other activities. Resort hotels often have game rooms, television rooms, and nightclubs. Along with their commercial counterparts, many resort hotels have facilities for conventions.

Apartment or residential hotels provide permanent homes for people who prefer living in apartments but also want many of the conveniences of hotels. In an

**HOTEL** Restaurant, Arizona Biltmore (1929), Phoenix, Ariz. *[Architect: Arthur Chase McArthur; consulting architect: Frank Lloyd Wright]*

apartment hotel, residents occupy their own complete apartment units of varying sizes and receive maid and maintenance services from the hotel staff. Linens are also usually available as are public dining and other facilities. Another kind of hotel is a youth hostel. These provide simple lodgings, food services, and recreational facilities for traveling young people, usually for no more than three days at a time.

Hotels are further classified as either European or American plan. The European plan means that there is a set charge for lodging with the cost of meals extra. In the American plan, which was derived from the custom in colonial days, the set charge includes both rooms and meals. Most hotels and motels use the European plan, while some, in particular resort hotels, have the American plan or offer a choice. Many hotels and motels are owned and operated as chains by established companies, but there has been a trend in recent years toward ownership by real estate investment interests and management by hotel companies.

**Elements** The major planning elements of a hotel are the guest areas, sometimes called the front of the

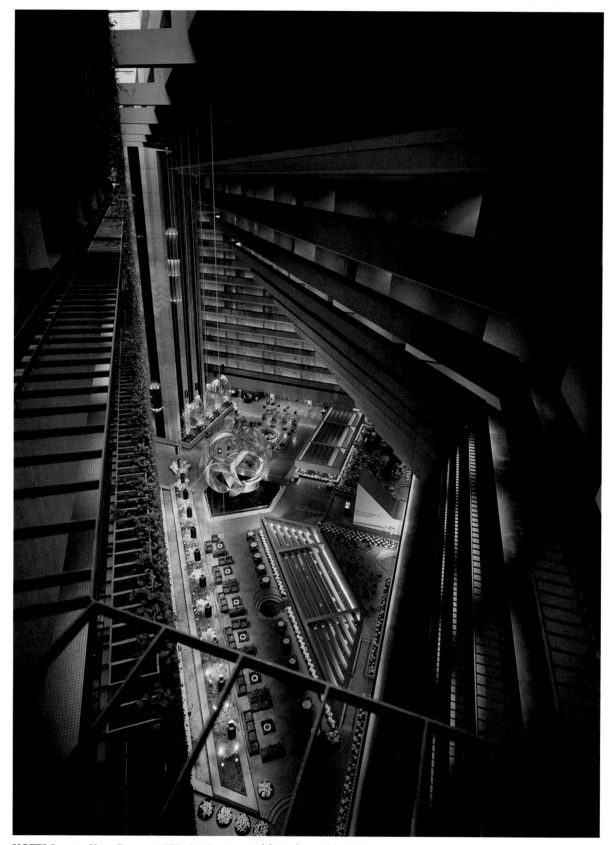

**HOTEL** Interior, Hyatt Regency (1972), San Francisco, Calif. *[Architect: John C. Portman]*

house, and the administration-service areas, sometimes called the back of the house. These major areas are kept as separate as possible. Guests experience only the guest area, while the administration-service area caters to their needs but is hidden from the guests.

The guest area of a hotel may be further subdivided into public areas and private areas. The private areas of a hotel are the guest bedrooms and baths, and often suites of two or more rooms. Public areas include the lobby; front desk, where guests register, obtain mail and keys, and pay bills; elevators and corridors; restaurants; shops; and other facilities. If convention facilities are included, they too are public areas but are often separated from public areas used by all guests. In many cities, hotels cannot provide adequate convention facilities, and in these cases convention centers replace many of the hotel functions. Few cities in the United States have sufficient hotel and convention facilities to house large numbers of visitors for major conventions.

The administration-service area of a hotel includes space for seven major types of activity: management; laundry services; food and beverage preparation and service; housekeeping services; mechanical and electrical spaces, including heating and air conditioning; maintenance areas, sometimes including carpenter and other shops; and storage for furniture, equipment, and supplies.

At one time, people went to hotels only because they needed a place to stay while traveling. They still go for that reason, but they have come to expect much more, such as comfort, a pleasant staff, a bit of luxury, good meals, and recreation. And hotels are being designed and built to satisfy these requirements.

**American Development** In the earliest times in America, travelers slept on the ground and cooked their meals over campfires. The more enterprising built crude shelters of tree branches or brought along skins or cloths that could be fashioned into tents. It soon became the custom for travelers to be invited into private houses along the way, for food, drink, shelter, and entertainment. The travelers supplied conversation and news about other places to isolated families and were in turn furnished hospitality without charge.

Early in the 17th century, public inns were established along well-traveled roads and waterways. Often called taverns or ordinaries, these inns provided meals, drink, and shelter for modest prices. About the middle of the 17th century, stagecoaches came into use, bringing with them an increase in the number of inns along the roads traveled. Toward the end of that century and the beginning of the next, the building of great toll roads, called turnpikes, flourished, creating a vast increase in stagecoach travel and in the building of inns along the

roads. The building of canals, starting in the late 18th century, and of railroads, starting in the early 19th century, brought with them the need for additional inns and eventually, hotels.

Starting in the early part of the 19th century, hotels as we now know them were built. Early examples were the Tremont House (1829) in Boston, the Astor (1836) in New York City, both designed by Isaiah Rogers (1800–69), and the St. Charles (1836) in New Orleans. In the middle of the century, with expansion of the railroads, many other hotels were built all over the country. Some were quite luxurious. During the latter part of the century and the first years of the next, the building of hotels was stimulated by new developments in steel skeleton-framed and fire-resistant structures. Some of the greatest, all now destroyed, were the old Waldorf-Astoria (1897), New York City, designed by Henry J. Hardenbergh (1847–1918); and the Great Northern (1892) by Burnham and Root, the Hyde Park (1891) by Theodore Starrett, and the Metropole (1881) by Clinton J. Warren, all three in Chicago.

Distinguished early hotels are still in existence in many cities, and some have been restored and remodeled to become urban showplaces.

In the 1920s and 1930s, there was another wave of hotel building, and after a lull of about 20 years, still another starting in the late 1950s and continuing, generally, until the present time. This has been a time for building numerous hotels and motels for the large chains. It has also produced some of the best hotels, including several Hyatt Regency Hotels, designed by John Calvin Portman, Jr. (1924– ).

**Related Articles** HOUSING; PORTMAN, JOHN CALVIN; RECREATION BUILDING; ROAD AND TRAFFIC DESIGN.

**Further Reading** Pevsner, Nikolaus: *History of Building Types*, Princeton University Press, Princeton, N.J., 1976; Rutes, W. A., and R. H. Penner: *Hotel Planning and Design*, Whitney Library of Design, an imprint of Watson-Guptill Publications, New York, 1985.

**HOUSE** A building in which people live, as an apartment house, row house, or duplex or single-family house. All these types of houses are discussed in other articles in this book except single-family houses, which comprise the type with which most people are familiar, since they live in them, or their neighbors, friends, or relatives do.

**Single-Family Houses** These houses also comprise the building type of which there is the greatest number in existence and the greatest number are built every year. In addition, single-family houses are likely to be the first building type with which an architect becomes familiar, early in the architectural school days. And

**HOUSE** Robie House (1909), Chicago, Ill. [*Architect: Frank Lloyd Wright*]

more often than not, such houses will be the building type designed first by a young architect starting out in practice. Because of this familiarity with houses, most people are apt to take their design for granted, as if the design of a house should be the simplest thing in the world.

In actuality, the design of houses is not simple. What could be more complicated than a building in which people of varied ages must live, in relatively close quarters, and perform such a great variety of functions as individuals and in small and large groups? What could be more complicated than a building in which most people spend more time than they do anywhere else during their lifetimes? What could be more complicated than a building in which people work, play, study, cook, eat, sleep, argue, fight, procreate, are born, are ill or injured, and die?

In a manner of speaking, a house is a multiuse building, incorporating many of the functions of a number of other building types. The proper design for all those functions is anything but easy. And to further complicate the situation, each family is different from any other and each individual in a family is different. It is no wonder that some of the greatest designers of houses maintain that to design houses properly, a designer should almost live with families, sharing in all their activities.

**Social Factors** In addition, other factors deeply affect the design of houses today. In the past, it was common for three generations (grandparents, parents, and children) to live in one house. Today this is very rare. In the past, a husband and wife would usually live in one house all their lives. And then the house would often be passed on to their children, who would then repeat the process. Today it is very uncommon for a husband and wife to live in one house only. People are more mobile today than in the past. Changing jobs or occupations often calls for moves from one place to another, and this might happen several times in a lifetime.

People are also more mobile, socially, today than in the past. Formerly, children tended to follow their father's vocation, often in the same places in which they grew up; today children aspire to increasingly better

**HOUSE** Exterior, Dow Residence (1941), Midland, Mich. *[Architect: Alden Dow]*

educations, followed by better jobs and higher incomes than those of their parents. And the parents, as their income increases, aspire to better houses in better locations. As a result, houses, which in the past were more or less permanent residences for their occupants, are today often transient residences for those who will eventually move on. Therefore house design must take into account both resale value and the fact that a house should be designed to fit the requirements of its occupants. Of course, a house can become so special that it is hard to find a buyer for it.

Recently, there has been a tremendous increase in the number of women working outside the home, including working wives, and in the number of women who are heads of households. This has deeply affected house design, partly because no one in these families is at home all or most of every day, and housekeeping, once the almost sole province of housewives, is now often a shared responsibility. Servants, once a fixture in the houses of the great middle class, have now become relatively rare. Whereas such households used to have live-in or daily servants, today's householders, excluding the wealthy, do without servants or have someone come in once or maybe twice a week. In some cases, these are maids working as individuals, but often the work is accomplished by cleaning service establishments.

As the hours of work for most people have decreased, a greater amount of time has been released for other activities. At one time, many thought this would produce a situation in which houses would have more use as recreation centers than before. In actuality, what has happened is a boom in recreational opportunities outside the home. Television, of course, tends to keep people home, but except for the occasional group that gathers to watch a game on TV or some other special, the use of television for recreation has been a more or less solitary occupation and has not had a great effect on house design. Perhaps the development of TV sets that can project images on walls or large screens will affect house design in the future.

**Convenience Appliances** Other factors that affect the design of houses are the great number of comfort,

319

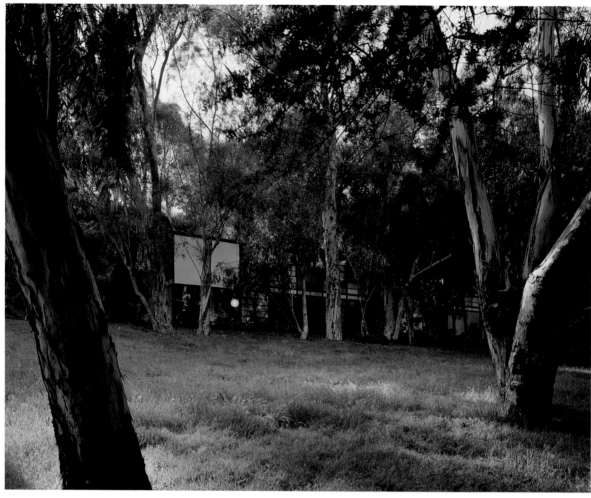

**HOUSE** Eames House (1949), Pacific Palisades, Calif. This was a revision of Case Study House No. 8, sponsored by *Arts and Architecture* magazine. *[Architects: Charles and Ray Eames]*

laborsaving, and convenience appliances available. In the past, many of these were optional, but now are considered necessities by many people. Heating and electric lighting have become standard in houses, of course, as have gas or electric stoves and ovens, sinks, and bathroom fixtures. In addition, many people would not live in a house without air conditioning and others would not want to give up automatic clothes washers and dryers, dishwashers, trash compactors, garbage disposals, food processors, electric mixers, coffee makers, microwave ovens, toasters, and a great variety of other electric appliances. Others feel they cannot get along without shower stalls, whirlpool tubs, light dimmers, stereo systems, compact disc players, videotape decks, barbecue facilities, and so on. And computers, printers, answering machines, and the TV (or sometimes several TVs) have become fixtures.

All this has resulted in another factor affecting the design of houses: the shortages and high prices of energy in the form of gas, electricity, and fuel oil. Now design-

ers must make efforts to reduce the total energy loads of houses they design and to make sure that energy will be employed sufficiently. Thus better use of materials, such as insulation, is required, and better design and orientation of houses for taking advantage of natural phenomena, such as solar and wind energy. Other factors and trends will have to be taken into account in the design of houses in the future, and those who design them will have to keep up with new developments.

**Elements** In a sense, the major elements of a house might be said to be the communal areas, those shared by family members and often guests, such as living rooms, dining rooms, playrooms, and so on, and the private areas, such as bedrooms, bathrooms, and so on. Through such consideration, some direction can be given to house design, since the shared areas have functions that are quite different from those of the more private areas. Kitchens were formerly more or less private areas in which a servant or a housewife worked, but today they have become more communal places

320

**HOUSE** Whiting Residence (1981), Sun Valley, Idaho. *[Architect: Neil Wright of Wright, Bryant & Johnson]*

where other members of the family work, eat, and entertain.

In another sense, the elements of a house might be said to consist of the following: living areas, in which individuals, families, and guests relax, talk, play games, and the like; sleeping areas, which often also double as areas for study, reading, and other pursuits; dining areas, which can be part of the living space, separate, or part of kitchens, and are used for both family dining and entertaining; bathrooms; work centers, in which meals are prepared, laundry done, and various other functions performed; storage spaces; and space for mechanical-electrical equipment. This is also a useful way to consider the design of a house.

It is, of course, entirely possible to design a house today along the lines of traditional plans, with separate rooms for the various functions, according to the needs, wishes, and financial status of those who will occupy it. Such a house might have only a living room, with a dining wing or alcove, a kitchen, and any number of bedrooms and bathrooms. This concept might be enlarged to include any or all of the following: a study, sometimes called a den; a separate dining room; pantry; breakfast room; breakfast bar in the kitchen; music room; playroom or family room; bar; laundry room; dressing rooms; servants' rooms; and so on. Such a house might have a carport, open on the sides, or a garage, for one or more automobiles. It might have porches, patios, decks, or other outdoor living areas. And it might have a swimming pool, a tennis court, a billiard room, or even a bowling alley.

**Deterrents** There are two major deterrents to the design of houses with separate rooms as in the past: the economics of house building which have driven costs very high, often beyond the means of many families, particularly young ones; and the trend toward informal living today. Because of these factors and the preferences of some people, the trend in recent times has been toward open planning.

In an open-planned house, the various spaces may no longer be separate rooms, each with four walls separating it from the other spaces, but may be organized in

**HOUSE** Forbes Residence (1991), Bloomfield Hills, Mich. *[Architect: Hugh Newell Jacobson]*

such a way that the various spaces are separated only by space dividers, low walls, planters, and other means that allow them to function together, flexibly and in a variety of ways. For example, a house might have a kitchen–work center that opens into the dining area which in turn opens into the living room, then to decks, porches, or patios, thus creating a complex of spaces in which people and their activities may flow from one space to another comfortably, easily, and flexibly. In such a complex of spaces, a person, or several, may cook meals yet continue to be part of a family gathering or social affair. In a plan of this sort, the kitchen–work center might also open into a family room or outdoor living area. In a similar manner, bedrooms may open into play or study areas that are private or shared, living rooms into libraries, and so on. The possibilities are almost endless, only dependent on the requirements of the occupants and the skill of their architects.

House design, then, is involved with understanding the needs and wishes of the occupants and their finances, relating the elements properly to each other, and provid-ing the best possible solution to the problems. The designer must make sure that if and when the time comes for the first occupants to move on, the house will attract potential buyers.

**Prefabrication** Recently, methods for reducing the costs of houses have included prefabrication, sometimes called precutting or preassembly. Prefabrication of hous-es involves construction or fabrication of the lumber and other materials that go into houses in factories rather than on the building sites. The prefabricated parts may then be assembled into components, such as whole or partial walls, often with windows and doors in place, which can be shipped to the building sites and erected. Many house components may be fabricated and pre-assembled, including tub and shower combinations, and even whole bathrooms and kitchen components. In their most complete form, prefabrication and preassembly can be used to manufacture entire houses which are then trucked to their sites and erected on previously prepared foundations. The most prevalent example of this today is manufactured housing. See the article entitled housing.

**Vacation Homes** In the past, some families maintained vacation places, sometimes very rudimentary houses, often called camps or cabins. Located in scenic spots, for example, in the mountains or on the seashore, these camps or cabins were places to get away from the everyday life at home and to rough it to an extent. People still have such places, but today the trend is toward much more elaborate vacation homes, with all or most of the comforts of primary residences. Sometimes these second, or vacation, homes are rented to vacationers at certain periods, while the owners use them at other times and during off-seasons. The design of vacation homes is very similar to that of other types, except that the emphasis is often on recreational features and easy maintenance.

**History** Shelter was of primary concern to primitive humans. Since no remains of the earliest shelters have survived, what they were like is a matter for conjecture. The first shelters were probably natural caves. Humans may then have dug their own caves, and later erected rudimentary tents made of poles and skins or huts of poles and brush, leaves, or thatch. As in houses built later, the primary considerations were the climate in which the people lived, the materials available, and the dangers present. Humans who lived in places where mud with proper characteristics existed, covered their huts of twigs or thatch with the mud which then dried to protect the interiors. In places like the Middle East, where trees

were scarce but clay was plentiful, people used sun-dried bricks for the walls of houses.

By about 4000 B.C., the lake dwellers of Europe built houses over the water on logs driven into lake bottoms. And by about 300 B.C., the Egyptians and others built sun-dried brick houses. A few hundred years later, the processes of hardening bricks in fire and glazing to make them more impervious to water were discovered.

The ancient Greeks built elaborate homes, often of stone, and usually with atriums, open courtyards or patios, in the middle. The Romans generally followed the ideas of the Greeks, but in addition to the private town house, or *domus*, developed the country house, or *villa*, and apartment, or *insula*. The Romans also introduced central heating, using hot air or water piped into houses, and were the first to use glass in windows. During the Middle Ages, house building continued and the concepts of fortified castles and walled towns were developed. In the Middle Ages, houses in town were generally built close together and often a number of families lived in one building. Also during this period, the building of half-timbered houses was begun. These buildings utilized heavy timbers with cross braces between them and with the spaces filled in with plaster, made of a mixture of clay and straw, or with brick.

During the Renaissance, an important development was the building of great palaces, most of which were

**HOUSE** Bartelt Residence (1993), Walled Lake, Mich. *[Architect: Arthur Smith (Photo: Gary Quesada/Korab Ltd.)]*

designed by architects. This started a trend toward the design of important houses by architects and the trend has persisted ever since.

**American Development** The earliest colonists in America built crude shelters very much like those of the American Indians. They dug caves in the sides of hills, dug pits in the ground and erected walls above using poles and brush or thatch, or drove logs in the ground close together and roofed them with branches, covered with thatch or grass. Gradually, the colonists started to build more permanent houses, first with wattle and daub, which utilized wattles, twigs, or other materials woven together, placed in the house frame and covered with daub, a mixture of clay or mud with straw or similar materials. In the French settlements, another method called *briquette entre poteaux*, using soft brick between timbers, was employed.

When the colonists were settled enough to build permanent homes, they turned to local materials, mostly timber and brick in the East, and brick or adobe in the Southwest. The designs of the houses followed those the colonists had known in Europe, and soon developed into styles that became known as New England Colonial, adapted from English buildings; Dutch Colonial in New York and other places settled by the Dutch, adapted from buildings in the homeland; Southern Colonial in the South, adapted to the needs and climate from English buildings; and French and Spanish Colonial, adapted from the buildings in those countries. Thus regional styles were created, derived from those of other places but changed to fit the specific requirements in America.

When the colonists began to migrate toward what later became the Western states, they built houses out of the materials they found at hand. Thus in many places, the pioneers built log cabins by laying timbers on top of each other and attaching them together at their ends for strength. When pioneers reached the great plains of the Midwest, where trees were in short supply, they often built sod houses, made from dirt, or dug caves in which to live.

As time went on, Americans built more and more elaborate houses as well as modest ones. Many of the great plantation houses of the South and the great town houses of the cities were among the best examples of architecture of their time. During the 1800s many improvements were made in houses, including heating, using iron stoves rather than only fireplaces; artificial lighting with kerosene and then with gaslights; and indoor toilets. During the early part of the 19th century, other developments that improved homes were electricity for lighting, heating, and appliances; and central heating, first with coal, then with gas or fuel oil, and finally with electricity. These were followed by air conditioning and a great variety of other types of laborsaving and convenience appliances and equipment.

A boom in house building began after the federal government established the Federal Housing Administration (FHA) in 1934 to help families who had not been eligible for loans for financial or other reasons obtain mortgage loans at reasonable interest and with reasonable monthly payments. The Depression and World War II slowed down house building almost to a halt; but after the war, a building boom swept across the country and very large numbers of houses were built. The rate of house building slowed yet again during subsequent periods, but single-family houses are still one of the most important building types.

One result of the boom in single-family house building has been that an ever-smaller percentage of smaller houses has been designed by architects. Their builders or owners make their own plans, or buy them from what are called plan services, often with unsatisfactory, even disastrous, results. The apocryphal story is that of the architect, who when told by a friend that he had designed his own house, asked if he had also removed his own appendix. Some builders and plan services have their houses designed by architects, who often make several basic designs, with variations, which assure more acceptable results and often very good designs.

**Related Articles** APARTMENT; PREFABRICATION; Articles on individual architects and firms; Articles on other individual building types.

**Periodicals** *Architectural Record,* 1221 Avenue of the Americas, New York, N.Y. 10020; *NAHB Journal of Homebuilding,* 15th and M Sts., N.W., Washington, D.C. 20005; *Professional Builder,* 5 S. Wabash Ave., Chicago, Ill. 60603.

**Source of Additional Information** National Association of Home Builders of U.S.A., 15th and M Sts., N.W., Washington, D.C. 20005.

**HOUSING** The term *housing* includes all types of human shelter, but this article is focused on subsidized housing, housing for the elderly, and manufactured housing. Changes in the makeup of the population, government policies, and funding have changed the thinking about providing housing for special social groups. This article addresses some options for housing designed for people with special needs.

**History** Housing for industrial workers began in the early 19th century in New England. In addition to the labor movement, social workers, government, and architects recognized the needs for housing long before the end of the century. Efforts to design so-called model tenements in New York dated from the 1870s. The influx of workers into the war industries during World War I resulted in the construction of temporary housing, which was demolished at the end of the war. Government-sponsored public housing started in the United States in the 1930s; the first two units were built in Greenbelt, Md., in 1936. These were two-story apart-

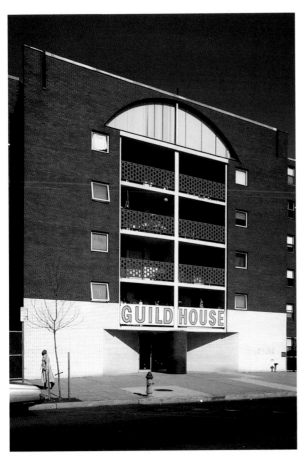

**HOUSING** Guild House, Friends Housing for the Elderly (1961), Philadelphia, Pa. [Architect: Robert Venturi]

ment buildings, built under the Public Works Administration (PWA). In all, 59 projects were built by the PWA in 36 cities before World War II. Starting in 1937, the newly created U.S. Housing Authority took up the task of providing public housing; in 1942 the work was carried on by the National Housing Agency; in 1947, by the Housing and Home Finance Agency; and since 1965, by the Department of Housing and Urban Development (HUD). Today public housing programs are administered by local housing authorities, which may build new housing, buy housing from developers, or lease housing, usually on a short-term basis. A number of government programs are aimed at enabling low-income individuals and families to afford rental housing and low-interest loans for home ownership.

**Low-Income Housing** The fastest-growing housing type is for single people living alone, now about one-quarter of all housing needs. Single-parent families represent about 12 percent of housing. It has become clear that many housing concepts of the past are no longer valid. Oscar Newman pointed out the need for housing and site security in his 1974 book *Defensible Space*. We have come to realize that putting too many people with serious problems together leads to disaster and despair.

The former decision process where developers and sponsoring agencies and their architects made decisions affecting the lives of those who had no other options is being replaced with more consumer involvement. Central planning is no longer a viable approach to housing. Separation of the rich and the poor leads to problems which are better addressed by mixing uses and social classes together.

Earlier public housing has had a spotty record, although some well-maintained low- or mid-rise housing has survived as viable housing. Subsidized housing in high-rise structures has not proven feasible, and housing experts continue to refer to the demolition of the Bruitt-Igoe high-rise buildings in St. Louis as a symbol of failure. Even a middle-class high-rise is difficult to supervise and maintain, so that high-rise living would appear to be reserved to the upper-income and elderly populations, where proper entry control and security can be afforded. High-rise apartments are difficult to integrate into an existing neighborhood. Recent efforts show that good design, without condescending to the occupants, leads to successful housing.

The history of federal funding of housing in itself has led to problems, particularly where large projects have been removed from the subsidized market by their developers who have paid off their federal loans in favor of renovation and marketing at current rates. Recent programs such as the Community Development Block Grants have allowed local governments freedom to develop housing as local needs suggest. Private nonprofit groups have taken up the cause of providing subsidized housing for special social groups. The increase in the numbers of homeless and low-income have resulted in entirely new types of housing, including shelters and transitional housing for individuals and families in crisis situations. Construction or purchase of housing units by government or a combination of nonprofit and government has provided some good prototypes of housing solutions, but the need for improving the U.S. housing

**HOUSING** Sycamore Place (1982), Columbus, Ind. [Architect: Gwathmey Siegel]

stock remains a critical problem. One successful program enabling the low-income to acquire their own housing is Habitat for Humanity, where "sweat equity" combined with no-interest loans gives the prospective home owners a true sense of ownership.

Prototypes of homeless shelters with supporting services, transitional housing, single-room occupancy housing, family housing, mixed-income developments, and retirement housing are leading the country to a better understanding of housing needs. Some of these projects combine recycled abandoned or poorly maintained buildings with new construction. There have been limited experiments in the European style cohousing, perhaps more well known as communes, where residents share dining and kitchen facilities, often with day-care centers and other facilities.

Special housing for AIDs patients reflects attempts to personalize and humanize their environment, which by association will have a beneficial design influence on all nursing home and hospital planning.

**Elderly Housing** Statistical studies indicate that about 80 percent of senior citizens remain in their own housing. Even the low-income find this preferable to homelessness or public housing, and programs for maintenance and repair of deteriorated housing are organized by volunteer groups for programs such as Christmas in April. Often existing housing can be modified for accessibility for those with special problems, and zoning laws may permit the creation of apartments in a private home or separate buildings on a house lot, sometimes called "echo housing" or "granny flats."

The elderly may be grouped by those with adequate finances and those who require subsidized facilities. As the elderly live longer, and as the post–World War II "baby boom" generation reaches retirement, the need for special facilities for the elderly becomes critical.

Approximately 5 percent of the elderly require intensive nursing care, which may be funded by Medicare or Medicaid programs. Although stays in nursing homes are frequently of short duration, some elderly require continuing care for many years. The remaining elderly seek retirement housing of varying levels of supported lifestyles. For the more physically able, retirement housing in either single-family or group units has been built. A discussion follows of manufactured housing as one option for retirement housing.

For the well-to-do, life-care facilities have been constructed with a combination of housing and related nursing facilities. The best of these allow independent living as long as health permits. For those requiring short-term hospitalization or maintenance nursing care, the life-care nursing facilities have proven effective support for the elderly. Sometimes retirement housing is near medical support facilities.

A special group are those with severe physical or mental problems, such as Alzheimer patients, who require specialized controlled living arrangements. Specialized facilities are now being built for these population groups. Another housing type for the terminally ill is called a "hospice." The Americans with Disabilities Act (ADA) has improved the accessibility of transportation and public buildings for those with physical limitations.

**Manufactured Housing** What was previously known as mobile homes is now called "manufactured housing." A manufactured house may be delivered in sections to be assembled on the site or, if small enough, may be brought on its own wheeled chassis. Widths of the fully finished units have increased to the present maximum 18 ft, and these units may be combined into housing up to 24 ft wide and almost any length. The manufacturer may provide additions such as carports, decks, and porches. Although there are zoning limitations on the location of manufactured housing, they are prevalent and, with proper site planning of large tracts, are good housing for the low-income and elderly. The advantage of low cost brings ownership to many who cannot afford other housing solutions. Since 1963, such homes are eligible for long-term financing and insurance. Both the U.S. Federal Housing Administration (FHA) and the Veterans Administration (VA) provide mortgage financing for manufactured housing.

The manufactured housing requires water, sewage disposal, and electrical power connections, as well as foundation support. Site planning is similar to normal housing developments. The layout of manufactured home communities must take into consideration setbacks from streets or adjoining properties, access to community streets, walk systems, and maneuvering for the off-loading and installation of the units. The older units require maintenance as does any other housing, and some older parks have had a poor reputation and have become eyesores. Since 1966, manufacturers must provide installation and maintenance procedure manuals to the owner. Potential damage caused by hurricanes or destruction by tornadoes has led to U.S. Department of Housing and Urban Development (HUD) regulations concerning setting, anchoring, and tie-down of manufactured housing. A model code for manufactured housing is one developed by the National Conference of States of Building Codes and Standards (NCSBCS) which includes reference to relevant standards.

**Related Articles** APARTMENT; COLLEGE AND UNIVERSITY BUILDING; DESIGN, ACCESSIBLE; FARM BUILDING; FULLER, RICHARD BUCKMINSTER; GOVERNMENT; HOSPITAL; HOTEL; HOUSE; MILITARY BUILDING; PREFABRICATION; PRISON.

**Further Reading** Newman, Oscar: *Defensible Space— Crime Prevention Through Urban Design*, Macmillan, New

York, 1974; Nolon, John, and Duo Dickenson: *Common Walls/Private Homes: Multiresidential Design,* McGraw-Hill, New York, 1990.

**Periodicals** *Architectural Record,* 1221 Avenue of the Americas, New York, N.Y. 10020; *Journal of Housing,* 2600 Virginia Avenue, N.W., Washington, D.C. 20037; *NAHB Journal of Homebuilding,* 15th and M Sts., N.W., Washington, D.C. 20005.

**Sources of Additional Information** American Association of Homes for the Aging, 1129 20th St. N.W., Washington, D.C. 20036; Manufactured Housing Institute, 1745 Jefferson Davis Highway, Suite 511, Arlington, Va. 22022; National Association of Housing and Redevelopment Officials, 1320 18th St. N.W., Washington, D.C. 20036; National Council of Aging, Inc., 600 Maryland Ave. S.E., W. Wing, Suite 100, Washington, D.C. 20024.

**HUNT, RICHARD MORRIS** American architect (1827–95). During his practice of architecture, lasting more than 40 years, Richard Morris Hunt established himself as the most influential architect of his time in the United States.

He was the first native-born American to be thoroughly trained in architecture. He was the first to establish an atelier, or studio, in which he personally taught young men to become architects. He was the pioneer of the Eclectic style in the United States, based on the principles of the École des Beaux Arts in Paris, where he had studied. He deeply affected the work of other architects, not only through his atelier but in his encouragement of students to go to Europe for training at the Beaux Arts. As a result of his early influences and those of later Beaux Arts graduates, a system of architectural education, based on Beaux Arts principles, was established in the United States during his lifetime and dominated the training of architectural students until well into the 20th century.

Hunt also wielded considerable influence on architecture in the United States through his building designs. He was an eclectic, who designed buildings in many styles for the most powerful and wealthy people in the United States. Hunt's buildings became well known, and the designs of a great many other architects were deeply influenced by them. Although Hunt designed buildings based on those of many historical periods, perhaps his most spectacular buildings were derived from French châteaus.

Hunt's influence also spread through his work for his profession. One of the founders of the American Institute of Architects, he worked very hard for that organization for many years.

**Works** During his professional career, Hunt designed a large number of buildings of many types, including

**HUNT, RICHARD MORRIS** Marble House (1892), Newport, R.I.

327

**HUNT, RICHARD MORRIS** The Breakers (1895), Newport, R.I.

apartments, libraries, art museums, and office buildings. He also designed monuments, but was perhaps most noted for the great mansions he designed in New York City, Newport, R.I., and other places for wealthy families. Among his first designs was a studio apartment building (1857) in New York City, considered to be one of the first multiple dwellings, if not the first, in the United States. He also designed several other apartment buildings, all since demolished. He designed a number of office buildings in New York City, all of them since demolished, except the Roosevelt Building (1874) and a number of town houses for members of the Astor, Vanderbilt, and other families, all gone now including the best one (1881) for William Kissam Vanderbilt (1849–1920).

The only other important buildings by Hunt remaining in New York City where he practiced and made his reputation are the Jackson Square Library (1887) and the Metropolitan Museum of Art, the central portion of which was completed before his death, with the remainder completed in 1902 by his son Richard Howland Hunt (1862–1931). The Metropolitan was the building for which Hunt himself wanted to be remembered. Also still in existence in New York City is Hunt's Vanderbilt Mausoleum (1886) in the Moravian Cemetery. And in that city is his base for the much-loved Statue of Liberty (1886), with the figure of Liberty

by the French sculptor Frédéric Auguste Bartholdi (1834–1904) and the structure of the sculpture by the French engineer Alexandre Gustave Eiffel (1832–1923), who designed the Eiffel Tower in Paris and helped design the Panama Canal. Hunt was one of the New York architects who controlled the eclectic designs of the World's Columbian Exposition (1893), Chicago, and he designed one of its most important structures, the Administration Building.

Two of Hunt's great mansions, both completed in 1895, the year of his death, still exist: The Breakers, Newport, R.I., for Cornelius Vanderbilt II (1843–99), and Biltmore, near Asheville, N.C., for George Washington Vanderbilt (1862–1914). The great landscape architect Frederick Law Olmsted (1822–1903) designed the grounds for the latter house. Biltmore is considered the most impressive of Hunt's house designs and is certainly the most ambitious. Another of his buildings, less prepossessing than the other two, was also finished in 1895, the Fogg Art Museum, Harvard University, Cambridge, Mass. The Museum was later renamed Hunt Hall, for its architect, after the building of the new Fogg Art Museum (1927), designed by Coolidge, Shepley, Bulfinch and Abbott.

Richard Morris Hunt took little heed of the changes that were beginning in architecture with the pioneering

**HUNT, RICHARD MORRIS** Biltmore (1895), near Asheville, N.C.

work of Henry Hobson Richardson (1838–86), who had been the second American at the Beaux Arts in Paris, Louis Henri Sullivan (1856–1924), Major William Le Baron Jenney (1832–1907), and other architects of the Chicago school who were laying the groundwork for what would become the modern movement in American architecture. Hunt continued designing eclectic buildings and so did his followers. Architects have continued to design in eclectic styles ever since, but the later buildings have not closely approached the great size, splendor, perfection, and scholarship of the buildings of Hunt and other early eclectics.

**Life** Richard Morris Hunt was born in Brattleboro, Vt., on October 31, 1827, into an artistic family that included his brother, the noted painter, William Morris Hunt (1824–79). As a young boy, he showed considerable artistic talent. He studied at the Boston Latin School, graduating in 1843, and then in Geneva, Switzerland.

In 1846 Hunt entered the École des Beaux Arts in Paris, the first American to go there, to study architec-

ture, painting, and sculpture simultaneously. He chose architecture as his lifework and was the first American to graduate from the Beaux Arts. He then traveled in Europe and the Middle East for two years. In 1854 he was appointed inspector of construction in Paris and worked on additions to the Louvre and the Tuileries, both of which had been under construction since the 16th century, and on other buildings.

On his return to the United States in 1855, Hunt established an architectural office in New York City, where he practiced the rest of his life, except for a few years spent in Europe in the 1860s. In 1857 Hunt established an atelier, or studio, in connection with his office, modeled after those in which the students of the École des Beaux Arts studied. In his atelier, Hunt trained a great number of young men, who were later to make their marks in architecture in the Eclectic style, based on Beaux Arts principles of design that he had learned in Paris. Among the most noted of his students were Frank Furness (1839–1912), George Browne Post (1837–1913), and William Robert Ware (1832–1915), who founded the first American architectural school at Massachusetts Institute of Technology, Cambridge, in 1868.

In 1861 Hunt married Catherine Clinton Howland and in 1862 they had a son, Richard Howland Hunt, who was educated at MIT, the École des Beaux Arts, and in his father's atelier, and who became an architect and his father's partner until the death of the elder Hunt. Another son, Joseph Howland Hunt (1870–1924), also an architect, later joined his brother in a partnership.

Early in his career, Hunt was unable to obtain commissions for important buildings, but after his trip to Europe in the 1860s he began to win numerous commissions, many for mansions for the wealthy, including the Vanderbilts, Astors, and Belmonts, but also for other important buildings. By the end of his career, Hunt was the most influential architect in the United States, successful in his practice and financially, respected by his profession and by the public.

In 1857 Hunt was one of the founders of the American Institute of Architects (AIA) under the leadership of Richard Upjohn (1802–78). Upjohn became the first president of the organization, serving for 18 years, and Hunt became the first secretary. After serving in that position for several years and also as vice president, Hunt became the third president of the AIA and served in that office from 1887 to 1890. Later, one of his students, George Browne Post, became president.

Toward the end of his life Richard Morris Hunt received a great many honors for his work in architecture, in his profession, and in education. He did not live to see the almost wholesale demolition of most of his New York buildings and many of those in other places. On the site of one of those demolished, the Lenox Library on Fifth Avenue in New York City, a monument to him was erected after his death on July 31, 1895. A more lasting monument appears on the great bronze doors he added to the masterpiece of Richard Upjohn, Trinity Church (1846), in New York City. The sculptor of the doors, Karl Theodore Francis Bitter (1867–1915), who was Hunt's friend and had executed the sculpture of the entrance of his Metropolitan Museum of Art, placed a sculpture, on the frame of the right-hand door, of the head of Hunt, complete with beret and Van Dyke beard.

**Related Articles** BEAUX ARTS, ÉCOLE DES; ECLECTIC ARCHITECTURE; EDUCATION; EXPOSITION; FURNESS, FRANK; POST, GEORGE BROWNE; UPJOHN, RICHARD.

**Further Reading** Stein, Susan: *The Architecture of Richard Morris Hunt*, University of Chicago Press, Chicago, Ill., 1986.

# I

**INSECT PROTECTION** Devices and methods used in buildings to control insects, protect building occupants from annoyance or injury caused by them, and protect building materials and components from damage or failure caused by them. While many insects, such as butterflies, are considered beneficial, many others are harmful to humans and their architecture. Houseflies, mosquitoes, and other insect pests are annoying; some bite or sting humans and animals; some carry diseases; and some damage or destroy materials. Termites and wood borers damage or destroy wood. The larvae of moths destroy certain fabrics, such as wool; silverfish damage paper, books, and other articles. Pests, other than insects, such as fungi, also harm buildings. Certain actions may be taken in the design and construction of buildings to prevent or minimize the dangers and damage caused by these pests.

Insects are small, six-legged animals, of which almost a million kinds have been classified by entomologists, zoologists who study them. Some entomologists estimate that there may be millions of insects that have not yet been identified. In any case, the kinds of insects outnumber other kinds of animals by at least 4 to 1. Of the insects identified so far, several thousand types are considered harmful, while the remaining million or so are not, and many types are beneficial. In architecture only a few types of harmful insects are of great importance, including those that bite or sting humans and animals; those that may carry disease; those that destroy furnishings, fabrics, and other interior elements; those that destroy wood structural members; and those that are just considered nuisances. In addition, harmful insects destroy plants, shrubbery, trees, and flowers. (See the article entitled garden.)

**Harmful Pests** Mosquitoes, houseflies, and other insects may carry disease, including such dangerous types as malaria, encephalitis, plague, typhoid fever, and cholera. Some insects, such as lice, fleas, bees, and wasps, inflict bites or stings, which are not only painful but in some cases cause sickness or even death. Although not insects, ticks also bite and may carry Rocky Mountain spotted fever. Some insects, including roaches and flies, spoil food. Moths and beetles eat clothing, carpets, upholstery, and other fabrics. Silverfish and some beetles destroy books and other paper items. Sometimes ants also cause problems in buildings.

**Wood Damage** A number of insects damage or destroy wood structural members and other components used in buildings. Certain types of beetles and wood wasps bore holes in unseasoned wood but not in seasoned wood. Powder-post beetles attack and destroy all wood. Carpenter ants chew holes in wood in which to make nests. Wood in contact with salt or brackish water is subject to destructive attack by various marine borers. By far the most destructive insect is the subterranean termite, which contrary to popular belief, is known to have caused great damage in wood buildings in every state of the mainland United States. Nonsubterranean termites are also very destructive in many states, including California, Arizona, New Mexico, Texas, Louisiana, Mississippi, Alabama, Florida, Georgia, and North and South Carolina.

**Pest Control** Only a few architectural methods are available for control of the more common insect pests, such as mosquitoes and houseflies. Provisions for tightly closed storage of food, clothing, and other materials eaten by insects helps considerably. Provisions for good housekeeping, minimizing dirt, spilled food, and other debris also help, as does good housekeeping practiced by the occupants of buildings. Elimination of standing water anywhere on or near building components, without cracks, crevices, or other openings through which insects may enter, is very important. This will also prevent other pests, such as mice and rats, from entering buildings. Certain electronic and other types of devices are available to trap or kill insects. In addition, building occupants often apply insecticides, or subscribe to extermination services, to control insects.

The only other important architectural device for control of common pests is woven wire cloth, usually called screening or sometimes fly screening, over all openings in buildings, including not only windows and doors but foundations and attic vents. Woven wire cloth or screening is usually made of 22-gauge wire woven to produce 12 openings per inch in each direction. The most commonly used types are made of steel or aluminum wire, but other types are available in bronze, copper, stainless steel, and other metals, and in plastics. Generally available in rolls, up to 6 ft in width and 100 ft in length, screening is ordinarily installed into metal or wood frames, often called screens or screen doors, with tacks, staples, or plastic or neoprene strips which hold the screening into slots in the frames. The least expensive types are steel, aluminum, and plastic; the most expensive are copper, bronze, and stainless steel. The cheaper types do not last as long or maintain their shape under impact as well as the expensive group.

Many beetles, borers, and wasps that attack unseasoned wood may be avoided by using only wood that has been properly seasoned. Other insects that attack dry wood may be controlled with insecticides, including types that may be used with oil on the wood. Treating lumber with preservatives can also help to control such insects. The major types of preservatives are creosote, creosote combined with coal tar, water-soluble metallic salts, and carbolic acid, generally called phenol, compounds. Although such materials may be brushed on the surfaces of wood, or the wood may be dipped in them, the most effective method is impregnating the wood with the substances under pressure, called pressure treating. While many of these materials are effective against most insects, the only effective method for marine borers requires pressure treatment with creosote and creosote–coal tar solutions. It also helps to prevent damage from insects if wood is kept completely dry or completely submerged in water.

**Termites** These insects are much more destructive and much harder to control than the other nonmarine insects. Subterranean termites live in the ground where they can obtain the moisture they need for survival. Emerging from underground colonies, they make their way to wood which they eat until it fails or crumbles. Nonsubterranean, sometimes called dry-wood, termites, found only in a narrow strip across the southern United States, do not require contact with the soil to live. They are almost as destructive as the other type but do not destroy wood as rapidly.

Control of termites requires a number of actions. Wood treatments, as outlined above, are helpful. So are well-ventilated areas around wood and screening of openings through which the insects may enter buildings. Wood must not come into contact with the ground or with moisture. Solid masonry walls, with portland cement joints, or concrete walls will bar their entry as will concrete slab floors. In some cases, properly sealed plastic is used on the ground in crawl spaces under buildings to prevent entry. All litter, particularly pieces of wood, should be removed from such spaces. And precautions should be taken to ensure that no paths are left open for the insects to reach wood members from the ground.

Poisoning of the soil under buildings and around foundations is known to provide protection for many years. Several chemicals are approved by the Environmental Protection Agency (EPA) for this use, and the cyclodienes used in typical mixtures (aldrin, chlordane, dieldrin, and heptachlor) are very long lasting. Poisoning should be considered only one factor in termite control.

In the case of subterranean termites, sheet metal guards, called termite shields, are often placed under the lowest portion, the sill, of the wood structures of buildings. Termite shields have turned-down edges to prevent the insects from reaching the wood. Termite shields are not necessarily effective against the nonsubterranean types. Treatment at regular intervals with insecticides is also recommended. If in spite of all precautions, termites enter the wood members of buildings, they must be promptly exterminated and the damaged wood replaced. Extermination can often be accomplished by fumigation with special poisons of the areas affected.

**Fungi** Although not insects, but plants, fungi can also damage and destroy various components of architecture. Whereas some fungi are beneficial, including mushrooms and the rare truffles, some, such as mold, mildew, and other decay-producing fungi, must be controlled in architecture. Fungi do not produce food for themselves by photosynthesis like most other plants, but live as parasites on living things or as saprophytes on dead organic matter. In order to damage or destroy components or objects in buildings, they need organic food sources: air, relatively warm temperatures, and adequate moisture. While some of the damage of fungi, such as the mildewing of articles placed on damp concrete floors on grade, may only be annoying, the great damage, even destruction, is of wood structures and other components of buildings.

Fungi cause wood to decay, reducing its strength and fire resistance, and eventually may cause it to fail. In order for such damage and destruction to take place, fungi must have all the conditions cited above. Wood continuously under water will not be attacked by fungi because of the lack of air. Wood that is continuously dry will not be attacked because of the absence of moisture. Even dry rot, a great destroyer of wood components in buildings, cannot occur unless the fungi that cause it have access to moisture.

Dry rot and other damage to wood from fungi can be prevented by taking proper precautions. In the first place, heartwood is more susceptible to attack than sapwood. And certain species of wood are more susceptible than others. For example, many cedars, cypress, redwood, and black walnut are quite resistant to decay caused by fungi. Almost as durable are such woods as Douglas fir, Southern yellow pine, and white oak. More susceptible are such woods as beech, birch, hemlock, hickory, maple, red oak, and spruce.

Other precautions to take against dry rot and other fungus infections of wood include pressure treatment as previously described for insect protection, adequate ventilation around wood members, and separation of wood from sources of moisture, including condensation. Proper maintenance, including periodic washing of wood or other architectural components with mildew-reducing solutions, proper painting, and so on, will also aid in preventing decay caused by fungi. If wood is attacked, the damaged portions should be replaced and the new wood properly protected to prevent recurrence.

Crawl spaces under buildings without basements should provide a minimum of 18 inches clearance under wood joists or other members. Openings in masonry or concrete walls for the ends of joists and other members should be large enough to allow adequate air space around their sides and ends. Crawl spaces should also be provided with an adequate number and sizes of screened vents for cross ventilation.

As in the protection of buildings and their occupants from other hazards, protection from insects and other pests is very important. Fungi, termites, and other pests cause great amounts of damage to buildings every year. And much of it could be avoided by proper design and construction.

**Related Articles** DOOR; FOUNDATION; GARDEN; WINDOW; WOOD; WOOD-FRAME STRUCTURE.

**Sources of Additional Information** American Institute of Timber Construction, 11818 S.E. Mill Plain Blvd., Suite 415, Vancouver, Wash. 98684; National Pest Control Assoc., 8100 Oak St., Dunn Loring, Va. 22027; U.S. Department of Agriculture, 14th St. and Independence Ave., S.W., Washington, D.C. 20250.

# INSULATION, THERMAL
Often simply called "insulation," materials used in buildings to decrease loss of heat in winter and gain of heat in summer. In architecture, the term *insulation* is also used for sound con-

trol or acoustical materials and for electrical insulation. (See articles entitled electric power and wiring; sound control.) All building materials resist the flow of heat to some extent. For example, masonry materials, such as brick, stone, and concrete, resist the flow of heat, mainly because they can absorb relatively high amounts of heat when the sun shines on them and the air is warm, store it in a heat sink, and then release it at night and when the air is cooler. When thermal insulation is spoken of today, the term usually means nonstructural materials that have the property of impeding the flow of heat, rather than storing it as in masonry.

**Kinetic Energy** Heat is a form of energy, called "kinetic," that results from the motion of molecules within various substances. The amount of kinetic energy or heat in a substance at a given time is dependent on how fast the molecules move; the faster, the more heat. Temperature, in degrees Fahrenheit (F) or Celsius (C), is dependent on how fast the molecules are moving, and is a measure of the average kinetic energy of the molecules. Heat, in British thermal units (Btus), joules (J), or kilojoules (kJ), is dependent on both the speed and the number of molecules in a substance, and is a measure of the total kinetic energy in the substance. Heat flows from a warm substance to a cool one in three ways: conduction, convection, and radiation. Conduction involves the movement of heat from molecule to molecule, as in heat that travels from a heated end of an object to the other end. Convection involves the movement of heat from one substance to a cooler one, usually in air, causing currents that rise as the air is heated. Radiation involves the movement of heat by means of waves that do not heat the intervening air, as in heat received from the sun. Heat transfer in buildings occurs in all three ways. The purpose of thermal insulation is to minimize the effects of the heat transfer.

Heat is measured in Btus, generally taken to be the amount of heat required to raise the temperature of 1 pound of water 1°F, or in joules. Heat flow, or thermal conductivity ($K$), is a measure of the amount of heat in Btus that will flow through a material 1 ft$^2$, 1 in thick with a temperature differential of 1°F between its sides, in 1 hr, or in joules per second, called watts (W). Today insulating materials are often taken to be those that have thermal conductivities of less than 0.5 Btu, or 0.5275 kJ.

Thermal conductance ($C$) is a similar measure applied to the thickness of an actual material, such as a brick or concrete block. The overall conductance ($U$) is a similar measure applied to a complete building component, such as a wall, a roof, or a floor. Resistance ($R$) is the reciprocal of conductivity or conductance ($K$, $C$, or $U$); for example, in a material with a $C$ factor of 0.5, the $R$ factor would be $1/0.5$, or 2. $R$ factors are very useful in the calculations of heat transfer, because, unlike the other values, $R$ factors of the various materials that make up a building component, a wall, for example, can be added together to determine the resistance of the entire component.

In buildings, heat losses in winter and heat gains in summer occur mainly through walls, ceilings, roofs, and floors. Glass in windows or doors is a very large source of heat loss or gain. Heat losses and gains through walls and roofs may be minimized by the provision of dead air spaces within them and by proper insulation in sufficient amounts. Heat losses and gains through glass can be minimized by reducing the number and sizes of such openings and by the use of double or multiple glazing, storm windows and doors, or heat-absorbing glass.

**Resistances** Some differences of opinion exist about the proper resistances that buildings should have today. Since the beginning of the fuel shortages in the second half of this century, many have maintained that very high resistances should be provided to minimize the use of fuels. However, many others believe that a given building should provide an interior climate that is healthy and comfortable at the minimum cost, including annual operating and fuel costs for heating and air conditioning and the original costs of the mechanical systems, the insulation, and other materials and elements used to produce thermal comfort, prorated over 10 years or more.

Resistances, sometimes referred to as desirable to produce comfortable interiors, range from 10 when the outside temperature is 30°F, to 17 when it is 0°F, to 25 when it is 30°F below zero. These resistances are necessary to produce interior wall temperatures of 68°F, which most people find comfortable in winter when air temperatures inside are about 70 to 75°F. In general, resistances of 24 for ceilings, 13 for walls, and 19 for floors over vented crawl spaces have often been considered acceptable. Some might maintain today that these $R$'s are too low in time of fuel shortages.

Resistances for materials ordinarily used today vary greatly, from about 0.0031 for 1-in-thick steel, which has little resistance to heat flow, to about 0.40 for whole face brick, to about 0.89 for window glass, to as much as 16 for some types of insulating materials. $R$-factor tables for materials, and tables of overall resistances for various types of walls, floors, roofs, and so on are widely available.

Overall resistances may also be calculated by adding the resistances of individual materials used in a wall or other building component to the resistances of air spaces within the component and the resistances of the film of air on the outside of the component and that on the inside. In a relatively common situation, such as in the walls of a wood-frame house with nominal 2 by 4 in studs, the materials might include ¾-in wood siding ($R$=1.05), building paper ($R$=0.06), ⅜-in plywood

sheathing ($R$=0.59), 3½-in glass-fiber insulation ($R$=15.75, at 30°F), and ½-in gypsum board ($R$=0.45).

In addition, for the outside surface air film in a 15 miles per hour wind, $R$=0.17; for the inside surface air film, in still air, $R$=0.68; and for the air space in the wall, $R$=0.84. The overall total resistance of this will be the sum of all the $R$'s of its components and will equal 19.59, over 80 percent of which is attributable to the insulation. With the same materials, except for nominal 2 by 6 in studs and 5½ in of glass-fiber insulation, the total $R$ would be 28.59. Both of these $R$ factors are well above the recommended figure of 13 for walls, mentioned previously. However, if the insulation were left out of this wall, the resulting $R$ would be only 4.84, well below that recommended. It should be remembered that additional insulation beyond a certain point produces diminishing returns in resisting heat flow. In the wall example above, an approximate 57 percent increase in insulation produced an approximate 46 percent increase in resistance. Further increases in insulation would produce further diminished results.

Savings in heat transmission can be accomplished by the use of insulating glass. While ordinary window glass has an $R$ of only 0.89, double glazing with a single air space has an $R$ of about 1.50, and triple glazing with two air spaces, about 2.20. Storm windows have $R$ factors of about 1.80; in addition, they help prevent wind infiltration, as does weather stripping.

**Insulation Forms** Thermal insulation for buildings comes in a number of forms: batts or blankets, usually enclosed on one or both sides with waterproof paper or other materials, in pieces or rolls; loose materials; rigid boards or sheets; reflective types; and plastic foams that may be made into boards or foamed into places in buildings.

Batts and blankets are made of mineral wool (sometimes called rock wool), glass fibers, and sometimes wood or other fibers. Loose materials include mineral wool, glass fibers, cork granules, and such materials as vermiculite and perlite which can be expanded by heating to produce trapped air pockets. Boards and sheets are made of cork, glass and other fibers, and cellular glass, sometimes called foamed glass. Reflective insulations are usually of aluminum foil, often fabricated to produce air pockets between sheets. Foamed insulations are generally of polystyrene or polyurethane plastics; the latter produces toxic gas in fires. Thermal insulating materials may be laid, nailed, blown, or foamed into place in buildings.

With the use of insulation in buildings, the problem of condensation of water vapor in the air is intensified. Water vapor acts in a manner similar to any gas and therefore very much like air. The flow is generally from warm places toward colder ones, from the interiors of buildings toward the exteriors in winter, and in the opposite direction in summer. In the winter, as warm air, laden with water vapor, moves from the interior toward the exterior, it may reach its dew point, at which it deposits condensation in the cooler insulation or exterior building components.

To counteract such conditions, vapor barriers are used in conjunction with insulation, always applied on the warm side. This means that vapor barriers should be on the inside of insulation in the winter and on the outside in summer. However, temperature differentials in winter can vary 60°F or more between outside and inside, while in summer they seldom vary more than 15°F. Thus vapor problems, in most instances, will be more serious in winter than in summer.

Vapor barriers are usually made from impervious materials, such as aluminum foil, bituminous-treated building papers, and plastics. If vapor barriers are used on the outside of insulation, they must have the capability of letting trapped vapor escape to the outside. Also walls, roofs, including spaces in attics, and other building components are often vented to the outside for the same purpose.

The use of insulation in buildings today has become a necessity in most areas of the United States, not only to provide comfort for the occupants but for reducing the initial costs of heating and air-conditioning systems and for lower operating costs and conservation of fuels. Insulation is widely used for piping and ducts. Efficient insulating materials are available as well as information on design and installation.

**History** Thermal insulation of the types used today did not exist during earlier periods of architecture. The masonry buildings of the past, with thick walls, resisted the inflow of heat in the summer and its loss in the winter. Windows and other openings were relatively small and contributed little to heat flow. To keep warm in winter in colder climates, people huddled around fires and stoves and wore heavy clothing indoors. In warmer climates, during the heat of the day in summer, people stopped work or other activities, for siestas. Also, since heating was relatively primitive, there was little need for efficient insulation.

Beginning in the 19th century came the development of better heating systems and of skeleton-framed walls that did not depend on thick masonry for structural strength. Thermal insulation was needed to allow the thin walls to resist heat flow as had the masonry walls of the past, but nothing much was done about the problem until after 1920. Then people began to wear lighter clothing indoors and to expect, at the same time, an increased degree of comfort. The advent of air conditioning increased the requirements for insulation and thin curtain walls further increased them, as have the fuel shortages of the 20th century.

In the 20th century, many new types of thermal insulation materials have been developed, including glass fibers, first produced in 1908 but not commercially until 1938, expanded minerals such as vermiculite and perlite, aluminum foil, and foamed plastics.

**Related Articles** CLIMATE; ELECTRIC POWER AND WIRING; ENERGY; HEATING, VENTILATING, AND AIR CONDITIONING; SOUND CONTROL; WATERPROOFING; WEATHER PROTECTION.

**Further Reading** *ASHRAE Handbook of Fundamentals,* American Society of Heating, Refrigerating and Air-Conditioning Engineers, Inc., Atlanta, Ga., 1985; Turner, W. C., and J. F. Malloy: *Thermal Insulation Handbook,* McGraw-Hill, New York, and Robert E. Krieger Publishing, Malabar, Fla., 1981.

**Sources of Additional Information** American Hardboard Association, 520 N. Hicks Rd., Palantine, Ill. 60067; American Society of Heating, Refrigerating and Air-Conditioning Engineers (ASHRAE), 1791 Tullie Circle, N.E., Atlanta, Ga. 30329.

**INTERIOR DESIGN** The process of developing concepts of the finishes, furniture, and furnishings to go into the interiors of buildings and individual rooms. People who program, plan, design, and execute interiors of buildings are called interior designers, a title that only came into wide usage after World War II. Formerly, interior designers were called interior decorators, as some still are today, a title that had been in use since the 19th century.

Before the latter half of the 19th century, interiors were usually designed by architects, cabinetmakers, or furniture designers, though some evidence exists of designs by others, including amateurs. Interior design, though it was not called that at the time, was the first design field in which women became prominent, dating back at least to the time, in France, of Jeanne Antoinette Poisson (1721–64), better known as Madame de Pompadour, mistress of Louis XV (1710–74), and of Marie Antoinette (1775–93), wife of Louis XVI (1754–93), who wielded considerable influence over the interior design of buildings for the nobility and royalty. The influence of women on interiors has remained strong since that time.

**Classification** Interior designers today may be classified into two major categories. First, there are the professionals who design interiors for fees, as architects usually design buildings, and who, though they may select and purchase furniture and furnishings for their clients, do so on a professional fee basis. Second are the commercial interior designers, often called decorators even today, who work for or own commercial firms, in which profits on the sale of furniture and furnishings are often paramount, with those for design services either

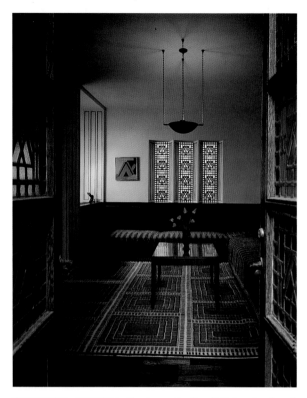

**INTERIOR DESIGN** Saarinen Studio (1930), Cranbrook Academy, Bloomfield Hills, Mich. *[Architect: Eliel Saarinen]*

nominal or absorbed by the firms in order to make sales. Interior-design operations of the first type are usually carried on by interior design departments of architectural firms, by independent professionals, and in some cases by subsidiaries or departments of commercial furniture or other firms. Independent interior designers often work with architects, but in other cases compete with them for work. Interior design operations of the second type are often found in department stores, furniture stores, home furnishings stores, and in smaller retail operations owned and operated by designers.

**Services** Most interior design operations offer a variety of services, including design and planning of interior layouts; design of walls, ceilings, and other interior elements; color coordination; design or selection of built-in elements such as bookcases, cabinetwork, and the like; selection of movable furniture, carpets, curtains, and other items for interior use; selection of wall coverings, flooring, lighting, and the like; purchase of items for clients; and administration of the construction work, including inspection to ensure that it is performed properly. Interior designers usually handle the design of interiors for buildings of all types, including houses, offices, banks, theaters, and schools. A few specialize in one type, such as offices, or a few types.

**Space Planning** A special type of interior work, closely related to interior design, is called space plan-

ning. By this is meant the activities involved, in an office building, for example, in the analysis of operational needs, flow of people from one department or office to others, flow of paperwork between various offices and departments, space requirements, and so on. This process goes much deeper into the organizations and operations of offices than do the usual procedures of interior design. However, the programs and schedules prepared by space planning may then be translated into interior designs.

**Open Planning** A relatively new type of interior design, often used in office buildings but adaptable to other types, is open planning, or in office work, office landscaping. Open planning was first espoused by early modern architects, such as Frank Lloyd Wright (1867–1959), in their house designs. Instead of placing four walls around every room, thus effectively cutting each off from the others, they designed spaces that had no walls on some sides, spaces that flowed into each other so that people could move easily from living areas to dining to cooking and to outside spaces.

In the newer concept of office landscaping, there are no interior walls, or almost none, thus creating an open space in which divisions between activities are accomplished by placement of special furniture: space dividers, planting, and other partial barriers which do not rise to the ceilings. For some functions, such as those that are similar or closely related, the concept seems to work very well. For others, for example, those in which one occupation that is noisy and outgoing is placed next to one that is quiet and introspective, the concept works very poorly. Whole systems of furniture, space dividers, and other elements for open office planning are available.

Although the processes involved in interior design may vary considerably, they are somewhat similar to those in architectural services. Generally, the phases include programming; space planning; design; preparation of procurement documents, working drawings, and specifications; and construction, including administration, inspection, and actual procurement of items of furniture and furnishings.

For people who are motivated toward creative work that is also functional, work that requires taste and professionalism and which also results in tangible results that are actually constructed, a career in the field of interior design can be very gratifying. Interior designers are motivated by much the same things that motivate architects. Yet their work is usually on a smaller scale, and often more concerned with the fine details of arts and crafts than that of architects. In other ways, interior design is very much like architecture. As is necessary for architects, interior designers must work with people, manage offices, study and analyze problems, prepare programs for their solutions, design interiors, make construction documents such as working drawings and specifications, and administer the construction process.

**Education** Preparation for higher education in interior design begins with a broad preparatory course in secondary school, including sciences, mathematics, social sciences, and humanities. Drawing and other art courses, if they are highly creative, may be helpful, but otherwise should be avoided. In a college or university or one of the specialized schools of interior design, the course consists of four years, sometimes less, of general college courses, together with others in design, history of art and architecture, interior design, sketching and rendering, drafting, lighting design, construction materials, furniture, furnishings, color, and so on.

Today three to four years of practical experience in the office of a professional interior designer is recommended after graduation, before an interior designer starts an independent practice. Another avenue for those who want to become professional interior designers is a two-year, general college course, followed by three years in a specialized school of interior design and three to four years of experience. After completion of such requirements, a person should have become fully qualified as an interior designer, and to become a member of the professional association, the American Society of Interior Designers (ASID), must then subscribe to the ethics of the organization. ASID was founded in 1931, but only in 1961 did it drop the name Decorators from its title and add Interior Designers.

**History** Interior design, though it was not called that until the 20th century, was practiced from the earliest times when humans first furnished their caves and decorated them with painted and sculptured walls. The ancient Egyptians, Greeks, and other Middle Eastern and Mediterranean people decorated the interiors of their houses and other buildings, often in elaborate styles. This practice was continued by the Romans.

During the early Middle Ages, interiors of buildings were mostly simple, utilizing hangings and furniture that was usually made of heavy oak, unadorned or decorated with paint. Very few early Gothic pieces of furniture or other interior furnishings have been preserved. Later, furniture and furnishings were given more attention and resulted in better designs, including those for tapestries, hangings woven with yarns of different colors to form pictures or designs. Tapestry weaving was highly developed in the Middle Ages, particularly in France, and a number of fine examples are still in existence, including *The Lady and the Unicorn* in the Cluny Museum, Paris; the *Burgundian Sacraments*, in the Metropolitan Museum of Art; and *The Hunt of the Unicorn*, in the Cloisters, a branch of the Metropolitan, both in New York City.

During the Renaissance, the art of tapestry making was further developed in Brussels, Belgium, and in Paris by the Gobelin family after 1663. The arts of furniture and interior design were also highly developed during the Renaissance period and the years immediately following. Italian designs were mostly derived from classical Greece and Rome, and designs in France and England, from the Italians. At this time, walnut came into use for furniture, partly replacing oak which had been widely used previously. Very few examples of Renaissance furniture and furnishings, other than tapestries and a few minor pieces, have survived and these are hard to authenticate.

By about the end of the Renaissance period, interior design was profoundly affected by a succession of styles, some of which lasted only a short time, and most of which were different in various countries. Some of these interior styles took their names from the architectural styles of the day, others from furniture styles, still others from various influences. Italian leadership in interior and furniture design began to wane, and was replaced by that of other countries, including France and England.

**French Styles** In France, at first the styles were named for the kings in whose reigns they occurred. Thus there was the Louis Quatorze style (1643–1715), named for Louis XIV (1638–1715); the Louis Quinze style

**INTERIOR DESIGN** "The Modern Room" (1935), Edsel B. Ford House, Grosse Pointe Shores, Mich. *[Architect: Albert Kahn; interior designer: Walter Dorwin Teague]*

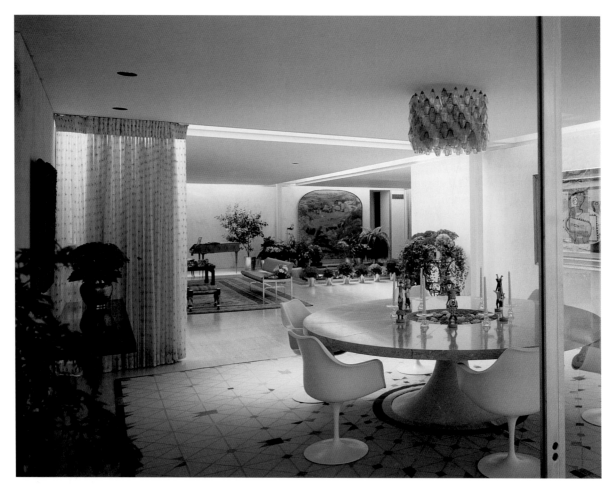

**INTERIOR DESIGN** Interior, private residence (1957), Indiana. *[Architects: Eero Saarinen with Alexander Girard]*

(1715–74), named for Louis XV (1710–74); and the Louis Seize style (1774–94), named for Louis XVI (1754–93). During the Louis XIV period, interiors and furniture and furnishings were based on classical designs and were very formal. During the Louis XV period, designs were still classical but were lighter, more delicate, more ornamented, and were done with more gaiety. During the Louis XVI period, designs were much more simple and subdued than before.

The succeeding styles in furniture and interiors included the Directoire, named for the Directory, the five men who ruled France (1795–99) after the overthrow of Louis XVI in 1792. This style was even more simplified and subdued than the one it superseded. The next great style was the Empire, named for the reign (1804–14) of Emperor Napoleon I, the title assumed by Napoléon Bonaparte (1769–1821), who had been First Consul in the Consulate, which took over the rule of France (1799–1804). The Empire style returned to grand forms in interiors and furniture, based on those of Imperial Rome, and lasted until about 1840. Later, a

Second Empire style (1852–70) was developed, but it was very heavy and often incongruous, unlike the style it tried to emulate.

**English Styles** In England, beginning with the Renaissance, furniture and interior styles took their names from the architecture of the periods. And the architectural styles were named for the reigning monarchs. The earliest was the Elizabethan style (1558–1603), named for Elizabeth I (1533–1603). This was a transition style between that of the Gothic in the Middle Ages and that of the Renaissance. Next came the Jacobean style (1603–25), named for James I (1566–1625), Jacob being an ancient form of the name James. This style was more in the spirit of the Renaissance and used forms derived from that period.

Next came the Stuart style (1625–1702), named for the Stuart rulers of England, not including James I. The Stuart style was predominant in England during the time of Charles I (1600–49), who was beheaded, through the Commonwealth (1649–60), when the country was ruled by Oliver Cromwell (1599–1658), and

**INTERIOR DESIGN** Law offices for Jaffe Snyder (1988), Detroit, Mich. *[Architects: Newman & Smith (Photo: Gary Quesada/Korab Ltd)]*

through the reigns of Charles II (1630–85) and James II (1633–1701); it ended in 1702, with the death of William III (1650–1702), who had reigned jointly with Mary II (1662–94). Architecture and interior design during the William and Mary era is sometimes called by that name. The Stuart style saw the development of great English Renaissance interiors and furniture as well as architecture.

The next style was the Georgian (1702–1830), named for the Hanoverian kings of England, George I (1660–1727), George II (1683–1760), George III (1738–1820), and George IV (1762–1830). Sometimes other names are used for styles in certain portions of this period; Queen Anne in the period (1702–14), when Anne (1665–1714) reigned, and Regency for the period 1811–20, when the Prince of Wales, later George IV, ruled as regent while George III was mentally and physically unable to reign. The Georgian style was based on concepts of design from the Renaissance, particularly in Italy. The style was predicated on rules of design, many of which were developed by English architects and other

designers from the books of an Italian Renaissance architect, Andrea Palladio (1518–80).

Later styles in England are sometimes called by the names of the architects or cabinetmakers who predominated in interior and furniture design at the time. Thus the graceful, ornate style of cabinetmaker Thomas Chippendale (*c.* 1718–79) and of his son Thomas (d. 1822) is often called the Chippendale style, while the delicate style of cabinetmaker George Hepplewhite (d. 1786) is often called the Hepplewhite style. These men were the greatest furniture designers and makers of their time and examples of their work are very much admired today.

Perhaps even more influential, certainly in interior design if not in furniture design, were the brothers Adam, who were architects, interior designers, and furniture designers. Of the four brothers, Robert (1728–92) and James (1730–94) were the most talented. They deeply influenced architectural and interior design, not only in England but in America as well, with their light, decorative designs. Another Englishman was Thomas Sheraton

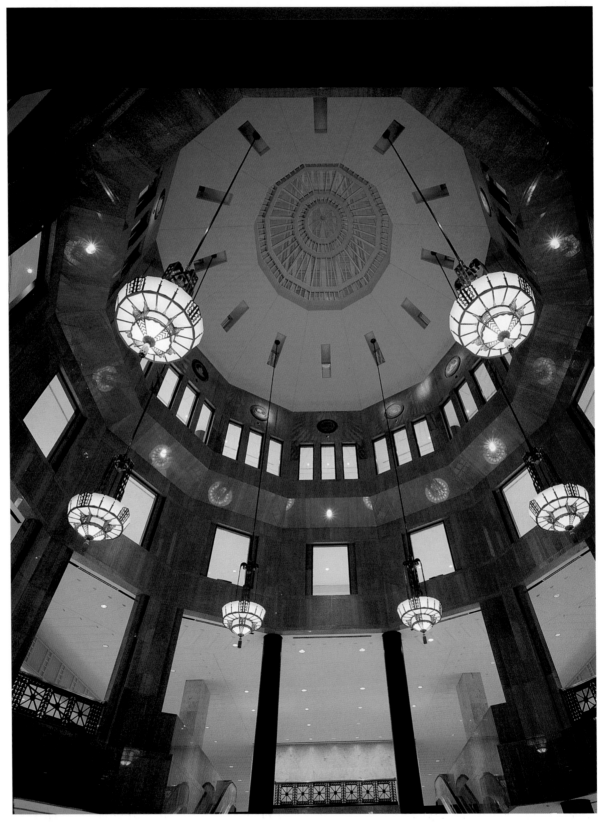

**INTERIOR DESIGN** Norwest Bank (1989), Minneapolis, Minn. *[Architect: Cesar Pelli (Christian M. Korab)]*

(1751–1806), who was strictly a furniture designer and who published widely admired books of his designs.

**American Development** In the earliest days in colonial America, interior design was almost nonexistent, the settlers using what little furniture and furnishings they had brought from home and later supplementing these with crude items made from native woods, pewter, and homespun fabrics. Early American homes were smaller than many of those in Europe, and the furniture the colonists made was usually smaller than the European prototypes. Since colonial architecture, for some time, usually reflected that of the buildings the colonists had known in Europe, so did interiors.

In New England the architecture, including interiors, was adapted from that in England and became known as New England Colonial. In the English Southern colonies, the source of inspiration was the same, but buildings and interiors were modified to meet the special requirements of the climate and for other purposes. In New York and other places settled by the Dutch, Dutch Colonial became the style, as did French Colonial and Spanish Colonial in places settled by people from France and Spain. Interiors in New England houses in the early days often had white or off-white walls, with colorfully patterned carpets and curtains. Furniture was simple and only a few pieces were used in rooms. On the other hand, in the South, much of which was settled by more affluent people, houses were larger and more splendid and were often furnished, at least partly, with furniture and furnishings imported from England.

The earliest furniture made in the English colonies in America was based on the Jacobean style, prevalent in the home country at the time of the earliest colonization. In America the style came later than in England, about 1650, and lasted until about 1670. Subsequent furniture and interior designs generally followed those popular in England, but they also ordinarily came to America later. Certain phases of the Stuart era were popular in America, such as the William and Mary style in the 18th century, and of the Georgian era such as the Queen Anne style, which became popular in America after the death of the queen and remained so at least until the middle of the 18th century.

The Chippendale style reached America about the middle of the 18th century. Fine furniture derived from it was made by American craftsmen, particularly in Philadelphia, in what came to be called American Chippendale. After this, the style of the brothers Adam became widely accepted in American architecture, including interiors, mainly because of the books they wrote about it; the Adam style never caught on in furniture in America because the brothers Adam did not publish their furniture designs. As had happened with

**INTERIOR DESIGN** Harvey's Place office (1992), Southfield, Mich. *[Designer: Alan Deal]*

Chippendale, the Hepplewhite style came to America in the late 1700s, after the Revolution, and was closely followed by the Sheraton style. Hepplewhite furniture was forceful and original, while the Sheraton was delicate and eclectic, based on the work of other men, including not only Hepplewhite but Chippendale and the brothers Adam. Many other styles were imported to America in the 19th century, including the French Directoire and Empire styles.

However, the greatest influences on American interiors in the late colonial period, and afterward, came from architects, many of whom were cabinetmakers and craftsmen, the others having studied the architecture of interiors in books. Also of great importance were the American cabinetmakers who designed furniture. Often using mahogany or walnut, such craftsmen were to be found in every colony. Some of the best were John Goddard (1724–85) of Dartmouth, Mass.; William Savery (1721–87) of Philadelphia; and the man usually considered the greatest craftsman Scottish-American Duncan Phyfe (1768–1854) of New York City. Phyfe produced furniture based on the ideas of Sheraton, but sometimes his work is referred to as the Phyfe style, rather than American Sheraton.

During the latter part of the 19th century and continuing to some extent in houses to the present, archi-

**INTERIOR DESIGN** Apartment interior, 880 Lake Shore Apartments (1993), Chicago, Ill. *[Designer: Krueck and Sexton (Photo: Marco Lorenzetti, Korab/Hedrich-Blessing)]*

tects designed buildings in a variety of eclectic styles based on those of the past. Interior design has generally followed the lead of architecture in these buildings, but in some cases has been eclectic even when the architecture was not. Thus there have been Classic Revival, Gothic Revival, Renaissance Revival, and almost every other imaginable revival in both architectural and interior design.

There have also been many fads, inspired by one thing or another. These have included a vast potpourri of styles, some more long lived than others, such as the Victorian style, named for Queen Victoria (1819–1901) of England; the Eastlake style, named for Sir Charles Lock Eastlake (1793–1865), an English painter and critic; the General Grant style, named for Ulysses Simpson Grant (1822–85), Civil War general and later president of the United States; and the Arts and Crafts Movement, espoused by interior and furniture designer William Morris (1834–96), who designed the Morris chair. All were interesting but derivative, and none contributed much to the future development of architectural or interior design. One of the most interesting fads was the Steamboat Gothic style, utilizing the elaborate ornament of river steamboats in buildings, some of which were thousands of miles from a river.

Also part of American architectural design, including interiors, of the late 19th and 20th centuries, was a vast outpouring of styles based on very exotic places and times that were far away and long ago. Thus buildings and their interiors were designed in styles based on the Romanesque, Gothic, Classic, and other eras in Greece, Rome, Egypt, France, Italy, Spain, England, Germany, and almost everywhere else, including Japan, China, India, and other countries.

Beginning in the latter half of the 19th century, American architects and those of other countries began to develop a type of architecture, including interior design, which has come to be called modern architecture. Led by Major William Le Baron Jenney (1832–1907) and other architects of what is often called the Chicago school of design, they turned away from designs based on those from the past toward architecture that was expressive of the time in which it was created. Although some of the earliest modern architects were not deeply involved in interior design, those who came a bit later, including Louis Henri Sullivan (1856–1924) and Frank Lloyd Wright, began to consider the design of interiors as integral parts of their buildings.

Wright, together with other young architects in the early 20th century, often designed the complete interiors of their buildings, including in some cases furniture and other furnishings. This practice has been continued to some extent today. For discussion of late-20th-century interiors, see the article entitled furniture.

Many present-day architects continue to perform the interior design of their buildings, or have interior design departments in their firms which handle this function. Other interiors are designed by independent designers. Not a small amount of interior design today, more often than not still called interior decoration and mostly for houses, is handled by amateurs or people who work part-time. Many of the professional designers work only in modern idioms. Others still attempt interiors intended to be period pieces, particularly in such building types as houses and restaurants. A specialized form of period work, requiring great scholarship and skill, is restoration and reconstruction of historical interiors.

**Related Articles** AESTHETICS; ART IN ARCHITECTURE; DESIGN, ARCHITECTURAL; FURNITURE; HISTORY OF ARCHITECTURE; PROGRAMMING.

**Further Reading** Abercrombie, Stanley: *A Philosophy of Interior Design*, Harper Collins, New York, 1991; Pile, John: *Interior Design*, Henry Abrams, New York, 1988.

**Periodicals** *Contract Interiors*, 1515 Broadway, New York, N.Y. 10036; *Interior Design*, 150 E. 58th St., New York, N.Y. 10022.

**Source of Additional Information** American Society of Interior Designers (ASID), 608 Massachusetts Ave., N.E., Washington, D.C. 20002; Institute of Business Designers (IBD), 341 Merchandise Mart, Chicago, Ill. 60654.

**IRON** A metallic element, mined from the earth, that has wide usage in architecture for everything from nails to structures. Iron, produced today in a blast furnace, is used in buildings mainly in cast and wrought forms. After having been refined into steel, the material has a great number of additional uses in architecture.

The second most abundant metal, surpassed only by aluminum, iron is found in most countries in the world. The Soviet Union leads in mining iron ore, with the United States second. Although every state in the United States contains iron ore, the richest deposits are in Minnesota and Michigan, near Lake Superior, where 75 percent of the U.S. iron is mined.

**Types** Two forms of iron are used in architecture: wrought iron, which has less than 0.1 percent carbon, usually much less; and cast iron, which usually has from 1.7 to 4 percent carbon. The most important use is in steel, which has up to 2 percent carbon. Wrought iron is relatively soft, malleable or easy to work by forging, bending, or other processes, and can be welded. Available in a variety of shapes, including pipe, plate, sheets, and bars, wrought iron is used in architecture mostly for pipe, furniture, fences, hardware, and sometimes ornamental ironwork. Cast iron is a hard, brittle metal that can be easily cast in many forms in molds, but generally cannot be worked by forging, bending, or other usual methods. Malleable cast iron, sometimes called malleable iron, is produced by heating cast iron and holding it at an elevated temperature long enough to relieve the internal stresses. This process, called annealing, produces a metal that can be machined and worked by other methods. Cast iron may be alloyed with other substances, including nickel, chromium, molydenum, and silicon, to produce types with added strength and corrosion or chemical resistance. Cast iron is available in pipe, sheet, plate, bars, and other shapes, and is used in architecture for many purposes, including pipe, plumbing fixtures, fireplace dampers, gratings, stairs, and ornamental ironwork.

**Production** The usual network for making iron from ore utilizes a blast furnace, a tall, round furnace made of steel lined with refractory brick. Usually operated continuously, 24 h a day, a blast furnace is charged with iron ore, crushed limestone, and coke. Wood is set on fire to start the coke burning, after which additional iron ore, limestone, and coke are added continuously, at the top, to keep the furnace operating. Burning is intensified by a steady blast of air, heated by gas in stoves, from nozzles near the bottom of the furnace. This blast of air gives the furnace its name. The hot air together with the burning of the coke produces carbon monoxide which rises through the iron ore and other materials, melting them and causing some of the carbon to combine with the molten iron.

The molten iron falls to the bottom of the furnace to a crucible or hearth, and every few hours is drawn off, or tapped. Impurities, called slag, float on top of the molten iron, now called pig iron, with 95 percent iron, up to 4 percent carbon or slightly more, and traces of impurities. The slag is also drawn off. The pig iron is tapped into special vehicles called ladle or bottle cars. The ladle cars transport the molten pig iron to casting houses, where it is cast into bars called pigs, or directly to an open-hearth or other type of furnace to be made into steel. Blast furnaces are of different sizes; the largest can produce as much as 2,400 tons of pig iron a day. A furnace that large would also produce about half that much slag, useful in architecture for such purposes as the manufacture of portland cement, aggregates for concrete, building streets, and others. Another by-product is gas drawn off from the top of the furnace, treated to remove useful substances, and then employed as fuel in steel making or other operations.

In addition to the above uses in architecture, iron has such other uses as inclusion as an alloying metal to increase the strength of aluminum, brass, bronze, copper, and other metals; as a color pigment in glazes for clay tile and porcelain enamel products; and as a preservative.

**Corrosion Protection** Although wrought and cast iron have some resistance to corrosion, they are almost

**IRON** Cast-iron facade, Haughwout Building (1857; later alterations), New York, N.Y. [Architect: J. P. Gaynor]

always protected with coatings. Several types of paint or other organic coatings may be used. Proper types should be carefully selected for the material to be painted and for the function of the product. Different paints or coatings are available for interiors, exteriors, and areas with chemical fumes, saltwater, air pollution, and so on. Iron may also be protected with asphalt coatings where extreme conditions exist.

Iron may also be protected from corrosion by treating it with phosphates to produce rust-resistant surfaces, by plating with other metals, and by galvanizing, a process that covers the iron with a thin coat of zinc. Galvanized iron is often painted. Properly selected or designed, installed, and protected, products of wrought or cast iron are very useful and reliable. Both can be used for ornamental objects. Wrought iron, in particular, was widely used for such purposes in the past. Still highly admired, it is not used so frequently for ornament today, to the regret of some people. Although the intricate and often delicate forms possible in wrought iron cannot be duplicated in cast iron, the latter material has had a place in architectural ornament in the past and might well be used more often today. And it is hard to imagine how the great variety of iron functional architectural components (stairs and grilles) could be effectively replaced by ones made from another material.

**History** Eventually, iron became the most useful metal in architecture, particularly after methods of making steel were developed. However, this took a long time

**IRON** Ornamental ironwork, Bradbury Building (1893; restored), Los Angeles, Calif. *[Architect: George H. Wyman]*

to get started. While copper was beginning to be used by about 5000 B.C. or even earlier, iron, in the form of meteorites, was not known to humans until about 1,000 years later. Another 1,000 years passed before experimental iron smelting was tried and almost another 2,000, before the beginning of the Iron Age, about 1200 B.C.

Before that time, iron had been used in Mesopotamia and Egypt, mostly for jewelry and other ornament, and sometimes for weapons. The earliest of these were of meteoric iron fashioned into primitive forms. Later, globules of iron were obtained by heating ores in primitive smelters. The globules were then reheated and hammered into wrought iron. The making of steel was discovered soon after the earliest production of iron. The ancient Egyptians and other people around the Mediterranean Sea developed improved smelters and discovered the method of hardening iron by quenching the hot metal in cold water. The ancient Greeks made wrought iron and steel and also cast iron, which was used only rarely.

When the first use of iron in architecture occurred is unknown, but the earliest uses are thought to have been for relatively small components. The Greeks used it for clamps and other fasteners to hold various components of stone and wood together or to fasten them to buildings. For example, iron dowels were sometimes used to join sections of stone columns. Iron was also used at times for structural members. The iron in Greek buildings rusted away long ago, but traces of it may be found on stone elements that have survived.

The Romans made iron, using simple hearth furnaces very much like earlier ones. Although they also made steel, the best kinds were imported from the early steel-making centers in India, Persia, and Damascus, Syria. In architecture, the Romans used iron for clamps and other fasteners in conjunction with masonry, which sometimes acted somewhat like the reinforcing of concrete or masonry today. The Romans also used iron for other parts of buildings, including hardware, nails, and structural elements, such as beams and girders.

During the Romanesque period of architecture, iron was widely used for such purposes as hardware and grilles and for strengthening doors with iron plates, nails, and heavy, strong locks and bolts. Little structural use of the material was made. During the Middle Ages, new types of more efficient forges were introduced in several places in Europe; they used forced drafts induced by bellows, instead of the natural drafts of chimneys. Except for modest amounts of steel, all these forges produced wrought iron. By about 1350, forges had been further developed into the first blast furnaces, producing cast iron, and thus establishing the basis for iron and steel production from that time on. The major uses of iron in architecture during the Middle Ages were in

grilles, placed in windows, to strengthen the masonry and glass and to prevent burglars from breaking in; for fastening together stone components; for hardware, including nails; and for relatively minor structural purposes. Iron was sometimes used, especially in Germany, for ornament.

During the Renaissance, iron continued to be used for purposes much like those of the past, but its use in structures increased spectacularly. In addition to its use for fastening stone components and similar purposes, iron was also used in chains placed around the great domes of the period to resist the outward forces, or thrusts, of the masonry. Some of these chains were plated with tin or enclosed in lead to prevent rusting. Iron bolts and other fasteners were used to construct timber trusses.

The early American colonists established blast furnaces for making iron during the first half of the 17th century. The first blast furnace was located at Falling Creek, Va., in 1621, and the second in Braintree, now West Quincy, Mass., in 1644. Furnaces were soon built at other places in Massachusetts, New Jersey, and Connecticut, and later in other colonies. The early blast furnaces produced only modest amounts of iron for local usage, mostly nonarchitectural, except for nails which were always in short supply in the colonies.

The art of making steel, which had been lost or ignored after ancient times, was rediscovered in 1740. In 1856 the English engineer Sir Henry Bessemer (1813–98) invented the Bessemer converter, an improved method for making steel, still in use today. In 1864 the open-hearth furnace, another improved method and still in use, was first used in England by Sir William Siemens (1823–83), who in 1878 developed the first successful electric furnace for making steel. An open-hearth furnace had been independently developed in 1864 by a French engineer, Pierre Emile Martin (1824–1915). These inventions were followed by other improved methods for handling iron ore, iron, and steel.

During the late 18th and early 19th centuries, new developments occurred in the use of iron as a structural material. For example, one of the first real applications of wrought iron as a reinforcing agent for masonry was in the Classic Revival Church of Ste Geneviève (completed 1790), later renamed the Panthéon, in Paris and designed by Jacques Germain Soufflot (1713–80). The English architect Thomas Rickman (1776–1841) built four Gothic Revival churches in Liverpool, England, including Saint George's (1814), in which almost every component was of cast iron, including door and window frames, structure, pulpit, and ornament. Iron was first used in a bridge for a span over the Severn River, at Coalbrook Dale, England, in 1781. It was designed by an architect, Thomas Farnolls Pritchard, constructed by

Abraham Darby III, and is still in existence. Other iron bridges soon followed.

**American Usage** Both cast and wrought iron were important building materials in 19th-century America, their use perhaps first popularized by the success of the Crystal Palace (1851), at the Great Exhibition in London, designed by Sir Joseph Paxton (1801–65), with a structure entirely of iron. In other buildings, iron was used for such purposes as grilles, fences, ornament, columns, and complete structures. Buildings with iron structures, and sometimes with other important iron components, were erected in many places in the United States during the 19th century, including notable examples in New York City and St. Louis. At first, these were structures of moderate height, usually only a few stories. A remarkable group of cast-iron buildings were constructed in New York City during the 1850s and 1860s, and somewhat later, designed by prominent architects and manufacturers, including James Bogardus (1800–74) and J. P. Gaynor. Many have long since been demolished, but a few examples remain, including Gaynor's Haughwout Building (1857).

In the late 19th and early 20th centuries, an even more remarkable series of iron buildings was constructed in Chicago by architects of the so-called Chicago school of design. Although iron had been used previously in Chicago for relatively tall buildings, the first skeleton frame of the material was used in the 10-story Home Insurance Building (1855), designed by William Le Baron Jenney (1832–1907), and later demolished. This was also the first use of Bessemer steel for beams in a building. Although masonry bearing walls continued to be used after that time, the end of their use in buildings was clearly in sight. Other iron-framed tall buildings soon followed. In 1874 the first use in the United States of Bessemer steel for any type of structure was in the Eads Bridge, St. Louis, designed by engineer James Buchanan Eads (1820–76), for whom the bridge was named. The Reliance Building (1895), designed by Burnham and Root, was the first tall building in which steel columns as well as other structural members were used. The steel in these early buildings was riveted to form the frames. Riveting became the most used American fastening system for steel structures for many years. Later welded steel structures were often used.

Today steel remains one of the most important architectural materials for structural purposes, including concrete reinforcing, and for a host of other uses. Stainless steels are also used for many purposes. Cast iron is extensively used for pipe, hardware, ornamental work, and many other purposes. Wrought iron is used mostly for corrosion-resistant pipe, railings, fences, and grilles.

**Related Articles** Bogardus, James; Bridge; Burnham and Root; Concrete Structure; Jenney, William Le Baron; Prefabrication; Steel; Steel Structure; Articles on various building components and systems.

**Source of Additional Information** American Iron and Steel Inst., 1133 15th St., N.W., Washington, D.C. 20005.

**JEFFERSON, THOMAS** American statesman, farmer, writer, and architect (1743–1826). The many achievements of Thomas Jefferson have been so well documented and praised that the excellence of his architecture has often been overshadowed. Yet in spite of the years spent in service to his country and in a host of other pursuits, in all of which he excelled, he designed some of the greatest buildings in American history. His architectural training, as did that of other amateur gentlemen-architects of his time, came almost entirely from books.

Unlike many other American architects of his time, Jefferson was able to augment the book learning by close study of the Georgian buildings of Williamsburg and later of French and Roman buildings during the five years he was U.S. Minister to France. In addition, he was a scholar of classical literature, having learned both Greek and Latin as a boy.

**Many-Sided Scholar** His deep interest in classical culture led him away from the Georgian style so prevalent at the time to an architecture derived from the Roman buildings he had seen and studied in books. An early proponent of Classic Revival architecture, Jefferson used both his own buildings and his official positions to influence the designs of buildings, particularly those of the new American republic. His own taste was classical, based on the strict principles of proportion and decoration of ancient Rome. As time went by, he became more and more anti-British in his architecture as well as in his politics and philosophy. Thus he played an important role in the evolution of American architecture as he had in its government.

For Jefferson, architecture was not merely a way to occupy himself pleasantly; he was most serious about it. He worked at perfecting his drawing skills until he became a very accomplished draftsman. He was one of the first American architects to use drawings as a means of studying designs. He prepared plans for his buildings and wrote specifications for them. He ordered materials, hired workers, supervised construction, and kept strict financial records.

Jefferson designed both buildings and town plans, among them a checkerboard scheme that envisioned squares of buildings alternating with open space squares, a revolutionary idea at that time. Among his town plans were one for Richmond, Va., and another for portions of Washington. He designed master plans and groups of buildings, including those for the University of Virginia at Charlottesville. He helped foster good planning through his support of the L'Enfant plan for Washington, and good architecture through his appointment, while president, of Benjamin Henry Latrobe (1764–1820) as surveyor of public buildings for the federal government.

Jefferson was an architectural scholar who collected the greatest library of books on the subject of that era. He was an architectural educator, helping to train young architects; his most notable student was Robert Mills (1781–1855), who spent two years studying and working with Jefferson. He was an innovator and inventor in the use of materials and systems, working out methods for manufacturing brick and other elements of buildings, and inventing systems of double glazing of windows to minimize heat losses, hot-air heating systems, and double doors that opened simultaneously.

**Works** It is in his own buildings, though, that Jefferson's genius as an architect is most apparent. His first work was his own house, Monticello, originally built (1769–75) in Georgian style, then remodeled and altered many times and drastically remodeled (1808) in Roman Revival style. In fact, Jefferson designed and redesigned, built, tore down, and rebuilt Monticello continually from

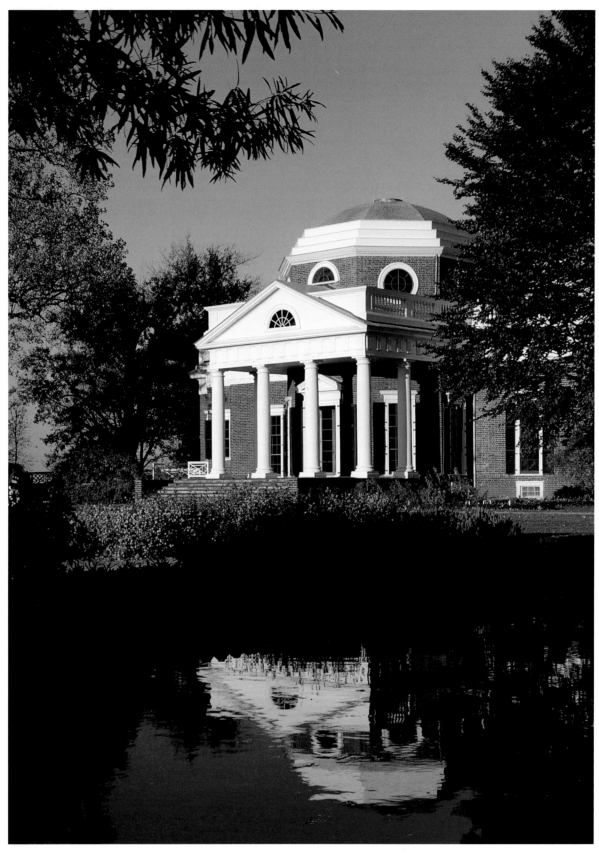

**JEFFERSON, THOMAS** Monticello (1769–75, remodeled 1796–1808), Charlottesville, Va.

1769 almost until the time of his death, except for periods when he was absent on governmental affairs.

Monticello is a magnificent building, some think Jefferson's masterpiece, in a beautiful setting on top of a hill near Charlottesville, Va. With a domed central element and porticoes on two sides, the two-story house was constructed of brick with wood trim, fabricated at the site under Jefferson's supervision. Underground passages led from either side to long wings that housed servants, and contained the kitchen, stables, an office, and other rooms. Sold after Jefferson's death to help settle his debts, the house deteriorated badly over the years, until it was bought by the Thomas Jefferson Memorial Foundation, which has had the house and grounds restored and many of the original furnishings reinstated.

Jefferson designed a number of other Virginia houses. Among the finest of those still standing are Belle Grove (1796) in Middleton and Poplar Forest (1820) in Forest. After the state capital of Virginia was moved from Williamsburg to Richmond, Jefferson designed a Capitol Building in 1784, loosely adapted from the Roman Maison Carrée (c. 16 B.C.) in Nîmes, France. After arriving in Paris as U.S. Minister, he did additional work on the design and had a model of the building made by a French architect, C. L. A. Clerissau. The drawings and models were sent to Richmond in 1786. The work on the building had begun in 1785 and was finished in 1791. Jefferson also designed a governor's house for Richmond, based on the Villa Rotunda (c. 1657) at Vicenza, Italy, but it was never built. The Virginia Capitol was the first building in the United States with a design adapted from a pure temple form and was some 20 years ahead of the first in France, the Church of the Madeleine, begun in 1806.

Jefferson's last great work, which, though he loved Monticello, he considered his finest, was the campus and buildings of the University of Virginia (1825) in Charlottesville. Here Jefferson designed what he described as an academic village. For his village, Jefferson produced a master plan with five major elements: two long ranges of buildings each consisting of five two-story pavilions in which professors lived and taught, interconnected with single-story dormitory rooms for students; at one end of the range is the focal point of the plan, the library, now called the Rotunda; behind each of the ranges, and separated from them by landscaped grounds, are two additional long buildings, each with three dining rooms separated by additional dormitories. The University of Virginia is still considered one of the greatest master plans in all American architecture.

For each pavilion, Jefferson chose the style of an actual great classical building or a design from the books of the 16th-century Italian architect Andrea Palladio (1518–80). For the Rotunda, the model was the Pantheon (A.D. 124) in Rome but half the size of that building. In 1851 Robert Mills, who much earlier had studied architecture with Jefferson, designed a large annex behind the Rotunda. In 1895 the annex caught fire and burned, the fire spread and the Rotunda was seriously damaged. Stanford White (1853–1906), of McKim, Mead and White, renovated the Rotunda in 1912, but in the process changed Jefferson's design considerably. The building has now been restored almost to its original design. And Jefferson's famous serpentine garden walls have been rebuilt to the design of the originals.

For the University of Virginia, Jefferson designed the campus and its buildings, supervised the construction, kept the construction accounts, and trained and directed the workmen. He went on to design the curriculum, select the books for its library, and to choose the faculty members. In the end, he came to call himself the father of the university, which he undoubtedly was in a sense. He might also be called the father of the Roman Revival movement as well as one of the two or three founders of the Classic Revival style in America.

**Life** Thomas Jefferson was born at the family home, Shadwell, in Albemarle (then Goochland) County, Va., on April 13, 1743. He was the son of Peter Jefferson, surveyor, colonel of militia, and landholder, and Jane Randolph, a member of one of the oldest and best families in Virginia. Jefferson's early education consisted of studying with his father and in local schools.

After his father's death, when young Jefferson was only fourteen, he continued his education at the school of the Rev. James Maury in Charlottesville. At age sixteen, he entered the College of William and Mary in Williamsburg, Va. By this time, he had already learned a considerable amount of French, Greek, and Latin and to play the violin. These were to become lifelong interests. In Williamsburg, Jefferson got his first introduction to architecture in the buildings of the colonial capital. This was another interest that would last all his life.

After graduation in 1762, Jefferson remained in Williamsburg to study law with George Wythe (1726–1806), a learned lawyer and judge. In 1767 he was admitted to the bar. He had by that time grown tall, 6'2", was freckled and red-haired. He had studied deeply in the arts and sciences and in music and literature. Formally trained as a lawyer, and having delayed as long as possible, he now entered the practice of law. By his own admission and the observations of others, it is certain that he never really enjoyed the law very much. But it was a stepping stone to the great career as a politician and statesman that lay ahead. And though he never really liked it, his career as a lawyer was most successful.

Dividing his time between Williamsburg and the family home, Shadwell, Jefferson began to pursue

**JEFFERSON, THOMAS** State Capitol (1791, with later addition), Richmond, Va.

another of his enthusiasms, architecture. He had studied the architecture of Williamsburg, most of which he did not like, and he had studied classical architecture in the library that had been assembled by William Byrd (1674–1744), at Westover. The finest of its day, it included 26 architectural books, particularly those of Andrea Palladio. Jefferson began to collect architectural books for his own library. Soon after his admission to the bar, he began the design of a house for himself, on the top of the 500-ft-high hill he called Monticello (little mountain), near Shadwell. The top of the hill was leveled and construction began in 1769 on the first phase, a one-room house, finished late that same year. This was the beginning of an architectural career as brilliant as that of any American of his time.

In 1770 Shadwell burned, destroying all of Jefferson's papers and library. Because of the loss of the papers, little documentation of his earlier years exists. Of the later years, the information is voluminous in his own journals, in the thousands of his letters that have been preserved, and from other sources. In addition, over 500 of his architectural drawings have survived. He immediately began to assemble a second library that eventually had some 6,000 volumes. This second collection was sold to the United States, at about half its value, to form the basis of the Library of Congress, replacing the books that had been burned by the British in the War of 1812. Jefferson moved to Monticello and continued work on his house.

During his lifetime, Jefferson designed a number of other houses, a church, two courthouses, all of them notable, and in addition to Monticello, two other masterpieces, the State Capitol at Richmond and the University of Virginia.

In 1772 Jefferson married a widow, Margaret Wayles Skelton. It was a happy marriage, producing a son and five daughters, but only Martha and Mary lived to maturity. Jefferson's wife died 10 years later, and he never remarried.

**Political Career** Jefferson's brilliant career as a politician and statesman started with his election to the Virginia House of Burgesses, where he served from 1769 to 1775, and ended with his two terms as president of the United States (1801–09). During the interim, he had been a delegate to the Continental Congress (1775–76) in Philadelphia, for which he wrote the Declaration of Independence, and again a delegate (1783–85); had been governor of Virginia (1779–81); and had written the Virginia Statute of Religious Freedom. He served as U.S. Minister to France (1785–89), during which he enlarged his architectural knowledge; as U.S. secretary of state (1790–93), during

**JEFFERSON, THOMAS** University of Virginia (1825), Charlottesville, Va.

the presidency of George Washington (1732–99); and as vice president (1797–1801), during the presidency of John Adams (1735–1826).

During all this time, Jefferson continued his architectural work. He had turned official Washington architecture away from the Georgian toward Classical Revival, in particular Roman Revival which he thought a fitting style for the new republic. He had, in fact, come close to becoming the designer of the White House, then called the President's House, placing second in a competition he had entered anonymously, which was won by James Hoban (c. 1762–1831). Later, as president (1801–09), he made designs for additions, including the garden front portico to the house.

In 1809, when his second term as president ended, Jefferson returned to Monticello to stay. Years before he had said, "All my wishes end, where I hope my days will end, at Monticello." He had turned away from politics, which he had served so well, as he had earlier turned away from law. He could now spend his days in the place he loved and in the way he wished to live, in study and contemplation, in invention and design and building, both on his own house and buildings for others. And the grand finale of his architectural work began.

**Model University** For many years, Jefferson had been thinking about the design of a model university. By 1805, while he was still president, he had come up with a scheme that envisioned a university as a small village in which professors and students lived and worked, with a great library as its focal point. He asked Benjamin Henry Latrobe and William Thornton (1759–1828), who had designed the U.S. Capitol, to think about the design and advise him. With some help from their ideas, Jefferson chose a building with a dome for the library, the central feature of the plan. The design of this building, however, was Jefferson's.

The construction of the university began in 1817 and was completed in 1825. Though somewhat aged, Jefferson supervised the work until its completion, in person, and with the aid of a telescope mounted on the terrace at Monticello.

During his last years, his happiness in being at Monticello and with his studies and work was marred by financial troubles with which he was never able to deal properly, and later with ill health.

In 1824 he entertained the Marquis de Lafayette (1757–1834), an old friend, at Monticello and at a formal dinner in the still-unfinished Rotunda. By 1825, when Lafayette returned from his trip to the Western United States to say his farewells, Jefferson was so weak that he had to receive him while lying on a couch. His condition worsened during the next few months, and on July 4,

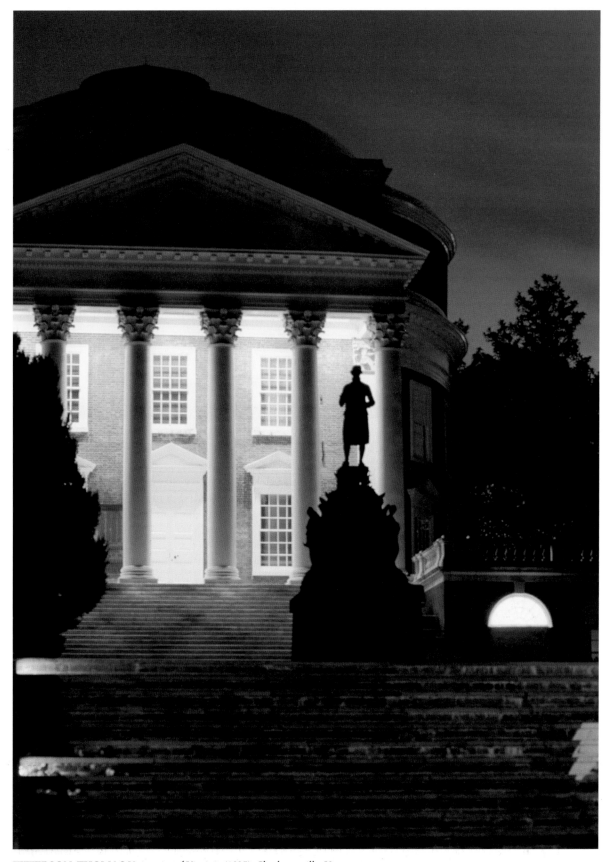

**JEFFERSON, THOMAS** University of Virginia (1825), Charlottesville, Va.

1826, the fiftieth anniversary of the signing of the Declaration of Independence, Jefferson died.

He had lived a life full of accomplishment, unequaled by that of any other American before or since. And he had written his own epitaph, which now appears on his gravestone at Monticello: "Here was buried THOMAS JEFFERSON Author of the Declaration of American Independence of the Statute of Virginia for Religious Freedom and Father of the University of Virginia."

**Related Articles** CLASSIC REVIVAL ARCHITECTURE; GEORGIAN ARCHITECTURE; LATROBE, BENJAMIN HENRY; MILLS, ROBERT.

**Further Reading** Kimball, Fiske: *Thomas Jefferson: Architect*, reprint of 2d ed., Da Capo, New York, 1968.

**JENNEY, WILLIAM LE BARON** American engineer and architect (1832–1907). Although trained as an engineer rather than as an architect, and though his talents were mostly in engineering rather than in architecture, William Le Baron Jenney became one of the most influential architects of his time. Probably because of his interest in and knowledge of structural engineering, Jenney was the first proponent of the early style for tall buildings of the group of architects who came to be known as the Chicago school. Never a school, in the real sense of the word, these architects, led by Jenney, began to design buildings late in the 19th century, utilizing iron and later steel skeleton structures. As time went on, they designed the exteriors of their buildings to express the structure underneath, instead of attempting to adapt older traditional styles to the new tall buildings. These then were some of the earliest antecedents of what was to become modern architecture.

Jenney led the way, both in his own buildings and in his influence on younger architects of the Chicago school. In fact, of the five most influential younger men, four, Louis Henri Sullivan (1856–1924), Martin Roche (1855–1927), William Holabird (1854–1923), and Daniel Hudson Burnham (1846–1912), had worked in Jenney's office. Only John Wellborn Root (1850–91) had not worked for Jenney, but he was influenced by his partner, Burnham. All were to become fine architects in their own right and all were to contribute to the progress of the Chicago school and the movement toward modern architecture. Much earlier than in any other American city, they were to establish solid principles for the design of modern skyscrapers.

**Works** What Jenney and the others were beginning to develop became apparent in his First Leiter Store (1879) and was further developed in the Second Leiter Store (1891), now a Sears Roebuck store, both in Chicago. The latter had a boldness and vitality not seen before. Jenney continued the development in other Chicago buildings, the Manhattan Building (1890), the

Fair Store (1891), now a Montgomery Ward store, and the Ludington Building (1891). In 1885 Jenney's masterpiece, the 10-story Home Insurance Company Building, was completed. This was a real breakthrough. Some call it the first skyscraper. The structure utilized cast-iron and wrought-iron columns, and wrought-iron and steel beams, the first use of Bessemer steel in a building, though it had been used previously in bridges. This was also the first building in which both floors and exterior masonry walls were supported by the metal skeleton. Considered the most important building of its era, and one of the most important in American history, the building was demolished in 1931.

The Isabella Building (1893) and the Association, or Central YMCA, Building (1893), both in Chicago, were the last of Jenney's buildings to maintain the high standards of design he had reached. It seemed that he had pioneered as far as he could, and the later buildings were anticlimax. Jenney had already proved himself an original structural designer, not overly concerned with the aesthetic qualities of his buildings, but a creative architect who was unafraid to break with precedent. He had set an example for innovative work to be done by later architects.

**Life** William Le Baron Jenney was born in Fairhaven, Mass., on September 25, 1832. The son of a wealthy whaling fleet owner, Jenney had a first-rate education in engineering, studying for two years at the Lawrence Scientific School at Harvard University. In 1853 he went to the École Centrale des Arts et Manufactures in Paris and was graduated in 1856.

He was a daring man, a trait he was to demonstrate in his buildings. Before going to Paris, he had participated in the gold rush of 1849, and later in the construction of a railroad in Panama. In 1861 he entered the Union Army as an engineer and served during the Civil War until 1866. His army career was exemplary. He rose rapidly in rank to major, a title he was to use the rest of his life, and served on the staffs of generals Ulysses S. Grant (1822–85) and William Tecumseh Sherman (1820–91).

Jenney went to Chicago in 1867, and opened his office the following year. He practiced in Chicago the rest of his life. His first buildings were not impressive, but he rapidly developed the style of architecture that was to become the hallmark of the Chicago school.

Jenney was considered by those who knew him to be an easygoing, impressive gentleman and gourmet. He enjoyed being a guest but enjoyed even more being a host. He was a cultured man, learned in science and history as well as in his chosen profession. He gave interesting lectures, among them a series at the Chicago University in 1883 that was published in *Inland Architect and Builder* in 1883–84.

In both the number and the consistent excellence of his buildings, 1891 was the high point in Jenney's career. In that year, he took in William B. Mundie (1863–1939) as a partner, an arrangement that was to last until Jenney's death. In 1905 he took in another partner, Elmer C. Jensen (1870–1955), who had worked for him since 1885. The firm then became Jenney, Mundie and Jensen, but only two years later, on June 15, 1907, Jenney died. Though mainly an engineer, he had not failed to make a lasting mark on architecture of his time and the future. He left a legacy in his buildings and in those he had helped train to carry on.

**Related Articles** BURNHAM AND ROOT; HOLABIRD AND ROCHE; MODERN ARCHITECTURE; SULLIVAN, LOUIS HENRI.

## JOHNSON, PHILIP CORTELYOU American architect (1906–    ). Having become an architect relatively late, after graduating in architecture from Harvard in 1943, when he was thirty-seven years old, Johnson nevertheless has had a great influence on the architecture of his time. As a writer, critic, and lecturer on architecture, and as director of the department of architecture of the Museum of Modern Art, New York City, Johnson and his ideas made a considerable impact on architecture and architects.

**International Style** With critic and historian Henry-Russell Hitchcock (1903–87), Johnson invented the term *International style* to denote what they considered to be important developments in modern architecture that were leading toward building designs that were simple, unadorned, and expressed their structure with modern materials. In their view, these trends, adopted by architects all over the world would lead to a modern architecture devoid of local or regional characteristics.

Johnson and Hitchcock collaborated on a book espousing this position, *The International Style—Architecture Since 1922*, published in 1932. And that same year, Johnson organized the first International Exhibition of Modern Architecture at the Museum of Modern Art. Johnson believed that the architecture of Ludwig Mies van der Rohe (1886–1969), who had emi-

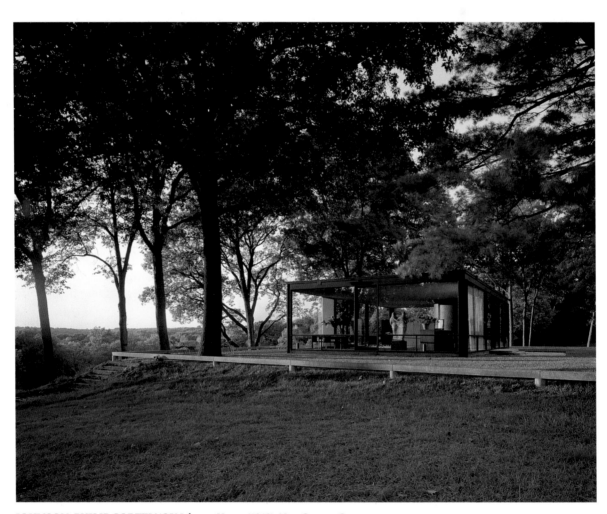

**JOHNSON, PHILIP CORTELYOU** Johnson House (1949), New Canaan, Conn.

grated to the United States from Germany and had become director of the architecture school at the Illinois Institute of Technology, Chicago, was the epitome of the International style. Mies decried the phrase and even the word *style* in his work, but the book and exhibition were very influential. Many architects and critics espoused the cause, but later many were to declare that while some of the principles may have been valid, there never really was an International style.

**Work** After becoming an architect, Johnson designed mostly houses for a while. He continued to write and lecture and he continued his interest in and espousal of the work of Mies. Johnson incorporated his principles in a house he built for himself (1949) in New Canaan, Conn. Three years were spent in its design and the resulting glass-enclosed house brought its architect much recognition and is still considered one of his best buildings.

Johnson continued to design other buildings, mostly houses, which demonstrated the principles of the International style. Some of his best houses of that period were the Hodgson (1951), Ball (1953), and Wiley (1953), all in New Canaan; Leonhardt (1956), Lloyd's Neck, Long Island, N.Y.; and the Boissonnas (1956) in New Canaan. Beginning with his houses, Johnson's influence began to spread by means of his designs as it had previously through his writing, lectures, and other work.

Johnson designed a new wing (1950) for the Museum of Modern Art, designed its sculpture garden (1953), and added another wing (1964). He also designed a number of nonresidential buildings, including the Kneses Tifereth Israel Synagogue (1956), Port Chester, N.Y.; University of St. Thomas auditorium and class-rooms (1957), Houston, Tex.; the Roofless Church (1960), New Harmony, Ind.; and two art museums, the Munson-Proctor-Williams (1960), Utica, N.Y., and the Amon Carter Museum of Western Art (1961), Ft. Worth, Tex. He designed buildings of other types, including the Nuclear Reactor (1961), Rehovot, Israel; the New York State Theater (1964) at the Lincoln Center for the Performing Arts, New York City; and the Kline Science Tower (1964), Yale University, New Haven, Conn. He also was associated with Mies van der Rohe on the great Seagram Building (1958), New York City, a commission which he helped Mies to obtain, and he designed an elegant restaurant, the Four Seasons, which is located in the building.

Philip Johnson has not designed a large number of buildings during his career, but those he designed through the 1970s have continued to have considerable influence on architecture. His early theories of an International style have been largely superseded. But few architects of Johnson's era have been able to

approach the crisp elegance, the sophistication of his best designs. And Johnson was still producing such designs with John Henry Burgee (1933– ) until the mid-1980s. During their years of collaboration, designs that should be mentioned include the IDS Center in Minneapolis (1973), the twin towers of Pennzoil Place (1976), Houston, Tex., and the later more controversial designs for AT&T tower in New York (1982), the all-glass head-quarters for PPG Industries in Pittsburgh, Pa. (1984), and the Spanish Colonial center for Fort Lauderdale, Fla. (1984).

**Life** Philip Cortelyou Johnson was born in Cleveland, Ohio, on July 8, 1906. He attended Harvard University at various times beginning in 1923 and graduated with an A.B. in 1930. He was interested in the arts, particularly in architecture, though he had no intention of becoming an architect. After the Museum of Modern Art was char-tered in 1929, Johnson became the first director of archi-tecture in 1930. In this position he became familiar with the modern buildings of the time and with the architects who were designing them. He also became familiar with

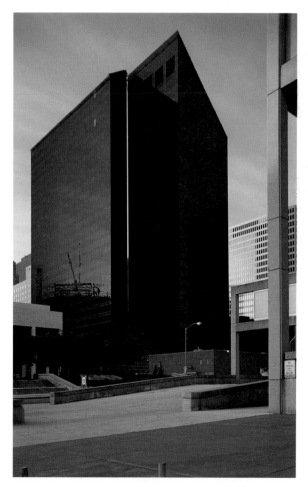

**JOHNSON, PHILIP CORTELYOU** Pennzoil Place (1976), Houston, Tex. *[Architects: Johnson and Burgee]*

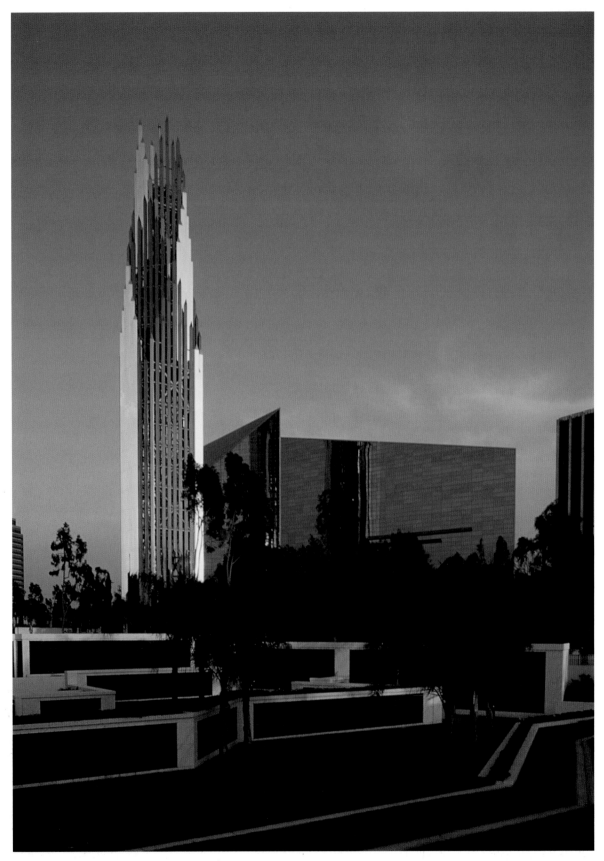

**JOHNSON, PHILIP CORTELYOU** Crystal Cathedral (1980), Anaheim, Calif. *[Architects: Johnson and Burgee]*

many of the architecture critics of the day, and he started to write critical articles and books.

In 1932 Johnson and Henry-Russell Hitchcock published their book on the International style, and it had great influence on the modern movement in architecture. Johnson continued to write critical articles on architecture. In 1936 he left his position at the Museum of Modern Art and traveled in Europe studying the new architecture firsthand. Returning to the United States, he entered the Graduate School of Design at Harvard University and received his architectural degree in 1943. At age thirty-seven, he had finally embarked on his career as an architect. Before graduation though, he had designed his first houses and continued designing others after leaving Harvard.

In 1946 Johnson returned to the Museum of Modern Art as director of the department of architecture and design, remaining there until 1954. He continued designing houses during this time, including his own famous glass house. By this time, he had become deeply interested in and impressed by the architecture of Mies van der Rohe and wrote the first important American book on his work, published in 1947 and revised in 1953.

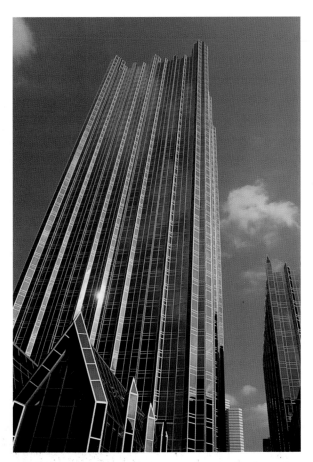

**JOHNSON, PHILIP CORTELYOU** Pittsburgh Plate Glass (1984), Pittsburgh, Pa. *[Architects: Johnson and Burgee]*

Johnson continued to write and to design houses, but after 1956 he began to devote a major portion of his energies and talents to other building types. Since that time, he has designed buildings of many types in a number of locations in the United States and abroad. Many of these have been significant examples of contemporary architecture. Some have felt that there was a period in Johnson's career during the late 1960s and early 1970s when his work was less interesting than it had been before. That may be, but his later work, designed in partnership with John Burgee (1933– ), has brought worldwide recognition. After 20 years in association with John Burgee, in 1992 Philip Johnson formed a new architectural firm at age 86. His fame is such that clients continue to seek his services for major projects. For the excellence of his architecture, Philip Cortelyou Johnson received the highest award of the American Institute of Architects, the Gold Medal, in 1978. In 1980, he received the prestigious Pritzker prize.

Through exhibitions at New York's Museum of Modern Art, lectures, and writing, Philip Johnson has promoted the careers of younger architects including Michael Graves (1934– ), Robert A. M. Stern (1939– ), and Peter Eisenman (1932– ). Alert to new trends and ideas, he was curator of the 1987 exhibit at the Museum of Modern Art in New York, "Deconstructivism in Architecture."

**Related Articles** CONTEMPORARY ARCHITECTURE; EXPOSITION; MIES VAN DER ROHE, LUDWIG; MODERN ARCHITECTURE.

**Further Reading** Hitchcock, Henry-Russell, Jr., and Philip Johnson: *The International Style—Architecture Since 1922,* reprint of 1932 edition, Norton, N.Y., 1966.

**JONES, FAY** The architect Fay Jones (1921– ) is identified with Arkansas, where he was born, educated, taught, and practices architecture. Although a well-regarded architect for his house designs, it was the Thorncrown Chapel of 1976 which brought him fame. Influenced by the buildings of Frank Lloyd Wright, Fay Jones has produced a body of work peculiarly American in spirit, in harmony with nature. Fay Jones also credits the influence of such figures as Charles Sumner Greene (1868–1957), his brother Henry Mather Greene (1870–1954), Bernard Maybeck (1862–1957), Richard Neutra (1892–1970), Harwell Hamilton Harris (1895-1981), and most particularly Bruce A. Goff (1904–82). Jones has received many awards, including the Gold Medal of the American Institute of Architects in 1990.

**Work** The international attention paid to Fay's Thorncrown Chapel (1980) shows his power to move people through his designs using wood construction. The Mildred B. Cooper Memorial Chapel (1988) in Bella Vista, Ark., and the Marty Leonard Community Chapel

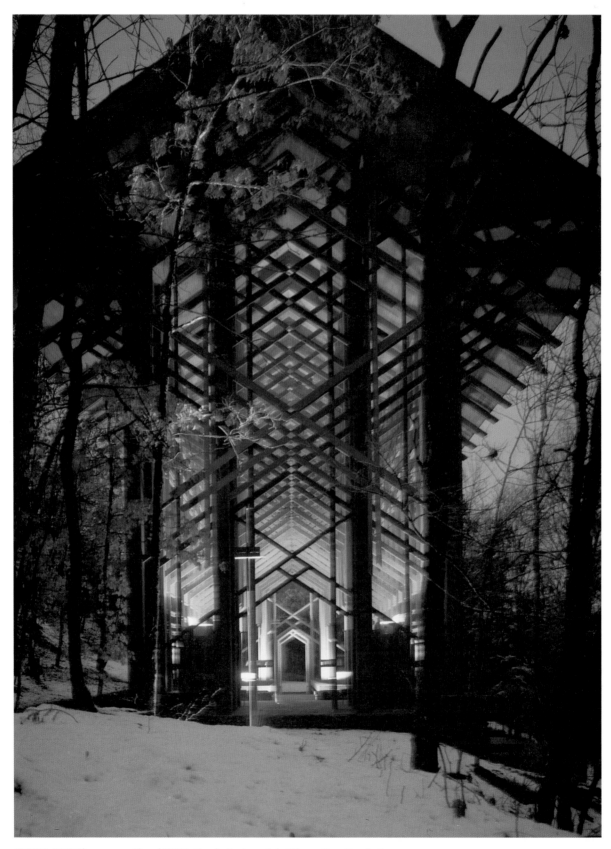

**JONES, FAY** Thorncrown Chapel (1980), Eureka Springs, Ark. *[Photo: Greg Hursley]*

(1990) in Fort Worth, Tex., continue the series of wood chapels.

His house designs have drawn equal attention, with the Davenport House (1984) in Evergreen, Colo., being particularly praised. Other houses include his own (1956) in Fayettesville, Pine Knoll (1964) in Little Rock, and Stoneflower (1965) in Eden Isle, Ark., with a dramatic cantilevered deck and cavelike lower floor. Other houses are built on lakes or bridge a stream. Some houses are modest in size, and for wealthy clients, may be very large. Among other details, Jones is particularly adept at custom wood lighting fixtures which seem integral to his buildings. Now in his seventies, his list of clients continues to grow.

**Life** Fay Jones was born January 31, 1921, in Pine Bluff, Ark. His family moved to Little Rock and later to El Dorado, Ark. He was directed toward architecture when at age 17 he saw a film on Frank Lloyd Wright's work for the Johnson Wax Company in Racine, Wis. At that time, there was no school of architecture in Arkansas, and Fay Jones entered the University of Arkansas School of Engineering. In 1941, he withdrew from the university and became a Navy pilot in the Pacific theater during World War II. In 1943, he married Mary Elizabeth Knox. In 1945 he became an architectural student at the Oklahoma A&M and received his degree in 1950. He met Frank Lloyd Wright in 1949 and spent the summer of 1953 at Taliesen at Spring Green, Wis. Prior to this, Fay Jones received a fellowship and graduate teaching assistantship in architecture at Rice University and later taught at the University of Oklahoma from 1951 to 1953. He values his time with the architect Bruce A. Goff, who was chair of the department of architecture at the University of Oklahoma from 1948 to 1955. Later in 1953 Jones returned to join the faculty of the University of Arkansas in Fayettesville, where he continues to live. In 1974, he was named Dean of the new school of architecture at the university. In addition to the awards for his architecture, Fay Jones is the recipient of many awards for his academic work, including several honorary degrees.

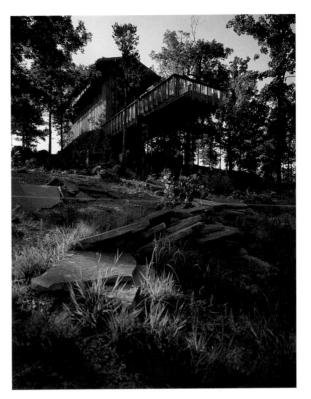

JONES, FAY Stoneflower, Robert Shaheen and Kurt Goodfellow Residence (1965), Eden Isle, Ark.

Fay's early clients were faculty members, and he built his own house in 1956. His work was published beginning in the late 1950s, and awards came as his work became known. He received the Rome Prize Fellowship in 1980, and he continues to visit and lecture at the American Academy in Rome, Italy.

**Related Articles** CONTEMPORARY ARCHITECTURE; WRIGHT, FRANK LLOYD.

**Periodical** *Architecture and Urbanism*, February 1991, no. 215. Special Feature: Fay Jones: Pinecote Pavilion, Thorncrown Chapel, and the Edmondson Residence.

**Further Reading** Ivy, Jr., Robert Adams: *Fay Jones,* American Institute of Architects Press, Washington, D.C., 1992.

# K

**KAHN, ALBERT** German-American architect (1869–1942). Emigrating with his family from Germany when he was eleven, Albert Kahn received his professional training from apprenticeship in an architect's office and from a year's study in Europe on a scholarship. Starting out as an eclecticist, Kahn continued to design in various styles all his life, except on industrial buildings or factories, in which he became one of the greatest pioneers of modern architecture. In the practice of architecture he was also a pioneer, developing one of the largest and most successful offices ever. His office became a complete entity, handling all phases of the architectural and engineering work for his buildings.

**Innovative Factory Design** Beginning in 1903, Kahn started a long series of innovative factories of reinforced concrete and steel. He introduced factories that were all under one roof and later factories that were all on one floor, revolutionary techniques at that time. At the time, factory design in most offices was relegated to junior draftsmen. Kahn introduced rigorous planning into his factories, designed by himself and by the best designers in his office, including Ernest Wilby, a good designer who worked with him from 1903 to 1908.

Kahn was the first architect to use industrial steel sash, which had to be imported from Europe, with a concrete frame. He helped develop buildings to house continuously moving assembly lines. Kahn originated the practice, later almost standard in factories, of maximum natural lighting and ventilation through the use of continuous bands of windows, skylights, and roof monitors. Over the years, Kahn introduced many structural innovations in both concrete and steel, including the use of long, flat-span trusses to provide interior spaces unobstructed by columns.

**Works** Among the milestone industrial buildings of Albert Kahn, the earliest was the Packard Motor Car Company Plant (1903), Detroit, in which he used steel sash in a concrete-framed building. This was followed by another first, a building for Ford Motor Company (1909) in Highland Park, Mich., in which the Ford production line was housed under one roof. Kahn added several other buildings at this plant, culminating in a building (1918) with cantilevered balconies inside to facilitate handling of materials and parts. In 1926 Walter Adolf Gropius (1883–1969), one of the European architects who had become interested in the work of Kahn, used similar balconies in his Bauhaus at Desau, Germany. Other important buildings of this era were the plants for Burroughs Adding Machine Company (1919), Detroit, and Fisher Body Company (1921), Cleveland, Ohio.

Starting in 1917, Kahn produced a number of buildings for the large Ford River Rouge Plant, Detroit. The first of these, called Building B, was revolutionary. A half-mile long, the building sheltered the entire assembly line for automobiles in a steel frame enclosed entirely with windows. In the De Soto Division Press Shop of Chrysler Corporation (1936), Detroit, Kahn produced an elegant design utilizing large trusses beneath which glass curtain walls enclosed the interior. In 1938 he produced similar elegance in the Half-Ton Truck Plant of the Dodge Division of Chrysler. This time, the effect came from long-span trusses, butterfly monitors on the roof, and curtain walls. The Ohio Steel Foundry Company Building (1938), Lima, Ohio, is similar in design.

Then came the great World War II war plants. Among these were the large bomber plant for Glenn L. Martin Company (1937), Baltimore, and the even larger, in fact the largest in the world, Willow Run Bomber Plant for Ford (1943), later converted to automobile manufacture and assembly. In the latter, because of wartime blackout regulations, Kahn turned away from glass-curtain walls to a windowless, artificially lighted factory. Other important wartime buildings were American Steel Foundries Cast Iron Plant (1941), East

**KAHN, ALBERT** Air view, Ford River Rouge Plant (1917), Dearborn, Mich.

Chicago, Ind., and American Locomotive Company Machine Shop (1942), Auburn, N.Y.

Albert Kahn, in a career that lasted 57 years, worked right up to the time of his death in 1942. He had accomplished a great deal. He had made factory buildings into architecture, his own best architecture. His other nonindustrial buildings, which seemed to him to be of a higher order, never actually approached the excellence of his factories. In the factories, he influenced the growth of modern architecture at home and abroad.

**Life** Albert Kahn was born in Rhaunen, Germany, on March 2, 1869, the oldest of six children of a rabbi and teacher. Kahn's family emigrated to the United States, settling in Detroit in 1880. As a youth, he wanted first to become a musician, then an artist. By the time he was sixteen, however, the family had eight children and to help out, Kahn took a job in 1885 as office boy in the architect's office of Mason and Rice in Detroit. He soon became a draftsman. In 1891 Kahn won a scholarship for a year of travel and study in Europe. In Florence, he met Henry Bacon (1866–1924), later to become a noted architect himself, and also on a scholarship. The two young men traveled together through Italy, France, Belgium, and Germany, sketching and studying.

Back from his travels, Kahn was to practice in Detroit the rest of his life. He returned to the office of Mason

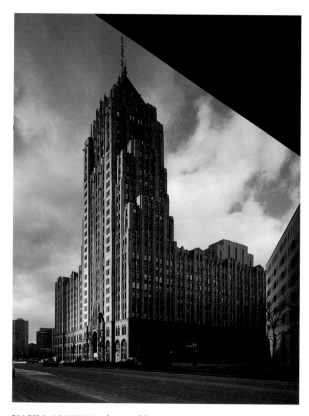

**KAHN, ALBERT** Fisher Building (1928), Detroit, Mich.

and Rice, where he remained until 1896. In that year, he married Ernestine Krolik and formed a partnership with George W. Nettleton and Alexander B. Trowbridge, who left in 1897 to become dean of the Cornell University College of Architecture. The two remaining partners continued on until the death of Nettleton in 1900. For a short time, he then had a partnership with his old employer, George D. Mason (1856–1948), but it was dissolved in 1902. During these years, the work of Kahn and the others was eclectic, and Kahn continued designing most of his buildings in this manner the remainder of his life. His industrial buildings were something else again. From a rather inauspicious beginning with a building for a machine company in 1901, Kahn was to design numerous industrial buildings for many of the great American companies, including Ford, General Motors, and Chrysler. Most were innovative and experimental, many of them daring and creative.

In 1929 a Russian commission visiting Detroit was so impressed with Kahn's work, they asked him to design a tractor plant (1930) in Stalingrad. This building was so successful that the Soviet government hired Kahn to help industrialize Russia. For this purpose, he sent over a group of architects and engineers from his office, under the direction of his brother, Moritz Kahn. In two years, they built 521 factories all over the Soviet Union and trained over 1,000 Russian engineers and technicians to handle the work.

For many years, Kahn was commissioner of the Detroit Institute of Fine Arts. In this capacity, he was able to have Paul Philippe Cret (1876–1945) of Philadelphia chosen as architect for the Institute Building (1927).

Kahn's office rapidly expanded, including about 400 people by 1938. The office was then handling about one-fifth of all the architect-designed industrial work being done in the United States. The office handled all the architectural, structural, and other engineering work. Improved techniques shortened the necessary time for making working drawings. When World War II began, the office expanded to about 600 people and was plunged into the design of a large number of factories for war production. In addition, the office did naval bases in Alaska, Hawaii, Puerto Rico, Midway Island, and Jacksonville, Fla.

Active all his life, the heavy burden and long hours of the war work proved too much. Under strain and overtired, he contracted a bronchial ailment and died on December 8, 1942. The organization he had built so well survived to continue the work he started and, as Albert Kahn Associates, is still in practice today.

**Related Articles** Bacon, Henry; Cret, Paul Philippe; Factory; Modern Architecture.

**Further Reading** Hildebrand, G.: *The Architecture of Albert Kahn*, MIT Press, Cambridge, Mass., 1974.

**KAHN, LOUIS ISADORE** Estonian-American architect (1901–74). Although he only designed slightly more than 100 buildings, many of which were never built, Louis Isadore Kahn was one of the most notable and influential 20th-century architects. Much of his time was spent in study, contemplation, and introspection. He wrote little, but he did manage to impart to his students and to others a philosophy, which some have called more poetry than philosophy, of an architecture that would serve people and at the same time be a high form of art.

**Philosophy** Louis Kahn's designs illustrate his philosophy. They are bold forms, composed of masses and voids, with the materials, the structure, and even the mechanical and other engineering aspects strongly expressed. He said he depended mostly on inspiration, not on knowledge. He favored no style, no methods, no technology. Instead, he sought to find out what the building wants to be; or what a brick wants to be. He was something of a mystic, even a guru, who led his students and other followers toward order in architecture, the sense of the relationships and bonds between all things. And a very creative and personal kind of architecture it

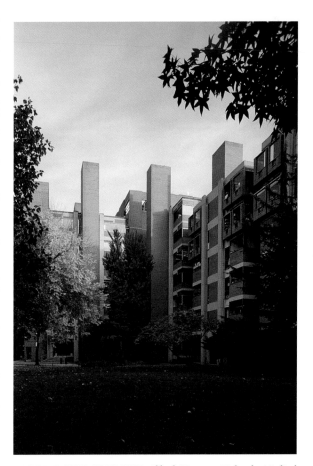

**KAHN, LOUIS ISADORE** Alfred Newton Richards Medical Research Building (1965), University of Pennsylvania, Philadelphia, Pa.

**KAHN, LOUIS ISADORE** Salk Institute for Biological Studies (1965), La Jolla, Calif.

produced. He worked closely, for the last two decades of his life, with the noted engineer August E. Komendant.

Kahn believed that in the complete set of laws of nature, which of course no one understands, there exists a force that can produce order in architecture as well as in everything else. During his career, he made a great number of speeches, or rather they might be called lectures, to students, fellow professionals, and others. His message was cryptic and had to be sensed more than understood. Those who received the message properly believe it is expressed in his designs. Although the believers are many, there are some who have doubts about this philosophy, if not about his buildings.

**Work** After he began his own practice in 1935, Kahn designed a small number of buildings during the next decade other than government housing projects. His first important commission was the Art Gallery (1953), Yale University, New Haven, Conn. This brought him to the attention of architects but brought only a few new commissions. Then came a wave of publicity about a new and controversial design on which he

was working, the Alfred Newton Richards Medical Research Building (1961; see illustration) at the University of Pennsylvania. Controversial the building may have been and still is to some extent, but many have come to consider it Kahn's best design and one of the best of its era.

Other commissions started to come in. Kahn designed about 20 houses, about half of which were built. During the next few years, he designed a number of notable buildings, including the Tribune-Review Newspaper Plant (1961), Greensburg, Pa., and the Indian Institute of Management (1963), Ahmedabad, India. Then he designed what has been called his masterpiece, the Salk Institute for Biological Studies (1965), La Jolla, Calif., for the world-famed inventor of the polio vaccine, Dr. Jonas Edward Salk (1914–   ).

During the next decade, Kahn designed other notable buildings, including Temple Beth El (1966), Chappaqua, N.Y.; the First Unitarian Church (1967), Rochester, N.Y.; the Olivetti-Underwood Factory (1970), Harrisburg, Pa.; the Kimbell Art Museum (1972), Fort Worth, Tex.; the

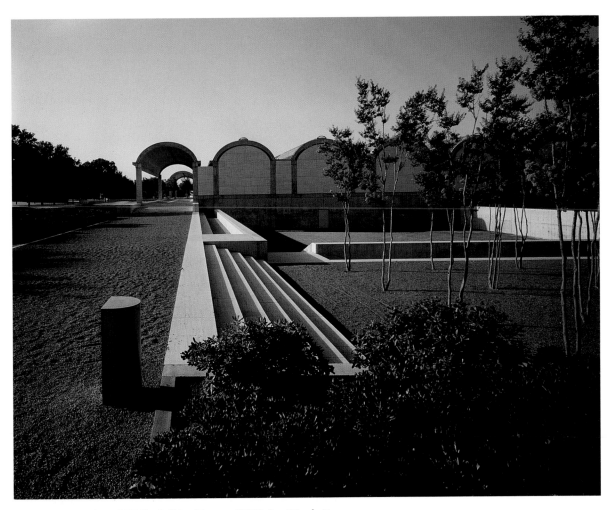

**KAHN, LOUIS ISADORE** Kimbell Art Museum (1972), Fort Worth, Tex.

Library and Dining Hall (1972) at Phillips Exeter Academy, Exeter, N.H.; and a great master plan and buildings for the capital at Dacca, East Pakistan, now Bangladesh, part of which was still under construction when he died. His last building was the British Art Center (1976), Yale University, New Haven, Conn.

**Life** Louis Isadore Kahn was born on February 20, 1901, on the island of Saaremaa (Oesel), Estonia. Although Estonia was later incorporated into the Soviet Union, Kahn always insisted he was an Estonian, not a Russian. In 1905 the family emigrated to the United States and settled in Philadelphia. In 1915 Kahn became a naturalized U.S. citizen. Having graduated from the Industrial At School of Philadelphia in 1917, he spent the next three year studying at the Pennsylvania Academy of Fine Arts, receiving a number of prizes for drawing and painting. He then enrolled in the architectural school of the University of Pennsylvania in 1920, was a student of Paul Philippe Cret (1876–1945), and graduated in 1924.

After working in an architectural office for a short time, he became the chief designer for the Sesquicentennial Exposition (1925–26) in Philadelphia. During the next few years he traveled and studied in Europe, returning to Philadelphia in 1929, during the Depression. In 1930 and later, he worked in the office of Paul Philippe Cret, who had been his teacher. In that same year, he married Esther Virginia Israeli, and they had one daughter. In 1931 he organized a number of unemployed architects and engineers into the Architectural Research Group, which studied planning, housing, and other problems.

In 1935 Kahn started his own practice and later was associated in practice with George Howe (1886–1955) from 1941 to 1943 and with Oskar Stonorov (1905–70) in 1942–43. Kahn served in various civic positions most of his professional life, starting with his appointment as consultant architect for the Philadelphia Housing Authority in 1937, and then for the U.S. Housing Authority in 1939. Never a man to let one area of activity satisfy him, Kahn continued his practice over the next years and still found time to serve as consultant architect to the Philadelphia Planning Commission, a

**KAHN, LOUIS ISADORE** Library and Dining Hall (1972), Phillips Exeter Academy, Exeter, N.H.

position he held six years starting in 1946 and then again in 1961. He became professor of architecture at Yale University, New Haven, Conn., in 1947, remaining there until 1952, with time out for a year as resident architect of the American Academy in Rome, Italy (1950–51). He was a professor at Massachusetts Institute of Technology, Cambridge, in 1956. In 1957 he was appointed professor of architecture at his alma mater, the University of Pennsylvania, a position he held until 1971.

Although Kahn was considered something of a mystic, private and reserved in manner and introverted, his philosophy and his architecture made him world famous. His buildings that were constructed, and even some of those that were not, had an impact on architects and architecture completely out of proportion to their number. His later life was filled with almost every honor that might come to an architect: seven honorary doctor's degrees; exhibits of his work; and election to the National Institute of Arts and Letters, to the Royal Swedish Academy of Fine Arts, and to fellowship in the American Academy of Arts and Sciences and the Royal Society of Arts of England. In 1971 the architects of his adopted country gave him their highest honor, the Gold Medal of the American Institute of Architects. The following year, the architects of Great Britain gave him theirs, the Royal Gold Medal of the Royal Institute of British Architects.

In 1974 Louis Isadore Kahn was at the pinnacle of his career. He had several interesting projects under way, including a redevelopment project in Iran and the buildings at Dacca, Bangladesh. Returning from a trip to Bangladesh and India, Kahn reached New York's Pennsylvania Station to take a train back to Philadelphia, collapsed with a heart attack, and died on March 17, 1974.

Since Kahn's death, critical scholarship has evaluated his work as of primary importance to 20th-century architecture. An indication of this are the national debates concerning proposed additions to the Salk Institute for Biological Studies at La Jolla, Calif., and the Kimbell Art Museum in Fort Worth. The 1991 exhibition of photographs shown extensively in this country and abroad and the accompanying publication have brought a new generation to appreciate the enduring quality of his design.

**Related Articles** CRET, PAUL PHILIPPE; EDUCATION; MODERN ARCHITECTURE.

**Further Reading** Brownlee, David B., and David G. DeLong: *Louis I. Kahn: In the Realm of Architecture*, Rizzoli, New York, 1991; Hochstim, Jan: *The Paintings and Sketches of Louis I. Kahn*, Rizzoli, New York, 1991; Latour, Alessandra, ed.: *Louis I. Kahn: Writings, Lectures, Interviews*, Rizzoli, New York, 1991.

**KOHN PEDERSEN FOX** Kohn Pedersen Fox Associates is a major American design firm of commercial buildings. Many cities in the United States and abroad contain examples of the firm's work. Known as a successful firm, it benefits from an unusually effective group of partners. William Pedersen (1938–   ) is the design partner, A. Eugene Kohn (1930–   ) an effective marketing partner, and Sheldon Fox (1930–   ) the manager of the firm. Patricia Conway (1937–   ) is president of the firm's interiors division, Kohn Pedersen Fox Conway Associates, Inc. Arthur May (1940–   ), William C. Louis (1942–   ), and Robert L. Cioppa (1942–   ) are other partners of the firm. The firm of Kohn Pedersen Fox was formed in 1976. The building which established them among the leading designers of high-rise buildings was 333 Wacker Drive, Chicago (1983). All the partners were previously with the firm of John Carl Warnecke and Associates.

**Work** Most of the company's buildings have been mid- to high-rise commercial buildings, but the firm's projects include a performing arts center design for Bucknell University (1982), Stanford University Business School expansion, Palo Alto, Calif. (1987), news broadcasting center for WABC TV Seven (1979), New York, a television studio building, ABC Studio (1984), New York, several bank offices, the Hyatt Regency hotel, Greenwich, Conn. (1986), and the U.S. embassy in Nicosia, Cyprus (1988).

From the large number of completed buildings, a few are selected as typical of the larger body of projects: 333 Wacker Drive, Chicago (1983) is located on a triangular site at the point where the city street grid meets the curved Chicago River, which is reflected in the building's curved glass wall, while the other facades relate to the city streets. The building sits on a pedestrian arcade with office floors above. The building form and relationship to its site brought this building much praise and established the firm as a major player in the development of the high-rise building.

The Procter & Gamble General Offices Complex, Cincinnati, Ohio (1985), was located next to the existing headquarters building, and the site is divided by a major street and bounded on one side by an interstate freeway access. This urban-edge location resulted in a two-tower solution set on an L-shaped base opening onto a series of gardens and plazas. The limestone exterior of the original buildings was used on the new, combined with granite and marble accents. Multiple glass types were used for solar control and to enrich the facades. Glass bridges link the complex. The entrance lobby pavilion is approached across the plaza, and the interior contains a fountain which provides effective sound masking. The complex makes an effective gate to the city and is visually rich without the possible corporate excess. The gardens and plazas do much to humanize what is in fact a very large-scale development.

A typical midtown New York City office tower is 70 East 55th Street (Heron Tower), New York (1986). This project was a 28-story midblock development and is a study in relating the building to its particular site just off Park Avenue. The building is a three-part design, with the street portion relating to the height of its Park Avenue neighbors and in scale with the plaza across the street. The shaft of the tower is set back from the street and rises to the twenty-first floor. The upper floors are recessed at the corners and terminate in a pair of towers. The street front is a subtle combination of light gray and green granite. The stone is used at the corners, forming quoins against the brick side walls. This building is a good example of integrating a new building into an existing neighborhood. Another example is the 125 Summer Street building in Boston (1988), in which a number of existing buildings were incorporated into the design, resulting in extensive retail space on the ground floor. The success of this building indicates what many cities are seeking in their design review process.

Several U.S. firms are involved in major developments in London. Kohn Pedersen Fox has prepared proposals and has proceeded with two buildings at Canary Wharf, a 71-acre site in the London Docklands, in London, England (1991), planned for a four-phase development. Less spectacular than other projects, these midrise buildings relate well to new neighboring buildings by other architects. The firm's ability to provide efficient, well-constructed buildings has provided it with a good reputation and continued opportunities to design more buildings of individual character.

**Lives** A. Eugene Kohn was born in Philadelphia, Pa., in 1930, received his architectural education at the University of Pennsylvania, and served as a lieutenant commander in the U.S. Navy before returning to civilian life. He was senior designer for Vincent G. Kling from 1960 to 1965, design director for Welton Becket Associates New York from 1965 to 1967, and president and partner of John Carl Warnecke and Associates from

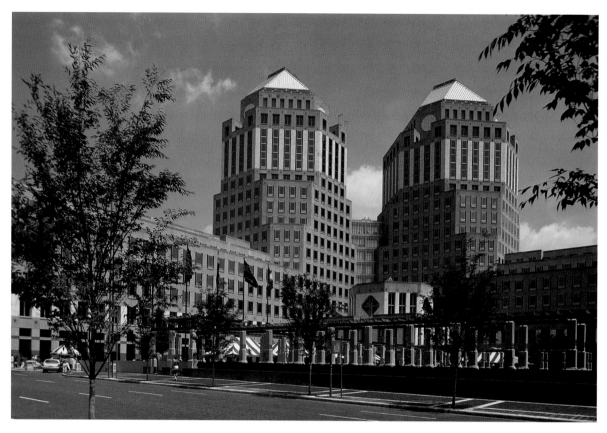

**KOHN PEDERSEN FOX** Procter & Gamble Headquarters (1985), Cincinnati, Ohio.

1967 to 1976, before the formation of the Kohn Pedersen Fox firm in 1976.

William Pedersen was born in St. Paul, Minn., in 1938. He received his architectural education from the University of Minnesota (1961) and the Massachusetts Institute of Technology (1963) and won the Rome Prize (1965) which allowed him to study for two years at the American Academy of Rome. His early architectural experience was with Pietro Belluschi, Eduardo Catalino, and I. M. Pei, and he was vice president of John Carl Warnecke and Associates before the formation of Kohn Pedersen Fox in 1976.

Sheldon Fox was born in New York City in 1930 and received his architectural degree from the University of Pennsylvania in 1953. After military service, Fox was with the firm of Kahn and Jacobs from 1955 to 1972 and was senior vice president of John Carl Warnecke and Associates until the formation of his new firm.

Patricia Conway was born in Reading, Pa., in 1937 and received degrees from New York University in 1959 and 1964 and a degree in Urban Planning from Columbia University School of Architecture in 1972. Her early career was in journalism. In 1982, she published *Ornamentalism: The New Decorativeness in Architecture and Design.* Ms. Conway was associate director of planning for John Carl Warnecke from 1972 to 1976 and joined in the formation of the new firm. In 1991, Patricia Conway was named dean of the Graduate School of Fine Arts at the University of Pennsylvania.

**Further Reading** Chao, Sonia R., and T. D. Abramson, eds.: *Kohn Pedersen Fox, Buildings and Projects 1976–1986,* Rizzoli, New York, 1987.

# L

**LABORATORY** A building, group of buildings, or room, used for scientific experiments or other research and testing. Laboratories, or research buildings, have become an important building type only in the last 50 years or so. Research and testing had previously been carried on mostly in buildings not specifically designed as laboratories.

**Types** Research is often divided into basic or fundamental, sometimes called pure, research and applied research. Basic research is concerned with the discovery of basic laws of nature, while applied research is concerned with the application of basic knowledge to practical problems or needs. Regardless of the type of research, laboratories must be designed to allow the activities to be carried out efficiently and effectively. Laboratories are used by many organizations that sponsor and perform research, including governments, associations, universities, businesses, and foundations. Laboratories are used in every discipline or field of human knowledge and endeavor, including the biological and chemical sciences, mathematics, agriculture, education, physical sciences, medicine, engineering, social sciences, business, and industry.

**Elements** The design of a laboratory begins with the classification of the research to be performed: (1) the principal science, as in chemistry or agriculture; (2) the activity, as either basic or applied research; and (3) the field of investigation, as in fuels or fertilizers. The major elements of a laboratory are the research areas, the administrative areas, the support areas, and the service facilities.

The research areas contain rooms, called laboratories, with necessary benches and other equipment for the type of work to be done. In many cases, laboratories require an environment in which temperatures, humidity, air purity, and other factors can be controlled. Frequently there are requirements for special services, such as steam, distilled water, compressed air, vacuum, and other systems. Offices or desk space and meeting rooms are needed.

Administrative areas contain offices and other related rooms. Support areas may include an auditorium, lecture rooms, library, computer room, cafeteria, and so on. Service areas include provisions for electrical and mechanical equipment, shops, and other rooms for service and maintenance. In addition, laboratories require special facilities for washing or cleaning equipment; disposal of harmful wastes; and receiving, storage, and

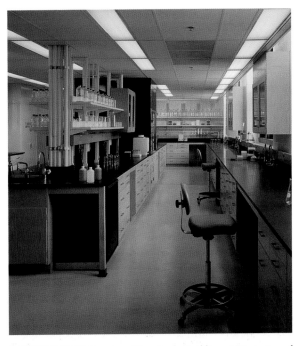

**LABORATORY** Interior, Chemistry Building, University of Michigan, Ann Arbor, Mich. *[Architects: Harley Ellington Pierce Yee Assoc. (Photo: Gary Quesada/Korab Ltd)]*

**LABORATORY** BASF Bioresearch Co. (1993), Worcester, Mass. *[Architects: Smith, Hinchman & Grylls]*

shipping. Some need special provisions for animal quarters, radiology, nuclear work, photography, and other operations.

The design of a laboratory is involved with the provision of all the many diverse requirements in a building, where the researchers and other staff may perform their experiments under controlled conditions, safely, effectively, and comfortably. Designs must allow for flexibility, not only of the laboratory building but individual spaces within the building. The complex and demanding requirements of laboratory design are challenging and rewarding to architects.

**History** Research has always been carried on by members of the human race. Until the 16th century, true research, which involves experimentation, did not exist on a wide scale. During the 16th century and afterward, researchers worked as individuals in small rooms, which might be called the first laboratories, of their own or provided by their patrons. One of these men, the English philosopher Sir Francis Bacon (1561–1626), was

the first to cite the need for organized research. His idea did not come to fruition until the latter part of the 19th century.

**American Development** In the American colonies, as in Europe and elsewhere at the time, there was no real research and no laboratories. The first laboratories were founded by individual American researchers, mostly inventors, starting in the late 1800s. They were followed by research activities in universities. One of the first real research laboratories was built by the Bell Telephone Company at about this time. A tremendous boost to organized research was given by the establishment of the U.S. National Research Council in 1916. Subsequently, a number of laboratories were built, but with the advent of World War II, laboratory construction boomed and today has become a major building type.

**Further Reading** Braybrooke, Susan, ed.: *Design for Research—Principles of Laboratory Architecture*, John Wiley, New York, 1986.

**LANDSCAPE ARCHITECTURE** Garden near Garden Grove, Calif. *[Sculptor: Isamu Noguchi]*

## LANDSCAPE ARCHITECTURE

**LANDSCAPE ARCHITECTURE** The art and science of the design, planning, and construction of outdoor spaces around buildings, including gardens, plazas, and outdoor furniture and fixtures.

A person who has been educated to practice landscape architecture is called a landscape architect, or sometimes a land planner or site planner. A landscape architect is primarily responsible for the design and construction of the outdoor spaces around and between buildings and in other places, such as parks and playgrounds. The work of a landscape architect on one project may entail only the land planning and landscaping for a single building; on another it may include similar work for a large residential development or other complex. Landscape architects design small city squares and great national parks. Some work on even larger projects, such as in city or regional planning.

**Functions** For buildings, a landscape architect's major responsibilities include establishment of proper relationships between buildings and between buildings and features of their sites, shapes and grades of the land, planning of various areas of sites, and design of walkways, driveways, walls, fences, steps, fountains, pools, and planting arrangements. In all of these functions, the landscape architect works closely with the architects, and sometimes with civil engineers.

Landscape architects perform another important function, the study and evaluation of land to determine its usefulness for buildings or other purposes. In this work, they consider the effects of the composition of the subsurface soil; the surface soil, or topsoil; surface characteristics of the topography, or form, of the land; vegetation; climate; views; landmarks; and water-supply proximity to other buildings.

**Work Phases** Landscape architects work for governmental agencies, as consultants, or in architectural firms. Some, including practitioners, teach. As consultants, they often are engaged by architects to handle the landscape work. When performing this function, landscape architects generally follow the same phases as the architects, that is, schematic, in which studies, preliminary drawings, specifications, and cost estimates are prepared; design development, in which refinements are made; and construction document, in which final drawings and specifications are prepared, from which the actual construction may be performed and a more refined estimate is made. Finally comes the construction phase, in which landscape architects inspect the site and landscaping work to ensure that it is properly constructed. A landscape architect may be called upon for other services when required on specific projects.

For people who are naturally imaginative and creative, yet practical and of sound judgment, landscape architecture can offer a fulfilling and exciting career. Not only does it offer ample opportunity for creative design, it also is a functional art in which the creative aspects can be put to practical purposes.

**Education** In addition to the usual college preparatory secondary school courses, students should take cours-

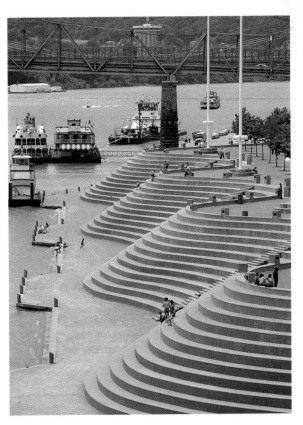

**LANDSCAPE ARCHITECTURE** Ohio River Quay (1980), Cincinnati, Ohio. *[Architect: Harry Weese]*

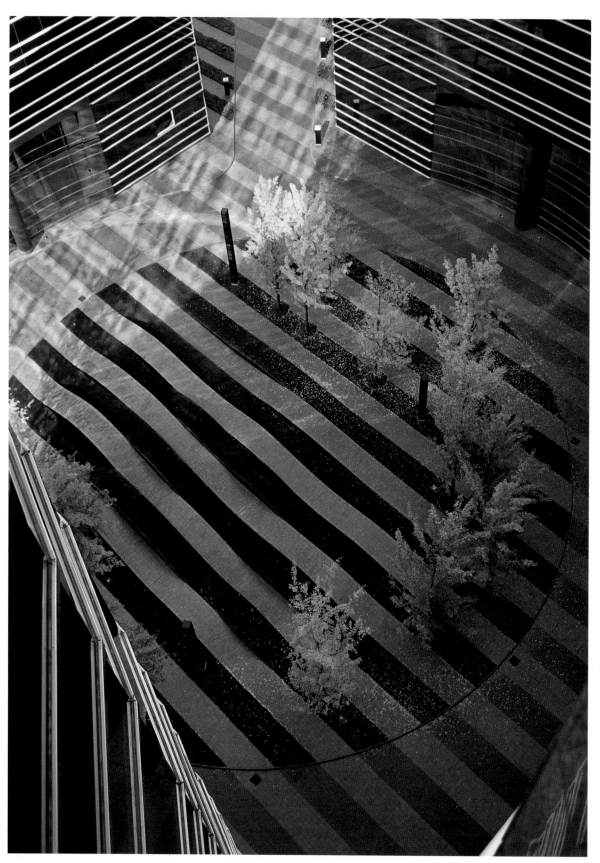

**LANDSCAPE ARCHITECTURE** Regency Court (1991), Dearborn, Mich. *[Landscape architect: John Grissim Assoc.]*

es in biology and botany if possible. In college, they take general courses in humanities, social sciences, mathematics, and sciences. They also take courses in design, history of art and architecture, site planning, construction materials, and specialized courses in landscape architecture. There are only a few landscape architecture schools in the United States, and most of these operate as part of architectural schools.

**History** The exact time of the beginning of landscape architecture, or landscape gardening as it was called for a long time, is hidden in ancient history. However, from hieroglyphs, tomb paintings, and other sources, it seems apparent that humans may have begun cultivating gardens for their pleasure as early as the Neolithic period, beginning about the 50th century B.C. in the Middle East. Egyptian nobles placed pools, trees, and other plants around their houses no later than the 26th century B.C. And the hanging gardens of Nebuchadnezzar II (d. 562 B.C.), king (605–562 B.C.), of Babylon, are famous.

Little is known about ancient Greek gardens except that they existed and that they contained trees, vineyards, and flowers. The Romans created numerous parks and gardens as well as private gardens, not only in Rome but in conquered areas, such as Constantinople, now Istanbul. Other early gardens of importance were established in such places as Persia, now Iran, and in Japan, beginning about the 3rd century A.D.

Little is known of the gardens of the Middle Ages, except that they were usually enclosed with walls, as were monasteries, castles, and towns, and were mostly simple in design and contained a small number of types of plants and flowers. During the Renaissance, landscape gardening flourished and the term landscape gardener came into use to denote a person who designed and constructed gardens. Great gardens, plazas, and parks, intended mostly for use of the nobility and the wealthy, were designed and constructed in cities and for town houses and country villas. In France and Italy, landscape gardening produced a great number of magnificent gardens, and in England, examples that were great but not as spectacular as those on the European continent.

During the 18th century, landscape gardeners in England designed gardens to produce an illusion of foreign, exotic, or old places, such as a Chinese or ancient Greek garden. This type of garden, which the French called le jardin Anglais, was soon built in France and elsewhere in Europe. These too were gardens for the wealthy and the nobility. And they soon became more picturesque than formal, designed to be beautiful, not functional.

**American Development** The early colonists started gardens soon after reaching America. Most were simple in concept and were built near private houses. New England gardens featured a device called a forthright, which was a path leading from the house lengthwise through the garden. After a few years, the colonists also began to build civic gardens, most of which were based on the formal models of earlier gardens in Europe.

One of the first American landscape architects, though he did not call himself that, Andrew Jackson Downing (1815–52), turned away from formalism toward more natural or picturesque landscape design. As the editor of The Horticulturist (1846–52), as the author of several books, and as the landscape architect for the U.S. Capitol, the Smithsonian Institution, and the White House, all in 1849 and all located in Washington, Downing exerted considerable influence on landscape architecture in the United States. Before his untimely death at age thirty-seven in a steamboat accident on the Hudson River, he also practiced architecture for a time in partnership with Calvert Vaux (1824–95), who later became the partner of the dominant figure in landscape architecture of the time, Frederick Law Olmsted (1822–1903). Olmsted was the first person to sign his drawings as a landscape architect and he designed a great many parks, including, with Vaux, Central Park, New York City. Olmsted rejected the idea that landscape design was only for the wealthy and powerful, and established the first parks in the United States that were intended for the people.

Olmsted continued to practice until the latter part of the 19th century and more than anyone else was responsible for the establishment of landscape architecture as a profession. He also deeply influenced landscape design. His son, Frederick Law Olmsted, Jr. (1870–1957), and his stepson, John Charles Olmsted (1852–1920), became famous landscape architects, as did his partner Charles Eliot (1860–97). His two sons, together with nine others, established the professional organization, the American Society of Landscape Architects, in 1899. And in 1900 the first professional school of landscape architecture was founded at Harvard University, Cambridge, Mass., and named for his former partner, Charles Eliot.

The profession of landscape architecture has since become well established and has made great progress, not only in the landscaping of individual buildings and groups of buildings but in land planning and city and regional planning. Some of the noted landscape architects of the 20th century are Garrett Eckbo (1910–   ), Daniel Urban Kiley (1912–   ), John Ormsbee Simonds (1913–   ), Lawrence Halprin (1916–   ), Hideo Sasaki (1919–   ), and Ian McHarg (1920–   ).

**Related Articles** ECOLOGY; FOUNTAIN; GARDEN; OLMSTED, FREDERICK LAW; PARK; PLANNING, CITY; SITE PLANNING.

**Further Reading** Tobey, George B., Jr.: *A History of Landscape Architecture—The Relationship of People to Environment*, American Elsevier, New York, 1973, available through Books on Demand, UMI, Ann Arbor, Mich.

**Periodical** *Landscape Architecture*, 1500 Bardstown Rd., Louisville, Ky. 40205.

**Source of Additional Information** American Society of Landscape Architects, 4401 Connecticut Ave., N.W., Washington, D.C. 20008.

**LATROBE, BENJAMIN HENRY** English-American architect and engineer (1764–1820). Often considered the first professional architect in America, Latrobe exerted considerable influence on the architecture of his own time and that which came later. He was one of the founders and leaders of the Classic Revival movement in American architecture. A designer and an innovator, he was also a voluminous writer, particularly of searching and thoughtful letters, and a talented artist. He was responsible for the architectural training of two men, who also became great architects, Robert Mills (1781–1855) and William Strickland (1788–1854). Most of all, he was a great architect. The buildings he did were excellent examples of the architecture of his time.

Latrobe was also a talented and inventive engineer, designing waterworks, canals, and docks as part of his practice. The experimental design of his buildings and other structures and his work with industrial machines, steam engines, water looms, water systems, and steamboats were ahead of their time. Many of the experiments that led him to disastrous financial losses later brought fame and fortune to others.

**Works** Emigrating to America from England in 1796, Latrobe began his practice with the Pennock House (1796), Norfolk, Va., and the Harvie-Gamble House (1799), Richmond, Va. In 1797 Latrobe won a competition for the new State Penitentiary (1800) in Richmond. This was a milestone, his first important big building; perhaps of even greater importance, it allowed him to meet Thomas Jefferson (1743–1826), an event that was to affect the lives of both men. Jefferson's interest in advanced prison design had been one of the reasons for the competition. Jefferson was interested in the prison and its architecture, and Latrobe was influenced by Jefferson's theories that design could lead to reform and hope rather than to punishment and despair. In 1798, Latrobe moved to Philadelphia.

In Philadelphia, Latrobe soon had a number of buildings to do, the most notable being the Bank of Pennsylvania (1801), the first real Classic Revival building in America; it was later demolished. In all of his early work, Latrobe worked in this style, with forms derived from those of ancient Greece and Rome, adapted to the needs, materials, and methods of the day. This was to continue in other important houses: Sen. John Pope House (1811), Lexington, Ky., and the Robert Carter Burwell House (1812), Clarke Co., Va.

As always, Latrobe had surprises in store; a notable example is his Gothic Revival Sedgeley House (1799),

Philadelphia, considered the first building in that style in America.

For perhaps his most important building, the Cathedral of the Assumption (1818), Baltimore, Md., Latrobe's ideas went through many phases. He later said he designed it seven times before it was completed, including one scheme utilizing the Gothic Revival style. In the end, the cathedral was in the Classic Revival style. Many consider this the best use of the style in any American building. He also designed another important building in Baltimore, The Exchange (1820).

Other notable churches are Christ Church (1805) and St. John's Church (1816), often called the church of the presidents, both in Washington, D.C. He also designed a number of important houses, notably the Taft House (1820), Cincinnati, Ohio, and Decatur House (1818), Washington, D.C., until recently the headquarters of the National Trust for Historic Preservation. Some also attribute another great Classic Revival house to him, Homewood (1801), now part of Johns Hopkins University, Baltimore, Md., partly because of its resemblance to the Taft House.

Another significant aspect of Latrobe's professional life was his work for the U.S. government. In 1803 Thomas Jefferson (1743–1826) appointed Latrobe surveyor of the public buildings of the United States, to superintend the construction of the Capitol Building (illustrated in capital, United States); that occupied a large part of his time until 1812, and also from 1815 to 1817. Latrobe made important contribution to the construction of the building and to its design, particularly in the south wing, in repairs and alterations of the north wing, and in many details. The interior of the central portion is primarily from his design. Latrobe also worked on the White House (see illustration in article capital, United States), or President's House, as it was then called. He redesigned the interiors and added terrace pavilions. Later, porticoes he had designed were added. And he designed the buildings of the Navy Yard (1804) in Washington.

Latrobe went to New Orleans in 1818. While there, he designed the Louisiana State Bank (1821), still in existence, and a tower (1820) for the Cathedral of St. Louis. The tower was demolished when the cathedral was rebuilt in 1850.

**Life** Benjamin Henry Boneval Latrobe was born on May 1, 1764, in Fulneck, Yorkshire, England. His father, an Irish-born Moravian minister whose antecedents were French, had moved to England before young Latrobe was born. His mother, also a Moravian, was born in Pennsylvania; she was descended from German nobility. Originally named Boneval de La Trobe, the Latrobe family was descended from French nobility. In later life, Latrobe again took up the use of Boneval as a third given name.

Benjamin Henry Latrobe attended the Moravian school at Fulneck until 1776, when he was twelve years of age. He had a good mind, did well in his studies, and showed considerable talent in drawing, particularly landscapes and buildings. From 1776 to 1784, Latrobe attended Moravian schools in Germany. After traveling in Europe, Latrobe returned to London in 1784, apparently determined to become an architect.

After a period of searching, during which he studied and wrote, he went to work in 1787 for a London architect, Samuel Pepys Cockerell (1754–1827). Little is known about his architectural experiences there. In 1791 he opened his own architectural office in London and work, mostly alterations and remodeling, came in almost immediately. Two of his houses still stand in England: Hammerwood Lodge (1792), Sussex, and Ashdown House (1793), Berkshire. The lodge was his first independent design. Both houses were forerunners of the Greek Revival buildings he designed in America. He also made designs for a canal that was never built.

On February 27, 1790, Latrobe married Lydia Sellon. They had a son and a daughter, but his wife died in childbirth with the third child in 1793. Latrobe suffered a serious nervous breakdown, and his practice came almost to a standstill.

In addition to his depression, which adversely affected his architectural practice, France and England went to war in 1793, and building construction came to a halt. Adding to his problems were his sympathies for the new American republic and for the French revolutionaries. In late 1795, he made up his mind to go to America. Sending his books and instruments ahead, he left England on November 25, 1795, and landed in Norfolk, Va., about the middle of March 1796. He had good letters of introduction and started practice immediately, designing the Pennock House within weeks of his arrival. A year later, after designing a few houses, he won the competition for the Virginia State Penitentiary.

After moving to Philadelphia in 1798, Latrobe received commissions for other buildings, including an important bank. On May 2, 1800, he married Mary Elizabeth Hazelhurst. Eventually they had three daughters and two sons, one of whom, John Hazelhurst Boneval Latrobe (1803–91), became an architect and lawyer. Another son, Henry Sellon Latrobe (1792–1817), by his first wife, became an architect and builder and worked as superintendent of construction for his father.

Latrobe soon was very busy. In addition to his architectural work, he was appointed engineer of the Philadelphia waterworks. That he was busy did not mean that he had an easy time starting his practice. He believed in complete architectural services, from the idea to the completed building, much as architects of today practice. But his practice was opposed by the powerful Carpenters' Company, whose members thought only they should design and construct the buildings of Philadelphia. In spite of their opposition, Latrobe received commissions for several houses and the Philadelphia waterworks during this period. He also spent a lot of time on buildings never built, competitions not won, and prospects for commissions never received.

Starting in 1798, Latrobe worked on several federal government projects, including a 165-ft-wide by 800-ft-long covered drydock, suggested by President Thomas Jefferson, in 1802. The drawings were finished in just a few weeks but, despite the architect's and Jefferson's satisfaction with them, the drydock was never constructed. Impressed by Latrobe's abilities, Jefferson appointed him surveyor of public buildings of the United States in 1803. The title implies more than it means. Actually, Latrobe's job was to take over the direction of the U.S. Capitol construction. Two talented architects, Stephen Hallet (1755–1825) and James Hoban (c. 1762–1831), had already tried to construct the building. Both had found working with its architect, Dr. William Thornton (1759–1828), impossible and had resigned. Latrobe soon found himself in the same position but he persisted longer than the others, staying with the work until 1812.

In 1807 Latrobe moved his family to Washington. He not only worked on the Capitol but also designed a lighthouse, buildings for the navy, and other projects for both the government and private clients. He also did work on the White House. By 1812, Latrobe's reputation had suffered, mostly because of the troubles with Thornton. Never able to handle his personal finances properly, he had also suffered losses in money and prestige in various schemes that failed.

Disillusioned and disheartened, he left Washington in 1813, moving his family to Pittsburgh, where he had become involved in a steamboat building venture with Robert Fulton (1765–1815), who had designed and built the first successful steamboat. The Pittsburgh venture was not fruitful. Latrobe managed to build up an architectural practice while there, but all his income from it and his capital disappeared in the ill-fated project. With Fulton's death in 1815, the venture failed. Financially ruined and deeply in debt, Latrobe had another nervous breakdown.

Early in 1815, Latrobe was recalled to Washington by President James Madison (1751–1836) to rebuild the Capitol, burned by the British in the War of 1812. Again he found himself embroiled in controversy and, late in 1817, resigned his position. Soon afterward he was declared bankrupt, and in 1818 moved to Baltimore where he had buildings under construction. After less than a year, Latrobe moved to New Orleans.

During much of his career, Latrobe acted as engineer and architect for waterworks, including those in

Philadelphia. Starting in 1810, with time out during the War of 1812, his waterworks in New Orleans had been under construction. He not only designed the waterworks but arranged for their financing and constructed the project. Latrobe's son, Henry, who had assisted him in the work on the Capitol and other buildings, was the construction superintendent and also designed and constructed buildings on his own. On September 3, 1817, Henry died, at age twenty-four, of yellow fever. The grief-stricken father went to New Orleans to take over the work on the waterworks, replacing his son.

His spirits revived by the new environment, Latrobe started designing buildings in New Orleans. At fifty-six, he had survived financial losses, controversy, the premature death of his first wife in childbirth and three other children, and the loss of his reputation. Then yellow fever struck him and he died on September 3, 1820, three years to the day after his son. He died worn out by overwork, despondent, and almost penniless. But all of his troubles and his tragic death could not obscure the greatness of his architecture.

**Related Articles** CAPITAL, UNITED STATES; CARPENTERS' COMPANY; CLASSIC REVIVAL ARCHITECTURE; JEFFERSON, THOMAS; MILLS, ROBERT; STRICKLAND, WILLIAM.

**Further Reading** Hamlin, Talbot: *Benjamin Henry Latrobe,* Oxford University Press, New York, 1955.

**LEAD** The heaviest metal, lead is widely used in construction. These uses include roofing, coated metals, paints and coatings, glass, and radiation protection. Lead had long been used in paints but has been banned from interior use for health reasons. Lead in the human body may build up to toxic levels, and is a particular hazard for children who may ingest dry paint containing lead. Lead fumes, vapor, or dust are also toxic if experienced in quantity.

The U.S. lead deposits have been mined since 1621 in Virginia, and lead was later discovered in the Mississippi Valley. The eastern deposits were relatively free of precious metals, but in the west, lead was associated with veins of gold and silver, which encouraged wider mining and use of lead. In the western United States, lead was found often mixed with zinc. The process for separating these two metals was not found until 1925. Since then, large quantities of both metals have been produced.

The ore is mined and crushed and ground to separate the ore from waste rock. The various metals can be separated by a flotation process, where the lead can be drawn off. After this process, the lead slag is smelted and sulfur eliminated to give the needed characteristics. Lead bullion can then be refined. Many products of a complex refining process may include copper, gold, silver, tin, zinc, arsenic, bismith, and sulphur.

Lead may be extruded, rolled, cast, or used in such a form as metal powder. Lead is graded, and only certain types are used in construction. Commercial types of lead include basic lead carbonate, lead coatings, lead oxides (litharge and red lead), sheet and strip, lead silicates, and lead sulfates. Alloys of metals containing lead include brass and bronze. Lead may be added to copper, iron, steel, and tin to improve their behavior. Coated metals containing lead are called "terne."

**Roofing** The use of sheet lead for roofing has a long history, and has been used because of its resistance to corrosion. Some lead sheet roofs have survived for centuries without failing. Most lead roofing is replacement roofing for historic structures or for roofs which are exposed to salt spray. The weight of lead roofing limits its use. The dull gray color absorbs considerable heat from solar radiation, which may be a problem in hot climates.

**Coated Metals** Thin coatings of lead may be applied to other metals used in construction. One such product is lead-coated copper, which may be used for roofing and flashing where the dull gray appearance of lead is preferred to the green of oxidized copper. Because lead is neutral, it can protect the metals underlying the lead coating. Terne is a lead coating over iron, steel, or stainless steel.

**Paints and Coatings** Basic lead carbonate has a long history as pigment for white paint and is still used in some exterior paints. It provides adhesion, toughness, durability, and elasticity to the paint. The newer lead silicates are used as a white pigment and may supplant the use of lead carbonate. Another product used since ancient times is red lead (lead oxide), now used to coat structural steel as one of the best rust-inhibitive paints.

**Radiation Protection** Sheet lead is an effective protection from x-rays and other radio interference and has found wide use in hospitals and dental offices where x-ray protection is important. It is also used to protect stored computer discs and tape from radio interference. Sheet lead is also used for many products used in nuclear facilities including lead bricks, lead plates and castings, laboratory table and sink tops, storage containers, and lead rubber gloves and aprons. It is also used as sheathing, nails, and lead plywood when radiation protection is needed.

**Other Uses** *Litharge* is lead monoxide and is used in making rubber, storage batteries, glass, and glazes. Litharge was first used by the Egyptians for glazes and by 800 B.C. in glass. Litharge is also used in chrome pigments and may be used as a stabilizer and binder in the manufacture of paints, plastics, and linoleum. When mixed with glycerin, litharge makes a strong adhesive used for joining glass, metals, and ceramics. Lead products are used in a wide variety of other products which benefit from the qualities contributed by this versatile metal.

**Further Reading** Hornbostel, Caleb: *Construction Materials—Types, Uses and Applications,* 2d ed., John Wiley, New York, 1991.

**LIBRARY** Cleo Rogers Memorial Library (1969), Columbus, Ind. *[Architect: I. M. Pei & Partners]*

**LIBRARY** A building or a room in which a collection of books, and sometimes other materials, is kept for reading and reference. Of all the building types, none is more important to the culture and civilization of the human race than the library. The books and other materials contained in libraries are essential to the understanding of history and progress and to the education of those who will provide the progress of the future. And a library is one of the most challenging and rewarding buildings to design.

A library may be a small room with a modest collection of books in a private residence or it may be a great public institution with books and other materials in the millions. Libraries may constitute limited collections made by individuals for their own pleasure and needs or they may be highly specialized and virtually complete collections of materials on limited subjects, used only by scholars.

**Types** There are many types of libraries owned by government on all levels, from national to local, by schools from kindergartens through universities, by businesses, and by religious groups. In fact, there is no field of human endeavor in which there are no libraries.

Public libraries are owned by and located in cities and towns for the use of people living there. These range in size from a few thousand volumes in the smallest localities to millions in the largest cities. Libraries in schools, colleges, and universities also vary considerably in size according to needs and to financial resources available. It has been said that an educational institution can be judged, in large part, by the quality of its library. In some schools, libraries are called by such names as instructional materials, instructional resource, learning resource, or information resource centers, apparently in an attempt to describe the expansion of such libraries to include media other than books, such as periodicals, cassettes, compact discs, videotapes, closed-circuit TV, moving pictures, slides, microfilm, and the like. Materials of this sort are now available in other types of libraries.

In addition to the libraries of colleges and universities, which are often research libraries, there are others for research supported by private organizations, foundations, associations, and government. Some of these are highly specialized. Other special libraries are maintained by businesses and other organizations for their own specific purposes. For example, newspapers, manufacturers,

**LIBRARY** Library, University of California (1970; addition 1987), San Diego, Calif. *[Architect: William Pereira; addition architect: Gunnar Birkerts]*

and professional associations often have libraries dedicated strictly to their own endeavors and needs. All states have libraries and the U.S. government has a great number in all of its departments and three national libraries, all in or near Washington, D.C.: the Library of Congress, the National Library of Medicine, and the National Library of Agriculture.

There are architectural libraries in architectural schools all over the country. Perhaps the greatest is the Avery Library, Columbia University, New York City. Another important architectural library is that of the American Institute of Architects in Washington, D.C.

Many public libraries, in addition to their main buildings, maintain branch libraries located in convenient places in neighborhoods of cities. An extension of branch units is the bookmobile, a van or truck that can be driven to various points in cities or elsewhere bringing books to those who find it inconvenient to visit the library building.

In addition to their primary functions of storing and lending books and other materials, libraries perform a number of other services. They often serve as archives for important papers, original manuscripts, biographical information, government records, and so on. Many provide Braille books and talking books, articles and books on tape, for those who are blind. Many sponsor performances, discussion groups, and other educational and entertaining programs for children and adults. Others stage exhibits of various kinds.

**Elements** The major elements in libraries are the spaces for books and other materials, readers, meetings, administration, and equipment and maintenance. Books, other than those in reading rooms or on display, are ordinarily stored in bookstacks, tiers of shelves specifically designed for library use. In some libraries, the bookstacks or stacks are open, making them accessible to readers; in others, stacks are closed and attendants must bring books to readers. In the stacks, as elsewhere in libraries, books are filed according to a system, ordinarily the Dewey decimal or that of the Library of Congress. Sometimes, especially in research libraries, cubicles, called carrels, are provided in which scholars may work.

Readers are accommodated in reading rooms. Some are general reading rooms, but others may be classified according to the types of materials available or by the people who use them. Thus there may be periodical reading rooms for newspapers and magazines, microfilm rooms, reference rooms, and children's and young adults' rooms. Books and materials used in a given type of reading room may be stored in stacks nearby, or in central stacks. Important parts of a library, located in the reading room or nearby, are the card files, now more frequently computerized, in which titles may be located, and checkout desks where materials may be signed out and returned. Meeting rooms and rest rooms must be provided in convenient locations. Some libraries have small kitchens adjacent to meeting rooms and some have auditoriums for large groups.

Administrative areas are generally of three types: offices for librarians and other employees; workrooms where books and other materials may be processed, cataloged, and repaired; and employee areas, such as lounges, rest rooms, and dining facilities. Equipment and maintenance areas must be provided for mechanical and electrical equipment and for the upkeep and repair of the building.

All the elements of libraries must be planned together in a manner that will make their use pleasant, comfortable, and rewarding for readers. At the same time, libraries must be efficient and easy to operate and must have provisions for protecting books and other materials. The planning and design of libraries that meet these criteria have been continuing concerns of architects for many centuries.

The impact of computerization on information access has grown rapidly, although the high costs of development and maintenance may require a fee structure for access. One feature of automated search is a standardized terminology. For architecture, the Art and Architecture Thesaurus (AAT) developed within the Art History Information Program of the J. Paul Getty Trust organizes terms applicable for indexing, cataloguing, and research of periodicals, books, images, and objects. This thesaurus uses hierarchical and alphabetical terms that may be linked to retrieve information. It is used by the Research Libraries Group's Research Libraries Information Network (RLIN). Other more general efforts include the Ohio College Library Center (OCLC) and the Library of Congress machine-readable catalogue (MARC) initiated in 1961 in accordance with the Anglo-American Cataloging Rules and now in advanced form used nationally.

**History** For at least 5,000 years before the birth of Christ, pictorial and written records were made on clay tablets in Mesopotamia. It is believed that libraries of these tablets were assembled at about the same time. A library from the 21st century B.C. has been discovered as have later ones. Papyrus scrolls are known to have existed as far back as 2500 B.C. and papyrus continued to be used well into the Christian era, not only by the Egyptians but by other people living around the Mediterranean Sea, including the Greeks and Romans. Many of these scrolls were assembled into libraries but almost all have disappeared because of the rapid decay of

**LIBRARY** St. Mary's College (1982), South Bend, Ind. *[Architects: Woollen, Molzan and Partners]*

papyrus. Leather was used instead of papyrus in some cases, and by the end of the 5th century A.D., parchment, the untanned skin of animals, had supplanted papyrus. Vellum is a very fine grade of parchment.

Some of the most famous ancient libraries were those of Ramses III, Egyptian pharaoh in the 13th century B.C.; Assyrian King Sennacherib in the 7th century B.C. in Nineveh; and the library of Alexandria, Egypt, founded by Alexander the Great and developed by pharaohs Ptolemy I and II in the 4th century B.C. The Greeks established the first public library in Athens, about 500 B.C., and Aristotle founded another great library. The Romans, starting with Julius Caesar, built at least 25 public libraries in Rome by the 5th century and also built libraries in the countries they conquered.

During the Middle Ages, the important libraries were in monasteries and churches. Although paper had been invented by the Chinese in the second century A.D., it did not reach Europe until about the 12th. By the 15th century, paper had mostly replaced parchment, and printing with movable type was invented by Johann Gutenberg about 1450. Thus began the age of libraries of books rather than handwritten manuscripts. One of the world's great libraries, that of the Vatican, in Rome, was founded about the same time. Other great European libraries were founded, including the Bibliothèque Nationale in Paris in the 14th century, and the Bodleian, at Oxford University, England, and the Laurentian, in Florence, Italy, both in the 16th century. Many other great libraries, all over the world, have been founded since.

**American Development** In the American colonies, the first libraries were private collections made by individuals for their own use and pleasure. The library at Harvard University, Cambridge, Mass., was founded in 1638 when John Harvard (1607–38) left his private library and money from his estate to help start both the university and its library. The first public library was founded in 1653 in Boston; many libraries were built in the years succeeding. The Library Company of Philadelphia was founded in 1731 by Benjamin Franklin (1706–90). It was the first of many subscription libraries which bought books with members' dues and loaned the books to them free.

In 1800 the Library of Congress was established, but the British burned its books during the War of 1812. The private library of Thomas Jefferson (1743–1826) was purchased to form the nucleus of what has become the largest library in the United States. The first tax-supported public library was opened in Peterborough, N.H., in 1833. The industrialist and humanitarian Andrew Carnegie (1835–1919), a Scottish-American who made a fortune in steel, gave millions of dollars toward the construction of more than 2,500 libraries in the United States. The building of libraries has continued in the United States ever since. Many libraries are notable examples of good architecture designed by talented architects.

**Related Articles** BOOK, ARCHITECTURAL; COLLEGE AND UNIVERSITY BUILDING; MAGAZINE, ARCHITECTURAL; SCHOOL; Articles on architects.

**Further Reading** Toan, Danforth: "Libraries," *Encyclopedia of Architecture—Design, Engineering & Construction*, John Wiley, New York, 1989.

**Source of Additional Information** American Library Association, 50 E. Huron St., Chicago, Ill. 60611.

**LIGHTING** The system that provides illumination in buildings and their surroundings. Lighting can be natural, as that received from the sun through windows, or artificial, as in electric lighting. For further discussion of natural lighting, see articles entitled climate; window. Beginning in the fourth quarter of the 19th century, electric lighting has steadily increased in importance in architecture. Today it is difficult to imagine what life was like before that time. And reliable electric lighting, at relatively low cost, deeply affects the design of buildings.

**Electromagnetic Energy** Light is a form of radiant energy that permits vision. Light is also considered to be one type of electromagnetic energy, similar to cosmic rays, gamma rays, x-rays, ultraviolet, infrared or heat, radio, and electrical waves. Each type of wave travels at certain ranges of velocity and each operates in a range of frequencies, or cycles per second, measured in hertz (Hz). The shortest waves, with the greatest frequencies, are cosmic rays, measured in a miniscule fraction of an inch and with frequencies of about $10^{22}$ Hz. At the other end of the spectrum are radio waves which may be miles in length and up to about $10^4$ Hz. Light waves fall somewhere in the middle between the two extremes, about $10^{15}$ Hz, and from slightly less than 400 to more than 800 nanometers (nm), or about 400–800 x $10^{-9}$ meters (m). Light is believed to travel at a speed of 186,282 miles per second (299,792 km/s).

**Color** The color of visible light is dependent on the wavelengths and frequencies. Light with the longest wavelengths and lowest frequencies, near the infrared or heat range, is red; as wavelengths decrease and frequencies increase, the color changes, in turn, to various shades of orange, yellow, green, blue, and violet until the visible light approaches the ultraviolet range. White light is produced when a source emits approximately equal quantities of light from all portions of the visible spectrum.

**Color Temperatures** Light is sometimes described by its color temperatures. This measure, named for English physicist William Thompson, Lord Kelvin (1824–1907), is based on the fact that when light-absorbing bodies are heated, they at first glow deep red, then brighter red, then shades of yellow until at the highest temperatures, they glow white, or at white-hot.

Color temperatures are measured in International System (SI) units, on the kelvin temperature scale in kelvins (K). (The degree Celsius has been adopted as a special name for the kelvin for use in expressing Celsius temperatures or intervals in the SI system.) The kelvin, sometimes called the absolute, scale, used mostly for scientific work, is related to the Celsius scale, ordinarily employed for most purposes in the metric system. In SI units, 0°C represents the freezing point of water; 100°C represents its boiling point. On the kelvin scale, 0 K is called the absolute zero and occurs at -273°C or -456°F. Thus 273 K is equal to 0°C, and 373 K is equal to 100°C. Some typical color temperatures include candle flames at about 1700 K; incandescent lamps from 2500 to 4000 K; and fluorescent lamps from 3500 to 6500 K. Blue sky overhead has a color temperature of more than 10,000 K as contrasted to the first rays of a sunrise at about 2000 K.

**Light Measures** Several measurements are used in lighting design. The most basic is luminous intensity, the light-emitting power of a source, measured in candelas (cd). Luminous flux is the measure of the flow of light, in lumens (lm). Luminance is the light emitted by a unit area of surface of a source, measured in candelas per square meter ($cd/m^2$). Illuminance, sometimes called illumination, is the light falling on a unit area of surface, measured in lux (lx), a quantity equal to lumens per meter squared. The quantity of light is measured in lumen-seconds (lm•s); light exposure in lux-seconds (lx•s); and luminous efficacy, formerly called efficiency, in lumens per watt (lm/W).

**Characteristics of Light** Lighting affects the eye and without those effects would have no purpose in architecture. Four basic characteristics of light primarily affect the eye: luminance, which is almost synonymous with brightness; size; contrast; and time. Visual tasks are dependent on these four factors and also on the perception of detail, low contrast levels, and levels of brightness. When lighting is being designed for various tasks or purposes, these characteristics must be taken into consideration. Various tasks require various combinations of characteristics. In terms of luminance or brightness, fine work requires greater brightness than that which is less fine. Reading type on a page generally requires less brightness than reading handwriting. In sewing by hand, some 10 times as much luminance is required as for reading type, if the work is with white thread on white cloth; black thread on white cloth may require as much as 30 times the luminance for reading type.

The size of objects is important in lighting and seeing. Larger objects are easier to see than smaller ones, but smaller ones can be made easier by moving them nearer the eye. Contrast required for various tasks varies considerably. For example, in reading type on a page, black type contrasted with white paper aids in the read-

**LIGHTING** Interior of renovated Dome, Michigan State Capitol (1879; alteration, 1993), Lansing, Mich. *[1879 architect: Elijah B. Meyers; restoration architect: Richard Frank; lighting design: Gary Steffy]*

ing. On the other hand, black type on a gray page is harder to read. However, high contrasts between the work being performed and the background are considered detrimental. It is therefore often considered best to have the brightness of the work no greater than 3 times that of the background. The time of viewing an object is important in seeing and lighting. An object will be seen better if viewed over a relatively long period of time than if viewed only briefly. An object viewed only briefly will require more brightness than one of the same size viewed over a longer period of time. Minimum levels of luminance have been established for various tasks, and tables of these quantities are widely available.

**Qualitative Characteristics** Another important consideration in lighting is the quality of the light. One of the characteristics of quality is glare, light received by the eye directly from light sources, causing discomfort and interference with good vision. The amount of glare is rated by brightness, size, and position of the glare-producing light source. Glare is generally controlled by reducing the brightness of the source or its size or changing its position. Reflected glare, from mirrors or other polished surfaces, must also be controlled.

Another qualitative characteristic of lighting is diffusion, the direction or directions from which light emanates. If light were perfectly diffused, it would come

**LIGHTING** Detail, interior of Christian Theological Seminary (1987), Indianapolis, Ind. *[Architects: Edward Larrabee Barnes/John M. Y. Lee]*

from all directions with equal intensities. At the other extreme would be the least diffused, a light emanating from a single direction. In architectural lighting for general purposes, such as the overall lighting of offices, classrooms, and the like, diffused lighting is most often used. For specific tasks, such as fine detailing in a drafting room, directional lighting is used to supplement the general lighting. Diffused lighting produces relatively uniform levels of light in rooms, tending to eliminate shadows and contrast, and therefore tending to make things look flat. Directional lighting produces shadows and contrasts. For many purposes, some combination of the two types will be found useful and comfortable. For example, in an art museum, sculpture might have diffused lighting for general vision, with directional lighting to illuminate the three dimensions with shadows and highlights.

Another important qualitative characteristic of lighting is color. When light strikes surfaces, portions of it are absorbed and portions reflected. White light striking a

black or white surface is partly absorbed and partly reflected in the entire spectrum of colors of which the light is composed. White light striking surfaces of other colors is selectively absorbed and reflected. For example, a white light striking a blue wall has various components of its spectrum absorbed, except the blue which is reflected and is seen to be blue. The attribute that is usually called a color is actually a hue: red, yellow, green, or others. Black, white, and gray, composed only of black with white, are colorless or neutral, and therefore have no hues. The brilliance or brightness of a color is called its value. In general, white is the most brilliant and black the least, with the various hues in positions in between the extremes. The saturation of a color is an indication of its vividness. For example, starting with a gray that has no hue and a relatively low brilliance or value, the addition of another color, such as red, changes the saturation or vividness of the gray, but does not change its brilliance. Saturation is sometimes referred to as chromaticity.

Colors strongly affect lighting; for example, the greater the value of a color, the greater its reflectance of white light, with white surfaces the most reflective, black the least, and the hues in between. Colors are also considered to have strong psychological effects. Colored light and objects may be used to alter the appearance of things. For example, bluish or greenish lights or walls make the interiors of buildings, their contents, and people look quite different from reddish lights. Many other psychological effects are created by colors, including the feeling that warm colors, like red, make rooms look smaller, and cool ones like blue, make them look larger. In addition, warm colors are thought to produce tensions in people, while cool colors have calming effects.

**Proper Lighting** This is of extreme importance in architecture today. Good lighting for various tasks and purposes helps prevent tension, tiredness, eyestrain, discomfort, and even illness in occupants. Proper lighting promotes efficiency in the work of the occupants, helps prevent accidents and reduce errors, and aids in good visual health by helping to prevent eye defects or to keep them from becoming worse. Improper lighting can produce any of the opposite effects or all of them, in combination. In addition, proper lighting can produce a great many kinds of exciting, ornamental, and esthetic effects in architecture, outdoors as well as in interiors.

**Sources** The most universal source of light is the sun which provides daylight. (See articles entitled climate; window.) Another important source, from the earliest times, is fire, still used in some parts of the world for certain kinds of lighting. Today the all-important sources of artificial lighting in buildings are various electrical devices. Such devices include various types of lamps, in the form of bulbs, tubes, and panels. The major types are incandescent, gaseous discharge, and electroluminescent lamps. Incandescent lamps generally operate on the principle of wire filaments, enclosed in glass bulbs, heated by electric currents. Gaseous lamps operate generally on the principle of gases, which conduct electricity through glass tubes. Electroluminescent lighting is based on the principle of direct excitement of phosphors in thin sheets or panels by electric currents.

For many years, incandescent lamps were the most important source of electric lighting in architecture. In general, they are sealed glass bulbs, in which tungsten filaments are located. The filaments are heated by electric currents, producing light and heat. Such lamps are not very efficient sources of light, dissipating some 90 percent of the electric power in heat. Most incandescent lamps are either frosted or coated inside with silica for diffusion of the light. Incandescent lamps are available in a number of shapes, with several types of bases, and in numerous capacities for uses in architecture. Very small lamps, similar to flashlight bulbs, are sometimes used for warning and control lights for mechanical and electrical equipment. From these very-low-wattage types, lamp capacities range up to 300 W and higher. For lighting in buildings, lamps have various types of bases, including the smallest for use with standard 120 V current, called the candelabra base, and the next larger, intermediate, both used for ornamental purposes. The most commonly used is the medium base, and the mogul base is used for very-large-capacity lamps.

Incandescent lamps are available in various specialized types, including ones with reflector surfaces inside; colored glass types; single lamps with two filaments, providing three different levels of lighting; safety lamps; and low-voltage lamps. Extended-service lamps have longer useful lives than regular lamps, up to 2,500 hours or more, but are not as efficient. Other types are also available for special purposes. One is the tungsten-halogen type, which is an incandescent lamp, with a tungsten filament enclosed in a quartz tube, filled with one of the halogens: iodine, chlorine, bromine, or fluorine. These lamps have useful lives twice as long as those of ordinary incandescent types, because the halogens prevent evaporation of the tungsten filaments.

While incandescent lamps are still widely used in architecture, particularly in residential buildings and for ornamental, stadium lighting, and other purposes; fluorescent lighting has come to be used very widely for many purposes in many building types. Fluorescent lamps are generally tubular types filled with inert gases, such as low-pressure argon, and mercury vapor. Passing electricity through the mercury vapor causes it to arc, producing ultraviolet light that excites the interior coatings of fluorescent phosphors in the tubes. The phosphors then emit visible light.

Fluorescent lamps require devices called ballasts to produce the very high voltages necessary to start arcs in the mercury vapor and to limit the current after the arcs have started. Fluorescent lamps are usually rapid-start, requiring about 1 s for starting, or instant-start. Fluorescent tubes generally come in lengths ranging from 24 to 96 in, representing wattages from 25 to over 200. They are available with regular or mogul bipin, single-pin, or double-contact bases. Fluorescent lamps also require starters, including a type in which a button must be held in momentarily, and others that start almost instantaneously. Most fluorescent lamps are straight tubes, but special types are also available in U shapes, circles, and panels. The efficiency of fluorescent tubes depends on many variables, such as frequency of starting, hours of burning, and temperatures. In general, they are more efficient than incandescent types.

A number of other gaseous discharge lamps are available for uses in architecture. Neon lighting, in which neon gas conducts the electricity to produce light, is used mostly for signs. High-intensity discharge lamps are used for special purposes. They operate on the principle of the production of light in high-pressure gases or vapors. Three types are currently available, in capacities up to 1500 W: mercury vapor, metal halide, and high-pressure sodium. All require ballasts and are used for street lighting and other purposes.

Electroluminescent light sources are generally available in sheet form for use with 120 V current. The sheets are made of phosphor materials, with aluminum foil and electrical leads enclosed in plastics. Emitting light from their entire surfaces, these light sources are used mostly for ornamental purposes and are available in several colors in addition to white.

A number of other types of light sources are sometimes used in architecture for lighting and other purposes, including ultraviolet, or black light, used for ornamental and other purposes; carbon arc lights, used in searchlights and motion picture projectors; and cold-cathode lamps, used for purposes similar to neon types. Other specialized types include infrared lamps for heating, laser lamps for security purposes, light-emitting diodes (LED) for indicators and controls, and ozone and germicidal lamps for sterilization of the air in buildings, such as hospitals.

**Luminaires** Literally thousands of types of lighting fixtures, sometimes called luminaires, are available today. They range from simple, utilitarian types to ones that are very ornamental. They may be fixed, as in ceiling fixtures, or movable, as in floor types. They may be acquired with lamps of any of the kinds previously discussed. There are indoor and outdoor types. Ceiling fixtures may be surface-mounted, recessed, or hung permanently or on tracks. There are types for installation on walls, poles, and in other locations. Lighting fixtures may distribute light in many kinds of patterns, asymmetrical as well as symmetrical. They may also emit light directly, indirectly, or in combinations. They may emit diffused direct light or combinations. Such fixtures may be square, round, rectangular, or other shapes. They may have reflectors, louvers, lenses, filters, or any of a number of other accessories. Light fixtures may also be mounted above a hung plastic luminous ceiling that emits light from a large area rather than a single point or line.

Luminaires generally illuminate in one of five ways: direct, in which most of the light is downward; indirect, in which 90 percent or more of the light is upward; semi-direct, in which 60 to 90 percent is downward, the remainder upward; semi-indirect, with 60 to 90 percent of the light upward, the remainder downward; and general diffuse, which directs approximately equal amounts of light upward and downward. Among the thousands of luminaires available, there are types for every imaginable architectural purpose. The best source of information on luminaire types is included in catalogs issued by manufacturers. Also available are many kinds of special switches, dimmers, timers, and other devices often used in conjunction with lighting systems.

**Lighting Design** The design of lighting for general and special uses within and outside buildings is quite complex and varies considerably between building types. In general, the purposes of such design are to provide functional, efficient, and economical lighting for all the general and special needs in buildings, together with pleasing ornamental architectural effects. Proper lighting levels, of the proper quality, should be provided for the various tasks and activities to be performed in buildings. Lighting design begins with analysis of the functions and problems in a proposed building, proceeds to selection of proper light sources including fixtures, then to calculation of the loads and to establishment of fixture patterns for the overall or general lighting. Supplemental lighting for special purposes or effects may then be calculated and sources and fixtures selected. Finally, the entire design must be reviewed, and altered if necessary.

The design of lighting, in all but the simplest applications, is ordinarily handled by lighting designers, many of whom are electrical engineers. Others were trained in architecture or other disciplines. Lighting designers must coordinate their work closely with that of other environmental designers, particularly with that of architects and electrical engineers who design electric power and wiring systems in buildings. Lighting design offers great opportunities for the achievement of ornamental and dramatic effects in architecture, in addition to the purely functional requirements.

**History** The first lighting in architecture was the natural light from the sun that came through openings in primitive huts and tents. Natural lighting has remained an important element of architecture to this day.

The first artificial lighting used by humans came from campfires and from burning branches removed from the fires. Later, fires inside huts and tents gave off light; for portable lights, torches of resinous woods, such as cedar, were used. Early humans had little use for such lighting, since they usually went to bed when the sun went down and arose with the sunrise. This continued to be the most usual practice for many centuries. In the early civilizations around the Mediterranean Sea, Egypt, the Middle East, and the mainland of Greece as well as in islands such as Crete, candles of wax or tallow were used as far back as 3000 B.C. People also used simple lamps, usually no more than a hollowed stone in which a wick and oil were placed. Later, improved lamps were made of pottery, seashells, and metals. The ancient Greeks and Romans used candles, lamps, and torches for lighting. Fuels were various oils, such as olive, castor, linseed, and others. The first use of petroleum is thought to have occurred in Mesopotamia.

The use of candles and lamps for lighting was quite widespread in Roman times, but during the Middle Ages less artificial lighting was used than previously. Oil for lamps and candles was scarce and expensive and therefore used mostly in churches, cathedrals, and castles. Some light was, of course, supplied by the great fireplaces used to heat Gothic castles, but the churches and cathedrals were unheated. During the Renaissance, artificial lighting was almost as little used as in the Middle Ages. Fireplaces gave some light, and lamps and candles were scarce and expensive, affordable only by wealthy people.

**American Development** In early colonial America, candles and oil for lamps were scarce and expensive. For the most part, people arose at sunrise and went to bed at sundown. Some light came from fires in fireplaces. In the 18th century, artificial lighting began to improve, mostly because of the increasing availability of oil from the sperm whales, pursued and captured by New England whalers. Candles also became more plentiful, but were still expensive. Most households had their own candle molds, in which they made their own, until candle-making machines were developed much later. Modest homes and other buildings were then lighted with candles in holders, while more important buildings and larger homes were often lighted with candelabra and chandeliers which often held a great number of candles.

In 1792 an English engineer, William Murdock (1754–1839), revolutionized artificial lighting when he first installed coal-gas lights, fueled with a by-product of the coking process. In 1802 he used this kind of lighting for the exterior of a factory and in 1806, in the interior of another. In the latter year, coal gas was first used for lighting in the United States. By 1824, natural gas was used, in a limited way, for lighting. By the middle of the 19th century, gas lighting was used in buildings all over the United States. The quality of the light from gas was greatly improved by the invention of the Bunsen burn-

**LIGHTING** Interior, Styling Dome, Chrysler Technology Center (1992), Auburn Hills, Mich. *[Architect: CRSS; lighting design: Stefan R. Graf, IlluminArt Lighting Consultants]*

er, which premixed air and gas, and the Welsbach mantle, a cloth hood treated with chemicals. Bunsen burners produced hot, blue, smokeless flames, and are still used in laboratories today. Welsbach mantles produced very hot, white, incandescent flames, and are still in use today in gas and gasoline lanterns, such as those used by campers. By the end of the 19th century, manufactured and natural gas were firmly established as fuels for lighting.

Rudimentary incandescent light bulbs had been made during the first half of the 19th century, but Thomas Alva Edison (1847–1931) produced the first practical type in 1879. Arc lights had been used on a limited scale for illumination previously. By the end of the century, electric generating plants had been built in many places in the United States, and electric lighting was beginning to replace gas lighting. The changeover proceeded rapidly, but the use of gas for lighting lingered on for some time into the early part of the 20th century. In 1881 a mile of Broadway, in New York City, had been lighted with carbon arc lights; other cities soon followed suit.

With the spread of electric lighting for buildings and cities came new kinds of lives for people, who now could use the night hours for purposes previously only possible in the daytime. And the new development changed architecture radically. No longer would buildings be con-

structed almost entirely for daytime activities. No longer would their occupants be dependent on daylight or the relatively inefficient light produced by burning gas. Eventually, the easy availability and efficiency of electric lighting led to what many think are excesses in architecture. In some buildings, there was little or no provision for natural lighting. In others, artificial lighting was provided in amounts considerably greater than needed for activities. Such buildings have been criticized for their often unnatural, even inhuman, interior qualities and in later years, for their waste of energy.

From the beginning of its use, electric lighting has been almost continually improved. More efficient incandescent light bulbs have been developed and the quality of the light improved. Other types of electric light sources have been developed, including the fluorescent tube, which produces high levels of light with less energy than do incandescent types. Fluorescent lighting in architecture has increased rapidly since World War II and has become the standard general lighting for many building types, including office buildings and stores. Along with the improvements and new developments in light sources, there have been corresponding improvements in lighting fixtures.

Today many types of light sources are available for architectural uses, including high-intensity lamps, electroluminescent lamps, and germicidal lamps. Neon and cold-cathode lamps, first invented in 1911, are widely used in signs on buildings and elsewhere, to the delight of some observers and with the opposite effect on others.

**Related Articles** CLIMATE; ELECTRICAL ENGINEERING; ELECTRIC POWER AND WIRING; ENERGY; INTERIOR DESIGN; WINDOW.

**Further Reading** Nicholls, James L.: *Interior Lighting: For Environmental Designers,* 2d ed., John Wiley, New York, 1983.

**Periodical** *Architectural Record Lighting,* quarterly supplement to *Architectural Record,* 1221 Avenue of the Americas, New York, N.Y. 10020.

**Source of Additional Information** Illuminating Engineering Society of North America (IES), 345 E. 47th St., New York, N.Y. 10017.

**LIGHTNING PROTECTION** System used to protect buildings from damage and their occupants from injury or death by lightning strokes. Compared to many other hazards, lightning causes relatively little damage to buildings and relatively few injuries and deaths. In the United States, about 350 people are killed and 1,500 injured each year by lightning. Of the fires in buildings each year, slightly over 1 percent are caused by lightning. However, lightning protection is a very important architectural consideration in certain kinds of buildings and other structures, including those that are isolated or relatively tall or with tall portions, such as church steeples.

**Lightning Stroke** A lightning stroke is an electrical current or spark of very high magnitude, as much as 15 million V and 8 mi long, between a cloud and the earth and can travel that distance in approximately 0.0004 s. Lightning occurs when clouds, or the waterdrops within them, become sufficiently charged with electricity. It is believed that as waterdrops fall through rising columns of air, they break up into larger particles with positive charges and smaller ones with negative charges. When enough electric potential has been built up, a stroke of lightning flashes from a positively charged portion of the cloud toward a negatively charged area, a different part of the same cloud, another cloud, or some object or area or a water body on the earth. When lightning strikes the earth, it may cause considerable damage to buildings, other structures, and trees, may start fires, and may kill or injure people.

**Need for Protection** Current practice in architecture does not require lightning protection for every building or structure. The need for lightning protection may be determined by a careful analysis of a building or other structure of such factors as exposure; height; monetary value; historical value; potential dangers to building occupants; and the frequency, duration, and intensity of thunderstorms in the area of the site. Buildings of relatively great height, such as tall offices or other types, and tall structures, such as water towers, chimneys, or steeples, usually require lightning protection. So do those in exposed locations, as in rural areas with no other buildings nearby. Valuable tall trees also need protection, particularly if standing alone.

**Air Terminals** The only known system of lightning protection involves the provision of air terminals, or lightning rods, at the highest points of buildings, other structures, or trees, to attract lightning strokes away from the other parts, connected to metallic downconductors, usually of copper or other alloys, which carry the electricity to the ground. Ordinarily, a number of air terminals are required. In addition, anything of metal on roofs should be connected by conductors to the downconductors. The downconductors are connected to adequate grounds in the earth. The grounds may be pipes (ground rods), ground plates, or loop (counterpoise) conductors of wire with an adequate number of electrodes. Radio and television antennas should always be grounded in a similar manner and provided with devices called "lightning arresters."

In steel-frame buildings, the frames may be used as conductors; and in concrete-framed buildings, the reinforcing bars in the concrete should be welded together to provide continuous conductors. In all types of construction, conductors should prevent electricity from passing through nonconducting portions, in which heat could start fires or where the great force could cause damage.

The design of proper lightning protection is specialized. Various standards and codes govern the subject, including the materials and equipment to be used, notably those of the National Fire Protection Association and the Underwriters Laboratories. Improperly designed or partial systems may increase the likelihood of lightning damage, rather than prevent it. Accordingly, most lightning protection systems today are designed by specialists in the field.

**History** Although humans have always held lightning in awe, its essential nature as electricity was not understood until Benjamin Franklin (1706–90) flew a kite in a thunderstorm in 1752. In that same year, Franklin also invented the first lightning rod and erected it on his house.

**Related Articles** BUILDING CODES AND STANDARDS; COMMUNICATION SYSTEM; CONCRETE STRUCTURE; COPPER ALLOY; FIRE PROTECTION; STEEL STRUCTURE; WEATHER PROTECTION.

**Source of Additional Information** Lightning Protection Inst., P.O. Box 1039, Woodstock, Ill. 60098.

# M

**MAGAZINE, ARCHITECTURAL** Periodical containing articles about architects, architecture, and related subjects. For many years, architectural magazines have been important to architects and other environmental designers, and they continue to be so today.

**Definition** A magazine is a periodical, published on a regular basis, usually weekly or monthly; each issue contains a collection of articles or stories, usually on diverse subjects, with illustrations. A magazine is distinguished from another type of periodical, a newspaper, by the fact that it usually does not attempt to cover daily news, is published on better paper, and is bound. Magazines published every week are called "weeklies," those published every month, "monthlies," those published every two months, "bimonthlies," and those appearing every three months, "quarterlies." Magazines may be published at other intervals, such as twice a month for semimonthlies or every two weeks for fortnightlies.

**Types** Sometimes magazines with broad audiences composed of members of the general public are called "mass" magazines, whereas those with limited audiences which have certain special interests are called "class" magazines. Magazines published for specific audiences of various professional, trade, or business groups are often called "trade" magazines or journals. In other instances, such publications may be called "business" or "professional" magazines. Architectural magazines today fall into the professional group. Many thousands of magazines of a great many types are published in the United States, and many millions are distributed every day through the mails or sold on newsstands.

In the past, a number of architectural magazines were published in the United States; today only three national magazines can be called architectural in the strict sense: *Architectural Record*, *Architecture*, and *Progressive Architecture*. All are monthlies, although

they may publish special extra issues, and all are distributed through the mails to specific audiences. In addition, a number of regional architectural magazines are published in the United States. These have audiences limited to certain geographical areas. Many other magazines, of interest to architects and other environmental designers, are published in such fields as construction, engineering, interior design, landscape architecture, and city planning. Many are listed in various articles in this book.

**Qualified Audience** Although magazine publishing, including architectural magazines, is quite complex, the general principles may be stated rather simply. All the architectural magazines serve the interests of certain specific audiences, sometimes called their "qualified" circulation. These audiences vary somewhat between the individual magazines but are generally composed of architects, engineers, and other environmental design professionals who perform services for buildings, and others in the building industry.

**Editorial Content** To these audiences, the magazines furnish editorial services of interest to them, along with advertising pertinent to architecture. The editorial content of magazines is the key to success. If able to attract subscribers in sufficient numbers, who wish to obtain the editorial content, if the subscribers actually read the content and are in a position to select and specify the products advertised, the magazines can then sell advertising to product manufacturers who wish to bring their promotional messages to the magazine audiences. A portion of the income of the magazines is obtained from subscriptions, but the major portion comes from the sale of advertising.

Good editorial content thus generates circulation among people of importance to both editors and advertisers and creates good readership. The audience or circulation may then be translated into advertising that produces product sales for manufacturers and others and income for the magazine. With increasing income, the editorial content can be further improved in quality as well as in quantity.

Architectural magazines are thus able to serve the interests of both readers and advertisers. To readers, the magazines present each month, or more frequently, a colorful package of information in text and pictures, generally covering the readers' professional interests, as the management and, in particular, the editorial staffs of the magazines view those interests. Each magazine has a ratio between the pages of editorial content and the pages of advertising. If this ratio falls too low on the editorial content side, readership may suffer; if too high on the editorial side, the profitability of the magazine may suffer. In national architectural magazines today, editorial-advertising ratios range from about 35:65 to 50:50.

In addition, each architectural magazine has what is called an "editorial mix," a balance between types of editorial content, news, feature articles, and so on. Each magazine strives to make its own mix the unique one preferred by its audience. A striking feature of architectural magazines is the high ratio of pictures to text, reflecting that architecture is a visual art and that architects usually react more strongly to graphic content than to reading matter. Recently, there has been a change to publishing color pictures throughout magazines.

**Organization** Although it varies somewhat among individual publications, the general organization of architectural magazines includes a management group, an editorial staff, and a business group. The management is directed by a publisher, who usually though not always has overall responsibility for the entire magazine. The editorial staff has responsibility for the editorial content and is usually headed by an editor or editor in chief. Next in authority is the managing editor, who usually handles the day-by-day management of editorial matters. The business group handles advertising, circulation, and other business matters.

Editors on architectural magazine staffs perform many kinds of tasks. One is to keep up with architecture, including design, practice, and other important matters. Architectural editors initiate articles, find authors for them, and aid in their writing; write articles themselves; obtain illustrations, including photographs and drawings; edit articles; and perform other related functions. Today most photographs in architectural magazines are taken by freelance architectural photographers, who usually license their photographs for one-time use in magazines. Other photographs are sometimes obtained from architects, and in some instances editors take their own. Drawings for use as illustrations are usually obtained directly from architects or other environmental

design professionals. Many are redrawn for reproduction, often by freelance illustrators.

Architectural magazines today have editorial staffs ranging in size from about 8 to 15 people, plus secretaries and assistants. In addition to the editor and managing editor, each staff has several classifications of editorial positions, starting with the highest, senior editors, followed by associate editors, then assistant editors. All have varying degrees of responsibility, according to their ranks, and all perform editorial functions that are generally similar. In addition, each magazine staff has an art director and assistants who are responsible for the design and layout of the magazine. Each also has a production editor or manager, who handles the details of actually producing the magazine, working with typesetters, printers, and so on as well as with the editors. In addition, some architectural magazines have part-time advisers, mostly environmental design professionals, called "correspondents," "contributing editors," or "editorial consultants." Sometimes the magazines utilize various news services.

**Sections** All architectural magazines are large in size, 9 by 10 3/4 in, and all are bound with a glue system that is fairly permanent and strong but not so strong as the sewn bindings of hardbound books. Each magazine issue has three major sections, the front, center, and back of the magazine, bound into a cover. The front of the magazine contains the contents page, or pages, with a masthead listing the staff, together with various combinations of editorials, news, and continuing features, or departments, interspersed with advertising pages. The center of the magazine is devoted exclusively to editorial content, including articles, picture features, and other matter. The back of the magazine generally resembles the front and contains departments, news, and advertising.

The resemblance among the national architectural magazines is somewhat superficial. Each has its own editorial mix, editorial philosophy, and special departments. The magazines have in common departments for publishing news, calendars of events, letters to the editor, notices of various kinds, book reviews, and others. Other departments may include product reports, product literature, law columns, and engineering or technical departments. One has regular departments devoted to building costs, construction statistics, and office management. All have advertisers' indexes and reader inquiry cards. All publish articles about new buildings, but the number of buildings covered in each issue and the pages devoted to the new buildings vary considerably. Two are mostly staff-written, with only occasional articles by others, and the third is primarily composed of articles written by people other than staff members.

**Processes** In general, magazine processes include planning issues, editorial preparation of articles (writing, illustrations, editing, and production), plant operations (typesetting, printing, and binding), and mailing operations. The planning process for an issue of a monthly magazine starts months in advance of the issue date and includes such considerations as estimated pages of editorial content and mix of articles and other content. Editors receive assignments and start to acquire or prepare articles. Other editors work on the content of the various departments assigned to them. Drawings are prepared or acquired, along with photographs. Some weeks before the issue date, layouts of articles are prepared, last-minute changes are made in articles, the content is copyedited to correct errors and to ensure that articles properly fit their assigned pages, and other adjustments are made. After the text and other manuscript of various departments and articles have been completed, the manuscripts are marked with instructions for typesetting and sent to typesetters, who set them in type and pull long proofs, called "galley proofs" or "galleys." Computers now are used to set type and to prepare page layouts. Electronic scanners are used to incorporate photographs, artwork, headlines and credits, and so on into the computerized text. Where they occur together, editorial and advertising pages are combined in the computerized page layouts.

When certain portions of the magazine have been dummied and everything else is in readiness, everything is sent to the printer to be made into pages. Ordinarily, these portions are sent out in multiples of 8 to 64 pages, which eventually will be printed at one time, or in one form, on offset presses. After the content has been made into pages, page proofs are pulled and read for errors. Then various forms may be approved for the actual printing. The printed press sheets are then folded into signatures. If necessary for special reasons, an editor or production person may examine actual press sheets as they come from the printing press to ensure quality. When all the signatures have been printed and folded, they are gathered together, bound into their covers, trimmed, wrapped in paper covers (sleeves), or now more likely plastic-wrapped, and mailed.

The business group of an architectural magazine usually consists of five major functions: circulation, management, advertising sales, advertising production, and general management. The circulation department, usually headed by a circulation director or manager, solicits subscriptions, manages subscription lists, and attends to processes, called "fulfillment," involved in delivery of magazines to subscribers. The advertising sales department, usually headed by a sales manager, solicits contracts for the publication of advertising in the magazine from building product manufacturers and other companies interested in the architectural market. Each national architectural magazine has from 5 to 12 salespeople who make direct calls and otherwise attempt to persuade advertisers of the importance of their magazine's coverage of the significant selectors and specifiers of architectural products and other items, of the completeness of their coverage of such people or the market, of the readership of the magazine, and of other reasons why the advertisers should place their faith in a particular magazine. The advertising salespeople, often called "space" salespeople, attempt to persuade both manufacturers and their advertising agencies. Space salespeople may be members of the staffs of architectural magazines or independent contractors, often called "magazine representatives," who sell advertising in more than one magazine.

Most advertising pages in architectural magazines are designed and prepared by advertising agencies. The advertising production departments of the magazines prepare the few that are not and also oversee the production processes of the advertising received from agencies. The magazines also have staffs who aid in the preparation and placement of the magazines' own promotional efforts, mostly in the form of direct mail campaigns and promotional pieces for sales purposes. Promotion departments ordinarily are headed by research or promotion managers. The business management department administers the general business affairs of a magazine.

**Editorial Services** Architectural magazines perform many editorial services for their readers, including furnishing news of the environmental design professions, the building industry, and related topics; and information on new building types, practice, legal matters, design, engineering, and many other subjects. All the magazines try to provide inspiration in addition to information. Advertising in the magazines, together with product reports and literature, keeps professionals up to date on building products, materials, and systems. In addition, the magazines sponsor award programs, round-table discussions, educational meetings, and other events of interest to architects and others.

Because of their wide-ranging interests, attendance at meetings and seminars, interviews, reading, and other activities, many architectural editors are good sources of many types of information. And many editors answer specific questions from members of design professions and others. Architectural magazines are also of great important to architects and others as media for the publication of their building designs and completed buildings. Such publication carries a certain amount of recognition, even prestige, and offers an opportunity to obtain tear sheets or reprints of the articles in the business development and public relations programs of architects.

Many architects, particularly young ones, often ask what they should do to get their buildings published.

There is no easy answer, but the most obvious one is to design good buildings. It also helps to know architectural editors, although it is possible, if a building is of sufficient excellence and out-of-the-ordinary interest, to have it published by simply mailing a description, along with drawings and photographs, to an architectural magazine. In any case, the availability of good photographs and good reproducible drawings can be very helpful in getting a building published. See articles entitled graphic design; photography, architectural.

Anther way to be published in architectural magazines is to write well-illustrated articles. In general, the procedure might start with an attempt to interest an editor in an outline, together with suggested illustrations. For a discussion on some writing details of this sort, see the article entitled book, architectural. Many architects gain recognition and sometimes prestige, along with publicity, by writing articles for nonarchitectural magazines, in particular those that reach audiences of potential clients in such fields as hospitals, schools, office buildings, hotels, and other building types. In many cases, editors of such magazines welcome well-written, timely articles directed to their audiences.

For many architects and other design professionals as well as people educated as journalists or in other disciplines, work on the editorial staffs of architectural magazines offers a chance to contribute heavily to their professions, to architecture, and to society in ways that are quite different from the work of most professional practitioners. For those with interests in language, graphic design, printing, people, and communication as well as in architecture and other types of environmental design, architectural magazines offer interesting and rewarding careers unlike any others in architecture.

Some knowing editor, a long time ago, described an editor as a person who is able to think and plan, organize, and execute. The editor must know writing and reporting, people, and production and must be able to establish and keep deadlines, write, and inspire good copy, bright headlines, and exciting article leads. The editor must believe that all articles can be better when shorter and must be willing to work toward that goal. It should be added that an architectural editor must also know and believe in good architecture.

**History** Although there is some disagreement about which was the first magazine, the most likely candidate is *Journal des savants*, first published in Paris in 1665. The first English magazine is considered to be *Gentleman's Magazine*, which began publication in 1731. The first periodicals in America, appearing in 1741, were *American Magazine* and *The General Magazine* of Benjamin Franklin (1706–90). Since that time, a great number of magazines are started every year, covering every possible subject, and a great number are discontinued each year.

**American Development** It is not easy to establish when the first American architectural magazine appeared. In colonial times, various building publications somewhat like magazines were published, some periodically. Unlike later magazines, these did not devote themselves to articles on diverse subjects. Most contained collections of drawings or patterns, often called "plates," from which various elements of architecture could be derived and constructed. The first real architectural magazine, if its title can be believed, may have been *The Architectural Magazine*, published for about five years beginning in 1834.

Next came the *Architectural Review and American Builder Journal*, which lasted only a short while after its debut in 1869. In 1876 *American Architect and Building News* was published by the James K. Osgood Co. of Boston. This magazine was later bought by the Hearst newspaper and magazine chain and renamed *The American Architect*. In 1938 it was bought by and merged into *Architectural Record*. In 1879 the *Inland Architect and Builder* was published in Chicago. By 1885, these three magazines had been joined by a number of others, including: *Building; Carpentry and Building; Builder and Woodworker; Decorator and Furnisher; Building Review;* and *The Builder*.

In 1891 *Architectural Record*, the first of the architectural magazines still published today, was founded as a general magazine for laypeople interested in architecture as well as for architects. A quarterly in those days, the magazine had a broad range of editorial content, including essays, critical and historical articles, poetry, and even a serialized novel by the first editor of the magazine, Harry W. Desmond.

In 1896 another magazine of importance was established; this was *Architectural Review*, not to be confused with the English publication of the same name. Later, its editor was an architect who had a distinguished career in architectural journalism, Henry H. Saylor (1880–1967). Saylor was editor of *Architecture* in the 1920s and 1930s and became the first editor of the *Journal of the American Institute of Architects* (*AIA*) in 1944, serving in that capacity until 1957. The AIA had previously published a magazine of the same title, from 1912 to 1928, under the editorship of Charles Harris Whitaker, and before that, from 1900 to 1912, the *American Institute of Architects Quarterly Bulletin*. In 1892 *The Brickbuilder* was started.

All the early magazines were not really professional magazines, but rather were intended for members of the general public who wanted to be informed about architecture, or for the building trades, such as brick masons, plumbers, and carpenters. In 1914, under the leadership of its editor-publisher, Dr. Michael W. Mikkelson, *Architectural Record* was converted from a magazine for the lay public to one for professional architects. Thus began a trend that has continued, with some exceptions, ever since. In 1917 *The Brickbuilder* became *Architectural Forum*, an important professional magazine for many years. And in 1920 *Architectural Review* spawned a new magazine, *Pencil Points*, slanted mostly to drafters, designers, and specification writers rather than to professional architects. The magazine had only three editors, Eugene Clute, Russell Whitehead, and Kenneth Reid (1893–1960), before becoming a more complete professional magazine and being renamed *Progressive Architecture*, the title it still bears today. Architect Thomas Hawk Creighton (1904–84) became its editor at that time, in 1946, and remained in the post until 1963.

By the late 1920s, the leading architectural magazines were *American Architect*, published by Hearst; *Architectural Record*, then edited by Mikkelson; *Architectural Forum*; *Architecture*, then published by Scribner's and edited by Saylor; and *Pencil Points*. In 1932 *Architectural Forum*, under the direction of editor-publisher Howard Myers (1894–1948), was purchased by Time, Inc. From a professional circulation of some 5,000 in 1932, the magazine grew to more than 70,000 by the time of Myers's death in 1948. Perry Prentice then became editor-publisher and continued the course toward becoming a large-circulation, generalized architecture magazine. In 1950 the name was changed to *The Magazine of Building*, though the *Architectural Forum* title was also retained.

In 1952 this magazine was split into two, *Architectural Forum*, once again, and *House and Home*, for professionals and house builders. In 1954 Douglas Haskell (1899–1979), who had previously been an editor of *Architectural Record* for 20 years and of *Architectural Forum* for 5, became the magazine's editor. As it turned out, he was the last in the Time, Inc., era, as the magazine was suspended in 1964. The other, *House and Home*, was sold to McGraw-Hill, Inc., and was published for a short period under the title *Housing* until it ceased publication. *Architectural Forum* again began publication in 1965, having been given by Time, Inc., to a nonprofit organization, Urban America, Inc., which published it, with Peter Jost Blake (1920–  ) as editor. In 1970 the magazine was sold to Whitney Publications and again published under the editorship of Blake until 1973, when it ceased publication.

*Progressive Architecture* suffered similar vicissitudes but has survived. Sold to a conglomerate, Litton Industries, resold and then resold again, it continues to be published today. After Creighton, its editors have been Jan Christopher Rowan (1924–85), Forrest Wilson (1918–  ), and the present editor, John Morris Dixon (1933–  ).

The *Journal of the American Institute of Architects* was often called the *AIA Journal,* from 1957 when Joseph Watterson (1900–72) became editor. From 1964, when William Dudley Hunt, Jr. (1922–87), formerly senior editor of *Architectural Record*, became its first publisher, serving until 1972, the official name became the *AIA Journal.* In 1965 Robert Earl Koehler (1924–  ) became editor, and he was succeeded by Donald James Canty (1929–  ) in 1973. In 1983, the magazine was renamed *Architecture.* Deborah K. Dietsch became editor in chief when the AIA sold the magazine to BPI Communications, Inc.

After becoming a strictly professional magazine in 1914, *Architectural Record* continued to grow, though not without periods of trial, until it became the largest and most successful architectural magazine in the world. In 1938 it absorbed *American Architect* and *Architecture.* Having become a monthly in 1902, the magazine added a new fillip in 1956, a thirteenth regular issue published ever since and now called *Record Houses.* In 1961 the magazine, together with its parent company, F. W. Dodge Corporation, was sold to McGraw-Hill, Inc., and has been published by that company ever since. *Architectural Record* noted its 100th year with a special issue in 1991 and is the oldest continuously published architectural magazine in the United States. Since World War II, the magazine's editors have been Kenneth Stowell (1894–1969), Harold Dana Hauf (1905–  ), John Knox Shear (1917–58), Emerson Goble (1901–69), Walter Frederick Wagner, Jr. (1926–85), and Mildred F. Schmertz (1925–  ). In April 1990, Stephen A. Kliment (1930–  ) was named editor, and continues in that position.

A number of other architectural, or architecturally related, magazines were started after World War II, only to cease publication a few years later. Among them were *Building Products, Architectural and Engineering News,* and *Architecture Plus.* One of the most influential, *Arts and Architecture,* was published from 1940 to 1960. Originally called *California Arts and Architecture* and edited by John Dymock Entenza (1905–84), it later expanded to a national circulation. Among the accomplishments of the magazine and its editor was the sponsorship of pioneering house designs, which were actually built and featured in the magazine, designed by many noted architects of the era.

The only primarily architectural magazines being published in the United States today are *Architectural Record, Architecture,* and *Progressive Architecture.* In addition to their chief editors, many of whom have been named previously, all three magazines have had many distinguished staff editors and famous authors. Some idea of the importance of the people who have written for architectural magazines might be gained from a sampling of the lengthy list of authors: critic Montgomery Schuyler (1843–1914), critic and historian Lewis Mumford (1895–1990), and historian Henry-Russell Hitchcock (1903–87), for *Architectural Record*. Mumford and Hitchcock also wrote for *Architectural Forum*, whose writers and editors include Jane Jacobs (1916– ) and Walter McQuade (1922– ). Although the other magazines have been mostly staff-written, the *AIA Journal* for most of its existence has usually published articles by outside authors, a list of whom would include most of the well-known American architects, other environmental designers, critics, and historians of the 20th century.

A number of provocative and important books have been made out of articles in architectural magazines. Some idea of their importance may be gained from the mention of only a few: first published in the *AIA Journal*, the *Autobiography of an Idea* by Louis Henri Sullivan (1956–1924), and, in *Architectural Record, In the Cause of Architecture* by Frank Lloyd Wright (1867–1959).

A large number of important series have appeared in architectural magazines over the years, including the critical series published by *Progressive Architecture* and *Architectural Forum*, beginning in the 1940s, the series on architectural philosophy in the 1950s, and the *Image of the Architect* series in the 1950s and 1960s in *Architectural Record*, together with its *Building Types* series, which has been running since 1937. Important series in the *AIA Journal* have been the *Urban Design* series written by Paul Spreiregen (1931– ) of the 1960s, which had great impact on the architecture and planning of cities, and the *Comprehensive Architectural Services* series of the same era, which pioneered concepts of broad areas of architectural practice which have been adopted today. Both series eventually were made into books. Another important series was the *Office Practice* series, which was spawned from the *Image of the Architect* series in *Architectural Record*, beginning in the 1960s. Edited by senior editor William B. Foxhall (1913–75), this series was also later made into an important book. For a number of years, the *AIA Journal* published the finest architectural book review department in the United States, under the editorship of Mary E. Osman (1913– ).

In addition to their editorial content, the architectural magazines serve their audiences in other ways. Over the years, they have sponsored numerous round tables, discussion meetings, and other important events. Notable among these have been the round tables of *Architectural Forum*, beginning in the 1940s, and of *Architectural Record* recently. The magazines have given aid to out-of-work or needy architects in bad times, for example, by engaging them to write articles,

as in the case of Louis Henri Sullivan for the *AIA Journal* and Frank Lloyd Wright for *Architectural Record*. Wright edited special issues of his work for *Architectural Forum*, which also helped architects in another way during the era of Howard Myers, by staging competitions for building design, with money prizes for the winning architects. A more recent example of this kind of service to architecture, architects, and the public is the international competition, called "Human Settlements," sponsored by *Architectural Record*, under the general editorship of senior editor Mildred Floyd Schmertz. Judged in 1976, the competition involved the design of complete urban environments for underdeveloped countries. An example of a continuing service to architects and architecture is the annual design award program of *Progressive Architecture*, published every year since the mid-1940s.

**Related Articles** BOOK, ARCHITECTURAL; CRITICISM, ARCHITECTURE; GRAPHIC DESIGN; LIBRARY.

**Periodicals** *Architecture*, 1130 Connecticut Ave., N.W., Washington, D.C. 20036; *Architectural Record*, 1221 Avenue of the Americas, New York, N.Y. 10020; *Progressive Architecture*, 600 Summer St., Stamford, Conn. 06904; Engineering, landscape architecture, interior design, and other related magazines are listed in various articles in this book.

**Sources of Additional Information** The following indices are updated regularly: *Architectural Index*, Architectural Index Inc., Boulder, Colo.; *Art Index*, H. W. Wilson Co., New York; *Avery Index to Architectural Periodicals*, Avery Library, Columbia University, New York; *Engineering Index*, Engineering Index, Inc., New York; *Reader's Guide to Periodical Literature*, H. W. Wilson Co., New York.

**MASONRY STRUCTURE** A system in which masonry units (bricks, concrete block, and stone) are used to form the structure of buildings, as opposed to masonry veneer in which the units only function as a covering or finish for walls or other building parts. Although the word *masonry* originally referred only to stonework, the term is used today to denote work with any materials that are held together with mortar, including brick, structural clay tile, other types of tile, concrete block, cement brick, gypsum block, glass block, and stone.

**Uses** Although masonry materials were often used in the past for the construction of roof structures, particularly domes and vaults, today the major structural uses are for bearing walls, which support their own weights, those of other building elements above them, and the live loads imposed by snow, wind on roofs, furniture and furnishings, and people. In such walls, masonry arches are sometimes used over openings, but steel or concrete lintels are more commonly used today. Brick walls may

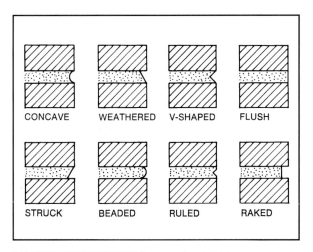

**MASONRY STRUCTURE** Sections of typical joints.

also be used in skeleton-frame buildings to resist lateral forces of wind on the structures. Masonry is often used in the foundations of buildings which may have wood-frame, masonry, or other types of wall structures, and is sometimes used, with reinforcing, in columns and beams. Masonry materials are often used for nonstructural, nonload-bearing walls, and for such purposes as curtain walls on the exteriors of buildings and partitions in their interiors.

**Types** The major types of masonry used for structural purposes in buildings today include brick, structural clay tile and facing tile, concrete block, and stone. These may also be utilized for nonstructural purposes. Other nonstructural masonry types include other kinds of clay tile, such as ceramic mosaics and other tiles intended for floor and wall coverings, gypsum block, and glass block.

Major considerations in the structural design of walls with masonry units include the strength and other properties of the types of units to be used; laying and bonding of the units so that they act together as an integral system; types and placement of mortar; height and thickness of walls; bracing or support for loads from the sides, called lateral support; support provided by foundations or footings; and reinforcement if used.

**Code Requirements** Requirements for masonry structures are contained in building codes and other codes and standards. In general, requirements begin with the allowable compressive stresses, those that result when masonry is pushed upon by weights, or loads, from above, the major stresses that masonry withstands. Such stresses are dependent on the type of masonry unit and the type of mortar used. They cover a wide range and apply to the gross cross-section of complete walls or other structural elements of buildings. Structural clay-tile masonry allowable compressive strengths are low, ranging from about 70 to 100 pounds per square inch

(psi), according to the type of unit and the mortar used. Concrete block masonry has similar allowable strengths. Solid brick masonry has allowable compressive strengths ranging from about 75 to 500 psi, according to the type of brick and mortar. Stone masonry has allowable compressive strengths ranging from about 80 psi for rubble work, with certain mortars, to 800 psi or more for ashlar granite work, with the strongest mortars.

The allowable compressive strengths for various types of mortars are determined by the portland or masonry cement used in them and the proportions of cement to hydrated lime or lime putty. The strongest mortar, designated M, is usually made with 1 part by volume of portland cement, 1 part masonry cement, and $4\frac{1}{2}$ to 6 parts aggregate. Sometimes type M mortar is made with $\frac{1}{4}$ part hydrated lime or lime putty, 1 part portland cement, and $2\frac{1}{2}$ to $3\frac{3}{4}$ parts aggregate. Type M mortar has an allowable compressive stress of 2,500 psi. Type S mortar has an allowable compressive strength of 1,800 psi, type N 750 psi, and type O 350 psi. In addition, there are high-strength mortars with high tensile as well as compressive strengths. Allowable loads for specific building locations must be determined from the applicable building and other codes and standards. Upon this basis and that of the actual loads to be supported, proper masonry systems may be designed.

The laying and bonding of masonry units to conform with codes and for proper practice generally requires the proper amount of mortar to be used, its proper placement, and the proper bonding of masonry units by laying them in positions that produce bonding or by the use of corrosion-resistant metal ties. Practices vary between masonry types. (See articles entitled brick; stone; tile.)

The thickness and height of masonry walls are also included in codes. In general, masonry bearing walls are required to be a minimum of 12 in in thickness, except that residential buildings not more than 3 stories tall or 35 ft high may have walls 8 in thick. Nonresidential buildings, taller than 35 ft, must have the lower portions of their walls thickened an additional 4 in for each 35 ft, or fraction, of additional height. Thus a 105-ft-high building would have 20-in walls for the lowest 35 ft of height, 16-in walls for the next 35 ft, and 12-in walls for the uppermost portion. Exceptions to these rules exist; for example, rubble stone walls must usually be 4 in thicker than the walls previously mentioned. Other exceptions also exist. Nonbearing masonry walls may generally be 4 in less in thickness than bearing walls, but not usually less than 8 in.

Another requirement for masonry bearing walls is that certain ratios between heights to thicknesses and lengths to thicknesses must not be exceeded. In general, the ratios are 20:1 for solid walls and 18:1 for walls with hollow units or cavity walls. Thus a 12-in solid wall should not be higher or longer than 20 times 12 in, or 20 ft. If the height or length exceeds 20 ft, the wall must be supported laterally, generally by the use of cross walls, buttresses, piers, floors, roofs, or other means. All must be solidly anchored or bonded to the supported wall. The unsupported height of piers should not exceed 10 times their smallest dimensions. In calculating the ratios for masonry work, the thicknesses of veneers are not included, unless they are bonded in such a way as to become integral portions of the structural walls. Nonbearing walls may have higher ratios.

Masonry walls may be reinforced by various means, including integrating them with reinforced concrete, and use of special joint reinforcement devices. Masonry is also used for retaining walls that resist the forces of earth on one side. The structural design of reinforced and retaining walls is ordinarily accomplished by structural engineers to suit the needs of individual buildings. Masonry walls may also be used for garden walls and similar purposes. For all masonry structures, proper design of foundations is required to prevent settling, cracking of walls, or other deterioration or failure. (See the article entitled foundation.) Other methods for preventing cracking are limitation of moisture penetration and movement in walls, use of control or expansion joints, and use of reinforcement.

In general, expansion joints are provided in long walls, where offsets occur, at junctions of walls, and other places where movement may be expected. Steel reinforcement may be placed in walls to limit movement resulting from temperature changes and other causes. Moisture penetration into walls may not only cause movement, but is undesirable because of its effects on strength and appearance and the need to prevent moisture from reaching the interiors of buildings.

**Moisture Resistance** Certain masonry products have better moisture resistance than others, and this factor should be taken into consideration in their selection. It is also important to use the recommended mortars, particularly in such cases as in masonry below grade. Mortar should solidly fill the spaces between masonry units. Several types of mortar joints are employed in masonry work, including concave or rodded, weather, and V-shaped, all considered good protection against water infiltration; flush joints, considered fair protection; and beaded, raked, and struck joints, considered poor protection. In brick of more porous types, concrete block, and sometimes other masonry structures, painting with special paints or coating with bituminous products, silicones, or other kinds of coatings or finishes are required to prevent moisture infiltration. In cavity walls, weep holes are required to allow moisture to escape from the cavities. For all types of masonry, proper flashing is required. (See the article entitled waterproofing.)

The preceding discussion about masonry structures must be considered as general, providing only guidelines for design and construction. In practice, governing codes and standards must be followed as well as principles of good design and construction to ensure that masonry structures will be adequate in strength, will resist cracking and moisture penetration, will properly perform the required functions, and will present the appearance desired for specific buildings.

**History** Masonry structure have been used in architecture since early primitive times. Their uses in the early civilizations around the Mediterranean Sea and in Europe are discussed under the titles listed at the end of this article.

The pre-Columbian American Indians living in Southwestern lands that later became part of the United States never developed the high level of stone architecture constructed in Mexico, Central America, and Peru. However, they did construct brick and sometimes stone walls in front of their cliff dwellings and well-designed pueblos of adobe. Some of these are still in existence, at least in part, mostly in Colorado, Arizona, and New Mexico. Stonework was usually laid without mortar and adobe was constructed much as it is today. Pre-Columbian use of these materials was for walls only; their builders did not know the principle of the arch.

**American Development** American colonists used stone and brick for construction early in the 17th century in the English colonies and even earlier in the Spanish. Used at first for relatively minor architectural elements, such as building foundations and chimneys, brick and stone were later used for columns; bearing wall structures; and arches, vaults, and domes. Brick and stone masonry was used for the structures of many buildings in the United States, particularly the more important ones, until nearly the end of the 19th century. Although supplanted to some extent by structural steel and reinforced concrete, they are still extensively used, but usually not in tall structures. During the 19th century, several innovations occurred in masonry work. Included in these innovations were hollow clay blocks, similar in purpose to the structural clay tile of today; reinforced masonry, making stronger structures possible; and both solid and hollow cement and sand-lime bricks, often marketed as artificial stone. Concrete block came into widespread use in the 20th century. All these materials are important masonry materials today. Walls of masonry with the exterior courses separated from those of the interior, called cavity walls, also were developed in the 19th century. They were then considered to be superior to solid walls in the prevention of moisture infiltration and in insulating qualities. For some years, cavity walls were used extensively, but they are used less frequently today.

More commonly used today are solid masonry walls of brick, structural clay tile and facing tile, concrete block, or stone; and used even more extensively are walls of building, sometimes called common, brick, structural clay tile, or concrete block, with exterior facings of stucco, face brick, stone, ceramic veneer (formerly known as terra-cotta), or structural facing tile, and the interiors covered with plaster or other materials.

**Related Articles** ARCH; BRICK; COLUMN; CONCRETE; DOME; FOUNDATION; GLASS; ROOF; TILE; VAULT; WALL.

**Additional Reading** Ambrose, James: *Simplified Design of Masonry Structures*, John Wiley, New York, 1991; Beall, Christine: *Masonry Design and Detailing*, 2d ed., McGraw-Hill, New York, 1987; Orton, Andrew: *Structural Design of Masonry*, 2d ed., John Wiley, New York, 1993.

**Sources of Additional Information** Brick Institute of America, 11490 Commerce Park Dr., Reston, Va. 22091; Building Stone Inst., 420 Lexington Ave., New York, N.Y. 10170; Facing Tile Inst., P.O. Box 88800, Canton, Ohio 44711; International Masonry Inst., 823 15th St., N.W., Washington, D.C. 20005.

**MAYBECK, BERNARD** American architect (1862–1957). Somewhat of an enigma as an architect, Bernard Maybeck has been called eclectic, mystic, romantic, bohemian, actor. He played all these roles; in short, he was a character. He selected the forms and themes of his architecture from wherever he found them. In one of his most famous buildings, the First Church of Christ, Scientist (1910) in Berkeley, Calif., elements of Byzantine, Romanesque, Gothic, Renaissance, Japanese, and perhaps even Chinese architecture may be found, along with that of Swiss and American wood buildings. He was a faddist, espousing vegetarianism and other prevalent movements. When he designed the terra-cotta cornice for an early building he worked on, he contrived a fanciful monogram of the initials of his future wife, which was repeated all around the top of the building. He also designed his own clothes, including high-waisted trousers to serve as vests.

Despite his apparent eccentricities, Maybeck was a gifted designer. His plans were ingenious and functional. The forms he used for his buildings were inventive in ornament and appearance, but no less inventive was his use of materials, structural systems, and other engineering aspects of his buildings. Through all the eclectic elements of his buildings, there is a glimmer of the modern movement in architecture.

**Works** In many of Maybeck's early buildings may be seen a preoccupation with the Craft Movement, begun in the 19th century by William Morris in England. As time went by, he never deserted the precepts of fine craftsmanship, but he did gradually abandon

**MAYBECK, BERNARD** Panama-Pacific International Exposition, Fine Arts Palace (1913), San Francisco, Calif.

the simplicities of wood architecture that occupied his contemporaries, the Greene brothers, most of their lives. Instead, he employed a much more complex and eclectic use of diverse forms and materials. In his first major building, Hearst Hall (1899), University of California, Berkeley, he pioneered the use of laminated arches, built up of glued layers of wood, which eliminated the need for columns in the entire central portion of the building. This was a structural milestone. Destroyed by fire in 1922, the building had an exterior of redwood shakes with the form of the great arches exposed on the front. He used laminated arches for many later buildings. Other buildings of about the same time still exist on the Berkeley campus: the Faculty Club (1902), now much enlarged, and the Hearst Memorial Gymnasium for Women (1925), designed in association with Julia Morgan (1872–1957), the architect of part of William Randolph Hearst's estate, San Simeon.

Maybeck continued his structural innovation in his Town and Gown Clubhouse (1899), Berkeley, where he utilized wood king-post trusses; in the Outdoor Art Clubhouse (1905), Mill Valley, with its posts and beams projecting outside and ornamented; and in the Hopps House (1906), Moss Valley, which had paired rafters with posts between them. At the time, he was designing other buildings, mostly houses, including a house for Mrs. Hearst, now destroyed, which cost $100,000, a very large sum for those days, especially when compared to the $4,000 to $5,000 houses he had been designing. In 1907 he turned his attention to a monolithic reinforced concrete structure in the Lawson House, Berkeley.

Then came Maybeck's greatest opportunity, one that many think produced his best building, the commission for the design of the First Church of Christ, Scientist (1910) in Berkeley. In this design, his creative powers, now fully developed, were employed to their fullest.

This is the church previously mentioned as combining parts of so many styles and cultures. In this building, Maybeck produced a rich and ornamental effect throughout the interior and exterior. His experiments with materials and structure continued: great carved wood trusses, exposed inside the building, intersect in the middle to form a Greek cross that reflects the floor plan. New materials, such as asbestos panels, metal factory windows, and reinforced concrete, are skillfully combined with redwood in a building of the present, but with its roots in the past. After this, his commissions declined. He did the charming wood-shingle Chick House (1913) in Berkeley and the Bingham House (1917) in Montecito.

Then he produced the splendid Palace of Fine Arts (1915) for the San Francisco Panama-Pacific International Exposition. The structure of the palace was formed with daring three-hinged steel arches that had been used in buildings only a few times before, but its exterior was as eclectic as any Maybeck had done previously. The palace made an immediate hit with San Franciscans. Unlike the other fair buildings, it was allowed to remain standing after the fair had closed. But though its structure was sound, the materials covering it were not and soon began to deteriorate. Gradually it turned into a ruin, which may well have been what Maybeck had intended. In 1967, with the aid of $2 million given by a San Francisco citizen, Walter Johnson, and matched by the State of California, the palace was rebuilt in more permanent building materials by architects Welton Becket and Associates, following the original Maybeck plans housed in the library of the University of California.

Maybeck had reached his peak. He did town plans for two small towns, but nothing came of the first one and only two buildings from the second. In 1923 he designed the Glen Alpine Cabins, Lake Tahoe, simple buildings of granite, with factory windows and corrugated iron roofs, integrated into the rugged landscape. In 1927 he did the Hearst Gymnasium, and found a new client who kept him going for a while. For this client, Earle C. Anthony (1880–1967), Maybeck designed an elaborate house (1927) in Los Angeles that had 21 levels and was constructed of stone from Caen, France, and roof tile from Barcelona, Spain. The cost was $500,000. He also designed two showrooms for Packard automobiles in Berkeley and San Francisco, built in 1928, for the same client. Though he continued to go to his office until 1942, when he was eighty, his last important commission was for the master plan and buildings of Principia College, Elsah, Ill. The eight buildings were not completed until 1938. Maybeck did not supervise their construction, and though the college shows traces of his better work, the vigor and creativity were gone.

Maybeck lived to see his work highly regarded and himself praised as one of the great pioneers of modern architecture. He felt that he could make things of the past come alive again, in harmony with the present in a world of his own creation. Many think that he succeeded.

**Life** Bernard Maybeck was born in New York City on February 7, 1862, the son of German immigrant parents. His father, a wood-carver, wanted his son to follow him into that trade, but his mother, who died when he was three, had wanted him to be an artist. Maybeck always remembered a childhood spent drawing instead of playing ball like other boys. He also took extra courses in French, German, and philosophy. Young Maybeck turned out to be an indifferent student and left school at seventeen, to be apprenticed to a wood-carver as his father had wished. This lasted only a short time, and he soon found himself working for his father, who directed a large New York wood-carving shop.

At eighteen, Maybeck was sent to Paris as an apprentice in furniture design. The shop in which he worked was across the street from the famous École des Beaux Arts. Becoming interested in architecture and architects, Maybeck, with his father's permission, entered that school of classical academic tradition. This seemed to suit him just fine, for he had become captivated with Classic Greece and the Romanesque and early Gothic eras, and their architecture. This romantic and eclectic approach to architecture stayed with him all his life, as did his pronounced flair for invention.

After passing his final examination at the École in 1886, Maybeck returned to the United States to his first architectural job with Carrère and Hastings, a New York firm, recently established by his roommate at the École, Thomas Hastings (1860–1929). This firm, later to become a leading eclectic office, was engaged in the design of the now-demolished Ponce de Leon Hotel (1888) in St. Augustine, Fla. Hastings and Maybeck produced a design that was a mixture of Spanish and Mexican forms which foretold the future of eclecticism of both men.

After the hotel was finished, Maybeck formed a short-lived partnership with James Russell in Kansas City, Mo., where he met Mark White and his sister, Annie, who was to become the architect's wife in 1900. Mark White worked with Maybeck for many years as superintendent of construction. Moving on to Berkeley, Calif., with the Whites in 1889, Maybeck worked a while for an architect, then as a furniture designer and carver, and then as a drafter with another architect, A. Page Brown (1859–96). In this office, he worked on the Church of the New Jerusalem (Swedenborgian), built in 1894 in San Francisco.

In 1894 Maybeck took a position teaching descriptive geometry in the department of drawing at the

University of California, Berkeley, and later taught architecture. These were the rudimentary beginnings of the College of Architecture at that university. While teaching at the university, Maybeck initiated and administered an international competition for a campus master plan, sponsored and paid for by Mrs. Phoebe Apperson Hearst, activities that took him to New York City and Europe and brought him considerable recognition and publicity. However, the competition cost Maybeck his job, for architect John Galen Howard (1864–1931), brought from New York in 1901 to supervise the work, took over as professor of architecture. While administering the competition, Maybeck had received several commissions, including one from Mrs. Hearst for Hearst Hall, later destroyed by fire.

Before his career ended, Maybeck designed at least 250 buildings. An innocent in money matters, Maybeck started offices in San Francisco on three separate occasions, commuting from Berkeley, but none was profitable. His wife, soon after their marriage, had taken over their financial affairs, both private and professional, and she managed to keep things fairly solvent until about 1910. During the next few years, to keep going, he sold, one by one, some lots he had bought some years before. Maybeck was then forced by his circumstances to take a job as a drafter with another architect, Willis Polk (1867–1924), one of his former students. Polk had received a commission to design the Palace of Fine Arts in San Francisco. Too busy to do the work, Polk asked his draftsmen to try their hands at its design. Maybeck produced a design that so impressed a member of the architectural commission, Henry Bacon, architect of the Lincoln Memorial, that Bacon insisted it be constructed. Polk gave Maybeck full charge of the work and also the credit. Although he grumbled about doing this work for drafter's wages, Maybeck went on to produce what many think is a masterpiece.

Maybeck maintained and visited his office until 1942. His name remained in the lobby directory and on an office door because the old man had told his young associate, William Gladstone Merchant, he never wanted to retire. During World War II, his fame obscured, Maybeck lived in a cabin he had designed, busying himself with various ideas and projects. After the war, he returned to the old Maybeck house in Berkeley. The late 1940s saw a resurgence of interest in his work, as it had in that of the Greene brothers. Yet his carpenter, Ivan Melvin, called him a real common man. As an architect his peers thought otherwise. In 1951 they awarded him the Gold Medal of the American Institute of Architects, their highest honor.

At age ninety-five, on October 3, 1957, Bernard Maybeck died. He left a legacy of highly original and creative buildings that have influenced architecture ever since.

**Related Articles** BEAUX ARTS, ÉCOLE DES; ECLECTIC ARCHITECTURE; GREENE AND GREENE; MODERN ARCHITECTURE; MORGAN, JULIA.

**Further Reading** Cardwell, Kenneth H.: *Bernard Maybeck—Artisan, Architect, Artist,* Peregrine Smith, Salt Lake City, 1977.

**McINTIRE, SAMUEL** American architect and woodcarver (1757–1811). Samuel McIntire became one of the greatest architect-builders of colonial times and the early years of the American republic. Although self-taught in architecture, he had great skill in working with wood that complemented his innate sense of the right way to develop the inherent qualities of wood into sensitive and beautiful elements of buildings. This was particularly apparent in his interiors, which are still considered as some of the most finely detailed and executed in America.

**Works** McIntire's buildings, most of which were houses for the wealthy of Salem, Mass., are usually con-

**McINTIRE, SAMUEL** Gardner-Pingree House (1805), Salem, Mass.

sidered to be Georgian in style, though certainly a rather late Georgian that is sometimes called Adam or Early Federal style. Perhaps his masterpiece was the Gardner-Pingree House (1805) in Salem. The exterior is a rather austere, restrained squarish building of three stories, beautifully proportioned and detailed. Inside, the art of McIntire comes into full play in the masterfully designed and executed fireplaces and mantels, doorways, and windows.

Another fine McIntire house is the Pierce-Nichols (1785), Salem, also noted for its fine proportions and details. Among others in Salem are the Elias Hasket Derby House (1780) and a remarkable series of houses on the west side of Washington Square. Two of McIntire's nonresidential buildings still exist in Salem: Assembly House (1783), remodeled about 1796, and Hamilton Hall (1807).

**Life** Samuel McIntire was born in Salem, Mass., in January 1757, where he subsequently designed and built his buildings. In fact, he never traveled very far from his birthplace. Trained as a wood-carver by his father, he became an architect and builder through the study of books and from experience. His work for the wealthy of Salem, most of them shipowners or otherwise involved in commerce of the sea, developed into a long and successful career. Starting out on his own he later employed his son, two brothers, and a nephew, all craftsmen, in his work. In 1792 he took part in the competition for the design of the U.S. Capitol, a prize that went to an amateur gentleman-architect, Dr. William Thornton (1759–1828). McIntire died in Salem on February 8, 1811.

**Related Articles** CAPITAL, UNITED STATES; COLONIAL ARCHITECTURE; GEORGIAN ARCHITECTURE.

**Further Reading** Cousins, Frank, and Phil M. Riley: *The Woodcarver of Salem—Samuel McIntire, His Life and Work*, AMS Press, New York, 1970; Kimball, Sidney F.: *Mr. Samuel McIntire, Carver—The Architect of Salem*, Essex Institute, Salem, Mass. 1940.

**McKIM, MEAD AND WHITE** American architectural firm. Charles Follen McKim (1847–1909), William Rutherford Mead (1846–1928), and Stanford White (1853–1906) formed the firm of McKim, Mead and White in New York City in 1879. It became one of the largest and most successful architectural firms in the world. The three partners practiced together more than 25 years, and produced more than 500 buildings. The firm continued until the 1960s, long after all three original partners were dead. Starting out as eclectic architects working in a number of styles, the firm gradually turned almost exclusively to buildings in a style developed from the architecture of the Renaissance and adhering quite strictly to the tenets of the École des Beaux Arts in Paris,

where McKim had been educated. Their buildings were noted for classical good taste, constrained and discriminating rather than inventive.

**Firm's Works** Important houses were those for H. Victor Newton (1881), Elberon, N.J., W. G. Low (1887), Newport, R.I., both with shingle exteriors; that for H. A. C. Taylor (1885), Newport, in Colonial Revival style; and the Villard residences (1884), New York City, originally six separate houses in Italian Renaissance style. The firm designed a great number of clubs, among the finest being the Century Association (1891); the Harvard Club and the Metropolitan Club, both in 1894; and the University Club (1900); all in New York City. Among the libraries designed were the Boston Public Library (1895), often considered the firm's best building; and the Low Library (1897) at Columbia University, and what has been called the jewel of Renaissance Revival style, the Morgan Library (1906), both in New York City. The firm designed many other notable buildings, including several others at Columbia University, the First Methodist Church (1882), Baltimore, Md., in Romanesque Revival style, and Pennsylvania Station (1910: see illustration in article railway station), New York City, now demolished. The firm was also deeply involved in the design of the World's Columbian Exposition in Chicago in 1893, and designed the Agricultural Palace for that fair.

**McKim's Life** Charles Follen McKim was born at Isabella Furnace, Chester County, Pa., on August 24, 1847, the son of a Presbyterian minister father and a Quaker mother. McKim originally planned to become a mining engineer and entered Harvard University, Cambridge, Mass. While spending a few months working in the office of an architect, Russell Sturgis (1836–1909), he decided that he would rather be an architect. In 1867 he entered the École des Beaux Arts in Paris and after three years of schooling and travel in France and England returned to American in 1870, to enter the office of architect Henry Hobson Richardson (1838–86), then practicing in New York City. He stayed there until 1872, working on, among other buildings, Richardson's Trinity Church (1877) for Boston, across from which McKim's firm would place its own Boston Public Library some 25 years later.

In 1872 McKim formed a partnership with William Rutherford Mead and William B. Bigelow, which lasted until 1878, when Bigelow retired. In 1879 Stanford White, who had been working in Richardson's office, joined the other two in partnership, with McKim as senior partner. McKim distinguished himself not only in architecture, but in his encouragement of patronage of the other arts by his wealthy clients and in his service to architectural education and to his profession.

Just as McKim, Mead and White built a reputation for buildings derived from those of the Renaissance, McKim acquired a reputation as a sort of Renaissance man. He felt that art and architecture were the prime civilizing influences on society. And he spent much of his time in fine clubs, often designed by his firm, in luxurious parlor cars, and in European travel, enjoying cultural activities and conversation while he persuaded potential clients to entrust their buildings to his firm and to allow him to commission sculpture, murals, and other art to go into the buildings. A tall, redheaded man, he was genial, dignified, urbane, and discriminating.

All his energies went into his professional and public life. He never really had much of a private life. Married in 1874, at age twenty-five, to Annie Bigelow, the sister of his partner, they had one daughter, Margaret. The marriage ended in divorce in 1878. He then married Julia Amory Appleton in 1885, but she died two years later. He did not see his only daughter for 20 years, until 1899, but later she became his companion. Busy all his life designing great houses for his friends and other clients, McKim never had time to design one for himself. All his time went into his practice, his profession, and his other interests.

In the architectural profession, McKim was one of the giants. Of his many services to his profession perhaps the most important one was serving as president of the American Institute of Architects for two years, 1901 to 1903. During his tenure as president, the notable house designed by Dr. William Thornton (1759–1828) for Col. John Tayloe, now called The Octagon (1800), was purchased to become the AIA headquarters with funds personally underwritten by McKim. It was also a time in which he served on the Park Commission of the District of Columbia, working to complete the planning of Washington that began with the plans Pierre Charles L'Enfant (1754–1825) had designed in 1791.

McKim worked all his life for the cause of architectural education, establishing scholarships and fellowships for students. With other architects, especially Daniel Hudson Burnham (1846–1912), who had also designed buildings for the World's Columbian Exposition in Chicago in 1893, McKim originated the idea for a postgraduate school for architecture and other arts in Italy. In 1895 this idea became a reality with the opening of the American Academy in Rome, called at first the American School of Architecture. McKim became its first president and continued in that position for 15 years.

In his later life, McKim received many honors for his work, honorary doctor's degrees from Columbia University and the University of Pennsylvania, hon-

**McKIM, MEAD AND WHITE** Newport Casino (now National Tennis Hall of Fame) (1881), Newport, R.I.

orary membership in the Royal Institute of British Architects, and its highest honor in 1903, the Royal Gold Medal.

On January 1, 1908, suffering from ill health, McKim left the office of McKim, Mead and White for an extended vacation. But he was never able to return to work, and on September 4, 1909, he died. On December 15, 1909, the Gold Medal of the American Institute of Architects, voted to him a year before, was received by the last surviving original partner of McKim, Mead and White, William Mead, and presented by him to the architect's daughter, Margaret McKim. To a large and distinguished audience, the major address was made by the President of the United States, William Howard Taft (1857–1930).

**Mead's Life** William Rutherford Mead was born in Brattleboro, Vt., on August 20, 1846. After graduating from Amherst University, Amherst, Mass., in 1867, Mead worked for a while in the office of an engineer and in 1868 for an architect, Russell Sturgis (1836–1909). During 1871 and 1872, he studied architecture at the Academia de Belle Arte in Florence, Italy.

After returning to the United States, Mead formed an architectural partnership, McKim, Mead and Bigelow, with Charles Follen McKim and William B. Bigelow. In 1878 Bigelow left the firm and was replaced the following year by Stanford White; the name of the firm was then changed to McKim, Mead and White. Unlike the other two partners, both of whom were noted for their design abilities, Mead was more talented in the management of the firm than in design. He was considered a very good critic of the design work of the others and helped them to improve their work. He occasionally made conceptual designs of buildings.

In 1884 he married a Hungarian, Olga Kilenyi. After the death of McKim in 1909, Mead took over the presidency of the American Academy in Rome, and remained in that position until he died. Mead withdrew from the firm in 1919, but continued as a consultant for the rest of his life. Having survived his partner, White, by 22 years, and McKim by 19, William Rutherford Mead died on June 20, 1928.

**White's Life** Stanford White was born in New York City on November 9, 1853, the son of Richard Grant White (1821–85), a noted writer, editor, and music critic. White showed considerable talent in drawing and the arts as a young child. After having attended private schools in New York City, he entered New York University, but stayed only a short time. At nineteen, White worked in the office of Henry Hobson Richardson, where he met his future partner, McKim, who was working there on Richardson's magnificent Trinity Church, to be located in Boston.

When McKim left the office in 1872 to start his own practice, White took over some of the work on the plans and details of the church. Most of McKim's ideas were eventually supplanted. In 1878 White left Richardson's office to travel and study in Europe, returning in 1879 to become a partner in McKim, Mead and White. He also

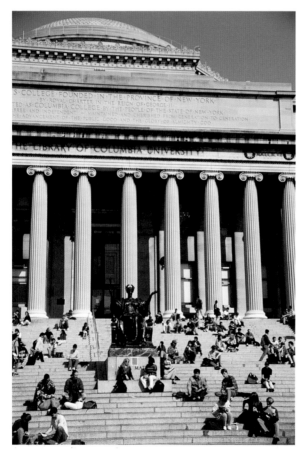

**McKIM, MEAD AND WHITE** Low Memorial Library (1897), Columbia University, New York, N.Y. The sculpture of Alma Mater (1903) is by Chester Daniel French.

returned to his studies and graduated from New York University in 1881.

White married Bessie Springs in 1884, and a year later they had a child who died the same year. They had a son, Lawrence Grant White (1887–1956), who later graduated from Harvard, became an architect, joined McKim, Mead and White in 1914, and became a partner in the firm in 1920.

Stanford White was a talented drafter and designer, not only of buildings but of interiors, picture frames, magazine covers for *Scribner's* and *The Century*, book bindings, and jewelry. A tall, well-built, redheaded man, White was a bon vivant, exuberant and flamboyant in his professional work and in his behavior. Considered Bohemian in his habits, he hobnobbed with a rather racy set, many of whom were connected with the theater, including the great actor John Barrymore (1882–1942). White and his wife lived apart after the first few years of their marriage, White staying in various apartments and studios in New York City.

White was considered a connoisseur of beauty in architecture, other arts, antiques, decoration, and women. Much of his work in the firm was devoted to ornamental or decorative details of buildings, and to their interiors, including furniture and furnishings. A collector all his life, he amassed a huge personal collection of art, antiques, and other art objects. He also selected and purchased such articles for clients of the firm.

In addition to his work on most of the buildings designed by the firm, White made designs on his own. One of his best was the Farragut Monument (1881), in Madison Square, New York City, for which White designed the base, and the famous sculptor Augustus Saint-Gaudens (1848–1907) did the sculpture, the first such collaboration between sculptor and architect in the United States. Another was also a monument, Washington Arch (1892), in Washington Square, New York City.

White was associated most closely with the design of certain buildings, houses, and clubs, mostly in New York City. The few that are still standing include the club for the Century Association (1891), the Metropolitan Club (1894), and the Hall of Fame (1900) at New York University.

White lived a full life, one that was full of triumphs and ended with scandal and tragedy. In 1890 his masterpiece, Madison Square Garden, was completed. This was a great complex that included a theater, a restaurant, a concert hall, a tower with studios, and a roof garden. White occupied one of the studios, while his wife lived in their country home on Long Island. White had a reputation for staging wild and voluptuous parties and associating with theatrical people, including chorus girls. In 1901 he met a sixteen-year-old artist's model and chorus girl, Evelyn Nesbit, with whom he became involved, she claimed intimately. Later Evelyn Nesbit married Harry Kendall Thaw, the profligate son of a wealthy Pittsburgh railway tycoon. Thaw, irresponsible, wild, and reckless, and some said a drug addict, was also madly jealous.

In 1905 disaster struck White; his great collection of art was totally destroyed in a New York City warehouse in which it had been stored. Then on June 25, 1906, while seated in the Madison Square Roof Garden, Stanford White was shot to death with a revolver held close to his head by Harry Kendall Thaw, who was obsessed with the idea that White had grievously wronged his wife and himself.

In the years following, three of White's finest buildings, Madison Square Garden (1890), the Herald Building (1893), and the Madison Square Presbyterian Church (1906), were demolished.

**Related Articles** ASSOCIATION, BUILDING INDUSTRY; BUILDING INDUSTRY; ECLECTIC ARCHITECTURE; EDUCATION; RICHARDSON, HENRY HOBSON.

**Further Reading** Baldwin, Charles C.: *Stanford White*, reprint of the 1931 edition, Da Capo, New York, 1971;

**McKIM, MEAD AND WHITE** Morgan Library (1906), New York, N.Y.

Granger, Alfred Hoyt: *Charles Follen McKim—A Study of His Life and Work*, reprint of the 1913 edition, AMS Press, New York; Moore, Charles: *The Life and Times of Charles Follen McKim*, reprint of 1929 edition, Da Capo, New York, 1970; Wilson, Guy: *McKim, Mead & White, Architects*, Rizzoli, New York, 1983.

**MEASUREMENT** The extent, degree, capacity, dimensions, or amounts of anything, determined by measuring it; also the act of measuring or a system of measures. In architecture, a number of measurements are employed, including not only the dimensions of buildings, sites, and components but also time, temperature, forces, and heat flow.

In the United States, two major systems of measurement are used in architecture. One is the English, now often called the customary system, since England has adopted the metric system. Of growing importance in the United States is the metric system, now often called the Système International D'Unités (SI), or International System of Units. As the last major nation to adopt this system, the United States is embarked on a voluntary conversion to the International System and its SI units. In other parts of the world, actions are being taken to convert the metric units of all countries to the International System of Units (SI).

Major types of SI units utilized in architecture are those of length, area, and volume. For engineering and other purposes in architecture, important SI units are utilized to measure quantities in mechanics, the branch of physics that deals with forces on bodies; in heat and related phenomena; and in electricity, lighting, and acoustics. For further discussion on forces and related measurements of bodies not in motion, see the article entitled structure; on heat measurements, articles entitled heating, ventilating, and air conditioning; insulation, thermal; on acoustical measurements, the article entitled sound control; on lighting measurements, the article entitled lighting.

**Customary versus SI Units** Architects and other environmental designers in the United States measure buildings and their components in feet, inches, and fractions of inches in the English, or customary, system. In SI units, buildings and their components are usually measured in millimeters (mm), very much simplifying the preparation of working and other types of drawings, since no fractions are required. Also, when millimeters are used exclusively on drawings, the use of the abbreviation mm is not required. In the customary system, a dimension might appear on a drawing as 2′-7½″. The equivalent SI unit measurement, in millimeters rounded off, would appear as 800. In drawings of larger elements of architecture, such as a site plan for a subdivision, the meter (m) may be used. And for even larger distances,

## SI BASE UNITS

| Physical Quantity | Unit | Symbol |
|---|---|---|
| length | meter | m |
| mass | kilogram | kg |
| time | second | s |
| electric current | ampere | A |
| thermodynamic temperature | kelvin | K |
| luminous intensity | candela | cd |
| amount of substance | mole | mol |

## DERIVED UNITS WITH COMPOUND NAMES

| Physical Quantity | Unit | Symbol |
|---|---|---|
| area | square meter | $m^2$ |
| volume | cubic meter | $m^3$ |
| density | kilogram per cubic meter | $kg/m^3$ |
| velocity | meter per second | $m/s$ |
| angular velocity | radian per second | $rad/s$ |
| acceleration | meter per second squared | $m/s^2$ |
| angular acceleration | radian per second squared | $rad/s^2$ |
| volume rate of flow | cubic meter per second | $m^3/s$ |
| moment of inertia | kilogram meter squared | $kg \cdot m^2$ |
| moment of force | newton meter | $N \cdot m$ |
| intensity of heat | flowwatt per square meter | $W/m^2$ |
| thermal conductivity | watt per meter kelvin | $W/(m \cdot K)$ |
| luminance | candela per square meter | $cd/m^2$ |

## DERIVED UNITS WITH SPECIAL NAMES

| Physical Quantity | Unit | Symbol | Derivation |
|---|---|---|---|
| frequency | hertz | Hz | $s^{-1}$ |
| force | newton | N | $kg \cdot m/s^2$ |
| pressure, stress | pascal | Pa | $N/m^2$ |
| work, energy, heat | joule | J | $N \cdot m$ |
| power | watt | W | $J/s$ |
| electric charge | coulomb | C | $A \cdot s$ |
| electric potential | volt | V | $W/A$ |
| electric capacitance | farad | F | $C/V$ |
| electric resistance | ohm | $\Omega$ | $V/A$ |
| electric conductance | siemens | S | $\Omega^{-1}$ |
| magnetic flux | weber | Wb | $V \cdot s$ |
| magnetic flux density | tesla | T | $Wb/m^2$ |
| inductance | henry | H | $Wb/A$ |
| luminous flux | lumen | lm | $cd \cdot sr$ |
| illumination | lux | lx | $lm/v^2$ |
| activity | becquerel | Bq | $s^{-1}$ |
| absorbed dose | gray | Gy | $J/kg$ |
| temperature | degree Celsius | °C | K |

## PREFERRED MULTIPLES AND SUBMULTIPLES

| Prefix | Symbol | Factor | Magnitude |
|---|---|---|---|
| exa | E | $10^{18}$ | 1 000 000 000 000 000 000 |
| peta | P | $10^{15}$ | 1 000 000 000 000 000 |
| tera | T | $10^{12}$ | 1 000 000 000 000 |
| giga | G | $10^{9}$ | 1 000 000 000 |
| mega | M | $10^{6}$ | 1 000 000 |
| kilo | k | $10^{3}$ | 1 000 |
| milli | m | $10^{-3}$ | 0.001 |
| micro | μ | $10^{-6}$ | 0.000 001 |
| nano | n | $10^{-9}$ | 0.000 000 001 |
| pico | p | $10^{-12}$ | 0.000 000 000 001 |
| femto | f | $10^{-15}$ | 0.000 000 000 000 001 |
| atto | a | $0^{-18}$ | 0.000 000 000 000 000 001 |

## CONVERSION FACTORS FOR THE MOST COMMON UNITS USED IN ARCHITECTURE

| Metric to Customary | | | Customary to Metric | | |
|---|---|---|---|---|---|
| **Length** | | | | | |
| 1 km | =0.621 371 | mile | 1 mile (int) | =1.609 344 | km |
| | =49.7097 | chain | 1 chain | =210.1168 | m |
| 1 m | =1.093 61 | yd | 1 yd | =0.9144 | m |
| | =3.280 84 | ft | 1 ft | =0.3048 | m |
| 1 mm | =0.039 370 1 | in | | | |
| | | | 1 in. | =25.4 | mm |
| **Area** | | | | | |
| 1 km² | =0.386 102 | mile² | 1 mile² | =2.59000 | km² |
| 1 ha | =2.471 04 | acre | 1 acre | =0.404 687 | ha |
| 1 m² | =1.195 99 | yd² | | =4046.87 | m² |
| | =10.7639 | ft² | 1 yd² | =0.836 127 | m² |
| 1 mm² | =0.001 550 | in² | 1 ft² | =0.092 903 | m² |
| | | | 1 in² | =645.16 | mm² |
| **Volume, modulus of section** | | | | | |
| 1 m³ | =0.810 709 x 10⁻³ | acre ft | 1 acre ft | =1233.49 | m³ |
| | =1.307 95 | yd³ | 1 yd³ | =0.764 555 | m³ |
| | =35.3147 | ft³ | 100 board ft | =0.235 973 | m³ |
| | =423.776 | board feet | 1 ft³ | =0.028 316 8 | m³ |
| 1 mm³ | =61.0237 x 10⁻⁶ | in³ | | =28.3168 | L |
| | | | 1 in³ | =16 387.1 | mm³ |
| | | | | =16.3871 | mL |
| **Capacity** | | | | | |
| 1 L | =0.035 314 7 | ft³ | | | |
| | =0.264 172 | gal (US) | | | |
| | =1.056 69 | qt (US) | 1gal (US) | =3.785 41 | L |
| 1 mL | =0.061 023 7 | in³ | 1 qt (US) | =946.353 | mL |
| | =0.033 814 | fl oz (US) | 1 fl oz (US) | =29.5735 | mL |
| **Second moment of area** | | | | | |
| 1 mm⁴ | =2.402 51 x 10⁻⁶ | in⁴ | 1 in⁴ | =416 231 | mm⁴ |
| | | | | =0.416 231 x 10⁻⁶ | m⁴ |
| **Plane angle** | | | | | |
| 1 rad | =57° 17′ 45″ | degree | 1 degree | =0.017 453 3 | rad |
| | =57.2958 | degree | 1 minute | =290.888 | μad |
| | =3437.75′ | minute | 1 second | =4.848 14 | μrad |
| | =206 265″ | second | | | |
| **Velocity, speed** | | | | | |
| 1 m/s | =3.280 84 | ft/s | 1 ft/s | =0.3048 | m/s |
| | =2.236 94 | mile/h | 1 mile/h | =1.609 344 | km/h |
| 1 km/h | =0.621 371 | mile/h | | =0.447 04 | m/s |
| **Acceleration** | | | | | |
| 1 m/s² | =3.280 84 | ft/s² | 1 ft/s² | =0.3048 | m/s² |
| **Volume rate of flow** | | | | | |
| 1 m³/s | =35.3147 | ft³/s | 1 ft³/s | =0.028 316 8 | m³/s |
| | =22.8245 | million gal/d | 1 ft³/min | =0.471 947 | L/s |
| | =0.810 709 x 10⁻³ | acre ft/s | 1 gal/min | =0.063 090 2 | L/s |
| 1 L/s | =2.118 88 | ft³/min | 1 gal/h | =1.051 50 | mL/s |
| | =15.850 3 | gal/min | 1 million gal/d | =43.8126 | L/s |
| | =951.022 | gal/h | 1 acre ft/s | =1233.49 | m³/s |
| **Equivalent temperature value (ᵗ°C=ᵗK-273.15)** | | | | | |
| ᵗC | 5/9 (ᵗF-32) | | ᵗF | =9/5 ᵗC+32 | |
| **Temperature interval** | | | | | |
| 1°C | =1 K=1.8°F | | 1°F | =0.555 556°C or K | |
| | | | | =5/9°C=5/9 K | |
| **Mass** | | | | | |
| 1 t (metric ton) | =1.102 31 | ton (2000 lb) | 1 ton | =0.907 185 | 1 (metric ton) |
| 1 kg | =2.204 62 | lb | | =907.185 | kg |
| | =35.2740 | oz | 1 lb | =0.453 592 | kg |
| 1 g | =0.035 274 | oz | 1 oz | =28.3495 | g |
| | =0.643 105 | pennyweight | 1 pennyweight | =1.555 17 | g |

NOTE: Underlined values are exact conversions.

## CONVERSION FACTORS FOR THE MOST COMMON UNITS USED IN ARCHITECTURE (Cont.)

### Metric to Customary / Customary to Metric

*Mass/unit length*

| | | | | | |
|---|---|---|---|---|---|
| 1 kg/m | =0.671 969 | lb/ft | 1 lb/ft | =1.488 16 | kg/m |
| 1 g/m | =3.547 99 | lb/mile | 1 lb/mile | =0.281 849 | g/m |

*Mass/unit area*

| | | | | | |
|---|---|---|---|---|---|
| 1 kg/m² | =0.204 816 | lb/ft² | 1 lb/ft² | =4.882 43 | kg/m² |
| 1 g/m² | =0.029 494 | oz/yd² | 1 oz/yd² | =33.9057 | g/m² |
| | =0.003 277 06 | oz/ft² | 1 oz/ft² | =305.152 | g/m² |

*Density*
(Mass/unit volume)

| | | | | | |
|---|---|---|---|---|---|
| 1 kg/m³ | =0.062 428 | lb/ft³ | 1 lb/ft³ | =16.0185 | kg/m³ |
| | =1.685 56 | lb/yd³ | 1 lb/yd³ | =0.593 278 | kg/m³ |
| 1 t/m³ | =0.842 778 | ton/yd³ | 1 ton/yd³ | =1.186 55 | t/m³ |

*Moment of inertia*

| | | | | | |
|---|---|---|---|---|---|
| 1 kg·m² | =23.7304 | lb·ft² | 1 lb·ft² | =0.042 140 1 | kg·m² |
| | =3417.17 | lb·in² | 1 lb·in² | =292.640 | kg·mm² |

*Mass/unit time*

| | | | | | |
|---|---|---|---|---|---|
| 1 kg/s | =2.204 62 | lb/s | 1 lb/s | =0.453 592 | kg/s |
| 1 t/h | =0.984 207 | ton/h | 1 ton/h | =1.016 05 | t/h |

*Force*

| | | | | | |
|---|---|---|---|---|---|
| 1 MN | =112.404 | tonf (ton-force) | 1 tonf | =8.896 44 | kN |
| 1 kN | =0.112 404 | tonf | 1 kip | =4.448 22 | kN |
| | =224.809 | lbf | 1 lbf | =4.448 22 | N |
| 1 N | =0.224 809 | lbf (pound-force) | | | |

*Moment of force, torque*

| | | | | | |
|---|---|---|---|---|---|
| 1 N•m | =0.737 562 | lbf·ft | 1 lbf·ft | =1.355 82 | N·m |
| | =8.850 75 | lbf·in | 1 lbf·in. | =0.112 985 | N·m |
| 1 kN•m | =0.368 781 | tonf·ft | 1 tonf·ft | =2.711 64 | kN·m |
| | =0.737 562 | kip·ft | 1 kip·ft | =1.355 82 | kN·m |

*Force/unit length*

| | | | | | |
|---|---|---|---|---|---|
| 1 N/m | =0.068 521 8 | lbf/ft | 1 lbf/ft | =14.5939 | N/m |
| 1 Kn/m | =0.034 260 9 | tonf/ft | 1 tonf/ft | =29·187 8 | kN/m |

*Pressure, stress, modulus of elasticity (1 Pa=1 N/m²)*

| | | | | | |
|---|---|---|---|---|---|
| 1 MPa | =0.072 518 8 | tonf/in² | 1 tonf/in² | =13.7895 | MPa |
| | =10.442 7 | tonf/ft² | 1 tonf/ft² | =95.7605 | kPa |
| | =145.038 | lbf/in² | 1 kip/in² | =6.894 76 | MPa |
| 1 kPa | =20.885 4 | lbf/ft² | 1 lbf/in² | =6.894 76 | kPa |
| | | | 1 lbf/ft² | =47.8803 | Pa |

*Work, energy, heat (1 J=.1 W•s)*

| | | | | | |
|---|---|---|---|---|---|
| 1 MJ | =0.277 778 | kWh | 1 kWh | =3.6 | MJ |
| 1 kJ | =0.947 817 | Btu | 1 Btu | =1.055 06 | kJ |
| 1 J | =0.737 562 | ft·lbf | | =1055.06 | J |
| | | | 1 ft[cdt]lbf | =1.355 82 | J |

*Power, heat flow rate*

| | | | | | |
|---|---|---|---|---|---|
| 1 kW | =1.341 02 | hp | 1 hp | =0.745 700 | kW |
| 1 W | =3.412 14 | Btu/h | | =0.745 700 | W |
| | =0.737 562 | ft·lbf/s | 1 Btu/h | =0.293 071 | W |
| | | | 1 ft·lbf/s | =1.355 82 | W |

*Heat flux density*

| | | | | | |
|---|---|---|---|---|---|
| 1 W/m² | =0.316 998 | Btu/(ft²·h) | 1 Btu/(ft²·h) | =3.154 59 | W/m² |

*Thermal conductance (heat transfer coefficient)*

| | | | | | |
|---|---|---|---|---|---|
| 1 W/(m²·k) | =0.176 110 | Btu/(ft²·h·°F) | 1 Btu/(ft²·h·°F) | =5.678 26 | W/(m²·K) |

*Thermal conductivity*

| | | | | | |
|---|---|---|---|---|---|
| 1 W/(m·K) | =0.577 789 | Btu/(ft·h·°F) | 1 Btu/(ft·h·°F) | =1.730 73 | W/(m·K) |

NOTE: Underlined values are exact conversions.

## OTHER MULTIPLES AND SUBMULTIPLES

| Prefix | Symbol | Factor | Magnitude |
|---|---|---|---|
| hecto | h | $10^2$ | 100 |
| deka | da | $10^1$ | 10 |
| deci | d | $10^{-1}$ | 0.1 |
| centi | c | $10^{-2}$ | 0.01 |

## MULTIPLES OF SI UNITS

| Physical Quantity | Name | Symbol | Magnitude |
|---|---|---|---|
| volume | liter | L | $10^{-3}$ m³=0.001 m³ |
| mass | metric ton | t | $10^3$ kg=1000 kg |
| area | hectare | ha | $10^4$ m²=10 000m² |
| pressure | millibar | mbar | $10^2$ Pa=100 Pa |

## SI SUPPLEMENTARY UNITS

| Physical Quantity | Unit | Symbol |
|---|---|---|
| plane angle | radian | rad |
| solid angle | steradian | sr |

## NON-SI UNITS USED WITH SI

| | |
|---|---|
| minute | min |
| hour | h |
| day | d |
| nautical mile | n mile |
| knot | kn |
| kilometer per hour | km/h |
| revolution per minute | r/min |
| degree (angle) | ° |
| minute (angle) | ' |
| second (angle) | '' |
| kilowatt hour | kW·h |

## METRIC UNITS NOT RECOMMENDED FOR USE

| Names of Unit | Symbol | Physical Quantity | Value |
|---|---|---|---|
| area | a | area | 100 m² |
| atmosphere | atm | pressure | 1.013 25 x 10⁵ Pa |
| bar | b or bar | pressure | 10⁵ Pa |
| calorie | cal | energy, work | 4.186 8 J |
| dyne | dyn | force | 10⁻⁵N |
| erg | erg | energy, work | 10⁻⁷ J |
| kilogram-force | kgf | force | 9.806 65 N |
| kilopond | kp | force | 9.806 65 N |
| maxwell | Mx | magnetic flux | 10⁻⁸ Wb |
| micron | μ | length | 10⁻⁶ m |
| millimicron | mμ | length | 10⁻⁹ m |
| oersted | Oe | magnetization | 7.957 747 x 10¹A·m¹ |
| quintal | q | mass | 100 kg |
| stere | st | volume | 1 m³ |
| stilb | sb | luminance | 10⁴ cd·m⁻² |
| torr | torr | pressure | 1.333 224 x 10² Pa |

CONVERSION FACTORS FOR THE MOST COMMON UNITS USED IN ARCHITECTURE *(Cont.)*

| Metric to Customary | | | Customary to Metric | | |
|---|---|---|---|---|---|
| *Calorific value* | | | | | |
| (mass and volume basis) | | | | | |
| 1 kJ/kg | =0.429 923 | Btu/lb | 1 Btu/lb | =2.326 | kJ/kg |
| 1 J/g | | | | =2.326 | (J/g) |
| 1 kJ/m³ | =0.026 839 2 | Btu/ft³ | 1 Btu/ft³ | =37.2589 | kJ/m³ |
| *Thermal capacity* (mass and volume basis) | | | | | |
| 1 kJ/(kg·k) | =0.238 846 | Btu/(lb·°F) | 1 Btu (lb·°F) | =4.1868 | kJ/(kg·K) |
| 1 kJ/(m³·K) | =0.014 910 7 | Btu/(ft³·°F) | 1 Btu/(ft³·°F) | =67.0661 | KJ/(m³·K) |
| *Illuminance* | | | | | |
| 1 lx | =0.092 903 | lm/ft² (footcandle) | 1 lm/ft² | =10.7639 | lx |
| *Luminance* | | | | | |
| 1 cd/m² | =0.092 903 | cd/ft² | 1 cd/ft² | =10.7639 | cd/m² |
| | =0.291 864 | foot lambert | 1 footlambert | =3.426 26 | cd/m² |
| 1 kcd/m² | =0.314 159 | lambert | 1 lambert | =3.183 01 | kcd/m² |

NOTE: Underlined values are exact conversions.

the kilometer (km) or 1,000 m is the proper SI unit rather than the mile as in the customary system. For land areas, as on building sites, the SI unit employed is the square kilometer (km²), and for smaller areas, the square meter (m²), while the acre and the square foot are ordinarily used in the customary system. The basic preferred module for the design and construction of buildings is 4 inches (in) in the customary system and 100 mm, slightly less than 4 in, in SI unit.

There are major differences between customary and SI units. SI units have rational relationships based on powers of 10, or decimals, with each other, while most customary units are based on arbitrary measurements, many of them derived from assumed dimensions of the human body. SI units comprise an organized system, in which only seven base units and two supplementary units may be used to derive all the many kinds of measurements needed in the world of today and in its architecture. Multiples of the base and derived units all use the same prefixes to denote the same powers of 10 by which the base and derived units are multiplied. For example, milli means 1/1000, or $10^{-3}$. Thus a millimeter is 1/1000 of a meter or 0.001 m, and a milligram (mg) is 0.001 gram (g).

Engineering and scientific calculations are greatly simplified by the use of SI units, not only because of decimalization but because of the greater coherence and versatility of the system. For example, 24 customary units for pressure and stress can all be expressed by one SI unit, the joule (J). In some cases, because of their usefulness and widespread acceptance, certain non-SI units are retained. They include the time units of minute, hour, and day; the angular measurements of second, minute, and degree; and the nautical mile.

**History** It is believed that crude measurements were used by humans in prehistoric times. The earliest were based on measurements of the human body and weights of plant seeds. Since the dimensions of the human body are anything but standard, different measurements were adopted in different places at different times. Even after the adoption of standard measurements, different countries and even cities and localities within countries continued to use their own standards. The result was a confused, even chaotic, situation, which exists to the present time.

Units of length are thought to have been the first measurements developed, mainly because they would have been needed in building huts and tents and for other purposes. The primary unit of length was the cubit, considered to be the length of the human forearm from the elbow to the tip of the middle finger. Other measures were the palm, the width usually taken across the palm at the base of the fingers; the digit, the width of a finger; and the foot, the length of that extremity. Although these measurements varied between localities, their relationships were somewhat as follows: 4 digits equal 1 palm; 4 palms, or 16 digits, equal 1 foot; 1 foot equals ²/₃ of a cubit; 6 palms equal 1 cubit; 4 cubits equal 1 fathom. All these are still used today in some places.

The earliest weights were used for the measurement of gold. They were based on the weights of plant seeds, and the term *grain* is still used in weighing gold and some other materials. Later such weight measurements were made equal to other quantities, such as the shekel, which varied in size from 120 to 218 grains (gr) in the ancient civilizations. Measures of volume were also developed very early and varied considerably between localities. By about 3000 B.C., attempts were made in the ancient lands to standardize the measures, at least within their own territories, by preserving specimen weights and measures in temples, by order of the rulers.

However, the variations between countries and localities persisted. For example, the Egyptian royal cubit, 20.63 in (524 mm), measured 7 palms or 28 digits, while the short cubit, 17.68 in (449 mm), was 6 palms or 24 digits long. The ancient Greek Olympic cubit, 18.23 in (463 mm), equaled 25 digits. An Olympic foot measured ²/₃ of an Olympic cubit, 12.15 in (309 mm), while the ordinary cubit, 12.45 in (approximately 316 mm), more often used, equaled 16 digits.

The Romans attempted to standardize measurements in their empire. In spite of this effort, their measurements continued to vary somewhat in different places and at different times. One set of Roman measurements included the digit (*digitus*), 0.73 in (slightly more than 18 mm); 4 *digiti* equaled 1 palm (palma), 2.9 in (approximately 74 mm); 4 *palmae*, 11.6 in (almost 1 foot or 296 mm), equaled 1 Roman foot (*pes*); 1¹/₂ *pedes*, 17.5 in (approximately 443 mm), equaled 1 cubit (*cubitus*).

After the time of the Romans, little or no attempt was made to standardize measurements, each nation, and often localities within nations, continuing to develop their own. By the 18th century, it is believed that there were almost 300 variations of the foot being used in Europe. A high degree of standardization was achieved in England in what came to be called the English system of measurement, and this system spread throughout the British Empire.

The first colonists who emigrated from England to America brought the English system, which was later somewhat modified and became the standard in America. Colonists from Spain, France, the Netherlands, and other places brought the systems of their own countries, and some of their measurements were absorbed into the American system.

The metric system was developed in France in the late 18th century; laws were passed in 1795 and 1799 making it the official system. Not until 1837 was the system made compulsory in France. And even today, some of the older terms for measurement, such as pound, are still used. Subsequently, the metric system was adopted in many of the nations of Europe and after World War II in China, India, and other Eastern countries. The major group of nations still using the older system in the second half of the 20th century included England, the British Commonwealth, and the United States. Although the metric system seemed, on the face of it, to be standardized; in actuality it was not. Practices and standards varied from nation to nation, even though all used the same or similar units of measurement.

In 1875 an International Bureau of Weights and Measures (BIPM) was founded for the purpose of imposing standards. In 1885 the United Kingdom joined the bureau. In the United States in 1866, Congress passed a law making the metric system legal, but optional. For many years, the system was used only for a few applications, such as optometry. However, after 1866, the United States began to base its standard measurements on the metric system and that is the practice today. Over the years, those standards have changed, the present one for the meter, for example, having been established only in 1960. In the same year, the General Conference on Weights and Measures (CGPM), the governing body of the international bureau, adopted an international system of units, called Système International d'Unités, or SI units. Not only are SI units standardized so that they represent the same measurements wherever they are used, but an attempt has been made to make relationships between units as simple as possible.

England began conversion to the metric system, using SI units, in the 1960s, leading to complete conversion of all measurements in the 1980s. Australia and Canada followed the English lead during the 1970s, as did other nations of the Commonwealth, leaving the United States as the only major holdout. For many years, efforts were made to have the United States convert to the metric system. All failed. In 1975 the U.S. Congress enacted a law calling for voluntary conversion, without any deadline for completion. Congress also created a U.S. Metric Board, with members to be appointed by the president. In 1978 the members were appointed. Over the years, the metric system has been taught to some extent in American schools, colleges, and universities and has been used in certain disciplines, such as chemistry. During the 1970s, the process of teaching the metric system accelerated on most educational levels, including engineering and scientific schools. And SI unit sizes are gradually being adopted by various industries. When the U.S. conversion to the metric system will be completed is still a matter of conjecture.

Since the 1970s, metric conversion has been achieved in certain industries, although this conversion does not affect most consumers except for wine and spirits, now sold in metric measurements, and the pharmacological industry. Industries involved in foreign trade have adopted metric measurements out of marketing need, including the automotive industry and the U.S. Department of Defense. Architects find it possible to design in metric measurements without too much effort, although some U.S. engineering calculations may require conversion to metric units.

**Source of Additional Information** American National Metric Council, 1620 I St., N.W., Washington, D.C. 20005.

**MECHANICAL ENGINEERING** A major branch of engineering concerned with the production, use, and distribution of mechanical power, including water, heat and air conditioning, and waste disposal in buildings. A mechanical engineer has been licensed or registered to perform professional services for work of this kind.

Working closely with the architect and coordinating the work with other engineers and consultants, a mechanical engineer is primarily responsible for designing the mechanical systems in a building; preparing the mechanical construction documents (working drawings and specifications); making estimates of the construction costs of the mechanical work; and inspecting the work while the building is under construction to ensure that the mechanical work is free of defects and is properly constructed.

**Mechanical Systems** The two major systems in buildings for which mechanical engineers are responsible are plumbing; and heating, ventilating, and air conditioning, sometimes referred to as HVAC. Plumbing includes all the piping, fittings and other devices, and fixtures required for supplying bathrooms, kitchens, laundry rooms, drinking fountains and water coolers, janitors' sinks, and the like, and also the piping and other devices for disposal of wastes. Heating, ventilating, and air conditioning includes all the ductwork or piping, devices, equipment, and controls for these purposes. In addition, mechanical engineers are often responsible in some buildings for refrigeration equipment and systems, fire protection systems, and other types of mechanical work.

In times past, mechanical engineering was not nearly so important as it is today. Systems were simpler then and the needs and wishes of the people who used buildings were relatively simple. Today elaborate heating and air-conditioning systems are thought of as necessities, along with a variety of kitchen, laundry, and other appliances, and many other increasingly elaborate systems. Other factors have heightened the importance of mechanical engineering today. Mechanical engineers are responsible for much of the equipment which requires energy in the form of electricity and fossil fuels. Thus mechanical engineers carry a considerable part of the burden for efficient use of energy in buildings and conservation of energy supplies.

Mechanical engineering has become more important, architecturally, in still another way in recent years. In the past, the norm in building design was to hide pipes, ducts, and equipment; yet for some time there has been a move to express the structure of buildings. Ducts and other items, in some buildings today, are openly exposed to become elements of the exterior, and sometimes interior, appearance of buildings. Thus the mechanical work previously carefully hidden or disguised can become a major esthetic design element. Mechanical work in buildings increases in both complexity and costs, with time, taking an ever large portion of total building construction budgets.

**Work Phases** The professional work of mechanical engineers in buildings is usually divided into phases that are the same as those of the other architectural and engineering work: schematic, design development, construction document, and construction administration. Mechanical engineers work closely with the architects and other engineers during all phases. During the schematic phase, mechanical engineers make studies of the building site, program, and problems, and prepare preliminary drawings, specifications, and estimates of construction costs of the mechanical systems. During the design development phase, they study the problems further and refine the drawings, specifications, and estimates. During the construction document phase, they prepare final drawings and specifications which will be used in the actual construction of the building and prepare further refined estimates of costs. During the construction administration phase, they assist the architects in the administration of the work and inspect the actual construction of the mechanical systems to ensure that they are properly constructed.

In addition to the major functions of the mechanical engineers, other services may be required, such as revisions in drawings, specifications, or estimates or preparation of as-built drawings after construction has been completed. In all their work on buildings, mechanical engineers strive not only to achieve the purpose of the systems for which they are primarily responsible but to cooperate with the architects and other engineers and consultants in the creation of buildings which, in their totality, achieve their purposes.

The education, registration or licensing, and practice of mechanical engineers today are similar to those of other professional engineers. (See the article entitled engineering.)

**Related Articles** BUILDING CODES AND STANDARDS; BUILDING INDUSTRY; COST CONTROL; DRAFTING; ENERGY; ENGINEERING; FIRE PROTECTION; HEATING, VENTILATING, AND AIR CONDITIONING; PLUMBING; SPECIFICATION; WORKING DRAWING.

**Periodicals** *Actual Specifying Engineer*, 5 S. Wabash Ave., Chicago, Ill., 60603; *ASHRAE Journal*, 345 E. 47th St., New York, N.Y. 10017.

**Additional Sources of Information** American Society of Heating, Refrigerating and Air Conditioning Engineers, Inc., 1791 Tullie Circle N.E., Atlanta, Ga. 30329; See also list at end of the article entitled engineering.

**MEIER, RICHARD** Richard Meier (1934–    ), American architect, is a leading designer with many awards including the 1984 Pritzker prize and the Gold Medal of the Royal Institute of British Architects to his credit. He acknowledges Le Corbusier and Frank Lloyd Wright as his major influences and describes his work as

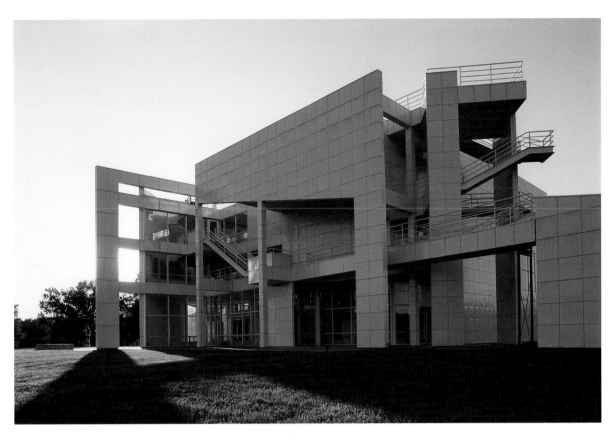

**MEIER, RICHARD** The Athenaeum (1979), New Harmony, Ind.

Neo Modern, or possibly Late-Modern Classicist. Many of his buildings are white objects in the landscape. He has been described as the leading designer of public buildings of his generation, several of which are European projects.

**Works** The early houses which received attention were the Smith House in Darien, Conn. (1967), the Saltzman House (1969) in East Hampton, N.Y., the Douglas House (1976) in Harbor Springs, Mich., and the Maidman House (1976) in Sands Point, N.Y.

Two recent houses are the Westchester House (1986), in Westchester County, N.Y., and the Ackerberg House (1986), in Malibu, Calif.

These large houses were balanced by Richard Meier's commissions for public housing agencies in New York. Although perceived as an elitist architect, Meier stresses his involvement in public and urban work. Influential proposals for multiple housing include the IBA Housing (1982), for Berlin, Germany, and the Spanish Quarter project (1987) for Naples, Italy, sponsored by the University of Naples.

Richard Meier's fame was ensured with the designs for the Bronx Development Center (1977), The Bronx, N.Y., the Athenaeum (1979) in New Harmony, Ind., and the Hartford Seminary (1981), Hartford, Conn. In recent years, his public work has been the greater part of his practice.

Richard Meier's museums are important works. The High Museum of Art (1983), in Atlanta, Ga., is a white building with a central sky-lit atrium. Access to the various floors is by curving ramps, inviting a comparison to Frank Lloyd Wright's Guggenheim Museum in New York City. However, in the Atlanta museum exhibition spaces are on adjoining galleries, avoiding the problem of displaying art on the ramps. The use of colored walls is particularly powerful in the otherwise white interiors. There is a quality in this museum of his residential work, and some critics have felt that the ramps are too narrow for a public building. The building, set among lawns and trees, is an important landmark structure in Atlanta.

The 1985 Des Moines, Iowa, Art Center (1985) project was an addition to an earlier building designed by Eliel Saarinen in 1948, with a 1965 addition by I. M. Pei. Richard Meier's addition consists of a new building to the north of the Saarinen building and two smaller additions to the earlier building. The smaller additions serve to emphasize the change of axis from the old to the new and provide needed space for the museum restaurant, opening into a previously little-used sculpture courtyard. The new addition provides new gallery space, with windows looking out at lawn and mature trees.

The Museum of Decorative Arts (*Museum Fur Kunsthandwerk*) (1985), in Frankfurt am Main,

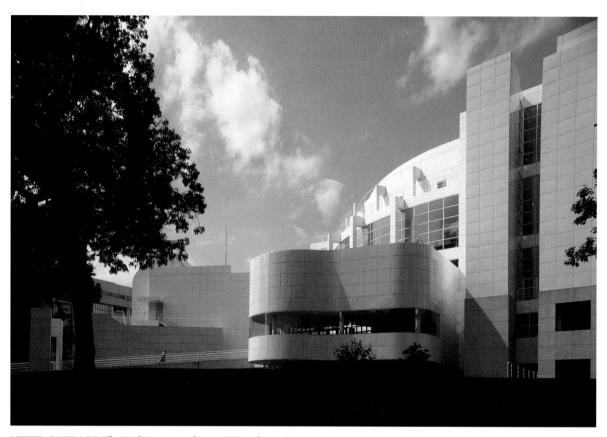

**MEIER, RICHARD** The High Museum of Art (1983), Atlanta, Ga.

Germany, is in an urban area of older buildings on the south bank of the River Main. The museum is an addition to the 19th-century Villa Metzler, the former museum, adjoining several other museum buildings. Together they are called the "*Museumsufer.*" The building is built at the east end of the site, with the remainder developed as a park open to the adjacent community, providing public access to the bridges over the Main leading to the center of the city. Because the site bends at the Villa Metzler, the addition consists of a grid overlaid with another grid varying by 3½ degrees from the other, parallel to other buildings facing the Main. This shifting of grids adds considerable interest to the building. Here again Meier uses white walls, large windows looking out on the park, and skylights over the circulation ramps connecting the exhibition floors on three levels. Another proposed urban museum is the Exhibition/Assembly building (designed in 1991) for Ulm, Germany, which is planned to reinforce the experience of the square in front of the cathedral and the city surrounding it.

The J. Paul Getty Center adjoining Los Angeles, Calif., is a major complex of art-related facilities on a high ridge overlooking the city. Only 24 acres of the 110-acre site will be developed. The largest building will be the Getty Museum, and other facilities will be in several related buildings. All buildings will be faced with limestone. Visitors will park in a parking structure in the adjoining valley and be transported up to the ridge by tram. The buildings will be surrounded by gardens and terraces. Commentary in anticipation of the reality concerns the huge scale of the development and the separation of museum functions into a series of study centers. This reflects an uneasiness with the size and multiple programs of the Getty Foundation rather than with Meier's buildings.

Richard Meier has received wide attention for his urban design and public building proposals for work in Europe and Israel. These include the Renault Administrative Headquarters (1981) for Boulogne-Billancourt, France, and an office building for Siemens (1983) in Munich, Germany. He designed a proposal for a large development called Progretto Bicocca (1986), for Milan, Italy, including industrial, housing, and commercial space on property no longer needed by the Fiat company. Meier's entry for the international competition for a new Supreme Court Building (1986) for Jerusalem, Israel, is of interest. Other European projects include a new City Hall and Library (1992) for the Hague, Netherlands, and the Exhibition, Training and Dining

410

Quarters (1991) for Max Weishaupt, GmbH, Schwendi, Germany, and the television studios and Corporate Headquarters for Canal+ (1991), in Paris, France.

Large projects in the United States include the Bridgeport Center (1989), for Bridgeport, Conn., the Eye Center (1986), Portland, Ore., and the Madison Square Towers (1987), New York, N.Y.

**Life** Richard Alan Meier was born in Newark, N.J. in 1934 and received his architectural education at Cornell University, receiving his degree in 1957. He worked for the firms of Davis, Brody and Wisnieweski, Skidmore, Owings and Merrill, and with Marcel Breuer. He opened his own office in New York City in 1963. For a period he worked in the studio of the artist Frank Stella, painting and making collages. He maintains offices in New York and Los Angeles, for which he designed the interiors. When time allows, Richard Meier has taught at Cooper Union in New York, at Yale University in New Haven, Conn., and at Harvard University in Cambridge, Mass.

In a period of shifting attitudes and theories of design, Richard Meier has developed his own style derived from the classic modern tradition. His interest in the placement of the building on the site, in a varied pedestrian experience, in the quality of light in buildings, and in the effective display of art are the strongest attributes of his work. Richard Meier describes himself as a fortunate architect.

**Further Reading** Meier, Richard: *Buildings and Projects 1966–1976*, Oxford University Press, New York, 1976; Meier, Richard: *Richard Meier*, Academy Editions, St. Martin's Press, New York, 1990; Meier, Richard: *Richard Meier, Architect: 1985–1991*, Rizzoli, New York, 1991.

**MIES VAN DER ROHE, LUDWIG** German-American architect (1886–1969). Although he was destined to become one of the world's most influential architects, Ludwig Mies van der Rohe had no formal education in architecture. A member of a quartet of architects that included Frank Lloyd Wright (1867–1959), Le Corbusier (1887–1965), and Walter Gropius (1883–1969) and that brought modern architecture to fruition, Mies saw only a small number of his designs built. He wrote very little, and what he did write was terse and to the point.

Yet in spite of his relatively small output, Mies profoundly affected the architecture of his time and of the future. He was fond of aphorisms, and some of them were widely repeated: "Architecture is the will of an epoch translated into space; living, changing, new," and "Form is not the aim of our work, but only the result."

**MIES VAN DER ROHE** Farnsworth House (1949), Plano, Ill. *[Photo: Jon Miller; © Hedrich-Blessing]*

**MIES VAN DER ROHE** 860-880 Lake Shore Apartments (1951), Chicago, Ill.

Later he was to refer to his buildings as "skin and bones," to his design philosophy as "less is more," and to say "God is in the details." But his great influence came from his architecture, not his aphorisms.

The buildings of Mies are predominantly rectangular. They have a clear, clean logic in their plans and appearance that makes their designs seem as rational as pure science. All the elements of a Mies design seem abstract, the lines and planes of the walls, roofs, and floors forming a functional composition that seems quite formal. It is as if he were seeking to reduce the building and all its details to the absolute reducible minimum. Though almost all his American buildings reveal their structure on the exterior, they all have a dignified subtlety and elegance that comes from considerably more than just their structure. His austere formalism had a powerful effect on the designs of architects, not only those who studied at the Illinois Institute of Technology, where he taught, but on architects everywhere.

**Works** The designs of Mies started having a degree of influence on architecture early in his career, mostly because of visionary projects that were widely published but never built. Then in 1929 he burst on the world

**MIES VAN DER ROHE** S. R. Crown Hall (1956), Illinois Institute of Technology, Chicago, Ill.

scene with one of the most published buildings of all time. This was the German Pavilion for the International Exposition, Barcelona, Spain. An abstract design of simple planes, the pavilion was not designed to house exhibits but to serve as an exhibit itself. It was considered a masterpiece of modern architecture and brought quick recognition to Mies. For the pavilion, he also produced another masterpiece, a chair (called the "Barcelona" chair) made of curved steel bands cantilevered to support cushions. This chair is considered by many to be the finest single piece of modern furniture, and it is still being produced. Demolished in 1930, the Barcelona Pavilion was reconstructed in the 1980s on its original site. A year later (1930), Mies produced the Tugendhat House, Brno, Czechoslovakia, also considered one of his best buildings, for which he designed another fine chair. The house suffered damage for many years, and the restoration of the famous building was started in 1986.

His first commission, after he came to America, was for the design of the campus and buildings at Armour Institute, which was later renamed the Illinois Institute of Technology (IIT; see illustration), Chicago. Beginning in 1939, this project occupied him for some 20 years and produced a unified group of buildings. Before he retired from IIT in 1958, he designed several other notable buildings. First came the Promontory Apartments (1949), Chicago, originally designed in steel but built of concrete, followed by the Farnsworth House (1950), Plano, Ill., a simple, elegant cube with glass walls. His 860 Lake Shore Drive Apartments (1951), two towers in Chicago, was another landmark design, followed by Commonwealth Promenade Apartments (1953), complex of four towers, also in Chicago. The only building by Mies in New York, the Seagram Building (1958) designed with Philip Cortelyou Johnson (1906– ), is one of the most notable skyscrapers of later years, in its plan, appearance, use of the site, and interiors. It contains an elegant restaurant, The Four Seasons, completely designed by Johnson right down to the tableware. Mies's last building completed before his death was the National Gallery (1968) in what was then West Berlin. Several other buildings were in the process of design at that time. The major legacy of Mies is to be found in his buildings and his students and in the influence they have had on architecture.

As time passes, some criticism of Mies's work concludes that the machine-made appearance of his buildings disguises the largely hand-built details. He has been accused of ignoring functional demands such as excessive solar gain through glass walls. He has been described as insensitive to neighboring structures and environmental concerns. Some of the buildings derived from the work of Mies have been inferior in concept and

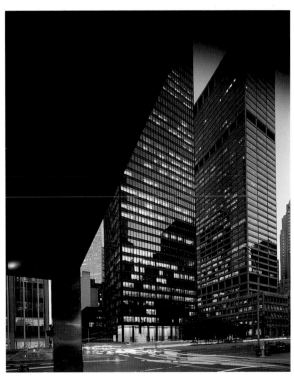

**MIES VAN DER ROHE** Seagram Building (1957), New York, N.Y.

execution, leading to a rejection of the Modern movement by many current architects. Perhaps Mies van der Rohe's lasting influence has been in the design of lobbies, convention halls, or open office floors. What remains appealing is his concern with theory, clarity of image, and carefully designed details.

**Life** Ludwig Mies van der Rohe was born on March 27, 1886, in Aachen, Germany, the son of a stonecutter and mason. Later he added his mother's name, van der Rohe, to his father's. As a boy, Mies learned stone masonry by working with his father. He attended the Cathedral School of Aachen and at thirteen entered the trade school there. At fifteen, his formal schooling ended when he left the trade school, but his education in the practical side of architecture continued. From age fifteen to nineteen, he worked as a designer and drafter of ornamental details in stucco for Classic style buildings. In 1905 he went to work for an interior and furniture designer in Berlin. In 1907 he left to embark on his architectural career and that same year designed a house in Classical style. In 1908 he went to work in the office of Peter Behrens (1868–1940), a pioneering German architect. While there, another future great architect, Walter Adolf Gropius, joined the firm, and later the great Swiss-French architect Le Corbusier (real name, Charles-Edouard Jeanneret) worked in the office.

Mies left the Behrens office in 1911, and went to The Hague, Netherlands, in 1912 to work on the design of a

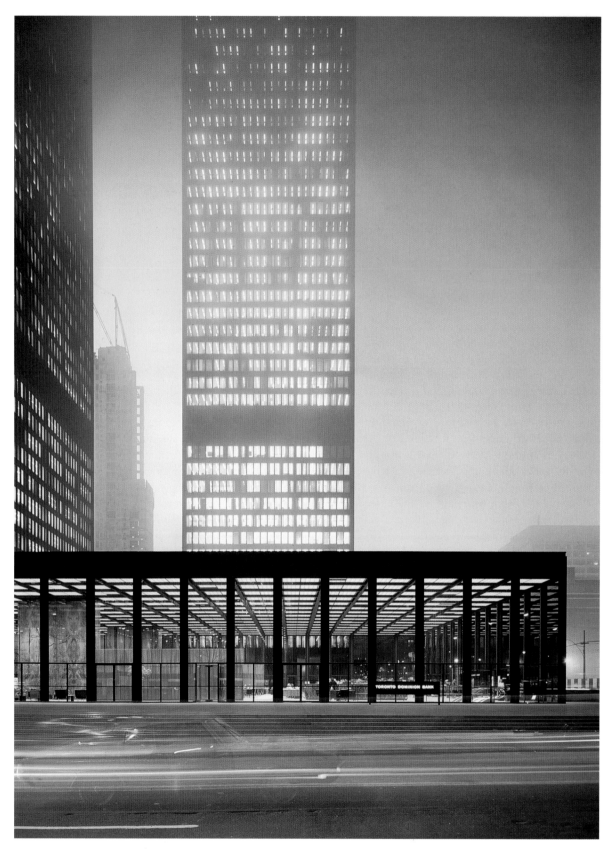

**MIES VAN DER ROHE** Bank, Toronto Dominion Centre (1968), Toronto, Ontario, Canada.

house for Mme. H. E. L. J. Kroller. Although he stayed for a year, finished the design, and had a full-size model of wood and canvas erected on the site, the house was never built. Here again, the style was traditional Classical. Returning to Berlin, Mies opened his own office, designed several buildings, all traditional, only one of which was built. In 1914 he was called into the German army in World War I, and served until the Armistice in 1918.

Returning to Berlin, he opened a practice in 1919. Lacking commissions for actual buildings, he spent his time designing exhibitions and writing. He also designed a remarkable series of five building projects, none ever built, but all different and all very much ahead of the times. These were schemes for a glass office building (1919), another for a glass skyscraper (1921), one for a concrete office building (1922), and two for country houses, one in brick (1923), the other in concrete (1924). These projects were widely published and established Mies as a pioneering visionary architect, though not a very practical one. He still designed projects, but most were never built.

In 1926 Mies was appointed first vice president of the German *Werkbund,* an organization of architects and industrialists attempting to improve the quality of industrial design in Germany. In this position, he directed the Second *Werkbund* Exposition (1927) in Stuttgart. To design the buildings, he brought in many of the best European architects, including Peter Behrens, Walter Gropius, Le Corbusier, and the fine Dutch architect Jacobus Johannes Pieter (J. J. P.) Oud (1890–1963). Mies designed one building. He served in this position until 1932.

In 1929 he designed a masterpiece, the Barcelona Pavilion, which brought him worldwide recognition, and the following year he designed his great Tugendhat House. Also in 1930, Mies was appointed director of the Bauhaus, the famous design and arts school, in Dessau. Political pressures caused the school to move to Berlin in 1932, and the following year it was closed by the Nazis.

Mies continued designing projects, including an innovative series of houses with courtyards, but again none was actually built. In 1937 he came to America, a very influential and famous architect, who by age fifty had designed many buildings, although only about 19 had been built. These include 11 houses, 2 apartments, and 6 exhibits destroyed at the end of the expositions in which they appeared. In addition, he had designed a monument that was built but was later torn down by the Nazis.

After a short time in America, in 1938 Mies was named director of architecture at Armour Institute, later renamed Illinois Institute of Technology. Soon after-

ward, he was commissioned to design a whole new campus and the buildings for the school. Starting in 1939, he designed the master plan for the school and eventually the buildings for the campus. He was occupied with the buildings at IIT and with the Architecture School for the next 20 years, until he retired, in 1958, to practice full-time in Chicago. He designed a number of other important buildings and continued to do so for the remainder of his life.

The profession that he embraced gave him numerous awards, including the Gold Medal of the Royal Institute of British Architects (1959). He had become an American citizen in 1944, and the architects of his adopted country, the American Institute of Architects, awarded him the Gold Medal in 1960. His last important building, the National Gallery (1968), was built in what was then West Berlin. On August 19, 1969, Ludwig Mies van der Rohe died, the last of the great quartet that had made modern architecture flower. He had outlived Wright by 10 years, Le Corbusier by 4, and Gropius by a little over a month.

**Related Articles** ART IN ARCHITECTURE; BAUHAUS, STAATLICHES; EDUCATION; GROPIUS, WALTER ADOLF; MODERN ARCHITECTURE.

**Further Reading** Blaser, Werner: *Mies van der Rohe: Continuing the Chicago School,* Birhauser, Cambridge, Mass., 1981; Tegethoff, Wolf: *Mies van der Rohe: The Villas and Country Houses,* The Museum of Modern Art, New York, 1985, distributed by the MIT Press, Cambridge, Mass.

**MILITARY BUILDING** A building for use in military defense, training, or war. Military buildings may be classified into two major types: those that have specialized uses in defense or in waging war, such as ancient forts or modern computerized missiles, and those usually employed for ordinary purposes that have been adapted to military functions. The use of modern military vehicles and automated weapons and defensive devices was dramatically demonstrated during the 1992 Desert Storm campaign.

Throughout history, architects have been deeply involved in the design and construction of military buildings. And it is only necessary to go back a few hundred years to find architects also deeply involved in the weapons of war and defense. Today architects are still engaged in the design and construction of military buildings and other structures, but not ordinarily with weapons. In the recent past, military construction formed a large and important part of the practice of quite a few architects and, for some, it continues to be important.

For various reasons, including their very specialized, often classified, nature, discussion of the specialized kinds of military buildings is beyond the scope of this article. Architects who become involved in such work are often required to obtain security clearance and have to work closely with the military services to determine how to program and design such buildings. In general, these architects find that work of this kind entails meeting many kinds of criteria, requirements, regulations, and specifications not ordinarily found in work for nonmilitary clients.

Architectural services for buildings of the second type more closely resemble those for nonmilitary clients. However, here again architects find a great number of special regulations and requirements. On the other hand, the design of such buildings has much in common with that of the same types used for nonmilitary purposes.

**Building Types** Military bases today are much like cities or towns and have requirements for many of the same types of buildings and other structures. Among the major building types usually found on military bases are apartments, banks, hospitals, houses and other types of housing, libraries, office buildings, parks, prisons, recreation buildings, religious buildings, restaurants, schools, shopping centers and stores, theaters, and warehouses. Other types of buildings often found on military bases include airport facilities, barracks that are similar to college dormitories in some respects, hotels, laboratories, museums, and railway stations. In addition, many military bases have buildings and structures so specialized that specific research must be accomplished by architects before they can be designed properly. Also certain structures, such as docks and bridges, are found on military bases, but are not ordinarily designed by architects today.

The military services also use buildings that are not located on the usual type of military base, including the college buildings of the service academies and office buildings, such as the Pentagon, in Washington, D.C. Architects who wish to design military buildings should establish contact with the various services to determine their requirements.

During periods when defense budgets are reduced, a list of military bases are proposed to be closed, often to the economic detriment of nearby communities. These bases may be of historic importance, and some have been successfully adapted as parks or museums. The National Park Service operates several such facilities in the United States.

**History** Since prehistoric times, human beings have made war on each other, seeking such goals as territory, wealth, power, and security. Therefore military buildings and other structures have been part of human life ever since. No one knows exactly what form military structures took at first. It is believed that they were simply rocks or boulders piled up for protection, probably followed by palisades or stockades made of tree trunks. In the Middle East, after people began to create towns, protective walls of mud or sun-dried bricks were erected. In Mesopotamia and other nearby areas, town walls might be 20 ft or more in thickness and were made of sun-dried brick, sometimes framed with timbers and erected on stone bases. Many of them had towers at intervals. Some had double walls and at strategic places within the walls, forts or citadels, with additional walls to protect the most important buildings. In other cases, the circumferential walls were augmented by crosswalls within.

The city of Babylon, rebuilt by King Nebuchadnezzar II (c. 605–563 B.C.), was heavily fortified with an inner wall protecting the principal buildings and outer walls surrounding the entire city. In the Middle East, forts were also built at important places away from cities, such as river fords.

The ancient Greeks also placed walls around their towns. In fact, it is thought that by the 4th century B.C., every sizable Greek city was protected by walls. These were constructed of mud brick, later of stone, irregular shapes at first, followed by squared stones. These thick walls usually had towers and also ditches outside.

The Romans built walls around their towns and those they conquered. These walls were usually of masonry and were erected in pairs about 20 ft or so apart with as many as three ditches outside. Some towns even had three walls. In between the walls, parapet walks were constructed of rammed rock and earth. The outer wall was quite high and had alternating solid and open sections, called crenelation, at the top. Such a wall is often called a battlement. The inner walls were lower, allowing easy access from inside the towns. Gates had elaborate baffles to delay or prevent entry by enemies.

**MILITARY BUILDING** Fort Pulaski National Monument (1829–47), near Savannah, Ga. [*Designer: Gen. Simon Bernard*]

Galleries at different levels, elaborate stairways, chambers, and towers served a similar purpose.

During the Middle Ages, early forts and fortified castles were constructed with wooden stockades placed on mounds and had wooden towers called keeps. Later stone was used for fortifications, at first in simple walls without towers, then in elaborate ones, with towers and galleries of wood, later replaced by stone, or hoardings, which projected from the tops to the outside. From the hoardings, objects could be dropped on invaders below.

By the 13th century, design and construction of castles and other fortifications had become much more complex. Walls were strengthened, elaborate towers of various sizes were placed in important locations, and certain areas of forts or castles were designed to be held by the defenders even if other parts fell to the invaders. About the 13th century, the French began construction of fortified towns, called *bastides.* The introduction of gunpowder into Europe in the 14th century, long after its first use in China, revolutionized warfare and fortifications. Walls were made wider to accommodate defensive artillery and lower to reduce the effects of the artillery of the attackers.

During the Renaissance, after the advent of artillery, forts and fortified towns were not usually constructed with high walls which would present excellent targets to enemy gunners. In their stead, the main walls were made stronger, of masonry, but just high enough to prevent scaling and were sloped. Massive earthworks and ditches were placed outside the walls, making it difficult for artillery to score direct hits on the walls. Rocks, trees, and other objects behind which enemies might be protected were removed for great distances beyond the mounds and ditches. And various obstacles were erected to impede the progress of the invaders, including stockades or palisades of poles, called *fraises,* cut-down trees with branches trimmed to points, or *abatis,* and wooden stocks with pointed ends placed radially, called *chevaux-de-frise.* Other types of fortifications were developed, including polygonal structures that were thought to be more easily defended than some other types.

In the late 16th and early 17th centuries, many systems of fortification were developed, though no radical changes were made like those necessitated by the introduction of artillery. The science of fortification was systematized during this period, in which an important role was played by the French engineer Sébastien Le Prestre Vauban (1632–1707). Vauban worked out a system of fortification unequaled by any that preceded it. His principles included provisions that fortifications must be strong enough to withstand cannon fire, that all parts

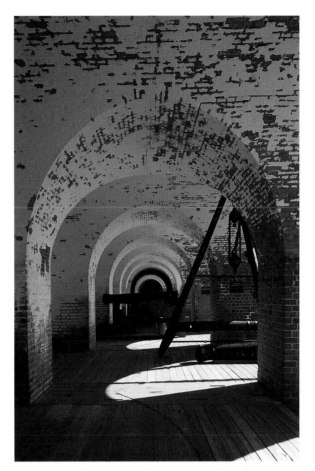

**MILITARY BUILDING** Fort Pulaski National Monument (1829–47), near Savannah, Ga. *[Designer: Gen. Simon Bernard]*

must be positioned so no hiding places were available to enemies, and that every part must be within reach of defensive musket fire from other parts. Acting upon these principles, Vauban took part in the erection of more than 30 new French forts and the improvement of about 300 others, with the result that his nation developed the best fortification system in Europe. Vauban also directed some 50 sieges during the almost unending series of wars fought by France during his lifetime. The work of Vauban had considerable influence on fortifications and upon military tactics and strategy in colonial America as well as in Europe.

**American Construction** In early colonial America, forts were among the first structures to be built. American forts generally were modeled after those of the European nations, mainly France, Spain, and England, which had established colonies in the New World. Over the years, forts and other military buildings and structures have continued to be built, each succeeding example reflecting the needs at the time and the prevailing theories of defense. Many of these forts and other military buildings and structures are still in exis-

417

tence, though some are in ruins. A number have been reconstructed.

Although anything approaching a history of military construction in America is far beyond the scope of this book, some understanding may be gained through examination of a place that might represent that history, in microcosm, the city and surrounding area of Pensacola, Fla.

**Pensacola** The site of Pensacola is thought to have been discovered in 1540, by the crew of a ship of the Spanish explorer Hernando De Soto (*c.* 1500–42). Tristan de Luna established a colony, called by its Indian name Ochuse, in 1559, but it was abandoned two years later, thus bringing to a temporary end a city that was six years older than the oldest existent in the United States, St. Augustine, Fla. Almost 140 years passed before another Spanish settlement was made in Pensacola in 1696. Although the original colony may have had fortifications, the first known structure of this kind in Pensacola was Fort San Carlos de Austria, completed in 1699, and constructed of two rows of pine logs with sand between them. Other forts of wood had earlier been built near what is now Jacksonville, Fla., and St. Augustine. About 1719, the Spanish built another fort on Santa Rosa Island, across Pensacola Bay from the present city. In 1719, when war broke out with the Spanish, the French attacked Pensacola, burned the town, and destroyed the fort.

In 1723, three years after the war ended, the French restored Pensacola to Spanish rule. The town was rebuilt but was again destroyed in 1754, by a hurricane. In 1763, as a result of the Treaty of Paris, Spain ceded Florida to Great Britain and Pensacola became a British colony. The entire Spanish population of the city, except for one man, deserted Pensacola. The city then became the British headquarters for West Florida and soon several forts were built, including Fort George and Fort Redoubt, about 1770. In 1781 a French and Spanish force headed by the governor of Spanish Louisiana, Bernardo de Galvez (*c.* 1746–86), attacked the British at Pensacola and erected Fort Bernardo a short distance from Fort George. From Fort Bernardo, the Spanish successfully bombarded the British fort and it surrendered. Galvez renamed it Fort San Miguel and Pensacola went back under Spanish rule.

About 1787, a more permanent Fort San Carlos was built by the Spanish. The earlier forts have long been demolished, but portions of this fort still remain. In 1813, during the War of 1812, the British invaded Pensacola and seized the forts. Within a few months, the British were defeated by General Andrew Jackson (1767–1845), returning the town to the Spanish. In 1818, during the so-called Seminole War, Jackson again entered the city, capturing the forts. In 1821 he returned to the city to receive West Florida from Spain and to become its first U.S. provisional governor.

After the War of 1812, the United States embarked upon a major construction program of permanent forts. At Pensacola, Fort Pickens was constructed in 1834, on Santa Rosa Island at the site of the earlier Spanish fort; in 1839 Fort McRee, across Big Lagoon was completed. Fort Barrancas was built in 1844, adjacent to the site of old Fort San Carlos, and Advanced Redoubt (*c.* 1859) nearby was begun a short time later. The engineer for all was Col. William H. Chase, U.S. Army. None of these forts ever fired a shot at a foreign enemy or were fired upon by one. However, they did figure in the American Civil War. Forts Barrancas and McRee were occupied by Confederate troops, as was the Navy Yard, which had been established in 1826, but Fort Pickens became one of the few forts in the South to be occupied by Federal troops throughout the war. The others were Fort Taylor (1845), Key West, Fla.; Fort Jefferson (1845), Garden Key, Fla.; and Fort Monroe (1827), Hampton, Va. Occasional artillery duels between the guns at Fort Pickens and those of the Confederates occurred early in the war. In 1862 the Confederates abandoned the city to the Federal troops who occupied it for the remainder of the war.

In 1898 improvements were made at Fort Pickens and, later, disappearing guns of the U.S. Army Coast Artillery were placed there. The fort protected the port of Pensacola during the Spanish-American War and World Wars I and II, but was later abandoned, to become a Florida State Park in 1949. From 1886 to 1888, the famed Apache Indian Chief Geronimo (1829–1909) was imprisoned in Fort Pickens.

All the forts built in Pensacola after the War of 1812 are still in existence, except Fort McRee of which only a few ruins remain underwater. Fort Monroe is still in use. The forts in the Florida Keys are also still in existence. Fort Jefferson was made into a prison after the Civil War; its most famous inmate was Dr. Samuel A. Mudd (1833–83), convicted of conspiracy in the assassination of President Abraham Lincoln (1809–65), because he set the broken leg of the murderer, John Wilkes Booth (1838–65). Mudd was later pardoned because of his services in a yellow fever epidemic. None of the forts was considered effective against rifled cannon, invented about the time of the Civil War.

The long military history of Pensacola continues today. In 1914 the old Navy Yard was converted into the Pensacola Naval Air Station and since that time has had a major role in the flight training of naval pilots and other flying personnel. In addition to the main base, there are three other naval flying fields in the area.

**U.S. Forts** Many old American forts are still in existence, at least partly, from all eras of colonial and U.S.

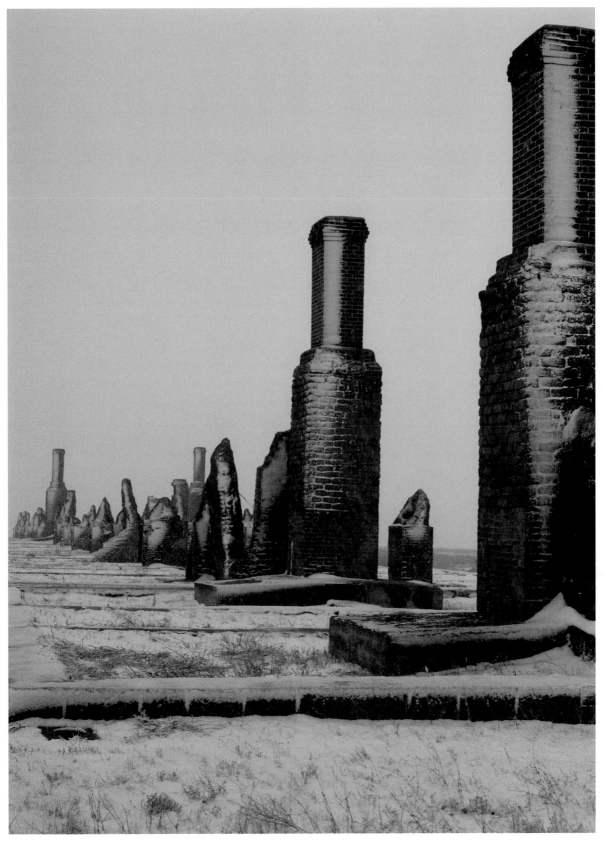

**MILITARY BUILDING** Ruins, Fort Union National Monument (1863–67), near Watrous, N. Mex. The fort was built to protect the Santa Fe trail and was in use until 1891.

history, or have been reconstructed. Among the old Spanish forts are the Castillo de San Marcos, St. Augustine, Fla., begun in 1672 and not completed until 1756, and Fort Matanzas (1742), near that city. The earliest English fort, a very small one made of earth and logs, believed to have been built about 1584, has been reconstructed at Manteo, N.C., on Roanoke Island. This is the site of the lost colony, the first English colony in America, established under the sponsorship of Sir Walter Raleigh (c. 1552–1618), who never saw it. Here Virginia Dare was born in 1587, the first English child to be born in America, but Virginia and other colonists vanished and were never found.

The remains of Frederica, an early and unusual English fortified town built in 1736, are located on Saint Simons Island, near Brunswick, Ga. In 1754 an early British fort was built by Colonel George Washington (1732–99). Called Fort Necessity and located near Farmington, Pa., the fort has been reconstructed. Two early French examples are Fort Ticonderoga (1755), Ticonderoga, N.Y., and Fort Pitt (c. 1750), Pittsburgh, Pa.

British fortifications as well as those of the Americans and their French allies, built in 1781, exist at Yorktown, Va. Here the British General, Lord Charles Cornwallis (1738–1805) surrendered to General Washington on October 17, 1781, ending the Revolutionary War. Fort McHenry, Baltimore, Md., built soon after the war, in 1790, was made famous during the War of 1812, when Francis Scott Key (1779–1843), held prisoner on a British ship, wrote the words to *The Defense of Fort McHenry*, later known as *The Star Spangled Banner*, in the early morning of September 14, 1814. A later fort, begun in 1827 but never finished, Fort Sumter, on an island in the harbor of Charleston, S.C., became famous as the scene of the first shots fired in the Civil War, on April 12, 1861.

Two forts which figured in the westward expansion of the United States are Fort Davis (1854), Tex., a base in the U.S. actions against the Apache and Comanche Indians, and Fort Laramie (c. 1834), Wyo., which protected the Oregon Trail and was the scene, in 1868, of a treaty ceding lands to the Indians. Many other historical and interesting forts and other military buildings and structures exist in other parts of the United States.

**Related Articles** APARTMENT; BANK; HEALTH-CARE FACILITIES; HOUSING; LIBRARY; OFFICE BUILDING; PARK; PRISON; RECREATION BUILDING; RELIGIOUS BUILDING; SCHOOL; STORE; WAREHOUSE.

**Further Reading** *Historic American Buildings Survey— Catalog of the Measured Drawings and Photographs of the Survey in the Library of Congress, March 1, 1941*, U.S. Government Printing Office, Washington, D.C., 1941, catalog supplement, 1959, catalogs by states; Robinson, Willard B.: *American Forts—Architectural Form and Function*, Amon Carter Museum of Western Art and the University of Illinois Press, Urbana, Ill., 1977, available from Books on Demand, UMI, Ann Arbor, Mich.

**MILLS, ROBERT** American architect and engineer (1781–1855). After graduating from Charleston College, Robert Mills obtained his architectural education while working for James Hoban (1762–1831), the architect of the White House; Thomas Jefferson (1743–1826); and Benjamin Henry Latrobe (1764–1820). Thus Mills became one of a growing number of men who early in the 19th century were trained for the professional practice of architecture in all of its aspects: design, engineering, and construction.

Mills became one of the most important architects of his time. A believer like his mentors, Jefferson and Latrobe, in Classic Revival architecture, in particular the Greek Revival style, Mills designed a great number of buildings during his career: houses, churches, courthouses, and other public buildings.

It was for his large public buildings and monuments that he became best known, imparting to them meticulously fine proportions, simple unadorned great masses

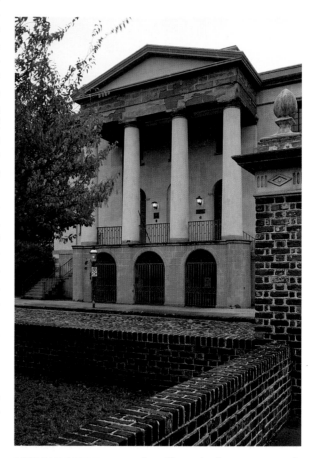

**MILLS, ROBERT** Fireproof Building, also known as Records Building (1826; later alteration), Charleston, S.C.

**MILLS, ROBERT** National Portrait Gallery, formerly U.S. Patent Office (1840), Washington, D.C.

that produced monumental effects unlike most buildings built before that time. His buildings were simple, yet bold, with excellent engineering.

**Works** Although it is unclear when Mills left the office of Latrobe, it is known that in 1808 he received his first important independent commission for the Sansom Street Baptist Church (1809), followed by the Octagon Unitarian Church (1813), both in Philadelphia. Neither building has survived. But the most important development at this stage of his career was his winning of a competition to design a church intended to memorialize 71 people who had died in a fire. This commission produced what many think is one of the architect's best buildings, the Monumental Church (1812), Richmond, Va., which fortunately is still in existence. The church is simple and straightforward in concept, inside and out, with refined, restrained details. The building has a dual purpose: a memorial to the dead and an active church. The porch and the main building seem therefore almost to exist independently of each other. The main church building is octagonal in plan, of brick and stucco, with a low dome of wood construction, plastered inside. The porch, of stone, is square in plan, much like a Greek Doric temple, a building type from which it is derived. In the center of the porch, a rather large funerary urn symbolizes the receptacle of the ashes of those who died in the fire. The

building became a milestone in the development of Classic Revival architecture in America.

Another milestone, though for a different reason, was the Record Office (1827), Charleston, S.C. This building, one of the most innovative of its time, came to be known as the Fireproof Building, for that is what Mills set out to accomplish. Here again Mills expressed his talent for simple, dignified classic forms, but it is in the function of the building and its engineering that his greatest accomplishments were made. Two stories high with a basement, the Fireproof Building contains eight rooms on each floor, all opening on halls and all with outside exposures. All the walls and partitions are brick covered with stucco, and the ceilings of the basements and first floor are brick vaults, covered with stucco. Thus no wood was used except for the roof structure, from which the second floor ceiling of suspended plaster was hung. The roof was covered with copper and all the windows and shutters were of iron. In the center of the building, a central stairwell extends from the basement to the second floor and is covered with a skylight in the roof. Here too the materials were incombustible, the stairs and landings of stone, the railings of iron. In this building then Mills established himself as a complete architect, dedicated to his profession and skilled in design, engineering, and construction.

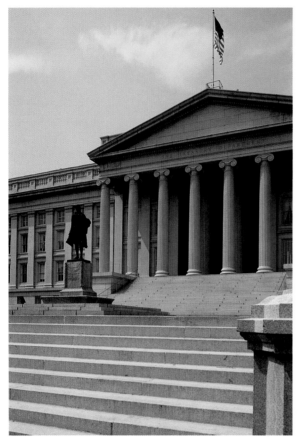

**MILLS, ROBERT** U.S. Treasury Building (1842), Washington, D.C.

Most of the important later work of Mills was accomplished in Washington, where he spent the remainder of his professional life after 1830. Appointed architect of public buildings, a post in which he served from 1836 to 1851, Mills designed a number of U.S. government buildings and monuments, among them the Patent Office (1840), now the National Portrait Gallery; the Treasury Building (1842); the Old General Post Office (1869), now the Tariff Commission Building; and the Washington Monument, a project not finished until 1884, long after the death of the architect.

Of the government work of Mills, the Treasury Building is considered his masterpiece. Here again, Mills demonstrated the simple, straightforward design that had become his style, but in a building of monumental size, three stories and basement, 190 ft deep and 336 ft long. The plan is simple, sort of like a letter E laid on its side with great courtyards in the spaces between the strokes. The long side of the E, the major elevation, has 30 gigantic Greek Ionic columns, each three stories high imposed on the basement. Behind this great colonnade are strictly utilitarian office spaces, designed for the functional purposes to which they are put, much as in the earlier Fireproof Building. As in that building, the architect paid considerable attention to engineering and

fire safety, using incombustible materials, in this case mostly Acquia stone, and vaulted ceilings. And as in that earlier building, Mills again provided a magnificent curved stair extending up through the building.

At one point, in 1838, it looked as if this magnificent building would never be completed. Mills had been the subject of mounting criticism in Congress, led by Levi Lincoln, a Massachusetts congressman. It was much the same position in which Latrobe had found himself when his work for the government had been attacked, and seemed to have stemmed from the same reason, politics and jealousy. The congressman had a young Philadelphia architect, Thomas U. Walter (1804–87), appointed to make a report on the Treasury Building. This report led to a bill in Congress to demolish the Treasury Building, before completion. After much debate and maneuvering, the bill was narrowly defeated, 94 to 91, and the building went on to completion in 1842.

**Life** Robert Mills was born in Charleston, S.C., on August 12, 1781, of a Scottish father and an American mother. He seems to have decided upon a career as a professional architect when quite young. After graduating in liberal arts from Charleston College at twenty, he began his architectural education in the office of Hoban who practiced for a while in Charleston, went with him to Washington in 1800, then to Monticello where he worked and studied with Jefferson for about two years. In 1804 he continued his education by visiting a number of architects, including Charles Bulfinch, in the Eastern United States, and studying their buildings firsthand. He entered the office of Latrobe and spent about five years there, working and learning. About 1808, he began his own practice, doing work in Philadelphia, Washington, Richmond, and Baltimore.

In 1820 Mills received an appointment as engineer and architect of the State of South Carolina, and moved his family back to Charleston. Returning to Washington in 1830, Mills was appointed architect of public buildings by President Andrew Jackson (1767–1845), in 1836. He held this post until 1851, a period that saw him design his three notable government buildings in Washington. Mills died on March 3, 1855.

**Related Articles** Classic Revival Architecture; Jefferson, Thomas; Latrobe, Benjamin Henry.

**Further Reading** Bryan, John M., ed.: *Essays by Robert L. Alexander, Douglas E. Evelyn and Pamela J. Scott, Robert Mills, Architect*, AIA Press, Washington, 1989.

**MODEL MAKING** The construction of three-dimensional, usually small-scale, representations of buildings, groups of buildings, or other architectural projects for study purposes or for presentation of design concepts to clients and others. Now the making of models has been largely replaced by computerized images which can produce realistic views incorporated into photographs of the site.

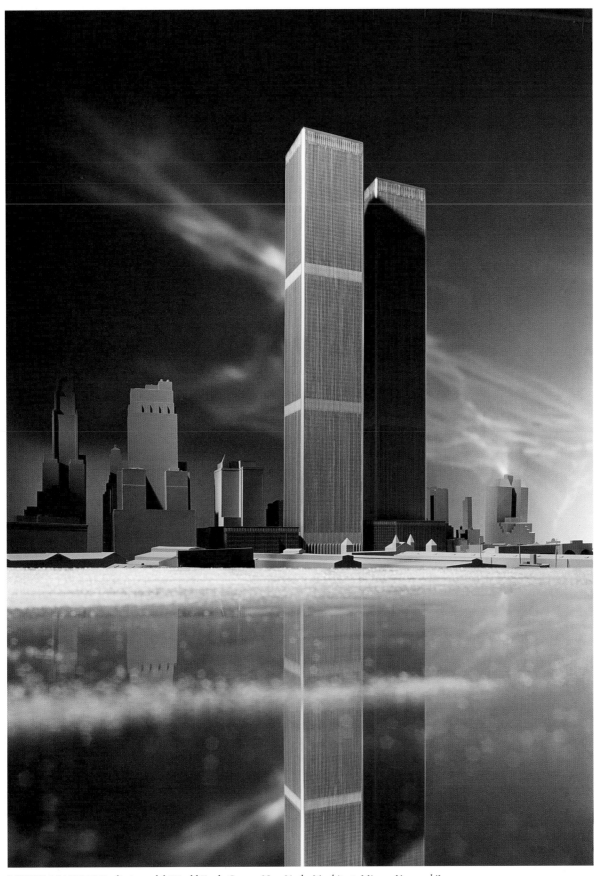

**MODEL MAKING** Realistic model: World Trade Center, New York. *[Architect: Minoru Yamasaki]*

**MODEL MAKING** Abstract or schematic model: proposal for urban development pattern. *[Architect: Theodore Waddell]*

**Types** In the last few decades, making images of buildings has become increasingly important in architecture. Models have come to be accepted as one of the best means of accomplishing many purposes. In architecture, models are of four major types: study models, finished models, working models, and mock-ups. Study models are usually made of simple, common materials assembled in a somewhat unfinished manner and without undue expenditure of time, to help designers visualize various aspects of their designs, such as relationships to sites, orientation, relationships between buildings in groups, form of buildings, materials, circulation of people around and within the buildings, and such details as room sizes, entrances, and so on.

Finished models are made from a variety of materials to simulate as closely as possible what a completed building will be like. They are constructed with care, usually require many hours of work, and are often quite costly to build. Though finished models may also be of help in the study of building designs, their major purpose is for presentation to clients and others of completed designs, in a way that drawings or renderings, which often supplement models in presentations, cannot duplicate. The major function of finished models is to sell the building design to potential buyers. Photographs of a model are often used, and some of these may be made by superimposing photographs of the model on photographs of its site and surroundings.

Working models, more rarely used than the types just described, are made when some movement of parts of a building, such as a stadium dome which may be opened or closed, must be studied or demonstrated. Mock-ups, either full-size or scaled-down, are used for purposes similar to those of working models and also for testing building elements or components, such as testing water infiltration through a new type of wall.

In addition to the four major types, other types of models are used in architecture, including structural models, showing structures or parts of them; landscaping models, showing grading of sites, planting, and other aspects; planning models, showing cities or portions of them; and interior models showing space planning of interior spaces, colors, materials, furniture, and furnishings.

Architectural students, and often those in related fields, learn how to make models as part of their curricula in professional schools. Therefore all architects have had some experience in model making. Other model makers learned their craft through experience or as a hobby. In practice, some architects make their own models, particularly study models, but also finished or presentation models and other types. However, finished or presentation models are more often made by specialists, who may have their own businesses or work for others. Some model makers are employees of architectural firms, but usually only the largest firms can afford staff members who perform solely this function.

**Tools** The tools of model makers are many and varied. There are numerous kinds of hand tools, such as knives, rasps, drills, tweezers, planes, strippers, scissors, and clamps on the market, many of them designed specifically for model makers. There are also many types of power tools available, some of which are regular shop tools but others specifically intended for model making, including hand-held electric tools that use as bits an array of grinders, cutting wheels, polishers, cutters, routers, and so on. There are special tools for plastics, wood, and metals, and there are several types of sprayers for paints.

**Materials** The materials used by model makers comprise a bewildering array. A skilled and inventive model maker may use almost any material available on the market for any purpose to help depict in miniature the actual materials and form of buildings. Such materials include most woods, metals, plastics, paper products, glass, and others. Also of importance are the great number of materials and other items produced to scale specifically for use in models, including materials that simulate structural steel shapes, brick, stone, wood siding and the like, roofing, windows, doors, landscaping, and many other elements of buildings and their sites. In addition, various glues, cements, and adhesives are used for the assembly of models, and paints and other coatings are used for finishes. First-class architectural models are the result of careful selection of the materials and other items and careful workmanship by skilled and creative model makers.

**Construction** The actual construction of models varies widely, not only because of the different purposes for which they may be used but because of the varied skills and techniques of architects and model makers. In general, though, the first step in making a model should be careful study of its purpose, followed by study of the proper size and scale of the model. Residential models are often built at a scale of ¼ in equals 1 ft, while larger buildings may be at a scale of ⅛ in to 1 ft. For even larger projects, such as a college campus or a portion of a city, smaller scales such as 1 in equals 50 ft, 1 in equals 200 ft, or even smaller must be used. In general, the smaller the scale of the model, the less detail is shown. Another important early consideration in model making is the choice of a proper base on which to construct it and a plastic cover for the model if it is to be displayed publicly or for a long period of time.

The actual construction of the model may proceed after the preliminary decisions have been made and the required materials have been collected. The first step, if required by the model to be constructed, is the preparation of the site of the building on the model base. This may require the building up of the form of the site into contours that represent the slope of the land. Then follows the gradual building up of the remainder of the model, starting with the large forms and proceeding to ever smaller details, until the whole model building has been completed, together with its landscaping and with figures of people, automobiles, and other things to indicate its scale.

**History** Model making is one of the oldest crafts practiced by humans, small-scale, three-dimensional representations of boats and other articles having been made at least as far back as the 40th century B.C. Some of these models still exist. Whether the earliest architects made models or not is uncertain. It is known that early Egyptian architects and others made drawings of buildings, and this practice has continued to the present time. These drawings have served several purposes. They have been a means of studying the designs of buildings and their parts; they have been used as a means of explaining or demonstrating the designs to clients; they have been used as guides to the actual construction of buildings; and they have served as a record of what has been built. In later times, they have also served to obtain publicity for architects' work.

Architectural model making was practiced in ancient Greece and Rome, and the practice was continued to an extent in later periods of history. However, the use of drawings, for the most part, to serve the purposes cited continued until the late 19th century. In the late 19th and in the 20th centuries, the use of study models made of clay and later claylike plastic substances came into wide usage. These models were valuable for study of form, of little or no use in study of volumes or space, and virtually useless in presentation of a building design to clients or others.

During the 20th century, many new model-making techniques have been developed, along with new materials. As a result, making architectural models has become quite widespread, not only for study and presentation purposes, but also in full-size models, or mock-ups, for testing and other purposes. A recent development has been building models for wind tunnel testing to determine building performance in hurricanes and other storms.

**Related Articles** COMPUTER; DESIGN, ARCHITECTURAL; RENDERING.

**Further Reading** Gurden, Ernest: *Architectural Delineation—A Photographic Approach to Presentation,* 3rd ed., McGraw-Hill, New York, 1992.

**MODERN ARCHITECTURE** Usually taken to mean the architectural movement that began in the late 19th century in opposition to the eclectic architecture then prevalent. In the strictest sense, the word *modern* may be defined as characteristic of the present or of the most recent era. Thus the phrase *Modern architecture* is a somewhat unfortunate choice to describe this movement, since what was modern in the 19th century is now historical. Some have suggested that the phrase *contemporary architecture* replace Modern architecture. Since the word *contemporary*, strictly defined, means living, occurring, or existing at the same time, its choice is also unfortunate.

For purposes of discussion here, the well-established phrase, Modern architecture, though somewhat inappropriate, is employed, because of its widespread usage to denote the architecture that turned away from past historical styles toward designs of buildings expressive of their own time. This article discusses Modern architecture from its beginnings in the 19th century through the end of the most significant work of the great Modern architect-theorists, Walter Adolf Gropius (1883–1969), Le Corbusier (1887–1965), Ludwig Mies van der Rohe (1886–1969), and Frank Lloyd Wright (1867–1959), after the middle of the 20th century. For a discussion of architecture after about 1970, see the article entitled contemporary architecture.

Inevitably, there is some overlap between the two eras and the two articles.

**Forerunners of Modern Movement** There is no general agreement about the beginning of the Modern movement. Some have placed it in the early and middle parts of the 19th century, with the advent of such buildings as the Crystal Palace (1851) in London, designed by Sir Joseph Paxton (1803–65); the Bibliothèque Ste Geneviève (1850) and Bibliothèque Nationale (1868), both in Paris and designed by Henri Labrouste (1801–75); and Les Halles Centrale (1858, demolished in 1970), Paris, designed by Victor Baltard (1805–74). Such buildings utilized materials and techniques developed during the industrial revolution, such as iron framing and large amounts of glass, and were considerably more functional than many buildings of the time. However, all used eclectic forms, in iron rather than stone or other materials of the past. Yet some prediction of things to come later can certainly be detected in them today, if not at the time when the buildings were constructed. Even before, some hints of the coming Modern movement were present in various factories and other industrial buildings constructed in Europe and elsewhere.

In the United States, the first glimmerings of the Modern movement may be seen in the work of James Bogardus (1800–74) and many others who designed and constructed cast-iron buildings in New York City and other places all over the country. In these buildings as well as those in Europe, the materials and techniques tended to be expressions of the industrial revolution and their purposes were functional, but the forms were eclectic.

**Beginning of Modern Movement** Therefore all these early buildings might be considered forerunners of the Modern movement, and its real beginning placed in the late 19th century, with the work of the architects who, reacting against eclecticism, began to develop new kinds of architecture. Their reactions to eclecticism took a number of different forms, but the two most important came to be known as the Art Nouveau style and the Chicago school of architecture. Other reactions, of lesser importance, included what came to be called the Craft movement.

**Art Nouveau** This style started out, about 1890, as a revolt of architects, artists, and artisans against the work of the past. It flourished in Europe for about 10 years and held on for about another 10 after that. Before it had run its course, Art Nouveau had affected not only architecture and interiors but furniture, jewelry, typography design, sculpture, painting, and other fine and applied arts. Its main characteristics were undulating, fluid forms and lines, sometimes extremely contorted into strange and exotic shapes resembling living organisms.

The earliest proponents of Art Nouveau were two Belgian architects, Victor Horta (1861–1947) and Henry Van de Velde (1863–1957). Other architects affected by the style include a Scot, Charles Rennie Mackintosh (1868–1928); a Spaniard, Antoni Gaudi (1852–1926); and a Frenchman, Hector Guimard (1867–1942). In painting, the style is perhaps best exemplified in the work of Henri Marie Raymond de Toulouse-Lautrec (1864–1901). Art Nouveau had very little effect on American architecture but did influence other arts, including the stained-glass designs of Louis Comfort Tiffany (1848–1933).

Art Nouveau affected the work of architects in other parts of Europe, including the Austrian pioneer, Otto Wagner (1841–1918), who started out as an eclectic architect and later became the inspiration of the movement known as the Austrian Secession. Wagner also influenced two younger architects who became the leaders of the Austrian Secession, Joseph Marie Ohlbrich (1869–1908) and Joseph Hoffmann (1870–1956). Another Austrian pioneer of Modern architecture, Adolf Loos (1870–1933), rebelled against the secession as well as against eclecticism. Other European pioneers of Modern architecture were Hendrik Petrus Berlage (1856–1934) of the Netherlands, Peter Behrens (1868–1940) of Germany, and Auguste Perret (1874–1954) and Tony Garnier (1869–1948) of France. Although the Art Nouveau architects had little effect on American architecture, other pioneer architects had great influence: their ideas of architecture for its own time, functionalism, use of modern materials and techniques, and discard of eclecticism reflecting and influencing the ideas of the American pioneers of the Modern movement.

The Craft movement had a considerable effect on the work of a few American architects, but very little on most architects. Originated by an English architect, William Morris (1834–96), the movement turned away from industrial machines to handcrafted elements of architecture, furniture, and other arts and crafts. Among the important American architects deeply affected by the movement were the Greene brothers, Charles Sumner (1868–1957), Henry Mather (1870–1954), and Bernard Maybeck (1862–1957), architects of creative buildings, all highly ornamented with handcrafted details and furnishings.

**Chicago School** The most important accomplishments in the establishment of the Modern movement in the United States were those of the architects of the so-called Chicago school. Sometimes their work is called the Commercial style, since most of it was devoted to office buildings, warehouses, department stores, and other commercial building types.

The prime mover of the Chicago school was Major William Le Baron Jenney (1832–1907), an engineer turned architect who began late in the 19th century to turn away from the eclectic architecture of the time. The

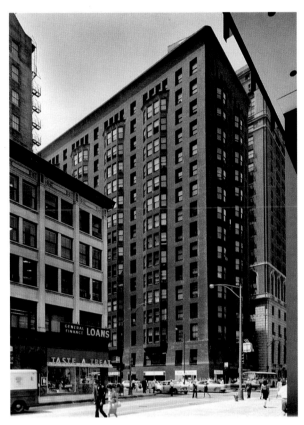

**MODERN ARCHITECTURE** Monadnock Building (1891), Chicago, Ill. [Architects: Burnham and Root]

prime impetus to the Chicago school was the great fire of 1871, which virtually destroyed the downtown area of Chicago. After the fire, the architects who came to be known as the Chicago school started to rebuild in a distinctly different manner. Iron had been used quite often for structures in Chicago before the great fire, but afterward for some years, architects turned back almost exclusively to brick and stone. Gradually, the use of iron, at least for the interior columns of some buildings, was resumed. Then several events came at once: some technological innovations and one purely architectural change.

The major technological changes included the invention of a safe elevator; the first was installed by its inventor, Elisha Graves Otis (1811–61), in the five-story Haughwout Building (1857), New York City, designed by J. P. Gaynor. The second technological change was the growing use of central heating. Together, the elevator and central heating helped establish the beginning of tall buildings, or skyscrapers. And central heating, along with new insulating methods, allowed the use of large areas of glass in walls. The important architectural change was the growing disenchantment with eclecticism that eventually led to the functional architecture later called Modern. Another factor that affected the architecture of the time was the development of methods

for making iron, and later steel, structural members fire-resistant, or fireproof, as it was called then, by enclosing them with masonry.

Led by Jenney in whose office most of them worked at one time or another, the Chicago school architects created a new kind of architecture in the late 19th century: functional with ornament used sparingly, of iron (later steel) skeleton-framed tall buildings with large areas of glass in exterior walls. In New York City and other places, architects had also begun designing tall buildings, many of them exceeding in height those in Chicago. But the Eastern buildings were eclectic, while those in Chicago were designed in forms more appropriate to the time and its technology and needs.

In the First Leiter Building (1879), Chicago, Jenney used brick columns for the exterior and iron columns for the interior. Six years later, his Home Insurance Co. building (1885, since demolished) was built with a complete skeleton frame, mostly of iron but with some steel beams. His former employees followed his lead. Daniel Hudson Burnham (1846–1912) joined in partnership with John Wellborn Root (1850–91), who had not worked for Jenney, to design some of the great Chicago buildings of the era. Two former Jenney employees, William Holabird (1854–1923) and Martin Roche (1855–1927), formed another firm that did masterful work. And the greatest of all of the former Jenney employees, Louis Henri Sullivan (1856–1924), outperformed them all in a series of fine buildings designed and built in the late 19th and early 20th centuries. (See articles entitled Burnham and Root; Holabird and Roche; Jenney, William Le Baron; Sullivan, Louis Henri.)

By the early 20th century, the Chicago school architects had developed a new kind of architecture, now called Modern, that was almost purely American, demonstrating few if any influences from the Modern movements taking place in Europe at that time. From the commercial buildings of Chicago and other places, the new architectural design spread to other building types. And the work of the Chicago school architects began to affect that of younger architects, including one destined to become a towering master, Frank Lloyd Wright. From the time of his employment in the office of Louis Henri Sullivan, Wright deeply affected architecture.

First acclaimed in Europe for his work, Wright eventually became the best-known and greatest architect of his time, some think of all time. In California, the Greene brothers and Bernard Maybeck, affected by the Craft movement in Europe, created masterfully detailed and crafted buildings, some of them, particularly in the case of Maybeck, very romantic, even mystical. Another California architect, Irving John Gill (1870–1936), believed to have been influenced by the emerging Modern architecture in Europe, particularly that in Germany, Austria, and the Netherlands, created a per-

**MODERN ARCHITECTURE** Chrysler Building (1930), New York, N.Y. *[Architect: William Van Alen]*

**MODERN ARCHITECTURE**  Empire State Building (1931), New York, N.Y. *[Architects: Shreve, Lamb & Harmon]*

sonal kind of architecture of excellent quality. Gill turned his back on handcrafts but not on craftsmanship. His architecture was strictly of its time, finely detailed, using modern technology and methods. (See articles entitled Gill, Irving John; Greene and Greene; Maybeck, Bernard; Wright, Frank Lloyd.)

**Modern Movement Established**  In the 1920s and 1930s, the Modern movement became firmly established not only in the United States but in Europe and else-

where. Eclecticism still held on strongly and has persisted, to some extent, ever since. Frank Lloyd Wright continued to be the towering figure in the United States, always dedicated to what he called organic architecture and increasingly influential with younger architects all over the world. In Europe, the towering figure was a Swiss, who practiced in France, Charles Èdouard Jeanneret, almost always called Le Corbusier. Others deeply affected Modern architecture, including a German, Eric Mendelsohn (1887–1953), who later became a British subject and still later practiced for a time in Israel and the United States; a Swede, Sven Markelius (1889–1972), and two Dutchmen, Jacobus Johannes Pieter (J. J. P.) Oud (1890–1963) and Marinus Dudok (1884–1974).

**U.S. Architect-Émigrés**  To the United States emigrated a number of remarkable people who were already, or were destined to become, accomplished architects. The first to arrive was a German, Albert Kahn (1869–1942), at age eleven; Kahn became a great pioneer of modern factory design. A Finn, Eliel Saarinen (1873–1950), already famous in Europe, arrived in the 1920s and deeply affected architecture in the United States. Another architect who had an important part in the development of Modern architecture, an Austrian, Richard Joseph Neutra (1892–1970), arrived about the same time, to become famous later, particularly for his houses and schools. Just before World War II, two German architects, already established and famous, arrived in the United States, Walter Adolf Gropius and Ludwig Mies van der Rohe, the former to revolutionize modern architectural education as he had already done in Germany and the latter, also an educator, to establish a spare, beautifully detailed architecture of planes and modern technology that had deep effects on the architecture of the time and afterward. (See articles entitled Gropius, Walter Adolf; Kahn, Albert; Mies van der Rohe, Ludwig; Neutra, Richard Joseph; Saarinen, Eliel.) Others also came to the United States, one of the most notable being an Austrian, Rudolph Schindler (1887–1953).

The architecture of Frank Lloyd Wright and some other American architects of the time was warm, often utilizing exotic forms and natural materials, with modern technological methods. The works of Mies, Neutra, Schindler, and often that of Gropius and others was composed mostly of simple, rectangular forms, using almost entirely modern materials, such as glass and steel. The work of Wright and others of his persuasion affected the architecture of other architects.

**The International Style**  However, the work of Mies and the others, and some architects in Europe, had an even wider influence at the time. So widespread did their ideas become that some thought that a new style was being created that would eventually become estab-

**MODERN ARCHITECTURE** Rockefeller Center (1940), New York, N.Y. *[Architects: Rienhard and Hofmeister; Corbett, Harrison and MacMurray; Hood and Fouilhoux]*

lished around the world. Called the International style in the 1932 book of the same title, written by the historian and critic Henry-Russell Hitchcock (1903–87) and Philip Cortelyou Johnson (1906–  ), not as yet an architect, the phrase caught on with architects and others. Although the phrase was later denigrated by most of those who were supposed to have developed the style, including Mies and Gropius, there was a great deal of truth in the idea at the time, and some truth even today.

**A Decade of Notable Architects** During slightly more than a decade starting in 1895, a number of people destined later to become notable architects were born. In Europe, they included the Finn Alvar Aalto (1898–1976), Spaniards José Luis Sert (1902–83) and Eduardo Torroja (1899–1961), the Englishman Edwin Maxwell Fry (1899–1987), the Italian Gio Ponti (1897–1979), and the great Italian engineer Pier Luigi Nervi (1891–1979). Modern architecture was making inroads in other places too, including Brazil in the work of Lucio Costa (b. 1902) and Oscar Neimeyer (b. 1907).

Born in approximately the same decade were Americans who later became notable architects, including William Wilson Wurster (1895–1973), Buckminster Fuller (1895–1983), Wallace Kirkman Harrison (1895–1981), Bruce Goff (1904–82), Philip Cortelyou Johnson, and three architects who established one of the world's most successful firms, Skidmore, Owings and Merrill, Louis Skidmore (1897–1962), Nathaniel Alexander Owings (1903–81) and John Ogden Merrill (1896–1975). (See articles entitled Fuller, Richard Buckminster; Harrison, Wallace Kirkman; Johnson, Philip Cortelyou; Skidmore, Owings and Merrill; Wurster, William Wilson.)

The same era produced a number of architects who emigrated to the United States and practiced there, including Pietro Belluschi (1899–1994) from Italy, Louis Isadore Kahn (1902–74) from Estonia, Marcel Lajos Breuer (1902–81) from Hungary, and Eero Saarinen (1910–61) from Finland, brought by his family to the United States when he was young. Others of importance are William Lescaze (1896–1969) from Switzerland and Serge Chermayeff (b. 1900) from the Soviet Union. (See articles entitled Belluschi, Pietro; Breuer, Marcel Lajos; Kahn, Louis Isadore; Saarinen, Eero.)

By the 1940s and 1950s, two trends, that of the organic architecture of Wright or something resembling it, and that of the International style, whatever it might be called, had been firmly established in the United States. Architects like Goff and Alden B. Dow (1904–83)

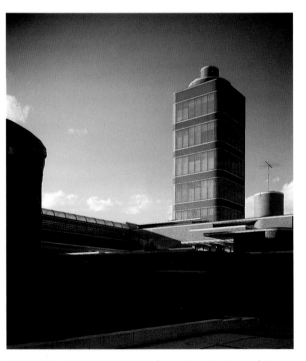

**MODERN ARCHITECTURE** Johnson Wax Co. Research Tower (1949), Racine, Wis. *[Architect: Frank Lloyd Wright]*

and others followed the Wrightian philosophies, while architects like Johnson, Skidmore, Owings, Merrill, Harrison, Breuer, and others followed the philosophies of Gropius and Mies. Other architects, such as John Ekin Dinwiddie (1902–59), Harwell Hamilton Harris (1903–80), and Belluschi, seemed intent on establishing regional styles on the West Coast, styles somewhat more akin to the ideas of Wright than of Gropius and Mies.

By this time, Wright's concepts had evolved into the use of free-form, sculptural shapes in his architectural designs. And other architects, including Belluschi and Breuer, some of whom had been going in other directions, sometimes used such forms. The trend was toward an architecture that was not only thought of as sculptural but was also sometimes called sensual or emotional. And ornament also began to come back into building designs. Some of the younger architects became involved in work of this kind, including Minoru Yamasaki (1912–86) and Paul Rudolph (1918–  ). Although he started out designing buildings much like those of Mies, Eero Saarinen turned to sculptural, emotional forms for many of his later buildings. Louis Isadore Kahn designed great sculptural buildings that have deeply affected architecture since that time. (See the article entitled Kahn, Louis Isadore.)

During this era, Le Corbusier and others went even further, developing a phase of the sculptural style that came to be called the Brutal style, not to be critical of it, but in recognition of its use of heavy sculptural forms, often in quite large sizes.

The era of great pioneers of the Modern movement in the United States—Jenney, Burnham, Root, Roche, Holabird, and Sullivan—came to an end when the last of them, Martin Roche, died in 1927. Before that, their influence had given way to that of the great masters of the movement: Wright, Mies, Gropius, and Le Corbusier. Wright died in 1959, Le Corbusier in 1965, and both Mies and Gropius in 1969. This was the end of another great era. By that time a group of younger architects, many of them in their thirties, forties, or early fifties, were making names for themselves. For a discussion of their accomplishments, see the article entitled contemporary architecture.

**Illustrations** The illustrations for this article show famous buildings of the Modern period beginning in the 19th century. The 16-story Monadnock Building (1891), Chicago, Ill., designed by Burnham and Root, was the last tall building with masonry bearing walls, which were 6 ft thick for the first story. By 1930, when the Chrysler Building, New York City, designed by William Van Alen, was completed, the record height for a building had gone from less than 20 stories to 75.

The height record of the Chrysler Building lasted only a year, until the 102-story Empire State Building

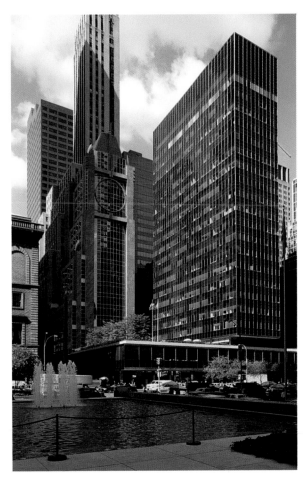

**MODERN ARCHITECTURE** Lever House (1952), New York, N.Y. *[Architects: Skidmore, Owings and Merrill]*

(1931), New York City, by Shreve, Lamb and Harmon, was completed. This record lasted until 1973 when the 110-story World Trade Center, New York City, designed by Minoru Yamasaki, in association with Emery Roth and Sons, was completed. Its height was equaled a year later by the Sears Tower (1974), Chicago, Ill., by Skidmore, Owings and Merrill. Rockefeller Center (1940), New York City, by Reinhard and Hofmeister; Corbett, Harrison and McMurray; and Hood and Fouilhoux, was the first great group, or urban complex, of tall buildings to be completed in the United States.

While the Chrysler Building, Empire State Building, and Rockefeller Center are all eclectic in design, Lever House (1952), New York City, designed by Gordon Bunshaft of Skidmore, Owings and Merrill, was an early metal and glass curtain-wall building, placed on its site to allow a great plaza on the ground level and another elevated above it.

In contrast to the urban settings of the other buildings mentioned, the Johnson Wax Co. Research Tower (1950) in Racine, Wis., was part of the complex

431

designed by Frank Lloyd Wright for Johnson Wax beginning in 1939. The tower consists of alternating circular and square floors. The exterior is brick and the glazing consists of glass tubing and gaskets behind plate glass. The building received international attention and is still a much-visited complex for the interest in Wright's experimental structures. Although no longer used for research, the tower is well maintained. Many other office buildings of all sizes are illustrated in other articles.

**Related Articles** Contemporary Architecture; Eclectic Architecture; Gropius, Walter Adolf; History of Architecture; Mies van der Rohe, Ludwig; Skidmore, Owings and Merrill; Sullivan, Louis Henri; Wright, Frank Lloyd; Various articles on other Modern architects.

**Further Reading** Condit, Carl W.: *The Chicago School of Architecture,* University of Chicago Press, Chicago, 1964; Giedion, Sigfried: *Space, Time and Architecture: The Growth of a New Tradition,* 5th ed., Harvard University Press, Cambridge, Mass., 1967; Hitchcock, Henry-Russell: *Architecture in the Nineteenth and Twentieth Centuries,* Penguin Books, Baltimore, Md., 1958; Jordy, William H.: *American Buildings and Their Architects,* vol. 4, *Progressive and Academic Ideals at the Turn of the Century,* and vol. 5, *The Impact of European Modernism in the Mid-Twentieth Century,* Doubleday, Garden City, N.Y., 1972, and Oxford University Press, New York, 1986; McCoy, Esther, and Randall L. Makison: *Five California Architects,* 2d ed., Hennessy, Santa Monica, Calif., 1987. See also listing in the article entitled history of architecture.

**MOLDING** Part of a building usually in the form of a relatively narrow strip primarily used as ornament around doors and windows, at the intersections of exterior walls with roofs and interior walls with ceilings, and in many other places. Moldings (sometimes spelled *mouldings*) are ordinarily rectilinear or curved or some combination of these forms.

In many of the past periods of architecture, moldings were one of the major ornamental elements of building interiors and exteriors. With the advent of the Modern movement in architecture, their importance declined to the point that today moldings are considerably smaller, simpler, and sparingly used. Most are made in stock sizes and shapes and their most frequent use is in covering joints between surfaces or materials in buildings.

**Materials** In the past, moldings were made of such materials as wood or plaster, but the highest development came in stone, which was often carved or otherwise ornamented. In some periods, certain types and systems of moldings were developed of which vestiges still exist today. In Modern architecture, moldings, when used at all, are apt to be of wood or metal, in simple, standardized or stock shapes, in relatively small sizes and unor-

namented. Many of the available moldings are named for their purposes, such as crown, corner, picture, base, rail, stop, and so on; others are named for their shapes, as round, half round, and quarter round. In recent years, the use of more elaborate moldings has had a revival.

**History** At the time of the great ancient civilizations around the Mediterranean Sea, moldings were not important ornamental elements in architecture. The scale of Egyptian, Middle Eastern, and Aegean architecture was so great that moldings would have seemed insignificant. They were used on columns, however, and in a few cases moldings of relatively large size were used on Egyptian buildings.

As they did in other architectural elements, the ancient Greeks developed moldings to a high degree of perfection. Refined and delicate, Greek moldings were usually carved into stone. So important were moldings to the Greeks that they developed a whole system, which has been followed to an extent in the moldings of subsequent architectural periods. The most important moldings of the Greeks were the fillet, a flat band; and seven curved types: astragal; torus, now called half round; ovolo, called quarter round, even though the Greek ovolo was more egg-shaped than like a quarter segment of a circle; cavetto, called cove; scotia; cyma recta, called crown; and cyma reversa, called ogee. Some moldings used on Greek buildings were plain; others had skillfully carved ornament on their surfaces.

The Romans used moldings that were largely derived from those of the Greeks. The major Greek types were all used, often with abundant carved ornament, and less skillfully executed than that of the Greeks. Roman moldings also differed somewhat in shape from those of the Greeks.

Both the Greeks and Romans often placed moldings of various kinds adjacent to each other to form highly

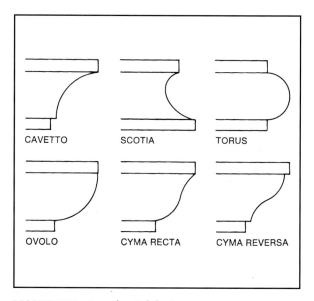

**MOLDING** Sections of typical classic types.

ornamental major building elements. The classic molding types have had a very important place in American architecture in almost every period, but most particularly during the Classic Revival and Eclectic eras.

Moldings in Early Christian architecture were usually rich but crude, often using acanthus leaf motifs. In Byzantine architecture, moldings were seldom used because mosaics, wall paintings, and other ornament almost completely covered every important architectural element. Romanesque moldings were mostly rather heavy and coarse, elaborately carved in stone, in designs adapted from those of the Romans. The moldings of none of these eras have had any appreciable effect on American architecture.

During the Gothic period of architecture, moldings at first were used sparingly and were simple in design, but later became very complex and vigorous, with quite extreme variations between different centuries and different countries. In Italy, moldings remained similar to those of Roman times; in Spain, they were usually somewhat crude, often in designs adapted from those in France; in Germany, they were intricate and highly detailed; and in France, they were large and bold, but not so ornate as in some other countries. Moldings were, perhaps, most highly developed in England, where rich, bold applications were made to a great number of architectural elements, including columns, arches, and openings. Often elaborately carved, English Gothic moldings utilized a number of motifs, including chevrons, cables, dogteeth, cones, flowers, and scrolls. These moldings were often deeply undercut and different types were frequently used together, sometimes passing behind and in front of one another. Gothic molding types, especially those of the English, were used in later architecture in Europe and America, particularly during the Gothic Revival and Eclectic periods.

During the Renaissance, moldings were mostly derived from those of the Classic periods, particularly the Roman era. Using combinations of the classic Roman molding types, or variations of them, Renaissance architects created complex moldings, often with alternating flat and curved bands, for many architectural elements, including cornices, the highest part of the elements supported by columns, and other parts of the building. Cornices often were designed to project out a considerable distance and were ornamented in such a way as to make them of considerable importance in building designs. Such combinations of classic moldings varied considerably among Renaissance buildings. Another ornamental feature, developed during this period, is a railing system, or balustrade, often used above the cornices of buildings.

**American Development** In early colonial America, moldings were used sparingly and were mostly of wood, in designs derived from those in Europe. In later archi-

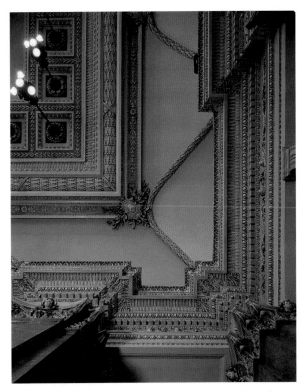

**MOLDING** Restored ceiling, Wayne County Building (1902), Detroit, Mich. *[Architects: John & Arthur Scott]*

tecture, moldings were adapted from those of historical periods of European architecture as shown in books, most of which were published in England, or as established through scholarly research of the older examples from which they were derived. By the end of the 19th century, the use of ornamental moldings was declining and in the 20th, came virtually to an end, but is now revived for preservation, restoration, and some post-Modern work. Today vestiges of the ornamental uses of moldings are sometimes found in the design of handrails for stairways and other building elements. The main use of moldings today is not actually ornamental but to cover joints that might otherwise be objectionable, between building materials or elements.

**Related Articles** ARCH; ART IN ARCHITECTURE; BOOK, ARCHITECTURAL; COLUMN; DESIGN, ARCHITECTURAL; HISTORY OF ARCHITECTURE; ORNAMENT; Various articles on American architectural history.

**MONUMENT** A building or other structure erected to commemorate a person or event, and sometimes to denote a natural geographical feature or historical site. Monuments range in size from simple grave markers to the gigantic carvings at Mount Rushmore in the Black Hills, near Rapid City, S.D. Some monuments have functional purposes; other are purely symbolic.

**Types** There are many kinds of monuments. A grave marker in a cemetery is used to commemorate a person

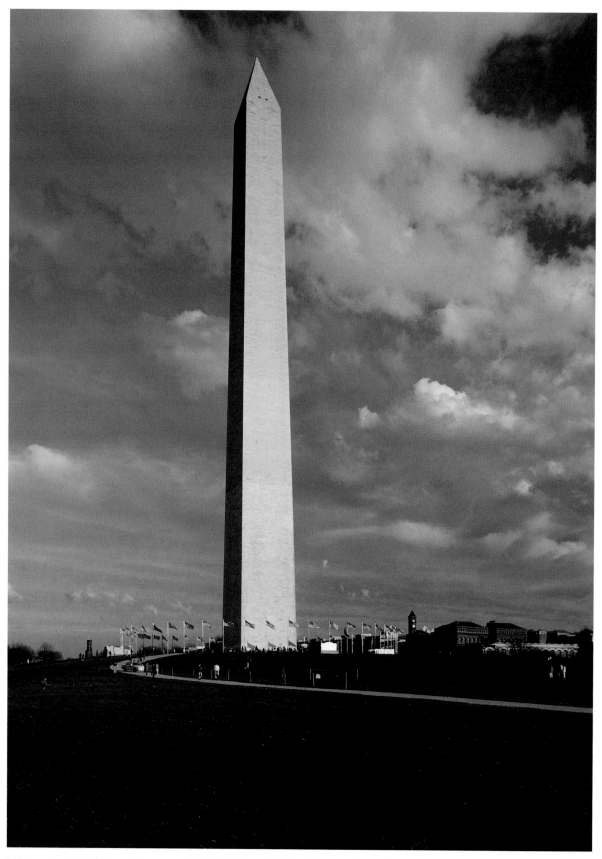

**MONUMENT** Washington Monument (1884), Washington, D.C. [Architect: Robert Mills]

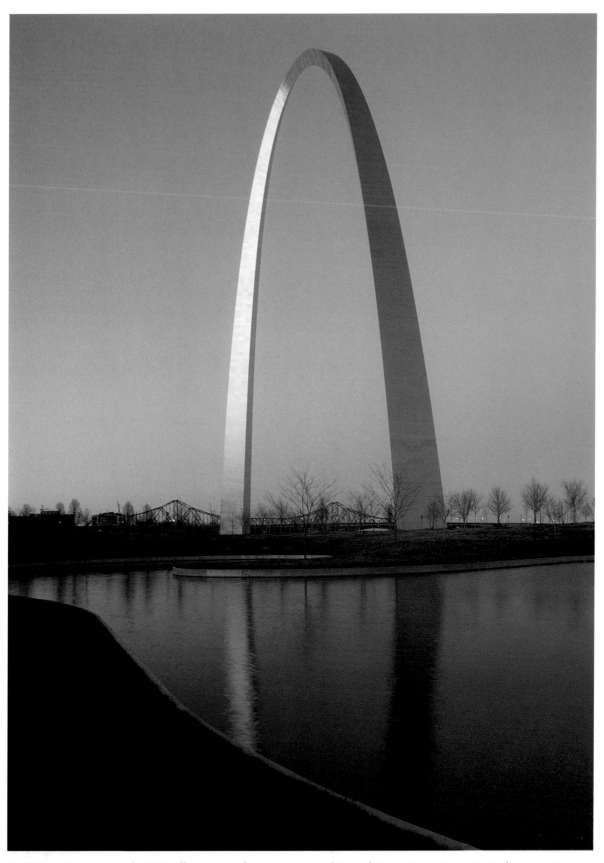

**MONUMENT** Gateway Arch (1964), Jefferson National Expansion Memorial National Historic Site, St. Louis, Mo. *[Architect: Eero Saarinen]*

who has died. Memorial markers, called "cenotaphs," are used in places other than where the person memorialized is buried. A mausoleum is a building in which the dead are entombed and which also acts as a memorial. Monuments may also be buildings, streets, highways, parks, sculpture, or pillars. And canyons, mountains, water bodies, and land areas are sometimes named as monuments.

**History** From the earliest times a great number of these types of monuments have been constructed. In prehistoric times, monuments were usually made of large stones and were called "megaliths." In France and Great Britain, such monuments were called "menhir" or, if a flat stone supported on two vertical stones, a "dolmen" or "cromlech." Single stones called "stele" were carved with sculpture and are among the major monuments of antiquity, particularly the funereal Greek stele. The Romans built numerous monuments, including columns, mausoleums, and triumphal arches. Many of these early monuments are still standing.

Monuments have been built all over the world. They vary a great deal, from the magnificent Taj Mahal

**MONUMENT** Vietnam Veterans Memorial (1982), Washington, D.C. [Architects: Maya Ying Lin, Kent Cooper]

(1653), in Agra, India, a mausoleum built by Shah Jahan (1628–58), to the awe-inspiring pyramids built in the 28th to 26th centuries B.C. at Gizeh, Egypt, near Cairo, to the Arc de Triomphe de l'Étoile (1836), Paris, designed by Jean François Chalgrin (1739–1811).

**American Development** In colonial America, few monuments were built other than grave markers or simple types. After the Revolution, Americans erected monuments for every conceivable historical event and person. Many of the monuments were designed by architects, whose names read like a Who's Who of American architecture. Among them were Louis Henri Sullivan (1856–1924), who designed a number of mausoleums, and Paul Philippe Cret (1876–1947), who designed monuments of many kinds.

Although monuments are to be found all over the United States, the biggest collection is in Washington, D.C. A selection of these will demonstrate the range of types. In and near the U.S. National Cemetery, Arlington, Va., in addition to the thousands of single grave markers, there are the Memorial Amphitheater (1920) designed by Carrère and Hastings, the Tomb of the Unknown Soldier (1931; renamed Tomb of the Unknowns in 1958 when two more unknowns, one from World War II and one from the Korean conflict were buried there) by Lorimer Rich (1891–1978), the Memorial Gate and Memorial Bridge, both designed by McKim, Mead and White and built in 1932, and the John F. Kennedy grave (1966), designed by John Carl Warnecke (1919–  ). Across the river in Washington are the three most famous monuments in the area: the Washington Monument (1885), designed by Robert Mills (1781–1855), the Lincoln Memorial (1922), by Henry Bacon (1866–1924), and the Jefferson Memorial (1943), by John Russell Pope (1874–1937).

Among the more notable recent additions to memorials in Washington, D.C., is that for the Vietnam War, designed by Maya Ying Lin and built in association with Kent Cooper. It was dedicated on Veterans Day, 1984, and has become one of the most visited memorials in the city.

**Related Articles** BACON, HENRY; CAPITAL, UNITED STATES; CRET, PAUL PHILIPPE; McKIM, MEAD AND WHITE; MILLS, ROBERT; POPE, JOHN RUSSELL; SULLIVAN, LOUIS HENRI.

**MOORE, CHARLES** American architect and educator (1925–93), combined teaching with a prolific career as designer. His architectural practice was as an individual and in association with individuals and firms in various parts of the country. Several of the small firms he established with student help have continued after he moved elsewhere. This need to move helped spread his love of architecture and implanted his love of design as seen in his approachable and whimsical buildings.

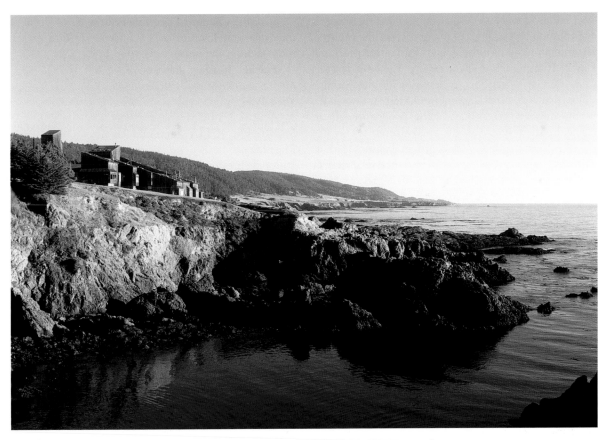

**MOORE, CHARLES** Sea Ranch Condominium (1965), Sea Ranch, Calif. *[Photo: Alan Weintraub]*

**Work** Charles Moore's career included the design of a series of houses for himself and other clients. Because of his moves to different parts of the country, he has been able to use his own houses to develop ideas seen in his later work.

The large group of private houses have received wide attention, including the 1974 book *The Place of Houses*, written with Gerald Allen and Donlyn Lyndon. Charles Moore was author and coauthor of several additional books. The careful analysis of historic sources can be seen in all his work. His condominium building (1965) for the development at Sea Ranch, Calif., is notable for its careful relation to the seacoast site. The shed-roof, wood-sided buildings were copied extensively but do not display the freshness of approach of Moore's early design at Sea Ranch.

In New Orleans, Moore designed the famous Piazza d'Italia (1978), classic forms lit by neon lights, and the temporary Wonderwall (1984) for the New Orleans World's Fair. For this project, Charles Moore worked with William Turnbull, and others. Other projects include several for the University of California, including the Faculty Club at Santa Barbara, Kresge College (1974) at Santa Cruz, and the Alumni Center at Irvine (1985).

**MOORE, CHARLES** Piazza D'Italia (1978), New Orleans, La. *[Photo: Norman McGrath]*

Charles Moore also designed museums and religious and educational buildings in many parts of the country. His foreign work includes public housing for the Tegel Harbor Housing in Berlin, Germany. The Beverly Hills Civic Center reflects his appreciation of the Spanish Colonial architecture of Southern California. Known for his drawings and renderings, Charles Moore brought an element of fantasy and play to architecture.

**Life** Charles Moore was born in Benton Harbor, Mich. in 1925. He received his architectural education at the University of Michigan, his MFA degree from Princeton University in 1956, and his Ph.D. in 1957.

**Teaching** Charles Moore has held the following positions: assistant professor, Princeton University (1958–59); associate professor, University of California, Berkeley (1959–62); chair, Department of Architecture, University of California, Berkeley (1962–65); chair, Department of Architecture, Yale University (1965–69); dean, School of Architecture and Planning, Yale University (1969–1970); professor, School of Architecture, Yale University (1970–75); professor, University of California at Los Angeles and visiting professor, School of Architecture, Yale University (1975); and O'Neill Ford Professor of Architecture at the University of Texas in Austin (1985–93).

In 1991, Charles Moore received the Gold Medal of the American Institute of Architects. He died at age sixty-eight in December 1993.

**Further Reading** Johnson, Eugene J., ed.: *Charles Moore: Buildings and Projects 1949–1986*, Rizzoli, New York, 1986.

**MORGAN, JULIA** American architect (1872–1957). Most famous for her commissions from the Hearst family for their estate named San Simeon on the California coast at San Luis Obispo, she was one of the earliest women architects in the United States, and the first to be licensed in California. Trained as a Beaux Arts architect, her long career was overshadowed by the post–World War II dominance of the International Modern style. Critics tended to see the California early modernists such as R. M. Schindler (1887–1953) and Richard Neutra (1892–1970) as more important figures.

**The Hearst Castle** Phoebe Hearst had provided Julia Morgan with a number of commissions and recommended Julia Morgan to her son, William Randolph Hearst. Hearst commissioned Julia Morgan to design his spectacular Casa Grande, the main building at San Simeon on a high hill overlooking the Pacific coast. The first buildings were the three elaborate guest houses,

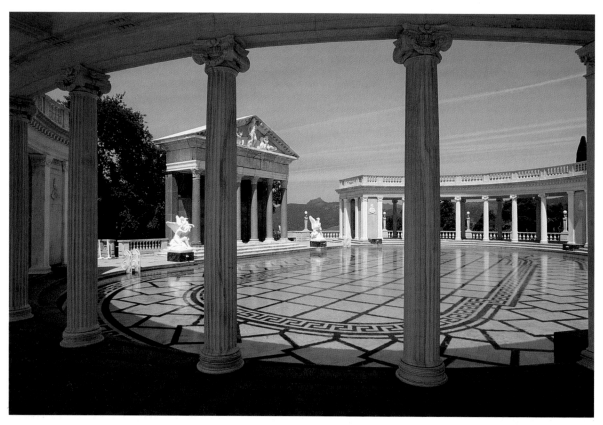

**MORGAN, JULIA** Neptune pool, La Cueta Encantada, The William Randolph Hearst Castle (1917–47), San Simeon, Calif. [Photo: Jane Lidz]

which were used during the 20 years of construction of the Casa Grande. All the buildings incorporated many of the art objects collected by William Randolph Hearst. Since 1958, the Hearst Castle has been a California State Museum and is now open to the public. Among other features are terraced gardens and the series of guest houses overlooking the natural landscape. The most spectacular design is the Neptune pool near the front entrance incorporating a classic temple facade. The scene of lavish entertainment of Hollywood stars, Casa Grande's interior contains a spectacular indoor "Roman" swimming pool. Hearst's companion, the comedienne actress Marion Davies, was hostess, since Millicent Hearst and the children spent most of their time in New York City and Long Island. Mrs. Hearst did not share her husband's pleasure in the company of the actors and actresses of the time, which kept him in California.

**Other Work** During her 47 years of practice (1904–1951) Julia Morgan designed over 700 projects, most of which were built. Among notable buildings were her work at Mills College, including the Bell Tower (1903), and Library (1905), the Asimolar Conference Center near Monterey, the Herald Examiner's newspaper plant in Los Angeles, and several projects for the YWCA in California, Utah, and Hawaii. In 1927, she collaborated with Bernard Maybeck for the Hearst Memorial Gymnasium for Women at the University of California at Berkeley.

For the Hearsts, she developed a series of houses at their great Northern California estate Wyntoon. She was involved with work here from 1924 to the 1940s. The buildings were "Bavarian" in style, and incorporated much of Hearst's German art. Although the buildings were picturesque, they were carefully spaced to reflect Morgan's Beaux Arts principles. Julia Morgan was adept at designing elaborate stage set effects and evolved a good working relationship with William Randolph Hearst.

**Life** Julia Morgan was born in San Francisco in 1872, and grew up in Oakland, Calif. She was the first woman to enroll in the engineering program at the University of California at Berkeley. There she studied under Bernard Maybeck (1862–1957), who encouraged her architectural interest and suggested she study at the École des Beaux Arts in Paris. At that time, there were no architectural programs in the western United States. In Paris, after two years of preparation, she was the first woman to be admitted to the architectural program in 1898. She obtained her certificate in 1902, and after travel in France and a visit to New York, returned to California, where she worked for John Galen Howard (1864–1931) before opening her own office in 1904.

Working long hours, Julia Morgan made her employees her family and kept them on the payroll even during the depression of the 1930s. Her early residential work was followed by larger projects in a number of architectural styles requested by her clients. She maintained this office until she was 79, closing it in 1951. She had her drawings destroyed in the belief that the finished buildings were sufficient evidence of her work. She died in 1957.

**Related Articles** BEAUX ARTS, ÉCOLE DES; ECLECTIC ARCHITECTURE; GREENE AND GREENE; MAYBECK, BERNARD; MODERN ARCHITECTURE.

**Further Reading** Bontelle, Sara Holmes: *Julia Morgan, Architect*, Abbeville Press, New York, 1988.

**MUSEUM** A building, or group of buildings, or a room in a building, in which are housed collections of rare and educational objects or works of art. Many museums also have gardens or other outdoor areas for display of certain objects.

**Types** Sometimes an art museum may be referred to as an "art gallery," a term also applied to stores in which works of art are displayed for sale. Other kinds of museums include those that specialize in archaeology, history, natural history, applied science, or other fields of knowledge. A general museum houses collections in a

**MUSEUM** National Air and Space Museum (1975), Washington, D.C. *[Architects: Hellmuth, Obata and Kassabaum]*

**MUSEUM** Walker Art Center (1971), Minneapolis, Minn. *[Architect: Edward Larrabee Barnes]*

**MUSEUM** Interior, Kimbell Art Museum (1972), Fort Worth, Tex. *[Architect: Louis I. Kahn]*

number of these fields. Some museums are specifically for children. Others limit themselves to some relatively small subject, such as the site of a battle or other event, a home of a famous person, or a single art style or period. In some cases, whole areas that preserve or re-create the environment in which people lived in the past operate as museums. Two of the most famous are the colonial area of Williamsburg, Va., and Old Sturbridge Village, Mass.

**Functions** Museums may be located almost anywhere, but for the most part they are in cities, on college and university campuses, and on historical sites. In addition to their functions in the preservation of objects and display to the public, most museums are cultural centers, in which experts engage in research; monographs, books, and other publications are published; theatrical and musical performances are staged; and many other activities are pursued.

Museums acquire their collections by outright purchase, trading with other museums, gifts, and searching for them in archaeological and other expeditions. Museums are financed primarily by governments on various levels, from the local to the federal, and by donations of money by individuals and other institutions.

**Elements** Although a somewhat small number of museums is built in any given period, museum design is

440

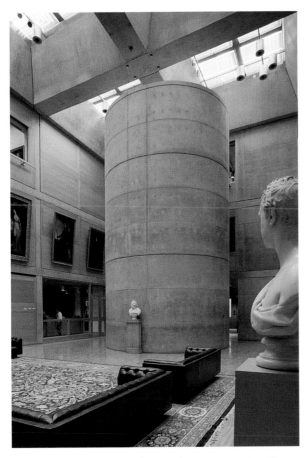

**MUSEUM** Interior, Center for British Art (1977), New Haven, Conn. *[Architect: Louis I. Kahn]*

**History of Museums** The history of museums dates back at least to the 5th century B.C. Some of the earliest were in Egypt and nearby countries. Museums of the kind known today began during the Middle Ages, but really became important during the Renaissance. Most of these museums came from collections of art or other objects made by private collectors and donated to institutions, such as universities. Probably the first of these museums was the Ashmolean (1683) at Oxford University, England. The establishment of museums speeded up in the 18th century and included the British Museum (1753), London, and the Louvre (1783), Paris. The fastest growth in the number of museums took place in the 19th century, when such museums as the Prado (1819) in Madrid, Spain, the Berlin museums (1830), the Victoria and Albert (1857) in London, and the Hermitage (1852) in St. Petersburg, Russia, were founded.

**American Development** The first museum in America was founded in 1759 in Charleston, S.C., but the great era of American museum building was also in the late 19th century. At that time, important museums such as the Smithsonian Institution (first building, 1849) in Washington, D.C., the Metropolitan Museum of Art (1870) in New York City, the Boston Museum of Fine Arts (1870), the Philadelphia Museum (1876), and the Art Institute of Chicago (1879) were built.

interesting and challenging to architects. And since museums seem to be constantly acquiring new objects, making changes in exhibits, and expanding their facilities, a goodly number of architects may be involved in their design. Although every museum presents different problems to its architect because of its location, size, type of collections, and other factors, all museums have several common elements, public and private. Public spaces include display areas or exhibition rooms which are the primary museum spaces, shops where souvenirs and other items are sold, and rest rooms. Often lecture rooms, auditoriums, and libraries, and restaurants, cafeterias, or snack bars are provided. Important private areas of a museum are administrative offices; spaces for preparation of exhibits and storage of objects not on display; shops for repairs and maintenance; rooms for scholars; and rest rooms, lounges, and other rooms for the staff.

Of primary importance in the design of a museum are provisions for flexibility in mounting and arranging exhibits, for expansion, and for lighting the displays, either with natural or artificial light or a combination of the two.

**MUSEUM** Holocaust Museum (1993), Washington, D.C. *[Architect: James I. Freed of Pei Cobb Freed & Partners]*

Since the end of World War II, many museums have been built in America. Among a few of the most notable are those designed by Louis I. Kahn (1901–74), including the Yale University Art Gallery (1953), the Kimbell Art Museum (1972), Fort Worth, Tex., and the Yale Center for British Art (1974) in New Haven, Conn. I. M. Pei (1917–    ) designed the East Wing of the National Gallery of Art (1978) in Washington, D.C., and, perhaps equally noted, the remodeling of the Louvre in Paris, including the pyramidal glass entrance pavilion in the Cour Napoleon (1989). One of the largest museum complexes is the J. Paul Getty Center in the Santa Monica mountains south of Los Angeles, scheduled for completion in 1994. The architect for this immense project is Richard Meier (1934–    ), also known for his High Museum of Art (1983) in Atlanta, Ga., among other museums. Frank Gehry (1929–    ), Robert Venturi (1925–    ), and Denise Scott Brown (1931–    ) are other contemporary architects who have designed notable museums.

**Related Articles** ART IN ARCHITECTURE; CAPITAL, UNITED STATES; COLLEGE AND UNIVERSITY BUILDING; LIBRARY.

**Source of Additional Information** American Association of Museums, 1225 I St., N.W., Washington, D.C. 20005.

# N

**NEUTRA, RICHARD JOSEPH** Austrian-American architect (1892–1970). Although his work has often been considered to parallel that of other great 20th-century architects—Le Corbusier, Mies, Gropius, and Wright—Richard Joseph Neutra started much later than they did. Neutra began his architectural practice in 1926, some 15 years after the first three architects above and 30 years after Wright. Although his career ran concurrently with theirs for more than 30 years, his work always seemed to be somewhat overshadowed by their work. Through his lifetime, Neutra's work was a source of some controversy. There were those who thought it derivative from that of the other architects and those who thought it creative and original in itself.

Time seems to have justified those who supported the latter view. Neutra's buildings have a grace and lyrical style all their own, related to the work of other architects but not derivative. Neutra was deeply concerned with the environment in which his buildings would exist. Experienced as a landscape gardener in his youth, he respected building sites and developed them as creatively as any architect of his time. He was concerned with technological progress. He respected industrial products, but did not worship them as some did. He was keenly interested in the biological sciences and his designs reflected that interest. Most of all, Neutra was interested in people, especially the people who would inhabit and use his buildings. And he was interested in large-scale planning and devoted a measure of his talents to master plans, city plans, and development projects. As a result, he designed some notable buildings of his era and strongly influenced the architecture of his time and of the future.

**Works** Opening his office in 1926, Neutra made a rather slow start, but Lovell House (1929; see illustration), Los Angeles, drew the attention of the world's architects. Often called the Health House because of the interest of Neutra and its owner in natural living and health, the Lovell House, with a steel skeleton, thin concrete walls, and glass, was hailed as a technological breakthrough and a masterpiece. Over the next few years, he designed several notable houses, including one for himself (1933) and the Von Sternberg House (1936), both in Los Angeles. He also designed a military academy and a school, his first of many, and several other buildings. The school, Corona Avenue (1935), was the first with one-room-deep classrooms, with glass on both sides, and a wall that could be opened with sliding doors to the outside. He also worked on ideas for prefabricated houses, but none was ever built. His great design for the Kahn House (1940) in San Francisco included furniture that he also designed. This was followed by other California houses, including the Nesbitt House (1942), West Los Angeles; another masterpiece, the Kaufmann House (1946; see illustration), Palm Springs; the Tremaine House (1948), Santa Barbara; the Moore House (1952), Ojai; and the Singleton House (1959), Los Angeles. During this period, he had designed a number of other California buildings, the most notable of which are Holiday House (1948), a seaside motel at Malibu, and Eagle Rock Club House (1953), Los Angeles. He also designed a pioneering housing development, Channel Heights (1942), San Pedro, Calif., and its furniture.

After the formation of Neutra's partnership with Robert Evans Alexander (1907– ) in 1949, the firm produced a number of buildings of other types, including the Child Guidance Clinic (1954) in Los Angeles, Miramar Chapel (1959) in La Jolla, Alamitos Elementary School (1957) in Garden Grove, all in California; the Lincoln Memorial Museum (1959), Gettysburg, Pa.; and the U.S. Embassy (1961), Karachi, Pakistan.

While in partnership with Alexander, Neutra continued to handle certain designs by himself. Two impor-

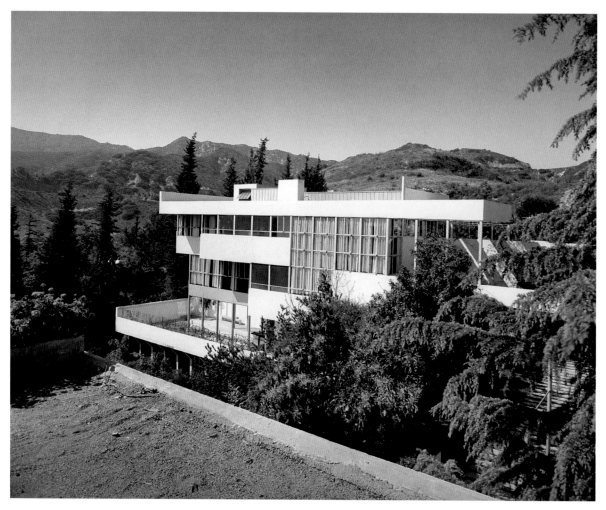

**NEUTRA, RICHARD JOSEPH** Lovell House (1929), Los Angeles, Calif. *[Photo: Julius Schulman]*

tant ones were the Gemological Institute (1956), West Los Angeles, and an open-air classroom school, based on what he called the ring plan, first projected in 1928 and finally built in Lemoore, Calif., in 1960. It is named the Richard J. Neutra School.

Neutra had a lasting effect on modern architecture, through his own designs and through the large number of books and articles he wrote.

**Life** Richard Joseph Neutra was born on April 9, 1892, in Vienna, Austria, the son of the owner of a small factory that made brass and bronze castings. As a boy, he became interested in architecture and enrolled at the Vienna Technical High School, the equivalent of a college in the United States. When he was sixteen, he left school to join the Austrian army artillery and served as an officer, in the Balkans, during World War I. Returning to Vienna in 1917, he went back to school to receive his degree. While still a student, he met the pioneering modern architect and critic Adolf Loos (1870–1933), and worked in his office for a time. The architectural design philosophy of Loos made a deep and

lasting impression on him. Loos also interested him in the United States, particularly its industrial design. He was greatly impressed by the designs of Frank Lloyd Wright (1867–1959), which were published in Europe at that time.

Since Austria was in the middle of a revolution when he graduated from school, Neutra went to Switzerland in 1919, where he worked for a landscape architect and gardener. Then he worked for the municipal government of Brandenburg, Germany, helping to resettle workers from the city to the country. While there, he designed a chapel and gatehouse for a cemetery. In 1921, interested in Eric Mendelsohn (1887–1953), he went to Berlin to visit and stayed to work in his office as a drafter. Neutra later collaborated with Mendelsohn on the design of buildings, including four exhibition houses in Berlin (1922), and in 1923, on a competition for a business center in Haifa, Israel, then Palestine, which they won. The building was never built.

Neutra married Dione Niedermann, a cellist, in 1922. The next year, alarmed by the inflation and turbu-

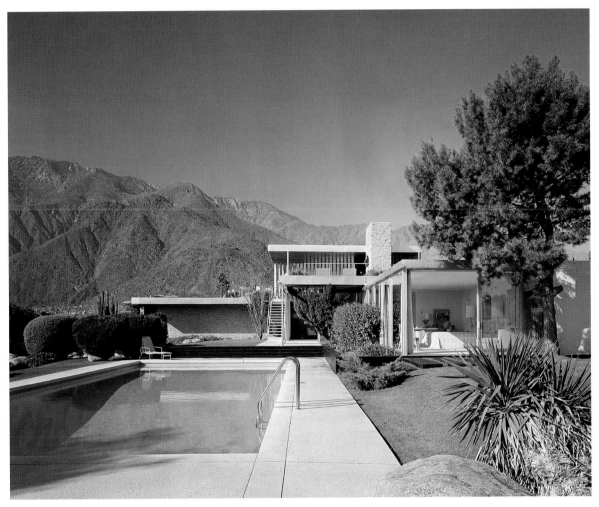

**NEUTRA, RICHARD JOSEPH** Kaufmann House (1946), Palm Springs, Calif. *[Photo: Julius Schulman]*

lent conditions in Germany, they went to the United States. For a few months, Neutra detailed Gothic ornament for buildings in New York and in November 1923, moved to Chicago, where he went to work for the office of Holabird and Roche, the large firm that had designed many of the tall (Chicago school) buildings. Soon after arriving in Chicago, Neutra visited Louis Henri Sullivan (1856–1924), who was then sixty-seven, ill, with less than a year to live. At Sullivan's funeral, in April 1924, Neutra met Frank Lloyd Wright, whose work had so impressed him in his youth. During the year Neutra visited Wright at Taliesin in Spring Green, Wis., several times and in 1925 stayed there to work with Wright for several months.

In 1926 Neutra went to Los Angeles to open his own practice, sharing office space with R. M. Schindler (1857–1953), a pioneering modern architect, fellow Austrian, and former drafter for Wright. The two architects collaborated on a few designs that were not built. That same year, a son, Dion (1926–    ), was born to Richard and Dione Neutra. Neutra's first design, on his own, was for the Jardinette Apartments (1927), Los Angeles, but it showed little promise of his later style. In 1928–29, Neutra taught architecture at the Academy of Modern Art, Los Angeles. The Depression slowed his progress as it did that of all architects. But he had begun to receive recognition for his work and commissions came in more rapidly. In 1930 Neutra became an American citizen. During the early postdepression years, he continued to design houses and other building types, including schools and apartments. From 1939 to 1941, he was a member and served as chairman of the California State Planning Board.

During World War II, commissions slowed and Neutra turned to nonessential materials (redwood, common brick, and glass) in his house designs. In 1942 Neutra's son, Dion, aged sixteen, came to work in his father's office and continued to do so with time out for his architectural education until 1960. After the war, in addition to houses, schools, and apartments, Neutra received commissions for other building types, including those for offices, clubs, churches, and clinics.

445

In 1949 Neutra formed a partnership with Robert Evans Alexander, architect and city planner, which was to continue for nine years until 1958, when Alexander left to organize his own firm.

In 1951 Neutra and Alexander were appointed planning consultants and architects to the government of Guam, a role that Neutra had played in Puerto Rico during the war years. The 10-year master plan for Guam was one of a number of planning projects handled by Neutra with Alexander.

In 1965 Neutra's son again joined the firm, which was renamed Richard and Dion Neutra, and they practiced together until the elder Neutra's death. The firm continued with Dion.

On April 16, 1970, at age seventy-eight, Richard Neutra died in Wuppertal, West Germany, while on a lecture tour. He had helped pioneer the development of modern architecture, in a very American way, though he had been born and educated in Austria. He was deeply concerned with the environment and sites of his buildings and with the people who occupied and used them. In 1977, seven years after his death, he was awarded the highest architectural honor of his adopted country, the Gold Medal of the American Institute of Architects.

**Related Articles** MODERN ARCHITECTURE; SULLIVAN, LOUIS HENRI; WRIGHT, FRANK LLOYD.

**Further Reading** Drexler, Arthur, and Thomas Hines: *The Architecture of Richard Neutra—From International Style to California Modern*, Museum of Modern Art, New York, 1982, distributed by H. Abrams; Neutra, Dione: *Richard Neutra—Promise and Fulfillment 1919–1932*, Southern Illinois University Press, Carbondale, Ill., 1986; Neutra, Richard: *Survival Through Design*, Oxford University Press, New York, 1954.

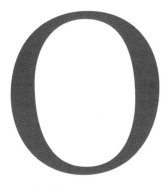

**OBATA, GYO** American architect (1923– ), heads the St. Louis firm of Hellmuth, Obata and Kassabaum (HOK), one of the largest and most successful firms in the United States. The high level of accomplishment reflects the design leadership of Gyo Obata. In addition to Obata, the other founding partners when the firm started in 1954 were George Hellmuth (1907– ) and George Kassabaum (1921–82).

In 1949 George Hellmuth formed a firm with Minoru Yamasaki (1912–86) and Joseph Leinweber (1895–1983) in Detroit (Leinweber, Yamasaki and Hellmuth) and another in St. Louis (Hellmuth, Yamasaki and Leinweber), most noted for their terminal (1957) designed for Lambert Field in St. Louis (1957), illustrated in the article entitled airport. When the firm split up in 1955, Hellmuth joined with two others in the former firm to start Hellmuth, Obata and Kasabaum (HOK). For the career of Yamasaki after 1955, refer to the article entitled Yamasaki, Minoru.

**Work** The firm is famous for several buildings including the Gallerias in Houston (1977, illustrated in the article entitled shopping center) and Dallas (1983), Tex.; the National Air and Space Museum (1976, illustrated in the article entitled museum, and the 1988 restaurant addition) on the Mall in Washington, D.C.; the Dallas/Fort Worth International Airport (1978); and the Camden Yards Twin-Stadium complex (1992), Baltimore, Md.

In addition to these well-publicized projects, international work includes the King Saud University (1984) with the Gollins Melvin Ward Partnership of London, U.K., the King Khalid International Airport (1983) in Riyadh, Saudi Arabia, as well as projects in Egypt, San Salvador, and Japan.

The firm is famous for the design of sports facilities such as the 75,000-seat Joe Robbie Stadium (1987) in Dade County, Fla., the Camden Yards Twin-Stadium complex for Baltimore, Md., and plans for the new Cominskey Park Stadium in Chicago.

The most prominent adaptive use project was the major renovation and redevelopment of the St. Louis Union Station (1985) including a retail mall and large hotel. The restoration of the Grand Hall and other public spaces in the old station (1894) ensures that this station now listed on the National Historic Register will remain a landmark in the city.

From the many office buildings designed by the firm, of special note is Levi's Plaza (1982), which successfully inserted a major low-rise development into downtown San Francisco. In competition with New York architects, the firm is well represented on the East Coast by such projects as the Aetna Group Division Headquarters (1984) in Middletown, Conn., the E. R. Squibb & Sons corporate headquarters and research facility (1972) in Lawrenceville, N.J., and the Mobil Oil U.S. Division Headquarters (1980) in Fairfax County, Va. A recent high-rise office structure is the 801 Grand Avenue building (1990) in Des Moines, Iowa (see illustration in article entitled office building). The list of important and varied projects demonstrates the firm's design quality under Gyo Obata's direction.

Additional projects for college buildings, health-care facilities, public buildings, and religious groups are of importance. Selected examples illustrated in this book include the Living World (1989) at the St. Louis Zoo (see article entitled zoological building), the Priory of St. Mary and St. Louis (1962), St. Louis, Mo. (see article entitled religious building), and the Temple of the Reorganized Church of Jesus Christ of Latter Day Saints (1992) in Independence, Mo. (see article entitled construction, building).

**Life** Gyo Obata was born in San Francisco in 1923 and grew up in Berkeley, Calif. His father, Chiura Obata,

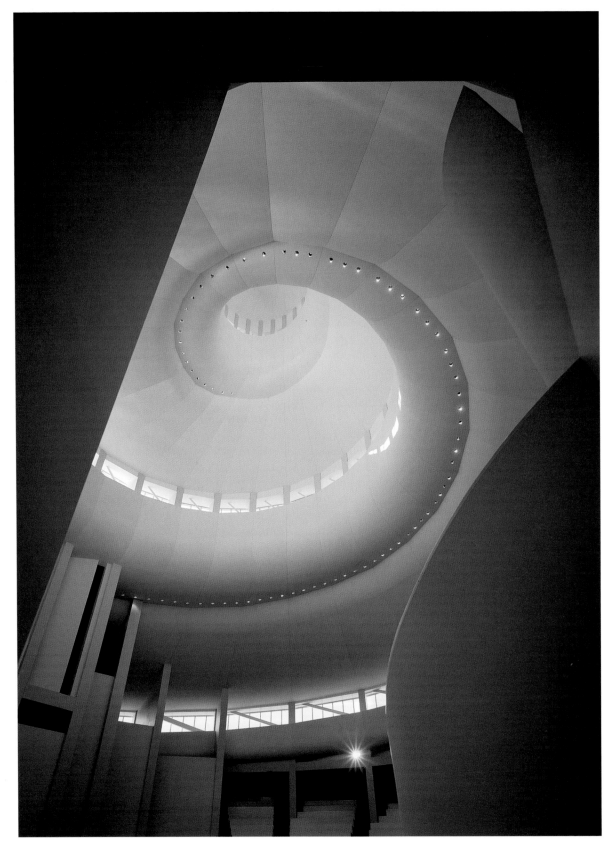

**OBATA, GYO** The Temple of the Reorganized Church of Jesus Christ of Latter Day Saints (1992), Independence, Mo. *[Architects: Hellmuth, Obata and Kassabaum]*

was a professor of art at the University of California at Berkeley. His mother, Haruko Obata, taught *ikebana*, the Japanese art of flower arranging.

Gyo Obata began architectural studies at Berkeley, was interned during World War II, but in 1942 was able to transfer to Washington University in St. Louis, Mo., and received his architectural degree in 1945. He studied at the Cranbook Academy of Art in Bloomfield Hills, Mich., under Eliel Saarinen, and received a master's degree in architecture from Cranbook in 1946. After a brief time in the U.S. Army, he joined the Chicago office of Skidmore, Owings and Merrill in 1947, and in 1951 joined Hellmuth, Yamasaki and Leinweber as a designer, and became principal in charge of design for the new firm of Hellmuth, Obata and Kassabaum (HOK).

A resident of St. Louis, Mo., Gyo Obata has contributed many buildings to St. Louis and has been recognized for the significance of his contribution to the urban renewal of the city. The firm has received many design awards from the American Institute of Architects, the Urban Land Institute, the Federal Design Council, and the General Services Administration.

**Related Articles** AIRPORT; MUSEUM; OFFICE BUILDING; RELIGIOUS BUILDING; SAARINEN, ELIEL; SHOPPING CENTER; YAMASAKI, MINORU.

**Further Reading** McQuade, Walter, *Architecture in the Real World, The Work of HOK*, Harry Abrams, N.Y., 1984; *Gyo Obata/HOK*, Dec. 1990 extra edition, *Architecture and Urbanism*, Tokyo, Japan.

**OFFICE BUILDING** A building in which business is transacted or professional services performed. A room, for the same purposes, in such a building is called an "office." Office buildings are one of the most representative building types of the 20th century, and almost all architects design them. In this era of social and technological change, new ways of working suggest that new work environments will evolve to handle the increasing complexity of commerce. Studies on the quality of the workplace result in recommendations for such spaces as lounges and public

**OFFICE BUILDING** John Deere & Company Headquarters (1963; later addition), Moline, Ill.
*[Architect (1963): Eero Saarinen; addition architects: Kevin Roche  John Dinkeloo & Associates ]*

areas where workers can interact and a greater attention to pleasant working environments not always achieved in office settings. Commitment to environmental concerns has been heightened by the "sick building" syndrome when ventilation and air quality is inadequate.

**Ownership** Offices are needed for almost all government and business functions. Office buildings may be government-owned, although in recent years some are built by developers on a lease-back arrangement where title eventually passes to the government agency concerned. Major corporations use a number of ownership formats, including buildings built and owned by the corporation or built to specific programs and leased from developers or other investors. In recent years, many corporations have sold buildings which they own in favor of lease arrangements, often for the same building.

A number of office buildings have been built by developers for specific tenants or in anticipation of finding tenants. Although many such ventures have been successful, problems can occur. With banks and insurance companies willing to finance such ventures during the 1980s, too many office buildings were built, often leading to bankruptcy or near-bankruptcy for developers and the lending banks or insurance companies. These doubtful real estate investments have resulted in failures to the point where the U.S. Government's Resolution Trust Company has been established to take over banks and become owners of vast quantities of insolvent real estate. Some insurance companies have also failed because of poor real estate investments.

A device for raising funds from investors is a Real Estate Investment Trust (REIT). Some of these have been successful, but others have failed. Several developers have taken groups of well-managed properties for investing in a new form of REIT to raise funds or to settle other debts.

**History** The earliest existing office buildings are in Italy and date from the 13th century. Typically, these early examples were combined market, town hall, and court. The market was at street level, with the other rooms above. Other early government buildings are most typically town halls. Such buildings as the Palazzo Vecchio in Florence, Italy, dating from about 1300 are typical of government buildings separated from markets. After this time surviving major northern European government buildings may be found in many of the older center cities. Perhaps the most famous is the Antwerp Town Hall in the Netherlands designed by Cornelis Floris and completed in 1565. The famous Uffizzi in Florence, Italy, dates from 1560 to 1571 and was originally built to house a variety of government offices. The Uffizzi has survived as one of the world's great art museums.

Another form of government office is the capitol or parliament, including offices and meeting rooms. By the

**OFFICE BUILDING** Sears Roebuck Tower (1974), Chicago, Ill. [Architect: Bruce J. Graham of Skidmore, Owings and Merrill]

18th century, a number of Parliament buildings were built. The early American examples include the Virginia State Capitol of 1790 designed by Thomas Jefferson, and the U.S. Capitol, in Washington, with William Thornton's modified design in 1794. Each state constructed state capitols, many of which survive. In Britain, the houses of Parliament designed by Sir Charles Barry were begun in 1835. In this century, the Brasilia Parliament buildings (1960) in Brazil were designed by Oscar Niemeyer, and the new Australian Parliament House (1988) in Canberra was designed by the American firm Mitchell/Giurgola.

In the 19th century, the diversity of government buildings reflected the growth of population. Some buildings of note include the various Washington, D.C., government buildings described in the article on Washington, D.C. Noted 20th-century examples elsewhere include Frank Lloyd Wright's Marin County Civic Center, San Rafael, California (1957–69), the Boston City Hall of 1969 designed by Kallmann, McKinnel & Knowles, I. M. Pei's Dallas City Hall (1977) in Texas, and the Hennepin County City-County Building (1975) in Minneapolis, Minn., designed by John Carl Warnecke.

The earliest banks in Italy date from about the time of the first government office buildings. These and stock exchanges were built beginning in the 15th century.

Although some of these early buildings survive, many were replaced with larger buildings over time. An example is the Bank of England in London, where the elegant John Soane buildings of 1788 to 1834 have been largely replaced. Noted American banks include Philadelphia's Second Bank of the United States (begun 1818) designed by William Strickland in classic temple form. Refer to the article entitled banks for further examples.

Commercial office buildings became dominant in the late years of the 19th century, particularly in Chicago after the fire of 1876 and in the cities of the East Coast. Such firms as G. B. Post in New York, Louis H. Sullivan, Burnham & Root, and Holabird & Roche in Chicago developed the concept of high-rise urban office buildings. In the 20th century, Frank Lloyd Wright, Mies van der Rohe, and Skidmore, Owings and Merrill were all famous for their high-rise office designs. Refer to articles about each of these architects.

**Structure** Although office buildings were traditionally nearly square or rectangular, current designs may take a variety of forms. The high-rise office building is usually built with a structural steel frame, although concrete has also been used for midrange building heights. Masonry bearing walls are limited in height because of the need for heavy walls on the lower floors. Typical of suburban development is the office park, which may contain a number of low-rise office buildings with associated parking and landscaping.

It took the development of structural steel in the late 19th century to allow the high-rise building with curtain walls hung on the frame. The development of structure for office towers is an interesting subject, including braced frames, clustered towers, and suspended structures. The layout of many office functions requires large open spaces free from columns, so a number of structural solutions have evolved for economically building such spaces.

**Issues** Fire safety of multistory office buildings requires protection of structural steel which otherwise may deform during fires. This is achieved by using masonry or plaster products to achieve the required protection. Exceptions to this might include water-filled columns, or, if the ceiling is high enough, no protection is required. Properly designed concrete structures achieve fire protection by the nature of the materials. Shafts, such as elevators or stairways, require fire-rated separation from the surrounding building.

For many years when energy was inexpensive, architects and engineers designed buildings with sealed exterior walls and interior climate control. Energy shortages have brought new consideration of lighting levels, ventilation rates, and more efficient exterior walls, perhaps with operable windows and many other techniques for reducing the energy consumed. Refer to the articles entitled building codes and standards and energy.

Flexibility of office space is desirable to accommodate tenants or changes in the operation of an office, such as is required for modern computers and communication systems. Such planning devices as open floor layouts and vertical electrical and communication shafts and closets on each floor for rewiring as needed have led to the concept of the "intelligent" building. Another trend is to use task lighting with reduced general illumination to reduce glare or reflections on computer monitors. The development of new office equipment including computer networking, not necessarily limited to a single building, suggests that further changes in office buildings can be anticipated.

Most codes now require some on-site parking facilities, either surface parking in suburban areas or parking structures adjoining or under an urban tower. Equally important is good access to public transportation. Some of the newer "edge cities" are deficient in this regard, relying exclusively on automobile use.

**Equipment** High-rise office buildings were made possible by the invention of the elevator during the late 19th century. Elevator use for large populations is a special engineering problem so that any passenger has a minimal wait for an elevator. In extremely tall buildings, elevators may be stacked with sky lobbies at about every 30 stories. This reduces the amount of ground coverage required for elevator shafts.

In the 19th century, office space was designed to take advantage of daylight, and large windows were the norm in these early buildings. With the development of electric lighting, floor areas could be used without regard to daylight. As recommended light levels increased, a greater percentage of energy was consumed for lighting. Recent attempts at reducing the energy used for lighting have been successful; some areas may be less brightly lit or supplemented with local task lighting.

Another invention required by office buildings is the telephone, and in later years the computer, modem, and fax (facsimile) machine.

**OFFICE BUILDING** Union Carbide Corp. World Headquarters (1982), Danbury, Conn. [Architects: Kevin Roche, John Dinkeloo]

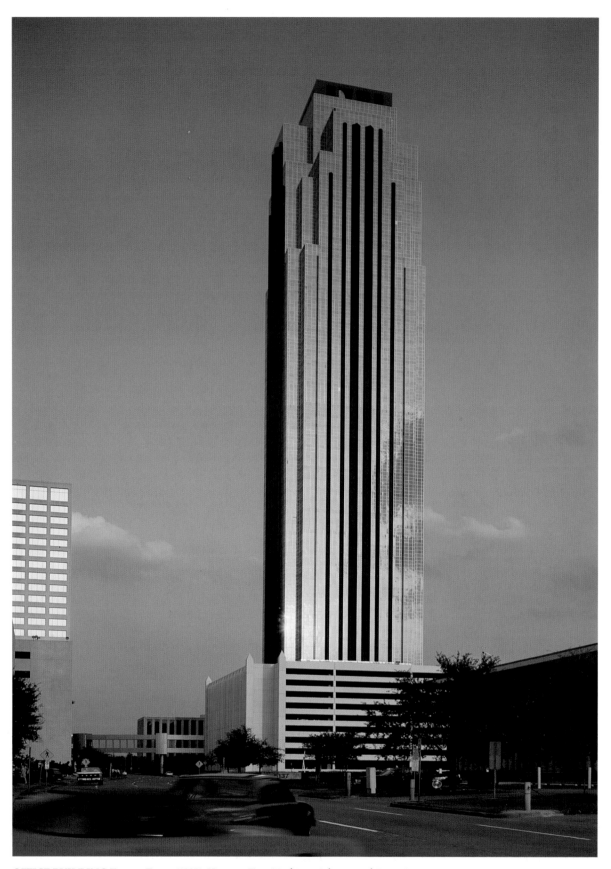

**OFFICE BUILDING** Transco Tower (1983), Houston, Tex. *[Architect: Johnson and Burgee]*

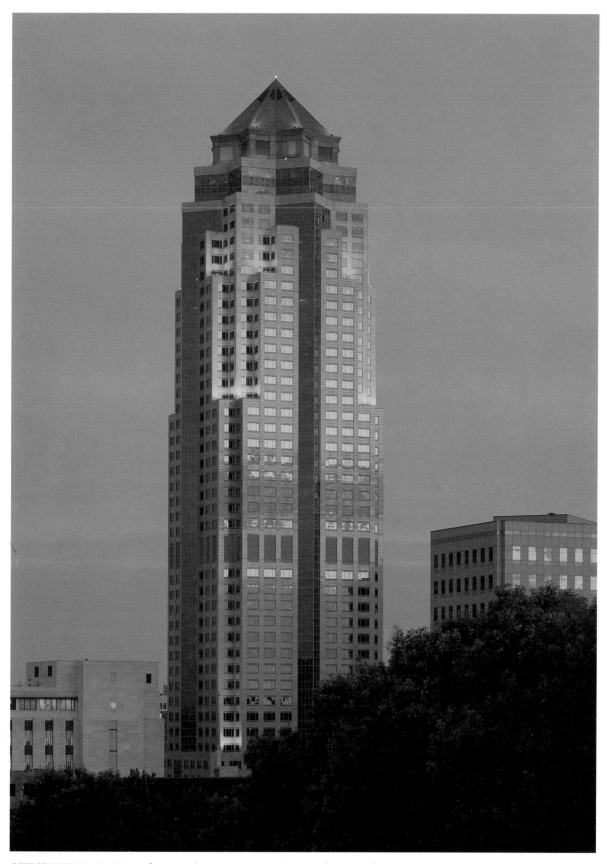

**OFFICE BUILDING** 801 Grand Avenue (1991), Des Moines, Iowa. *[Architects: Hellmuth, Obata and Kassabaum]*

**Space Planning** Office buildings are generally open floor spaces which are fitted out to suit the needs of the particular client or user. The process used to arrive at space use is called "space planning." The first requirement is programming the uses for space, including definition of the goals and objectives of the user, collecting data about the operation to be housed, and a projection of requirements for proper functioning, such as appropriate relationships between people and departments. The need for accurate budgeting for work to be done and furniture to be reused or purchased is necessary for a successful project.

Offices, whether headquarters or branches of major corporations or smaller businesses, have similar needs. A current trend is a growth in professional/technical staff whose requirements are not those of the typical corporate office. The need for workstations designed to support electronic technologies affects lighting, ventilation, and air conditioning (particularly as buildings are better insulated), special electrical power, and cabling at about twice previous figures.

All offices have growing needs for information management. Paper use is an issue because of the need for efficient storage, accessing, copying, and routing of paper. Records management now includes computer printouts, diskettes, large-format items as well as microfilm. Proper filing procedures are critical for office efficiency. Mail handling may now be largely automated, and careful study of distribution and pickup may include electrically guided cars programmed to stop at predesignated mail stops. Many offices have needs for a library for publication and document storage now often accessed through on-line search programs utilizing computers. Specialized spaces might include teleconferencing rooms.

Many office planning needs affect building and systems requirements. Older office buildings, including those designated as historic structures, require major retrofitting to adequately meet modern office requirements. In some cases, only the facades of older buildings survive as street fronts to what is basically new construction behind, whereas in others interior courts or additions may be used to introduce new systems into older buildings.

**Office Building Design** Current interest in older office buildings of the 1920s and 1930s has led to a movement away from the modernist style to a more eclectic approach in an effort to fit into existing urban streets. Features of several new buildings are their elaborate entrance lobbies and atria. The forms of the buildings are less boxy and more articulated with broken profiles and skylines. The most structurally complex are the very tall, slender buildings. Architects of the newer office buildings include Murphy/Jann, Swanke Hayden Connell, Skidmore, Owings and Merrill, Kohn Pedersen Fox, Roche/Dinkeloo, Cesar Pelli, John Burgee, and Pei Cobb Freed. In a tight rental market, these more elaborate designs are more likely to attract tenants.

**Related Articles** FACTORY; INTERIOR DESIGN; LABORATORY; STRUCTURAL ENGINEERING.

**Further Reading** Kay, Gersil Newmark: *Mechanical and Electrical Systems for Historic Buildings*, McGraw-Hill, New York, 1991; Goldberger, Paul: *The Skyscraper*, Alfred A. Knopf, New York, 1981; Huxtable, Ada Louise: *The Tall Building Artistically Reconsidered*, Pantheon Books, New York, 1982; Pevsner, Nikolaus: *A History of Building Types*, Princeton University Press, Princeton, N.J., 1970; Pulgrim, William L., and Richard E. Stonis: *Designing the Automated Office*, Whitney Library of Design, New York, 1984.

**Periodicals** Refer to the architectural magazines and interior design magazines for current articles on office buildings of all sizes.

**OLMSTED, FREDERICK LAW** American landscape architect (1822–1903). Usually considered the first professional landscape architect in the United States, Olmsted is thought to be the first person to have placed the words, *landscape architect*, on a set of plans. These plans were for his masterpiece, Central Park, the designs for which were begun in 1857 by Olmsted and his partner, Calvert Vaux (1824–95).

**Professional Innovations** Olmsted was not the first person to design landscaping, a practice which goes back to ancient times. But he was the first to practice landscape architecture, called landscape gardening earlier, as a profession. One of his most important innovations was charging fees for his work, in a manner similar to the practice today in landscape architecture, rather than working for wages, as landscaping employees would, or taking profits on the cost of the work, as landscaping contractors would. In this and other ways, Olmsted pioneered the character of landscape architecture and the professional role of landscape architects, as they are known today.

Olmsted was a pioneer of landscape architecture in other ways. Landscaping had been largely the province of landscape gardeners, who worked mainly for the nobility and other wealthy patrons. Most of their work was for gardens and other landscaping of palaces, large country estates, and great city gardens and plazas, which were designed to be beautiful but not functional. Thus landscape gardening was mostly for the wealthy and powerful. Olmsted also designed landscaping for the estates of the wealthy and for gardens and plazas, but his main interest was design of great public parks, intended for public use. He also designed suburban developments intended for low-income and middle-income families.

**OLMSTED, FREDERICK LAW** Gardens and grounds (1888–95), Biltmore estate, Asheville, N.C. This property was the first example of forest management in the United States. *[Architect: Richard Morris Hunt]*

Having started out as a farmer, Olmsted never lost his admiration for nature. And he brought this quality into his designs. English gardeners before him, in the early 19th century, had tried to impart natural qualities into their designs for country estates, but often what they achieved was only designed naturalness, contrived through their talents to look like what they thought nature should look like. Olmsted also tried to keep nature in his designs, but he had had experience with nature as it really exists, and had a great respect for it. In his designs, natural scenery was left alone as often as possible and then enhanced by the addition of designed landscaping elements. In this way, he was often able to create a sort of rural atmosphere that was beautiful and functional.

Thus Olmsted was ahead of his time in many ways. He was an intellectual and a socially conscious person who believed in simplicity, not pomp and circumstance. His abilities and philosophy transcended those of the new profession of landscape architecture, which he had pioneered.

**Works** Olmsted applied the principles of professional landscape architecture to the design of a great many projects, including estates, plazas, suburban housing developments, an exposition, and parks. His greatest

works are undoubtedly parks. And the greatest of these is his masterpiece, Central Park. He and Vaux won the competition for its design in 1857, and Olmsted worked another 20 years continuing to design and build its elements. The result was a park that has brought pleasure to millions of people and stands today as one of the world's great monuments to creative design.

Olmsted designed many other parks all over the United States. Some of the most notable parks are Prospect (opened 1867), Brooklyn, New York City; in Boston, Franklin (1875) and the Fenway, together with its parkway system, the first in an American city, starting in 1879; and others in Buffalo, N.Y., Chicago, and elsewhere. Among his most important designs of other types are the grounds of the U.S. Capitol, including the west terrace (1875), and the site plan for Stanford University, Stanford, Calif., beginning in 1886, with the first buildings by Shepley, Rutan and Coolidge, the successor to that of Olmsted's friend and associate, Henry Hobson Richardson (1838–86). Another important project was landscaping the immense estate, Biltmore, of George Washington Vanderbilt (1862–1914), near Asheville, N.C. The building (1895) was designed by Richard Morris Hunt (1827–95) and the grounds, beginning in 1888, by Olmsted. His last great project was the design for landscaping the grounds for the World's Columbian Exposition (1893) in Chicago.

**Life** Frederick Law Olmsted was born in Hartford, Conn., on April 26, 1822, the son of a merchant and a descendant of one of the founders of that city. His mother died when he was three years old and his father married again when the child was five. His early education was in dame's schools, named for the ladies who conducted them, and then in a series of other schools to which he was sent by ministers with whom he lived. By 1842, when he was twenty, Olmsted had been instructed by some 12 schools and tutors. Not much had come out of it but he had developed three interests that he would retain the rest of his life: nature, reading, and travel.

Olmsted joined the crew of a sailing ship, the bark *Ronaldson*, in April 1843 and sailed from New York around the Cape of Good Hope to China. He arrived back in New York a year later, very tired and ill. For about a year and a half, he lived on farms and studied farming while recovering, then attended lectures at Yale for about three months and returned to rural life. In 1847 he moved to a farm which his father had bought for him near Guilford, Conn. Still restless, he left there in 1848 to move to another farm bought by his father in Staten Island, N.Y., and farmed there until the early part of 1850. Olmsted then spent the next six months traveling in Europe. Back from his travels, Olmsted brought awakening enthusiasms for public parks, stirred by those he had seen in England, and for social issues, particularly the plight of the poor, sailors, and slaves.

**Social Issues** Now determined to become a writer, Olmsted published his first article, on the subject of cruelty to sailors in 1851, and his first book, *Walks and Talks of an American Farmer in England,* in 1852. The book was concerned more with social problems than with the practice of farming. He continued to travel and to write about his travels the rest of his life. In 1852–53 and again in 1854, he traveled in the South and wrote a series of articles on the effects of slavery in those states for the *New York Daily Times.* In 1856 his book on the same subject, *Journey in the Seaboard Slave States,* was published.

**Central Park** Most of his efforts went into writing until 1857, when he met an English architect, Calvert Vaux, who had moved to New York City to practice. The meeting changed Olmsted's life. Having determined sometime before to build a great public park in New York City, Central Park, the Board of Park Commissioners appointed Olmsted its superintendent. That same year, work on the site began, and a competition was held for the design of the park. Vaux talked Olmsted into collaborating on an entry, which they called Greensward, in the competition, and in 1858, they were awarded the commission for park design.

Olmsted and Vaux worked on the design and construction of the park until 1863, resigned, and then were reappointed in 1865. By 1876, they had essentially finished the main features of the park and in that year, Olmsted was dismissed, Vaux staying on until 1883. Vaux did some further work on the park later and Olmsted continued to make recommendations for important design improvements for many years.

**Family** In 1857 Olmsted's younger brother, John Hull, died at age thirty-two. The brothers had always been very close, and Olmsted was grief-stricken. In 1851 John had married May Cleveland Bryant Perkins, and they had three children. In 1859 Frederick Olmsted married his brother's widow. They had a son a year later, but the baby died before his first birthday. A daughter followed in 1861. A second son was born in 1866 but died on the day he was born. In 1870 a third son was born and christened Henry Perkins. The elder Olmsted was determined that this son should become a landscape architect and carry on the tradition that had been started. Accordingly, he renamed him Frederick Law Olmsted, Jr. (1870–1957), when the child was four years old. The boy did become an important landscape architect, city planner, and college professor.

**Later Life** During the Civil War, Olmsted served as secretary of the Sanitary Commission, a group formed to investigate and improve health conditions in the Union camps and hospitals. In 1863 he resigned as secretary of the commission and went to California, where he had taken a position as superintendent of the development of the Mariposa, a 70-square-mile estate, near the future Yosemite Park, which contained great mines and a number of villages. His work on the development of the estate was not too successful, but he gave considerable aid to the proposals for reserving Yosemite and the Mariposa Big Tree Grove, with its ancient sequoias, for future designation as U.S. parks.

When Olmsted had first started working with Vaux, the two men had formed a firm called Olmsted, Vaux and Company, which continued until 1872. Over the years, they designed the landscaping for a great many estates, suburban developments, and parks. Olmsted was later associated with other landscape architects and architects, including Henry Hobson Richardson. Beginning in 1878, he moved part of his practice to Cambridge, Mass.; in 1881 he left New York City and moved to Cambridge permanently. His nephew and stepson, John Charles (1852–1920), began working in his office in 1875, and in 1884 became a partner, with the firm renamed F. L. and J. C. Olmsted. In 1893 another noted landscape architect, Charles Eliot (1860–97), joined the firm, and it was renamed Olmsted, Olmsted and Eliot.

By 1895, Olmsted was having serious mental problems, and John Charles became senior partner.

Olmsted's memory began to fail, and he began to show signs of increasing senility. In that year his son, Frederick Law, Jr., joined the firm. The elder Olmsted's condition continued to worsen until September 1898, when he was committed to McLean Hospital, Waverley, Mass. Frederick, Jr., had been appointed his father's legal guardian and often stayed with him in his cottage at the hospital. With Frederick, Jr., at his bedside, Frederick Law Olmsted died on August 28, 1903. He had accomplished much: his great design for parks, especially Central Park; his devotion to the solution of social problems; and his tremendous influence on the establishment of the profession of landscape architecture. He had received numerous honors, including honorary doctor's degrees from both Harvard and Yale. But perhaps the greatest honor was the founding by his two sons, along with nine other landscape architects, of the American Society of Landscape Architects on January 4, 1899, a little more than three months after he had been committed to the mental hospital and 3¹/₂ years before he died. A year later, the first professional curriculum in landscape architecture was started at Harvard University and named for his former partner, Charles Eliot.

**Related Articles** LANDSCAPE ARCHITECTURE; PARK; PLANNING, CITY.

**Further Reading** McLaughlin, Charles Capen, ed.: *The Papers of Frederick Law Olmsted, vol. 1, The Formative Years, 1822–1852,* Johns Hopkins University Press, Baltimore, 1977; Olmsted, Frederick Law, Jr., and Theodora Kimball, eds.: *Forty Years of Landscape Architecture—Central Park,* MIT Press, Cambridge, Mass., 1973.

**ORNAMENT** An element of a building primarily intended as embellishment or decoration. While the line of demarcation may be blurred between ornament and art in architecture, ornament is usually taken to mean elements that are integrated into buildings, while artworks generally are complete, or almost complete, within themselves independently of the buildings in which they are placed.

However, the distinction is not quite that clear. A carved molding may certainly be called ornament and freestanding sculpture art, but sculpture attached, or engaged, partly integrated into a column or wall might be classified either way. For a discussion of artworks not integrated in architectural elements, see the article entitled art in architecture. See also the article entitled molding.

Ornament of many kinds has been a very important element in architecture from very early times. Various civilizations developed a great array of styles and forms of ornament, each often derived to some extent from those preceding but each with specific attributes peculiar to its own era.

**ORNAMENT** Detail, Niagara Mohawk Power Co., Syracuse, N.Y.

**History** In the earliest times, little ornament was used on buildings, but by the time of the great ancient civilizations around the Mediterranean Sea, beginning about 3000 B.C., ornament had come to be of considerable importance.

The Egyptians used ornament extensively in their buildings, around openings, on walls, on floors, and in other places. Most of the ornament consisted of stylized or conventionalized symbolic depictions of natural objects, including the sacred beetle (scarab), feathers, palm leaves, lotus blossoms, papyrus, the sun, and people. Such ornament was ordinarily carved into building elements and often painted with primary colors. In Mesopotamia, ornament generally followed the precedents of the Egyptians, using stylized, natural forms in pavings, on walls, and around openings. In Crete, both stylized and naturalistic forms of ornament were used, mostly painted on walls and other architectural elements.

These earliest forms of ornament have affected the architecture of America very little, except for an occasional use of Egyptian types mainly during the Eclectic era.

457

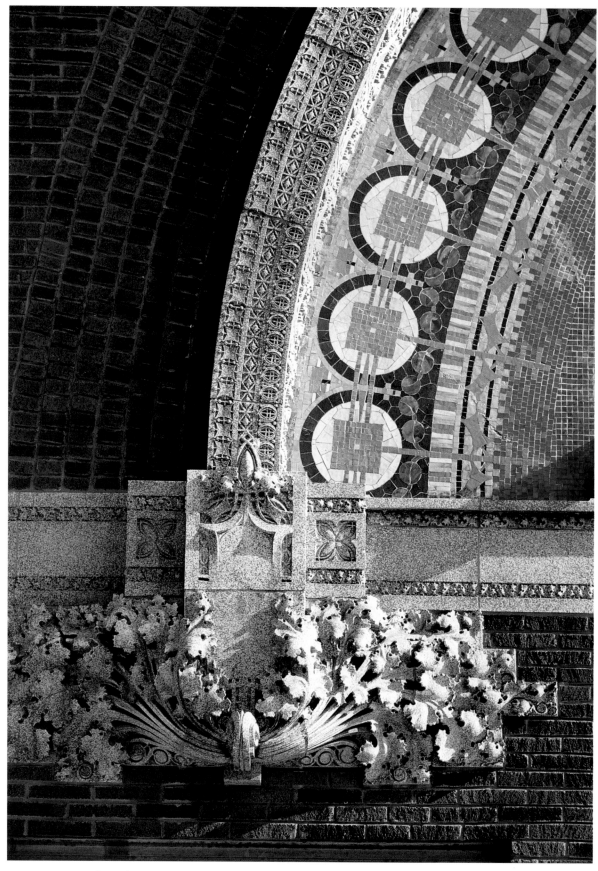

**ORNAMENT** Detail, People's Savings and Loan Association (1917), Sidney, Ohio. *[Architect: Louis Sullivan]*

some cases overpoweringly so. Using many kinds of subjects, including geometric, natural, and religious, as depictions of saints and symbols, such as doves, anchors, peacocks, and olive branches, Early Christian and Byzantine ornament has had considerable effect on the architecture in some countries, for example, the former Soviet Union, but very little in America.

Romanesque ornament was often heavy and crude, mostly utilizing forms derived from vegetation and sometimes from animals. It has not had a great effect on American architecture. On the other hand, Gothic ornament has had important effects on the architecture not only of America but of other countries, on church architecture especially, during the Gothic Revival and Eclectic periods. Gothic ornament was mystical and religious in nature and was developed to a high level of excellence, using plant, animal, and human forms somewhat realistically or conventionally. Many Gothic churches and cathedrals were almost literally covered with a profusion of ornament, much of it sculpture attached, or engaged, to walls and other building elements. Figures of animals, monsters, and people, often grotesque in appearance, called gargoyles, are interesting works of Gothic art. Used as ornamental waterspouts for roofs, they were usually carved in stone for major buildings and made of lead for minor ones. Perhaps the highest form of Gothic ornament is the

**ORNAMENT** Use of color; Pacific Design Center, Phase I (1975) and II (1988), West Hollywood, Calif. A future Phase III will be red. [Architects, Phase I: Cesar Pelli at Gruen Assoc.; Phase II: Cesar Pelli & Assoc.]

The Greeks greatly admired architectural ornament and used it extensively in their buildings. Beautifully executed, Greek ornament was derived mainly from natural and geometric forms and was often highly stylized. Among the preferred forms were acanthus leaves; anthemia, derived from palms or honeysuckle; egg and dart, or egg and tongue; bead and reel; fluting; scrolls; birds' beaks; and dentils, bands of small, separated blocks. It is believed that much of the ornament as well as the buildings were originally painted in bright colors.

The Romans also used ornament extensively, much of it derived from the Greeks and some executed by Greek artists. While ornament in Greece was ordinarily delicate, refined, well executed, and located with esthetic discretion, that of the Romans was often somewhat coarse, not always well executed, and placed almost anywhere imaginable.

Greek and Roman ornament have had an important effect on the architecture which came later, including that of America, in most periods up to the modern movement.

In both Early Christian and Byzantine architecture, ornament was often very elaborate and decorative, in

**ORNAMENT** Detail, Reston Town Center (1991), Reston, Va. [Architects: RTKL]

stone figures of many of the cathedrals, particularly those in France.

During the Renaissance, there was a great outpouring of building ornament of every kind imaginable, not only based on religious subjects and symbolism but on subjects that had preceded Christianity: pagan gods, classical mythology, and other aspects of Greek and particularly Roman life and beliefs. Ornament was produced in a vast variety of materials, including stone and metals. Many elements of architecture were ornamented during the Renaissance, including door and other openings, doors, walls, and columns. However, the overwhelming accomplishments in ornament in the Renaissance are to be found in the work of the large number of great artists of the period, many of whom were also architects. Using every conceivable material and medium, these artists produced a profusion of murals, sculpture, and other works of art, never equaled in volume and scarcely in excellence, in any period before or since. Renaissance ornament is closely related to the art in architecture of the period. (See the article entitled art in architecture.)

**American Development** Early American architects in the colonies used ornament derived from that which was current in their homelands. During the various periods of architectural revival, ornament was derived from the Classic, Gothic, Renaissance, and other earlier periods. Toward the end of the 19th century, with the beginning of the Modern movement, ornament came to be used with less frequency, until it virtually disappeared from American buildings in the 20th century. Important buildings using ornament were designed by such architects as Louis Henri Sullivan (1856–1924), Bernard Maybeck (1862–1957), the Greene brothers, Charles Sumner (1868–1957), Henry Mather (1870–1954), and Frank Lloyd Wright (1867–1959). Their efforts had some considerable effect but not enough to prevent most modern buildings from being designed with little or no ornament.

Modern architecture tended to rely on natural materials, colors, and patterns, such as window walls and space frames. However, some decorative Art Deco ornament was built, although this work was limited to pre–World War II building. In recent years, architects have renewed interest in ornament, including preservation of buildings from the past, and the post-Modernist interest in classic forms has resulted in more decorative buildings by such architects as Robert A. M. Stern (1939– ) and Michael Graves (1934– ).

**Related Articles** Arch; Art in Architecture; Column; Design, Architectural; History of Architecture; Molding; Various articles on American architectural history.

# P

**PAINT** A liquid which, upon being applied to a surface in a building, dries to form a protective and decorative coating. Paints and other coatings today often contain pigments, which impart color, opacity, and other properties, suspended in a liquid vehicle of oil, plastic, or other material. Paints and other coatings often have additional ingredients. In addition to its protective qualities, paint is mostly used for the effect of the colors obtained. For a discussion on other kinds of finishes that may be used to impart textures, patterns, and colors to architectural elements and surfaces, see articles entitled construction materials; plastics.

**Composition** A great variety of paints and other coatings for use in architecture exists today. Paint and other coatings are made up of liquids in which various materials have been dissolved. The liquid or vehicle, in which the other materials may be contained, allows paint to spread on surfaces where it will harden into a protective coating when it dries. Vehicles usually contain solvents or thinners, binders, plasticizers, and driers that control the spreading, drying time, and other characteristics of the paint. Suspended in the vehicle are pigments, such as titanium dioxide, that give paints their hiding power. Other pigments impart color, and inert substances make paints last longer and give them other desirable characteristics.

The major types of vehicles are natural such as rosin, opal, or shellac, or synthetic resins, such as alkyd plastics. Solvents or thinners in paints are either water (water-based paints), or organic liquids (oil-based paints).

**Properties** In general, paints and other coatings used in architecture should have certain basic properties, including proper workability, flow and spreading characteristics, fast drying, good adherence and hiding power qualities, stability, flexibility, durability, hardness, fade-

resistant colors, and stability under exposure. Exterior paints and coatings, in particular, should have good resistance to abrasion and to the effects of weather and the sun. In addition, certain paints and coatings for special purposes should have such properties as heat resis-

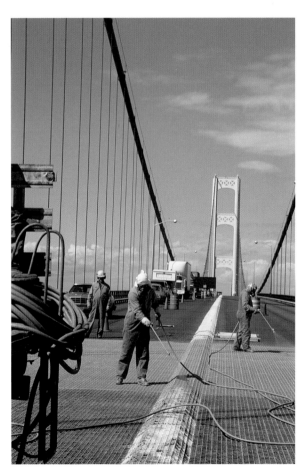

**PAINT** Undercoating, rust-proofing, Mackinaw Bridge, Mich.

461

**PAINT** Bowling Alley, Drummond Isle, Mich. *[Architect: Charles Moore]*

tance, fire retardation, rust inhibition, and resistance to chemicals, mold, and fungus.

**Types** Selection of the proper paint or coating for use in architecture must be made from a vast and bewildering array of types and formulations. In addition to oil-based and water-based paints, other types of coatings include varnish, enamel, lacquer, shellac, stains, bituminous, cement-mortar, sealers, primers, and waxes. Varnish is a transparent coating, usually made of drying oil and natural or synthetic resins. Enamel is a coating with a varnish vehicle and pigments. Enamels may be applied in the field or in a factory, where they are baked on and are called baked enamels. Lacquer is a quick-drying coating with nitrocellulose as its basic ingredient. Shellac is a fast-drying, transparent coating made with resins, obtained from lac insects, dissolved in denatured alcohol.

Stains utilize various vehicles, such as water, alcohols, or oils, together with small amounts of pigment that color but do not obscure the grains of woods. Bituminous coatings have bases of either coal-tar pitch or asphalt. Cement-mortar coatings generally consist of water as a vehicle, with portland cement, pigments, and other ingredients. Sealers are special coatings for use on wood, knots in wood, or other purposes, in preparation for other coatings. Primers are used for similar preparation of surfaces, such as plaster, for application of further coatings. Waxes are natural coatings, obtained from bees or plants, used mainly to protect other coatings. In addi-

tion, many other types of materials are often used in conjunction with paints and coatings: putties and wood fillers, to repair minor defects in materials; glazing compounds, for installation of glass in windows; caulking compounds, for sealing against moisture penetration in buildings; and a variety of thinners, driers, and paint and coating removers.

When selecting paints or other coatings for specific purposes in architecture, first consideration must be given to the functions, qualities, and appearances required; to the materials to which they will be applied; and to the circumstances of the applications, such as interior or exterior uses. Also to be considered is the question of whether the paint or coating will be applied on the job at the building site or in a mill or factory. Painting of materials at building sites is usually done with brushes, rollers, or spray guns. Mill or factory painting may be accomplished by any of these methods or by one of several others, including dipping, coating between rollers, and silk screening. Mill or factory paint may also be baked on. Finish painting may be handled in a mill or factory or materials may be only primed there, to be finish-painted at the building site.

**Special Coatings** For painting masonry, brick, concrete block, and concrete, several types of paints and coatings, with widely varying characteristics, are available, including bituminous; cement-mortar; oil-based; water-based; varnish-based; various types made with plastics, such as epoxies, alkyds, urethanes, vinyls, and acrylics; and paints with synthetic rubbers. A special kind contains silicone for water-infiltration resistance. Many of these paints and coatings are also suitable for plaster. There are also special paints for concrete floors.

Several types of paints and coatings for iron and steel include those with coal-tar pitch or oil bases; and those that utilize various plastics, such as alkyds, phenolics, epoxies, polystyrenes, urethanes, vinyls, and synthetic rubbers. Primers used for painting these metals usually contain red lead or other ingredients for inhibiting rust. For such metals as aluminum, copper alloys, and galvanized iron, special paints and coatings are available.

There are many types of paints and coatings for use on wood. For exteriors to be painted white or in colors, types formulated with alkyds, epoxies, latex, or oil bases are generally used. Alkyd, latex, oil-based, water-based, and vinyl paints are also used for painting interior wood. Stains may be used for exterior or interior work, as may varnishes, when transparent coatings are required. Urethane coatings are sometimes used for the same purpose indoors. Lacquers, either clear or colored, are used indoors, where high-gloss, hard finishes are desired. There are special varnishes for interior wood floors and for exterior floors. Many paints and coatings may be obtained in various degrees of gloss, from flat, sometimes called matte, to semigloss to high gloss. Many are available in a wide variety of ready-mixed standard colors, and other colors may be mixed for special purposes.

Special paints and coatings may be obtained for other materials or conditions. For example, fire-resistant paints and coatings are incombustible and therefore do not contribute to the spread of flames. Heat-resistant paints and other coatings are used for the finishing of boilers, in which high temperatures are encountered. Fire-resistant paints are used to protect building elements by swelling up when flames touch them. Other special paints and coatings are also available, formulated for resistance to mold, fungi, marine borers, and other pests. Some ordinary paints may also be obtained with ingredients for such purposes.

Many factors must be considered when selecting paints for various architectural uses. Hiding power for opaque paints, measured by what is called the index of refraction, is of utmost importance. White lead, the most used material for obtaining hiding power in the past, has now been supplanted by titanium dioxide, which has a greater degree of hiding power, from 6 to 8 times that of white lead, which is harmful to human health. Other requirements for paints and coatings are contained not only in federal regulations but in various building and health codes.

Paints and other coatings vary in appearance and color under different types of lighting. A paint in natural light does not have the same hue under artificial light. And paint under fluorescent lighting looks quite different under incandescent.

After the proper paint or coating has been selected for the material on which it is to be used, it must be properly applied. Thickness and number of coats, drying times, effects of temperature and humidity during the time of application and drying, proper preparation of surfaces to ensure that they are dry, clean, free of grease, and so on, and proper priming are all of utmost importance to ensure good workmanship and long-lasting painted or coated surfaces.

To ensure that the proper paints and other coatings are selected and that they are applied properly, specifications of manufacturers, associations, government sources, and others should be consulted. For special problems, manufacturers can often help.

**History** Paints existed before humans constructed their first buildings. Although the time of the first use of paint is unknown, wall paintings in a number of caves in Europe date back at least to about 15,000 B.C. in the late Paleolithic, or Old Stone, Age. Primitive humans also painted designs on such things as clay pots and on their bodies for religious or ceremonial purposes.

By the time of the great civilizations around the Mediterranean Sea, beginning about 3000 B.C., paints were used extensively. The ancient Egyptians are thought to have been the first people to develop a wide range of colors, which they made from minerals and other materials mixed with such substances as bitumen, eggs, and waxes to make them adhere. By about 1500 B.C., paints were also used in ancient Greece and Crete. Generally, these early people used paint for ornamental purposes rather than for protection of the building materials. Paint making, as well as its use, was considered an art and was a jealously guarded secret. The Romans used paint, mostly for ornamental purposes, and some think they were the first to use white lead in paints.

By about the 5th century A.D., the art of making paints had largely disappeared, not to be rediscovered until about the 15th century when the Middle Ages were coming to an end. Paints at that time were used on public buildings to some extent. Artists had not only continued to use them all along for paintings but mixed their own paints, using secret ingredients.

In the 18th century in the United States and in Europe, manufacturing paints for utilitarian purposes, including protection of buildings, began. The first of these paints were made with hand-ground pigments and various natural materials as vehicles. Most could be thinned with water. About the end of that century, paint materials were first made with machinery. The materials were then mixed by painters. In 1867 the first complete, ready-mixed paints were offered on the market.

Many new paints and other coatings have since been developed, including sundry kinds of synthetic pigments and vehicles. Today many types for general and even specialized purposes are available.

**Related Articles** ART IN ARCHITECTURE; ORNAMENT; PLASTICS; WATERPROOFING; Articles on various materials, systems, and components of architecture.

**Further Reading** Weismantel, G. E.: *Paint Handbook,* 2d ed., McGraw-Hill, New York, 1980.

**Source of Additional Information** National Paint and Coatings Assoc., 1500 Rhode Island Ave., N.W., Washington, D.C. 20005.

**PARK** A tract of land set aside for the enjoyment and recreation of the public, in or near a city or town or in a natural or wilderness area. A park may be a small open area with a few trees and plants in a city where people may stop for a while to relax; a much larger landscaped area in which facilities are provided for many types of sports, cultural activities, and other pursuits; or a vast national park with provisions for hiking, camping, and enjoyment of nature in the wilderness. In any case, parks have become what many people view as necessities in the world of today. A playground is a special area set aside for games and play by children and others. Playgrounds may be located in parks, school yards, or other places.

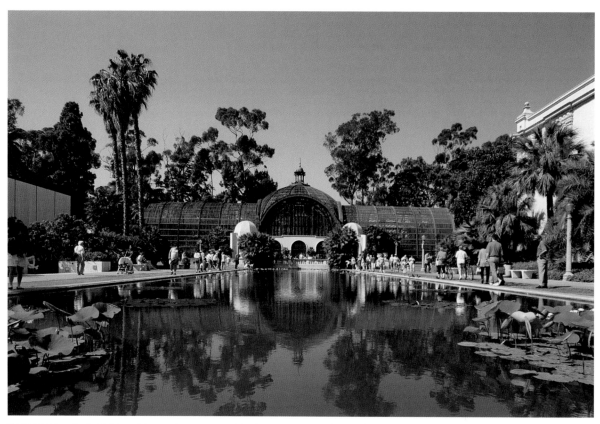

**PARK** Balboa Park (1880s and later), San Diego, Calif. This 1,400-acre park was the site of the 1915 Panama-California International Exposition and the 1935 California-Pacific International Exhibition. The 1915 California Building (now the Museum of Man) is shown in the article entitled Cram, Goodhue and Ferguson.

**Types** Parks today are of many kinds. Some are specialized, such as those located at historic sites or those established as nature trails for nature study, seashores, or wilderness areas. Other parks are general purpose and may include not only natural areas but facilities for several different activities, such as recreational sports, games, athletics, educational pursuits, contests, concerts and other performances. Some parks have restaurants; others have overnight facilities for recreational vehicles and lodges or cabins or camp sites.

Parks are an important part of architecture. They are designed by landscape architects or city planners, and architects and engineers are usually involved in the design of their buildings and other structures. However, parks are of so many types, purposes, and sizes that generalizing about the elements of their design is almost impossible.

**Purposes** Perhaps the best way to start examining the design of parks is to determine their purposes. The primary purpose of any park is recreation, or enjoyment by people. Recreation is an elusive concept. For one person, it may consist of quietly sitting in the sun or shade, contemplating nature. For another person, it may mean participation in a game, such as chess, with one oppo-

nent, or in a card game with several participants. For still another person, recreation may mean active participation in sports, individually or as a member of a team, or in dramatic performances or concerts. And recreation may mean a vast number of other pursuits. To further complicate the subject, one person may find recreation in quiet contemplation on one occasion and in very active games or sports on another. Many park planners try to provide for a whole spectrum of recreational pursuits.

It might be said that parks provide, in general, opportunities for visual, mental, and physical recreation and that, in doing so, parks cater to the emotional needs of people. To accomplish these goals, a park must have a purpose. The park must be designed to function properly for these purposes, and each part must be in the proper relationship with the others. For example, bicycle riders or joggers should not interfere with those who are resting or reading. Finally, a park should provide experiences to its users, including aesthetic experiences.

**Elements** In beginning the design of a park, consideration must be given to existing factors, including such natural elements as soils, topography, presence of water bodies, subsurface characteristics, vegetation and wildlife, seasonal temperatures, and precipitation.

Consideration must also be given to human-made factors, such as boundaries, streets and roads, utilities, and so on. Consideration must also be given to aesthetic factors, such as views and surroundings.

In general, a park might be divided into major elements for such purposes as nature study, group sports and games, picnics, camping or sleeping, circulation of automobiles and pedestrians, parking, service and maintenance, and areas left in the wild state. Not every park contains all these elements, and they vary in importance in parks of different types. Some parks may have other elements, such as provisions for boating and other water sports.

**Design Goals** After studying the purposes and the existing conditions of a park, a program outlining the goals of the design and criteria and methods for meeting the goals may be prepared. Based on the program, the design of a master plan for the park can proceed.

Locations for the various activities may be established, taking into consideration the sizes of areas needed, orientation to views and to prevailing winds and the sun, operating needs, supervisory requirements, circulation, safety, budgets, and other factors. Playing fields and other important spaces may be located by park planners, as may buildings, parking lots, and other structures. Areas to be left in the natural state may be selected. Site changes and landscaping of the park may be determined.

Then the elements may be properly related to each other, to the site, and to the overall concept of the park. If all these factors have been properly handled in the design and construction of the park, it will then have become a place where people can find recreation and a place where people and other elements of nature can coexist and commingle, in harmony.

**Playgrounds** Although often reserved for children, playgrounds may also be used by young adults and older people. Ordinarily, a playground for very young children contains only play spaces, with simple devices such as swings, slides, seesaws, sand piles, and perhaps carousels operated by pushing. For older children and young adults, playgrounds often have facilities for sports and athletics, such as basketball, football, and softball or baseball. For adults, facilities for tennis, horseshoes, and other games may be provided, and many of these may also be used by younger people. In some cases, playgrounds have swimming pools and facilities for track and activities.

Playground facilities are often divided into elements that are somewhat separated from each other on the basis of the age groups that use them and by the nature of the uses. Playgrounds must be designed to be functional and safe. The major problem in their design is the provision of the proper facilities in the proper relationships to each other and to the overall plan. Playgrounds

**PARK** Samuel Paley Plaza (1967), New York, N.Y. *[Landscape architects: Zion and Breen]*

are usually located in parks or in school yards, but some are separate entities.

American landscape architects, city planners, and architects have designed many notable parks, most of them during the late 19th and 20th centuries. Others will be designed and built in the future, and the design professionals who create them will find in their design very satisfying and fulfilling experiences.

**History** Since ancient times, certain areas have been set aside for recreational purposes. In Egypt and the Middle East, these were areas such as hunting preserves, whose use was restricted to the rulers and the nobility. The first public areas for recreational purposes are thought to have been established by the ancient Greeks; most of these were for athletic purposes and had groves of trees for people to walk through. The Romans built small parks; although a few were open to the public, most constituted hunting preserves, which were restricted to the ruling classes and the wealthy. This practice was continued for many centuries. During the Renaissance, parks were mostly promenades or formal gardens, and few were open to the public.

**PARK** Bryant Park (1884; altered and restored), New York, N.Y.

During the 18th century in England and Scotland, the practice of establishing great hunting preserves for the nobility continued, often at the expense of farmers and shepherds who were displaced from their homes to make way for the preserves. City parks of the time, in London and other cities, were not public, being restricted to certain classes of people or requiring admission fees for entry. During the 19th century, many of these became public parks, and many hunting preserves and other parks of the nobility were converted to public use.

**American Development** The first city park in colonial America is thought to have been the Boston Common, established in 1634. Commons were located in other New England cities, and later other types of public parks were built. These parks were generally formal in concept, suitable for walking or sitting but not very much else. Such was the situation when Frederick Law Olmsted (1822–1903) won, with his partner, Calvert Vaux (1824–95), the competition for the design of Central Park in New York City.

Olmsted, the first person to call himself a landscape architect, and Vaux set out, in 1857, to create the first park in the United States that was planned from the beginning. They created a masterpiece that was planned not only in a natural, almost rural, manner but provided the public with a park in which all who wished to do so

could find recreation. Olmsted designed many other parks in such cities as Buffalo, N.Y., Washington, D.C., Philadelphia, and Boston. He also helped establish the national park system, by his recommendations for the Yosemite Valley in California, which ultimately became Yosemite National Park in 1890. The first national park, Yellowstone National Park, Wyo., had been founded in 1872.

Olmsted was devoted to the establishment of city parks as natural, rural retreats for those who could not go to the country. At that time, others involved in park establishment and planning followed his philosophy, which came to be known as one of "passive recreation." Beginning in the early 20th century, some planners believed that parks should provide active recreation, playgrounds, areas for sports and athletics, nature study, arts and crafts work, and other activities. These opposing viewpoints resulted in two types of facilities: parks that were natural and passive, and recreation areas for the more active pursuits. Parks were planned properly, recreation areas planned almost not at all. This situation persisted until the end of World War II. Then the two opposing camps tended to merge their interests, also merging passive and active recreation in park design. In recent years, the great numbers of visitors to national parks have led to a restriction on the numbers of visitors to environmentally fragile sites. Some believe that vast areas should be left as wilderness for future generations.

In the United States today, there are parks of many kinds: small and large, owned by cities and towns, counties, states, and the federal government. In addition to the above-mentioned purposes, they serve as places for educational pursuits; musical, dance, and dramatic performances; contests; and other activities. Or as some park planners put it, they provide refreshment for mind and body.

There are literally tens of thousands of parks in the United States, occupying millions of acres. The 100 largest cities alone have more than 7,000 parks and the states more than 2,000, occupying more than 5 million acres. The national park system has about 40 national parks, about 20 national battlefield parks, military parks, national memorials and monuments, and historic sites.

Some of the most notable city parks in the United States, in addition to those already mentioned, are Prospect, Brooklyn; Lincoln and Jackson, Chicago; Rock Creek, Washington, D.C.; Golden Gate, San Francisco; Fairmount, Philadelphia; Druid Hill, Baltimore; and Belle Isle, Detroit.

**Related Articles** GARDEN; LANDSCAPE ARCHITECTURE; OLMSTED, FREDERICK LAW; PLANNING, CITY; RECREATION BUILDING.

**Further Reading** Ramsey, Charles G., and Harold R. Sleeper: *Architectural Graphic Standards*, 9th ed., John Wiley, New York, 1994; Molner, D. J., and A. J. Rutledge: *Anatomy of a Park—The Essentials of Recreation Planning and Design*, 2d ed., McGraw-Hill, New York, 1986.

**Sources of Additional Information** National Parks and Conservation Assoc., 1701 18th St., N.W., Washington, D.C. 20009; National Recreation and Park Assoc., 3101 Park Center Dr., 12th Fl., Alexandria, Va. 22302.

**PATRON, ARCHITECTURAL** The client who hires an architect to achieve more than a serviceable building does so out of a limited group of motivations. The patron may have more than one motivation to seek architectural excellence. These motivations include social standing, civic pride, religious faith, a better-than-average return on investment, a corporate image, or simply aesthetic appeal.

The architects who are employed by patrons tend to be design leaders, whose imaginative approach has brought them some fame. However, their buildings do not achieve wide recognition unless each building's purpose serves a real function. The most successful buildings survive over time by the use of suitable materials, allowing the buildings to weather well.

The best efforts result when the patron and the architect can work together for a recognized goal. Architectural patrons may be found in several areas of

**PATRON, ARCHITECTURAL** Private patrons; residence of W. Watts Sherman (1876), Newport, R.I. *[Architect: Henry Hobson Richardson]*

society, including religion, commerce, government, social betterment, and cultural life. Each generation has identified those who have earned the honorific title of patron of architecture.

**Government Patrons** Some of the most successful public buildings have been the result of public competitions. In antiquity, the buildings of the acropolis in Athens, Greece, were the subject of a competition selected by public vote. In 1401 a well-known competition was held for a pair of doors on the Baptistery in Florence, Italy, won by the sculptor Lorenzo Ghiberti (1378–1455). Later, the follow-up winner, Filippo Brunelleschi (1377–1446), was selected by a competition to design the dome on the Florence Duomo, a design that is still admired.

Competitions are not peaceful ways to select an architect to design a new building, and perhaps the most important element is who gets to select the winner.

**PATRON, ARCHITECTURAL** Corporate patron; IBM Rochester (1959; later addition), Rochester, Minn. *[Architect: Eero Saarinen]*

**PATRON, ARCHITECTURAL** Corporate patron; Parkside Elementary School (1962; addition, 1992), Columbus, Ind. *[Architect: Norman Fletcher of The Architects' Collaborative]*

Architectural competitions may be open internationally or be restricted to selected designers. In recent years, international guidelines have been promoted to ensure fairness to those who enter competitions. Occasionally, losing entries have become famous and have increased the fame of such architects as Le Corbusier (League of Nations) and Eliel Saarinen (Chicago Tribune Tower).

Below are a list of some of the famous and more successful public competitions from around the world:

The White House and Capitol, Washington, D.C., 1792
Houses of Parliament, London, Great Britain, 1835
The Paris Opera, Paris, France, 1860
The Reichstag in Berlin, Germany, 1882
The Eiffel Tower, Paris, France, 1886
The Austrian Saving Bank, Vienna, Austria, 1903
Stockholm Town Hall, Sweden, 1903
Helsinki Station, Finland, 1905
The Peace Palace, The Hague, The Netherlands, 1905
Chicago Tribune Tower, Chicago, Ill., 1922
Termini Station, Rome, Italy, 1947
Sydney Opera House, Australia, 1956
Congress Building, Kyoto, Japan, 1962
Amsterdam Town Hall, The Netherlands, 1967
Centre Pompidou, Paris, France, 1970
Vietnam Memorial, Washington, D.C., 1981

**PATRON, ARCHITECTURAL** Private patrons; Rothko Chapel (1971) for John and Dominique de Menil, Houston, Tex. The building houses a series of paintings by Mark Rothko. *[Architects: Barnstone & Aubry; sculptor of* Broken Obelisk: *Barnett Newman]*

**PATRON, ARCHITECTURAL** Universities as patrons; Arts and Architecture Building (1963), Yale University, New Haven, Conn. *[Architect: Paul Rudolph]*

Some government agencies achieve high-quality building programs by setting up design controls to ensure that the appropriate architects have an opportunity to design major public works. Awards programs are a way for architects and the government to recognize good design.

**Social Standing** Most lavish private homes of more than average interest are built as a public statement. Newport, R.I., has a large group of ostentatious houses from the gilded age designed by the best architects of the period.

**Corporate Image** The use of architectural programs to enhance the image of a corporation is well documented. Such clients as the telephone companies, IBM, and Disney as well as smaller corporations have achieved public recognition for the quality of their building programs.

**Development** In some periods developers recognize the benefits of innovative design as a way to financial success. Las Vegas hotels are designed to attract the largest group of visitors. One of the leading developers making use of quality design has been Gerald D. Hines in Houston, Texas, and other cities.

**Aesthetics** Cultural organizations have perhaps the clearest record for support of architecture. The list of notable museum buildings, concert halls, and art centers provides design architects with compatible building programs. Many of these are illustrated in this book.

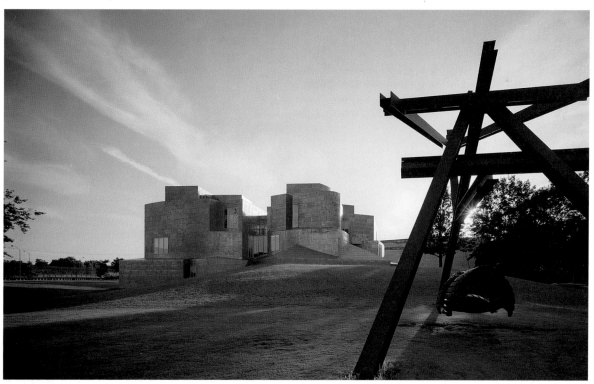

**PATRON, ARCHITECTURAL** Cultural institutions as patrons; Center for the Visual Arts (1993), University of Toledo, Toledo, Ohio. *[Architect: Frank Gehry]*

Occasionally there will be a patron who commissions buildings out of a conviction that a community will benefit from the best design thinking. A famous example of such a program is represented by Columbus, Ind., where architectural fees for public buildings have been underwritten by the Cummins Engineering Company and its president, J. Irwin Miller.

**Religious Faith** Religious groups have been a traditional patron of art, music, and architecture. Although less prominent than in past years, excellent work is continuing. Buildings of Islam as well as churches and synagogues are often major buildings in their communities and are desirable architectural commissions.

**Related Articles** ECLECTIC ARCHITECTURE; HOUSE; MUSEUM; OFFICE BUILDING; RELIGIOUS BUILDING; THEATER.

**Further Reading** de Haan, Hilde, and Ids Haagsma: *Architects in Competition—International Architectural Competitions of the Last 200 Years,* Thames and Hudson, New York, 1988. This article was written in response to con-

**PATRON, ARCHITECTURAL** Corporate patron; Team Disney Building, Buena Vista, Fla. *[Architect: Arata Isosaki]*

versations and less to published material. Although we have avoided reference to magazine articles, the Dec. 1990 (vol. 79, no. 12) issue of *Architecture Incorporating Architectural Technology* is pertinent and may be referenced.

**PEI, IEOH MING** I. M. Pei (1917–   ) is a leading architect of his generation. Born in China, he received his architectural training, and has practiced, in the United States. Known as a late Modernist architect, his firm has enjoyed great international renown, for a variety of building types.

**Works** Pei worked during his early career for the developer William Zeckendorf, and his firm Webb and Knapp, from 1948 to 1960. Of the many projects credited to Pei the design of the Society Hill residential complex (1964) in Philadelphia, Pa., and the Earth Sciences Building at MIT (1964) are of particular note. The plan for Southeast Washington, D.C., was immense in scale, and only partly realized, but many other major projects were constructed in Atlanta, Syracuse, N.Y., and Manoa, Hawaii. Overseas projects included the U.S. Chancery (1969) in Montevideo, Uruguay, and the Luce Memorial Chapel (1963) in Taichung, Taiwan.

Pei's first independent project was the National Center for Atmospheric Research (1967), near Boulder, Colo. Pei was appointed architect of the John F. Kennedy Library (1979) in Cambridge, Mass. Due to public resistance, the original site was abandoned in favor of a point of land in Boston Harbor.

Pei has been identified with a number of projects in Texas, including the Dallas Municipal Administration Center (1977) and the Morton H. Meyerson Symphony Center (1989), and his partner Henry Cobb was designer for the Allied Bank Tower (1986).

A project which caused the firm serious problems was the John Hancock Building (1976), Boston, Mass. The failure of the exterior glazing resulted in a series of lawsuits that threatened the future of the firm. Fortunately, projects in Singapore and college and muse-

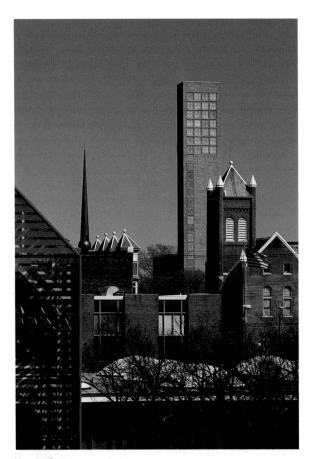

**PATRON, ARCHITECTURAL** Corporate patron; Columbus, Ind. Shown in illustration are Irwin Union Bank & Trust Company (1954; 1973) *[Architect: Eero Saarinen; additions: Kevin Roche],* First Christian Church (1942) *[Architect: Eliel Saarinen],* Spire of St. Peter's Lutheran Church (1988) *[Architect: Gunnar Birkerts].* For over 30 years, Cummins Engine under the leadership of J. Irwin Miller, has supported architectural excellence in Columbus, Ind.

um work kept the firm busy while the legal problems were addressed.

The design of the East Building of the National Gallery (1978), Washington, D.C., brought major attention and praise to the firm. The central atrium was immediately appreciated by the public, and critical comment did not interfere with the recognition of Pei's firm as a major design force.

The Jacob K. Javits Convention Center (1986) for New York City's west side was on 21 acres, including five blocks between 11th and 12th avenues. Pei's partner James Freed was identified as lead designer. The glazed space frame was technically complex, and politically difficult—because of publicity and delays concerning bolt failure attributed to faulty manufacture—with the final building recalling the great glazed halls of the 19th century.

Probably the best-known project is Pei's commission for the remodeling of the Louvre Museum in Paris, France. The needs of the museum required a below-grade building under the Cour Napoléon, with access from above. The choice of the glazed pyramid centered on the court caused tremendous public discussion and argument, lasting until the project was completed. The classical form of the pyramid has been accepted as an appropriate solution to an almost impossible challenge, and the museum

**PEI, IEOH MING** Dallas Municipal Administration Center (1977), Dallas, Tex.

**PEI, IEOH MING** East Wing of the National Gallery (1978), Washington, D.C.

**PEI, IEOH MING** Bank of China (office building) (1990), Hong Kong. *[Photo: Paul Warchol]*

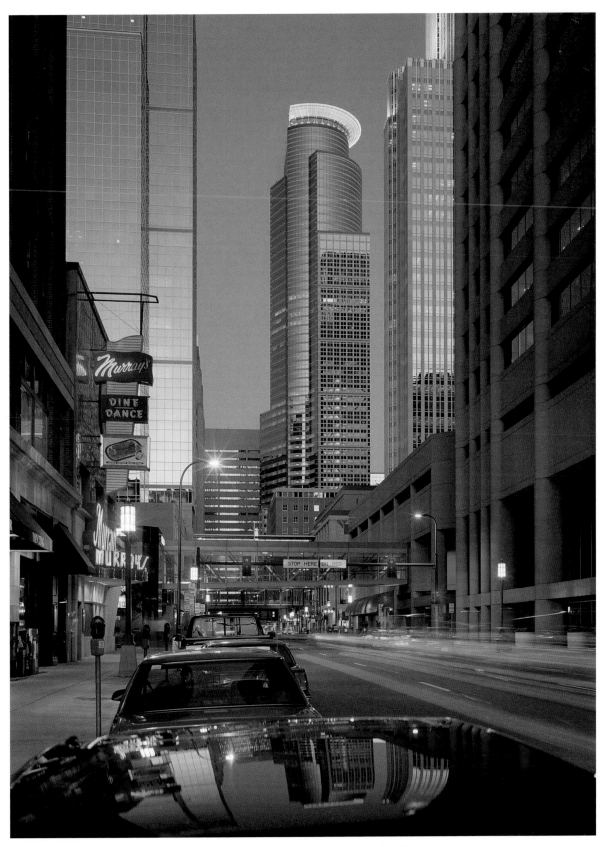

**PEI, IEOH MING** First Bank Place (1992), Minneapolis, Minn. *[Architect: James I. Freed of Pei, Cobb, Freed and Partners (Photo: Christian M. Korab)]*

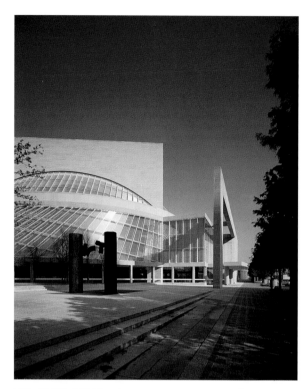

**PEI, IEOH MING** Morton H. Meyerson Symphony Center (1989), Dallas, Tex. *[Photo: Greg Hursley]*

has been provided with its first adequate entrance and other services requiring 600,000 ft² of new space.

**Life** Ieoh Ming Pei was born in Guangzhou (formerly Canton), China, in 1917, the son of a successful banker. In his youth he lived in Hong Kong and later in Shanghai. He studied at the St. John's Middle School in Shanghai. Although his father favored a British education, Pei was allowed to enroll in the University of Pennsylvania's architectural school. In 1935, he transferred to MIT as an engineering student but was quickly encouraged to continue with architecture by William Emerson, dean of the architecture school. He received his degree in 1940 and intended to return to China, but his father advised he stay in the United States during the war. He married Eileen Loo in 1942. After working briefly for the engineering firm of Stone & Webster, he enrolled in the Harvard Graduate School of Design and, along with teaching and some time in defense work, received his master's degree in 1946. After graduating, he expected to return to China but again was advised to remain in the United States. In 1948, he accepted a job with William Zeckendorf to initiate an architectural unit with Zeckendorf's real estate firm, Webb and Knapp. Henry Cobb joined them in 1950, Eason Leonard in 1952. Ulrich Franzen was also a part of the Pei operation at that time.

**PEI, IEOH MING** Holocaust Museum (1993), Washington, D.C. *[Architect: James I. Freed of Pei, Cobb, Freed and Partners]*

By 1955, the architectural firm was identified as I. M. Pei & Associates, who worked exclusively for Webb and Knapp. During this period Pei gained wide experience in large-scale urban projects and assembled a large staff. When Zeckendorf's financial problems grew unmanageable by 1960, they became an independent architectural firm. After 1966, the firm was called I. M. Pei and Partners. Internationally active, he has achieved many honors, including the Gold Medal of the American Institute of Architects. His firm is now named Pei, Cobb, Freed and Partners. I. M. Pei retired from active management of the firm at age seventy-three in 1990 but maintains an office there.

**Further Reading** Wiseman, Carter: *I. M. Pei: A Profile in American Architecture,* Harry N. Abrams, New York, 1990.

**PELLI, CESAR** Cesar Pelli (1926– ), American architect and educator. Pelli was born in Tucuman, Argentina. His present firm, Cesar Pelli & Associates in New Haven, Conn., was formed in 1981 with Diana Balmori and Fred Clark (1947– ) joining him as partners. As a successful design practice, the firm's work is memorable and shows a change in the late 1980s from late Modernism to a shift in materials and forms reflecting a response to historic buildings, particularly those of the 1920s and 1930s. Each new project of this firm is of design interest.

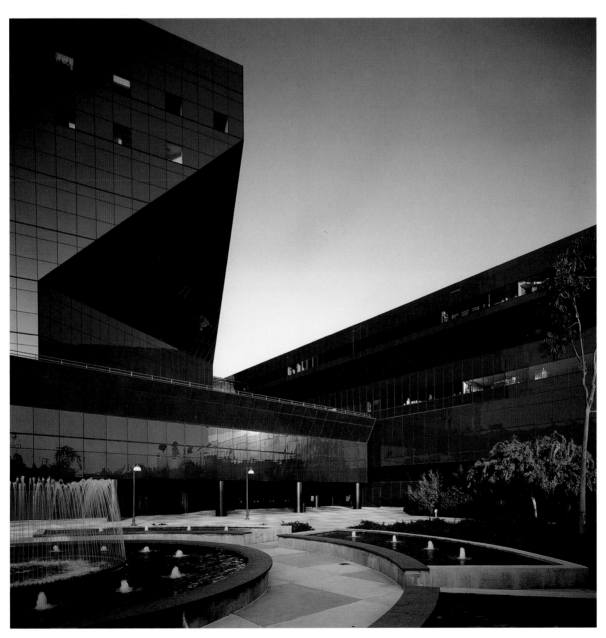

**PELLI, CESAR** Pacific Design Center, Phases I (1975) and II (1988), West Hollywood, Calif.

**PELLI, CESAR** Herring Hall (1984), Jesse J. Jones Graduate School of Administration, Rice University, Houston, Tex. *[Photo: Greg Hursley]*

After working for 10 years with the firm of Eero Saarinen in Bloomfield Hills, Mich., and Hamden, Conn., in 1964 Cesar Pelli joined Daniel, Mann, Johnson & Mendenhall (DMJM) in Los Angeles as director of design (1964–70). Notable projects credited to Pelli during this time were the Comsat Laboratories, Clarksburg, Md. (1969), the Kukui Gardens—832 low-cost units of housing near downtown Honolulu (1969), and the Worldway Postal Center at the Los Angeles Airport, in California (1970).

From 1968 to 1976, Pelli was partner for design at Gruen Associates. Selected projects of this period include the San Bernardino City Hall in California (1972), the Commons and Courthouse Center (1973), at Columbus, Ind., the Rainbow Center Mall and Winter Garden (1977) at Niagara Falls, N.Y., and the U.S. Embassy (1975) in Tokyo, Japan.

In January 1977, Pelli was appointed dean of the Yale University School of Architecture. Shortly after becoming dean, Cesar Pelli was named design architect for the

Museum of Modern Art Gallery Expansion and Residential Tower in New York City. That year, he formed his own firm with Diana Balmori and F. W. Clarke III. In 1984, Pelli resigned as dean at Yale because of the increasing demands of his practice.

**Work** The Museum of Modern Art Gallery Expansion and Residential Tower (1984), New York City, was needed to accommodate an increasing collection and public attendance not anticipated in the famous earlier buildings. The Residential Tower was planned to underwrite the operating costs of the museum. The new galleries are organized around the museum garden court. The tower is faced with a curtain wall utilizing eleven shades of ceramic glass.

Pacific Design Center, Phases I (1975), II (1988), and III (proposed) are landmark structures in Los Angeles, Calif. The original building houses offices and showrooms in a blue-glazed curtain wall building known locally as the "blue whale." How to design the additions was the problem presented, and Pelli's solution was to

**PELLI, CESAR** Cleveland Clinic Building (1984), Cleveland, Ohio.

design buildings of differing shape and color. The second phase is a square green building with truncated corners sitting on a blue base matching the earlier building. Phase III is proposed to be red.

The World Financial Center and World Financial Center Plaza (1987) were awarded on the basis of a competition. A mixed-use group of buildings include four office towers of 34 to 51 stories, two octagonal gateway buildings, a winter garden, and a 3½-acre landscaped plaza on the waterfront at the tip of Manhattan, New York City. The project is tied to the city by two overhead bridges spanning Water Street.

The Carnegie Hall Tower (1990), in New York City, was a study in accommodation to an urban site involving an addition to the landmark Carnegie Hall and an office tower. The street front was designed to be a good neighbor to Carnegie Hall, with the tower set back from 57th St. The design of the tower, although using modern structure, was carefully related to the earlier building through devices of color, scale of openings, and, to cap

the building, a decided change at the top of the tower, complete with a modern cantilevered cornice. The Carnegie Hall Tower has received the 1994 AIA Honor Award.

Canary Wharf Tower, Retail and Assembly Room Building, and Docklands Light Railway Station, London, England, is part of a major development of the old dock areas of London, and an international group of architects have been commissioned to design various buildings. The Cesar Pelli 50-story tower, part of the completed Phase I of Canary Wharf, is the dominant center of the complex, sheathed in stainless steel, with the lower buildings clad in limestone.

At Rice University in Houston, Tex., Cesar Pelli has designed Herring Hall for the Graduate School of Administration, fitting in the university's Beaux Arts campus plan. The use of patterned brick with limestone makes a lively addition to the university, as does the addition to the adjoining Lee Student Center, completed in 1986. Other university projects are the Boyer Center

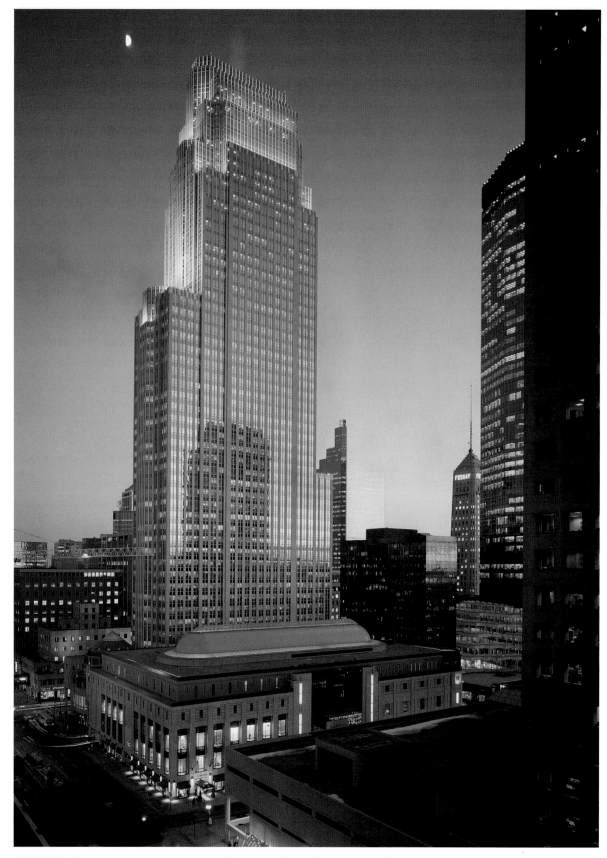

**PELLI, CESAR** Norwest Center (1989), Minneapolis, Minn. *[Photo: Christian M. Korab]*

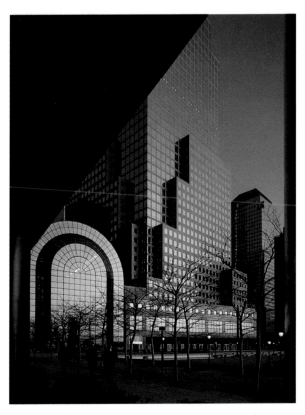

PELLI, CESAR World Financial Center (1987), New York, N.Y.

for Molecular Medicine at Yale University in New Haven, Conn. (1991), the Trinity College Academic Building (1990), in Hartford, Conn., and the Frances Lehman Lobe Art Center at Vassar College (1992), Poughkeepsie, N.Y.

Smaller projects have included exhibitions, a temporary arch for the Galveston Mardi Gras in 1986, a prototype house exhibited at the Leo Castelli Gallery in New York (1980), and the related house in Maryland (1989).

**Life** Cesar Pelli earned his Bachelor of Architecture degree from the University of Tucuman, Argentina, in 1950. He received a scholarship to and earned his master's degree from the University of Illinois in 1954. After graduation, he worked for Eero Saarinen and was project designer for such buildings as the TWA terminal at Kennedy Airport in New York City and the Samuel F. B. Morse and Ezra Stiles Colleges at Yale University in New Haven, Conn.

Diana Balmori studied architecture at the University of Tucuman, Argentina, and urban history at the University of California at Los Angeles, receiving a Ph.D. with highest honors in 1973. Ms. Balmori is principal for landscape and urban design projects and is principal of her own affiliated landscape and urban design firm, Balmori Associates.

F. W. Clark III was born in Houston, Tex., and received his Bachelor of Architecture degree from the University of Texas at Austin; on graduation he joined

Cesar Pelli at Gruen Associates. He joined the Pelli firm upon receipt of the commission for the Museum of Modern Art and the Residential Tower, moving to New York and then to New Haven. He was named principal in the firm in 1981. His responsibilities, in addition to project principal for many of the urban and institutional commissions, have increasingly been directed to management of the firm.

**Further Reading** Gandelsonas, Mario, and John Pastier, *Cesar Pelli: Buildings and Projects 1965–1990*, Rizzoli, New York, 1990.

**PHOTOGRAPHY, ARCHITECTURAL** Photography, as an interpretive and artistic medium of image making, has become an inseparable part of modern life in general and of the world of architecture in particular. Photography's role in the practice of architecture can be defined as follows: (1) working and communication tool during the design development stage; (2) valuable aid for promotion and marketing; (3) versatile form of art installed in buildings; and (4) major contribution to history, research, and education of the architect.

Skillful model photography during the design development can verify the validity of a proposed scheme for the designer as well as sell it to the client. Eero Saarinen's office pioneered such a process. The study of

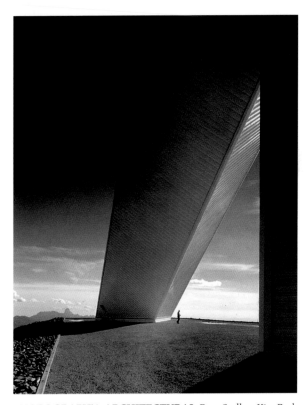

**PHOTOGRAPHY, ARCHITECTURAL** Ezra Stoller: Kitt Peak Solar Telescope, Kitt Peak, Ariz. [*Architects: Skidmore, Owings and Merrill*]

479

**PHOTOGRAPHY, ARCHITECTURAL** The camera as a tool for design development. Model photography during the study of the TWA terminal at Kennedy Airport by Eero Saarinen (1957). This image was created from half a study model such as seen in the accompanying image with the help of a mirror, cutout people, smoke, and moderate airbrushing.

the TWA terminal for the Kennedy Airport presented complex problems of form and space. Models were built expressly to undergo scrutiny by the camera, images were taken to duplicate the condition of being there, and slide shows thereof helped in the decision making both for the architect and the client. This method was developed to such a degree that renderings were replaced by the higher credibility of photographs. This intensive use of photography has been carried to new heights by the office of Roche/Dinkeloo, using in-house photographers and designers with both camera and model-building skills. In fact an elaborate model shop was built mostly to stage settings for photography.

The camera in the hand of the architect has other practical ends. It can record progress on the construction site, Polaroid images complement notes with visuals, and some architects are apt to undertake study shots to convey their suggested views to the professional hired for the finished photography.

Sketching, the traditional way to record observations and travel impressions, has been largely replaced by the

camera, the result of which can be made into slide shows for didactic or marketing purposes.

**PHOTOGRAPHY, ARCHITECTURAL** TWA terminal study model (1957). Eero Saarinen in company of Kevin Roche and Cesar Pelli.

**PHOTOGRAPHY, ARCHITECTURAL** Model photography with computer imaging. First Bank Place, Minneapolis, Minn. *[Architect: Pei Cobb Freed & Partners].* The lighting of the model (tallest building at right) was to match that of the existing skyline photograph and dubbed in with imaging technology. *[Photo: Harr, Hedrich-Blessing]*

Video camera work, though not strictly photography, can yield interesting results if used for similar purposes as a still camera.

Photography plays an important role when the building is finished. But even before, during the construction period a camera can help in advance publicity with sophisticated model photography. The combination of high-precision models and computer-imaging capabilities can now produce a truly convincing picture of the future building, resulting in an excellent marketing tool. An in-depth photographic coverage has a wide range of promotional uses for both the architect and the owner, in publications, magazines, books, exhibits, and to solicit new work. Specialized photography is also used by advertisers for building products and services, including the hotel industry and health-care, educational, and similar institutions.

Finally, photography finds its way to being displayed in buildings as permanent art in traditional framed form or as murals, often converted into lasting materials, etched in metals, glass, or plastics.

There is also a photographer of a certain kind, sometimes a trained architect or art historian whose pictures are inspired by various aspects of architecture. These photographers may deal, dubbed often by their own writing, with historic, vernacular, sociological, urban, or environmental subjects, and their chosen form of

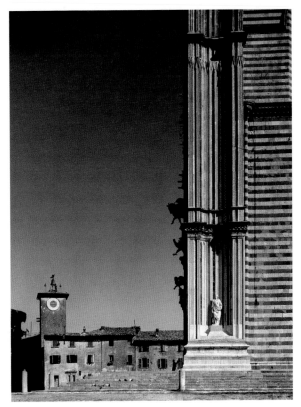

**PHOTOGRAPHY, ARCHITECTURAL** Orvieto Cathedral (1310), Orvieto, Italy. *[Photo: G. E. Kidder Smith]*

481

expression may be books, exhibits, lectures, or activist involvements. Some of the currently active such photographers are: G. E. Kidder-Smith, Norman Carver, Jr., Steven Brooke, Cervin Robinson, Evelyn Hofer, David Plowden, Balthazar Korab, and others.

Most of the routine photography nowadays is done in color, putting a greater technical and budgetary burden on the photographer as well as the client. Still, the merits of black-and-white work are well recognized. An aesthetic and ethical debate dealing with the photography of architecture is a frequent editorial subject, ranging from such simple questions as the use of people in pictures to the more involved ones as the critical responsibility of the photographer when interpreting a building.

"Architecture has become inseparable from the photography of it. We know most buildings through the photography that appears in books and magazines. And even when we visit noted buildings, we can't help being affected by the photos we have seen of them. As in so many other areas of our social and political life, images seem more real than the things themselves. Buildings have begun to merge with their likenesses." Thus begins an in-depth article by Thomas Fisher in the August 1990 issue of *Progressive Architecture* about the state of the art and craft of photography of architecture.

"One could even argue that Modern and post-Modern architecture, for all of their differences, succeeded in part because of their memorable imagery, powerfully conveyed on the printed page. What we think of as architectural has become what we see as photogenic" is the highly quotable conclusion of Fisher in the same article.

**Technique** Due to the complexity of the subject one should refer the interested reader to the large number of publications dealing with the topic. Suffice it to say here that the development today, in contrast with the cumbersome 8-in by 10-in format used in the earlier days, tends toward favoring 4 by 5 view cameras. However, the excellent quality of 35mm equipment with a wide choice of lenses, including the shifting, parallel correcting ones, and the high-resolution and color quality of the films on

**PHOTOGRAPHY, ARCHITECTURAL** Julius Shulman: Kaufmann House (1946), Palm Springs, Calif. *[Architect: Richard Neutra]*

**PHOTOGRAPHY, ARCHITECTURAL** Ken Hedrich: Chrysler Building (1933), Century of Progress, Chicago, Ill.
*[Architect: Holabird & Root (Photo: courtesy of Chicago Historical Society, Hedrich-Blessing collection)]*

the market, make this format suitable for most editorial usages. Note that a large percentage of the illustrations in this volume were produced from 35mm originals.

The main technical problem today is color fidelity, hard to achieve due to the complexity of mixed-light sources. A sound experience and skill is needed to deal with the color problem. An arsenal of lights, filters, gels, screens, expert assistance, a full command of light sources on site, not to mention the sun and the moon and infinite patience is required to accomplish a quality expected by the ever-more-demanding picture editors.

**History** A static subject such as the outbuildings of Nicephore Niepce's backyard in France lent itself well to an eight-hour exposure needed for the first photograph ever taken in 1826. All through the development of photography, architecture remained a favorite subject to many such as Eugene Atget (France), Pompeo Pozzi (Italy), August Sander (Germany), Frederick Evans (Great Britain), Berenice Abbott (U.S.A), and more. It was, however, in America that the high specialty with a strong pictorial approach was developed by Ken and Bill Hedrich from Chicago, Ezra Stoller from New York, and Julius Shulman from Los Angeles just to mention the most important early practitioners. They were followed by an ever increasing number of newcomers spawned by the building boom of the recent years and a great popularity of the study of photography among the young. Starting from the 1960s one can experience a gradual lib-

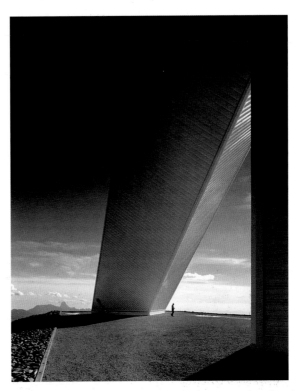

**PHOTOGRAPHY, ARCHITECTURAL** Arthur Drexler selected this photograph of the Renaissance Center in Detroit in a moody light as the theme image for his 1979 exhibition "Transformations in Modern Architecture" at the Museum of Modern Art in New York. *[Photo: Timothy Hursley/Korab Ltd.]*

**PHOTOGRAPHY, ARCHITECTURAL** Christian M. Korab: "Christian M. Korab's depiction of Cesar Pelli's Norwest Center recalls the Stieglitz tradition." *[Fisher, Thomas, "Image Building," Progressive Architecture, August 1990.]*

eration from the stylized legacy of the masters of the 8 by 10 format, tending toward an editorial flexibility and diversity made easier by the improvements of photo technology in any of the smaller film sizes. At the same time, from the other side of the Pacific, Yukio Futagawa proceeded with the characteristic industry of the Japanese to catch up with the Americans and to cover the architecture of the whole world.

**Related Articles** PRACTICE OF ARCHITECTURE; RENDERING.

**Further Reading** Molitor, Joseph W.: *Architectural Photography*, John Wiley, New York, 1976; Robinson, Cervin, and Joel Herschman: *Architecture Transformed*, MIT Press, Cambridge, Mass., 1987; Shulman, Julius: *The Photography of Architecture and Design*, Whitney, New York, 1977.

**PLANNING, CITY** The art and science of the design, planning, and construction of cities and parts of cities; also called "town" or "urban" planning. City planning principles can also be extended to include areas larger than cities, as in regional planning. Persons who practice city planning are often called city planners or urban or town planners, though some prefer to be called simply planners.

**Modern Planning** City planning is an ancient calling, but as practiced today, it is a product of the 20th century. Early in the century, planners were mostly privately sponsored, but this changed rapidly to sponsorship by local, municipal, or country governments. Early in the century, planners were mostly concerned with the major visual elements of cities, parks, boulevards, civic centers, and parkways. Today planners are concerned with the total fabric of cities, not only the physical aspects, now seen in three dimensions rather than two as before, but the economic, social, legal, and human aspects. Previously, planners devoted much attention to streets and squares, public buildings, docks and harbors, and railroads. Today they are still concerned with these factors but also with transportation of all kinds; buildings of all kinds, including housing; utility distribution; and all other aspects of urban life.

**Practitioners** In the past, most planning was performed by architects, engineers, and landscape architects. Today many planners come from those professions, but there are also planners trained as economists, sociologists, geographers, and so on, reflecting the attention given to factors other than the physical planning of urban areas.

**Planning Commissions** Planning was given a big boost with the creation of planning commissions in urban areas during the first part of the 20th century. Two of the first were those of Hartford, Conn., started in 1907, and Chicago, founded in 1909. The idea spread to other communities all over the United States. The commissions were not very effective, because the laws affecting planning were loosely constructed or nonexistent. Starting in 1916, when New York City adopted the first zoning law in the United States, regulations for land use and building heights, bulking, and uses gave planners the tools with which to enforce their plans.

**Work Areas** The work of planners may be divided into five major areas: preparing master plans, ordinances and regulations, and improvement programs for urban areas; preparing regional master plans for larger areas; planning of portions of urban areas, such as shopping centers, neighborhoods, and so on; planning for urban renewal, slum clearance and redeveloping older areas; and planning new towns.

To accomplish this work, planners generally follow a process that includes development of long-range goals and objectives; study and analysis of existing conditions, physical, economic, and social; study and analysis of the problems; preparation of master plans covering aspects such as land use, transportation, buildings, and other facilities; and putting the master plans into effect, with the aid of zoning and subdivision regulations, codes, ordinances, and other means.

**PLANNING, CITY** Original plan of Washington, D.C. (1791). *[Planner: Maj. Pierre Charles L'Enfant]*

Most planners today work for planning commissions that are government agencies, mostly at the municipal level. Others practice as consultants who perform services for municipalities which do not have their own planning staffs or wish to have special studies made. Planners make studies of many kinds, including projections of future employment patterns; population growth; movement of people, industries, and businesses into and out of areas; needs for transportation and utilities; and so on. They then translate these studies into reports and master plans that define the future needs and character of cities and demonstrate how the needs can be met and the character fulfilled in the best manner. They also make studies of portions of cities or specific problems and translate these into reports and plans to meet the needs or problems. Planners also are concerned with zoning and building codes, and with development and redevelopment that take place in cities. Regional planners are concerned with the same subjects as city planners, but perform their work for whole regions rather than single cities.

Planning offers careers to many types of people, since it involves social and economic planning, and the physical planning of cities, in a manner similar to the work of architects, landscape architects, and engineers. A great variety of functions are performed by planners, some by people who are essentially creative, others by those who are primarily studious, and still others by those who are active by nature. All must be interested in urban life and in the process of improving urban life and its setting, the cities.

**Education** Preparation for planning may be acquired in a number of ways. Many architects, landscape architects, and engineers, in particular civil engineers, ultimately find their true careers in planning. All these professionals take some related courses in college. More than 30 universities offer degrees in planning in the United States. Some are attached to architectural schools; others are not. Many are graduate schools, which require an undergraduate degree in some related field before a student may be accepted. A few schools allow architec-

**PLANNING, CITY** The new town of Reston Master Plan (amended 1987), Reston, Va.

**PLANNING, CITY** Lake Anne (1965), Reston, Va. *[Architects: Conklin and Rossant, and others]*

tural students to specialize in planning, after their first few years of general architectural training.

**History** Humans founded urban settlements during prehistoric times. Although the first of such settlements have not been accurately dated, it is known that by the beginning of the Neolithic period, about the 80th century B.C., some humans left the nomadic life and had begun to settle in villages in Mesopotamia, Egypt, and other Middle East areas. Some of the villages grew into cities. These early villages and cities were located on easily defended sites.

During the Neolithic period, large cities were developed, not only in the Middle East but in India and China. Two of the greatest, Nineveh and Babylon, are believed to have been founded in early Neolithic times, to have flourished about the 20th century B.C., and to have been destroyed sometime during the 7th century B.C.

Most early cities were not planned, in the meaning of today. They were founded in locations where natural resources, such as minerals, existed, near trade routes or water bodies, or near populated rural areas, which were food sources. Then these cities developed without planning around temples and forts. Some early cities were planned, mostly with public areas at their centers and with two main streets, one running north and south and the other east and west. Other streets divid-

ed the cities into what has come to be called a gridiron or grid plan, in which the blocks of the city form squares or rectangles bounded by streets on all four sides. The gridiron plan was used for many thousands of years and can still be seen in most American cities. An early gridiron-plan city, still in existence, is Alexandria, Egypt, founded about 332 B.C. by Alexander the Great (356–323 B.C.).

The Romans founded cities in many conquered places. Some cities, not including Rome which just developed naturally and haphazardly, had grid plans. Typical examples are Gloucester and Lincoln, England; Florence and Turin, Italy; Cologne, Germany; and Barcelona, Spain.

During the Middle Ages, cities declined somewhat and their place was taken to some extent by monasteries and castles. The cities that existed grew in an unplanned manner, mostly with narrow, crooked streets, behind protective walls. Starting about the 11th century in Italy and spreading to the rest of Europe later, a resurgence took place in cities. Many new ones were built. Most had plans based on the grid, unlike such older cities as Paris and London. Some of the new ones were *bastide*, or fortress, towns. They were laid out with a regular pattern of streets and blocks, gridiron fashion. Such towns were built in many places in Europe. Monpazier, France,

**PLANNING, CITY** Phase I, Reston Town Center (1990), Reston, Va. *[Architects: RTKL Associates, Inc.; landscape architects: Sasaki Assoc.]*

founded in the 13th century, typifies their planning: a walled and fortified town with blocks approximately 125 ft wide by 150, 250, and 300 ft long, separated by major streets 24 ft and minor ones 16 ft wide. Through the blocks ran alleys about 6 ft wide. Near the center was a market square surrounded by arcades, with the nearby church the major architectural feature.

During the Renaissance, planning of towns and cities followed the principles of the *bastides* for a time. But the Renaissance was also a time of great theorizing about city planning as well as architecture. Some important books dealing with the subject were written by the Italian architects Leon Battista Alberti (1404–72) and Andrea Palladio (1518–80), and the philosophers, Italian Tommaso Campanella (1568–1639) and the Englishmen, Sir Francis Bacon (1561–1626) and Sir Thomas More (1478–1535).

Many projects for new towns and for replanning of older ones were developed during the Renaissance. Most of these projects were never executed, but some notable examples that were built include partly replanned open-space areas, such as the great plazas in Italy at San Marco, Venice; the Campidoglio by Michelangelo Buonarroti (1475–1564), and San Pietro by Giovanni Lorenzo Bernini (1598–1680), both in Rome. Pope

Sixtus V (1521–90), with the help of architect Domenico Fontana (1543–1607), replanned a portion of Rome.

Later great plans for European cities include that of Sir Christopher Wren (1632–1723) for rebuilding London after the Great Fire of 1666. This plan, with radial major streets, was never adopted nor were those prepared by two nonarchitects, John Evelyn (1620–1706), a minor government official and writer, and Robert Hooke (1635–1703), philosopher and scientist. Other important city plans of the era were those for Bath, England, by architects John Wood, Sr. (1704–54) and his son John Wood (1728–81), and the replanning of portions of Paris by Baron Georges Eugéne Haussmann (1809–91).

Others who deeply affected city planning were the Englishmen, Sir Patrick Geddes (1854–1932), planner and sociologist, who worked for slum clearance through planning, and Sir Ebenezer Howard (1850–1928), who originated the concept of the modern garden city, an urban area surrounded by a rural one. The first garden city, Letchworth, England, was begun in 1903. Laws enabling cities to carry out planning were passed in Europe in the second half of the 19th century, in Italy in 1865, and in England in 1875.

**American Development** Planning in colonial America began with the founding of St. Augustine, Fla., in 1565 by the Spanish. This city was given a plan, more or less on the grid pattern, but quite irregular. Later Spanish towns followed the gridiron plan more strictly, as the plan for San Antonio, Tex., founded about 1730 as the villa of San Fernando de Bexar; Pensacola, Fla., first settled in 1559, destroyed and rebuilt several times since; and Santa Fe, N. Mex., founded in 1609. French settlements in what eventually became the United States started much later, Detroit, Mich., in 1701; New Orleans, La., in 1721; Mobile, Ala., in 1702; and St. Louis, Mo., in 1764, all with grid plans.

The earliest English colonies in America had plans that were somewhat similar to the *bastides,* fortified cities of the Middle Ages in Europe, but much more primitive. Jamestown, Va., founded in 1607, is thought to have originally had a stockade of logs around a triangular plan, within which the buildings were located. The first permanent New England settlement, at Plymouth, Mass., founded in 1620, is thought to have originally had two rows of houses with a street separating them, all surrounded by a stockade. St. Mary's, Md., founded in 1633, is thought to have had meandering streets that followed Indian trails. A good early plan was that of New Haven, Conn., in 1638, a square plan with nine large squares, the central one being referred to as the town common.

Both Virginia and Maryland passed new town acts in the 17th century, and these resulted in policies for planned towns in these states. Many new towns were planned as a result of these acts and a number were established, mostly utilizing grid plans. Most of the new towns were planned by administrators, who were amateur planners, rather than by architects or others who practiced planning. Some of the most important were Norfolk (1682) and Richmond (1737), Va., and Baltimore (1729), Md., all with grid plans; and Annapolis (1694), Md., planned by Sir Francis Nicholson (1655–1728), with major streets radiating from the center rather than on a grid plan. Later, Nicholson also planned Williamsburg (1699), Va., reverting to the grid plan. Nicholson had an interesting career, as the governor at various times of Virginia, Maryland, South Carolina, and Nova Scotia, and lieutenant governor of New England.

In New England, most early towns had grid plans that were modified to fit the topography and other natural features and to accommodate farms nearby. New England town plans often had central open spaces, called greens or commons, where townspeople could congregate and around which meeting houses and other public buildings were often built. Before 1635, at least 20 towns had been established in what is now Massachusetts, including Salem, founded in 1626, and Boston, in 1630. Many others soon followed in Massachusetts and in the other New England states. Towns were built in the other colonies, beginning in the 17th and continuing into the

18th century. New Amsterdam, which became New York City, was founded in 1624. Philadelphia, founded in 1682, was planned by William Penn (1644–1718), with the aid of a surveyor, on a grid system with five great squares reserved for parks. Another grid town plan was that for Savannah, Ga., founded in 1733 by James Edward Oglethorpe (1696–1785).

None of these early significant plans were designed by architects, engineers, or planners, who had formal training in the subject or practiced any of the design professions. They were able administrators who had the knowledge, ability, and foresight to envision what cities of the time should be like and the power to see their plans realized. This was a situation that lasted for a long time in the United States, as settlers spread westward and built new towns in the territories that eventually became states.

The most striking attempt to plan a new town of the time was that for what eventually became the city of Washington, D.C., the nation's capital. President George Washington (1732–99) chose a French engineer, who

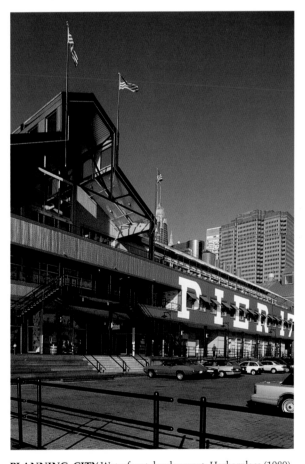

**PLANNING, CITY** Waterfront development, Harborplace (1980), Baltimore, Md. *[Architects: Ben Thompson and Assoc.].* Related development includes World Trade Tower (1977) *[Architect: I. M. Pei],* National Aquarium (1981) *[Architects: Cambridge Seven]*

had served as an engineering officer in the Continental Army, Pierre Charles L'Enfant (1754–1825), to design the plan in 1791. L'Enfant made the plans for the city, the results of which are so apparent today. In 1792 L'Enfant was dismissed after a series of disputes about the work. He had designed a magnificent plan, with locations for the most important government buildings, from which radiated broad avenues. Great open spaces and vistas were envisioned, the greatest of them being the mall which stretched from the Capitol building, or Federal House as it was then called, to a great monument at the other end behind the White House, or President's House as it was called. L'Enfant's original map was mislaid, and the surveyor of the capital city, Andrew Ellicott (1754–1820), redrew it from memory, not exactly as L'Enfant had laid it out, but close.

Thus the city was actually laid out according to the map of Ellicott and the work continued later according to a revised plan of 1797. For the next 100 years, development continued in the city in a haphazard manner, with few planning and no zoning controls. By 1900, L'Enfant's envisioned mall had turned into a shambles of disorganized planting, railroad tracks, and a railroad station. In 1900 a new plan was devised under the leadership of architects Daniel Hudson Burnham (1846–1912) and Charles Follen McKim (1847–1909), landscape architect Frederick Law Olmsted (1822–1903), and sculptor Augustus Saint-Gaudens (1848–1907). From that time, the city of Washington has been developed following this plan and the later work of a great many other talented architects and planners on various commissions.

In the years following the planning of Washington, many new towns were planned and new plans made for older cities. Much of this work was by architects and engineers, who had an interest in planning. Most of the plans were of the gridiron type.

Thomas Jefferson (1743–1826) had long been interested in city planning and had proposed plans for both Washington and Richmond, Va., that were never used. Early in the 19th century, Jefferson proposed a radically new type of plan, which came to be called the "checkerboard plan." It consisted of a gridiron pattern with blocks for buildings alternating with open squares in both directions. This was a fresh concept and it was put into practice in the town of Jeffersonville, Ind., in 1802, but within 15 years a decision was made to sell lots in the open squares, and the original concept of the plan was destroyed. The same thing happened in Jackson, Miss., after its founding in 1822, and the checkerboard plan was never used again, in spite of its seeming merits.

During much of the 19th century, cities became overcrowded, land speculation reached new heights, and little was done in the way of planning. An exception was the significant work of Frederick Law Olmsted and his partner Calvert Vaux (1824–95) in the planning of suburbs and towns, which followed the natural contours and other features of the land on which they were built. Late in the century, attention once again turned to good planning, and its leading exponent was the architect Daniel Hudson Burnham.

Starting with the classic Beaux Arts eclecticism of the World's Columbian Exposition in Chicago in 1893, Burnham, who had been chief consulting architect of the fair, proposed for Chicago and other cities new designs based on those of the fair. Burnham's proposals and those like them later came to be known as the City Beautiful Movement. As an attempt to revamp modern city plans to something approximating those of older, great European cities with their wide boulevards and impressive public buildings, the movement made a great stir for some years and then disappeared under the onslaught of more progressive city planning principles.

Burnham designed inventive plans for many cities, including the one for Chicago. His theories have been superseded, not because of any inherent flaw in the ideas but because of the increasing desire and need to make cities more efficient, a state often, but not always, achieved by making them less beautiful. More importantly, Burnham had established city planning as an essential part of American life, a place it has occupied ever since.

Speaking at the first international meeting of planners held in 1910 by the Royal Institute of British Architects, Burnham made it plain that planning was here to stay. The first national conference on planning in America had been held in Washington the year before. In 1917, five years after Burnham's death, the American City Planning Institute, composed mainly of architects, engineers, and landscape architects, was organized and it eventually became the present-day American Institute of Planners. A few years later, the first specialized college courses were established at Harvard University, Cambridge, Mass. Since then, the profession of planning has grown rapidly to the point where there is scarcely a government body in the United States on any level that does not have a planning commission, and many have professional planners on staff.

The work of planning goes on. Some of the most significant work of the 20th century was that of Clarence S. Stein (1882–1975) and Henry Wright (1878–1936), both planners and architects. Drawing on the garden city theories of Ebenezer Howard and his predecessors, Stein and Wright planned important new towns such as Radburn, N.J., and Chatham Village, Pittsburgh, both built in the 1930s. Stein went on to plan other projects that came to be called "greenbelt" cities, taking the garden city ideas to a new level of achievement. During the second half of the 20th century, a number of new towns have been built, including Columbia, Md., and Reston, Va.

Other noted planners of the 20th century include Albert Mayer (1897–1981), Edmund Norton Bacon

(1910– ), Christopher Tunnard (1910–73), Kevin Lynch (1918–84), and Ian McHarg (1920– ). Of great influence on the planning of cities has been the writing and philosophy of Lewis Mumford (1895–1990).

**Related Articles** BUILDING CODES AND STANDARDS; BURNHAM AND ROOT; CAPITAL, UNITED STATES; ENGINEERING; HOUSING; JEFFERSON, THOMAS; LANDSCAPE ARCHITECTURE; OLMSTED, FREDERICK LAW; PARK; ROAD AND TRAFFIC DESIGN; STEIN, CLARENCE S.; SURVEYING.

**Further Reading** Reps, John W.: *The Making of Urban America: A History of City Planning in the United States*, Princeton University Press, Princeton, N.J., 1991; Whittick, A.: *Encyclopedia of Urban Planning*, McGraw-Hill, New York, 1974, reprinted by Krieger, Melbourne, Fla.; Whyte, William H.: *City: Rediscovering the Center*, Doubleday, New York, 1988.

**Periodicals** *American City*, Pittsfield, Mass. 01201; *Nation's Cities*, 1612 K St., N.W., Washington, D.C. 20006.

**Sources of Additional Information** American Institute of Planners, 917 15th St., N.W., Washington, D.C. 20004; American Planning Assoc., Suite 704, 1776 Massachusetts Ave., Washington, D.C. 20036.

**PLASTICS** In the last 30 years, plastics have become a major component of buildings, including a long list of products and applications. Based on raw materials such as petroleum, natural gas, coal, and cellulose, plastics are typical of the scientific contribution to contemporary life. This article is introductory in nature and is designed to indicate the broad scope of the plastics industry. Fortunately, the field of manufactured plastics may be divided into two major groupings, those which are thermosets and those which are thermoplastics. Thermoplastics can be softened and hardened repeatedly by heating and cooling, and result in rigid products. Thermosets are created by heating only once to complete their molecular structure. The response to temperature and heat determines which plastics are appropriate for a given use in building.

**Uses** For building, nonstructural uses of plastics include wall and partition coverings, windows, skylights, doors, thermal insulation, moisture barriers, flooring, gutters and downspouts, hardware, cabinetwork, furniture and moldings, masonry surfaces, piping and plumbing fixtures, ducts, lighting fixtures, electrical fittings, and solar energy collectors. Structural or semistructural uses include shells, sandwiches, building panels, translucent panels, tanks, structural shapes, tension and air-supported structures. Other uses include adhesives, coatings, sealants, and gaskets.

**Additives** The property of plastics can be modified by the use of additives. Plasticizers are used to make thermoplastics flexible and may contribute to the resistance of a product to weather or fire. Fillers may be used

to aid in molding and in other desirable attributes, as well as reducing the cost of a product. Since many plastics are clear or translucent, dyes may be used to provide color. Some phenolic plastics may be dark. Stabilizers are used to increase the ability of plastics such as polyethylenes to resist sunlight or other weathering and ultraviolet rays. All additives must be selected for compatibility with the base plastic resin.

**Thermoplastics** The large group of thermoplastics has many uses in buildings. This listing only suggests the wide application of thermoplastics, and the reader is referred to the additional reading references for more information.

ABS (acrylonitrile-butadiene-styrene) is used for pipes and fittings, especially drain, waste, and vent. Other uses include refrigerator door liners and tanks, faucets, shower heads, and bathtubs and surrounds.

Acetal is used for plumbing exposed to moderate heat, including outdoor exposure.

Acrylic (PMMA) plastics are a group, but polymethyl methacrylate (PMMA) is the most used for glazing, lighting fixtures, and decorative items. Acrylic skylights are vacuum formed. Other uses include plumbing trim, spandrels, and illuminated signs. Thin films and sheets provide protective overlays for metal and other materials.

Cellulosics are made from processed natural materials such as wood pulp or cotton. Rayon is a cellulose product as is cellophane. Cellulose nitrate is used for lacquers and tool handles, although this material is flammable. Cellulose-acetate-butyrate is used for skylights, curtain walls, small structures such as bus shelters, and for outdoor signs.

Fluoroplastics are resistant to corrosion and may be used to line pipes subject to corrosive materials. One compound is used for bearing pads under trusses and others for strong industrial finishes and for glazing solar collectors.

Polyamides (nylon) is a group of resins which are used for hardware parts, handles of power tools, or casters for furniture.

Polybutylene is used for pipes for water as a part of a plumbing system and piping for solar collectors.

Polycarbonates are used for glazing, including laminates for security glass, and for lighting fixtures and decorative items.

Polyethylene is used for vapor barriers and under concrete slabs. Piping is used for irrigation systems and for plumbing.

Polyethylene-based resins are used for electrical items such as boxes for outlets, fuseboxes, and a variant may be used in pumps and plumbing.

Polypropylene is used in various forms, including piping, packaging, and a foam version for molded seats and panels.

Polystyrene's main use is for thermal insulation in a foamed product.

Poly(vinyl chloride) (PVC) and variants are the most commonly used plastic in building. It is used for latex paints, adhesives, and other coatings. Variants include piping, siding, window frames and sash, gutters and downspouts, and interior trim. Interior uses include tile, wall coverings, upholstery, and refrigerator parts.

Styrene-acrylonitrile (SAN) is a tough and dent resistant group of plastics, used for hardware knobs and housewares.

**Thermosets** Epoxies are brittle by nature but may be reinforced with glass fibers or other reinforcement. The most common uses are for reinforced plastics, laminates, flooring such as terrazzo, joint fillers or adhesives used with metals, masonry, and concrete. Epoxies are widely used for protective coatings.

Melamine Formaldehyde (MF) and Urea Formaldehyde (UF) are used for plastic laminates and in foam products for thermal insulation and for adhesives in the manufacture of plywood and particle board.

Phenolics, Phenol-formaldehyde (PF), was one of the earliest groups of plastics used in building. It is used for the backup sheet for plastic laminates and for waterproof adhesives for plywood and particle board. Phenolics are the binders for glass and mineral-fiber insulation. In a foam version, phenolics are used for thermal insulation.

Unsaturated polyesters are low in cost and are widely used instead of epoxies. Applications include building fascias, bathroom components, wall liners, structural shapes, molded forms, translucent panels, pipe, tanks, hoods, ducts, and solar collectors.

Polyurethanes are often used as foams for insulation boards, coatings, pipes, and pipe linings. Flexible foams are used for upholstery, mattresses, and automobile seating.

Silicone (SI) is strong and able to withstand high temperatures and weathering. In buildings, silicones are used for sealants.

**Fabrication** Plastics may be made into many forms by compression molding, injection molding, transfer molding, extrusion, and blow molding for hollow forms such as bottles.

Films and sheet are made by such processes as calendering (between rollers), casting and extrusion, or drawing or blowing where an extruded tube is increased in diameter by blowing, and then cooled, cut, and flattened.

Foams are created by extrusion, bead expansion, and liquid foaming. Polystyrene with a gas-foaming additive may be extruded through a hot die. This activates the foaming additive, resulting in large forms which are then cut to the desired dimension and shape. Beads or pellets containing gas-foaming additives may be heated in a mold or cavity, where they expand to fill the cavity and weld to each other to produce a foam slab which can be cut as desired. Liquid foaming is used for such plastics as polyurethane, which may be foamed and poured into a cavity such as a stud space. The gas formed expands the plastic to fill the space while hardening. Syntactic foams and multifoams include preformed bubbles of glass, ceramic, or plastic in a plastic resin matrix. Reinforced foams are made using additives such as glass fiber, carbon black, and metals which change the character of the foam to increase its mechanical properties, but at a cost. Structural foams are poured into a mold which allows the foam to expand and to form a solid surface against the mold.

**Composite Plastics** Composites may be grouped by the addition of fibers, particularly glass fiber; laminates incorporating printed paper, fabric, or metals and sandwiches where two facings are bonded to a foamed plastic core; or particulates such as polymers used as an additive to concrete, even substituting for portland cement in such items as bridge paving, building panels, and to resurface old materials such as concrete floors, roads.

**Behavior** Properties of plastics which require consideration include strength, stiffness, toughness and hardness, thermal expansion and contraction, thermal conductivity, surface temperatures, light transmission, permeability by water, temperature dependence, composite properties, durability, both interior and exterior. Understanding the behavior of plastics allows the selection and use of appropriate materials. Problems occur with inappropriate uses, and the use of plastics in building is controlled by building codes. Some foamed-in-place insulations have been banned in some localities because of gases released during curing.

One of the most serious aspects is the behavior of plastics in fires. Plastics by nature are combustible. There has been extensive study of flame spread and smoke development for various plastics. Additives include flame retardants, but these may increase smoke. Protective coatings may be used to delay ignition and to reduce flame spread.

**Further Reading** *Modern Plastics Encyclopedia*, McGraw-Hill, New York, 1976–77; Wilkes, Joseph A., and Robert T. Packard, eds.: *Encyclopedia of Architecture— Design, Engineering and Construction*, 5 vols., s.v. "phenolic resins," "plastic laminates," "plastics," "plastics, ABS," "polyamides (nylon)," "polyesters," "sealants," John Wiley, New York, 1989.

**PLUMBING** A system in a building consisting of piping, fixtures, appliances, and other parts through which natural and manufactured gas and hot and cold water are supplied, and through which the wastes of these systems are removed. Until the 19th century, plumbing systems were either very simple or nonexistent in buildings.

Today such systems are considered necessities and may be quite complex. Plumbing systems are now major elements of architecture and among the most expensive systems in buildings.

Plumbing, generally taken to mean systems in and closely related to buildings, primarily consists of the piping and other devices required to supply gas and water, the appliances and fixtures in which these substances are used, and the waste disposal system. Supply systems conduct water to kitchens for cooking, drinking, and dishwashing; to laundry rooms for clothes washing; to bathrooms for bathing, washing, and use in toilets, or water closets; to drinking fountains; to hose outlets for outdoor use; and to many other kinds of outlets, fixtures, or appliances. A very important supply problem is water for fire fighting and for fire-sprinkler systems. (See the article entitled fire protection.)

**Central Water Systems** Water is generally supplied to buildings in cities and towns from central water systems usually operated by municipalities. The runoff from precipitation drains into streams, rivers, and lakes or soaks into the ground. Water is drawn directly from rivers and lakes or from reservoirs that are like artificial lakes constructed for water storage. Most large cities obtain their water supply from such sources. Many smaller cities and towns, and some of the larger ones, obtain their supplies from wells drilled to tap underground water sources. Water obtained from any of the sources is often stored in water tanks, or towers, as well as in reservoirs.

While some water obtained form these sources is pure enough for human use, most of it must be treated in settling tanks, with filters and chemicals. After treatment, the water is pumped into the main system that supplies buildings and other users. At building sites, water ordinarily flows through meters which measure quantities for which building owners and users then pay. In rural areas, central water systems are not ordinarily available. Buildings in such areas usually rely on private water systems, consisting of wells equipped with pumps and storage tanks. Shallow wells, less than 25 ft deep, may be used where the level of water in the ground, or water table, is high. Where greater depths are needed, deep wells are required. Shallow wells are often dug, while deep wells are usually drilled. For impure water obtained from wells, private systems for chlorination, or chlorinators, are available. Systems are also available for changing hard water to soft (water softeners), and for reducing the acidity of water.

**Sewage Systems** Waste disposal or sewage systems outside buildings in cities and towns are usually municipally operated. From the buildings, sewage and waste flows into collecting systems which carry them to plants removing and treating solids to form sludge, which may be further treated and dried for use in fertilizers. The liquid materials are filtered and treated with chemicals to form a liquid, called effluent, which is safe and can be discharged. In rural areas, private sewage disposal systems are required. Today there are two main types: grease-trap and drain-field systems, and septic tanks and drain-field systems. Grease-trap systems are used mostly for wastes that contain grease, such as that from kitchen sinks and dishwashers. In the trap, grease remains while the effluent flows into the field system of clay tile or other types of piping to be discharged into the ground. In a septic tank, bacteria act upon sewage changing it into harmless solids that remain in the tank, gases which escape, and effluent that flows into the ground through drain fields. In both grease traps and septic tanks, solids must be periodically removed.

In order for a private sewage disposal system to be installed, health and other codes require that the ground be capable of absorbing the effluent that will be discharged into it. This is often determined by a percolation, or perc, test, in which a hole of a specified diameter and depth is made in the ground, water poured into it, and the distance it drops in 30 min recorded. If the water drops enough within the allowable time, a septic system will be allowed; if not, its use will not be permitted. Much of the rural land in the United States cannot pass percolation tests because of its clay composition, high water tables, and other reasons. Therefore buildings cannot be constructed in many rural areas unless patented private sewage disposers are employed. Several types are available, but have not been widely accepted under various health and other codes. In some localities soil survey maps and test borings are used, sometimes in conjunction with perc tests, for the determination of soil suitability for septic systems.

Rural water and sewage systems, as well as other types, must be kept separate at all times. Until the 19th century, the fact that the relationship of water supply to sewage contributed to the spread of disease was unknown. For rural systems, certain code and good practice requirements specify the distance that must be maintained between wells and septic systems. In other installations, care should be taken to eliminate the possibility of contamination of water supplies by sewage.

**Gas Services** Gas supplies in buildings furnish either natural or manufactured gas for heating, cooking, clothes drying, and other purposes. In cities and towns, gas services are usually supplied by the municipalities through mains and meters into buildings. In rural areas, gas is ordinarily supplied to buildings in containers of manufactured, liquefied gas, sometimes called bottled gas. When the contents of one have been exhausted, another is obtained or the first refilled.

**Piping System** For water supplies entering buildings, complex systems of piping and fittings are required to direct the water to the places where it will be used.

Piping is often of steel, wrought iron, or copper, with the latter considered the best. Today plastic piping is also used for many purposes. In some buildings, such as wood-frame houses, piping is often concealed in floors, walls, and other elements, but in other buildings, particularly large ones, special spaces, called pipe chases, are provided. The piping is joined with a variety of fittings, such as elbows, couplings, and tees, for connecting pipe lengths and making turns. In small buildings, the pressure of the water flowing from the mains is sufficient to distribute it to the places where it will be used. In larger buildings, especially tall ones, pumps are used to raise the water to upper floors, where it is stored in tanks and from which gravity causes it to flow downward.

In the supply system, cold water flows to all the fixtures in buildings, including bathtubs, wash basins, water closets, bathrooms, kitchen sinks and dishwashers, laundry tubs and clothes washers, drinking fountains, hot-water or steam heating systems, and hose outlets. In certain buildings, fire, building, and other codes require water reserves to be held for fire-fighting purposes. Sprinkler systems in such buildings must also be supplied. Cold-water supply lines are connected with hot-water heaters (gas or electric), which are of three major types: storage tank heaters, with heating coils inside of them; tankless heaters, which operate when a demand for hot water is made on them; and hot-water tankless heaters that are installed in or in connection with boilers used for heating the interiors of buildings. (See the article entitled heating, ventilating, and air conditioning.) Often hot-water pipes are covered with special insulation to avoid heat losses during transmission, and insulation is often used for cold-water pipes to keep condensation from them and to avoid freezing in exposed locations. Shutoff valves are installed at various points in the water supply systems to allow stopping the flow of water to certain portions of the system for specific fixtures, repairs, or other purposes. Sewage, or sanitary drainage, systems are completely separate from water supply systems. Fixtures in buildings are equipped with traps, curved sections of pipe that hold water which prevent sewer gases from entering the interiors of buildings. From the traps, fixture branch piping, of cast iron, copper, plastic, or steel, takes the waste from fixtures and allows it to flow, by force of gravity, to pipes called waste stacks and then down to the main drains, all made of the same materials. In order to let air enter the system so that waste will flow freely and discharge gases from it, vertical pipes of the same materials, called vents, are provided. These rise above the roofs to discharge gases. In the sewage lines, cleanouts, with removable threaded plugs, are provided to allow cleaning of the system if clogs occur. The main drain passes through a main trap to the outside sewer on the site, made of clay tile, cast iron, or plastic pipe, to the public sewer lines or to the lines of private septic tank and grease-trap systems.

**Fixtures** A great variety and number of fixtures are available, including various kinds of sinks of porcelain enamel and baked enamel steels, stainless steel, and others; tubs and showers of many types and sizes; and other fixtures. These come in many colors and finishes. There is a wide variety of appliances: hot-water heaters of various types and capacities; dishwashers; gas-fired and electric stoves; separate ovens and stove tops; clothes washers and dryers, both gas-fired and electric; water softeners; built-in grilles; and microwave ovens. These appliances are available in a range of colors and finishes, for both domestic and commercial use.

Plumbing systems in buildings are designed by mechanical engineers. Building, health, and other code requirements are very strict today for both design and construction, specifying how many fixtures may be attached to drain lines, types of traps to be used, types of piping and sizes required, vents required, and many other things related to such systems.

**History** In the most ancient primitive buildings, there was no plumbing. Water for drinking and other purposes was supplied by springs or other water bodies, used at its source, and later carried and stored in clay and other vessels. By the time of the great ancient civilizations around the Mediterranean Sea, methods had been developed for obtaining water from wells, springs, cisterns, and other sources; transporting it through aqueducts and conduits made of brick, hollow timbers, or stone; and lifting it with primitive machines, using ropes, buckets, and levers. The water was used not only for all human needs but for animal needs and for irrigating farmlands. Later pottery pipes were used for conducting water and still later, lead and bronze pipes. Similar pipes were also used to drain away waste water and sewage. Remains of such systems have been found in many places, including Mesopotamia, Crete, Mycenae, on the Greek mainland, and in Egypt. These early people also had primitive latrines or toilets, showers, and bathtubs.

The ancient Greeks built water and drainage systems, using mostly terra-cotta pipes, but sometimes lead or bronze ones. The Romans built remarkable water supply and drainage systems that were never equaled until modern times. They also built plumbing systems, with many things in common with those of today. To supply water, the Romans built a vast system of aqueducts, wells, cisterns, reservoirs, and conduits, resulting in the most plentiful and reliable water system up to that time. From the sources, the water was conducted to settling tanks, in which sediment was allowed to settle out, then to water mains of wood, strengthened with iron, terra-cotta, bronze, or lead, from which fountains, baths, and buildings were supplied. Since the Romans had no reliable method of purifying water, they kept the supplies from various sources separate, using the purest for drinking and the others for sundry purposes.

The Romans had sewage disposal systems, and the overflow from baths, fountains, and other places was often disposed of by the systems. The water supply, plumbing, and sewage disposal system of Rome was complete and highly developed. In other parts of the Roman Empire, such systems were constructed, but usually on a smaller scale and not so elaborate as that in Rome. In other places, the supplies of water were not always adequate to the needs, and sometimes water had to be rationed.

The public baths, or *thermae*, constructed by the Romans are well known. Often quite complex, they contained not only hot and cold baths, but often rooms for exercise, recreation, and other pursuits. They also had central heating with hypocausts, through which hot air and smoke circulated under floors. Not so well known are the Roman toilets, or *foricae*, which had groups of seats located over water flowing in channels. *Foricae* were located in various places in Rome, including apartment buildings. The sewage flowed, untreated, into the Tiber River, through a great sewer, the construction of which had begun in the 6th century B.C. Private bathtubs, very much like those of today, were used in the residences of wealthy people. And the Romans had provisions for water to be used in fire fighting.

After the time of the Romans, the systems for water supply, plumbing, and sewage disposal declined in number and quality. In some cases, the aqueducts and other parts of Roman systems were maintained, but in others they were not. Water from the roofs of buildings poured into open gutters, which also carried sewage. Wells and other water sources were often polluted with sewage or other refuse. Cleanliness became less important to people than it had been in Roman times and standards of hygiene worsened. All these negative factors contributed to the spread of the plague and other epidemics through Europe during the Middle Ages.

Beginning about the 13th century, conditions began to improve. Water supplies became more reliable, and sewage was discharged through pipes or directly into rivers and other water bodies. Since there were shortages of metals, pipes were often made of wood. Public baths were again instituted, and toilets were used to some extent, but often their contents were thrown on the street or emptied into moats, rather than disposed of properly.

During the Renaissance, conditions improved somewhat and better concepts of hygiene were adopted. Roman aqueducts were repaired and new ones constructed. In palaces and other residences of the nobility and wealthy, bathrooms were constructed, often with elaborate tubs filled and emptied with buckets. Pots were used for toilets or people went to outside privies. Sewage was not handled properly for the most part, and epidemics of diseases carried in sewage were frequent. Often the sewage was discharged into streams, which were also used for water supplies, thus compounding the disease problems. Major sewage systems were not constructed until the 17th century in Paris and the 19th century in London.

**American Development** In early colonial America, water supply, plumbing, and sewage systems did not exist. Water came from natural sources, such as springs, and then from wells and cisterns. Outdoor privies were constructed or pots were used inside and emptied out-of-doors. Baths were taken in washtubs. Such conditions existed well into the 19th century. During that century, public sources of water, including reservoirs, were established in many places. Pumps and piping were installed to conduct the water to buildings. The quality of water did not improve much but the quantity available did. There were no sewers, but later elaborate systems were built, discharging directly into rivers and other water bodies. For places without sewers, cesspools and later septic tank systems were developed. Primitive types of toilets, or water closets, were introduced early in the 19th century.

During the same century, water filtration plants, using sand, came into use and were followed by chemical treatment plants. The relationship between water and sewage, in the spread of disease, was recognized and sewage treatment plants were constructed. Water closets became more efficient and gradually the inside toilet replaced the outdoor privy. By the late 19th century, inside bathtubs with water connections and drainage were installed, along with wash basins or lavatories, which were often placed in bedrooms. About the same time, sinks, with running water and drains, were installed in kitchens. The goal became a bathroom and kitchen with plumbing in every house.

In later years, one bathroom per house became the exception, with many houses containing several, including private ones connected to individual bedrooms. Equipment for kitchens and bathrooms has become increasingly more prevalent and elaborate during the 20th century, with the addition of built-in tubs and shower enclosures in bathrooms, and dishwashers, food disposers, and other appliances in kitchens. People today find other uses for plumbing, for example, in heating and air-conditioning systems; for ponds, fountains, and other purposes; and for swimming pools near or in houses. There has been a similar increased use of plumbing and appliances in buildings of most other types.

**Related Articles** DAM; ENERGY; ENVIRONMENTAL PROTECTION; FIRE PROTECTION; FOUNTAIN; GARDEN;

HEATING, VENTILATING, AND AIR CONDITIONING; MECHANICAL ENGINEERING.

**Further Reading** Stein, Benjamin, and John E. Reynolds: *Mechanical and Electrical Equipment for Buildings,* 8th ed., John Wiley, New York, 1992.

**Sources of Additional Information** American Society of Mechanical Engineers, 345 E. 49th St., New York, N.Y. 10017; Cast Iron Soil Pipe Inst., 5959 Shallowford Rd., Suite 419, Chattanooga, Tenn. 37421; Plumbing, Heating and Cooling Information Bureau, 35 E. Wacker Dr., Chicago, Ill. 60601.

**POPE, JOHN RUSSELL** American architect (1874–1937). A good student and an inspired man, John Russell Pope became one of the foremost architects in the United States. Some count it a misfortune that he lived in an era when architecture was changing radically from the eclectic styles that had dominated it for so many years to the Modern movement.

Pope started his career under the tutelage of an architect, William Robert Ware (1832–1915), who had been influenced by the principles of the École des Beaux Arts in Paris. Then he won a scholarship given by another Beaux Arts architect, Charles Follen McKim (1847–1909), to the American Academy in Rome, a school McKim had helped found and of which he was president. Pope then attended and graduated from École des Beaux Arts. Coming back to the United States, he met McKim and, highly impressed, fell almost completely under the spell of the Beaux Arts philosophy and the man.

Thus Pope had very little choice, except to become an architect who based his work on Beaux Arts principles and produced buildings in the Eclectic style. Whether he had a choice or not, Pope designed buildings in this manner throughout his lifetime. And Pope was very good at it. The only others of his time about whom this may be said were Cass Gilbert (1859–1934) and Paul Philippe Cret (1876–1945). Although many of the buildings of these three architects were notable, some are anachronisms since they were built in the 1930s and 1940s.

Pope started out as a talented and scholarly architect, who designed striking and popular buildings in a variety of styles. He ended by becoming one of the most successful architects in the United States, practiced almost 40 years, and designed a great number of buildings of many types, including public buildings, colleges, churches, houses, and museums. He also designed a large number of monuments.

**Works** Although Pope practiced in New York City, his most important buildings were constructed in other places. Of his work in New York City still in existence, the two most important commissions involved remodeling and additions to existing buildings. Pope remodeled the home of Henry Clay Frick (1849–1919), steel industrial-

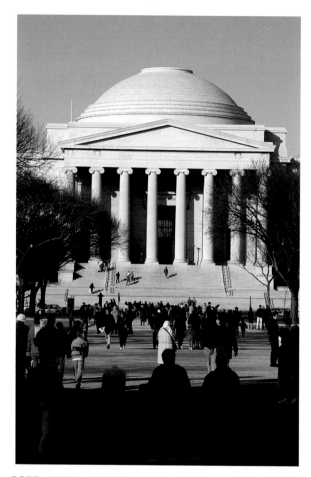

**POPE, JOHN RUSSELL** National Gallery of Art (1937), Washington, D.C. *[Architect: John Russell Pope; associate architects: Eggers and Higgins]*

ist, originally completed in 1914 by Carrère and Hastings, into an art gallery (1935) to house the Frick Collection and added a library. The building is now known as the Frick Museum. He also added to the complex of the American Museum of Natural History a building called the Roosevelt Memorial Building (1936), named for President Theodore Roosevelt (1858–1919). The original portions of the complex (1877) were by Vaux and Mould. The only other important Pope buildings in New York City are the Spence School (1929) and the house of William Kissam Vanderbilt II (1878–1944), now the headquarters of the Rumanian delegation to the United Nations.

Pope designed plans for a number of campuses, including those of Yale University, New Haven, Conn.; Johns Hopkins University, Baltimore, Md.; Syracuse University, Syracuse, N.Y.; and Dartmouth College, Hanover, N.H. He designed buildings and monuments in many locations, including Syracuse and Plattsburgh, N.Y., and Baltimore. One of his most important monuments was the American Battle Monument (1937), Montfaucon, France.

The greatest collection of Pope's works is in Washington, where he designed the Temple of the Scottish Rite (1910), Washington International Center, or Meridian House (1915), Constitution Hall (1930), and the National Archives Building (1935). Three of his most important commissions were not completed until after he died: the National City Christian Church (1939); the National Gallery of Art (1941), given to the city by the industrialist and financier Andrew Mellon (1855–1937); and the Jefferson Memorial (1943). The last-named two were the last great Eclectic buildings in Washington.

**Life** John Russell Pope was born in New York City on April 2, 1874, the son of an artist. After studying at the College of the City of New York, now City University of New York, Pope enrolled in 1891 in the architectural program, established in 1881 at Columbia University, New York City, by a former student of Richard Morris Hunt (1827–95), William Robert Ware. In 1894 Pope graduated with a bachelor of philosophy degree, which seems unlikely enough, from the architectural program in the Columbia University School of Mines, which seems even more unlikely.

In 1895 Pope won the McKim scholarship, allowing study at the American Academy in Rome. Winning another scholarship the following year, Pope was able to stay two years in Rome, studying architecture. He then entered the École des Beaux Arts in Paris, where both Hunt and McKim had studied. Completing the architectural course in two years, Pope graduated in 1900. Returning to New York, Pope worked for a while in the architectural office of Bruce Price (1845–1903), the father of Emily Price (1873–1960) who later became famous on her own, using her married name Emily Post, as the foremost authority on etiquette in the United States.

Pope then established his own office in New York and soon had a successful practice that brought him commissions, not only in many parts of the United States but in England and France. He practiced almost 40 years and became one of the most respected architects in the United States. He was active in many organizations and served on several national commissions, including the National Council of Fine Arts, to which he was appointed by President Woodrow Wilson (1856–1924), and the National Board of Consulting Architects, appointed by President Herbert Clark Hoover (1874–1964). He received many honors, including election to membership in the National Institute of Arts and Letters and the National Academy of Design. Pope served as president of the American Academy in Rome from 1933 until August 27, 1937, when he died.

**Related Articles** BEAUX ARTS, ÉCOLE DES; ECLECTIC ARCHITECTURE; EDUCATION; HUNT, RICHARD MORRIS; MCKIM, MEAD AND WHITE.

**PORTMAN, JOHN CALVIN** Hyatt Regency Hotel (1969), Atlanta, Ga.

**PORTMAN, JOHN CALVIN** American architect and developer. John Portman (1924–    ) is known for his large-scale building in Atlanta, Ga., as well as major groups of buildings in many cities of the world. His success as developer has made him a unique figure in the architectural profession. The scale of the projects is beyond compare. His interest in the pedestrian experience makes these projects a lively experience, appealing to the public. His design goes for the big dramatic effect, and in this he is typically an American designer. As director of a conglomerate of corporations, he has a financial understanding that has made him a successful businessman.

**Works** Initially identified with the huge Peachtree Center (1981–1986 and later) in Atlanta, Ga., Portman's most famous early design was the Hyatt Regency Atlanta (1969) built around a dramatic atrium rising through the building. This 19th-century concept was new to contemporary hotel design. In addition, the elevators were pulled out into the atrium, enclosed with glass-walled cabs that provided a moving sculpture. These devices have been widely emulated. Connected to the Peachtree Center, other buildings include office towers, a retail mall, restaurants, athletic club, urban plaza, pedestrian bridges, and parking. Peachtree Center also connects to the Westin Peachtree Plaza (1976) and the Atlanta Marriott Marquis (1985) also designed by Portman, and the Merchandise Mart (1961), Apparel

497

Mart (1979), and Gift Mart and INFORUM Technology Mart (1989). The One Peachtree Center Tower (1992) is the latest 60-story office tower to be added to the complex.

In San Francisco, John Portman was developer for the major Embarcadero Center (1981, expanded in the late 1980s). The Hyatt Regency San Francisco was separated from the original Embarcadero Center construction but has since been connected to the more recent additions to the complex. The hotel (1973) is another memorable structure, with sloping walls of rooms adding visual excitement to the exterior and the interior atrium. The entire complex combines plazas, planting, sculpture, and fountains for a memorable urban experience.

A more problematic urban development is the Renaissance Center, Detroit, Mich., where the 35-acre site was separated from the city by Jefferson Boulevard, a 13-lane freeway. The solution, to develop a city within the city, has many dramatic features as well as planted areas and trees set high above surrounding streets. Criticism has focused on the separation of the development from the rest of downtown Detroit.

Other projects have included major hotels in many cities. The Westin Bonaventure (1977), Los Angeles, Calif., is a group of four dark glass cylinders, sitting on a concrete base, containing parking, conference rooms, and the central atrium. This circular theme has been widely used by Portman, as in the Hyatt Regency O'Hare (1971), the Westin Peachtree Plaza in Atlanta (1976), and several of his office towers. More conventionally rectangular, the Portman–San Francisco (1987), San Francisco, Calif., fits appropriately into the city environment.

Internationally, major building complexes include Marina Square (1987), Singapore, and Shanghai Centre (1990), Peoples Republic of China. The Singapore project included three hotels and a large shopping mall on 23 acres of reclaimed land on Singapore Bay and was developed in association with S. P. Tao. The Shanghai project includes apartment towers, a 48-story hotel, offices, a thousand-seat theater, a retail village accessible from neighboring streets, and a large exhibition space.

Portman was asked to prepare a proposal for the city of Genoa, an aging Italian port associated with Columbus. The new-world proposal (not built) was a dramatic waterfront development of the Porto Vecchio with a proposed landmark tower completely dominating the city.

University work has included two buildings at Emory University, Atlanta. The Emory University Physical Education Center (1983) was built partly underground to reduce the apparent mass of the building. The Emory University Student Center (1986) was an addition to an older building, with the facade exposed in the new building.

Portman's redesign of the underground concourse at Rockefeller Center in New York is an appropriate contribution to the 1930 complex most closely related to his own large developments.

Criticism of his work relates to the speed of construction, which required design of large-scale, simplified forms which at times can appear overwhelming. His attention to pedestrian movement and varied experience helps to offset the huge scale of the buildings. His attention to water effects, sculpture, and painting enrich the pedestrian environment.

**Life** John Calvin Portman, Jr., was born in 1924 and has lived most of his life in Atlanta, Ga. After serving in the Navy during World War II, he received his architectural degree from the Georgia Institute of Technology in 1950. He opened his own office in 1953, and in 1986 merged with the established Atlanta firm of H. Griffith Edwards to form Edwards and Portman. When Edwards retired, the firm became John Portman and Associates. Married to Jan Portman, he is the father of six children.

John Portman designed a home in Atlanta named Entelechy I and in 1986 a vacation home at Sea Island, Ga., which he named Entelechy II. Both of these large homes are filled with paintings, sculpture, and extensive gardens. He has been honored with many awards and serves as a member of the National Council of Architectural Registration Boards (NCARB).

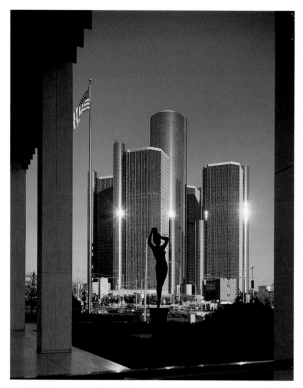

**PORTMAN, JOHN CALVIN** Renaissance Center (1977), Detroit, Mich.

**Related Articles** COMPLEX, ARCHITECTURAL; CONTEMPORARY ARCHITECTURE; FINANCE; PLANNING, CITY.

**Further Reading** Riana, Paolo: *John Portman*, L'Arca Edizioni, Milan, and The American Institute of Architects Press, Washington, D.C., 1990.

**POST, GEORGE BROWNE** American architect (1837–1913). George Browne Post was an eclectic architect who designed buildings of many styles derived from the past. He learned his architecture from the pioneer of the Beaux Arts principles of design in the United States, Richard Morris Hunt (1827–95). Perhaps because of his earlier training as a civil engineer and because of his inquisitive nature, Post made a greater number of contributions to architecture than many other Beaux Arts architects, who were preoccupied with scholarship, past styles, and ornament.

In spite of the eclectic nature of his building designs, George Post was an architectural innovator. He was one of the first New York City architects to design tall office buildings, later known as skyscrapers, including the 25-story St. Paul Building (1900) in New York City. He was one of the first architects to use elevators. He pioneered in the design of modern hotels, most of them for the Statler chain in cities around the United States, and was a good planner. He also took a deep interest in good materials, sound construction, and meeting the needs of his clients.

**Works** During the more than 40 years he practiced, Post produced a great number of buildings of many types, including office buildings, banks, hotels, apartments, college buildings, and houses. He also designed a remarkable series of New York City buildings for national marketing groups: the Produce Building (1884), considered one of his best designs, and the Cotton Exchange (1885), both since demolished; and the New York Stock Exchange (1903), still in use.

Post designed a number of houses, the best of which was that for Cornelius Vanderbilt II (1843–99), built in New York City in 1880, enlarged in 1894, and since demolished. Other important New York City buildings by Post include the Williamsburgh Savings Bank and the Western Union Building, both completed in 1875; the Long Island Historical Society Building (1878); the old Times Building (1889), now part of Pace College; the Old Borough Building (1897), Brooklyn; and the Vincent (Astor) Building (1890), Fordham University. In 1900, he designed a master plan for the College of the City of New York, now the City University of New York, and later designed buildings for the campus (1907). These buildings are still in existence, except for the Western Union Building, which was demolished.

Post designed buildings in other parts of the country, including Newark, N.J., Pittsburgh, Detroit, and Cleveland. He also designed the Manufacturers' and Liberal Arts buildings for the World's Columbian Exposition in 1893 in Chicago. His last important building, completed in 1917, four years after his death, was the State Capitol of Wisconsin, Madison.

**Life** George Browne Post was born in New York City, on December 15, 1837. He attended Churchill's School, a military institution, in Ossining, N.Y. After graduation, he entered New York University, graduating in 1858 with a degree in civil engineering. He then entered the architectural atelier, or studio, of Richard Morris Hunt, who was the acknowledged master of the Eclectic style based on the principles of the École des Beaux Arts in Paris, where Hunt had studied. In 1860 Post left the atelier to form an architectural practice in New York City, in partnership with Charles D. Gambrill (1832–80), who later was the partner of Henry Hobson Richardson (1838–86).

In 1861 the office was closed when Post went on active duty as a captain in the U.S. Army, during the Civil War. He served until 1865, participating in battles, and was eventually promoted to colonel. After the war, Post returned to New York City and opened a new office,

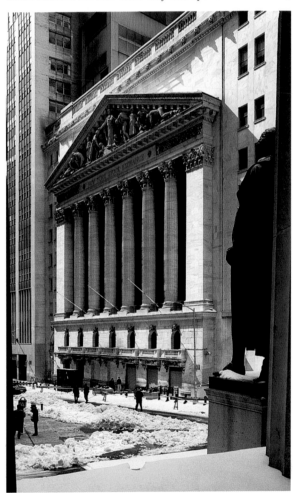

**POST, GEORGE BROWNE** New York Stock Exchange (1903), New York, N.Y.

this time without a partner. Soon commissions began to come in, and before long Post was one of the busiest architects in the city. He became one of the most successful of his time, always practicing in New York City and designing most of his buildings to be constructed there.

In 1863 Post married Alice Matilde Stone. They had two sons, William Stone Post (1866–1940) and J. Otis Post (1874–1951), who became architects. In 1904 both sons were taken as partners by the elder Post, and the firm was renamed George B. Post and Sons, which it remained until the death of the father. The brothers continued the firm for many years afterward, designing buildings of many types. They also continued the hotel work for the Statler chain, begun by their father, and designed the Statler-Hilton (1924), New York City. This hotel, originally called the Pennsylvania, was immortalized for big band fans by a song using its telephone number, "Pennsylvania Six-Five Thousand," written by band leader Glenn Miller (1904–1944).

George Browne Post was much admired, and he received many honors. He was very active in architectural, arts, and other types of organizations. He was elected president of the American Institute of Architects in 1896 and served in that position until 1898. He was a

**PRACTICE, INTERNATIONAL** Berlin Museum (1968), Berlin, Germany. *[Architect: Mies van der Rohe]*

member of the National Institute of Arts and Letters, the American Academy of Arts and Letters, and several other organizations. In 1911 Post received the highest honor the AIA can bestow on an architect, the Gold Medal. After a life that was active right to the end, George Browne Post died on November 28, 1913.

**Related Articles** ECLECTIC ARCHITECTURE; HUNT, RICHARD MORRIS.

**PRACTICE, INTERNATIONAL** For many years, U.S. architects have practiced in other countries, and foreign architects have been commissioned for buildings in the United States. This type of practice is simply called "international practice," and is very different from dealing with clients at home.

Clients for U.S. architects' foreign work might be the U.S. Department of State for embassies or other U.S. government activities including military bases and aid programs. Another client might be a multinational corporation such as a bank or manufacturing company. During the oil boom, many projects were commissioned and built in oil-rich developing nations. Another source of international work for U.S. architects would be international competitions.

Projects vary as to the economy of the country, from those for countries with a per capita gross national product on the lower end to those for developed countries

**PRACTICE, INTERNATIONAL** Carpenter Center for the Visual Arts (1963), Harvard University, Cambridge, Mass. *[Architect: Le Corbusier with Sert, Jackson and Gourley]*

**PRACTICE, INTERNATIONAL** King Fahad University of Petroleum and Minerals (1969–85), Dhahran, Saudi Arabia. [Architects: CRSS]

with high standards of living. The developed countries tend to have architects who compete with U.S. firms for most projects. One way of operating abroad is to associate with a local professional firm that is better able to cope with the local building industry, codes and standards, as well as language, culture, and politics. Sometimes the U.S. architects act as the executive or consultant to local firms; sometimes complete service is offered, similar to normal practice.

One of the issues in working abroad is to design appropriately for the local culture and climate. In areas subject to interruption of electric service, for instance, it may not be possible to rely on air conditioning, and the building should be designed to operate with simpler modification of the climate. There is considerable literature on weather and climate conditions available for reference.

**PRACTICE, INTERNATIONAL** Grand Louvre, Phase I (Cour Napoleon and Richelieu wing connections) (1989), Paris, France. [Architect: I. M. Pei (Photo: André Biro)]

Another issue in many countries is the availability of building materials and labor. In difficult climates, prefabricated buildings may be a rational response. Sometimes maintenance of a building may be a problem, resulting in inoperative elevators, blocked roof drains, to say nothing of floods, earthquakes, and special soil conditions.

Each country has specific codes and standards or uses those developed by another country. Some of these might be the British Standards (BS), the French Association Française de Normalisation (AFNOR), the U.S. American Standards Institute (ANSI), the American Society for Testing and Materials (ASTM), or the Japanese Industry Standards (JIS).

Practice issues may include the local lack of understanding of professional services. It is necessary to provide clear descriptions of work to be done and to reference published national contract forms. There has been some work in establishing international forms of agreement for services developed by the International Federation of Consulting Engineers (FIDIC). There are many special considerations involved in operating outside the home country, and the architectural press frequently publishes articles on such subjects as legal remedies for obtaining payment of fees. Currency variations and taxation for the country of origin and the country of activity are typical issues to be addressed. The last decades have produced many commissions for U.S. architects all over the world.

Some well-known buildings have resulted from international practice. In the United States, a few examples of the work of foreign firms include the Carpenter Center for the Visual Arts (1963), Harvard University, Cambridge, Mass., designed by Le Corbusier in association with Sert, Jackson & Gourley; the Arthur M. Sackler Museum (1984), Harvard University, Cambridge, Mass., and the Extension of the School of Architecture, Rice University, Houston, designed by James Stirling Michael Wilford and Assoc.; the Canadian Chancery (1989), Washington, D.C., by Arthur Erickson; Team Disney office block (1991), Buena Vista, Fla., and additions to the Los Angeles Museum of Art (1992), by Arata Isozaki; the Alice Pratt Brown Hall Shepherd School of Music (1991), Rice University, Houston, designed by Ricardo Bofill/Taller de Arquitectura, with Kendall/Heaton Assoc., Inc., architects. In addition, the Italian Pietro Nervi was engineer for several U.S. buildings.

The list of U.S. architects working abroad is extensive, and this list is only a sample. In Japan, U.S. architects designed the following: the Bancho House, Tokyo (1990), Robert A. M. Stern, architect; the Momochi District Apartment Building (1989), Fukuoka, Japan, Michael Graves, architect; the Minato Mirai 75-story Landmark Tower, Yokohama (1993), The Stubbins Associates,

**PRACTICE, INTERNATIONAL** Australian Parliament House (1989), Canberra, Australia. [Architects: Mitchell/Giurgola & Thorp (Photo: Heide Smith)]

architects; Koizumi Sangyo Building, Tokyo (1990), Eisenman Architects with K Architects and Assoc., architects; Osaka Aquarium, Osaka (1990), Cambridge Seven Assoc., architects; and the Fukuoka City Mixed-Use Building (1989), Kiushu, Japan, Tigerman McCurry, architects, with Yoshihide Kato, Zenitada Corp.

In Great Britain, work includes some projects in London: the work at Canary Wharf, interrupted by the bankruptcy of the developer, with buildings by Cesar Pelli and Skidmore, Owings and Merrill; at Broadgate and Bishopsgate, more buildings by Skidmore, Owings and Merrill; at Spitalfields, others planned by Swanke Hayden Connell, and the Sainsbury Wing of the National Gallery (1991), designed by Venturi, Scott Brown and Assoc.

In Paris, American work includes the additions to Le Grande Louvre (1989) by I. M. Pei, and the Canal+ headquarters building (1992) by Richard Meier & Partners, architects.

Highlights of American work elsewhere include Edward Durell Stone's design for the American Embassy in New Delhi (1959), the Australian Parliament House (1988) designed by Mitchell/Giurgola, architects; and the Haj terminal, King Abdul Aziz International Airport, Jeddah, Saudi Arabia (1982) engineered by Jazlur Rahman Khan of Skidmore, Owings and Merrill. Another project in Jeddah is the National Commercial Bank (1983), designed by Gordon Bunshaft of Skidmore, Owings and Merrill.

Many other major projects have been built, and many more will be added to the list of important buildings. Architectural design services remain a substantial U.S. export.

**Related Articles** EISENMAN, PETER; GIURGOLA, ROMALDO; GRAVES, MICHAEL; MEIER, RICHARD; PEI, IEOH MING; PELLI, CESAR; SKIDMORE, OWINGS AND MERRILL; STERN, ROBERT A. M.; TIGERMAN, STANLEY; Also other contemporary architects.

**Further Reading** Baden-Powel, Francis, "International Practice," vol. 3, *Encyclopedia of Architecture, Design, Engineering and Construction*, John Wiley, New York, 1989.

**PRACTICE OF ARCHITECTURE** The application of architectural skills to a client's problem. For this purpose, offices are organized around the necessary specialized skills required for contemporary practice. Although the design skills are what is popularly understood as the practice of architecture, many other skills are required. A list of these skills would include marketing and marketing communications, programming, project and business management, specifications writing, estimating and cost management, construction contract administration, and proficiency in the planning and design of specialized building types such as hospitals, high-tech manufacturing plants, or high-rise office buildings. In general, offices can be classified as having more emphasis either on the art of architecture or on the business of architecture.

**Office Structure** Several studies have been undertaken concerning organization of the architectural practice. The result has been a recognition of a variety of approaches to organization not counting the small-office, nonstructured "do-it-all" operation that cannot survive in a larger firm.

**Departmental Structure** This traditional approach divides the staff by their functions, such as design, production of documents, and construction administration. Each department would have an administrator with responsibility for hiring, training, client relations, quality control, and profitability. Problems with this structure are that most projects require action by all departments, and clients often have difficulty identifying who

**PRACTICE OF ARCHITECTURE** Embassy of Singapore (1993), Washington, D.C. [Architects: RTKL Associates, Inc.; structural engineers: RTKL Associates, Inc.; mechanical and electrical engineers: RTKL Associates, Inc.; landscape architects: RTKL Associates, Inc.; interior designers: RTKL Associates, Inc.; contractor: Whiting-Turner Contracting Company]

is in charge at various times in the design and construction of a project.

**Project Manager** Such an organization has a project manager who is responsible for meeting the project goals and who follows the project until completion. Conflict can occur if staffing of a project does not match the staffing capability available. And the employee may be uncertain as to which project manager has priority in a given situation.

**Project Team** In this organizational form, people with appropriate skills are assembled to suit the needs of the project or multiple projects. The leader might be called "project manager," "director," or "architect." Teams change according to needs, resulting in internal mobility of the staff, often upsetting to the individual, between teams. A client or market may desire stability in the team, which can conflict with individual interests or firm needs.

**Studio** Efforts to establish permanent project teams can be described as studio organization, because each team is responsible for hiring, business development, quality control, and profitability. If workload fluctuates, having a permanent team may be too costly, and it may produce unwanted competition and divisiveness among employees.

In summary, aspects of each organization may be adopted by firms at different times. For instance, some firms may have a unified design group but divide the production into a series of teams, or the studio concept may apply except for construction administration or perhaps also production of documents.

**Management** Some firms depend on an individual to lead the firm, but almost all firms require others to assist in management, where functions are to ensure coverage in the owner's absence, educate the staff on the firm's goals, provide a link between clients and staff, provide opportunities for staff to become part of management, and free the owner or owners to do what they prefer to do most, such as marketing or design.

A responsibility of the architectural firm is to promote the education of interns in the firm. The Intern Development Program jointly developed by the American Institute of Architects (AIA) and the National Council of Architectural Registration Boards (NCARB) offers curriculum and training programs for preparation for licensing. Support and encouragement of continuing education for all architects is another responsibility of the firm.

**Social Structure** Architecture is a social art, and firms should encourage public education and communication and the involvement of the public in decisions affecting a community. The patron of architecture is now likely to be a public board or industrial and commercial clients. Involvement in low-cost housing has led to neighborhood revitalization and a greater involvement for architects in community and urban design.

The character of architectural firms is changing as more women and ethnic minorities become members of the profession. The formerly small group of wealthy clients is now more likely to represent a wider income range.

The place of architecture in the economic structure depends on the strength of the building industry. Low interest rates and a strong economy are stimulants to building. The level of construction worldwide as well as in the United States determines the amount of work available. History showed that the 19th-century growth of cities and industries was a great stimulus to the growth of the profession of architecture. Although building has declined as a percentage of the national economy, demand for architectural services has increased, and architecture with other professions has become part of the service economy. New roles and markets for services have been created. More architects are involved in design and production activities, leading to more specialization.

Although computers are widely used by the architect, the effect on office organization and functions has been minor. Refer to the article entitled computer for the many uses of computers in architecture.

**Intern Development** The period from graduation from an accredited program in architecture to having enough experience to be admitted to licensing exams is called the "internship" period. The intern development program established by the American Institute of Architects (AIA) and the National Council of Architectural Registration Boards (NCARB) has established the requirements for experience in three categories: design and construction documents, construction administration, and office management. A supplemental area encourages interns to become involved in special activities, from a long list including such items as computer applications and teaching. Seminars, self-study guides, and sponsored programs are used to help the candidate prepare for licensing. The responsibility of firms for maintaining such programs is a professional responsibility.

**Societal Influences** The practice of architecture and the role of the architect has been affected by changes in society. Historically clients were the church, the state, and powerful individuals. Now the clients are as likely to be commercial organizations. As more women and minorities enter the profession, the profession will change to be more representative of U.S. society.

**Financial Influences** The success of the profession depends on a healthy building industry. The level of construction both nationally and internationally determines the amount and type of work that will involve architects. The increased complexity of building has resulted in many persons performing functions that previously were done by few.

Within the firm, architecture is a balance between aesthetic and business concerns. The architect coordinates and directs the many individuals from whom input is needed. Because architecture is complex, careful organization and management are critical. A project requires many skills, and individuals in an office usually become specialists in some areas. This specialization may make it difficult for an individual to change emphasis or to move into other areas.

The difficulty involved in an individual architect's starting an independent practice means that most firms start small. Surveys indicate that a vast majority of firms remain small, although a disproportionate level of income goes to the few largest firms.

**Related Articles** BUILDING CODES AND STANDARDS; CAREER; COMPUTER; CONSTRUCTION CONTRACT ADMINISTRATION; COST CONTROL; DESIGN, ARCHITECTURAL; EDUCATION; ENGINEERING; FEASIBILITY STUDY; GRAPHIC DESIGN; INTERIOR DESIGN; LANDSCAPE ARCHITECTURE; MODEL MAKING; PLANNING, CITY; PRESERVATION; PROGRAMMING; REMODELING; RENDERING; SITE PLANNING; SPECIFICATION; WORKING DRAWING.

**Further Reading** *General references:* American Institute of Architects (AIA): *Architect's Handbook of Professional Practice*, latest edition, AIA, Washington, D.C.; Callender, John H.: *Time Saver Standards for Architectural Design Data*, 6th ed., McGraw-Hill, New York, 1982; Merritt, Frederick S., ed.: *Building Design Construction Handbook*, 4th ed., McGraw-Hill, New York, 1982; Ramsey, Charles G., Harold R. Sleeper, and John R. Hoke, eds.: *Architectural Graphic Standards*, 9th ed., John Wiley, New York, 1994. *Business practices:* Bockrath, Joseph T.: *Contracts, Specifications and Law for Engineers*, 4th ed., McGraw-Hill, New York, 1985. *Business development:* Coxe, Weld: *Marketing Architectural and Engineering Services*, 2d ed., reprint of 1983 edition, Krieger, Melbourne, Fla., 1990; Jones, Gerre L.: *How to Market Professional Design Services*, 2d ed., McGraw-Hill, New York, 1983; Spaulding, Margaret, and William D'Elia: *Advanced Marketing Techniques for Architecture and Engineering Firms*, McGraw-Hill, New York, 1989.

**Source of Additional Information** The American Institute of Architects, 1735 New York Ave., N.W., Washington, D.C. 20006.

**PRE-COLUMBIAN ARCHITECTURE** The buildings and other structures by the American Indians and their ancestors before Christopher Columbus landed in America in 1492. The ancestors of the American Indians are believed to have come to America across a strip of land connecting what is now Alaska and the former Soviet Union. The land connection has disappeared and Bering Strait is located there. Although the exact time

**PRE-COLUMBIAN ARCHITECTURE** Pueblo Bonito (*c.* 1100), Chaco Canyon National Monument, near Bloomfield, N. Mex. [*Architect: unknown*]

**PRE-COLUMBIAN ARCHITECTURE** Cliff Palace (*c.* 1100), Mesa Verde National Park, Colo. *[Architect: unknown]*

these people reached America has not been established, and it is not known what they called themselves, it is believed that the migrations started at least 20,000 years ago and continued for quite a long time.

Traces of these early people have been found in North America, including caves they occupied in the west and tools they used as far back as 15,000 B.C. in what is called the Folsom culture. No remains of these early humans have been found. Their architecture, if they had any other than caves, also remains a mystery. However, it is believed that they began to construct crude huts from limbs of trees and brush and tents from limbs and animal skins sometime before 5000 B.C. The remains of none have been found.

**Medicine Wheels** The earliest construction of the Indians still in existence in the United States are medicine wheels, though their real purpose has not been firmly established. Found in many places in the Western United States and in Canada, they are geometric arrangements of stones, roughly in the shape of wheels with spokes. Thought to have had astronomical and religious purposes, some of these wheels are 200 ft or more in diameter and are thought to have been built about the time of the pyramids in Egypt, about the 27th century B.C., or earlier. It is believed that there may be literally millions of these located in the area stretching roughly from Texas into southern Canada.

**Mounds** Other early structures made by Indians are mounds of various kinds. Some are thought to have been constructed as early as 300 B.C., while others have been dated as late as A.D. 1200. Thousands of these mounds have been found in many places in the United States, the greatest number in the states of Ohio and Illinois, with lesser numbers in Indiana, Wisconsin, Arkansas, Kentucky, Tennessee, Iowa, Louisiana, and Georgia. The mounds are of three major types: burial; temple, earthen pyramids on top of which temples were built; and effigy, shaped like crude representations of animals, birds, or snakes. The effigy mounds probably had religious significance, but their exact use is not known.

Some of the most notable mounds still in existence are Effigy Mound, near Lake Koshkonong, Wis.; Azlatan, near Madison, Wis.; Etowah, near Cartersville, Ga.; and Cahokia Mounds, near East St. Louis, Ill. Among the many important mounds in Ohio are Great Serpent, Hillsboro; Mound City; Newark Earthworks, Newark; Fort Ancient, Lebanon. Hopewell mounds, for which the culture of the Mound Builders has been named, are to be found in many locations in the eastern half of the United States.

**Early Buildings** The earliest buildings of most of the Indians in America, other than that of the Pueblos, have not survived because of the perishable materials used in their construction. However, their construction has been documented quite well because the types continued to be built by Indians long after the colonization of America by Europeans. The architecture of the Indians was regional in character, and varied considerably from place to place, in order to fit the climatic conditions and the way of life of the users.

**Later Buildings** Later Indian architecture may be divided into five major groups: Eastern Forest, Great Plains, Pacific Northwest, California, and Southwest. Eastern Forest Indians lived by farming or by combining farming with hunting. The farmers in the Southeast

generally built houses of wood, with thatched roofs and walls plastered with mud. In Florida, the Indians built chickees: open-sided thatched huts. The farmer-hunters of the Northeast built two main types of buildings: dome-shaped wigwams, huts made of limbs or small trees, covered with bark; and longhouses, made in a similar manner, but large enough for several families to live together.

The Indians of the Great Plains were hunters or farmers, and sometimes combined both pursuits. The nomadic tribes lived in tepees, or tipis, cone-shaped, often highly ornamented tents, constructed of poles and covered with animal, often buffalo, skins. A single tepee required some 15 to 30 poles and an equal number of buffalo hides. More sedentary Indians built earth lodges, often partly underground and covered with logs, brush, and dirt. In the Pacific Northwest, where the Indians were generally sedentary fishermen, wood dwellings of split planks were constructed and were highly ornamented.

California Indians, sedentary for the most part, gathered seeds, roots, and nuts for food. Some tribes lived almost entirely on acorns. Their major type of dwelling was the wickiup, a framework of poles in a sort of beehive shape, covered with brush and sometimes with dirt. Many of the Indian tribes also built communal build-

**PRE-COLUMBIAN ARCHITECTURE** Cahokia Mounds (before 1250), E. St. Louis, Ill. Posts are modern reconstruction. *[Architect: unknown]*

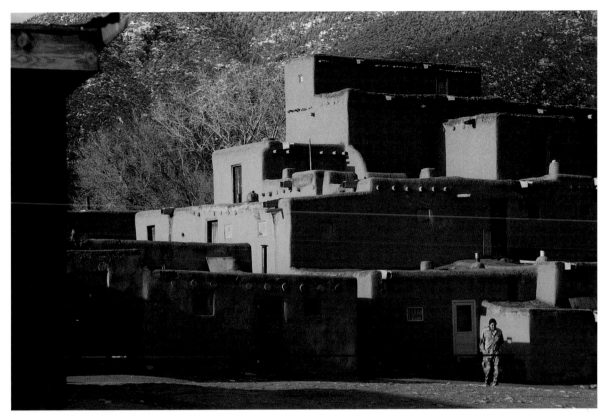

**PRE-COLUMBIAN ARCHITECTURE** Taos Pueblo (*c.* 1300, rebuilt *c.* 1700), Taos, N. Mex. *[Architect: unknown]*

ings, or meeting houses, of various types. In the Southwest, some of the earliest Indians, who were semi-nomadic, lived in slab houses, or pit dwellings, made of logs and mud, partly underground, and sometimes lined with stone slabs. Others lived in hogans, houses made like log cabins, with earthen roofs.

**Basket Makers** The crowning architectural achievements of the early Indians are the magnificent structures of the Southwest. The origins of the people who constructed these buildings have not been firmly established. It is known that they descended from a culture called the Basket Makers that has been traced to approximately the time of the birth of Christ. The Basket Makers were pit dwellers and are the earliest definitely known ancestors of the people who later became known as the Cliff Dwellers and still later as the Pueblo Indians. Perhaps more to the point is the name by which the Navaho called them, Anasazi, the ancient ones.

Beginning about A.D. 500, the culture of the Basket Makers advanced considerably until, by about 700, they had learned to construct remarkable buildings of adobe brick, and sometimes stone; these were not only single residences but apartments with a great number of units, and structures of other types, including ceremonial chambers, called kivas. The buildings of the Basket Makers came to be known as pueblos, the name by which

they are still called. Although the Basket Makers built pueblos on level sites, some of the most spectacular were located on the sides of cliffs and in canyons. In these pueblos, they were relatively safe from enemies. They farmed areas near their cities and hunted elsewhere.

By 1100, these Indians had a very highly developed culture, making pottery and many other kinds of vessels, implements, tools, and weapons; and clothing of skins and woven from cotton and other fibers. But in their architecture, they reached their highest level of accomplishment. Sometime before 1300, these Indians began to leave their cliff and other pueblo homes. No one has determined exactly why they left or where they went. Two theories have been advanced for their departure: increasing attacks by enemies and a severe drought that is known to have occurred during the last quarter of the 13th century. In any case, by 1300, all had departed, probably to be absorbed into other related tribes in the area, now known as the Pueblo Indian tribes.

They left a magnificent and spectacular architectural heritage. Some of the greatest of the cliff and other dwellings existing today, at least in part, include: Chaco Canyon, N. Mex., and the Mesa Verde, Colo., perhaps the most magnificent of all (see illustrations); also in New Mexico, Gila Cliff, and Aztec, a misnomer since the Aztecs had nothing to do with this pueblo; and in

Arizona, Canyon de Chelly, Kayenta, Montezuma Castle (which the Aztec chieftain never saw), Sunset Crater, Tonto, Walnut Creek Canyon, and Wuptaki.

When the Spanish explorers arrived in the Southwest during the 16th century, they found many descendants of the Anasazi, or their relatives, living in pueblos located on mostly level sites rather than in canyons and on the sides of cliffs. An exception was Acoma, N. Mex., constructed on top of a massive butte and still in existence. Another famous pueblo, still in existence and still inhabited, is located in Taos, N. Mex. Some 30 other pueblos, including those at Laguna and Zuni, N. Mex., are still in existence in Arizona and New Mexico, mostly along the Rio Grande Valley.

Although the architecture of the American Indians has generally influenced that of succeeding eras very little in the United States, the great pueblos of the Southwest did have considerable influence on the early Spanish architecture of that region. And adobe is still widely used in the region for buildings that continue to reflect the early Spanish culture and that of the Anasazi, who preceded them.

**Related Articles** COLONIAL ARCHITECTURE; HISTORY OF ARCHITECTURE.

**Sources of Additional Information** See listing in the article entitled history of architecture.

**PREFABRICATION** A system of construction in which standardized components or elements of buildings are manufactured and assembled in factories instead of on building sites. Prefabrication has always been of some importance in architecture. Recently, because of rising costs of construction at building sites, scarcity of skilled craftspersons, the greater precision and efficiency of factories, and the possibility of lower costs, prefabrication construction has become increasingly more important.

Prefabrication is sometimes called industrialized construction, since components are manufactured in factories. Prefabrication is also sometimes called systems building and the use of prefabricated units, systems design or the systems approach to design. The integration of prefabrication systems into the total construction of buildings is often called an industrialized building system.

**Types** Three major types of prefabrication are important in architecture: components; systems composed of components; and complete, or nearly complete, buildings. A component is usually a relatively small unit, made to be used with other units of the same kind and others in the construction of buildings. A system is a number of such components, joined together in a manner allowing the whole to perform some function or functions. However, it should be remembered that small components, like bricks, may be joined together in a sys-

tem, such as a wall, that in turn may be considered a component of the structural system of a building. The structure then becomes a component of the entire building system, which is in turn a component of the environment in which it exists.

Thus prefabrication can be seen to be concerned with a large array of products and materials, ranging in size from the smallest manufactured item, such as a nail or other fastener, through a whole spectrum of sizes and complexities, to complete buildings. It is not too difficult, at least in theory, to imagine an even greater extension to groups of buildings and even entire communities.

In practice, prefabrication is of importance in architecture on a somewhat smaller scale. Increasingly, architects and other design professionals must design buildings with manufactured or prefabricated products, over which they exercise no design prerogatives except selection, the products having previously been designed by others beyond the control of architects. Architects may also design with products that are precut to size, such as wood studs or steel beams. In such cases, architects exercise some control over the products to be used. At the next level of complexity, products or components are combined in a process sometimes called preassembly into systems, some of them relatively small and simple, such as windows, some large and complex, such as entire curtain walls for tall buildings. Some of these systems, including most windows today, were designed by others, with architects only making selections from stock types. In other cases, such as curtain walls, architects may either select or design systems, the choice often being determined by function, aesthetics, and economics.

**Design** Practicing architects may design complete prefabricated buildings, but most are designed by the staffs of the companies that produce them. These companies occasionally commission practicing architects to make designs for prefabricated buildings. Because of this situation, many architects are convinced that prefabricated buildings are not good architecture, and that these buildings are in competition with their own. The prefabricated building companies reply that they can provide buildings that are perfectly adequate for many purposes and are acceptable to certain clients at lower cost than those designed by architects; they are more speedily erected, saving the time, energy, and money expended in having buildings designed by architects and constructed by contractors or others. Architects reply that no stock building can be as good as one designed by a competent architect.

Short of selecting complete prefabricated buildings from catalogs, architects and other design professionals find that they must be up to date on the latest components and systems. And many also find that methods may be discovered for combining prefabricated components in new and imaginative ways. As the cost of on-site fabrication and assembly of buildings and their parts continues to rise because of continuing inflation, the use of prefabricated components and systems may be expected to increase. And architects will have to deal with that fact in their designs. Some think this will necessitate a systems approach to design. Others hope that architects will be called upon more frequently to design the components and systems, as they have occasionally in the past. Admittedly, such architects will have to learn the principles of design for industrial production in order to accomplish good designs in this field. A few have done so in the past and some people believe that a greater number of future architects may specialize in design for fabrication of entire buildings as well as components and systems.

**History** Although prefabricated building construction is often thought of as quite modern, actually such practices began soon after humans constructed their first huts. When the first builder cut poles that were properly sized and transported them to a building site to be erected, the practice of prefabricated construction had its rudimentary beginnings. This was followed by making sun-dried brick in standard sizes so that they could be combined together to make walls and other systems.

Other prefabrication methods were developed over the years, using mostly craft labor and rudimentary machines for the production. Not until after the beginning of the industrial revolution in England, about the middle of the 18th century, did prefabrication, or industrialized building, as practiced today actually start. However, some prefabricated wood houses had been produced in England and shipped to the American colonies and other places early in the 17th century and, by the end of the first quarter of the 18th, such houses were produced in the colonies.

By the middle of the 19th century, buildings were prefabricated not only of wood but also of cast and wrought iron in England, New York, and other places and shipped to countries as far away as Australia. In 1851, with the construction of the Crystal Palace, at the Great Exhibition in London, designed by Sir Joseph Paxton (1801–65), the practice of prefabrication was given a great impetus. For this building, English engineer Sir Charles Fox (1810–74) devised a structural system, with standardized sizes of iron columns and other structural members, including only three sizes of trusses, and with 300,000 panes of window glass all of the same size. All fit into a planning unit or module of 8 by 8 feet. All the parts of the Crystal Palace were prefabricated, transported to the site, and erected with the aid of machinery. For this very large building, of some 754,000 ft² of ground floor area, the whole process of fabrication and erection was accomplished in nine months, a feat

made possible by its modular design, standardized parts, and prefabrication.

The design, prefabrication, and erection of the Crystal Palace was so well done that it was later dismantled and erected again at Sydenham, England, only to be destroyed by fire in 1936. Although the Crystal Palace was not really appreciated as a work of architecture until some 50 years after it was built, it nevertheless had an almost immediate effect on the use of iron and glass in buildings and on standardization and prefabrication of buildings and their parts. Others soon followed, including major ones at the Paris expositions of 1855 and 1889.

By the end of the 19th century, iron and timber prefabricated buildings were relatively common. Some systems even lent themselves to the construction of any of a number of types of buildings, including churches, houses, and stores. Some not only included prefabricated structures, but fronts or facades as well. Prefabrication of iron structures and facades for office and similar buildings was further developed by several people and companies in New York City in the latter half of the 19th century. The best known and most successful was an American inventor, James Bogardus (1800–74), who designed and fabricated a number of such buildings in New York City and in other American cities. Beginning in 1905, another important system of prefabrication, precast concrete, had been used in buildings.

**U.S. Prefabrication** During the early part of the 20th century, in the United States considerable progress was made in the standardization of building components, such as windows and doors. Some prefabricated buildings were constructed for war workers during World War I, but they were mostly crude and of a temporary nature. After the war, various attempts were made to develop new prefabrication systems for complete buildings. One of the most interesting was a design for an aluminum building, called the Dymaxion House, made in 1927 by Richard Buckminster Fuller (1895–1983). Designed to be constructed on assembly lines in aircraft plants, idled after World War II, the first prototype was manufactured in 1946. The revolutionary building went into production.

Earlier, the production of trailers, begun in the 1930s, led to the development of mobile homes, now called "manufactured housing," fabricated in factories and transported mostly by truck to their sites. Never truly mobile, since most of them are never moved again, manufactured housing has become the most successful housing prefabrication system in the United States. Several million people live in them, and relatively large numbers are sold each year.

A large number of other prefabricated systems for houses have been developed in recent years. Although many of these systems, like those of manufactured housing, leave much to be desired in terms of aesthetic design, many have been successfully marketed in the United States and elsewhere. Like manufactured housing, other prefabricated house systems, because of their lower costs as compared to conventional construction, have made it possible for millions of Americans to own their homes.

One of the most important developments in prefabrication has been the gradual increase of open system components and other building elements. As opposed to a closed system, in which components and elements may be interchanged only with those in the same system, open system components and elements are designed and manufactured to fit together properly in a great variety of ways and systems.

Great impetus was given to open system prefabrication in the 1930s and 1940s by the development of a dimensional coordination system for buildings and their components and other elements. Called modular coordination, the system was started by an American manufacturer, Albert Farwell Bemis (1870–1936), in the 1920s and later continued by the Modular Building Standards and the American Standards associations. Their work resulted in standards for building components and building dimensions, based on a module of 4 in. The system was later adopted in other countries. In countries using the metric system, a module of 100 mm (millimeters), slightly less than 4 in, was adopted. Modular standards have gradually made it possible for building components to fit together properly in generally open systems. And the standards have also made design, detailing, and drafting for buildings more efficient.

At the end of World War II, interest in prefabricated housing was revived because of the nationwide housing shortage. Of the experimentation, only the Lustron House (1946), a steel and porcelain enamel house produced in an aircraft factory using automated assembly techniques, still exists. Although some 5,000 were built, distribution problems were too great, and the failure of this program gave a bad name to prefabrication.

Some of the most interesting and well-designed prefabricated houses were those designed by Carl Koch (1912–   ), including his Acorn and Techbuilt houses, introduced in the 1950s.

In prefabricated systems for buildings other than houses, considerable progress has been made in the 20th century, particularly after World War II. Industrial and other types of buildings of precast concrete, timber, and metals have been developed and are widely available. Components such as curtain walls of metals and other materials have come into widespread use and have been considerably improved over the years. Completely fabricated in factories and often delivered to building sites in large assemblies, such curtain walls are not only

improvements over older types of walls but may often be more inexpensively manufactured and can be erected quickly. Just how quickly, if need be, was demonstrated by the erection, perhaps mostly as a publicity stunt, of an entire aluminum curtain wall on a tall building in New York City in a single day in 1954.

Precast concrete units have been widely used in buildings in recent years. These include both very large wall and other structural panels, and complete rooms, prefabricated in their entirety and lifted into place in buildings like blocks. Similar systems have been developed in other materials. Experiments with plastics resulted in a prototype Monsanto House, designed by Marvin Goody (1957), seen by thousands at Disneyland Park in Buena Park, Calif.

Many interesting and important improvements in design for prefabrication have recently taken place in many parts of the world, including England, the former Soviet Union, and the United States. One of the most interesting and important was a program called School Construction Systems Development (SCSD), during the 1960s. Under the direction of Ezra D. Ehrenkrantz (1932–   ), the SCSD program produced, with cooperation of manufacturers of various components and systems and with funds provided by Educational Facilities Laboratories, a series of 13 schools in California, designed specifically as demonstrations of a systems approach to building prefabrication. These schools were notable not only for their rather complete use of prefabrication but for the integration of lighting, heating, and other comfort systems within the overall systems of structure and other elements.

For the Montreal World's Fair (1967), Moshe Safdie designed the Habitat housing project. This was a widely publicized modular concrete construction. Habitat preceded the U.S. Operation Breakthrough program of 1969. The Operation Breakthrough's search for innovation involved many proposals, which were faulted for being insufficiently analyzed. However, the impact on the construction industry has continued.

Today in the United States, as elsewhere, prefabrication of all kinds is growing rapidly. Hundreds of thousands of manufactured housing units are produced each year, and it is estimated that about one-fourth of all American families now live in prefabricated houses of some kind. What are sometimes called pre-engineered buildings, for many purposes, are widely available. And the number of prefabricated components and systems increases as time passes. Many architects believe that the advent of widespread prefabrication is not an unmixed blessing. Admitting that factory production of building components has many desirable aspects, they are less than happy as they envision the possibilities for a faceless, dehumanized, standardized environment.

**Related Articles** Bogardus, James; Building Industry; Fuller, Richard Buckminster; House; Articles on various building components and systems.

**Further Reading** Dietz, Albert G. H., and Laurence Stephan Cutler: *Industrialized Building Systems for Housing*, MIT Press, Cambridge, Mass., 1971; Gale, M., and E. Gollon, Jr.: *Cast-Iron Architecture in New York*, Dover Publications, New York, 1974; Russell, B.: *Buildings Systems: Industrialization and Architecture*, John Wiley, London, 1981; Watkins, A. M.: *The Complete Guide to Factory Made Houses*, E. P. Dutton, New York, 1980.

**Sources of Additional Information** Manufactured Housing Inst., 1745 Jefferson Davis Hwy., Suite 511, Arlington, Va.; Metal Building Manufacturers Assoc., c/o Charles M. Stockinger, Thomas Assoc., 1230 Keigh Bldg., Cleveland, Ohio 44115.

**PRESERVATION** Taking appropriate actions to prevent further changes or deterioration in a site, building, group of buildings, or other structure. Thus preservation accepts sites, buildings, or other structures generally as they exist and does not attempt to make changes for historic or similar reasons. An architect who does preservation work on buildings is often called a "preservationist," as are other people interested in the subject.

**Definitions** Some confusion exists about the precise meanings of some of the processes related to preservation work. Repairs are work performed on a building in order to correct problems that may further injure it. *Restoration* is the rehabilitation of a building in a manner that will closely approximate its state when it was first constructed or at some other time in its history. *Reconstruction* means the construction of a new building that resembles an old building as closely as possible, on the basis of studies of historic, archeological, and other types of evidence. *Remodeling* means rehabilitation of, or making changes in, a building without any particular regard to its history or original form. A variant is preserving or restoring the exterior of a building while remodeling the interior, or in extreme cases, called *facadism*, building a new building behind older facades. See article entitled remodeling. *Adaptive use* involves changing a building that was originally designed for certain functions into one to be used for different functions. A restored or preserved building operated as a museum is not normally considered adaptive use. See article entitled adaptive use. A variation may be a modern addition to a historic building.

In preservation work, it is often said that the best and most honest procedure is that of preservation, if at all possible, followed in descending order of desirability by repairs, restoration, and reconstruction. A wide range of opinion exists on the subject of specific buildings that should be preserved, restored, or reconstructed. At one extreme end of the range are those who have no interest in their historic or architectural heritage and do not care if anything is saved. At the other extreme are those who think everything from the past is worth preserving.

Yet even among those who are dedicated, there is considerable difference of opinion. Some believe that the buildings worth saving are those considered to be excellent architecture. Others believe that buildings of historic interest should be saved. The most widely held and accepted view is that buildings, groups of buildings, other structures, and sites that make cultural contributions to society should be preserved, that those of historic or architectural significance, or both, should be saved. This philosophy still leaves room for debate, some maintaining that sites of single events, such as the Wright brothers' first flight at Kitty Hawk, N.C., the birthplace of a president, or some other place, should be preserved, restored, or reconstructed, while others may disagree. The debate will no doubt continue.

Many architects are involved in some kind of preservation work. To do effective work in this field, they must be scholars as well as architects. For such work to have authenticity, architects must understand the background of the building upon which they will work, not only the architectural background but the historic, together with the lives, manners, goals, and other characteristics of the people who first constructed the building and those who occupied it. Such pursuits are of great interest to some architects, but not to others. Those of no particular historic bent, who are not willing to spend time in study and research, and who are not willing to sublimate their own creative talents to those of the architect or other designer of the original building, should leave preservation work to persons who do have the requisites.

**Research** The process of preservation, restoration, or reconstruction begins with research. The amount and depth of the research required varies considerably. For example, if only repairs and modest rehabilitation are to be undertaken, the research might be minimal. On the other hand, if a reconstruction is to be attempted, research might begin with the remains, if any, of the foundation of the former building and extend to searches of old records, documents, books, and many other sources limited only by the abilities and imagination of the researcher.

Research is of three major types: historic, archeological, and architectural. Historic research involves investigation of every source that might yield information on the building, its builders, and those who lived in it or used it and their times. Archeological research involves investigation of the site of the building for artifacts and other remains that may then be identified, preserved, restored, cataloged, and studied. Architectural research is involved with the character and dates of the building, its details, and site.

Such research is usually initiated at the beginning of a project and often proceeds during the entire process until the construction work has been completed. Based on the initial research, a program may be prepared for the work, outlining the goals to be achieved and methods for reaching them. First, the importance of the building must be established, along with the facts of its plan, structure, size, location, and so on. Next, the use to which the building will be put must be determined. Although many of these buildings are used as museums, the trend today is often toward other and more vital uses, such as offices, homes, information centers, and so on. Care must be taken not to destroy the architecture of these buildings in order to provide such uses.

Once the use has been determined, the next important decision is the date or era to which the building will be returned. In some cases, this may be the time in which it was originally constructed; in others, it might be some time of historic importance. In still others, a decision might be made to retain some elements of each of the various eras in a building's history. The selection should be made with extreme care and should be based on thorough and painstaking research. After the purpose has been determined, the use to which the building will be put must be examined in detail. If it is to become a museum, what are the requirements for large groups, offices, storage, or spaces of other types?

**Preparatory Phases** Other than the requirements for scholarly research and the translation of the research into period construction that will appear authentic, architectural services in preservation, restoration, and reconstruction are generally similar to those for other buildings. There is one great difference and that is the necessity for keeping scrupulous records, written and graphic, of everything discovered about the buildings through research and during the construction.

PRESERVATION Michigan State Capitol (1879; restored), Lansing, Mich. *[Architect: Elijah E. Meyers; 1993 restoration architect: Richard Frank; lighting designer: Gary Steffy]*

After the completion of a program for a building, the next steps are preparing a schematic design, along with preliminary specifications; developing them more fully, during the design development phase; and preparing contract documents, working drawings, and specifications from which the work can be constructed. Cost estimates are also prepared.

Contracts for the construction are then bid or negotiated and the actual construction may begin. All these phases are similar to those for other buildings, except that in this work, there are unusual requirements for old materials and objects to be found or reproduced and for a very high level of craftsmanship. During the construction phase, architects ordinarily spend more time than they would on that of a new building of relatively the same size and complexity. As construction work proceeds, parts of the building are revealed, often furnishing bits of information that will be useful in later work or problems that could not have been foreseen. Old parts must be carefully removed, numbered, cataloged, and stored. A major problem, of course, is in finding contractors interested in this sort of work and skilled craftspeople to execute the work.

PRESERVATION Restoration, Governor's Palace (1720; addition, 1751), Williamsburg, Va. *[Architect: uncertain but may have been Sir Christopher Wren; 1751 addition architect: Robert Taliaferro]*

After a building has been completed, there remain a few other services the architect may perform, including sometimes the interior design and furnishing of the building. Another important service is the provision for display of features of the building, such as characteristic details, various types of construction, unique features, and the like. Information on good operating and maintenance practices should be furnished to the owner. An architectural record should also be prepared, completely illustrating and documenting the work that has been performed, including what was done, and why and how. Copies of such reports should be filed in the Historic Buildings Survey section of the U.S. Library of Congress, Washington.

**Historic Sites** Literally thousands of buildings and other structures of historic or architectural importance have been preserved, restored, or reconstructed in the United States, including whole towns, or parts of them, as in the Vieux Carré, New Orleans, La.; Williamsburg, Va.; and Sturbridge Village, Mass. Many thousands of others have been destroyed for economic reasons, as the old Pennsylvania Station (1910), New York City, designed by McKim, Mead and White; or allowed to collapse into ruins, as the great houses of Rosewell Hall (1740) in Gloucester, Va., by an unknown architect, and Belle Grove (1857), Iberville Parish, La., designed by James Gallier, Jr. (1827–68), two of the many truly great houses that have been lost through neglect. Many other buildings are still in need of preservation or restoration, and their chances of survival are probably better today than at any other time in the history of the United States, mainly because of laws passed in recent years by the states and the national government and efforts of dedicated preservationists. In spite of these efforts, many significant buildings continue to be demolished all over the country.

**Laws** Preservation began early in the United States, though at first it was almost completely confined to sites and buildings of importance in the early history of the country. About the middle of the 19th century, preservation work accelerated as a result of the efforts of governments and individuals. By the early 20th century, various laws had been passed attempting to encourage preservation, among them the National Antiquities Act of 1909. Also organizations dedicated to preservation were founded about that time or somewhat earlier, including the Society for the Preservation of New England Antiquities and the Association for the Preservation of Virginia Antiquities.

Starting in 1933, the work of preservation has been helped enormously by the Historic American Buildings Survey (HABS). Beginning in that year, HABS has systematically collected data, photographs, and drawings of buildings and other structures all over the United States

and its territories. Administered by the National Park Service of the U.S. Department of the Interior, under an agreement with the American Institute of Architects and with the Library of Congress, where the records are deposited, HABS has collected information on more than 16,000 buildings. In 1935 the National Historic Sites Act was passed, establishing a list of a number of sites to be protected and preserved.

In 1949 the National Trust for Historic Preservation was chartered by the U.S. Congress for such purposes as the collection and provision of information, consulting services, publishing of materials, grants, and preservation and maintenance of a number of historic buildings. With over 100,000 members, the National Trust does much to encourage and promote preservation. In addition, there are many other groups, on local, state, and national levels, involved in such work. Several hundred government programs are involved in preservation in some way and most states have preservation commissions.

In 1966 the National Historic Preservation Act gave a giant boost to preservation. It expanded the list of historic sites into a National Register of Historic Places that now includes some 15,000 properties considered significant. In general, these properties must be more than 50 years old, but significant later ones may be exempted from this requirement. The act also established an Advisory Committee on Historic Preservation, composed of people in government and in private life, to advise the president and Congress. Most importantly, the act established funds for grants to the National Trust and to the states for preservation work, millions of dollars of which have been spent since the first grants in 1968. Many other federal and state programs that encourage preservation and aid in its funding have since been established.

**Tax Credits** Since 1976, federal tax laws have encouraged the preservation of historic structures. The

**PRESERVATION** Reconstruction, Oneida Museum, Green Bay, Wis.

National Register of Historic Places, maintained by the Department of the Interior, includes buildings, districts, or structures of certified importance. The tax credit of 20 percent applies to rehabilitation of certified historic buildings for income-producing purposes. They also allow depreciation of improvements over 31.5 years for nonresidential properties and 27.5 years for rental residential properties. Work on historic structures must conform to the Secretary of the Interior's Standards for Rehabilitation.

Nonhistoric buildings built before 1936 receive a 10 percent tax credit for rehabilitation of structures. The only requirements are that 50 percent of the building's exterior walls be kept as exterior walls, at least 75 percent of the building's existing external walls be retained in place as either external or internal walls, and that at least 75 percent of the building's internal structural framework remains.

The 1986 tax law places limits and restrictions on rehabilitation tax credits, and consultation with a tax lawyer is recommended.

For people who have a deep interest in history as well as architecture, preservation work can be very rewarding. Some people, including a number of architects, specialize in this work. In order to prepare themselves to handle the many requirements, specialized training is required, especially in general history, archeology, and the other social sciences as well as architectural history. Many architectural schools offer electives of value in preservation work, and a few offer specialization in the field and specialized degrees.

**Related Articles** ADAPTIVE USE; ARCH; COLUMN; DOME; REMODELING; SOCIAL SCIENCE; VAULT; Various articles on history and architects.

**Further Reading** Howard, Hugh: *The Preservationist's Progress: Architectural Adventures in Conserving Yesterday's Houses*, Farrar, Straus, and Giroux, New York, 1991; Kay, Gersil Newmark: *Mechanical and Electrical Systems for Historic Buildings*, McGraw-Hill, New York, 1992; Maddex, D., ed.: *All about Old Buildings: The Whole Preservation Catalog*, National Trust for Historic Preservation, The Preservation Press, Washington, D.C., 1985; Murtagh, William J.: *Keeping Time: The History and Theory of Preservation in America*, Sterling, New York, 1991; National Trust for Historic Preservation, Tony P. Wrenn, and Elizabeth D. Mulloy: *America's Forgotten Architecture*, Pantheon Books, a division of Random House, New York, 1976; Technical Preservation Services, National Park Service, U.S. Department of the Interior: *Respectful Rehabilitation*, The Preservation Press, Washington, D.C., 1982.

**Periodicals** *Historic Preservation* and *Preservation News*, 1785 Massachusetts Ave., N.W., Washington, D.C. 20036.

**Sources of Additional Information** Preservation Action, 1350 Connecticut Ave., N.W., Suite 401, Washington, D.C. 20036; The Historic American Buildings Survey, National Park Service, Department of the Interior, Washington, D.C. 20240; Library of Congress, Division of Prints and Photographs, Washington, D.C. 20450; National Trust for Historic Preservation, 1785 Massachusetts Ave., N.W., Washington, D.C. 20036.

**PRISON** A building, or group of buildings, in which people convicted or accused of breaking the law may be confined. Prisons, including jails and other types, have been designed by architects since about the 16th century. Although they never comprised a building type of great numbers, prisons have been an important fact of life since that time, and a number of architects have contributed to improvements in their design.

**Types** Prisons may be classified into three major types: lockups, jails, and correctional institutions. Lockups are usually part of the police stations operated by municipalities and are used for holding people, temporarily, for investigation, hearings, or trials. Jails are usually operated by cities or counties and are used both for temporary detention, as in lockups, and for people serving sentences of less than one year. Correctional institutions, sometimes called prisons or penitentiaries, are usually operated by a state or federal government and are used for those serving sentences longer than one year, and in the case of federal institutions, for those convicted of federal crimes. There are several specialized types of correctional institutions, including maximum-security and minimum-security prisons and special detention facilities for children, formerly called reform schools or reformatories, now usually called juvenile halls or homes. There are also special institutions for convicts who are physically or mentally ill.

**Controversial Principles** Prisons are controversial as are the concepts of law and order, punishment, and rehabilitation. Authorities have debated these principles for a very long time. On the one hand, there are those who espouse retribution and punishment, including prison terms, for those convicted of breaking laws. Some argue that such punishment acts as a deterrent to crime. On the other side are those who believe that the risk of punishment does not deter crime and that prison sentences may help make hardened criminals out of wrongdoers, who happened to commit crimes but who have not actually embarked on lives of criminality. The social costs of imprisonment are very high indeed, but are immeasurable. The economic costs are more easily understood. It costs more for a person to spend four years in San Quentin, a California state prison, than four years at a private college or university. In 1993, it cost $23,500 per year to keep a drug addict in jail.

**PRISON** Metropolitan Correctional Center (1978), Chicago, Ill. *[Architect: Harry Weese and Assoc.]*

Because of the controversies surrounding the whole subject of law and order and of justice, design philosophy for prisons has also become quite controversial.

**Elements** The design of prisons may be as simple as the provision of a few cells in a small police station lockup to the major problems of large maximum-security prisons, which in addition to housing prisoners in cells must have most of the elements of a complete city. The major elements of all but the smallest prisons are housing, dining services, recreation, reception and discharge, visiting, and administration.

Housing for inmates may be of several types, dependent on the type of institution and its security requirements. Housing units include interior cells usually back to back in the center of cell blocks and exterior cells on outside walls. Cells are usually barred and are equipped with toilet fixtures. Other types of housing include individual rooms, and dormitories, shared by up to 30 inmates. Near the inmate housing, other facilities are often provided, including dayrooms for recreation.

Dining services must be provided not only for the inmates, but for the prison staff. Such facilities may include central dining halls, localized dining halls near

the various cell-block units, and dining in the cells. The latter is considered the least desirable.

Correctional services include facilities for counseling, clinical testing and treatment, academic and vocational education, and inmate work areas. Inmate services include libraries, commissaries, barber and beauty shops, and chapels. Medical services include facilities for medical, psychiatric, and dental care of both bed and ambulatory patients. Recreational facilities include provisions indoors for sports, physical education, games, movies, and other activities, and provisions outdoors for exercise, sports, and games.

The reception and discharge element has provisions for booking prisoners in and out, storage of prisoners' clothing and other property, medical examinations, issue of prison clothing, and fingerprinting and photographing. Visiting facilities may be closed, with inmates and visitors completely separated physically, but able to see each other through tempered glass and to talk using telephones; and open, either indoors or outdoors, allowing normal contact. Administration includes offices and other facilities for the warden, guards, and other officials of the prison.

The proper design of a prison involves provision of all the elements required and establishment of proper relationships between them. In addition, the design must provide adequate security against escape by inmates, for inmates from each other, prison property, and the administrative personnel. The degree of security required varies considerably between institutions of different types. For example, a maximum-security prison is completely surrounded by a strong wall or fence, with guards patrolling it and others manning towers that overlook the entire facility. Inmates are housed in individual cell blocks each with its own toilet facilities. On the other hand, a minimum-security prison might have

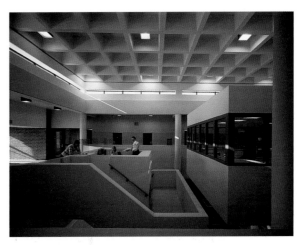

**PRISON** Interior, Minnesota Correctional Facility (1982), Oak Park Heights, Minn. *[Architects: Gruzen Sampton Steinglass]*

no walls, fences, or towers and the inmates might be housed in open dormitories or individual rooms. Sometimes a single institution houses inmates of varying security risks, and various areas of the complex have provisions for security at maximum, medium, and minimum levels.

In any prison, there must be provisions for proper communications, often including closed-circuit television and paging and public address systems as well as telephone and alarm systems. In addition, provision of secure locking systems and control of their keys is a necessity.

**History** In the earliest times, there were no prisons. Punishment of criminals took other forms. Beginning about the 12th century, prisons were established for certain kinds of offenders. Some of the great castles incorporated dungeons or keeps. The Tower of London, completed in the late 12th century and added on to later, is one of the best-known fortress-castles incorporating a keep in which, for centuries, illustrious prisoners were jailed. Prisoners in the Tower include two wives of Henry VIII (1491–1547), Anne Boleyn (born 1507, beheaded 1536) and Catherine Howard (born about 1520, beheaded 1542). Other famous inmates were the great English statesman and writer Sir Thomas More (born 1478, beheaded 1535), Lady Jane Grey (born 1537, proclaimed queen in 1553, imprisoned in the Tower 10 days later, and beheaded in 1554), and Sir Walter Raleigh (would-be colonizer of North Carolina and Virginia, born about 1552, beheaded 1618).

Another famous early prison was the Bastille (built in the 14th century) in Paris. It too jailed many famous prisoners, including a French government official, Nicolas Fouquet (1615–80), thought to be the model for *The Man in the Iron Mask*, written by Alexandre Dumas (1802–70), and the great writer Voltaire (1694–1778), the assumed name of François Marie Arouet. The prison was destroyed by a mob on July 14, 1789, the date marking the beginning of the French Revolution, and later celebrated as the French national holiday, Bastille Day.

Other prisons were built later, but in the 16th and 17th centuries a new method was widely employed: the prison ship or galley rowed by prisoners. Houses of correction were used, starting in the 16th century, mostly for people awaiting trials. Another innovation was the debtor prison for confining those who owed money. In most of the early prisons, sanitation was almost nonexistent and overcrowding was the rule. Treatment of prisoners was inhumane and corporal punishment was widely practiced. Prison reforms later changed these conditions, starting about the end of the 18th century, by which time imprisonment had been adopted as the most generally used method of punishment.

**American Development** The early colonists in America built jails, houses of correction, and debtors'

prisons, and conditions in them were no better than they were in Europe, until prison reforms started in the 1800s. A number of famous American architects designed prisons, including the Walnut Street Prison (1776), Philadelphia, by Robert Smith (1722–77), since demolished; the Virginia State Prison (1800), Richmond, by Benjamin Henry Latrobe (1764–1820); Moyamensing Prison (1835), Philadelphia, by Thomas Ustick Walter (1804–87); the Tombs (1838), New York City, designed by John Haviland (1792–1852), and later destroyed; and the Allegheny County Jail (1888), Pittsburgh, by Henry Hobson Richardson (1838–86). Many of the early prisons were Egyptian in appearance, which their architects seemed to think was proper to their purpose, but Richardson changed to Romanesque. Early American architects also designed jails, as have their later counterparts. Then, and today, jails were often associated with courthouses and almost every early American county seat had a building of each type.

The number of court convictions exceed the capability of governments to build prisons, with the result that many facilities are overcrowded. In 1992, about 436,000 people were held in the local and county jails each day. The time required to obtain sites and funding for new prisons emphasizes the severity of the problem.

New prisons tend to be more normal in environment, with the corrections officer moving among the prisoners instead of being behind a protective, glassed-in control booth. Also, a wider range of prisoners includes youth, women, and the elderly who need specialized facilities. A greater emphasis on education and job training has affected the design of prisons.

**Related Articles** LATROBE, BENJAMIN HENRY; RICHARDSON, HENRY HOBSON; WALTER, THOMAS USTICK.

**Further Reading** American Institute of Architects Committee on Architecture for Justice: *Justice Facilities Review, 1992–93*, AIA Press, Washington, D.C., 1993.

**PROGRAMMING** The process involved in developing a statement of the requirements, conditions, and goals, and of methods of satisfying these aims, in a proposed building. An architectural program is a report containing information of this type. Before a problem of any kind, including an architectural design problem, can be solved, it is necessary to know what the problem is. Then steps may be taken to solve it. Thus in architecture, the process of design is the solving of architectural problems, and the process of programming is the determination of the problems to be solved. This is also the case in other types of design involved in architecture. For example, interior designers, landscape architects, and city planners prepare both programs and designs.

**Scientific Method** Although not always recognized as such, even by architects, architectural problem solving utilizes what is known as the scientific method, a system for problem solving thought to have been first used by the Italian astronomer and scientist Galileo Galilei (1564–1642), called simply Galileo. The scientific method involves five major steps for orderly problem solving: statement of the problem; formulation of a hypothesis, or tentative theory; collection of data through observation and experimentation; testing and interpretation of the data; and drawing conclusions.

In architecture, the process is often broken down somewhat differently into six steps: definition of the problem; establishment of objectives; collection of data; analysis of the problem; consideration of possible solutions; and solution of the problem. The first four steps of the problem-solving process are included in architectural programming. The last two steps, which are involved in the solution of the problem, are included in architectural design. In other words, the steps in architectural programming might be said to include establishment of goals to be achieved and needs to be met, collection and analysis of data, development of concepts expected to lead to the solution of problems, and a statement of the problems.

The process in programming is collection and analysis of data, or the separation of the problem and the information gathered into their constituent parts or elements so that they may be studied. The process in design is composition, or synthesis: putting together the component parts or elements to form a whole, in other words, a building. In the complex world of architecture today, good building design depends on good programming, even for smaller building types such as houses.

In practice, architectural programming occurs in three major ways: by building owners, if they have competent staffs and construct numerous buildings; by architects, based on data furnished by their clients; and by architects, who handle the entire process. Although some buildings are still designed today without adequate programs, many architects believe so strongly in programming that they will not undertake commissions that do not include it; and many prefer to handle the processes themselves to ensure they are performed properly and thoroughly. In all these cases, it is necessary for architects to work closely and smoothly with clients' representatives.

**Data Classifications** The goals and needs of owners of proposed buildings must be clearly understood by architects performing programming functions. These are determined through conferences, study, and analysis. Many types of data are ordinarily required in programming; the amounts and types required depend on the type of building, its size and complexity, and other factors. The kinds of data required may be generally classified into six major groups: area or regional characteristics of the surroundings of the building site; the site itself; user needs and goals; budgets and other financial information; concepts for problem solving, or design; and schedules. Each of these categories may include many types of information. For example, site and related information ordinarily includes property boundaries, easements, and locations of natural features (rocks and trees), walkways, streets, curbs, pits, ditches, electrical and telephone posts and services, elevations and contour lines, subsoil conditions, views, prevailing winds, and so on. The programmer must determine which items of information will be required in each category and then gather the data.

After going through all the steps of programming, the program itself may be prepared. A program may be used for several purposes. First, it is used to demonstrate to the client what is involved in the project, and the program itself is subject to approval by the client. Second, the program may be used to explain the project to those expected to finance it, those who will use it, and others. Finally, the program serves as a guide for design by the architects and other design professionals involved in the work.

A program may take one of several forms, according to the preferences of those who prepare it and those who will use it, and the requirements of the project. However, as a guide, programming activities can be organized in a manner similar to the following outline.

*Outline of Programming Activities*

1. Establish goals
   a. Obtain management approval
2. Collect, organize, and analyze facts
   a. Collect quantitative data
   b. Select pertinent data
3. Uncover and test concepts
   a. Initiate qualitative ideas
   b. Collect further data as needed
4. Determine needs
   a. Need vs. desire
   b. Budget restrictions
5. State the problem
   a. Designer involvement

Program activities for specific buildings may vary considerably from the outline, but most will generally follow its concepts. As may be seen in the outline, the final category of information in a program constitutes a set of premises upon which the design of a building may be based. Thus a program is not an end in itself, but a tool used in the process of designing and constructing buildings. Also a program should not be thought of as a self-contained product or a procedure that takes place before design, and that design is another self-contained procedure that follows programming. In fact, the two are closely related and intertwined.

Some architects view programming procedures as part of the design process and believe that both should be performed by the same people, while other architects believe that programming (mostly analysis) and design (mostly synthesis) require different kinds of talents. In the first instance, programming and design might be performed by an architectural designer. In the second, a programmer would do the programming, a designer the design. The most important thing, however, is the preparation of informative and well-studied programs upon which creative designs may be based, regardless of who performs the various functions and how they are accomplished. Programming is also widely used in architectural schools for design problems to be solved by students. Sometimes a design professor furnishes a program to students; in other cases, students prepare the programs.

Programming has become such an important, even essential, part of architecture today that it is hard to imagine how architects functioned without it. Yet it is believed that no architectural programs were prepared for buildings until about the middle of the 19th century. And it is only in the past few decades that programming of the sort described above has come into widespread use. Today no important building, and very few minor ones, would be started without first preparing a program. And the process of programming has been greatly eased and expanded by use of computers for storage and retrieval of large amounts of data.

**Recent Developments** Programming became a recognized activity with the publication of William Pena's *Problem Seeking* (1969). The work of his firm, CRSS Architects, was pioneering in this field. The third edition of the book was published in 1987. As this has become a legitimate area of activity, the publication of research and case studies has led to some observations that are outlined here.

As in all of architecture, the computer has had a profound effect on programming, because it is now possible to build up databases linking postoccupancy evaluations to programming and design. Many involved in programming emphasize the need for user research and participation rather than limiting input to management or owners. In office buildings, for instance, facility managers provide expert input to programming. Much new insight results from special design challenges such as those for special groups, for example, those suffering from dementia; other challenges include unusual safety requirements, building security, and issues relating to energy conservation. The materials used in programming include literature, photo record review, walk-through inspections, executive interviews, and data analysis. Despite the definition of specific steps and activities, programming and design are continuous activities, not separate steps. For some clients, facility programming is an ongoing process in that needs change continuously.

There has been some difficulty in involving architects in programming. This is described as an education issue in that faculty in the schools of architecture have not all been well trained in programming, and there is need to educate architects in this activity. Also, programming expense must be paid for, and clients need to recognize the value of programming. This suggests the building professions need to prove the worth of programming. Successful projects result in educated clients.

Programmers must understand that the architect's aesthetic goals need to be identified and set during programming. In addition, programmers need to be more subjective and less dependent on data collection. The architectural designer should be involved in determining important issues of human, institutional, and cultural values which will shape the research for a program.

Each client presents special issues. It is important that in a client organization decision makers be involved in the programming process. It is frequently observed that many projects may present value conflicts which need to be recognized and addressed. An example might be in correctional facilities, where a variety of valid opinions exist that are often contradictory. It is important for the programmer to respond to the specific client goals. Other building types have other value conflicts, such as the need for a pleasant environment versus building security needs.

Programming has become a recognized profession, although only a few universities offer degrees in the field. As architects and architectural faculty become more involved in programming, it will be recognized that programming is for architecture, not merely for buildings.

**Related Articles** COMPUTER; DESIGN, ARCHITECTURAL; FEASIBILITY STUDY; PRACTICE OF ARCHITECTURE.

**Further Reading** Paterson, John: *Information Methods for Design and Construction*, John Wiley, New York, 1977; Pena, William: *Problem Seeking*, AIA Press, Washington, 1987; Preiser, Wolfgang F. E., ed.: *Professional Practice in Facility Programming*, Van Nostrand Reinhold, New York, 1993; Sanoff, Henry: *Methods of Architectural Programming*, Van Nostrand Reinhold, New York, 1977.

**PUBLIC BUILDING** A type of building, or group of buildings, owned and operated by a governing body, and often occupied by a governmental agency. Government buildings exist on every level, from the borough or town to the city, county, state, and federal.

Some government buildings are similar to those in use by private organizations. Other government buildings are uniquely related to functions that are purely governmental. Some of the major types are city and town halls, courthouses, fire and police stations, state capitols and related buildings, embassies, and the Capitol and other buildings of the national capital, Washington, D.C.

**The U.S. Capital** The capital of the United States is unique. It contains a great many public buildings of all sorts, many of them magnificent buildings by talented architects, others not up to that level. The greatest is undoubtedly the U.S. Capitol, upon which construction work and design and redesign have been going on since the competition for its design was won by an amateur architect, Dr. William Thornton (1759–1828), in 1792. For further discussion on the many interesting and important government buildings in Washington, see the article entitled capital, United States.

**State Capitols** State capitols are not an important building type today since none is being built. The latest was the State Capitol of Hawaii (1969), designed by John Carl Warnecke (1919–    ) in association with Belt, Lemmon and Lo. Many of the capitols were designed by eminent architects, starting in colonial times, and some are distinguished architecture. One of the most notable of the early buildings is the Colonial Capitol (1705), Williamsburg, Va., burned in 1749, and reconstructed in 1931. It may have been designed by the noted English architect Sir Christopher Wren (1632–1723). Others are Independence Hall (1745), Philadelphia, formerly the State House of Pennsylvania, designed by Andrew Hamilton or Edmund Woolley (1696–1771); the Maryland State House (1772), Annapolis, by Joseph Horatio Anderson (d. 1781); the Massachusetts State House (1798), Boston, designed by Charles Bulfinch (1763–1844); and the Capitol of Virginia (1791), designed by Thomas Jefferson (1743–1826). Notable later capitols include those of Tennessee (1859), by William Strickland (1788–1854); Rhode Island (1901), by McKim, Mead and White; Minnesota (1905), by Cass Gilbert (1859–1934); Wisconsin (1917), by George Browne Post (1837–1913); and Nebraska (1928), by Bertram Grosvenor Goodhue (1869–1924).

**Governors' Residences** State governments build many types of buildings, including office buildings and colleges. Some notable residences for governors include the Governor's Palace (1614), Sante Fe, N. Mex.; the Governor's Palace (1749), San Antonio, Tex., reconstructed in 1931; the Governor's Palace (1720), Williamsburg, Va., reconstructed in 1933, all by unknown architects; and the Governor's Palace (1767), New Bern, N.C., by John Hawks (1731–90), burned in 1798, and reconstructed in 1959.

**Town and City Halls** These halls are still being built today, thought not in great numbers. Their major elements are departments requiring considerable contact with the public, those requiring contact on occasion,

**PUBLIC BUILDING** United Nations Headquarters (1953), United Nations Plaza, New York, N.Y. *[Architects: Wallace K. Harrison (United States), Le Corbusier (France), Oscar Niemeyer (Brazil), Sven Markelius (Sweden), and others]*

those requiring contact for special purposes, city council chambers, offices for officials including mayors and city managers, storage, rest rooms, locker rooms and related facilities, and mechanical and electrical equipment spaces. Often a city or town hall also has courtroom facilities.

Such departments as those of tax collectors require frequent contact; departments such as building permits or city planning require contact on occasion; police and fire departments require contact for special purposes. In the design of city and town halls, emphasis must be put upon providing the special kinds of facilities needed by different departments, placing them in the proper relationships to each other, and locating them according to needs for contact with the public. In localities where town meetings, gatherings of voters, are held, special provision for this purpose must be made in town halls.

City and town halls were constructed in Europe in very early times and this tradition was later followed in America, when towns and cities started to grow. A great number of architects have designed such buildings and continue to do so today. In colonial America, there were no town halls in most of the country, other than New England, since the earliest local seats of government were usually counties.

519

A number of early town halls are still in existence, including that in Marblehead, Mass. (1727); Fairfield, Conn. (1794), later restored; Wilmington, Del. (1798), designed by Peter Baudry; and the Cabildo (1799), New Orleans, La. Later city and town halls of note include that in New York City (1812) by Joseph François Mangin (d. 1818) and John McComb, Jr. (1761–1853); the old City Hall (1850), New Orleans, La., by James Gallier, Sr. (1798–1868), now called the Gallier Building; the Old Boston City Hall (1865), by G. J. F. Bryant (1816–99) and Arthur Delevan Gilman (1821–82); Baltimore (1875), by George A. Frederick (1842–1924); Philadelphia (1890), by John McArthur, Jr. (1823–90); and San Francisco (1915), by Bakewell and Brown.

A striking and innovative new city hall (1969) for Boston was designed by Gerhard M. Kallmann (1915– ), Noel M. McKinnell, and Edward F. Knowles (1929– ) in association with Campbell, Aldrich and McNulty.

**Customs Houses** Customs houses are much like other office buildings and the principles of their design are similar. This is a venerable building type and American architects have designed notable examples since colonial days. An early Customs House (1715) by an unknown architect still exists at Yorktown, Va. Other interesting examples that survive include the Customs House (1770) at Williamsburg, Va., by Robert Smith (1722–77); the Exchange and Customs House (1771), Charleston, S.C., by Samuel Cardy (d. 1774) and William Rigby Naylor (d. 1773); and the Customs House (1841), New York City, by Ithiel Town (1784–1844) and Alexander Jackson Davis (1803–92), later used as a subtreasury building and now called the Federal Hall National Memorial. Over the years, a number of mints have been built in various locations, including Charlotte, N.C., Denver, Colo., New Orleans, and San Francisco.

**Courthouses** These constitute an important building type. The highest court in the country is the U.S. Supreme Court, in Washington, which occupies a building, completed in 1935, designed by Cass Gilbert (1859–1934). Other federal courts include district courts, which hold trials for federal cases, and courts of appeals, which hear appeals from district courts. Special federal courts include the Court of Claims and the Customs Court. On the state level, the highest courts are the state supreme courts, and some states have appeal courts on the next lower level. Trial courts include county and municipal courts and, on the lowest level, the courts of justices of the peace, police courts, and special courts, such as those for probate proceedings.

The design of courthouses, on all levels, includes all or most of the following elements: one or more courtrooms; one or more judge's suites; court officers' offices; jury rooms; and witnesses' rooms. In addition there may

**PUBLIC BUILDING** Fire Station #4 (1967), Columbus, Ind. *[Architects: Venturi & Rauch]*

be libraries, press rooms, assembly rooms, conference rooms, and other spaces. Criminal courts also require holding cells for the accused and related facilities for the use of marshals and other law officers. The design of courthouses is quite complex. There are a number of diverse functions to be performed in them. There are times when the performers must come together, as in the courtroom during trial appearances, and times when they must be strictly separated from each other, as when juries or prisoners are not in court.

Courts have existed from ancient times. At first the courts were held by rulers or religious officials in their palaces, in churches, or in other locations. By the Middle Ages, it had become the custom in England for officials to travel around the country holding court in various local buildings. By the time of the English settlements in America, special courthouse buildings were constructed and this practice was followed in the colonies. In many cases, the judges still traveled to the localities to hold court and this practice still exists, to some degree, today. For the most part, courthouses and the judges and other officials hold court in fixed locations at the municipal, county, state, and federal levels.

In colonial America, a courthouse was built in almost every county. Some still exist, including a remarkable series in Virginia, thought to have been designed by Richard Taliaferro, pronounced Toliver (1705–79). If he were in fact the architect, he was prolific indeed. In addition to many other buildings, he designed at least eight courthouses, including four that still exist in the counties of Charles City (1730), King William (1746), Hanover (1750), and Isle of Wight (1750). Many interesting courthouses have been designed since by architects all over the country.

New and renovated older courthouses reflect the changes in court operations and are now better referred to under the general heading of "corrections architecture." Special types of facilities include prisons and prison hospitals serving many special segments of the population, including women, youth, the elderly, the sick, and mentally ill. Prisons are now likely to be referred to as "correctional facilities." Specialized courts include juvenile and family law courts and tax courts.

**Fire Stations** Firehouses are an interesting building type. There are two major types: those operated by paid fire department employees, and those operated by volunteers. The design of both types is essentially the same, the major difference being in the facilities required for the personnel. The main elements of a fire station are the apparatus room, where the fire vehicles are housed, and the personnel areas. In an apparatus room, space is provided for one or more vehicles. Since hook-and-ladder aerial trucks might be 70 ft long, they require considerable space. Also in the apparatus rooms are the watch station, or room, rack or tower for drying hoses, facilities for storing and drying fire-fighting clothing, rest rooms, mechanical and electrical equipment areas, and sliding poles. Facilities for the personnel include sleeping quarters, cooking and dining areas, lockers, rest rooms and showers, study rooms, libraries, and recreational facilities.

In a fire station manned by volunteers, frequently a hall for meetings and social events is provided, and space for rescue vehicles is often required. In these stations, sleeping facilities are not usually required, unless the fire company employs paid drivers.

The history of fire fighting is as old as the history of the use of fire by humans. Pumping machines of various sorts were used in ancient Egypt in the 2d century B.C., and the Romans later invented improved machines. Hand-held squirt guns were used in 17th-century England, until mechanical pumps operated by levers and treadles were introduced about the middle of the 17th century. Soon afterward, machines of this sort were brought to colonial America. Horse-drawn, steam-operated fire vehicles came into use in both Europe and the United States about mid-19th century, but they were gradually replaced by engine-powered vehicles in the 20th century.

**Police Stations** These stations may be in separate buildings or incorporated into city or town halls. They usually have lockups or jails and police courts incorporated into them. Police stations may be quite small, in small towns, or quite large, in large cities. In either case, the major elements are administrative operations, divisional operations, prisoner facilities, public facilities, rest rooms and other personnel facilities, courts, storage, and mechanical and equipment spaces.

Administrative operations include offices and other facilities for the chief and other officials, and spaces for training, photographing and fingerprinting, communica-

tions, and record keeping. Divisional operations require spaces for the various law-keeping divisions, including detectives, juveniles, public safety, and others. Prisoner facilities include receiving, processing, and booking areas; cell blocks; cooking and dining facilities; and other spaces. Public facilities are those used by people who come to the station on business, and include waiting rooms, information centers, traffic violation bureaus, and complaints sections. Personnel facilities include such spaces as lounges, locker rooms, rest rooms, gymnasiums, lunchrooms, and snack bars. Police court requirements are similar to those of other courts but simpler, and in addition to the courtroom may include judges' chambers, offices, prisoners' rooms, and other spaces. Major aspects of the design of police stations involve the proper relationships between the various elements and proper precautions to prevent prisoner escapes and to protect police officials and the public as well as the prisoners.

There has been some sort of police authority since ancient times. In England, in the 9th to 11th centuries, the kings appointed people, called reeves, to represent them in the counties, called shires. From the combination of these words into shire reeve comes the present-

**PUBLIC BUILDING** City Hall (1969), Boston, Mass. *[Architects: Kallmann, McKinnell & Knowles]*

day word *sheriff*. For police protection, all men over sixteen had to stand what was called watch and ward duty under the direction of the sheriffs. By the early 19th century, cities had watchmen, and by the second quarter of the century, paid police had been organized, thus creating the need for the first police stations.

The American colonists followed the English system of watch and ward for many years. In 1838 Boston hired a paid police force of six men, and New York followed with a larger one in 1844. Since that time, the construction of police stations has followed, and their development has closely paralleled that of courthouses.

**Recent Public Buildings** Many other kinds of public buildings have been constructed in the past and are being constructed today. Interesting, varied, and important public buildings constructed in the recent past, include the United Nations Headquarters (1950, library 1963), New York City, designed by an international team of 15 architects, headed by Wallace Kirkman Harrison (1895–1981) of the United States, and including Le Corbusier (1887–1965) of France, Oscar Niemeyer (b. 1907) of Brazil, and Sven Markelius (1889–1972) of Sweden. Another joint effort is the Chicago Civic Center (1967) by an association of firms: C. F. Murphy; Skidmore, Owings and Merrill; and Loebl, Schlossman, Bennett and Dart. Other important buildings are the Marin County Civic Center (1972), San Rafael, Calif., completed many years after the death of its architect, Frank Lloyd Wright (1867–1959); the twin-towered World Trade Center (1973), New York City, by Minoru Yamasaki (1912–86) and Emery Roth and Sons; and the Post Office and Federal Building (1976), Saginaw, Mich., by Smith, Hinchman and Grylls. The Portland Building, Portland, Ore. (1982), was designed by Michael Graves (1934–    ), and the Federal Judicatory Building (1992) in Washington, D.C., was designed by Edward Larabee Barnes (1915–    ) with John M. Y. Lee & Partners for a prominent site next to Union Station in Washington, D.C.

Other public buildings include post offices, federal, state, and county office buildings, public colleges and universities, town centers, community and recreation centers. Many museums are built with public funds. Federal reserve banks are a specialized building type. Famous federal building programs include the TVA development of dams along the Tennessee River valley and the buildings of the National Park Service. New architectural attention is given to buildings for utilities, such as water and power, and waste treatment.

Transportation systems are often built by government or regional government agencies and include such building types as airports, parking structures, dock and terminal facilities, subways and light rail.

**Embassies** One of the most interesting kinds of public buildings constructed in the second half of the 20th century has been a series of U.S. embassies. A truly remarkable demonstration of good American architectural design was disseminated all over the world in these new embassies built in many countries. Although they vary in their degree of excellence, the embassies make an impressive list: The Hague, Netherlands (1956), by Marcel Breuer (1902–81); Athens, Greece (1961), by Walter Adolf Gropius (1883–1969) and The Architects Collaborative; Havana, Cuba (1953) and Rio de Janeiro, Brazil (1954), by Harrison and Abramovitz; Rabat, Morocco (1961), by Morris Ketchum, Jr. (1904–83), Francis X. Gina (1910–    ), and Stanley Sharp (1914–    ); Seoul, Korea (1957), by Ernest Kump (1911–    ); Karachi, Pakistan (1961), by Neutra and Alexander; Stockholm, Sweden, and Copenhagen, Denmark, both 1954, by Ralph Rapson (1914–    ); Djakarta, Indonesia (1958), by Antonin Raymond (1888–1976) and Ladislav Rado (1909–    ); Amman, Jordan (1957), by Paul Rudolph (1918–    ); London, England (1956), and Oslo, Norway (1959), by Eero Saarinen (1910–61); Baghdad, Iraq (1956), by José Luis Sert (1902–86); New Delhi, India (1954), by Edward Durell Stone (1902–78); Bangkok, Thailand (1959), by John Carl Warnecke (1919–    ); and Accra, Ghana (1958), by Harry Weese (1915–    ).

Because of world terrorism and political unrest, new consular buildings reflect an emphasis on security. A recent example is the U.S. Embassy for Amman, Jordan (1992), designed by Perry Dean Rogers & Partners, which includes a chancery, ambassador's residence, and a club for visiting U.S. citizens within a secured compound.

**Related Articles** Capital, United States; Individual architects and firms; Various building types.

**Further Reading** Hitchcock, Henry-Russell, and William Seale: *Temples of Democracy—The State Capitols of the USA*, Harcourt Brace Jovanovich, New York, 1976; Pare, Richard, ed.: *Court House*, Horizon Press, New York, 1978.

# R

**RAILWAY STATION** A building for the arrival, loading, handling, and departure of railroad trains and their passengers, crews, and freight. There are two major kinds of stations: passenger and freight. Each station is usually operated by one railroad company, but some stations are used by more than one railroad company and are often called "union" stations.

Today railway station design is almost completely a thing of the past, except for remodeling and construction of a few small stations. Railway stations, particularly those in large cities, in the golden era of railroading, were almost like complete cities with facilities for almost every need of passengers and visitors. Today a few of these great stations still exist, and several have been restored to their former glory. As European railway stations have been rebuilt, so we may see a new generation of U.S. railway stations, often in conjunction with other transportation systems. Some older rail lines are being renovated to again carry passengers in an effort to relieve automobile traffic.

**Elements** In the small railways stations of today, the major elements are few: a waiting room, a ticket office, a baggage room, rest rooms, mechanical and electrical equipment spaces, and canopy-covered platforms. Sometimes there is a newsstand or a snack bar. The design of these stations is straightforward, mainly consisting of placing the various elements in an efficient relationship with each other. This is a far cry from the complications and complexities of the great terminals of the past.

**History** The history of railroading began in England with the invention of the first steam locomotive in 1804, with the first locomotive to pull cars in 1814, and with the first regularly operated railroad in 1825. Since that time, many railway stations, large and grand or small and modest, have been built all over the world.

**American Development** The first railroad locomotive in the United States started operating in 1825 and the first scheduled railroad in 1830. The railroads started building stations soon afterward. None of the earliest stations has survived. Many of the buildings constructed in the era of railroad expansion during the second half of the 19th century have been demolished.

The grand era of railroad station design came in the late 19th century and the first quarter of the 20th. A large number of stations were designed by many of the best U.S. architects; Frank Furness (1832–1912) and Henry Hobson Richardson (1838–86), made a specialty

**RAILWAY STATION** Pennsylvania Station (1910; demolished 1964), New York, N.Y. *[Architects: McKim, Mead and White]*

523

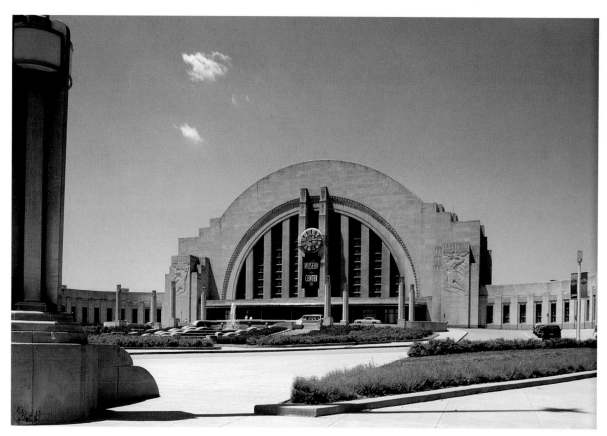

**RAILWAY STATION** Cincinnati Union Terminal (1933; later alteration), Cincinnati, Ohio. *[Architects: Fellheimer and Wagner]*

of their design. Some stations were very large, and some were quite opulent. A number of these are still in operation, including Union Station (1908), Washington, D.C., by Daniel Hudson Burnham (1846–1912), later remodeled; Grand Central Station (1913), New York City, by Reed and Stem in association with Warren and Wetmore, often threatened but still standing; Union Station (1926), Chicago, by the successors to Daniel Hudson Burnham—Graham, Anderson, Probst and White; and Union Station (1926), Richmond, Va., by John Russell Pope (1874–1937).

In recent years, public support for renovation and preservation of railroad stations has resulted in the adaptation of several for public purposes. Of note are the St. Louis Union Station (1894) designed by Theodore C. Link, remodeled by Hellmuth, Obata and Kassabaum (HOK), Burnham's Union Station in Washington, D.C. (1908), restored (1988) and reused as a shopping and restaurant center by Ben Thompson (1919–    ), and the Cincinnati Union Terminal (1933), Cincinnati, Ohio, designed by Fellheimer and Wagner, most recently renovated for use as a cultural center. In New York City, the loss of Pennsylvania Station (1910, demolished 1964–65), designed by McKim, Mead and White, has resulted in recent proposals for the conversion of the nearby surplus General Post Office (1913),

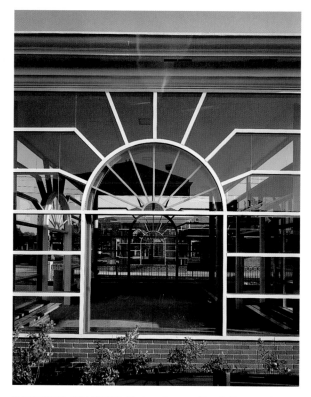

**RAILWAY STATION** Shaker Square Rapid Transit Station (1986), Cleveland, Ohio. *[Architect: Gould Assoc.]*

also designed by McKim, Mead and White, as a new Pennsylvania Station.

**Rapid Transit** Related to the regular railways are rapid transit systems, including subways, elevated railroads, and light rail. The first elevated railroad in the United States was built in Chicago in 1892, the first subway in Boston in 1897, followed by New York in 1904. A subway system was built in Chicago, starting in the 1930s. Until recently, these were the only U.S. cities with such rapid transit systems.

In the past few years, other cities have studied the possibilities of more efficient public transportation, and two have constructed systems: San Francisco's first part opened in 1972, and Washington's first part opened in 1975. Harry Weese (1915– ) designed the stations for the Washington system, called Metro. More than 14 architects and 8 landscape architects participated in the design of the San Francisco system, Bay Area Rapid Transit, or BART. From the beginning of BART, in 1960, to 1966, Donn Emmons (1910– ) served as consulting architect, and from that time to 1970, the position was held by Tallie B. Maule (1917–74). An effort has been made over the past few years to improve the grim and dreary appearance of the subway stations of the old New York City system.

Other cities, including Atlanta, are planning rapid transit systems, but there is considerable doubt that they can be constructed and operated economically. More likely are the light rail systems which have been proposed or built in several cities.

**Related Articles** AIRPORT; HOTEL; RESTAURANT; Articles on individual architects and firms.

**Further Reading** Lancaster, Clay, and Lawrence Grow, eds.: *Waiting for the 5:05—Terminal, Station and Depot in America,* Main Street/Universe, New York, 1977.

**REAL ESTATE** Land and all things, such as buildings, trees, and minerals, more or less permanently attached to it. The concept of property has been a part of human affairs since prehistoric times. Although hard to define precisely because of the different interpretations given to the concept in various societies and in various periods in history, property, in general, means things of value that are owned or which people have rights to use, enjoy, and dispose of. Property is generally divided into two major types: personal property, or personalty, and real estate, or realty. In the United States, real and personal property may be owned by individuals, groups of people, partnerships, corporations, governments, associations, religious groups, and others. Most types of personal property may be bought, sold, or given away freely without the necessity of contracts. Real estate in the United States may be sold or given away only by written contracts.

**Functions of Agents** Real estate is a very important part of the building industry and has a considerable effect on architecture. Real estate agents of various kinds, acting for owners and sometimes for themselves, actively engage in buying and selling land and buildings, in real property leasing, in development of projects, and in management of real property. In the performance of these functions, real estate agents are frequently involved with architects. They often represent owners, or themselves, in the assembly and development of land. By placing evaluations on land and other real property, they affect the financing of building projects. They ·advise owners on building projects and they often procure the financing for them. Sometimes they engage in the construction of buildings.

The basic function of real estate agents is selling real property for owners. A person who performs this function is often called a real estate broker. A broker may have real estate salespeople who are responsible to and work under the direction of the broker. Some people in the field specialize in real estate appraisal, evaluation of land and other real property; in real estate counseling, advising owners and others on purchases, sales, and similar matters; or in real estate management, administration of leasing, maintenance, and business matters for real properties.

**Developers** Often called entrepreneurs or promoters, developers actively promote the creation of building projects, including the assembly of land on which they are to be built and their financing, design, construction, and leasing or sale. Developers are often engaged in real estate work of other kinds, or come into development by way of such work, but this is not always the case. Anyone with the knowledge and business acumen necessary for putting together projects that are often large in size and quite costly can become a developer. And this includes some architects, who act as developers or who join with others to create developments.

A developer may promote a development, which is ultimately sold to others, in the expectation of profits; but perhaps the more usual case is that in which the developer retains total or part ownership in the completed development. Sometimes developers sell all or a portion of a development to others and then lease it back from them; this is called a sale–lease back transaction. When a developer sells a project and contracts to buy it back on a long-term basis, the transaction is called a sale–buy back or installment-sale contract. Architects also may participate in these processes.

In a typical development by a group, the major interests may be an investor, who supplies the equity capital, sometimes called the front money, to get the project started; a real estate agent, who assembles the land; a mortgage banker, who obtains the long-term financing, secured by a mortgage, a lien on the property; an architect, who performs the architectural services; and a contractor, who constructs the building. Also sometimes involved in such a group are an attorney to handle the legal aspects, an economist to ensure the feasibility of the project, and engineers and other consultants. Often the users of a development may also be involved, for example, in the case of the major tenants of a shopping center.

In a development by an individual developer or a development company, all the risks are taken by the developers, and the ownership or potential for profits is all theirs. For the other functions, architects, contractors, and others are engaged to perform their own functions as they would in any building project. When the development is handled by a group, or team, such as previously described, each participant performs specific functions for which each receives a fee, salary, or other payment; all share in the risk and divide the profits or ownership.

A development organization may be a single proprietorship, a partnership, a corporation, or a real estate investment trust (REIT). A joint venture, which may also be used, is like a partnership for one specific project or a series of projects. An REIT is an institution organized, usually by large developers or mortgage lenders, to spread the risk of development over a relatively large number of projects. The excessive building during the 1980s led to failure of some development companies, banks, and insurance companies and to losses for those who invested in REITs. Others have been successful investments.

**Development Stages** Developments ordinarily go through a number of important stages: establishment of the concept; determination of users' requirements; determination of approximate building size and costs and land requirements; feasibility and economic analysis of the venture; securing of land options; determination of financing sources; development of programs, schematic designs, and refined cost estimates and economic analyses; proposal to users; project design and preparation of construction documents, working drawings, and specifications; construction; and delivery of completed project to the users. Many developments have much more complicated steps than those outlined. In all cases, each step must be performed properly, efficiently, and with knowledge and foresight if a development is to be successful.

**Regulations** In the past, real estate transactions were not well regulated and real estate agents were neither well regulated nor well trained. Today there is a body of laws and regulations governing the actions of real estate agents and the functions they perform. Local real estate boards, located in every sizable municipality and the state associations of the National Association of Real Estate Boards (NAREB) govern the actions of their members in matters of ethics and other conduct. Real estate brokers must be licensed and must pass examinations to obtain their licenses. And for a person to use the title realtor, it is necessary to be licensed and a member of NAREB, who subscribes to its code of ethics. Real estate salespeople must also be licensed. In the United States, more than a half-million people are licensed real estate brokers and salespeople. An increasing number of brokers and salespeople have taken courses in real estate in the more than 250 U.S. colleges and universities offering such study. And an increasing number have graduated from one of the more than 50 colleges and universities offering degrees in real estate.

**Related Articles** BUILDING INDUSTRY; FEASIBILITY STUDY; FINANCE; PROGRAMMING.

**Periodical** *National Real Estate Investor*, 461 Eighth Ave., New York, N.Y. 10001.

**Sources of Additional Information** American Society of Real Estate Counselors, 430 N. Michigan Ave., Chicago, Ill. 60611; National Association of Real Estate Boards, 155 E. Superior St., Chicago, Ill. 60611.

**RECREATION BUILDING** Any of a wide variety of building types, where people may congregate to enjoy cultural pursuits, participate in athletics, watch sports, or engage in other activities. Recreation buildings are closely related to outdoor facilities used for similar purposes.

Recreation is a very personal thing. To some, it is represented by a quiet chess or card game. To others, it is flying an airplane, racing automobiles, or surfing. Recreation for many consists of spectator sports, either by attending games and other events or watching them on television. For others recreation is found in travel, gardening, studying, or collecting stamps, coins, or any of an almost boundless list of articles. Many pursuits provide recreation to some people but are actually the vocations of others, who seek recreation in different activities. Because of the great variety and number of recreational pursuits possible, a discussion of recreation buildings must necessarily be quite general, touching only on buildings and related outdoor areas that are primarily and specifically recreational in nature.

**Classifications** The major recreational facilities may be classified as follows: those for participant sports and athletics; those for spectator sports; clubs; camps; community recreation centers; and a miscellaneous category that would include amusement parks, fairgrounds, gambling casinos, dance halls, and other types. For further discussion of specific cultural recreation building types and open recreation areas, see titles listed at the end of this article.

There is no hard and fast line of division between recreation facilities of the various types, two or more

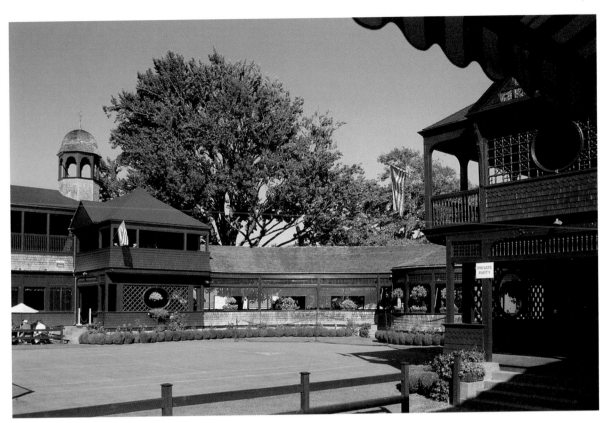

**RECREATION BUILDING** Newport Casino, now National Tennis Hall of Fame (1881; later alterations and additions), Newport, R.I. *[Architects: McKim, Mead and White]*

often being combined in one facility. For example, a golf club usually provides facilities for recreational golfing, a participant sport, and for tournaments, a spectator sport. And a country club may provide for both these functions and also have facilities for other sports, dining, dancing, card playing, other games, and so on.

**Ownership** Recreation facilities are owned and operated in several ways: by governments on all levels, federal, state, county, and municipal; by church groups; by associations or other organizations; by corporations or other businesses; and by individuals. Recreation facilities may be open to the public at large or to segments of the public, such as the inhabitants of a neighborhood or city; or to members and their guests as in most clubs; or they may be intended only for the private enjoyment of a family or an individual and guests.

**Participant Sports** There is a long list of participant sports, for which indoor or outdoor facilities are often provided. Some of them are bicycle riding; boating, in marinas, boat ramps, and other facilities; bowling; fishing boats, docks, camps, and other facilities; golf; hunting camps and other facilities; rifle and pistol ranges; skating, ice and roller; softball; skeet and trap shooting; swimming; and tennis. Of course there are a number of others and new ones are being invented all the time.

Some of the later additions include the use of vehicles of various kinds, such as dune buggies, four-wheel-drive recreational vehicles, go-carts, hang gliders, motorbikes, motorcycles, skateboards, and snowmobiles. Many think these latter pursuits are nourished by thrill-seeking and intoxication with speed and noise, and as these fads become unfashionable, they will be replaced by new ones. Some of these pursuits have become problems since may of their devotees have been known to destroy public and private property and natural resources and to create public nuisances.

**Spectator Sports** The major spectator sports are football, baseball, and basketball; but boxing, soccer, tennis, horseracing, and ice hockey are also popular. Facilities for these sports may be buildings, often called arenas, in which the contests take place indoors, and other structures, often called stadiums or parks, in which the games are played out-of-doors. A recent development has been stadiums that are completely or partly roofed, and in a few cases stadiums in which the roofs may be opened or closed as occasion demands.

**Clubs** Clubs, for recreational and other purposes, include youth clubs, adult clubs, golf clubs, tennis clubs, country clubs, and other types. Among the most important clubs for youths are the Young Men's Christian

527

**RECREATION BUILDING** Leonard Natatorium, Macalister College, St. Paul, Minn. *[Architects: The Leonard Parker Assoc.]*

Association (YMCA), Young Women's Christian Association (YWCA), and the Young Men's Hebrew Association (YMHA), the last named often combined into a club for both men and women (YM&YWHA).

**Camps** In addition to sports camps, such as those for fishing or hunting, many other camps exist for those traveling with trailers or campers and for those who like to vacation in more or less natural surroundings, in cabins, tents, tent campers, travel trailers, or on the ground. Such camps range from those that have small parking spaces for camping or travel vehicles, with hookups for electricity, water, and plumbing, and other facilities such as shower rooms, coin-operated laundries, and stores, to primitive camping sites accessible only to hikers or sometimes four-wheel-drive vehicles.

**Community Centers** Community recreation centers provide facilities in which people of all ages can engage in numerous activities, including sports, games, dances, craft and artwork, meetings, and so on.

**Amusement Parks** Among the miscellaneous recreational types, a popular one today is the amusement park. In the past, such parks were relatively simple, providing a few rides, such as a ferris wheel, carousel, and roller coaster; a midway where games could be played; a few concessions selling hot dogs, soft drinks, and cotton candy; and

perhaps a fun or ghost house, and a few sideshows featuring jugglers, snake charmers, and the like.

Now amusement parks have become much more complicated and contrived. An attempt has been made in many parks to fabricate an illusion of some exotic place far away or in some olden time, or both. These are often called theme parks. In some, for example, Disney Land, Anaheim, Calif., and Disney World, near Orlando, Fla., the result has been a sort of fantasy environment, based on the creative motion pictures of the Disney artists and technicians. In other theme parks, the result has often been only a vast potpourri of contrived fake buildings, shops, games, overpriced food and drink, shows of little or no artistic merit, and rides that must be made ever more elaborate and scary to hold their appeal.

Amusement parks can be more creative than such theme parks, with better architecture too. This is demonstrated by some examples around the world, perhaps the most famous of which is Tivoli Gardens, founded in 1843, in Copenhagen, Denmark. Here, in an imaginatively conceived park, light, landscaping, buildings, fountains, pools, rides, displays, top-quality ballet, drama, pantomime, concert and circus performances, and other interesting and provocative things have been combined in such a way as to bring mirth, laughter, even

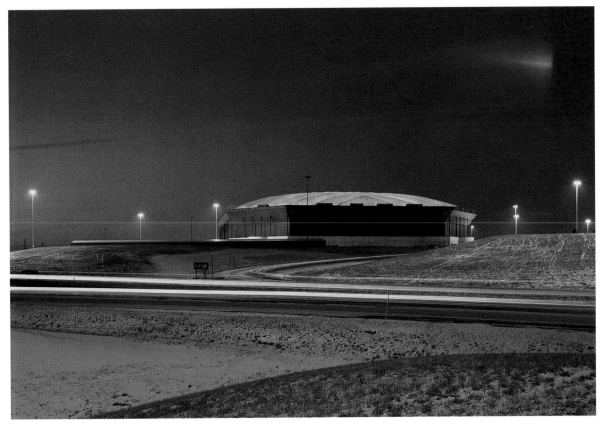

**RECREATION BUILDING** Silverdome (1976), Detroit, Mich. *[Architects: O'Dell, Hewlett, Luckenbach]*

a degree of happiness to those who visit the park. Perhaps, if given a chance, architects of today might design amusement parks of such delightful fantasy and fun through flights of creative imagination, rather than parks contrived to be something of which they can only be pale and unconvincing copies.

**Design Problems** The major problems in the design of recreation buildings and related facilities of any kind are proper provision for the functions to take place in them and for the age groups that will use them, in comfortable, attractive, and safe surroundings. There are so many types of recreational facilities that the designer must become familiar with the rules and requirements for the type to be designed. For example, there are standards for football fields to which the designer must adhere and there are specific requirements for the needs of players, officials, coaches, concessions, and spectators. In a bowling alley, there are different specific requirements.

Requirements vary considerably between clubs of various types. And the same holds true for the great number of other types of recreation facilities. In attempting to satisfy the specific requirements, the designer must also remember that recreation facilities are intended for the enjoyment and entertainment of people in their leisure time. In their design, recreation buildings should reflect those sometimes elusive pursuits.

**History** One of the basic needs of human beings is for recreation, activities engaged in for pleasure, relaxation, and excitement by choice, but no one knows when such activities started. It can be presumed that primitive humans engaged in recreational activities, but no records have been found indicating what they were. From the earliest historic times, it is known that many recreational activities were pursued, including dancing, music, games, festivals, and contests between animals and between animals and humans.

The ancient Minoans practiced a form of bull fighting as far back as 3000 B.C. and the custom was carried on by both the Greeks and Romans. The ancient Egyptians had a number of recreational pursuits, such as games of various kinds and athletics, including wrestling, and by about 1500 B.C. had developed races by horse-drawn chariots. The ancient Greeks and Romans continued all these activities. In addition, the Greeks developed drama and music, as these arts are understood today. They also enjoyed athletic contests that were highly developed in Olympic Games, which began in 776 B.C. The greatest athletic event in ancient Greece, the games were abolished at the end of the 4th century A.D. In 1896 the

**RECREATION BUILDING** Lake Harriet Pavilion (1991), Minneapolis, Minn. *[Architect: Milo H. Thompson of Frederick Bentz/Milo Thompson/Robert Reitow]*

Olympics were revived and the first modern games were held in Athens.

The Romans loved recreational activities and were very inventive in the establishment of some of the more barbarous types, including battles between gladiators and between gladiators and wild animals, and throwing criminals and Christians to wild animals. The Romans also played games, attended theaters, and visited the public baths, where entertainment was furnished by acrobats, magicians, and other performers. Both the Greeks and the Romans built theaters. And the Romans built very large amphitheaters for certain spectacles, and what they called circuses, arenas in which chariot races were held.

During the Middle Ages, recreation of any but the simplest sort was not available to the peasants or serfs. The lords amused themselves in many ways, including such games as dice, chess, and checkers; plays and festivals; and jousting, in which two knights fought, and tournaments in which two groups of knights did combat. After the Middle Ages, recreational pursuits of all kinds began to flourish and new ones were started. For example, the kind of circus of today was started in the 1700s in England.

Many other kinds of recreational pursuits have since been invented and many have required new kinds of buildings and other structures. Some have been interesting and important works of architecture; others simply reflected the evanescent fashions and fads of the day, or lacked any distinguished features.

In the 20th century, with the trend toward continuing reduction of the hours people must work to make their living, there has been a plethora of recreational pursuits, and requisite buildings or structures have been built in ever-increasing numbers. Some pursuits have many redeeming features; but many people believe that others cater to mere escapism that comes from too much idle time and a failure to engage in more meaningful activities.

**Related Articles** BOTANICAL BUILDING; HOTEL; LIBRARY; MUSEUM; PARK; THEATER; ZOOLOGICAL BUILDING.

**Further Reading** Ramsey, Charles G., and Harold R. Sleeper: *Architectural Graphic Standards,* 9th ed., John Wiley, New York, 1994; DiChiara, Joseph, and John Hancock Callender: *Time-Saver Standards for Building Types,* 3rd ed., McGraw-Hill, New York, 1990.

**Sources of Additional Information** American Society of Golf Course Architects: 221 N. LaSalle St., Chicago, Ill. 60601; National Recreation and Park Assoc., 1601 N. Kent St., Arlington, Va. 22209; National Spa and Pool Inst., 2111 Eisenhower Ave., Alexandria, Va. 22314.

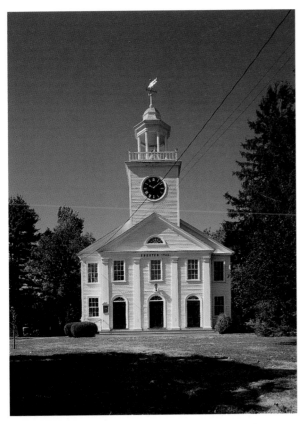

**RELIGIOUS BUILDING** Second Unitarian Church (1742), Hingham, Mass. *[Architect: unknown]*

**RELIGIOUS BUILDING** A building, or group of buildings, such as a church, a synagogue, sometimes called a temple, or a mosque, in which people worship, or other buildings used for religious or secular purposes by the worshipers, or for housing religious orders.

**World Religions** In order of their number of members, from the largest to the smallest, the major religions of the world are Christianity (Protestant, Roman Catholic, and Eastern Orthodox), Islam, Hinduism, Confucianism, Buddhism, Shinto, Taoism, and Judaism. While some of the other religions are established in the United States in a relatively small way, the major religious bodies in this country are Protestant, with some 70 million members, Roman Catholic, with some 50 million, Judaism, with about 4 million, and Eastern Orthodox, with about 4 million.

**U.S. Religious Bodies** The major U.S. religious bodies operate more than a quarter-million churches and synagogues and a large number of schools, hospitals, colleges and universities, seminaries, monasteries, and other institutions. There are some 300 Protestant denominations in the United States and about 15 Eastern Orthodox denominations, usually divided along national lines, including Greek, Russian, Syrian, and so on. Some of the Eastern Orthodox churches include the

word *Catholic* in their titles. Judaism, in the United States, is divided into three groups: Orthodox, Conservative, and Reformed. Thus for these major U.S. religions, religious buildings constitute a major building type. The other religious groups in the United States construct very few buildings, although some are of high quality.

**Common Elements** Buildings of the major religious groups in America all have some things in common. The churches or synagogues are all designed for the worship of God. Most have provisions of some sort for other purposes, including religious instruction, social activities, and the like. All have ritualistic requirements of some kind. But their requirements are quite different in many ways. Therefore the only way to understand the design of buildings for the various religions or denominations is to examine each individually. For a discussion on buildings constructed for purposes other than worship and related activities, see articles entitled college and university building; school.

**Synagogues** The places of worship of the Jews, the followers of Judaism, are synagogues. Practices vary in other religions, but almost every synagogue has three major elements: a sanctuary, for worship and other ritual events; an educational center; and a social center. The sanctuary, or synagogue proper, is not considered a place of mystery, and should be bright and well lighted. The

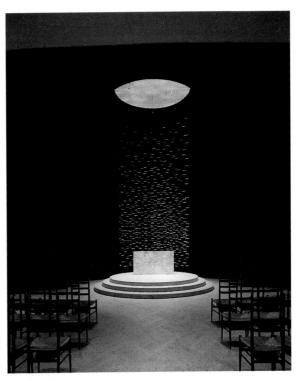

**RELIGIOUS BUILDING** Interior, MIT Chapel (1955), Cambridge, Mass. *[Architect: Eero Saarinen]*

531

**RELIGIOUS BUILDING** Mission Church of San Francisco de Asis (*c.* 1813; later alterations), Taos, N. Mex.

service consists of prayers, readings from sacred texts, songs, responsive readings, and sermons.

In practice, the three groups of Judaism (Orthodox, Conservative, and Reformed) have certain practices that are the same and others that are different. The focal point of the sanctuary for all three is the sacred Torah, the scrolls containing the first five books of the Old Testament of the Bible. The Torah is kept in the ark, a niche or chest, usually located on the eastern wall. A paroche or curtain covers the ark. An eternal light hangs near the ark and on one or both sides are placed seven-branched candelabra, called menorahs. The Tablets of the Law usually hang above the ark. A raised platform (bema, bimah, or almemar) is provided, and on it are located a table or desk on which the Torah is placed to be read. In Orthodox services, the reader faces the ark; in the Reform, the congregation; and in the Conservative, either way. Sometimes the table or desk is used also as a pulpit by the rabbi and the cantor, who chants the liturgical music. In other cases, one or two pulpits may be provided. The Orthodox place the bema in the center of

the sanctuary, the other groups at the end in front of the ark. Choirs, and sometimes pianos or organs, are often involved in Conservative services, always in the Reform, but never in the Orthodox. Choirs may be visible or concealed. Seating is provided for the congregation in the sanctuary, and the usual practice today is to provide a center aisle for weddings and other ceremonies. In addition, there is a vestibule or foyer and cloakroom. In some synagogues, chapels are provided for smaller groups.

Other elements of a synagogue are the educational center, which has classrooms for religious instruction, and the social center, which not only serves for plays, meetings, dances, and so on, but also is used in Jewish rituals which require festive meals during Passover and on other holidays. Social centers have banquet rooms, kitchens, and stages. In addition, synagogues have offices, libraries, and other facilities. Synagogues are often decorated with stained-glass windows, sculpture, tapestries, and other works of art. Until recently, these were expected to be purely symbolic, but today some representational art is allowed in Reform synagogues.

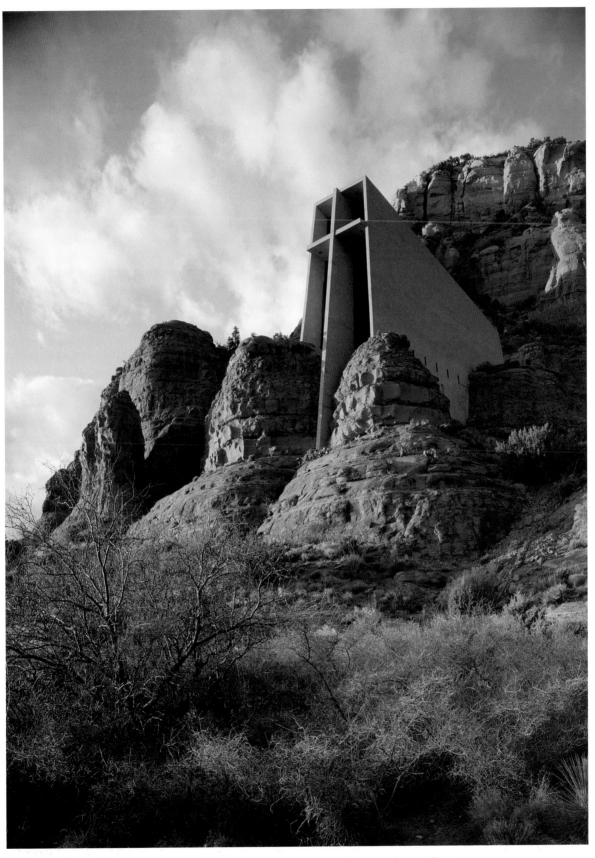

**RELIGIOUS BUILDING** Chapel of the Holy Cross (1956), Sedona, Ariz. *[Architects: Anshen & Allen]*

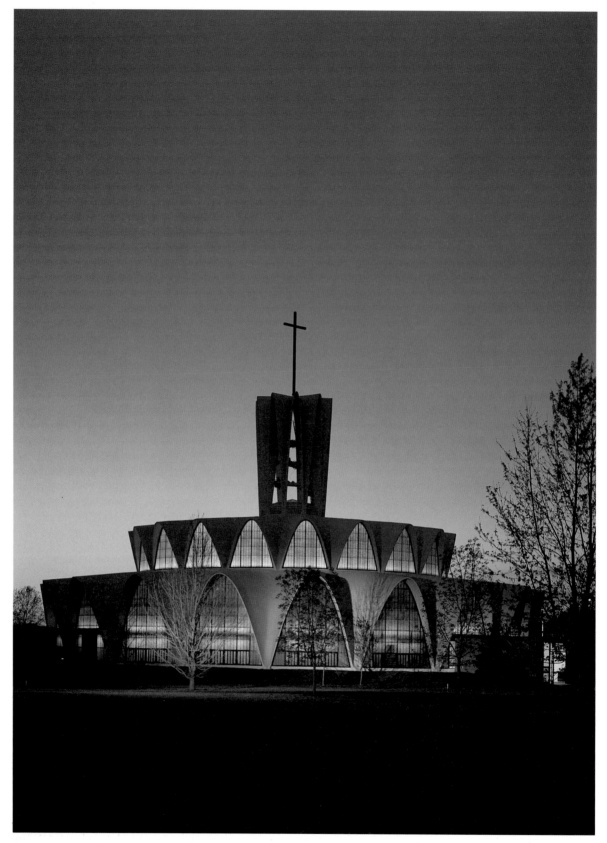

**RELIGIOUS BUILDING** Priory of St. Mary and St. Louis (1962), St. Louis, Mo. *[Architects: Hellmuth, Obata and Kassabaum; landscape architect: Hideo Sasaki]*

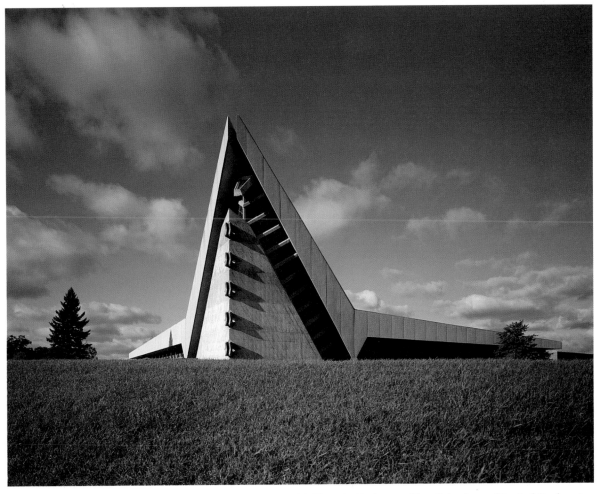

**RELIGIOUS BUILDING** Shaarey Zedek Synagogue (1962), Southfield, Mich. *[Architects: Albert Kahn, Inc. and Percival Goodman]*

**Roman Catholic Churches** Whereas Roman Catholic churches often have such elements as classrooms, parish halls for gatherings, rectories in which priests live, and others, the only major element is the church itself. The church is considered a sacred place, set apart from other things, in which there is a Divine Presence, the Holy Eucharist. Therefore the design of a Roman Catholic church involves mainly the provision of a building in which the liturgy can be performed properly. The major element is the church proper, divided into the sanctuary, in which the priests perform their functions, the choir, and the body of the church or nave in which the congregation gathers. The choir may be placed in any of a number of places, in the sanctuary, at the back of the church, and others. The body of the church contains chairs or pews for seating the congregation, though in the early church the congregation often stood during services.

The sanctuary is usually elevated higher than the floor of the nave and is divided from it by the communion rail, at which communicants kneel or stand to receive the Holy Eucharist or Communion. The central and most important element of the sanctuary is the altar, which may be placed against a wall or may be freestanding. The altar cross, which must have the figure of the crucified Christ, may be placed on the altar, suspended above it, or mounted on a staff behind the altar. Although not required, a canopy is often placed over the altar. On the altar is permanently fixed the tabernacle, a strong vault or box, in which is kept the Holy Eucharist or Sacrament. It is covered with a tentlike veil. A sanctuary light, sometimes more than one, burns continuously near the tabernacle, but not over the altar. At one side is located the credence table which holds articles used in the masses and other services. Sermons may be delivered from the predella, a space in front of the altar used also in celebration of Mass, from a lectern, or from a special place, a pulpit, provided specifically for sermons. Two other important furnishings of the sanctuary are priedieux, kneeling benches with shelves in front, for use by priests, and sedilia, benches on which priests and others may sit at times during Mass.

535

**RELIGIOUS BUILDING** St. Meinrod Monastery (1983), St. Meinrod, Ind. *[Architect: Woollen, Molzan and Partners]*

Other important elements of Roman Catholic churches are a vestibule, called the narthex; baptistery, where baptisms are held; confessionals, small rooms in which priests hear confessions; and sacristy, in which various church articles are stored and in which priests don their robes or vestments. Often an atrium or courtyard is located in front of the church, providing a division between the church and the outside world. A church may have one or more chapels, additional altars and shrines, and other elements. Churches usually have depictions of religious history and beliefs on their walls, windows, and elsewhere. These may include sculpture, paintings, stained glass, carvings, mosaics, and other art forms. Although some are relatively plain, many are highly ornamental. Additional elements of Roman Catholic churches, such as church schools, parish houses, and the like, are similar to those of other denominations or those used for lay purposes.

**Eastern Orthodox Churches** There is some resemblance between Eastern Orthodox churches and Roman Catholic churches. Some of the latter churches are small, simple, and restrained, but Eastern Orthodox churches are always richly ornamented, with spacious interiors and high curved ceilings, in keeping with the doctrine that they are the dwelling places on earth of God, the Eternal King of Heaven, and therefore should have royal splendor.

Orthodox churches are always built on east-west lines, with the sanctuaries on the eastern ends. They often have domes and belfries, each of which is always topped with a cross. Some churches have vestibules at the western ends, above which are located choir lofts. Inside, the nave is divided into a rear section for the congregation and a front section, the chancel, for the priest and cantors, or chanters of liturgical music. The chancel is always elevated higher than the rest of the nave. Behind the chancel is the sanctuary, separated from the

rest of the church by a screen, called an iconostasis, with tiers of icons or pictures of Jesus Christ, Mary, Mother of God, and saints. The sanctuary represents the dwelling of God, the Most High, Holy of Holies. In it are located the altar or holy table, representing the table on which Jesus and the Apostles had the Last Supper, the cross on which Jesus was crucified, the sepulchre in which he was buried, and the throne on which he sits at the right hand of God, his Father.

**Protestant Churches** Architecturally, Protestant churches are more difficult to describe than those of the other denominations. There are some 300 denominations, each with beliefs that vary from the others, and each with liturgical requirements that also vary considerably. Therefore it is only possible to describe the major requirements of Protestant churches and to furnish some particulars of the churches of some of the predominant denominations in the United States. As in buildings of other religious groups, Protestant churches may have such facilities as social, educational, and other types. Their design is similar to that for the other groups and those for lay purposes.

In general, Protestants can be divided into Episcopal, Presbyterian, and Reformed groups. These three groups vary in their doctrines and in the way they are administered or governed. They also vary in the degree of ritual, from the most elaborate, the Episcopal, to the least, the Reformed, which includes the church denominations usually called Congregational. Architecturally, the churches designed for the three groups vary from the often more elaborate and ornamented churches of the Episcopal to the quite simple for the Reformed churches, which are often called simply meetinghouses.

The main body of the church, for all Protestant denominations, is divided into two elements: the nave where the congregation is seated and the chancel, sometimes called the sanctuary, where the ministers or priests and other officiants perform their functions. In most churches, the central focal point of the chancel is an altar, sometimes called the Lord's Table. Often a cross is placed on, over, or near the altar. Also located in the chancel are a pulpit and sometimes a lectern, which often holds the Bible. In some denominations, such as the Church of Christ, Scientist, and some of the reformed groups, the central focal point is the pulpit instead of an altar. Also the baptismal font is placed in the chancel where it can be seen by the entire congregation in meetinghouses for reformed groups and churches for other denominations, such as the Lutherans, instead of in some other location.

A Protestant church often has a vestibule or narthex. In churches in which the priests or ministers wear special garments or vestments, there are sacristies or vesting rooms. Where choirs also wear vestments or robes, there is a choir robing room. In Protestant churches, choirs may be located in a number of places, such as

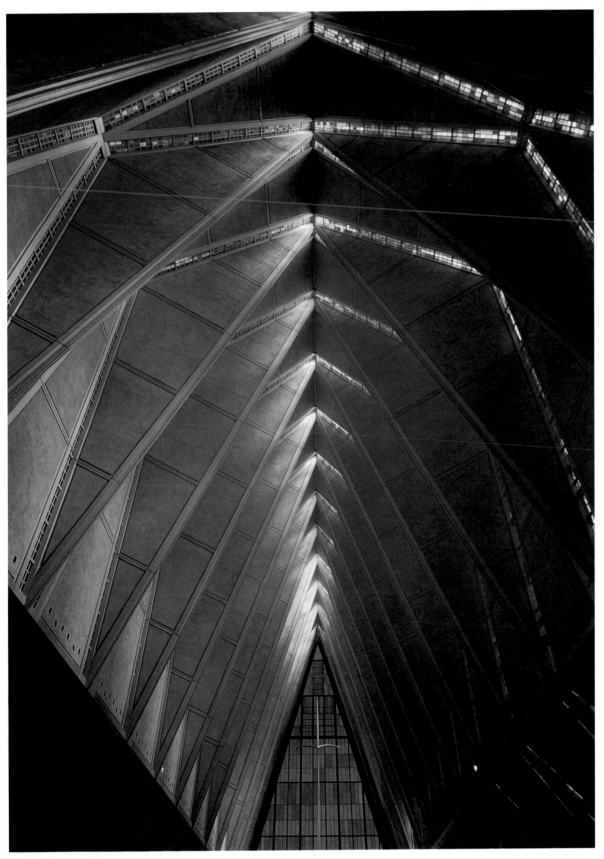

**RELIGIOUS BUILDING** Interior, Chapel (1962), United States Air Force Academy, Colorado Springs, Colo.
*[Architect: Walter Netsch of Skidmore, Owings and Merrill]*

behind the altar, in the nave in front of the altar, in the rear of the church, in a loft above the main level of the nave, or in an alcove, at the side of the chancel. The organ console, if there is one, is usually located within or near the choir, in a position that is unobtrusive but allows the organist to see the entire chancel and also give cues to the choir.

In some churches, communion rails, at which communicants kneel to receive Communion or the Lord's Supper, are provided. Most Protestant denominations practice baptism, usually of infants or small children by sprinkling or pouring water taken from a container (a font) on the head. In some denominations, fonts may be located in or near the narthex or in a separate room, called a baptistery. Baptist denominations practice baptism only of older persons and by total immersion, submerging people completely in water.

Many Protestant denominations use ornament in their churches, including stained glass, sculpture, mosaics, paintings, and so on. Other denominations use little or no ornament. In addition to the main body of the church, many denominations provide other kinds of facilities, such as chapels, parish halls, banquet halls, and others for use by members for both religious and lay activities.

In the past, churches of most denominations were ordinarily rectangular or cruciform, in the shape of a cross, in plan. Today many denominations allow the plans of their churches to be almost any form that can be made to function properly for the rites and services to be held. One development, which has often been used in recent years, is the concept of a central plan, in which the altar is located in the middle of the church with the congregation seated around it. Such plans may be circular, hexagonal, or other shapes.

Churches and synagogues form an important building type and many architects design them. Buildings of this sort can be challenging and gratifying to design. To design a church or synagogue properly, an architect must understand the tradition of rituals of the particular religious group. Since these vary so widely, adequate time must be spent in research to determine the specific requirements. Once these have been determined, many denominations today allow considerable freedom to their architects.

**History** Although no real facts have been established, it is believed that primitive humans practiced some type of religion. There is reason to believe that the first religious activities involved worship of natural objects, or naturism, and that this was followed by animism, the belief that all natural objects have souls. The next step may have been spiritism, which includes the belief that the spirit or soul lives on after death and may have contact with the living. The important early religions are believed to have been based on such principles. They also included fetishism, the belief in the magical powers of objects of nature, or the possession of people and objects by spirits other than their own. Polytheism was the worship of a number of deities, each responsible for certain natural phenomena, and in the simplest form these deities resembled people. Henotheism was the belief in one deity, but did not preclude belief in others. Monotheism is the belief in one God, to the exclusion of others.

The ancient Egyptians practiced polytheism in some localities, worshiping gods each of whom rules over certain natural phenomena, such as air, moisture, earth, and sky. In other localities, the people worshiped one god. Some of the earliest religious buildings, temples, were built in Egypt, starting about 2700 B.C., and many later ones are still in existence. The earliest religious building ruins are located in the Middle East, in what was Mesopotamia. The ancient Greeks practiced polytheism, as did the early Romans in a somewhat different form. Both cultures produced great religious architecture, some of which is still in existence. Although Christianity was introduced into Rome and Greece in the first century A.D., it was not established as the state religion in Rome until the 4th century, and polytheism did not die out in Greece until the 6th century.

Of the major religions of the world today, Hinduism and Shinto are thought to be the oldest, beginning about 2500 B.C. Hinduism is polytheistic, having three gods, as is Shinto, with many gods. Three major religions were founded about the 6th century B.C.: Buddhism, Confucianism, and Taoism. Islam was founded in the 6th century A.D.

Judaism, the oldest monotheistic religion, is believed to have been founded by Abraham, to have been given form by Moses about the 13th century B.C., and to have been developed into a form closely resembling that of today by the 5th century B.C. In the United States, Judaism is divided into three groups: the Orthodox, who believe in strict interpretation of the Torah, the first five books of the Old Testament, and Jewish traditions and laws; the Conservative, who believe in Jewish law and tradition, but allow interpretations of some religious doctrines; and the Reform, who believe that people of each generation have the right to accept or reject traditions.

Christianity was founded by Jesus Christ and is therefore almost 2,000 years old. For almost 1,000 years, there was essentially one Christian religious body. Beginning in the 9th century, differences began to develop between the Western church in Rome and the Eastern in Istanbul, then called Constantinople. In the 11th century the two bodies separated, forming in the West, the Roman Catholic church, and in the East, the Greek

Orthodox, which later spread to other countries and became known as the Eastern Orthodox Church. Beginning in the 16th century, during the Protestant Reformation, large numbers of people left the Roman Catholic church to form Protestant churches, and later these divided to become the approximately 300 denominations in existence today.

Throughout their history, the Jewish, Roman Catholic, Protestant, and Eastern Orthodox groups have built churches and synagogues. Early Christian churches were built in Rome and other places. Christian churches in what came to be known as the Byzantine style were built in the domain of the Eastern Orthodox. These were followed by the great churches in the Romanesque style and then by the magnificent Gothic style cathedrals of the Middle Ages. Many of these early churches and cathedrals are still standing. The products of unknown master builders, these buildings are among the world's finest architecture. During the Renaissance, the building of churches and cathedrals continued, and their architects were the greatest of the time, including Filippo Brunelleschi (c. 1377–1446), Leon Battista Alberti (1404–72), Donato d'Agnolo, called Bramante (1444–1514), and Michelangelo Buonarroti, called simply Michelangelo (1475–1564). From that time on great churches and synagogues have been designed by many, including some famous, architects, and their designs have produced some of the best architecture.

**U.S. Religious Buildings** In the United States, the early colonists built churches and synagogues soon after they arrived. The first church in America is believed to have been built at Jamestown, Va., in the early 1700s but was later destroyed and another built on its foundation, only to be partly destroyed. Other old churches still in existence include St. Luke's, sometimes called Old Brick (c. 1682), Smithfield, Va.; Christ Church (1732), Lancaster, Co., Va.; and the Old Ship Meeting House (1681), Hingham, Mass. The first synagogue in America, Touro, was built at Newport, R.I., in 1763, and was designed by Peter Harrison (1716–75). The first Spanish colonial churches in what is now the United States were probably built in the Southwest near the end of the 16th century in what later became New Mexico. Since that time, numerous churches and synagogues have been built all over America. Many architects have designed them and the building continues. Some of these buildings in every era are considered among the finest examples of American architecture.

**Related Articles** ART IN ARCHITECTURE; COLLEGE AND UNIVERSITY BUILDING; HEALTH-CARE FACILITIES; HOUSING; RECREATION BUILDING; SCHOOL.

**Further Reading** Clausen, Meredith L.: *Spiritual Space: The Religious Architecture of Pietro Belluschi,* University of Washington Press, 1992.

**Sources of Additional Information** Guild for Religious Architecture, 1777 Church St., N.W., Washington, D.C. 20036; Stained Glass Association of America, 1125 Wilmington Ave., St. Louis, Mo. 63111.

**REMODELING** Making repairs or additions to a building without regard to its history. Several other terms referring to changes to buildings are related to this subject and, for this book, require definition. In general there is some confusion about the use of these terms, perhaps because a project may involve work described by more than one.

**Definitions** *Adaptive use* describes work to allow a change in use of an existing, often historic, building. Refer to the article entitled adaptive use for further information. *Preservation* is limited to actions taken to prevent further damage to an existing historic building, with minimal replacement of materials and systems. Refer to the article entitled preservation. *Reconstruction* refers to new construction based on historic research of documents, archaeological investigation, and written records. The Governor's Palace (1720; burned 1781; reconstructed 1930) and the Capitol (1704; burned 1747; rebuilt 1753; burned 1832; reconstructed 1934) at Williamsburg, Va., are well-known examples of reconstructed buildings. *Rehabilitation* is closer to remodeling in that it refers to introduction of new materials or systems into an older building. This is often a part of remodeling or adaptive use. *Restoration* is the renovation of a building to a specific period in its history. This may include new work replacing lost parts of the original building, or later additions may be removed.

**Types of Work** Remodeling may involve rehabilitation of only portions or all of a building. It may involve only rehabilitation of the building so it will perform its

**REMODELING** George C. T. Woo Residence (1984), Dallas, Tex. This house was built over an existing house. [*Architect: George C. T. Woo & Partners*]

**REMODELING** George C. T. Woo Residence (1984), Dallas, Tex. *[Architect: George C. T. Woo & Partners]*

current function better, or it may be concerned with what has come to be called adaptive use, or recycling, of a building to change it to new uses, for example, from a hotel to an apartment building. Some remodeling projects are very small, involving only relatively small amounts of work and relatively low budgets; others may be quite extensive and involve millions of dollars in expenditures.

**Practitioners** Traditionally, remodeling work and additions to existing buildings have been the kinds of commissions, other than modest houses, which architects starting out in practice were most likely to receive. This is still the case, but it should not be inferred that only young, beginning architects do this kind of work. In fact, most architectural firms perform remodeling and addition work to some extent, if only for their established clients. And it is estimated that more than 75 percent of the architectural firms in the United States do some of this work on a regular basis. Some do remodeling work only as a service to their regular clients and do not expect to make appreciable profits on it. Other firms take on any remodeling and addition work which they can obtain and make profits that compare favorably with those for new buildings.

**Building Types** In any case, remodeling and addition work seem to be plentiful, and commissions for this type of work often seem easier to obtain than those for new buildings. Although the situation varies at different times, remodeling and addition work are usually available for most building types. However, such commissions are ordinarily most plentiful in certain types, such as offices, schools, houses, religious buildings, and stores. Not so plentiful, but still numerous enough to be attractive to architectural firms, are such types as apart-

ments, hospitals, banks, factories, and public buildings. It might be assumed that most of these commissions would be for buildings of some considerable age, as is usually the case in preservation work, but actually that is not always the case. Surveys have shown that of the buildings remodeled at any given time, about one-half were less than 25 years old and about one-third were less than 15. It has also been shown that over one-third of these projects involved major additions of floor area.

It may therefore be seen that remodeling and addition work comprise a quite important part of architecture today. This kind of work is prevalent for several reasons. One of the most important is economic; building costs have gone up so radically in recent years that it is often possible to remodel an existing building much less expensively than it would be to construct a new one. In many cases, the structures and exteriors of older buildings are satisfactory, needing only minor work, and could not be duplicated by new construction for anything approaching the cost of remodeling. In such cases, the major work is usually renovation of the interiors and provision of up-to-date systems, such as heating, air conditioning, electrical, lighting, and elevators. Many other reasons exist for remodeling and addition work, including needs for changes in function, improvements for comfort and efficiency, increasing profitability, and needs for meeting code requirements set after a building had been constructed.

**Remodeling Requirements** Remodeling or addition work is usually handled by architects in a manner similar to that in which they handle new work. However, remodeling or addition work may often be considerably more complicated, and there may be problems not found in work on new buildings. These include factors related to the existing condition of buildings, some aspects of which may be hidden; the need sometimes for demolition; requirements for nonstandard materials to match or blend with existing ones; needs for changing certain elements of building, such as plumbing or electrical systems or structures and materials., to conform to building and other code requirements from which the buildings were formerly exempt; requirements for cutting, patching, and refinishing work and for removal of old materials and equipment from the building and the site.

Remodeling and addition work differs from that on new construction in other important ways. There will often be more concern with the economic and technical advisability, or feasibility, of a remodeling or addition project than a new one. Budgets for remodeling or addition work are often more difficult to prepare than for other jobs, because of the unknowns that are always present regarding the condition of existing buildings.

In spite of all of the problems, many architects find remodeling and addition work challenging, satisfying, and profitable. Because of its complications, such work usually brings higher fees to architects, sometimes up to twice as much as for new work with the same budget. For these reasons, many architects actively seek commissions for work of this type. Others are able to find clients such as chain stores or chain hotel organizations which seem to be continually expanding their operations, making acquisitions of existing businesses and their buildings or seeking new markets. For many of these clients, remodeling and addition work also seem to go on continuously. Such continuing clients do much to make an architectural practice function more smoothly, efficiently, profitably, and most importantly, with continuity.

**Architectural Services** Very few, if any, architects have specialized departments to handle remodeling and addition work. Instead, services for these commissions are performed by the same people who handle such services for new buildings. And the services performed are generally the same as those for new buildings: programming; schematic design, along with preliminary specifications; design development; preparation of contract documents, working drawings, specifications, and others; and construction contract administration, including inspection of the work to ensure conformance with the contract documents. In addition, construction budgets are prepared early and gradually improved as more information becomes available during the architectural processes.

Some differences do exist in the manner in which services are performed for remodeling and addition work as compared to those for new buildings. In the first place, it is almost always necessary to make measured drawings of existing buildings. These are done by making actual measurements which are noted on sketches of floor plans and elevations. From this information architectural drawings may be drafted. Often much of the information that would ordinarily be in the specification may be placed instead on the working drawings. Specifications often vary more from job to job in remodeling and addition work than in new. There is usually an increased need for special conditions, such as patching, cutting, refinishing, demolition, and removal, not required for new work.

Another important difference is that remodeling and addition work often require more time and effort in the programming, schematic design, and design development phases than does new work. Remodeling and addition work also often require architects to spend more time on the construction site than they would for a new building of comparable size. And remodeling and addition work require, for proper execution, contractors, subcontractors, and craftspersons who are both experienced in and enjoy such work.

Sometimes a contractor may be selected very early, at the time of the schematic design phase or earlier, to allow the architect to obtain advice and counsel on materials, systems, and construction methods while the project is being designed. As in preservation work, as-built drawings, showing the work as actually constructed, are often required in remodeling and addition work.

Other design professionals, such as engineers and interior designers, often become involved in remodeling and addition work. In fact, the largest expenditures on some jobs of this type are for new or improved mechanical and electrical systems. And some jobs consist almost entirely of interior renovation and improvements.

**Related Articles** ADAPTIVE USE; CONSTRUCTION CONTRACT ADMINISTRATION; COST CONTROL; DESIGN, ARCHITECTURAL; FEASIBILITY STUDY; PRACTICE OF ARCHITECTURE; PRESERVATION; PROGRAMMING; SPECIFICATION; WORKING DRAWING.

**Further Reading** Kay, Gersil Newmark: *Mechanical & Electrical Systems for Historic Buildings,* McGraw-Hill, New York, 1991; Weaver, Martin E.: *Conserving Buildings: A Guide to Techniques and Materials,* John Wiley, New York, 1993.

**RENDERING** A drawing that illustrates floor plans, exteriors, interiors, or details of a building or a group of buildings. The word *rendering* is also used to denote the process of making such a drawing. Renderings have two main purposes. They are a means by which an architect or other designer visualizes and studies the design of a building, and they portray the appearance of a building to the owner of the building and to others. Renderings of the latter type are often called presentation drawings.

**Terms Defined** Delineation is often used as a synonym for a rendering, but more properly means any drawing, or the act of making a drawing. Other terms are important in rendering. Entourage is the landscaping and other features around a building in a rendering, and sometimes applied to the same elements around an actual building. An esquisse is a sketch or rendering, made in a relatively short time, to show the most important and general features of a building or a portion of it. A rendu is another name for rendering, and sometimes used for the color of a rendering. A wash is a method of applying watercolors in a rendering, usually in relatively large areas, as in a sky, by wetting the paper and letting the color flow from the brush onto the wet paper. A graded wash, in which the color is graded from dark to light, as often actually seen in the sky, is made by putting a small amount of color in the water on the paper and gradually adding more color as the wash proceeds across an area, or by starting with a dark color and gradually diluting it with water. A stretch is the preparation of watercolor paper for a rendering by soaking it in water, stretching it

**RENDERING** First Bank Place (1992), Minneapolis, Minn. *[Architect: James I. Freed of Pei, Cobb, Freed and Partners (Rendering by Carlos Diniz)]*

by hand onto a drawing board, then fixing it with vegetable glue. After drying, the stretch prevents buckling and rippling when watercolors are applied to the paper.

**Characteristics** Renderings may be quite small or very large. They may be in full color or in a single color. They may depict a complete building or group of buildings or only a small detail, such as a doorway. They may be made with quick, sketchy drawing techniques or controlled, painstaking techniques that take many hours. They may show only an impression of a building or a complete and realistic picture. They may have two dimensions as in a rendering of a floor plan or they may utilize perspective, a method that simulates depth, or three dimensions, in a rendering that has only two dimensions.

**Renderers** All architects learn to make renderings as a part of their education. And many continue to make

sketches at least as part of their study of the design of their buildings. Some architects also make presentation renderings as part of their professional work, and in some architectural offices, one or more people may specialize in making these drawings. A person who makes renderings is called a renderer or delineator. Some renderers have their own specialized, free-lance offices and make renderings for architects, owners, or others. Some renderers, in architectural offices or in free-lance work, are not architects but learned their craft in architectural or art schools.

Much of the knowledge and many of the abilities required by artists in other fields are the same as those for renderers. All must have basic art knowledge and skills of drawing, perspective, shades and shadows, color, textures, form, and composition. In addition, a renderer must acquire a deep knowledge and understanding of architecture, in school, through experience, or from other studies.

**Computers** Computer-aided design and drafting (CADD) software is now widely used in preparation of presentation drawings. Typically, computer images are created and then used as a basis for a hand-drawn or painted image. With the aid of scanners, computers are also used to process photographs of scale models of a proposed building, which can be integrated into a photograph of the building site. Some of the resulting images may be so convincing as to fool the eye into believing the building already exists. Future uses of the computer will allow development of new techniques for preparing presentation drawings.

**Tools** Renderers use all the basic equipment and tools employed by architectural and other drafters: drafting tables, T squares, triangles, scales, pencils, and so on. In addition, they use a wide variety of other equipment and tools similar to those used by other artists, working with watercolors, inks, charcoal, special papers, and the like.

Pen and India ink, pencil, and watercolor, or combinations of these, all on paper, are the traditional rendering media. Renderers often use other media for all or a portion of their renderings: pastels; charcoals; Chinese ink, like India ink except that it comes in a stick which the renderer grinds and mixes with water; tempera, watercolors that are opaque rather than transparent like regular watercolors; and others. Sometimes a renderer will use a photograph as part of the rendering, for example, in a rendering of a building superimposed on a suitable photograph of its actual site. Montages, in which various pieces of other materials or other appropriate elements are arranged, are sometimes used; for example, in an interior rendering where it is considered important to show actual colors, materials, and textures of furniture, carpets, and curtains.

Other tools used by the renderer are brushes, watercolor, and others; a wide variety of pencils, black and a variety of colors; special papers; and a host of other items, some of which are artists' tools; some are everyday items like sponges, blotters, and cheesecloth; and others that are limited only by the ingenuity and needs of the renderer. In the past, when watercolor was the usual medium for a color rendering, special papers were used that when wet could be stretched onto a drawing board. These papers tighten as they dry, preventing curling or buckling when watercolors are applied. Today such renderings are often done on illustration, or poster, board made of a fine quality paper bonded to a cardboard backing.

**Preparation of a Rendering** The actual processes used in making renderings are as varied as the media in which they are done, the buildings they portray, and the knowledge, skill, and ingenuity of the renderers. Some idea of these processes may be gained through a generalized example of the preparation of a rendering. First, the renderer must determine the purpose of the rendering, what should be shown and how this is to be accomplished. The renderer then thinks the problem through, usually with the help of study sketches. Next, a medium, or combination of media, a size for the rendering, and a point of view for the people who will see the rendering might be selected. A perspective of the rendering would then be drawn, together with major landscaping or other required features and, when satisfactory, transferred to the final rendering paper. At this point, the techniques begin to vary widely. Some renderers start by lightly painting in the sky and lawn, continuing on to the general form of the building, then to details and to the final touches in the landscape, gradually developing each element of the rendering to its finished appearance. Others work directly on the whole rendering, in the manner of many painters. Some do much of the detail work with pen and ink or with pencil. Some execute sharp, crisp lines for building corners and the like; others use a looser style. The variations are endless.

**History** Rendering has a very long tradition stretching back to prehistoric times. The Egyptians developed architectural symbol hieroglyphs and drew floor plans and elevations of buildings on papyrus, stone, or wood. The development continued in ancient Greece and Rome, though few examples of the drawings exist today, and through the work of monks and master masons (architects) on the Gothic churches and other buildings of the Middle Ages. These renderings represented little more than did the floor plans and elevations of the earliest times, though of course the later ones were more complex and complete.

The preparation of accurate drawings of buildings had its beginning in the Italian Renaissance. Early studies of perspective drawing were codified in the writings of Lorenzo Ghiberti (d. 1455), Leon Battista Alberti (d. 1472), Piero della Francisca (d. 1492) and Leonardo da Vinci (d. 1519). Paper became widely available. The invention of the printing press allowed architectural renderings and other materials to be widely disseminated, thus affecting architecture everywhere. And the first rules were formulated for the proper use of perspective to simulate the three-dimensional character of buildings. Renaissance architects used these new techniques extensively, making possible the construction of a building from drawings by an architect, who might appear on the site only occasionally rather than remaining there almost constantly as in the Middle Ages. Renaissance architects were deeply interested in rendering, and studied and practiced it with great skill. This interest has remained with architects, the subject studied and the skill actively sought, to the present day.

**American Development** The earliest drawings in America that would now be called renderings were done by amateur architects, who were self-taught from European books in their libraries. Later architects were knowledgeable and skillful in rendering, which they had learned in Europe before emigrating to the colonies. Shortly before the middle of the 19th century, American-born architects obtained their education, including rendering, in Europe. Many continued to do so even after American architectural schools had been established. One of the notable European schools, the École des Beaux Arts in Paris, trained many American students. This school strongly emphasized rendering in its curriculum. This emphasis continued in U.S. schools of architecture until about the middle of the 20th century by means of architectural projects prepared and judged by members of the Beaux Arts Institute of Design in New York. Today the trend in rendering is toward newer techniques, including photography to complement or supplement the older methods, and others such as acrylic plastic paints, computer-assisted drawings.

**Related Articles** AESTHETICS; DESIGN, ARCHITECTURAL; DRAFTING; EDUCATION.

**Further Reading** Burden, Ernest: *Architectural Delineation—A Photographic Approach to Presentation*, 3rd ed., McGraw-Hill, New York, 1992.

**RENWICK, JAMES, JR.** American architect (1818–95). Although James Renwick, Jr., had been educated as an engineer, thus following the profession of his father, he wanted to become an architect from an early age. Completely self-taught, he learned architecture from books, notably those of the French-English architect-theorists August Charles Pugin (1762–1832) and his son Augustus Welby Northmore Pugin (1812–52), both of whom wrote about the glories of Gothic architecture. To

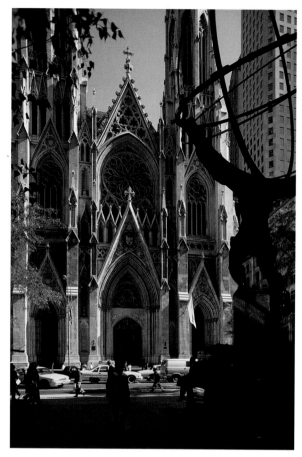

**RENWICK, JAMES, JR.** St. Patrick's Cathedral (1879), New York, N.Y.

the knowledge he gleaned from books, Renwick added practical experience working in construction.

From a socially prominent New York City family, Renwick started out in architecture in 1843, by winning the commission for the design of Grace Church (1846), the home parish of many of the wealthiest and most fashionable families in the city. For this church, he produced a fine design in Gothic Revival style, based on his studies of the books by the Pugins and others. Grace Church has New York landmark status. He soon received other commissions and he eventually became one of the most successful American architects of his time. He was also one of the most consistent in design philosophy, never deserting the Gothic Revival style in any important way.

**Works** Although Renwick designed buildings of many types, including hospitals, schools, houses, and museums, he is remembered for his churches. Among the best of these churches still in existence in New York City are Grace Calvary (1846), St. Stephen's (1854), Riverdale Presbyterian (1863), St. Ann's (1869), and All Saints (1894). He did churches in other cities, including a little gem in Washington, Oak Hill Chapel (1850), but

his masterpiece is St. Patrick's Cathedral, New York City, for which he received the commission in 1853. Delayed by the Civil War, St. Patrick's was essentially completed by 1879. Renwick added a rectory in 1884.

Other Renwick buildings still in existence in New York City include the Cleveland E. Dodge House (1863), known as Greystone and now a conference center for Teachers College, Columbia University; Cathedral High School (1869); and the Graymore Friars' Residence (1869), formerly St. Joseph's Church School. In Washington, the finest Renwick works are the first building of the Smithsonian Institution (1849); and St. Mary's Episcopal Church (1887).

James Renwick, Jr., practiced architecture for more than 50 years and designed many buildings, some of which are heralded as among the best examples of Gothic Revival architecture of all time in the United States. During his long career, Renwick had another important accomplishment: he trained a large number of young men who worked in his office. Some of these trainees became important architects, including Frank Furness (1839–1912), George B. Post (1837–1913), and Bertram Grosvenor Goodhue (1869–1924), who worked with Renwick from 1884 to 1891 and became thoroughly indoctrinated in Gothic Revival design. Having become disenchanted with the style late in life, Goodhue designed a notable building with Modern overtones, the Nebraska State Capitol, Lincoln, completed in 1928 after his death. Another esteemed architect who trained in Renwick's office was John Wellborn Root (1850–91), who worked there in 1869 and 1870, after graduating in civil engineering. Root became more deeply involved in the Modern movement than did Goodhue, and much earlier. With his partner, Daniel Hudson Burnham (1846–1912), Root designed some of the pioneering tall, skeleton-frame buildings in Chicago that presaged the architecture of today. Goodhue's influence on Modern architecture was minimal because he started too late; Root's influence was never fully realized because he died at age forty-one.

**Life** James Renwick, Jr., was born in New York City on November 1, 1818, and named for his father, an engineer, professor at Columbia University, and amateur watercolorist. When he was young, Renwick exhibited artistic talent and expressed a desire to become an architect. Entering Columbia University, he graduated in 1836 and took an engineering position with the Erie Railroad. In 1839 he took a job as superintendent of the construction of the Croton Reservoir, completed in 1843 on a prominent site in midtown Manhattan, but demolished in 1900 to be replaced by the New York Public Library (1909) by Carrère and Hastings. On this job, Renwick gained his first experience in architecture and building construction.

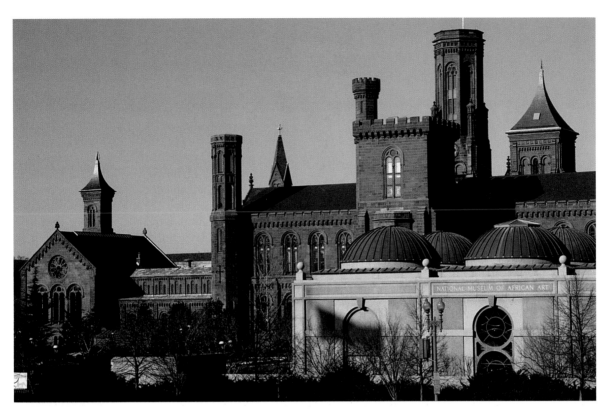

**RENWICK, JAMES, JR.** Smithsonian Institution Building (1855) behind the Sackler Gallery, Washington, D.C.

In 1843, the year the reservoir was completed, Renwick entered and won a competition for Grace Church, which started him on an architectural career that became one of the most successful of the time. By the early 1870s, Renwick had become one of the most famous architects in the United States, and received more commissions than he could handle. To help with the buildings, Renwick took in a partner, Joseph Sands (d. 1880), and the firm became Renwick and Sands. After the death of Sands, James L. Aspinwall (1854–1936) became a partner and a short time later, Renwick's nephew, William W. Renwick (1864–1933), who had been trained in architecture in his uncle's office, became a partner. Still later, after William H. Russell (1854–1907) had become a partner, the firm became Renwick, Aspinwall and Russell. Regardless of what name it operated under, the firm did a large amount of work, most of it in and around New York City.

Other than in New York City, the most important Renwick buildings are in Washington, D.C. One of them, the Old Corcoran Gallery (1859), later used by the Court of Claims, was restored in 1972 by architects John Carl Warnecke (1919–    ), exteriors, and Hugh Newell Jacobsen (1929–    ), interiors. The building was then renamed the Renwick Gallery in honor of its original architect who, during his lifetime, had been an avid oriental art collector. A house on Fifth Avenue, New York

City, was the last building by James Renwick, Jr., completed shortly before he died on June 23, 1895.

**Related Articles** BURNHAM AND ROOT; CAPITAL, UNITED STATES; CRAM, GOODHUE AND FERGUSON; GOTHIC REVIVAL ARCHITECTURE.

**RESTAURANT** A building, or rooms in a building, in which food and drink are prepared and served. Restaurants are an important building type, and almost all architects design them as individual buildings or groups of rooms in buildings of other types. Restaurants may be very small to very large, serve low-cost, simple meals or snacks to very costly, sumptuous dinners. Their buildings or rooms and their interiors, furniture, and furnishings may be quite simple, even severe and relatively inexpensive, to very ornate and expensive. Restaurants may be located almost anywhere, by roadsides, in hotels, in shopping malls, in office buildings, and so on. Restaurants serve fixed-price meals, with one price covering everything, or a la carte, with separate prices for each item; some offer both.

**Types** There are many kinds of restaurants, including hotel and motel dining rooms and coffee shops, take-out food, and complete restaurants. A cafeteria is a special type with food displayed on counters by which patrons pass with their trays to be served or to serve themselves. A variant of this is called a "scramble" sys-

545

tem, where the patrons are free to move among counters to find the menu of their choice. In the past, fountain lunch counters were often found in drugstores, and in cities, Automats, where coins were inserted to open glass doors to obtain food and drink items. Now large-chain fast-food restaurants are found in most communities. A variant is shopping mall food courts where a variety of menus may be ordered from a diversity of food suppliers, with centralized seating shared by all. Some fast-food restaurants have seating, others offer only take-out orders.

**Merchandising** The success of any type of restaurant depends on good merchandising. The location must be right. The exterior must be inviting to the prospective clientele. The interior must satisfy the expectations of the clientele, as must the meals and beverages served. Patrons must be served in the manner they expect. The cost of dining must be appropriate to the level of quality of meals and service. Even when all these requirements are satisfied properly, there is no guarantee of success for a restaurant. There are too many intangibles, too many fads, too many fickle aspects of human nature. A badly designed restaurant, in a good location, serving popular meals at reasonable prices may well be a huge success, while one that is well designed, but lacking in some of the other aspects, may fail. Thus the construction of restaurants may be something of a gamble. To decrease the risk, architects and restaurant owners and operators must be very scrupulous in their study of the various factors and in the planning of everything from the building, its interiors and furnishings, to the menus to be served, the service to be provided, and the ambience.

**Common Elements** There are considerable differences in the design of various kinds of restaurants. A fast-food operation is different from a fancy French restaurant in important ways. However, all restaurants have some elements in common, including the dining areas, the serving areas, and the production areas. These elements and their relationships with each other must be properly designed. Important factors are the type of restaurant, type of menu to be served, type of service, volume of service, equipment to be used, traffic patterns, and storage.

In a regular restaurant, regardless of location, serving full meals, the dining areas ordinarily have provisions for separate tables for one or two people, four people, and larger groups. In a simple restaurant, as little as 10 to 12 ft² of floor space per diner might be allowed; in a fancier one, as much as 20 ft². In some restaurants, banquette seating, which resembles sofas placed along walls, is used. This type of seating can only replace a portion of the movable chairs. Other seating arrangements include booths, often used in simpler establishments or coffee shops, and counter seating, used mostly in lunch-

**RESTAURANT** Azur Restaurant (1989), Minneapolis, Minn. *[Architect: Shea Architects (Photo: Christian M. Korab)]*

rooms, sandwich shops, and coffee shops. Cafeterias, Automats, and vending machine restaurants may have any or all of these types of seating, as may fast-food operations, some of which provide no seating at all.

The serving areas of restaurants vary considerably. The menus to be served, the expected volume, and, most importantly, the type of service, all affect the design of serving areas. In a regular restaurant, in which waiters or waitresses serve tables, service stations are located in various parts of the dining areas. In the service stations, provisions are made for the preparatory work of waiters and waitresses, and for easy access to tableware, napkins and tablecloths, condiments, butter, and so on. In a cafeteria, the serving area is a counter on which food and beverages are displayed in containers that may be heated or cooled as required, located between the dining and production areas. Fast-food serving areas are similar, but with fewer requirements for heating and cooling. Where food is served at counters, the counters are the serving areas.

The production areas also vary considerably because of the differences between types of restaurants. All types must provide for certain necessary functions, including receiving, storage, preparation, cooking, serving facilities, and sanitation. The spaces required for each of these functions depend on the size, menu served, and volume of the individual restaurant.

All restaurants must have facilities for receiving and for dry, low-temperature, freezer, and other types of storage. Preparation areas of restaurants may be quite simple, as in a fast-food operation where only a few simple foods are served. In a large, full-service restaurant, these facilities might be quite extensive and include specialized areas for preparation of meat, vegetables, salads, and sandwiches. Cooking facilities required also vary considerably between restaurants. In a fountain lunch, for example, a limited number of cooking appliances are located on the work area, or back bar, separated by an aisle from the counters. In a full-scale restaurant, the appliances required are determined by the menu served. One restaurant might limit the types of cooking, while another might do all types, including roasting, broiling, baking, grilling, frying, baking bread and pastries, and so on. Facilities must be provided for all these types and also for steam tables to keep meals warm and for plate warmers.

The serving facilities required in the production areas of restaurants also vary considerably from what amounts to almost none at all at a lunch counter to full facilities, including pickup points in the cooking area, pantries, cold food service areas, and checkout areas.

Sanitation requirements of all restaurants are similar, though they vary in size and complexity. Typical facilities include dishwashing, pot and pan washing, and waste disposal. In addition to the major elements, restaurants have requirements for cashiers; guest rest rooms; and locker, lounge, rest rooms, and dining facilities for employees. And some restaurants have provisions for entertainment; some have dance floors. Such establishments are often called nightclubs and may offer full food service or only drinks and snacks.

Except in the restaurants of chain operations, which tend toward standardized designs, each restaurant presents a unique set of problems to its designer. If it can be made to satisfy the wishes of the clientele it expects to attract, the design problems will have been properly solved. If it fails, at least a part of the problem will undoubtedly have been in its design.

A bar or cocktail lounge is an establishment in which alcoholic and other drinks are served, and sometimes light meals or snacks. A bar or cocktail lounge may be part of a restaurant or it may exist independently. In either case, the required elements are similar to those of restaurants, as are the design considerations. In an establishment of this sort, the bar is a counter similar to that of a lunch counter, though often more ornate. Bars also have work areas, or back bars, as in lunch counters. The cocktail lounge portions provide seating at tables, in booths, and so on as in restaurants. Sometimes entertainment is provided, such as music by a piano player or a small group. And sometimes the piano may have a

counter around it to form a piano bar. Nightclubs often operate in a manner similar to that of cocktail lounges, but ordinarily provide more elaborate entertainment.

**History** The first restaurants, called taverns or ordinaries, were located in the inns of 16th-century England. At first only travelers staying in the inns were served, but later others were allowed to come in, usually for one meal a day at a fixed time and price. A tavern or ordinary was later called a coffee house in England, and in France a *café*, the French word for coffee. In the 18th century, in France a café came to be called a *restaurant*, the French word for a restorative.

**American Development** The first restaurants in America were taverns or ordinaries similar to those in England at the time. They were located in inns along well-traveled roads and waterways, and later in towns and cities. Some of the early taverns are still in existence in various parts of the country, including the Fraunces Tavern (*c.* 1750), New York City, and Gadsby's (1752), Alexandria, Va. As the building of turnpikes, canals, and later, railroads progressed, so did the building of inns and taverns.

The first restaurant of the sort known today was established in New York City, about 1834, by Lorenzo Delmonico (1813–81). Although no longer in its original building or location, Delmonico's Restaurant is still in existence. Soon after its founding, other restaurants were established in New York City and elsewhere. And many great restaurants have been designed during the years following. The first cafeteria, called the Exchange Buffet, was opened in New York City in 1885. Fast-food restaurants were first established early in the 20th century, multiplied after World War II, and have mushroomed everywhere.

**Related Articles** HOTEL; RECREATION BUILDING.

**Further Reading** Dorff, Martin E.: *Restaurants That Work: Case Studies of the Best in the Industry*, Whitney Library of Design, New York, 1992.

# RICHARDSON, HENRY HOBSON American
architect (1838–86). Known as a romantic because of his espousal of the Romanesque Revival style, Richardson was nevertheless a creative architect who adapted the Romanesque into his own personal and logical style. His was the first of the styles of the Eclectic era in architecture which was developed by an American architect and not adapted from the European revivals.

Although he lived less than 50 years, practiced only about 20, and designed fewer than 100 buildings, he became the most influential, some think the greatest, architect of his time. He is now acclaimed one of the greatest American architects of all time. Richardson has often been called the first modern architect, but he never really was that. He was a traditionalist, taking his inspi-

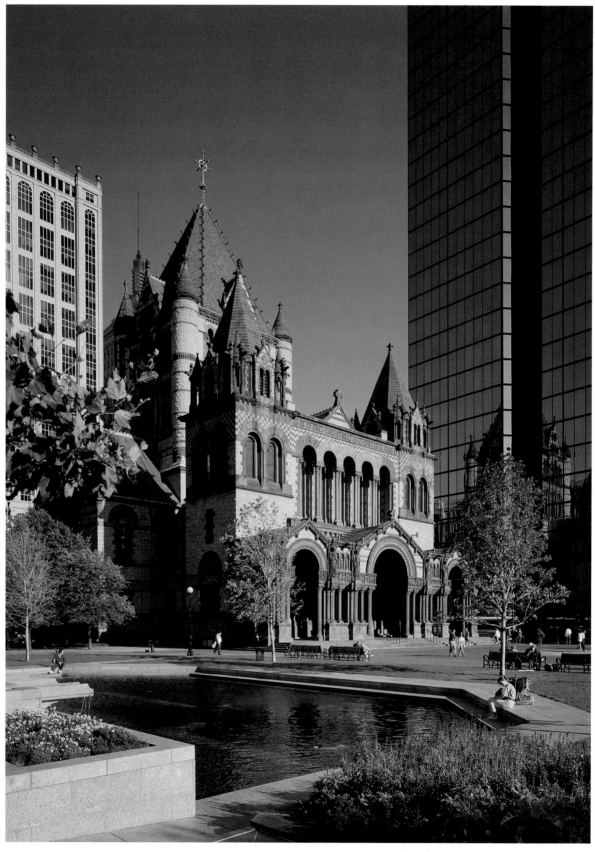

**RICHARDSON, HENRY HOBSON** Trinity Church (1877), Boston, Mass.

ration from the architecture of the past and recasting it into buildings that were peculiarly and personally his own. He was not an innovator who invented new forms or used new materials or techniques.

**Appraisal** Richardson's buildings were designed to utilize the techniques and materials of the past, in particular masonry, mostly stone masonry, and wood, in a controlled and masterful manner. He was deeply concerned with the spaces within his buildings and the forms of the masses that composed them. Many of his buildings have a sculptural quality that was almost nonexistent in other buildings of his day, a quality that sometimes seems a prediction of the sculptural architecture of many other later architects. Richardson's buildings are bold in form and in details, also qualities of much of today's architecture. They are consummately three-dimensional, as opposed to much of the architecture of his time that seemed as if it had leaped from the two dimensions of the drawing board to two dimensions in the buildings. Richardson spent a lot of time with the craftspeople working on his buildings, altering his designs as the actual job conditions warranted until he had everything the way he wanted it.

Richardson's architecture was accepted very well in his own day, by clients and by the public. Even the architects of the day were impressed. In 1885, a year before his death, they voted his Trinity Church the best building in America; it received 84 percent of the votes. And four of his other buildings were named among the 175 best buildings.

In 1870, his philosophy of architectural design still tentative and unformed, Richardson acquired his first assistant, Charles Rutan (1851–1915), who was associated with him the rest of his life. Another, Charles Follen McKim (1847–1909), just back from the École des Beaux Arts and destined to become a famous architect himself, joined the firm and stayed until 1872. Commissions continued to come in and Richardson won competitions for others, the most important of which were the Brattle Square Church in Boston and the Lunatic Asylum, now known as the State Hospital, in Buffalo, N.Y., which was not finished until 1878.

The eventful year in Richardson's life was 1872. In that year he received the commission for Trinity Church. In that year, McKim left to start his own practice and another young architect, who later made his own name, Stanford White (1853–1906), joined Richardson to stay until 1878. White afterward became a partner, with McKim, in the firm of McKim, Mead and White. Also, in 1872 Richardson moved part of his practice to Boston, and in the spring of 1874, moved the rest of his firm and his family to Brookline, Mass. For the next 15 years, the firm produced some of the finest American buildings, and Richardson became a famous architect.

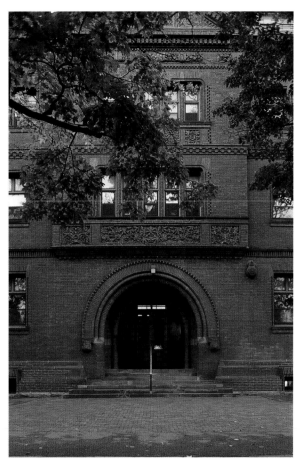

**RICHARDSON, HENRY HOBSON** Entrance, Sever Hall (1880, later alterations and additions), Harvard University, Cambridge, Mass.

By 1882, Richardson was tired, overweight, and ill. That summer, he returned to Paris for his only visit since he had worked there. He also went to London, consulted doctors about his health, and journeyed on to Italy and Spain. Everywhere he went, he collected photographs of Romanesque architecture. Returning to the United States, he received more commissions than he had ever had at one time in the past. As his health deteriorated, his designs became increasingly erratic.

In 1884 two young architects joined his firm, George Foster Shepley (1860–1903) and Charles Allerton Coolidge (1858–1936). On April 27, 1886, after a long illness, Richardson died at age forty-seven. A successor firm, Shepley, Rutan and Coolidge, was formed to finish the work on hand. The engineer Charles H. Rutan (1851–1915) was the third partner in the new firm. The firm, now known as Shepley, Bulfinch, Richardson and Abbott, is still in existence. Thus this firm has had one of the longest-lasting practices in America. In 1973, in recognition of its work, it received the Architectural Firm Award of the American Institute of Architects.

After his death, Richardson's architecture had little influence on the work of most architects, who now espoused an academic eclecticism. There were some notable exceptions. John Wellborn Root (1850–91), one of the Chicago pioneers of modern tall-building design, was influenced by Richardson's work. And Louis Henri Sullivan (1856–1924), the greatest of the early Chicago modern architects, admired and was deeply affected by the Richardson designs. Frank Lloyd Wright (1867–1959) was also impressed with and learned from Richardson's buildings.

During his career, Richardson designed a number of significant buildings. This is not to say that all his buildings were great. Many were below the standards of his best work. And the best examples intermingle with the others from the beginning to the end of his professional life.

**Works** The first important designs by Richardson were for the Church of the Unity, Springfield, Mass., and Grace Church, West Medford, Mass., both completed in 1869, both in a Victorian Gothic style. Richardson designed a great number of churches afterward, though he never considered himself a very religious person.

After designing houses, offices, a school, a bank, and so on in other styles, it is appropriate that his first building in the Romanesque style should be a church, this time the Brattle Square Church (1872), Boston. It is also considered one of his more significant buildings. He then designed a number of other buildings, including a school, a hospital, a courthouse, and houses. Next came the building many think his masterpiece, Trinity Church (1877; see illustration), Boston, the first full expression of his Romanesque style.

Over the next few years, he designed a number of buildings, including three important Massachusetts

**RICHARDSON, HENRY HOBSON** Detail, Allegheny County Courthouse and Jail (1888), Pittsburgh, Pa.

**RICHARDSON, HENRY HOBSON** Crane Memorial Library (1883), Quincy, Mass.

libraries: the Winn Memorial (1878), Woburn; the Ames Memorial (1879), North Easton; and the Crane Memorial (1883), Quincy. He also designed the City Hall (1882), Albany, N.Y., and two important buildings at Harvard University in Cambridge, Mass.: Sever Hall (1880) and Austin Hall (1883), which house the law school.

Over the years Richardson, designed a number of houses. Among the best are the Sherman House (1875), Newport, R.I.; the Stoughton House (1883), Cambridge, Mass.; the Brown House (1882), Marion, Mass.; and the Sard House (1883), Albany, N.Y.

During the last few years of his life, Richardson designed a great number of buildings, 30 of them in the last three years. He was an extremely popular architect, who took on a greater number of commissions than he could handle properly. These last buildings, 20 of which were incomplete at the time of his death, include some of the best of his work and some of the worst. Certainly three of the best, completed after his death in 1886, are the Marshall Field Wholesale Store and Warehouse (1887), Chicago, since demolished; the Allegheny County Courthouse and Jail (1888), Pittsburgh; and the Glessner House (1887), Chicago. Many think these three measure up to his Trinity Church and were the forerunners of what would have been a whole new creative era in his life, had he not died at age forty-seven.

**Life** Henry Hobson Richardson was born on September 29, 1838, at Priestley Plantation, St. James Parish, La., which is located about halfway up the Mississippi River from New Orleans to Baton Rouge. His father, a prominent businessman, died when the boy was sixteen. Richardson then spent the summers on the plantation and the winters in New Orleans, where he attended a private school. After a year at the University of Louisiana, now Tulane University, Richardson went to Cambridge, Mass., to be tutored for entry into Harvard University. After a rather undistinguished undergraduate career, he graduated from Harvard in 1859, with a degree in civil engineering, now determined to become an architect. In June of that year, he went to Paris. In the fall, he took the examinations for the École des Beaux Arts in Paris and failed everything except mathematics.

Richardson stayed on in Paris for a year, studying. In November 1860, he tried again and was admitted, becoming the second American to study there. Entering an atelier or study group, he began his architectural education, but after two years the Civil War in America disrupted his financial support. Going back to Boston, he could not find work, perhaps because as a Southerner, he would not take a loyalty oath to the Northern States. Returning to Paris, he worked as a drafter in the office of Theodore Labrouste and possibly in others until 1865, when he returned to the United States. Urged by his family to come to New Orleans and by his friends to Boston, he did neither. He went to New York City, thus establishing once and for all that his career would be in the North instead of in Louisiana, to which he never returned.

The next few years were uneventful. Richardson worked for a while for a builder, then designed gas light fixtures for Tiffany's, and did other odd jobs. He was in extremely bad financial straits and was forced to sell his library, except for his architectural books. His first real break came in 1866 when he won a competition for the design of the Church of the Unity. In January 1867, Richardson married Julia Hayden, who had been his fiancée since his Harvard days. In October of that year, he formed a partnership with Charles Gambrill (c. 1832–80) that lasted with ever-decreasing effectiveness until 1878. In 1867 Richardson won the competition for Grace Church. The newly married couple settled in Staten Island, an unlikely choice of a home for an architect who never had any real commissions in the New York City area.

Commissions in Massachusetts began to come into the office in increasing numbers and even a few from places such as Buffalo, N.Y. One, a little building, the Agawam National Bank (1870), Springfield, Mass., since destroyed, gave the first hint of a later predilection for the Romanesque Revival style.

**Related Articles** BEAUX ARTS, ÉCOLE DES; ECLECTIC ARCHITECTURE; MCKIM, MEAD AND WHITE; MODERN ARCHITECTURE; PUBLIC BUILDING; RELIGIOUS BUILDING.

**Further Reading** Gorman, J. F.: *H. H. Richardson: Architectural Forms for an American Society*, The University of Chicago Press, Chicago, 1987; Hitchcock, Henry-Russell: *The Architecture of H. H. Richardson and His Times*, rev. ed., MIT Press, Cambridge, Mass., 1975.

**ROAD AND TRAFFIC DESIGN** The process of developing designs for facilities for vehicular traffic. Road and traffic design, or engineering, affects architecture in many ways. Since automobiles and other vehicles have become such an important part of life today, the design of facilities for them is of major concern in regional and city planning, which produce the total background or setting in which architecture exists. Streets and other vehicular facilities, such as parking adjacent to sites, also strongly affect the design of buildings placed on the sites. Provisions for vehicular facilities on building sites are of great importance and, in the case of architectural complexes, such as housing developments or shopping centers, can become dominant features of the designs.

Roads are strips of land on which vehicles travel. Roads within cities and towns are usually called streets, while major roads between urban areas are usually called highways, a name they acquired when roads were first constructed with their surfaces higher than the level of the ground.

**U.S. Roads** Several types of roads and highways are used in the United States. Local roads are used in smaller areas; secondary roads are used to connect smaller communities and for access to the primary highways that connect larger communities. The term *freeway* is used for a major highway, which theoretically allows free flow of traffic and which has controlled access at specific locations, called interchanges. Freeways are sometimes called superhighways or expressways and may require toll payments. When freeways pass through urban or congested areas, they are often elevated above or depressed below city streets. These are called grade separations.

Freeways that charge tolls were originally called turnpikes and some are still called that today. A parkway is like a freeway except that it is located in a landscaped, parklike setting and often only automobiles are allowed to use it. An interstate highway is a freeway, without tolls, connecting major urban areas of the United States. Freeways almost always have median strips, open land between the set of traffic lanes going in one direction and those going in the other, often with fencing or other devices to control accidents. Bypass highways are located so that traffic may go around or past towns and other urban areas. Circumferential highways, sometimes called beltways, go around large cities, allowing access to various neighborhoods or local areas directly, without passing through other areas of the cities.

Streets are very much like other roads, but are located in urban areas. Arterial streets handle major portions of the traffic; they are often larger than other streets and may have medians. Sometimes arterial streets are called avenues or boulevards.

**Pertinent Factors** Road, highway, and traffic design, planning, engineering, and construction are quite complex, because of the great number of important factors that must be taken into consideration. Long-range studies must be made of subjects, such as where people live or goods are produced, where they will go, how they will get there, and so on. The future of urban, suburban, regional, and larger areas must be studied. Traffic counts must be made and projected to indicate needs for the future. Utility requirements, lighting, landscaping, drainage, safety, grading, and other factors must be studied. Decisions must be made on the preparation of the land, surfacing intersections, bypasses, grade separations, and other questions.

**Government Finance** Road, street, and highway construction is financed by governments, towns and cities on the urban level, and mostly states but sometimes counties on the rural level. The funds come from several sources: taxes, bond issues, tolls, and federal monies. The interstate system has been paid for, 10 percent by the states and 90 percent by the federal government, from a highway trust that receives money from taxes on items related to highway usage, such as vehicle fuels, tires, and tubes, and by trucks and buses.

**Design Professionals** Several design professionals are involved in the design, planning, and engineering of roads, highways, and streets: city and regional planners, highway and traffic engineers who have civil engineering degrees, landscape architects, and architects. The major functions in the analysis of their design and in their programming are often performed by city planners and traffic engineers; the major functions in their engineering, by highway engineers. Landscape architects often design the landscaping and architects become involved in relation to the buildings and building complexes they design.

**History** The history of roads goes back to prehistoric times, the first examples being trails and paths thought to have been made originally by animals and used by humans to track the animals. Later humans made their own trails while seeking water, food, and fuel.

During the Neolithic period, starting about the 40th century B.C., rudimentary roads were built and used for pack transport, first by women who carried the loads, while the men, presumably, protected the women. Following their domestication, some animals were trained to carry packs. The first is thought to have been the ass, beginning very early in the Neolithic period. The first vehicles for transport were sledges which slid on runners when they were pulled by humans and, later, by oxen or other animals.

After the invention of the wheel about 3500 B.C., road building began in earnest. Some of the first surfaced roads utilized what is called the corduroy system, logs or brushwood laid on the ground parallel to each other, to cross soft ground. These were followed by rut roads, made with grooves cut into the ground in which the wheels of vehicles could run. Roads were paved with stone no later than the 25th century B.C. Although travel by water continued to be used extensively, roads were built by the ancient Egyptians and by other people in the Middle East, and streets were paved in both Mesopotamia and Egypt with flagstones, some of which were set on brick bases with a mortar made of bitumen. Roads were also built in many other places, including China.

The ancient Greeks were not noted as road builders; most of the roads they built were rudimentary types, such as rut roads. The Romans were great road builders, not only in the extent of the network of roads they constructed all over Italy and their conquered territories but in the technical excellence of their work. The Roman roads were of two main types: paved; and sanded or graveled. Both were well designed and constructed. In one type of paved Roman road, for example, the surface of the ground was excavated to a proper level, then sand was laid down with cement mortar on top of it; on top of this were laid successive layers of stone slabs or blocks in mortar, concrete, and a surfacing of stone set in mortar or concrete. The roads were sloped from the centers to the sides for water drainage, and ditches were dug alongside to take away the water.

The Romans are thought to have built more than 50,000 miles of roads, some in Africa and Persia and some as far away as England. The first of their roads and perhaps the most famous was the Appian Way, begun in 312 B.C. This road runs 162 miles from Rome south to Terracina. Many Roman roads are still in use today.

During the Middle Ages and the Renaissance, road building came almost to a stop, even though many architects of the Renaissance period were interested in road design. Most of the roads that were built were unpaved, primitive tracks, often passable only by pedestrians, horseback riders, and pack animals. Starting in the reign of Louis XIV (1638–1715) of France and continuing through the era of the Emperor Napoleon (1769–1821), good roads were built in France for military purposes. In the rest of Europe, roads were not improved very much until the 17th century and later.

In the late 18th and early 19th centuries, two Scottish engineers revolutionized road building. First, Thomas Telford (1757–1834), also noted for his bridge designs, designed and built a network of good roads in Scotland, constructed of layers of stone with gravel. Then another engineer, John Loudon McAdam (1756–1836), developed even better and less costly methods of road building. For the more costly hand-laid stone foundations used previously, McAdam substituted thin packed layers of crushed stone by a method that was named for him, macadam, and which is still used today. Concurrent with the improved roads came the establishment of stagecoach travel, and in England, the building of the first toll roads, or turnpikes as they came to be called.

**American Development** In colonial America, the first roads were primitive trails. Until the end of the 18th century, most roads were unpaved and followed trails made by Indians. Travel was almost entirely by foot or horseback, later by stagecoach. The first hard-surfaced road, of crushed stone and gravel, in the United States was the Lancaster Turnpike, 62 miles long, constructed in Pennsylvania in 1795. Early streets were unsurfaced, but cobblestones and wooden blocks were used later and still later stone was used. In 1873 the first brick street was constructed in Charleston, W. Va. Bituminous paving was also used about that time. The first concrete street was built in 1893, and the first concrete road in 1908, in Detroit.

With the advent of automobiles, road and street building accelerated in the early part of the 20th century. In the 1920s a great deal of this sort of construction was carried on; then the activity slowed down during the Depression and World War II and accelerated again after the war. Since the 1950s, the Federal Interstate Highway System has added many thousands of miles of roads all over the United States. In all, there is a total of some 4 million miles of roads and streets in the country today.

**Related Articles** ENGINEERING; HOTEL; PLANNING, CITY.

**Periodical** *Traffic Engineering,* 1815 N. Ft. Myer Dr., Arlington, Va. 22209.

**Source of Additional Information** Institute of Transportation Engineers, 1815 N. Ft. Myer Dr., Arlington, Va. 22209.

**ROCHE, KEVIN** Irish-born American, late Modern architect (1922– ) known for a series of important corporate headquarters buildings and urban high-rise office buildings, as well as museums and other building types. Influences on his work include Mies van der Rohe and Eero Saarinen.

With John Dinkeloo, he inherited the firm of Eero Saarinen and started the firm of Kevin Roche John Dinkeloo and Associates with a number of major projects, leading on to a major practice.

**Work** The first project of the new firm was the Oakland Museum (1968), Oakland, Calif. The building is a series of terraces and garden areas, with the galleries partially underground. The regional museum contains museums of art, natural history, and cultural history. Perhaps the most famous project of the firm was the Ford Foundation Headquarters (1968), New York City,

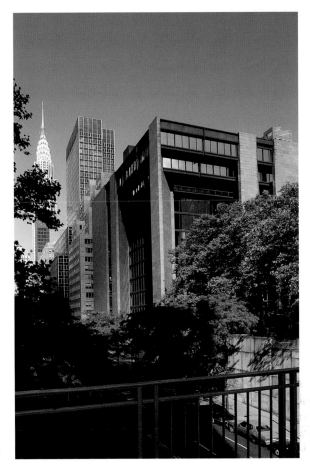

**ROCHE, KEVIN** Ford Foundation Building (1967), New York, N.Y.

containing an 8,500 ft² interior garden along 42d street. The vertical concrete surfaces contrast to the steel and glass wall.

The redevelopment area of New Haven, Conn., contains the Knights of Columbus Headquarters (1969), visible from the New England Turnpike. The 23-story building contains a central core and four corner cylindrical towers supporting the floors. It adjoins the Veterans Memorial Coliseum (1972), also designed by the firm.

Among several corporate headquarters projects are the Richardson-Vicks Inc., Headquarters (1974), Wilton, Conn., where two floors of offices are placed between parking below and on the roof. The effect is a preservation of the natural contours of the land on a wooded site. John Deere & Company (1979), West Office Building, is a successful addition to the earlier Eero Saarinen building. The atrium between the original and new office areas is particularly appealing. The Union Carbide World Headquarters (1982), Danbury, Conn., and the General Foods Corporation (1982), Rye, N.Y., are spectacular buildings which received wide attention when published.

The work for the Metropolitan Museum of Art in New York City started with a new master plan involving

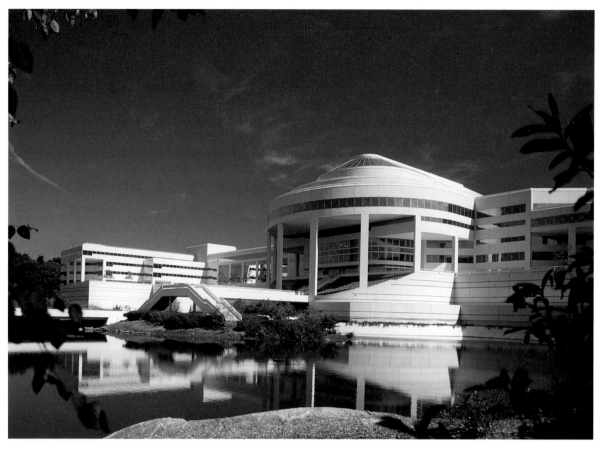

**ROCHE, KEVIN** General Foods Corporation Headquarters (1982), Rye, N.Y.

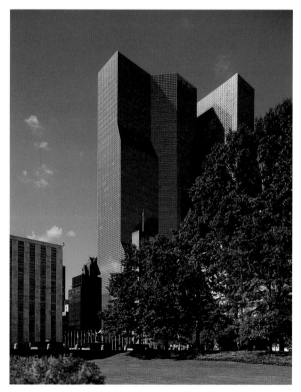

**ROCHE, KEVIN** United Nations Plaza (1983), New York, N.Y.

a number of additions and alterations to the historic buildings. These were added over a number of years and include a new street development along 5th Ave. with two large fountains and improved access to the museum. Additions include the Robert Lehman Pavilion (1974), the Temple of Dendur Pavilion (1976), the Michael C. Rockefeller Primitive Art Wing (1976), the American Wing (1980), the Bookshop (1980), the Andre Meyer Galleries (1980), and the Southwest Wing (1985). A total of 6.88 million ft$^2$ were added to the museum. An attempt was made to reduce the height of the buildings in Central Park as contrasted to the formal front along 5th Ave.

Commercial office projects of note are the minimalist sculpture of the United Nations Plaza One and Two (1983), New York City, and the E. F. Hutton Building (1986), New York City, with its gigantic granite columns forming an arcade at street level.

Important buildings have been built in smaller cities. The Worcester County National Bank, Worcester, Mass. (1974), is a landmark building in that city. Several projects have been built in Columbus, Ind., including the Post Office, the Irwin Union Bank and Trust (1972), the Cummins Engine Company Corporate Headquarters, and the Cummins Engine Company Sub-Assembly Plant. In Fort Wayne, Ind., Kevin Roche John Dinkeloo

**ROCHE, KEVIN** Cummins Engine Headquarters (1984), Columbus, Ind.

and Associates designed the 26-floor One Summit Square Complex. For Ashland, Ky., the firm designed the Kentucky Power Company Administration Building.

The Denver Center for the Performing Arts is a major grouping of performing arts facilities incorporating the Boetcher Concert Hall designed by Hardy Holzman, Pfeiffer, and another existing auditorium and arena. Kevin Roche John Dinkeloo Associates designed the Helen G. Bonfils theater. The most dramatic feature is the 70-foot glazed arcade giving access to parking.

**Life** Kevin Roche was born in Dublin, Ireland, in 1922. He received his architectural education at the National University of Ireland in 1945 and came to the United States in 1948. After working for Sir Maxwell Fry (1899–1987) in London, he came to Chicago to study at the Illinois Institute of Technology under Mies van der Rohe. In 1950 he joined the firm of Eero Saarinen in Bloomfield Hills, Mich. In 1954, he became principal design associate and worked with Eero Saarinen until Saarinen's death in 1961. The surviving partners, Kevin Roche, Joseph Lacy, and John Dinkeloo, continued under the name Eero Saarinen and Associates. Several major projects of the Saarinen firm

**ROCHE, KEVIN** 750 7th Ave. (1991), New York, N.Y. [Photo: courtesy of Roche & Dinkeloo]

completed after Eero Saarinen's death included the St. Louis, Mo., Arch, the TWA Terminal at Kennedy International Airport in New York, the Dulles International Airport near Washington, D.C., the Deere & Company Headquarters in Moline, Ill., and the CBS Headquarters Building in New York City. In 1966, with the retirement of Joseph Lacey, the firm became Kevin Roche John Dinkeloo and Associates, with offices in Hamden, Conn. In 1981, John Dinkeloo died, but the firm name continues. The firm received the AIA Firm Award in 1974. Kevin Roche received the Pritzker Prize for 1982 and the Gold Medal from the American Institute of Architects in 1993.

**Further Reading** Dal Co, Francesco: *Kevin Roche*, Rizzoli, New York, 1985.

**ROOF** The weatherproofed topside of a building, including its structure and covering, or roofing. One of the major structural systems that protect buildings, their contents, and occupants from the effects of weather, roofs have always been important elements of architecture.

**Forms** Roofs come in many different forms, a traditional response to climatic conditions. In relatively arid areas of the world, roofs have tended to be flat. In other areas, with relatively large amounts of snowfall or rainfall, roofs have usually been sloped to drain off the precipitation. Today these principles still apply in architecture; however, improved materials and structural methods have made it possible for architects to use just about any form of roof they wish in almost any climate.

**Sloped Roofs** These roofs are often covered with shingles or tiles, which come in small units and depend on their overlaps and the slope of the roofs to prevent leaking. The slope of a roof is usually referred to as its pitch, meaning the ratio between the vertical rise of the roof and its horizontal span. For example, if a roof spans 10 ft and rises 5 ft, it is said to have a half-pitch, one in the ratio of 5:10. For convenience, roof pitches are usually expressed in rise per foot of span; therefore a one-half pitch would be expressed as 6:12, denoting a 6-in rise in a 12-in span. Pitches may also be expressed in ordinary fractions, in which case the 6:12 example would be a $\frac{1}{2}$ pitch. Some other commonly used pitches for roofs include: 0 for a roof that is flat or nearly flat; 3:12, or a $\frac{1}{4}$ pitch; 4:12, or a $\frac{1}{3}$ pitch; and 5:12. Sometimes roof pitches may be even greater than the above.

**Types** The simplest roof is a flat one, though it usually has some slight slope or pitch. If it has a steeper slope, in only one direction, a roof is often called a lean-to or shed type. A roof that slopes in two directions from the top or peak toward the outsides is called a gable type and its form makes triangles at the ends, which the ancient Greeks termed pediments. A butterfly roof also slopes in two directions, but from the outsides down to

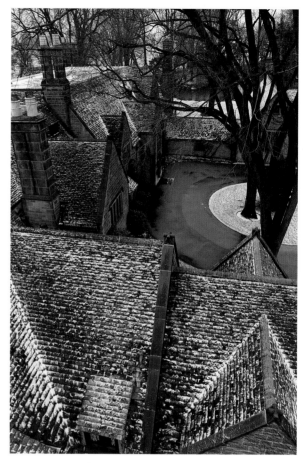

**ROOF** Stone roof (Cotswold stone), Edsel B. Ford House (1926), Grosse Pointe, Mich. *[Architect: Albert Kahn]*

its center. A hip roof has slopes on all four sides, the shorter ones usually being called the hips. A gambrel roof slopes up from only two sides, but has two different pitches on each side, the lower portions of the roof having steeper pitches than the upper portions. A gambrel roof is sometimes called a mansard roof, but often the latter term is applied to a roof sloping from all sides, like a hip type but with two different pitches on each of the four sides. Other types are the sawtooth roof, often used in factories or other large-area, low-rise buildings to permit the entry of more light, and sometimes air, than would otherwise be possible; and the monitor roof, which has raised sections with windows on their sides for the same purpose.

For the usual types of sloped roofs, the line along which two slopes meet at their highest level is called the ridge, the line along the lowest level is called the eave and, if it projects beyond the wall, is often called an overhang. The trough where two roof planes intersect is called a valley. The top of a wall that projects above the eave of a roof is called a parapet. A wall that projects through a roof surface, for fire-resistance purposes, is called a fire wall.

**Other Forms** Today there are a great variety of other roof shapes, made possible by advanced structural methods, particularly in reinforced concrete, steel, and aluminum. These include various shapes of vaults and domes in several geometric shapes, such as segments of spheres and cylinders, conoids, hyperbolic paraboloids, and hyperboloids. Many other roof forms are possible through the use of relatively new structural systems, such as lamella, laminated-wood arch, thin concrete shell, stressed-skin, suspension, and space frame.

**Elements** The major elements of a complete roof system are the roof structure and the deck or other surface upon which is placed roofing, the material used to weatherproof the roof deck. Two other elements are often used: a vapor barrier, laid on the deck to prevent moisture from the heated interior of a building from reaching the roofing; and thermal insulation, placed over the vapor barrier to retard the flow of heat into the building interior in hot weather and out of it in cold. A fifth element, almost always necessary to complete the weatherproofing of a roof, is flashing, a device usually made of metal but sometimes of other materials, used to prevent water infiltration where roof planes meet and where roofing meets the edges of roofs, chimneys, or other building elements. Associated with flashing are devices to direct the flow of water from roofs, including gutters and downspouts and other types. For further discussion on vapor barriers, see articles entitled insulation, thermal; waterproofing. The latter article also covers flashing, gutters, downspouts, and so on. For further discussion on roof structures of various materials, see articles entitled concrete structure; steel structure; wood-frame structure. See also the article entitled roofing.

Roof systems are one of the most important determinants of architectural design, primarily because their forms have a great deal to do with the overall appearance of buildings; and because of their textures, colors, and patterns. Architects of today design roofs in a variety of

**ROOF** Manhattan roofscape.

forms and may choose roofing from a great variety of types. The architectural treatment of roofs, their slopes and how they intersect, also strongly affects the appearance of buildings. A great deal of attention is therefore paid to the aesthetic design of roofs.

In addition, a great deal of attention must be paid to proper structural design, detailing, and workmanship. Roof structures, including roof decks, must be strong enough to withstand the loads to which they will be subjected. They must be stiff enough so that undue deflection will not weaken their structures, lessen their weatherproofing qualities, or cause other problems. They must be designed and constructed in accordance with the fire-resistance qualities required in building codes. In many roofs, expansion joints must be provided to prevent damage to the materials when they expand and contract with changes in temperature.

In addition, roofs are often the location for building elements of many kinds, including penthouses for elevator or other types of machinery, water tanks, ventilators, skylights, scuttles for roof access, and dormer windows. All such elements must be properly designed, structurally as well as aesthetically, and must be properly flashed

**ROOF** Cable-supported roof, Town & Country Shopping Center (1983), Houston, Tex. *[Architect: Kober Assoc.]*

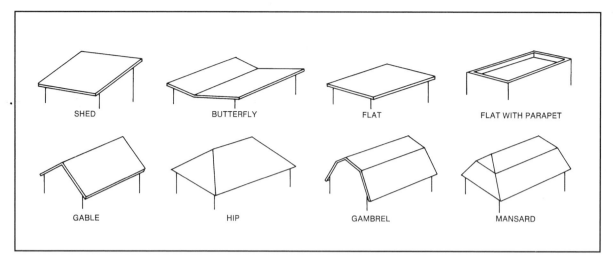

**ROOF** Types.

or otherwise protected from water infiltration. Flat roofs are often used for terraces or other areas for various types of activities. If they are to be used in this manner, special provisions must be made so that their structures will withstand such loads, and they must be surfaced so that the roofing will be protected from damage.

**History** Ancient primitive buildings had roofs constructed of poles set in a conical shape. In Mesopotamia, roofs were flat and constructed of wood, or had vaults or domes constructed of brick, at first sun-dried and later kiln-dried. In Crete, wood also was used for roof structures, which were generally flat, and sometimes had slabs of gypsum over the timbers. Roofs in Egypt were generally constructed of stone slabs and were flat, making it possible to use them for various activities.

In ancient Greece, roof structures were generally framed in timber, in low-pitched, gable shapes. The Romans used a variety of roof forms (gables, vaults, and domes) constructed of a variety of materials, including wood, stone, and concrete. Early Christian buildings generally had gable roofs, made with wood members. Byzantine architecture utilized mostly domed roof structures of brick, stone, and concrete. In Romanesque architecture, barrel-vaulted roofs of stone were used along with timber roofs; sometimes both types were used for various portions of a single building.

During the Gothic period in architecture, roofs were constructed mostly with timber trusses, which were sometimes exposed on the interiors and sometimes placed over stone vaults. When exposed, the trusses were usually ornamented with carvings, especially in England. Gothic roofs were generally in gable shapes, with low pitches in Italy, medium pitches in England, and high pitches in France.

During the Renaissance, roof structures of several types were used, including gable roofs, with trusses of timber, and domes and barrel vaults of brick, stone, and sometimes concrete. In Italy, except for domes, roofs were generally low-pitched and were often concealed from view by railings or balustrades, or other ornamental architectural features. In the countries north of Italy, domes were often used as were gable, high-pitched roofs. Hip roofs, used only rarely before, were also sometimes used, as were flat roofs and the type of roof with two pitches, called a gambrel or a mansard roof, after the French architect Francois Mansart (1598–1666), who used it often and who even developed a type with three pitches. Renaissance roofs, particularly in France, often had many dormers and ornamental chimneys.

After the Renaissance, roofs used on buildings varied widely and included all the types previously used. As time went on, stone and brick were gradually abandoned as roof structural materials in America as well as in Europe and other places, to be replaced today by three major materials: steel, reinforced concrete, and wood. During the various revival and eclectic periods of architecture, roof styles were derived from those of the past.

After the beginning of the Modern movement in architecture in the 19th century, flat roofs were used quite widely and the trend has continued to the present time. A type not ordinarily used in the past is the lean-to or shed roof, previously used only on the most ordinary buildings. Today many types of roofs are used, including all of those of the past. In addition, various curved and other shapes may be used in concrete, steel, and other materials. Also roof structures today may be space frames, made up from relatively small members of various materials in a variety of shapes; laminated timbers; and other types.

**Related Articles** ARCH; CONCRETE STRUCTURE; DOME; INSULATION, THERMAL; MASONRY STRUCTURE; ROOFING;

STEEL STRUCTURE; VAULT; WATERPROOFING; WOOD-FRAME STRUCTURE.

**Further Reading** Griffin, C. W., Jr.: *Manual of Built-Up Roof Systems*, 2d ed., McGraw-Hill, New York, 1982; Publications of the following associations.

**Sources of Additional Information** Asphalt Roofing Manufacturing Assoc., 6288 Montrose Rd., Rockville, Md. 20852; National Roofing Contractors Assoc., 10255 W. Higgins Rd., Rosemont, Ill. 60018-5607; Cedar Shake and Shingle Bureau, 515 116th Ave., N.E., Bellevue, Wash. 98004; Roofing Industry Educational Institute, Building H, Ste. 110, 14 Inverness Dr. E., Englewood, Colo. 80112-5608; Single Ply Roofing Institute, 20 Walnut St., Wellesley Hills, Mass. 02189.

**ROOFING** The materials used to make the top of buildings weatherproof. Roofing is the outer element of a roof system that also includes a structure of some sort with a deck over it, upon which the roofing may be placed. The system often includes a vapor barrier placed over the deck to prevent moisture from coming up from heated areas below and insulation over the vapor barrier to decrease the amount of heat entering a building interior in summer or escaping in winter. For further discussion on these other elements of complete systems, along with roof flashing, see articles entitled insulation, thermal; roof; waterproofing. Roofing is usually measured in squares, the amount that will weatherproof 100 ft$^2$ of roof structure.

**Types** The large number of roofing products may be grouped by materials and application techniques. The major ones are built-up roofing; cold-applied roofing; metal roofing; single-ply roofing; asphalt, slate, clay tile, concrete tile, and wood shingles; and spray-applied foams. In general, roofing is considered a system, which includes a structural deck, thermal insulation and roofing material to keep out moisture, as well as flashing to protect joints with other materials. Roofing systems are complex and require good judgment and the cooperation of contractors and material manufacturers to produce a satisfactory roof.

Built-up roofing for low-slope roofs consist of asphalt or coal-tar pitch and felt membranes installed at the job site. These roofs have given years of satisfactory service and represent a major roofing system, with estimated many billions of square feet of roofing in place in the United States. Cold-applied roofing has been used for repairs or temporary sealing of a leaking roof, or may be applied as a new surface over existing built-up roofs.

Metal roofs have been in use since ancient times, and the technology is well understood. These roofs require special detailing to maintain weatherability, such as standing seams to allow the roofing to be attached to the decking. Sometimes batten seams are used for decorative effects. Materials available for metal roofs include aluminum, copper, and zinc, which all may be left exposed to the weather because a thin film of oxides form which protect the metal beneath. Stainless steel changes little in appearance when exposed. Steel must be protected from the weather by coating with other metals, paint, or ceramics. Steel roof products are the most used because of lower cost.

Single-ply roofing systems can be grouped by their chemical makeup and include vulcanized elastomers (EPDM and neoprene), nonvulcanized elatomers (CSPE, PIB, NBP), thermoplastic materials (PVC, EIP), and modified bitumen roofing membranes. These products are manufactured in large flexible sheets, which may be used loose-laid for nearly flat roofs, or mechanically attached, and for steeper slopes, fully adhered. Nearly flat roofs may require stone ballast to hold the roofing in place. Joints must be sealed with heat or compatible adhesives, and specific fasteners, coatings, and flashing are required for a complete roofing system.

Steep roofing applications are generally tile or shingles, where the overlap of small units provides weather protection. Asphalt shingles are the most common in use, for new and replacement roofs. Asphalt shingles should generally be used on slopes of 4 in to the foot or greater. Slate roofing is selected for durability and appearance, with several colors and textures available from different quarries. The natural cleavage of the slate determines the smoothness of the surface, and sometimes ribbons of a different color are experienced. Exposed to the weather, some slates will change slightly in color compared with others. The weight of slate roofs is a structural consideration. Clay tile has an ancient history and is selected for color and texture of the roof. Tiles may be rolled or flat in shape. A more recent type of tile is concrete roofing tile extruded under high pressure, and installed similarly to clay tile. Wood shingles are often made of cedar because of its ease in splitting, and its natural resistance to weather. The shingles may be machine-sawn, machine-split, or hand-split for varying appearance. Wood shingle roofs are normally installed on plywood sheathing or to wood strips nailed to rafters.

Spray-applied foams consist of a number of proprietary products. Urethane foams require protection by an elastomeric liquid-applied coating. The advantage of these systems is to provide thermal insulation, sometimes in combination with conventional insulation products. The use of spray-applied foams in the field may vary depending on climate conditions and care in application.

**Characteristics** The selection of roofing for an individual building presents an architect with an almost endless variety of types, forms, appearances, textures, colors, life expectancies, fire resistances, and costs. Built-up roofs are restricted to the colors available in the gravel or other materials with which they are covered, unless the roofs are surfaced with tile or some other material for use as roof terraces or for some other purpose. Natural materials, such as slate or wood (generally cedar but also available in redwood or cypress) have color, texture, and weathering characteristics peculiarly their own. Each of the metals has its own color and other characteristics. Galvanized iron should be painted and thus has unlimited color possibilities. Most other roofing materials have limited color and texture ranges, except for asphalt shingles.

Life expectancies for roofing range from about 15 years for wood shingles, somewhat more for asphalt shingles, up to about 20 years for some built-up types, and somewhat more for such materials as slate, clay tile, copper, stainless steel, terneplate, and a few other metals. Fire resistance of roofing materials ranges from the lowest for wood shingles, which are combustible, and asphalt shingles, which have little resistance, through the metals which are incombustible to concrete tile and slate, which are quite fire-resistant. The fire resistance of built-up roofs varies considerably with differences in structures, decks, types of application, and surfacing materials. Building codes determine which roofing materials meet fire resistance requirements.

The cost of roofing materials varies widely from the lowest, roll roofing, through intermediate levels, including asphalt shingles, usually considered to be the lowest-priced acceptable material for houses, to very high-priced types such as flat-seam roofs of several metals.

**History** In the primitive cultures of early history, roofing is thought to have been of animal skins or brush, thatch, or other vegetation. In Mesopotamia, roofing was usually of clay and reeds or bitumen on masonry. In Egypt, roofing was not employed on top of roof structures, but the stones of the structures had channels cut in to take away rain.

Roofing in ancient Greece was of marble or terra-cotta (clay) tiles. In Rome, roofing was of terra-cotta tiles, but sometimes marble tiles or bronze were used. In Byzantine architecture, no roofing at all was used for many buildings; in others, metals, such as lead, were sometimes used.

During the Middle Ages, in the Romanesque and Gothic periods, slate and lead were the major roofing materials. During the Renaissance, both materials were used, as were tile and slabs of other kinds of stone. By the end of the Renaissance, many of the various kinds of roofing materials used today had been developed. Notable exceptions are galvanized iron, which dates from about the middle of the 19th century; asphalt and aluminum at the end of that century; and the use of plastics in the 20th century.

**Related Articles** ROOF; Various articles on individual building materials.

**Further Reading** Griffin, C. W., Jr.: *Manual of Built-Up Roof Systems*, 2d ed., McGraw-Hill, New York, 1982.

**Sources of Additional Information** See listing in the article entitled roof.

# S

**SAARINEN, EERO** Finnish-American architect (1910–61). Eero Saarinen was the son of a famous architect-father and a talented artist-mother. Eero Saarinen was almost preordained to become an architect. Originally, he decided to become a sculptor, but later he changed his mind, becoming one of the most sculptural architects. He was also one of the most inventive, particularly in the forms of his buildings.

After graduating from Yale University School of Architecture in 1934, he joined his father in 1937 in a partnership, Saarinen and Saarinen, located in Bloomfield Hills, Mich., and the two worked together until the death of the father in 1950.

In 1948 Eero Saarinen won the competition for the design of the Jefferson National Expansion Memorial in St. Louis, with a giant stainless-steel-covered arch that came to be known as the Gateway Arch. The favorable publicity his design received brought in commissions independently of his father. After the death of his father, he started his own firm, called Eero Saarinen and Associates. In the little more than a decade he had left to live, Saarinen designed a number of buildings, many of which received sensational receptions in the press and among architects. Most of the buildings were sculptural in form, and each seemed to have been designed with little or no reference to those that preceded it.

**Works** Among Saarinen's first works were the Kresge Auditorium and the Chapel (both 1955) at the Massachusetts Institute of Technology, Cambridge, Mass. These were followed by the U.S. embassies in London (1956) and Oslo, Norway (1959); two 1956 buildings for International Business Machines (IBM), a manufacturing plant at Rochester, Minn., and the Thomas J. Watson Research Center at Yorktown Heights, N.Y.; the John Deere Administration Center (1957), Moline, Ill.; two buildings at Concordia College

(1958), Fort Wayne, Ind.; the Ingalls Hockey Rink (1958) at Yale University, New Haven, Conn.; the University of Chicago Law School (1960), Chicago; and the TWA Terminal (1960) at John F. Kennedy, then Idlewild, International Airport, New York City. Several of his most interesting buildings were completed after his death, including the Samuel F. B. Morse and Ezra Stiles colleges (1962) at Yale University; the CBS Buildings (1956) in New York City; and the Gateway Arch (1965). His great and pioneering design for Dulles Airport, Chantilly, Va., was not finished until 1963. Many people think it his masterpiece.

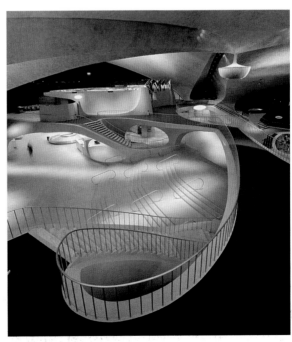

**SAARINEN, EERO** Interior, TWA Terminal (1960), John F. Kennedy International Airport, New York, N.Y.

**SAARINEN, EERO** Kresge Auditorium and Chapel (1955), Massachusetts Institute of Technology, Cambridge, Mass.

In addition to these major works, Saarinen is also known for the design of furniture, including the pedestal furniture (1957) and the "Womb" chair (1948), both manufactured by Knoll Associates. He was also architect for a number of houses, perhaps the most successful being that for Irwin J. Miller (1957).

**Appraisal** Eero Saarinen was something of an enigma to the public as well as to his fellow architects. He never quite seemed to fit into any mold or pattern. Each building design seemed to present him with a specific challenge which he then answered in an original way. He always seemed to be searching for something new or better or both. And he never seemed to find it, at least not for long. He never seemed to have been interested in developing a style in his work, unless it was the style of treating each new problem as if there were no precedents for its solution. His accomplishments startled and surprised many people. He was always fresh and intriguing. Many people called him a genius, but others are still not completely convinced. One sign of professional appreciation is the awarding of American Institute of Architects 25-year awards to such Saarinen projects as the General Motors Technical Center (Saarinen and Saarinen, 1953) and the Dulles International Airport. In addition to the illustrations accompanying this article, refer to the index for other Saarinen buildings in other articles.

**Life** Eero Saarinen was born on August 2, 1910, in Kurkkonummi, Finland. His father, Eliel Saarinen (1873–1950), was already a famous architect in Europe. Something of a prodigy, who could sketch with either hand, Eero Saarinen had little formal training in his early years. But he designed, drew, painted, and modeled. In 1922, when he was twelve, he won a contest for a design with matchsticks. In that same year, his father placed second in the competition for the design of the Chicago Tribune Tower and received great acclaim for the design, which many critics thought superior to that of the winner.

As a result of the prominence that came from the Tribune Tower competition, Eliel Saarinen moved to the United States, and Eero and the rest of the family joined him in 1923. In 1925 the family moved to Bloomfield Hills, Mich., where Eliel designed the Kingswood School for Girls (1929), for which Eero designed sculptural wood furniture. Having decided to become a sculptor, he then enrolled in 1929 in the Grande Chaumière in Paris. After a year, he changed his mind and transferred to the architectural school at Yale University. Graduating with honors in 1934, he won a two-year traveling scholarship and went to Europe.

After returning from Europe, Saarinen went back to Cranbrook in 1936, to serve as a design instructor and in

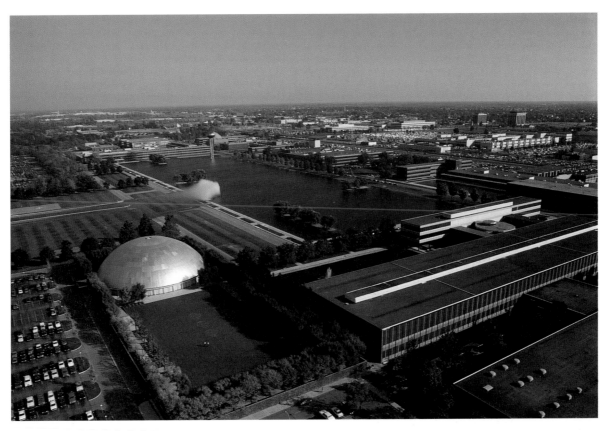

**SAARINEN, EERO** General Motors Technical Center (1957), Warren, Mich.

1937, to join his father's architectural firm, which was renamed Saarinen and Saarinen. Some of the notable buildings they did together are the Kleinhaus Music Hall (1938), Buffalo, N.Y.; the Crow Island School (1939), Winnetka, Ill., in association with a Chicago firm destined for success, Perkins, Wheeler and Will; and the First Christian Church (1942), Columbus, Ind. In 1939 he married Lily Swann, a student of ceramics at Cranbrook. In 1940 he and Charles Eames (1907–78) won two first prizes for furniture design in a competition of the Museum of Modern Art in New York City. During World War II, Saarinen served with the Office of Strategic Services from 1942 to 1945. Even during his wartime service, he found time to work with his father on building designs.

After the war, the Saarinens received commissions for important buildings and other projects, among them campuses for several colleges. The largest and most comprehensive project was the General Motors Technical Center, Warren, Mich. The design of this more than $100 million complex, with associated architects Smith, Hinchman and Grylls, began soon after the war but was not completed until 1957, seven years after the elder Saarinen died. In 1948 Eero Saarinen won the competition that established him as an individual architect, the Gateway Arch, which was not finished until 1965, after his death.

In 1953, having been divorced, Saarinen married Aline B. Louchheim (1914–72), an art critic and later a television commentator. After winning the Gateway Arch competition, Saarinen received a great number of commissions for buildings of all types. For each one, he seemed to be able to come up with a design unlike that of any of the others. The large number of projects required a large staff, which eventually reached about 100 people. Among them were some talented younger men, including the Irish-American architect Kevin Roche (1922– ) and John Gerard Dinkeloo (1918–81), who later formed a successor firm to that of Saarinen, and have themselves since designed many notable buildings.

At age fifty, Eero Saarinen seemed to have everything. His architectural design was inventive and virile. Commissions were pouring in. His personal life was happy. Honors were coming in, including election as fellow of the American Academy of Arts and Letters. Then tragedy struck him down at age fifty-one at the peak of his powers. On September 1, 1961, he died after brain surgery. The following year he was awarded, as had been his father, the highest honor of the American Institute of Architects, the Gold Medal. The posthumous award was accepted in his name by his widow, Aline Saarinen.

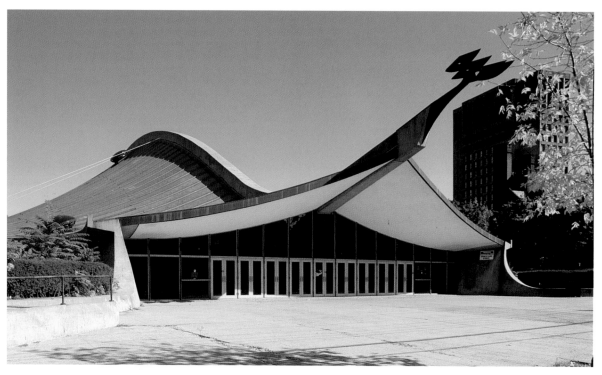

**SAARINEN, EERO** Ingalls Hockey Rink (1958), Yale University, New Haven, Conn.

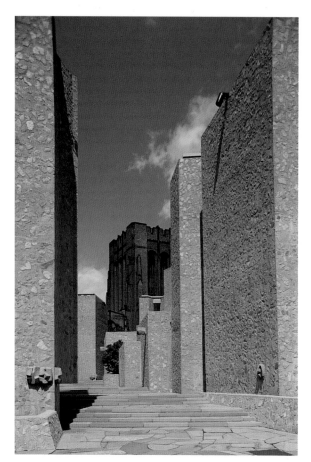

**SAARINEN, EERO** Ezra Stiles and Samuel F. B. Morse Colleges (1962), Yale University, New Haven, Conn.

**Related Articles** CONTEMPORARY ARCHITECTURE; MODERN ARCHITECTURE; SAARINEN, ELIEL.

**Further Reading** Saarinen, Eero, and Aline B. Saarinen, eds.: *Eero Saarinen on His Work—A Selection of Buildings Dating from 1947–1964*, Yale University Press, New Haven, Conn., 1968; Temko, Allen: *Eero Saarinen*, Braziller, New York, 1962.

**SAARINEN, ELIEL** Finnish-American architect and planner (1873–1950). Originally having expected to become a painter, Eliel Saarinen changed his mind and instead became one of the foremost architects, planners, and educators of his era. His buildings and city plans left their mark on the development of modern architecture. His philosophy, as expressed in his books, and especially as expressed in the school he built, Cranbrook Academy of Art, Bloomfield Hills, Mich., had an even greater effect on modern architecture.

Only about six years after Walter Adolf Gropius (1883–1969) started the Bauhaus, the influential German school of modern design, Saarinen instituted a similar program in the United States, at Cranbrook. There were differences in philosophy between the two schools, of course. The Bauhaus, for example, was perhaps more dedicated to design for machine-made products. Cranbrook was more dedicated to humanism. In both schools, the emphasis was on the integration of all the design arts, not just architecture alone. And both schools attracted talented faculty members and students, who went on to great accomplishments in their chosen fields.

Saarinen had a considerable reputation in Europe before he arrived in the United States in 1922. The only thing known about him in America was his masterful design for the Chicago Tribune Tower, which won second place in the competition but engendered a great deal of publicity. In Finland, he had designed a number of notable buildings and city plans. And he continued to do so in the United States.

**Works** He designed almost the entire educational complex at Cranbrook, including the Kingswood School for Girls (1929), the Cranbrook School for Boys (1930), and the Cranbrook Academy of Art (1941) with pool sculpture by Carl Milles. His son, Eero Saarinen (1910–61), joined him in a partnership, Saarinen and Saarinen, in 1937, and together they designed a whole series of interesting buildings, including the Kleinhaus Music Hall (1938), Buffalo, N.Y.; the pioneering Crow Island School (1939), Winnetka, Ill., in association with Perkins, Wheeler and Will; the Tabernacle Church of Christ (1940), Columbus, Ind.; the Tanglewood Opera House (1944), Lenox, Mass.; Christ Lutheran Church (1949), Minneapolis, in association with Hills, Gilbertson and Hays; and the more than $100 million General Motors Technical Center, Warren, Mich., in association with Smith, Hinchman and Grylls, completed in 1957, seven years after Eliel Saarinen died.

Eliel Saarinen left a legacy for future architects and all those who enjoy architecture, in his buildings, in his

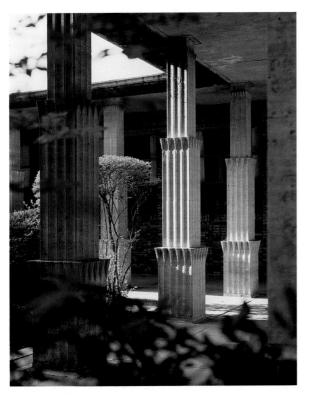

**SAARINEN, ELIEL** Detail, Kingswood School for Girls (1929), Bloomfield Hills, Mich.

books, and especially in the students whose careers he helped to mold.

**Life** Gottlieb Eliel Saarinen was born in Rantasalmi, Finland, in 1873, the son of a Lutheran minister. The family moved to Ingermanlandia, Russia, about 30 miles south of St. Petersburg, when young Saarinen was two years old. Here he spent his childhood in a rural atmosphere, while his father ministered to the Finnish-speaking peasants of the area, recently released from serfdom. From an early age, he drew and painted and thought he would like to become an artist.

Saarinen went back to Finland to attend high school in Wiipuri. Passing through St. Petersburg on his trips to and from school, he spent many hours in the Hermitage, one of the world's greatest art museums. These visits strengthened his desire to become a painter but he also had reason to believe that architecture might prove to be more practical. In 1893 he enrolled simultaneously in the Polytechnic Institute in Helsinki as an architecture student and in the University Art School as a painting student. Before graduating in 1897, Saarinen had made up his mind to practice architecture. But he never lost his deep interest in painting and the other arts.

Even before he left school, Saarinen started an architectural firm in 1896, in partnership with Herman Gesellius and Armas Lindgren. His Finnish Pavilion for the Paris Exposition of 1900 brought him recognition in Europe as a talented architect and his National Museum (1902) and Central Railroad Station (1904), both in Helsinki, firmly established his reputation.

In 1902 Saarinen and his partners designed and built a studio house with 38 rooms, Hvittrask, on a bluff overlooking a lake 18 miles from Helsinki. In 1904 he married Loja Gesellius, a sister of his partner, and in 1905 their first child, Eva-Lisa, always called Pipsan (1905–79) was born.

Loja was a talented artist, who did sculpture, weaving, and photography. Pipsan later became a noted designer. In 1910 a son, Eero, Finnish for Eric, was born and he, like his father, became a famous architect. The house-studio was the early training school in the arts for both children. Surrounded by such activities, they too soon began to design, paint, draw, and model. And all these pursuits became a family affair, a situation that continued during the later part of their lives. The house-studio was also a center of cultural pursuits, attracting a number of the great men of the time who came not only for the good conversation but for recreation. Among the regular visitors were Eliel Saarinen's good friends, Jean Sibelius (1865–1957), the Finnish composer, and Carl Milles (1875–1955), the Swedish sculptor, who later joined Saarinen at Cranbrook. And they were often joined by others, including the Russian writer Maxim Gorki (1868–1936), the Austrian composer Gustav Mahler (1860–1911), and another close friend of

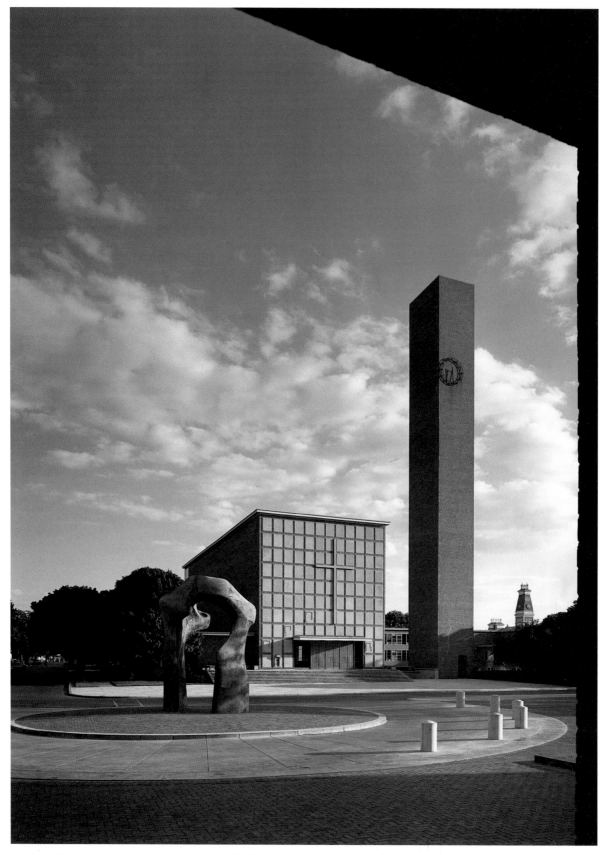

**SAARINEN, ELIEL** First Christian Church (formerly the Tabernacle Church of Christ) (1940), Columbus, Ind.

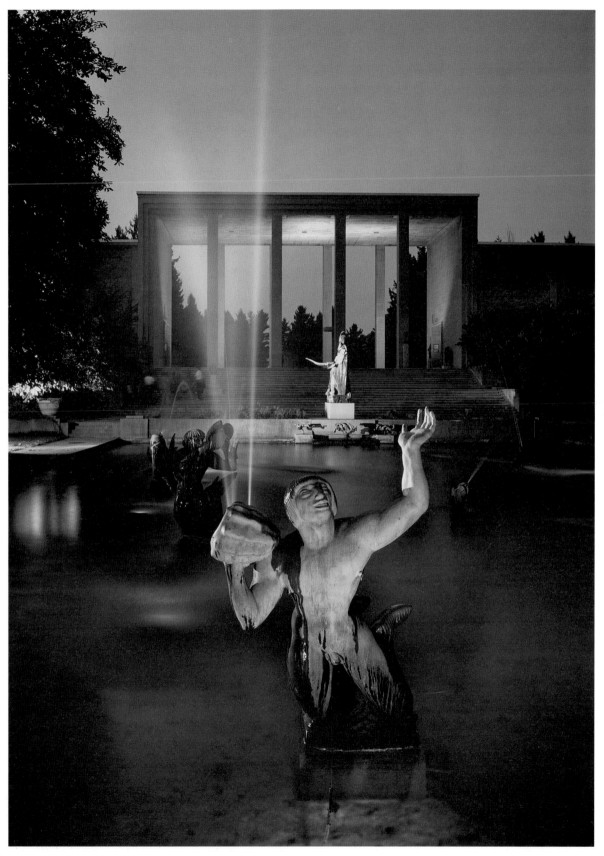

**SAARINEN, ELIEL** Cranbrook Academy of Art (1941), Bloomfield Hills, Mich.

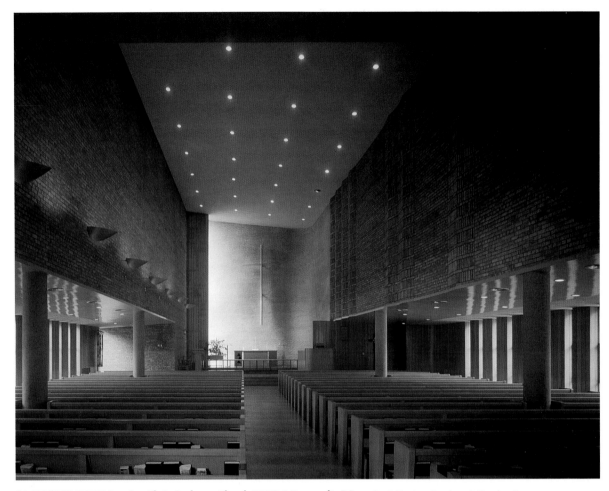

**SAARINEN, ELIEL** Interior, Christ Lutheran Church (1949), Minneapolis, Minn. [Architects: Saarinen & Saarinen]

Saarinen's, Julius Meier-Graefe (1867–1935), the German art critic and writer.

In 1907 Saarinen left the partnership but continued to practice architecture; and having become involved in city planning, he designed plans for Reval and Helsinki, Finland. In 1922 he won second prize in the Chicago Tribune Tower competition, with a design that many people preferred to the winner. Having come to America to receive his prize, he decided to stay and later brought his family to New York and then to Michigan a short time later. Named director of the Cranbrook Academy of Art (see illustration) in 1925, a position he held the rest of his life, Saarinen transformed the school into an institution where all the design arts were integrated and taught together.

Saarinen started another architectural practice in Bloomfield Hills, and soon the work again became a family affair. On one early project, the Kingswood School for Girls, Saarinen designed the building; his wife, Loja, did the rugs, draperies, and furniture coverings; his daughter, Pipsan, designed the auditorium and dining hall interiors; and his son, Eero, designed the furniture.

In time, Saarinen designed the campus and buildings for the entire Cranbrook complex.

The reputation of Cranbrook spread and soon the school began to attract students who would later become noted designers themselves. Some of them were Charles Eames (1907–78), designer; Harry Bertoia (1915–78), sculptor; Harry Weese (1915– ), architect; and Ralph Rapson (1914– ), architect and architectural educator.

His partnership with his son, Eero, produced a number of notable buildings and lasted until Eliel Saarinen died on July 1, 1950. He had accomplished a great deal in architecture, in planning, and in education. By that time, he had gained worldwide recognition for his work in all three fields. In 1947 the architects of his adopted country awarded him their highest honor, the Gold Medal of the American Institute of Architects.

**Related Articles** BAUHAUS, STAATLICHES; EDUCATION; HOOD, RAYMOND MATHEWSON; MODERN ARCHITECTURE; SAARINEN, EERO.

**Further Reading** Saarinen, Eliel: *Search for Form—A Fundamental Approach to Art,* reprint of 1948 ed., Dover, New York, 1985.

**SCHOOL** L. Frances Smith Elementary School (1969), Columbus, Ind. *[Architect: John M. Johansen]*

**SCHOOL** A building, or buildings, in which students are given organized instruction at levels below that of a college or university. The main purposes of schools are to impart knowledge and skills to young people, and to teach them how to live productive, useful, and satisfying lives as members of society.

**School Systems** For many years in the United States, school education was divided into the 8-4 system: elementary, the first eight grades, followed by secondary, the last four grades. Elementary education was the minimum that was considered acceptable, and secondary education, in high schools, was considered highly desirable. A secondary education is now considered the minimum. And those who achieve only this minimum are expected to learn at least the rudiments of trades or skills at which they can work after graduation, in addition to the academic and physical education they receive. For students expected to enter college, the emphasis has been on academic preparation for further education.

During the first half of the 20th century, the trend was toward further subdividing school systems, in order to help meet some of the stresses students face in adolescence and in the process of maturing. Thus the so-called 6-3-3 plan was introduced, with elementary schools providing grades 1 through 6; junior high schools the last two elementary grades, 7 and 8, and one of the secondary, 9; and senior high schools providing 10 through 12. There has been a trend toward the addition of another grade to precede the first, kindergarten, intended to prepare young children, usually five-year-olds, for elementary school, thus making K-6-3-3 school systems. Kindergartens have existed for a long time in the United States, but only recently have come to be considered a mandatory part of education in some communities. Often kindergartens are located in elementary schools. This system spread all over the United States,

though not all school systems adopted the exact system in its entirety. For example, some systems combined the two higher schools into junior-senior high schools, the K-6-6 system. Recently, there has been a tendency to separate grades even further. In many systems, other types of schools have been added, and the types are elementary, K-4; middle 5-8; and high 9-12; the K-4-4-4 system. And some systems have gone even further, to elementary, K-4; middle, 5-6; intermediate, 7-8; and high, 9-12; the K-4-2-2-4 system

For a number of years, proposals have been made for ungraded education or continuous progress schools, where all students advance at their own rates. Individualized programs are expected to increase as computer programs make this possible.

Most secondary schools offer both practical and academic training to students, thus preparing them either for vocations or for further education. In some school systems, particularly in large cities, some high schools specialize in vocational training, along with academic courses. Such institutions include trade schools, technical schools, business schools, and agricultural schools.

**Other Types** Other kinds of schools include community, neighborhood, regional (central or consolidated), and special schools for students who are retarded, handicapped, or unusually intelligent. In community schools, facilities are provided for regular use during nonschool hours for athletic, social, educational, and other activities by children and adults, including the elderly. More of this type of facility can be expected in the future. Other schools may be used occasionally for such purposes. Neighborhood schools serve small community areas where students can ordinarily walk to and from school. Regional (central or consolidated) schools serve larger areas, such as counties, where students usually ride buses to and from school. Special schools for the retarded, handicapped, or unusually intelligent are sometimes provided in communities, but the trend today seems to be incorporation of these students in the general school system. Accessibility needs will result in schools equipped with elevators, escalators, and exterior ramps as well as stairs.

In the future, students and their parents may be able to select the kinds of educational programs from those available in their communities. Specialized schools for science or art and a better fit between vocational schools and actual employment needs will be offered, including time at actual work locations.

In addition to the above schools, preschool facilities have grown as, increasingly, both parents work outside the home. Many communities offer preschool for three- and four-year-olds, as well as day care from infancy for working parents. Many day care and preschool facilities are business- or government-sponsored; others are privately operated. The federal Head Start program for disadvantaged children is often housed in existing community facilities which may need modification to provide proper environments for early childhood education.

**Ownership and Operation** School systems owned and operated by government bodies, usually towns, cities, or counties, are public schools; private schools are owned by private organizations that are usually nonprofit; parochial schools are owned by church organizations. Some private and parochial schools are called "preparatory" schools, reflecting that their primary function is to educate students to enter colleges and universities. Private and parochial schools are administered by individuals, often called "principals" or "headmasters," appointed by the governing boards which set policies. Public schools are usually administered by principals, appointed by superintendents of education, the top administrative officers of these systems, often called "school districts." Superintendents are normally appointed by boards of education, the top policy-making bodies in the public school districts. Members of boards of education, often called "school boards" and sometimes "boards of trustees" or "school trustees," may be elected by the voters or appointed by city councils, county commissioners, or other community officials.

**New Schools** In the United States, some 100,000 elementary schools have changing enrollments projected to peak in the year 1998, when 35 million students will be in kindergarten through 8th grade. The figure for grades 9 to 12 is expected to peak about the year 2000 with over 14 million students. After 2000, the school population is expected to drop to more moderate levels. The need for new schools varies considerably over the years, due mainly to fluctuations in the birth rate at various times. Therefore, although schools are a very important building type, the number being designed and built at various times fluctuates considerably. Demographic and economic changes are other factors affecting new construction of schools. Education is now compulsory in all the United States, but the length of time students must attend or the ages that they must attain before leaving school varies among the states. These factors also affect the number of schools built in a given period in various localities. In spite of the variations, schools constitute a building type designed by a great number of architects, and in many cases constitute an important part of their practice.

**Facilities** The design of any school begins with the establishment of an educational program, stating the educational concept, its goals and purposes, the activities to be carried on, and the detailed area, space, and equipment requirements. Based on the educational program, study can then be made of the major facilities of schools: instructional, academic, and vocational; athletic, physical education, and recreational; service; administrative; and maintenance and mechanical-electrical equipment.

Academic and vocational instructional facilities include classrooms, laboratories, workshops, libraries, auditorium, band and choral rehearsal rooms, and sometimes art studios, theaters, and lecture halls. Athletic, physical education and recreational facilities include such indoor spaces as gymnasiums and swimming pools and such outdoor areas as playing fields and stadiums. Closely related to the instructional elements are the service facilities, such as cafeterias, restrooms, student lockers, student lounges, and parking lots. Administrative facilities include offices for principals, teachers, and counselors, faculty lounges, and sometimes dining rooms, first aid or health rooms, and conference rooms. Maintenance and mechanical-electrical facilities include spaces for janitorial services and heating, air conditioning, and other mechanical and electrical systems.

**Educational Improvement** In some schools, several functions may be performed in one area of the building, often called an "all-purpose" or "multipurpose" room. Here any two, or all three, functions of an auditorium, a cafeteria, and a gymnasium may be provided. One method for converting spaces to multipurpose uses is provision of movable partitions, folding or accordion doors, or other means for subdividing large rooms for use by either small or large groups.

A widely adopted method to improve the learning processes in schools is the conversion of libraries into learning resource centers (LRC), instructional materials centers (IMC), or information resource centers (IRC). In this concept, libraries take on responsibilities for materials and activities, in addition to the more traditional ones, for example, computers; audiovisual materials including tapes, records, cassettes, closed-circuit TV, videos, films, and other media. In such centers, provisions are often made for listening rooms, audio laboratories, video laboratories, and other activity areas.

Another trend intended to improve the education of students involves the provision for different kinds of learning experiences. Some experiences seem to be more meaningful if performed by an individual alone, such as reading a book, whereas others, such as laboratory experiments, are better when participated in by two or more students, as in discussions or lectures.

Educators and educational psychologists are continually studying and researching new methods for the improvement of education. One result has been the concept of team teaching, which involves the education of students not by a single teacher in a single subject but by a team of several teachers who can bring to students various aspects of larger areas of learning.

Another method, first tried in the 1920s but mostly developed since the middle of the 20th century, involves what is often called "programmed" learning, frequently using teaching machines. Programmed learning uses devices that enable students to receive pieces of informa-

**SCHOOL** Troy High School (1993), Troy, Mich. *[Architects: Perkins & Will]*

tion in some kind of order and then to make responses, repeating the process over and over with increasing amounts of information and degrees of difficulty. The simplest form is a book, or other printed material, arranged in such a way as to elicit response from a student, who is then directed to another section or chapter to learn whether the response was correct and whether to proceed or go back for another try. Computers are increasingly used for this type of learning. There are many variations of this system. Other systems, in ascending order of sophistication, are student-operated machines that display information and receive responses; audiovisual systems that present visual programs on film, film-strips, or slides with sound on records or tapes, to which students respond using microphones; and increasingly, computer systems.

**Elements** Architectural requirements for schools vary widely according to the type, the number of students, the grade levels, and many other factors. In general, the elements required are fairly simple for a nursery school and range through various levels to the most complex in high schools.

Nursery schools ordinarily have only a few facilities, often all contained in one or a few rooms and a playground. Inside the schools are areas for group activities, reading and listening, art activities, play, storage, restrooms, and sometimes cubicles for individual tutor-

ing. Often included are observation areas where teachers and others may observe children while remaining unseen by them.

In elementary schools, the most important educational elements are classrooms, one or more libraries or resource centers, gymnasiums and cafeterias or multipurpose rooms, and playgrounds. In higher elementary and lower secondary schools, provisions must also be made for laboratories, shops, music rooms, auditoriums, and athletic facilities outdoors. In high schools, facilities are similar to those of the other schools, with the addition of more elaborate athletic facilities and sometimes theaters, art studios, observatories, and automobile education driving ranges. In boarding schools, where students live while school is in session, provisions must also be made for dormitories, dining rooms, and housing for administrators and teachers.

**History** Education has been a very important human activity since prehistoric times. At first, teaching the young was handled within families and by the tribe elders. By about 3000 B.C., with the invention of writing, schools began to appear, but they were mostly for boys. In ancient Greece, schools became highly developed, but in early Rome most teaching was done at home until about the 2d century B.C. The Romans then established schools, with emphasis on what they called the liberal arts: arithmetic, astronomy, geometry, grammar, logic, music, and rhetoric. The phrase *liberal arts* is still in use today but now generally means all the natural and social sciences and the humanities. From about the 2d century A.D., the Romans established public schools which eventually replaced most of the private schools. During the Middle Ages, church schools were established. All types of schools (church, public, and private) flourished during and after the Renaissance.

**American Development** The earliest schools in colonial America were set up soon after the colonists arrived. They were mostly one-room schools, in which up to 40 students of varying ages were taught. The one-room school was the most predominant type until well into the 19th century. In 1990, 729 one-teacher schools were still in use. Gradually, the colonists set up other types of schools, including trade schools. Beginning about the end of the first quarter of the 19th century, various states established public school systems to augment those operated by churches and other organizations. These school systems were supported by taxes, and children could attend without charge. The first elementary schools were started in the early 1800s; the first public high school was opened in Boston in 1821. During the remainder of the 19th century, public school buildings continued to grow, and by 1900, students in public high schools outnumbered those in private and parochial schools, as has been the case ever since.

Gradually, during the 19th century, many one-room schools were expanded to make room for additional students. Some of the expansion was done without much planning and resulted in buildings that were often unsatisfactory for their purposes, unhealthy, and unsafe. The first graded elementary school was opened in Boston in 1848. By 1860, there were only about 300 high schools in the United States, and the figure had doubled by 1900. Early in the 20th century, educators and architects developed principles that led to better schools designed for their functions, with safe and healthy environments for students. The biggest period of improvement was since 1940, the date of the influential Crow Island School of Winnetka, Ill., designed by Perkins, Wheeler & Will with Eliel and Eero Saarinen. A noted program of the 1960s was the California School Construction Systems Development (SCSD) program using a series of prefabricated systems to allow flexibility and to speed up construction. An experiment of the 1970s was to seek available spaces in the community which could be adapted to education, provided at less cost and made more quickly available than new buildings. The concept of community schools, housing social agencies and adult programs, also started in the 1970s and now may be found in several communities.

A great many architects have designed schools, and some have produced innovative improvements. One of these is the so-called open plan which, instead of having self-contained classrooms, provides larger spaces that can be readily subdivided into modular areas for different activities by groups of varying sizes. Many teachers found open plan spaces hard to use. Other ideas have been one-room-deep classrooms with windows on both ends, allowing better control of sunlight and ventilation. Another is the cluster plan which consists of pavilions for instruction connected with open or closed corridors.

**Future Trends** Lifelong learning will encourage use of schools by the community. Sizes of schools may be smaller, particularly with the increased technology of computers and television. Schools will be open for more hours to serve adults as well as children. Teachers will have better working spaces, including telecommunication, computers, space for planning, preparation, and counseling. There may be a move toward ungraded education and less dependence on fixed schedules. Students and parents may have greater selection of programs. Technology will continue to change education. Flexibility will become increasingly important as curricula, technology, class sizes, and educational approaches change. Energy use will continue to be studied, and schools will be more responsive to local climates. Regional differences will be reflected in the use of materials and construction. More construction dollars will be spent to renovate existing schools.

As progress continues in both educational psychology and architecture, better schools will be possible in the future. To their architects, they will present challenging design problems.

**Related Articles** HOUSING; LABORATORY; LIBRARY; RECREATION BUILDING; RESTAURANT; THEATER.

**Further Reading** Graves, Ben E.: *School Ways—The Planning and Design of America's Schools*, McGraw-Hill, New York, 1993.

**Periodicals** *American School & University Magazine*, 491 N. Broad St., Philadelphia, Pa. 19108; *School Product News*, 1111 Chester Ave., Cleveland, Ohio 44114; *The School Administrator*, 1801 N. Moore St., Arlington, Va. 22209; *Architectural Record*, 1221 Avenue of the Americas, New York, N.Y. 10020; *Architecture*, 1130 Connecticut Ave., N.W., Suite 25, Washington, D.C. 20036; *Progressive Architecture*, P.O. Box 1361, Stamford, Conn. 06904.

**Sources of Additional Information** American Assoc. of School Administrators, 1801 N. Moore St., Arlington, Va. 22209-9988; National School Boards Assoc., 1680 Duke Street, Alexandria, Va. 22314-3407; Assoc. of School Business Officials/International, 11401 North Shore Drive, Reston, Va. 22090-4232; Council of Education Facility Planners/International, 941 Chatham Lane, Suite 217, Columbus, Ohio 43221; International Society for Educational Planning, c/o Educational Administration, Purdue University, G-10 South Campus Court, W. Lafayette, Ind. 47907; state departments of education.

**SECURITY SYSTEMS** Systems or devices used in buildings to prevent burglaries, vandalism, or other criminal acts. Security systems used in buildings today are of four major types: those intended to prevent intrusion into buildings, those that detect and give warnings when intrusions occur, those that safeguard valuables after intrusions occur, and those that make records of intrusions. The types used and the extent of their use depend, to a large extent, on the degree of risk of human life or property involved and the value of property to be protected. In high-risk areas, such as certain central areas of cities, more safeguards must be taken than in certain low-risk rural or other areas. Certain types of safeguards may be effective in cities, while suburban or rural areas may require other types. More safeguards are ordinarily required for buildings in which money and high-value, easily marketed items, such as television sets or jewelry, are stored than in those in which only low-value or difficult-to-market items, such as supplies in a barber shop or paperwork in a real estate office, are located.

**Site Security** Some buildings require controlled access to sites for protection from hostile acts, unauthorized entry, and access and egress control. Guard booths, fenced enclosures for vehicle inspection, sliding gates and vehicle barriers, and on-site traffic control barriers and lift gates are devices that can be used. Combinations of trenches, berms, and fencing can provide perimeter protection. The use of proper site lighting will assist guard surveillance.

Entry to buildings may include metal detectors and x-rays, turnstiles accessed with card readers, or one-way turnstiles. These items are in addition to a comprehensive building security system. Airport security systems include x-ray inspection of luggage and metal detection checks for all boarding passengers.

**Security Measures** Guarding the interior of a building against intrusions generally involves strong doors, windows, and other openings; strong and reliable hardware; and similar architectural elements. Guards are also employed for security purposes. Intercom systems, with units at building entrances, allow voice identification of visitors before allowing them to enter; and peephole devices in doors or closed-circuit television systems allow visual identification before allowing entry. In a well-lighted, low-crime area, with reliable police protection, elements of this sort may provide adequate security for most buildings in normal times. In times of riots and other disorders, such as those that occurred in Washington in April 1968, in New York City during the blackout in July 1977, and in Los Angeles in April 1992, architectural measures cannot provide total security for buildings and their occupants.

**Warning Devices** Criminals have been known to brag that no amount of security of the types suggested can prevent them from burglarizing buildings. Certain types of systems and devices are therefore often used in buildings to give warning when intrusions occur. Guards may also perform this function, and sometimes watchdogs are used. The usual method of protection by guards involves making rounds within, and sometimes around the outsides of, buildings. The simplest method uses a series of boxes with time clocks inside, which a watchman opens, inserts a key, and records the time. More sophisticated systems employ similar boxes connected electrically to a central location, in which lights on a board show the progress and locations of guards. Some guards carry portable telephones which may be plugged into jacks along the inspection route, or carry portable radios or walkie-talkies.

Other systems used for detecting and warning of intrusions include types that operate by contact, photoelectric cells, proximity, or radar. Contact systems use wires, pads, metallic tape, magnetic switches, and other devices that set off alarms or give other warnings when they are touched. A photoelectric cell performs similar functions when a light beamed on a receiver is interrupted. Proximity devices are generally used to safeguard single items, such as files or safes. They trip alarms or give other warnings when a person comes near. Radar systems emit signals which give alarms when motion occurs in their paths. Other similar types of security systems employ ultrasonic signals or magnetic fields which, when interrupted, give warnings. Closed-circuit television is also often used for detection and warning of intrusions.

Any of the intrusion types of security systems can be used to sound alarms and transmit information to central places in buildings. They may also be connected with police stations or private security organizations, activating alarms or signals that show an intrusion has taken place and where it has occurred.

**Safes and Vaults** The major types of devices used for safeguarding valuables are safes and vaults of various kinds and sizes. Such devices may be very small and simple in construction for use in houses, stores, and so on, or very large and complicated, as those used in banks and other places where large quantities of money and other valuables are stored. Safes may be freestanding or built into floors, walls, and other building elements. Attempts are often made to conceal their existence. Vaults are ordinarily constructed of heavy, fire-resistant materials with complicated doors that are very difficult or impossible for intruders to open. Often safes and usually vaults are interconnected with sophisticated electronic and other security systems. Many vaults are also electronically timed, so that they cannot be opened except at regular intervals and under specific conditions set by the users.

Devices for recording intrusions and other criminal acts include closed-circuit television systems, which can

573

be used to monitor such activities as well as to record them on video tape, and automatic cameras. Either may be hidden or exposed according to the needs of the buildings in which they are used.

Security systems may have sizable effects on the operating costs of buildings, since insurance rates vary considerably in individual cases. Security systems for buildings are quite specialized and are usually designed by specialists in consultation with architects and building owners. In many cases, they involve secrets which architects must protect, unlike the architects of ancient Egypt who were often put to death after designing royal tombs and pyramids.

**Architectural Security Devices** Special construction using lead sheet is used to limit radio waves, protect computer data storage, and protect against unwanted x-ray exposure. The increase in electronic financial records and automatic transfers has resulted in the need for computer security systems.

Special security doors and windows are manufactured for use in prisons and psychiatric hospitals. The design of buildings for safety include consideration of site lighting, location and construction of entrances, and avoiding exterior spaces where people can hide unseen.

**History** Security, the provision of protection of people and their property from invaders, burglars, and other risks, has always been a factor in architecture. The earliest settlements that later became towns and cities were usually founded on easily defended sites. Later walls and other fortifications were provided to protect towns and cities. The practice of building walls around towns and cities continued until about the 15th century. The practice of protecting towns and cities with forts continued even longer, until after the American Civil War.

Other types of security measures began early, including devices to bar doors against intruders, followed by locks of various kinds. Windows were barred or shuttered for the same purpose. The need for security against burglars and other intruders has varied considerably during different periods of history. For example, the Romans were able to police their cities quite well. This fact was reflected in more open plans and larger windows during the era of Roman supremacy. In contrast, after Rome began to decline a period of lawlessness existed in Europe. Walls were built for protection against enemies; windows were small and protected by bars and other devices; doors were strengthened with iron bands and heavy hardware. During the Renaissance, when there was less lawlessness, windows were made larger and had fewer security devices. The building of walled cities began to decline, not so much because there was less danger from enemies but because gunpowder rendered them ineffective.

Since the Renaissance, the situation has fluctuated between periods of war and peace, and greater or reduced incidence of lawbreaking. Today the provision of security for the occupants of buildings and their property is of considerable concern in architecture.

**Related Articles** ENGINEERING; FIRE PROTECTION; HARDWARE; MILITARY BUILDING; PLANNING, CITY; WINDOW.

**Further Reading** Hopf, Peter S.: *Handbook of Building Security Planning and Design,* McGraw-Hill, New York, 1979; Keogh, James, and John Koster: *Burglarproof, a Complete Guide to Home Security,* McGraw-Hill, New York, 1977; Robinson, Robert L.: *How to Burglarproof Your Home,* Nelson-Hall, Chicago, 1978.

**SEISMIC DESIGN** The provision of structural qualities intended to allow buildings and their elements and systems to resist the effects of earthquakes. The theory of plate tectonics shows the earth's crust is divided into several major plates, some 50 mi thick, that move slowly and continuously over the interior of the earth. Earthquakes are initiated when a geological fault on or near a plate boundary slips abruptly due to accumulated pressure or strain, resulting in vibrations that radiate from the line of fracture. Faults exist in many places on earth; some are hidden beneath the surface, but others are visible, as is the San Andreas fault in California, the largest in the United States, stretching some 600 miles. The San Andreas fault is a part of an earthquake-prone area, the circum-Pacific belt, that stretches along the edge of the Pacific Ocean, including New Zealand, Japan, the Aleutian Islands, and the coast of Alaska, Canada, the U.S. mainland, Mexico, and Central and South America. Another major earthquake zone, the Alpide belt, stretches from Burma to the Alps in Europe.

**Seismic Forces** The ground motion or vibration caused by earthquakes travels in the form of primary waves (P), which travel at about 18,000 mph. These waves alternately push and pull the ground. The next waves are the secondary (S) waves that have a sideways motion to the forward direction of the P waves. Other ground motion effects are waves that move from side to side with no vertical motion and the more complex waves that move both vertically and horizontally. Since vertical movement tends to cause less damage than the horizontal, seismic design is predominantly that of dealing with dynamic horizontal forces.

Other earthquake-induced effects include ground surface fault ruptures. In California, these faults have been mapped, and laws have been passed limiting development directly over the faults. Buildings are not designed to protect against fault rupture. Another effect is the liquefaction that may take place during earthquakes where the ground loses its strength and behaves as a viscous fluid, similar to quicksand. This effect is experienced in areas with large deposits of sands and silts and where ground water is within 30 ft of the surface.

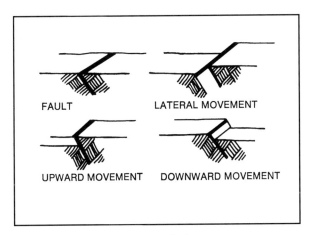

**SEISMIC DESIGN** Movements in faults.

Here again, even careful foundation design cannot protect against this effect. One documented case of liquefaction was the 1811 and 1812 earthquakes in New Madrid, Mo., estimated at 7.2 on the Richter scale.

Landslides may be generated by ground motion. This has been a concern in Japan, where steel nets are used to protect highways from possible rock slides. Site-specific damage may be caused by tsunamis, waves caused by undersea earthquakes. Some tsunamis have reached a height of 80 ft. Coastal areas along the Pacific coast and coastal areas of Hawaii and Alaska are subject to damage. In May 1960, Hilo on the island of Hawaii was largely destroyed by a series of tsunami, and, in September 1992, the coast of Nicaragua was inundated by a tsunami, with a large loss of life and property. In Japan, some specially shaped concrete barriers have been erected to protect areas against storms and possible tsunami.

**Measurements** Seismic activity in a region is studied from data derived from geological evidence, such as faults, history of earthquakes and their locations, and determinations of the quantitative measurements of earthquakes in the area. Measurements for earthquakes have not been made absolutely uniform. However, the major measure is the magnitude or size of an earthquake, usually on the Richter scale, a logarithmic scale that measures the energy of earthquakes from 1.5, the smallest that can be felt, to 8.5 or 9 for a very devastating earthquake. This scale was named after American seismologist Charles R. Richter (b. 1900). Another measure is the Mercalli scale, where the effects of ground movement are described in words on a scale from I to XII. The term *seismicity* means the frequency of earthquakes in a region.

**Instruments** *Seismology* is the science of earthquakes, and a *seismologist* is a scientist engaged in studying this activity. A *seismograph* is an instrument for the detection and recording of the magnitude of earthquakes on the Richter scale. Such instruments, in groups of three, measure vertical movement in earth-

quakes and movements along north-south and east-west lines. They can also be used to determine locations, called "epicenters," of earthquakes.

**Buildings** Earthquakes can result in serious damage to buildings. The vibration of a building is called a "period" or "frequency." If the building mass has the same frequency as the ground motion, movement can be accelerated by several times. In the 1985 earthquake in Mexico City, such effects caused buildings to fail. In general, buildings are inefficient vibrators because of the building mass, shape, connections, materials and nonstructural elements, but in severe earthquakes forces experienced can exceed those assumed in building codes. Protection against maximum forces is uneconomic and would cause problems in planning and appearance.

Building movement under seismic forces displays the property of ductility. Steel will resist such forces, but other brittle materials such as unreinforced masonry or inadequately reinforced concrete may fail suddenly. The duration of the ground movement will affect the amount of stress on building structures. Some earthquakes have been timed for a period over 2 minutes, such as in the Alaska earthquake of 1964. Another effect on buildings is torsion forces, which are difficult to calculate and are generally controlled by designing symmetrical building forms, although provisions can be made for nonsymmetrical building forms.

The stiffness of a structure is another factor addressed in design. This relates to the horizontal forces applied to a structure, where such forces are transferred to columns. Many buildings are designed to be flexible. In these buildings, contents damage will occur. Sometimes later additions cause inadvertent stiffness, and such items as partitions may be destroyed in an earthquake.

**Seismically Safe Structures** Resistance to seismic forces can be designed using shear walls, braced frames, and moment-resisting frames. Shear walls are vertical elements and should be approximately equal in length in all building directions and are most effective as outside walls. These buildings can be economical, resulting in a very stiff building where stresses can be kept low. Failure of shear wall buildings is very rare, and any cracked walls are easily repaired. Wood structures with plywood shear walls are inexpensive versions of braced-frame buildings.

Braced frames are most common in steel-framed buildings and can be economically designed using story-height diagonal braces. These members are designed to take both compressive and tension forces during an earthquake.

A more complex system is the use of moment-resisting frames, where the connections between beams and columns are designed to dissipate seismic forces. These buildings are designed with steel or reinforced concrete but are difficult to achieve with wood or precast concrete. The moment-resistance frame is expensive and requires special care in design and inspection. These structures are flexible and may contribute to extensive damage to nonstructural items during an earthquake.

It is a common misconception that a well-designed building will be fine after an earthquake. In reality, occupants are often left without power or water and may be physically isolated because of damage to roads and bridges.

**Hazardous Buildings** In many places in the world loss of life and extensive seismic damage occurs from hazardous building systems such as unreinforced masonry bearing walls of brick, stone, adobe, or concrete block. In California, these all predate 1933, when steel reinforcing was first required. In Los Angeles, a 1981 ordinance required that owners of unreinforced masonry buildings either strengthen or demolish them within a specified time.

Extensive damage caused by the January 1994 earthquake in Los Angeles is in large part attributed to the failure to upgrade existing structures to meet existing regulations. Other failures have been experienced with concrete tilt-up walled buildings, and in the Mexico City earthquake of 1985 several nonductile reinforced concrete frame buildings failed. These were widely used in Latin America as well as in the United States. In California, this problem was observed in the 1971 earthquakes, and codes were revised in 1973 to require ductile design of concrete frames. Since 1950, more than 90 percent of deaths from California earthquakes can be attributed to nonductile concrete failures.

A large effort in California is the ongoing retrofit of buildings subject to seismic damage. For the 1957 University Hall at the University of California at Berkeley, the nonductile concrete structure was revised by Hansen Murakami Eshima, Architects, who added steel bracing on the exterior of the building and a new concrete colonnade to stiffen the lower story. This building is only 1 mile from the active Hayward fault. The 1989 Loma Prieta earthquake affected San Francisco, Oakland, and San Jose. Abandoned, damaged structures and lots left vacant from the subsequent demolition of buildings are still to be seen.

Often additional loss of life and further damage occur from fires following earthquakes, sometimes involving broken gas lines.

**Seismic Codes** As experience is gained, the building code provisions for earthquakes have become refined. The earliest codes include Italy (1908), Japan (1923), and California (in 1927 but not enforced until 1933). The Uniform Building Code is the U.S. leader in developing provisions for seismic design and is used in the western states. These provisions have influenced the other U.S.

building codes as well as foreign ones. Revisions continue to occur, and the reader should refer to the latest edition of the codes. See the article entitled building codes and standards.

**Innovations** Engineers have experimented with new concepts for seismic design. One of these is to introduce rubber bearings under columns to isolate them from ground motion. These bearings are designed to move horizontally several inches, and space around the foundations must accommodate this movement. The remainder of the building has much reduced seismic forces, and contents are less subject to failure. Another development is to introduce eccentric braced frames, where diagonal bracing members connect to beams leaving a short section before connections to columns. These short sections absorb stresses, reducing the need for fixed joints and protecting the columns. This is economical and is in use in newer buildings.

**History** Earthquake damage has occurred worldwide. Fortunately, many of the most active areas have low populations. These areas include Greenland, Siberia, northern Canada, most of Australia, the Amazon basin, the Sahara, and Antarctica. All areas of the United States are subject to seismic forces except parts of the southeastern United States. California experiences many earthquakes each year, most of them causing little damage. Major earthquakes occur less frequently, with Richter readings over 6. Experience predicts 80 earthquakes between 6 and 6.9 on the Richter scale in 100 years, 12 earthquakes measuring 7 to 7.9, and once in a hundred years an earthquake measuring over 8 on the Richter scale. The most severe earthquake ever recorded was about 9 on the Richter scale. The severity of the earthquake is not the only criterion for analysis, but also the cost and effort needed to recover and reconstruct in heavily populated areas.

Some notorious earthquakes in this century include San Francisco (1906), over 500 deaths; Messina, Italy (1908), where 75,000 deaths occurred; Avezzano, Italy (1915), 29,970 lost; Kansu Province, China (1920), where an estimated 180,000 people lost their lives; Tokyo-Yokohama, Japan (1923), with 143,000 deaths; Kansu Province, China (1932), 70,000 lost; Quetta, Pakistan (1935), 60,000 lost; Agadir, Morocco (1960) 12,000 lost; Iran (1962) 10,000 lost; Alaska (1964), 114 lost; Iran (1968), 11,588 lost; Peru (1970), 47,194 lost; Iran (1972) 5,057 lost; Mexico City (1985) over 4,200 lost; Loma Prieta, Calif. (1989); and Los Angeles, Calif. (1994).

Improved building technology has limited loss of life due to seismic forces in the United States, and greater understanding of structure will lead to further application of seismic design principles to all new buildings.

**Related Articles** BUILDING CODES AND STANDARDS; FIRE PROTECTION; STRUCTURE; WEATHER PROTECTION.

**Further Reading** Dowrick, David J: *Earthquake Resistant Design for Engineers and Architects*, 2d ed., John Wiley, New York, 1988; Okamoto, Shunzo: *Introduction to Earthquake Engineering*, reprint of 1973 edition, Columbia University Press, New York, 1985.

Numerous reports of scientific studies have been published by organizations, such as the American Institute of Architects; American Society of Civil Engineers; and the Seismological Society of America; by universities, including the California Institute of Technology, Pasadena; University of California, Berkeley; and Massachusetts Institute of Technology, Cambridge; and by many institutes and conferences, notably in New Zealand and Japan. In the United States, the Federal Emergency Management Agency (FEMA) has recently published a reference guide on seismic design for architects.

**Source of Additional Information** Seismological Society of America, El Cerrito Professional Building, Suite 201, El Cerrito, Calif. 94530.

**SERT, JOSEP LLUIS** Architect and educator (1902–83). Born José Luis Sert in Barcelona, Spain, Sert came to the United States in 1939. As an architect and urban planner, he formed the firm of Sert, Jackson & Associates in 1957 in Cambridge, Mass. His first building of note, a studio for his friend the painter Juan Miro

on the island of Majorca, Spain, dated from 1956. His next major project was the U.S. Embassy in Baghdad, Iraq, in 1960. After his late start, the number of his projects greatly increased, and his clients included Harvard and other universities, European clients, and the New York State Urban Development Corporation.

Proud of his Catalan heritage, in the 1970s Sert changed the spelling of his name from the Spanish José Luis to the Catalan Josep Lluis. His work shows the influence of Le Corbusier, and the indigenous Catalan building of his youth.

Sert's friendship with major artists of the early 20th century inspired him in his architecture. His buildings look best in the strong sunlight of the Mediterranean coast and sometimes look less appealing in the gray and rainy weather of Cambridge, Mass. His work is reflective of a deep respect for the needs of the human individual in relation to building, community, and the environment.

**Work** Sert's fame as an architect is based on projects at Harvard and the two art museums in France and Spain. Few architects have made an impact on a city as did Sert in Cambridge. The Undergraduate Science Center for Harvard is typical of these buildings, with fenestration reflecting Le Corbusier's "Modulor" system of proportions and setback upper stories. Related designs for the Peabody Terrace Married Student

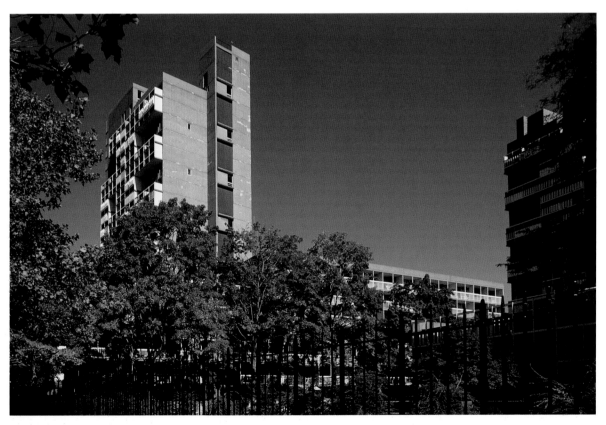

**SERT, JOSEP LLUIS** T. G. Peabody Terrace (1964), Harvard University, Cambridge, Mass.

Housing and the Holyoke Center make a major series of award-winning projects.

His design of the Museum of Contemporary Art for the Foundation Maeght at St. Paul de Vence, France (1964), was seen by Sert as a prototype for expansion into a village.

Sert's houses in Punta Martinet, Ibiza (Balearic Islands) were a villagelike group based on the island's vernacular style and were completed in 1971.

Probably his most appealing work is the Miro Foundation in Barcelona (1975), which is responsive to the hot sun of the Mediterranean using light hoods to bring indirect light into the galleries. The building contrasts a sense of age and newness, of rough surfaces and smooth, which in itself is a work of art, suitable for the exhibited works it contains.

**Life** Josep Lluis Sert grew up in Barcelona and received his architectural degree from the Escuela Superior de Arquitectura in 1929. Sert invited Le Corbusier to lecture to a group of fellow architectural students in Barcelona, and after this meeting Sert was invited to go to Paris to work in the atelier of Le Corbusier. Sert worked there for two years beginning in 1929 and became active in the early years of the International Congresses of Modern Architecture (CIAM), for which he later served as president from 1946 to 1956. Interested in urban planning, he worked on proposals for Barcelona in 1933 to 1935 and designed the Casa Bloc (1936), a 200-unit low-rent housing project. When the Spanish Civil War broke out in 1936, he sided with the Republican government and was asked to design the Spanish pavilion for the 1937 Paris Exposition. Picasso's painting *Guernica* was first displayed in this building. Sert became friends with many artists in Paris, and Alexander Calder, Julio González, Alberto Sanchez, and Joan Miró contributed works to the Spanish pavilion exhibitions. With the fall of the Spanish government, Sert came to the United States and founded Town Planning Associates (TPA) in 1941 with Paul Lester Wiener and Paul Schulz. TPA produced redesign proposals for Bogota, Columbia, and plans for several new cities, some in collaboration with Le Corbusier. In 1943 he published his influential book *Can Our Cities Survive?*, based on the 4th CIAM Congress, and in 1944 Sert became professor of city planning at Yale University.

When Walter Gropius resigned as chair of the department of architecture at Harvard University in 1953, he recommended Sert as his successor. Sert succeeded Joseph Hudnut as dean of Harvard's graduate school of design, as well as chair of the department of architecture. In 1956 Sert also became planning consultant to the university. During Sert's time at Harvard (1953–69), he established the first degree program for urban studies in the United States.

By 1955, Sert opened his new firm with Huson Jackson and Ronald Gourley in Cambridge. His earlier firm, TPA, was dissolved in 1958. While he was dean at Harvard during a period of expansion, Sert, Jackson & Associates were commissioned to design a number of new projects, including the Holyoke Center and Peabody Terrace housing complex. Sert was instrumental in bringing Le Corbusier to design the Carpenter Center at Harvard. This building is the single example of Le Corbusier's work in the United States. Sert also received commissions for the Maeght Foundation in St. Paul de Vence, France, and the Joan Miró Foundation/Center for Studies of Contemporary Art in Barcelona.

Sert resigned his position at Harvard in 1969, at age 67. At this time his office had a large volume of projects, and Sert remained active until 1977. In 1981, at age 78, Sert was awarded the Gold Medal of the American Institute of Architects. Josep Lluis Sert died in 1983.

**Further Reading** Freixa, Jaume, ed.: *Josep Lluis Sert: Works and Projects,* Editorial Gustavo Gili, S.A., Barcelona, 1979, Spanish/English edition, 1989.

**SHOPPING CENTER** A building, or group of buildings, in which a number of stores and service establishments are located, with provisions for automobile parking nearby, often in a suburban location but may be in a city or town.

**Big Stores** Shopping centers are just like big stores which contain a collection of smaller stores. They therefore resemble the downtown shopping areas cities and towns have had for many years and which the developers of shopping centers have tried hard to replace. Shopping centers are different from their downtown counterparts in some ways. First, there probably never would have been any shopping centers if there had not

**SHOPPING CENTER** Northland Center (1948), Southfield, Mich. *[Architect: Victor Gruen]*

been a mass movement of people out of cities and towns to suburbia. And there might not have been any real suburbia if it had not been for the proliferation of automobiles. In a sense then, shopping centers had their genesis in the widespread use of automobiles and have been automobile-oriented ever since. In fact, the earliest centers had large parking areas which almost dominated the stores that face them. Later centers have turned inward, the stores facing spaces for people and turning their backs on automobiles. In many suburban areas, new "edge cities" have been formed as office space and hotels are built in close proximity to existing and enlarged shopping centers, often convenient to airports. Thus the shopping mall has become the new pedestrian minicity and is at the center of major employment areas. Almost all urban growth now takes place in these peripheral cities. As population grows, shopping malls are built in conjunction with stations of subway systems and near major highways.

**Merchandising Principles** Since shopping centers are essentially stores, they must be designed to sell goods effectively if they are to be successful. Like any store, a shopping center must arouse the interest of potential customers and lure them inside. Then customers must be attracted into the individual stores whose interests are served by selling products. Merchandising principles apply to both stores and shopping centers, but the latter must draw potential customers who arrive in automobiles as a rule rather than on foot as is often the case in downtown stores. (See the article entitled store.) In major metropolitan areas, new shopping malls may be planned to fill special roles in retailing, such as those containing discount stores, or to attract higher-income individuals. The major discount stores, often in separate buildings with their own parking areas, may provide serious competition to established shopping centers.

A shopping center contains individual stores, any of which may offer any combination of staples or demand goods, convenience products, and impulse or luxury items. In addition, the whole shopping center functions much like a large department store, with the individual stores acting like departments. Thus the merchandising of the entire shopping center is important, but once inside, the individual stores must also be merchandised. Customers must be able to move easily through the entire shopping center, must be attracted into various individual stores and then be lured through their interiors.

**Types** The two major types of shopping centers are the neighborhood or community center and the regional center. Neighborhood or community centers often contain only a few stores, usually including a supermarket and a drugstore and sometimes one or more branches of department stores. These centers serve limited marketing areas in cities, towns, or suburbia. Regional centers serve large marketing areas, sometimes drawing customers from many miles away. The keystones of these centers are department stores, of which there may be one to four or more in a single center. During recent years, several department stores have gone out of business, with the surviving stores part of major corporations with nationally located stores. There may be as few as 50 other stores in a regional shopping center, though some have up to 100 or more. A regional center may contain stores of almost every possible kind, from small specialty shops, such as florists, candy stores, or bakeries, to service establishments, such as barber and beauty shops or banks, to large, complete department stores. Supermarkets are not usually found in regional shopping malls. In addition, regional centers may also have entertainment facilities, such as multiple-motion-picture houses or bowling alleys. Many have dining facilities, such as restaurants, cafeterias, or food courts. Some have professional offices for doctors, dentists, and others; branch libraries; post offices; gasoline service stations; and almost every type of commercial operation imaginable.

**Master Plans** The major types of master plans for shopping centers include row or strip developments, in which stores are lined up along sidewalks with automobile parking often facing a street or highway, and cluster developments, in which the various elements containing stores are arranged around a pedestrian area in the middle, with parking around the perimeter of the cluster. Cluster developments, usually called "shopping malls," have open spaces or enclosed malls in the middle between the stores. Shopping centers may be one-story or two-story affairs, the most usual today, and some have more than two stories. Sometimes existing malls are enlarged with additional floors and new stores. Many malls are filled with stores of national retailers, giving a similarity to shopping malls throughout the country.

One of the most important principles in the design of a shopping center with a mall is the design of the mall itself. It must be made into an attractive pedestrian area, with appealing shops on the sides, their fronts facing inward toward the mall. Many malls have comfortable seating areas, shrubbery, flowers and trees, sculpture, fountains, and even elaborate recreational facilities.

Another important aspect of shopping center design is provision for efficient automobile parking facilities and easy access into the center. Parking may be provided at ground level outside, on the roof, or in parking garages. For shopping centers, a great deal of space is required for parking, ranging from about 2.5 car spaces per 1,000 ft$^2$ of leasable store area in a downtown center to 6 or more car spaces per 1,000 ft$^2$ in suburban centers.

Because of the many types of stores and other establishments that may be included, the complexities of pro-

**SHOPPING CENTER** Galleria (1970), Houston, Tex. *[Architects: Hellmuth, Obata and Kassabaum]*

viding for buildings, for automobile traffic and parking, and for pedestrian traffic, shopping centers have become a sort of universal building type. They test the design abilities of architects who must somehow put all the pieces of the puzzle together so that the whole functions properly as well as all the various parts. Not all shopping malls succeed, often due to the difficulty of access and limited parking.

**History** No one knows when the first shopping center of ancient times was built, but the ancient Greek merchants brought their wares to the *stoa,* a long *portico* through which passersby could be sheltered and shop too. A stoa was built around an *agora,* or public meeting square, and connected important buildings. The agora was the center of public life and therefore was always amidst a lot of traffic, the first consideration in the location of any commercial building. Later the Romans built shopping centers, perhaps the first being the one erected adjacent to the Roman Forum about A.D. 110. Other shopping centers, of various kinds, were later built in European cities.

**U.S. Centers** The first shopping centers resembling those of today were built in the United States in the last few decades before World War II. After the war, the rate of movement of people from cities and towns to suburbs increased rapidly. And suburban shopping centers were not far behind. At first, these were neighborhood or community centers, but starting about the middle of the 20th century, big regional centers were constructed. The trend has continued ever since. Soon after the construction of regional centers began in earnest, great redevelopment projects, intended to slow the movement from cities to the suburbs, helped revitalize the centers of cities. And urban shopping centers quickly followed. This trend too has continued. Thus shopping centers of all types remain a very important building type today.

**Related Articles** GARAGE; GRAPHIC DESIGN; ROAD AND TRAFFIC DESIGN; STORE; WAREHOUSE; Other individual building types.

**Further Reading** Lion, Edgar: *Shopping Centers—Planning, Development and Administration,* John Wiley, New York, 1976, also available through Books on Demand, UMI, Ann Arbor, Mich.

**Source of Additional Information** International Council of Shopping Centers, 445 Park Ave., New York, N.Y. 10022.

**SITE PLANNING** The process of developing a concept or design for the land on which a building or other structure is to be constructed, or for other purposes, such as parks or playgrounds. Site planning is concerned with many factors, including building location, grading, planting, location, and design of other features of sites, and with the circulation of pedestrians and automobiles and other vehicles. Site planning is ordinarily one of the first processes in the design of architecture and is performed by architects, city and regional planners, engineers, and landscape architects. These professionals also engage in site selection, making investigations and analyses of sites to determine their suitability or feasibility for use as building or other project sites, and to make selections between alternative sites.

**Preparatory Phases** The first steps in both site selection and site planning are collection of data and their analyses. These procedures develop important information upon which a selection of a site may be made, if required, and which will become part of a program for a building or other project.

Based on the analysis and the program, a land-use plan may then be prepared. A land-use plan shows only the general aspects of a site, such as areas for various functions or activities; the densities, or number of people or families to be accommodated per acre; the circulation of people, goods, and so on; and other important relationships or linkages between the activity areas. All these phases of site planning begin with the concept of the larger area or total environment in which a site exists, and then proceed to the specific environment of the site itself.

The major factors studied in both cases may be classified as natural, constructed, and aesthetic. Natural features include soils and other geological conditions, topography, water bodies, vegetation, wildlife, climate, and others. Constructed features include boundaries, streets and roads, sidewalks, existing buildings or other structures, utilities, and so on. Aesthetic features include views, surroundings, and others. Many questions must be studied and answered concerning all these features and their interrelationships.

**Topographic Maps** One of the important tools for site planning is a topographic map, showing natural and constructed features of the site. Maps of this sort may be obtained from the U.S. Geological Survey, or they may be prepared at larger scales and showing more details from information derived by surveying the site. Topographic maps contain such information as property lines; easements; rights of way; storm and sewage systems; woods; water bodies; rock out-croppings; elevations and contours of the land and other objects; locations; and information on first-floor elevations of existing buildings, walls, driveways, parking lots, and other structures.

Contour lines are used on topographic maps and other drawings to indicate levels or elevations of the land, slopes, and similar information. A contour line represents a constant elevation above some selected reference level, or plane, called a datum. A vertical distance, called a contour interval, is selected between contour lines for each map or other drawing. For example, a contour interval might be 2 ft. Thus adjacent contour lines will be 2 ft apart from each other vertically. Contour

**SITE PLANNING** Location and site plan, Embassy of Singapore (1993), Washington, D.C. *[Architects: RTKL Associates, Inc.]*

lines that are close together indicate relatively steep slopes, while those that are farther apart indicate more gentle slopes. In a map with contour lines at 2 ft vertical intervals, if two consecutive lines are 4 ft apart horizontally on the map, the indication is of a slope that rises 2 ft, vertically, in a horizontal distance of 4 ft. The slope, the ratio of the horizontal distance to the vertical, would then be 4:2 or, as it would usually be expressed, its equivalent of 2:1, a very steep slope. Another related term is grade, expressed as the percentage the height, called the rise or fall, is of the horizontal distance. Thus the 2:1 slope is equivalent to the 50 percent grade.

**Creative Elements** After a program and a land-use plan have been prepared, the process of planning a site can proceed further. Major considerations are locations of buildings or other structures and provisions for vehicular and pedestrian circulation into and on the site and into the buildings. Parking is another important consideration. All these elements must be handled efficiently and economically, with proper consideration given to safety and comfort, to protection of the site and the environment, to sun orientation, and to visual design factors. As in all architectural design, the visual considerations include creative use of shapes, volumes, textures, colors, and other factors to produce design elements that are properly balanced, in proportion, and in the proper scale to each other and to the whole design. Natural visual elements include the land itself, along with rocks, plants, water, and others. Constructed visual elements may include paving, walls, outdoor stairs, fountains, pools, sculpture, lighting, and benches and other outdoor furniture. In addition, there may be requirements for playing fields and other facilities.

Visual elements of the above sort are part of every site plan; all must be combined in a manner that will create a harmonious and aesthetic overall design. In addition, the site planner must design the elements for proper construction and for efficient maintenance. The planner must also properly handle the technological aspects of the site plan, including grading of the site, water protection and drainage, utility services, roads, streets, parking, noise, sewage disposal, and other construction items.

It would be difficult to overstate the importance of proper and creative site planning, for buildings of all types and sizes and particularly for building complexes. Site planning not only affects the individual buildings and complexes, but also the areas that surround them and the entire environment. The changes made in sites affect the ecology of the area as well as the human and aesthetic qualities. Therefore site planning is a subject to be taken very seriously and should be performed only by those with adequate knowledge, experience, and creative ability to accomplish worthwhile results that can lead to overall designs of high excellence.

**Related Articles** DESIGN, ARCHITECTURAL; ECOLOGY; ENGINEERING; FOUNTAIN; GARDEN; LANDSCAPE ARCHITECTURE; PARK; PLANNING, CITY; PRACTICE OF ARCHITECTURE; PROGRAMMING; SPECIFICATION; SURVEYING; WORKING DRAWING.

**Further Reading** De Chiara, Joseph, and Lee E. Koppelman: *Site Planning Standards*, 3rd ed., McGraw-Hill, New York, 1984; Parker, Harry: *Simplified Site Engineering for Architects and Engineers*, John Wiley, New York, 1954.

**SKIDMORE, OWINGS AND MERRILL** American architectural firm, founded by Louis Skidmore (1897–1962), Nathaniel Alexander Owings (1903–84), and John Ogden Merrill (1896–1975). Founded in 1936 by Skidmore and Owings, the firm became Skidmore, Owings and Merrill (or SOM) in 1939. From this beginning, the firm grew to become one of the largest and most influential in the world, with offices in New York City, Chicago, San Francisco, Washington, D.C., and Portland, Ore.

Most noted for large office buildings, the firm has designed many other building types and continues to do so. Their work is characterized by sophisticated and artful handling of big buildings for big businesses and other

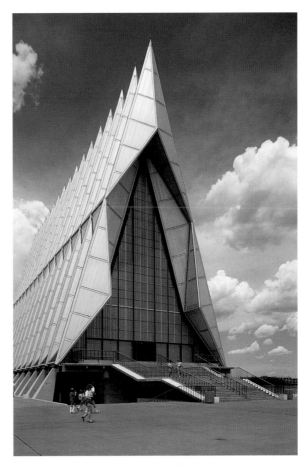

**SKIDMORE, OWINGS AND MERRILL** Chapel (1963), Air Force Academy, Colorado Springs, Colo. *[Architect: Walter Netch of Skidmore, Owings and Merrill]*

institutions, by clear, careful handling of plans and exteriors and interiors down to the smallest details, and by use of glass and metal-curtain walls, prefabricated and sometimes preassembled in factories.

While the work of the firm has sometimes been criticized for a degree of sameness of their buildings, actually there is considerable variety but it is subtle. In a way, the work of SOM, in theory is much like that of Holabird and Roche in the late 1800s and early 1900s in Chicago. Both firms attempted to perfect their designs, with each succeeding design growing or evolving from those that preceded. By such evolutionary architecture, SOM, like Holabird and Roche, has produced a body of work that is of consistently high quality. The firm has also proved that a large office can produce good work, an idea that many architects have not accepted very readily.

**SOM Works** During the early years of the SOM practice, commissions were often for small buildings or remodeling jobs. For a firm later to be recognized as a world design leader, there was little to indicate the future. Then the firm was given the commission for the important New York City Building for the 1939 World's

Fair in that city. Other commissions came in, and then World War II began. By that time, the firm had become well known enough to be asked in 1942 to design a huge new complex for a secret government project in Tennessee. As it turned out, the firm designed a whole town for 75,000 people who would work on and support the Manhattan Project, which produced the atomic bomb. The town was Oak Ridge, Tenn., and SOM worked on the buildings for several years, finishing after the end of the war. Commissions then flowed in at an ever-increasing rate for some of the most important buildings in the United States. And the commissions have flowed in ever since.

After the war, SOM designed buildings of various types and was recognized as a competent architectural firm. Then in the early 1950s, they produced a building that brought them worldwide acclaim, one that is still acknowledged as one of their best ever, if not the best. This was Lever House (1952), New York City. SOM had the vision to design this great building, but they would never have been allowed to design it in the way they did except for the vision of another architect, turned soap

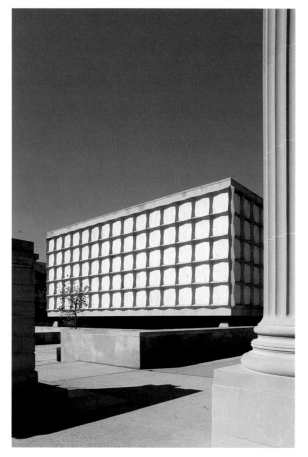

**SKIDMORE, OWINGS AND MERRILL** Beinecke Rare Books and Manuscript Library (1963), Yale University, New Haven, Conn. *[Architect: Gordon Bunshaft of Skidmore, Owings and Merrill]*

company executive, the president of Lever Brothers, Charles Luckman (1909– ). Later Luckman returned to architecture and built a large and successful practice of his own.

After Lever House, there were steady commissions, some for elegant small buildings like the Manufacturers-Hanover Trust Bank (1954), New York City; others for large elegant buildings, some in the suburbs like the Connecticut General Life Insurance Co. offices (1957), Bloomfield, Conn., and some in the city like the Inland Steel Building (1958), Chicago. Then followed the Crown-Zellerbach Building (1958), San Francisco, and the Reynolds Metal Co. Building (1958), Richmond, Va. Then came a commission that many architects had sought, but SOM got, the design of an entire campus and buildings for the new U.S. Air Force Academy (1962), Colorado Springs, Colo. The Academy, and particularly its Chapel, received wide recognition. Soon SOM was involved in the design of another complete campus and its buildings, the University of Illinois Chicago Circle Campus (first phase completed in 1965), in Chicago.

In succeeding years, SOM has designed a number of other notable buildings. Among them are the Union Carbide Building (1960) and the Chase-Manhattan Bank (1961), both in New York City; the John Hancock Center (1969), Chicago; the Library (1971) at Northwestern University, Evanston, Ill.; the Weyerhaueser Headquarters (1971), Tacoma, Wash.; and the Sears Roebuck Tower (1974), Chicago. The last-named is either the world's tallest or second tallest building, according to whether you ask its proponents or those of the World Trade Center (1973) in New York City. In either case, the Sears Roebuck Tower is considered by many to be SOM's best building effort so far.

**Skidmore's Life** Louis Skidmore was born in Lawrenceburg, Ind., on April 8, 1897. He served in England during World War I as a private in a construction group. After the war, Skidmore entered the architectural school at Massachusetts Institute of Technology and graduated in 1924. In 1926 he won the coveted Rotch Traveling Fellowship on his second try. This is one of the oldest and most respected awards in architecture, having been awarded almost every year since 1884.

Skidmore used the fellowship for travel in England, France and other European countries, and the Near East, remaining away from the United States almost three years. During his travels, he met Eloise Owings, the sister of his future partner, in Paris where she was studying fashion design. In 1929 she and Skidmore were married. He and Owings then did some architectural work together, but nothing much came of it once the Depression started.

In the early 1930s, when word circulated that there would soon be a great fair in Chicago, Skidmore sought

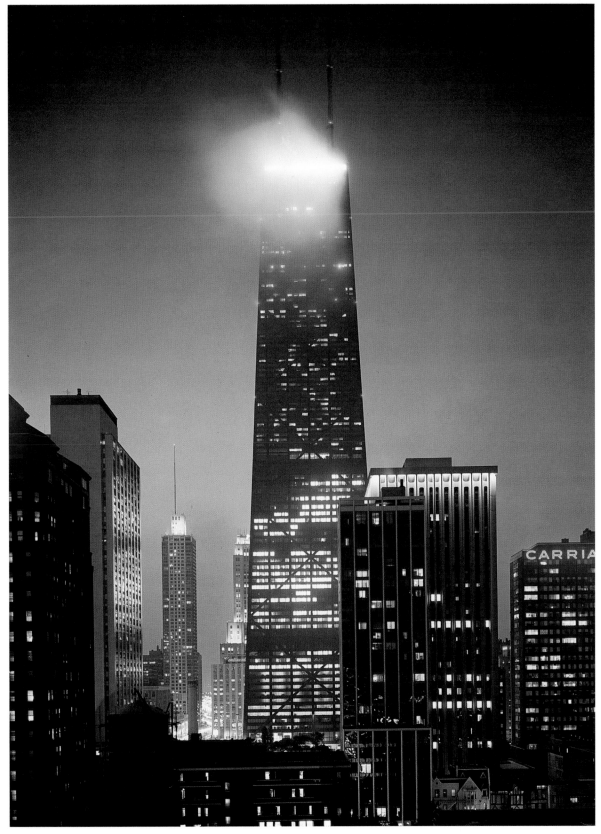

**SKIDMORE, OWINGS AND MERRILL** John Hancock Center (1970), Chicago, Ill. *[Architect: Bruce J. Graham of Skidmore, Owings and Merrill]*

**SKIDMORE, OWINGS AND MERRILL** Hirshhorn Museum (1975), Washington, D.C. *[Architect: Gordon Bunshaft of Skidmore, Owings and Merrill]*

out the leaders of the architectural commission, Raymond Mathewson Hood (1881–1934) and Paul Philippe Cret (1876–1945). Skidmore was appointed chief of design for the fair and took his brother-in-law to Chicago with him to help. The next three years were spent working on the Century of Progress, as the Chicago World's Fair of 1933 came to be known.

After the fair closed, Skidmore and Owings opened an office together in Chicago in early 1936. This was the beginning of what later became one of the largest and most influential firms of the 20th century. Some months later, they opened another office in New York and Skidmore took charge of it. Plagued with ulcers most of his life, he still managed a very busy schedule in New York, but once in a while had to retreat completely away from it all to recuperate. In spite of his physical problems, he managed to establish the office solidly.

In 1956, after the firm had been in existence for 20 years and both it and the partners had become hugely successful, Skidmore retired to a house with an orange grove beside a lake in Winter Haven, Fla. In 1957 he was awarded the highest honor his profession can give, the Gold Medal of the American Institute of Architects. He spent his last five years mostly staying at home with his wife, enjoying the lake and the orange grove. On September 27, 1962, Louis Skidmore died.

**Merrill's Life** John Ogden Merrill was born in St. Paul, Minn., on August 10, 1896. He attended the University of Wisconsin for two years (1915–17). He served as an officer in the U.S. Army during World War I from 1917 to 1919, then transferred to the architectural school at Massachusetts Institute of Technology, from which he graduated in 1921. In 1918 he had married Ross MacKenzie and they had three children, one of whom, John Ogden, Jr. (1923–   ), became an architect and later a partner in Skidmore, Owings and Merrill.

Merrill worked in various offices and a short time for the Federal Housing Administration. In 1939 he joined Skidmore and Owings in their partnership and its name was changed to its present form. In 1942 he moved to Tennessee to take charge of the highly secret buildings at Oak Ridge, remaining there until 1945, and directing the work after that from the Chicago office of the firm.

Having been divorced from his wife, Merrill married Viola Berg in 1946. During 1947–49, after having become expert in the technology of buildings and building codes, he directed a major revision of the Building Code of the City of Chicago. In 1948 he retired from practice and went to live in Colorado Springs, Colo. On June 7, 1975, John Merrill died.

**Owings' Life** Nathaniel Alexander Owings was born in Indianapolis, Ind., on February 6, 1903. Impressed by the cathedrals of France on a trip he had won as a boy scout in 1920, he decided to become an architect. First, he entered the architectural school at the University of Illinois, Urbana, and stayed a year. After passing the entrance examinations to the U.S. Military Academy at West Point, he became very ill and had to give up the appointment. Recovering, he went to Oklahoma to work for a pipe company.

Failing in his new ambition to enter the architectural school at Cornell University, Ithaca, N.Y., he was admitted to its College of Agriculture, later transferred to architecture and graduated in 1927. After graduation, Owings went to New York City where he worked for a while in the office of York and Sawyer. When Louis Skidmore, his brother-in-law and partner-to-be, was named chief designer for the Chicago World's Fair of 1933, Owings went along to work with him.

In 1931 Owings married Emily Hunting Otis and they had four children. After the close of the Chicago Fair, Owings and his wife traveled in Japan and China and then went to Paris where Owings and Skidmore planned the future architectural firm that would bear

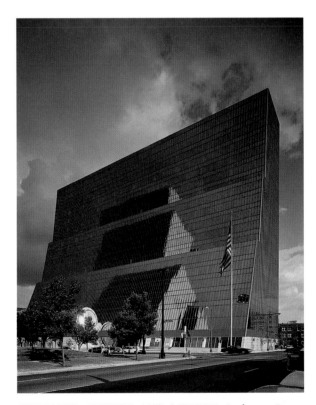

**SKIDMORE, OWINGS AND MERRILL** Lutheran Center (1983), Minneapolis, Minn. *[Architect: Edward Charles Bassett of Skidmore, Owings and Merrill]*

their names. Early in 1936, they opened their first office in Chicago.

Divorced from his wife in 1953, Owings married Margaret Wentworth Millard on the last day of the year. Having gone to San Francisco to direct the SOM office there, Owings built a house (1957) in Big Sur, on the coast of California, and moved there to live. Much of his time in the last decades was spent in important civic work, including the President's Council on Design of Pennsylvania Avenue; beginning in 1963, the California Highway Scenic Roads Commission (1963–67); and the U.S. Interior Department Advisory Board on National Parks, Historic Sites, Buildings and Monuments (1966–72), serving as chair (1970–72). Owings was awarded the Gold Medal of the American Institute of Architects in 1983. On June 13, 1984, Nathaniel Owings died.

**Famous Employees** A great number of noted architects have worked for or have been partners in Skidmore, Owings and Merrill over the many years of its existence. One of the more noted was Gordon Bunshaft (1909–90), who in his lifetime became more famous than the name partners, and who in 1988 was awarded jointly with the Brazilian Oscar Niemeyer the prestigious Pritzker prize, nine years after Bunshaft's retirement from the firm. Many of the firm's most famous buildings beginning with Lever House (1952) in New York and ending with such projects as the National Commercial Bank (1981), Jeddah, Saudi Arabia, are associated with his name. Bunshaft retired in 1979.

Other well-known design partners have included Edward Charles Bassett, Myron Goldsmith (1918– ), Bruce J. Graham (1925– ), Walter E. Hartman (1916– ), Walter Netsch (1920– ), and the engineer Fazlur Rahman Khan (1929–82). A younger generation of partners continues the firm.

**Related Articles** AIRPORT; ART IN ARCHITECTURE; CONTEMPORARY ARCHITECTURE; EXPOSITION; LIBRARY; MODERN ARCHITECTURE; OFFICE BUILDING; PUBLIC BUILDING; STONE; WOODWORK; WURSTER, WILLIAM WILSON.

**SOCIAL SCIENCE** The field is generally known as environment and behavior, but may also be called environmental psychology, people-environment studies, and design-behavior studies. With roots in the nineteenth century, serious research began in the late 1960s.

**Theory** There is no one recognized theory in the field, rather a diversity of approaches. They may be grouped as philosophical approaches, over-arching theories, or theories within specific areas of environment and behavior.

Philosophical approaches use terms like *interactional, organismic,* and *transactional. Interactional* refers to environmental factors, psychology, and time, and the interactions between them. A postoccupancy evaluation would be a study of this type, explaining how people and groups interact with the physical environment as expressed in attitudes, satisfaction, performance, or other factors. Organismic approach is related to psychological systems in which people and environment affect each other. Studies of schools, hospitals, and dormitories would be of such relationships. Transactional approach is similar to the Aristotle view of causation. This might be shown in subjective and experienced people-environment relationships expressed as meaning, feelings of attachment, and orientation of people to places. These studies would include the response of individuals to their homes or residential spaces.

Over-arching theories attempt to separate the theories that relate to the field as a whole, contrasted to theories that apply to a subdiscipline. One such over-arching theory is the transactional, contrasting the environment with psychological, behavioral, cultural, social, political, and economic factors.

Subdisciplines would include Gestalt theory, where people perceive the environment as a whole rather than the sum of its parts. Developmental theories concern how children acquire mental images of spaces and places as they develop. Another subdiscipline is the arousal theory, where there appears to be an optimal level of arousal, for example from noise, but where overstimulation can interfere with performance, such as in overcrowded conditions in cities.

All these theories are important because they tend to influence research. The field is changing from descriptive research to one recognizing multiple complex responses to the environment in respect to time. Research methods include postoccupancy evaluations, gathering data from a sample group, unobtrusive observation, and obtrusive interviews and questionnaires. Quantitative analysis is based on standard measurements of numerical data, and other approaches may include direct observations, evidence of use such as furnishings and decorations in a home or the graffiti on public walls, or what individuals have added or subtracted from the environment. Archival materials might include architectural criticism, diagrams, photographs, and other materials.

**Building Types Research** Interior design and furniture arrangements include studies of personal space, which have affected airport and office design among others. Design to provide for personal space, which includes issues of size and shape of rooms, degree of openness, access to the outside, complexity and displacement, and brightness, is an architectural response.

Housing research includes analysis of the concept of home, housing for children, for students, for low-income people, for disabled people, and for the elderly.

Institutional research includes research in correctional facilities, hospitals, mental-health-care facilities, schools, and office buildings.

Research also includes work on large-scale architecture and urban design. Research has affected the design and changes of public plazas in and around mixed-use and office building projects. An example would be the restrictions on high-rise building in San Francisco, Calif. The impact of environment and behavior studies on architecture has been immense, and the public has benefited from the better understanding of the issues involved. Most schools of architecture now include courses on social and behavioral factors. Perhaps the biggest hurdle is to translate research into practical application for particular building types.

**Further Reading** Lynch, Kevin: *The Image of the City*, MIT Press, Cambridge, Mass., 1960; Sommer, Robert: *Personal Space: The Behavioral Basis of Design*, Prentice-Hall, Englewood Cliffs, N.J., 1969; Stokels, Daniel, and Irwin Altman, eds.: *Handbook of Environmental Psychology*, John Wiley, New York, 1987; Whyte, William H.: *City—Rediscovering the Center*, Doubleday, New York, 1988.

**Periodicals** *Environment and Behavior*, Corwin Press, Inc., 2455 Teller Road, Newbury Park, Calif. 91320; *Journal of Architectural and Planning Research*, Locke Science Publishing Co., Box 146413, Chicago, Ill. 60614-6300; *Journal of Environmental Psychology*, Academic Press, Ltd., 24-28 Oval Road, London NW1 70X, England.

**Source of Additional Information** Environmental Design Research Assoc., P.O. Box 24033, Oklahoma City, Okla. 73124.

**SOUND CONTROL** The materials and other physical characteristics in buildings, or rooms, that determine the loudness or volume, intensity, and quality of sound. Sound consists of the waves, or oscillations, that occur when an object vibrates. These sound waves travel through air or some other material causing vibrations in the eardrum or tympanum, stimulating the auditory nerves and the brain. Acoustics, the science of sound, always involves a source, a transmission, a path, and a receiver of sound. When the science is applied to buildings, it is called architectural acoustics and when applied to rooms in buildings, room acoustics. Architectural acoustics is concerned with two major considerations: the design of buildings for wanted sounds to be heard properly, and for unwanted sounds, or noise, to be controlled or excluded. A third consideration, often of importance, is reduction of the level of reverberations of sounds.

**Sound Characteristics** When objects vibrate, sound waves are generated. The major properties or characteristics of sound are frequency, wavelength, magnitude, intensity, and velocity. Frequency is the times an object

**SOUND CONTROL** Anechoic Chamber, Engineering Building, University of Michigan, Ann Arbor, Mich.
*[Architect: Smith, Hinchman & Grylls (Photo: Gary Quesada/Korab Ltd.)]*

vibrates or a sound wave oscillates in a given period of time. One cycle per second is called a hertz (Hz), and human hearing encompasses an approximate range of 20 to 20,000 Hz. Wavelengths are measurements of the distance between similar points on two successive sound waves, or the distance sound travels in one cycle, or hertz. Humans can hear sounds of approximately 0.5 in. on the high-frequency side. The magnitude of sound is its power, or energy, measured in watts (W). The intensity of sound refers to its power per unit of area, often expressed in watts per square meter (W/m²).

A decibel (dB) is an abstract number often used to express a certain level of sound value. For every 10 points rise in the decibel scale, the intensity increases tenfold. Thus, 50 dB has 100,000 times the intensity of 0 dB. The loudness of a sound is the apparent power of the sound perceived by the eardrum and transmitted to the auditory nerves and brain. A sound with a certain intensity may seem louder to one person than to another. The velocity of sound is the rate at which it moves through a material. Velocity of sound varies considerably between materials, from about 1,100 feet per second (ft/s) in air at 32°F and normal atmospheric pressure, to some 4,700 ft/s in water and 16,400 ft/s in steel. For comparison,

light, which may travel in a vacuum, which sound cannot do, has a speed of 186,281 miles per second (mi/s).

Other characteristics of sound are important in architecture. The threshold of hearing or audibility, below which the normal ear cannot hear sounds, is considered to be at an intensity level of 0 dB, and the threshold of feeling, at which sound affects feeling in the ear, and of pain, at which sounds can actually hurt, is considered to be at an intensity level of 130 dB. A person who cannot hear sounds below the threshold of pain is considered to be totally deaf. Other approximate intensity levels include an average office at 50 dB, speech from 3 ft away at 70 dB, a shout from 5 ft at 90 dB, rock band at 120 dB or more, and near a jet engine at 140 dB. The Occupational Safety and Health Administration (OSHA) allows a 90-dB maximum level for industrial workers who work eight-hour days. Continued exposure to sound intensities of more than 85 dB will damage the hearing of many people.

Sound attenuation is a reduction in the intensity caused by distance from the source or absorption or blocking of the sound by materials or objects between the person hearing the sound, or the receiver, and the source. For sound sources at distances, the intensity of sound is reduced by one-quarter each time the distance between the source and receiver doubles. In sound absorption and blocking, or barrier, materials and objects, various degrees of attenuation occur.

Two or more sounds may combine as in an orchestra. Sound may be reflected as well as absorbed or blocked. Background noise levels affect sounds heard and perceived. Another important consideration in architecture is the reverberation time of sound, its persistence after the sound has stopped issuing from a source. The quality of sound is also important, particularly in concert halls, theaters, and similar building types. The quality of sound is largely determined by the tones that issue from the source of the sound. For example, the tones from a violin are quite different from those of a trumpet. Each instrument produces certain fundamental tones at various frequencies, along with overtones at different frequencies. Overtones are often spoken of as harmonics, the second harmonic vibrating at twice the frequency of the fundamental tone, the third at three times the frequency, and so on. Other factors affect the quality of sound, including resonance, the production of large vibrations by small forces, such as in a piano or cello.

**Architectural Acoustics** In general, architectural acoustics deals with the provision of good conditions for sound in buildings. This involves the design of buildings for good speech conditions, privacy, and freedom from distracting noises. In such buildings as theaters, concert halls, opera houses, and similar types, architectural acoustics also must provide good conditions for listening to drama and music.

For the provision of good conditions in most buildings, acoustical design involves controlling the amount of sound through absorption or sound insulation, through blocking of sound, and through control of background noises. Good acoustical conditions may also be achieved, at least partly, through design of machines, such as furnaces and boilers, refrigerators, air-conditioning systems, and the like, for quiet operation.

**Sound Absorption** Sound is absorbed most readily by materials that are fibrous or porous, such as heavy curtains, upholstered furniture, carpets, and the like. Human bodies also absorb sound readily, each person absorbing more sound than a yard of thick carpet. Many sound-absorbing materials are available for use in ceilings of buildings, including tiles made of fiberboard, glass fibers, and others, and acoustical plaster. Standard systems are available for installation of such materials in ceilings or for their use in suspended ceilings. Measures of their effectiveness are sound absorption coefficients, in these materials from about 0.38 for low frequencies in the range of 125 Hz to more than 0.95 for higher frequencies of about 4,000 Hz. As a contrast, concrete ranges from about 0.01 to 0.0 Hz. Sound-absorbing qualities of materials are often referred to by noise reduction

coefficient (NRC) numbers, which are averages and range from the lowest, 0.0, upward. Good sound-absorbing, acoustical materials may have NRC numbers from about 0.65 to 0.95, while concrete has 0.0. Heavy carpet on concrete has an NRC number of 0.30, while the same material with a foam rubber backing or pad has an NRC number of 0.55. Medium-weight curtains have an NRC of about 0.55 and heavy-weight, 0.60.

**Sound Isolation** Sound blocking, or isolation, is accomplished by the use of relatively dense, heavy materials which reflect sound away from the spaces to be protected. While sound isolation is very important in all building types, it is especially needed in such buildings and spaces as airports, offices in conjunction with factories, and the like. Concrete, with an NRC number of 0.0, provides excellent sound blocking. Other good sound-isolating materials are brick, concrete block, and heavy plate glass, with 0.05, and plaster, gypsum board, stone, and tile, with 0.0.

**Standards** Standards have been established for sound absorption and sound isolation in various building types. The standards for sound absorption involve recommended reverberation times for various types of buildings. For example, the optimum reverberation time, in seconds, at frequencies between 500 and 1,000 Hz include approximately the following: elementary classrooms 0.6–0.8; moving picture houses 0.8–1.2; auditoriums 1.5–1.8; concert halls 1.4–2.1; and so on.

Noise criteria (NC) curves are used for the determination of acceptable noise levels in various kinds of buildings. Some NC values, with their approximate decibel ratings, include concert halls, NC 15–20, 25–35 dB; sleeping rooms, NC 20–30, 30–40 dB; private offices, NC 30–35, 40–45 dB; stores, restaurants, and the like, NC 35–40, 45–50 dB.

The NC curves measure acceptable levels of background noise in various kinds of rooms. Too much background noise may make it impossible to hear and understand conversation and other wanted sounds or to enjoy properly dramatic, musical, and other performances. Too little background noise is also undesirable, for such reasons as privacy of conversations. The aim in controlling background noises then is to achieve the proper balance for the functions to be performed in architectural spaces.

**Other Noise Sources** Much of the noise to be dealt with in buildings comes from outside sources, such as automobile traffic, or sources in adjoining rooms. Such noises are usually controlled by the methods previously discussed. Other annoying noises to be controlled in buildings are those from various kinds of mechanical equipment, such as pumps, elevators, and air-conditioning components. Such noises can be controlled, at least partly, with sound-blocking materials. However, it is considered better practice to control as much of this noise as possible at the source. Mechanical equipment, such as pumps, fans, air-conditioner components, and others, are often mounted on springs or on concrete or other supports mounted on springs. Neoprene or other resilient pads are also often used. These do not prevent the vibrations of the machinery that produce noise, but help prevent the noise from being transmitted through the building frame. Noise transmitted through ductwork can be minimized by proper design of the airflow through them, by glass-fiber duct linings, and by mufflers. Other methods are sometimes used for controlling noises from mechanical equipment, including special floor systems.

**Special Acoustical Problems** Auditoriums, including lecture halls, concert halls, opera houses, theaters, and the like, present special acoustical problems. The programs to be presented in such buildings or the range of types of performances must be determined. Sizes of audiences are important, as are the relative levels of sophistication of the performances and the audiences. In general, large auditoriums are more difficult to design, acoustically, than are smaller ones. And auditoriums in which professional opera, drama, or music is to be presented to audiences with extremely high expectations for perfection have quite different acoustical requirements than elementary or high school auditoriums.

The acoustical design of auditoriums involves room acoustics and noise control. Many factors affect room acoustics, including size or volume of the room; shapes of floors, walls, and ceilings; sound absorption; reverberation characteristics; sound reflection; sound scattering or diffusion; and sound flow around objects or diffraction. The acoustical design of auditoriums is quite complex and is usually handled by acoustical specialists. In addition, the design must assure that noises are strictly controlled. Acoustical design for auditoriums often involves the provision of electronic sound systems, consisting of microphones, amplifiers, loudspeakers, and other equipment. (See the article entitled communication system.)

Building types, other than auditoriums, often present specific acoustical design problems. For example, schools house a number of widely varied activities. Provisions must be made for such activities as lectures, quiet studies as in libraries, outdoor and indoor athletics, physical education, and others. Each type of activity presents acoustical problems that must be solved not only for that activity but for other different activities located nearby. Churches, offices (particularly open-planned types), houses and apartments, and many other building types also present varied acoustical problems that must be solved.

Sound control and acoustics in buildings today is a highly complex subject, only discussed in a very general manner in this article. Because of the complexities, acoustical design is generally handled by specialists,

acoustical consultants, who are usually engineers or physicists. Architects and other environmental designers also contribute importantly to good acoustical design, since the shapes of rooms, the materials used, the design and placement of mechanical equipment, and other architectural and engineering considerations have great effects on the acoustics of buildings.

**History** There is little evidence that attention was paid to acoustics and sound control in the buildings of the early civilizations around the Mediterranean Sea or before that time. In early huts and tents, little could be accomplished, and if it could have been, would probably have been considered unnecessary. In the buildings of ancient Mesopotamia, Crete, and Egypt, sound blocking was a natural result of the massive masonry used in construction, but no attention seems to have been paid to other acoustical factors.

In ancient Greek theaters and those of the Romans that followed, excellent acoustics were achieved, some experts think by accident. In achieving good sight lines from the audiences to the stages, such theaters were usually designed in semicircular or similar forms and had seating that inclined upward away from the stage or orchestra, as it was called. Behind the orchestra, there ordinarily was a wall, sometimes with a canopy, called a *skene*. The combination of the shape of the theater, the inclination of the seating, and the sound-reflecting qualities of the *skene* as well as the absence of distracting noises near the theater produced very good acoustics.

After the time of the Romans, little or no attention was paid to acoustics for several centuries. Theater construction stopped during the Middle Ages and when it was revived, during the Renaissance, theaters were mostly small and had good sight lines, which incidentally produced good acoustics.

The first printed references to acoustics were published in 1486, even though written by a first-century A.D. Roman architect, Marcus Vitruvius Pollio, usually called Vitruvius. His book *De architectura*, now often called *Ten Books on Architecture*, discussed many elements of architecture, including the acoustics of Greek theaters. It had some effect on the architecture of the time when it was published, but has had considerable importance since that time.

The beginnings of the modern science of acoustics may be taken to be the 17th century, when the French mathematician Marin Mersenne (1588–1648) first measured the velocity of sound in 1640, or when the German mathematician Athanasius Kircker (1601–80) published books on sound, music, and acoustics. Other developments in the science of sound and in acoustics also took place in the 17th century, but they had little or no effect on the acoustics of buildings of the Renaissance and Baroque periods and those that followed, until the 19th century.

In the late 19th century, a number of influential books on acoustics were published, including the two volumes, in 1877 and 1878, of *The Theory of Sound* by the English physicist Lord Rayleigh (John William Strutt; 1842–1919). The science of architectural acoustics began with the work of American physicist Wallace Clement Ware Sabine (1868–1919), who was a professor at Harvard University, Cambridge, Mass. Sabine not only developed important principles of acoustics but applied the principles to the first building in America to be specifically designed acoustically for the performance of music, the Boston Music Hall, now known as Symphony Hall (1900), designed by McKim, Mead and White.

Since the time of Professor Sabine's work in acoustics, the science has advanced very rapidly. Many new techniques have been developed for providing proper acoustics, not only in theaters, opera houses, symphony halls, and other buildings requiring excellent sound but also in other types, such as office buildings. Progress has also been made in sound control of other sorts, including sound blocking and noise control. Today acoustics and sound control are routinely part of architectural design. In the case of structures, such as theaters, acoustical specialists ordinarily handle acoustical design and testing and often they are consulted on other types of acoustical problems.

**Related Articles** AIRPORT; HEATING, VENTILATING, AND AIR CONDITIONING; RECREATION BUILDING; RELIGIOUS BUILDING; THEATER.

**Further Reading** Beranek, Leo L., ed.: *Noise and Vibration Control*, 2d ed., McGraw-Hill, New York, 1992; Egan, M. David: *Architectural Acoustics*, McGraw-Hill, New York, 1988.

**Periodical** *Journal of the Acoustical Society of America*, 355 E. 45th St., New York, N.Y. 10017.

**Sources of Additional Information** Acoustical Society of America, 500 Sunnyside Blvd., Woodbury, N.Y. 11797; National Council of Acoustical Consultants, 66 Morris Ave., Springfield, N.J. 07081.

**SPECIFICATION** The process involved in preparing a written document (the specifications), which describes the materials, workmanship, and final results expected in building construction, along with legal considerations, insurance requirements, inspection and testing procedures, and other requirements. Specifications are sometimes referred to as specs.

The written descriptions of the specifications amplify and augment the graphic descriptions of the working drawings, sometimes called the plans. Together, the working drawings and specifications and other required items are often called the contract documents, since they are part of the contracts between owners and contractors for the construction of buildings.

**Contract Documents** For the construction of buildings, contract documents consist of the agreement (or contract) between an owner and a contractor, the working drawings, the specifications, the general conditions of the contract, any supplementary conditions or addenda issued before the contract is signed, and later modifications signed by the parties to the contract.

An agreement, general conditions, specifications, and working drawings are the basic parts of a set of contract documents. The others are used as required. Sometimes, contract documents, with the exception of working drawings, are collected into what is called a project manual, which also includes several other items, a copy of the invitation or advertisement for bids, instructions to bidders, and sample forms for insurance and bonds. Formerly, general conditions were considered part of the specifications, but the practice today is to consider these as two separate documents, though they are bound together into project manuals. This is because the content of the general conditions today is confined to questions, such as the responsibilities of and relationships between owners, contractors, subcontractors, architects, and others involved in the construction, and with other business and legal requirements. The content of the specifications may then be confined to the technical requirements for the construction of buildings.

The general conditions of the contract for construction has 14 parts: (1) contract document requirements; (2) the functions, responsibilities, and rights of the architect, (3) the owner, (4) the contractor, (5) the subcontractors; (6) rights to award separate contracts for portions of the work and related requirements; (7) miscellaneous requirements, including laws, damages, bonds, royalties, patents, tests, and so on; (8) time, scheduling, progress, and related requirements; (9) payments to the contractor on completion of the job; (10) safety requirements for people and property; (11) insurance requirements; (12) changes in the work; (13) correction of defective or incorrect work; and (14) termination of the contract.

**Formats** Today specifications are based on a format (1964) originally developed by the Construction Specifications Institute (CSI) with the American Institute of Architects (AIA), Associated General Contractors (AGC) of America, Consulting Engineers Council (CEC) of the United States, Council of Mechanical Specialty Contracting Industries (CMSCI), National Society of Professional Engineers (NSPE), Producers' Council (PC), and the Specification Writers Association of Canada. Thus the UCI format for specifications has the backing of many of the major building industry associations.

The 16 divisions of what is now called the CSI *Masterformat* are almost universally used. The

*Masterformat* includes a section-numbering system suitable for automated master specifications. The 16 divisions are (1) general requirements, (2) sitework, (3) concrete, (4) masonry, (5) metals, (6) wood and plastics, (7) thermal and moisture protection, (8) doors and windows, (9) finishes, (10) specialties, (11) equipment, (12) furnishings, (13) special construction, (14) conveying systems, (15) mechanical, and (16) electrical.

In each of the 16 divisions, sections vary in number, according to needs, from 6 to more than 20. For example, in the furnishings division (12), the 8 sections are artwork, cabinets and storage, window treatment, fabrics, furniture, rugs and mats, seating, and furnishing accessories. All these sections, as those in other divisions, are broad in scope; other sections may be added as required. Each section is further subdivided into subjects of narrower scope. For example, in division (12), artwork section, are ceramics, paintings, sculpture, and stained glass; but here too other subjects, such as frescoes, photomurals, and so on, may be added if required.

In a set of specifications, reference is often made to the general and other conditions in the various divisions and in the sections. In addition, each specification section is often divided into three parts: general provisions, materials, and execution of the work. In some specifications, the sections contain slightly different parts: general provisions; materials; fabrication, installation, and testing; closeout and continuing requirements; and submissions of samples, test results, shop drawings, and the like.

**Philosophies** There are two major philosophies of specification writing: the procedure, sometimes called the prescriptive, specification system; and the performance specification system. In the procedure system, materials to be used and methods of construction are specified. In the performance system, the results expected in the construction are specified, but not the materials or means to be used to arrive at the results. Although some specification writers prefer one system over the other, both are generally used to some extent in most specifications, since certain construction requirements can be better expressed in one way, while some are better expressed in the other.

**Materials or Products** One of the most important aspects of specifications is the information they contain on materials or products. There are two major methods for the handling of products or materials: closed or open specifications. In a closed specification, certain materials or products are specified by name, with no substitutions allowed. This method is used where it is thought that only these products will be acceptable.

In an open specification, certain options are available in the products or materials used. Open specifications may contain provisions of several kinds: a list of all acceptable products or materials, giving the contractor options; a list of products or materials, with the provisions that a contractor may apply to the architect for approval of substitutes, or equals, before or at the time of bidding or during the construction; and a descriptive specification, which lists the qualities, functions, sizes, performance, and so on of products or materials, any of which will be approved if the requirements are met. All these types of material or product specifications are used by architects at various times.

After approval of the designs and outline specifications by an owner, the preparation of working drawings and final specifications may begin. Working with the outline specifications and the working drawings as they progress, a specification writer develops checklists and other information to be included in the final specifications. In smaller offices, and to some extent in larger ones, specifications previously prepared for similar projects may be used as guides in the preparation of new specifications. In larger offices, a master specification is often maintained for guidance. As the actual writing of the specification proceeds, the writer will need to confer with the project architect or other person in charge of the project, and with those actually preparing the working drawings. It may be necessary to seek information from other sources, including manufacturers' catalogs, standard specifications prepared by governmental and building industry technical groups, books, magazines, building codes and ordinances, and other sources.

**Reproduction Systems** When the specifications have been prepared, they must be checked for accuracy and completeness, carefully proofread, and then reproduced and bound. For relatively small and simple projects, specifications are often reproduced by photocopying or similar methods. For larger and more complex projects, specifications are often printed, sometimes by letterpress but more often by offset process. Binding of specifications usually entails only stapling the pages, along with the other parts of the project manual, into covers. Many larger offices today have their own reproduction systems, while smaller ones often obtain such services from commercial sources. Some offices also use automated systems involving computers with attachments for printing the specifications on paper or diskettes, which allow recall, editing, and automatic typing of the specification contents.

**Specification Writing** Ordinarily, specification writing begins early during architectural services. When the design of a building has been developed to a point at which its major elements may be determined, preliminary or outline specifications are usually prepared. In a small office, an architect might prepare these; in larger offices, specification writers are usually specialists in this work. Recently a computerized Master Outline specification has been issued by the AIA Master Systems. Other

**SECTION 08522**

**FIXED ALUMINUM WINDOWS**

**PART 1 - GENERAL**

**1.01 SUMMARY**

A. Related Documents: Conditions of the Contract, Division 1 - General Requirements, and Drawings apply to Work of this Section.

B. Section Includes:
1. Fixed aluminum window systems, complete with reinforcing, shims, anchors, and attachment devices.
2. Accessories necessary to complete Work.

C. Products Furnished But Not Installed Under this Section: Inserts and anchoring devices which are to be built into structure.

D. Related Sections:
1. Section 01018 - Exterior Wall Design Requirements.
2. Section 01411 - Exterior Wall Testing.
3. Section 01430 - Mock-Ups.
4. Section 07920 - Sealants and Calking: Perimeter sealants and backup materials.
5. Section 08805 - Glass and Glazing.
6. Section 11014 - Window Washing System.
7. Section 12511 - Horizontal Louver Blinds.

**1.02 REFERENCES**

A. Aluminum Association (AA):
1. - Designation System for Aluminum Finishes.

B. American Architectural Manufacturers Association (AAMA):
1. - Aluminum Curtain Wall Design Guide Manual.
2. 605.2-85 Voluntary Specification for High Performance Organic Coatings on Architectural Extrusions and Panels.

C. American National Standards Institute (ANSI):
1. Z97.1-84 Specifications and Methods of Test for Safety Glazing Material Used in Buildings.

RTKL DC ASSOCIATES PC
© COPYRIGHT 1991

---

D. American Society for Testing and Materials (ASTM):
1. A36-87 Structural Steel.
2. A123-84 Zinc (Hot-Dip Galvanized) Coatings on Iron and Steel Products.
3. B209-88 Aluminum and Aluminum-Alloy Sheet and Plate.
4. B221-88 Aluminum-Alloy Extruded Bars, Rods, Wire, Shapes, and Tubes.
5. B308-88 Aluminum-Alloy 6061-T6 Standard Structural Shapes, Rolled or Extruded.
6. C509-84 Cellular Elastomeric Preformed Gasket and Sealing Material.
7. C542-82 (1984) Lock-Strip Gaskets.
8. C716-87 Installing Lock-Strip Gaskets and Infill Glazing Materials.
9. C864-84 Dense Elastomeric Compression Seal Gaskets, Setting Blocks and Spacers.
10. C920-87 Elastomeric Joint Sealants.
11. C1036-85 Flat Glass.
12. C1048-87 Heat Treated Flat Glass-Kind HS, Kind FT Coated and Uncoated Glass.
13. E283-84 Test Method for Rate of Air Leakage Through Exterior Windows, Curtain Walls, and Doors.
14. E330-84 Test Method for Structural Performance of Exterior Windows, Curtain Walls, and Doors by Uniform Static Air Pressure Difference.
15. E331-86 Test Method for Water Penetration of Exterior Windows, Curtain Walls, and Doors by Uniform Static Air Pressure Difference.
16. E773-88 Test Method for Seal Durability of Sealed Insulating Glass Units.
17. E774-84a Sealed Insulating Glass Units.

E. Consumer Product Safety Commission (CPSC):
1. 16 CFR 1201 Safety Standard for Architectural Glazing Materials.

F. Federal Specifications (FS):
1. TT-P-645A Primer, Paint, Zinc Chromate, Alkyd Type.

G. Flat Glass Marketing Association (FGMA):
1. 1986 Edition Glazing Manual.

H. Steel Structures Painting Council (SSPC):
1. SP2 Hand Tool Cleaning.
2. SP3 Power Tool Cleaning.
3. Paint 12 Cold-Applied Asphalt Mastic (Extra Thick Film).

RTKL DC ASSOCIATES PC
© COPYRIGHT 1991

1.03   SYSTEM REQUIREMENTS

A.   General Standard:  In addition to requirements shown or specified, comply with applicable provisions of AAMA Aluminum Curtain Wall Design Guide Manual for design, materials, fabrication and installation of component parts.

B.   Design Requirements:

1.   Metal stick framed systems with interior and exterior exposed metal framing.

2.   System manufacturer is responsible for design and engineering of window systems, including necessary modifications to meet specified requirements and maintaining visual design concepts.

3.   Design glazing system for interior glazing at vision areas and exterior glazing at spandrel areas.

4.   Design perimeter conditions into system that will allow for installation tolerances, expansion and contraction of adjacent materials, and sealant manufacturer's recommended joint design.

5.   Drawings are diagrammatic and do not purport to identify nor solve problems of thermal or structural movement, glazing, anchorage or moisture disposal.

6.   Requirements shown by details are intended to establish basic dimension of unit, sight lines and profiles of members.

7.   Do not assume glass, sealants, and interior finishes contribute to framing member strength, stiffness, or lateral stability.

8.   Engineer assemblies to be free from rattles, wind whistles and noise due to thermal and structural movement and wind pressure.

9.   Attachment considerations are to take into account site peculiarities and expansion and contraction movements so there is no possibility of loosening, weakening or fracturing connection between units and building structure or between units themselves.

10.   Design anchors, fasteners and braces to be structurally stressed not more than 50% of allowable stress when maximum loads are applied.

11.   Provide for expansion and contraction due to structural movement without detriment to appearance or performance.

12.   Design system to drain exterior face of wall, water entering joints and condensation occurring within windows by drain holes and gutters of adequate size to evacuate water without infiltration to interior.

13.   Provide continuous interior gutter system at sill which drains to exterior through weep holes.  Head members shall also have gutter system which drains directly to exterior or drains internally to sill below.

14.   Provide baffles at weep hole locations.

15.   Provide concealed fastening wherever possible.

16.   Metal faces are required to be visually flat under all lighting conditions, subject to acceptance of Architect.

17.   Provide uniform color and profile appearance at components exposed to view.

C.   Performance Requirements:

1.   Air infiltration:  Air leakage shall not exceed 0.06 cfm per square foot of surface area when tested in accordance with ASTM E283 at differential static pressure of 6.24 psf.

2.   Water infiltration:  No uncontrolled leakage when tested in accordance with ASTM E331 at test pressure of 6.24 psf.

D.   Structural Requirements:

1.   Wind loading:

a.   Basic zones:   Resist wind pressure of 25 psf positive and 25 psf negative.

b.   Corner zones:   Resist wind pressure of 40 psf positive and 60 psf negative for areas extending 12 feet from corners.

2.   Deflection under uniform loading:   When tested in accordance with ASTM E330 at design pressure, maximum deflection of exterior member shall not exceed L/175 of span or 3/4 inch, whichever is less.

3.   Parallel to wall and corner mullion deflections:   75% of glass edge bite or 3/8 inch, whichever is less.

E.   Thermal Requirements:  Engineer framing systems to accommodate expansion and contraction movement due to surface temperature differential of 180°F without causing buckling, stress on glass, failure of joint seals, excessive stress on structural elements, reduction of performance or other detrimental effects.

F.   Interface:

1.   Furnish inserts and anchoring devices which need to be preset and built into structure to appropriate trade.

2.   Supply on timely basis to avoid delay in Work.

3.   Instruct other trades of proper location and position.

4.   Furnish setting drawings, diagrams, templates and installation instructions.

1.04   SUBMITTALS

A.   General:   Submit in accordance with Section 01300.

B.   Proposal Drawings and Data:

1.   Submit with proposal engineering drawings, details, and information necessary to support and clarify proposal.  Include alternative suggestions.

2.   Draw alternatives at 1/4 full size (3"=1'-0") and details of window system.

3.   Include data indicating manufacturer's name, product type and performance information of products proposed for use.

4.   Furnish proposals containing following minimum details and data:

a.   Head, sill and jamb of window system at junction of building structure.

b.   Typical intermediate mullion and corner mullions.

c.   Anchorage system.

d.   Connections between components.

**SPECIFICATION** Portions of specifications for fixed aluminum windows, Embassy of Singapore (1993), Washington, D.C. [Architects: RTKL Associates, Inc.]

design professionals, such as engineers, ordinarily prepare specifications for the types of work they handle, and these are then delivered to the architect for approval and to be bound with the other divisions.

Recently, even more sophisticated methods for specification preparation, using computers, have been developed. Some computer specifications were developed in architects' offices. Others are national in scope and are available on a subscription or fee basis. The two most widely known are *Masterspec* produced by AIA Master Systems and *Spectext* issued by CSI. Both are issued in printed form as well as for computerized operations. In addition to the master specification systems, several guide specifications have been developed and maintained by federal agencies including the U.S. Army Corps of Engineers and the U.S. Naval Facilities Engineering Command.

**Specification Specialists** Specifications are generally prepared by architects, especially in smaller offices, by specialists in specification writing, either in architects' offices or those of other design professionals, or by specialists who have their own consulting firms. Effective writing of specifications requires considerable knowledge of the building industry, not only of products, materials, systems, and workmanship but of construction procedures, design and working drawing preparation, construction contracts, law, and construction contract administration.

While courses in specification writing as well as in related subjects are available in professional schools, none are detailed and complete enough to suffice for the proper writing of specifications. Therefore specification writing is often performed by professionals and other construction industry people with an interest in and a deep knowledge of the subject gained through experience working with seasoned specification writers. Many of these are architects, engineers, technicians, or construction people, who chose to become specification writers.

**History** It is believed that the use of specifications began in the 18th century. Until well into the 19th century, such specifications were quite simple and often were organized according to the crafts which performed the work. A textbook by T. L. Donaldson, *Handbook of Specifications*, published in London in 1860, divided the work into two major headings: carcase (or carcass) of a building, and its finishing. The subdivisions under carcase were excavator, bricklayer, mason, slater, founder and smith, and carpenter. Under finishing were joiner, plasterer, painter, glazier, paperhanger, ironmonger, smith and bellhanger, and gasfitter.

At the end of the 19th century, specifications were often divided into three sections: masonry, carpentry, and mechanical work. In 1915 the AIA published the first edition of its general conditions and this document

has subsequently gone through a number of revisions. In 1963 the Construction Specification Institute published its CSI format for construction specifications and in 1966, the Uniform Construction Index, based on the CSI format, was published. In 1969 Production Systems for Architects and Engineers, Inc., was founded for the primary purpose of developing the master (computerized) specification it now makes available to the building industry. As previously described, the national master specifications are undergoing frequent updates by the two major organizations. These are the AIA Master Systems' *Masterspec* and the Construction Specifications Institute's *Spectext*.

**Related Articles** COMPUTER; ELECTRICAL ENGINEERING; INTERIOR DESIGN; LANDSCAPE ARCHITECTURE; MECHANICAL ENGINEERING; PRACTICE OF ARCHITECTURE; STRUCTURAL ENGINEERING.

**Further Reading** *Architect's Handbook of Professional Practice*, latest ed., American Institute of Architects, 1735 New York Ave., N.W., Washington, D.C. 20006; *Manual of Practice*, and *Masterformat*, Construction Specifications Institute, 601 Madison St., Alexandria, Va. 22314; Meier, Hans W. J.: *Construction Specifications Handbook*, Prentice-Hall, Englewood Cliffs, N.Y., 1975; Rosen, Harold J., and Tom Heiniman: *Construction Specifications Writing: Principles and Procedures*, 3rd ed., John Wiley, New York, 1990.

**Periodical** *The Construction Specifier*, 1150 17th St., N.W., Washington, D.C. 20036.

**Sources of Additional Information** AIA Master Systems, a Division of the American Institute of Architects, 1735 New York Ave., N.W., Washington, D.C. 20006; Construction Specifications Inst., 601 Madison St., Alexandria, Va. 22314-1791.

**STAIR** A part of a building that allows people to walk from one floor level to another. Stairs are usually constructed on an angle, with a series of steps consisting of treads, horizontal members to walk on, and vertical members, one to each tread, called risers. A stair is also sometimes called a staircase or a stairway and the portion of a stair connecting two floor levels, a flight of stairs. The horizontal distance covered by a flight of stairs is often called a run, and the same term is sometimes used for a single tread. The vertical height of a flight of stairs is called the rise, but the same term is also applied to the height from one tread to another.

**Types** The simplest form of stair is a ladder, still used sometimes today. Almost as simple is a straight-run, unbroken flight type that rises in a certain direction from one floor level to another. Many other stair forms are possible and are often used for reasons of design, appearance, or space limitations. The next simplest form is one that rises a certain distance, usually to the halfway point between floors, where it meets a platform, called a landing, from which it then rises the remainder of the distance in another direction, usually at right angles to or in the opposite direction from the first.

Many other geometrical forms may be used for stairs, including circular, elliptical, and other curves, and helical, sometimes called helicoidal, or spiral, stairs that wind around poles or are constructed with reinforced concrete or other structures that are self-supporting. Treads of curved stairs are called winders.

**Construction Methods** Stairs may be built to fit into spaces or shafts, called stairwells, or without stairwells. A special kind with no well, called a dog-legged stair, rises to a landing in one direction then resumes its rise in the opposite direction.

The usual construction for stairs involves inclined structural members, called stringers, which span the distance from floor to floor or between floor and landings. Such stairs may be closed underneath or open. If they are open, the underside is called a soffit. Risers may also be closed or open. In open-rise stairs, the vertical spaces between treads are left open rather than being filled in with various materials as in a closed-rise type. Other construction methods may be used, including cantilevers, in which treads project out from a supporting structure. Stairs are usually provided with handrail systems, often called balustrades, which consist of rails of various materials supported by posts at the ends and at landings, called newels, and smaller posts in between, called balusters or banisters.

**Construction Materials** The most usual materials for the structure of stairs are wood, reinforced concrete, steel, and sometimes aluminum. One special system consists of preformed steel tread and riser assemblies, called stair pans, which are usually supported by steel stringers. Concrete or another material is poured into the pans to form treads. Many materials may be used for treads and risers, including wood, usually oak or pine but sometimes others, steel grids, marble or other stone, terrazzo, ceramic and quarry tile, and carpeting. Sometimes metal devices, called nosings, are placed on the front edges of treads to protect them from wear and for safety reasons. Specially formed treads, incorporating abrasives or made of rubber or other materials (nonskid treads), are often used for safety.

Many special types of stairs are available for specific purposes, including ships' ladders of steel, cast iron, and aluminum; prefabricated steel stairs for utilitarian purposes; disappearing stairs of wood, aluminum, or other materials for access to such places as attics and available with mechanical or electrical operators; and fire escapes.

**Code Requirements** The design of stairs is governed by building code requirements and other standards for construction, inclines, widths, ratios of rise to run,

handrails, number required in various building types, sizes, and other particulars. Such codes and standards also govern the requirements for spaces at stair ends and doors necessary for the exit of people from stairs during fires or other emergencies.

In addition, certain concepts of good practice in stair design have been developed over the years. Of utmost importance are the proper inclines. In general, outdoor stairs are not made as steep as those indoors, since those on the exteriors of buildings must be used in bad weather. For interior stairs, certain rules of thumb are sometimes cited, such as that the dimension of a riser plus that of a tread should equal 17 or $17\frac{1}{2}$ in or that the dimensions of a riser multiplied by that of its tread should equal 70 or 75. There is also a definite relationship between the relative height of risers to the width of the tread. Building codes now call for risers of 7 in with 11-in treads for stairs. For other proper ratios, a stair designer should consult various stair tables and diagrams that are widely available. A special riser-tread ratio is sometimes used for monumental buildings, in which the intent is to slow walkers to gain certain effects as they approach. In such buildings, risers are often made very low and treads are made very wide. Many people find such stairs uncomfortable. Similarly, many people find that the steeper stairs become, the harder they are to climb.

Accidents relating to stair and ramp design have led to a consensus of safety requirements including proper handrails, correct ratio of tread to riser, slip-resistant surfaces or steps and ramps, adequate lighting, good maintenance, guardrails and toeboards, and no stair with fewer than three risers in a run.

**History** Although none are known to exist, it is thought that the first structures of more than one story constructed by humans were provided with vines for climbing from one level to another. Later rudimentary ropes were probably used for this purpose and in time primitive ladders made from limbs of trees. The time when the first real stair was constructed is unknown. However, by about 3000 B.C. when the great early civilizations around the Mediterranean Sea were well established, stairs were in common use.

Most of the earliest stairs still in existence are monumental exterior types leading to great temples and other important buildings. Stairs of this type are still in existence in such places as the Palace of Persepolis (486 B.C.), Iran, and many places in Greece. An early interior stair is in the Palace (c. 1600 B.C.) of King Minos, Crete, a place where buildings were as many as four stories high, all levels being served by stairs. The Romans constructed buildings of considerable height, up to about 160 ft, with all levels served by stairs; a number of Roman examples have survived at least in part.

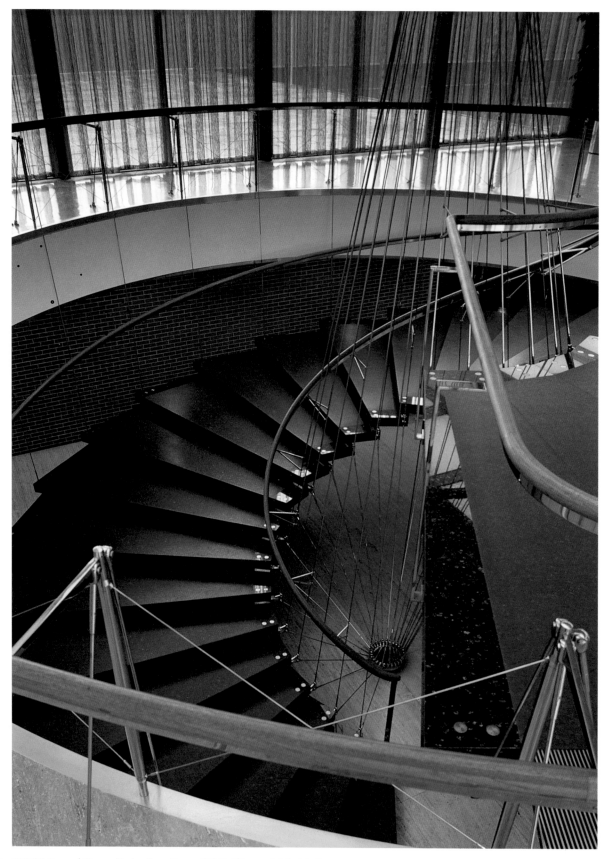

**STAIR** General Motors Technology Center (1957), Warren, Mich. *[Architect: Eero Saarinen]*

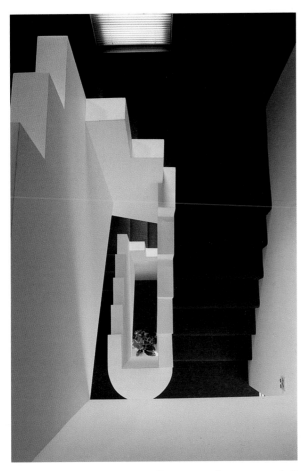

**STAIR** Woo Residence (1984), Dallas, Tex. *[Architect: George C. T. Woo & Partners]*

Gothic exterior stairs were usually of stone, while interior ones might be of stone or wood. Stairs of this period were usually not emphasized as architectural features and were often in spiral forms that wound around central columns. During the Renaissance, stairs became important elements of architecture and many fine examples were constructed in many places in Europe. A small sampling of the most notable are double stairs of the Palais de Chambord (1547), France; Palazzo Farnese (1549), Caprarola, Italy, designed by Giacomo Barozzi Vignola (1507–73); and Ashburnum House (1662), Westminster, England, thought to have been designed by John Webb (1611–72). An interesting situation exists at the Chateau de Blois (1524, with later additions), France, where a late Gothic stair was built about 1504 and an early Renaissance example in a tower about 1524.

Many notable stairs were constructed in the years following the Renaissance, including the Baroque example in the Opera House (1874), Paris, designed by Jean Louis Charles Garnier (1825–98), and the Art Nouveau stair in the Tassel House (1893), Brussels, Belgium, by Victor Horta (1861–1947).

**American Development** In early colonial America, stairs were strictly utilitarian. Later notable curved stairs and other types were constructed in many houses and other buildings during the Colonial period and during the years after the Revolution. Many of these stairs were well designed and graceful, but much simpler than the ornate types often constructed in Europe at the time. In the Classic Revival and Eclectic periods of American architecture, the design of stairs, along with that of other architectural elements, was generally derived from past periods. Some monumental stairs were used for important buildings and this practice continues to an extent today.

Most stairs today, though often well-designed architectural elements, tend to be consistently simple and utilitarian rather than important architectural features. In buildings taller than two stories, except for stairs required by building codes for fire and disaster exits, elevators and sometimes escalators have virtually replaced all stairs. An exception is sometimes made in the lobbies of certain buildings and outside the entrances of others. Public buildings are required to have exterior ramps or other means of access for the physically challenged to supplement exterior stairs.

**Related Articles** DESIGN, ACCESSIBLE; FIRE PROTECTION; VERTICAL TRANSPORTATION.

**STEEL** An alloy of iron with varying quantities of carbon and often with one or more other substances, used in numerous forms and for many purposes in buildings. The three most common forms of ferrous metals in architecture are wrought iron, cast iron, and steel. The main difference between them is in the amount of carbon they contain. Wrought iron contains the least, less than 0.1 percent carbon but usually much less; cast iron the most, usually from 1.7 to 4 percent carbon; and steel falls in between the two types, with up to 2 percent carbon usually.

**Production Methods** Steel is made from the product of blast furnaces, called pig iron, which contains approximately 95 percent iron, up to 4 percent carbon, or slightly more, and traces of other substances. Molten pig iron, often with scrap steel and iron added, is processed in a Bessemer converter or an open-hearth, electric, or oxygen furnace, thus removing impurities which are taken off as slag, leaving steel with the amount of carbon required. Metals may be added to the molten steel to produce alloys of various kinds.

About 90 percent of the steel made in the United States comes from open-hearth furnaces. In general, a batch of steel, called a heat, is made by charging the furnace with limestone and scrap steel. The mixture is melted by fires fueled with oil, gas, or other fuels. After the mixture has been melted, molten pig iron is added. After a few hours, if test samples indicate that too much carbon is present, iron ore is added and a small quantity of spiegeleisen or spiegel, pig iron with 20 percent manganese and 5 percent carbon, is added to help remove oxygen from the steel and make it stronger. When samples of the mixture indicate that the heat is ready, the molten steel is tapped into ladles, into which manganese is added. Impurities, in the form of slag, float on the top and flow off into a smaller ladle. The molten steel is then poured into molds to form ingots, and small amounts of aluminum are added to remove oxygen. The entire heat will have taken some 8 to 10 hours and have produced some 50 to 500 tons of steel.

Steel is also made by other methods, including Bessemer converters, today largely supplanted by oxygen furnaces that produce considerably less air pollution. Another method utilizes an electric furnace, in which electric currents cause electrodes inserted into the furnace to arc to the scrap steel and alloying metals and back to the electrodes. Electric furnaces are used mostly for making stainless and other special-alloy steels.

At the end of a steelmaking process, the molten steel is poured into molds to form ingots. The ingots are again heated to an even temperature in a soaking pit, from which they go to a semifinishing mill where they are rolled, while hot, through rollers to form rough shapes called blooms, billets, or slabs, depending on their shapes and sizes. These shapes go to finishing mills where they are rolled again to produce structural shapes, bars, sheets, strips, plates, or other shapes. These shapes may be used as they come from the finishing mills, as is usually the case with structural shapes, or may be further processed into final products.

**Classifications** Steels for use in architecture are generally classified as carbon or alloy steels. Carbon steels have at least 95 percent iron, up to 2 percent carbon, and unspecified amounts of other substances. Alloy steels have quantities of other substances in amounts large enough to impart such properties as strength or rust resistance, different from those of carbon steel. Some of the major alloying substances, in addition to carbon, include silicon, manganese, aluminum, boron, chromium, nickel, molybdenum, and vanadium. Many different alloys are available with widely differing characteristics, making alloy steel a versatile architectural material. Stainless steels are special alloys that contain more than 10 percent chromium to impart resistance to corrosion or rusting.

**Carbon Steels** In general, carbon steels may be worked in several ways (rolled, cast, wrought, and forged) and they can be welded. They are used in architecture for such purposes as structural members, concrete reinforcing rods, mesh and cable, rough hardware, windows, doors, and many others. Since they rust readily, they are painted with rust-inhibiting primers and

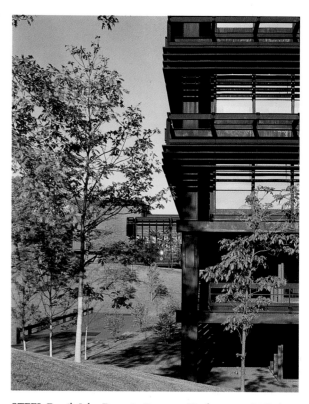

**STEEL** Detail, John Deere & Company Headquarters (1963; later addition), Moline, Ill. The exposed steel is Cor-Ten corrosion-resistant steel. *[Architect: Eero Saarinen]*

usually finish coats. Carbon steels are generally available in a number of sizes and forms, such as sheet, strip, plate, bar, pipe, tubing, and structural shapes, including I beams, wide-flange beams, and H beams, angles, channels, pipe columns, and bar joists. Carbon steel sheet is often formed into light-gauge structural shapes, such as studs and joists.

Development of structural steel alloys has increased the working stress of steel members. In 1874, wrought iron was rated at 12,000 psi. The working stress for modern A36 carbon steel is rated at 24,000 psi, and stronger steels are available where needed.

**Alloy Steels** Alloy steels vary in their workability, based on the amounts and types of alloying substances. Alloy steels are used where high strength and corrosion resistance are required, for such purposes as elevator cables, high-strength bolts and other fasteners, and sometimes special structures.

Stainless steel comes in several types, classified according to the alloying substances used and their amounts. Stainless steel may be worked by casting, forging, bending, rolling, drawing, and extrusion, and may be welded or soldered. Stainless steel is used in many applications in architecture where high quality, strength, and corrosion resistance are considered important, including curtain walls; windows; doors; countertops;

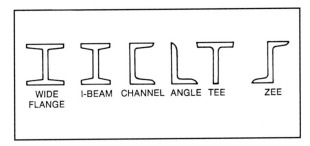

**STEEL** Typical rolled shapes.

grilles; and kitchen, laboratory, and other appliances. Stainless steel generally comes in sheets, bars, structural shapes, strips, and plate. Sheet is available in several finishes, ranging from an as-fabricated finish through matte satinlike finishes to polished mirrorlike finishes. The first major use of stainless steel in architecture was in the Empire State Building (1931), New York City, designed by Shreve, Lamb and Harmon.

Recently, another type of high-strength, low-alloy steel, called weathering steel, has been used quite often in architecture. Alloyed with 0.20 to 0.55 percent copper, 0.30 to 1.25 percent chromium, and small quantities of niobium, formerly called columbium, these steels need no painting; their surfaces gradually oxidize to brownish colors and after a time cease to oxidize further. Many architects believe this to be one of the most important

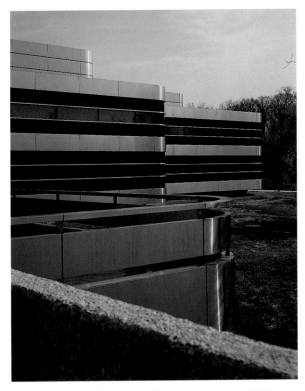

**STEEL** Stainless steel, Industrial Technology Institute (1987), Ann Arbor, Mich. *[Architect: William Kessler Assoc.]*

technical developments in the 20th century, a material that can be exposed like redwood, cypress, stone, or bronze to gradually achieve a natural coloring that is unique. Care must be taken, in using this material, to prevent contact with other metals, such as aluminum, which will be corroded by galvanic action, or with copper, which will cause the steel to corrode. Water, in the form of runoff from one material to another, will also cause corrosion for the same reason. Runoff from weathering steel may stain or discolor some materials, such as stone. For the most part, all other types of steel used in architecture must be painted or otherwise protected by such measures as galvanizing, aluminizing, porcelain enameling, plating, or other surface treatments.

Architects and other environmental designers often design buildings, other structures, and their components of steel. Many steel products come in complete forms, from which the ones to be used may be selected. Others, such as sheet metal for flashing, must be designed and detailed for each application. For structural uses, tables of properties, allowable loads, and so on are widely available, thereby helping to simplify the structural design of most relatively uncomplicated building structures. For others, structural engineers perform the structural design.

**History** The making of primitive steel is thought to have started in the civilizations around the Mediterranean Sea sometime after 3000 B.C. Steel was used only to a small extent, while wrought iron and later cast iron were used much more extensively in early architecture. Fine steels were made in various places, but they were used mostly for swords and other weapons and ornament. The secret of steelmaking was lost, not to be rediscovered until the 18th century. Since that time, steel has become increasingly important in architecture, for structural and many other purposes. For further discussion on the history of steel, see the article entitled iron.

**Related Articles** BURNHAM AND ROOT; CONCRETE STRUCTURE; IRON; JENNEY, WILLIAM LE BARON; PREFABRICATION; STEEL STRUCTURE; Articles on various building components and systems.

**Source of Additional Information** American Iron and Steel Inst., 1133 15th St., N.W., Washington, D.C. 20005.

**STEEL STRUCTURE** Building construction system using steel in the form of columns, beams, and other members for the structure of a building. Structural steel construction refers to the use of hot-rolled members, of not less than $1/8$ in thickness, such as I beams, wide-flange beams, columns, angles, channels, tees, zees, and others. Such structural steel shapes are classified into heavy structural shapes, those that have at least one dimension of 3 in or more, and light structural shapes or bars. Light-gauge steel, for structural systems, includes such members as beams, joists, and studs made of sheet steel which has been bent, cold, or otherwise fabricated, for use in relatively small buildings.

**Uses** Steel members may be used in building structures in many ways, ranging from a single pipe column to take the load of a floor or roof in a wood-frame house to the complete framing of tall buildings. A method often used for relatively small, low-rise buildings consists of bearing walls of masonry or other materials, with floors and roofs framed with steel members. For buildings in which large open, columnless spaces are required, steel may be used for long spans, utilizing trusses of various kinds, large girders, arches, space frames, rigid frames, or long-span joists. For relatively small buildings, often only one story, light-gauge members may be used for walls, floors, and roofs. In some cases, such members are fabricated to produce a slot into which nails may be driven to fasten finishing and other materials.

It can be seen that steel is a versatile structural material that can be employed in buildings in a great variety of ways. One of the most important today is in the construction of skeleton-framed buildings. In such buildings, mostly heavy structural shapes are used to form complete structures of walls, floors, and roofs. Often steel decking is used in roofs that are finished with fire-resistant materials, such as concrete or plaster. Skeleton-framed steel buildings generally have columns, beams, and girders attached together to form strong frames. Usually, the connections between members are made by riveting or welding, but sometimes in smaller buildings or for relatively minor connections, by bolting. Forces from the sides of skeleton-framed buildings, lateral loads, such as those from wind or earthquakes, are usually resisted by either diagonal steel bracing or by masonry or concrete transverse walls, called shear walls. In many cases, masonry or concrete serves the additional purpose of providing fire resistance for the steel framing members.

While regular steel heavy structural shapes may be used for the construction of floors and roofs in buildings with walls of masonry or other materials, a more usual method employs open-web steel joists. These are prefabricated, flat trusses made of small steel sections, such as angles, tees, and bars. They are available in various depths, lengths, and strengths. Open-web joists, used for relatively short spans, are often called bar joists, and those for longer spans, up to 144 ft, are usually called long-span joists. They are used in relatively close spacing, in a manner similar to that of wood joists in a house, and are usually covered with corrugated steel or other types of materials upon which concrete is poured. The undersides may be left exposed in such building types as factories or warehouses and plastered or otherwise sur-

faced in shopping centers or other building types in which finished appearances are important. In high-rise buildings, steel is protected from fire by concrete, masonry, or other materials, achieving protection from heat of 4 h for columns and 3 h for floor construction.

Light-gauge steel members are available in such sections as channels, zees, angles, and others, and in I sections, made by welding two channels together or two angles to a single channel. Such members come in various sizes and gauges, and special types may also be designed and fabricated. The design of buildings using stock light-gauge steel is somewhat similar to the design of buildings with stock wood-framing members. For special types, a considerable amount of calculation is required, and the procedures are quite different from those involved in design with structural steel sections.

Other important steel structural materials, widely available, are light-gauge roof and floor decking. Such components come in several types, among the most important being the ribbed and cellular types. Ribbed types, in several gauges and in a variety of widths and lengths, are generally used for roof decks and are often covered with insulation and built-up roofing. Cellular types are made in such a way that spaces are provided in which electrical wiring or other systems may be installed and easily modified. The cellular types come in various sizes and strengths and are used for both floors and roofs, usually with concrete placed on top of them. Their bottom sides may be finished with plaster or other materials. There are also special types with perforated metal undersides, above which acoustical materials may be installed.

Many other applications of steel in structures may be made. For example, steel pipe, available in many sizes and strengths, is often used for columns. Sometimes pipe columns are filled with concrete for added strength. Steel, in the form of reinforcing bars, welded wire fabric, and wire rope or cable, is widely used for reinforcing concrete. (See the article entitled concrete structure.)

**Assembly Systems** An interesting and important use of steel in building construction is assembly of relatively small steel members into systems that can span great distances. A type that has been used for centuries in architecture is the truss, an assembly of relatively small members into a system, composed of triangles, the most rigid geometrical shape possible, for long spans. In steel, five types of trusses are generally used: the Pratt, Fink, Warren, scissors, and bow string. The five vary in shape and in the way the members are arranged. The scissors and bow-string trusses were named for their shapes, the others for their designers, American engineer Thomas Willis Pratt (1812–75), German-American engineer Albert Fink (1827–97), and English engineer James Warren (d. 1848). A later type of truss, the Vierendeel, does not depend on triangles for its rigidity but on strong, welded joints between its members.

Other assemblies of relatively small members, used to span great distances, are steel arches, of which there are three major types: three-hinged, two-hinged, and hingeless. All are constructed with triangles, like trusses. Three-hinged arches have hinge pins at the base while the crown is rigidly connected. Three-hinged arches are simpler than the two-hinged to design and easier to erect. Two-hinged arches are usually heavier than the three-hinged type. Hingeless arches have no pins, but are rigidly connected. They may be economical for structures built on ground with good bearing strength and where the arches will carry relatively light loads. Another type of steel structural member for long spans is the rigid frame, which may be two-hinged or hingeless for single spans. Rigid frames are assembled from steel structural shapes.

**Space Frames** Many other types of steel structures are used today, including space structures or space frames. Strictly speaking, a space frame is any structure in three dimensions and thus includes rigid skeleton frames of buildings and other types. Today the term usually denotes various types of structures, including folded plates, domes, arches, grids, and others, in which the entire structure of a roof, for example, is made up of relatively small members designed and connected in a manner allowing the entire structure to act as an assembly to carry loads. These loads are then transferred directly to columns, foundations, or other structural elements. In other types of structures, for example, trusses, the loads on the roof are ordinarily carried by the roof deck, then transferred to purlins or other structural members, then to the trusses, and finally to the columns. Space frames are capable of spanning long distances in two directions, utilize relatively small steel sections, and are simple to fabricate as compared to many other systems. Space frames also make possible structural forms of buildings that would not ordinarily be possible when other systems are used.

**Other Developments** Many other types of structures utilizing steel are possible today, including suspension systems, in which roofs of buildings are hung from cables, as in suspension bridges. Steel is a very versatile structural material and new and modified uses of it continue to be developed. Tables of data and other information are widely available. Computers have simplified calculations and have made additional data available to structural engineers for use in calculations. Many of the procedures used today were very difficult, or impossible, to handle before the advent of computers.

Among the most recent developments is weathering steel, which can be exposed without painting or other treatment. This steel weathers to brownish colors that

**STEEL STRUCTURE** Construction photograph, Federal Reserve Bank (1972), Minneapolis, Minn. [*Architect: Gunnar Birkerts*]

protect it from further oxidation or rusting. Other important developments have been the use of huge trusses in buildings to resist the lateral forces of wind and earthquakes, and the design of tall buildings based on the structural principle of a tube or group of tubes.

For all but the simplest uses of steel in structures, calculations in structural design may be quite complex. Therefore the discussion here has only covered general guidelines and principles of design and construction. In practice, the applicable building and other codes must be followed, as must good principles of design and construction. Experienced and highly competent structural engineers usually design all but the simplest steel structures. And architects using steel in their buildings must have a keen understanding of its properties, characteristics, and uses in order to exploit the material to the ultimate.

**History** Steel making was discovered very early in history, perhaps by 3000 B.C. The early civilizations rarely used steel, preferring wrought iron for architectural and other purposes, most of which were relatively small at first. Probably because steel did not come into widespread use, the methods for making steel were later lost or ignored. In 1740 steelmaking began again. However, steel did not become a structural material for buildings until the late 19th century, with its use for some beams in the Home Insurance Building (1885), in Chicago, designed by William Le Baron Jenney (1832–1907), and later destroyed. In 1895 steel columns were first used in the Reliance Building, Chicago, designed by Burnham and Root. From that time, steel has been a very important structural material, not only for tall buildings but for most other types.

The Reliance Building had 4 floors when it was first built, and was later expanded to 14. Only a few years later, in 1907, the steel-framed Singer Building, New York City, designed by Ernest Flagg (1857–1947), with 47 stories and 612 ft high, was completed. This was the

603

**STEEL STRUCTURE** Typical trusses.

record height for a building until about 1909, when the 700-ft-high Metropolitan Life Insurance Building, New York City, designed by Nicholas Le Brun and Sons, was completed. The record did not last long. In 1913 the Woolworth Building, New York City, designed by Cass Gilbert (1859–1934), was completed, with 55 stories and 760 ft high. Its record lasted the longest, until 1930, when the Chrysler Building, New York City, designed by William Van Alen (1882–1954), was completed with 75 stories, 1,049 ft high, including its spire. A year later, this record was broken by the Empire State Building (1931), designed by Shreve, Lamb and Harmon, 102 stories and a height of 1,250 ft to the top of its never-used dirigible mast. Later a tall television antenna was added on top. At the present time, the height record is a tie between the World Trade Center (1973), New York City, designed by Minoru Yamasaki (1912–86), in association with Emery Roth and Sons, and the Sears Tower (1974), Chicago, designed by Skidmore, Owings and Merrill. Both buildings have 110 stories and are 1,454 ft tall. How long their record will stand is a matter for speculation. In any case, it is important to know that all the above buildings were framed in steel. Some think that the era of the design of buildings so tall, or taller, is over. Others disagree. One who disagreed was Frank Lloyd Wright (1867–1959) who, in 1958, proposed a mile-high skyscraper, with 528 floors. It was never built, but Wright always insisted it was feasible. Not all architects or engineers were convinced.

While American architects were building ever-higher steel-framed skyscrapers, other important developments were also taking place in structural steel usage. In fact, some of these developments were necessary before tall buildings could be designed and constructed. The connection of steel structural members with rivets was derived from the method of making boilers. The steel-skeleton frame was derived from earlier wrought-iron and cast-iron frames. At first, steel buildings used masonry walls to resist the forces of wind, or lateral forces, and sometimes these forces were even ignored, a practice definitely not followed today.

Before the beginning of the 20th century, another method for providing lateral bracing had been developed: riveting all structural members to form a rigid frame. In a rigid frame, all the beams, girders, columns, and other structural members are rigidly connected together to form a complete system which resists loads. This became a standard method in architecture. Another technique was later developed for this purpose, the provision of diagonal bracing, which has also become a standard method. Steel trusses have been used in a number of buildings to provide diagonal wide bracing.

Of course, tall steel-framed buildings would not have been feasible if Elisha Graves Otis (1811–61) had not invented a safe elevator, first used in an office building in 1857. The development of central heating and later air conditioning were also necessary for tall buildings to function properly.

In the years after the early steel-framed buildings, many new developments were made. Most of them would not have been possible without improved mathematical methods for calculations of structural members and complete structures. In addition, stronger and better steels have been developed. Improvements have also been made in testing structures by means of mock-ups and models. Until the advent of computers in the second half of the 20th century, it was still very difficult or impossible to perform some of the calculations required for complicated structural designs. Computers have now made possible many advanced and sophisticated structures.

Beginning in the 1960s, a new concept of the structure of tall buildings was developed. Instead of considering the frame as a rigid structure assembled of columns, beams, and so on, it is thought of as a tube perforated by windows. Considerable savings of steel can be achieved in structures of this type. In fact, the concept is a tube within a tube, the inner one the elevator and systems core, usually of reinforced concrete, surrounded by an outer tube of structural steel. Used in the John Hancock Center (1970), Chicago, designed by Skidmore, Owings and Merrill, the tubes are braced with diagonal steel members on the exterior of the building.

In the Sears Tower, mentioned above, the concept was a perforated bundle of nine tubes, with diagonal bracing. In this building, the tubes are in sets of two or three, each set terminating at a different height, the lowest at the 50th floor, the highest at the 110th. The tube concept has also been used in other buildings. The structures of both of these buildings were designed by Pakistani-American engineer Fazlur Rhaman Khan (1929–82), of the staff of the architects of the buildings.

Although electric arc welding had been invented in 1881, it was not used in a steel building structure until 1920. Beginning in the 1930s, welding became an important method in steel construction. It allows savings in the amount of steel used, simplifies difficult connections, and, theoretically at least, makes possible connections as strong as the members themselves. Welding is widely used today in making connections in steel-framed buildings. Welding is particularly well adapted to connections required in many types of curved or oddly shaped structures. Such structures include space frames of various types, arches, vaults, domes, and others. High-strength bolts are also used for similar purposes.

Other types of steel structures used in architecture today include two-hinged and three-hinged arches; rigid arches; latticework structures, called lamella; geodesic domes, invented by R. Buckminster Fuller (1895–1983); and cable-suspended structures. When the ingenuity of architects and engineers is combined with the versatility of structural steel and with the great information retrieval and calculation capabilities of computers, it can be expected that new types of structures will be developed in the future.

**Related Articles** BRIDGE; COMPUTER; IRON; OFFICE BUILDING; STEEL; STRUCTURAL ENGINEERING; STRUCTURE; VERTICAL TRANSPORTATION; Various articles on individual 19th- and 20th-century architects, and on building components and systems.

**Further Reading** Gaylord, Edwin H.: *Design of Steel Structures,* 3rd ed., McGraw-Hill, New York, 1991; *Manual of Steel Construction,* latest edition, American Institute of Steel Construction, New York; Parker, Harry, and Harold D. Hauf: *Simplified Design of Steel Structures,* 6th ed., John Wiley, New York, 1990; Schueller, Wolfgang: *High Rise Building Structures,* John Wiley, New York, 1977, reprint of 2d edition, Krieger, Malabar, Fla., 1986.

**Sources of Additional Information** American Iron and Steel Inst., 1133 15th St., N.W., Washington, D.C. 20005; American Institute of Steel Construction, 1 E. Wacker Dr., Suite 3100, Chicago, Ill. 60601-2001.

**STEIN, CLARENCE S.** American architect and planner (1882–1975). Although he started out as an architectural designer, working mostly in eclectic styles, Clarence Stein soon found that his major interests and

talents were in planning. He chose to devote his career to planning some of the most progressive communities in the United States. And he became a leader of the cause for good community and regional planning.

**Community Planning** With his partner, architect and planner Henry Wright (1878–1936), Stein pioneered many ideas that were in opposition to the meaningless, ugly, inconvenient, and uncomfortable sprawl of cities and their suburbs. Stein and Wright were a long way ahead of their time. They advocated and designed master plans for communities in which houses could be located properly on their sites and in proper relationships to each other, to vehicular and pedestrian travel, to open space areas, and to landscaping. In their designs, varying functions, such as automobile and pedestrian traffic, were separated for convenience and safety. Communities were set in what came to be called greenbelts, areas of trees and other natural elements that protected them. Schools, shopping areas, and so on were located in specific areas so that their activities could function without infringement on others. Groups of houses were arranged into neighborhood units, in which families could achieve a sense of freedom and identification. The houses faced open areas and trees, shrubbery, and grass.

The result of these theories and practices were communities that were far superior to those being built elsewhere in the United States then. And far superior to most of those being built today. Stein and Wright had a

**STEIN, CLARENCE S.** Area plan (1930), Radburn, N.J. *[Planners: Clarence S. Stein and Henry Wright (Stein & Wright)]*

**STEIN, CLARENCE S.** Plan (1930), Radburn, N.J. *[Planners: Clarence S. Stein and Henry Wright (Stein & Wright)]*

vision of something better and they made it work. This is not always the case in the developments of today.

**Works** The first important development by Stein and Wright was Sunnyside Gardens (1924), Queens, New York City. This was followed by Phipps Garden Apartments (1931), also in Queens, and Hillside Homes (1935), in the Bronx, New York City. Then followed two new communities for which Stein and Wright acted as master planners. The first was Radburn, N.J., for which they started planning in 1928 and which was built in the early 1930s according to their plans but with buildings designed by others. The second was Chatham Village, Pittsburgh, also built in the early 1930s and with buildings by others.

After the death of Henry Wright in 1936, Stein continued to act as planner and architectural consultant for other new communities. He did not design buildings for these, but had considerably more success in affecting the quality of their architecture than he had exercised in the early projects. He planned a series of three communities,

based on his earlier greenbelt ideas, for the Farm Security Administration of the U.S. government: Greenbelt, Md.; Greendale, Wis.; and Greenhills, Ohio. All were notable for their plans but not for financial success. In the early 1940s he planned Baldwin Hills Village, its buildings designed by Robert Evans Alexander (b. 1907), Los Angeles, and in the early 1950s was associated with British planner Gordon Stephenson on the planning of Stevenage, England. In the latter community, he was able to establish, for the first time, a town center free of vehicular traffic. In 1951 Stein acted as planning director for his last great project, the new industrial town of Kitimat, British Columbia, Canada.

**Life** Clarence S. Stein was born in Rochester, N.Y., on June 9, 1882, the son of a successful businessman. Frail and often ill as a child, Stein moved with his family to New York City when he was a boy. After graduating from high school, he entered the architectural school at Columbia University, New York City, in 1908, stayed a short while, and transferred to the École des Beaux Arts in Paris, studying there until 1911.

Upon his return from Paris, Stein went to work in the office of Bertram Grosvenor Goodhue (1869–1924) in New York City in 1911, and worked there until 1918. While with Goodhue, he participated in the design of numerous buildings and designed the master plan for a mining village in Tyrone, N. Mex. In 1918, during World War I, he served in the U.S. Army Corps of Engineers as a first lieutenant.

Having become deeply concerned with housing, particularly for low-income families, Stein started his own architectural practice in 1919 and became involved in the work of New York state committees on housing and planning. At first, he designed buildings as would any other practicing architect but later devoted more and more time to planning, particularly new towns and other developments. In this work, he was one of the earliest pioneers in the United States.

In 1924 his first important housing, Sunnyside Gardens, Queens, New York City, was completed; others followed over the years. From 1918 to 1921, he served as associate editor of the *AIA Journal*, using the magazine as a medium to espouse the cause of good planning and conservation, including the proposal for the Appalachian Trail made in 1921 by the noted and farsighted forester and planner Benton MacKaye (1879–1976). Thus began Stein's lifelong dedication to the cause of planning, not only his own but that of others, including MacKaye; the famous historian, writer, and critic Lewis Mumford (1895–1990); Catherine Bauer (1905–64), who later taught at the University of California and was married to William Wilson Wurster (1895–1973); and Henry Wright, who was his partner in planning most of the great communities. Stein arranged for Wright to work out the Regional Plan of New York State in 1923, a classic example of creative planning, still much admired.

In 1928 Stein was married to Aline MacMahon, an actress. He later helped organize a group to promote planning on all levels, the Regional Planning Association of America. Many of the foremost planners of the day were active in this organization. Stein did everything he could for the cause. He wrote articles, lectured, made movies on planning, sent reports and memos to government officials, and edited *Town Planning Review* from 1951 to 1959. He had also embarked on a busy professional career that gradually found him making master plans for communities that are still models of good design. Gradually, he also stopped designing buildings; in his greatest communities, he did not design a single building.

Plagued by illness much of his life, Stein nevertheless accomplished a great deal. Many honors came to him, including the Gold Medal, the highest honor of the American Institute of Architects, in 1956. When he died on February 6, 1975, at age ninety-two, he had come to be considered not only a pioneer of planning but a sage as well.

**Related Articles** BEAUX ARTS, ÉCOLE DES; CRAM, GOODHUE AND FERGUSON; HOUSING; MODERN ARCHITECTURE; PLANNING, CITY.

**Further Reading** Stein, Clarence S.: *Toward New Towns for America*, MIT Press, Cambridge, Mass., 1967.

**STEIN, CLARENCE S.** Block plan (1930), Radburn, N.J. *[Planners: Clarence S. Stein and Henry Wright (Stein & Wright)]*

**STERN, ROBERT A. M.** American architect, educator, and author (1939–  ). Robert A. M. Stern was born in New York City and received his B.A. degree from Columbia University (1960) and his architecture degree from Yale University (1965). Known particularly for his residential designs, he is identified with the post-Modern movement. He uses the term *Modern Traditionalism*. In recent years, larger projects have dominated his practice. Stern is comfortable with the moneyed American past and designs for the affluent present.

**Work** In his earlier house designs, Robert A. M. Stern used traditional forms and materials, combined with modern details and interiors. As his work advanced, his houses are more traditional in feel, both exterior forms and interior design. His seashore buildings are often shingled, with white trim, and large shingled roofs with dormers. Close analysis of these houses indicates that Stern has not created an old house but has used the traditions of earlier houses as a base for inventive variation. Several have received design awards. Multiple-housing projects include condominium units, apartment houses, such as one of the villas designed for Berlin at Tageler Hafen containing 2 one-bedroom units and 4 two-bedroom apartments in a building reminiscent of an earlier German lakeside summer community and the classicist work of the German architect Bruno Paul (1874–1957). Stern's development designs have groupings of large homes for an affluent market.

In addition to individual houses, Stern has designed apartment remodeling in New York City, as well as interiors for doctors' offices, athletic clubs, and showrooms. Temporary structures have included exhibition design and a temporary clubhouse at Swan Valley, Breckenridge, Colo. (1985). As one of the group of architects designing for the Disney corporation, Stern has designed the Lake Buena Vista, Fla., employee-hiring facility, a mock Venetian palace, the Yacht and Beach Club Resorts reminiscent of pre–World War I resort hotels, and two hotels for Euro Disney near Paris (1991).

Several larger projects have included commercial and educational facilities. The Prospect Point Office Building at La Jolla, Calif. (1985), reflects the local Spanish Colonial architecture of the area, using stucco walls and clay tile roofs. Bancho House (1990), Tokyo, Japan, is a remodeled five-story office building topped by a new two-story penthouse, reflecting his study of the British embassy across the street. Detailing is reminiscent of the work of English architect Sir John Soane (1753–1837). The penthouse looks out on the gardens of the Imperial Palace. In the United States, the high-budget Ohrstrom Library for St. Paul's School, Concord, N.H., fits comfortably among a group of 19th- and early-20th-century buildings. The associations evoked in this building recall a number of historic prototypes while remaining of the present.

**STERN, ROBERT A. M.** Lawson House (1981), E. Quogue, N.Y. *[Photo: Peter Aaron]*

**Life** Born on May 23, 1939, in New York City, Robert Arthur Morton Stern has been associated with New York throughout his career. After college, he became program director of the Architectural League of New York (1965–66) and then worked briefly for the office of Richard Meier before becoming special assistant for design in the Housing and Development Administration of the City of New York. In 1969, he and the architect John Hagmann formed a partnership, Stern & Hagmann Architects, which was dissolved in 1977. Since then the firm has been known as Robert A. M. Stern Architects.

Robert A. M. Stern has been involved in architectural education since early in his career, and is professor at the Graduate School of Architecture, Planning and Preservation at Columbia University. In 1984 he became the first director of the Temple Hoyne Buell Center for the Study of American Architecture at Columbia University. He has also been associated with the Institute of Architecture and Urban Studies and was president of the Architectural League of New York from 1973 to 1977.

Robert A. M. Stern is also an author of a number of books, including the *New Directions in American Architecture* first published in 1967 and revised in 1977. More recent works include *New York 1900*, coauthored with Gregory Gilmartin and John M. Massengale, and *New York 1930* with Gregory Gilmartin and Thomas Mellins. His book *Modern Classicism*, with Raymond W. Gastil, was published in 1988. The Public Broadcasting System aired a 1986 television series presented by Stern called "Pride of Place: Building the American Dream." In 1990 he published an entertaining children's book called *This Is the House That Bob Built*, showing a Stern house as seen by a child. It is probable that additional books will be written by and about Robert A. M. Stern.

Having known Robert Venturi (1925– ) before the publication of the influential *Complexity and Contradiction in Architecture* (1966), Stern has been seeking his own response to historic buildings. As Robert A. M. Stern has commented, after all considerations of style and theory, the viewer can only respond to the actual building.

**Further Reading** Arnell, Peter, and T. Bickford, eds.: *Robert A. M. Stern 1965–1980: Toward a Modern Architecture after Modernism*, Rizzoli, New York, 1981; Aslet, Clive: *American Houses of Robert A. M. Stern*, Rizzoli, New York, 1991; Rueda, Luis R., ed.: *Robert A. M. Stern: Buildings and Projects 1981–1985*, Rizzoli, New York, 1986.

**STONE, EDWARD DURELL** American architect (1902–78). Edward Durell Stone is a controversial architect about whose work architects and other people seem to have widely divergent views. Nevertheless, Stone put his mark on the architecture of his time, in the many important buildings he designed, in his espousal of refined ornament in his later years, and in his establishment of sunscreens, usually grilles, as a major element of his buildings. He also became well known for his dedication to the cultural aspects of his buildings and their proper harmonization with their surroundings.

**Works** Starting with his first commission, for the Mandel House (1933), in Mt. Kisco, N.Y., Stone designed numerous fine houses all over the country. It took a rather long time for him to become established in the design of other building types, but beginning in the early 1950s, he produced a steady stream of notable buildings. Some of them are the El Panama Hotel (1946), Panama City, Panama; U.S. Embassy (1954), New Delhi, India, which many consider his best building; Stanford University Medical Center (1955), Palo Alto, Calif.; Stuart Company offices (1956), Pasadena, Calif.; U.S. Pavilion (1957) at the World's Fair, Brussels, Belgium; the National Geographic Society Building (1961), Washington; and the John F. Kennedy Center for the Performing Arts (1969), Washington.

**Life** Edward Durell Stone was born on March 9, 1902, in Fayetteville, Ark. As a boy, he was a good student and was interested in building things like boats, furniture, and birdhouses. His older brother, Hicks (1888–1928), was an architect who practiced in Boston. In 1920 Stone went to the University of Arkansas, but dropped out in 1923 to join his brother in Boston. He then worked in architectural offices, including that of Coolidge, Shepley, Bulfinch and Abbott, and studied architecture nights at the Boston Architectural Club, since 1944 the Boston Architectural Center.

In 1926 Stone won a competition for a scholarship to Harvard University and stayed there a short time and then transferred to Massachusetts Institute of Technology and stayed until 1927. Having won the Rotch Traveling Scholarship, Stone went to Europe in 1927, and remained there until 1929. Returning to America, Stone went to New York, where he worked for several firms until 1933, when he opened his own office.

In 1931 Stone married Orlean Vandiver and they had two children. These were Depression times and architectural commissions were very few. After Stone first opened his office, he designed a few houses that brought him considerable attention, including one for Henry R. Luce (1898–1967), the noted publisher of *Time*, and later *Life*, magazines. Luce commissioned Stone to design a plantation house and several other buildings (1936) in Moncks Corner, S.C. He was then chosen to design, with Philip L. Goodwin (1885–1957), the new Museum of Modern Art (1939), New York City, to which wings were added in 1951 and 1964 by Philip Cortelyou Johnson (1906–  ), and incorporated into the gallery expansion and tower (1984) by Cesar Pelli (1926–  ). After that, commissions started to come into his office in increasing numbers.

When World War II started, Stone entered the U.S. Army Air Force in 1942, and was released as a major in 1945. Returning to New York, he reestablished his prac-

**STONE, EDWARD DURELL** Museum of Modern Art (1939; alterations and additions, 1951, 1954; addition, 1982), New York, N.Y. *[1939 Architects: Philip Goodwin & Edward Durell Stone; 1951, 1964 additions: Philip C. Johnson; 1984 addition and tower: Cesar Pelli]*

tice, this time in Great Neck, Long Island, and again started designing houses. Soon commissions for other types of buildings started to come in and his career, other than as a house architect, began.

In 1951 Stone was divorced from his wife, and in 1954 he married Maria Elena Torchio, the American-born daughter of an Italian father and Spanish mother. They had two children but were subsequently divorced. He then married again, this time to Fiona Campbell and they had one child.

Stone eventually built one of the most successful architectural practices of his time, and designed a great number of important buildings all over the world. His life was not always easy, with two divorces and a long struggle with the problems of alcohol. But he always kept the good humor he was noted for and weathered all his troubles to keep on producing architecture. He also received many honors, including doctor's degrees and membership in the American Academy of Sciences and the National Institute of Arts and Letters. On August 6, 1978, Stone died.

**Related Articles** CONTEMPORARY ARCHITECTURE; MODERN ARCHITECTURE.

**STONE** Rock used in the construction of buildings for walls, floors, and other purposes. Rock is the hard, solid mass, composed of minerals, that makes up the earth's crust. Soil is composed of rock particles, often mixed with organic matter. Rock used for construction purposes is often called building stone after it has been cut, sized, or otherwise processed for use in architecture. Stone has been a very important building material from the earliest time and until the 19th century was the primary structural and ornamental material for monumental and other notable buildings. Today stone is still widely used for various purposes in buildings, but not often for complete structures.

**Types** Rock occurs naturally all over the world and stone suitable for architectural uses exists in many places. Rock may be classified into three types: igneous, sedimentary, and metamorphic. Igneous rock was formed by the cooling of molten rock or magma, from within the earth. Sedimentary rock consists of various rock materials that were deposited in layers, or strata, by the action of water, held together by cementitious materials. Metamorphic rock is another type that has had its appearance and sometimes its composition changed by the action of pressure, heat, or chemical action.

**Building Stone** Stone used for buildings comes from all three types of rock, including granite from igneous, limestone and sandstone from sedimentary, and marble and slate from metamorphic. Many varieties of these stones are found in the United States, with widely vary-

ing characteristics and properties of strength, maximum and minimum usable sizes, colors, textures, and the like. Some types are occasionally imported from other countries, including a few from quarries that were first worked by the Greeks and Romans. Thus architects and other designers have a wide choice of available building stones.

Among the most important are limestone, granite, sandstone, slate, and marble. Limestone is a hard, durable type that is relatively easy to work and comes in various shades of buff and gray. Granite is a very hard, very strong type that is relatively hard to work. It comes in a range of gray tones, usually with visible specks of mica, quartz, and other minerals, giving it a mottled appearance, and it can be highly polished. Sandstone is moderately hard, easy to work, and comes in a variety of colors. Some sandstones do not weather well, but others are very weather-resistant. Slate may be split into thin forms for use in shingles and flooring; it comes in a limited range of grays, blue-grays, greens, and almost black. Marble is a strong, very durable stone that comes in a variety of colors, often with streaks of other colors. For many centuries marble has been considered the finest building stone, and even today many people would agree. The world *marble* is sometimes loosely applied to limestones, particularly dolomitic types, which can be highly polished.

**Quarrying** Stone is quarried in very much the same manner as it was in ancient times, except for the use today of power machinery and explosives. Rough stone is blasted from quarries with explosives, broken into usable sizes, and used in its rough form or finished. Cut stone is quarried by drilling and cutting channels or sawing and using wedges to break huge blocks, weighing up to 50 tons, from the bedrock. These blocks are then sawed into smaller ones. Smaller blocks are cut into the desired shapes and sizes and finished by polishing or other methods to enhance the texture and color. The final operations may be completed at the quarries or by stone fabricators, located elsewhere.

**Other Building Stones** Rough stone, called fieldstone, just as it comes from the ground and with no cutting or finishing may be used in walls and other building elements. However, the major types used for such purposes are rubble and dimension stone. Rubble, rough and irregular in shape but sometimes roughly squared, is used for walls and other purposes usually, but not always, uncoursed. Dimension stone comes in specific sizes, square and finished to be used in walls, for wall facings or veneers, and other purposes. In larger sizes, dimension stone is often called cut stone and in smaller ones, ashlar, which may be laid in walls in courses and in patterns of large and small pieces. Laid without continuous joints, such stonework is called random ashlar.

Another type of stone, frequently used in architecture, is flagstone, relatively thin, flat pieces, from about 1 to 2 inches thick, that may be either irregular or squared. Flagstone is used, inside and outside of buildings, for flooring, walkways, terraces, stair treads, countertops, and other purposes. Crushed or broken stone is used for a variety of purposes, including aggregates in concrete and terrazzo, and for walks, roads, and surfacing built-up roofs and asphalt building products. Powdered stone is used in paints, resilient flooring, and other products. Relatively massive stone, either rough or finished, used for such purposes as monuments or sculpture, is often called monumental stone.

**Characteristics** Stone comes in a great variety of colors, including red, green, blue, yellow, gray, and various color combinations. Some stones, such as granite, have specks of various minerals that sparkle in the sunlight. Other stones, such as marble, often have streaks of various colors in a monotone background. Cut stone may be obtained from any of several surface textures, including relatively rough finishes imparted by the type of saws used. These include shot-sawed, gang-sawed, and chat-sawed types. Other types of textures may be imparted to stone by bushhammering, peen hammering, and other methods. Stone may also be tooled, by hand or machine, imparting grooves or striations in the face; this very expensive method is rarely used today.

Polished stone may be obtained in various degrees of smoothness. From the least smooth to smoothest, the methods include machined, stone directly from a planer; Carborundum finished, produced by using a Carborundum machine instead of a planer; wet rubbed, treated with abrasives; rubbed and honed; and honed and polished.

**Bonding Methods** Stone is erected in buildings in several different ways, by laying it in mortar, by attaching it with anchors, and sometimes by the use of adhesives. Stone used for structural purposes, as in bearing walls, is laid in mortar either in solid walls or as veneers bonded to back-up materials, such as brick or structural clay tile. Bonding may be accomplished by either laying the stone, and other materials when used, in mortar to interlock with each other, forming a strong integral wall, or by use of metal wall ties. When stone is used as a veneer for other wood-framed structures, it is laid in mortar and tied to the structures with metal ties. Mortar for use with stone, other than fieldstone, must be made with nonstaining cement and white sand to avoid discoloration. When used in curtain walls, stone is usually connected to building frames with metal anchors. High-strength adhesives are sometimes employed to attach thin-stone panels. Stone for flooring, walkways, and the like are ordinarily set in cement seating beds; flagstone is sometimes set in sand beds.

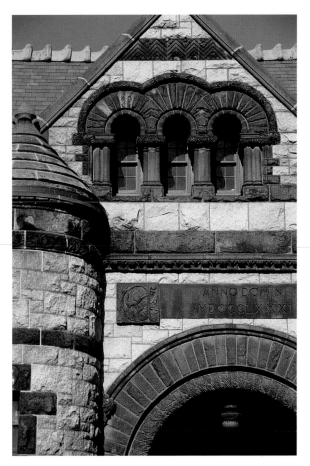

**STONE** Detail, Crane Library (1883), Quincy, Mass. *[Architect: Henry Hobson Richardson]*

In recent years a new series of products have come onto the market in response to the high cost and weight of full-thickness natural stone. These products are thin sections of stone bonded to other materials to strengthen the panels for use on the exterior or interior of buildings. Structurally reinforced stone panels up to 50 feet$^2$ may have only $5/16$ in of marble or granite on the surface; for interior use, the stone may be reduced to $3/16$ in thickness. Stone is also used as aggregates for terrazzo, and marble chips bonded with polyester resins may be used for flooring.

Stone is one of the most important architectural materials. Its long life, beauty, and strength have appealed to architects from almost the beginning of building construction. Many architects today believe that no other material can satisfy specific kinds of requirements in certain elements of buildings as well as stone. However, stonework is relatively expensive, compared to other materials, and must be used with care. It is subject to discoloration and deterioration by water-borne or airborne pollution. Some stones are easily stained by such materials as bronze and other copper alloys, steel, and even some types of wood.

To use stone properly, architects and other environmental designers should familiarize themselves with the properties and characteristics of the various types and follow the recommended practices for their uses. Careful selection must also be made of the proper colors, textures, finishes, and variations in the stone. Samples of stone to be used are always required, as are accurate shop drawings for its fabrication. Delivery problems and shipping costs should be determined, as well as the availability of skilled labor near the locality of building sites.

**History** Although the time of its first use has not been firmly established, stone is believed to have been used, in crude form, as early as 4000 B.C. In the ancient civilizations around the Mediterranean Sea, stone was used for almost all important buildings in areas where it was to be found. Thus in Mesopotamia, where there was little stone, brick and other clay products, such as terracotta, became the primary building materials. In Egypt, where it was plentiful, stone was used. The first important use of stone in construction was for the stepped Pyramid of Zoser (2778 B.C.) in Akkara, Egypt, constructed from relatively small blocks of limestone. Later the Egyptians used very large blocks, in what is called Cyclopean stonework, laid without mortar, named after the mythological one-eyed giant, Cyclops.

The largest stone buildings ever built are the pyramids (c. 2723–2563 B.C.) at Gizeh, Egypt. The largest of the three, the Great Pyramid of Cheops, was originally 480 ft high and 756 ft on the sides at its base. These pyramids were originally encased in fine limestone, but much of their covering has deteriorated or been taken away. As was customary in Egyptian construction, no mortar was used for setting the stone, but a thin lime mortar was used as a lubricant to help in the placement of the blocks. Although many theories have been advanced, no one really knows how the Egyptians, with only simple machinery, were able to construct these pyramids made with pieces of stone that averaged 2½ tons in weight. For columns, obelisks, sculpture, and other important architectural elements of the sort, the Egyptians mostly used single or monolithic stones. Many kinds and qualities of stone were available in Egypt, but the main kinds used were limestone, granite, and sandstone. In ancient Crete and early ancient Greece, stone was used along with wood, brick, and other materials.

As it had been in Egypt, stone was the major building material used for important buildings in ancient Greece. And the Greeks brought the design of stone buildings and their elements to a level of perfection never equaled except, perhaps, in the Gothic cathedrals of the Middle Ages. Stone was plentiful in Greece, a good deal of it being marble, including the famous Pentelic marble, often used in fine buildings, and the equally famous Parian marble, often used in sculpture. The Greeks designed marble building elements to perfection, cut them to perfection, and erected them to very small tolerances for error, usually without mortar.

Instead of the monolithic elements of Egyptian architecture, the Greeks generally built up columns and other architectural elements in pieces. Columns were made with pieces of stone, called drums, which were placed one above the other without mortar, but with very precise joints. The drums were joined to each other with wooden dowels at first and later with iron ones. Sometimes the Greeks covered the buildings with stucco made of fine marble dust, and highly polished. Stone sculptures and carved ornaments of the finest quality were placed by the Greeks on all their most important buildings. As had been that of the Egyptians, Greek architecture was trabeated, or post and lintel.

The Romans also used stone extensively in their architecture. Although they had sources of fine travertine limestone at Tivoli, Luna marble at Carrara, and marble from Siena, most of the other stones were of lesser quality, at least in appearance. Therefore, for stone that was exposed on buildings, the Romans often imported marble and other stone from all over their empire, including the famous quarries in Greece. Stone was used in walls and other architectural elements in a manner similar to that of the Greeks, except that the Romans generally laid it in walls in mortar and often used monolithic stone for columns and similar elements.

The Romans also used rubble stone set in thin beds of mortar. A more widespread use of stone by the Romans was in facings or veneers for buildings constructed of other materials, mainly concrete. Unlike the Egyptians and Greeks, the Romans used the trabeated,

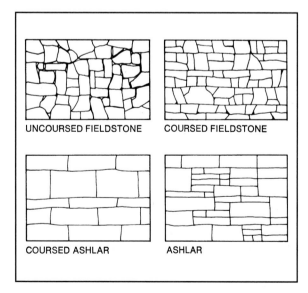

UNCOURSED FIELDSTONE    COURSED FIELDSTONE

COURSED ASHLAR    ASHLAR

**STONE** Typical coursing.

or post and lintel, structural system sparingly, preferring the arcuated structural system, employing arches, vaults, and domes. For such structures, the Romans used stone as well as concrete and brick. They also used stone for sculpture and architectural ornament, often utilizing Greek artists for its creation.

In Early Christian architecture, stone was generally used in a manner similar to that of the Romans, including the use of vaults. Often Roman buildings were stripped of columns and other elements that were then reerected in Early Christian churches. In Byzantine architecture, brick was the material used for most buildings, since almost all stone had to be imported. Unlike Early Christian architecture, which utilized mainly vaults, Byzantine architecture used mainly the brick dome as a structural system. Imported monolithic stone columns were sometimes used, but the major use of stone was in ornamenting almost every available surface, including floors, with patterns made with marbles and other stones of various colors, sizes, and shapes.

During the Romanesque period of architecture, if stone was available, it was used much in the manner of the Romans. In other places, brick was often used. During the Middle Ages, architectural design in stone again became, in Gothic architecture, the dominant material for buildings, using the arcuated structural system, mainly with arches and vaults. However, some buildings were constructed of brick in places where stone was scarce. Stone for use in Gothic architecture was generally cut into smaller pieces than had been done in the past. Most of the stone came from local quarries near the buildings to be constructed, or was transported by ship from quarries located near a waterway to buildings which were also near a body of water.

In Gothic architecture, stone was generally finely cut and fitted, particularly exposed stone. In some cases, especially in large elements such as buttresses, stone rubble laid with lime mortar was used for the structure, with facings of fine cut stone. When using hard stones, such as granite or sandstone, ornament and sculpture were usually more simple and restrained than when using more easily carved stones, such as marble. In Italy, where marbles of various colors were available, some buildings were ornamented with two or more colors of stone, sometimes in strips, or other patterns, producing very rich effects.

During the Renaissance, stone was used extensively, no longer in the rubble method of the Middle Ages but in ashlar, with large pieces of stone, accurately cut and placed in horizontal courses. In Italy, all the fine stones that had been quarried and used by the Romans were employed and new quarries were developed. Local stones were quarried in many other places in Europe. Although stone walls and other elements were sometimes used, a

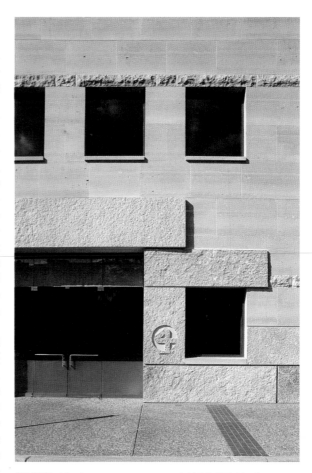

**STONE** Mankato stone exterior, WCCO-TV Headquarters, Minneapolis, Minn. *[Architects: Hardy, Holzman and Pfeiffer]*

more usual method utilized stone facings on building structures of brick or other materials. Another method used brick walls with stone quoins at corners and adjacent to window and door openings.

**American Development** In colonial America, wood and then brick were the major building materials. However, rough stone was often used for foundations of early buildings and for fireplaces and chimneys. Good building stone can be found in many locations in the United States today. A number of these locations were soon discovered, and quarrying sandstone and granite began early in the 17th century in what is now the State of Connecticut. Quarrying coquina, a soft limestone with shells embedded in it, began in Florida a short time later.

By the end of the 18th century, sandstone was quarried in Virginia, North Carolina, Ohio, Pennsylvania, Maryland, and New Jersey. Granite was quarried in New Hampshire and Massachusetts; limestone in Pennsylvania, New Jersey, and Ohio; and marble in Pennsylvania, Vermont, Massachusetts, and Connecticut. By the middle of the 19th century, stone of various kinds was quarried in New York, Michigan, Nevada, Kentucky, Maine, Utah, Tennessee, and Georgia. Stone is still quarried today in most of these places and in others, such as Missouri, California, Colorado, and Arizona.

As time went on, cut stone was used increasingly in the American colonies, mostly for elements of buildings, such as fireplace facings and mantelpieces, stairs, door and window sills, and quoins in conjunction with brick, but sometimes for complete walls of important buildings. Rubble stonework continued to be used to some extent. Cut stone became an important building material during the 19th century, with the development of transportation by railways and canals. Limestone, granite, marble, and sandstone, in particular the variety called brownstone, were all used as structural materials for many of the most important buildings during the Georgian, Classic Revival, Gothic Revival, and Eclectic periods of architecture in the 19th century.

With the beginning of the modern movement in the 19th century, stone was used less frequently for structures. However, it continued to be widely used as facings for buildings constructed of other materials and for elements, such as stairs. Today stone is used on infrequent occasions for bearing walls and other structural elements. The major uses are in thin slabs for curtain walls and veneers; for sculpture, slate roofs, flooring, stairs, garden walls, and monuments; and in such relatively small building elements as chalkboards, countertops, sills, toilet partitions, and so on. Crushed or broken stone is often used as aggregates in concrete and terrazzo, for driveways and walks, as a finish for built-up roofing, and for other purposes.

**Related Articles** ARCH; BRICK; COLUMN; DOME; FIREPLACE; FLOOR; MASONRY STRUCTURE; MONUMENT; ROOF; VAULT; WALL.

**Source of Additional Information** Building Stone Inst., 420 Lexington Ave., New York, N.Y. 10017.

**STORE** A building, sometimes called a "shop," or a room in a building, in which merchandise is sold. Stores constitute one of the most important building types. Stores may have one, two, or many floors. They may be very small or very large, simple and utilitarian or complex and ornate, but all stores have one thing in common: They must be designed to sell goods or they do not succeed.

A look around any city, town, shopping center, or shopping mall reveals a myriad of stores, offering every conceivable product: women's apparel, men's apparel, specialty apparel, such as sportswear and footwear; specialty stores of all kinds; fitness centers, barbers and beauty shops; domestic goods; entertainment; books, cards and gifts; specialty foods; restaurants of all types;

services such as eye care, drug stores, tailors, dry cleaners; banks; and department stores which sell a wide range of merchandise. Whatever the types, whatever the size or combination, the sole purpose of all these establishments is to sell goods to make money. Thus the architectural design problem begins with the question of how to provide spaces in which the products may be merchandised successfully.

The growth of the suburban shopping mall reflects the public's desire to drive on major roads and to park conveniently. This trend has hurt the older downtown centers with congested traffic and limited parking unless the parking issue has been addressed. Convenient access by public transportation has supported many urban stores. Many poorly located older local retail businesses have failed in competition with suburban malls and the growth of national or area chain stores. Stores that have continued have often expanded as tenants in suburban shopping malls. Well-located malls have succeeded more than those which are far from their markets, or where road access is difficult. Some older centers in limited market areas or in competition with newer centers have closed.

**Classifications** Stores are classified as wholesale, those that sell to retail stores and others, who then sell to consumers; and retail, those that sell to consumers. Wholesale stores vary somewhat between industries,

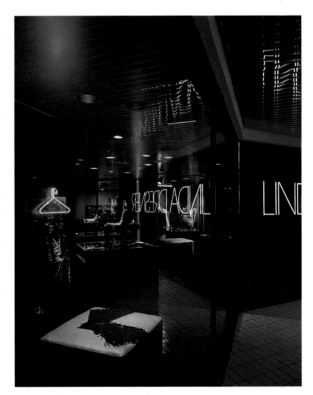

**STORE** Linda Dresner (1985), Troy, Mich. *[Designer: Arthur Smith]*

but all tend to be quite similar, in that they must have showrooms appropriate to the goods offered and to the needs of the business people who are the buyers, adequate warehousing, and often libraries of catalogs.

There are many types of retail stores, which vary considerably. The simplest is the specialty shop which offers only goods of a certain type, such as jewelry, groceries, baked goods, women's wear, and so on. At the other extreme are the large generalized stores that offer many types of goods. One of these is the department store which has specific areas or departments, much like many specialty shops gathered into one store. Some department stores are operated as discount houses, which theoretically sell to consumers at lower prices than are available elsewhere. Another large store is the supermarket, a grocery store in which many types of food and drink are offered in departments, as in a department store.

**Special Types** A special type of store is a mail-order house. These stores may be organized somewhat like large department stores, with a wide range of products, or like single-goods specialty shops. If their business is only by mail order, their merchandising will be entirely by means of advertising mail promotions and catalogs. In other cases, a mail-order business is an adjunct to a regular store and customers have a choice of buying either way.

Another special type is the chain store, one of a group of stores owned and operated by one company or other companies under franchises from the chain. Chain stores exist in the bakery, grocery, drug, clothing, shoe, department, and other industries. Most stores, including chains, are owned by corporations or individuals and operated for profit. A cooperative store is owned by a group of people, its members, and operated for their convenience and benefit, without the store itself making profits. In the past, most generally found in rural communities, cooperatives are now often also located in urban areas. The three major types of cooperatives are marketing, for the selling of goods produced by the members; service, for example, for the purpose of providing loans to its members, operation of cooperative apartments, and the like; and the consumer cooperative, the only type that is actually a store. In the latter type, products are purchased, wholesale, for resale to members and sometimes to the general public.

**Merchandising Principles** The first principles of merchandising goods in stores are that the interest of the potential customer must be aroused and that the store then satisfy the interest. These principles also apply to the architectural design of stores for merchandising. Their actual application in stores varies somewhat according to the types of goods offered. Such goods might be divided into staples, or demand goods, those that consumers regularly need and buy; convenience

goods, those bought at irregular intervals or for special needs; and impulse goods, often luxury items, that consumers might not really need, but to which they are attracted sufficiently to purchase.

At the one extreme in merchandising are the staples, which in a sense are simply collections of needed products conveniently located for easy pickup by shoppers. At the other extreme are the luxury or impulse items that must be sold by the personality, glamour, or other means of the products themselves and the manner in which they are merchandised. Some stores fall at one of the extremes; for example, some supermarkets handle staples only and some specialty shops, only luxury items. Most stores fall in between. Although they may offer products at one extreme, such as staples, they also offer some convenience and impulse or luxury items.

The major considerations in the design of a store of any kind are location, the site, type of merchandise, exterior and interior character, and proper planning of the spaces. Merchandising experts say that the location of a store is all-important. Without a proper location, nothing else can work. However, it is also important that the building be designed properly for its site and for the merchandise offered, a factor intimately related to the type of clientele to be attracted. All these factors must be properly handled in the establishment of the character of the store and in its plan in order to ensure its success.

**STORE** Sandra Collins Craft Store (1992), Birmingham, Mich. *[Architect: Lou Gauchi]*

**Elements** The major elements of a store are the selling areas and the work areas. Both must be planned to operate efficiently and effectively not only as individual units but together. The selling areas begin with the storefront, which establishes the image the store presents to potential customers. The shop windows, if any, should be attractive and contain interesting displays. The entrance should be inviting. The graphic design of signs should help draw customers inside. Inside the store, displays should be arranged for the convenience of both the customers and the salespeople. In addition, they must allow easy and unobtrusive restocking of shelves from the storage areas. As customers are drawn through the store, in some cases primarily by the demand for staple products, they must be motivated to pass convenience items and impulse or luxury goods, inventively placed and displayed. On the other hand, impulse items, such as jewelry, often have the most visual appeal for customers. Next most important are high-impression items, such as women's and men's clothing, and last are the more mundane articles, such as stationery. In any store, the proper placement and display of these types of merchandise must be accomplished. The spaces must also be planned for easy flow of customers, who are drawn from one department, or type of article, to another.

The exterior of the store having established its character and having drawn customers in, the interior must maintain the character and also provide proper fixtures for display of products and proper lighting to show them to their best advantage. Interiors and displays may range from the simple and straightforward through the entire range to the very dramatic. The important thing is to achieve the proper character for the store, the clientele, and the merchandise. The psychology of sales is a study on which much talent, time, and money are continually being spent. To design effective stores, architects must also study this psychology and apply its principles in their designs.

Other important adjuncts of selling areas of stores are cash registers and wrapping stations. These should be conveniently, but safely, located. In a supermarket, there are usually a number of such stations, called checkout counters, located near the exits. In department stores, stations are located in various places convenient to the selling departments. In a small specialty shop, the counter might be out of the way, almost concealed from the customers. Other important spaces related to the selling area are fitting rooms, near clothing sales areas, customer rest rooms and sometimes lounges, cafeterias or other food operations, credit offices, tables for writing cards, and so on. The type of store will determine which of these should be included.

The work areas of stores vary considerably in size but all contain offices and stockrooms. Some stores need large and elaborate storage areas, others only minimal facilities. In addition, certain stores have special requirements, such as alteration rooms for clothing stores, preparation rooms for florists, and special gift-wrapping areas for gift and jewelry shops. All stores require space for electrical and mechanical equipment, janitorial spaces, and the like.

In the past, many stores utilized some forms of automated equipment, such as dumbwaiters for transporting goods from stockrooms to selling areas and pneumatic tube systems for sending sales slips and other paperwork back and forth between sales areas and business offices. Today the trend is toward more use of automation, with certain stores now operating with computer-controlled stocking of shelves and others experimenting with such ideas. Another ubiquitous item is the growing use of electric scanners that read price codes on products, feed the prices into computers, add up the totals, provide inventory control, and furnish the salesperson and customer with a printout indicating the transactions. In less sophisticated systems, the salesperson punches the transaction into a computer terminal and receives the completed sales slip back. Such systems can be expected to become better and more widespread in the future.

**History** Merchandising, at first by barter or trade, has been practiced from the time of the earliest primitive humans. In the beginning, there were no buildings specifically devoted to merchandising. But stores are still one of the oldest building types, having become well established by the 4th century B.C. Stores, in some instances specialty shops, were common in ancient Greece and Rome. Though barter was again prevalent after the time of the Romans, retail stores later became the major means of merchandising. And retail stores of all kinds have proliferated ever since.

**American Development** The early colonists established stores soon after arriving in America. One of the interesting early types was the general store, which came into existence in America in the early 19th century, stocked a little bit of everything, and was a place for people to gather as well. Such stores are still found in rural areas, operated in almost the same manner as in the past. Almost every form of store existed in the early days of merchandising, though it is impossible to date their beginnings accurately. In later times, some of the older practices were again adopted and improved upon. Cooperatives were first founded in the United States in the early 19th century, though the greatest growth of consumer cooperative stores did not occur until after World War I. Some of the chain stores of today were founded in the mid-19th century, but have had their greatest growth in the 20th. Present-day department stores and mail-order stores both started in the late 19th century. Supermarkets, of the type known today, started in the 20th century in America and later spread to other countries around the world. Shopping centers of current types began in the first half of the 20th century and since midcentury have been built all over the United States.

Since the beginning of architecture in the American colonies, many architects have designed stores. Many of these have been well designed and successful in their time, some for quite a long time. In a few instances, store design has produced significant buildings, but for the most part the requirements of the fashions of the time and the changing tastes of people have made specific store designs short-lived, to be soon replaced by other merchandising ideas.

**Related Articles** GRAPHIC DESIGN; SHOPPING CENTER; WAREHOUSE.

**Further Reading** Redstone, Louis G.: *New Dimensions in Shopping Centers and Stores*, 1973, reprint by Krieger, Melbourne, Fla., 1983.

**STRICKLAND, WILLIAM** American architect and engineer (1788–1854). The son of a successful master carpenter, William Strickland spent his early life in and around buildings under construction. Along with another young man destined to become a noted architect,

Robert Mills (1781–1855), Strickland served his apprenticeship with Benjamin Henry Latrobe (1764–1820). Before he was twenty-one, he established himself in an architectural practice that became one of the most successful of the time.

**Works** Strickland's first major building, the Second Bank of the United States (1824), Philadelphia, established him as an important architect. An early Classic Revival building, it also established him as one of the leaders of that movement in architecture. During the next few decades, he designed a number of important buildings in Philadelphia, among them churches, houses, theaters, and other types. Two of his most notable buildings in that city were the Naval Asylum (1833), later called the Naval Home, and the U.S. Mint (1833), both demolished. An even more important building, the Merchants' Exchange (1834), has survived. In 1828 he restored Independence Hall and added the present steeple.

During his career, Strickland handled the engineering for a number of nonbuilding projects. Among these were the survey of a route for the Chesapeake and Delaware Canal (1823), consulting engineer for the Delaware and Raritan Canal (1825), design of the Brandywine Shoal Lighthouse (1827), and the engineering of Delaware Breakwater (1840), Lewes, Del.

**STRICKLAND, WILLIAM** Second Bank of the United States (1824), Philadelphia, Pa.

Important buildings designed by Strickland for locations other than Philadelphia include the U.S. mints at Charlotte, N.C. (1835) and New Orleans (1836); the Athenaeum (1838), Providence, R.I.; and the Tennessee State Capitol (1859), Nashville. He designed numerous buildings and consulted on the U.S. Capitol and other buildings in Washington.

Strickland was one of the most successful American architects. There were good reasons for this. His building designs were accepted and admired. He was a good engineer who insisted on sound practices, good materials, and first-rate workmanship. He was admired for his ability to estimate building costs accurately and to construct buildings within their budgets and within their time schedules. More could scarcely be expected from him as an architect. And his performance might well serve as a model for all those who are or wish to become architects.

**Life** William Strickland was born in Navesink, N.J., in November 1788, the son of a carpenter. Moving the family to Philadelphia in 1790, the father later became the carpenter for the Bank of Pennsylvania (1801), designed by Benjamin Henry Latrobe. This building is considered to be the first in the Greek Revival style in the United States. The young Strickland played around it during the four years it was under construction, and in 1803, at age fourteen, was apprenticed to its architect. Latrobe thought his apprentice to be intelligent and talented but also undependable. After two years Strickland proved him right by leaving the office without notice and going to New York to sketch. In 1808 he returned to Philadelphia and designed his first building, Masonic Hall (1811), in that city.

A talented artist as well as architect, Strickland supported himself during this time mostly by doing engravings for books and magazines, designing theatrical scenery, and surveying. On November 3, 1812, he married Rachel McCollough Trenschard and they had six children. During the War of 1812, he helped survey the defensive positions for Philadelphia and helped supervise the building of redoubts around the city. Attempting to get his architectural practice started after the war, he entered several competitions and finally won that for the Second Bank of the United States. Strickland's former employer, Benjamin Henry Latrobe, won the second prize and promptly claimed that Strickland had stolen his design. The controversy is still debated by architectural historians to this day. In any case, this building established Strickland's reputation as an architect and led to a successful professional career.

Strickland, a convivial man, attracted people and formed lasting friendships, which helped him to acquire architectural commissions and honors. He joined many social and intellectual societies, including the American Philosophical Society and the Pennsylvania Academy of Arts, and served as a director of the latter organization for 28 years. He continued painting and sketching all his life. He liked to travel and made several trips to Europe. He was well thought of as an engineer and served in a number of official engineering capacities. As a result, he was elected a member of the Royal Institution of Engineers in London. He composed songs. He wrote essays not only on architecture but on other subjects, including art criticism. He was one of the founders in 1836, and first president, of the American Institution of Architects, the first national architects' organization, which later failed.

In spite of his many other activities and pursuits, Strickland produced a number of notable buildings. He played an important part in the development of Classic Revival architecture in the United States. In 1845 Strickland moved, with his family, to Nashville, Tenn., where he had been selected to design the Tennessee Capitol, his last major building, finished in 1859, five years after his death. During the years in Nashville, he also designed two churches, one of which is in an Egyptian style, and three monuments. He is believed to have designed a number of houses in and around Nashville. His son, Francis Strickland (1818–95), became an architect and joined his father in the work on the Tennessee Capitol and other buildings. In 1851 Strickland became ill and Francis carried on the work. On April 6, 1854, William Strickland died and, by resolution of the state legislature, was buried in a vault in the Tennessee Capitol building he had designed.

**Related Articles** CLASSIC REVIVAL ARCHITECTURE; LATROBE, BENJAMIN HENRY; MILLS, ROBERT; PUBLIC BUILDING.

## STRUCTURAL ENGINEERING

Within civil engineering, one of the major engineering branches, a specialty field that deals with the engineering design and construction of buildings and other structures to withstand the weight, winds, rain, and snow, and other forces to which they are subjected. Although people who practice structural engineering are actually civil engineers, who have been licensed or registered to perform professional services for work of this kind, they are often called structural engineers. And what they design is the structure of buildings, the framework of walls, columns, beams, floors, roofs, and so on that will withstand the forces to which buildings are subjected.

For the smallest and simplest buildings, such as houses, architects often design the structures along with their other work. For larger and more complex buildings, structural engineers design the structures.

Structural engineers and architects work closely in the design of buildings, perhaps even a bit more closely than do architects with mechanical or electrical engineers. Structure so often strongly influences the form of buildings and is so interwoven with the other aspects of architecture that it is difficult, if not impossible, to produce a good design without their close cooperation.

**Service Phases** Working with the architect, a structural engineer performs services in phases that are like those of the architect, but which are confined to the structure from the foundation to the roof. In the schematic phase, a structural engineer starts by studying the site, the building program, and problems; analyzing the work of the architect; and seeking possible structural solutions. Based on the architectural design studies of the architect, the structural engineer prepares structural design studies that lead to schematic or preliminary drawings showing the proposed structure, preliminary estimates of costs for the construction work, and preliminary specifications that outline elements of the construction of the structure. Still working closely with the architect and with the other engineers and consultants as required, in the design development phase the structural engineer refines the drawings, estimates, and specifications. Upon approval of this work, the structural engineer then prepares, in the construction document phase, the structural contract documents, drawings, and specifications that will be used to construct the structure, and a further refined estimate of costs. After the actual construction has begun, during the construction administration phase, the structural engineer assists the architect in administration and inspects the structural work of the building to guard against defects or mistakes and to ensure that the structure is properly constructed.

During construction, the structural engineer may also have to make supplemental drawings and specifications and perform other services to ensure that the construction moves forward efficiently, on schedule, and within the budget for the building. Upon completion of the building, the structural engineer then makes a final inspection of the work and sometimes prepares as-built drawings, which show the building as it was actually constructed.

Education for structural engineering, together with experience, registration or licensing requirements, and methods of practice, are similar to those for other engineering specialties. (See the article entitled engineering.)

Excellence in architecture today is as much a result of excellence in structural engineering as of almost any other factor. To achieve a high level in architecture, structural engineers and architects must work closely and in harmony. Each must understand a great deal about the work of the other and both must work toward the end of buildings designed in their totality, not just in their parts or details. In addition, the structure is often expressed in the appearance of buildings today.

**History** Until the late 19th century, much of the structural engineering for buildings was done by architects, some of whom were also very talented engineers, who designed bridges, waterworks, and other structures as well. Since that time, many professional structural engineers have made considerable contributions to architecture. Some of them are Othmar Hermann Ammann (1879–1965), Charles S. Whitney (1892–1959), Frederick Severud (b. 1899), Paul Weidlinger (1914– ), Mario Salvadori (1907– ), Tung Yen Lin (1911– ), Lev Zetlin (1918– ), John Skilling, William J. Le Messurier, and Fazlur Rahman Khan (1929–82).

**Related Articles** BUILDING CODES AND STANDARDS; BUILDING INDUSTRY; CONCRETE STRUCTURE; CONSTRUCTION CONTRACT ADMINISTRATION; COST CONTROL; DRAFTING; ENGINEERING; MASONRY STRUCTURE; SPECIFICATION; STEEL STRUCTURE; STRUCTURE; WOOD-FRAME STRUCTURE; WORKING DRAWING.

**Further Reading** Gaylord, Edwin Henry, and Charles N. Gaylord: *Structural Engineering Handbook*, 3rd ed., McGraw-Hill, New York, 1990. See also listing in the article entitled engineering.

**Periodical** *ASCE News*, 345 E. 47th St., New York, N.Y. 10017-2385.

**Source of Additional Information** American Society of Civil Engineers, 345 E. 47th St., New York, N.Y. 10017.

**STRUCTURE** The parts of a building that in the proper combination withstand the weight, wind, rain, and snow, and other forces to which a building is subjected. Structure may also mean a building or something else that has been constructed.

Structure, in the sense of the combination of parts in a building which resists forces, is obviously of great importance in architecture. Without a properly designed and constructed structure, a building may fail in some way or even collapse. If the structure has been properly designed and constructed, it will be strong enough to withstand all the forces to which it may be subjected. Some architects and engineers believe that the structure should be just that strong and no stronger. In addition to the function of providing strength in buildings, many architects believe that structure is one of the primary determinants of architectural design.

**Forces** From an engineering point of view, the primary purpose of structures is resistance to forces, which are the actions of one body upon another, mainly by compression (pushing) or tension (pulling) which cause or tend to cause the body to move. The major forces on the structures of buildings include those imposed by the weights of the buildings themselves, by the people and objects that occupy them, by snow or rain, and by wind. Earthquakes also product great forces on building structures.

Structures for some buildings may be designed by architects, but for most, including all the more complicated ones, structural engineers perform the structural design functions. In either case, structures are designed by using the principles of a branch of physics often called structural mechanics, which is divided into statics, which deals with equilibrium in bodies produced by balanced forces, and strength of materials, which deals with the behavior of bodies which are acted upon by such forces.

In order to work with forces, it is necessary to determine their magnitudes, lines of action, points of application, and directions. When a force, or system of forces, acts upon a building structure, it produces a load in the structure. In this way, a column in a building, for example, may support a certain load placed upon it by the weights above it and other forces, must resist the load without failure, and must transfer it to a foundation and eventually to the ground. In the column the load produces stresses, which are the internal forces within the column that must be resisted.

**Stress** There are four main kinds of stress: tension, compression, shear, and torsion. A tensile stress is produced by pulling on an object and tends to stretch the object. A compression stress comes from pushing on an object and tends to crush it. A shearing stress causes parts of an object to tend to slide past each other or split away from each other. These are the most important stresses dealt with in building structures. The fourth, torsion, is of lesser importance and is caused by twisting forces.

**Loads** There are several kinds of loads on building structures. Dead loads are permanent loads imposed by the weights of the buildings themselves. Live loads are the less permanent loads caused by people, furniture, and so on. Dead loads on a structure may be calculated by adding their weights together. Live loads are determined statistically and experimentally and are specified in building codes. Snow loads are live loads, but are often added to the dead loads since they act only vertically on structures. In some cases, the live loads of heavy rains must also be dealt with. Another kind of load is that imposed by wind. Wind loads are usually considered to act horizontally, though this is not strictly the case. In calculation, wind is customarily considered to act at right angles to roof structures.

Since maximum snow loads and maximum wind loads cannot occur at the same time, the usual assumption for maximum loading on a building structure may be the dead load plus maximum snow load, dead load plus maximum windload and minimum snow load, or dead load plus maximum snow load and minimum wind load. To these must be added live loads, including those of people and objects within the building. In addition, many other loads must be dealt with in certain structures, including those of earthquakes; those caused by pressure of the earth or of water against foundations and basement walls and the like; unusual loads imposed by heavy machinery or other equipment; loads imposed by motion, including that of vehicles or people; and so on. The actual loads to be dealt with in the design of any building structure will be those specified in the appropriate building code for the locality in which the building will be constructed and which conform to good practice in structural engineering.

**Structural Failures** Thus a person who designs the structure of a building must make sure that it conforms to a building code and to good practice. In a sense, this means primarily that neither the structure itself nor any of its parts will fail to perform properly. Failure in a building structure may bring to mind a roof that collapsed or some other dramatic destruction of a building or any of its major parts. In actuality, a structure may fail in any of a number of ways, ordinarily considered to include failures in stability, strength, or stiffness, or because of changes in the materials of the structure.

Stability in a structure means that it has been designed not to tip over, fall down, or move about unduly. It must be noted that buildings do move and this factor must be dealt with in their design. In general, the taller a building is the more it will move. Strength in a building structure is concerned with its ability and that of all its parts to resist, without breaking, the loads placed on them. Stiffness means that a structure and all its parts can resist failure by deformation, any change in the shape or size of the structure or its parts. In some members of structures, such as beams, a deformation of this sort is called deflection and causes them to sag. Excess deflection may cause problems, such as the cracking of plastered ceilings, but can also be extremely dangerous in a structure. Deformation of columns or other members, or buckling, may be equally dangerous. Stiffness in building structures is so important that it often determines the design of certain members.

Changes that may take place in the materials used in building structures are of two major types: those caused by the nature of the materials used, and those caused by deterioration of the materials. In the first instance, a structural designer must thoroughly understand the materials used. Concrete and masonry shrink; wood sags. All materials change sizes, expanding and contracting as temperature rises and falls. And different materials expand and contract at different rates. Each material has its own unique characteristics that must be understood and dealt with.

Deterioration modifies, usually lowering, the loads that structures and structural members can take. Deterioration in building structures may result from many causes, including water infiltration, dry rot, insect activities, fire, chemical changes, abrasion, corrosion,

SPACE FRAME

LAMINATED WOOD ARCH

VIERENDEEL TRUSS

RIGID FRAME

THREE-HINGED ARCH

HINGELESS ARCH

FOLDED PLATE

HYPERBOLIC PARABOLOID

**STRUCTURE** Contemporary types.

**STRUCTURE** Hajj Terminal (1982), King Abdul Aziz International Airport, Jedda, Saudi Arabia. *[Architects: Fazlur R. Khan of Skidmore, Owings and Merrill]*

and bacterial action. These threats must be understood and allowed for in structural designs or their occurrence must be prevented.

**Structural Systems** In the past, structural systems used in architecture were mostly limited to the trabeated, or post and lintel, system using walls, columns, and beams; and the arcuated system, based on the principles of the arch. Today these systems are still widely used, but a vast array of new systems and extensions of old ones are available. The same is true of materials for structures. In addition to wood, brick, and other traditional materials, structures may now be constructed of many types of steel; precast, prestressed, and other forms of concrete; laminated timbers; aluminum; and other materials.

Structural designers today may also utilize new types of domes and vaults, concrete slabs, space frames, lamella systems, laminated wood arches, thin shells, folded plates, stressed-skin systems, suspension systems, rigid frames, a variety of trusses, and other systems. Many of these types of structures were difficult or impossible to design properly in the past. Today new methods of calculation and testing have been developed. The advent of the widespread availability of computers has made complicated calculations feasible which in the past were too time-consuming to be attempted or were virtually impossible.

In practice, not every structure or part of a structure need be calculated. Load tables and other data are available for every structural material and many structural systems. For relatively simple structural problems, such as the sizes of steel beams or wood floor joists to carry given loads under ordinary conditions, a designer of a structure may select proper sizes from tables. In somewhat more complicated problems, it may be necessary for the designer to make a series of calculations. And in the most complex problems, a design may require complicated calculations whose solution may only be practical with computers.

**Structural Expression** Many architects today maintain that structure is one of the primary determinants of architecture, that it should be expressed in buildings, or even exposed in them. Others disagree. This is a difference of opinion that has occurred throughout history. It is only necessary to note the expression of structure in Gothic cathedrals as opposed to the hiding of the structure in many Renaissance buildings to understand the wide divergence of approach. This is not to deny that the structure of a building will, to some extent, determine its total form and effect, but to question the relative importance of the structure in that determination. Many people, including architects, are often confused by discussions on such subjects involving principles of structural honesty, expression, fitness to purpose, and similar subjects frequently engaged in by architects, architecture critics, and others.

Many people find great beauty in objects that are almost pure structural expressions, in fine bridges, for example. Many would agree that great beauty may be found in buildings that express, in more subtle ways, their well-designed, carefully crafted structures. And many architects today attempt to create beauty in their buildings in just such a manner. Other architects exploit the structures of their buildings by exaggeration of the structures to produce sculptural effects or by details that seem to have been designed to look right rather than for the ultimate in structural efficiency. Other architects design buildings in which the essential facts of structure are denied in their appearance.

It would thus appear that many approaches to the structural design of buildings may be taken. It is essential that the approach to structure produce a strong, safe building. The overall influence of structure on the sum total of the architecture of that building is determined by design preference, by the era in which the building is constructed, and by many other social, historic, and cultural factors.

**History** The first building structures made by humans are thought to have been caves. These were followed by simple structures of limbs or poles taken from trees and covered with animal skins or with brush, leaves, or thatch; and mud houses. Since that time, structures for buildings have changed radically over the years into the sophisticated types that are used today.

The earliest wood building structures had pyramidal forms in which the end of limbs or poles were placed around a circle on the ground with their opposite ends leaning inward to form a peak in the middle at the top. In some cases, the limbs or poles were bent into curves, as they rose upward, to increase the headroom inside.

**Structural Developments** After this primitive beginning, the next big development in building structures was the post and lintel, or trabeated, system, still being used today. The most familiar post and lintel buildings today are wood-frame houses, but many steel-framed and concrete buildings also utilize this system.

In the Middle East, another type of structure was developed in about the 25 century B.C. This is the arcuated system, based on the use of arches instead of posts and lintels to support the weights imposed on buildings. Such structures also utilized vaults and domes, which are based on arch principles. In Egypt, though the arcuated system was used occasionally, the trabeated system was most generally used. In Mesopotamia, where stone was almost nonexistent and wood scarce, the arcuated system was often used, but mostly for relatively minor purposes at first.

The ancient Greeks used the trabeated system for the most part. Stone was plentiful and could be quarried in relatively large pieces, and timber was also available. The Greeks, who were so creative in many disciplines including architectural design, were seemingly content to use a structural system from the past and to add to it very little in the way of innovation.

**Roman Engineering Feats** The Romans had a quite different attitude toward building structures. Although not considered as creative in architectural design as the Greeks, the Romans were talented engineers and builders. While the Romans did not usually invent new methods, they were masters of the refinement of older techniques and of their extension to perform daring structural feats not thought possible before. The Romans borrowed the principles of arcuated structures, including arches, vaults, and domes, from the ancient Etruscans, who inhabited west-central Italy. From the ancient Greeks, they borrowed the principles of trabeated, or post and lintel, structures. They then combined the two systems to produce buildings and other structures of great size and complexity. The Romans used all types of available materials, mainly brick, wood, stone, and concrete, utilizing each alone or in combination with others as the occasion demanded.

One of the most striking characteristics of Roman architecture is the great spans they achieved using concrete to form barrel, or semicircular, vaults. Many Roman buildings had vaults spanning as much as 90 ft. The dome of the Pantheon (second century A.D.) spans almost 143 ft and is still the largest masonry dome in the world. The Romans also built very tall buildings and other structures. The Flavian Amphitheater, usually called the Colosseum (A.D. 82), is almost 158 ft high. The great aqueduct near Nîmes, France, the Pont du Gard (about A.D. 14), is 155 ft high, and other Roman buildings and structures approach these heights.

The Romans also surpassed, in sheer size, the buildings constructed previously. The Circus Maximus (1st century A.D.), used mainly for chariot races, measured 650 ft wide by 2,000 ft long, and seated 255,000 spectators, more than twice the number of the largest stadiums in the United States. The Temple of Jupiter (second century A.D.) in Baalbek, Lebanon, amply demonstrates the Roman penchant for size. Although the temple is of modest height, 126 ft, the substructure or platform on which it rests is almost 40 ft. high and some of the stones in it measure about 64 by 11 by 14 ft, and each weighs about 725 tons.

Although the Romans used domes extensively and for long spans, they almost always placed them over circular or polygonal substructures because of the problems in building them over square structures. Pendentives, a method of using curved wall surfaces to make the transition from a square structure below to a round dome above, were used by the Romans but only on relatively small and minor buildings.

**Domes** In Byzantium, later renamed Constantinople and still later Istanbul, now part of Turkey, the art of building with domes became highly developed beginning about the 4th century. The Byzantines often used pendentives to allow their domes to cover square spaces below. They also developed a system of smaller domes and partial domes which would resist the forces of the main dome. They developed drums, circular structures placed beneath domes to raise them higher and to permit windows below the bases of the domes. The greatest expression of Byzantine architecture is thought to be the Church of the Holy Wisdom (537), Istanbul, formerly called Santa Sophia but now more generally called the Hagia Sophia.

**Skeleton System** During the period immediately preceding the Middle Ages, no great structural innovations were made. However, the beginnings could be detected of what was to become a revolutionary change during the Middle Ages. The structural systems of the Romans and others who came before them were based mainly on the principle that great masses of stone or other materials could be made to resist the forces of each other by placing them in opposing positions in sufficient quantities. Now a structure system was developed that discarded the principles of great opposing masses and replaced it with one in which each structural member was designed to perform its exact purpose without excess bulk or weight.

Thus, beginning about the 9th century, master buildings began to develop the system which would result in the great soaring, relatively light, skeleton structures of the Gothic style. This was an arcuated system, using the principles of the arch to produce great vaults, at first round and later pointed. These vaults were

**STRUCTURE** Minneapolis Convention Center. *[Architects: The Leonard Parker Assoc. et al.]*

constructed at right angles to each other so that each of a pair of intersecting vaults resisted the forces of the other. Eventually, the system became so sophisticated that the major functions of the intersecting vaults could be performed by ribs at the intersections, while the spaces between the ribs could be filled with light materials having only minor structural purposes. As time went by, all the structural members were gradually reduced to the minimum sizes that would serve their purposes, making possible the high, light structures of the great Gothic cathedrals in many places all over Europe.

During the Middle Ages, progress was also made in the use of wood for structures. For example, in earlier buildings, wood-framed roofs ordinarily utilized timbers that were placed as rafters or joists, each acting almost independently in carrying the loads placed on the roofs. During the Middle Ages, various types of timber trusses were developed, thus strengthening and lightening roof structures and allowing longer spans than before. These trusses were designed so that a number of pieces of timber could be fastened together in a manner that allowed the entire structure to work as a unit in resisting the loads placed upon it.

**Scientific Calculation** The Renaissance was marked by a reawakening of interest in classic Greece and Rome and a turning away from the Middle Ages. It has been said that Renaissance architecture was mostly based on aesthetics and therefore the major contributions to architecture were in ornament and aesthetic design. The architects of the time deserted the Gothic structural forms, for the most part, including ribbed vaults and pointed arches, to return to semicircular arches and especially domes.

Perhaps the most important development in structures, during the Renaissance, was the introduction of scientific methods of calculation. Renaissance architects utilized these methods to design the structures of the great vaults and domes. Among the most dramatic

results were the development of revolutionary methods for designing domes, including the use of chains to resist forces in them and the construction of domes with double, later triple, shells. They also developed the first timber trusses with diagonal members to withstand forces, a method which is still used today. The science of mechanics and strength of materials became established during the Renaissance, paving the way for the future development of structural engineering. The testing of materials, now standard procedure, also began at that time.

**Iron Structures** After the Renaissance period, scientific and engineering study of structures and related subjects accelerated and considerable progress was made. New developments in structures were not far behind. In 1781 the first major structural use of cast iron was made in a bridge at Coalbrook Dale, England, still in use. Many others soon followed. The first important structural uses of iron, both cast and wrought, in buildings occurred in France in the late 18th century, as framing for roofs. Soon afterward, iron began to be used in buildings in England and in 1803, William Strutt built what was probably the first building, a mill, with a complete iron frame. From this beginning, the use of iron for building frames spread all over Europe and to the United States. The construction of the great Crystal Palace (1851), London, designed by Sir Joseph Paxton (1801–65), with an iron frame combined with glass, had a considerable effect on architecture all over the world.

After the time of the Romans, concrete as a structural material fell into disrepute. In the early 19th century, methods were developed for making what came to be called portland cement, a product still very much in use today. As time went by, concrete again began to be used in building structures, but only in a limited way. Concrete was not to equal the importance it had in Roman times until the 20th century.

During the latter half of the 19th century, the use of cast-iron structural frames for buildings increased. New methods for making wrought iron were introduced, as were methods for rolling beams of this material, leading to its increased use in buildings. Another development was the construction of iron trusses.

**Reinforced Concrete** In the early 19th century, iron was experimentally embedded in concrete, thus creating a composite material in which the concrete could withstand compressive forces and iron, tensile forces. In this way, a new type of structural material, eventually to be called reinforced concrete, was developed, possessing the best qualities of both concrete and iron. By the second half of the 19th century, reinforced concrete was used for the structures of both bridges and buildings. Later new and improved methods of calculation made it possible for reinforced concrete to achieve its current prominence as a 20th-century structural material. Beginning in 1905, precast concrete has also been widely used in buildings. Although steel had been developed many years before, the Eiffel Tower (1889), in Paris, designed by Alexandre Gustave Eiffel (1832–1923), was designed with a wrought-iron structure.

**New Structural Frames** Beginning in the 1800s and continuing in the present century, structural innovations have occurred regularly and rapidly. About 1830, the invention of the balloon-frame system revolutionized wood structures. This system utilized relatively small, light-wood members which could be erected by semiskilled labor quickly and efficiently. Instead of relying only on the strength of individual posts or columns, beams, and so on, a balloon-frame building has walls, floors, and roof constructed in such a way that all act together to resist forces. For well over 100 years, the balloon frame was the preferred structural method for houses in the United States and in other places. It has now largely been replaced by a similar but even newer and simpler method called western, or platform, framing.

Another great and important innovation was the invention of the metal skeleton frame. Until the late 1800s, buildings generally had heavy masonry bearing walls which supported the weights of the floors and other elements above them. The Home Insurance Building (1885), in Chicago, since demolished, designed by William Le Baron Jenney (1832–1907), became the first building in which the entire structure was of skeleton construction, utilizing both cast and wrought iron and the first Bessemer steel used in any building. This was the beginning of the era of tall, skeleton-framed buildings that still continues today.

**Structural Theory** Other important developments have taken place since the beginning of the 20th century. New structural theory has been developed that allows the design and construction of ever more innovative structures. New testing methods have been developed. And the widespread use of computers in structural design, beginning about the middle of the century, has made possible calculations that were virtually impossible before. Structural theory has now become so complex that only computers can make the most complicated calculations possible or practicable.

New types of structures have been developed in the past few decades. Among the most important are curved structures of various kinds, including domes and shells of concrete and other materials in such shapes as segments of spheres or cylinders, hyperbolic paraboloids, hyperboloids, conoids, and others. Another type of relatively new structure is the space frame, an assembly of relatively small structural members into a three-dimensional framework that for its own weight can resist relatively large forces. Among the best-known space frames are the geodesic domes designed by R. Buckminster Fuller (1895–1983).

Other types of structures developed during the last few decades include prestressed concrete, pneumatic structures inflated by air pressure, long-span systems, and many others. Also having an impact on structures is the advent of prefabricated and industrialized systems and those in which structural systems are integrated with lighting, heating, air-conditioning, and other service systems.

The use of structures in America parallels their use elsewhere. In the earliest colonial times, the first buildings had wood structures, followed by ones of brick and stone. As wrought and cast iron began to be used in Europe, these materials were also employed in structures in the United States. The same is true of concrete structures and those of other types.

**Related Articles** ARCH; BUILDING CODES AND STANDARDS; CONCRETE STRUCTURE; CONSTRUCTION MATERIALS; DESIGN, ARCHITECTURAL; DOME; FIRE PROTECTION; MASONRY STRUCTURE; SEISMIC DESIGN; STEEL STRUCTURE; STRUCTURAL ENGINEERING; WEATHER PROTECTION; WOOD-FRAME STRUCTURE; Various articles on building systems, components, and materials.

**Further Reading** Ambrose, James: *Building Structures,* 2d ed., John Wiley, New York, 1993; Ambrose, James: *Simplified Design of Masonry Structures,* John Wiley, New York, 1991; Ambrose, James, and Dimitry Vergun: *Simplified Building Design for Wind and Earthquake Forces,* 2d ed., John Wiley, New York, 1990; American Institute of Timber Construction: *Timber Construction Manual,* 3rd ed., John Wiley, New York, 1986; Orton, Andrew: *Structural Design of Masonry,* 2d ed., John Wiley, New York, 1993; Schuller, Wolfgang: *High-Rise Building Structures,* John Wiley, New York, 1977, reprint of 2d ed., Krieger, Melbourne, Fla., 1986; Thorton, Charles H.: *Exposed Structure in Building Design,* McGraw-Hill, New York, 1992.

**SULLIVAN, LOUIS HENRI** American architect (1856–1924). Although not recognized as such during his own lifetime, Louis Henri Sullivan has now come to be regarded as the first great Modern American architect.

**Appraisal** Sullivan struggled to free architecture from adherence to styles of the past, from decoration for its own sake, from suppression of the functions of buildings to their appearance. Instead, he formulated principles that called for architecture which fulfilled the needs of people in their own time, which expressed such social needs in buildings that reflected the technology of their own times. His oft-quoted dictum, that form follows function, was probably first used by sculptor and writer Horatio Greenough (1805–52). In any case, it became a major principle in the philosophy of later Modern architects, including Frank Lloyd Wright (1867–1959) who worked and studied with Sullivan. In this, as in his buildings and in his famous writings, *Kindergarten Chats* (1901–02) and *Autobiography of an Idea* (1924), Sullivan was something of an enigma.

He did not always adhere to his own dictum in his buildings, and his writings contain much that is ambiguous. He struggled mightily to become an architect, achieved a high level of important work for a relatively brief period of about 12 years (1888–1900), and sank into almost anonymous, debt-ridden obscurity, made worse by alcohol. He was rescued, at least partly and temporarily, by the publication of the *Autobiography* in the *AIA Journal,* during 1922–23, shortly before his death. Later his reputation was restored and enhanced by the many talented architects, in Europe as well as the United States, who acknowledged him to be the progenitor of Modern architecture. In this vein, it is interesting that the American Institute of Architects, which had partly supported him with payments for his *Autobiography,* finally gave him its highest award, the Gold Medal, in 1946, 22 years after his death.

The enigma of his life, his buildings, and his writings, and the late-coming recognition do not detract from his importance. His buildings are important, not only for their overall designs but for his dedication to function and use of ornament. His philosophies are important. Their threads can be found running through architecture to this day. The miracle is that he was able to accomplish what he did, under adverse circumstances, in a short period of time, in only some 30 buildings and two major books.

**Works** In 1879 Sullivan went to work for Dankmar Adler (1844–1900) and afterward formed a partnership with him. The first important building that felt the imprint of what was to become Sullivan's style and philosophy was the Borden Block (1880), Chicago. In this building, now demolished, could be seen the beginnings of the architect's experimentation with newer types of structure and with what was to become his manner of handling the form and ornamentation of tall buildings. This was followed by another early example, the Chicago Joint Board Building (formerly Troescher) built in 1884 in Chicago, in which these themes were further developed and refined. The Auditorium (1890), also in Chicago, went still further, especially in the use of ornament in the interior.

During the years following the Auditorium, Sullivan as an individual, and Adler and Sullivan as a firm, continued to innovate and mature. This period produced a number of notable Chicago buildings, including the Garrick Theater in the Schiller Building (1892) and the Transportation Building (1893) at the World's Columbian Exposition (1893), both demolished later, and the Stock Exchange Building (1894). Sullivan also

found time to develop further his use of ornament on some tombs, such as those for the Ryersons (1889) and the Gettys (1890) in Chicago, and for the Wainwrights (1892) in St. Louis. The Ryersons' tomb was designed for the family which had commissioned Adler and Sullivan to design the Ryerson Building (1884) in Chicago, now demolished. The Wainwright family had commissioned a building by the architects, the Wainwright Building (1891), St. Louis, still in existence and considered one of their masterpieces. The Wainwright is considered to be the first tall building to be designed so that its steel skeleton frame is expressed in the exterior appearance. Soon to follow was the Prudential Building (formerly Guaranty), built in 1895 in Buffalo. This was the last building of Adler and Sullivan. Their partnership dissolved, and Sullivan continued on his own.

It has been said that the career of Louis Sullivan was marked for decline by the dissolution of his partnership with Dankmar Adler. It is true that within five years or so, his private practice had almost disappeared and after that he produced only a few small buildings. But within the five years, he produced what is now considered one of his best buildings, and perhaps the most Modern, the most noteworthy example of his philosophy and style.

**SULLIVAN, LOUIS HENRI** Interior, Charnley House (1891), Chicago, Ill. *[Architects: Adler and Sullivan (Photo: Nick Merrick/Hedrich-Blessing)]*

**SULLIVAN, LOUIS HENRI** Guaranty Building (1896; later alterations; restored, 1983), Buffalo, N.Y. *[Architects: Adler and Sullivan; architects, restored: Cannon Design; dePolo/Dunbar]*

This is the Carson, Pirie, Scott Department (formerly Schlesinger and Mayer) Store (1904; see illustration), Chicago, highly praised for the restrained (almost spare) purity of its exterior appearance, but has also been criticized for its lack of architectural character in the interiors. Other important Sullivan buildings, produced on his own, are the Condict (formerly Bayard) Building (1898), his only New York City building, and the Gage buildings (1899), Chicago.

During his later years, Sullivan produced a series of small, Midwestern banks, some of which are admired for their architectural form, and all, in varying degrees, for their use of ornament. The best is the earliest, Security (formerly National Farmers') Bank, built in 1908, in Owatonna, Minn. Others are People's Savings Bank (1911), Cedar Rapids, Iowa; Poweskiek Co. (formerly Merchant's National) Bank (1914), Grinnell, Iowa; People's Savings and Loan Association (1917), Sidney, Ohio; and Farmer's and Merchant's Union Bank (1919), Columbus, Wis.

**Functional Architecture** During his lifetime Sullivan was an outspoken advocate, in both his buildings and his writings, of what came to be called Modern architecture. He turned away from the styles of the past, and the mixing of such styles, eclecticism, to what he thought of as functional architecture that expressed in its appearance the uses to which it was to be put, the materials of which it was made, and the new skeleton struc-

tures that supported it. He also became one of the leading proponents of the Chicago school of architects, a group composed of Jenney and the younger architects who had worked for him, the most noted, Sullivan, Holabird, Roche, and Burnham and others influenced by him, including Adler and Root. With some help from a few others, these men invented and developed the architecture of the early Modern Chicago tall buildings, or skyscrapers. They strongly influenced the architecture of the future. In this, Sullivan played a leading role, one not really appreciated in his lifetime but more apparent in the years after his death.

**Life** Louis Henri Sullivan was born in Boston, on September 3, 1856. As a youth, he spent most of his summers on the farm of his maternal grandparents near Boston and lived with them other times. Here he acquired an interest in and curiosity about nature and craftsmanship, interests that continued the rest of his life and that were reflected in his architecture. Having decided early that he wanted to be an architect, he entered Massachusetts Institute of Technology in 1872, at age sixteen. He stayed about a year, thus beginning what was to be a sketchy education at best.

He went to New York where he visited Richard Morris Hunt (1827–95) and then to Philadelphia, where

**SULLIVAN, LOUIS HENRI** Detail, Carson, Pirie, Scott Store (1899; addition, 1904), Chicago, Ill. *[Architects: Adler and Sullivan]*

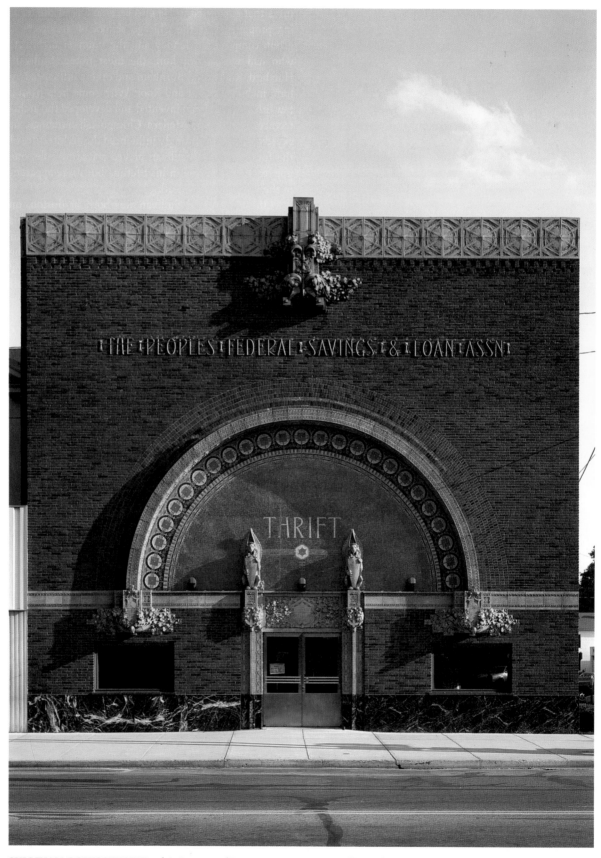

**SULLIVAN, LOUIS HENRI** People's Savings and Loan Association (1917), Sidney, Ohio.

he was hired as a draftsman by the firm of Furness and Hewitt. Lack of work caused him to leave this firm shortly after he was hired. He then went to Chicago where his parents were living and to work for William Le Baron Jenney (1832–1907) for a short time, leaving in 1874 to continue his education at the École des Beaux Arts in Paris. This attempt lasted only about six months and, much disillusioned, he was back in Chicago by early 1875.

After having worked as a draftsman in several Chicago offices, he joined the firm of Dankmar Adler, a moderately successful Chicago architect, in 1879. The talents of the practical-minded, engineering-oriented Adler were perfectly complemented by those of the romantic, design-oriented younger man. In 1881 Sullivan was made a full partner in the firm, renamed Adler and Sullivan, a partnership that was to last almost 15 years and produce some of the masterpieces of that era.

Frank Lloyd Wright joined the firm in 1887 and remained until 1893. This association between Sullivan and Wright profoundly affected the lives and the architecture of both men. Wright always acknowledged his debt to Sullivan, whom he called his master. And Sullivan's own philosophy and work derived much of value from Wright.

During the panic and subsequent depression of 1893, building construction came to a virtual standstill. The firm of Adler and Sullivan held on until 1895, when it was dissolved. During the next five years, Sullivan did not exactly prosper. But these were the years that saw the flowering of his talents.

Sullivan's career then went downhill. His designs had never become acceptable enough to bring him an adequate number of clients. He sank into despondency brought on by the slipping of his practice and by drink. At the time of the climax of his career, in 1899, he married Margaret Hattabough, but she left him in 1906, and the marriage ended in divorce in 1917. From 1900 until his death, Sullivan produced only a few buildings, interesting in their designs but modest in size, a few stores and offices, a few small banks, a church in Cedar Rapids, Iowa, and two houses. He died in Chicago, in April 1924, in obscurity, his philosophy and buildings admired by only a few, his accomplishments not yet fully appreciated.

**Related Articles** FURNESS, FRANK; HUNT, RICHARD MORRIS; JENNEY, WILLIAM LE BARON; MODERN ARCHITECTURE; RICHARDSON, HENRY HOBSON; WRIGHT, FRANK LLOYD.

**Further Reading** Sullivan, Louis: *The Autobiography of an Idea*, Dover, New York, 1956; Sullivan, Louis: *Kindergarten Chats on Architecture, Education and Democracy*, Dover, New York, 1980; Twombly, Robert: *Louis Sullivan—His Life and Work*, University of Chicago Press, 1986.

**SURVEYING** A branch of civil engineering concerned with measuring land, determining points on the land and their relationships, areas, and relative heights or elevations. Another kind of surveying is the detailed analysis of materials and equipment with which to construct buildings. This type of surveying is called quantity surveying in Great Britain. For further discussion on quantity surveying, see the article entitled cost control.

**Types** There are many types of surveying, including hydrographic surveying, which is concerned with shore lines and bottom contours of water bodies; land surveying (including geodetic), which takes into account the curvature of the earth and is used for large areas; and plane surveying, in which the earth is considered flat, and is used for smaller areas. Other types are named according to their purposes: topographic surveying, for establishing heights or depths, called elevations, of earth features and for producing data for contour maps that have lines of constant elevation; route surveying, for highways and railroads; mine surveying; underground surveying, for locating underground features, such as pipes or tunnels; and construction or engineering surveying, for constructing buildings and other structures. Types of surveying are also classified by the major instruments employed, such as plane table, transit, and photogrammetric surveying.

**Instruments** A plane table is a drawing board on a tripod with an alidade, a combination ruler and telescope; it is used for rapid work not requiring a great degree of accuracy. A transit is an optical instrument with a telescope that can be elevated or depressed and turned horizontally, mounted on a tripod and with a plumb bob for accurate positioning. A transit is fitted with accurate scales with verniers, devices for reading small fractions of degrees, and spirit levels, and can be used to measure vertical and horizontal angles accurately. A transit can also be used for measuring distances and elevations by sighting at a surveyor's rod held by an assistant at distant points. Photogrammetry involves the use of photography in surveying. A theodolite is similar to a transit, but much more accurate.

Other important tools of surveyors are measuring devices, including Gunter's, or surveyor's, chain; the engineer's chain; and the steel tape. A Gunter's chain is 66 ft long and is divided into 100 links. Gunter's chain came into widespread use because it was useful in laying out land. An acre, 43,560 ft$^2$, is exactly 10 square chains; or a piece of land 1 chain wide by 100 chains long contains 1 acre. More prevalently used today is the steel tape, which comes in lengths of 50, 100, and 200 feet. For very precise work, tapes made of invar, an alloy of nickel with steel, are used because they are less affected by temperature changes than regular steel tapes. Surveyor's rods of this material are also used for the same reason.

Another instrument used in surveying is the level, a device much like a transit except that it can be used only for measuring elevations, not for distances or angles. Land and construction surveying are the types most used in architecture, for several purposes, including the layout of housing and other developments, such as roads and streets, and in the establishment of property lines in subdividing land. A most important use of surveying in architecture is in connection with the actual design and construction of buildings. Before proceeding with the design of a building, an architect needs accurate information on the boundary lines and topography of the site; location of streets, curbs, pavements, and utilities; location of buildings or other structures on or adjacent to the site; and location of trees and other major landscaping features. At the beginning of construction, a building must be accurately laid out, as to its position, shape, size, and height. As the construction proceeds, surveying is used to check progress, to correct errors, and to make adjustments, until the building has been completed and its grounds have been landscaped.

**New Technology** Recent changes in surveying include the use of total stations, which consist of a theodolite (transit), electronic infra-red beam distance meter, and a small computer to record survey data which may be downloaded to an office computer. The Global Positioning System (GPS) allows engineers to determine true positions from readings taken from two or more satellite positions, which can then be downloaded to a computer to precisely fix the point ($x$, $y$, and $z$ axis) where the readings were taken. Field electronic calculations are used by COGO computer programs to collect and sort data from the field to generate a computerized drawing of a site plan. Other computer programs provide readings of an original survey and a new site plan for automated cut-and-fill calculations. Computerized drafting programs allow multiple overlay site drawings for different purposes, such as paved areas, utility lines, and site drainage. Current zoning laws now identify provisions for the protection of the environment, including flooding, chemical pollution, water detention and retention ponds, and the protection of wetlands. Refer to the article entitled environmental protection.

**Career** For a person who likes to work out-of-doors with precision instruments, often on a great variety of projects, such as buildings, dams, bridges, and highways, surveying offers attractive career opportunities. Since surveying theory and practice are based on mathematics, in particular geometry and trigonometry, a person considering this field should have aptitudes and education in those subjects. Professional engineers, in particular civil engineers, study surveying and many continue to do surveying after graduation. Another way to learn surveying is in technical schools and through experience in the field.

In most of the states, surveyors must become registered or licensed to practice surveying. Typically, the requirements for licensing or registration include six years of acceptable experience, for two years of which acceptable work in an accredited engineering school may be substituted. Candidates for licensing or registration must also pass written examinations lasting one or two days in basic sciences and mathematics; in the principles, theory, and practice of surveying; and in law and ethics. Land surveying boards of the states are often part of the same bodies that regulate architectural and engineering registration or licensing, but in some cases are separate organizations.

**History** Surveying is an occupation of humans that dates back to ancient times and which had been developed to a high degree of sophistication by the ancient Egyptians. Surveying has held an important place in the history of architecture ever since.

**American Development** In early colonial America, surveyors laid out township lines and divided the townships into lots. As people pushed west to settle, the early pioneer surveyors were often the first to arrive, braving the dangers of wild animals, weather, and unfriendly Indians. Surveying has always been considered an honorable profession, and many early Americans who were to make their marks later in other fields started as surveyors. Some of the most famous were George Washington (1732–99), Thomas Jefferson (1743–1826), and Daniel Boone (1734–1820).

By the time Washington did his first surveying in the Shenandoah Valley of Virginia in 1748, almost all the major present-day instruments, except the steel tape, were available, though mostly in elementary forms. Since that time, more accurate instruments have become available and old methods have been improved, and new ones developed, such as photogrammetry, which utilizes photographs, especially aerial photographs, for making surveys.

**Related Articles** CONSTRUCTION, BUILDING; COST CONTROL; REAL ESTATE; STRUCTURAL ENGINEERING.

**Further Reading** Breed, Charles B., and George L. Hosmer: *Principles and Practice of Surveying—Elementary Surveying,* 11th ed., John Wiley, New York, 1977; Davis, R. E., and F. S. Foote: *Surveying: Theory and Practice,* 6th ed., McGraw-Hill, New York, 1981.

**Periodical** *Surveying and Mapping,* Woodward Building, Washington, D.C. 20005.

**Sources of Additional Information** American Congress of Surveying and Mapping, 54410 Grosvenor Ln., Bethesda, Md. 20814-2122; American Society of Civil Engineers, 345 E. 47th St., New York, N.Y., 10017.

**THEATER** A building or outdoor structure in which audiences watch actors, musicians, and dancers perform. Theaters are sometimes called playhouses.

**Types** An opera house is a kind of theater in which operas, or musical dramas are presented, while a concert hall is a theaterlike building for the performance of music alone by orchestras, bands, instrumental soloists, or singers. Some theaters have specialized purposes, as a ballet theater, primarily intended for dance performances. Sometimes buildings in which motion pictures are shown are called motion picture theaters. Also buildings in which radio and television shows are enacted are sometimes called theaters, though the more proper term is studio.

Some theaters are used for only one type of performance, such as operas or plays, but others may be used for several or all types. An amphitheater is an outdoor theater often semicircular or elliptical in plan. An arena theater is one in which the seating for the audience surrounds the stage in the middle. Sometimes a theater in which plays are performed is called a legitimate theater.

An auditorium is a room in a building, such as a school, college, or university, used for theatrical and musical performances, meetings, instruction, or other similar gatherings of relatively large groups of people. The word *auditorium* is also used for the part of a theater occupied by the audience. The auditorium is often divided in sections, including the main area or orchestra, on the main floor; the balcony, a gallery projecting over part of the orchestra, or sometimes more than one; the loge, the front part of the lowest balcony; and private seating areas, sometimes called boxes.

**Elements** All the above types of buildings are essentially theaters and their design, though it varies in details, is similar. The two major parts of a theater are the public areas, sometimes called the front, and the pro-

duction areas, called backstage. The major element in the front of a theater is the auditorium which the audience occupies; the major element backstage is the stage, on which the performance takes place. These two elements may be combined in theaters in three major ways: in a proscenium theater; a thrust-stage, or open-stage, theater; and an arena theater.

In a proscenium theater, there is a wall between the stage and auditorium, with an opening framing the stage on which the performance is held. The audience sits in rows of seats on one side of the wall; the stage is on the other. A curtain covers the opening and is lifted or drawn aside when a performance begins, and closed when an act or a performance ends. Behind the wall, on either side of the opening, are spaces on the stage called wings. Above the stage is a space called the flies, or fly loft, used for scenery and other equipment which may be raised or lowered by ropes and other rigging.

In a thrust-stage, or open-stage, theater, the stage projects into the auditorium, allowing the audience to be seated around the stage on three sides. One advantage of the open stage is the possibility of action that is more three-dimensional than that on the more traditional proscenium stage.

An arena stage takes the principles of the open stage full circle, by placing the stage in the middle of the auditorium, completely surrounded by the audience. This is often called theater-in-the-round. Some theaters have been designed so that they can be converted from one type to another as occasion demands.

Other elements of the backstage areas are dressing rooms for the actors; property rooms for storage of props; storage rooms, called docks, for scenery; rehearsal rooms; green rooms, in which performers may relax or receive visitors; shops for making and repairing costumes, props, and scenery; and offices. In addition, the-

631

aters have prompters' boxes at the front of stages and sunken spaces in front of the stages, called orchestra pits.

In addition to the auditorium, the front of a theater must have a lobby or foyer, or both, for circulation of the audience into and out of the theater and, nearby, rest rooms, ticket office, and checkroom. Some theaters also have lounges, restaurants, bars, and cocktail lounges.

In a proscenium theater, the performers enter and leave the stage via the wings. In an arena theater, this is accomplished by openings between groups of seats, called vomitories, at various points in the auditorium. In an open-stage theater, performers may make entrances and exits through the back of the stage and through vomitory tunnels under the auditorium.

**Design** In the design of any theater, the major considerations are circulation of the audience, seating and sight lines of the audience, good acoustics, safety, lighting, and proper relationships between the various front and backstage elements. The audience should be able to enter the theater with ease, have adequate space in the foyer or lobby, with rest rooms and other conveniences nearby, and easy access to their seats through adequate aisles and spaces between rows of seats. The stage should be in the proper relationship with the auditorium to allow good sight lines from any seat in the house. For the same purpose, seating in theaters is placed on inclined floors, rising away from the stage, and often the rows of seats are curved. Ratios have been established between the depths of auditoriums and their widths for optimum viewing for different kinds of theaters.

Good acoustics are all-important in theaters. The acoustics of theaters are affected by many factors, such as the shape of the stage and the auditorium, the materials, the placement and size of the audience, and so on. The design of theater acoustical systems is therefore very complex and is usually performed by specialists.

Many disastrous theater fires have occurred in the past, some with the loss of a considerable number of lives. Today there are stringent codes and regulations governing design for safety in theaters. The number and position of exits, the widths of aisles, the number of seats next to each aisle, and the locations of storage rooms are all fixed by law. Panic bars, which open doors when pushed from inside the building, are required. Scenery, curtains, and other materials must be made nonflammable and fire-resistant. High-risk areas must be protected by automatic sprinkler systems. Exit lights must be provided.

Lighting in theaters is of two major types: the lighting of the public areas and the lighting of the stage. In the public areas, lighting is similar to that in other building types used by the public, except that in the auditorium, provisions must be made for dimming the lights,

bringing the house lights down at the beginning of performances and up at intermissions and at the end of performances.

Stage lighting is a complex art. Many types of lights are used in a great variety of positions, colors, and conformations, designed and timed to fit the action taking place on the stage. The lights are controlled by electricians, trained for this work, who operate complicated switchboards, called control boards or consoles. The design of stage lighting for theaters is complex and is performed by specialists in this field.

The major relationships between the front and backstage elements of theaters are those between the lobby or foyer and auditorium, between the auditorium and stage, and between the stage and other backstage areas. These must be designed to work effectively and efficiently for the audience, the performers, and the stagehands and other workers backstage. For example, a very important aspect of theater design is the provision for easy changing or moving of sets, scenery, and props.

**Special Needs** Theaters of various types have some special requirements. For example, a motion picture house must have an adequate projection booth from which the projectors can project films. Today almost every type of theater has a projection booth. In drive-in motion picture theaters, automobile parking, with individual sound speakers, must be provided for the audience, along with a projection house that is sometimes combined with a snack bar or other refreshment facility; in some, seating areas are provided for those who walk in.

In some theaters, special stages are provided. Some roll into and out of place, and some revolve, allowing several sets to be installed in advance and brought onstage when needed. Amphitheaters present special problems to designers, since it is more difficult to provide proper acoustics, lighting, and so on, outdoors. Auditoriums, particularly those in schools, colleges, and universities, often have requirements for band, choral group, and other practice rooms and are also used for purposes other than performance.

Each theater must be designed to function properly for its purpose or purposes and to accommodate performances, the audience, the performers, and other workers. Thus theaters are one of the most intriguing of building types to the architects and others who design them, as well as to those in the entertainment industry and those who comprise the audiences.

**History** Drama is one of the oldest art forms, having had its beginnings in ancient times, probably originating in religious rites. In every historic era and in every part of the world, some sort of drama was performed. Theaters also date back to ancient times, though in Egypt

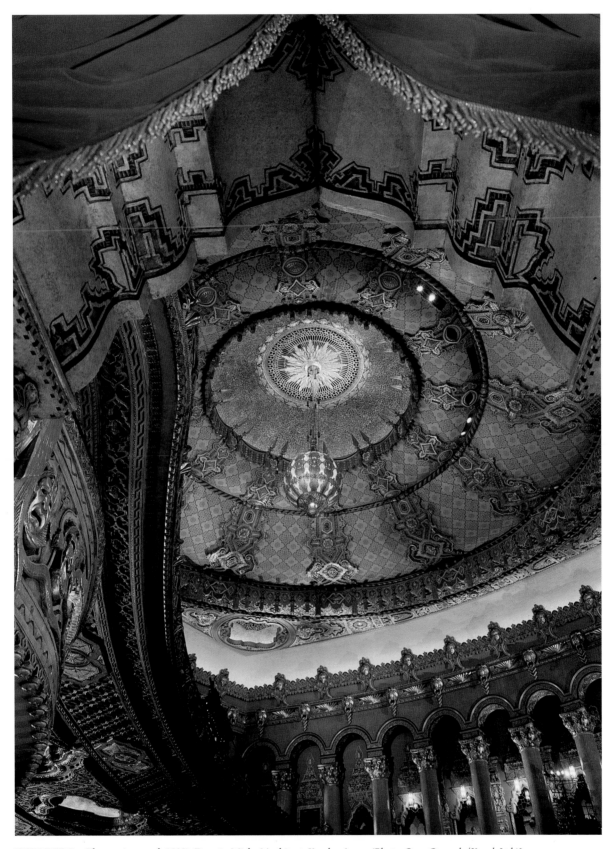

**THEATER** Fox Theater (restored, 1988), Detroit, Mich. *[Architect: Kessler Assoc. (Photo: Gary Quesada/Korab Ltd.)]*

**THEATER** Arena Stage (1961), Washington, D.C. *[Architect: Harry Weese]*

and the Near East performances took place in palaces or other buildings rather than in structures specifically designed as theaters. The ancient Greeks built theaters, or amphitheaters, usually in natural, bowl-shaped depressions on the sides of hills where thousands, sometimes tens of thousands, of spectators sat on the ground or on wood seating later replaced by stone to watch performances on the stage below. At first, the performances consisted of dancing and singing by groups of people. Sometime in the 6th century B.C., the Greek poet Thespis, who is thought to have invented tragedy, is believed to have stepped forward from such a group and recited a monologue. Soon after that, Thespis or perhaps the Greek playwright Aeschylus (525–456 B.C.) added another actor, creating a dialogue on the stage. This was the beginning of the plays of today, and ever since then, actors have often been called "thespians." The Greeks built many great theaters, quite a few of which are still in existence. One of the most famous to survive is the Theater at Epidaurus from about 350 B.C., seating 17,000. Some of the world's greatest playwrights were

early Greeks, including the tragic writer Sophocles (*c.* 496–406 B.C.), Euripides (5th century B.C.), and the writer of comedies, Aristophanes (*c.* 448–380 B.C.).

Although there were theaters in ancient Rome, the Romans preferred other pleasures, and the theater declined. The Romans were the first to build theaters on flat land, with the seating raised on masonry arches and vaults. In other parts of the world, theater flourished, particularly in India and China. During the Middle Ages, the theater was revived during the 9th century, for the most part in performances connected with religion. During the Renaissance, other types of theater were revived in Europe. The first covered theater in Europe was built in the city of Vicenza in 1580. Surviving Italian theaters include the Teatro Olimpico at Sabbionetta, Italy (1588), and the Teatro Farnese at Parma (1618).

The first theater in England, called simply The Theater (1576), London, was built by the English actor James Burbage (d. 1597). In this building were probably performed the first plays of William Shakespeare (1564–1616). The most famous Elizabethan theaters

**THEATER** Mummers Theater (1970; renovated, 1992), Oklahoma City, Okla. *[Architect: John M. Johansen; renovation architect: Elliott & Assoc.]*

were the Swan Theater (1596), the Globe, identified as Shakespeare's theater (1600), and the Red Bull Theater (1662). The Globe Theater was built in 1598, destroyed by fire in 1613, rebuilt in 1614, and demolished by the Puritans in 1644. Another famous London theater, Covent Garden, was built in 1732, later disintegrated, was reconstructed in 1792, destroyed by fire and rebuilt in 1810, destroyed by fire again and rebuilt in 1858.

Later many theaters were built all over the world. Opera as it is known today was invented in Italy in the 17th century, and the construction of opera houses as well as of concert halls began. Few of the early theaters still exist, for many reasons, but mostly because theaters were very apt to be destroyed by fire or other violent events. Surviving opera houses include the Teatro San Carlo of Naples (1737), Teatro della Pergola in Florence (1738), and, most famous, the Teatro alla Scala of Milan (1778). The Paris Opera (1876), designed by J. L. Garnier (1825–98), is known for its elaborate public spaces.

**American Development** In colonial America, theater was popular, but the first permanent building was not built until 1766, in Philadelphia. It was followed by the Chestnut Street Theater (1794) and the Walnut Street Theater (1809), the oldest still existing in the United States, both in Philadelphia. Theaters were then built all over the United States, in every city and in many towns. Although the building of theaters has slowed down at various times, they have continued to comprise an important building type to the present time. A great number of architects have designed theaters and some of them have been significant architecturally.

Efforts were made by many in the late 19th century to discover ways to photograph motion and project motion pictures. No one knows which person was first successful, but the first showing in the United States was made in 1896 by Thomas Alva Edison (1847–1931). Shortly before that time, showings had been held in France. This was the beginning of the motion picture industry, though the early showings were all in theaters designed for other purposes.

The first theater designed specifically for motion pictures, The Electric Theater, was opened in Los Angeles in

635

1902. Cinema houses have since been constructed all over the United States. With the advent of sound in 1927, the process speeded up until every hamlet in America had its own movie house, and sometimes more than one. Many architects designed these buildings, some quite ornate, in almost every conceivable exotic style. The construction of motion picture theaters slowed down starting in the 1950s, mostly due to the inroads made by television in the entertainment industry. By the 1970s interest in motion pictures began to revive and so did the building of motion picture theaters. The advent of television and videotapes has affected attendance at the motion picture theaters. One result has been the construction of multiplex facilities which contain from 4 to 12 smaller theaters, each with fewer than 300 seats.

Beginning late in the 19th century, there was considerable dissatisfaction with commercial theaters. As a result, all over Europe and the United States, little theaters were started. These new theaters were free of some of the restrictions of commercial theaters since they received financial support from individuals and organizations without the necessity for making profits, so essential to the commercial theaters. The first little theaters in the United States were established in Provincetown, Mass., and New York City in 1915. Later, little theaters were built all over the United States, many of them with financial help from the Federal Theater Project from 1935 to 1939.

Today there are many thousands of theaters of all types across the United States in cities, towns, suburbs, and rural areas. They exist in separate buildings and within other structures, including office buildings, shopping centers, and airports. Many are located in schools, colleges, and universities. Some are part of large theater complexes that contain several buildings, as in the Lincoln Center for the Performing Arts (1968), New York City, and some are in buildings that contain several theaters under one roof, as in the John F. Kennedy Center for the Performing Arts (1969), Washington, designed by Edward Durell Stone (1902–78).

The buildings of Lincoln Center, designed under the general direction of Wallace Kirkman Harrison (1895–1981) are New York State Theater (1964), by Philip Cortelyou Johnson (1906–   ); Philharmonic Hall (1962), by Max Abramovitz (1908–   ); Vivian Beaumont Theater (1965), by Eero Saarinen (1910–61); Julliard School of Music (1968), by Pietro Belluschi (1899–1994); Library-Museum of the Performing Arts (1965), by Skidmore, Owings and Merrill; and the Metropolitan Opera House (1966) by Harrison.

Other contemporary theaters are the Arena Stage (1961) designed by Harry Weese (1915–   ) in Washington, D.C., and the Tyrone Guthrie Theater, Minneapolis, Minn., which can be described as a three-quarter arena stage. The Guthrie Theater was designed by Ralph Rapson. Theater design has been influenced by major figures in theater. The cost of building theaters for the performing arts is expensive and cannot be supported by ticket sales alone. Usually major theaters and opera houses are nonprofit organizations formed for the purpose of operating a center, perhaps financed by government, educational, or cultural groups.

Another recent trend in theater design is the adaptation of older theaters or movie theaters for the legitimate stage and the conversion of surplus buildings for theater purposes.

**Related Articles** Fire Protection; Lighting; Sound Control; Articles on individual architects and on other building types.

**Further Reading** Izenour, George C.: *Theater Technology*, McGraw-Hill, New York, 1988; Izenour, George C.: *The Roofed Theater—Then and Now*, John Wiley, New York, 1988; Jewell, Don: *Public Assembly Facilities—Planning and Management*, John Wiley, New York, 1978, reprint of 2d ed., Krieger, Melbourne, Fla., 1990.

**THORNTON, WILLIAM** English-American architect (1759–1826). Although William Thornton was a medical doctor, he did not practice professionally. He was a dilettante, an amateur artist, philosopher, linguist, scientist, and sportsman. He is remembered today for another of his amateur pursuits: architecture. And in architecture, he is remembered almost entirely for one building, the original designs for the United States Capitol in Washington.

**Works** To base Thornton's reputation as an architect, amateur or otherwise, on the Capitol alone, even though it is one of the greatest American buildings, does him an injustice. After coming to the United States, Thornton settled in Philadelphia, where he designed his first building for the Library Company (1789; since demolished) of that city. He eventually moved to Washington where he produced designs for a number of notable buildings, mostly houses. Some of his important houses, all still in existence, are Octagon House (1800), designed for Col. John Tayloe III (1771–1828), now preserved by its owners, the American Institute of Architects; Tudor Place (1815), a Classic Revival house considered by many to be Thornton's best building, both in Washington; and Woodlawn Plantation (1805), near Mount Vernon, Va. Thornton also designed St. John's Church (1804) in Georgetown, Washington, now much modified. This church should not be confused with that of the same name across from Lafayette Square, near the White House, built in 1816 from designs by Benjamin Henry Latrobe (1764–1820).

In spite of all his other accomplishments, Thornton's name is mostly associated with the design of the U.S.

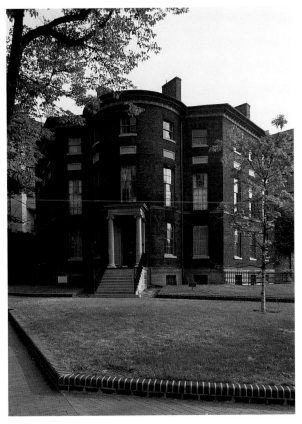

**THORNTON, WILLIAM** Octagon House (1800; restored, 1994), Washington, D.C. *[Restoration architects: Mesick Cohen Waite]*

Capitol (see illustration in the article capital, United States), the commission for which he won in a competition in 1792. The construction of the Capitol began the next year, but it soon became apparent that Thornton did not have the knowledge to direct the work. The runner-up in the competition, a French architect, Stephen Hallet (1755–1825), was appointed to direct the construction. Thornton, having been appointed a city commissioner in 1794, remained involved in the construction until 1802. After that, a number of architects worked on the building, changing and making additions to many of the elements of Thornton's original design, but retaining the major element of a central dome with porticoes front and back and wings on either side.

**Life** William Thornton was born on May 20, 1759, on the island Tortola, now in the British Virgin Islands, but then considered part of the British West Indies. When he was fifteen, he went to England to attend school and in 1781 entered the University of Edinburgh, Scotland, and studied there until 1784. In that year, he transferred to the University of Aberdeen, Scotland, and received a medical degree in 1784. He came to the United States in 1787, settled in Philadelphia, and became a U.S. citizen in 1788.

He was married in 1790, and while on his honeymoon in Tortola, learned of the competition for the U.S. Capitol. In 1792, though he had no training in architecture, he won the competition. Two years later he moved

**THORNTON, WILLIAM** Woodlawn Plantation (1805), near Mount Vernon, Va. A property of the National Trust for Historic Preservation.

to Washington and lived there the remainder of his life. In 1794 he was appointed a city commissioner and in 1802, commissioner of patents of the federal government, a position in which he served until his death.

All his life, Thornton pursued a great variety of interests. He made inventions, among them boilers and firearms; he painted; he attempted to found a national university in Washington. One of his major interests from the time he was in his thirties was in the abolition of slavery. In the 1790s, he proposed that colonies should be set up in Africa, to which ex-slaves could be repatriated. He was one of the first members, and a very active one, in the American Colonization Society, organized in 1817 for just such a purpose. In 1822 the Society managed to establish a small colony for this purpose at Monrovia, West Africa, which eventually grew into the present-day Republic of Liberia.

Thornton had a reputation among some of his contemporaries as a cantankerous and unreasonable man. The architects, including Hallet, James Hoban (*c.* 1762–1831), and Benjamin Henry Latrobe (1764–1820) who had tried to work with him on the construction of the Capitol, all had trouble with him. To his friends, Thornton seemed just the opposite, a scholar and gentleman, talented but eccentric, full of humor, generosity, and humanity. On March 28, 1826, Thornton died in

Washington, his adopted city, and was buried in the Congressional Cemetery.

**Related Articles** Capital, United States; Classic Revival Architecture; Latrobe, Benjamin Henry.

**TIGERMAN, STANLEY** American architect (1930– ). Stanley Tigerman is in a partnership with his wife Margaret McCurry. The firm is named Tigerman McCurry, with offices in Chicago, Ill. Known for exhibition design as well as furniture, he has written and lectured frequently. Tigerman is known for his witty and trenchant comments on the state of architecture and U.S. society as expressed in his buildings. His work has been widely published and exhibited internationally and has received several design awards. Stanley Tigerman is the author of a number of books.

**Works** Houses include remodeled barns such as Frog Hollow (1974) in Berrien, Mich., and one in Burlington, Wis. (1972), and a series of private homes of a wide variety of materials and plan forms, the earlier ones often with humorous names such as Daisy (1978), Porter, Ind.; Hot Dog (1975), Harvard, Ill.; House with a Pompadour (1979), Dunes, Ind.; Animal Crackers (1978), Highland Park, Ill.; and the Metal and Glass House (1975) in Glencoe, Ill. All these houses have logical plans, which with their exterior appearance suggested the names.

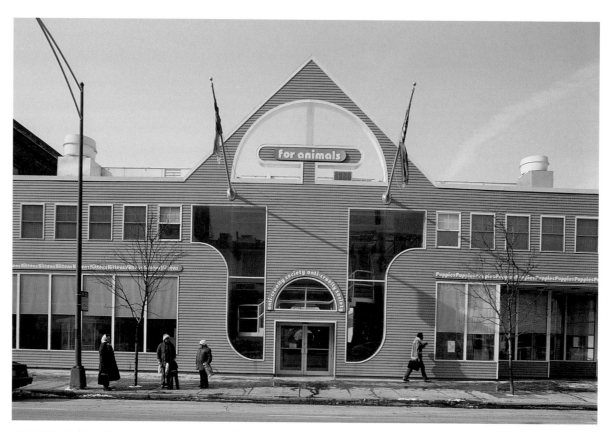

**TIGERMAN, STANLEY** Anti-Cruelty Society Addition (1978), Chicago, Ill.

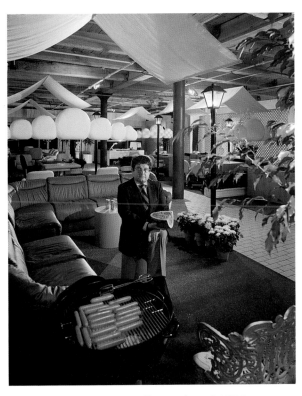

**TIGERMAN, STANLEY** "Office Landscape" (1981), a concept installation. Stanley Tigerman is shown in the photo.

Later housing includes an urban villa, Tegeler Hafen, IBA (1988) in Berlin, Germany, and the Fukuoka City mixed-use apartment building (1989), Kiushu, Japan.

Urban projects include the Illinois Regional Library for the Blind and the Physically Handicapped (1978); the Anti-Cruelty Society Addition (1978) (illustrated), and the Self-Park Garage (1986), all in Chicago. Restaurant designs include the Hard Rock Cafe (1985), adjoining an existing Commonwealth Edison Sub-Station in Chicago.

Exhibits include Fourth Federal Design (1978) at the Building Museum, Washington, D.C.; Chicago Architecture 1872–1922 (1988) at the Art Institute of Chicago; and the Frankfurt Museum Court Exhibition (1984), Frankfurt, Germany. Showrooms include those for Knoll International Park and Showroom, Houston (1982), and the Formica showroom at the Merchandise Mart, Chicago (1986). Furniture design includes a prototype double chaise lounge for Formica (1986); a chair for Herman Miller (1987); jewelry for Cleto Munari (1987); and china, flatware, decorative objects, and household accessories for Swid-Powell Designs (1989). Several of these are also credited to Margaret McCurry.

**Life** Born in 1930, Stanley Tigerman was briefly at the Massachusetts Institute of Technology, worked for George Fred and William Keck, and served in the U.S. Navy beginning in 1950. He worked for Skidmore, Owings and Merrill beginning in 1957 and returned to college in 1959. Tigerman completed his architectural education at Yale University in 1960 and 1961. He worked for Paul M. Rudolph in New Haven, Conn., returned to Chicago and a brief time at Skidmore, Owings and Merrill, before opening his own firm. He speaks of the strong influence of Mies van der Rohe in Chicago, and the difficulty of finding his own style. In his writings, he suggests influences of the de Stijl movement of the 1920s, Paul Rudolph's brutalist architecture, megastructures, socially conscious concerns, Modernism, Surrealism, Architecture of the Absurd, historical allusions, and post-Modernism.

He has been a visiting professor at Yale and Harvard among others and was a resident architect at the American Academy in Rome. He is director of the School of Architecture at the University of Illinois at Chicago and maintains his office in Chicago.

**Further Reading** Tigerman, Stanley: *Versus: An American Architect's Alternatives*, Rizzoli, New York, 1982; Underhill, Sarah Mollman, ed.: *Stanley Tigerman: Buildings and Projects 1966–1989*, Rizzoli, New York, 1989.

**TILE** A baked clay unit used in building construction for flooring, wall coverings, roofing, structural systems, and other purposes, often laid with mortar in a manner similar to that for brick. The word *tile* is frequently used to denote other materials that are made in relatively small units, such as vinyl tile flooring. However, tile is most closely related to various products made of baked clay.

**Types** Clay tile used for flooring and wall coverings may be obtained either unglazed, with integral color throughout, or glazed, with ceramic materials in various colors fused to the surfaces. Other types include quarry tile, which is an unglazed tile in earth colors, generally used for flooring. Roof tiles are available in glazed and unglazed finishes, in various shapes, often named for the countries from which they were derived, including Greek, English, Spanish, and French. Structural clay tiles, in the past often called hollow tiles because of their conformation, are used for various building components, including the structures of walls, and are often finished with stucco, plaster, brick, or stone. Structural facing tiles have colored, glazed surfaces that may be left exposed. Clay tile pipes are used for drainage and other plumbing and sewage purposes. Terra-cotta is a baked clay product used for finishes on buildings and may be flat or molded. Because of the relative ease of molding, terra-cotta has often been used for ornamental purposes in architecture. However, it is seldom used today, except in thin tiles, usually called ceramic veneer, which may be obtained with graphic or ornamental designs. Clay flue linings are often used in chimneys.

**Floor and Wall Tiles** Clay floor and wall tiles are used today for those purposes and sometimes for facing fireplaces and countertops. Tiles of this type are made of clay, usually ball clays (in the industry sometimes called plastics), fillers, often flint or silica, which impart strength and resist shrinkage during firing, and solvents, usually feldspar, called fluxes. The exact proportions of these materials vary among the various types of tile.

Floor and wall tiles are made by either the dust-press or the plastic process. Each process requires a number of operations. In general, the dust-press process involves shaping the mixture of clay and other materials in steel dies under great pressure, after which the shaped tiles are fired. The plastic process involves shaping the mixture by extrusion through dies or by hand molding, after which they are fired. The dust-press method produces more precise shapes and sizes than the plastic method, which produces tiles that look somewhat handmade. The surfaces of floor and wall tiles may be unglazed or glazed. In unglazed types the color is integral throughout the body of the tiles and their appearance comes from the materials used. Glazed tiles have ceramic materials fused to their faces in an additional firing. Glazed tile may be almost any color and may have surface textures, such as mottled or stippled. Glazes may be polished or bright, or matte. Floor and wall tiles are also classified by their degree of fusing of the materials, or vitrification, which largely determines their degree of water absorption. From the least impervious to water to the greatest, tile may be nonvitreous, semivitreous, and vitreous or impervious.

The major types of floor and wall tiles, often called ceramic tiles, include glazed wall tiles, ceramic mosaic tiles, and floor tiles. Glazed wall tiles are usually made by the dust-press method. Nominal sizes usually available are $5/16$ in thick, $4\frac{1}{4}$ and 6 in square, and $4\frac{1}{4}$ by 6 in. They also come in other sizes and in octagonal shapes. A special type is the weatherproof glazed wall tile, made by either method, and used in locations where freezing occurs. These tiles, in matte finishes, may also be used for flooring in areas with moderate traffic.

Ceramic mosaic tiles, usually unglazed, may be used for interior or exterior floors and walls. They come in two types: porcelain, made by the dust-press method, and vitreous or impervious; and the natural clay type, made by either method. Ceramic mosaic tiles are generally small in size, of nominally $\frac{1}{4}$ in thickness, and 1 or 2 in$^2$ or 1 by 2 in. Because of their small size, they are often furnished with paper attached to their faces to hold them in place while they are being set. Porcelain types come in a wide range of colors, while the colors of the natural tile are generally determined by the types of clay used.

Other than those previously mentioned, floor types include quarry tiles and pavers. Both are available in squares and rectangles, in nominal sizes ranging from 3 to 9 in, and in thickness from $3/8$ to $3/4$ in. Both types are unglazed. Quarry tiles are made by the plastic method and pavers by either method. Both types may be used for interior or exterior installations and both are resistant to wear from heavy traffic. Quarry tiles are generally restricted in color to those produced by the clays from which they are made. Pavers are similar to ceramic mosaics and may be obtained in a variety of colors. In all types of floor and wall tiles, special shapes may be obtained for use in corners, for bases at the bottom of walls, caps at the tops, and so on. Also special fixtures, such as soap dishes, are available for use with tile.

Many other types of tile are available for special purposes, including faience, majolica, and delft. Faience tiles are named after the town of Faenza, Italy, where they were first made during the Middle Ages. They are highly ornamental, resembling Persian tile, usually with striking opaque glazes. Majolica, named for the island of Majorca where it was first made in the Middle Ages, is a special kind of faience, with brilliant, enameled ornament fired on its face. Delft tile, named for the town of Delft, the Netherlands, where it was first made in the 16th century, is a faience, often in blue and white and with ornament derived from oriental sources.

Floor and wall tiles are available in various grades, which are different for the particular types of tile. When tiles are being selected or specified for use in buildings, a determination of the proper grades should be made. Floor and wall tiles may be installed by either of two methods: one using mortar and the other, adhesives. Joints between individual tiles are grouted with special groutings or caulking materials or with portland cement mixed with sand or other materials.

**Roof Tiles** Clay roof tiles are available unglazed, in mostly earthly colors, or glazed in a variety of colors, in rounded and other shapes, and as shingles. Sizes of the various shapes of roof tiles range from about 8 to 12 in wide and from about 11 to 18 in long. Shingles are generally 12 or 15 in long and 6, 7, or 9 in wide. The minimum pitch of roofs using shaped tiles is $4\frac{1}{2}$ in rise to 12 in of length, or run; for shingles, the minimum is 6 in rise to 12 in run. Clay roof tiles and shingles are generally installed with noncorrosive nails, and some types have interlocking features. Special shapes are available for use on roof ridges and similar purposes.

**Structural Tiles** Structural clay tiles may be obtained with unfinished faces to be used as backup for exteriors of brick or other materials, which combine to support loads, or as structural facing tile, in which the tile itself supports the entire load and is finished with stucco or other materials. Structural facing tiles may also be obtained with unglazed or glazed finished faces, and with smooth, scored, combed, and other textures. Unglazed types are generally in earth colors derived from the types of clay used, and glazed tile may have any of a number of colors, in solid, mottled, or other finishes that are either shiny or matte. Structural tiles may be obtained as loadbearing for use in masonry structures or nonload bearing for other uses. There are also special types, such as fireproof tile, used to protect steel structural members.

Structural tiles are generally available in nominal sizes of 4 in thick by 12 in long and various heights and 8 in thick and high by 16 in long. Other sizes may also be obtained. Many special shapes are available in structural facing tiles for corners, jambs of doors and windows, bases at the bottom of walls, caps at tops, and so on. Some of the types of structural tile come in several grades for various uses. Structural clay tiles are usually installed in mortar, composed of portland cement, lime, aggregate, and water. The proportions of these materials, the time of their mixing, and the placement of the mortar must be strictly controlled.

Terra-cotta, or ceramic veneer, ordinarily comes in nominal sizes of $3/8$ to about 4 in in thickness and in pieces up to about 3 by 4 ft. It may be obtained unglazed, in various earth colors determined by the clays used in its manufacture, and in various textures and finishes. If glazed, many colors are possible. Ceramic veneer is usually installed with mortar and special setting clips. Clay flue tiles for use in the lining of chimneys generally come in round, rectangular, and square forms, in various sizes, from which the proper size may be selected based on the size of the fireplace to be served. Clay pipe comes in unglazed form, usually called drain tile, for use in drains and underground sewage disposal systems, in sizes, based on the inside diameter from 3 to 24 in. A perforated type is also available. Vitrified clay pipe, used for storm sewers, sewers, and other purposes, comes glazed or unglazed and in sizes from 4 to 42 in. Both types have bell and spigot ends for fitting together. Various fittings such as Y's, tees, and so on are available for both types.

Clay products constitute such a variety of types and have such a wide usage in architecture that it is virtually impossible to generalize about their selection. In types for structural purposes, attention must be paid to load bearing characteristics. The degree of water infiltration allowable in specific installations must be determined and tile with sufficient vitrification selected. For exposed installations, colors, textures, finishes, and shapes are important. Since many types of tile come in various grades, selection must be made of the ones that fit the purposes intended.

Proper mortars or adhesives must be selected and the tile installed under the proper conditions and in the correct manner on walls or other bases that have been correctly prepared. If proper selections and safeguards are followed, all clay tile products will give many years of almost maintenance-free service.

**TILE** Typical roofing types.

**History** Clay or ceramic materials, such as terra-cotta and tile, have been used in architecture from early primitive times, about 5000 B.C., or even earlier. When the first of such materials was used has not been established, but early types have been found in the oldest remains of civilizations around the Mediterranean Sea, including those in Mesopotamia, Crete, Egypt, and Greece. At first tile and terra-cotta were sun-dried, but later they were kiln-burned.

The ancient Egyptians used both tile and terra-cotta, but not as extensively as in Mesopotamia and other areas of the Middle East. Nor did the Egyptians reach the high level of excellence in the use of color, carvings, and moldings achieved in the Middle East, where clay was abundant but other materials were not. The Mesopotamians developed terra-cotta and tile into a high art, ornamenting many of their walls and other building elements with elaborate depictions of animals and people made of these materials. The ancient Greeks used terra-cotta and other clay materials, not so much for ornamental as for functional purposes, such as roofs, sewers, and water conduits. As ornament, the Greeks used terra-cotta for cornices and similar purposes.

The Romans used tile and terra-cotta extensively, not only for ornament and roofs, as had their predecessors, the Etruscans, but also for piping, flooring, in hollow forms for conducting hot air and smoke to heat buildings, and in the form of hollow boxes for construction of vaults and domes. Roman terra-cotta and tile were often unglazed and uncolored, but that was not always the case. Along with brick, tile and terra-cotta were used only infrequently during the Middle Ages. Exceptions occurred in Italy and Germany and, particularly, in Spain

**TILE** Poolhouse using Pewabic pottery (1929), Grosse Ile, Mich. *[Restoration architect: Alan Deal]*

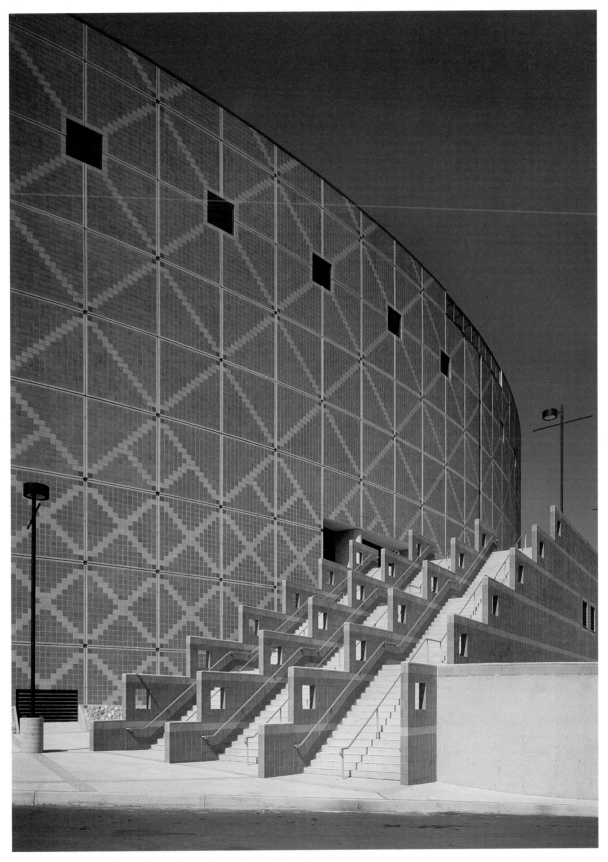

**TILE** Palace (1988), Auburn Hills, Mich. *[Architects: Rossetti Assoc.]*

and the Muslim countries, where ornamental tile work has been of high excellence since very early times.

During the Renaissance, tile and terra-cotta were widely used, not only for ornamental features of buildings but, in the case of terra-cotta, as a sculptural medium by many of the leading artists of the time. The art of making fine tile spread from Spain to Italy, England, and other countries, in particular to the Netherlands. Terra-cotta was used in England for a time, but by the end of the 16th century, its use had been virtually discontinued there. It continued to flourish in Italy and elsewhere for a time, but by the end of the Renaissance was no longer widely used in Europe.

**American Development** In the American colonies, neither tile nor terra-cotta was used. Later tile was imported, particularly delft from the Netherlands, and used mostly for ornamentation and fireplace facings. Tile was later manufactured in America and its use for other purposes grew. The use of terra-cotta was revived in the late 19th century, first for use in Victorian and other buildings and then for ornamental uses in cornices and other elements of early tall buildings. With the modern movement in architecture, the use of terra-cotta for ornamental purposes came to an end,. except in latter-day Eclectic buildings. Today structural clay tile, tile pipe, and other types are used for functional purposes. Clay roofing tile is mostly used for buildings designed to reflect a Spanish influence or that of some other country. Ceramic tiles are widely used in bathrooms and kitchens and for other purposes. Ceramic veneer continues to be used to some extent.

**Related Articles** BRICK; FLOOR; MASONRY STRUCTURE; PLUMBING; ROOF; WALL.

**Sources of Additional Information** Ceramic Tile Inst., 700 Virgil Ave., Los Angeles, Calif., 90029; Facing Tile Inst., 1750 Old Meadow Rd., McLean, Va. 22101; National Ceramic Manufacturers Assoc., 59 E. Main St., Moorestown, N.J. 08057; National Clay Pipe Inst., 350 W. Terra Cotta Ave., Crystal Lake, Ill. 60014.

**TOWN, ITHIEL** American architect and engineer of bridges (1784–1844). Ithiel Town was partner to Alexander Jackson Davis (1803–92) from the period 1829 to 1835. Town became a wealthy man from his bridge patents and was known for the size of his library. His work shows the influence of the new Greek style, thought by Thomas Jefferson and others to be suitable for the new nation, and he also designed in the early American Gothic style which was becoming popular in the period before the Civil War.

**Works** By 1813, Ithiel Town was practicing in New Haven, Conn., and is known as the architect of the Center Church (1815), modified from a scheme by the Boston architect Asher Benjamin (1773–1845). Town's

design of the tower was an early example of his structural skills. He also designed the Trinity Church, in the early American Gothic style. Both of these churches face the Green in New Haven. He designed meeting houses for Plainfield and Thompson, Conn. (1815), and a hotel in New Haven (1816).

The period from 1816 to 1825 was devoted to bridge design. In 1825, he returned to New Haven and resumed his architectural practice, including a house for Mrs. Eli Whitney (1826). Yale College awarded him an honorary master's degree. However, a bank failure in New Haven and resulting depression led Town to move his office to New York City. The following ten years were the most productive of his career. He introduced the Doric temple form to New York City in the New York Theatre (1826) and is credited with the design of what became the typical American temple-form house with wings for his Northampton, Mass. house (1827). Town is credited with the New Haven State House (1831), another temple-form building, later destroyed, and the Third Congregational Church (1829) in New Haven.

The firm of Town and Davis designed the state capitols for Indiana (1835, later destroyed) and North Carolina (1840). The latter was started by William Nichols and finished by David Paton. The firm designed

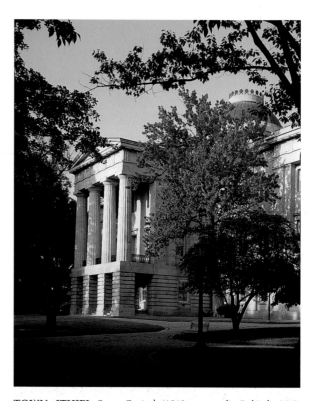

**TOWN, ITHIEL** State Capitol (1840; restored), Raleigh, N.C. *[Architects: William Nichols, Jr.; Town & Davis; David Paton]* Town and Davis were designers for both the Indiana (1835) and North Carolina (1840) Capitols.

the New York Customs House (1842), later called the Subtreasury Building and now known as the Federal Hall National Memorial on Wall Street in New York City.

Town and Davis were among the first to use Greek columns and antae for townhouse doorways in New York. Their churches were often in Greek temple form, including two examples in New York City and one in Middletown, Conn. An early American Gothic church was the Christ Church Cathedral in Hartford, Conn. (1828). The first house in the Gothic style was Glen Ellen (1834) in Towson, Md. The firm designed buildings for New York University (1837).

**Town and Davis** The firm of Town and Davis was one of the earliest American architectural firms and was founded in 1829. For the period 1832–33, James H. Dakin (1811–52) was added to the firm, while Davis worked on projects in Baltimore and Washington. The firm designed in several styles, including the most popular Greek, as well as Gothic, Tuscan, and Egyptian.

The firm had the largest architectural library in America, which had been assembled by Ithiel Town. He remained the head of the firm and acquired most of the major commissions. Davis was the more skilled designer, but both partners and the younger James H. Dakin worked together on the projects. Although the credit for a particular project may be difficult to determine, Davis's records and drawings have been preserved. As the firm prospered, James Gallier, Sr., John Sole, and Charles B. Dakin (1811–39), younger brother of James H. Dakin, were hired as drafters, and Davis taught a number of students in the office from 1829 to 1832. Most of the projects were built without their direct supervision, but Town and Dakin supervised some of the major works, including the Indiana Capitol (1835). Town and Davis shared the expenses and income, and each earned additional income, Town from his bridges, and Davis from drawings. Records indicate that when J. H. Dakin joined the firm, he received 40 percent of the fees and Town and Davis each received 30 percent. When Town received an additional bridge patent in 1835, the firm was dissolved, although Davis continued to prepare drawings for Town, and they collaborated on the competition for the Illinois State Capitol (1837) and worked together on the drawings for the Ohio Capitol (1839). Near the end of Town's life, he joined with Davis for the completion of the Wadsworth Athenaeum in Hartford, Conn. (1844). Based on plans by Henry Austin, the facade design is credited to Davis.

Town traveled in England, France, and Italy during 1829 to 1830, sending back additions to his library. The papers of the firm of Town and Davis are in the Alexander J. Davis collections of the Avery Architectural Library, Columbia University, New York, the Metropolitan Museum of Art, and the New York Public Library.

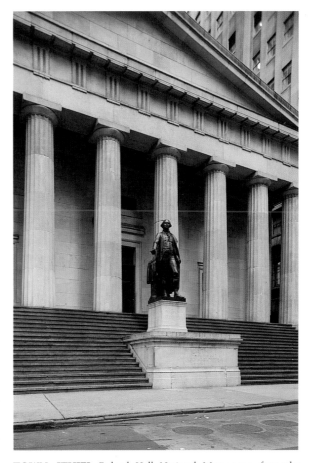

**TOWN, ITHIEL** Federal Hall National Monument, formerly Subtreasury Building, originally U.S. Customs House (1842; later alterations and restorations). *[Architects: Town and Davis; alterations architects: John Frazee and Samuel Thompson; sculptor, statue of Washington (1883): J. Q. A. Ward]*

**Life** Ithiel Town was born in Thompson, Conn., in 1784. His father died when Ithiel was eight, and he thereafter lived with his uncle. In his youth, he taught briefly at a country school, became a carpenter, and by 1816 was working with the Boston architect Asher Benjamin (1773–1845).

Town associated with Isaac Damon to build several bridges over the Connecticut River, and Town then worked in the South, mostly in North Carolina, where he developed his lattice truss which he patented in 1820. This form of truss was widely used for covered bridges, and he acquired considerable wealth from his designs and licensing his patent. He used some of these funds to start his famous library, which eventually grew to some 11,000 books and 25,000 prints.

Town's travels convinced him of the appropriateness of the Greek style, and by age forty he was again practicing architecture in New Haven. The failure of New Haven's Eagle Bank in 1825 led Town to move his office to New York City. He was associated with Martin E.

Thompson from 1827 to 1828 and was partner with Alexander Jackson Davis from 1829 to 1835. Town's 1835 bridge patent was the cause of dissolving the firm. He moved his library to his new house in New Haven in 1836. After the financial panic of 1837, Town sold most of his library, and the contents are known from catalogues published at the time of the auction sales of his books.

Town and Davis attended the 1836 meeting in New York establishing the American Institution of Architects. The list of architects who attended this famous meeting also included Isaiah Rogers (1800–69), John Haviland (1792–1852), Minard Lafever (1798–1854), Asher Benjamin (1773–1845), Thomas U. Walter (1804–87), William Strickland (1788–1854), and others. Although this organization apparently never became active, it is seen as the predecessor organization to the American Institute of Architects. Ithiel Town was an Honorary and Corresponding Member of the Royal Institute of British Architects (1836), and made his last trip to England and France in 1843. He died in New Haven in 1844.

**Related Articles** BRIDGE; DAVIS, ALEXANDER JACKSON; GOTHIC REVIVAL ARCHITECTURE; STRICKLAND, WILLIAM.

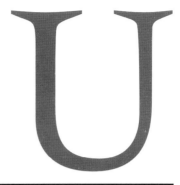

**UNDERGROUND BUILDING** Earth-sheltered structures have an ancient tradition which has received new attention in recent years as an approach to energy conservation. This is possible because temperatures even with shallow coverage average between 44 and 66°F (7 and 18°C) in the United States. Seasonal variations are slight, offering warmth in cold weather and coolness in hot. Another advantage of underground buildings is safety from tornadoes, military attack, or vandalism. In some areas it has been possible to use the ground over structures for other uses in urban areas or college campuses.

The Pusey Library at Harvard University (1976), Cambridge, Mass., designed by Hugh Stubbins and Assoc., was placed underground to allow a major addition to the Harvard University Library System with minimal disruption of the open space of Harvard Yard. The security of the structure was well suited to storage of rare books and special collections, manuscripts, and maps.

The Civil and Mineral Engineering Building (1983), University of Minnesota, Minneapolis, Minn., designed by BRW Architects, achieved similar benefits and was a test of energy conservation. Three floors were built with cut and cover. Below this space, a limestone strata was preserved as a roof over two additional floors of mined space.

Occasionally it is possible to use excavations in exposed stone strata. An example of this are the extensive warehouse and manufacturing areas in Kansas City, Mo. The spaces were mined for building stone at earlier dates, but the use of the mined space has proven advantageous because of constant temperature of about 50°F.

The largest group of earth-sheltered buildings are houses, and it is estimated that there are over 6,000 such houses in the United States, built since 1975. Most of these have partial walls exposed to light to overcome the psychological problems of living underground. Frank Lloyd Wright (1867–1959) was a pioneer in design of solar housing, with earth berms banked against the north walls and a curved glass wall facing south for the Herbert Jacobs House near Madison, Wis., and the proposed E. L. Marting House (1947). Special issues of concern for earth-covered buildings are the presence of poorly draining soils, expansive clay soils, or rock which

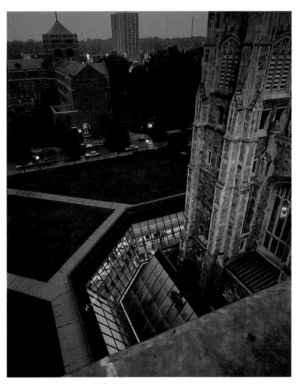

**UNDERGROUND BUILDING** University of Michigan Law School addition (1981), Ann Arbor, Mich. *[Architect: Gunnar Birkerts (Photo: Gary Quesada/Korab Ltd.)]*

**UNDERGROUND BUILDING** Interior, University of Michigan Law School addition (1981), Ann Arbor, Mich. *[Architect: Gunnar Birkerts (Photo: Gary Quesada/Korab Ltd.)]*

may prove uneconomical to remove. Water leakage is a potential problem, particularly in areas of high water tables. It is possible to build to eliminate ground water, but special construction is needed. Repairs are particularly expensive for underground leaks. Another factor regarding earth-sheltered buildings is the extra loads carried by earth-covered roofs, and lateral pressures from the earth.

Other issues are psychological, including limited natural light, lack of exterior views, possible claustrophobia related to underground spaces, and problems of temperature and humidity control, and lack of ventilation. All these problems may occur in conventional buildings, but being underground results in different perceptions. From a health point of view, the lack of daylight, lack of fresh air, and indoor pollution may be concerns which must be addressed in building design. Also, control of high humidity must be addressed to allow control of the possible growth of such items as bacteria, viruses, fungi, and mites.

Many devices may be used to make earth-sheltered buildings pleasant. These include naturally lighted entrances, use of high ceilings, light wells, or even optical devices to allow a view of the surface. Interior design using warm, bright colors, finished surfaces, use of

plants with special lighting are helpful, as is the use of artworks in lieu of windows. These buildings require careful design of mechanical systems to provide fresh, clean air at comfortable temperatures.

**Related Articles** CONTEMPORARY ARCHITECTURE; ENERGY; HOUSE.

**UPJOHN, RICHARD** English-American architect (1802–78). Starting out as a cabinetmaker and carpenter, Richard Upjohn studied architecture and drawing. In an earlier era, he might have gone on to become a craftsman-architect as had many before him. But by the time he began practicing architecture in 1833, it had become possible for a career to be made in architecture alone. Thus Upjohn became one of the earliest professional architects in America.

**Architectural Influence** Although he designed a relatively large number of buildings of many types, it is as a church designer that he made his reputation. He designed more than 100 churches, located in many parts of the United States, remodeled and renovated many more, and influenced the design of many others, mainly through his book on church design, *Upjohn's Rural Architecture*, containing drawings of a prototype church and other buildings, originally published in 1852.

While his commercial and residential work were often exceptions, his designs were almost always in the Gothic Revival style, using forms and details derived from the churches and cathedrals of the Middle Ages. Upjohn's use of this style influenced the architecture of his time, and the architects then as well as those who later turned to Gothic themes in the era of Victorian

**UPJOHN, RICHARD** Kingscote (1839; addition 1881), Newport, R.I. *[Architect: Richard Upjohn; addition architects: McKim, Mead and White]*

architecture. He also had a lasting influence on architecture and its practice through his many years of work for the benefit of the profession.

**Works** It has been said that the reputation of Upjohn rests on his design of one building, Trinity Church (1846), New York City. Although there is some truth in this assessment and Trinity certainly is his masterpiece, Upjohn designed a number of other notable buildings. Among them are the Church of the Ascension (1841), New York City; Christ Church (1842), Brooklyn; Grace Church (1848), Brooklyn; St. James' Church (1850), New London, Conn.; St. Mary's Church (1854), Burlington, N.J.; St. Paul's Church, Buffalo, N.Y.; and the Chapel at Bowdoin College (1853) in Brunswick, Maine.

**Life** Richard Upjohn was born in Dorsetshire, England, on January 22, 1802, the son of a surveyor. His mother died the same year. His father moved the family to Newfoundland in 1808 but soon returned to England. After showing an aptitude for drawing, Richard was apprenticed to a cabinetmaker at seventeen. While serving his apprenticeship, he began to study architecture, a pursuit he continued after he started his own cabinetmaking business. On November 14, 1826, he married Elizabeth Parry; their son, Richard Mitchell (1827–1903) became an architect.

In 1828 Upjohn brought his wife and son to the United States, first settling in Manlius, N.Y., and then moving to New Bedford, Mass., where he worked as a draftsman. In 1833 he began his career as an architect with the design of a house in Bangor, Maine. During the next few years, he designed several other houses, and in 1834, moved to Boston. Soon afterward, he designed his first church, St. John's (1839), Bangor, Maine. This was the beginning of a great career in church design. Largely because of the success of the Bangor church, and through his friendship with the newly appointed rector of Trinity Church, N.Y., Dr. Jonathan Wainwright, Upjohn was called to New York to design a new building for the congregation. This church, Trinity (1846), firmly established Upjohn as one of the most important American architects and one of the finest church architects of all time. Over the succeeding years, he designed churches all over the United States and also did a number of other buildings, including houses and university and commercial buildings.

Upjohn formed a partnership with his son, Richard Mitchell, called Upjohn and Co., in 1853; the firm name was changed several times, to Richard Upjohn, in 1858; and finally R. and M. Upjohn, in 1864, reflecting the growing importance of the younger man in the firm.

During the later years of his life, Upjohn began to devote more and more of his time to his profession and

**UPJOHN, RICHARD** Trinity Church (1846), New York, N.Y.

less to his own practice. He then took a step which ensured his deeper involvement with his profession. On February 23, 1857, a group of architects met in the Upjohn office to discuss the foundation of an architectural organization that would have a great effect on architecture. Out of this meeting came the professional organization, the American Institute of Architects. Upjohn was elected its first president, a post in which he served for 18 years.

In 1872 Upjohn dissolved his partnership with his son, who carried on his own practice afterward. Retiring to an old house he had bought in Garrison, N.Y., Upjohn spent his last years mostly relaxing with his grandchildren and painting in oils the scenery around the house and the Hudson River. On August 17, 1878, Richard Upjohn died, honored and respected by his profession. Much of his great architecture survived him, as did his architect-son, Richard Mitchell, and architect-grandson, Hobard B. (1876–1949). A great-grandson,

Everard Miller (b. 1903), studied architecture but instead became a professor of fine arts at Columbia University.

**Related Articles** ASSOCIATION, BUILDING INDUSTRY; BUILDING INDUSTRY; GOTHIC REVIVAL ARCHITECTURE; RELIGIOUS BUILDING.

**Further Reading** Upjohn, Everard Miller: *Richard Upjohn—Architect and Churchman*, DaCapo Press, New York, 1968; Upjohn, Richard: *Upjohn's Rural Architecture—Designs, Working Drawings and Specifications for a Wooden Church and Other Structures*, reprinted, Da Capo Press, New York, 1975.

VAULT A structural element of a building using the principles of the arch extended to form a curved roof over an interior space.

As the arch, the vault was originally constructed of masonry, stone, brick, or tile units, shaped so that when assembled they formed a strong structural system that transferred weight down through the vault units to walls or columns. As in the arch, this weight produces forces that thrust outward at the base of the vault as well as downward. To prevent the vault from collapsing, the outward, or lateral, thrusts must be resisted by thick walls or by special structural elements called buttresses. In some cases, vaults are placed side by side so that the lateral thrusts of adjacent vaults resist each other. A flying buttress is a special type, much used in the Gothic architecture of the Middle Ages, consisting of sloping structural elements supported on an arch that transfers the lateral thrust of the vault to a pier.

**Elements** Other terms are important in vaults. A crown is the top of a vault. A haunch is the middle part of a vault between the crown and the spring line. A spring line is the lowest part of a vault, where it begins to rise. The rise of a vault is the height from the spring line to the bottom of the crown. Its span is the width between the interior sides of a vault.

**Types** Masonry vaults are of three main kinds: barrel, groined, and ribbed. The simplest, the barrel vault, sometimes called tunnel vault, is semicircular and spans the space between two walls like a continuous arch. A groined vault is formed when two vaults intersect, the groin being the ridge or rib formed at the intersection. In a ribbed vault, ribs only are constructed where the groins would otherwise be, thus creating a skeletonlike structure much lighter in appearance and actuality than a groin vault. The spaces between the ribs may then be filled with relatively light materials, including glass.

Vaults have also been constructed of homogeneous materials, such as concrete, from the time of the Romans. Today such vaults would be built of reinforced concrete. Vaults of reinforced concrete perform in much

**VAULT** Interior, Union Station (1894; restored), St. Louis, Mo. *[Architect: Theodore C. Link]*

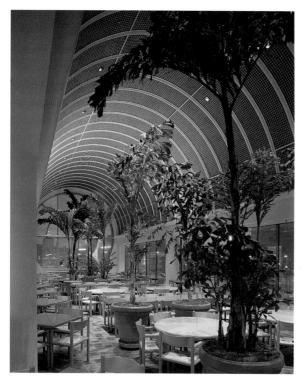

**VAULT** Interior, Lutheran Brotherhood (1893), Minneapolis, Minn. [*Architect: Edward Charles Bassett of Skidmore, Owings and Merrill*]

the same way as those of masonry, except that the side thrusts may be eliminated, thus also eliminating the need for heavy piers and buttresses.

**History** The use of vaults as structural elements began at about the same time as arches, in Mesopotamia

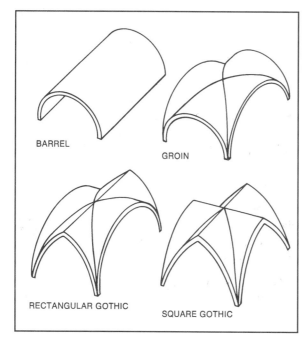

BARREL

GROIN

RECTANGULAR GOTHIC

SQUARE GOTHIC

**VAULT** Typical masonry types.

about 6,000 years ago. This tradition was continued by other cultures, including the Egyptian, but not the Greek, and was further developed by the Romans, particularly masonry and concrete barrel and groined vaults. The development of the masonry ribbed vault reached its apex in the Gothic architecture of the Middle Ages, notably in the great cathedrals. In the Renaissance period, vaults were used extensively, though most were the barrel form.

**American Development** Vaults of masonry have been used in American architecture since colonial times, especially in churches and other buildings in which a monumental effect was desired. Later reinforced concrete vaults came into widespread usage, for the achievement of similar monumental effects and where relatively long distances were spanned by the roofs.

During the height of the Classic Revival movement in America, vaults of masonry, designed to strict engineering standards, were used by many architects in a daring and innovative manner. Their use continued during the Gothic Revival and Eclectic periods in American architecture and into the 20th century.

**Related Articles** ARCH; CONCRETE STRUCTURE; DOME; MASONRY STRUCTURE; STEEL STRUCTURE; WOOD-FRAME STRUCTURE.

**VENTURI, ROBERT** American architect, author and theoretician (1925–   ). Robert Venturi is partner in the firm Venturi, Scott Brown and Associates. Robert Venturi is credited with a comprehensive shift in architectural thinking on the basis of his 1966 seminal book *Complexity and Contradiction in Architecture*. The small book is credited with causing a move away from classic Modern design to one more responsive to historical influences, called post-Modern. A second edition of this work was published in 1977. Venturi's wife, Denise Scott Brown (1931–   ) is also an author, and has collaborated with her husband on such books as *Learning from Las Vegas* with Steven Izenour. John Rauch (1930–   ) was the business partner of the firm. For many years, the work of the firm was not generally appreciated by the architectural profession, and the favorable shift of opinion dates from the 1980s.

**Work** The much-published house for Venturi's mother, Vanna Venturi (1962), was the first project to exemplify his theoretical search for continuation of a classical approach to design.

The Guild House (1965) for the Friends Housing for the Elderly in Philadelphia, Pa., made good use of a minimum budget by careful design of the entrance and selection of window openings of various sizes in a symmetrical building.

The Franklin Court, Philadelphia, Pa. (1976), is an evocation of the demolished house of Benjamin Franklin. The steel "ghost" structure is supplemented with an

**VENTURI, ROBERT** Franklin Court (1976), Philadelphia, Pa. A monument to Benjamin Franklin on the site of his demolished home. *[Architects: Venturi, Scott Brown and Assoc. (Photo: Matt Wargo)]*

underground museum. This project was timed for the bicentennial celebration of the United States.

Work at Princeton University, Princeton, N.J., includes the Gordon Wu Hall, Butler College (1980), and the Fisher/Bendheim classroom building (1991) for economics and international finance.

Restoration and renovation work has included the Furness Library at the University of Pennsylvania in Philadelphia, Pa. A new building for the university is the Clinical Research Building (1991) designed by Payette Associates, Inc., in association with Venturi, Scott Brown and Associates. A related building is the renovation and addition to the Thayer School of Engineering (1991), Dartmouth College, Hanover, N.H., also in association with Payette Associates, Inc.

On the basis of an international competition, Venturi was selected to design a major addition (1991) to the National Gallery in London, U.K. This project was highly debated while it was in design, and the consensus is that its exterior was an appropriate response to the 1838 National Gallery. The rear elevations of the new wing are more functional, suitable for the streets on which they face. The interior entrance, cafe, grand stair, and top-lit galleries are the public spaces of a complex program which includes a new lecture theater and temporary exhibition galleries on the basement level.

**Life** Robert Venturi was born in 1925 in Philadelphia, Pa., and received his architectural education at Princeton University, receiving his B.A. in 1947 and the M.F.A. in 1950. He received the Rome Prize and spent at year at the American Academy in Rome. His early employment included employment with Oscar Stonorov in Philadelphia, Pa., with Eero Saarinen (1910–61) in Bloomfield Hills, Mich., and with Louis I. Kahn (1901–71) in Philadelphia, Pa. He started his own

career as a partner in Lippincott, Venturi, Cope & Lippincott from 1958–61, then in the firm of Venturi & Short from 1961 to 1964. In 1964 he joined with John Rauch to form the firm Venturi and Rauch. In 1967 he married Denise Scott Brown, and she joined the firm as partner that year. Robert Venturi and Denise Scott Brown have a son, James. In 1980 the name of the firm was changed to Venturi, Rauch & Scott Brown, and since 1989, Venturi, Scott Brown and Associates. Robert Venturi was the 1991 recipient of the Pritzker Prize.

Denise Scott Brown was born Denise Lakofski in Nkana, Zambia, in 1931. She studied at the Kingsmead College, Johannesburg, South Africa, the University of Witwatersrand, and the Architectural Association School in London, U.K. In 1958, she emigrated to the United States and has been a naturalized citizen since 1967. She attended the University of Pennsylvania from 1958 to 1960 and earned a master's in city planning degree and a master's in architecture in 1965. In 1955 she married the architect Robert Scott Brown who died in 1959. She married Robert Venturi in 1967, and joined the firm as partner. Her teaching experience includes the University of Pennsylvania and University of California at Berkeley and at Los Angeles. Denise Scott Brown seeks to integrate architecture to the social concerns of the urban planner, as reflected in her work for the firm. In addition to her teaching, she has written many articles and coauthored books with her husband.

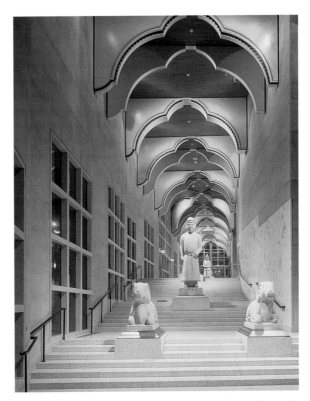

**VENTURI, ROBERT** Seattle Art Museum (1992), Seattle, Wash. *[Architects: Venturi, Scott Brown and Assoc. (Photo: Matt Wargo)]*

**VENTURI, ROBERT** Bard College (1993). *[Architects: Venturi, Scott Brown and Assoc. (Photo: Matt Wargo)]*

John Rauch was born in 1930 in Philadelphia, did his undergraduate studies at Wesleyan University in 1951, and transferred to the University of Pennsylvania at Philadelphia, where he received his bachelor's in architecture in 1957. John Rauch served in the U.S. Army from 1951 to 1953 and was in the Army Reserves from 1953 to 1955. He became partner with Robert Venturi in 1964 as the business partner of the firm.

**Further Reading** Moos, Stanislaus von: *Venturi, Rauch & Scott Brown: Buildings and Projects,* Rizzoli, New York, 1987; Schwartz, Frederick, ed., with essays by Vincent Scully and Robert Venturi: *Mother's House: The Evolution of Vanna Venturi's House in Chestnut Hill,* Rizzoli, New York, 1992; Scott Brown, Denise: *Urban Concepts,* Architectural Design Profile 83, St. Martin's Press, New York, 1990; Venturi, Robert: *Complexity and Contradiction in Architecture,* Museum of Modern Art, New York, 1966.

**VERTICAL TRANSPORTATION** A system for transferring people or objects between floors in buildings. A stair is the most common and rudimentary of such devices used in buildings today. When vertical transportation is mentioned today, the reference is usually to electrical or hydraulic devices, such as elevators or escalators. Many other devices are used for such purposes. (See the article entitled stair.)

**Vertical Transportation Devices** An elevator is a conveyance that lifts and lowers people and objects in a building by means of a car, cage, or platform in a vertical shaft. In England and some other places, an elevator is called a lift. The word *elevator* is used in England to denote a platform that can be raised or lowered vertically for such uses as construction of buildings. In the United States, such a device is generally called a scaffold and may or may not be motorized. A special kind of scaffold is sometimes attached to buildings for use in window washing and maintenance.

Temporary elevators for lifting workers and materials during building construction are sometimes called hoists. The word *hoist* may also be applied to lifting machinery, such as that employed in factories or warehouses and in other ways. An escalator is an inclined device for vertical transportation of people on moving stairs. A similar device is a moving ramp. The principle of escalators and moving ramps has also been applied to the movement of people and objects horizontally on moving sidewalks.

A stairlift is a device, used mostly in houses or other residential buildings, for transporting handicapped, ill, or elderly people up and down stairways. A stairlift is like a motorized chair that rides on the railing of a stairway. A dumbwaiter is like a small elevator and is used for raising or lowering objects in buildings. Other vertical transportation devices include pneumatic tube systems for conveying paperwork between various building locations, and many kinds of conveyors for materials and other objects. Information on various kinds of dumbwaiters, conveyors, hoists, and so on are included in articles in this book pertaining to building types and systems in which they are used.

Elevators may be used in all buildings two stories high or more. In buildings higher than two stories, they are considered necessities. Escalators are generally used in buildings where large numbers of people move in a single direction or where it is considered desirable to direct their movement in one direction. Ordinarily escalators are one story high, though some are higher, and groups of them are generally used for only a few stories. At first escalators were mostly used in transportation buildings, such as railway stations, airports, subways, and the like. Stores soon found them useful for directing shoppers through various floors and departments. Today escalators are often used in many other types of building, including hospitals, schools, hotels, and sports arenas and amphitheaters. Elevators, of course, have uses in almost every building type.

**Elevator Mechanisms** Although elevators may be used for transporting both people and materials, a distinction is often made between passenger and freight elevators. There are two major types of elevator mechanism: hydraulic, for buildings from two to about six stories; and electric, for buildings from two to any number of stories. Electric elevators are of two major types: geared traction and gearless traction. Geared traction elevators are often used in buildings of medium height and in which the elevator speeds do not exceed 350 feet per minute (ft/min). In taller buildings, elevators with speeds up to 1,000 ft/min or more, gearless traction elevators are usually used. Hydraulic elevator installations are limited by the fact that the hydraulic cylinders that furnish the lifting power must extend into the ground a distance equal to or greater than the height to which the elevator rises. Also their speeds are limited to a maximum of about 150 ft/min.

The major components of an electric elevator system are the hoistways, the vertical spaces in buildings in which elevators operate; the penthouse, a room on the roof of a building or above the top floor the elevator serves, in which various machinery is located, including electric motors that power the elevators, motor generators, and control panels; and the elevator cars. Inside the hoistways are guide rails which cause cars to move vertically without moving sideways or twisting. Elevators are hung from their tops on metal cables, called roping, which are raised or lowered by the electric motors above, with the aid of counterweights that help balance the cars and reduce the effective weight to which the motors are subjected.

A number of limit switches, safety devices, car leveling devices, buffers, and other components ensure safe, smooth, efficient operation of the cars. The whole operation is activated when a passenger pushes a button, and is usually controlled by computers or other automated devices, instead of elevator operators as in the past. Hydraulic elevators are similar to the electric, except that the operating mechanisms are hydraulic rather than electric; there is a need for pits underneath and shafts for the hydraulic plungers, but no penthouses are needed.

**Passenger Elevator Design** The proper design of elevator systems for buildings is quite complex and highly specialized. Some electrical engineers design such systems, while others are handled by elevator specialists. Proper elevator design begins with consideration of the characteristics of a building, such as the number of floors, heights of stories, critical periods of elevator travel, number of people using the building or the building population, and so on.

After determinations of this sort, consideration is given to such time factors as interval, the average time a

**VERTICAL TRANSPORTATION** Elevators, Hyatt-Regency Hotel (1967), Atlanta, Ga. [*Architect: John Calvin Portman*]

passenger must wait for an elevator, often taken to be a maximum of 30 to 40 seconds (s), but sometimes longer; and average round-trip time. The average round-trip time includes loading time in the lobby, door closing times at each stop, transfer times at each stop, the times taken for unloading and loading, until the highest stop is reached, and similar times for the return trip to the lobby and the opening of the door at that level.

After the time factors and the number of people to be served have been determined, the number of elevators and their capacities may be calculated. A number of other design decisions remain to be made, including location of the hoistways in the building; lobby arrangements and access, control, and operation of the elevators; and specific floors to be served. In some buildings, particularly relatively tall ones, elevators are zoned, that is, certain cars serve certain levels of the building exclusively. For example, some cars might serve only the second through seventh floors, others the eighth through fourteenth, and so on. Another method, sometimes used, is called the skip-floor system. In this system, cars stop at alternate floors. For example, in a medium-rise to high-rise building with two-story individual apartment units, elevators might stop on the living levels but not on the bedroom levels. A recent variation of this system utilizes double-decker elevator cars, each two stories tall.

Groupings of elevators usually range from two cars, side by side, up to eight elevators in two groups of four, across from each other. Though not generally recommended, larger groupings are sometimes used. Other important considerations in elevator design for buildings are locations in floor plans, provision for incoming and outgoing traffic, and traffic peak times. Also special considerations must be made in certain building types, such as commercial, apartment, institutional, multiuse, parking garage, and others.

**Escalator Design** The design of escalators starts with basic considerations similar to those for elevator design, including building population, number of floors, heights of stories, times of travel and use, and so on. In addition, it is considered desirable to locate escalators so that they are readily seen by potential passengers. Since escalators are essentially devices that run continuously in one direction, they are usually built in pairs, one going up, the other down. Their directions can be reversed if, for example, traffic flows upward in the morning and down in the evening. When escalators are the primary form of vertical transportation, they must be supplemented by elevators for handicapped people, mothers with baby carriages, and people with other problems.

Escalators are rated by their width at the approximate hip level of people and by their speed, which generally ranges from 90 to 120 ft/min. From these factors, their carrying capacity can be determined. Escalators

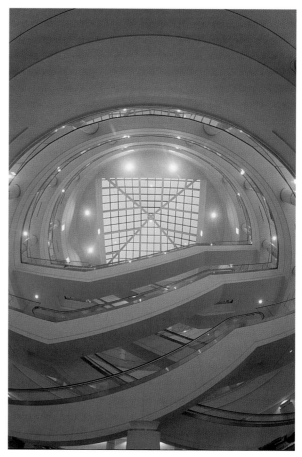

**VERTICAL TRANSPORTATION** Escalators, Chrysler Technology Center (1992), Auburn Hills, Mich. *[Architect: CRSS]*

generally occupy relatively large amounts of space. Therefore they are usually grouped, either side by side or crisscrossing each other. Escalators are usually thought to be superior to moving ramps, which take more space because of their relatively low inclines, and because escalators are considered safer.

**Freight Elevator Design** Freight and materials-handling elevators, including dumbwaiters, are usually designed in a manner similar to that of passenger elevators, except that the basis is the size and weight of loads to be carried rather than the requirements of people. Also passenger elevator cars are better finished than those used for materials. Materials-handling elevators may range in size from cars of about 1 ft$^2$ of floor area to about 9 ft$^2$ for dumbwaiters and, for freight elevators, up to almost any size and to carrying capacities of more than 50 tons. For freight elevators, attention must be paid to needs for loading and unloading. As is the case with other elevators, specialists are usually required for the design of freight and other materials-handling elevators.

**History** Devices for raising people and objects from one level to another have been used by humans from early ancient times. The earliest and most rudimentary were vines, ropes, and ladders, which were developed into stairways. Later, devices powered by humans or by animals were used. The earliest types of elevators usually employed systems of ropes, winches, pulleys, and windlasses, which lifted and lowered platforms carrying people or objects. These early elevators were very limited in the amount of weight that could be handled and the heights to which people and objects could be lifted. They were also quite dangerous for the ropes often broke and the elevator crashed down. The earliest passenger elevator is thought to have been invented about 253 B.C. by the Greek mathematician and scientist Archimedes (c. 287–212 B.C.), who also invented the pulleys with which the elevator operated.

Very little progress was made in elevator design for almost 2,000 years after Archimedes' invention. During that period, crude devices were used for lifting people and objects, but they had no safety devices to stop a fall when ropes broke. Most were powered by animals, usually horses by the late 18th and early 19th centuries. In the early 19th century, steam replaced horses as the source of power and later in that century hydraulic power was used. The real beginning of the elevators of today was in the second half of the 19th century. It is a matter of conjecture whether the desire to construct buildings of more than four or five stories in height led to the modern elevator or whether the development of safe elevators led to the design of tall buildings.

The first elevator with a safety device to keep it from falling if the ropes broke was demonstrated by its inventor Elisha Graves Otis (1811–61) in The Crystal Palace of the New York Exposition of 1853. Until the Otis invention, elevators were mostly used in factories and warehouses. In 1857 Otis installed the first of his new, safe elevators in the five-story Haughwout Building (1857), still in existence in New York City, designed by J. P. Gaynor. After that, elevators began to be widely used in stores and hotels at first, and later in other building types. For some years, both hydraulic and steam-pow-ered elevators were used, but the hydraulic type was faster and could lift to greater heights. In 1889 the first electric elevator was installed in a New York City building by the company of Otis's sons, which later became the Otis Elevator Company of today. In 1894 the same company installed the first automatic push-button elevator. In 1900 the Otis Company installed the first escalator in a building of the Paris Exposition. It was later removed and installed in a Philadelphia department store, where it operated until 1939.

As the heights of office buildings increased in the early 1900s, hydraulic elevators, which could not reach the heights accomplished by electric types, were superseded, except for their use in relatively low-rise buildings. This situation still exists today. Other improvements in electric elevators followed: automated and computerized systems, increased safety factors, smoother operation, and considerably higher speeds. Improvements in escalators have also been made and their principles adapted to moving sidewalks for horizontal movement of people and objects. Such improvements continue to be made even today.

Elevators may be very plain in design, very elegant, or anything in between. Many materials may be used and many unusual applications are possible. One has been the provision, in some very tall buildings, of intermediate lobbies to which express elevators take passengers, who then board locals to reach the next group of floors above the lobbies. Elevators can run up the outside of buildings or up the walls of interior open spaces. Such elevators are often, at least partly, glass-enclosed. Elevators need not run straight up, but may be placed on inclines. Other innovations may be expected in the future.

**Related Articles** AIRPORT; APARTMENT; COMMUNICATION SYSTEM; ELECTRICAL ENGINEERING; OFFICE BUILDING; STAIR.

**Further Reading** Strakosch, George R.: *Vertical Transportation—Elevators and Escalators*, 2d ed., John Wiley, New York, 1983.

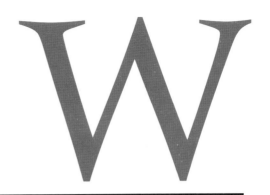

WALL A part of a building, usually vertical or nearly so, that encloses it or subdivides it into rooms. A wall that helps to support the weight of the building is called a bearing wall, while an exterior wall that does not is called a curtain wall. An interior wall, bearing or curtain, is often called a partition. Many of the important aspects of walls are discussed in other articles. For example, for further discussion on the structures of bearing walls, see articles entitled concrete structure; masonry structure; steel structure; wood-frame structure. For openings in walls, see articles entitled door; window. See also the article entitled weather protection.

**Types** In addition to the walls of buildings, others are used in architecture, including garden walls or similar types for enclosing outdoor areas, and retaining walls for preventing earth from sliding down into areas. A cavity wall is made of masonry with a separation between the masonry units on the exterior side and those on the interior side. A party wall is shared between two buildings or units of a building. A fire wall has a certain degree of fire resistance, often measured in terms of the hours, from one to four, it can be expected to withstand flames, before failing. A parapet wall extends above the roof of a building. Fire walls usually have parapets extending about 3 ft above roofs. A window wall is a curtain wall made entirely of glass with metal frames. A spandrel wall in a multistory building occupies the spaces between strips of windows.

**Functions** Although they may seem quite simple elements of buildings, walls are actually among the most complex because of the great variety of functions they serve. Exterior walls are expected to protect buildings and their occupants from a great many inconveniences, discomforts, and dangers, including intruders, insects, dirt, odors, animals, rain and other precipitation, winds, hot and cold temperatures, lightning, fires, condensa-

tion, floods, noise, sunlight, and earthquakes. In addition, exterior walls are expected to provide privacy inside buildings. On the other hand, exterior walls are also expected to allow access to the interior for occupants, visitors, and other people; light; solar heat; breezes; warm or cool temperatures; and pets. At the same time, exterior walls are required, in many cases, to permit views from the interiors of buildings to the outside. Exterior walls are also expected to allow passage from the interior to the outside for occupants, visitors, and other people; pets; air; heat; odors; light; and sometimes to permit views from the outside in. As if all these diverse, sometimes conflicting, functions were not enough, exterior walls are also very important determinants of the appearance of architecture.

Not only are exterior walls expected to have the flexibility to perform all or most of the above functions but

WALL Pre-Columbian dry stone wall, Chaco Canyon National Monument, New Mexico [Architect: unknown]

they are also expected to be easy to maintain and repair and to be economically feasible. If bearing walls, they must also support the construction above them in buildings. Interior walls may have all the above functions, in some cases, but in most will not be quite so complex. Interior walls are expected to provide the desired architectural effects.

**Exterior Wall Finishes** Building exterior walls may be enclosed with any of a great many materials, including most of those used in architecture. Bearing walls of masonry, concrete block or brick, clay brick, structural clay tile, stone, and others may be used. Many of these materials, such as brick or stone, may also be used as veneers for walls of other materials, such as concrete block or structural clay tile. Reinforced concrete may also be used for walls. Masonry walls of certain materials, such as structural tile and concrete block, may be finished with stucco. Others, including those of building brick, are often painted.

Masonry materials, such as stone or brick, may also be used as veneers for light wood-frame walls. Also used for such purposes are many wood materials, such as shingles or shakes; siding of various types; board and batten, consisting of relatively wide boards placed vertically with small strips or battens, sheets of plywood; asbestos-cement shingles or boards; aluminum shingles or sheet; plastic shingles; corrugated or sheet plastic materials; stucco; galvanized iron; and many other materials. Glass is an important material in such walls, for fixed as well as operating windows, and sometimes for doors, and also in the form of glass block.

**Exterior Curtain Walls** These walls, usually with metal frames, may be obtained with panels of aluminum, porcelain enamel, stainless steel, copper alloys, stone, thin-veneer brick, architectural terra-cotta, now usually called ceramic veneer, clay tiles of various types, glass, plastics, concrete, steel, and other materials. Often prefabricated in relatively large units, such curtain walls may have insulation, windows, exterior and interior finish materials, and other components completely assembled. Delivered to the sites of buildings, the complete assemblies are erected into walls, with only the installation of weatherproofing and fire-resistant backup walls if required to be added on the job.

If properly designed, such curtain walls have a number of advantages over past types. They efficiently protect from weather and are light, preassembled, and have long useful lives, strength, and flexibility. They also eliminate much handwork on building sites and may be easily erected from inside buildings.

**Interior Building Walls** These walls or partitions may be constructed of and finished with any of the materials used for exterior bearing walls: brick, stone, wood, frame, concrete, and so on. Nonbearing walls may also be constructed of such materials, but may also utilize others, attached to wood or metal studs, including gypsum board, plaster on plaster lath, hardboard, fiberboard, particle board, plywood or solid-wood paneling, and ceramic tile. Some of these materials have integral ceramic, laminated plastic, baked enamel, or other finishes. For materials that do not have integral finishes, paint or other coatings, wallpaper or cloth, various types of fiber cloth, plastics, fabrics, cork, and other finishes may be applied.

**Nonbearing Partitions** Solid gypsum boards and solid plaster on metal or gypsum lath are also used for nonbearing partitions. Another type of nonbearing partition, called a movable partition, is often used in buildings, such as offices, where frequent floor layout changes may occur. Such partitions are available from manufacturers as complete systems with framing members, wall finish materials, door and frames, and sometimes with integral electric fixtures and conduits for electrical and telephone service lines. Although most types might not be movable in the strictest sense, they do permit considerable flexibility in the arrangement of interior spaces. And many of the components are salvageable for further use after changes have been made.

A special type of nonbearing partition often used in architecture is a folding partition, actually a large folding door that may be closed or opened to convert a large space into smaller ones and vice versa. Another special type, used in open-planned offices, sometimes called office landscaping, is a space divider that acts as a low partition and at the same time as bookshelves, storage, or other office furniture. Partial partitions of other types are also often used, including ones constructed in a manner similar to that of full-height types. Partial partitions of this sort may be any desired height; they may be solid or have glass or plastic from about waist level to the tops.

Hollow types of bearing and nonbearing exterior and interior walls often serve another purpose, the concealment of piping, ductwork, conduits, vents, and chases or other spaces required for plumbing, heating, air-conditioning, electrical, telephone, and other systems.

**Design** Both exterior and interior walls come in a wide variety of types, finishes, acoustical ratings, and fire resistances, and with an equally wide choice of accessories, such as windows, doors and other openings, solar shades, provisions for mechanical and electrical systems, and other characteristics. This often bewildering array presents architects and other environmental designers with some of their most intriguing and baffling problems. At the same time, the proper design of walls for both function and appearance is one of the most challenging and gratifying of design experiences. Some authorities have suggested that architects and other designers should consider walls as filters. In this sense,

**WALL** Exterior wall detail, IBM Corporate Computer Center (1972), Sterling Forest, N.Y. *[Architect: Gunnar Birkerts]*

walls may act, flexibly, as barriers, limits, or passages for people, precipitation, temperature, light, views, sounds, odors, and other factors. A perfect wall would function as a barrier, limit, and passage, in various combinations at various times, subject to the will and needs of the occupants.

In addition, walls must be designed with adequate strength to function properly and, in some cases, to provide protection from fires, hurricanes, earthquakes, and other dangers. And all the many functions must be properly performed, while the walls also serve as one of the most important determinants of the appearance or aesthetics of buildings. To architects, who customarily design walls except in unusual cases, the challenge is a great one.

**History** During the most ancient times, humans are thought to have provided their crude shelters with walls of thatch, leaves or brush, or animal skins. By the time of the great ancient cultures around the Mediterranean Sea, beginning about 3000 B.C., quite functional walls had been developed. Walls in Mesopotamia were usually of sun-dried then kiln-dried brick; they were thick and massive to shield the interiors of buildings from the hot sun. In Crete and other places, in and around the Aegean Sea, the lower portions of walls were usually of stone with timber framing above and sun-dried brick between the timbers. Walls were often covered with stucco outside and painted inside.

In Egypt, walls were usually of massive, thick limestone or sandstone or of sun-dried then kiln-dried brick. Walls were usually carved in low relief and often had thin coats of painted stucco. In ancient Greece, walls for the most important buildings were of carefully and skillfully cut and placed stone, with the units usually con-

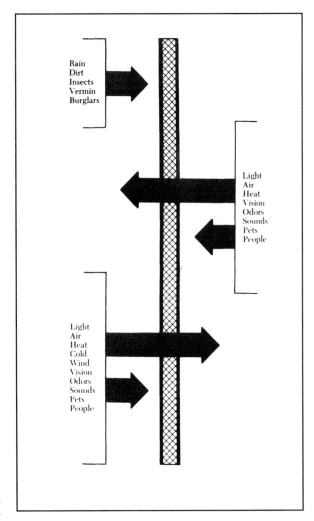

**WALL** The wall as a filter.

nected together with cramps and dowels of lead or iron, and set without mortar. In some instances, coarse-grained stone was used and covered with stucco made with marble dust. For houses, stone was often used for the lower parts of walls with stucco-covered brick above.

The Romans used stone and sometimes brick in their walls, but their favorite material was concrete. Often the Romans would cover concrete walls or those of other materials with thin veneers of stone or with plaster or stucco. Roman walls were usually massive, thick bearing walls. Early Christian architecture made use of the Roman methods, employing brick or stone that was often covered with stucco or plaster. Byzantine walls were usually of brick, and highly ornamented with marble or glass mosaics. During the Romanesque period, walls were generally along the lines of those of the Romans, but usually of somewhat heavy, rough construction.

During the Gothic period, walls were generally of cut stone set in lime mortar for cathedrals and other

**WALL** Former construction method contrasted with a metal curtain-wall product.

important buildings. For less important buildings timber was used in a system called half-timbered. In the half-timbered system, heavy posts and diagonal members make up the structure of walls. To fill in the spaces between the timbers, bricks or more often wattle and daub, a sort of plaster made of a mixture of clay with straw or sticks, were used. In some Gothic buildings, walls were load bearing, but in others, such as many of those in the cathedrals, the main loads were carried by columns or pilasters with vaults overhead. The walls acted as curtain walls supporting only their own weights. In many cases, particularly in cathedrals and other religious and public buildings, walls were ornamented with carvings or sculpture. Brick walls were rarely used during the Gothic period.

During the Renaissance, walls for important buildings were usually of brick or carefully and accurately cut and placed stone. Those of brick were often covered with facings of stone, but sometimes brick and stone were combined and left exposed. Brick was sometimes used for main walls, with stone quoins at the corners of buildings and around windows and doors. Stucco or plaster was frequently used to cover walls constructed of other materials and was often ornamented. Some of the greatest artists of the Renaissance painted frescoes or other types of murals on the interior walls, mostly of religious buildings.

After the Renaissance, the design of walls of buildings in America as well as elsewhere generally followed the precedents of the past historic styles from which they were derived. Most were bearing walls constructed from the materials that had been used in the past, such as stone, brick, wood, stucco, and so on. In the 19th century, with the beginning of the modern movement in architecture and the use of metal skeleton frames, bearing walls were gradually superseded in many building types by curtain walls of various kinds. The Monadnock Building (1891) in Chicago, designed by Burnham and Root, pushed the use of bearing walls to the limit: 16 stories, requiring 6-ft-thick walls for the first story. This was the last tall brick bearing-wall building. After that, bearing walls were largely outmoded, except for smaller buildings, such as houses.

Although curtain walls had always been used in architecture, the tall skeleton-framed buildings ushered in many new developments in this type of wall. At first, brick and stone were used for curtain walls in much the same way they had been used previously in bearing-wall buildings. Later thin walls, sheathed with various materials, such as copper, bronze, thin-stone slabs, stainless steel, aluminum, or glass, were developed. For walls of this type, building codes required a backup of masonry or other fire-resistant materials, thus effectively reducing the value of the prefabricated, production-line nature

of the new walls. Later some of these requirements were relaxed, making it possible to produce curtain walls in relatively large units, complete with windows, insulation, and sometimes interior finishes, deliver them to building sites in large assemblies, and erect them quickly and efficiently on building structural frames.

Today walls for buildings may be constructed of a great variety of materials, in various sizes and shapes, plain or ornamented. Many of the types are available as stock items from manufacturers, while others are designed individually by architects.

**Related Articles** CLIMATE; DOOR; FIRE PROTECTION; GLASS; INSULATION, THERMAL; PREFABRICATION; SOUND CONTROL; STRUCTURE; WATERPROOFING; WEATHER PROTECTION; WINDOW; Articles on various materials, components, and systems.

**WALTER, THOMAS USTICK** American architect (1804–87). Thomas Ustick Walter received his architectural training from William Strickland (1787–1854), a great Classic Revival architect, who had in turn received

**WALTER, THOMAS USTICK** Interior, Dome of U.S. Capitol (1850), Washington, D.C.

663

his training from the noted architect Benjamin Henry Latrobe (1764–1820), who had been one of the founders and early leaders of the Classic Revival movement in America. It was only natural then that when Walter became an architect, he would design buildings in the Classic Revival style, derived mostly from ancient Greece.

**Private Practitioner** Walter had an unusual career as an architect, divided into three major stages: the first as a private practitioner, the second as a government architect, the third in semiretirement. At twenty-eight, he won a competition for a very important building, Founders Hall, Girard College for Orphans, Philadelphia, winning the commission over some of the greatest architects of the time, all older than he. In this building, completed in 1847, Walter achieved what many think is the climax of the Greek phase of the Classic Revival style. Soon Walter was recognized as a leading American architect and began to receive important commissions for churches, public buildings, office buildings, banks, and houses.

Before the Girard College competition, Walter had received only one important commission, the Moyamensing Prison (1832), Philadelphia, a building that he designed, oddly enough, in Gothic Revival style. Later when he added a Debtors' Wing (1835) to the prison, he utilized an Egyptian style, thought by architects of the time to be appropriate for places where people would be incarcerated. Among Walter's designs for houses, the most notable was that for the Greek Revival Andalusia (1836) near Philadelphia, the home of the banker Nicholas Biddle (1786–1844). Another important Greek Revival building, still in existence, is Hibernian Hall (1935), Charleston, S.C.

**Government Architect** In 1850 Walter's professional life entered the second stage. In that year he won the competition for a new dome to replace that of the U.S. Capitol (see illustration), in Washington, D.C. Appointed architect of the Capitol the following year, Walter took over the construction of the dome, which is now a dominant feature of the Washington scene. Of cast-iron construction, the dome established Walter as a leader among architects of the time and as a talented engineer as well. During his tenure as architect of the Capitol, Walter confined his architectural practice to work on the Capitol and on other Washington government buildings. In addition to the great dome, completed in 1863, Walter also extended the wings, completing that of the House of Representatives in 1857 and the Senate in 1859.

While in Washington, Walter did alterations, extensions, and remodeling of a number of other buildings, including the Treasury Building; the Old Patent Office, now the National Portrait Gallery; and the Old Post Office, now a multiuse building with stores and shops.

**Semiretirement** In 1865 Walter's career entered the third and last stage. Having resigned from his government office because of ill health, Walter practiced architecture only sporadically for the more than 20 years before his death. He spent the last 10 of those years as president of the American Institute of Architects, of which he had been a cofounder in 1857.

**Life** Thomas Ustick Walter was born in Philadelphia on September 4, 1804, the son of a brick mason and builder. Having had little formal schooling, he entered the office of William Strickland in 1819, when he was fifteen, but left after a short time to study mathematics, science, and construction on his own. In 1822 he went back into Strickland's office as an apprentice and remained there for several years.

In 1830 Walter started his own practice and the following year obtained his first important commission, Moyamensing Prison. In 1832 Walter won a competition for an even more important building, Founders Hall at Girard College. The other architects competing were a distinguished group: Strickland, his former employer, who placed second; Isaiah Rogers (1780–1869) of Boston, who placed third; Ithiel Town (1784–1844) and Alexander Jackson Davis (1803–92) of New York City; and John Haviland (1792–1852) of Philadelphia. This was quite a conquest for a young, beginning architect and brought Walter considerable recognition.

After winning the competition, Walter received commissions for other buildings in Philadelphia and elsewhere. In 1836 he was one of the founders of the American Institution of Architects, in New York City, and later, after this organization had failed, helped found the American Institute of Architects, also in that city, in 1857, along with Davis who had been an original member of the earlier group, Richard Upjohn (1802–78), and 11 other architects. Upjohn became the first president of the AIA, serving 18 years until 1877, when Walter became the second president and served until his death 10 years later.

In 1850 Walter won the competition for the design of a new dome for the U.S. Capitol, Washington, to replace that originally designed by William Thornton (1759–1826) and completed by Charles Bulfinch (1763–1844).

In 1851 he was appointed architect of the Capitol by President Millard Fillmore (1800–74) and retained that position for 15 years until 1865. He replaced Robert Mills (1781–1855), who had served in the position since 1836. It is ironical that in 1838, when Walter was thirty-four, he had written a report recommending that the unfinished U.S. Treasury Building (1842) of Mills be demolished. This did not happen but in a further irony, Walter designed additions to the Treasury Building that were completed in 1869. During the 15 years, he worked not only on the Capitol but on a number of other government buildings. After resigning his Washington position because of ill health, Walter returned to Philadelphia. Although he was associated for a time with John McArthur, Jr. (1823–90), the designer of the Philadelphia City Hall (1890), Walter never returned to full-time practice.

Walter married Mary Anne Hancocks, and they had 11 children, including a son, Thomas Ustick Walter, Jr., who became an architect. He in turn had a son, Thomas Ustick Walter III (1864–1931), who also became an architect. Walter's wife died in the birth of her eleventh child, and later, he married Amanda Gardiner, by whom he had two children.

Walter was honored in his later years for his work, receiving several honorary degrees, including a Ph.D. from Harvard University in 1867. When he died on October 30, 1887, at age eighty-three, he had been out of his position as architect of the Capitol for some 22 years, yet the government still owed him $25,000 for his work. The profession he had served so well, represented by the AIA, petitioned Congress, 10 years later, to pay his heirs the money he was owed. Congress granted the heirs not the full amount but $14,000.

**Related Articles** CAPITAL, UNITED STATES; CLASSIC REVIVAL ARCHITECTURE; MILLS, ROBERT; STRICKLAND, WILLIAM.

**WAREHOUSE** A building, or a room in a building, in which objects are stored. In addition, warehouses must have provisions for receiving and shipping. Warehouses are important elements of factories for handling both raw materials and finished products. They are also important in many other kinds of businesses, such as retailing and wholesaling products. A bonded warehouse is one in which goods may be stored without paying taxes or duty until the goods are withdrawn. Similarly, a warehouse in a free zone or free port is one in which goods may be stored without payment of customs duty until shipped.

There has been a trend to regional warehouses where retail goods can be collected and easily distributed to retail stores in metropolitan areas. Often these warehouses are built in suburban or semirural areas where land costs are lower. A major criterion for such is a good road system easily accessible by trucks.

**Design** Warehouses are utilitarian and thus are not often highly regarded as an architectural building type. However, these buildings require a considerable amount of design skill to make them economical and efficient.

Some of the major considerations are open floors as free of columns and other obstructions as possible; proper heights, widths, and lengths for efficient storage and handling; strong structures to withstand heavy loads on floors; and flexibility of layout to facilitate changes and special storage problems.

**Mechanical Handling Devices** Perhaps the most important consideration in the design of warehouses today is the provision of mechanical handling devices appropriate to the products to be handled. Most warehouse handling is performed with the aid of such devices, which include forklift trucks, tractor trailers, conveyors, and overhead systems. Forklift trucks have prongs that may be inserted under pallets, portable platforms on which products are stored, lifting and stacking and removing the pallets as required. Forklifts may also place pallets on tractor trailers for long horizontal movements. Conveyors of many kinds are used, including belts, chains, chutes, and elevators. Overhead systems include monorails and various kinds of cranes. Recently, there has been a trend toward automation in warehouses, with mechanical handling devices activated by computers or other electronic devices.

Warehouses may be single-story or multistory. The decision about which type to construct is based mainly on the articles to be stored, the size of the site available, and which type will be most economical.

**History** Since prehistoric times, some storage has been used, at first in caves and later in simple structures. With the expansion of trading activities during the Middle Ages, warehousing, as now known, started. Early warehouses were built along waterways which were the major means of transportation. Later they were built along roads and railroads and then near airports.

**American Development** The earliest warehouses in colonial America were built beside the docks in Atlantic seaboard towns to handle the storage of goods arriving from Europe and goods to be shipped there. Gradually, as river transportation developed and roads and canals were built, warehouses also appeared along these trade routes. And the growth of cities, with their increasing mercantile activities, brought warehouses into urban areas, a trend that has been somewhat reversed in later years.

**Related Article** FACTORY.

**WATERPROOFING** Moisture protection, which involves procedures used to prevent damage to buildings from water or vapor.

**Definitions** Terminology includes *dampproofing* which describes materials of low permeability used to prevent moisture from entering a wall, foundation, or slab on grade. *Waterproofing* describes the use of materials with high permeability used where a foundation may be subject to water pressure called hydrostatic conditions. *Water table* refers to the below-grade standing water elevation, which may vary over time. *Condensation* refers to water changing from vapor to a liquid. This occurs when the air is saturated to 100 percent humidity. *Surface water* is water which travels over the surface of the ground, sometimes caused by an impervious surface. *Moisture protection* is the generic term for keeping water out of a building.

**Sources of Water** Water includes rain, snow, and ice, surface water, ground water, high water tables, and condensation on surfaces or in the building enclosure. Not normally addressed are such things as broken water lines, blocked drains, or improper operation of sprinklers.

Most building materials are not impervious to moisture and require attention as to their use. Some of these materials may expand at differing rates, requiring design of joints to accommodate movement without admitting water.

**Systems** The roof system is the most needed for moisture control in most climates. Proper flashing to other surfaces or for roof penetrations is a part of the roof system. Because of temperature differences between the air and the interior, release of water vapor is necessary by use of roof vents or cap vents. Gutters and downspouts are used to carry water from the roof to the ground and must be properly sized and maintained to fulfill their function. In areas subject to freezing, it may be necessary to add waterproof membranes at the perimeter of roofs under roofing shingles to prevent damage from ice dams.

Masonry walls have always been a problem when exposed to wind-driven rain. Cracks between the masonry unit and the mortar joint are almost impossible to avoid. Results of moisture in masonry include possible spalling of the masonry and efflorescence from chemical reaction of the mortar and the masonry. To control these conditions, the theory of masonry walls is to allow water which may enter the wall to be collected and drained out at the bottom through weep holes. High-rise curtain wall design uses a similar theory. In some high buildings, wind-driven rain may actually flow up the wall. In addition to wind forces, thermal changes between sunlit and shaded surfaces add stress to the wall and may open up joints.

Openings in walls such as doors and windows require proper installation to keep out water. Sealants are needed between frames and adjoining materials, as is flashing at the sill to allow water running down the window or door to exit without damaging the building. Condensation on the surfaces of glass or metal may be controlled by double or triple glazing with thermal separated frames.

Where ground meets a building is a vulnerable spot for water entry. Problems can occur if the ground does not slope away from the building and if backfill has been improperly placed or contains inappropriate material such as trash, rocks, clay, or organic materials.

**Foundations** Materials can be grouped as two types, those to remove water and those to seal the foundation to prevent moisture from entering. The first group includes footing drains, which allow water to be drained away from the wall. A similar system is to use foundation mats designed to drain water off the wall to be collected in the footing drains. The other group are impervious materials applied to the structural foundation. Historically this might have been tar but now is more likely to involve adhesives and sheet materials. Depending on the site, these materials may be required for slabs and walls treated to form a continuous membrane. An additional concrete slab may be required over the continuous membrane. Sometimes this work is limited to elevator pits, sump pumps, and other low-lying spaces.

Also used are spray-on materials including bentonite, or liquid applied rubbers and urethanes protected with a polyethylene sheet and polystyrene insulation or other board. Areaways must be provided with drainage provisions. The specification of foundation weatherproofing should be considered a system, and selection should be carefully made, since remedial work is very expensive.

**Historic Buildings** Many older buildings were built without adequate knowledge about moisture protection. Typical problems include decay of wood, spalling brick, surface salts, deterioration of stone and metals. The U.S. National Park Service has several publications of use for preservation of existing buildings.

**Insulation and Vapor Barriers** Because of differences between outside and inside temperatures in many climates, buildings are insulated. Under some conditions dewpoint temperatures may occur in the wall. For this reason vapor barriers are introduced into the wall construction. Placement of vapor barriers in the wall is determined by analysis of climate and construction. Sometimes water vapor can be added or subtracted from the interior air. In times of high relative humidity, condensation may occur on cool surfaces, with the possibility of molds and mildew. Increased ventilation can be provided, and water vapor can be lowered using a dehumidification system.

**Related Articles** BRICK; CONCRETE; CONCRETE STRUCTURE; DOOR; FLOOR; FOUNDATION; INSULATION, THERMAL; MASONRY STRUCTURE; PAINT; ROOF; ROOFING; STONE; WALL; WINDOW.

**Further Reading** *ASHRAE Handbook of Fundamentals,* American Society of Heating, Refrigerating, and Air Conditioning Engineers, New York, 1985; *The NCRA Roofing and Waterproofing Manual,* 3d ed., National Roofing Contractors Association, Rosemont, Ill., 1989; Smith, B. M.: *Moisture Problems in Historic Masonry Walls: Diagnosis and Treatment,* U.S. Department of the Interior, National Park Service, Preservation Assistance Division, undated.

**WEATHER PROTECTION** The provisions employed protect buildings and the occupants from discomfort, damage, injury, or death from the effects of weather, the natural atmospheric phenomena of temperature, wind, sun, humidity, and precipitation in the form of rain, sleet, snow, and hail. Weather, or meteorology, is the science concerned with such phenomena over relatively short periods of time, while climatology is the science concerned with the same phenomena over periods of many years.

Both climate and weather are important considerations in architecture. One set of concerns deals with the usual or relatively normal effects of climate and weather, including protection of buildings and their occupants from heat, cold, precipitation, and humidity, and controlling the admission or exclusion of the sun into buildings. Much of the work of architects and other design professionals is devoted to such considerations and to ways in which weather phenomena may be excluded, controlled, or modified to provide general protection for buildings and protection and comfort for the occupants. For further discussion on considerations of this sort, see titles listed at the end of this article.

**Catastrophes** Another important concern of architecture is the disastrous effects that weather may have on buildings and the occupants. Along with earthquakes and fires, weather causes the most damaging catastrophes for both buildings and their occupants. Catastrophic weather events include lightning strikes and heavy snow on buildings. (See articles on fire protection; roof; seismic design; structure.)

Other than the above weather events, the most dangerous are high winds and flooding; flooding may be caused by winds, heavy precipitation, earthquakes, and volcanic eruptions. Catastrophic events are often interrelated in other ways. For example, earthquakes frequently cause fires when gas lines are broken. Similar things may happen during or after other catastrophes. Heavy snows or rains may cause flooding and mud slides which engulf or severely damage buildings.

**Winds** The major damage to buildings and injuries or deaths of people caused by strong winds result from the tremendous forces of the winds themselves and wind-driven water. It is generally considered impractical or economically infeasible to protect all buildings against all possible catastrophes. However, buildings and their occupants can be protected in high-risk areas by proper measures against the hazards of high winds and flooding.

High winds occur in storms, disturbances of the atmosphere in which differences primarily in temperature and atmospheric pressure cause masses of air to move rapidly in a counterclockwise direction in the Northern Hemisphere, clockwise in the Southern Hemisphere. This circular motion of air is usually called cyclonic and the effects it produces, cyclones. All cyclonic winds revolve around centers of relatively low pressure and the winds blow inward toward the low. Anticyclonic winds blow outward from centers of high pressure. For the most part, such conditions produce only ordinary weather, not storms. When a storm develops, its winds gain in velocity and pick up moisture that eventually may be deposited in the form of precipitation. The high winds of storms over oceans or other sizable bodies of water build tremendous waves and drive them to create unusually large tides, especially when a storm occurs at the same time as normal high tides.

Winds are usually measured on the Beaufort scale, which has been in use since 1805. Numbers on the Beaufort scale range from 0, when air is completely calm, to 17, the strongest possible wind. Another method, employed particularly in boating and other marine activities, classifies dangerous winds and their accompanying sea conditions as warnings, including small-craft warnings when winds are near but do not exceed about 31 miles per hour (mph), gale warnings 32 to 54 mph, whole gale warnings 55 to 73 mph, and hurricane warnings above 73 mph (12–17 on the Beaufort scale). Gale winds may cause damage to buildings and injury to people, and whole gale winds even more extensive damage to buildings and trees and injury or death to people. The major damage to buildings and injuries and loss of life to people are caused by winds of hurricane force. Such winds are found in three major types of storm: hurricanes, cyclones, and tornadoes.

**Hurricanes** A hurricane may be defined as a large, violent storm, with winds of 74 mph or more, sometimes with gusts to more than 200 mph, which revolves counterclockwise in the Northern Hemisphere. Hurricanes, which are intense tropical cyclones, are formed over the ocean in tropical regions and generally move northward, at first somewhat toward the northwest, then in a northerly direction, and later somewhat toward the northeast. Hurricanes usually begin as tropical disturbances and progress to tropical storms, with winds exceeding 40 mph.

In the center of a hurricane is a region of almost complete calm, some 20 miles (mi) in diameter, around which the high winds spread out as far as several hundred miles. Hurricanes usually move relatively slowly, some 10 to 30 mph, but they are erratic and hard to predict both in velocity and direction of movement. Occurring mainly between June and November, they are most frequent in September. When hurricanes travel over water, they often intensify and accelerate. Over land, friction slows them down and dissipates their energy, raising the pressure and slowing the winds. However, heavy rains may continue for some time. It was formerly believed that only buildings and people on the coasts of the Gulf of Mexico and the Southern Atlantic states were dangerously exposed to hurricanes, but many hurricanes have taken their greatest toll in the Eastern and Middle Atlantic states.

**Cyclones** Another type of cyclone, called extratropical, revolves counterclockwise around a center in the Northern Hemisphere and may develop winds that can reach hurricane force. Such cyclones in the United States usually originate over the Western states, from which they move generally from the Southwest toward the Northeast. A cyclone of this type may be less than 100 mi in diameter or it may be large enough to cover the entire United States. Large cyclones usually move only 100 or so mi per day, but smaller ones may move more rapidly. While cyclones may cause damage, injury, and death in the same manner as hurricanes, most pass over the country without causing problems of this kind.

**Tornadoes** An extremely intense storm, like a small cyclone, usually only a few hundred yards to a few miles across, is called a tornado or sometimes a twister. Tornadoes characteristically have tall, narrow, funnel-shaped clouds, move relatively fast, from 25 to 40 mph, and have very short lives of only about half an hour or so. During their short life span, they are, for their size, the most destructive of all storms, with winds up to several hundred miles per hour.

Tornadoes occur in all parts of the world. In the United States, they occur most frequently in the Midwestern states, but there have been numerous occurrences in many other places, including the states of the Deep South. Although properly designed and constructed buildings may withstand the effects of tornadoes, light-framed houses and other less sturdy types may not. In any case, in areas where tornadoes occur regularly and frequently, concrete storm cellars or other refuges are often provided for protection of people.

Tornadoes at sea are called waterspouts. A typhoon is what a hurricane is called if it originates over the Pacific Ocean. Typhoons usually occur from July to October, form in the North Pacific Ocean, and travel northwest and then northeast, bringing death and destruction mainly to the islands of the Pacific and Eastern countries, such as China, Japan, and India.

**Blizzards** A blizzard is an intense winter storm with heavy snowfalls, high winds, and usually quite low temperatures. Blizzards ordinarily occur when very cold Arctic air meets warmer air from the South, forming low-pressure areas called cold fronts along the lines where the masses of air meet. In the United States, blizzards are most common in the Midwestern states but may occur in states to the south and east of that area. The snow and low temperatures, made worse by the wind-chill factor, cause blizzards to be extremely dangerous and disruptive to human activities. The greatest dangers to buildings and their occupants, other than failure of heating systems, is from the heavy snow loads that may be deposited on roofs and from high winds. For a discussion of snow loads, see the article entitled structure.

**Protection for People** People may be protected from severe storms by evacuation before a storm strikes, in shelters, by locations of buildings on less hazardous sites, and by proper building design to resist the effects of wind, water, and other hazards. Another method is the modification or prevention of storms, an activity that, though still in its infancy, has been the subject of considerable research and some practical applications. Recently, the National Weather Service, in cooperation with weather services of other nations, has greatly improved its prediction of storms. Through its hurricane watches and warnings, tornado watches and warnings, and marine advisories and warnings, the Weather Service has made it possible for people to anticipate violent storm activities and to evacuate or take shelter. A watch alerts people to the possibilities of storm activities and a warning indicates that people should evacuate or take shelter. Through the use of radar, airplane surveillance, weather satellites, and other techniques, the loss of lives has been dramatically reduced.

**Building Protection** Protection of buildings from severe storms is mainly a matter of proper location away from hazardous areas and proper structural and architectural design. Very little can be done about the predilection of people to build in high-risk hurricane areas, such as along the beaches of the Gulf of Mexico and Atlantic coasts, the tornado areas of the Midwest, and high-risk areas elsewhere. However, proper structural design of buildings and their location above storm tide levels may prevent major damage during intense storms. In some cases, as in the disastrous mud slides in southern California caused by torrential rains, some experts believe that nothing can prevent major damage short of location of buildings in safer areas.

**Wind Damage** The structural and architectural design of buildings to resist intense activities of wind and water are governed by requirements in various building and other codes. However, some experts think that these requirements do not go far enough. The criteria to be used in the design of any building in a hazardous area should be based on the records from that area, from which probabilities of similar occurrences can be derived. In any wind storm, the least consequential dangers are the loss of TV antennas, roofing, and the like, followed in gravity by loss of glass and windows or walls, proceeding to structural damage, and finally to building collapse. The winds tend to make buildings overturn, slide from their foundations, or for whole buildings or part of them to be lifted upward. Also winds may hurl debris against buildings, damaging them. In addition, in some cases, particularly in tornadoes, relatively high air pressures within buildings as compared to extremely low pressures outside can cause buildings literally to explode.

**Wind Resistance** In general, the major factors affecting the design of buildings for wind resistance are the forces of winds that may be encountered, including those in high-velocity gusts, and building shapes, dimensions, and height-width ratios. All these must be carefully considered. For example, a tall narrow building must withstand greater forces than a short wide one. In order to overcome the effects of strong winds, a building structure must be properly designed, particularly in matters that might cause it to be deformed or deflect, in proper anchoring of the building and its elements to prevent uplift or overturning, and in the proper design of enclosure elements, such as roofs, walls, and windows, particularly the glass in windows, to withstand the great forces to which they will be subjected.

**Storm Damage** The effect of water in severe storms, sometimes called storm surge, can cause coastal areas to be inundated with tides as much as 24 ft or more above normal. When the storm-driven tides coincide with normal high tides, they can reach even greater heights. Storm surges tend to cause buildings to overturn or slide and can also cause erosion or scouring under foundations. Other damage, injury, and loss of life can occur in the inundation by the flood waters or can be caused by the extremely strong forces or currents and wave action and by debris hurled against buildings by the force of the water.

**Storm Resistance** Proper use of codes and standards will aid in the design of storm-resistant structures. Also the use of proper materials and structures is important. For example, reinforced concrete structures, if properly designed, are thought to be able to resist even the most destructive of storms: hurricanes and tornadoes. Specialized design for storm resistance, by experts, is certainly appropriate in many cases. Adequate insurance against the perils of storms to buildings should be carried. Policies today as well as in the past usually insure against most hazards, except the effects of flooding. Until somewhat recently, flood insurance was not available, and those who incurred damage by water found themselves, often to their dismay, not covered for risks of this sort. In other cases, flood insurance, though available, was not carried because of its extremely high cost. Today in some areas of the country, flood insurance, at reasonable rates made possible by federal government sponsorship, is available.

**History** The hazards of violent weather have always been a factor in human life. Almost every year, a number of people are injured or killed and vast amounts of property damage occur. The first recorded hurricane spawned in America occurred on February 12, 1493, and was noted by Christopher Columbus (1451–1506) on the return trip of his first voyage to America. Since that time, almost 1,000 have occurred, taking a vast toll in human life and injury and in property damage. Since the beginning of the 20th century, more than 100 hurricanes have struck the Gulf and Atlantic coasts from Texas to North Carolina and others have hit the Middle Atlantic and Northeastern states. The worst in U.S. history, in terms of lives lost (6,000), occurred in Galveston, Tex., on September 8, 1900. Loss of lives has recently gone down, primarily due to earlier warnings, but loss of property has been in the billions of dollars. Hurricane Andrew in August 1992 left 160,000 people homeless in southern Florida. Failure to provide proper bracing and anchorage of wood-frame buildings unnecessarily added to the damage.

Flooding is a common occurrence along many river valleys, but severe flooding occurs less frequently. One such severe flooding occurred along the Missouri and Mississippi rivers during the summer of 1993. Major floods have been mapped to record the 100-year flooding level along rivers subject to severe flooding. Problems occur when construction is allowed in the flood plain area. Debate continues on the value of levees to restrain the flood waters, since this tends to narrow the river channel and increase the velocity of water.

A great number of tornadoes are reported in the United States each year and they too take a heavy toll in lives, injuries, and property damage. During the second and third quarters of the 20th century, the number of tornadoes reported each year in the United States has varied from less than 50 to a high of more than 1,000 in 1973, and deaths each year, from about 25 to more than 900. The average number of tornadoes per year for the period is about 400 and the average number of deaths, about 175.

Other storms, including blizzards, have also caused many injuries, taken many lives, and damaged a great deal of property. Such extreme hazards require the utmost attention of architects and other design professionals.

**Related Articles** BUILDING CODES AND STANDARDS; CLIMATE; CONSTRUCTION MATERIALS; DESIGN, ARCHITECTURAL; FIRE PROTECTION; HEATING, VENTILATING, AND AIR CONDITIONING; INSULATION, THERMAL; LIGHTNING PROTECTION; STRUCTURE; WATERPROOFING.

**Further Reading** Ambrose, James, and Dimitry Vergun: *Simplified Building Design for Wind and Earthquake Forces,* 2d edition, John Wiley, New York, 1990; Tannehill, Ivan Ray: *Hurricanes, Their Nature and History, Particularly Those of the West Indies and the Southern Coasts of the United States,* 9th ed., Princeton University Press, Princeton, N.J., 1956, reprint of the 1938 edition, Greenwood, Westport, Conn.

**Sources of Additional Information** U.S. Dept. of Commerce, National Weather Service, National Oceanic and Atmospheric Admin., National Meteorological Center, 5200 Auth Rd., Camp Springs, Md. 20746.

**WINDOW** An assembly, usually including a frame, glass, and hardware set into an opening in an exterior wall of a building for control of the entry of light, air, and solar heat into the interior. Windows have been used in architecture since its beginning, but in the earliest times were not considered important features; later they became important for both functional and ornamental reasons. Today windows are very important functionally and in many cases are major determinants of the architectural design of buildings, both in their exteriors and interiors.

**Types** Windows may be classified by the ways in which they operate, by the materials used, and in other ways. The major types used today include projected; fixed; double-hung, which have two operating units, called sash, which slide vertically inside or outside each other; casements, with hinges at the sides, and often used in pairs, swinging horizontally out and sometimes in; horizontal sliding; and pivoted, either at the center top and bottom, called vertical pivoted, or at the center of the sides, called horizontal pivoted. There are also single-hung windows, in which only one sash moves.

Projected windows come in various types. Most swing out at the top, though some are hinged at the bottom and others may swing in. They range from a single sash hinged at the bottom, called a hopper window, or at the top, through awning windows which have several sash that swing out from the top, and jalousie windows which are like the awning type but in which the sash are smaller and are glass without complete frames. Fixed windows may be used in conjunction with other

types or individually; when they are relatively large, they are often called view or picture windows. Some windows combine, in single assemblies, two or more of the above types. For example, an intermediate window may have a fixed glass portion at the top, an outward projecting section in the middle, and an inward projecting hopper at the bottom. Two or more individual window units of various kinds may also be combined, for example, a view window with operating windows at either side.

**Window Unit** A window unit is a complete assembly in a frame, together with weatherstripping and hardware, and often with insect screens and storm sash, which may be closed to lessen the effects of bad weather. Storm sash and insect screens may also be applied separately. A sash is a single window assembly, fixed or operating, that ordinarily fits into a window frame, consisting of jambs at the sides and head, and usually a sill at the bottom with a stool on the interior side, and often with casings for trim around the frame. Trim on the interior side at the bottom beneath the stool is called an apron. The vertical side pieces of a sash are called stiles and the horizontal top and bottom ones, rails. Narrow horizontal or vertical bars, called muntins, subdivide sash into what are often called lights. A mullion is a vertical element separating two window assemblies.

**Construction Materials** The major materials used in window construction are wood, including pine, fir, cypress, cedar, and redwood; aluminum; steel; stainless steel; and bronze. In recent years, plastic windows have been added to the list. Wood, plastic, aluminum, and steel windows are used mostly in houses, and steel has been used for factories and other utilitarian buildings. Windows of any available material may be used in buildings of other types, but stainless steel or bronze is often used for permanence and minimal maintenance.

**Classification** Windows are sometimes classified by such terms as basement or utility, residential, commercial, or monumental. Basement or utility windows are simple, economical types, usually projected from the top, or hoppers, often used in garages, service stations, or other utilitarian buildings. Residential windows may be any type described above, but are usually of somewhat lighter weight and sometimes less rugged construction than commercial or monumental types. Commercial, sometimes called industrial, windows are often used in commercial and industrial applications where strong, economical types are most appropriate. Monumental windows are usually heavy, of rugged construction, and often of stainless steel or bronze, for use in monumental, important buildings. A clerestory window is placed high in a wall system, often in a wall that rises above an adjacent roof.

**Special-Purpose Types** Many types of windows are available for special purposes, including security, detention, and psychiatric. Security windows are heavy, strong, usually of steel, and built to make unlawful entry difficult. These windows usually have inward projecting sash and continuous muntins, horizontally and vertically, welded together for strength and extending over the entire window unit, including the operating sash. Detention windows are heavy and strong, available for various degrees of restraint needed to prevent escape of prisoners from jails. Psychiatric windows are like detention types, designed to restrain mental patients but without the forbidding heavy appearance of regular detention windows.

Many other special types of windows are available, including sound insulation types and complete storefront systems with both windows and doors, for use in stores and other commercial establishments. Another type of special system is a curtain wall, an assembly of various wall materials complete with windows, wall finishes, insulation, and in some cases interior finishes. Many curtain walls have strips of windows with other materials over and under them, called spandrel covers. In other cases, windows are used to form an entire wall, which is often called a window wall. Windows in both types of walls may be fixed or operable, or in various combinations.

**Glazing** Glazing for windows is usually accomplished with window glass for small panes and heavier float glass in larger ones. Sometimes double glazing, or triple in severe climates, is used for retarding heat losses from buildings in winter and heat gains in summer. The technology of glass and glass coatings allows a selection of the energy-effective glazing for a particular location or orientation of a building. Refer to the article entitled glass. Usually the double- or triple-glazed sash is facto-

**WINDOW** Etched glass window at Oak Hill, Chauncey M. Brewer House (1859), Marshall, Mich.

ry-produced, although double glazing may be accomplished by the use of two panes of glass in a sash. Historically, the use of storm sash has been widely practiced to provide some level of weather protection, and later styles are incorporated into sash where storm sash and insect screens can be raised or lowered at will or taken off and stored when not needed.

Sometimes tempered glass, made by a heating and cooling process to give it strength, or laminated glass with two or more layers separated by and adhered to plastic materials, or acrylic plastic glazing are used where greater safety against breakage is required. Glazing of all kinds is usually set into a window sash with glazing mastics or compounds or with special plastic or neoprene gaskets. In older wood windows, panes were often held in by small metal devices, called "glazier's," or "push" points, over which the glazing compound was placed. Newer wood windows are now often factory-glazed. In metal windows, glass is often held in by metal clips or beads and sealed with glazing compounds or gaskets.

**Standard Units** Window units are available in a great variety of standard sizes, and others may be fabri-

**WINDOW** Typical contemporary types.

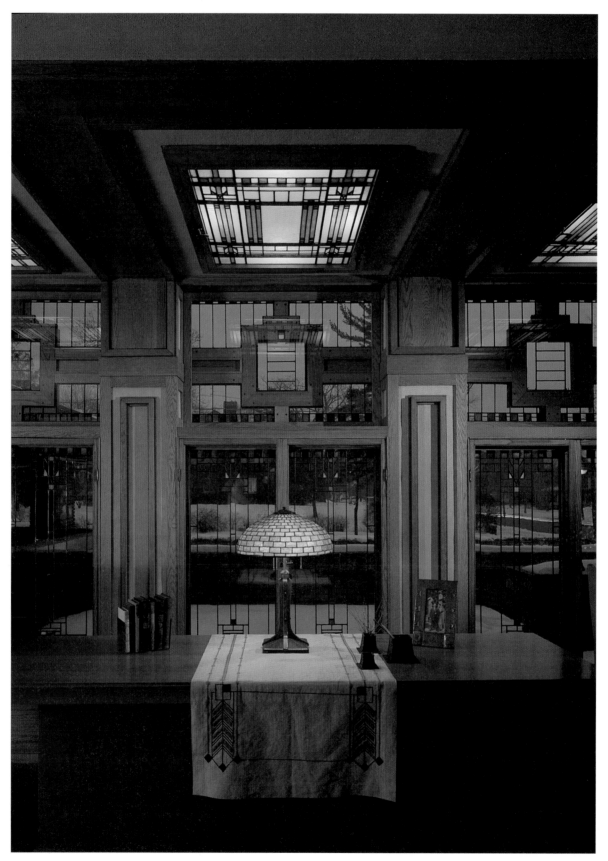

**WINDOW** Meyer S. May House (1909), Grand Rapids, Mich. *[Architect: Frank Lloyd Wright]*

cated to special sizes. For maintenance or historic preservation, special windows may be fabricated to fit existing openings. Many windows come complete with glazing and weatherstripping in place and standard operating devices, though some are available unglazed or weatherstripped. It is also possible to obtain special operators, including both mechanical and electrical types. Many types of panes are available for windows, but wood sashes today often have plastic, wood, or metal fake muntins that fit over large panes to simulate older muntins in windows with small panes.

**Finishes** The finishes available in windows vary between materials. Although wood windows may have natural finishes, they are most often painted, and today some types have the wood parts covered with plastic or metal and do not need further finishing. Regular wood windows are obtainable, finished or unfinished. Steel windows are usually galvanized or otherwise treated at the factory and then painted. Aluminum windows may have no special finish other than a clear coating of plastic or other material applied at the factory to protect them during shipping and erection. More recently, anodized or painted aluminum windows are used more frequently. Stainless steel windows need no special applied finishes, but it is possible to obtain them with various surface textures. Bronze windows need no finishes; in fact, one of the qualities most admired in this material, other than its long life, is the patina it acquires as it weathers.

**Functions** The size, number, and placement of windows in buildings have a considerable effect on the appearance of buildings, when viewed from the inside as well as from the outside. The proper use of windows also has a great deal to do with the comfort and well-being of building occupants, with the benefits to be derived from solar energy and winds, and with conservation of other types of energy. Therefore windows are a very important part of architecture today and must be carefully designed, detailed, and constructed, not only as individual units but as major elements of entire walls. In addition, the design of related elements, such as solar screens, sunshades, and others, must be carefully integrated with the windows and walls. Finally, proper provisions must be made for cleaning, maintenance, and repairs, operations often provided in many buildings today by mechanized scaffolds which may be lowered from the roofs.

**History** The earliest primitive people who constructed buildings are thought to have covered windows with crude flaps of animal skins or brush. By the time of the Mesopotamians and Egyptians, windows had become highly developed, but were rarely used because doorways usually admitted sufficient light. Windows were usually rectangular and had lintels of stone or wood over them.

For protection, stone or carved wood grilles were often placed over the openings. Later crude shutters or lattices were used. The Greeks used windows sparingly, almost not at all in temples. Windows were rectangular and simply designed, but were sometimes narrowed at the tops. Some ornamentation was used around openings.

Most Roman windows had semicircular arches at their heads, though some were completely rectangular in shape. The Romans often used mullions in window openings to separate windows. In many of the ancient civilizations, attempts were made to develop window coverings that would keep out heat, cold, intruders, and so on, yet admit light. Such materials include thin sheets of stone, shell, horn, mica, oiled paper, pierced stone, and cloth. Although glass had been invented about 2500 B.C., it was not used in windows until the time of the Romans, who used it occasionally and in small panes.

In Early Christian architecture, windows were usually small and had either flat or semicircular heads; their openings were often filled in with ornamented and pierced sheets of stone or plaster. High windows, or clerestories, were also used at this time. Byzantine windows usually had arches at their heads and often were filled in with thin sheets of stone or in some cases glass. Romanesque windows usually had semicircular arched heads and were surrounded by series of ornamental moldings. Circular types called wheel windows and later, when stained glass came into use, rose windows, were also used. Glass had come to be widely used, particularly in important buildings, by the time of Romanesque architecture.

In Gothic architecture, windows were developed to a high degree of excellence. Gothic windows generally had pointed arches at their heads and their surrounds were often ornamented. Wheel and rose windows were widely used, particularly in France, and other types were developed, including lunettes, crescent or other shapes, usually placed over doorways; and lancet windows, tall narrow types, with pointed arches above, most often found in English Gothic buildings. Glass had come into common use in cathedrals and other religious buildings by the beginning of Gothic architecture and in other important buildings by the 14th century.

The crowning glory of Gothic windows is stained glass, combined with tracery, ornamental stone, or wood shapes made to support the glass in devices of lead called cames. Although the glass used in Gothic architecture had imperfections, such as air bubbles, and was only available in relatively small panes, craftsmen used it to create scenes and designs, particularly in Gothic cathedrals, that are now considered masterpieces. Many examples are still in existence. In the Gothic era, pictures were painted on windows. Bay windows of varied shapes that project outside of walls were also used. Special kinds include bow windows, in which the projecting shapes are segments of circles in plan, and oriel windows, which project from upper stories. Casements and dormers were also used.

During the Renaissance, the design of windows, like that of other architectural elements, turned away from the Gothic era to classical architecture, particularly Roman. With greater law enforcement than had prevailed in Gothic times, windows could be made larger. In northern Europe, they were actually made larger to admit additional light, but in the relatively hot southern countries, such as Italy, they were kept small. Windows of the era ordinarily had semicircular, arched heads and, unlike those of the Gothic era, were placed symmetrically in building walls, often in groups that were superimposed one over another. Window designs were usually formal, with surrounds that were often ornamented with flanking columns or architraves, a series of ornamental moldings. By the 16th century, window glass was commonly used in buildings of all types, including houses. Panes were larger than those in previous times, but often smaller ones were used by choice.

Renaissance architects used windows of many types derived from classical examples and developed others of their own. Although used to some extent previously, round windows, called by various names, *oeils-de-boeuf*, bull's-eye, oxeyes, or oculis, became popular for use in attic walls. During the Renaissance, important types of windows still in use today were developed, including double-hung windows, developed in England, and French windows, sometimes called French doors, that usually come in pairs, open and close like casements, and start at the floor. Another important development was the Palladian window, or Palladian motif, used for windows, doors, and other architectural purposes. First used by the Italian architect Andrea Palladio (1508–80), the motif consists of a three-part opening, the center part of which is arched and supported on freestanding round columns, each of the outer two with a horizontal head, supported by one of the columns on one side and on the other by a rectangular pilaster or column. This motif was used extensively by architects in the Classic Revival and Eclectic periods.

After the Renaissance, in America as well as in Europe, windows were derived from those of past eras. Newer materials came into use, including wrought and cast iron, but window design remained much the same as in previous periods.

During the 19th century, considerably more emphasis was put on the interior environments of buildings than had been placed on such aspects in most periods of the past. Glass had become widely available and architects designed buildings with greater numbers of windows, particularly in such utilitarian buildings as mills and factories. During the latter part of the 19th century, with the beginning of the modern movement, windows became one of the most dominant elements in architecture. The early modern architects were frankly fond of glass as a material and most later architects have agreed with them.

Long ribbons of windows appeared on buildings. One of the most effective designs was used in many of the buildings of the so-called Chicago school of architects in the late 19th century. It consisted of a three-part window system, with a fixed pane of glass in the center, now often called a view or picture window, flanked by operating windows. This idea was later repeatedly used for every type of building, including speculative houses, and though somewhat outmoded is still used to some extent. Other later developments were curtain walls and the all-glass wall, often called a window wall, both of which have also been used extensively.

Today windows are mostly free of ornament, are available in many materials, and may be glazed with window, float, sealed multiple panes, or heat-absorbent or mirror glass that reflects heat and images. Several manufacturers offer windows with curved tops, semicircular forms, or full-circle windows and a variety of decorative muntins. Windows may be obtained in systems, such as window or curtain walls, or individually. Windows can be fixed or movable in any number or combination and may have such special attachments as built-in blinds or sun controls of various types.

**Related Articles** ART IN ARCHITECTURE; CLIMATE; DOOR; GLASS; HARDWARE; HEATING, VENTILATING, AND AIR CONDITIONING; INSECT PROTECTION; INSULATION, THERMAL; LIGHTING; ORNAMENT; PLASTICS; SECURITY SYSTEMS; WALL; WEATHER PROTECTION; Various articles on building materials and systems.

**Further Reading** *Repairing Old and Historic Windows: A Manual for Architects and Owners*, Preservation Press, Washington, D.C., 1992.

**Sources of Additional Information** American Architectural Manufacturers Assoc., 2700 River Rd., Suite 18, Des Plaines, Ill. 60018; National Fenestration Rating Council, 962 Wayne Ave., Suite 750, Silver Spring, Md. 20910; Stained Glass Assoc. of America, 4050 Broadway, Suite 219, Kansas City, Mo. 64111.

**WOOD** The material in the interior of trees under the bark which is cut into lumber and other forms and used for many purposes. One of the most important uses of wood is in buildings, a practice which began in prehistoric times and continues today. Wood is used in buildings for structures as in wood-framed houses; for finish materials as in floors, wall paneling, and exterior siding; for elements of buildings as doors and windows; and for furniture.

**WOOD** Swainson Cottage (1965), Manistee, Mich. *[Architect: William Kessler and Associates]*

**Classification** Types of wood are classified into what are called softwoods and hardwoods, in spite of the fact that some softwoods are harder than some hardwoods and vice versa. For example, Douglas fir, classified as softwood, is harder than poplar, a hardwood. The term *hardwood* is applied to wood taken from deciduous trees, those with broad leaves that are shed in the fall. Softwoods are taken from coniferous trees, usually having needlelike leaves, which are evergreen. Among the important hardwoods used in building construction for flooring, wall paneling, woodwork, and furniture are walnut, birch, oak, and maple. Among the most important softwoods, sometimes used for similar purposes but more prevalently used for building structures and related purposes, are fir, pine, spruce, and hemlock.

**Uses** Wood is a very versatile material. It is used in many forms in buildings as lumber, 2 x 4's, and so on; as heavy timber, 5 x 5's or larger, for structural purposes; as boards, either plain or machined into patterns, for floor-ing, exterior siding, wall paneling, and the like. Layers of wood can be glued together or laminated, to form relatively large, strong structural elements, such as beams or arches. Wood can also be laminated into large panels, plywood; and as thin sheets, wood veneers, may be laminated to backup wood for use in furniture. Wood chips or shavings can be chemically or mechanically broken down and recombined with filler adhesives to form boards, panels, or other products, or used as an ingredient of plastics.

Wood is more easily worked than most other building materials. It can be sanded, planed, sawed, or drilled with relative ease. It may be fastened to itself and to other materials, with nails, screws, bolts, or adhesives. Wood comes in an almost endless variety of colors and patterns, and with a wide variation of properties of hardness, strength, and durability. It can be given a great range of surface textures and can be finished with paints, stains, plastic or other coatings, and in some cases, as redwood, left unfinished to weather naturally.

**WOOD** Pavilion on Lake Pepin (1991), Wis. *[Architect: James Stageberg (Photo: Christian M. Korab)]*

**Types** Wood for building construction comes in three primary types, classified according to the amount of work done on it before it comes to the market. Rough lumber has been sawed, in a sawmill, into shapes with straight sides and rough edges. Rough lumber is not used to any great extent in building construction today. Dressed lumber has been processed, in a planing mill, to make the sides and edges smooth. Worked lumber, sometimes called factory or shop lumber, has been dressed and further machined to give it a pattern for decorative or other purposes or to provide for joining pieces together. The last two types are widely used in building construction.

**Grading by Usage** Lumber for building construction is graded according to its uses. Yard lumber is intended for general building purposes, such as house construction. Structural lumber is most often used in heavier structures, and comes in larger sizes, generally 2 in or more in both thickness and width. Factory or shop lumber is that intended mainly for further machining into worked lumber which will have patterns in it.

**Quality Grading** Lumber is also graded by its quality, that is, by its relative freedom from defects, such as knots. Yard lumber is graded select, with a minimum of defects and suitable for exposed, finished parts of buildings; and common, with defects that detract from its appearance but which do not prevent its use for structural and other parts that are not exposed. Select lumber is further graded (1) suitable for natural finishes and (2) suitable for paint finishes, with two further subgrades in each category. Common lumber is further graded (1) for standard construction and (2) for less exacting purposes, with three further subgrades in the (1) category and two in (2). Structural lumber is graded according to its strength, the weights it can hold up or resist safely and efficiently. Hardwood lumber is graded from the best, most free from defects to the least, in the following grades: first; seconds; selects; No. 1 common; No. 2 common; sound wormy; No. 3A common; No. 3B common.

**Hardwood Dimension Lumber** This is hardwood lumber that has been sawed into small pieces, free of defects. Plain blocks of such wood are called rough hardwood dimension; if further trimmed, sanded, or otherwise worked, they are surfaced hardwood dimension; and if machined into parts, as in legs or arms of chairs, they are called completely fabricated hardwood dimension.

**Sizes of Lumber** The sizes of lumber are given in inches for the thickness and width and in feet for the length. These sizes are not the actual sizes, but are called the nominal sizes, those of the lumber before it was dried or seasoned and before it went through the planing mill. The actual sizes are less. For example, a 4-in board actually measures $3\frac{1}{2}$ in today, and for many years in the past measured $3\frac{5}{8}$ in. Lumber is sold by the board foot which is a nominal dimension of 1 in thick by 1 ft wide by 1 ft long.

**Processing Lumber** Trees are brought from the forest to a sawmill, where the logs are moved first to debarkers, which remove the bark, then to a series of saws that cut the log into various sizes of lumber, and finally to a machine called a trimmer which squares up the ends. Lumber may be plain-sawed, quarter-sawed, or rift-sawed. In plain sawing, all boards are sawed from the log in the same direction, parallel to each other. In quarter sawing, one quarter of the log is sawed at a time, with the saws working parallel to each other and generally toward the center of the log. Rift sawing is similar, except the saw cuts are at slight angles to each other. The first method produces strong lumber and costs less because there is less waste. The others produce lumber with edge grain that is pronounced and ornamental.

**Seasoning** Newly sawed lumber, called green lumber, has a high moisture content. It must be dried or seasoned to reduce the moisture. During this process, the lumber shrinks. If green lumber were used in a building, there would be warping or other distortion. To prevent this from happening, lumber is seasoned either by air drying, stacking it outdoors to be dried by the sun and wind, or by kiln drying, in which the lumber is subjected to controlled heating to drive out the proper amount of moisture. The recommended average moisture content in the United States varies from 6 percent in dry areas to 11 percent in humid areas.

**Planing** After having been seasoned, all lumber other than that to be used as rough lumber is further processed in planing mills. Here the lumber is moved through machinery with knife blades that shave and smooth the rough lumber. Factory or shop lumber is further worked in milling and other machines to produce patterns for various purposes.

**Wood Treatment** Wood may be attacked by fungi or by insects such as beetles, bees, ants, and termites. Termite infestation has been experienced in most areas of the United States and is most likely in California or the southeastern states. In marine conditions, wood may

**WOOD** Typical joints for siding and other components.

be attacked by a number of sea creatures, including marine borers. Chemical treatment of wood is required to control these infestations. Decay of wood requires moisture, moderate temperatures, and oxygen, and may be detected by sighting of sawdust, insect droppings, or insect wings. Wood can be inspected by jabbing it with a pointed knife or awl. Decayed wood may crack or crumble or be soft and mushy. When wood is tapped, hollow or dead sounds may indicate internal damage. For definitive information, laboratory tests of samples may be used to determine the cause of decay. Sonic devices may be used to check soundness of utility poles, and large structures may make use of x-ray inspections.

Chemical treatment of wood must be applied under conditions that ensure proper penetration of the chemicals. The Environmental Protection Agency requires that treated wood be labeled to identify the treatment used. Care should be taken by carpenters to limit their exposure to the sawdust from treated wood. Pressure treatment of wood may be used to control the amount of preservative used. Other treatments may be brushed or sprayed on wood, or fence posts may be placed in tanks of preservatives.

The chemicals used are dangerous, and over the years limitations have been placed on those approved for use. Such materials as creosote, pentachlorophenol, and arsenic may not be sold over-the-counter. The most common processes and materials include creosote-type preservatives, which have been linked to cancer and are limited in application. Organic solvent types, such as copper naphthenates, give the familiar green color to treated wood, and the pentachlorophenols allow treated wood to be painted or stained. Water-based types include a number which may be used for specific installations, such as wood in contact with the ground or in the water. Sometimes the chemicals may leach out over time, but they have advantages when used under proper conditions. One such common proprietary process is Wolmanizing.

Other wood treatments may be used to provide fire-retarding qualities, either by chemicals or by the use of intumescent paints. Note that good construction practices will reduce hazards to the structure and to people and will identify where wood treatment is cost-effective.

**Veneer Wood** One other method for preparing wood for use in buildings, making veneer wood, has increasingly become more important. In this case, instead of being sawed, the log, called a peeler log, is held against a long blade of a machine and rotated in such a way as to peel a thin veneer from it. The veneer thus produced is then laminated, under pressure, with adhesives to other sheets of wood to form plywood and similar products.

**History** Wood has been used in architecture from earliest prehistoric times. The earliest primitive structures are believed to have been similar to those of the American Indians. The development of wood uses and forms has continued ever since, through all the great styles or movements in architecture. Even in an era like the Middle Ages, in which stone was the major material, great roof structures of wood, handled in a skillful and craftsmanlike manner, were used for cathedrals and many other important buildings. And of course, wood never ceased to be used widely for humbler structures.

**American Development** Wood has played a large part in the architecture of America from the earliest times to today. The Pre-Columbian Indians used wood in the form of branches and logs for wigwams, longhouses, and other structures, and continued to do so well after the establishment of the colonies. The colonists found great forests, which provided ample lumber, the most easily usable material for their earliest buildings. Sawmills, using waterpower, were established in Virginia and New England in the early 17th century; waterpower was replaced with steam by the middle of the 19th. Most of the early colonial buildings were of wood used in a simple manner, but later in a much more sophisticated way, often in forms adapted from buildings of stone and brick in Europe. Wood has continued to be one of the most important building materials in the United States, and notable architecture in wood has been produced in every era and is still being produced today.

**Related Articles** BUILDING TRADE; CEILING; CONSTRUCTION, BUILDING; CONSTRUCTION MATERIALS; DOOR; FLOOR; FURNITURE; HOUSE; MOLDING; PREFABRICATION; ROOF; ROOFING; STRUCTURAL ENGINEERING; STRUCTURE; WALL; WINDOW; WOOD-FRAME STRUCTURE; WOODWORK.

**Sources of Additional Information** American Forestry Assoc., 1319 18th St., N.W., Washington, D.C. 20036; American Plywood Assoc., 1119 A St., Tacoma, Wash. 98401.

**WOOD-FRAME STRUCTURE** Building construction system using wood in the form of studs, beams, girders, joists, rafters, and other members for the structure of a building. Wood is one of the most ancient and versatile structural materials used in architecture. The major structural methods used today are light wood framing, utilizing small thicknesses, nominally 2 inches (in), of lumber to form the structures of relatively small buildings, such as houses; heavy timber, sometimes called mill or warehouse, construction, in which much larger structural members are used for relatively large buildings; plank and beam framing, which utilizes relatively large beams and sometimes posts, with roof and floor decking of nominal 2-in planks. Other methods are also used, including wood piling. For further discussion on wood piling, see the article entitled foundation.

**Advantages and Disadvantages** Wood, in the form of lumber and timber, has marked advantages as a structural material in buildings. It is plentiful in most places and is renewable by replanting trees. Many species of trees furnish structural lumber and timber. Thus a wide variety of characteristics, including strengths, may be obtained. Wood is the most easily worked of all building materials, easy to saw, plane, drill, shape, and fasten, with almost all tools and machines. It is also easy to finish. Wood is one of the most inexpensive structural materials, is strong and durable if handled properly in design and construction, and has insulating qualities. Wood is also one of the favorite materials of many people, including architects and other environmental designers, for its warm appearance and other esthetic qualities. A major disadvantage of wood is that it is subject to damage when attacked by certain insects, such as termites, and to deterioration and damage from water and from attacks by various fungi that cause it to decay and eventually fail. All these negative qualities can be avoided through proper design, construction, and maintenance. Perhaps the greatest disadvantage is that wood is combustible; therefore it cannot be used for buildings of certain types, occupancies, and sizes.

**Wood Species** The major woods used for structural members, both softwoods, are Douglas fir and southern pine (the Georgia pine). In addition, many other softwoods may be used, including various hemlocks, cedars, spruces, redwood, and larch. Each of these types of wood has specific characteristics and properties that must be taken into consideration in the design of structures of various kinds. For basic characteristics and properties, along with sizes, grading, and other information, see the article entitled wood. Engineering data, including allowable stresses in types of wood, load tables for such structural members as joists, rafters and decking, and so on, are widely available. Modern forest management ensures future supplies of wood.

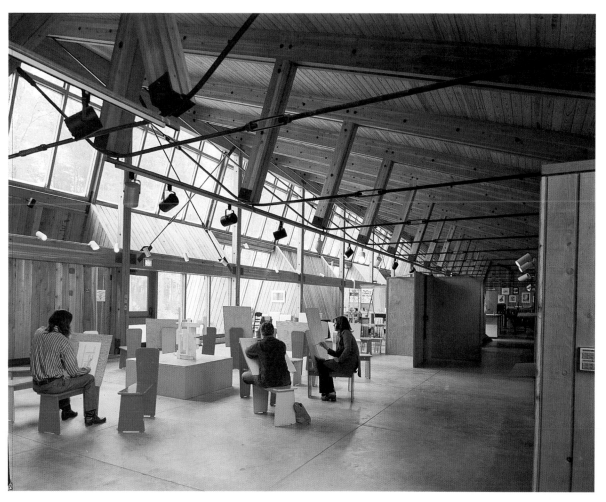

**WOOD-FRAME STRUCTURE** Northwestern Michigan College (1978), Traverse City, Mich. *[Architects: The Architects' Collaborative]*

**Light Wood Framing** This framing system is often used for construction of houses and other relatively small buildings, one to three stories in height. Ordinarily, light wood-frame structural members are a nominal 2 in in thickness by various depths and lengths. The vertical structural members used for walls, called studs, are usually 2 x 4's erected on 16-in centers, or for one-story buildings sometimes on 24-in centers. In walls with 2 x 6 studs, 24-in centers are often used. Other primary light wood-frame structural members, such as floor and roof joists and rafters, are usually 2 in thickness, range up to 14 in depth and up to 24 ft or more length. Such members may also be of 3 or 4 in thickness. Fabricated wood trusses are frequently used in light wood framing for joists and rafters.

**Balloon Frame** There are two major methods for light wood framing: the balloon frame and the western, or platform, frame. The balloon frame, long the standard method in the United States, utilizes studs that are two stories high in two-story buildings. In this method, usually two 2 x 6's or other sizes of lumber, called the sill,

are bolted to the foundation. The studs are nailed to the sill. The horizontal structural members, floor and roof joists, are nailed to the sides of the studs. A plate, two wood members the same thickness and depth as the studs, is nailed along the top of the stud wall. Rafters if used are nailed to the sides of the roof joists. Diagonal wood or plywood sheathing is nailed to the outside of the studs. Wood subfloors are nailed on top of the floor joists and wood roof decking nailed to the top of the rafters in pitched roofs or the roof joists in flat roofs. Wood or metal bracing is used between joists. Wood firestops, the same thickness and depth of the studs, are nailed in place at each floor level and at the mid-heights of the studs. Similar fire-stops are nailed between joists at the outer ends.

**Western Frame** Today western, or platform, framing has supplanted the balloon method to large extent. Western framing utilizes studs that are only one story high. A sill, usually only one wood member, is bolted to the foundation as in the other type. The first-floor joists are then nailed directly to the sill and the subflooring nailed to the joists. On top of the subfloor, a sole plate, sometimes called a shoe, is nailed and the studs are nailed to it. On top of the studs, a double plate is nailed as in the balloon method. The same process is repeated for the second floor and if required, the third. Cross-bridging is used between joists as before, along with a roof deck. One of the major advantages of this method of framing, as compared to the balloon, is that the framing of walls may be completely assembled and then tilted into place.

Although both methods of light wood framing utilize mostly lumber in small sizes, usually of nominal 2 in thickness, in certain cases heavier timbers are used for girders, columns or posts, and similar members carrying heavy loads. Sometimes steel structural members are used instead. Light wood framing is also often used in conjunction with masonry exterior walls, and in this case is usually called ordinary construction.

**Heavy Timber Construction** This system utilizes structural members larger than the nominal 2-in thickness of light wood framing. Heavy timber construction has considerable fire resistance since the heavy wood members retain much of their strength for long periods of time in fires because of the slow rate of surface charring. In order to qualify for a fire-resistant rating, heavy timber construction must be accomplished with structural members of certain minimum sizes or greater, with approved connectors and details, with no concealed spaces under floors and roofs, and with fire-resistance-rated wall, floor, and roof construction. Typical of the nominal sizes for heavy timber structural members are the following: 8 in for columns supporting floors and 6 in for those supporting roofs; 6 in wide and 10 in deep for beams and girders; and other minimums for other members. In heavy timber construction, either solid or glued laminated timber may be used. Bearing walls in heavy timber construction must have fire-resistance ratings of two or three hours and nonbearing walls must be incombustible, and have fire-resistance ratings of from one to three hours if separated from other construction by less than 30 ft. Buildings of many types, in quite large sizes, may be built with heavy timber construction. Although the most common use of the system is for utilitarian buildings, such as factories and warehouses, it may also be used for many other types in which open, columnless spaces and long roof spans are needed.

**Plank and Beam Framing** This framing system is often used for houses and other buildings of relatively small sizes. In this system, the vertical supports may be walls constructed in a manner similar to western framing or wood posts. Instead of joists, beams of relatively large size of solid wood, built-up with smaller members attached to each other or of laminated wood, are used on centers usually of 6 to 8 ft. Nominal 2-in-thick tongue-

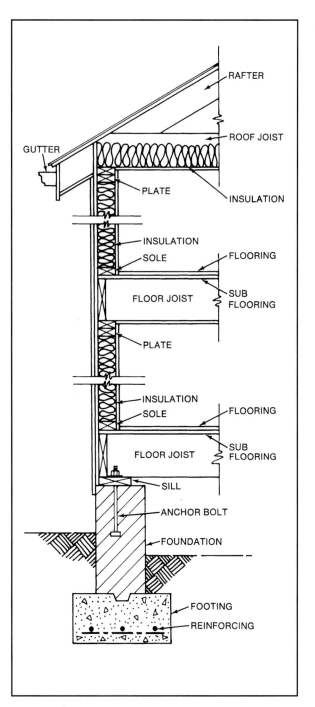

**WOOD-FRAME STRUCTURE** Section of western, or platform, frame.

and-groove planks are attached to the top of the beams to form floors and roofs. Many architects and other people prefer the architectural effects achieved with the exposed beams and planks and the additional ceiling heights that can be obtained at little or no extra expense. On the other hand, concealment of piping, electrical wiring, and ductwork is more difficult than in the more conventional light wood framing systems.

Another structural system, sometimes used for the more utilitarian types of buildings, such as factories or frame buildings, utilizes round timber poles for columns. Often a reinforced concrete floor slab, supported by the ground, is used. Simple connections are possible and simple wood trusses may be used for roofs. This system is one of the most economical of structures available for buildings today.

**Special Structural Elements** Many types of special structural elements are used in conjunction with the above systems, including trusses, trussed rafters, arches, stressed-skin panels, structural diaphragms, and shell structures. Most of these were developed in the 20th century, except for trusses which go back to ancient times.

A truss is a special kind of structural element used to span long distances. Trusses are made up of relatively small members into rigid shapes, usually composed of triangles; several kinds of trusses are used today, including the Pratt, flat Pratt, bowstring, Belgian, Fink, Warren, Howe, scissors, and sawtooth. The shapes of most of these are illustrated in the article entitled steel structure. Wood trusses may be constructed in two major ways: with wood members only, bolted or fastened together with special connectors; or with compression members of wood combined with steel rod tension members. Large trusses, spaced 8 to 20 ft apart, are used in buildings, such as factories, in which great columnless spaces are required for spans up to 80 ft or more. For smaller buildings, lighter trusses, often called trussed rafters, are used. Trussed rafters are made of small lumber, are placed at 2-ft to 4-ft intervals, and usually span up to 32 ft, though they can be made to span greater distances. Trussed rafters are often prefabricated, trucked to building sites, and erected.

Wood arches may also be used for long roof spans. Often of glued laminated timber, though sometimes built up in other ways, the arches are generally available in several shapes, including A frame, like a gable end; Gothic, curved and pointed; radial, like a segment of a circle; parabolic; three-centered; and Tudor. Such arches may be used for spans up to 100 ft or more. Often left exposed beneath roof decks, laminated arches are used for several building types, including churches and assembly buildings. Many architects and other environmental designers often prefer laminated arches for their building designs, not only for their long spans but for their appearance.

Other structural members made of glued laminated wood are also available, including roof beams, which may be straight, curved, or pitched in one or two directions. Roof beams of this type may span up to 60 ft or more. Columns and other members may also be made of glued laminated wood. Plywood is the most commonly

**WOOD-FRAME STRUCTURE** House in Canada (1965). *[Architect: Harry Weese]*

used glued laminated material, for a great many purposes in architecture. As a structural material, plywood is mostly used for wall sheathing, subfloors, roof decking, and the like. In addition to carrying the normal weights or loads in such structures, plywood also may be designed to act as a diaphragm to resist loads from the sides, or lateral loads. Plywood is also sometimes used to construct stressed-skin panels, made by gluing plywood to the tops, and usually the bottoms, of wood frames. Used for strong walls, floors, and roofs, and also for box beams, stressed-skin panels are very strong for their weight and the amount of materials of which they are composed.

Shell construction with wood generally utilizes hyperbolic paraboloids: strong, thin, double-curved shapes used for roofs of buildings. Such structures in wood are usually constructed with laminated or solid wood structural members on the perimeters. Sheathing may be solid wood or plywood attached to the top or bottom, or sandwiched between the perimeter members. Roofs with other types of curves may be constructed of wood, but the hyperbolic paraboloid is one of the easiest to design. It is also relatively easy to fabricate and construct because, though it may seem unlikely, the double-curved surface is actually composed of straight lines that slope but do not curve.

**Fasteners** Fasteners or connectors for wood structures are extremely important. For light wood frame buildings, the most generally used fastener is the common nail. Standards of good practice have been established for the types, sizes, and number to be used for various purposes, and the driving methods. Many timber structural elements, such as trusses and others, are connected with bolts and nuts, usually in combination with washers. Today trusses and similar components are frequently connected with special connectors or plates which are often used in conjunction with bolts and nuts, or with nails. These special fasteners not only speed up fabrication but produce stronger joints than bolts and nuts alone. Many kinds of special items of steel or iron are used in conjunction with wood construction. Various kinds of steel or iron plates are used for such purposes as splicing wood members; anchoring wood members to masonry or concrete, bearing plates under beams, and other members; and hangers for beams, joists, and other members. Most types are available from stock, but others must be fabricated for the exact purpose intended. A great number of other fasteners, including wood and lag screws, spikes, and rods, are often required.

For many architects and other environmental designers, the use of wood in building structures is both interesting and satisfying. And some believe that some of the methods, such as laminated wood exposed inside buildings, produce very fine architecture. The information in this article provides only general guidelines for design in wood. Engineering tables are widely available for use in determining various wood structures. However, for all but the simplest structures, such as light wood frame houses, structural design in wood must be accomplished by informed and experienced architects or structural engineers.

**History** Wood was one of the earliest structural materials used by primitive humans to construct huts and tents. And wood has continued to be an important construction material to the present time. While all the earliest wood structures have long since disappeared as have many that came later, it is thought that the early buildings were simply sticks or branches set in the ground in a circle at the bottom and tied together at the top in the form of a tepee. Over the crude frame were placed branches or leaves or skins of animals. Later, primitive people constructed more elaborate buildings with vertical and horizontal structural members of wood, and sometimes gable roofs, in the system that is known as the post and lintel, or trabeated.

In the ancient civilizations in and around the Mediterranean Sea, Mesopotamia, Egypt, Crete, and the mainland of Greece, wood structures were also used, though stone and burned-clay units were the major building materials. Wood was used structurally in all these places for posts, lintels, and rafters in earliest times and later, mostly for small buildings and for relatively minor uses in important ones. Because of the ravages of time, insects, and weather, none of these early wood structures has survived.

The Romans also used wood extensively. Although none of their wood buildings has survived, there is evidence of them in the works of writers of the time and from archeological excavations. The Romans used structural wood for columns, beams, trusses, joists, roof and floor structures, and complete buildings. They also sometimes constructed wood bridges. Roman wood buildings used the trabeated system, developed elsewhere, with few innovations.

During the Middle Ages, wood structures were used quite extensively for the roof structures of cathedrals and other important buildings and for complete structures of less important types. Some buildings were constructed with split logs, but many were of roughly dressed timbers. Some were highly ornamented with carvings.

One of the major uses of wood in Gothic structures was for the framing of roofs of timber buildings and over the stone vaults of others. Often made of oak, these roof structures were usually joined together with mortise and tenon joints and with wooden pegs. Rafters were usually connected to each other with tie beams to increase their strength and stability and sometimes diagonal bracing was also used for the same purpose, thus creating an assembly that resembled a truss. Some of the roof structures were quite elaborate, particularly in England, where curved ribs were sometimes used in assemblies. The English also used a very ornamental system, called a hammerbeam roof, which had short hammer beams at the side from which rafters and arched ribs rose. Also of importance in Gothic architecture were half-timber buildings, in which wood posts and diagonal members formed the structure, with the spaces in between filled with plaster, brick, or other materials.

During the Renaissance, wood was not as important a structural material as were brick and stone. Wood continued to be used, much in the manner of the Middle Ages, in half-timber structures, in roofs, and for other purposes. Renaissance architects sometimes used trusses, somewhat like those of the Romans. Wood trusses were often used for domes, which were then roofed outside and plastered inside.

**American Development** In early colonial America, wood was the most used structural material, particularly in the English and other colonies of the Middle Atlantic and New England areas. The methods of construction were those the colonists had known in the countries from which they emigrated. Later a method called the braced frame was developed. This system utilized large heavy posts and horizontal members called girts, with diagonal bracing. Wood structures have continued to be used in the United States since that time. However, brick and stone and later reinforced concrete and fire-protected steel have become the structural materials used in centers of cities where fire risks are so great.

Wood has continued to be the major structural material used in houses to the present time. Early in the 19th century, a system for wood framing of relatively small buildings, called the balloon frame, was introduced in the United States and was later used elsewhere. The balloon frame is believed to have been invented by a contractor, G. W. Snow (1797–1890). The balloon frame made it possible for a house to be constructed with small pieces of lumber instead of heavy timbers, nailed into place instead of fastened with mortise and tenon joints. The system was fast and inexpensive and could be erected by relatively unskilled carpenters. Soon the balloon frame became the major method for constructing houses. It continued to be widely used in the 20th century. Today western, or platform, framing, a similar and even simpler method, has replaced balloon framing to a large extent.

Heavy timber, often called warehouse or mill, construction has been used mostly for factories and other utilitarian buildings for a long time in the United States and continues to be used. Plank and beam structures are often used in houses today. Laminated wood structural members, such as columns, beams, and arches, are often used not only in houses but in other types of buildings. Wood is often used for the structures of prefabricated houses and other building types.

**Related Articles** BUILDING CODES AND STANDARDS; FACTORY; FOUNDATION; HOUSE; INSECT PROTECTION; PREFABRICATION; STRUCTURAL ENGINEERING; STRUCTURE; WOOD.

**Further Reading** American Institute of Timber Construction: *Timber Construction Manual*, 3d ed., John Wiley, New York, 1986; Breyer, Donald E.: *Design of Wood Structures*, 3d ed., McGraw-Hill, New York, 1993.

**Sources of Additional Information** American Institute of Timber Construction, 11818 S.E. Mill Plain Blvd., Vancouver, Wash. 98684; American Plywood Assoc., P.O. Box 11700, Tacoma, Wash. 98411.

**WOODWORK** A part of a building made of wood by carpenters or cabinetmakers, in particular a finished part rather than the rough work in wood framing in walls. Work in wood on buildings is generally accomplished by two trades: carpentry and cabinetmaking. Carpentry is often classified as either rough, concerned mainly with

**WOODWORK** Swan Turnblad House (1907), Minneapolis, Minn. *[Architect: Christopher A. Boehme & Victor Cordella]*

the wood framing of buildings; or finish, concerned with such work as sheathing, exterior, and interior finish, setting windows, hanging doors, and installation of stairs, flooring, moldings, and the like. Cabinetmaking is concerned with the construction of special items of wood, such as built-in furniture, cabinets, wall paneling, and so on. Although there is some overlap between these trades, woodwork is usually the responsibility of cabinetmakers, and in some cases, finish carpenters. Millwork consists of elements of wood, such as windows, doors, and moldings produced in a woodworking plant.

Woodwork in buildings today consists mainly of furniture and storage, stairs, moldings and other trim, and wall paneling. In the past, wood windows and doors and their frames were often made by cabinetmakers or carpenters. Today most of them are made on assembly lines in factories and put into place in buildings by carpenters, who usually also install the trim around them. For further discussion on doors, moldings and other trim, stairs, and windows, see articles listed at the end of this article.

In the past, such items as built-in dressers, chests of drawers, bookcases, special closets, kitchen cabinets, and

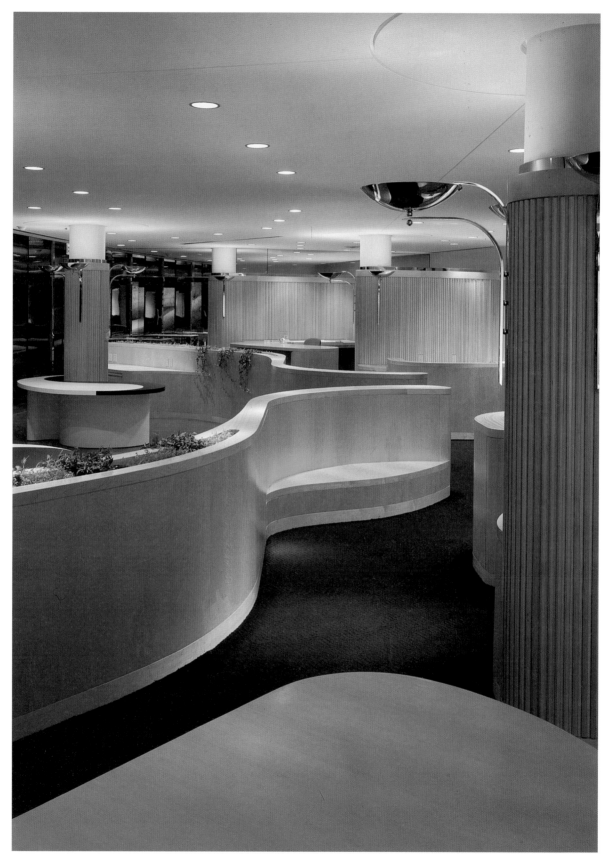

**WOODWORK** Holtzman & Silverman Office Building (1989), Southfield, Mich. *[Architect: Gunnar Birkerts]*

so on were often built on the job, in place, in buildings. Later many of such items were specially constructed in woodworking shops for specific buildings. Both methods are still employed to some extent today, but a far more prevalent practice is the selection of such items from standard lines of stock types mass-produced in factories. This is particularly true of kitchen cabinets. Also many items of this sort, again particularly storage cabinets, are produced in metals today rather than in wood.

**Prefabricated Cabinets** Prefabricated kitchen cabinets, of wood or metal, are available in a variety of sizes, types, qualities, and finishes. Stock kitchen cabinets are of two major types: base cabinets with countertops, placed on the floor to form storage spaces and work areas; and wall cabinets. Base cabinets are generally 36 in high, 24 to 25 in deep, and 12 to 42 in or more wide. Wall cabinets are generally 13 in deep, 15 to 30 in high, and in widths similar to those of floor cabinets. Special types of cabinets are available for sinks, built-in ovens and stovetops, tray storage, recycling bins, and other special uses. Metal cabinets have largely been replaced with wood or laminated plastic cabinets, with countertops of laminated plastic, stainless steel, ceramic tile, wood, or stone. For most installations, other than the simplest, the countertops are made to order with backsplashes. Wood cabinets may be obtained unfinished, primed for painting, prepainted, stained, or otherwise finished, in several types of wood including birch and maple.

**Prefabricated Units** Prefabricated dressers, chests of drawers, closets, bookcases, and other items are also available in many combinations and in several woods. Storage and other units for offices, libraries, and other building types, made of steel or wood, come in a variety of types and sizes.

When cabinets, storage units, and the like are to be used in buildings, care must be taken to ensure accurate dimensioning, use of proper finishes, and, above all, proper construction and craftsmanship. In the case of prefabricated units, such considerations may be a matter of observation and understanding of manufacturers' specifications and their actual products. When such work is to be specially designed and constructed for specific uses in individual buildings, extreme care must be taken in the preparation of working drawings and specifications covering the work and in checking large-scale shop drawings from which the items will actually be fabricated.

**Cabinetwork** A major consideration in cabinetwork is selection of the proper woods. Softwoods, such as pine and fir, are often used for cabinets or other items to be painted, and sometimes redwood, cypress, or cedar for those to be stained or given natural finishes. Aromatic cedar is often used for lining clothes closets. For other pieces to be stained or given natural finishes, hardwoods

**WOODWORK** Typical cabinetwork joints.

are generally used, including birch, walnut, maple, oak, and mahogany. Although in the past solid woods or solid cores with thin veneers were usually used for cabinetwork, today plywood is generally used. For cabinetmaking and similar purposes, wood should be clear and free of blemishes. (See the article entitled wood.)

Another important consideration in cabinetwork is proper construction. Dimensions should be accurate, corners square, and parts properly fitted. Joints between various wood members are important. In rough carpentry, butt joints, in which one member with a flat end is simply nailed or otherwise fastened to another, are commonly used. In cabinetwork, special joints that are stronger and better finished are used, including tongue and groove, mortise and tenon, rabbet and dado, and dovetail types, all often fastened together with glues or other adhesives.

**Hardware** Many types of hardware are available for use in cabinetwork and other woodwork, including hinges, locks, slides, and so on, in such metals as brass, bronze, and stainless steel. Special devices may be obtained for almost every conceivable purpose, including shoe, tie, hat, and belt racks; umbrella holders; extension hangers; and pants, blouse, and skirt hangers. Special extension drawer slides are also available, as are adjustable shelf standards.

**Paneling** As in other woodwork, paneling in the past was mainly made of solid woods, often softwoods for surfaces to be painted and hardwoods for those to be

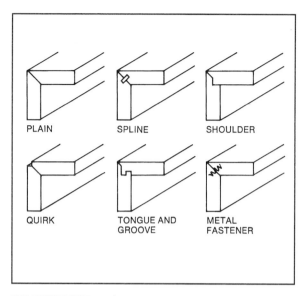

**WOODWORK** Typical corner joints.

stained or given natural finishes. In other cases, special veneers were used. Today some solid or specially veneered wood paneling is still used in buildings. Many exotic woods from all over the world are available for this purpose, in addition to the more generally used American woods, such as birch, walnut, oak, and maple. For the most part today, paneling in buildings is made of plywood, in which a great number of widely varied woods are available. In many cases, plywood paneling is installed in big sheets with very simple butt joints, often with V grooves or with specially made divider strips. Joints may be recessed or have strips called battens over them. Solid or specially veneered wood paneling may also be installed in large pieces, with various kinds of joints. Such paneling may also be installed in smaller pieces, in square or other shapes, with framing and molding around them.

In the past, many types of ornament were used in conjunction with wall paneling and other woodwork, including wood carving and marquetry, the inlaying of pieces of wood, and sometimes other materials, glued to a background. Such techniques are rarely used today.

**History** Because of the discovery of various early woodworking tools, it is believed that humans worked in wood almost from the time of the lower Old Stone, or Paleolithic, Age, perhaps as far back as 500,000 B.C. By the time of the New Stone, or Neolithic, Age, people were making excellently designed and crafted objects of wood and had even invented a kind of primitive mortise and tenon joint.

By about 3000 B.C., in Egypt, Crete, the Middle East, and Greece, fine woodworking had become a widely practiced craft. So accepted were various wood forms of the time that these ancient people often copied them

later in stone and other materials. From that time, woodworking has been an important part of architecture. It was practiced in Roman times; highly developed, particularly in carving, during the Gothic period; and further developed during the Renaissance.

Except for the magnificent era of Gothic wood carvings, the great age of woodworking was in the 18th century, when some of the finest furniture and other wood objects were produced in England, France, and other places, including America. The traditions that started then were continued to some extent in the 19th century, but by the end of that period, machines had replaced handwork in wood and the end of the great era had virtually come. The early architects of the Modern movement turned away from ornament in wood, as they had in other materials, to plain unadorned surfaces, usually in natural finishes. Some of the early Modern architects resisted this trend and produced ornamental woodwork still thought to be of the highest excellence. Among those who designed such work are the Greene brothers, Charles Sumner (1868–1957), Henry Mather (1870–1954), Bernard Maybeck (1862–1957), and Frank Lloyd Wright (1867–1959). Other modern architects have designed excellent built-in furniture and other objects of wood, using simple forms, for the most part simple and unadorned. This trend continues today, although more traditional detailing and decoration have been revived.

**Related Articles** CEILING; DOOR; FURNITURE; GREENE AND GREENE; INTERIOR DESIGN; MOLDING; ORNAMENT; PAINT; PREFABRICATION; STAIR; WALL; WINDOW; WOOD; WOOD-FRAME STRUCTURE.

**Source of Additional Information** Architectural Woodwork Inst., 2310 S. Walter Reed Dr., Arlington, Va. 22206.

**WORKING DRAWING** Plans, elevations, details, and other data that show how a building or other structure is to be constructed. Such information is presented graphically in the working drawings and supplemented by verbal information in the specifications. Working drawings and specifications, together with related items, are called the construction contract documents. They are not only guides for construction work but form part of construction contracts between owners and contractors. Because of their importance and legal status, working drawings as well as other contract documents must be prepared with skill, thoroughness, and care.

Generally, working drawings for the engineering portions of buildings, mainly structural, mechanical, and electrical, are prepared by engineers and their assistants, in close coordination with each other and with the architect. Various other portions may be prepared by other design professionals, such as landscape architects, interi-

**WORKING DRAWING** Architectural working drawing of plan at garden level and plan at entry level, Embassy of Singapore (1993), Washington, D.C. [*Architects: RTKL Associates, Inc.*]

**WORKING DRAWING** Heating, ventilating and air conditioning (HVAC) working drawing of plan at entry level, Embassy of Singapore (1993), Washington, D.C. *[Architects: RTKL Associates, Inc.]*

or designers, and so on. All the rest of the working drawings are prepared by architects and their assistants.

**Production** The preparation of working drawings and specifications is usually called production in architectural and other design offices. In the smallest offices, production might be handled by an architect if a sole proprietor, or by one or more partners. In somewhat larger offices, there may be a production department, with a few drafters and a specification writer. In still larger offices, the organization of production varies somewhat. In general, there is a production department under the direction of a principal or an upper-level employee of the firm, with a title such as director of production and overall responsibility for the entire production system. Under this individual might be a chief specification writer who directs the work of that department and a chief drafter who directs the preparation of working drawings. Often there is also a separate cost control department. And sometimes construction contract administration is included in the production department.

**Methods** Of the several methods for the actual production of working drawings, two systems are the most important. One system selects a job captain to direct each individual project, along with drafters. These people handle the production of working drawings for the job until they have been completed. The other system also employs a job captain to direct the work, but it is actually performed by drafters-specialists, each preparing only certain specific types of drawings for all or a number of the jobs in the office. Many variations of these systems are possible.

In most architectural offices, the individual responsible for an entire project, including all the processes such as production, administration, design, and so on, is an architect, who is called by some title such as project architect or partner-in-charge. Thus those who actually prepare working drawings are under the direction of a director of production, a chief drafter, and job captains, but the drafting they perform is directed toward the end result of producing contract documents for projects that are the responsibility of the project architects.

In architectural offices with engineering, landscape architecture, or interior design departments, production of such drawings is usually separate from architectural production, but closely related. When independent consulting engineers and others perform such work, their organizations are approximately similar to those of architects. In either case, each profession produces its own portion of the drawings, coordinating them with the others.

**Elements** For a very small building, such as a modest house, a set of working drawings may consist of only a few sheets. From this size, sets may range up to more than 300 sheets for a very large and complex building. Regardless of the size or complexity of buildings, all

**WORKING DRAWING** Structural working drawing of plan at entry level, Embassy of Singapore (1993), Washington, D.C. [*Architects: RTKL Associates, Inc.*]

working drawings contain several elements: plans, elevations, sections, details, schedules, and notes.

Plans are drawings that show horizontal views of a project. The most important plan, and usually the first one to be drawn, is the main floor plan. From it, many elements of a building may be developed. Other plans shown on working drawings include those of other floors, site or plot, roofs, foundations, and other elements. A special type is a reflected ceiling plan which shows a ceiling as if it were reflected in a mirror laid on a floor.

Elevations are drawings that show vertical views of buildings, mainly depicting the exteriors or facades and the interior walls. Sections are drawings that are made by theoretically slicing through a wall or other building element, either horizontally or vertically, to show its construction and other features. A wall section is a vertical section through a wall; a building section is a vertical section through a building. Building sections may be either full or part. A section elevation is a building section that shows an elevation. A detail is a drawing, usually at relatively large scale, showing some feature of interest, and may be a section or another type. A schedule is a list or table that gives types and other information about such items as windows or hardware. Notes are used to amplify and explain what may not be clear in the graphic work on working drawings.

**Subcategories** Ordinarily, working drawings sets are divided into subcategories, including architectural, structural, mechanical, electrical, and sometimes landscaping and others. Some production departments number the sheets of working drawings to indicate this division: A for architectural, S for structural, and so on. In sets of this type, architectural drawings would have numbers such as A-1, A-2, and so on, and structural drawings and the others would be numbered similarly.

A typical set of working drawings would include such individual drawings as plans—site, floor, for all floors including basement levels, roof, and possibly reflected ceilings; elevations—all exterior and important interior walls; sections and details—included as required to explain the building properly; and schedules—for such items as doors, windows, hardware, and room finishes, along with notes as required.

In the structural section would be included individual drawings of the structure, similar to those listed above, along with roof and floor framing plans and other specialized drawings and schedules of lintels, footings, piling, columns, beams, and so on. The mechanical and electrical sections would include drawings similar to those in the architectural section, but usually with outline of walls and so on drawn more lightly and the various systems shown diagrammatically and by symbols.

Schedules in these sections would include fixtures, equipment, appliances, and the like.

**Sheet Composition** All the sheets of the working drawings are cross-referenced to each other and various individual drawings, for example, sections and details are cross-referenced to the plans or elevations to which they refer. The first sheet of a working drawing set is called the title sheet; it contains, in addition to the title of the project, important general information, such as the names, addresses, and telephone numbers of the owner, architects, engineers, and others; a vicinity plan; a table of symbols; and other items. On each sheet in the set is a title block, giving the name and location of the project, the professionals involved and their addresses and titles, and the number of the individual sheet, and the seals and signatures of the architect and other professionals who certify the working drawings as having been drawn by them or under their direction. Also space should be provided for information concerning reissues or revisions of each sheet.

**Standards and Procedures** The preparation of working drawings requires great skill in drafting and considerable knowledge of the building industry, architecture, and construction. Accordingly, it takes some years of experience for a drafter to become competent in this work. Even skilled drafters may not always produce drawings that are of consistently high standards, without proper guidance. In addition to that given by directors of production, chief drafter, and others, many architects supply their drafter with office manuals that specify standards and procedures. Included in such a manual is information on symbols and abbreviations to be used, line types and weights, lettering sizes, types and quality, dimensioning practices, layout of drawings, coordination of the work, building industry regulations and standards to be followed, and so on. All these and others are factors in the systematic production of high-quality working drawings.

**Additional Drawings** In addition to the above types of drawings, production departments often prepare others, including preliminary working drawings which serve as the basis for the final documents, revisions of drawings, measured drawings of existing buildings, and supplemental drawings needed during construction; and as-built drawings showing how buildings were actually constructed.

**History** At the beginning of the 20th century, almost every working drawing was done in ink on tracing cloth. While some are still done with pen and ink, most working drawings today are done with pencil on tracing paper or sometimes cloth. Until a few years ago, this still meant that every line on every drawing had to be done by hand and every letter hand-lettered. This was a laborious, sometimes boring, process that was painstakingly repeated for every new job in production.

**Tools and Techniques** In the past few decades, many improvements have been made in drafting instruments and equipment, including new types of pencils, fountain drafting pens, and tracing papers. There have also been changes in techniques, many of which not only reduce the tedium of drafting but speed the process and facilitate the production of better drawings.

One technique involves the development of standard details that can be used more or less intact on succeeding jobs. Some firms have experimented with systems of detail drawings from which relevant examples may be selected for specific jobs, reproduced over and over, and bound into relatively small books which supplement the larger and more general drawings. Another method, in more widespread use, involves reproduction of details or other drawings, without redrawing, on clear materials that may be affixed to sheets of working drawings with clear tape or by other means. Typed or printed notes, tables, and other text may be affixed in a similar manner.

A quite extensive array of pressure-sensitive products are also available today, including alphabets and numbers, symbols, screens, patterns and tones, and lines. Generally, these are rubbed onto a drawing, covered with clear plastic, and burnished to ensure adhesion. Other types are available with adhesives that are not pressure-sensitive. Some of these materials also take typing or printing, which may then be affixed to drawings. Some offices utilize machines that reproduce details and other data, ready to be adhered to drawings. And many offices make drawings on sheets of plastic, rather than making them on tracing paper.

Other methods for improving the production of working drawings are in use today and others will no doubt be developed in the future. Some present-day methods include freehand detailing, in which details are drawn without drafting instruments on small pieces of drafting paper laid over grid sheets. Much faster than conventional detailing, the freehand method produces individual details that are then affixed to sheets of the working drawings. These working-drawing sheets may be reduced to half-size or less, photographically. The smaller sheets are easier to use and often less expensive to reproduce. Other photographic methods are also being used to reduce both the time required and the bulk of the sets of working drawings. The most revolutionary new drafting method involves the use of computers with working-drawing programs used as input, the output being complete or partly complete construction contract drawings.

**Computer** Many architectural and engineering firms are using computers to generate working drawings as well as many other applications of computers in contemporary offices. As of 1993, estimates were that about a quarter of architectural firms exclusively use computers to produce working drawings. A minority of firms prepare working drawings entirely by hand. The remainder of firms use a combination of computer-generated drawings and hand drawing for preparation of working drawings. It is expected that the trend to computerized working drawings will continue as the benefits of increased productivity are recognized and that earlier drawing techniques will become little used. Computer-directed plotters for producing full-size drawings on film or paper are necessary adjuncts to the creation of computerized drawing. For additional information, refer to the article entitled computer.

**Reproduction Techniques** From the latter half of the 19th century, blueprinting was the method used for reproducing working drawings. Its use was so common until a few years ago that many people still speak of the working drawings as the blueprints, even though they are not reproduced that way any more. And for some reason, the curious phrase that architects "draw blueprints" has persisted among certain laypersons, even though architects never did draw them.

Today the most common method for reproduction of working drawings is an ozalid system which is similar to blueprinting, but instead of producing white lines on a blue background, produces blue or black lines on essentially white backgrounds. These prints are sometimes called ozalids, but more often they are referred to as blue-line or black-line prints.

Blue-line and black-line prints are produced by processes in which the drawings, on tracing paper, are used as negatives to make prints on sensitized paper by exposure to ultraviolet light. The image on the print is then fixed by passing it through alkaline ammonia vapor. Additional negatives called vandykes, or sepias because of their color, may also be made by this process. Photographic processes are sometimes used for large complex jobs, in which 100 or more sets each numbering hundreds of sheets of large size must be reproduced. Generally, these processes involve reducing the size of the drawings, photographically, to half-size, preparing printing plates, and printing on offset presses. Other new methods, including chronflex, have also been developed in recent years.

**Legal Status** The legal status of working drawings and other construction contract documents is often misunderstood. Although there are variations, their legal status according to most agreements or contracts between owners and architects is that of instruments of service from which owners' buildings or other structures may be constructed. The ownership of working drawings remains with the architects, whether the building is constructed or not.

**Related Articles** Computers; Drafting; Engineering; Interior Design; Landscape Architecture; Practice of Architecture; Specification.

**Further Reading** Allen, Edward: *Architectural Detailing—Function, Constructibility, Aesthetics,* John Wiley, New York, 1993; Spence, William P.: *Architectural Working Drawings—Residential and Commercial Buildings,* John Wiley, New York, 1993; Wakita, Osamu A., and Richard M. Linde: *The Professional Practice of Architectural Detailing,* 2d ed., John Wiley, New York, 1987.

**WRIGHT, FRANK LLOYD** American architect (1867–1959). One of America's, and the world's, most famous architects, Frank Lloyd Wright had a profound and lasting effect on architecture. His professional career spanned 70 years, starting with an architecture of revivals of past styles and continuing through the era that saw the beginnings of what is now called Modern architecture, a movement in which Wright played a major role. It did not end before he had made a solid contribution to the establishment of the Modern movement that evolved into the architecture of today.

**Assessment** Wright lived so long and had such a profound effect on architecture that a considerable mythology about him has been created. His architecture was daring and controversial and so was his life. To separate the man and his architecture from the myths is not easy. It must be admitted that he was one of the most inventive and creative architects of his time, or any time. His was a most unusual life and philosophy: the poetic dreamer-artist, the pragmatic engineer, the freethinking individualist, the reformer, the evangelist. Through all his leanings was a strong reverence for life and nature. These attitudes and convictions recur again and again in this architecture. Above all though, he was an artist whose preferred medium was architecture.

Wright's architecture was always far ahead of its time and the work of most other architects. Just when others started to approach his position, he was off on another creative burst that again widened the gap.

Wright was a structural innovator, experimenting with great steel and concrete cantilevers and with types of poured concrete in many of his buildings. He was one of the first architects to take concrete block seriously, designing buildings of custom-cast blocks with patterns. He introduced open planning in buildings, letting spaces flow into each other instead of rigidly enclosing them with separating walls. He was interested in machines, and utilized factory-manufactured products in his buildings.

In all his work can be seen certain recurring forms; some he had learned in his childhood: circles, cubes, cantilevers, penetrated building elements, and walls with balconies enclosing space. There is also masterful use of ornament, most often machine-made but handcrafted whenever it seemed more appropriate to do so.

In everything, he was always the pioneering architect very much in the forefront of Modern architecture. His influence spread around the world and is still being felt. His designs and philosophy remain a subject of debate to this day. But there is no disagreement about his stature in world architecture. He was a giant.

Wright lived and practiced architecture for so long that historians have had a difficult time putting him and his work into perspective. Therefore his architectural career has sometimes been divided into periods, as was done with the Spanish painter Pablo Picasso (1881–1974). In Wright's case, the periods may be called the early (1893–1910), the mature (1910–45), and the late (1945–59).

**Early Period** After working for Louis Henri Sullivan (1856–1924) for six years, Wright started his own practice, designing houses that gave only slight promise of how his architecture would later develop. Among other buildings he designed during his early period, two masterpieces stand out. They are the Larkin Building (1904), Buffalo, since destroyed, and the Unity Church (1907), Oak Park, Ill. Harbingers of future development, both

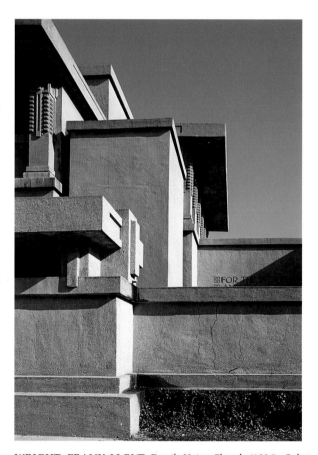

**WRIGHT, FRANK LLOYD** Detail, Unity Church (1906), Oak Park, Ill.

utilize cubistic forms. The Larkin Building had great balconies in a central hall rising the full height of the building and glassed-over on top. Unity Church was an early reinforced concrete building.

Another of Wright's masterpieces was his Robie House (1909), Chicago, one of the last of a long series of houses Wright designed in the Midwest, which he called Prairie houses. All these houses are low and horizontal in profile, and have widely projecting roof eaves and rows of windows. Other notable Prairie style houses are those for Ward W. Willits (1902), Highland Park, Ill.; Arthur Heurtley (1902), Chicago; Darwin Martin (1904), Buffalo; and Avery Coonley (1909), River Forest, Ill., a portion of which burned in 1978. All these finely designed houses illustrate the development and maturing of Wright's architectural philosophy. He had made the first steps toward what he called "organic architecture," an architecture that grew like living organisms by adaptation to specific environments, sites, uses, and materials, one that must change or evolve with changing conditions. By the end of Wright's early period, he was a success, artistically and professionally.

**Mature Period** The second or mature period of Wright's career began with his desertion of his family.

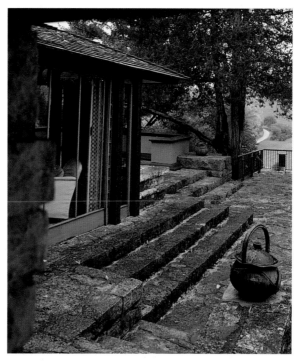

**WRIGHT, FRANK LLOYD** Exterior, Taliesin East (1911; rebuilt in 1915 and 1925), Spring Green, Wis.

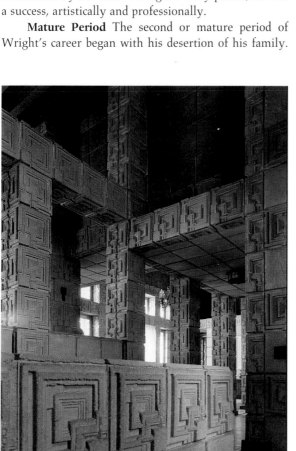

**WRIGHT, FRANK LLOYD** Interior, Charles Ennis/Brown House (1924), Los Angeles, Calif.

This heralded a turbulent time filled with tragedy and triumph. Between 1910 and the end of World War II, the productive periods in his work were interspersed with periods of almost complete idleness. In 1911 he built his home and studio, Taliesin, in Spring Green, Wis. It burned twice and was rebuilt each time, in 1915 and 1925. Like Jefferson at Monticello, Wright built, rebuilt, altered, and added to Taliesin the rest of his life.

Two notable designs of the mature phase of Wright's career were for buildings that are quite different. The first was for Midway Gardens (1914), Chicago, a great indoor and outdoor amusement center where large numbers of people could dance, attend concerts and other performances, drink and dine. The other was for the Imperial Hotel, Tokyo, which occupied most of Wright's time from 1916 until its completion in 1922. Hailed as an engineering triumph that survived the great earthquake of 1923, the Imperial Hotel foundation later settled unevenly and was demolished in 1968. Midway Gardens, after a period of success, could not survive Prohibition and was demolished in 1923. Wright also designed some houses during this period, the most notable of which is the Millard House (1923) in Pasadena, Calif. In the 1930s commissions were scarce, and most of those that came in were not built. Later in that decade things started to pick up again. As he had with his Prairie houses, he started a whole new series of houses which he now called Usonian, a term for the United States, used by Samuel Butler in his 1872 novel, *Erewhon.* Many of these were

**WRIGHT, FRANK LLOYD** Fallingwater, Edgar J. Kaufmann House (1936), Bear Run, Pa.

in California, but some were built in other places. In most, he experimented with custom-designed concrete block, a pioneering effort at the time.

Then came a flurry of creative activity toward the end of that decade. He designed a residential masterpiece, the Kaufmann House (1937; now open to the public), called Fallingwater, because it was built over a stream and waterfall at Bear Run, Pa. Fallingwater was followed by a striking design for the Johnson Wax Company Administration Building (1939), Racine, Wis.; the campus and buildings for Florida Southern University, Lakeland, Fla., started in 1940 and completed in 1952; and his own winter house and studio, Taliesin West (see illustration), Scottsdale, Ariz., started in 1938 and worked on until he died.

**Late Period** The World War II years saw little building activity. After the war, entering his late period, Wright found all the commissions he could handle. He designed houses again, among them the notable one for his son, David, in 1952 near Phoenix, Ariz. Another great building of the era is the Johnson Wax Company Factory and Laboratory Tower (1949), adjoining the Administration Building which Wright had previously designed. In religious work, the Unitarian Church (1947), Madison, Wis., was followed by the Beth Sholom Synagogue (1959), Elkins Park, Pa. Along the way, he

**WRIGHT, FRANK LLOYD** Usonian house, George D. Sturgis House (1939), Brentwood Heights, Calif.

**WRIGHT, FRANK LLOYD** Exterior, Taliesin West (1938–59), Scottsdale, Ariz.

**WRIGHT, FRANK LLOYD** H. C. Price Tower (1953), Bartlesville, Okla.

proposed a mile-high skyscraper, The Illinois, in 1958, which he claimed to be structurally possible and economically sound. It was never built. A little gem of a building is the V. V. Morris Gift Shop (1950) in San Francisco.

In 1953 the H. C. Price Tower, a 16-story building interspersing professional office spaces with duplex apartments, was built in Bartlesville, Okla. In 1943 he started designing a revolutionary art museum, the Guggenheim, for a site in New York City. A model of the building was first exhibited in 1945, but over 10 years passed before construction was started. The building, which features a continuous ramp around an interior court, was completed in 1959, the year Wright died. He left a number of unfinished projects; some were completed by his students at the Taliesin Foundation. Included was his last important building, the Marin County Civic Center (1972), San Rafael, Calif.

A giant figure, Wright deeply affected architecture. He was a man of his own time who had visions of the future and set out to find it in his architecture.

**Life** Frank Lloyd Wright was born in Richland Center, Wis., on June 8, 1867. His father deserted the family when Wright was sixteen; his mother was a strong-willed woman who decided that her son was to become an architect.

In 1876 Mrs. Wright learned about a new kindergarten teaching method originated by Frederick Froebel. The student, using a basic set of blocks, folded paper, and other simple materials, thought about the object to be built, named the object, drew plans for it, and finally constructed rudimentary buildings, furniture, and other objects. Although young Wright was past kindergarten age, he started to study in this manner when he was seven, under his mother's tutelage, and continued to do so for some years. Wright always maintained that the work with the Froebel system constituted his only early training and that it deeply affected his architecture. When Wright was sixteen, he enrolled in civil engineering at the University of Wisconsin, at Madison, but dropped out after less than two years.

At eighteen, Wright worked for a short time in the office of James Lyman Silsbee (1845–1913) and then went to Chicago to work in the office of the man he would always call master, Louis Henri Sullivan. As a designer and drafter in the office of Adler and Sullivan, Wright worked on some of their best buildings, including the Wainwright Building (1891) in St. Louis. He also absorbed much of the philosophy and design principles of the master, and the engineering knowledge and talent of the partner Dankmar Adler. It seems evident in the later work of Sullivan that in return the student influenced the master. While working with Sullivan, Wright designed a shingled house (1889) for himself in Oak Park, Ill. It showed little indication of his future directions in design. Here he later set up his practice. The chief of his drafting room was Marion Mahoney Griffin (1871–1961), later a respected architect.

However, the Charnley House (1891), Chicago, designed for Adler and Sullivan, and his first commission after setting up his own practice in 1893, the Winslow House (1893), River Forest, Ill., do hint at his future development. These houses marked the beginning of a long and productive life and an architectural practice that lasted 66 years. It was a life marked by periods of scandal and tragedy, and others of great happiness and satisfaction; a career marked by periods of frustration and failure, but predominantly by accomplishment and success.

During his early career, Wright worked mostly in a studio attached to his home in Oak Park and later in downtown Chicago. This was a very productive period for him. He designed a number of excellent houses, gradually developing what he named his Prairie style, and several other of his greatest buildings, including the

**WRIGHT, FRANK LLOYD** Guggenheim Museum (1959; additions and restoration, 1992), New York, N.Y.
*[Restoration and additions architects: Gwathmey Siegel]*

Larkin Building and the Unity Church. In 1889 he married Catherine Lee Tobin and by 1909 the family had six children. That year, Wright, as had his father, abandoned his family. He then went to Europe for a year with Mamah Borthwick Cheney, the wife of one of his clients.

After returning to America, Wright stayed for a short time in Oak Park, then went to Spring Green, Wis., where he had inherited his family's farm on which he had grown up. Here, in 1897, he had designed a fanciful windmill, which he had named Romeo and Juliet. Here Mrs. Cheney, now divorced, joined him. His wife, Catherine, did not divorce him until 1921. Wright designed a home and studio on a hill, and called it Taliesin, the Welsh word for shining brow and the name of a 6th-century Welsh bard. This was the beginning of a new life for Wright and his entry into the second period of his architecture, the mature years.

Then on August 14, 1914, tragedy struck, while he was in Chicago working on the Midway Gardens. Mamah Borthwick Cheney, her two children, and four workers were murdered by a crazed servant, who then set fire to Taliesin, destroying it.

In 1915 Wright rebuilt his Spring Green home, naming it Taliesin II. Important commissions came in, including that for the Imperial Hotel in Tokyo. While designing the hotel, Wright made a number of trips to

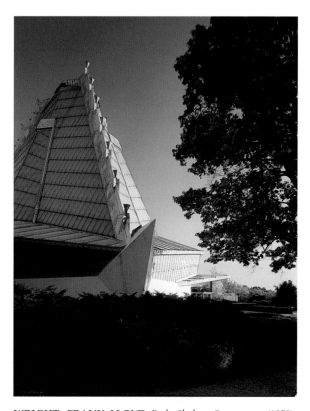

**WRIGHT, FRANK LLOYD** Beth Sholom Synagogue (1959), Elkins Park, Philadelphia, Pa.

Japan and lived there from 1918 to 1922, while it was being constructed. Accompanying him was a divorcée, Miriam Noel, whom he married in 1923. In 1923 Wright's mother, with whom he had always been very close, died at age eighty-one. He then returned to Taliesin II, in 1924, this time to remain.

The marriage to Miriam Noel lasted only a few months, but they were not divorced until 1927. Miriam later accused him of desertion, bigamy, and other charges. In 1925, another tragedy struck. Taliesin II caught fire in a storm.

After his divorce, Wright, in 1928, married Olgivanna Milanoff, who had been a member of the Russian Ballet Company. They then started to build Taliesin III, on which he worked the rest of his life. His former wife, Miriam, continued to press him, through publicity in the newspapers and legal actions, and even had Olgivanna, their daughter, and Wright jailed for several days. In the end, Wright was cleared of all charges, but by then he had been ruined financially and professionally.

In 1928 he was declared bankrupt and all his possessions at Taliesin sold, under the terms of the mortgage on the property. Wright fought back. He paid off the mortgage, and he was working on several designs for important buildings, including a glass skyscraper, a retirement town in the Arizona desert, and a New York City apartment. None was ever built. The stock market crash in 1929 and the ensuing Depression stopped all building. During these years, Wright supported his family by giving lectures and writing for the most part, while his architectural practice went into almost total decline.

Things started to get better in the mid-1930s. He did another remarkable series of houses, as he had in his early days, and other important buildings. He also designed Taliesin West, which he started to build in 1938 and continued to work on until he died. In 1932 Wright established the Taliesin Fellowship at Spring Green. This was a combination school and apprenticeship program in which architectural students could study and work. It was also a sociological experiment in communal living, in which the participants worked the Taliesin farm and performed maintenance and other chores. After building Taliesin West, the Fellowship was in residence there in the winter and in Spring Green in the summer. Many notable architects studied with Wright, as referenced in other articles.

By the late 1930s, both Wright and his buildings had admirers all over the world. He received recognition and honors from everywhere—Europe, Asia, and South America—except his own country. In the United States, Wright's students and other admirers were dedicated and outspoken, but not so the architectural profession. He had received honors from architectural professions all over the world, but the Gold Medal of the American

Institute of Architects was late in coming. It was presented to Wright, who never joined the AIA, in 1949, when he was eighty years old. The opening sentence of his acceptance speech was, "Well, it's about time!"

Work was scarce during World War II, but in 1945 Wright embarked on the final phase of his long career. This was a period of considerable activity, and he produced a number of great buildings. He had always been ahead of his profession in creative and innovative designs during the first 50 years of his practice, and he continued to hold his lead during the last years. Daring and imaginative all his life, he could not stop now, and he worked until just a few weeks before he died, on April 9, 1959. He had practiced 66 years, produced several hundred buildings, some think as many as 600, all innovative, many masterpieces. The exact number of his buildings is hard to determine. Many designs were never built, and he disavowed some of his own buildings. He had created a band of dedicated disciples who would carry on the philosophy of his design. Considered arrogant and overbearing by some, he was loved and respected by his disciples. He had led the way for architecture, his way, all his life. He had become one of the world's greatest architects (some think *the* greatest).

**Related Articles** MODERN ARCHITECTURE; SULLIVAN, LOUIS HENRI.

**Further Reading** Many books concerning the work of Frank Lloyd Wright have been published. Titles listed here are some recent additions to the literature, with new titles being added yearly. *Fallingwater: A Frank Lloyd Wright Country House*, Abbeville Press, New York, 1986; Hitchcock, Henry-Russell: *In the Nature of Materials—The Buildings of Frank Lloyd Wright, 1887–1941*, reprint of 1942 ed., DaCapo, New York, 1975; Hoffman, Donald: *Studies and Executed Buildings by Frank Lloyd Wright*, Rizzoli, New York, 1986; Lind, Carla, *The Wright Style*, Simon & Schuster, New York, 1992; *Nine Commentaries on Frank Lloyd Wright*, MIT Press, Cambridge, Mass., 1989; Pfeiffer, Bruce Brooks, ed.: *Frank Lloyd Wright: Collected Writings*, Vol. 1, *1894–1930*, Vol. 2, *1930–32*, Rizzoli, New York, 1992; Secrest, Meryle: *Frank Lloyd Wright: A Biography*, Alfred A. Knopf, New York, 1992; Sergeant, John: *Frank Lloyd Wright's Usonian Houses*, Watson Guptil, New York, 1984; Tafel, Edgar: *Years with Frank Lloyd Wright—Apprentice to Genius*, reprint, Dover, New York, 1985; Twombly, Robert: *Frank Lloyd Wright—His Life and His Architecture*, John Wiley, New York, 1978.

**WURSTER, WILLIAM WILSON** American architect and educator (1895–1973). Although he has been most widely admired for his achievements in the education of architectural, planning, and other environmental design students, William Wilson Wurster was also an accomplished architect.

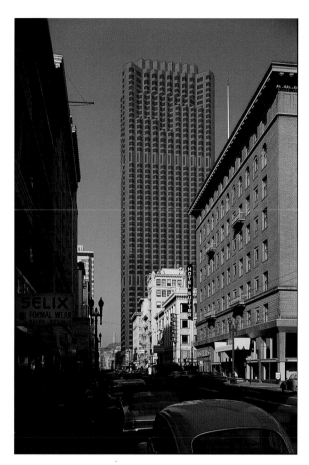

**WURSTER, WILLIAM WILSON** Bank of America Building (1971), San Francisco, Calif. *[Architects: Wurster, Bernardi and Emmons in association with Skidmore, Owings and Merrill and Pietro Belluschi]*

Beginning in the 1920s, Wurster started designing simple, livable houses in a manner that later was called the ranch style. For the rest of his life, he was preoccupied with house design, in particular warm, human-scaled, modest dwellings. He was deeply concerned with house sites, the surrounding landscapes, construction materials, and the institutions and culture of their locale. These principles deeply affected architects and architecture in an era when many buildings were designed to be different, daring, or provocative.

**Works** The principles of Wurster's house designs also deeply affected his design of other buildings. In every building, there is a sense of rightness that very few architects have managed to achieve. Wurster achieved it from the first, in the Gregory House (1927), near San Francisco. And many of his other houses, scattered all over northern California, still exist to testify to his principles. Other than the houses, his most notable buildings, all done by the partnership of Wurster, Bernardi and Emmons, are the Center for Advanced Study in Behavioral Science (1955), Palo Alto, Calif.;

U.S. Consulate (1959), Hong Kong; Golden Gateway Redevelopment (1967), San Francisco; the redevelopment and restoration of Ghirardelli Square (1969), San Francisco, in association with DeMars and Reay; and his last important building, the Bank of America headquarters (1971), San Francisco, in association with Skidmore, Owings and Merrill and Pietro Belluschi (1899–1994).

**Architectural Education** Wurster achieved many accomplishments in education. As dean of the architectural school of the University of California, Berkeley, for many years, he established it as a leader in architectural education. He founded the College of Environmental Design at the university in an attempt to integrate and interrelate the teaching of architecture with the other environmental design professions. He deeply influenced the design philosophies of several architects, including John Ekin Dinwiddie (1902–59) and Gardner Dailey (b. 1895). In recognition of his services and those of his wife, Catherine Bauer Wurster (1905–64), to the University of California, the College of Environmental Design was renamed Wurster Hall.

**Life** William Wilson Wurster was born in Stockton, Calif., on October 20, 1895. Deciding early that he wanted to become an architect, Wurster enrolled in the architectural school of the University of California at Berkeley and graduated with honors in 1919. His architectural career had started even earlier when he went to work, at fifteen, as an office boy for a Stockton firm.

After graduating from college, Wurster worked for architects in San Francisco and Sacramento, spent a year traveling in Europe, and then worked in New York City for Delano and Aldrich in 1923 and 1924. In 1926 he started his own firm in San Francisco and practiced as an individual until 1943. In 1940 he married Catherine Bauer, a noted planner and writer. They had one daughter.

In 1943 Wurster formed a partnership with Theodore C. Bernardi (1903–93), in San Francisco, and a year later Donn Emmons (1910–   ) joined the firm which was renamed Wurster, Bernardi and Emmons. In 1944 he was named dean of the School of Architecture and Planning, Massachusetts Institute of Technology, Cambridge, a position he held until 1950. From 1950 to 1959, Wurster was dean of the College of Architecture, University of California, Berkeley, and then founded the College of Environmental Design in 1959 at that university and became its first dean, remaining in that position until 1963.

Tragedy struck Wurster when his wife, Catherine, who had worked closely with him for many years and was a professor of city planning at the University of California, was lost while on a hiking trip in the mountains near San Francisco and died on November 22, 1964.

After retiring from the faculty at Berkeley in 1963 as dean emeritus, Wurster devoted most of his time to his architectural practice. He received many honors in the United States and in other countries, including an honorary doctor's degree from the University of California and fellowships in the American Academy of Arts and Sciences and the Royal Academy of Fine Arts of Denmark. In 1969 he received the highest honor, the Gold Medal, from the American Institute of Architects. William Wurster died on September 20, 1973.

**Related Articles** EDUCATION; MODERN ARCHITECTURE.

# Y

**YAMASAKI, MINORU** American architect (1912–86). A controversial architect, Minoru Yamasaki seems to have dedicated supporters and equally dedicated detractors. On the one side, some people are convinced that his buildings are works of art, sensitive to form, materials, and human needs. On the other side, many think that he has been too playful, even capricious, and that his buildings are merely ornamental, decorative forms for their own sake. Yamasaki said that the social function of an architect is to create a work of art. This, his detractors say, proves their point. His supporters, perhaps defining works of art differently, claim that his ornamental forms express the function and structure of his buildings as well as the delight which should be an integral part of great architecture.

**Appraisal** In spite of the controversy, Yamasaki has exerted a considerable influence on the architecture of today. In a time when many modern buildings were designed as plain, even sterile-looking, products of the industrial age, Yamasaki steadfastly designed buildings with ornament, with sculptural forms particularly in the details, and with gaiety or serenity as the occasion demanded. It may be true, as some claim, that he has not developed a group of followers or disciples. And Yamasaki, unlike many of his contemporaries, stuck closely to the practice of architecture, rather than combining it with teaching, writing, or lecturing. Yet many people find his buildings, of which he has produced a rather large number, delightful and exciting. And the work of some architects today reveals their interest in relieving the monotony of design of machine production with sculptural form and ornament. Some architects believe this would happen more often if the costs of construction had not soared to the point where ornament is often not feasible.

**Works** After working in the offices of other architects for more than 15 years, Yamasaki joined a partnership in 1949, Hellmuth, Yamasaki and Leinweber. The firm soon had some important commissions, including one for the Lambert–St. Louis Airport (1956; see illustration in article airport), which won several awards and established Yamasaki's reputation as a designer.

He has since designed more than 85 important buildings of many types. Among the most important are several buildings at Wayne State University, Detroit, including the McGregor Memorial Community Conference Center (1958); Reynolds Metal Company Building (1960), Detroit; Air Terminal (1961), Dhahran, Saudi Arabia; Federal Science Pavilion (1962; see illustration in article exposition), at the World's Fair, Century 21, Seattle; Michigan Consolidated Gas Company Office Building (1963), Detroit, in association with Smith, Hinchman and Grylls; International Business Machines Co. Building (1964), Seattle, in association with Naramore, Bain, Brady and Johanson; Woodrow Wilson School of Public and International Affairs (1965), Princeton University, Princeton, N.J.; the Century Plaza Hotel (1966), Los Angeles; Congregation Beth-El Temple (1974), Bloomfield, Mich.; and Federal Reserve Bank (1973), Richmond, Va. Yamasaki's last important buildings are the twin towers of the World Trade Center (1973; see illustrations in articles column; model making), New York City, in association with Emery Roth and Sons.

**Life** Minoru Yamasaki was born in Seattle, Wash., on December 1, 1912, the son of an immigrant Japanese farmer. A top student, he graduated from Garfield High School in 1929. While in high school, he became fascinated with architecture through watching the work of his uncle who was an architect. Determined to rise above

**YAMASAKI, MINORU** Exterior, McGregor Memorial Community Conference Center (1958), Wayne State University, Detroit, Mich.

the tenement surroundings in which he had been born and to become an architect, Yamasaki worked summers in fish canneries in Alaska, saved his money, and entered the architectural school of the University of Washington.

After graduating in 1934, Yamasaki went to New York City where he worked for eight years in several offices, including Shreve, Lamb and Harmon, Harrison and Fouilhoux, and the noted industrial designer Raymond Loewy (1893–1986). In 1941 he married Teruko Hirashiki and they had three children. He also taught architectural design at Columbia University from 1943 to 1945. He was able to escape internment as a Japanese-American during World War II with the help of the architects for whom he worked. And by bringing his parents to New York to live with him, he also saved them from internment. In 1945 he went to Detroit to

work for the large and successful firm of Smith, Hinchman and Grylls, remaining until 1949.

In 1949 Yamasaki went into practice in Detroit, in partnership with Joseph William Leinweber (1895–1993) and George F. Hellmuth (1907– ). The partnership lasted until 1955, when Hellmuth withdrew to form another partnership in St. Louis. Yamasaki and Leinweber continued their partnership until 1959. Yamasaki then formed a successor firm, Minoru Yamasaki and Associates, in Rochester Hills, Mich., near Detroit, until his death in 1986.

Soon after the Hellmuth, Yamasaki and Leinweber partnership was formed, the firm received a significant commission for a new airport in St. Louis. Its design brought quick recognition to the firm, resulting in many commissions. In 1953 Yamasaki became dangerously ill with ulcers which necessitated surgery. He recovered

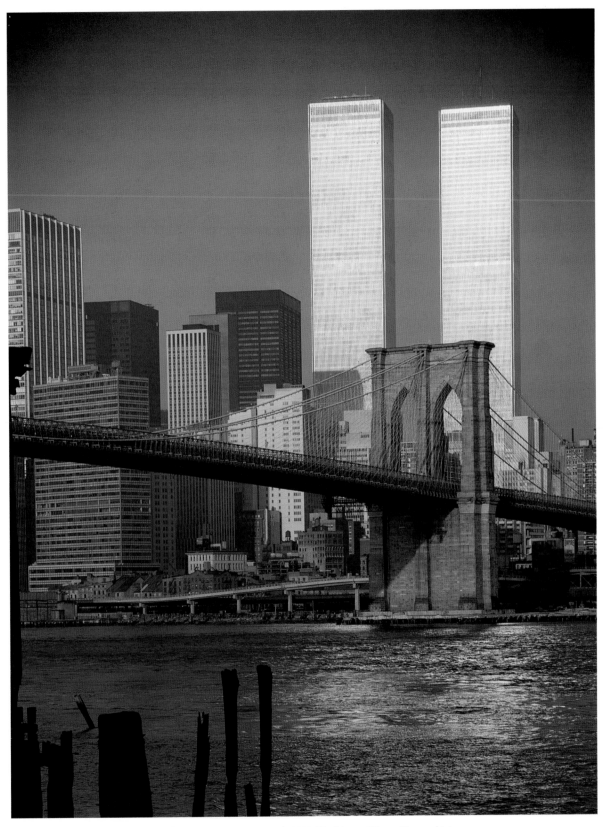

**YAMASAKI, MINORU** World Trade Center (1973), New York, N.Y. *[Architects: Minoru Yamasaki, in association with Emery Roth and Sons].* The Brooklyn Bridge is shown in the foreground.

and built a good-sized and successful practice. In 1961 he was divorced from his wife, but remarried her years later. Minoru Yamasaki died in 1986.

Minoru Yamasaki received many honors, including a number of honorary doctor's degrees, awards for several buildings, and fellowship in the American Academy of Arts and Sciences.

**Related Articles** CONTEMPORARY ARCHITECTURE; MODERN ARCHITECTURE.

# Z

**ZOOLOGICAL BUILDING** A building, or group of buildings, housing a collection of wild, and sometimes domestic, animals for study, display, and enjoyment. Such buildings are ordinarily located in zoological gardens, familiarly called zoos, areas set aside for keeping animals. In the past, most buildings for zoo animals were cages with bars or wire to keep the animals from escaping and to protect animals and visitors. Some cages were glassed-in, for example, those for snakes, which can escape through bars, and for monkeys, which are susceptible to human diseases. Nonswimming animals were sometimes placed behind moats or ditches, filled with water. Fish were kept in tanks; aquatic mammals, such as seals, and water birds were provided with pools. All were severely restricted to relatively small areas of activity. A later trend has been toward keeping the animals in large enclosures, which resemble the natural habitat of the animals as closely as possible.

**Thematic Classification** Zoo displays are often classified according to themes. The most important themes are systematic, zoogeographic, ecological, behavioral, and general. In the systematic zoo, the earliest type, cats are kept together, hoofed animals together, and so on. The zoogeographic type places animals together according to their place of origin, North American, African, South American, and so on, or by even smaller geographic locations, such as a single state or region. The ecological exhibit groups animals together according to habitat, such as desert, prairie, forest, and the like. In such exhibits, predators are often separated from their prey by barriers that are invisible to visitors. A behavioral exhibit displays animals that share certain habits, such as flying, burrowing, or swimming. The general zoo simply brings together the most popular animals, without regard to any classification. Many zoos utilize more than one theme in order to bring variety into their exhibits. And some arrange special exhibits, for example, exhibits where children may intermingle with and pet animals. Some of the most successful zoos are combined with botanical gardens to form more logical, complete, and natural exhibits.

**Elements** Zoos contain three major elements, for animals, visitors, and management and maintenance. The first precedence is given to the animals, which require special considerations according to their individual needs. Some of the specialized buildings include mammal houses, aviaries or bird houses, and aquariums for fish and other aquatic animals. In addition to walks among displays, visitor facilities include parking lots, rest rooms, and concession stands. Administrative and

**ZOOLOGICAL BUILDING** National Aquarium (1980), Baltimore, Md. *[Architects: Cambridge Seven]*

**ZOOLOGICAL BUILDING** Interior, The Living World (1989), St. Louis Zoo, St. Louis, Mo.
*[Architects: Hellmuth, Obata and Kassabaum, Inc.]*

maintenance facilities include offices, food preparation areas, animal hospital, reserve animal areas for those not being exhibited, and employee quarters.

Zoos comprise a limited building type since relatively few exist in the United States, and almost none have been built in the recent past. In existing zoos, some new buildings are being built and others remodeled. They are interesting and rewarding problems for the architects who design them.

**History** It is believed that the dog was the first wild animal to be captured and kept by human beings, during the Paleolithic, or Old Stone, age, 10,000 to 20,000 years ago. The first known zoo, or it might have been called a menagerie, was started by Egyptian Queen Hatshepsut about 1500 B.C. Menageries and aviaries were kept by other members of the ruling families of Egypt in ancient times, and in ancient China and Rome. During the Middle Ages and later, menageries were kept for exhibit of animals, often in unsanitary and crowded cages that were repugnant to many visitors. The first modern zoo, and botanical garden, was the Jardin des Plantes (1626) in Paris; it is still in existence. The first zoo in the United States was established in Philadelphia in 1859. Other notable examples are the Bronx Zoo in New York City, and the zoos of San Diego, Chicago, and Cincinnati. The National Zoological Park in Washington, D.C., was founded in 1890.

**Related Article** BOTANICAL BUILDING.

## ABOUT THE AUTHORS

Robert T. Packard, AIA,
is a prominent architect, writer, editor, and author. He was
formerly a staff member of the American Institute of Architects,
associate editor of the five-volume *Encyclopedia of Architecture,* and
editor of *Architectural Graphic Standards,* Seventh Edition.

Balthazar Korab
is a renowned architectural photographer and has
published several books with the National Trust for
Historic Preservation.

R 720.973 PAC
Packard, Robert T.
Encyclopedia of American
 architecture

For Reference

Not to be taken from this room

BAKER & TAYLOR